PUBLISHER'S NOTE

MICRO-OFFSET BOOKS are published in editions of from 100 to 250 copies. The titles issued in this series consist largely of reprints of out of print and scarce books required by those doing research work, and for which only an extremely limited sale is possible. Copies of the original edition have become practically unobtainable at any price; the occasional one that might prove available generally is priced far beyond the means of most libraries or scholars.

It thus becomes necessary to employ some method of reproducing these books in very small editions and at a moderate price.

Our method of reprinting such volumes hence makes available again titles that might otherwise prove unobtainable, perhaps for all time.

JAMES IREDELL
Associate Justice of the Supreme court of the U.S.

LIFE AND CORRESPONDENCE

OF

JAMES IREDELL,

ONE OF THE ASSOCIATE JUSTICES OF THE SUPREME COURT
OF THE UNITED STATES.

BY
GRIFFITH J. McREE.

"Hereditary honor is accounted the most worthy ; but reason speaketh in the cause of him who hath acquired it."—*Dean Bolton.*

VOL. I.

NEW YORK
PETER SMITH
1949

ENTERED, according to Act of Congress, in the year 1857, by
D. APPLETON & COMPANY,
In the Clerk's Office of the District Court of the United States for the Southern District of New York.

Reprinted 1949

LIBRARY
FLORIDA STATE UNIVERSITY
TALLAHASSEE, FLORIDA

Lithographed In The United States of America
N. Y. LITHOGRAPHING CORP., NEW YORK 3, N. Y.

In Memory

OF THE

HON. JAMES IREDELL,

LATE GOVERNOR OF THE STATE OF NORTH CAROLINA, SENATOR OF THE UNITED STATES,
ETC., ETC.,

THIS RECORD OF A FATHER,

WHOSE GENIUS HE INHERITED, AND WHOSE VIRTUES HE EMULATED;

IN MEMORY

OF HIM TO WHOSE PARENTAL CARE
I AM INDEBTED FOR THE GREATEST OF ALL BLESSINGS—

AN ADMIRABLE WIFE,

THIS VOLUME IS AFFECTIONATELY INSCRIBED,

BY

GRIFFITH J. McREE.

PREFACE

IMPRESSED, years ago, with a high opinion of the interesting character of the papers of Judge Iredell, and especially of their value as " materia historica," a vague purpose to prepare a biography of that eminent man, at the suggestion of the Hon. David L. Swain, soon assumed the consistency of a resolute determination.

But slight liberties have been taken with the original papers introduced into the volume : ancient have been made to conform to modern usages, as regards punctuation, capitals, and orthography : in no instance, however, has an attempt been made to make an illiterate appear an educated man. The papers of Judge Iredell are so perfect that I have not presumed to amend or correct them in the least degree ; not an i needs dotting—not a t to be crossed. I doubted about the propriety of this course ; but adopted it by the advice of the venerable Dr. Cogswell, of the Astor Library, whose opinion has with me the weight of the highest authority.

I have endeavored to state facts ingenuously : any error that I have committed, if pointed out, will be promptly corrected, and proper atonement made.

Fatigued by the transcription of the manuscripts of others, in hours stolen from the labors of my farm, and often consequently unfit for original composition, I am fully sensible that I can only claim for myself the merit of persistent industry. If the papers I present, vindicate the claim of North Carolina to a place in the front rank of the foremost States in the War of the Revolution, even if the publication be unattended with profit, I shall be content.

To Dr. Cogswell, upon whom I had no claim, for polite attention, for information kindly imparted, for frank advice, and for a generous proffer that would have surprised me from any other quarter, I desire publicly to tender my thanks. Distinguished for the universality of his attainments, in a ripe old age his heart is still warmed by the sunshine of generous youth. In a position for which he is admirably qualified, and which he values because of the opportunities it offers him to render services to others, none who know him will hesitate to concur in the wish—" That thy days may be long in the land."

To Dr. Hawks of New York, Gov. Swain, Dr. Carruthers, Joshua G. Wright, T. C. McIlhenny of North Carolina, for words of encouragement or services rendered with a courtesy that heightened my sense of obligation, I offer my grateful acknowledgments.

G. J. McREE.

WILMINGTON, NORTH CAROLINA,
    August 5th, 1856.

CONTENTS.

	PAGE

CHAPTER I.
England.—Birth.—Parentage, etc.. 1

CHAPTER II.
America.—Edenton; its People.—Study of Law.—Letters from England.................. 29

CHAPTER III.
Custom-House.—McCulloh.—Study of Law.—Letters.—Journal.—License............... 54

CHAPTER IV.
Difficulty of Speech.—War of the Regulation.—Letters from Great Britain.—Lyric.—Letters from Mr. Iredell.—The Circuit.—First Argument.—Letter from H. E. McCulloh........

CHAPTER V.
Historical Summary.—Courtship.—Letters from Sir N. Dukinfield.—Letter from Mr. Iredell.—Letters from England.—Letter from Mr. Iredell.—Journal, etc......................

CHAPTER VI.
Mr. Iredell at 21.—Journal.—Letter from Miss Macartney.—Journal.—Letters.—Marriage, etc...

CHAPTER VII.
Political Condition of the Province.—Iredell a Political Writer.—Collector.—Deputy for the Attorney General.—Letters from McCulloh, Dukinfield, Brother and Uncle.—First Provincial Congress in North Carolina.—William Hooper.—Society at Wilmington.—A. Neilson.—Address.—Hewes.. 183

CHAPTER VIII.
Letters from T. Iredell, Neilson, A. Iredell and Sir N. Dukinfield.—Iredell and Political Summary.—Letter from Iredell.—Last Speech and Flight of the Governor.—Letter from A. Iredell.—"Principles of an American Whig."—Letter from Hewes and Mrs. Iredell.—Political Events.—Letters from Hewes and Neilson.—Proclamation.—Letters from Johnston.—Congress at Hillsboro.—Letters from Johnston, Neilson and Hewes.............................

CONTENTS.

CHAPTER IX.

Letter from Hooper.—Battle of Moore's Creek.—Letters from J. Johnston and Hewes.—Prov. Congress.—Letters from Johnston and Thomas Jones.—Custom-House Closed.—Letters from Johnston and Thomas Jones.—British Retreat—Iredell's Essay.—Attack on Fort Sullivan.—Letters from Hewes.—Theft of unpaid Bills of Credit.—Letters from Iredell, Jones, J. Johnston and Charlton.—Defeat of Mr. Johnston.—"Creed of a Rioter."—State Constitution.—Letters from Johnston.. 268

CHAPTER X.

North Carolina enjoys Peace.—Letter from McCulloh.—First Session of the Assembly.—Letters from Iredell and Mrs. Blair.—La Neuville.—Letters from Iredell and Chief Justice Howard.—Letters from Iredell and La Neuville.—Iredell a Judge.—Letters from Hooper and Maclaine.. 340

CHAPTER XI.

The State.—Letter from Maclaine.—The Circuit.—Letters from Iredell, and Charge to the Grand Jury at Edenton.—Letters from Iredell.—Resignation as Judge.—Letters from Caswell, Nash, Iredell, and Hooper.—North Carolina Signs Articles of Confederation.—Letter to British Commissioners.—Assembly.—Letters, etc... 373

CHAPTER XII.

War in the South.—Letters from Iredell.—Confiscation.—McCulloh.—Letter from Iredell.—Sir George Collier at Norfolk.—Letters from Mrs. Blair.—Iredell Attorney-General.—Letters from Iredell and Hooper.—Schools in North Carolina.—The Circuit........................ 407

CHAPTER XIII.

Letters from Iredell.—Assembly.—The Circuit.—Letters from Iredell.—South Carolina subdued.—Condition of North Carolina.—Letters from Iredell.—Rocky Mount.—Hanging Rock.—Battle of Camden.—Assembly.—Letters from Iredell.—Second British Invasion.—Battle of King's Mountain.—Cornwallis Retreats.—Letters from Iredell.—Arrival of Greene.—Army.—Admiralty Suit.—Letter from Johnston, Delegate to Continental Congress........... 442

CHAPTER XIV.

Cowpens.—Letter from Robert Smith.—Assembly.—C. Johnston to Iredell.—S. Johnston to Iredell.—Spencer to Iredell.—Hooper to Iredell.—Pierce Butler to Iredell.—Battle of Guilford.—Letters.—Council Extraordinary.—Letters.—People of Edenton fly.—Greene's Campaign in South Carolina.—Letters from Butler, Johnston, Mrs. Blair, etc.—Trick played General Gregory.—Assembly.—Governor Burke.—Letters.—Negro Invasion.—Battle of Eutaw Springs.—Capture of Governor Burke.—Battles of Elizabethtown and Lindley's Mill.—Yorktown.—Evacuation of Wilmington.—Rejoicing.. 481

Appendix.. 565

LIBRARY
FLORIDA STATE UNIVERSITY
TALLAHASSEE, FLORIDA

LIFE AND CORRESPONDENCE

OF

JAMES IREDELL,

ONE OF THE ASSOCIATE JUSTICES OF THE SUPREME COURT OF THE UNITED STATES.

CHAPTER I.

ENGLAND, BIRTH, PARENTAGE, ETC.

JAMES IREDELL was born at Lewes, Sussex County, England, Oct. 5th, 1751, N. S. His grandfather was the Rev. Francis Iredell, of Dublin, Ireland, who married Eleanor Macartney. His father, Mr. Francis Iredell, a merchant of Bristol, married on the 1st August, 1750, Margaret McCulloh, of Ireland.

There is a tradition in the Iredell family that the true name is Ireton : that they are collateral descendants of Henry Ireton, son-in-law of Oliver Cromwell ; and that when at the Restoration, the body of the republican General was dug up and exposed upon the Tyburn gibbet, prudence dictated to the family such a change of name as would enable them to escape the clamor and fury of the royalists.

Ireton died in 1651. Now a tradition in a family, three generations of which are known to have been cultivated people, for so short a period, has certainly great weight.

Of Ireton, Hume remarks—" A memorable personage, much celebrated for his vigilance, industry, capacity, even for the strict execution of justice in that unlimited command, which he possessed in Ireland. He was observed to be inflexible in all his purposes ; and it was believed by many, that he was animated with a sincere and passionate love for liberty, and never could have been induced, by any motive, to submit to the smallest appearance of regal government."

If men transmit to their posterity moral and intellectual as they do physical qualities, the subject of this memoir bore a strong family likeness to the stern Republican.

In a letter to Judge Iredell from his brother, the Rev. Arthur Iredell, from Newhaven, Sussex, England, dated July 3d, 1792, he says:

"I inclose you a card with Tom's Arms, as I received them from the Herald office. Removing the star between the quarterings, and in the bend of the arm, they will be yours, who, as the eldest of our family, bear them without any distinguishing addition. Our paternal ancestors had not taken the pains, or put themselves to the expense of *buying a coat*. They had of late, at least, used, as in your seal, the arms of *Ireton*, to which, though that is possible, I could discover no right. I therefore thought it right to get a grant of *confirmation* of those arms, with the addition only of a sword between the bendlets, to the descendants of our grandfather Iredell. The Macartney arms we are entitled to quarter; our grandmother, in failure of her brothers, and their issue, having the right of a co-heiress to them. I mean some time or other to record our little pedigree, when I can get at dates, &c. Pray gather as much as you can from our mother about her family. Did not McCulloh once tell you he had a pedigree as long as Cadwallader's? By the by you are entitled to the McCulloh and Ferguson Arms, if I could send them to you; but the Ulster King at Arms in Ireland has been written to in vain. After all, arms in America may be treated with as much contempt as in France. I am sure you will pardon me if they are."

Whether the connection with Ireton be true or not, is of little consequence. Iredell was as illustrious in North Carolina for devotion to Republicanism, as Ireton in his native land; and still more remarkable for amiable qualities, learning and genius.

The American representative of the Iredells placed but slight value upon coats of arms as conferring distinction; yet the following curious table is in his handwriting,—one of the instances of that precision and laborious habit which will fully appear hereafter.

"*The Genealogy of James McCulloch, Esq., of Grogan, from Sir Cullo O'Niel, first Laird of Myrton in Scotland, who was a son of the family of Claneboys, in Ireland.*

"James McCulloch, of Grogan, son of William McCulloch, Esq., of Brandalstown, son of Alexander Laird of Myrton, son of Simon Laird of Myrton, son of Henry of Killerar, and Margaret of Myrton, which Henry was son-in-law of Sir Alexander Laird of Myrton, son of Sir Eleseus Laird of Myrton, son of Sir Norman Laird of Myrton, son of Sir Alexander Laird of Myrton, son of Sir Gulfred or Godfrey Laird of Myrton (who assumed the surname of McCullo) son of Sir Cullo O'Niel, first Laird of Myrton.

"MEMOIRS RELATIVE TO THE HOUSE OF MYRTON.

"About the beginning of the fourteenth century, the Irish, being desirous to shake off the English yoke, invited Robert de Bruce, King of Scotland, to assist them in their intended enterprise, and in case of success, determined to make Edward de Bruce King of Ireland.

"Edward de Bruce, in consequence thereof, landed in the North of Ireland at the head of 6,000 veteran Scots soldiers, in the year 1315, and drove the English out of Ulster the first campaign; having defeated them in several engagements,—and possessed himself of Carrick-fergus, Connor, and other places of importance. He then marched his army through Ireland several times, and forced the English into their strongholds and fortified places; but always returned to Ulster to take up his winter quarters.

"Edward de Bruce, about the year 1316, preferred Cullo O'Neil to be Captain of horse in his army. Robert de Bruce, King of Scotland, came to Ireland with reinforcements to his brother Edward, whose army was then near Dundalk, and King Robert marched his forces near Newry, in order to join him; but the English having received considerable reinforcements from England and France, with several gentlemen volunteers under Bermingham Earl of Lowth, in a manner surprised Edward de Bruce near Dundalk, who could not be prevailed on to quit his post, and to retreat to his brother, King Robert's army, though his little army was greatly diminished by the fatigues of the preceding campaign, and the English army was treble their number; but would at all events give them battle. The action happened in the month of October, 1317, and the English forced the centre of Edward de Bruce's army, who, with the assistance of his guards, endeavoring to stop their progress, was killed by one of the gentlemen volunteers named Malpass, under the command of Sir Walter Larpulk; Captain Cullo O'Neil then killed Malpass, and recovered and brought off Edward de Bruce's sword, and made his retreat to the King of Scotland's army. King Robert retreated to Connor, where he wintered his army, and quitted all his brother's posts in Ireland, and carried back his army to Scotland the following spring.

"Captain Cullo O'Neil, and many other Irish officers of Edward de Bruce's army, went with King Robert de Bruce to Scotland, who knighted Captain Cullo O'Neil, and preferred him to be his standard-bearer and secretary of state; and gave Sir Cullo O'Neil lands in Lorn, as likewise the lands of Myrton and Achawan, which comprehend Killerar and Ardwell in Galloway. Sir Cullo's charter is dated at Dunstaffnage, holding in fee blank form, the reddendo being a rose to the king to smell at when he comes to Myrton. Sir Cullo O'Neil died in the year 1331, and left his estate of Myrton and other lands in Galloway to his eldest son Sir Godfrey, who assumed the surname of McCullo, and Sir Godfrey McCullo had his charter renewed at Perth in the year 1332, by David de Bruce, then king of Scotland. Sir Godfrey McCullo died in the year 1358, and was succeeded by his eldest son Sir Alexander McCullo, who died in the year 1399, and was succeeded by his eldest son Sir Norman McCullo, who had his charter renewed at Rothsay in the year 1400, by Robert the Third, king of Scotland, and was knighted in 1429 by King James, and died in 1445, and was succeeded by his eldest son Sir Eleseus McCullo, who died about the year 1448, and was succeeded by his eldest son Sir Alexander McCullo, who died about the year 1524, without issue male; and was succeeded by his son-in-law Henry McCulloch of Killerar and Margaret his daughter (which Henry was descended from Thomas, second son of Sir Norman McCullo), who got their charter renewed by King James the Fifth in the year 1525, and died about the year 1561, and was succeeded by their eldest son Simon McCulloch, who got his charter renewed by Queen Mary, daughter of James the Fifth, and died in the year 1592, and was succeeded by his eldest son William McCulloch, who died about the year ——, and was succeeded by his eldest son Alexander McCulloch, who, finding his estate much embarrassed by family debts, borrowed some large sum of money from a Doctor McCulloch in London, the repayment of which he secured by heritable bonds, and put his estate of Myrton &c. into the hands of his brother-in-law, John McCulloch Laird of Ardwell, designing that the rents thereof should clear his debts,—and after having fixed his affairs in such manner, Laird Alexander came to Ireland with his family to Sir Henry O'Neil, who gave him lands near the main water, where he resided until the time of his death, which happened in the year 1643, and was succeeded by his eldest son, William McCulloch, Esq. of Brandalston, who died in the year —— and left two sons, to wit, James of Grogan and Henry of Brandalston. John Laird of Ardwell turned out a bad trustee to Laird Alexander and his family, having bought up for his own use all the old family debts, and heritable bonds affecting Myrton estate, &c. and under color thereof, Ardwell and his family continued possessors of Laird Alexander's Scotch estates,—and had a son named Alexander who was knighted by King Charles the Second. But, how William of Brandalston came to submit to such frauds, I have not been able to trace.

"The Genealogy and Memoirs of the House of Myrton herein contained, I transcribed from an old manuscript, which I found among my father's papers; but made small alterations in the diction of the Memoirs, but none in respect to facts.   J. McC.

"October 24, 1767.

"N. B. The manuscript is not attested by any persons, but I believe the contents to be true.

"Mem. The above is a copy of a transcript of the original Memoirs, in the handwriting of James McCulloh Esq. of Camdey, and now in the possession of Henry Eustace McCulloh, Esq. who favored me with a sight of it.   J. I.

"N. Carolina, June 9, 1772."

"James of Grogan, the last mentioned of that name in the foregoing Genealogy, had among other children the three following—William, James, Henry, and a daughter married to Charles Macartney, Esq. of Dublin. William had issue, James, (now of Camdey, near Dundalk in Ireland, in whose possession the Memoirs are, and from whom the copy referred to was obtained,) who is yet a bachelor. William, a merchant in Dublin, who is now a widower. By his wife (whose name was Coleman), he had three children, now living,—two daughters and a son—Henry, (late Secretary of this Province), two of whose daughters are now living there.

"James married Mary, the daughter of James Ferguson, M.D., of Belfast in Ireland, by whom he had issue two daughters, Margaret and Jane. Margaret was married on the 1st August, 1750, to Mr. Francis Iredell merchant in Bristol, a son of the Rev. Mr. Iredell of Dublin. Their issue is as follows:—

James, born 5th October, . . . 1751 (N. S)
Francis, born 21st December, . . 1752
Charles, born 1756
Arthur, born 1758
Thomas, born 8th December, . . 1761

FAC SIMILE OF MSS OF JUDGE IREDELL

To the Honorable the General Assembly of the State of North Carolina

The Memorial of James Iredell one of the subjects of the said State, on behalf of Henry Eustace McCulloh Esquire, at present non-resident out of the same —

Humbly sheweth,

That Henry McCulloh Esquire, father of the said Henry Eustace McCulloh did many years past purchase and settle at a very great expence a large tract of Land in the back-parts of this State, to the extreme impoverishment and distress of his private fortune and with the distant and precarious hope of its proving advantageous to his Posterity, by means at the same time highly conducive to the well-being and prosperity of this Country.

"Besides these, who are now living, they had three sons and a daughter who died—one son, named Thomas, born between Francis and Charles; a daughter named Mary, born between Arthur and Thomas; and two sons, named William and Henry, youngest of all. The Rev. Mr. Francis Iredell married Eleanor, the daughter of ——— Macartney, Esq., who had two brothers, one named ———, a Judge in the King's Bench (and afterwards in the Common Pleas) in Ireland, and another named ———, father of ———, who was the father of Sir George Macartney, and two other children, daughters. The brothers and sisters of Eleanor were, James, a merchant in Bristol, never married, who died in April, 1770; Charles, a merchant in Dublin, who married a daughter of James McCulloch, Esq., of Grogan, and by whom he had several children, one only of which is living, Margaret Macartney. He died in or about the year 1750.

"Isabella, the sister of Eleanor, was married, and died 26th December, 1765. The issue of Judge Macartney was only one son, named James, who married, and had two sons and four daughters; his two sons and one daughter died in his lifetime, so that his estate, which was £6,000 a year, descended to his three daughters, one of which only is married, whose husband's name is Greville, and the issue of his deceased daughter, who was married to William Henry Lyttelton, Esq., brother of Lord Lyttelton, and many years Governor of Jamaica, by whom she had three children.

"Jane, the other daughter of James McCulloch, Esq., was never married, and lives with her mother, in Belfast.

"Mr. Francis Iredell has one brother, Thomas, living in Jamaica, never married.

"I forgot to mention that James McCulloch, Esq., of Grogan, had, among many other children by a first wife, a daughter married to ——— McCulloch, a Scotchman, who had issue Alexander McCulloch, Esq., of Halifax County, in North Carolina, and who is first cousin by half blood to James and William McCulloch in Ireland, Mrs. Iredell, Miss Macartney, and Henry Eustace McCulloch, the only surviving child of Henry McCulloch, Esq., the brother of William and James, and Mrs. Macartney, by the whole blood."

Mr. Francis Iredell, of Bristol, being stricken with paralysis, and unable to supervise his business, was soon reduced to poverty.

However we may declaim about the heartlessness of the world, no man is ever utterly abandoned by his kind. God has established for us a law of mutual dependence; and his kind providence has so ordered that even the most unprincipled and vicious are not entirely friendless in their hour of punishment, or remorse, or wretchedness. However monstrous the outcast may be, in some one human heart the spark of charity will kindle into flame at the sight of his misery. Verily he "tempers the wind to the shorn lamb;" and "in his wrath forgets not mercy."

The Iredell family, in their day of prosperity, had not repelled by arrogance; but had conciliated friendship by amenity of manner and amiability of temper. When adversity assailed, and the wreck of their fortunes floated at the mercy of the blast, they were not without support and succor.

Many stepped forward to their aid, with tender concern, to offer counsel and shelter. They were allied by blood to Sir George Macartney, the Earl of Wigton, the Fergusons and McCullohs, and by marriage to Gov. Lyttelton*—all people of rank and consideration. Many others of humbler social position extended to them the warmest sympathy. The most powerful of their connections from influence and talent, was Sir George Macartney. This gentleman was created an Irish baron in 1776; in 1785, declared Governor-General of Bengal; in 1792, was advanced to the dignity of an Earl, and selected as the Ambassador Extraordinary of Great Britain to the Emperor of China. He married Jane, daughter of the Earl of Bute.† Though from early manhood warmly sustained by the family of Lord Holland, he was chiefly indebted for his elevation to his own merit. It must be acknowledged that he possessed virtues which qualified him for the most eminent situation in the service of his country. By his active agency, as soon as Mr. Francis Iredell so far recovered from his severe illness as to be capable of business, he received some small appointment under the Crown that nearly sufficed for his modest wants; and in a few years three of his sons were indebted to the kind offices of the same relation for official positions.

Mr. Henry McCulloh was the grand-uncle of the subject of this memoir. He and his son, Henry Eustace McCulloh, especially, were destined to shape the career and determine the character of the boy. The former, at a very early period, became connected with the Province of North Carolina. He had been Secretary of the Province, and had been appointed his Majesty's surveyor, inspector, and comptroller of the revenue and grants of

* Afterwards Lord Westcote; his first wife was Mary, daughter of James Macartney, of Longford, Ireland.
† Lempriere.

land; and speculated largely in crown lands with a view of paying for them by importing settlers.* It is said that he obtained, by fraud, grants for about one million of acres of land. It is further said, that subsequently the son, Henry Eustace McCulloh, settled his father's accounts with the Crown with so much tact and address, as to retain sixty-four thousand four hundred well-selected acres, without the payment of a single dollar. Upon what authority this statement is based is not known. It is so improbable that I cannot but doubt. If McCulloh sought a settlement "propris motu," his action implied a degree of honesty inconsistent with fraud. If he was prosecuted by the Crown, it is incredible that in the latter half of the eighteenth century, the era of Hardwicke and Mansfield, Johnson and Burke, the law-officers of the King should have so compounded rascality.† The charge is rebutted by the fact that Henry McCulloh always resided within reach of the English courts; and further, by the general affection and regard cherished for him by his friends and relatives. None are such accurate judges of character as those most intimate with a man—those brought into frequent contact with him, and enjoying a daily intercourse. About the year 1736, Henry McCulloh began to introduce emigrants from Ireland to occupy his lands, and soon the number swelled to between three and four hundred. They settled at first in the counties of Duplin and Bladen, but gradually spread westward. The fortune of the elder McCulloh, which was large, was greatly embarrassed by this enterprise, as he furnished the settlers the means of crossing the Atlantic. He died in the year 1778.

Henry Eustace McCulloh, after the usual term at the Inner Temple, was regularly called to the bar. He came to North Carolina about the year 1761,‡ and resided here constantly until the year 1767, during which time he was chiefly occupied as agent for his father, and served as a member of Governor Dobbs' Council. He was Collector of the Customs for Port Roanoke for many years, and for a long time had also the honor of representing the Province at the several Boards in England, his father attending to this business while he was absent in America. Before I dismiss him for the present, it may be well to trace his history to the end, though the chronology of the narrative be violated. He returned to England in 1767; but came again to North Carolina in 1772, where he remained until June, 1773,

* Life of Caldwell, Williamson's Hist. N. C.
† McCulloh's affairs with the Crown were finally settled, to McCulloh's satisfaction, before the King in Council.—Letter from M. to Iredell.
‡ McCulloh's Memorial to General Assembly.

when he once more returned to England. Death having removed all of his father's children, but himself, he obtained from him, in 1772, a conveyance of all his property here. He was a man of more than ordinary ability and culture; cunning, rather than wise. Of loose morals, with a decent regard for appearances, he veiled his vices from the public eye. He had no instrumentality in the appointment of young Iredell to office in America; but knowing him to be a youth of great promise, he employed all his arts to win his confidence and secure his subservience to his interests. He not only devolved on him all the duties of his collectorship, but employed him as agent to transact his private business. Through the agency of Mr. Iredell, he was enabled to enjoy, uninterrupted for long periods, the pleasures of a London life. He made Mr. Iredell no compensation for his services. Time after time he would hint to him that he intended making him his heir. Often he would amuse him with the hope that he would resign his office in his favor; but always found a ready excuse to evade the performance of his promise. His sagacity early detected the small cloud, surcharged with the thunders of the revolution, that was destined to spread over the continent. It was not until thus warned that he resigned his office. His property was confiscated by the State. After this loss, his letters to Mr. Iredell became abject and piteous. The latter, true to the generous instincts of his nature, forgiving McCulloh's errors, made, without success, strenuous efforts to procure his pardon and the restoration of his estates. The services he rendered him were manifold and valuable. At the close of the war, and after he had abandoned all hope of recovering his American lands, with shattered fortunes, but still with an income of twelve hundred guineas per annum, McCulloh retired to a country-seat in the vicinity of London, where he died in the year ———, as false to his kinsman in death as he had been in life.

Mr. Francis Iredell had a brother, Mr. Thomas Iredell, who was unmarried, and resided on a large estate that he owned in the island of Jamaica. He was too remote to render prompt succor to his brother in his misfortunes. He was embarrassed at that juncture by the failure of several successive crops. Prudent, industrious and economical, and forgetful of the maxim, "bis dat qui cito dat," he thought only of repairing his losses. He was a man of consideration in Jamaica, and more than once thought of for the post of Governor. James Iredell, in case of his death without issue, would have been his heir-at-law. He was first in his affection. Mr. Thomas Iredell was a high-churchman, and a stanch adherent of the Tory Government. He was intelligent, and well educated; but arrogant, of violent prejudices, impracticable. The part that James played in the American Revolution so excited his displeasure, that he thenceforth declined all intercourse with him, and when he died, left the whole of his estate to a younger brother. The following letters shed much light on the situation, difficulties and prospects of the family.

TREMBLAY, Feb. 10, 1767.

MY DEAR YOUNG FRIEND:—I have sent by the bearer a box of books belonging to you or your brothers. My compliments to your papa and mamma. They and theirs have my best wishes. Fear not; but trust in God, and he will take care of you all. Make him your friend, and your portion will yet be a happy one. Send me word if you can, what ships are to sail soon for (Ireland) Dublin. I want to send letters thither.

Believe me, dear Jemmy,
Your truly affectionate friend,
D. LEWIS.*

"Non, si male nunc, et olim sic erit."—HORAT. Lib. 2, Odes, 11.
"Tho' now 'tis cloudy, 'twill clear up again."—NORRIS.

MASTER JAMES IREDELL, Bristol.

LONDON, 5th March, 1767.

MY DEAR JEMMY:—I received your letter dated the 28th of February, and have been very sensibly affected by your father's misfortunes; the ill state of health he labors under, and the melancholy prospect there is for his family. What adds to my concern is, that I am so circumstanced, that it is really not in my power, at present, to assist him. Please God my son arrives in time, I shall consult with him what may be proper to be done for you, as it would give me great pleasure to put you in a road to provide for yourself. In the meantime, if you do not go to Jamaica (which I think will be no bad scheme), I would have you endeavor to get into some counting-house or office, in order to keep you employed in some business or other. Mrs. McCulloh recovers slowly. She is not yet able to walk. She joins me in her love to your father, mother, and all the family.

May God in his mercy grant you relief.

I am, dr. James,
Your affectionate friend and servant,
HENRY McCULLOH.

MR. JAMES IREDELL, Bristol.

* Mr. Iredell's Teacher.

DEAR JAMES:—I had the pleasure of receiving yours last night, when I returned from Mr. McCartney's, where I had dined, and spent the evening. I almost wished I had not been engaged there, as Mr. Garrick played last night, and the Royal Family was there. I believe, had I been sure of a place, I should certainly have tried to make an elopement; but I heard a lady say she had sent three times to the house, and could not get a place in any part of it; so I thought I had better be content where I was sure of meeting good company. We had a private concert and cards there. The Governor* dined with us. We talked a good deal about your uncle and all of you. The Governor tells me he is soon going to Portugal. Mr. Cust tells me in his letter, that he is so taken up that he can't attend to the arbitration, unless it can be deferred till June—so we must get somebody else. I am very glad to hear your father is so much better. God grant he may soon get entirely the better of his disorder. Your account of poor Mr. Bon's misfortune gave me great concern; but you don't tell me whether it's for a large sum or not, or whether he had met with any losses lately to bring it on. I pity Mrs. B. from my heart, as I think she seems to be in a very weak state of health, and this must be a great shock to her. Mrs. Parry, who is in town, insists on my dining with her to-day. She calls on me in her coach to take me first an airing in Hyde Park, and in the evening to the Opera. I am sure I am greatly obliged to her. My Aunt McCulloh seems to me to be in a very bad way. Give my duty to my uncle, and love to your papa and mamma, and believe me to be, dear James, your ever affectionate kinswoman,
MARGARET MACARTNEY.

KING'S SQUARE COURT, Soho, March 17, 1767.

P. S.—I had almost forgot to tell you that Miss Macartney broke her right arm about four months ago. I think that misfortune incident to the family. Love to all inquiring friends.

MASTER JAMES IREDELL,
Queen Square, Bristol.

KING'S SQUARE COURT, SOH .

I received, my dear James, your letter Saturday night; and yesterday went to my uncle in the morning instead of going to church, to ask his advice. He seems to think it a very good scheme, if at the Wells, as my cousin and all of us have a large acquaintance, especially amongst the Irish. He thinks

* Sir George Macartney.

that the house of Mrs. Wilcox, corner of Dowry Square, would be a good one, and says that he will write to her about it. He makes no doubt but that she will let you have it for little or nothing the first year by way of trial. He intends writing this week if he can, or the beginning of next week, and if Mrs. Wilcox likes the proposal she will speak to you. I have been kept at home these two days in expectation of Mr. Vesey. Last Friday he sent me a note to let me know he would wait on me on Saturday about 12 o'clock. I stayed at home till half-past five in the afternoon; but he neither came nor sent any apology—which I think very rude—nor have I heard any thing of him since. I have more hopes than ever of the Arbitration, but must see Mr. Vesey before the day is fixed. I spent the evening Friday, in Hanover Square, and am going there this evening. They sent their coach for me Friday, and I am to have it again to-night. I think their life seems wrapt up in Master Lyttleton. He is a very fine boy, three and a half years old. The Governor did me the honor of calling on me one morning last week, but I was just gone out to dine at Mrs. Parry's. I was sorry I had not seen him. Lady Rodney came from Greenwich on purpose to see me last Saturday. She insisted on my dining with her. Yesterday, accordingly, I went, and spent a very agreeable day. Thursday I saw Mr. Garrick play Ranger in the Suspicious Husband, and Saturday saw Mrs. Pritchard in Lady Macbeth for her own benefit. Thus you see in what manner I spend my time; but yet you have not the least reason to fear my having any reluctance to return to Bristol, for when I am there I can make myself happy in entertaining my friends with what I have seen; as much as I am at present in the real enjoyment of them; and that's saying a great deal, considering the many inducements I have to like this place. And now I must tell you, sir, that you are much obliged to me for this long letter, whatever you may think of it, for I refused dining this day with Mrs. Parry because I would not delay answering yours. I am glad to hear your father is much better. Give my love to him and your mamma. Tell her to take a little more care of her health; and that I hope she will live to enjoy many more years of happiness. Tell her also I have bought a pair of candlesticks, which, if she likes them and the terms, are for her—if not I will keep them myself. I am, my dear James, with duty and love where due,
Yours most affectionately,
March 13th, 1767. MARGARET MACARTNEY.

Call on the Miss Gresleys, and give my love to them. I wrote my uncle this post.

DUBLIN, 25th April, 1767.

DEAR COUSIN:—I received your favor of the 7th inst., and also your father's of the 19th of February, inclosing a copy of a letter from him to your uncle in Jamaica, which, according to your desire, was forwarded to your grandmother. I am persuaded it is needless for me to assure you that the unhappy situation of your family gives me the deepest affliction. I sincerely congratulate you on the prospect of your father's recovery from his very distressing indisposition. In consequence of your desire, I sent your letter to my brother, which he has returned to me. We join in thinking that the very best method that could be taken by every branch of your family, would be to get some discreet person of your Uncle Macartney's acquaintance (chosen by general consent) to open up to him the present situation of his affairs with every particular circumstance relating thereto, at such time as he is clearheaded—if any such time there is—and leave him to order his own affairs in such manner as may seem best to him, in their present circumstances. This we think would be the best way to prevent animosity and contention hereafter. I showed your letter to Mr. and Mrs. Paumier as desired. Please present my affectionate compliments to all friends with you. I am, dear cousin,
Yours very affectionately,
WILLIAM McCULLOH.

KING-SQUARE COURT, SOHO, 11 Sept. 1767.

DEAR SIR,—I have your favor of the 14th. An unexpected prospect of bringing on our affair before the King in Council, this month, agreeably detains my father and myself here, and we do not now imagine we shall see our friends your way till the beginning of next. The delay is certainly a disappointment, but business of this kind must be watched. My father desires me to inform you that you must for the present, at least, give up your hopes of going to India, as he finds every vacancy long filled, and the greatest interest necessary. You may assure yourself he has it much at heart to give you a good opening into life, and he directs me to inform you that he has thought of the Comptroller of the Customs' place at Newbern, in North Carolina, for you. It is an office to be created, none having been yet appointed,—he had reserved it in view for a near friend in Carolina, but his desires to serve you preponderate with him. The method of application he proposes is, that you make friends with some of the managers of the Bristol election to recommend you to my

Lord Clare, and to name the manner proposed; and if that is done, my father thinks you need not fear success. The salary paid here is £30 a year, which it is proposed your father should receive for his use; to this I am sure no objection can arise from you. The fees may amount to near £100 per annum now, a genteel office, easy, though requiring residence. You may at first view object to the country, but permit me to assure you life may be passed there very happily, without too great an exercise of philosophy: another thing is, that if your genius leads to the bar or trade—the first especially, you may promise yourself a fair field for success, as it is a most growing country. Add to this, that the natural weight which my father's property and my connections give us there, shall be of service to you in case this event takes place. You will inform us of the steps you take. Please to make our kind respects to Mrs. Wilcocks, and inform her of the alteration in our plan. Be so kind also as to see Miss Macartney, and to tender her my compliments and her uncle's affectionate remembrance.

My father joins me in affectionate compliments to your father and mother. I am, dear sir,

Your most assured humble servant,
HENRY E. McCULLOH.

You must conceal your age and the value of the employment from Lord Clare. Your friends may say it is worth about £50 per annum. Your success depends on being properly recommended to him.

LONDON, 17th Nov. 1767.

DEAR JAMES,—I did not imagine I would be near three months in London without hearing oftener than once from you. I have wrote you twice, but it is true I should have done so oftener to make good my promise,—but do assure you, since my arrival here, the greater part of my time has been taken up in a constant series of business which has prevented my writing to many friends. However, Mr. Jem (excuse the term) you can't plead this excuse—therefore I take it rather unkind your not letting me hear oftener from you, as you must have known from Mr. Hunter of my being in London. You will say I have made a long stay here. I must say so also; but yet London is so agreeable a place, that the time has appeared very short. However, I have at length fixed upon leaving this to-morrow by way of Chester, in company with my old school-fellow, Dick Weld. Some little time ago I was in hopes of having it in my power to return by Bristol; but now I am obliged to be in Ireland immediately, therefore must rest satisfied until another favorable opportunity offers for seeing my good friends at B———l. You will of course expect some little description of London, but time will not allow my saying any thing at present. When I get to Greenmount, and get my secretary settled,—after all fatigue and hurry—will then endeavor to give you some little entertainment. If I have not the pleasure of seeing you before you depart for the Eastern world, I heartily wish all possible success and happiness, and that you may in time prove a second Nabob. I shall expect to hear from you, without fail, very shortly. Let me know your schemes, and what you have in view. Direct to me at Antrim. My best wishes and respects to your father and mother, and all the little ones. My compliments to Miss Macartney. I wish her all happiness, whether in the married or single state. I must conclude with my best wishes for your welfare.

Dear James, your most affectionate friend, &c.,
SKEFFINGTON THOMPSON.

DEAR COUSIN:—I received both your favors of the 11th of December and 25th of January. The letters which you mention were all properly forwarded and delivered. I would have answered you much sooner in regard to Mrs. Paumier; but she and Mr. Paumier have been in the County of Fermanagh, at Mr. Leslie's, since the middle of September. As they were expected home before Christmas, I delayed writing till I could let you know particularly how she was. She and Mr. Paumier came to town a few days ago. They are both now in good health and spirits. They were delayed in the country by Mr. Paumier's being ill with the gout and cold, and she with the rheumatism. Mr. Crawford left this yesterday for London. My brother continues at Drogheda school, and is very well. My dada and sister join in affectionate compliments to all friends with you. I am, dear cousin, Your very affectionate humble servant,

ANN McCULLOH.
DUBLIN, 8th February, 1768.

KINGS SQUARE COURT, SOHO, 3d March, 1768.

DEAR SIR:—I can readily imagine that our long silence relative to Jemmy's affair, has long ago induced you to think our applications unsuccessful. The friendships of this life consist too much of profession and appearance; but the motives which influenced my father, were not to be discouraged by the difficulties he met with. The office which was intended for Jemmy, would have been obtained had not an unexpected engagement to Governor Tryon interfered. This disappointment gave us great uneasiness, but the Collection falling vacant, application was made for that, and there also rendered useless from the same cause,—a prior engagement. Thus disappointed, a third essay was made, which was to get Jemmy appointed Comptroller of the Customs at Port Roanoake (Edenton) in the place of the late Comptroller preferred; and this, we have the great pleasure to acquaint you, has succeeded. *The warrant for his appointment issued the 29th ult.*, and is now in our hands. I can but heartily congratulate you on this event, as I know nothing (his age &c. considered) which could have been wished more happy. The office is genteel, requires little or no duty, so that he will have time to apply himself to business; it is worth upwards of £100 sterling a year. His situation will be in the most agreeable part of the province, in the midst of my friends and connections, and consequently, in the way of my advancing happily his opening into life, of which (if he properly co-operates) his prospects are most fair and happy. He cannot, unless it is greatly his own fault, miss of doing extremely well, and we are the more pleased, as it may put him in a situation to be of the greatest service to you all. We have been at some expenses in this matter, and very willingly, and shall take upon us the care of providing the securities. I don't know but I may see Bristol soon. If I should be disappointed, I will write you what my father advises as to the time of Jemmy's going over. In the mean time, I think you had better use your interest with your friends at your custom-house to permit Jemmy to attend, and make himself acquainted with the nature of his office. It is with great cheerfulness we acquaint you, that you are only obliged to us in the above transactions for our kindest wishes, and our ready attention to, and information of circumstances. Sir George Macartney's behavior upon the occasion has been extremely kind and generous. He had the goodness to apply to the Duke of Grafton, in person; and it is to him, and his interest alone, you are indebted for this appointment. It is but strict justice to him, to mention also, that he applied in the two instances before mentioned. This attention and generous exertion of interest reflects great honor on him, and justly demands your most grateful sentiments. My father advises that you write to Sir George upon the subject, informing him that we have acquainted you of Jemmy's appointment, and that this happy alteration in your prospects is entirely owing to him. You may inclose the letter open to me, to seal and deliver; though if we should conceive it improper in point of expression, we shall use the kind right of friendship in advising you of it. I mentioned in a letter I wrote some time ago to Miss Macartney, that our affair was happily settled. Our doubts and uncertainties as to Jemmy's affair, was the reason I did not write you before. I write this in great haste, and will beg your excuse for my not going further than to mention our hopes that you have been all well. My father joins me in our kindest love to you, Cousin Peggy, and the boys. I am sorry to say he has been very unwell for some days, and still continues so. I shall expect the pleasure of hearing from you soon. By my next it is probable I may come to some determination as to my trip to Bristol. I will beg your care of the inclosed. Wishing you and yours every manner of happiness,

I am, dear cousin,
Your affectionate humble servant,
HENRY E. McCULLOH.
MR. FRANCIS IREDELL.

BELFAST, April 23d, 1768.

MY DEAREST JEMMY:—I received your letter of the 17th of March last Sunday, which gave your aunt and myself unspeakable pleasure. To hear that you were so happily provided for, gives us very great joy. We are all under great obligations to Sir George Macartney, your good uncle, and his son, who have all behaved so generously and friendly to you. I hope you will always bear a grateful sense of their favors and goodness to you, and behave yourself suitably, to deserve the continuance of them. I beg, my dear, you may be careful what company you take up with, and be directed by your cousin in every thing, who knows the province and the people. I beg you may take care of your health. I would be glad to know when your cousin intends going over; it had been your great advantage had you gone with him.

I am glad that your father has got his deliverance, and that your mamma and he are well. I spoke several times to Mr. Jones about Raeney, but he can get no satisfactory answer from him; always puts him off with excuses. I don't know what can be done with him. I am glad that Mrs. Agnew sent the money. I wish the letter she wrote to you had been sent over, wherein she recollected that it had not been paid. Mr. Agnew's son intends going to Bristol, Bath and London soon, in company with his Aunt Stewart and her daughter, who lives in Dublin. He is very well; but it is thought he will be the better to travel, and not to stay too much at Killwaughter. I hope you will write me when you go to Carolina. I will pay for a letter from you with great pleasure. May God Almighty bless and direct you in all your ways. I hope, my dear, you won't forget to pray to God daily; acknowledge Him, and he will direct you in all your ways. My blessing to my son and daughter, and all your brothers. Your aunt sends her love, and wishes you a good voyage and all manner of prosperity, which we will not neglect to pray for, and am, my dearest Jemmy,

Your most affectionate grandmamma,
MARY McCULLOH.

P. S.—Mr. Jemison told me of a brig going to Bristol, which returns here. I hope your mamma or Frank will write by her. He sends this letter under cover to Mr. Hunter, who will let you know when the brig returns. I would be glad to know if the butter was good. There is an affair which has happened this week which has given real concern to a great many. Poor Mr. William Haven has been obliged to stop payment. It is talked that he is in great debt, and been feared for some time, though I knew nothing of it. I shall long greatly for a letter, in hopes to hear how all affairs are. The sloop is ready, just waiting for a fair wind.

Mr. JAMES IREDELL, Bristol.

The grandson of a clergyman, and educated in the tenets of the Church, James Iredell was early imbued with a sense of religion. The following essay, found amongst his papers, and endorsed "written when I was very young," evinces the strength of his conviction:—

Nothing is a stronger argument of the profligacy and degeneracy of the present age, than the general turn to infidelity which universally prevails. Strange! that in an affair of so great importance as religion confessedly is, any should be so weak as to conceive a prejudice against it, without giving it that impartial examination which is due to *every* object of speculation, and which religion more particularly claims, as including within itself every thing of moment to our present and future happiness. The man who is singular enough to profess a value for religion, is too frequently considered as a *morose*, or an *unreflecting* being, whose conduct is unsocial, or whose principles are unsound,—adopted from education, and preserved by prejudice. But this is not the rational way of condemning opinions. It does not follow that every thing we receive from education is wrong; nor that because we still continue to revere truths our fathers taught us to revere, that this must be the effect of prejudice. As no one will pretend to deny, it is not necessary for me to prove, that as our judgments ripen, we become gradually capable of thinking for ourselves,—and of confirming, or condemning, former opinions. Reason faithfully exerted will seldom lead us astray; for if truth be the only object of our inquiry, it will be indifferent to us where we find it. I am not an advocate for carelessly receiving every thing upon trust—such an adoption of principles is irrational as well as infirm; but when we examine, let us do it with all the caution of a confined capacity,—let us be content with that proof which the nature of the thing will only admit of; but let us not reject the whole of a system of the purest principles of practice, and the highest objects of belief, because we may sometimes meet with a difficulty our reason cannot thoroughly comprehend, considering that many things in this natural world are equally amazing and incomprehensible. If that part we do understand conveys to us the utmost purity of thought, and teaches us the most rational sentiments, though some part of revelation may seem difficult and mysterious, yet if it has nothing directly contradictory to the dictates of reason, let us pass it by with awful reverence, supposing our capacities too limited to comprehend it, and resolve it into the wisdom of the Almighty, whose ways are above our ways, and past finding out. If we strongly possess ourselves with the divinity, the rationality, and the moral excellence of its *internal* evidence, we need fear very little from *external* shocks. We shall not easily believe, that a person born of low parents, and meanly educated, could early form a plan so consistently, so extraordinarily, and (if we reject the divinity of his mission) so *impiously* carried on, that his conduct should be entirely irreproachable, his life a pattern of the most exalted morality,—and yet that his designs should be blasphemous to his God, and an imposition upon all mankind; that he should give up every prospect of happiness, and subject himself to every hardship of life; that he should expose himself to persecution, hatred and revenge; that he should set up in opposition to opinions the most favored, and to practices the most indulged; that he should preach doctrines of the sublimest virtue; and the only objects of his attack should be, unworthy sentiments of religion, and the immoral lives of men,—enforcing every precept with his own example, and for what end? can you, can I, can any one believe it was for any other end than the declared one, the glory of God and the good of mankind; and that the many miracles he performed, and truths (hitherto unthought of or unknown) he related, confirm him in the divinity of his mission. Oh! easy, unpardonable credulity! that any one can believe such a man, with such designs—can be an impostor. Whether is it more rational to believe, that a religion every way worthy of God for its author, revealing truths which could not be discovered by the most learned Pagan philosophers, inculcating doctrines whose sublimity their theology never reached, and attested by miracles which nothing less than Divine power could enable to perform, was really introduced from heaven, and had God for its author and support;—or that it was framed by a man who propagated it with a lie (its own doctrines strictly condemning the least deviation from truth), and that of the most horrid nature,—a lie against the God of truth—that he was not only an enthusiast himself, but made many others so; that he associated with him twelve poor illiterate men, whom he possessed with the same enthusiasm; that the miracles they wrought, where every suspicion of deceit must be precluded, was owing to the assistance of demons; that this enthusiasm caught many thousands, and in time millions, in this very belief, in opposition to their immediate interest in this world; and that though the whole powers of the earth were exerted in vain to crush it, yet it still spread with the most astonishing success; and after lives which had experienced every cruelty or persecution which the rod of power could inflict, enthusiasm still made them submit to deaths of ignominy and torture, and seal with their dying lips the sincerity of their profession; and lastly, that at this day, the Christian religion is professed by the greatest part of the most civilized in the world; and all this, the effect of an imposture carried on by deceit, and propagated by enthusiasm, bidding defiance to the outward repulses of kingdoms, and the most favorite inclinations of individuals. Is it possible that any man on earth can be so lost to reflection as to think—so immersed in sensuality as to wish—or so inclinable to scepticism as to believe—the Christian religion, under these circumstances (and they are all capable of proof), is an imposture?

For my part, I am free and ready enough to declare that I think the Christian religion is a Divine institution; and I pray to God that I may never forget the precepts of his religion, or suffer the appearance of an inconsistency in my principles and practice.

LONDON, 5th September, 1768.

DEAR JEMMY:—I received a letter from you on Saturday. I am glad to hear you are not likely to be delayed; as Mr. Reeves will not agree to what was proposed, let him take the ten guineas, out of the balance to be paid in on account of Campbell, or if that balance should be insufficient, let him draw on me for the difference, and the bill shall be duly answered. If he scruples taking your bill on me, apply to Mr. Spann for the cash, and give him a bill on me. It is true every disbursement is at this time very disagreeable to us, but this is absolutely expedient to complete the endeavors we have exerted for you; as to provisions, &c., I imagine you will easily contrive that.

I shall now (in much hurry) by way of journal, mention some of the steps you have to pursue. When you get to Boston, wait immediately on Mr. Fulton; deliver my letter, recommend yourself to his patronage, and urge him to assist you in procuring your deputation as soon as may be; if any questions arise concerning your age, insist you was 21 in May last. Deliver my letter to the Commissioners, and my father's memorials on which you are to obtain an order, which you will either deliver or forward to Messrs. Ancrum & Shaw when you get to Carolina. You will of course make it your business to see Murray: of him, get what money you will want for your necessary expenses, and the fees of your deputation; we expect you will not make any greater use of our letter of credit than absolutely necessary. See Mr. Stewart the Cashier-General, and endeavor to settle with him the easiest and quickest method of remitting your salary, £30 sterling per annum, to your father or mother at Bristol. I conceive a power of attorney might be given to Mr. Murray to receive and remit it for you; and I recommend, if possible, a settlement of this matter before you quit Boston: it may be remitted half-yearly. The moment you have settled all your necessary business, ship yourself on board the first vessel, bound for the northern part of North Carolina,—if none offering, —on any for Wilmington, or in the last choice, on any for Norfolk in Virginia. You will find you have letters of credit for every one of these places. You cannot but be sensible how much depends upon dispatch, and I hope you will not squander away in pleasure or amusement, a moment of your time. Write your friends from Boston, fully. You can agree with the vessel that carries you to Carolina, to take your pay there.

Suppose you arrived at Ocrocock Bar (North Carolina), endeavor to learn if the Governor is at Newbern. If he is, go up immediately there; carry your deputation, and qualify yourself before him; and then you may immediately proceed to Edenton, and take possession of your office; this would be a fortunate circumstance, and by no means omit informing yourself at the Bar. When at Newbern, make no use, nor deliver my letter to Haslaine, but apply yourself to one Williams, a merchant there (a Quaker), a particular friend of mine, who will supply you with what money you want, and show you every civility. If the Governor should not be at Newbern, proceed up to Edenton, deliver my letters, and be directed by Mr. Johnston, or Mr. Brownrigg, where the Governor is, and the best and quickest way to get to him; lose no time, and return immediately after, for your taking possession of the office. That once done, you may look about you, and endeavor to improve the introduction you have received from me. You will find a great many very worthy people; and the country in its disposition, extremely hospitable and kind to strangers. It is your business to endeavor to oblige all, and to list yourself of no faction either public or private. You will be very happy in an intimacy with Mr. and Mrs. Brownrigg. You will find the gentlemen of Edenton very agreeable; particularly cultivate the notice of Mr. Hewes. It is unnecessary to observe you should be obliging to Mr. Hardy, and look on him as your superior both in years and office. You know our intentions as to your situation with Mr. Johnston. If he takes you under his care, you will be very happy; and in that expectation, I need not enlarge on the course of your studies, or rules for your particular conduct. I hope you will always have both too much sense and too much pride, to disgrace the introduction you have, by keeping improper company. Your office will barely support you genteelly, for the present it is what should content you: you know it is intended as an opening for better things. (Indeed, my dear Jemmy,—when you reflect upon the past and the future,—you have great reason to be thankful to that Providence which has blessed the endeavors of your friends to serve you.) I would have you by all means board yourself, but in this Mr. Johnston will direct. I hope you will not have too much idle time on your hands, and that you do not wish it. You must apply yourself closely to the business of the Collector's office. I have wrote Mr. Hardy you would ease him of the laboring oar. Endeavor to make yourself master of the subject. Be ready ever to oblige and do the business of the vessels, but keep no company with the master. Your own prudence and caution can only improve the circumstances of your life; every thing depends upon your application and behavior, for four or five coming years, and when you consider the alternatives are either poverty, contempt, and repentance,—or prosperity, friends, comfort and ease,—I hope you will want no incentive to a propriety of exertion. I am duly sensible how strongly passion prompts at your time of life; but be certain, that if it should now prove too strong for your reflection, all is over with you. Avoid the first occasions of evil; for no man can say, thus far will I go, and no farther. But I must stop, else I shall moralize a letter into a sermon.

I have wrote your cousin Benjamin McCulloh to supply you with a horse: on this you can take many excursions which will, in all probability, make life both agreeable and healthy to you. You will take care to deliver the various letters from me, as you pass their routes. If you should not pass Halifax in going to the Governor, it is probable you will, about Christmas, make an excursion to see your relations and friends that way.

I expect you will write me once or twice a month, very fully, and send me all the information you can in my affairs. When you see Mr. Campbell, urge him to ship to some correspondent, such a cargo as will answer the bill protested; and inform Mr. Brownrigg, I have never heard of the bill from him, and I trust in his friendship, he has long ago provided for it: write me their answers. See to the care and disposal, if possible, of some furniture I left at Edenton. Get Messrs. Lowther & Co. to send me an account of the things sold, and if any opportunities offer of purchasing good bills that way, desire them to invest what office money they may have in hand, therein. Write me fully of every occurrence in which I may be concerned that way.

When you see Col. McCulloh, acquaint him the bill remitted me by Mr. Hamilton proves bad, that there is a necessity he exerts himself to put me in cash for his affair immediately. Tell Ben, I have not heard from him since March; urge him to remit me every farthing in his power; assure him the money I brought over is long since expended, and that I am now supported upon the credit of the remittances I am looking for from him; desire him to reflect I had above £2,500 sterling to pay away to Selwyn & Co.: desire him to write me often and fully of every thing he has done, and to give you a summary thereof, to transmit me; learn also what you can of what Mr. Frohock is and has been doing; whether he has remitted or wrote me, and do you write me fully of every particular.

Acquaint Ben I desire his endeavoring to receive all the hogs he possibly can from the people indebted to me in Orange and Granville, to drive into Virginia to be disposed of for cash, or bills of exchange: that I would have him make up about 100 barrels of pork fit for this market, the hogs to be corn-fed, the pork clean packed in tight double-hooped barrels (no heads of the pork included), to be pickled, not dry-salted, and to endeavor to send them down to Edenton, together with 100 barrels of Indian corn to be shipped on board some proper vessel, consigned to Mr. Spann of Bristol; that I would have him particularly attentive to this object, and to advise as to the same with Mr. Montfort and Mr. Lowther; the liberty of importation here closes the 1st of May next.

When no opportunity offers from Edenton, forward your letters to me, to the care of Mr. John Driver, merchant, near Suffolk in Virginia. Direct to us at the Tennis Court Coffee-House, White Hall, London, and do not use more covers than necessary, as you know it increases the postage. I repeat I expect to hear very often, and to have very long letters from you. It is all we at present expect from you, and if we are disappointed, you may assure yourself we shall take it very ill of you. Be always as full in your information as you can. I write this letter in the greatest hurry, and very probably may omit some things material. What I can say can only serve as outlines; your own reason and prudence must direct you in the use of circumstances and things as they occur. You may depend on hearing often from me; and I shall freely use the privilege of my years and affection, to offer at all times to you any observations which I conceive may be of service to you in your future walk of life.

I expect to hear from you before you sail, though I scarce wish you may receive my answer. It is probable by the time you get to Edenton, you may meet a letter from me. If we both live, we shall meet there, by October 1769. If we have parted for the last time,—be it so,—be assured though, while I live, you shall ever find me disposed to serve you. I pray God, the common Father of Mankind, to take you under his protection, to watch over, protect, and bless you! Forget not your duty to Him as your first Benefactor, and endeavor to think and act so that you may ever be able to put your trust in Him. The mummery of form and nonsense are an offence to most thinking minds; but never lose sight of that religion, which will make you firm and constant in your duty towards God, and just and beneficent towards your fellow-beings.

For the present, my dear Jemmy, I shall take my leave of you, with my best wishes for your happiness and success in life; to which your uncle joins his, and his blessings to you. Him, in all probability, you will never see; though I make no doubt you will ever retain a tender sense of the affection he has shown you.

I can't conclude without observing that you must by no means suffer your imagination to dress up fairy scenes of ease, elegance, and pleasure where you are going. In a young country you must not expect the appearance of luxury or riches. It is best to be agreeably disappointed, and I am very hopeful you will be so.

Once more adieu! Remember my love to your father and mother, and I will write them soon. Believe me ever, truly,
Your affectionate and assured friend,
HENRY E. McCULLOH.

In accordance with McCulloh's suggestion, and in obedience to an impulse of his own, Mr. Iredell readily assented to the appropriation of his salary to the support of his father and mother. That he should devote so large a portion of his small income to so laudable an object, illustrates in a forcible manner his filial piety and his generous nature. The salary, as long as he remained an officer of the customs, was annually transmitted. After a perusal of McCulloh's letters, and a knowledge of the relations that subsisted between him and his kinsman, the reflection presses upon the mind that few young men have ever been so exposed to moral peril as was Mr. Iredell. McCulloh was his official superior, his elder, his connection,—an accomplished man of the world. Few similarly situated could have resisted the charm of his blandishments, or the infection of his example. His apparent success, his command of money, the throng that paid him court, threw around him a glare as well calculated to dazzle, as the ease of his address and softness of his manner were to attach. That the youth did remain pure and true, there is no doubt. The prayers taught him at his mother's knee were never forgotten; the lessons engraven upon his heart by the weight of a father's authority, defied all assaults. However at fault for a time, his strong sense would soon detect the right path, and his brave heart beat with manly vigor as he trod it with confident step. From his advent in America to the close of his life, so discreet and blameless was his conduct, that, by the concurrent testimony of all his acquaintance, his fame was ever unspotted—his honor unsullied,—not even suspicion ever rested upon it longer than the moist breath upon a mirror. Doubtless his sagacity early penetrated and understood the character of Henry E. McCulloh; but disparity of age, and their relative positions, exacted from him a prudent forbearance and studied respect, enforced by his dependence and thoughts of the loved ones who leaned on him for support. McCulloh, though generally kind in his intercourse with him, was not always so. Once he was so rude that Mr. Iredell declined his business. Struck by the young man's spirit, and alarmed for his interest, he was prompt to atone, and to soothe his wounded feelings, by infusing into his letters an additional warmth. As the softer metal, now heated by fire and now plunged into water, hardens into steel, so the young man's virtue was corroborated; the attrition of the world could only thenceforth impart to it an exquisite polish.

The following letter, written on the eve of Mr. Iredell's departure for America, is as remarkable for beauty of penmanship, as for its admirable sentiments and excellent counsel.

BRISTOL, September 10th, 1768.

MY DEAR SIR:—As you are so shortly to remove from your native country to a very distant land, in such a situation as your mind must necessarily be on this occasion, I apprehend that the subject of this friendly epistle might be serviceable. It hath pleased the good Providence of God to make a comfortable provision for you. I hope you will ever retain a deep and affecting sense of the divine goodness. You are going to an unknown region, and you know not, my dear friend, what events may await you. But you have this consolation—that you can remove nowhere but you will have the same God and the same Providence to attend you. It is an unspeakable comfort to reflect, that wherever we are, if we do but our duty, God will bless us! You are removing from kind parents, from a most tender and affectionate mother; and think, *what* must be their satisfaction to hear from time to time that you are sober and virtuous! And can you deny a parent these satisfactions! A great deal, almost *every thing is dependent upon your conduct. The eyes of great numbers are very anxiously fixed upon you. You have given your relations and friends reason to expect great things from you.* God hath *blessed you with excellent abilities, which you have worthily improved.* O, my dear friend, let me conjure you by every thing sacred, by the regard you owe your friends, by the duty you owe your parents, and the gratitude you owe to your God, not to disappoint us. Form, I entreat you, no connections abroad, but such as will redound to your reputation and credit. Keep two great objects in view,—to acquit yourself with honor and applause in your station, and to assist your parents and brothers. Let these two great objects fire you with a noble and virtuous ambition. I will not say, my dear friend, what I expect from you. *I know your intellectual endowments, and the proficiency you have made in useful knowledge.* Frustrate not my hopes, I beseech you. I am persuaded you will not frustrate them. May the blessing of Almighty God attend you. I will not cease to offer my fervent prayers to God for your virtue and welfare. In your absence may God comfort your parents, to whom you have been a great consolation. Shun vice, embrace virtue, and make God your friend, and he will never leave you nor forget you. Wishing you a prosperous voyage and every felicity, I am, dear sir,
Your affectionate friend,
E. HARWOOD.*

---

* The passages italicised are not so marked in the original. Edward Harwood, a dissenting minister, was born in Lancashire. He died 1794, aged 65. He wrote various works, but he is best known as the author of a "View of the Various

Soon after the date of this letter, Mr. Iredell embarked for America to fulfil the promise of his youth. As the ship that bore him away receded in the distance, eyes moistened with tears strained after him, and fond hearts grew sick and faint. He was not forgotten. The affection of his English friends watched his career with eager hope, and exulted in his triumphs. The scion of a race who boasted that since the Revolution they had ever been a Whig family, he was gone, under the same name and in a new revolution, to do his duty as a man; to win renown as a patriot.

APPENDIX TO CHAPTER I.

The paper below was found in Judge Iredell's office:—

The admirers of the works of the late ingenious Mr. Sterne will, doubtless, be pleased with the following letters; the first was wrote by doctor Eustace, late of this town, deceased, a man of wit and understanding; the other, in answer to it, by Mr. Sterne. They are both taken from original manuscripts.

DOCTOR EUSTACE TO MR. STERNE.

SIR,—When I assure you, that I am a very great admirer of TRISTRAM SHANDY, and have been, ever since his introduction to the world, one of his most zealous defenders against the repeated assaults of prejudice and misapprehension, I hope you will not treat my unexpected appearance in his company as an intrusion. You know it is an observation as remarkable for its truth as its antiquity, that a similitude of sentiments is the general parent of friendship. It cannot be wondered at, that I should conceive an esteem for a person whom nature had most indulgently enabled to frisk and curvet with ease through all the intricacies of sentiment, which, from irresistible propensity, she had compelled me to trudge through without MERIT OR DISTINCTION.

The only reason that gave rise to this address to you, is my accidentally having met with a piece of SHANDEAN statuary—I mean, according to the vulgar opinion; for, to such judges, both appear equally destitute of regularity or design. It was made by a very ingenious gentleman of this province, and presented to the late Governor DOBBS; after his death, Mrs. DOBBS gave it to me. Its singularity made many very desirous of procuring it, but I had resolved, at first, not to part with it, till, upon reflection, I thought

---

Editions of the Greek and Latin Classics," which has passed through several editions, and has appeared in almost every European language. After presiding over a congregation at Bristol, he came to London, where he lived by correcting the press, by teaching the classics, and by his various publications. It is said that he refused very liberal patronage to join the Church of England.—*Lempriere.*

it would be a very proper, and probably not an unacceptable compliment to my FAVORITE author, and, in HIS HANDS might prove as ample a field for meditation as a BUTTONHOLE or a BROOMSTICK.

I am, &c.,
JOHN EUSTACE.*

MR. STERNE'S ANSWER.

LONDON, Feb. 9, 1768.

SIR,—I this moment received your obliging letter, and SHANDEAN piece of sculpture along with it; of both which testimonies of your regard I have the justest sense, and return you, dear sir, my best thanks and acknowledgments. Your walking stick is in no sense more SHANDAIC than in that of its having MORE HANDLES THAN ONE—The parallel breaks only in this, that in using the stick, every one will take the handle which suits his convenience. In TRISTRAM SHANDY, the handle is taken which suits their passions, their ignorance or sensibility. There is so little true feeling in the HERD of the WORLD, that I wish I could have got an act of parliament, when the books first appear'd, "that none but wise men should look into them." It is too much to write books and find heads to understand them. The world, however, seems to come into a better temper about them, the people of genius here being, to a man, on its side, and the reception it has met with in France, Italy and Germany, hath engag'd one part of the world to give it a second reading, and the other part of it, in order to be on the strongest side, have at length agreed to speak well of it too. A few Hypocrites and Tartufe's, whose approbation could do it nothing but dishonor, remain unconverted.

I am very proud, sir, to have had a man, like you, on my side from the beginning; but it is not in the power of any one man to taste humor, however he may wish it—'tis the gift of God—and besides, a true feeler always brings half the entertainment along with him. His own ideas are only call'd forth by what he reads, and the vibrations within, so entirely correspond with those excited, 'tis like reading HIMSELF and not the BOOK.

In a week's time, I shall be deliver'd of two volumes of the sentimental travels of MR. YORICK through France and Italy; but, alas! the ship sails three days too soon, and I have only to lament it deprives me of the pleasure of sending them to you, being, dear sir, with great thanks for the honor you have done me, and with true esteem,
Your oblig'd and humble servant,
LAU. STERNE.

---

* Dr. Eustace was a resident of Wilmington, N. C.

CHAPTER II.

AMERICA, EDENTON, ITS PEOPLE, STUDY OF LAW, LETTERS FROM ENGLAND. ÆT 17–18.

IN the month of November, 1768, Mr. Iredell arrived at Boston, Mass. He immediately exhibited his Warrant to John Robinson, Wm. Burch, I. Henper, Henry Fulton, and Chas. Paxton—"Commissioners for managing and causing to be levied his Majesty's Customs and other Duties in America." And after giving bond in the sum of £500, was deputed and empowered by them to act as Comptroller of the Customs at Roanoke (Edenton) in North Carolina.

"LONDON, 26th Jan. 1769.

DEAR JEMMY:—I had, yesterday, the pleasure of receiving your letter dated Boston, 4 Dec. I am sorry for the delay and disappointment you met. You certainly did right in taking your passage via Virginia, though it would have been much more fortunate could you have proceeded to Ocrocock. I am glad to find you met so agreeable a reception at Boston, and hope the letters you carried, have introduced you to every necessary assistance and civility since; and that you have long ere this taken possession of your office. I shall depend upon hearing very often and fully from you, and shall think very unkindly of any omission you may be guilty of that way.

My leisure will not permit me at present to write you a long letter. My father and myself have our health but middling. I had a letter from your mother a few days ago, which mentions the family to be all well. You omitted in your letter to me any mention of what I principally recommend to you,—laying a foundation to assure the regular receipts of your salary to your parents. I trust, though, you did not omit the thing itself, and that you will never be capable of forgetting the discharge of any part of that great first duty.

I suppose by the time you will receive this letter, you will begin to be familiarized to scenes that must have appeared strange to you at first, and that you do not conceive your lot to be very unhappily cast. If it is not among the first, consider, thousands and ten thousands do not enter into life with prospects so good,—prospects which I hope your own good conduct will happily realize. I wish it may suit Mr. Johnston to take you under his care. I depend you will endeavor to make yourself master of the business of the office. I shall expect very full, particular, and faithful information from you of every thing your way in which my interest may be concerned. The mistake Porter mentioned to you, Mr. Hardy had long ago my orders to correct. I desire you will write me very fully of the present state of the office, and your opinion of things.

Mr. Berry's fees as Comptroller were 1 and 2 dollars. The Comptroller's fees were established by act of Parliament only,—there was consequently the greatest difficulty in procuring them at all. Desire Mr. Hardy to make up the fees to you 10s. and 20s. proc. out of mine, and let things rest on this footing for the present.

I make no doubt you will receive many very agreeable civilities from Mr. and Mrs. Brownrigg,* whom you will soon find to be two of the best people in the world. Present my very affectionate remembrance to them. Acquaint Mr. Brownrigg, I have not as yet been so happy as to hear any thing of his bill :—that I am cruelly distressed, and depend upon his honor and friendship, not to meet further delay.

Make my compliments to all my friends your way. I am much disappointed in not having had the pleasure to hear from them.

I am still here, anxiously looking out for letters and from my agents, on the receipt of which I propose sallying out in quest of adventures. My first course will be for Bath and Bristol, from whence I propose writing you. Your bill in favor of Mr. Murray has been presented and paid. *My father and myself both think you made a very moderate use of your credit*, and sincerely wish our good wishes and intentions towards you may be attended with the desired success.

I am very truly,

Your assured and affectionate friend,

HENRY E. McCULLOH.

---

* Mr. Brownrigg was an emigrant from Ireland, ancestor of the wife of the Hon. John L. Bailey, of Hillsboro', N. C.

P. S. If my lots in Edenton would sell for a good bill of £100 sterling I would let them go willingly. I depend on having long letters from you once a month at least. Opportunities often offer from Virginia.

Near the close of the year 1768 Mr. Iredell arrived at Edenton. He was then just seventeen years old ; at that age when pleasures are enjoyed with the keenest relish. Frank, ingenuous, of pleasing appearance, and winning manners, and educated in the best schools of England, he was kindly received and warmly welcomed. He arrived at a season of gayety and festivity, when families gather about the social altar, and neighbors interchange those courtesies, that, as flowers that bloom by the way, divert the mind from the fatigue, and care, and anxiety of life. On such occasions in North Carolina, "room for the stranger" is the impulse of every heart, while the ready grasp of the hand and the genial smile assure his hesitation, and calm his embarrassment.

The ancient borough of Edenton is situated on the northern shore of the Albemarle Sound. It was founded in 1716,* and named in honor of Eden, the Royal Governor ;† and is nearly opposite the points where the rivers Roanoke and Chowan discharge their waters into the Sound. It was the centre of a region of such remarkable fertility, that it might well have been styled the granary of the province : it was also the place of concentration, and market-town for the opulent planters of a large district of country. The territory north of the Albemarle is intersected with deep creeks and rivers, whose mouths expand into estuaries. Ordinarily the banks of every stream, on one side, are bold and bluff, affording fine sites for residences ; while on the other, the view is bounded by impenetrable swamps. In 1769 its population was sparse and scattered. Brave old forest trees, with the long moss waving from their branches like the pennons of sturdy knights in battle array, covered the arable lands, save where, here and there, the smoke curled above the roof of the settler. Here dwelt the first inhabitants of North Carolina ; and a little to the south-east lies Roanoke Island, where Sir Walter Raleigh left his first colony in America, in 1585 ; and where was born Virginia Dare, the first child of English parentage who ever gambolled upon the soil of the New World. The climate was humid and unhealthy, but soft and

---

* C. H. Wiley, N. C. Reader, Wheeler, Jones.
† Gov. Eden died in 1722. His daughter Penelope married Gov. Gabriel Johnston. That amiable gentleman, Tristram L. Skinner, of Chowan, is her lineal descendant.

luxurious. Game and fish were abundant ; and cattle, and sheep, and swine throve and multiplied upon the spontaneous fruits of the earth. If there was little of the parade and pomp of older communities, if many of the appliances of luxury were wanting, ease and abundance were the reward of but a slight degree of frugality and industry. No palatial dwellings existed—tapestry and plate were wanting ; but the homes of the planters were comfortable, and ample for all the purposes of hospitality ; while their tables groaned beneath dainties beyond the reach of wealth on the other side of the Atlantic. The inhabitants visited and traded oftener in boats than in any other vehicles ; were familiar with the use of the oar, and could spread with dexterity, to the wind, the sails of almost any species of craft. He who supposes them an untutored people is grossly deceived. They were not refugees from the justice of the Old World ; nor were they of desperate fortunes, or undisciplined minds. The letters that will appear in the course of the narrative will demonstrate that they were equal in cultivation, ability and patriotism to any of their contemporaries. The men were bold, frank, generous, and intelligent ; the females tender, and kind and polite. The strength of the former was developed by manly labors. The taste of the latter was improved, and their imaginations exalted by the varied forms of beauty that surrounded them : the sparkling water of the Sound—the smaller streams, now of the color of the amethyst, now of the topaz, and again black as the Stygian wave*—the woods resonant with the mock-bird's melody—the wild flower of every hue and tint, now blazing as flame, and now emulating the spotless snow. Verily it was and is a goodly land, with its clustering grapes† and perfumed air.

The town of Edenton possessed a population of about four or five hundred.

About eight miles south, across the Sound, was Tyrrel County, where resided Col. Richard Buncombe :‡ a little to the south-west was Plymouth, its capital, on the Roanoke River. About six miles west, over the Sound, was the County of Bertie, watered by the Roanoke and Cashie Rivers and Salmon Creek ; and here on one side of Salmon Creek, was Dukinfield, where resided Mr. and Mrs. Pearson, the latter the mother of Sir Nat. Dukinfield : on the oposite side resided Col. John Dawson. About thirty miles south-west, on the Roanoke, dwelt Dr. Cathcart.

---

* Dyed by roots, shrubs and decaying leaves.
† The Scuppernong is indigenous here.
‡ Wheeler, Diary of W. Avery.

Eleven or twelve miles to the north-east is Hertford, the county seat of Perquimans. Through this county flow the Cheopim, Little and Perquimans Rivers. On Harvey's Neck, between the Cheopim and Perquimans River was the home of Col. John Harvey. In 1769 the town of Edenton was the Court end of the Province. Within its limits and in its immediate vicinity there was, in proportion to its population, a greater number of men eminent for ability, virtue, and erudition, than in any other part of America. Samuel Johnston, Joseph Hewes, Thomas Barker, Thomas Jones, Jasper Charlton, Stephen Cabarrus, Robert Smith, Charles Johnson, John Johnston, William Cumming and Sir Nathaniel Dukinfield possessed talents and attainments that, when combined, not only enabled them to determine the politics of their District, but gave them a potent influence in the Province. Considering the intimate personal, professional, and political relations of these various gentlemen with Mr. Iredell, it may be well to pause for a brief glance at their history.*

Col. Richard Buncombe was a native of St Kitts.† He was educated in England, and possessed a large fortune. In 1776 he was appointed Colonel of the 5th Regiment of the Cont. Line of N. C. This Regiment he raised in his own county, and kept for more than twelve months at his individual charge. In the battle of Germantown he was severely wounded, and taken prisoner ; and died of his wounds soon after, at Philadelphia. He was distinguished for his martial appearance, his courage, and unbounded hospitality.

Of " lawyer Pearson, an English gentleman," little is known, save that he married the mother of Sir N. Dukinfield, and thus became master of large estates.‡ His seat was called Dukinfield.

Col. John Dawson, a lawyer and a Virginian, married the daughter of Gov. Gabriel Johnston. Mr. Avery,§ who visited him in 1769, was "highly pleased with the family, as well as surprised at the good sense and accomplishments of Mrs. Dawson."‖ Col. Dawson's mansion, Eden House, was noted for its "splendid hospitality" and the "refined society" generally assembled there.

Dr. Cathcart¶ was a "gentleman of extraordinary fine sense

---

* To these a few years subsequently Dr. Hugh Williamson, the historian, was added.
† Diary of Waightstill Avery, 1767. Jones' Defence N. C. passim. Wheeler's Hist. N. C.
‡ Avery.
§ W. Avery was a native of Connecticut, educated at Princeton, a signer of the Mecklenburg Declaration of Independence—Attorney-General, 1777, &c. &c. He was intelligent, honest and patriotic.
‖ University Mag., Aug. 1855.
¶ Avery.

and great reading." His "two daughters were possessed of the three greatest motives to be courted: beauty, wit and prudence, and money; great fortunes, and toasted in most parts of the Province"*

Col. John Harvey was Speaker of the House of Commons from 1766 to 1769.† He was Moderator of the first Convention of the people in 1774. He had great intellectual power, decision of character, and firmness of principles. At the time of his death (June 3, 1775) he was the undoubted leader of the Whig Party.

Of Joseph Hewes, one of the Signers of the Declaration of Independence, it is unnecessary to speak: his history is known to the Union. I need only say that he was affianced to Miss Isabella, the sister of Mr. Sam. Johnston. The death of that amiable lady, before the consummation of their nuptials, left him so bereaved, and the recollection of her grace and virtue was so vivid, that he never married. He was always regarded by the Johnstons as a member of their family. Thomas Barker was as generous as a man as he was able as a lawyer. He was one of the four Commissioners appointed to revise the Statutes in 1746. He was the early friend and legal instructor of Gov. Samuel Johnston.

Jasper Charlton and William Cumming, "two gentlemen Attorneys, both Deists," were men of ability and scholarship.‡ The former was one of the Commissioners selected in 1776 to revise the Statutes; more than once office was tendered to him and promptly refused. The latter represented the State in the Continental Congress, 1784.

Thomas Jones was one of the very first men in the Province in genius and learning. He was a native of England, a member of the Bar, and drew the draft of the Constitution adopted at Halifax, 1776.

Robert Smith was an Attorney. He was also the mercantile partner of Mr. Joseph Hewes. He was appointed a Lieutenant in Col. Howe's Regiment in 1775—Captain in the fourth, 1776. He represented Edenton in the Commons, 1780 and 1781. He never married. At his death he left a large portion of his means to trustees to found an Academy.

Charles Johnston, an Englishman, lived on the Chowan at Bandon. He was member of the State Senate in 1781-84 and 1790-92, and member of Congress in 1801. His courage, his patriotism and intelligence were universally admitted.§

* One of these young ladies married Gov. S. Johnston, and was the mother of Mr. Jas. C. Johnston, of Hayes, near Edenton.   † Wheeler.
‡ Avery, Jones.   § The grandfather of Dr. C. E. Johnston, of Raleigh.

Sir Nathaniel Dukinfield, of Dukinfield, in the county of Chester, G. B. owned large tracts of land in Bertie and other parts of the Province.* He was a member of Gov. Martin's Council: was gay, good-humored, and popular; and was soon to be to Mr. Iredell a dangerous rival for the hand of the lady who was afterwards the latter's wife.

In 1772 he went to Great Britain, where his friends prevailed on him to purchase a commission in the British Army. When the war broke out he could not be induced to serve against America; and when his Regiment was sent out, he contrived to remain behind, though he hazarded his reputation as a soldier and gentleman. His property was confiscated by act of Assembly in 1779.

Stephen Cabarrus, a native of France, was a man of active mind, generous feelings and liberal sentiments.† He was a merchant. He was member of the Commons 1783-87, from the town; from 1788-93 for the county; and again 1801-1804. He frequently presided over the deliberations of the House. In consequence of Mr. Iredell's connection with the Johnston family, it is indispensable that a more extended account of them should be given. If I go more into details than is, apparently, essential, I trust I may be pardoned; as otherwise, the narrative and accompanying letters cannot be well understood.‡

The Johnstons are an ancient family, and derive their surname from the Barony of Johnston, in Annandale, Scotland. By successive creations from 1420 to 1701, the head of the race attained the dignity of a Marquis.

Gabriel Johnston was a native of Scotland, and had received his education in the University of St Andrews.§ After spending a few years in the acquisition of medical knowledge, he was appointed Professor of Oriental Languages in the Seminary in which he had been reared; but his office, which was a sinecure, not suiting one of his practical and enterprising genius, he removed to London, and became a political writer. His contributions appeared in the "Craftsman," a periodical opposed to the Ministry, and very ably conducted. Among its writers were Bolingbroke and Pulteney, afterwards Earl of Bath.‖ Pulteney's true name was William Johnston. He married the heiress of the Earl of Bath, assumed the latter's name, and succeeded to his estates and title. He was the brother of Sir James Johnston, and Commodore Johnston, prominent and influential members of Parliament during the latter quarter of the eighteenth century. Sir James, the elder brother, was the proprietor of immense estates in the counties of Westmoreland and Cumberland, and returned

* Mrs. Pearson's Memorial to Gen. Ass.   † Wheeler.   ‡ New Peerage, 1784.
§ C. H. Wiley, Wheeler.   Preface to Rev. Stat. Iredell & Battle.
‖ Wraxall's Memoirs.

five or six members to Parliament. These gentlemen were Gabriel Johnston's relatives. To their influence, and that of his friend Spencer Compton, Earl of Wilmington, Gabriel Johnston was indebted for his appointment as Governor of North Carolina. He arrived in the river Cape Fear in Oct., 1734; and in November took the oaths of office. He was the ablest of all the Colonial Governors, not less distinguished for his energy and prudence than his extensive classical and scientific attainments. Gov. Johnston's* brother was Surveyor-general of the Province. He resided in the county of Onslow, where he owned large possessions.† The capital of the county, situate near its southern border, was called Johnston. The following table, prepared for me by an accurate and valued connection, ‡ exhibits the descendants of the Surveyor-general.§

John Johnston, who married Helen Scrymsoure, emigrated to this country from Dundee in Scotland, about the year 1736. He had issue.

I. Samuel, who married Miss Frances Cathcart (daughter of Dr. Cathcart), and had issue, Penelope who married John Swann, and died without issue, Gabriel, Fanny, Helen, all of whom died unmarried, and James C. Johnston.

II. John, who married Miss Williams, and had issue.

1st. John, who married a Miss Cotten, and had issue, Samuel Iredell, who still survives, and Ann, who married Mr. Wynne, and died without issue.

2d. Samuel, who married Miss Thompson, and left four children, John, Sam, William and Thompson, all of whom are now dead.

3d. Harry, who died a young man.

4th. William.

5th. Alexander.

* The true mode of spelling the name is Johnstone.   † Wheeler.
‡ Dr. Samuel T. Iredell.
§ After the death of Mr. John Johnston, Mr. Edward Starkey, Treasurer of the Province under Gov. Dobbs' Administration, acted as guardian for his children. He was a kind-hearted and intelligent man; an industrious and successful farmer. He was a regularly ordained Minister of the Church of England, a disciple of Burnet rather than of Laud. Though whiggishly inclined, he cherished the images of his Majesty when imprinted on gold or silver. On Sundays he generally read the services of the Church to his family and neighbors, who assembled at his house for worship; he was, however, more devoted to the accumulation of wealth than the interests of religion, more intent upon the cure of bacon than the cure of souls. On inclement days every species of domestic manufactures were carried on in his hall; tailors, shoemakers, saddlers, all plied their trades; while the treasury of the Province lay in his saddlebags in a corner of the same chamber. He had a great contempt for Provincial Bills of credit, though rather partial to English coin. Tolerant in his views, he had much popularity, and often represented his county in the Provincial and State Assemblies. Being a capitalist, it is said that he governed many in the Assemblies by lending them money. In 1776 he was a member of Gov. Caswell's Council.—Wheeler.

6th. Elizabeth, who married Mr. Phil. Alston, and had six children, John, James, Phil., Sandy., Ben., and Mary.

7th. Annie, who married Mr. Hunter, and died, without issue.

III. Penelope, who married Parson Stuart and died without issue.

IV. Jane married George Blair, and had five children.

1st. Helen married Samuel Tredwell, and had four children, Elizabeth, Margaret, James and Frances.

2d. William died without issue.

3d. Margaret married Dr. Hosmer, and had one child, Jane; she, after the death of Dr. Hosmer, married Dr. Sawyer, and had seven children, Annie, Lemuel, Samuel, Helen, Margaret, Mathias, and Mary.

4th. Samuel Blair died without issue.

5th. George Blair married Miss King, and had issue, George and Elizabeth.

V. Annie died unmarried.

VI. Isabella died without issue.

VII. Hannah married James Iredell, and had issue, Thomas, Annie, Helen, and James.

The two sons of the Surveyor-general were both men of mark. John, the youngest, lived in the county of Bertie. He was one of the Committee of Safety for the Edenton District in 1775, and was a member of the Provincial Congress 1776, and also for the subsequent Congress in the same year that adopted the Constitution of the State. He was Senator in 1787-88-89, and again in 1800; and Commoner in '95, '96. He was a man of clear head and sound heart.

Samuel Johnston, the eldest son, was born at Dundee, Scotland, Dec. 15th, 1733. He read law under Mr. Barker, and acted as Clerk of the Superior Court of Chowan, 1767-72: anterior to the War he was also Naval Officer, under the crown. For ability, learning, wealth, and character, at the time of Mr. Iredell's arrival, he was prominent in the Province. He bore the greatest weight of care and labor lightly as the mountain its crown of granite. His powerful frame was a fit engine for the vigorous intellect that gave it animation. Strength was his characteristic. In his relations to the public, an inflexible sense of duty and justice dominated. There was a remarkable degree of self-reliance and majesty about the man. His erect carriage and his intolerance of indolence, meanness, vice, and wrong, gave to him an air of sternness. He commanded the respect and admiration, but not the love of the people. Lofty, unbending, and impracticable, as he appeared in the world, in the bosom of his family he manifested the utmost sensibility and tenderness of feeling. The chords of his heart were as delicately strung as those of the harp that trembles at the slightest breeze.

When the embarrassment of public affairs and the necessities of the times demanded the wisest men in the Councils of the Province, he was promptly elected to the Assembly, 1770-71. It appearing that the public officers had collected a much larger amount of money than was necessary for the redemption of the bills issued by the Assemblies of 1748-1754, to the great oppression and distress of the people, Mr. Johnston introduced a bill to discontinue those illegal taxes, which was immediately and unanimously passed. The decision of this question separated the popular House, for the first time, as a distinct party from the Governor and his adherents. In 1774 he was one of the Committee to prepare an answer to the remonstrance of the Governor, relative to the Attachment Law, concerning which a long controversy had subsisted between the Governor and the Assembly. The Act gave to the citizens of the Province, the right of attaching the property of non-resident or absent debtors, and gave them priority over all others. It met with violent opposition in England, and was negatived by the Crown; but was obstinately insisted on by the Assembly. During this year he carried on an able correspondence with Alex. Elmsly,† and others, in London, concerning the Province; and, with four other prominent citizens, projected the first provincial Congress, in opposition to the Royal authority. Of this body that assembled in Newbern, Aug. 25, 1774, in defiance of the Proclamation and menaces of the Governor, he was a conspicuous member. At the close of their session, it was agreed that Col. Harvey, or in case of his death, Mr. Johnston, might, at any time, call them together. He was a member of the Provincial Congress convened April, 1775, at the call of the Moderator; and also of the Assembly that met at the same time and place. The same persons at one time sat as an Assembly under the Royal authority; at another, as a revolutionary Congress. At this session he was one of the committee to respond to the last violent, minatory speech of Gov. Martin. After the death of Col. Harvey, Mr. Johnston succeeded as Leader of the Whig Party, and summoned a Convention, to meet at Hillsborough, Aug. 20, '75. Of this assembly he was made President, and Chairman of the Committee to prepare a plan for the regulation of the Province. A Provincial Council was elected, in which was vested the Executive power

* Jones.
† Alexander Elmsly had practised law in N. C.: he was related to the Bookseller in the Strand, of the same name.

during the recesses of Congress: it consisted of two members from each of the six districts of the Province; and Mr. Johnston was elected from the Province at large, and placed at its head. On the 8th of Sept, he was elected Treasurer for the Northern District, the Province being divided into two Districts for financial purposes; and gave bond in the sum of £50,000 proc.* "He was more celebrated as a skilful financier than any other citizen of the State." In performance of the delicate trust committed to him, " he contributed the most important services to his country." February, 1776, he was one of three appointed by the Provincial Council, in their behalf, to confer with the Committee of Safety of Va. on their mutual interest. Congress assembled, at his summons, at Halifax, April 4th, '76, and on the 8th instructed their Delegates in the Continental Congress "to concur with the Delegates of the other Colonies in declaring independence." On April 13, he was appointed Chairman of the Committee to prepare a civil Constitution; but the labors of the Committee were abortive. He was a candidate for a seat in the Congress that assembled in Nov. 1776; but lost his election. It is said that " the whole force and energy of the Radical party of the State, was directed to the single object of defeating Sam. Johnston in the Chowan election." † Mr. Johnston's conservatism had been misunderstood and misrepresented. He was proclaimed the representative of the Aristocratic principle; and as inclined to Monarchy. Though no believer in the infallibility of the popular voice, at the very time when he was violently assailed, he wrote his most confidential friend :‡ "After all it appears to me, that there can be no check upon the Representatives of a people in a democracy, but the people themselves; and in order that the check may be more efficient, I would have annual elections." He was anxious to secure the rights of property, individuals and minorities, against the tyranny of majorities, the capricious fluctuations of the masses. To effect this, as far as practicable, he was disposed to limit and restrain the powers of the Legislative Assemblies by organic, Constitutional Law, that the people should be taught to revere as the Ark of their Safety. He had also much at heart the independence of the Judiciary, and their selection by the Legislature rather than by the popular voice. Though defeated Mr. Johnston yet attended the Congress. Every conservative feature of the Constitution then adopted may be regarded, in a great degree, as the fruit of his wisdom, counsel, and influence.

He was a member of the Continental Congress, 1780-82; and was elected Governor in 1787. A warm Federalist, and a

* Jones Wheeler.   † Jones.   ‡ Judge Iredell.

consummate statesman, he earnestly advocated the adoption of the Federal Constitution. While Governor, he presided over the Convention of 1788, called to consider that instrument; and participated in the debates with great vigor and eloquence. The Constitution was then rejected; but he subsequently had the honor of presiding over a second Convention, 1789, that added North Carolina as a segment to the incomplete circle of the Union. He was the first Senator from the State, 1789-93.*

As a lawyer he was ever highly esteemed—his patience, his industry, his logic were signal. Amongst his contemporaries at the Bar, he was second to Judge Iredell alone. As early as 1776 he was one of a Committee to revise the Statutes of the State. He was appointed Judge of the Superior Courts, Feb. 1800, but resigned Nov. 1803.

He owned many plantations, at different points, but generally resided at Hayes, near Edenton, or at the Hermitage near Williamston, Martin Co. He died in 1816, and was buried at Hayes.

Soon after Mr. Iredell's arrival at Edenton, he addressed himself with such energy and assiduity to the mastery of the routine of the Custom-house, that he soon accomplished his object, though his "was the laboring oar."† As soon as his familiarity with the business gave him sufficient command of time, he commenced the study of law under Mr. Sam. Johnston's direction. He soon gained his esteem—an esteem that ripened into friendship—a friendship that deepened into an attachment, that endured for his life; and that, after his death, lavished its beneficence upon his family. The sagacity of Mr. Johnston soon detected the youthful Comptroller's extraordinary merit. If Mr. Iredell's integrity ever wavered under the insidious counsels of Henry E. McCulloh, he had, in the sterner virtue of his preceptor, a ready monitor and sure support.

Never was youth subjected to a severer discipline, or so immersed in a sea of care and trouble: but the habit of decision, industry, and precision, that he speedily acquired, conduced greatly to his improvement, and fitted him for future usefulness. His office, and the multifarious transactions intrusted to him by his selfish and heartless kinsman, made him acquainted with every form of business, every species of trade, every affair of practical life, while his legal studies shed over them a luminous light.

LONDON, 10 May, 1769.

DEAR JEMMY.—I have the pleasure of acknowledging the

* Elliott's Deb. in Con.   † Letter from McCulloh.

letters from you dated in Jan., Feb., and March. I am much obliged to you, for your attention in writing me; and very happy that you find every thing so much to your satisfaction.

I make no doubt you will carefully improve your prospects; and assure you nothing in the power of my affection and friendship shall be ever wanting to you. I am much pleased at your having fixed your residence at Mr. Hardy's; Mr. Hardy* is a very good, kind person, and you will find him both sensible and honest, and possessed of much good-nature. I would have you cultivate Mr. Johnston's friendship and good opinion by every means in your power. I recommend this to you as a circumstance which merits your first and most constant attention. On your conduct and application, for four or five of the ensuing years of your life, depend your future prosperity and happiness on this side of time. I know how strongly pleasure solicits the senses at your time of life; beware the taste,—there is poison mingled in the cup: the time for pleasure and repose, is when the difficulties of the journey are conquered, not when we first set out. You do not want for sense to know these things, and I hope will not want resolution to practise them. I wrote you in January, in answer to your letter from Boston, and acquainted you that Capt. Hardy should, out of the Collector's fees, make up your 10s. on every country—20s. on every foreign vessel. I have given up thoughts of quitting England, (if I am not absolutely compelled) whilst my father lives—this a circumstance to yourself. I may think of resigning my office, perhaps in your favor; though in that case I should expect that you would suffer me to come in with you for a reasonable participation of the profits. I have fixed on nothing certain; I only mention these things in confidence to your good sense (this to you only). In two or three weeks I will write you from Bristol; I propose paying a short visit there some time this month: then I will write you more fully. My father has had his health very poorly of late, owing in a good measure to the disappointments we meet. Make my compliments to Mr. Brownrigg,—acquaint him I have not heard from him; I beg you would inform yourself of the circumstances which have prevented my receiving his bills, and how the matter stands, and write me fully. I believe Mr. B. has been disappointed; but his conduct on this occasion has been neither kind or proper. Whatever money you were supplied with by Capt. Hardy for your travelling expenses you have no occasion to repay him; I make you a compliment

* McCulloh's Deputy. Also a merchant.

of it. Remember me kindly to him. I am extremely sensible how happy I am in having the office under his management. I intrust you to make my compliments to all my friends and acquaintance your way. I have wrote them so often in vain, that I am quite discouraged. The information you send me, gives me little or no insight into my affairs. I can gather nothing as to what Ben* intends to do, or whether Mr. Montfort† could send me my money which has been so long in his hands. As to the corn and pork schemes, they are in the right : as to other things, I have too much reason to complain. Hereafter you may be enabled to render me some useful services, and I don't doubt your good will. No part of Mr. Campbell's protested bill, is yet replaced to me. I give you one piece of advice,—keep yourself clear of party in every shape. *Be all things unto all men.* When distraction is the topic, be silent. You will find much occasion for observing these rules. I heard lately from Bristol, and that every body was well. For the present I will conclude myself, what I truly am,

Dear Jemmy,
Your very affectionate,
HENRY E. McCULLOH.

"Tell Capt. Hardy he would infinitely oblige me by investing what proc. he receives in the office on my account into good bills if possible ; and that I will readily allow him £5 for negotiating them. If he cannot procure bills let him endeavor to lodge the proceeds with some merchant at Suffolk or Norfolk for bills at a sight of even six months ; and on the best terms he can. I would have him also send whatever cash he has for me directly to Mr. Driver to ship for me. Please direct Capt. Hardy not to pay over any more money on my account to my cousin, Ben McCulloh, for which this is his authority. His not being able to go to Virginia prevents him from turning it into bills for me. I beg leave to recommend what I write to Capt. Hardy, and desire you will assist yourself, with the strictest attention, and write me fully. You may acquaint the person who seemed to doubt of his consent as to her marriage that I shall be very happy to hear it, if for her advantage, and that I shall not withdraw my kindness.‡

H. E. McCULLOH.

* Ben. McCulloh represented Halifax in the Provincial Congress that formed the Constitution, Nov. 1776.
† The father of the wives of Willie Jones and Col. John B. Ashe, ladies remarkable for beauty and wit. His son Joseph was appointed an Ensign, April, 1776.
‡ The mother of his illegitimate son, George McCulloh. This amiable young man, after receiving an excellent education in England, was cruelly neglected by his father.

I am now at the 14th. I hope you have endeavored successfully to recommend yourself to the notice of Col. Harvey, my worthy and good friend. Present him with my sincere and affectionate respects, and acquaint him that I defer writing him in daily expectation of hearing from the Committee of Correspondence ; that in any event I will write him in about ten days, and that I have the most lively sense of his partiality and kindness, and ever will, while life is lent me. Inform him that I trust next winter will be very favorable to America, and that assurances are given by Government that the Session will open with the kindest intentions to remove the present causes of complaint.

If Capt. Hardy cannot procure bills, and the money is to be sent into Virginia, I shall depend upon your going with it yourself, and making the best agreement you can for me. Write me very often and fully, I entreat you, and of what is done with the things I left at Edenton. If my schooner can be sold for a bill of £100 sterling (good) payable here, I would have you do it. Mr. Shaw is going out to India ; I have asked him to take Frank,* which he says he will : he cannot in honor refuse.

One thing I had almost forgot ; pray write me fully in what manner you have settled the remitting of your salary to your mother. I hope your friends will have no occasion to blame you for a want of attention to your first of human duties : and that you have taken due care to have it remitted half yearly. Should you not have provided duly for this mother, you will offend all your friends here very much.

If Molly should get a husband, inform me what is to be done with the youngster. If she continues to take good care of him, I will continue my allowance. Write me a little of family matters now and then. Adieu. Be happy as I wish you !

H. E. M.

P. S. If you go to Virginia, make use of my name at Mrs. Mead's.

St. Dorothy's, Jamaica, 20th June, 1769.

DEAR NEPHEW :—I received several of your letters from England, which I did not reply to, having answered them in those I wrote your brother. I am much pleased with your two letters from N. Carolina. I fear many opportunities may have

* Mr. Iredell's brother.

offered since I received them ; but vessels bound to your province are so little talked of, and my abode so distant from Kingston that I seldom hear of them ; but I will take care to be better informed in future, as it will give me a particular pleasure to keep up a correspondence with you. I am glad to hear the climate is so agreeable, and wish and hope the summer season may prove more favorable than you seem to expect. It was a fortunate circumstance having so good a friend as Mr. McCulloh in the province ; as a proper introduction at first, is of singular advantage. Your resolution of assisting your father is truly natural, and cannot be enough commended. The afflicting situation of him and his family has given me more concern than any thing I ever met with. The situation of my own affairs will not allow me to do at present what my heart prompts, and what fraternal love urges so strongly ; yet so soon as I can, I will make both him and my sister independent by a settlement on my estate. I could wish to have it in my power to assist you by throwing something in your way from hence. I take it for granted you consume most of our commodities—sugar, molasses, rum, coffee, &c. We sometimes, also, ship off negroes, generally for running away, which I am told they cannot do with you, your woods affording them no sustenance ; besides the terror of the Indians, who, it is said, never spare them. Let me know the price of these articles, with the freight and charge on them. Returns to this island may be made in black and white oak—what are commonly called here picked or drawn, with other kinds of lumber, herrings and lamp-oil. Herrings, I am told, are very cheap in your neighborhood.* I should also be glad to know the prices of these several articles—freight, &c. Although I do not know Mr. McCulloh, I beg you will present my best compliments to him, and remain with much truth,

Your most affectionate Uncle,
THOMAS IREDELL.

St. Dorothy's, July 10, 1769.

"DEAR NEPHEW :—I have already wrote you by this conveyance, and have determined to make trial of a run-away negro I now send you. His name is Spencer. Dispose of him as you can ; and by first opportunity remit nett proceeds in red oak hogshead staves, and about 20 barrels of herrings. Consider my former letter particularly as soon as you can ; and

* The Edenton district is still celebrated for the fine herrings caught in its waters. They are well cured, and the best to be had in America, for the table.

give me an account not only of such articles as I have mentioned, but also of every other article imported from, or exported to this island. I am told the gentleman who carries on the herring fishing is a Mr. Brownrigg, brother to Councillor Brownrigg of this island, with whom I am intimately acquainted. He is a gentleman greatly esteemed here, and married into a very genteel family—the widow of a man of fortune. Besides £400 a year jointure, she had in her own right upwards of £3000. Pray make my compliments to Mr. McCulloh.

"Dear nephew,
"Your affectionate Uncle,
"THOMAS IREDELL."

London, July 14, 1769.

"DEAR JEMMY :—I wrote you in May, to which I refer. I have received your favor of the 11th same month, and I am very glad to hear of your health, &c. I returned from Bristol about three weeks ago, and left all friends well. I suppose they will have wrote you since I saw them. Your delicacy about what I desired Hardy to give you is misplaced ; however, it is not worth mentioning. I have thought of endeavoring to resign the office, perhaps in your favor : if I do, I shall make the terms for you, and will not doubt your punctual and honorable compliance. Sound Mr. Johnston whether the Comptrollership would be agreeable to him, and what sum he would give to have it in his own hands, and write me an answer by the first opportunity. I have not the most distant intentions of leaving England during the lifetime of my father, and much wish my lots were disposed of ; I recommend their sale to your attention. Transmit me a particular account how the things I left at Edenton were disposed of : pray oblige me, and draw out the account in a full manner. Sir George Macartney is out of town. I will seal your letter and forward it to him. On Wednesday I set out on my Continental tour. We have our carrosse ready at Calais, and have every reason to flatter ourselves with every thing agreeable. I propose crossing the Alps, and being back in November. I recommend the contents of my last letter to you, especially on the subject of bills, taking it always with you. I would never have any thing done which could give umbrage to my cousin Ben. Captain Fortune will deliver you sundries as per bills of lading to be inclosed you ; the letters your way, you will carefully deliver : let the things for Mr. Montfort, and the letters, be sent him by a cart and under the care of a careful driver ; I will not have them intrusted any other way : Mr. Hardy will assist you in this affair. I recommend it to you, to curb your natural flow of spirits, and to behave yourself with more circumspection. The people you are among are very observing. I am pleased to hear a great many kind things said of you, but have reason to fear you give too great a loose to your vivacity. Your time of life is the hour of application and reserve. Be not offended with the freedom I use, but make the use you ought of it. I shall write you a short letter at present, as I am hurried to death. Be careful as to the letters and things I send to your care. Don't let my trip to France be an excuse for not writing : my friend's letters will be forwarded to me. I depend upon hearing very often and very fully from you. I will leave a space for any thing which may occur, and conclude myself what I truly am,

Your affectionate and assured friend, &c.
HENRY E. McCULLOH.

The foregoing letters not only disclose McCulloh's character, but show the nature and variety of the services rendered by Mr. Iredell. There are a large number in my possession ; but only such parts shall be extracted as seem to possess a public or peculiar interest.

BRISTOL, 20th August, 1769.

With what pleasure, my dear James, do I take up my pen to scribble a few lines to you. I am flattered into a belief that my letters will afford you some amusement ; but I can't help being surprised that none of my letters have yet reached you. I suppose you have before this heard that there was a great uproar at Bath on Derrick's death, and that the place of Master of the Ceremonies was contested by Brereton and Plomer. The latter gained it by seven votes ; but was obliged to give it up, for peace sake to a third—a Captain Wade, son of Field-General Wade. All things, for a time, seemed quiet ; but within this fortnight hostilities seem to be recommenced. Brereton has quarrelled with a Mr. Gardener, who was greatly against him, and fought (not as gentlemen, but as bruisers). This piece of intelligence I gained in London where I have been for near five weeks, which prevented my sending a large packet, as I designed, by this vessel. There I saw Sir George Macartney, who asked after you. He is now one of the Privy Council of Ireland. The whole subject of discourse in town was Mr. Samuel Vaughan, who had offered to give the Duke of Grafton five thousand pounds to secure the reversion of the place he held in Jamaica to his son, and yet run counter to the Government. By the Duke's publishing the letter it exposed him greatly : it was in the papers a few days ago that he had shot himself ; but it is now contradicted. Now for news more in the ladies' way. The theatre has sustained a great loss in Mr. Powell, who is *now* allowed to be one of the greatest actors this age has produced. Curiosity led me, when in town, to see Mr. Sheridan in the character of Hamlet. Though I am quite an enthusiastic admirer of Sheridan as a reader, yet the tone of his voice, and his person, and his action, were so much inferior to Powell, that I thought it would not admit of a comparison. I likewise saw Foote in his Devil on Two Sticks ; and never was so highly entertained in my life—it is a very satirical piece, and in general, the satire very just. I also saw the Al Fresco at Vauxhall very well ridiculed at Saddler's Wells. I also went to Ranelagh. Above five thousand people there—the fireworks were very good ; but, as it was impossible to get a box till near 12 o'clock, I was greatly tired of strolling about. In my way from London, as I came in the post coach, I was greatly entertained by hearing the history of Captain Dunkelly, the late king's natural son, told by himself. I dare say you remember him at the Wells. He is so like the Royal Family that he can't be seen once without being known. I just saw your cousin Harry before he set out for Paris where he still is. Lord Wigton, poor man, seems breaking very fast. I dare say your brother wrote you word that Miss Beaton is going to be married to Mr. Holland, who served his time with Mr. Cruger, and is soon to be taken into partnership with him. Your brother Frank is to go with Mr. Shaw to the Indies, and Sir George has promised, if possible, to get Charles in one of the men of war that are going there. I also hope to get Arthur* a pair of colors ; and then all that are fit are provided for. Few people have had friends that have had it in their power to provide for a family better than you've all been provided for. God grant, my dear James, you may all prosper, and be blessed with grateful hearts to thank the Allwise Disposer of all things for thus raising friends to assist you in your distressed situation. That you may prosper in all your undertakings is the sincere wish of

Your sincere friend and kinswoman,
MARGARET MACARTNEY.†

The following essay is an unusual instance of maturity of thought, as well as fervent piety, in a young man of eighteen :—

* Mr. Iredell's brother.
† First cousin to Mr. Iredell's mother.

Sunday Morning, 17 Sept, 1769.

The interests of religion are too important to all mankind to be lightly considered by any. They respect a futurity which concerns us all, and have no less an object than eternal happiness to engage our attention. And lest our hopes should be insufficient to influence our conduct so that we might attain that object, our fears are directed to another of so terrifying an appearance, as to deter every wise man from the least chance of a connexion with it. No one yet has been so presumptuous as to brave the terrors of the Almighty upon a principle of heroism, or thought it honorable to oppose his Maker ; yet it is too much the practice of the present age to act contrary to His will, and believe it of very little consequence to do so, trusting to Divine mercy with the most entire confidence, as if it was equally indifferent whether the laws of God are observed or broken. But let us not be deceived ; for God will not be mocked. The Divine will is fully declared ; the terms of salvation are plainly offered ; and the gospel frequently and particularly acquaints us with the extent, and prescribes the limits of Divine mercy. Imperfection is the lot of humanity ; and God will mercifully overlook errors we commit as men. Even our sins will be forgiven if heartily and truly repented of. Are not these gracious instances of goodness ? and shall any man dare to abuse this goodness ? Can any one expect the favor of the Almighty, who pays no respect to his laws and thinks they may be dispensed with, when they counteract some seeming pleasure or advantage ? This is indeed the height of folly, and it is amazing men of sense can fall into it ; yet such is the consequence of prevailing impiety which has almost annexed shame to virtue, and made many afraid to appear good, even when a conscientious principle has restrained them from vice, —with grief and sorrow of heart I speak it,—religion is a subject for the derision of those who can exercise their wit on nothing else. Many who would be afraid of exposing themselves on any other topic, fearlessly take up this ;—since wit itself seems slow in attacking irreligious folly, and suffers the most absurd reasoning to flow on in uninterrupted dulness, when attempted to prejudice us against religion. Its friends are heard with proud contempt ; and no one's understanding have we so ill an opinion of, as his who thinks it applied to the noblest use in the defence of the laws of that Great Being from whom we received it. What can account for this infatuation ? Are we to receive our principles as we do the cut of our clothes, because some men dare to make a bold stroke ? But let us not debase, by enslaving, our understanding, (that noble distinction between men and brutes,) since every man has a reason of his own for his guide ; but let us bring every thing to that test, and after a fair, impartial consideration, we shall not be liable to any gross deception. This is the only laudable, the only useful exercise of the noblest privilege a man possesses. And if it may appear to us that the generality of mankind too slavishly submit their opinion to the guidance and influence of men whose understanding they may think superior, do not let us be governed in the same manner. Many of superior sense may be too much influenced by caprice, and adopt opinions upon inefficient grounds, or with a prejudice not carefully guarded against. If on account of a seeming singularity either in principle or practice we meet with many disagreeable occurrences, it is our duty to bear them with becoming fortitude, and to hope for a reward of steady perseverance in virtue, on a day when prejudice shall be undeceived, and rewards and punishments distributed without any distinction but of virtue and vice, and according to the different degrees of either. Then we shall all be on an equality, except that the most virtuous will be the most distinguished. Folly, prejudice, and all the evils attending upon them, will have done their worst. The reign of vice will then be over, and all its power of conferring honors and rewards— its usurped authority which was once exerted with such arbitrary sway—will then be punished with a severity not more rigorous than just.

"The proud distinctions of the earth shall fall,
And he's the greatest who was least of all."

Oh, dreadful yet pleasing day, when the doom of so many millions shall be irrevocably determined ! The choice of either happiness or misery is now at our option ; to-morrow may be too late. This moment is ours, the next is in the womb of futurity. Who would hesitate a moment when his all, so great an all, is at stake ? If we are still careless and supine, and live as if this world were to be our eternal home, we may be surprised at an hour when we think not, and the consequence may be most fatal. Not one virtuous excuse for delay can be named. If we are convinced of the necessity of a virtuous life *here* to entitle us to happiness *hereafter*, it is our duty to commence it immediately, or forfeit the hopes of immortality. By delaying it we show that we have not virtue enough at present, and subject ourselves to immediate danger. And if we are not willing to shake off evil habits now, how can we be assured of our inclination to remove them when they have gained strength by time, and are then made more necessary to our happiness. The consequence of one delay will be such a succession of delays as will rivet our habits to us so closely as to be immovable. If we are resolved to indulge ourselves in every sinful gratification till we are capable to sin no longer, this will show a propensity to vice that will not leave us, probably, when we act virtuously, merely of necessity. Such a proneness to evil (not a natural disposition, but the consequence of habitual indulgence) will render us very unfit for a reformation that will be effectual. But the event may happen sooner. The thread of life may be easily broken, and with it the ready promises of repentance. Nor is this thought a strained one. It is obvious to all, and instances to confirm its justness familiar to every one's eyes.

Death is the common lot of humanity; its power extends to all, and amidst all the skeptical criticism of the age, this is universally admitted. Surely this is a proper object for frequent and serious attention. Different periods of a man's life are allotted to different pursuits, each proper for its own period, but there is no period of life when death is not near us; and, consequently, we ought always to be prepared for his coming. I am sensible this is a common argument, and often pressed upon our practice; but its being common does not take away its force—it rather adds to it. The plain precepts of religion suffer much by a too anxious desire of refinement. The most obvious arguments are the most useful; and this argument must be apparent to a mind that is in the least seriously attentive; and if we were to bestow our thoughts purposely upon it in private, it might well be imagined, when we hear of many persons around us going off the stage of life, who were lately as hearty and healthy as ourselves, that we would bestow some moments' consideration upon an event which may be so nearly related to our own case. Instead of this, what is generally our conduct? We hear of a man's dying a natural death, as we do of an accidental one—perhaps shed a tear of tenderness to his memory, or pity to his fate, but never apply the instance to improve our lives, and as an argument to be always ready.

I am not ashamed to think seriously of religion, and hope no example will ever induce me to treat it with indifference. Youth is as much concerned to practise and revere it as any in the more advanced stages of life, and I have drawn up the foregoing plain but useful remarks as thinking it the best way of employing my time on this sacred day, when I have had no opportunity of attending public worship. I hope these reflections will be ever present to me; but lest they may not always be properly attended to, let me resolve to peruse them frequently. If they are still strong in my memory, a perusal may be a very useful way of reviving them; and if (which God forbid) I may lose a reverence for the sacred truths of religion, these reflections must occasion the most cutting remorse, and may be a means of recalling me to reason.

JAMES IREDELL.

Extracts from a letter from Henry E. McCulloh, dated London, Dec. 23d, 1769.

DEAR JEMMY:—I acknowledge the receipt of several letters from you, since my return from France; particularly yours of the 5th Sept., and 9th Oct. I wrote you once in Oct., and once in Nov. The middle of next month I shall write you very fully; this goes by a chance opportunity. I am obliged to you for your writing so frequently.

I wrote you samples in case the office comes to your hands: the instruction is not new. If the event takes place, I shall give you directions how to act, so as not either to hurt the office or your conscience. You are a young man and I hope not above receiving directions,—though I am far from finding fault with your delicacy.

If Molly * takes care of the child, *tant mieux pour elle*,—it may be *tant pis*; remember, that those folks are my friends. Inform Mr. Lowther I am happy to think the office is in his hands.

Your mother has taken a house at Bath, and I believe goes on swimmingly. I have not as yet heard they have received any thing from Mr. Murray.

Use no unnecessary covers in your letters to me; postage you know to be very dear, but don't cease to write me often.

BRISTOL.

I had the pleasure, my dear James, of receiving your very entertaining epistle, and am much obliged to you for it. So very much, that I shall not just sign my name, as you very gallantly desired; but send you a full sheet of paper, which, though filled with nothing more than mere female *chit-chat*, will, I flatter myself, be agreeable to you from the partiality I am convinced you have for me. You know Bristol so well that you will not be surprised when I tell you, that for some months after your departure, (when the players had left us,) we found an insipid kind of sameness. There was nothing but tea visits and cards going on —the latter of which excludes conversation. As to myself, I have spent my time much as I used to do while you were with us— with my friends, the Miss Gresleys, every evening. We used to dance cotillionets—cotillions we *dared* not call them, as we were but four, which, you know, is just half what there ought to have been. Your uncle had an attack last Christmas from his old disorder, which we thought would have carried him off, as there was some danger of a mortification ensuing. However, he soon

* His mistress.

got the better of it. I have been ill and was near two months at Mrs. Parry's at Hanham, and found much benefit from the country air. Since which I have been near six weeks backwards and forwards at Mrs. Paumier's, at Bath. A most ridiculous time it has been. Derrick's death made a most violent uproar, as Mayor Brereton and Mr. Plomer (our master of ceremonies) both set up for master of ceremonies at Bath. Each had a strong party to espouse their cause. You may easily conjecture I was for our old townsman; but as each party was equally vehement, and as fate had thrown me amongst the Breretons, I declared neuter, though they might easily see which side I inclined to. At last it was determined a third should be appointed, and Capt. Wade was the man. Brereton got five hundred pounds, and his wife two hundred a year, and Plomer six hundred pounds —so that the candidates were well off. Had either succeeded, Bath would have been a seat of perpetual discord; and whatever party had lost, would have been raising perpetual cabals to the prejudice of the person chosen by the other. This quarrel has been of service to the Hotwells, as many families have come there sooner than they intended. You say, my dear Jemmy, you have no talent for the descriptive. I assure you it gives me the greatest pleasure to read your descriptions of people and places; but I desire, for the future, you'll write longer letters to me. Write close, and not, as your Cousin Harry once told me, as if you had learnt to write in the Six Clerks' Office. Though you are designed for the Law, you need not write to your friends as if you were to be paid so much a line.

Now, as I speak of your Cousin Harry, I must tell you that we expect him here every day. In my next I shall be able, I hope, to afford you some amusement, as our Playhouse opens next Friday night. I intend to keep a kind of journal to send to you. Do you the same with descriptions of every person and thing you meet with. If I go to Mrs. Hoare's, at Stourton, as I have some thought of this summer, I will give you a description of the place. I am afraid you will hardly be able to read this, as I am not only obliged to write fast as possible, for the vessel, just about to sail, but am also tired, as I have written down five sides of paper to Marianna Smith, who is now in London on her way to the West Indies. I suppose you have heard by your father of the stoppage of the Warmly Company, and that in consequence of that, Mr. Champion has failed. As I am almost come to the end of my paper, I think it time to give you a little advice, which is to take care of yourself, and not dance too much. Pray, likewise, return my compliments, and Miss G——'s, to the gentlemen of Edenton; and tell them, if it's possible to get some dresses we have

ordered in time, we'll certainly wait on them the 12th—according to invitation; but inform them, at the same time, not to do things in the *true English taste*, as variety is one of the most pleasing things in the world, and would be a greater inducement to any person to go a length of way to see any thing, than any other argument that could be produced. Of one thing, however, rest assured, my dear Jemmy, which is, that I am and ever will be your most

Affectionate friend and kinswoman,
MARGARET MACARTNEY.

P. S.—Your uncle desires his love to you; and Miss Gresley and all friends desire to be remembered to you.

CHAPTER III.

CUSTOM-HOUSE, MCCULLOH, STUDY OF LAW, LETTERS, JOURNAL, LICENSE. ÆT 19.

During the year 1770, Mr. Iredell was actively employed. From his induction into office until April, 1776, he prepared all the accounts, returns and exhibits, and kept the books of the Custom-house. He not only performed the greater part of the drudgery of McCulloh's deputy, but kept a vigilant watch over the general interests of the Collector. The books and papers are still in existence, remarkable for accuracy and beauty of penmanship; they bear honorable testimony to his industry and fidelity.

He also transacted a multiplicity of affairs, delicate and difficult, for McCulloh. He sold and leased lands for him, collected his rents and fees, and made remittances by bills of exchange, and cargoes of corn, pork, etc. He made, on horseback, journeys to Suffolk, Halifax, and as far west as Salisbury, to confer with Mr. Frohock,* one of McCulloh's agents. He wrote to his principal frequent and long letters. McCulloh would, sometimes, rate him soundly for not writing oftener, and hint that he was indebted to him for office, and held at his pleasure; at others, would assure him of his love, his intent to resign in his favor, his purpose to make him his heir. He occasionally made Mr. Iredell small presents; but never paid him any fair or reasonable compensation for his arduous and valuable services. McCulloh remained in England for years at a time, living in luxurious ease. He was very seldom at Edenton, and his visits to the Custom-house never lasted longer than a few hours, while his indefatigable subordinate toiled painfully for a bare subsistence.

---

* Frohock, Clerk of the Court, his "plantation and house, the most elegant and large within one hundred miles."—*Avery's Diary*. He was a man of talent and education. As agent of McCulloh, who represented George Selwynn, claimant of large tracts of land, he had given rise to popular disturbances. He was afterwards a tory. Selwynn was the celebrated wit.

Every moment of leisure Mr. Iredell devoted to his legal studies, or to such intercourse with intelligent gentlemen and cultivated ladies as was calculated to refine and improve. He was a diligent student; he copied Mr. Johnston's arguments* and pleas in interesting cases. He read carefully and attentively the text-books, referring to the authorities quoted, and collating and digesting kindred passages from all the writers within his reach; he attended the courts, returned to his chamber and wrote out arguments of his own applicable to the cases he had heard stated.†

Extracts from a letter of H. E. McCulloh. London, January 26, 1770.

Your brother Frank is appointed a Cadet in the Indian Service, and is going out in about six weeks with Mr. Shaw, and yet I do not think you have any occasion to envy him. Mr. Shaw seems to me, to act upon a point of honor rather than inclination, and a Cadetship is (God knows) a chance for the £20,000. However I am glad it is so, and I have had much trouble to bring it about. As soon as Sr. G. M. returns from Ireland we shall endeavor to get the office in your name, (of this be silent,) and then I shall write you fully. I hope this will be done, though I cannot ensure success. Endeavors shall not be wanting. Your mother complains of not hearing from Mr. Murray. You should write to him and rub up his memory. I hope you are sensible of the necessity of your application to business, and that unless you *can* and *do* apply closely at this *period*, the *hopes of yourself* and of your *friends* are vain. Lay this to *your heart*.

February 13, 1770.

It gave me great pleasure, my dear Jemmy, to find by your last letter to your father that you had received some of mine. I began to be very uneasy lest they had miscarried, yet I thought it rather extraordinary, that not one out of seven letters that I had wrote should come to hand. The last I sent by a private hand from Bath, October 21st, where I had been led by curiosity (the prevailing passion of our sex it's said) to see Paoli. Many were the perils I encountered by so doing. In the first place, our

---

* Mr. Johnston's argument on the Act of Parliament "for the more easy recovery of debts in his Majesty's Plantations in America," in my opinion, surpasses, in learning and power, any cotemporary effort. His argument, also, on a bond given to Richard Spaight, Secretary of the Province, by Wm. Mearns, in consideration of the latter's appointment as Clerk of the C. Court of Currituck, fully sustains his reputation as a lawyer.

† The Manuscripts are before me.

---

chaise broke down in the midst of the dirty road leading to Russelton Common, when we had the satisfaction of being laughed at by some, and pitied by others. To render it still more provoking we found we should lose our dinner. There we stood above an hour while the chaise-boy was trying to tie the chaise together—when Dame Fortune, who was ever reckoned very changeable in her disposition, once more changed sides, and good-naturedly sent a chaise by, with Mr. and Mrs. David in it, who were going to dine at Mrs. Bush's, whose house was not one hundred yards from the place of accident—so we got to Bath just in time to dress. I went to the ball—stood till I was near fainting from the excessive heat—got a most violent headache—saw the General, and came home again. Now for a little Bristol news. Miss Smith (Mrs. Tyndal's sister) has bade adieu to England. She is gone to settle with her brother at St. Vincents. I have not yet heard of her arrival. Miss Davis, our neighbor, is married to a Mr. Forrester, and gone to settle in Barbadoes. N. B. Your brother Charles has this moment left me, as Capt. Smith, of the Blaiz-Castle is just gone down. I have given Charles a letter to Mrs. Forrester. Miss Gresley has taken a house in Calvert street. The occasion of their leaving the Square is that Mr. Hellier is going to quit his house—indeed, the poor man, I believe, is able to keep it no longer. It's a very distressful thing to see two old people who are unable to assist themselves in such circumstances. She seems to me almost a way-child. I suppose you have heard of poor Holland's death. The stage has received two great shocks by his and Powell's demise. I was sorry for them, as you know I am a great friend to theatrical amusements. Next summer, if we have any plays, King comes down as manager in Powell's place and Smith in Holland's; but at present there is some doubt, owing to a circumstance not known to the public till lately, though suspected for more than two years. Mr. Edgar held, with Powell and Holland, some share in the profits accruing to them as managers. The successors to these gentlemen don't choose to admit him to be on the same terms with them; and he, at present, does not seem inclined to give up a connection which, I suppose, he has found lucrative. How the point will be determined is yet uncertain; but, as Mr. Edgar's claim seems to be of an extraordinary nature, it seems probable it will be carried against him. I am obliged to write as fast as possible, as I am, at present, going through a course of lectures on Experimental Philosophy, under Mr. Arden. He has a very fine apparatus, and I think, is clear and makes himself understood. There are above fifty subscribers. I had almost forgot to tell you that Mr. Joe Whitechurch is married to the widow Purnell—a sister-in-law of Miss Purnell that used to be at Mr. Beaton's. She is a woman of good fortune, and Mr. Smith, of Wrington, has taken him into partnership. Jem Whitechurch is gone to Barbadoes. Mr. and Mrs. Smith are always inquiring after you. Mr. Maskelyn intends writing to you by the next opportunity. I desire, when you write to me, that you take a large sheet and fill it quite full. As to your not being clever at description and characters, all I can say is, I like them and long to know all the beautiful prospects you have seen, and every thing possible about the climate, and people, and what fruits, and other things are produced there. I think this may be useful to both you and myself, as there is not a more pleasing and instructive amusement than inquiring into the works of nature; it is a large field of entertainment, and worthy the attention of a human—or more correctly speaking, a rational creature. One thing I beg is that when you write to your father, or indeed to any one, not to put your letters under cover when you can avoid it, as it makes them pay double postage. I shall always, with pleasure, pay for letters from you, but remember I expect that all your paper is to be filled, the more sheets the better. Your last might have done well enough were we no farther separated than Bath; but letters should be proportioned to the distance friends are apart. I endeavored to let you know the duty of a correspondent, and from the length or shortness of your future letters, I shall, in some degree, judge of your esteem for me. Your uncle* has had a very severe attack lately, but is now pretty well recovered—indeed it's quite amazing to everybody that he holds it so long. Now for a subject more interesting to you. Your mother is now settled, and for the time, I think, has had great success. I hope it will continue. No doubt your father has wrote you about Mr. Shaw, so I shall say nothing on that subject. I have myself thought that it would be better for Frank to go to Jamaica, for even if your uncle would do nothing for him (which is unlikely) he might obtain a Clerk's place, which would be infinitely better than wasting his time as he now does, for at his time of life people are very apt to form a habit of idleness, which they can never get rid of. Your father is of my opinion, but your mother and Frank think otherwise. Mr. Blackford thinks it the best thing he could do. Now, if you approve, propose it as a scheme of your own, when you write to him, not of my suggestion, but as if the idea had struck you when you found he did not go with Mr. Shaw. I don't know whether I told you that I had given Halifax his freedom, so that

---

* Macartney.

he has left me. Sally desires her respects to you, and also Nance, who now lives with me. Miss Gresley drinks your health. Pray is the ball-room ready yet? What inducement do you offer those ladies and me to settle in Edenton? Is there a house ready for our reception? If not, haste to prepare one. You must likewise be our beau, to gallant us about. I am now forced to conclude, as I have hardly time to dress for dinner, and am engaged to Mr. Spann. Your cousin Harry has been very ill, but is now better. Adieu, my dear James; believe me, with the greatest sincerity,

Your ever affectionate kinswoman,
MARGT. MACARTNEY.

LONDON, March 20th, 1770.

DEAR JEMMY:—I hear dollars are plenty your way.

The sixpenny duty, I will depend, has been regularly collected, accounted for, and paid. No Collector's salary can be paid till he produces a certificate from the Com. Office, that he has fully accounted with them and paid his balances.

Mr. Hulton acts for the Receivers.

Mr. Lowther gives me great pleasure in informing me, you apply yourself to business. You must have sense enough to know that every thing depends on the turn you now take, and you may depend on a friend in me, who will rejoice at, and endeavor to promote your interest and happiness. Sir George Macartney is in Ireland. I have wrote to him on the subject of assisting me as to obtaining the Office for you, but received no answer. For the present that matter must be postponed, though I hope something may be done on Sir G——'s return. I am sufficiently secured as to absence, which makes me the easier on this head for the present. I hope, on what I wrote Mr. Lowther,* the parties will all be satisfied that the Office remains as it is. I depend you will give close attention, and take upon you the drawing out the lists and accounts and other writing part. You have great reason to be thankful that you have sense enough to prefer the little certainty, and humble but happy prospects you possess, to those flattering hopes with which some of your friends endeavored to fill you. Frank's dream is over; the circumstances I suppose you will have from your family; they reflect no honor on the titled party, and the conduct of the other is highly equivocal. I had much trouble in this matter to no purpose.

* Mr. Tristram Lowthe. was a lawyer and gentleman of refined manners: vide Life J. B. Skinner.

I shall write Mr. Campbell in a few days. I am sensible how much I am obliged to him for the flattering testimony I received, of the good opinion of the late Assembly.

I am pleased to find your letters so well written.

H. E. McCULLOH.

BATH, April 30th, 1770.

This packet, my dear James, will give you an account of my dear uncle's demise.* Though it's been an event long expected, yet I have no doubt but the filial tenderness you are possessed of will render it an affliction to you, who knew so well his affectionate regard for you. His last moments, my dear Jemmy, were as composed and easy as we could suppose the separation of body and soul to allow. As his life had been uniformly good, it was a blessed and desirable change for him. God grant that at our latter end we may have as comfortable a prospect before us. I have been here a few days, as a change of air and place was judged absolutely necessary for my health, which the fatigue I have undergone has greatly impaired. For seven nights following, I never had my clothes off. My spirits have almost failed me. I shall return to Bristol this week, give up my house, and then I have some thoughts of paying a visit for a short time to Ireland. It was very fortunate for me that my dear Miss Kerr arrived just as your uncle was in the greatest danger, and seeing how ill I was would not leave me. Her tender care in some measure relieved the distress of my mind—but why should I thus return to a subject I intended to avoid? Mrs. Pope is in great trouble. She has just heard of the death of Mrs. Colvill, in the East Indies. She died in childbed. It must be a great loss to him. The account was sent by Mrs. Vansittart (Miss Stonehouse)† to her father. I had a letter a few days ago from your cousin, H. McCulloh. I find he has not yet resigned his Collectorship. Whenever he does I hope it will be in your favor. That place, my dear James, would make you pass your life not only in a comfortable, but in an affluent way. Although happiness is not centred in riches, yet they add greatly to our comfort, as every generous mind must have great satisfaction in having the power to relieve the necessities and soften the afflictions of its fellow-creatures. Although those that *feel* sensibly for others, know many hours of pain, yet would I not sacrifice the sweet satisfaction of recollection for all I ever endured. I am quite of Sterne's opinion, "the tender sensations are the most valuable parts of humanity, and whoever endeavors

* Macartney.
† Daughter of Sir James Stonehouse, a physician and divine of great eminence.

to detract them from the soul, endeavors to rob her of the most precious gift of Heaven. If we had no feeling for each other, society and every good office would be at an end. I acknowledge myself an enthusiastic admirer of his writings—there is such a vein of benevolence runs through them. I can see his faults. He certainly, like many others, mistook his talent. The tender, the pathetic, was his forte. When he degenerates (as I must call it) into jesting strain, then I am displeased. Won't you think it very daring in me to criticise an author so admired? To you I am not afraid to tell my sentiments, as I am apt to flatter myself you are too partial to see my faults. Were I not of that opinion I should not, perhaps, have thought of scribbling so long a letter at a time I am so incapable of affording the least amusement. Miss Gresleys have left the Square for some time, and taken a house in Culvert street. I found a great loss in them, as it was impossible for us to be so much together as we used to be. Perhaps I ought to join with Pope in saying, every thing is for the best, as it has been a kind of weaning to us; and had I been constantly with them they would have missed me more at my departure from Bristol. The reason of their leaving was a melancholy one. Poor Mr. Hellier, by losing his business, was no longer able to keep the house. I am afraid the old couple have hardly bread to eat. As soon as things are settled with his creditors, I hope to raise a little money for him. It is a distressing thing to have the infirmities of old age and poverty come on together. Mr. Caldwell, of Belfast, has lost his daughter. She died in Bristol, where she had been some time on a visit to her uncle. Mr. Dean's sister is to be married in a few days, to a gentleman at Chandor, and the town says that your old friend, Bob Shute, is to have Miss Cheston. Whether there is any truth in the report I know not. By the first ship that sails from Bristol, Mr. Maskelyn will write you. Direct my letters in the usual manner, as I shall leave orders for them to be sent after me. I dare say it will give you pleasure to hear that your old schoolfellow, George Kerr, enjoys good health in the Indies, and has had great preferment. He is now a Captain in full pay, besides his Company of Sepoys and Brigade Major. His sister had three letters from him in January, and the distance of place between the date of the first and last was more than a thousand miles. Notwithstanding he is so harassed, he was in perfect health. He has made a very pretty addition to Lizzy's fortune. I was not surprised at it as he was so good a youth. How goes on the Law, my dear James. I hope one day to see you cut a great figure, and remember I expect your advice, gratis. I wish you would favor me with descriptions both of places, and the people you meet

with. You say you've no turn that way; but I know to the contrary. If you will write me Journal-wise—I will, if it will amuse you, do the same. Mrs. Harper is now here. She has married off her three beautiful granddaughters. Miss Bell, I think, was rather too young; but it was an advantageous match —so not to be slighted. Mrs. Harper is too fond of the good things of this life to neglect so powerful a consideration. She is ten times more miserly, if possible, than she was before, though her income is increased £200 per annum, by leasing Belgrove to Jack Bagnell. She has not now brought even a footman with her. It's amazing how a woman, who has been used to keep a regular set of servants, can (when it's no inconvenience in point of fortune) do without them. Everybody, almost, has, or ought to have, a necessary kind of pride of living according to their rank in life. Miss Gresleys present their compliments, with good wishes for your health and happiness. I have scribbled a long letter with very little in it; but you'll look on it as another proof of the love I have for you. I shall now conclude with an assurance that I am, with sincerity and affection, yours,

MARGARET MACARTNEY.

In the spring of 1770, Mr. Iredell seized three vessels, for violating the Acts of Parliament, relative to the Revenue; libels were filed by Mr. Thomas Jones. In the case of the sloop Lovely Peggy, the record of which is before me, William Brimmage, Judge of the Court of Vice-Admiralty,* no defence being made, decreed the sale of the vessel; and that the money arising therefrom, should be distributed according to law—i. e., one third to the King, one third to the Governor, and one third to the Comptroller, the cost and charges of the suit being first deducted. The sloop, tackle, and furniture sold for £27 5s. The Judge's fees amounted to £10 8s. 8d.; the Clerk's (Alex. Gallatly), to £8 17s. 7½d.; the Register's (Wm. Halsey), to £9 14s.; in all, £29 0s. 3½d.

The Comptroller's charge, styled "Incidents," amounted to £29 9s. 6d., besides the fee of one guinea paid Mr. Jones. As the fund was exhausted by the officers, he applied to the Commissioners at Boston. With an utter disregard of justice they declined payment, while the Collector reproved his rashness, and thought him rather zealous than wise.

* In the body of the decree he is also styled Commissary. The following affidavit relating to Brimmage was found among Judge Iredell's papers.

NEW BERN, Jan. 15, 1778.

Personally appeared before me, George Danison, and made oath that about the 10th and 11th inst., being with Wm. Brimmage on the road between Bath and New Bern,

LONDON, 5th May, 1770.

DEAR JEMMY:—I thank you for your punctuality in writing me, and for the accounts transmitted me. I shall take no other pay for the balance of your account with Mr. Lore than your future exertions for my service.

In the account of fees, from 24th October to 9th January 1770, is only £38 proc—is there no mistake?

I hope to hear from Messrs. Lowther and Hardy, in answer to the letters I have wrote,—and if they persist in refusing the office.

Be assured I shall ever be happy to hear of your well-doing. Application is the master-key to every thing in business, and I rejoice that you seem sensible it is. The good opinion of those with whom we live is a most desirable thing. I would by no means recommend to you to encourage a system of Informations. When forced no one will blame you for doing your duty, but the laws of trade in such a country as Carolina should ever have the most gentle and liberal construction put upon them. I hope the office in its present hands will not incur a suspicion of our severity. I think that custom has prescribed limits that a Judge should not overrule, and moreover that our right as well as interest is good. Mr. Brimmage, I trust, will determine like another Daniel.

Your uncle Macartney died about a fortnight ago. It was but civil in him. I have heard no further nor lately from Bristol. I propose to pay our friends there a visit in the summer. My father keeps his health very well, and proposes spending two summers near the sea-side. I have had my health but poorly

---

said Brimmage and this deponent being at Moore's, a dispute arose between them relative to our present government, wherein said Brimmage declared he did not like our present form of government, nor never liked a Republican Government, and never thought it any more than a mob government, that in his opinion the more arbitrary government was the better,—at the same time he declared he was a friend to the country, and intended pleading at the bar as usual,—the day following he repeated the same sentiments. Said Brimmage further declared that the whole dispute originated in New England, that the old Oliverian spirit had been carefully handed down among them, which now had showed itself, and which they did not pretend to deny. And he did not doubt, that (if America maintained their Independency) in the space of twenty years the Southern Colonies would each have crowned heads, and the Northern States might remain Republics; that he made no doubt Great Britain would send over the next campaign double the number of troops, and push every point,—this deponent then told said Brimmage he could not think it in the power of Britain to make up the deficiencies in their Army that had been killed and taken the last campaign, without the assistance of Russia. Said Brimmage answered that Great Britain was the Superior Force of the world, which he repeated several times.

Sworn to before me, January 15th, 1778.
WM. TISDALE, J. P.

The above deposition was made and signed in the presence of
SAM'L SPENCER, afterward Judge.

---

this winter,—a good thumping remittance would set all to rights, and perhaps give me spirits to go a courting, tho' it still continues to be all talk and no cider with me on that head. Mr. Shaw's friends are all out of the India direction. Sir G. M——y still continues in Ireland, verifying the old saying that a prophet has no honor in his own country. I have a friend in a corner with Lord North, who I hope will secure matters for the present, and bring them about hereafter. If you ever talk on the subject or are asked any questions, your answer is, my leave of absence is continued from the treasury. If you see Col. Harvey let him know I desired to be particularly remembered to him, and that I shall write to him, and the Committee of Correspondence very soon.* I am glad to hear of Sir N. Dukinfield's safe arrival, and present him with my compliments. If he chooses the plan Chuston drew for Dukinfield, he may have it, paying the charge, or what less you may agree for. It was my direction to Mr. Chuston to have no copy of it whatever. Speak to Sir N. D. on this business. I am sure the plan will be worth much more to him.

H. E. McCULLOH.

PINDAU VALLEY IN CLARENDON, JA.

DEAR NEPHEW:—I wrote you the 10th of November last by the snow Elizabeth, bound to South Carolina, inclosing two letters written some months before, which had been neglected in a Counting-house in Kingston; since which I have received your very pleasing letter of the 30th November. I am sorry to hear that you have already been attacked by the endemic disorder of your Province, which, I fear, must be the fate of all those who breathe a warm, moist air, and such I take that of Edenton to be. You have, without doubt, physicians who understand to prescribe, but unfortunately for their patients, those gentlemen more commonly understand their trade better than their profession; and it is more for their interest (how criminal soever it may be) to exercise the one than practise the other. In short if your doctor has not some friendship for you, you must pay severely both in pocket and person. If I may prescribe a safe preventive medicine that may serve but cannot hurt, I would advise you to take, on an empty stomach, every morning, half a pint of chamomile tea; and to begin and continue such a course during the fever season, or rather a little before it sets in. Nor is this unlikely to be of service, for chamomile flowers, reduced to powder, was the common febrifuge before the bark was discovered,

---

* Appointed by General Assembly.

---

about one hundred years ago. The account you give me of domestic affairs, gives me much pleasure. I have heard nothing from home for near twelve months. I begin to think they will not trouble me with letters, as it is not in my power to do much for them. However their neglect shall not make me forget my duty, whenever I have opportunity and ability to serve them. I think your brothers cannot fail of doing well in the East Indies, if they live, and are not greatly wanting to themselves; and as there is room for any number of your people there, one or both of them doing well, may be the means of drawing up the other boys after them. I long much for your answer to my former letters, as I shall for an answer to this. The more particular you are with regard to my brother, sister and family, with their state of health, prospects both for themselves and the boys, the greater pleasure you will give me, for as I hinted above, I despair of hearing of them through any other channel. I write this from my estate, near fifty miles from Kingston, so that I do not know when I may meet with an opportunity of sending it away. It is more than probable when it goes you may receive a few more lines from me.

I am, &c.

Extract from a Letter from H. E. McCulloh, dated June 20.

I did not expect to hear that the office was still complained of on account of the fees,—as I directed, and now direct, that such fees as are generally complained of, should be moderated to give satisfaction, and I repeat my directions that it be done, and that the office consult Col. Harvey, Mr. Johnston, and some of the chief gentlemen in the trade, on the subject. I would not give cause of complaint to any one,—and I strictly desire you will have the above directions carried into execution without delay. I write a few lines to Col. Harvey, and mention this matter to him. I desire you will, on the receipt of this letter, take a ride to his house, and consult with him. I wish Ben very happy, I have not heard from him on the subject. Make my compliments acceptable to Mr. Johnston; I beg leave to offer him my sincere congratulations on his marriage, and to assure him of my very sincere wishes for his happiness.*

Extract from a Letter from Mr. Thomas Iredell, dated St. Dorothy's, Ja., July, 1770.

From almost three years dry weather, we have been in a distressed situation, particularly for provisions this last year, and

---

* From a letter from Mr. McCulloh, dated 20th September, 1770, instructing Mr. Iredell to direct to him in future as the Provincial Agent of North Carolina, I infer that he began to act in that capacity during that year.

---

if it was not for supplies from your continent, must have starved. But I hope we are within a few weeks of plenty, as we have had fine rains and there are great crops of corn on the ground.

If I can meet with a safe conveyance, I will send you some books out of my small collection, both good and useful, and which I am sure you will be glad to peruse.

MR. IREDELL'S JOURNAL.

Edenton, 22d August, 1770.—As I spend too much time in an idle, unprofitable manner, I have thought of an expedient, which may perhaps correct my conduct a little. I am determined to set down the history of every day, and shall have ambition enough to deserve a good account of myself, so that, by this method, I shall review the conduct of my time; and frequent self-examination may be a good means of producing a habit of industry and application, which I hope will be of the greatest utility to me in my future walk of life.

It is now past 8 o'clock at night, and as it is a great cruelty to punish by an ex post facto law, I shall do myself the justice of delaying my journal till to-morrow morning.

Thursday, 23d August.—It is now near 7 o'clock, and I am just up—the morning too is very fine, and reproaches me in all the pomp of beauty. Indolence in any is shameful, but in a young man is quite inexcusable. Let me consider for a moment whether it be worth my while to attempt making a figure in life, or whether I will be content with a mediocrity of fame, and circumstances. And though it may be my duty to be satisfied with the latter, and my inclination would very well compound for a genteel competency; yet I know no motive to restrain a laudable and well-directed ambition to excel in some worthy and useful accomplishment. But nothing is to be acquired without industry, and indolence is an effectual bar to improvement.

Thursday, ten o'clock.—Just come home to dinner, 10 minutes past seven. I have not done as much as I ought to have done; read a little in Littleton's Tenures, and stopt in the middle of his Chapter on Rents, whereas if I had gone through it, it would have been better and more agreeable than losing three or four games at Billiards. N. B.—If you do play at Billiards, make it a rule not to lengthen. I went into my office to do some business there, but was prevented for want of red ink. I am now waiting for dinner, and will employ the intermediate time in finishing my Chapter on Rents.

Three o'clock.—Dinner hour—as we sat at table our reflections turned on a very melancholy incident which had happened a few hours before—a child of Dr. Lindners, who lived almost next door to us, died after an illness of only three days; a fine girl about six years old, her father and mother both absent—her father's illness occasioned her mother to go and attend him. She left all her children in perfect health, and now, will have the melancholy news of her daughter's death, before she knew she was out of order. The condition of those poor parents is much to be lamented, yet who is exempt from affliction?—it is the debt we all pay for our existence. Death has been very busy in his attacks of late—perhaps, in turn, he may pay me a visit. If so, God's will be done. Let me endeavor to regulate my conduct in such a manner as to have no gloomy fears at his approach.

Six o'clock.—This afternoon have been lying on the bed—not asleep though—it is but very seldom ever the heat of this climate encourages such indolence—reading a volume of the Spectator, which is ever new, ever instructing, ever entertaining. I hope they will be transmitted with honor to the latest ages. Their authors have gained an immortality of fame, and are deservedly ranked in the first class of fine writers, as well as good men. Strength of reasoning, elegance of style, delicacy of sentiment, fertility of imagination, poignancy of wit, politeness of manners, and the most amiable pattern of human life, appear through the whole in so conspicuous a manner, as at once to improve and delight. There have been other books wrote in imitation of these inimitable writings (the Tatler, Guardian, &c., are all the production of the same elegant Penman), but I own I have never read any of them with pleasure, except the Rambler, who has many fine thoughts, which are even agreeable through the medium of his cloudy and obscure style.

Nine o'clock.—Just stepped over to Mr. Jones' piazza; chatted a little with Mrs. Jones and Mrs. Hall, and then went up to Town. Met with Mr. Skinner at Mr. Smith's; received from him a packet for Mr. Johnston; was desired to inform him there would be an opportunity for Philadelphia in eight or ten days. Shut the windows of Mr. Johnston's and our office, afterwards drank tea at Mrs. Barker's, with her and Miss Elbrek.* By the way, this young lady is pretty enough, sings charmingly, and is very affable and engaging; but she wants a thousand nameless excellencies, which I think I can see elsewhere. Called at Bennet's, and talked of a new hat. As I was walking home called in at Horniblow's to see *who and who were together.* Mr. Hewes and Jackson playing Backgammon, Mr. Worth and Mr. Littlejohn looking on,—just saw the hit and came away. *Mem.*

---

* Miss Elbrek afterwards married Dr. Dickinson, who lived in the Cupola house.

I have not been much in a tavern these twelve months, and think an evening equally agreeable and more improving at home, besides the expense, which my finances will not afford; have been at home some time; resumed my Spectator; read a great many entertaining and improving things, particularly Mr. Addison's Discourses on Fame, in the 4th volume, which are incomparably elegant and sublime. Surely the writings of such great, learned, and good men, are more than a counterpoise to the libertine writings of professed Deists, whose immoral lives made them dread an account hereafter. How nobly superior is the dignified virtue of a good man, to the sensual and selfish actions of men of pleasure, whose desires centre in their own gratifications of loose and animal enjoyment; who consider this world as a medley of different interests and different pursuits, according to the uncontrolled dictates of every one's imagination, unrestrained by the principles of sense and reason. Whereas the other reflects that he is only one among millions whom God has placed in this world for the mutual help and support of each other; he knows it is not his duty to think himself abstracted from the general service of mankind; he takes all opportunities to make himself a useful member of society, and to answer the ends of his creation; for himself he desires to obtain nothing at the expense of virtue or honor, or to seek for any profit or advantage, by schemes inconsistent with the public, or any private, good; or by any deviation from order and decorum. He is not so bold as to trample on divine or human laws, because his duty exacts strict obedience to them—in short, he is willingly obedient to the laws of his Maker, from a sense of duty, and from a conviction that *His* Laws are at the same time the wisest direction he can follow, even for his own interest, knowing that the great Lord of the universe can have no views exclusive of our ultimate happiness. Reason instructs him in the necessity of human authority for the civil government of mankind, which will teach him a dutiful submission to the laws of his country; and we, who live in a land of freedom, and have been educated in free and liberal principles, obey the more willingly laws instituted for our own advantage; happy in the security of our lives and fortunes, which are protected by law, and cannot be forfeited but for the breach of laws that existed before we incurred the forfeiture; at a time when licentiousness is at an amazing and dangerous height, we shall be careful to guard against popular prejudice, though we must not blindly oppose the public voice, because it may appear too tumultuous. Let us view things impartially, and not approve or condemn any conduct on the whole, on account of a few improper circumstances attending it. I have strangely wandered,

but as it is now pretty late, and I find myself drowsy, I will go to bed.

Friday morning, seven o'clock.—Just up at the same hour I was yesterday morning, and yet I do not condemn myself so much, though I do not altogether approve of it. It rained the whole morning very hard, and it gave a turn to many reflections; however, I must break through this custom; it will never do.

Nine o'clock.—Breakfast just over. What have I done besides? No Littleton this morning. Why—must I say it?—why, to say the truth, I have wrote the whole of my Journal from three o'clock yesterday to this morning. What was it owing to? how were you otherwise employed? Come, this question is no disagreeable one, as it will lead to a proper explanation. Well, then, I did not write last night because I was afraid a candle would bring mosquitoes into the room, and I employed myself in reading in the 4th volume of the Spectator, till I went to bed.

One o'clock.—Come home to dinner; this morning pretty well employed; read a good deal in Littleton's Tenures, and afterwards a little in the Edinburgh Magazine for 1758; among other things read a few speeches in the Debate on the Seaman's Bill, the opposition to which shows, in an uncomfortable view, how the best schemes may be misrepresented, and what fine abilities are sometimes prostituted to the purposes of Faction.

But there was another circumstance I met with, must not be omitted. In an Extract from H. Walpole's Lives of Royal and Noble Authors, among the rest, is an account of Villiers Duke of Buckingham. Mr. Walpole taking occasion to speak of his astonishing quickness, gives this as an instance: In some part of a play that was acting, the Lover makes a speech to his Mistress, which begins with this line:

My wound is great, because it is so small.

To which the Duke instanter—

Then 'twould be greater, were it none at all,

which damned the Play.

In the life of Anthony Ashley Cooper, Earl of Shaftesbury, this anecdote is recorded,—that when a Bill was depending in the House of Commons for allowing persons indicted of High Treason to be heard by Counsel, as he was speaking in its favor, he hesitated for some time,—and then, with a noble presence of mind, and fine turn of sentiment, he took occasion from that very circumstance to fortify his argument; observing that if he, innocent and pleading for others, was daunted at the augustness

of such an Assembly, what must a man be who should plead before them for his life.

Nothing else material happened to me this morning.

Nine o'clock.—As I was sitting in Mr. Johnston's office, after dinner, I saw Mrs. Blair* and Mrs. Clarke pass along. I thought it a proper piece of politeness to attend them to the boat, as they were going over the creek,† and when I had handed the ladies in, they very obligingly expressed a desire that I would go over, which did not require much insisting upon. I went there and spent a very agreeable afternoon, though I had not the pleasure of seeing Mrs. Johnston, as she was indisposed—though but slightly I hope,—the more I am acquainted with that family, the greater is my esteem and love for them.

Upon my return I understood a fellow was to exhibit specimens of his dexterity in Balancing that evening. I afterwards went there with Miss Polly Jones, and really he was surprisingly clever; but the house was too confined for many of his pranks; he had a little recourse to sleight of hand, but here he performed miserably. It was at Mr. Jones's ware-house; the people who were there were the dregs of the town, except a very few. I came home about eight o'clock, and since have employed myself in reading my Spectator again, and will now go to bed.

This morning up between 6 and 7—was writing a little, and reading in Littleton's Tenures till breakfast, which is just over. The adventures of the day will be recorded hereafter.

One o'clock.—Could not quite escape a shower of rain, and now I am to mention how I bestowed my time this morning. I sat a little in Mr. J.'s office, and then went to the barber's to be shaved, returned immediately, and was soon after interrupted, disagreeably, by J. B. Beasley, who stayed there the whole morning. I afterwards bought a piece of linen, of Miller, which will cost me very dear, but I had rather been expensive about my person than in any other way. I mean, *simplex munditiis.* I am called to dinner and must desist.

Six o'clock.—Most of this afternoon at the billiard-table; I played a good deal, but came off clear, which is more than I usually do, though I know very well I frequently lose through carelessness. I will go and see how Mr. Jones does.

Nine o'clock.—Mr. Jones is very poorly, has a fever on him, and is very low-spirited. I hope it is only a slight disorder; the loss of such a man would not only be irreparable to his family, but very sincerely regretted by every one who knows him, and

---

* Sister to Mr. Johnston.
† Mr. Johnston's seat, Hayes, to the south, is divided from the Town by a navigable creek. Mr. Johnston married Frances, daughter of Dr. Cathcart.

more particularly by his intimate friends, who know him to be one of the best as well as most agreeable men in the world. It is now time to go to bed.

Sunday morning, seven o'clock.—Up about my usual time, and I have now to dress for church and go to see Mr. Jones.

Monday morning, six o'clock.—I have a good deal to do in my Journal, to account for the passing my day yesterday. I called to see Mr. Jones; found he had a very restless night, and that his fever was still on him, and what was worse, himself very much dejected. Cumming was there very seasonably, however, to cheer him a little; afterwards went up town; had my hair dressed; went to church with Mrs. Blair, the Miss Johnstons and Mr. Hewes, nobody to make the responses but Mr. Hewes and myself, and neither of us had a prayer-book,—Mrs. Barker very obligingly lent hers; no singing; Jackson was not at church, and the rest of the singers were too bashful to give out a Psalm; as this was, I think, owing to false modesty, I had a great mind to give out a Psalm myself, as I am very fond of church music, but I was irresolute, and took too much time to consider the propriety of it. Mr. Bruce's text was, (I forget the chapter and verse,) "Fervent in spirit, serving the Lord;" the sermon took up about twenty minutes, a very reasonable length; walked home with the Miss Johnstons, parted with them at the corner, thinking they were going to Mrs. Blair. Mr. Hewes asked me to dine with him; I sat down in his parlor; he went to look for Mr. Corrie, and found the Miss Johnstons. He and the Baronet * attended them to the boat; so would I, had I known they were going home; dined afterwards with Mr. Hewes; Mr. Worth, Mr. Smith, Mr. Littlejohn, Mr. Rome, and Nat. Allen † dined there too. After dinner Sir N. D., Mr. Hewes and myself went over to Mr. Johnston's, drank tea, and spent the evening there very agreeably. Mrs. Johnston was too unwell to be with us. Mrs. Dawson and her family were all there, and I had the pleasure to find they were all pretty well recovered again. In the afternoon the gentlemen took a walk to see Mr. Johnston's new ditch, respecting which there is a circumstance worth remembering. Mr. J. asked me whether I would go with them or stay with the ladies; as this was a puzzling question, because a preference seemed to imply a choice, I answered that politeness readily dictated an answer to that question, and was thinking to stay with the ladies, but he said I might as well go with him, and as my disposition in these trivial things is very pliant, I awkwardly con-

* Sir N. Dukinfield.
† Nephew to Mr. Hewes and father of Senator Allen of Ohio.

sented, upon which Hannah* was a little out. We soon returned and spent a very happy evening. Sir Nath'l stayed there. Mr. H. and I came over about 10 o'clock, and I went to bed directly.

Monday, two o'clock.—I was a good part of this morning with Mr. Jones, and extremely happy in finding him so well; went up town about 11 o'clock; did a little business in our own office, and then went to Mr. Johnston's, whence I am just come. N. B.—The New Bern Post is come in and no letter from Mr. Berry. I wonder at it.

Tuesday morning, seven o'clock.—I have to account for yesterday afternoon and evening. Soon after I went up town, met with Col. Buncombe and Mr. Steenberger, and staid most of the afternoon with them; called and sat some time with Mr. Jones, whom I had the pleasure to find much better; went in the evening to hear Mr. Hardsen sing and see Godwin dance, and was really very agreeably entertained, though I had a fever on me the whole time, the first I have felt this year; came home the moment they had done and went to bed. Am now just up; Jack came to ask me to dine with his master to-day; I do not feel myself very well, but hope I shall be able to go. I am always sorry at any opportunity I lose of being in company so perfectly agreeable.

Wednesday morning, nine o'clock.—Just after breakfast yesterday walked up town with Mr. Johnston; called at the barber's to have my hair dressed; walked over to Mr. Hewes' piazza, and chatted for some time with three or four gentlemen there; had not intended to go if Mr. Johnston had not been there; *as he was*, I thought going immediately from the barber's to his office would have had too much the appearance of affectation; went soon after to his office, and staid there the most of the morning; about 12 o'clock felt feverish; came home; on my way just called to see Mr. Jones; pretty well, considering; my fever continued to increase, and I really found myself very unwell, was obliged, very reluctantly, to send an apology to Mr. Johnston; could eat no dinner, but after a comfortable nap of three or four hours found myself much better; went over in the afternoon to see Mr. Jones, much the same, I think; read a little in a Magazine, and went to bed between 9 and 10 o'clock, and find myself very well this morning; nothing in particular to relate this morning; read a little in Littleton's Tenures, not much though, being interrupted.

Half past one.—Received a letter from Mr. McCulloh, dated June 15th, no new particulars; referring to others he has wrote of late; most of this morning employed in reading in Mr. John-

* Miss Hannah Johnston.

ston's office; was a little while in Miller's store with Mrs. Dawson* and Miss Anne. Just trudged home in the rain; escaped a wetting by the favor of Mr. Corrie's coat. *Mem.* Rub your teeth every morning with salt and water.

Friday, Sept. seven, half past one.—For several days past have been very unwell, and obliged to discontinue my Journal, which I now take up again. This morning have been very idle. I sat up late last night, and am not perfectly well; I went to see Godwin dance, which he did very agreeably; afterwards, the ladies danced a little with us; I was happy in having Miss Elbeck for my partner.

Won by the amiable graces of Miss Hannah Johnston, Mr. Iredell soon became an avowed suitor for her hand. No doubt, he omitted no opportunity of commending himself to her notice and favor. The following verses were about this time addressed her by him.

> In what soft language shall my soul convey
> Its dreams by night, and anxious cares all day,
> To her, the object of my fond desires,
> To call my wife whom my proud heart aspires;
> In whom each female excellence we view,
> The just decorum of the happy few,
> Possessed of elegant angelic minds,
> Where truth with goodness, grace with virtue shines.
> May you, the dearest mistress of my love,
> No more the pangs of dire affliction prove,
> But ev'ry day and ev'ry hour employ
> Some new occasion for a rising joy:
> And might the penner of this wish impart
> The rapt'rous feelings of his faithful heart,
> He'd hope to share the bliss, which you possess,
> And being blest, have some sweet pow'r to bless.

Miss Hannah, though her face was pleasing, had no pretensions to extraordinary beauty. She was distinguished, above all others in her region, for the dignity of her manners, and the stateliness of her carriage. When she appeared on the street, the thought "*Incedit regina*," involuntarily occurred to all who beheld her. Her mind had been well cultivated; she was acquainted with the various branches of polite learning; but her especial characteristic was the predominance of sound, practical, good sense. She seemed haughty to the stranger, but was not so; her unassuming nature and affability being universally recog-

* For a notice of the daughter of that accomplished lady, vid. Sketch of Joseph B. Skinner by Thos. H. Skinner, D. D., a "picture of surpassing loveliness and beauty."—*Un. Mag.* Mrs. Dawson was the daughter of Gov. Gabriel Johnston and grand-daughter of Gov. Eden.

nized and admired by her friends. She was a consummate mistress of all those arts that relate to housewifery, arts too often now unknown, neglected or forgotten, but arts that rendered the Carolina matron of the olden time, what God intended her—a helpmate for man, in the best sense of the word. It is unnecessary that I should enlarge upon her merit, as the reader will presently have an admirable likeness, sketched by a master-hand. Mr. Iredell's letters to her, for their esteem soon ripened into mutual affection, not only breathe the tenderest love, but possess a chastity of expression and exquisite delicacy of sentiment rarely equalled, never excelled. They constitute the noblest tribute to the maiden's purity and excellence.

The Parliament of Great Britain had resolved in 1764, that it "had a right to tax America," and though its temerity had been sternly rebuked by the resistance of the Colonies to Mr. Grenville's famous Stamp Act, yet had it turned a deaf ear to the warning, and persisted in its claim. The Stamp Act had occasioned the first organization of an American Congress—an assembly that insisted upon all the rights of Englishmen for the Colonists, including the right of self-taxation, and pointed the way to the Confederation.* At the repeal of the Stamp Act, great was the exultation of the Colonies; but soon was their joy clouded by gloom. The fond hope that British passion had subsided, was disappointed, and Parliament resolved again to renew a contest destined to produce the most calamitous results. In 1767† Mr. Townshend brought forward his scheme to raise a revenue in America, to provide a permanent income for the Governors and the Judges, that they might be independent of the Colonies, and to sustain an Army. Indignant remonstrances being unheeded, the Colonists zealously prepared other modes of resistance and defence. In 1769 the North Carolina Assembly passed resolutions maintaining their right to tax themselves, to petition and remonstrance, and to be tried by a jury of the vicinage. Though dissolved by the angry Governor, the members immediately reassembled in their private capacity, and entered into an agreement to import no articles from Great Britain, save those of prime necessity. Party lines began to be strictly drawn between the Tories and the Whigs. In 1770 riots occurred in Boston: troops fired on the people. The story of the "Boston Massacre" spread over the country with the speed, the fury, and the blaze of a prairie-fire. The sympathies of North Carolina were deeply excited, and the passions of her citizens inflamed at the outrage. Mr. Iredell was an interested, and intelligent observer of events. He had resolved to make America his home for life, and though a King's officer, soon became imbued with the views of the Amer-

* Hildreth, 1765.   † Hildreth.

ican leaders: felt that his future was identified with their future, and determined to participate in their defeat or success, to share in their disgrace or glory. He soon formed intimacies with the leading men of the province, men whose thoughts were to irradiate subsequent darkness, and whose voices were destined to cheer and sustain the people in the hour of disaster. Ere long he began with them an active correspondence, and his part was so well supported that a learned gentleman and most competent judge writes, "He was the letter writer of the war. He had no equal amongst his cotemporaries."*

The following letter is without date, but I am warranted by its references to other letters in referring it to this year.

Extract from a Letter from Mr. Thomas Iredell.

"As to your politicks, I have time to say little. I believe with you the spirit of enthusiasm has possessed your people pretty generally, but in what sense of the word (for it has several) I will not determine. I suspect an agreement among the great at home would soon knock in the head those visionary notions that have led your people to such unwarrantable lengths, and that no Parliament nor Ministry will ever give up the power of taxing, though they may that of internal taxation. But be this as it will, the less you meddle with politicks the better. As you are a King's officer, stand neuter at least. I am on the look-out for another runaway. When he is taken he shall be sent to you."

By and with the "approbation, and recommendation" of Chief Justice Howard, Mr. Iredell received from Gov. Tryon a license to practice Law in all the Inferior Courts of the Province the 14th of Dec., 1770. He took the prescribed oaths the 19th of the same month, before Thomas Jones, Clerk, at Edenton.

APPENDIX TO CHAPTER III.

The following letter found with Judge Iredell's papers, is without date. I have no knowledge of the difficulty referred to other than is contained in the letter. As Sir Nat. was only in North Carolina 1770—72, it belongs to that interval of time. Though not germane to my subject, it has interest as material for history, and because of the writer.

---

* Hon. David L. Swain, President of the University of North Carolina, in a letter to me, 1855. With a broader and nobler sense than any of his predecessors, of the relations of his post to literature, Gov. Swain has indelibly impressed his image on the heart of the State. He is ever ready to open the rich stores of his varied learning to the honest inquirer, and prompt to extend a friendly hand to every literary enterprise.

To Sir Nat. Dukinfield:

Dear Sir.—Pardon the trouble I am about to give you touching an affair that has very much disgraced the Magistracy of this County. You must know then, Sir, that last Tuesday was the day appointed by law for holding the Inferior Court of Tyrrell, on which day appeared six Attorneys, the Sheriff of the County and the Clerk, at the Court House, who continued there until Thursday evening with the Grand and Petit Jurors, Plaintiffs and Defendants with their witnesses, as also Constables, etc. During which time only two Justices appeared, viz., Col. Buncombe and John McKildo; of course no Court could be held for want of a third magistrate. Until Thursday the people attended with becoming patience and decency, at length they grew clamorous, damned the absent Justices, (I think with propriety,) prevailed on McKildo to adjourn the Court over to the next term, and then went to their respective homes. Some gentlemen of property in this County then met together and agreed, upon the persons set down in the inclosed list to be only placed in the Commission of the Peace for this County, and that the same should be transmitted to the Governor and Council. I immediately offered my service on this occasion, and have taken the liberty to state with truth the ill conduct of the Justices who neglected the publick business in so shameful a manner. The Sheriff and Clerk will attend the Council board. It will be further necessary for me to add, that no County tax is laid, no list of taxables is returned, no Sheriff qualified; *in totidem verbis*, all is confusion, anarchy, and uproar. Pray therefore lend your helping hand to remove this injury from a good people, and restore peace to his Majesty's ancient County of Tyrrell.

THOMAS JONES.

CHAPTER IV.

DIFFICULTY OF SPEECH; WAR OF THE REGULATION; LETTERS FROM GREAT BRITAIN; LYRIC; LETTERS FROM MR. IREDELL; THE CIRCUIT; FIRST ARGUMENT; LETTER FROM H. E. McCULLOH. ÆT. 20.

When Mr. Iredell first appeared at the Bar, "he had a difficulty to encounter which but few experience, and fewer surmount as he did. He had a natural impediment in his speech, which would have abashed and discouraged weaker minds, if possessed of but half his delicate sensibility. Yet like Demosthenes, one of the greatest orators of Ancient Greece, and perhaps of the world, he had the address to render it, in the opinion of the nicest observers, rather an advantage, as subservient to his power of recollection, and that ingenuity which he so often employed in the management of a cause, while by the multiplicity of his authorities and strength of his arguments, he often bore down all opposition." *

He did not spring into a lucrative practice, as a horseman vaults into his saddle. Years passed away before the number of his cases equalled his expectations: but his was a sanguine temperament, and hope gave life and energy to industry.

He was remarkable for his vivacity. In the rapid flow of ideas, thoughts seemed to crowd and jostle each other in their struggle for expression; but time soon calmed the riot of his spirits, and their exuberance was subdued into the genial warmth that ever rendered him the delight of the household, the charm of the social circle.

During this year the line of division between the adherents of government and the popular party continued to grow wider and more distinct. A great commotion occurred in the interior, known as the "War of the Regulation," which was suppressed, though not without bloodshed. The most prominent gentlemen

---

* Funeral Sermon by Rev. Chas. Pettigrew.

in the Eastern parts of the Province burying, for the nonce, their quarrels with the Governor, gave him a prompt and efficient support in this contest with the insurgents. Very conflicting opinions are entertained of the motives, conduct, and character of the Regulators; but it belongs to general history, rather than this work, to sift evidence and to render a righteous verdict.

In June Gov. Tryon was transferred to the government of New York; and was succeeded by Gov. Martin, who arrived in the fall.

Extract from a Letter from Master Arthur Iredell, a boy of thirteen years.

Bath, March 12, 1771.

Dear Brother:—Bath is at present pretty full, and I make no doubt but in a month it will be quite. Miss Linley (a great singer at Bath) is to be married to Mr. Long (a gentleman of £8000 a year) as soon as the writings can be drawn, by which he is to settle 1200 a year upon her, and to give her father 1500 for the remaining part of her prenticeship, as it seems she has four years to serve, but I think that very unreasonable. It was enough to give her 1200 a year; he is upward of sixty, and she sixteen.

There has been for a long time a dispute subsisting between two anonymous writers, under the signatures of Humanus and Spectator. Spectator charged Humanus (who is thought to be Dr. Rigges) with doctors not attending, as they ought, at St. Peter's Hospital; almost at the conclusion of the dispute, Humanus attacked Dr. Harwood, with being the author of Spectator. Dr. Harwood wrote, the next Saturday, a very spirited letter, which was so home, that Humanus could only answer with evasion. Humanus had charged Mr. Lee and Mr. Rouguet before he did Dr. Harwood; but for particulars we refer you to Fasley's Newspaper, which we send by this ship. You will then see that Dr. Harwood came off with flying colors.

Mr. Poulteney, who has an estate (very considerable) about Bath, which was left him by the Earl of Bath, and for which he changed his name from Johnston to Poulteney, has built a very handsome bridge over the river by Bathwick; and his intention for doing it, was to pass a Bill through the House of Commons, for leave to make a road from Bath to Devizes, by which you would avoid Kings-down Hill (which is a very steep one), and which would have been of great service to the city; but some gentlemen of Bath, who had estates by the London road, have obliged Mr. Poulteney to drop it. The Duke and Dutchess of Kingston are at present here; the Dutchess has introduced a fashion of going with her work-bag at the Rooms, and having her servants play the French horn there. There are likewise in Bath the Dukes of Northumberland and Queensbury; Earls of March, Plymouth, and family; Lords Mountstewart, St. John, Clare, Col. Nugent, and a great many people of Fashion.

We hope soon to see Charley in Blue and White, as Sir George promised to give him a commission."

In the year 1771 Sergeant Kempe, an eminent lawyer and devoted friend, assumed the charge of Arthur Iredell's education. The lad became a member of his family, and always accompanied him when, in his vacations, he retired to his country seat at South Malling. The Iredell family only had to supply Arthur with clothes the first year. Afterwards, by the kindness of the Sergeant, he earned £50 per annum, copying briefs, a sum that sufficed for his apparel. He was sedulously instructed by Mr. Kempe himself. In March '72 Arthur, in a letter to his brother, says,—"I have read Pliny the Consul's Letters: and have learned by heart the quarter part of the Latin Grammar. I have begun Porson on the Creed, which Mr. Kempe says I must abridge. So you see I am at the same time to enlarge my religious, as well as grammatical, knowledge." After he had received sufficient preparatory training he was entered in the Temple as student of law. Eventually, after some years' study, he was sent to Trinity College, Cambridge, where he took his degree, Feb. 1782; and was soon after admitted to Deacon's Orders. By the influence of Mrs. Catharine Macartney, in 1782 he was appointed by Mr., afterwards Lord Crewe, Tutor to his only son; and obtained also a curacy in the neighborhood of Crewe Hall.[?] By the refined and distinguished society generally assembled in that elegant mansion, he was most courteously treated, and made the acquaintance of many of the most illustrious men of the day.† Lady Crewe, the zealous friend of Mr. Fox, was a most beautiful and accomplished lady, second in charms, it is said, only to the Dutchess of Devonshire. Mr. Iredell enjoyed for years an intimate intercourse with that lady; and even after he ceased to be Tutor, was always at home in her house. In 1788 he was curate at Guilford, under the patronage of Lord Onslow. In 1791 Mr. Kempe, who was to him a second father, exerted his interest with the Duke of Richmond, and the Rev. Mr. Iredell was preferred to two Livings in the vicinity of Lewes,

* In 1784 a splendid entertainment was given at the mansion of Mr. Crewe, in Lower Grosvenor Street. Ladies as well as gentlemen were habited in blue and buff. A toast being offered by the Prince of Wales,—" True blue and Mrs. Crewe," which was rapturously received, that lady proposed another, not less laconic,—" True blue and all of you."

† Mr. Crewe was raised by Fox to the peerage in 1806. Wraxall's Post. Memoirs, p. 14.

Sussex Co. He became Rector of New Haven, and Glynde. In '93 he resided at Ringmer Park: in '96 at Glynde. His income was subsequently augmented by his appointment to a sinecure civil office. He married, Jan. 1792, Miss Anna Shrab, who brought him a considerable fortune. By the death of his uncle, he succeeded to a large estate in Jamaica. I propose to lay many of his letters before the reader. They are written with spirit and scholarship, and are running commentaries upon the men, the women, the politicks, and the gossip of the day; they also reflect much light on occurrences in America, of which he was always a profoundly interested observer. Mr. Iredell was one of the Executors to Mr. Kempe's will, and also one of the Guardians of his child.

Mr. James Iredell's fraternal affection was a beautiful trait in his character; and was marked by a tenderness almost feminine. All the letters he received from his little brothers were carefully preserved. On one is endorsed, "from my brother Tommy, aged 10 yrs. 3 mos.;" on another, with evident and exulting pride, from my "brother Arthur, aged 15."

Dublin, March 20th, 1771.

My last letter, my dear James, conveyed to you the melancholy account of your uncle's death, which I find you had not received when you wrote to me. Since that time I have been quite a rambler. The latter end of June I left Bristol, and went to London to join my friend Miss Kerr and Dr. Weld, with whom I had agreed to pay a visit to this kingdom. This you know has been long my intention. My time in London was spent, as it is generally done by those who pay it a short visit, in a continual hurry. I spent one day with Lord Wigton (Lord Fleming that was) and his new-married lady. She is an exceedingly pretty, agreeable woman, and brought him twenty thousand pounds—no bad thing for one that wanted it. As I have been unreasonable enough to expect a description of people, and places from you, I will also attempt the same for you. Now as the word pretty can't possibly convey an idea of a person, I will draw Lady W.'s picture as well as I am able—though perhaps after it's done, like many limnings I have seen, it might as well pass for any body else. In the first place, as to person, she is rather taller than I am; her face rather round than long; most beautiful complexion, both red and white; her eyes dark, as also her hair which is exceedingly fine; a very handsome head, and arm. Now, how do you like your new cousin? I spent two or three days with my friend, Mrs. Butler, at Turnham-green. Just before I left Eng-

land I went on a little party of pleasure for twenty miles about London. As you have never seen the seat of Mr. Hamilton, of Rayner-Hill, (Cobham,) a slight description may afford you some entertainment. Such as it appeared to me, will I, if possible, give you an idea of it. The house is not worth mentioning, but the improvements are delightful. The first view is from a shrubbery in an octagon form, in which is the tulip tree, and many others that come from your part of the world, and which are seldom met with in England; from this you come into a fine lawn on which he intended building. The river Mole winds round the greatest part of his estate, and serves as a boundary to it; in this river he has cut little islands and planted them with the most beautiful flowering shrubs. Cobham Church is a very pretty object from this place. The second view is from the vineyard, which of course lies to the south; from this vineyard he makes excellent champagne. The third view is from a Gothic Temple; from this place you see an excellent Chinese bridge over an extensive piece of water that Mr. H. has thrown into his garden by a simple piece of mechanism, which is a wheel in the form of a cork-screw that raises sixty-three hogsheads of water in a minute,—you, who have gone through a course of lectures, will easily comprehend the manner it works in—a tower just rising out of a thick wood; a marquee, or tent, in the most elegant form, made of white canvas, done round with blue fringe and tassels, and drawn up in festoons; a distant view of the ruins of a Roman gateway. There is also a beautiful Grotto, not quite finished; from this we walked up a wood, as wild as any you have described in America, to a Hermitage that was formed of old pines. We entered the room and found every thing within answer the outward appearance; an oakwood table, a couple of chairs, a straw-mattress on a couch, by way of bed, and a wooden candlestick. The place seemed formed for contemplation. From this we went into another room furnished in the same rustic manner. The beauty of the prospect cannot be described—the ripe corn waving in some places, while the different shades of green from the adjoining hills and meadows variegated the scene. On this excursion we spent three days very agreeably; went to the Duke of Newcastle's and to Woodburn-farm, the seat of Mrs. Southcote; but it would only be a repetition were I to say any thing particular on them. Your cousin Harry was of the party; but you are not acquainted with any of the rest, therefore it is needless to mention them. The 20th of July I left London. You need not be told that the company of my dear Lizzy Kerr made the journey agreeable to me. We travelled to Holyhead, and, thank God, had a safe though not quick passage. I went immediately

to your cousin Wells' but staid there only two days, till I went to the Black-rock to Mrs. Paumier's. It's unnecessary to tell you that I have experienced the greatest affection and civility, much the greatest share of which I must attribute to the love they bore my father. It must be to that, joined to the natural generosity and hospitality for which they are famed, as many of them I had never seen, scarce heard of. About five weeks after I came here I had the pleasure of being bridesmaid to my dear Eliza, who was married to your old school-fellow, Isaac Weld. I know it will give you pleasure to hear George Kerr goes on so well. Please God to spare his life, I dare say he will make a great figure. He sent his sister Weld last year £500. After the marriage, we went a little tour of three and twenty miles round Dublin. The first day's journey was to Drogheda; the next morning we went on to Slane, where there is the completest flour-mills in Europe. They are really very curious; the mechanism Mr. Weld explained to us; and at the same time there is such an elegant neatness reigns through the whole that it must give pleasure to any person to behold. We walked through Lord Cunningham's improvements, dined at Slane, and went on to Navan, and finding ourselves not tired with all the exercise we had taken, called in a blind harper and danced till supper. Next morning breakfasted at Trim, and afterwards went to see an old ruined castle at that place. We went to the top of it, though with some difficulty. When we were there, though we had a most extensive prospect, I wished myself down again, as it really looked dreadful standing on the broken battlements at such a distance from the ground. From this we went to Lord Mornington's at Dangan. Here we saw a most elegant little chapel, the windows, painted glass; that over the altar was John baptizing our Saviour, the heavens opening and the dove descending; the next was Moses delivering the law to the children of Israel, a most venerable, striking figure; the next St. John Evangelist, sitting on a spread eagle, a scroll in one hand and a pen in the other; the last Paul preaching. The expression in the faces, the due proportion, each figure being the natural size, together with the richness of the colors, made them strikingly beautiful. The branch, that hung from the ceiling, was of burnished gold, as were, also, the tall candlesticks that stood on each side of the altar, and those that stood on the communion-table. We went through his improvements, which are really exceedingly pretty. From this we went to Summer-hill, Mr. Rowley's. The house is magnificent, and esteemed a highly finished piece of architecture. In one of the rooms, over the chimney-piece is a beautiful piece of carved work in white marble, the Judgment of Hercules.

It's reckoned quite a masterly performance. After seeing the house, strolled above two hours round the domain, and it was with regret we left it then, though the moon was up and we had eight miles to go to the place where we had to sleep. Here, while supper was getting ready, we danced. The next day we went to Caston, the Duke of Leinster's. Here, indeed, elegance and taste were displayed. This nobleman lives in a truly princely magnificence. He has every thing within himself. This day ended our tour. We returned to Harold's Cross in the eve. The next week was entirely taken up with receiving visits, and the fortnight after in paying them, at the end of which time I went to pay a visit to the Fews. Here I staid five weeks, and thence went to pay Sir Archibald and Lady Acheson a visit, thence to Carmeen, Mrs. Langs, where having staid some time, I returned to Dublin, after being absent three months. Here I have gone through all the ceremonies, been presented at the Castle, and been at grand assemblies of Lady Jane Macartney, Lady Strangford, etc., etc. Now I think I have been as good as my word in giving you an account of my time. I must now take notice of some parts of your letter. First, as to—it's not Mr. Barry, but Baddely. Mrs. Farr, of Clifton, I hear is dead ; but I must leave Bristol news for your brother and mother. You ask me what Mr. and Mrs. Smith it is that make so many inquiries. It's Mr. Smith, whom you may remember at our house, and the Gresleys. Joe Smith, and his wife, I am not much acquainted with. Mrs. Mallard (Miss Beaton) has a son. Your friends here make many inquiries after you ; and it gives them, and all of us, great pleasure to think you are so happily settled. I am afraid, James, the fine young ladies you are so often in company with will render you inconstant to me ; but, seriously speaking, guard your heart with watchful caution till you are better able to maintain a wife and family. I should be extremely sorry to hear you had an *entanglement* on your hand, as the very wisest in that case are apt to act a *foolish* part ; but remember I expect to be your second wife. Your friend Joseph Whitechurch is a father ; but whether it is a boy or girl, I protest I don't remember. You tax me with telling, only, the lady is a fortune, without pointing out any other accomplishment. You'll allow in this expensive age, that that is one at least, and a necessary one ; but the cause of my silence was entirely owing to my not being acquainted with the lady. I never saw her but once, therefore cannot say any thing on the subject of her being—extremely sensible—very agreeable—"*et toute la chose necessaire*" on these occasions. What's the reason you write such short letters of late ? If you grow so polite, I must certainly get small gilt-paper instead of these monstrous sheets, to be on equal terms. I fancy the long letters I write frighten my correspondents. Let me not omit mentioning a circumstance concerning your brother Frank. He has at present an offer of going out to Africa as a writer in the African Company's service. All his friends here think it's the best thing he can do. Sir Geo. Macartney was with me yesterday, and I find it is his opinion also. He is to get Charles a midshipman's place, aboard a man-of-war. Your cousin, Jemmy McCulloh, of Antrim, sails in the packet this morning for London, from whence he is to proceed to the East Indies as a surgeon in the Company's service. I believe you were acquainted with him when you were here. His mother is lately dead. Cousin William McCulloh is just recovered out of a dangerous fever. The girls are well. Willy is still at Drogheda school ; they fear he will have a disagreeable operation soon to go through, as they have some cause to think he has a polypus growing in his nose. My cousin James (at the Fews) has not been very well lately, but is now pretty well again. As to politics, I suppose you would not thank me for any account I could send you. You, no doubt, have intelligence of what passes here. The Speaker's resignation of the chair surprised some people. His friends, they say, are displeased at his leaving them in the lurch, however, all parties seem to agree in saying, the man that has it is much fitter for the employment. Mr. Perry was bred to the bar, and is reckoned a most eloquent speaker in the House. How goes on your law study ? I expect to see you make a shining figure some day or other. I have now almost filled my paper, therefore must think of making a conclusion. Is the ball-room almost finished, and every thing in readiness for our reception ? I think you ought to build a house and get a little land around it, a couple of cows, etc., and if you made it comfortable, in all likelihood we might be tempted to stay. This is not the first time I have amused myself with imaginary schemes, but in serious earnest be assured I should be happy in serving you, and be assured that I am with the truest affection, my dear James, most sincerely your friend and kinswoman,

MARG'T MACARTNEY.

The following verses are without signature or date. I suppose them to be original because of the personal allusions. I assign them, perhaps arbitrarily, to this year, because it is in youth that the bubbling fountains of the heart are most apt to gush into the tinkling melody of song ; and, further, because the only verses known to be Mr. Iredell's were written ere yet the bright visions of hope had faded into the dull realities of life, as the golden-shower of the Roman-candle turns, in the urchin's hand, to blackened cinders. He did not often strike the lyre, but sometimes in his joyous moods his fingers played with its strings, and awakened notes pleasant and musical, if not strictly artistic.

> Cease ye party jangling swains,
> Leave your flocks, and quit your plains,
> Friends to country, or to court
> There's nothing here shall spoil your sport,
>   Ever welcome to our feast,
>   Welcome ev'ry friendly guest.
>
> Be it peace, or be it war,
> Both or either, I don't care,
> Prithee Colin what have you,
> Or I, with peace or war to do ?
>   Ever welcome, &c.
>
> Let the Nymphs with voice and hand,
> Hearts and ears at once command ;
> Goodall smile, and Charlton sing,
> And Davis touch the trembling string.
>   Ever welcome, &c.
>
> All the rip'ning sun can bring,
> Beauteous summer, beauteous spring,
> In one varied scene we show
> The ripe, the fair, the bud, the blow.
>   Ever welcome, &c.
>
> Comus jesting, wine inspiring,
> Beauty warming, Bacchus firing,
> Rage and party-malice flies,
> Peace returns, and discord dies.
>   Ever welcome, &c.

I propose now to let Mr. Iredell speak for himself awhile. The amiable graces of his character, and the excellence of style displayed in his letters, cannot, I trust, fail to prepossess the reader in his favor. The following letter to his brother, while exhibiting a generous warmth that wins our sympathies, is an earnest of that vigor of thought and expression, which in after years was to render him the ablest Judge in the highest tribunal known to the American Law.

Edenton, 15th June, 1771.

MY DEAR FRANK :—I have been lately obliged with a long letter from you, which, though it increases my regard for you, adds to my concern for your situation. Your account of the unkind treatment you met with in Ireland exceeds any thing I could have expected. To be in a manner turned out of a near relation's house, to be refused the loan of half a guinea in a case of so extravagant necessity, with equal haughtiness and ill-nature, and to have your most innocent, and best-intentioned actions censoriously misrepresented,—oh ! my dear Frank, this is too much—under such a load of indignity you must have been very unhappy. I feel for you, and the only consolation I can offer is, that you could never be so treated but by people who know nothing of the tender sensations of humanity, and who must for this behavior incur the hatred and contempt of the worthy part of mankind. Let your conduct be always guided by the principles of virtue, and you need not doubt acquiring the esteem of the wise and good. The capricious or evil tempers of mankind are out of our power ; those who are not under their influence despise them, and pity, without condemning, those who are. But, my dear Frank, it is over now, and if possible, bury it in oblivion. Avoid despondency as a great evil, and seek, when in your power, to shake it off by an unremitting habit of application and industry.

I think Sir George Macartney appears to have acted kindly ; and I believe it was not his fault that you have not yet obtained some place worth your acceptance ; as none would be that did not immediately procure you the conveniences of life, and point to future advantages. It is possible before this letter reaches you something may be concluded on. I am all anxiety on your account, and often am uneasy for you. I know not what to think of the proposal of your going to Africa ; it is an unhealthy, disagreeable country, I believe, and would remove you far from us all. And yet Gov. Dwayner seems to be a man of great goodness, and would deal candidly. At this distance I can judge of nothing ; but recommend you to the fatherly goodness of God. May a happy way of disposal be found for you, and when found, may your conduct insure the happiest success. What would you say, Frank, to a pair of Colors ? Sir George would readily procure them for you ; and it is a very genteel provision. It might be a very comfortable one, provided you did not give into the extravagance and gayety of the army.

As it is probable you may very soon be introduced into life as your own master, allow me to give you a little advice, dictated by experience and prompted by affection. On every occasion then associate with the genteelest company that are not too much above you ; for with them you will receive neither pleasure nor instruction. But be cautious of giving into any expense inadequate to your income ; to which purpose, spend nothing inconsiderately. Let your dress be always neat, but plain ; a poor man dressed richly will never command respect. Circumstances that might otherwise be concealed, will then be remembered; and he will only be an object of ridicule. At the same time consider decency as a virtue, and recollect the anecdote of Swift, who refused alms to a poor man because his hands were dirty, dismissing him with this reproof, that the poorest man might procure water. At first you may be inclined to spend money in trifles, but many trifles will require a large sum, and therefore, before you lay out any thing, seriously consider whether you can afford it. I am the more particular on this head, because for want of using this caution, I have not kept within bounds, though I have never been wilfully extravagant. Do not, however, learn to be a miser. Be generous where you can; and charitable where you ought—but first, you are to take care of necessaries; when these are secure you may then think of other things. With respect to the rules of conduct and behavior, I hope you want little direction. You have had a virtuous education, which, I flatter myself, will influence you through life. Be assured a good man knows more real pleasure than the most refined voluptuary; and will ever be treated with more respect. Vice has always for its attendants misery and repentance—had not these be better exchanged for joy and satisfaction? I need not, I believe, be very particular here. You have given me agreeable proofs of a disposition inclined to my wish; and will readily perceive the strength of my observations—but let me desire you to let no false flashes of wit, or impertinent raillery of religion, shock your principles, or stagger your belief. Men of this cast laugh at Religion, either because they know nothing of it, or care nothing for it. Men of shallow understandings, or bad hearts, are those who generally rank themselves in the list of Free-thinkers. Can any have credit for their judgment, in a case where they are entirely ignorant, or materially interested? And you know it is the interest of bad men, that there should be no future state. But there are two very dangerous vices, against which I must very particularly caution you—gaming and drinking. The incitement to the first is the hope of gain; what incitement the other has God knows, I know not. Now how many men have made fortunes by gaming? or have any?—and how many have been ruined by it? Millions! God forbid, any friend of mine should add to the number. Between two persons of equal skill, the chance is equal, and one must infallibly lose; and when we again consider the innumerable sharpers to be met with in all disguises, I would point at a gaming-house as a place of utter destruction. Private gaming is almost as bad; avoid it, and to do it effectually, learn no game, and then you can withstand solicitation. This is my method, and I never play cards at all, but to make one among particular friends, by way of amusement They are cursed things, and the four knaves of cards have done as much mischief as all the knaves in the world besides. Drinking I hope you have a natural aversion to; it is not only unjustifiable, but criminal, I mean when taken to excess. How it first happened that men drank more than was necessary for their support is astonishing. I will only say, it disorders the understanding, debilitates the constitution, ruins an estate, and is a prelude to every other misfortune.

I have but just room to desire that you will think favorably of my design in writing this letter, which was dictated by a tender regard to your best interest. God grant you may pass honorably and happily through life, and this will be a means of making our dear parents, myself, and all your friends happy.

I am ever, dear Frank,
Your very affectionate brother,
JA. IREDELL.

EDENTON, 15th June, 1771.

MY DEAR CHARLES:—I take up my pen to write you with much pleasure, more especially as I am told you wish to receive a letter from me. I am much obliged to you for your honorable and affectionate thoughts of me, and can truly assure you of mine in return. I am happy in hearing you are about being provided for, and hope it will be to your wishes and advantage. I should be very glad to see you in blue and white, and flatter myself your dress *alone* will not be suited to your profession. Be very industrious in learning every branch of naval knowledge, and whatever else may be of use to you. You will engage, my dear Charles, in no soft, effeminate employment; and the rugged paths of honor are difficult and craggy. This you must be sensible of, and therefore not be disappointed by scenes entirely new, perhaps not thought of by you. The greater the difficulty, the more glory in surmounting it, is a soldier's maxim, and should be ever present with him. There does not appear any improbability of war, and you may soon be called into action; here will be the trying scene, and though all your friends will wish and pray for your safety (and none will, I am sure, more fervently than myself), we shall have your honor very much at heart, and would even rather that you should die with glory, than live with infamy. God forbid, my dear Charles, that I should ever see the day when you will be no more. I can hardly refrain from tears while I write. I love you with the most affectionate sincerity, and hope to enjoy many happy years of friendship with you. My regard for you only induced me to hint at an unhappy incident which *might* happen, though it is not probable that it *will*. The officers of the Navy who are killed are comparatively few to those who survive; but as it is uncertain to whom the chance may happen, and all are liable to it, all ought to be prepared for it. This may teach you how peculiarly necessary it is, that your behavior be very circumspect, as you may so suddenly be snatched out of life. From the moment you enter on board a Man of War, consider your life as devoted to the public service; and though, at first, there may be something shocking in the thought, if properly improved it may be productive of much advantage to you. Your thinking so will not accelerate danger, and will better fortify you against it. In an engagement (which I suppose you would not wish always to avoid) suffer no womanish fears to unman, and if you feel any apprehensions sometimes, let a sense of honor, duty, and reputation, prevail with you to disregard them. Never give way to them; for that will be to purchase infamy, perhaps to forfeit life. Remember the truest courage does not arise from animal insensibility, but by the superiority of the mind over the weakness of the body. Do not therefore mistake timidity for cowardice, but as giving you an opportunity for the more honorable exertions to suppress it.

I have not time, my dear Charles, to write so particularly as I could wish, and hope you will consider what I have wrote as proceeding from a kind intention. Your welfare is an object of much concern to me; and God grant my wishes and prayers for your happiness may be perfectly answered!

I will conclude with desiring the favor of you to write me, and with assuring you that I am ever

Your very affectionate brother,
JA. IREDELL.

N. B. I forgot, as an incitement to your good conduct, to lay before you the prospect of advancement, which generally in the Navy is the reward of merit. Once more, my dear Charles, adieu! God help you.

15th June, 1771.

MY DEAR FATHER:—I returned yesterday from a distant County Court, and my time to write is very limited. I have just finished two letters to my brothers Frank and Charles which I will enclose to you. Since my last I have been favored with a letter from my mother, dated the 15th March, which gave me much pleasure, and for which she has my sincerest thanks. A day or two after, I received a little box, which you were so obliging as to send me. I am much obliged by so many instances of your goodness, and hope it will be rewarded with many years of happiness.

You must excuse, sir, my writing a long letter now, indeed I have no subject for one. But there have happened some scenes lately that you must be made acquainted with (and then follows an account of the Battle of Alamance*). We know nothing of a certainty since; there are various reports, but none to be depended upon. God knows how it will end; it is a matter of some doubt; at worst, a Regiment must be sent for from New York, but much mischief may be done in the mean time. How horrid are the miseries of civil war, but how much more horrid to have property insecure, and lives held at the will of a parcel of banditti!

I can acquaint you, with pleasure, that I am extremely well, and hope to continue so through the summer. I beg that I may hear very often, and particularly from you, as I am always anxious. Tell Atty that I have not time to write him now, but will by some other opportunity—that I am much obliged to him for his pretty letter, which has not above two or three faults, and those trifling ones; and that I trust he is not wanting in application to his learning, since he took all my books from me, pasted the leaves where my name was written, and inserted his own on another. I beg you to remember me to him with great affection. I should be sorry if I have deprived him of any books he wanted.

I have only to desire my very affectionate remembrance to my mother, and my love to my dear little brothers Tommy and Billy. Can Billy write? If he can, will you let me see some of his handwriting? I am, dear father,

Your very dutiful and affectionate son,
JA. IREDELL.

DEAR SIR:—I have lately been favored with your letter by Capt. Dayly of the 12th March, and have since had good opportunities of forwarding the letters enclosed. Though your letter was short, it gave me much pleasure as it was kind and friendly; and for some months past I have been very unhappy in the thought of having incurred your displeasure. I trust, however, two or three late letters have undeceived you, and taken off any impressions to my disadvantage. I will only add now, that I have never intentionally acted wrong; and have kept myself entirely free from vices. Under these circumstances, I flatter myself you will be inclined to overlook the imprudences of youth, which have been occasioned for want of acquaintance with man-

---

* The above letter is copied from Judge Iredell's letter-book; the omission of the account of the battle is greatly to be regretted.

kind; and this, I think, is the hardest censure any part of my conduct has deserved.

I have not much to add—nothing new has occurred in your affairs here—those in the back country must necessarily be in confusion. I saw your son George about two months ago. He is really a fine little fellow, and grows more like you every day. He is in breeches and looks very well. I will observe your directions about having him sent to school. I believe he is taken great care of. Col. Harvey is still very unwell. I have not seen him lately, having been prevented at a time when I intended it. Mr. Johnston is very well; about three months ago he had a very fine daughter. He always inquires very kindly after you, and proposes soon to write to you. Mr. Hewes is very well, so, indeed, are all your friends here. Mr. Lowther is going to live in New York. He will not be here, I believe, more than a month longer. The partnership is dissolved, and it is not certainly known whether any of the parties will ever renew the connection.

I will take leave now, sir, to conclude, but first desire my most dutiful respects to my uncle, and express my best wishes for his and your happiness.

H. E. McCULLOH.

EDENTON, 31st July, 1771.

MY DEAR FATHER:—I just, very fortunately, hear that a ship is lying at the Bar bound for Bristol, and that she is not to sail for eight or ten days; so that I have it in my power to convey this letter to her. Since my last, I have not been favored with any from you; but expect Capt. Todd in every day, by whom I expect to hear from you very particularly. I should be very happy if I knew you have all been as well as myself; for I have not had the least complaint the whole summer. It is a happiness I cannot be too thankful for, as I am almost the only exception to a general illness. We have not had any dangerous disorders; but agues and intermitting fevers have been very common. I am on the point of flying from them, as I shall go in a day or two to Col. McCulloh's, and perhaps thence into the back country: but that is rather doubtful. You will have heard long ago that all affairs there are effectually accommodated; and however disagreeable the means were, they were justified by the necessity, and have had the most happy influence. Regulation is a name scarcely remembered, and all busy spirits are at peace. Six Regulators were hanged as traitors, among whom was a man of some consequence; and these examples of deliberate justice, with others before of Governmental rigor, will intimidate the thoughts of any future sedition. The ringleaders have all absconded; most of them fled at the first fire.

I am at present a good deal engaged; and have not much to add on any subject. I wish impatiently to receive matter for future letters from some of yours. Be assured you shall always find me a regular and faithful correspondent; and I trust in your goodness and affection.

I am too often troubling you, but I will hope for your excuse of this last request, as it will be of particular, perhaps necessary, service to me. It is that you will be so obliging as to procure Dr. Blackstone's Commentaries on the Laws of England for me, and send them by the first opportunity. I have indeed read them through by the favor of Mr. Johnston who lent them to me; but it is proper I should read them frequently, and with great attention. They are books admirably calculated for a young student, and indeed, may interest the most learned.* The Law there is not merely considered as a profession, but as a science. The principles are deduced from their source, and we are not only taught in the clearest manner the general rules of law, but the reasons upon which they are founded. By this means we can more satisfactorily study, and more easily remember them, than when they are only laid down in a dictatorial, often an obscure manner. Pleasure and instruction go hand in hand, and we apply to a science, difficult indeed at best, with less reluctance, when by a well-directed application we may hope to understand it with method and satisfaction. I would take leave to add one more desire, that you would be pleased to send me the Tatlers and Guardians, the Spectators I have, and these with the others, will often afford me agreeable desultory reading. They are inimitable writings, and I can never be tired of perusing them. And now, sir, I believe I must take my leave of you. But first desire you to present my most respectful and affectionate duty to my mother, and to remember me very tenderly to all my brothers. Pray, likewise, give my best compliments to Mrs. Aldworth. Will you do me the same favor by Dr. Harwood; assure him of my most respectful remembrance, and that nothing could give me greater pleasure than a letter from him. If I am thus favored, I will take the liberty of requesting a continuance of our correspondence; and will observe it very faithfully on my part. God grant you may all be happy; my thoughts and wishes are ever with you.

I am, dear father
Your most dutiful and affectionate son,
JA. IREDELL.

* Blackstone's Commentaries had but recently been published: they did not, at first, meet with the general approval accorded them subsequently. Mr. Iredell's early appreciation of their great merit was creditable to his sagacity and taste.

SAMUEL MUNCKLEY, ESQ., SIR:—My father has mentioned to me the obliging readiness with which you undertook to negotiate my salary for him, in a manner at once expressive of his own gratitude, and engaging mine. Be assured, sir, I shall ever have the most tender sense of the many obligations you have conferred on my father and myself. I do not forget, at the same time, the great kindness of other gentlemen, who assisted my father and his family in distress; and I would beg the favor of making my particular acknowledgments to them through you, sir,—more particularly to the Collector to whom I am best known, and from whom I have received personal obligations. Mr. Nat. Coffin, my agent at Boston, has desired me to request that you would be so obliging as to acquaint him with the receipt of his remittances to you; as his doubts of their safety often make him uneasy. I have only to add, sir, that I hope you will excuse this additional request, and believe that

I am ever with very great respect,
Sir, your most obliged and obedient servant,
JA. IREDELL.

Extract from a Letter, dated 19th Aug., Spanishtown, from Mr. Thomas Iredell.

"I am glad to hear your brother Frank is to be provided for in the African service. You do not say what part of the coast he is going to. The Gold Coast is by no means unhealthy. Prudence and temperance will preserve a man in any climate, whose occupation does not too much expose him to its inclemency: and there is this advantage attending the prudent, temperate man, that as these virtues do not fall to the common lot of men, so they are the source of advantage to those who possess them; especially in a bad climate, where promotion is, of course, quick in favor of such men. The scheme for your brother Charles, considering his turn for it, is a very good one. Should there be war, as he has friends, he will stand no bad chance of being advanced. I have received the remittance for Spencer, and am well satisfied with what you have done in that business. The freight is enormous, but there is no help for it. I observe you are attending the Courts. I wish you much success in that pursuit; but observe to you that it is a profession dangerous to virtue in all countries, but more especially in your Colony, where persons can with so much ease, qualify themselves for its practice. I think you must have a great many of those people vulgarly called petty-foggers; indeed no free country, where the laws are generally intricate, is without them; they are very pickpockets, and their company and example carry contagion along with them. I promise myself the good principles instilled into you will preserve you from infection, for what is gained by the loss of integrity and honor cannot enrich, but makes a man poor indeed."

EDENTON, Oct. 3d, 1771.

MY DEAR MOTHER:—I am indebted to you for a very long letter, and sit down now with an intention of paying you. It is now more than a month since I had the very great pleasure of hearing from you by Capt. Todd, who likewise did me the favor to bring from you my valuable presents. I thank you, my dear parents, most kindly for them all; but should receive them with great reluctance, if I thought the purchase of them put you to any difficulty. Every thing was just as I could have wished, except the shoes, which were most of them too large, and all the pumps were; which was the greatest loss of the two, because all that are made in this country spoil the silk stockings. My foot has not grown much, neither do I suppose that it will, although I hope to be a little taller than I am. The hat is very pretty, but the silver band is rather too showy for me. However, I do not like to take it off, as it came from you; but I must reserve it for very particular occasions. And now, madam, it is time I should take some particular notice of your letter. After passing by your expressions of joy on hearing from me, for which I give you ten thousand thanks, you recommend to me one of Lady Huntingdon's * Chaplains for a Carolina Parsonage. To say the truth, this country is not very fond of parsons. Most parishes are full, and those that are not are very indifferent about it. It is a proposal that would never take, and might be the means of injuring a worthy man by a cruel disappointment, for we never take men upon *trust*. They generally have twelve months' trial before they are admitted to induction. So much, my dear mother, for this matter; and I have too good an opinion of your understanding to suppose you are turned Methodist. Be not afraid of the pistols you have sent me. They may be necessary implements of self-defence, though I dare say I shall have no occasion to use them. All *mobbing* is at an end here, and we are once more at peace. It is a satisfaction to have the means of security

* Selina, Countess of Huntingdon, was distinguished for her enthusiastic piety; she was the patroness of Whitfield, who often preached in the drawing-room of her mansion in Park Street.

at hand, if we are in danger, as I never expect to be. Confide in my prudence and self-regard, for a proper use of them, and you need have no apprehension. They are extremely neat, and I thank you, madam, for the trouble you have had about them.

When I went lately to Col. McCulloh's * I had then no intention of going further, as Captain Todd had not come in, whom I was impatient to see, and I returned a very few days after he arrived. Ben McCulloh did not go into the back country till the 22d of last month. Every thing there is in quiet and order. Mr. McCulloh and you I observe have very little connection with each other. I am sorry for it, and am afraid you each of you misunderstand situations. Believe me, my dear madam, when I say that I think the present circumstances of my uncle and cousin are difficult and distressing. This may account for many things, when added to it you make allowance for a particular temper fretted by disappointments. Were it in their power, I do believe they would assist you; but as it is not, they wish, perhaps, to avoid thinking of distress they cannot alleviate. Their not writing to you may, I dare say it does, appear to you unkind; and yet the motive may be a desire not to appear ostentatious of friendship without being able to give essential proofs of it. I wish this may be the case, and should be sorry to think their hearts were alienated from you because you are unhappy enough to be in the shade of adversity. You desire I will be explicit with regard to the collection. I will be so, and am sorry your advice came so late; but hope what I have done is not very censurable. You knew, from the first, I had a distant promise of that office; and about a year and an half ago I had much more sanguine hopes of it than I have now. Lately Mr. McCulloh has mentioned *danger* in offering at a transfer, and has therefore declined it. In the mean time I am pressed by the narrowness of my income, which occasions very disagreeable difficulties in my situation. His office he could at any time part with for a considerable sum, and this I dreaded he might be tempted to do, in his present distressed state. These things urged me to press him for a change in my favor, and I told him I would only reserve £200 proc (about £130 st.) to myself, and remit the rest (nearly as much more) to him. This may appear to you a disadvantageous proposal, but it is far otherwise. By this means I secure myself a genteel provision, upon which I can live comfortably; and my salary then will be £40 st. which will be yours. The purchase money will be little, and Mr. Mc-

* Alexander McCulloh was a member of Gov. Dobbs' Council in 1765. The wife of the venerable Mr. Wm. Boylan, of Raleigh, is one of his descendants.

Culloh is not rich enough to make presents; besides you remember he always mentioned terms. Offices are not now to be had untaxed, and he has the best bargain who has the least incumbrance. I cannot expect every thing at once—shall be only twenty Saturday; and all I wish for, at present, is enough to live upon independently. I can never hope to make a fortune here, and all the prospect I have is to live with ease and comfort. This is the case with all who come here. They are generally prisoners for life.

As my dear Frank is, I suppose, in Africa, I will answer the material part of his letter in this. The first question is, what relation Sir Nat. Dukinfield is to Mrs. Richards? I can only answer by saying his father and the late Sir Samuel's father were half brothers, and Mrs. Richards was sister to Sir Samuel, I believe. Mrs. Alice Macartney has behaved with admirable goodness. I thank her with my whole soul. Pray is that the lady whom I once saw in Bristol a day or two? She used to live in Granby Row, Dublin. Capt. Todd seemed much pleased with the civility he received from you, and gave me very agreeable accounts. I most heartily wish my brother Frank may realize the flattering prospects in his view. I must endeavor to keep up a regular correspondence with him, and pray your direction for that purpose; though I believe I shall have no other way than to send my letters to you. The only repugnance I have to this method is that it can happen so seldom. I write now by chance to Virginia, and know not how the letter will be forwarded. So poor Charles, it seems, is gone a voyage to Jamaica!* I cannot conceive why his appointment to be a Midshipman is postponed. I am well assured he will meet a most affectionate reception from my uncle, the kindness of whose letters to me gives me a great idea of the goodness of his heart; and his delay in giving any effectual assistance to my father has been occasioned, I am afraid, by difficulties of which we know little. I have not heard from him lately, but hope to do so in a few days. If Charles is at home, remember me to him very affectionately. How much am I obliged by his wish to come with Capt. Todd, which he might, perhaps, have been permitted to do, had there been a certainty of his return. In case he takes another trip, suppose it was to James River, I think that would do as well as any other, and I should be inexpressibly happy in seeing him. He might be able to tell you something too about Edenton, and my situa-

* Charles Iredell afterward entered the Navy. He was in several engagements in the Fleet under Sir Edward Hughes, in the East Indies, in 1782. He was killed in action in 1783. At the time of his death, he had attained, it is believed, the rank of Lieutenant.

tion here. Tell Atty I love him dearly, and wish for an opportunity of answering his letter; but that I beg in the mean time, as he has not so much difficulty in this respect as myself, that he will favor me with long, and particular letters. Can my dear little Tommy write me a letter? Mention me to him and Billy in the most affectionate manner.

The season has been sickly. Most people have been affected by it. I have myself more severely than I ever was before; but I thank God I am now as well as ever. I have but just recovered, but think I never was better in my life than at this moment. I was the more particularly concerned, that I had been prevented writing, because it was a time of the year that I thought would make you uneasy. My first wish is to remove every thing of that kind from you. I wish I could make you as easy in every thing else as about myself. I do not think of any thing to add to what I have written, but my most affectionate respects to my father, from whom I wish to hear more particularly than I usually do. Adieu, my dear mother,

Believe me ever your very dutiful and
affectionate son,
JAMES IREDELL.

During the course of this year, with healthy but vehement ambition, Mr. Iredell prosecuted his studies, and regularly attended the Courts. The latter was no easy task, but environed with perils from which a carpet-knight would have shrunk aghast. Upon horseback, often alone, through the dense forests, and across the almost trackless savannahs, now struggling with the rage of the suddenly swollen stream, and now fevered by a burning sun, the lawyer of that day travelled his weary circuit. Accommodations, by the way, were generally despicably vile; inns or taverns, in the true sense, had no existence. After the fatigue of a long day's journey, the wayworn traveller was often content with a bench by the hearth of some primitive log-cabin. With frame invigorated by manly exercises, and untainted by the vices of more cultivated climes, our young lawyer bore every discouragement and annoyance, not only with an elasticity of spirits that threw a gleam of sunshine upon the gloomiest scenes, but with a vivacity and good humor that enabled him to extract from them even amusement. Books he had not, save a volume or two stuffed into his saddle-bags with a scanty supply of apparel. At this period too, in what was then called the "back country," now the interior of North Carolina, the gentlemen of the Bar were objects of obloquy and denunciation to a generally poor and illiterate people, and frequently experienced at their hands the grossest outrages. It not only required, on their part, prudence, but also a courage equal to any emergency, to avoid indignity. The people justly complained of the burden of their taxes—a burden augmented by the extortion of illegal fees by the officers of the Courts; but, with a blind prejudice, many of them only saw in the profession, those who defended their oppressors, and who prosecuted them when their opposition broke out into acts of violence. Uncultivated settlers, who subdue the wilderness, are apt to look with suspicion upon the proprietor of the soil, when he demands rent for his land, or its value. Unfamiliar with those principles by which civilized communities can only be bound together, and with a wild sense of what they style natural justice, they insist that the first occupant has an indefeasible right to property that his labor has rendered productive; grants from Crown or State they regard as frauds, and the attorneys employed to bring ejectments or sue for use, as the venal instruments of tyranny, banditti, hired by gold to despoil them of the fruits of their honest industry.* With the feeling of independence fostered by the peculiarity of their life in a new country, they are little disposed to render tribute where tribute is due. The same causes that disturbed the peace of society then, still animate the same class of people to resistance to law, and urge them to violence and bloodshed. The squatter on the frontiers of the Union, looks rather to his rifle than authenticated parchment for a title to his home; and is more prompt to pay the demand of a legitimate owner in bullets than in the current coin of the realm. Anti-Rent disturbances, even in the State, proudly termed by its citizens the Empire State, have but recently shaken society to its centre, and polluted the altars of Justice with the blood of her ministers. The life of a briefless barrister is sad and melancholy. Years ordinarily must elapse before he can participate in the profits of his seniors; meanwhile, he encounters an expense under which he staggers. The discouragement, the hope deferred, often drive to despair, and many a bright intellect has disappeared for ever beneath the wave of a reckless, mad debauchery. Mr. Iredell early fixed his eye upon the glittering heights of his profession, and so self-assured was he of his capacity and industry that he never faltered in his purpose—he was resolute to win; and with

* Many large landed proprietors cared only to secure their titles, having no expectation of present gain, and looking to the future, solely, for profit. "I have known a person possest of 100,000 acres of land, which since my memory would not have paid a debt of £1,000 upon an 'Elegit' of fifty years; and yet the annual quit rent of those lands to the Crown amounted to £2,000 proc., and that gentleman has since made many thousands by the sale of those lands, which were then £2,000 worse than nothing."—*Mr. Johnston's argument on the Act for the more speedy recovery of debts in the Plantations.*

VOL. I.—7

such men, to resolve is to compel success. If unemployed in the Court House, he peopled his chamber with Judge, Jury, and spectators; he argued causes before his imaginary court, and reported his own arguments. Of these forensic displays, the following is a specimen. A question was agitated in the Superior Court of Edenton whether a sheriff's sale might be pleaded in bar to an action of detinue brought against a vendee for property purchased there, and which the plaintiff alleged at the time of the sale belonged to him, and not to the person as whose goods they were sold by the sheriff, in virtue of a writ of execution. Mr. Iredell was not employed in the cause, and indeed had not then received his Superior Court license; but here is the argument—curious, and interesting, at least, as the earliest recorded effort of one, who in a very few years became the brightest ornament of the Carolina Bar.

The question whether a sheriff's sale shall be absolutely conclusive against every other, is confessedly of great importance, as the decision will, one way or other, affect all the property in this Province; although I can by no means think it a question of such difficulty as it has been represented. Viewing it in the light of reason, and by way of analogy to other similar cases, there cannot be a doubt about its determination; and it must be viewed in this light, unless some cases expressly in point, with a judicial decision after a solemn argument on this point *only*, can be produced to silence us. I am confident no such cases can be shown; if any should, I will desire to speak to them. But I rest secure in this confidence, and as it is a circumstance which could not naturally happen often, I think we have no fixed decision to follow, nor any other light to guide us than what our reason can point to, in referring to general maxims of law and cases somewhat analogous to this, and even I can meet the gentlemen on their favorite ground,—the security of private property, and the protection which the law will certainly afford to titles purchased under its sanction.

Now it is a maxim in law which cannot be denied me, and which is the firm foundation on which I will rest my arguments, that every man who is legally possessed of any property has a right to the enjoyment of it, till it is taken from him in a legal manner. The premises are not denied, but the conclusion that I mean to draw. It is my business, therefore, to establish my conclusion, which seems to me as clearly to follow from the premises as any proposition in Euclid is capable of mathematical demonstration.

It is needless to enumerate before so learned an audience the several ways of acquiring property, and the rules of determining, in general, doubtful cases. But it is a known principle, that the title of a purchaser is only that of a vendor. This brings me to the ultimate question, what right a sheriff has to attach the property of *one* man, under color of an execution against the property of *another*. It is immaterial, it would be unworthy the dignity of this Court to mention that the sheriff may do so under a mistake, and therefore some line should be drawn between designed and inadvertent error. The right must be considered in the whole, and not with a view to the propriety of its exercise, which can never come within legal restrictions; and it would be absurd to make the security of any man's property dependent on the degree of a sheriff's capacity or care.

Every act of a sheriff must be either derived from his general or special power. I beg this may be attended to. It will not surely be asserted that a sheriff's sale is in virtue of his *general* power, because without a writ it would be an act of open violence, and he might, perhaps, be punished as a felon; he certainly would as a trespasser. His power then being only derived from a writ directed to him, is a *special* one, and therefore is strictly, absolutely confined within the terms of its direction. The moment he does or attempts any thing the writ has not directed him to do, he acts without any authority; he departs from the power he was legally possessed of, when obeying the terms of the writ, and assuming one which that did not give him, and which he could no otherwise be entitled to, his acts are not warrantable because they are not legal: for he could not justify himself under a *special* power against a charge for departing from it, and having no other sanction to protect him, he falls for having done contrary to his duty. The cases cited out of Dr. Blackstone do not contravene the doctrine we contend for. The particular circumstances he mentions, in which the wisdom of the law has made purchasers absolutely secure, required such a regulation; but he himself treats it as a practice only justified by the necessity. Now the instances cited from Dr. Blackstone are particular exceptions (which cannot judicially be extended farther) and a case of a sheriff's sale is not within them. It therefore stands upon general principles of justice, it not being necessary that these should be in this case sacrificed to motives of conveniency, which Dr. Blackstone gives as the only reason for what the law determines about the others. In the one case, that of a sale in a market overt, the amazing concourse of people unknown mostly to each other, and the great variety of sellers and purchasers which the necessities of mankind call together at such a place,

render it necessary that fair purchases, there, should be validated. A man who buys, knows nothing of him who sells; but as his being in possession is an evidence of his being the owner, it would be hard that he should be liable to have what he fairly bought taken from him, when he could have no redress against the seller. Is this any way similar to the case of a sheriff, an officer of the greatest notoriety to every body, and who has given security for the faithful discharge of his trust? Is a man injured in a sale from him? he cannot be at a loss to find the person or recover damages. He then is absolutely restored "in statu quo," and all the injury he suffers is that not being permitted to enjoy property which another has a legal right to. There is no kind of similarity that I can conceive between a market overt and a sheriff's sale, which is always on the spot where the goods are taken; and a fluctuating market overt would be a strange idea. So that he is neither within the *number* or *reason* of Dr. Blackstone's exceptions.

I come now to consider the terrible consequences they affect to draw, if a sheriff's sale should be in the least impeachable, and if property, purchased as they say, under a public confidence, should be shaken. Now I boldly deny the probability of all these consequences, and I engage to represent their doctrine as teeming with most calamitous mischief, and as strongly arbitrary in its nature. There is no such thing as dealing in any possible circumstance without some kind of confidence. Human wisdom may make us as cautious as we can be, but will never put us upon a certainty. Why should sheriff's sales be precluded from the general predicament? Is it because *there* a purchaser can usually be more confident than at any other sale? The notoriety of an execution, the neighbors' acquaintance with the property, and the great concourse of people generally attending it (many of whom, if there is mistake or fraud, can probably correct it), seem to render a purchaser absolutely safe: besides, too, the honor and interest of a sheriff being at stake, and which in any doubtful case he may legally secure by summoning a jury. But there is a possibility that a sheriff may mistake, and innocent, unwary purchasers ought not to suffer. True, but how will you remedy the possibility? Is there any situation in which the best and most cautious man may be absolutely secure? But is the possibility of this evil (which I am sure is a very remote and very improbable one) to be avoided by intrusting to the sheriff the absolute control over every man's property? For I aver (and no man can deny) that if their doctrine is established, a sheriff may do as he pleases with any property in his county. For if his sale (independent of the legality of it) is

to confer an unquestionable title, it may be as well without as with it; for it is no part of our inquiry now *how* the sale arose; you are satisfied with finding it was done by a sheriff. This is an evil unknown to any other part of our law. This is a power vested in no other subject, nor even in a king, for all his acts must be either justified under his prerogative or acts of Parliament. Shall we then allow a power of this kind to a sheriff? I am so ashamed of the idea, I will not offer to confute it. Besides, does *the law*, or will *you*, pay no regard to legal titles, unless they are derived from a sheriff's sale? Is the property which I have to-day to be rendered precarious, in order to insure a title to another to-morrow? I have a right to all my property specifically, until I am legally deprived of it. I may have some kind which to me, from an accidental circumstance, is more valuable than to another, and am I to lose it at the caprice of a sheriff? A satisfaction in damages may not be adequate to me. To a man who purchases, it is: for having at first no right to the property, he cannot be injured by its being restored to the right owner. And surely it is much more natural that a purchaser, so deceived, should have a remedy against the sheriff, between whom and himself there was a privity of connection, than that a person who had nothing to do with either of them, should have an executive and inadequate remedy only to have recourse to.

Most of these considerations are so extremely obvious, and their consequence as to the determination of this cause is so important, that it has amazed me, they should either be overlooked, or not sufficiently regarded, by the gentlemen on the other side. But they have continually had a phantom before them that has dazzled, if not blinded their understanding. A sheriff's sale was of too sacred a nature to be profaned by the impious claim of any other title. His judgment must be supposed infallible, or at least the possibility of its having any defect was of too slight a nature to be guarded against. His *mistake* or his *crime* (for they make no exception) can be equally valid to convey a title with a *legal writ of execution*. All men must bow to his *sovereign authority*, and humbly request that he would not dispose of their family pictures, jewels, rings, &c., which no sum of money, much less the mere pecuniary value, which was all that would be allowed, could ever compensate for. It will at the same time behoove others, who may have a longing desire to any specific part of another man's property, to make interest with a sheriff to help him to it. And not one legal title upon earth can exempt it from his rapacity. Are not all these absurdities evidently deducible from the doctrine on the other side, and which needs only to be seen in its naked and real aspect to be hated for the most hideous deformity? On our side, reason, propriety, and the nature of the thing, concur with the principles of law, to assert and vindicate our claim; and I trust in your Honor's wisdom and integrity, a cause so supported cannot fail of success."

This argument has the ring of the right metal; it is free from the redundant verbiage in which young gentlemen are wont to indulge: it is closely reasoned, and its style is terse and clear, possessing much of the neatness and perspicuity of the maturer efforts of the future judge. On the 26th Nov. 1771, Mr. Iredell was licensed by Gov. Martin to practise in the Superior Courts. He took the oath prescribed by law before Samuel Johnston, Clerk at April Term, 1772.

Extracts from a letter of H.E. McCulloh, dated Nov. 5th, 1771. London.

"I have of this date wrote fully to Mr. Coffin, at Boston, on the subject of my office, incidents, and attempt of the Currituck officers. I also enclosed the Commissioners a Warrant from the Lords of the Treasury for my leave of absence for two years from my former term. I have too good a friend in my Lord North to fear any attempts against my office. Respecting the attempts of the Currituck officers, you on the spot must judge and act on such circumstances as happen, advising always with Mr. Johnston. Should they act within my district, their acts and papers are void and a nothing, and you must seize any vessel that may break bulk within the district under such authority.

Mr. Brownrigg had also an Italian chair of mine to dispose of, and Mr. Campbell a very good fiddle.

My father's health continuing, I have very serious thoughts of crossing the Atlantic next summer, for a trip of five or six months. I proposed spending a couple of months this winter at Bath, but there is a "hiatus valde deflendus" in the pocket which prevents.

My affairs at present " sont beaucoup derangeés," but I hope for good things."

CHAPTER V.

HISTORICAL SUMMARY, COURTSHIP, LETTERS FROM SIR N. DUKINFIELD, LETTER FROM MR. IREDELL, LETTERS FROM ENGLAND, LETTER FROM MR. IREDELL, JOURNAL, &c. ÆT. 20–21.

THE destruction of the Gaspé,* an armed schooner, on the 10th of June, led to an act of parliament for sending to England for trial, all persons concerned in destroying His Majesty's ships, dockyards, or military stores. This act but added fuel to the flame of colonial resentment; and the Boston committee published "the boldest and most comprehensive exposition as yet set forth of Colonial rights and grievances." In North Carolina there was no meeting of the Assembly, but at an election for members of the Assembly, the Whigs were triumphantly successful.† In defiance of the express prohibition of the popular House, the Governor appointed commissioners to run the southern boundary line of the province. The feud between the executive and the people was fast becoming irreconcilable.

A very strong intimacy subsisted between Mr. Iredell and Sir Nat. Dukinfield; they were rivals for the hand of the same lady; but the contest was so generously conducted, and the deportment of each so marked by magnanimity, that, so far from their friendship being shaken, their mutual esteem was increased. Sir Nat's proposal met with a courteous, but prompt refusal, for Mr. Iredell had already won the young lady's heart, who strikingly manifested her good sense by preferring talent and virtue to the more brilliant offer of her titled suitor. The future fully vindicated the wisdom of her choice. The baronet's disappointment so affected him, that he deserted the province, to which he never returned: subsequently, when his estate was confiscated, most ably and eloquently did Mr. Iredell plead his cause. They regularly corresponded until the close of 1791.

WINGFIELD, 13th Feb., 1772.

... OH! my dear friend, how terrible is love, when pure and sincere, and free from lust and passion! I find myself greatly

* Hildreth. † Jones.

to have been mistaken when I have sometimes formerly thought myself in love. Never, I'm sure, did I discover any thing like the present. I have wrote to her, inclosed to my mother, and told her I hoped for permission to renew my addresses if she should be disengaged on my return. Though she did not yesterday really say that her affections were engaged, yet I suspected that to be the case. But, if upon your discovery of your passion for her, she should even (but I cannot suppose it) object to you, I hope you will let me know; or what reception you meet with. Indeed, she has shown her good sense if she has chosen you to be the happy man. You are much more deserving of her than myself. I can never expect so much happiness, 'tis too much for any mortal. How unfortunate is this. I can scarce support my existence. But I must endeavor to remove as much as possible the great grief which at present overwhelms me. Berry, thank God, suspects nothing of the real cause of my misery. He supposes it arises from leaving my mother and friends; but that is nothing in comparison to the real cause. I must dispel this additional curse, and totally insupportable. Excuse, my dear friend, the overflowings of my heart in this unconnected manner; 'tis some alleviation to me while I am unbosoming myself to you.

Believe me, my dear Iredell,
Your sincere,
NAT. DUKINFIELD.

EDENTON, 19th Feb., 1772.

MY DEAR FRIEND:—My time has passed very unhappily ever since I saw you. It can only be equalled by the severity of *your* distress. I feel for you with all the warmth of friendship, and anxiety of fear; and how to act in the very critical scene before me, is an afflicting thought. I did not know, my dear Sir Nathaniel, how sincerely I loved the dear girl who has engrossed both our hearts, until the night before your declaration to her. Heaven knew how miserably I passed it, and with what uneasy doubt I awaited the event. The unhappiness of your situation took off all thoughts of my own, till I became a prey to my reflections—then I felt what you only can imagine. Your letters from Mrs. Brownrigg's and Norfolk affect me extremely. I am nearly as unhappy as you can be. I know not how I will act, for I cannot answer for myself. My conduct to you shall be guided by the nicest sense of honor, and by as tender a regard for your happiness as is consistent with my own, and that of one much dearer to me. I have not seen her since you. They are still at Mrs. Dawson's, but are to be here, I am told, on Friday. I wish to God you were here too, that our fates might be decided. The most dreadful certainty is preferable to doubt. Whatever I do, and every circumstance relating to her, I will faithfully and regularly acquaint you with. And yet, Sir Nathaniel, if I can command myself so far as to withhold a declaration until your return, my conduct must suffer greatly in her opinion. I have for a long time past behaved to her with a particularity of attention that has engaged the eyes of the world, and which the delicacy of her sentiments must construe, as I intended it, into an indirect address. Such an application would have with me all the force of an express one, and now, when I have reason to believe she has loved me so far as to refuse you— to withdraw my attention, to become or appear more cool as her goodness advances upon me, and suddenly to change my behaviour on the first appearance of competition, would be a disgrace and meanness my heart revolts at. Suffer me to add, it would bring on me an insupportable affliction, without materially serving you. I know, and you must believe the greatness of her mind to be such, that she will not marry any man to whom she does not give an exclusive preference over all others, much less give her hand to one man when her heart is possessed by another. You and I both conclude her affections are engaged, and a thousand agreeable circumstances which crowd upon my memory convince me I am the happy owner of them. Oh! ecstatic would be the thought, could you be happy. To her, disguise and affectation are crimes, and I knew, I assured you so, that from her first answer you would have a final one. This, my dear friend, I wish you would consider such, and try while you are in England to dissipate your thoughts of what I think I must call a forbidden good. There is nothing in the repulse you have received at which to be chagrined or piqued. Here pride can require no sacrifices to appease it. I know few women who would at first have refused Sir Nathaniel Dukinfield,—perhaps none whose affections were not absolutely pre-engaged. And though the answer you received from Miss Hannah Johnston gave you so high an idea of her exalted sentiments as to justify your passion, it was such as to convince you a pursuit cannot be successful. There is a consistency and delicacy in her whole conduct which assures me that the man who is *once* happy enough to be beloved by her, will *always* be so, unless any part of his subsequent character should be different from his former. All the merit I can plead is a sincerity of heart and innocence of intention which never yet deserted me, and I trust never will. I have never sought, nor perhaps could have put on any disguise, and such as I am, with all my faults and follies, I am fully known to her. If under these circumstances the agreeableness of your understanding and the goodness of your mind were not sufficient to overbalance her tenderness for me, (the vanity of egotism is here extorted by candor,) I cannot think they ever will. It is an happiness for me that I was first acquainted with her, and have loved her longest. I have indirectly paid my addresses to her these two years, and should long since have made a declaration, would my circumstances have permitted me to marry. I dare say she never thought of your doing it, for it was generally imagined you loved her sister best. The faithfulness of my attention and a kind of negative merit (all I can flatter myself with being possessed of) perhaps inspired her with some esteem for me, which may have improved into tenderness, and now seems to be ripened into love. Oh! happy, happy Iredell, could I say, did not your afflictions interpose to grieve me. What shall I do, my dear Baronet? I am utterly at a loss. My friendship for you is perfectly sincere, and will dictate every thing possible for your quiet. But I cannot think of giving up my love to it. Had it indeed happened, as I assured you, that your addresses had been favorably received, I would have offered no interruption to your happiness, and great as the resignation would have been, should have humbly kissed the rod and acquiesced. But when I think as I now do, that she will not, cannot accept of your affection, because hers is engaged to me, love, honor, (every thing but friendship, and that, in this instance, is not compatible with the other two,) urge me to a declaration, at least compel me to an attachment. You will judge, by this letter, my mind is not at ease, that I will do every thing for you that is possible, or can be expected from me; but I cannot promise that I will make no declaration. I dare not do it, lest I should either be tempted to violate it, or make myself more miserable than I am already, and more I cannot well be. I will write to you by all opportunities, and beg, entreat, you will endeavor to conquer a passion (I am sorry for your sake to say, my dear friend) I think cannot be returned. God bless you, and grant you every felicity you ought to, and can have.

I will add no more than that poor Tom Hodgson paid the last debt to nature between 12 and 1 o'clock this morning. His disorder was a kind of fever, which reduced him to a state of weakness, in which he died. My mind is greatly disturbed. Adieu! my excellent friend! believe me to be, with the most tender respect,

Your very affectionate
JA. IREDELL.

Sir N. Dukinfield.

NORFOLK, March 5, 1772.

DEAR IREDELL:—My impatience on account of Capt. Lawton is now relieved by his coming here to day. He intends going to the vessel, which lies in Hampton Roads, to-morrow, to be ready to sail, so that I shall not be detained much longer, I hope. I believe I should not have written to you again till in England, had it not been to have acquainted you that I have repeated my letters to Miss Hannah Johnston through my mother, who is the only person besides yourself who knows of it; and I have desired her to deliver my letters with the greatest caution and privacy. She will be a most valuable acquisition to any one who can obtain her; and I cannot think of relinquishing her upon a single refusal. But if I find that her affections and yours are engaged to each other, I shall then desist my own importunities, in hopes, nevertheless, of being continued as a *friend*. I shall endeavor all in my power to make you both happy. But till that time I can't entertain an idea of quitting my pursuit. I am, my dear friend,

Yours sincerely.
NAT. DUKINFIELD.

I hope Mr. Jones keeps the secret.

MANCHESTER, 2d June, 1772.

MY DEAR FRIEND:—I have now been upwards of three weeks in England, and on Sunday last came down to Manchester, when I received your favor as well as several others. I will immediately relieve you from the state of uneasiness which you must be in, by resigning to you Miss Hannah Johnston, and then give you my reasons for it. I received a letter from my mother and Mrs. Dawson. I told you in my former letters that I had wrote to Miss Johnston through my mother's care. My mother tells me she offered the letters, which were not accepted; that Miss H. said she could not accept them; that it was entirely out of her power; and when my mother pressed her to receive them, she said it was useless; that she was quite determined. Both from my mother's and Mrs. Dawson's letters I find that 'tis in vain for me to think any more of this matter. Mrs. Dawson gives me much pleasure in assuring me of Miss Hannah's friendship, and that nothing will add more to her happiness than that I should never think of, or hope for more. Now, my dear Iredell, as I am fully convinced of what I had too great reason to expect, and that I may be no hindrance to such an happiness as you must in all probability enjoy, I promise you that henceforth I will not entertain a thought which may lead to a greater regard for Miss H. than friendship; for as her happiness was my con-stant view, I am determined to do nothing which may in any degree prevent it. It will give me great pleasure to hear of your declaration and success; and I hope to be of the company when your happiness is completed. Give me leave to offer myself for your valet when that time is fixed; it will, I do assure you, afford me great satisfaction, for though I cannot be a principal, I should be glad to be in some manner concerned. I own to you that I am much more easy since I received the letters, from a state of uncertainty is a most unhappy one. How could I, my dear friend, ever think of desiring you not to declare your passion till I should return—was ever any thing so unreasonable? But I ask your pardon, and hope to God you may have done it before this time and with success. Miss H. was sufficiently acquainted with our friendship to think that we have communicated our thoughts to each other, especially as I told her that I had asked you if you had made any protestations of regard for her. Therefore I could not but think (if I could at that time have thought at all) that it would be slighting her in a very great degree to neglect it after the discovery of her inclinations. What other woman would have refused to receive my letters?—the curiosity to read them would have been a sufficient inducement to most. But she showed her usual greatness, as she was well convinced she could give no other answer than she had already done. But I acquiesce, in hopes of being witness to the happiness of two, for whom I have the greatest regard. I am sorry to have been the cause of so much uneasiness to you both; but let my sincere wish for your mutual felicity be a sufficient atonement.

Mr. and Mrs. Richards and Mrs. Hale were in London with Lady Dukinfield when I arrived. I sent your letters to your father and Mr. Maskelyn by the post. I have, however, promised to visit Bristol this summer, and will then see your relations. I expedite my business here as much as possible, and I hope to return by November. Mr. McCulloh will be in Carolina before me, he intends to sail in July. Present my compliments when they will be acceptable. I am, dear Iredell,

Your sincere friend,
NAT. DUKINFIELD.

P. S. What success had Berry?

Friday, 19th April.

MY DEAR HANNAH:—I promised you I would write to-day, and I luckily find an idle moment for that purpose. Upon what must I write? I know not. I did, I believe, say something of a dissertation upon letter-writing. But that was too great a presumption for me to be serious in. I wanted an excuse to pass an occasional half hour happily, and you were kind enough to indulge me. Oh! that you would go still further. Do let me earnestly beg it. I leave it to your *goodness* only.

Come, my dear madam, I will tell you how I write letters, by way of show that I have not dropt my design. I just sit down and carelessly let my thoughts flow from my pen without too much anxiety about the expression, though taking care to keep that equally free from meanness and bombast—this is all the art I know. Practise it yourself, and let me have the happy sight of your performances.

Those write letters best who have an habitual justness and propriety of thinking; and, my dear Hannah, you must excuse my saying, that I think (from judgment not passion) you are unequalled in these particulars. There is in most ladies a remarkably easy flow of expression, and in all yours I discover the most exact propriety. I therefore know what to expect in a letter from you. I have this morning had a letter from Sir Nathaniel, a pleasing one it would have been, had it not acquainted me that he is to live in England, and this I regret for my own sake, not for his. Forgive my transcribing a short paragraph from it. "I am extremely glad you have such a prospect of happiness. I don't know any couple so deserving of each other as yourselves, and as it was not my good fortune to be the happy possessor of Miss Johnston's affections, I rejoice exceedingly that such felicity was destined for you. Happy may you long continue to be together!" He desires me too to let him know what you thought of his persisting to write to you. I am sure I cannot tell him now.

This letter, my dear, is sadly blotted and written. But the case was this with me: I was obliged either to write in this manner or not at all. Which would you be best pleased with?

Well, God bless you. I must now leave off. Once again, oblige me as I wish.

Ever most affectionately yours,
JAMES IREDELL.

Miss HANNAH JOHNSTON.

Wednesday afternoon.

MY DEAREST HANNAH:—Being greatly disappointed in my wishes and intentions of seeing you this afternoon, I snatch a moment to commune with you in this manner, as a kind of secondary pleasure to that of being personally with you. You can easily, I hope, conceive the severe feelings I have in being deprived of this happiness. It is indeed still more severe to me, as you do not know the cause why I have not gone over this afternoon; for the badness of the weather yesterday and to-day seemed to preclude the propriety of a visit, though I should not have regarded it, had I been at liberty to consult my own inclinations merely. My cousin Betsy McCulloh is now with us, and I make it a point to stay with her, not only out of a proper complaisance, but from a very affectionate regard her merit, yet more than her relationship, claims from me. Her situation has been difficult and trying, and yet notwithstanding this circumstance, and every disadvantage attending the method of her education, she is really a very fine, as well as a very good girl. I should abhor myself was my attention only directed to those of my relations who are in affluent circumstances, and did I aggravate unhappy and unavoidable misfortunes by a cruel slight of the innocent objects of them. How strange is it, my dear Hannah, that the regards of the generality of the world are chiefly attracted by adventitious advantages, which are often both gained and lost independently of either merit or demerit, and which at best only relate to appearances; and not to any influence of principles which either fix the mark of a good or ill mind! God knows what would have been my own situation, had misfortune appeared a crime to all; and had that very circumstance, which laid a claim to protection, been the bar to my receiving it! What would become of some of the sweetest feelings of the heart, should the principle of contemning distress become general? To relieve or alleviate distress is surely the most delightful pleasure in the world, and next to it is that fine sentiment of tenderness and compassion, which none but generous minds can feel, and which is fully compensated for the little pain often attending it by a thousand trivial circumstances, which nature certainly intended not only to mitigate, but to reward it. I know perfectly and pleasingly well how experimentally you can decide upon the truth of this observation, which you will read, I doubt not, not only without censure, but with great satisfaction, since it comes from a heart you honor with a kind preference.

But, my dear girl, I must break off. The ladies are in the piazza. I don't expect to get a peep at you, but shall indulge a hope that you may be looking at me, and by that means at once oblige me with some kind thoughts, and discover the reason of my not being with you this afternoon. Adieu! God bless you, my dear Hannah! So prays

Your ever affectionate
JAMES IREDELL.

Thoughts on the death of Mr. Blair.

"Let the melancholy train of my thoughts have vent. Let me unburthen, as to a kind of second self, the great grief which overwhelms my heart. Let me regret for others, ill-deserving such affliction, if it was to be uncompensated, the loss of a husband and a father—a man who not only held those ties by nature, but by the tenderest affection, and most anxious solicitude for the welfare of those who were so connected with him. Let me endeavor to conceive *their* distress, the afflicting misery of *their* situation, bereaved at once, and suddenly, of a dear, how dear a friend, and of a most tender guardian. From the thought, though but for a moment, of distress like this, I can the more readily pass to consider the condition of those amiable friends who sympathize in their affliction, and feel for their own loss but as for a secondary one. How amiable, but how unhappy, a sight was it for me to see the dear Miss Johnstons—a continual succession of tears and sighs—the tender effusions of grief for themselves, their sisters, and their young relations. Admirable girls! lovely women! may your lives be happy as you deserve. You cannot wish them happier. Mrs. Dawson will have a complicated share of distress to struggle with. When the sympathetic goodness of her heart has time to subside into reflection, how cruel will be the remembrance, how cutting the thought, that she has once passed in her own person a scene like that which Mrs. Blair suffers. For two such women to have occasion for grief like theirs, would be (would it not?) an unprovidential allotment, was this world to terminate our existence. No! a hereafter will reconcile all. Then the best will be the most happy. Upon that future state to which we are all hastening, must our thoughts direct themselves. Nothing is more uncertain than a life here, nothing more transitory than the enjoyment of it. One day happy in conversing with a friend, in all appearance promising to live many years,—another, viewing him on the bed of sickness,—a third on a *death-bed*. Gracious God! This is affliction in the extreme. Yet thou ordainest it, and we submit. Thou canst not, thou dost not, forbid the tear of sorrow, or the heart of grief. Otherwise it would not be that the best people have usually the most sensibility. Humanity requires, and religion does not forbid, that we should mourn for the loss of valuable friends. This even adds an increased motive to be good and virtuous—to direct our steps according to thy precepts. To reflect, and to feel, how fleeting are all our joys here, and how liable we are at all times, even when we think ourselves most secure, to be deprived of the comforts and blessing of life, must (it is the only consolation left) lead us to consider, that soon, perhaps very soon, we may pass the verge of this world, and enter (if we be not wanting to ourselves) into immortal happiness in another. We are too apt to think our stay here momentous to our welfare. There cannot be a more mistaken notion, as every day's experience testifies. Here one sorrow quickly succeeds another, and the happiest days are not without alloy. Yet even these would have less, did we possess a philosophic indifference for the shadowy advantages of this world, and look forward, with the confidence of a good conscience, to the blissful prospects of another. Young as I am, I have seen much affliction,—have been witness to much unhappiness,—and in some, a personal, an immediate sufferer—in all I trust (I should despise myself if I was not) a distressed sympathizer. I have passed through a school of misery, which I cannot, however, now regret for myself, as it has given my mind a turn of sobriety and reflection. May I daily endeavor to improve its disposition, and cultivate it with virtuous resolutions, and may I be enabled to carry these resolutions into practice, and by an uniform intention of doing my duty, make the tenor of my conduct here, deserving of happiness."

Mr. Blair was the husband of Miss Hannah Johnston's sister, and these consolatory lines, were, I presume, designed for that lady's eye.

Extract from a Letter from Mr. Iredell to H. E. McCulloh, dated March 5th, 1772.

"In answer to our crave upon the subject of our extraordinary incidents, we are now told by the Commissioners, in a letter equally strange and sophistical, that they do not approve of those seizures having been made, and that, as the amount of the sales was insufficient to reimburse the expenses, they would not allow any part of them to be incurred by the Crown. No *reasons* of disapprobation are given, and though the Commissioners are made, by an act of Parliament, judges of the propriety of granting, they cannot decently, I apprehend, altogether defend the justice of its intention. To you, sir, I need only add, that I am conscious of the rectitude of my conduct in this instance, and that I will not very patiently submit to be ill-treated. I *could have*, I *had* no lucrative view in seizing them, and think cases similar to mine clearly within the meaning and expression of the act. I will repeat my application to them, and if it should be unsuccessful, will ask the favor of your advice whether I shall not send a memorial to the Lords of the Treasury.

"The conduct of the Currituck Officers has been very flagitious, and a great injury to your office. It has been wanton in encroachment. Severely as I felt the insult, what could I do? The Commissioners had deserted me in similar instances, and in the face of their disapproving letter, to seize would have been imprudent. I never will again, willingly, risk such a pecuniary enthralment. I advised with Mr. Johnston as you desired, and he thought, for the reasons above, and as complaints had then been referred to the Governor upon this subject, supported by affidavits which raised his indignation, and had obtained his interference, seizure would be improper. Mr. Johnston had at that time a letter from the Governor* which spoke very indignantly of their conduct, and enclosed a letter to Pierce, supposed to contain an order for him to give a personal account of himself to his Excellency, and to produce the powers under which he acted. Probably too it had a rod for Malcolm. A current and received report that they had very extraordinary powers from the Commissioners, was the only reason, I believe, which prevented a suspension. I have very little doubt that it will follow, or that the measures adopted will have the effect to prevent any material repetition of their insolence. The Governor is a man of too much spirit to suffer any usurpation by those over whom he has control."

"I have written to you very lately by Sir N. Dukinfield, and since by a letter to Liverpool at the express request of Mr. Hardy, who was at that time very ill, and in consequence of many severe fits of sickness is determined to leave this country in the summer. He therefore desires that you will appoint another Deputy immediately, and Mr. Johnston advises you to appoint Mr. Charles Bonfield, who has a long time acted as his clerk, with an unexceptionable capacity and integrity. I am sure you could not have a more faithful or diligent agent, and hope he will succeed Mr. Hardy. I have written more fully on this in the letter to which I refer. It gives me much concern to find, by some parts of your letter, that you still had difficulties. I hope in God they will soon be all removed. You have earned an easy and happy provision, and might, without unreasonableness, expect it. However I may have trifled hitherto, I will do so no more. I feel the satisfaction of doing business, and am determined to apply to it. Necessity, I hope, will be no greater spur than inclination. Young men must be active, industrious, and modest in expectation. They have no right to look for the advantages and comforts of life by easier methods than their friends before them; happy, if they can obtain them by the same."

* Martin.

EDENTON, 20th July, 1772.

MY DEAR FATHER:—I wrote to you a hasty letter lately, and therein promised you to write again soon, and very particularly. I mean now to do so, and that I might be the more accurate, have reviewed some of the last letters I received from you, and minuted down such particulars, in the order they occurred, as I had not either before taken notice of, or might deserve a more full explanation. I must take notice, however, sir, that there is a very long lapse of time between September and February, during which there were no letters written to me; a circumstance which long gave me uneasiness, and prepared me for some heavy blow, though I had no idea of any so severe as my dear Billy's death. Lovely angel! such I now believe you to be; but such indeed I thought you upon earth. Oh! unhappy separation! what a dreadful loss! do I not daily feel it? I never can, I never shall think but with the greatest affliction on a misfortune by which I lost the dearest of brothers, and one of the finest boys in the world. He was all I could have wished him, and would have been, in all human probability, an honor and a blessing to us all. But the stroke of fate is not ours. My tears and tenderness cannot recall him, neither would it be now desirable that he should, if he could, return. He is, I trust, exceedingly, inexpressibly happy. This is all my consolation; no other could alleviate a weight of grief which oppresses my heart every moment I think of him. An accidental recollection of any pleasing circumstance in his behavior stings me cruelly, because I know (too certainly I know) such never will return. May we, his afflicted, surviving brothers (my eyes swim with tears while I write) strive as much as possible to make our dear parents, and one another, amends (but how inadequate with all our endeavors will they be) for this severe distress, by being still more solicitous to approve ourselves worthy and good men; and as much as we can, such men as my dear Billy would have probably taught us to be.

My mind is not now fit to talk on matters of business, such as many parts in those letters which are yet unanswered, are. But I will endeavor to go through them as well as I can. There will be, perhaps, an incoherency in my manner of answering them; but I was afraid, by modelling the form, of losing the substance. My debt to Mr. McCulloh is about £200 proc, not sterling, by any means. I have occasionally acquainted you how this arose; and if it be candidly considered for a moment, that when I came here, a stranger to every rule of purchasing for myself, that I stood in need of many things, and that my income was little more than £60 sterling to provide me with every thing, I shall meet with some compassionate allowances for falling a little in debt. To you, my dear sir, as it becomes me, I will be more particular. My board and lodging only cost me £15 proc, my washing £10, the maintenance of a horse, which I must either keep or occasionally hire one, which will be near as expensive, because I attend some County Courts (where by the by I have always hitherto lost money, for that, as well as any other business, must be succeeded in by time only), £15, a barber (without whom I cannot do, though I almost always wear my hair without dressing) £4, and other necessary expenses occasionally arise, besides the expense of clothes, which in this country are immoderately dear, and of which we must have a good deal, on account of the great heat in the summer. To give you an idea from this article of the rest, I will mention, that a suit of clothes which in England would be made up for £5 sterling will here cost £15 proc at least, and our exchange is only at 60. A reflection on these things will satisfy you I am not so culpably to blame.

The business of Mr. McCulloh's office, by multiplied and teasing directions, is rendered a most laborious one. For three years past my whole time has been devoted to it without recompense, with a rigidity of attention that has left nothing to be found fault with.

My mother desires to know who are my greatest favorites. Without reserve or hesitation, I declare, Mr. Johnston's family and some near connections of his here. They are all united by the tenderest ties of affection, and ever preserve an uninterrupted harmony of agreement, which is maintained by a general share of good sense, cultivated understandings, and engaging manners, that I have never seen excelled, if equalled. They are truly families of love, and are known to be so by all their acquaintance. At another time, when I am more at leisure, I will be more particular. At present I will just say that the families I speak of, are Mr. Johnston's, in which are himself, Mrs. J., a fine little girl of theirs, and two of his sisters, who are the most amiable and agreeable women I know. Mr. Johnston's eldest sister, Mrs. Blair, a few months ago lost her husband. She has five remarkably fine children, and is herself a most valuable and respected woman. Mrs. Dawson lives over the Sound, which is just before us, and is the daughter of Gov. Johnston; she has been a widow upwards of two years, and has three charming children, two girls and a boy. This lady is about 28, and in point of excellence of understanding, goodness of heart, and a most polite, attractive behavior, she is generally allowed to be above all kind of competition. She is *indeed* out of the circle of her relations. I could mention some others, but will only name Mrs. Brownrigg, who is now too unhappily a widow. Her husband will be long regretted by her and all who knew him. The sweetness of her temper, and amiability of her disposition, surpass all praise; you would greatly love, did you know her. She too has five children. Though I seem to have restricted myself to the mention of the above, I must say there is a gentleman in this town who is a very particular favorite of mine, as indeed he is of every body, for he is one of the best and most agreeable men in the world. His name is Hewes. He is a merchant here, and our member for the town: the patron and greatest honor of it. About six or seven years ago, he was within a very few days of being married to one of Mr. Johnston's sisters (elder than the two young ladies now living) who died rather suddenly; and this unhappy circumstance for a long time embittered every satisfaction in life to him. He has continued ever since unmarried, which I believe he will always do. His connection with Mr. Johnston's family is just such as if he had been really a brother-in-law, a circumstance that mutually does honor to them both. But I must go to my minutes, otherwise I shall run away with my paper on one subject. I am very sorry you have not had regular remittances; my directions to that purpose have always been very express, and I lately renewed them with much energy. I never for a moment thought of taking the least part of my salary, which shall be yours, whatever difficulties I myself contend with. I had much rather have such, than know you to have any. God knows you have had your share. I hope I may prophetically say, in the words of Horace, "non, si male nunc et olim, sic erit." Now for a word or two on the subject of the Collection: you much mistake the value of it, it is barely that value in Proc, which you suppose it in Sterling, 4 or 500l. I have made no express agreement with Mr M.: I only offered terms in a letter; but, I believe, there is no good reason to expect they will be complied with; his letters evade the notice of them. I have lately given him leave to do as he pleased with the office, without supposing himself under any restraint from having given me hopes to expect it.

I will engage to give him any security he can require; for indeed (though I would not distress him) it would be an object of much consideration to me, as I might probably hold it for a great many years. However, be it as it may, I am content, and think, without it, I shall be able in a little time to have a sufficient income. I have not, upon my honor, now, with the utmost frugality. And yet, sir, your very obliging intimation of providing for me in England (although of all things it would be my fondest wish) seems liable to strong objections. In England, I must in any way be some years in a dependent and consequently an insecure situation. Here, I have a tolerable certainty of something, though a mean one, and a probable expectation, by the fruits of my own industry (all I depend upon with assurance), of procuring in the course of a few years a genteel independency—what I mean by which is, a moral certainty of acquiring such an income every year as will maintain me genteelly. A young country is the fittest for a young man without a fortune; and however unpromising or disagreeable it may be at first, a steady attentive perseverance will in all likelihood be at last successful. These, sir, are seriously my thoughts; they have often been directed to this object, and I think must have had great weight to oppose the almost irresistible temptations I have, to wish a return home; but it is a matter of too much importance to have within my consideration any thing but the great end itself, a means of competent support. How much have my wishes yielded to my reason in this point, and how great is my regret that what you and I so much desire cannot, with propriety, be sought for.

Mr. Kempe's goodness to Atty is admirable. I enclose a letter to him, such as you desired. My thoughts there you will, perhaps, think clash with what I have said here: but pray consider, sir, I have been here between three and four years, waiting for something I have not got yet; that without my little place I could not have lived here; and that now I have reason to expect success in some way or another. I cannot on this occasion resist the seeming vanity (though real pleasure) I feel, in relating what Mr. Johnston said to me about this near three years ago. He very obligingly told me he thought it would be an injury to me to have Mr. McCulloh's office upon terms as (they not being known to all my friends) I should be in appearance greatly provided for, and they would think there was no occasion to do any more for me; and if any thing fell in this country, that it would be worth my while to apply for, my having that office might be an obstacle to my success: he told me at the same time (and from him praise is sweet indeed; for no man is more averse to flattery, though in that instance he certainly judged too partially) he would not give up my prospect of making money in the law for any place less than such a one as the Chief Justice's, or one of the first offices in the country. You will not suspect me of vanity in mentioning this to you. It may, perhaps, give you pleasure, especially when I say Mr. Johnston is remarkably sparing of praise, even in the absence of any one, and much more so in one's presence. His thoughts are wise and secret, his words few and faithful; in these particulars I mean, for he is a most agreeable man, as well as he is equal to any in the country in solidity of understanding, and superior to most (his equal can hardly be found) in the integrity of his heart and conduct. I most heartily rejoice at Atty's happy situation. I very sincerely congratulate him on it, and if I have not time, or may, perhaps, think it will swell the packet too much to write him, acquaint him of my dearest, tenderest affection. Assure him of my most friendly wishes, and beg that he will write to me often, and I will to him sometimes, for it is much easier to write to me than for me to write to him. My declining to write often, arises only from the infrequency of a good opportunity; for if I send a large packet, it will pay heavy postage, unless the opportunity be a very choice one. I have not had any letters from my uncle or Charles, but lately wrote to them both. It is a long time since I heard *from* my uncle, but this, I know, is because he knew of no opportunity; for I have many letters by me which show him to be the kindest, best of men, and I love him with great excess of affection and respect. Do you and he correspond together now, sir? I hope in God you do; and am sure his delay in giving any effectual assistance to you was occasioned by difficulties we know little of: an encumbered West India estate, with the tax of high living, is no nabobship; and an unfortunate crop is a very severe shock to such a one. My uncle has had many such from continual droughts.

Where is Miss Macartney now?—going to be married—to whom? If it be to her advantage and happiness, I greatly wish to hear it is so.—I have had no letter from her a long time. Pray write as much as you know about her. To Mrs. Aldworth I cannot be mentioned with too much warmth of regard. I am infinitely obliged by the kindness of her remembrance, and ever shall be happy to hear of her being well. I beg it as a very particular favor, you will always let me know how she is. I wish too you would tell me something about the Miss Bagwells that were. Mrs. Aldworth will be obliging enough to acquaint you. I am a good deal shocked to hear of Jemmy Agnew's death; he was a very fine boy and his death must have affected his father greatly. I beg you to mention to me the cause. Tell my grandmother and aunt my heart feels the most respectful and affectionate attachment to them; that I owe them a thousand obligations for the kindness of their thoughts towards me; and that nothing prevents my writing to them but my never having an opportunity. I have been often greatly obliged, my dear sir, by your goodness in sending political information to me. The last paper parcel you sent I have not yet received, neither can I find where it is; Mr. Granberry has it not. I am sorry I troubled you with a request about books not so easy to procure. I hope you have not sent them, and beg, entreat, you will not in that case do it. You will oblige me very much though, by sending me the pamphlet of Junius' Letters. It gives me a pleasure I cannot express to hear you are well. God grant you may long continue so. I hope long before now you have got that place you had in expectation. I think, my dear father, you have some right to solicit, or at least expect a better one. I wish the interest you proposed to stir for me would be exerted for yourself. Sir George Macartney I think might, and I believe would, look out for a place of 2 or 300l. a year, the duty of which would be easy or might be executed by a clerk or deputy. That lady who so obligingly gave money to Frank, and would have procured a pair of colors for Arthur, would befriend you too. Lord Clare might be applied to; and it seems to me a matter easily practicable. Suppose it even in London, you could live more agreeably there than in your present way; or indeed any where in England. Greatly happy should I be, if you might succeed in this. If I could see you and my mother with an easy genteel provision, it would be a satisfaction that would enliven every joy and alleviate every care of my own.

I thank my mother with my whole soul for the tenderness of her letters to me. I hope I shall not intrude on her goodness by desiring her to repeat them. I beg you to remember me in a proper manner to my mother and Tommy, though they may be assured themselves (as they will read this letter) that my heart yearns greatly towards them. With a very heavy heart I am obliged now to think of my dear *dead* (oh! what horror in that word, dead) brother. The rest all away too: but I hope God in his mercy will preserve and protect them all. To his goodness I likewise commend your happiness which, as it is either increased or abated, gives proportional joy or sorrow to, my dear father,

Your very dutiful and affectionate son,

JA. IREDELL.

MANCHESTER, 6th Sept., 1772.

MY DEAR FRIEND:—Your letter dated 16th April I received in June, which I believe I answered the same month when at Liverpool. The lesson which you learnt from me, and are pleased to do me the honor to call it an useful one, I have entirely neglected since I came into England—the copying of letters. Last week I returned from the assizes, at Lancaster, where I attended upon the Grand Jury—(here follow amusing accounts of a trial for defamation, Miss Dawson vs. Miss Kennedy, two young ladies of Liverpool; and also a similar case between two apothecaries. Judge Willes presided. The report is full of humor, but of so coarse a character as to be unfit for a page that may, perchance, meet the eye of some fair countrywoman.)

I can almost fancy that I can see you laugh, stamp, and rap out at reading my letter, and that Mr. Jones is enjoying it with arms akimbo. I hope at least it will have that effect. Jo Hewes will, I dare say, damn over it. I hope you are all well. I beg you will present my respectful compliments where you know they will be acceptable. When or how you will receive this scrawl I can't tell. I shall send it in a few days by a gentleman to Liverpool. I have a great deal of pleasure from your letters, and for want of new ones, I often read over those I already have. I shall be very glad to receive more. I hope to see you well and happy; till when, or till you hear from me again, believe me, my dear Iredell,

Your very sincere friend,

NAT. DUKINFIELD.

BRISTOL, Sept. 10th, 1772.

MY DEAR JEMMY:—I did not hear till late last night that there was a ship to sail this morning for Edenton, otherwise you should have had a long letter from me, in return for two very agreeable epistles of yours that remain unanswered. My reason for not writing sooner was, that there are so few opportunities of forwarding letters from Ireland, and not from want of inclination or affection. My life has, during my residence in that kingdom, been quite a rambling one, continually from one place to another. I have been in England three months, and purpose staying the winter. Be assured I shall neglect no opportunity of letting you hear from me, and hope you will act by me in the same manner. You have no doubt heard of the death of poor George Kerr—a charming character has he left behind him; it was a great shock, you may be sure, to my dear Eliza, who, I thank God, is well and happy. She has one beautiful little girl, and is now near the time when we expect another addition to the family. You have also, without doubt, heard of the very great accession to Mrs. Rock's fortune, about a year and a half ago—above 4000l. a year. There has been another change in the family. Mrs. Rock is now a widow. She has just received an account of her husband's death in Jamaica. I have been on a visit to her ever since the news came, as I thought my company at this time, as she is confined, would be more useful to her, than when she can again have all her friends about her. You desired me to send you some account of Irish politics. It is a task I am totally unfit for, yet will I, with pleasure, undertake it, if it can conduce to your entertainment. The greatest part of last winter party ran very high. Mr. Ponsonby, you know, had resigned the chair, which I apprehend he did rather too hastily, and that he would not have been sorry to have resumed it again. The House of Commons was more like a Bear Garden than a Senate: and the Patriots, instead of being of service, prevented the business of the nation from going on, while they employed their time in disputing about trifles. The Court, without doubt, struggled hard for a majority; but Lord Shannon, coming about to their side, weakened the opposite party so much, that they were no longer of consequence. My Lord Townshend still remains there, though the people have been continually expecting a new Lord Lieutenant. Sir George also continues, but "entre nous" tired of his place. Three thousand a year, however, is not to be thrown away, because we have a little trouble. Now we speak of Sir George, I must take some notice of the paragraph in your letter relating to Lady Jane. How such a report could rise I can't imagine. She is one of the prudentest, best of women, universally esteemed, and behaves with the greatest propriety. And now for a word concerning poor Mrs. Barry, who has paid her debt to nature. If her name was inserted in the Magazine, in the way you mention, it was a mistake of the printer, as she, during her life, acted with so much discretion and propriety, that even envy and malice itself could not advance any thing against her. In some theatrical strictures lately come out, wherein the author is very severe in criticising the merits and characters, they totally acquit her of any fault in private life, and give her some degree of merit as an actress. Our set this year are tolerable for comedy. Mrs. Buckley, whom you may remember, carries away the *Bays*; indeed she well deserves it, as she has great merit. Will you not be surprised when I tell you that Miss Cheston was married last Tuesday to Mr. Bensley, who purchased Holland's share of the Bristol Play House. He is, without doubt, a good actor, and, I have heard, a man of sense. Their acquaintance began last summer, by her being thrown from her horse by the carelessness of a postchaise-driver. So gratitude, I suppose, for saving her life, was the cause of her falling in love with him. They are at present at Mr. Stevenson's, but next week go to London as the Playhouse opens there the 21st. My uncle McCulloh is at Bath. Cousin Harry, without doubt, you will have heard from before this reaches your hands, as I hope, he is by this time safely landed in America. If I have time I will write him by this conveyance although I know it will not reach him till Xmas—as he is not, I find, to be with you till the meeting of the Council. I have scribbled this so fast that I cannot be certain whether it will be legible. Your father and mother will send you an account of all domestic concerns ; and have no doubt acquainted you with the whole affair concerning Doct. Harwood. I shall then only add that he has returned to Bristol. Miss Gresleys and all friends here well, and desire to be remembered to you.

I am, my dear Jemmy,
Your truly affectionate cousin, and sincere friend,
M. MACARTNEY.

P. S. How goes on the Law study ? Write to me soon, and let it be a long letter. The first ship that sails shall bring you one—Adieu.

BRISTOL, 12th September, 1772.

DEAR SIR :—It is with particular pleasure I embrace this opportunity of acknowledging the safe receipt of, and thanking you for the sundry letters you have been so kind as to favor me with since your residence in Carolina. How I came to be so very remiss as not to make this acknowledgment sooner, I can hardly account, or at least not to my own satisfaction. Sometimes when modes of conveyance have offered, an unremitting hurry in business has prevented me from writing, and for these twelve months past my mind, from various melancholy causes, has generally been too much out of tune to think of almost any thing. Within the short space of ten fleeting months, I most unfortunately lost a father, an only sister, and an only brother ! all most deservedly endeared by nature's *tenderest, strongest* ties ; and these, dear Jem, in my opinion, are the severest trials a mind of sensibility and feeling can possibly experience. Let those unhappy advocates, then, care and sorrow, plead my excuse with you for my past seeming inattention, and accept my promise of being a better correspondent in future. It has given me the greatest satisfaction to have heard, from time to time, by your friends, that all has been well with you. I rejoice in your happiness, and shall always be glad to promote your prosperity. I make no doubt but your conduct will invariably be such as will lead you to paths of honor and profit ; for a wise man will endeavor to *excel*, as well as to succeed in every thing he undertakes, and most particularly so when he stands in any degree connected with the public business of his country. Most good men in this kingdom sincerely rejoice at the peace and tranquillity that seem again to reign throughout the whole British empire in America, and most sensible men wonder *how the devil himself* could ever raise and fo-

ment the sad and discordant tumults that not long since so disgracefully triumphed over reason, truth, and justice. As Posthumus says, " politician I am none, nor like to be," but plain common-sense alone will clearly show every man who calmly listens to her dictates, the wide, very wide difference between right and wrong. That *modern patriotism* by which *modern popularity* is acquired I very sincerely despise, and happy for the public tranquillity, it seems (notwithstanding all the newspapers say) to be held *almost* universally, in pretty nearly the same degree of contempt. The letters which you intended I should have received by Sir N. Dukinfield came to me by post from London, whence I conclude Sir Nathaniel changed his plan of operations, and left Bristol quite out of the question, otherwise I should have been happy to have paid him all the respect and attention due to my friend's friend, and I thank you for the introduction. This city is much improved since you left it, our streets are all new paved after the London method, and a new street is now building in a line from the lower end of Corn-street to the draw-bridge, in consequence whereof St. Leonard's church, and a considerable part of Marsh-street have been taken down ; but of these and such like particulars, you have, perhaps, been before informed by others of your correspondents, therefore I need not enlarge. I have the pleasure to enclose you a letter from our dear and most amiable friend, Miss Macartney, who is now in this part of the world, and with warmest wishes for your health and happiness I remain most truly and sincerely, dear sir,

Your assured friend,
G. MASKELYN.

EDENTON, 22d October, 1772.

MY DEAR FATHER :—About three weeks ago I had the agreeable satisfaction of receiving my mother's letter of the 26th of June, which gave me the pleasing intelligence that you were all well, and that you, sir, were in possession of the place you had in expectation. Nothing could have made me more happy than these circumstances, but that the advance in your interest had been something ; however, you have been unhappy enough to require that, I devoutly thank a kind Providence for the mercies he has already extended to us. May every day of your future life be easy and happy, and may it be the constant (I hope too it will be the successful) study of myself and all my brothers to add to the happiness of you and my mother by regulating our conduct according to the strictest principles of honor and virtue, which you took such affectionate pains to instil into us, and

which is the only certain, I am sure, sir, it is the only laudable way to acquire success and reputation. Pray give me always the fullest intelligence you have about Frank, and I could wish by good opportunities you would enclose me copies of his letters, which Tommy will oblige me by transcribing. I feel much anxiety for his situation, and hope you will always mention me to him in the warmest terms of affection. I likewise desire you to assure Atty of my unabated, most affectionate attachment to him. I received a letter from Charles a few days ago dated February. It came here from Florida. He has wrote you since, so I can give you no new particulars of him. His letter evinces the great goodness of his heart, and I love him dearly. I was surprised though he did not write more correctly. Mr. McCulloh was obliged to go immediately into the back country, so was not at Edenton. I went to Halifax, and spent five most happy days with him. I had the great pleasure of seeing him in, perfect health, and with the most lively flow of spirits. He gave me the most endearing proofs of great kindness and affection ; spoke to the Governor (who happened to be there) of me in the kindest terms, mentioned my relation to him and Sir George Macartney, and said he should think himself particularly obliged by any notice or favor shown to me, and that he was confident, no part of my conduct would ever discredit the strength of his recommendation. To all his friends he most affectionately mentioned me, and in about two months I am to go with him to the Assembly, in order to have the same kindness and attention shown me. Indeed I owe him all the affection and gratitude my heart can feel. He went from Halifax into the back country near a fortnight ago, and is to be here about Christmas. He intends this winter to transfer his office to me if possible. He attempted it without success last winter, an order of the Treasury interfering, by which the Lords restrict themselves from admitting any transfer of an office from any one to another, except they are the nearest relations, such as father and son and one of the same name ; but I am to write to Sir G. M., and by his interest Mr. McCulloh thinks it can be effected. When he comes here at Christmas the letter for that purpose will go home. The terms are not yet precisely adjusted, but they will be very easy. I will write you more fully of this soon. I hasten now to relate to you a circumstance of the utmost moment to my happiness, and which I can now do with equal joy and confidence, as it meets with the entire and pleased approbation of Mr. McCulloh. Startle not, my dear father ; think of what I have just mentioned, and do me the justice, for once, of supposing I have a tolerable regard for myself. I have then, sir, presumed to offer my addresses to Miss

Hannah Johnston, Mr. Johnston's youngest sister, and I add with unspeakable happiness, they have been successful. My mother was always for my having an English wife. My mother does not know in England such a young lady as this. I cannot be particular about every thing now, but just take this short sketch of her, which I am able to draw with the greatest truth, after an intimate acquaintance with her of three years. Her person is a very agreeable one ; she is a little taller than myself, and though her face is not what is generally called handsome, there is an expression of goodness and benignity in it that is infinitely charming. Her understanding is uncommonly excellent, and it has been improved by much useful and elegant reading, of which she is fond to a degree that does her honor. Her heart is the best that I ever knew, and her temper the most mild and amiable. Her conversation (of which, however, she is very sparing among all but her intimate friends, and even with them too diffident to be properly communicative) such as you would suppose to flow from a young lady whose mind is disposed to every good and benevolent action ; whose thoughts are the results of the truest wisdom, and who is neither capable of thinking or expressing an ill-natured or detracting thing. And, sir, to show you that in this instance, greatly as my passions are affected, they have not had entire sway, I add, she is possessed of a prudence and economy which is as pleasing in itself as it will be useful and necessary to me ; she perfectly understands the use of her needle, and is a professed enemy to the feminine weakness of attachment to fine clothes and gaudy appearances, the want of which she supplies with the more desirable caution always to wear a dress of decency, neatness and propriety. I have at all hours and times, with the most unreserved intimacy, gone to Mr. Johnston's, and never saw her habited than with the most perfect decorum—a circumstance not universal with her sex, nor even so general as to make me think this unworthy of mention. There is a reverence for one's self which all of the least dignity of mind would ever study to preserve, and this disposition in her leads to an undeviating regard to all the lesser rules of life as well as the greater. I declare, upon my honor, I never recollect once to have observed the minutest departure from decorum in her conduct, or a single impropriety in her sentiments since I have known her, but all is indeed, without any exaggeration, excellence itself. In short, sir, she is a young woman whom I fondly, passionately love, and whom my cooler reason tells me is every thing I could wish. I present her to you as a daughter. Oh ! did you know her, how rapturously would you congratulate yourself and me. Mr. McCulloh honors me because I have had the good fortune to be approved by her, and indeed this is the best recommendation I could possibly have. Her family is, without exception, the first in this country in every respect, and in none more distinguishingly than in possessing an uncommon share of good sense, and the most admired rules of conduct. Her brother is a man the most universally and justly respected of any in this Province, and with pleasure and pride I say it, very intimately and generously my friend. As to you, sir, it is my duty to mention every thing, I believe her fortune too is a very genteel one, though I do not exactly know how much. Mr. McCulloh spoke to me of it in the warmest terms of admiration, and added that in this country, provided he had a competent income, the sooner a young man married the better; and it is now certain that if the change can be effected (of which there is little doubt) I shall be in a few months in possession of his office, when I am sure I can marry with propriety. But now, my dear and most honored father, it is incumbent on me to give you my reason why I proceeded so far in this matter without your knowledge or approbation, and I confess I should have thought it criminal to do so, could you thoroughly have known all the circumstances; but this was impossible, and I could think of no way so satisfactory to you as that it should be approved of by Mr. McCulloh. For I know of no objection you could possibly suggest, after it was determined I should live in this country, but that I was too young, and you doubted the prudence of my choice. The first, Mr. M.'s sentiments will satisfy you about, and I hope some favorable ones of your own as to me. The second it was impossible for you to know but from me or him, and he approves it highly, and I flatter myself the particular description I have given will make you easy if not happy. When I mentioned to her lately the friendly and affectionate reception I had from Mr. M., and the warm approbation he gave to my hopes of an union with her, she in the sweetest manner expressed her doubts lest you and my mother should be displeased, as my marrying so young might appear a disadvantage to me. I told her I knew it would be quite the contrary, and that I believed I should now be able to convince you so too, as my opinion had the sanction of Mr. M.'s concurrence, whose thoughts upon this subject I believed would conclude yours, as he was intimately acquainted with the country, and knew better than any one else the prudential advantages of it in which my friends were chiefly concerned, though I knew full well how fondly you and my dear mother would participate of my private happiness, and I trusted you would depend on the propriety of my expectations for the certainty of success. I likewise expressed to her, as I now do to you, my anxious wish that you could but know her, in order to judge properly of my happiness. She said, with a modesty and diffidence of herself, that appears in all her sentiments, it was fortunate for her you could not, as she had a high opinion of you and my mother, and she was sure she should suffer greatly by a near acquaintance. Oh! could that be put to a trial how happy I should be, and I may really add, how happy would you be, to see me married to a lady of a most excellent understanding, great goodness of heart, a most mild and amiable temper, admirable prudence, and who in every action shows an unerring desire to do her duty in all the occurrences of life; at the same time unconscious of any uncommon merit, although it is almost unequalled—excelled it cannot be. If you believe the account I now send you, you must deem me very happy; and I hope you do me the justice to believe I have some discernment and delicacy of choice. Young, very young, it is true I am, but I have had the advantage of a very early introduction into life, and think I can now be careful to avoid the commission of any great error. I assure you, my dear sir, that in this country, a young man without the joys of a private family has a very dull, and I may add a less improving life. Were it not for my tender connexions in England I could live in this country with perfect happiness, blessed with such a partner as I have chosen; and I flatter myself from what I have written (which again I assure you is not the least exaggerated) you will approve and sanctify my choice with equal readiness and pleasure. You cannot judge of things at this distance but as I represent them to you, and my heart is not capable of deceit. Make me happy then by your warmest approbation. I am sure, unless it be my own fault, you will have increasing reason always to bless the dear girl who will make me completely so. These hopes are formed on no visionary basis, and the reasons why I expect to be always happy with her are, because she is possessed of an uncommon share of good sense, to give me the delight of most rational and agreeable conversation; of a goodness which will be ever directed to please and make me happy, (and this I hope to repay with the same kind of attention on my part); of a temper the most excellent that I ever knew, and a prudence and discretion which will guide her with the most perfect propriety as to all the lesser rules of life. I need add no more but that your approbation can alone make me more happy, and this I think you now will not for a moment withhold. Oh! give me the earliest intelligence of it.

Your dutiful and affectionate son,

J. IREDELL.

MR. IREDELL'S JOURNAL.

Wednesday, 11th Nov., 1772.—After a long intermission of my Journal, first occasioned by sickness, and since by indolence, I enter upon the task again, with the same faithful intention to be perfectly honest, and set down my conduct such as it is, good or bad, or more probably both. And certainly I may propose much satisfaction from this procedure, as it will be a means of checking any improper purpose the hope of secrecy might otherwise tempt me to. And, however the weakness of human nature may lead our thoughts astray, it is the duty, as it will be found not only the greatest advantage, but highest pleasure, of us all to regulate our actions so strictly as that they may bear the test of the most minute observation, and if we find inclinations beginning to rebel against the law of reason and virtue, the means I now adopt may serve to compel one to act rightly as far as he is able. But I must exercise myself strictly at first, or I may be induced to relax.

Thursday, 12th Nov., 7 o'clock in the morning.—Just looking over the foregoing part of my Journal, I am not much pleased with it. I pay a compliment to myself when I speak of my dear Hannah's discernment of merit. And yet does she not possess it in a great degree? To deny it would be impossible—it is universally allowed—and yet to acknowledge it would be indirectly to praise myself, who am blest with her particular preference. I own I stagger. I *know*, I *feel* my own imperfections, and wonder at the fact, though devoutly grateful for the blessing. But, perhaps, her great and condescending goodness is pleased with my uprightness of intention, and from habitual, indulgent thoughts of me has acquired some tender feelings. Oh! may I study to deserve a continuance of this happiness, may I (gracious God, can I) be a tender promoter of hers? My will is all I can trust to. I greatly fear my power does not equal it. And yet she is kind now. May I not therefore hope, a constant series of attentive, affectionate conduct will have the chance to succeed? I hope it will. But I must now account for the passing my time this day.

It is no new thing for me to remark that I rose but a little before breakfast, which being early with us is less inexcusable, though perhaps not entirely so. I believe I ought to rise earlier, and employ my time till then a little usefully. However, I let it pass without a censure now. After breakfast went up town, and going to do business in my office could not find my penknife; supposed I left it in my desk, and returned to look for it there, when in searching my pockets for the key I found my knife.—Haste spoils many things. Better to take two minutes and do a thing right, than risk the doing it wrong by taking only one. Returning up town, met Col. Little and talked with him about half an hour, then went and did business in my office. Hearing Mr. Johnston in the street, went to speak to him,—had the pleasure to find him well, and that Penny had lost her ague,—obliged to leave him and clear a Captain out. Soon after came home to dinner,—afterwards went with the Doctor to read a Bristol paper of the 12th September.

A remarkable revolution in Sweden. The people have had the infatuation to make their Prince absolute. Strange! that though their present King is a very great and very good man, that they should give up their freedom, in exchange for which they only receive a certainty (or perhaps a probability, for power is very intoxicating) of a wise and just administration during the present reign; and unhappily the example of all absolute governments shows too strongly the weak guarantee their subjects have for happiness, or even for a miserable existence. Nine out of ten of all the absolute monarchs of the world have been tyrants, and at least nineteen out of twenty have done as much mischief by their folly and weakness as the others by their wickedness. The happiness of millions is of too much consequence to be trifled with, and that it should depend upon the caprice of one man,—at best a fallible one, probably a weak, and perhaps a wicked one,—is even in idea shocking and absurd. That a whole people should acquiesce in such a state, though it may be unhappily born to it, is wonderful; but that it should be solicited with eagerness, and adopted with satisfaction by men asking to be slaves, though living, and in a capacity of continuing, free, is a procedure I cannot account for. That free and generous Swedes should do so too! Oh! human nature, how art thou degraded. Suppose your Nobles were tyrannical and oppressive, could not your King together with the Orders of the State, which represent the people, keep them in order? Yes; the very act which you have committed, and which you must forever blush at, shows it. If you could new-model your Constitution from a free to an absolute government, could not you change it from an unequal one, if it was such, to a more equal one? Could not you, in short, with the same ease have *lessened* that you have *entirely destroyed*, the power of the Nobles? Good God! how are thy good gifts despised!—a large share of freedom voluntarily resigned for the

---

' Certain passages relative to Miss Johnston, though alike honorable to that lady, and Mr. Iredell's gallantry, are suppressed from deference to the wish of the family. In other respects the journal is transcribed with fidelity.

comfortable situation of having life, liberty, and property dependent on the will of a single man! I will only add one thing more on a subject which affects me greatly as a member of society in general. I am sorry that a man of such generous virtues, such patriotic intentions as the great Gustavus (for great the present one indeed is,) should be induced, for the temporary opportunity of doing his subjects more extensive good, to risk their future happiness on the most precarious tenure in the world. Happy, happy Englishmen, who have a constitution that might last to eternity, were not the seeds of its decay in the vices and luxury of mankind, which, alas! begin already to have too melancholy and conspicuous an influence. Nothing can destroy the liberties of Great Britain but the corruption of its inhabitants, but that is too general. However, its fall must be gradual. The Crown may influence in small things, but I trust that period is at a great, a *very* great distance, when it can find temptations for any prostitution. Temporary ills, not immediately affecting the liberty of the subject, may be suffered, but it is not supposable that men of large estates and endearing ties of relation will risk the loss of the one, or the servitude of the other, for a paltry place or pension! or prefer the glitter of a day to the solid, certain possession of happiness and wealth for themselves for life, and their posterity for ever. It is truly said, England can never be undone but by its Parliament, and even on the low scale of self-interest this must be a work of difficulty and time. Though I flatter myself, all the English exalted principles of liberty have not entirely lost their influence.

I have been reading Millott's History, a pretty little compact one, comprising a detail of the great facts, interspersed with many just observations, and delivered in elegant, perspicuous language.

The rest of my time, this afternoon and evening, has been employed in thinking of my dear Hannah, and now and then pleasing myself with a look at the smoke from the chimney of the room where she stays. How greatly do I long to see, to talk to her! I fear the little accident which has confined her to her room so long has been very painful. I hope it is now nearly recovered from. I greatly flatter myself with the hope of going with her to Mrs. Dawson's, Saturday.*

---
* Lines prepared by Mrs. Dawson to be inscribed on the tomb of her son, who died January 16, 1796, at the age of 31. She herself has since unfortunately died July 16, 1797.

Behold around this hallow'd gloom
His trees belov'd their boughs entwine,
With duteous shade to guard his tomb,
And grateful form a sylvan shrine!
There shall my pensive steps repair,
At morning dawn and twilight grey,
And bending o'er his earthy bed,
Sad rites of love and pity pay.
But what avails the tender tear,
The pensive sigh, the heart-felt moan,
With fond regret why seek thee here,
To brighter scenes for ever flown!
From pain and death for ever freed,
From darkness dire and ills severe
Escap'd; and sure some glorious meed
For patient sufferance waits thee there.

While kindred bands around thee throng,
A seraph fair, in life belov'd,
With strains harmonious as thy own,
By heavenly melody improved,
Shall joyful hail, and point the way,
To where her own blest mansion shines,
To the same orb thy soul convey,
And raptur'd say, this seat is thine!
And may no traces of our grief
Obtrude to damp thy well-earn'd peace,
And those fond hopes afford relief,
And bid our selfish sorrow cease!
Yet shall remembrance haunt the shores
And groves, thy lov'd retreat on earth,
And every friendly scene restore
Thy form, thy tenderness, and worth.

Friday, 13th, three o'clock.—Not up, this morning, till near breakfast, but my rest being broken in the night by thoughts which kept me for hours awake, and the morning being a bad one, I forgive myself. After breakfast employed myself constantly in doing business in my office till dinner, which I came to with great satisfaction, resulting from the reflection that I employed my morning properly. How pleasing is it to be approved by one's own heart! I hope it will always be my endeavor to deserve and procure this pleasure. I must not omit one trifle: Dinner not being ready immediately as I came in, I was going to walk in the piazza, and Charles Ackley said I might as well look out of the window as from there. How easily is my attachment perceived! I should abhor myself if I was capable of disguise.

Monday, three o'clock.—I have been prevented writing in my Journal since Friday, by Mr. Jones' having my pen and ink. Now for an account of the intermediate time: All Saturday morning employed in writing Mr. Jones' catalogue of books. In the afternoon had the pleasure of seeing Mr. Johnston, who very obligingly took notice I never came over to see his family, and asked me to dine with him next day. Cleared a Captain out and came home with Mr. Jones, and spent the evening with him. Yesterday morning went up town, had my hair dressed, returned with Mr. Jones, and afterwards went with him to see Mr. Charlton. I ought to have read something instructive, but improperly neglected it. Came from Mr. Charlton's, thinking to overtake Mrs. Clarke, but missed. Soon after I was at home saw a lady coming over the creek,—went to the bateau and found that it was Miss Anne; walked up town with her to Mrs. Blair's, who was just come over. Some time after went with them to Mr. Johnston's to dinner. Spent a most happy day, and came over between 9 and 10. Mr. Hewes, Mr. Smith and myself were intercepted by Mr. Jones, who was then up. Staid with him till 11 o'clock. Heard in the evening many discharges of guns on account of Horniblow's being married to Nancy Rainbough. Was told she was averse to the match, forced to it by her father and mother. Is it true? Can such cruel parents exist? and a too easy, too compliant daughter with the desires of parents, in a point they have no right to *command*. But I hope it is not so. I please myself with thinking I have reason to believe it is not. Otherwise her lot must be miserable. The married state, to parties whose minds are in unison, and whose hearts are connected by the ties of affection, is the most blissful situation the mind of man can conceive; when otherwise, how dreadful!

This morning after breakfast went up town, and finding Mr. Jones at a loss for somebody to copy his catalogue, undertook and did it. Coming out of the Court House saw Mr. Johnston and Hannah—went to them with pleasure,—stayed some time in Littlejohn's store, and left them at Mrs. Blair's. Entered Capt. Walton and did business in my office till between one and two. Drank two congratulating glasses of wine and bitters with Horniblow,—received a kind invitation to dine with him to-morrow, which I gladly accepted, although I had entertained some hope of going with Hannah and Mrs. Clarke to Eden-house; had not certainly determined it, but wished greatly it might so happen. Came down to Mr. Jones'—had the mortification to find the ladies were gone over—drank glass of Mr. Jones' raspberry which gave me rather too much spirits. Quite sober now. Mr. Jones and Worth gone to Hertford Court. I have eaten my dinner and now go up town.

Monday, half past six.—All this morning have been with Mr. Johnston. We drank tea with Mr. Charlton and afterwards came down town together. Mr. Johnston's boat not being come over, invited him to go and stay at Mr. Bondfield's, and as we were going there met Mrs. Littlejohn and Miss Mary Blount going from Mr. Jones'. Mrs. Jones asking Mr. Johnston to walk in, I too abruptly left him to accompany the ladies, as it was late. Returned in haste, fearing my hurry in leaving him might have appeared disrespectful; found Mr. Johnston still at Mr. Jones', but he seemed with his usual goodness to expect no apology. I had not, therefore, the prudence to make it; not considering that though Mr. Johnston might be too kind to take it amiss, I should have showed myself concerned that I might have given him cause. I frequently act contrary to my judgment through irresolution. God knows, no man living can more highly venerate another than I do Mr. Johnston, who deserves all the respect and attention that can be shown him. But he knew my motive and will excuse it. What is the reason that most men in this country are so unobservant of those little offices of attention to a sex immediately under our protection? The trouble at least is very little, the pleasure often very great, and the reward so agreeable as to make it really a piece of self-interest for a gentleman to show respect to the ladies.

Thursday morning, half past nine.—My journal is two days behindhand, various circumstances having contributed to cause this intermission. I will try to recollect the material passages of my conduct on them. Thursday morning had a good deal of conversation with Mr. Monfort, which broke the morning in such a manner I could do no business; so went to see Mr. Charlton, and staid with him till dinner time, then went to Horniblow's, where there were many gentlemen to eat a wedding dinner with him. Not much like one though, as there was no bride at table. Heartily tired of very insipid, disgusting conversation, I took a walk with Mr. Hewes to his wharf, and spent a happy afternoon with him afterwards at his own house. This gentleman I greatly love and respect; and I feel much concern that he has imbibed some prejudices which cannot stand the test of a fair inquiry, and which, if justly founded, would destroy the strongest ties of moral and social virtue, and would leave unconquerable difficulties in the room of those which only *seem* such, for want of a due attention or a competent knowledge of the subject. As a man and gentleman, possessed of an excellent understanding, and blest with a good heart, Mr. Hewes is deserving the honor and respect universally shown him. How happy am I in being intimately connected with that family, which is admired by all the world, for their improved minds, exemplary conduct, and agreeable deportment; happy in themselves and their friends, and in being beloved and respected by all mankind. In the evening of that day alternately read in Blackstone's Commentaries, and conversed with Charles Bonfield, whom I love for his honest, upright mind, though he sometimes plagues me with doubts that he wants apprehension often to have cleared up to him. By the by, my positiveness and heat in argument is generally misconstrued. If I know any thing of my own heart, it is oftener occasioned by a surprise and concern that other people's apprehension should not equal mine, than from any other cause. I think a truth or maxim self-evident to me ought to be so to others. Yesterday employed myself all the morning in waiting to see Miss Hannah Johnston, who was going to Miller's. About eleven had the happiness of seeing her in the street; went with her to Mrs. Blair's and staid until Mrs. Clarke came; afterwards rode with them to Miller's, and there had the mortification to be obliged to part with them, which cost me a very severe pang ; flatter myself Miss Hannah felt a little reluctance too. Found, when I returned, no business to do but what I could have done to-day—wished I could have known it when at the ferry ; but this was impossible, and I erred on the right side. My first object I hope will always be to do my duty, and then, as far as is consistent with that, I may indulge myself in innocent satisfaction. Was all the afternoon in my office—came home, where I found Mrs. Hutton ; after walking to Mrs. Hardy's with her, I returned and read a great deal in Blackstone, which I have been doing this morning ; will endeavor to continue with an assiduity, which, I am sure, will be rewarded with equal pleasure and improvement. Let me try what steady application will accomplish.

Saturday, half past one.—Just came home to dinner, which not being ready, I employed my intermediate time in bringing up my Journal. Thursday was all the morning in my office ; in coming home overtook Mr. Johnston, and had a little conversation with him about the Currituck office ; interrupted by Mrs. Hutton, trudging along to go and seize Mrs. Johnston. In the afternoon, willing to pursue the subject I was upon with Mr. Johnston, went to his house, but found him just gone on horseback. As I knew not how to overtake him, staid in the parlor, till his return, and afterward spent the evening with him. A happy one it indeed was. How greatly do I love and venerate this excellent man. Came home and went to bed. The next morning read Blackstone till breakfast ; afterwards went up town for a little while, and soon after returned to accompany Mrs. Johnston to Mr. Hewes', where she went to see Mrs. Harnett, who with her husband* had come here the evening before in their way home from the northward. Staid there most of the morning,—snatched half an hour to myself about noon, dined at Mr. Hewes', then went to Mr. Charlton, who had sent for me ; was

---

* Cornelius Harnett of Wilmington, a patriot and scholar. After the flight of the Royal Governor, as President of the Revolutionary Council, he was virtual Governor of the Province. Mr. Quincy styles him the "Samuel Adams of N. C." He was Mr. Adams' equal in ability : in polite learning, and elegance of taste, and refinement of manners he was his superior. He compared with Adams as Falkland did with Pymm.

made very happy in seeing him and his wife so much so, having just heard from his brother Ben. Drank tea with Mr. and Mrs. Harnett at Mr. Jones', and spent the rest of the evening at Mr. Johnston's. Went up town this morning before breakfast, hoping to do some business, but Ned had neglected to make me a fire as he promised ; a rashness in promising and an indifference about performing, is too common among ourselves, and therefore no wonder negroes so often are guilty of it ; but either in white people or negroes, it is a fault deserving of severe censure. Had the intelligence of Mr. Granberry's death ; a man who very industriously, and with a fair reputation, has raised a very handsome fortune for his family, and just when he might begin to enjoy it with them, is snatched away. How many repeated instances have we of the uncertainty of life, and the instability of all worldly treasures, and yet we act as if this world was certainly to be our home : and God knows we have not a sure moment to enjoy any thing in it. This being the case, would it not be wiser to be properly careful about the Goods of Fortune, with a mind rightly disposed for the probable or even possible events of it, hoping for the best, prepared for the worst, and resigned to all, than to have an anxious solicitude to obtain unbounded wealth and dignity ; advantages few can even *hope* to possess, and when possessed, incapable of *themselves* giving any substantial satisfaction, and when added to other ingredients of happiness, giving no more than what a small degree of either may as well. Grant me, gracious God, but enough to live comfortably myself, and if I am blest with a family, to provide happily and honorably for them, and I will bow down with reverence and gratitude to thy goodness ! Oh ! may I seek to deserve the happiness I flatter myself is before me, by enjoying it with reason, and making this an additional motive to be good and benevolent in all my actions. This morning the whole time in my office, except about five minutes I went to look if the Miss Johnstons were coming over. Afterwards came home to dinner.

Sunday, eleven o'clock.—Yesterday afternoon in my office, and finished all my business there. Coming home, Mr. Jones and Corrie took me into Smith's to drink punch with them,—staid a very little time, stole away, and read Blackstone all the evening. This morning, been doing very little, mostly walking with Corrie, and looking for the Miss Johnstons ; just met Tom, who told me they came yesterday by Miller's ferry. In doubt whether to go and dine there. My own inclinations strongly solicit me, and I know no reason why I should decline it.

Monday, one o'clock.—Going to the wharf yesterday, understood Mr. Johnston was just going over the Sound, and suppos-

ing therefore they had dined at his house, deferred my going till the afternoon. Talking with our folks in the piazza till dinner. Some time after went and spent a very happy afternoon and evening with the Miss Johnstons ; would have been *entirely* happy, but that my dear Hannah seemed unwell. Came home about ten, and went immediately to bed. This morning read a good deal in Blackstone's Commentaries before breakfast ; after, went and spoke some time to Mr. Hewes ; came home and transcribed some observations from Dr. B. on the subject of our conversation,—carried it to him, and we went together to see Mr. Charlton, from whom I am just come. Having nothing to do in my office I don't much condemn the manner of spending my time this morning. I forgot one thing,—I had the happiness of hearing Mr. Granberry was alive Saturday, so that there is reason to hope for his recovery. Monday afternoon and evening spent at Mr. Johnston's. Tuesday morning employed partly in doing the business of my office, and partly in writing letters home. In the afternoon pursued the same business,—went to Mr. Charlton's to give to a little boy there, just going to Ireland, a letter to my grandmother. Afterwards inquiring very anxiously for Mr. Blount who was just come from Newbury, and I understood had letters for Mr. Johnston, and I hoped for me. Late in the evening met him, received the letters he had for Mr. Johnston and me—mine were from Miss Macartney and Mr. Maskelyn, two very kind agreeable ones. Carried Mr. J. his, believing them to be important, though they did not happen to be so. It being very rainy staid at his house all night. In the morning I rose very early, impatiently wishing for a long time to see some of the family, and at last when we went to breakfast, my dear Hannah did not appear, being unwell. My spirits greatly affected by this circumstance. Some time after came over, and till dinner employed myself in my office. In the afternoon, after being about ten minutes with Charles Bondfield at the wharf, came home and read in Blackstone till interrupted by a captain who wanted to enter. Obliged, very reluctantly, to go up town with him, whence I am but just come. It pleases me very much though, that I can be displeased with an intrusion when I am reading a dry subject of law. Go on thus and you will do very well. Mem.—To-day I have written two short answers to my letters that I received yesterday, and then promised to write very soon more particularly. Wed. 25th Nov., 5 o'clock, Thursday morning. Till breakfast, reading Blackstone. Went immediately after to my office, where I had not been above half an hour before I saw Mrs. Brownrigg's Sampson pass by. Heard by him his mistress was at Mr. Hardy's, where I went and staid upwards of two hours. Com-

ing into town met Mrs. Johnston, Miss Annie and Mistress Kisbiss in Littlejohn's store ; went with them to see Mrs. Brownrigg, where having been near an hour, I attended them to the boat, and was obligingly expected to go over, but a very unlucky pre-engagement to Mrs. Hardy prevented. Dined at Mrs. Hardy's, drank tea at Mrs. Barker's, and spent an idle evening at home.

Friday, 27th.—In the morning at my office till between twelve and one, when I waited on Mrs. Brownrigg, thinking and wishing that she would go immediately over the creek, but she went first to Mrs. Hutton, who returned with her to Mrs. Hardy's, where I waited very anxiously for a long time before they were ready. At last we went over. At first, my dear Hannah not appearing, I was afraid she was unwell, and that I should not see her ; tantalized with hearing her speak,—the room-door open, every body going in, and I, out of a proper sense of decorum, dared not go too. As we were sitting at dinner she had the goodness to come in, which made me very happy. But I was under a cruel restraint the whole day. I am always much happier at Mr. Johnston's with none but his own family, than with a crowd of company. In the evening we all came over, and I spent a most agreeable time at Littlejohn's till near ten ; his wife and he are very happy, and behave kindly to themselves and others. How did the sight of them, with their little girls, fire my wishes. Came home about ten, staid up near an hour, chatting with our family at home, and then went to bed.

Saturday, 28th.—Yesterday morning mostly engaged in sending a canoe to Mr. and Mrs. Jones ; the next partly employed in reading, but chiefly with Mrs. Brownrigg, who, in a very tender conversation I had with her, made my heart bleed for the cruelty of her situation. A woman of the greatest goodness and best heart in the world, to be vilely calumniated by her unnatural father and brother—monsters that ought to be banished society for such infamy. Had from her a perfect and pleasing assurance that a report circulated with equal cruelty and confidence had not the least foundation in truth. My heart was greatly affected with her distress. I had not the folly to offer consolation, but sympathy, and assured her in the most tender and respectful manner I could, that she might at any time freely depend on any services I could render her. She is a woman I have always esteemed, and I revere her husband's memory with all that fondness of attachment he so well merited. Soon after parted with Mrs. Brownrigg, who should not have gone with a servant only, but I had business to do in the afternoon that could not be postponed. All the afternoon my spirits greatly depressed in thinking of that dear injured lady.

Sunday, 29th.—Done nothing this morning but write my Journal from Wednesday. Went to church, dined with Mr. Hewes. Soon after dinner there came in a very agreeable young gentleman, Mr. Blair, who lives in Jamaica, and gave me very agreeable accounts of my uncle. Went and staid an hour in the afternoon with Mrs. Blair, and afterwards spent the evening with that gentleman at Green's.

Monday, 30th.—This morning wrote letters to Sir N. D. and my uncle ; did a little business (all I had to do) in my office ; came home and dined, and this moment go to spend a happy afternoon at Mrs. Blair's, with her own and all Mr. Johnston's family.

Dec. 1st, two o'clock.—After spending a very agreeable afternoon at Mrs. Blair's yesterday, attended Mrs. Johnston, Miss Annie and Nancy West to the boat, and then returned to Mrs. Blair's, where I staid the rest of the evening in a most happy manner with herself and her sister Hannah, Mr. Pearson being there part of the time. Just called to dinner. In the afternoon went to Mrs. Blair's and drank tea. Mrs. Johnston, hearing her father and sister were come, went over the creek. Afterwards went with Mr. Hewes to Horniblow's, where I did not wish to stay five minutes, but Corrie being there, out of complaisance to him, staid until nine o'clock. Before breakfast reading Blackstone. Afterwards saw Dr. Cathcart,—had the pleasure to find him very well, and to hear that Miss Peggy and all the rest of the young ladies were at Mrs. Blair's ; went there, thence attended them to the boat, came in the evening to town with Miss Annie, and staid the rest of it with her at Mrs. Blair's together with Mr. Hewes.

Thursday.—All the morning doing business in my office. In the afternoon went with Mr. Jones to Mr. Charlton's ; went about sunset to Mrs. Blair's, where I had the happiness to find my dear Hannah,—staid and spent a most happy evening there.

Friday.—Most of the morning in my office, the rest with Robert Smith. Went with him in the afternoon to Mr. Johnston's, and staid till ten o'clock at night. Came over to town, went to the court-house, and danced with the children there till one o'clock.

Saturday.—All the morning after breakfast in my office reading Blackstone. In the afternoon cleared out Capt. Dunlap for Scotland, and spent the evening with Mr. Jones.

Sunday, 6th.—After breakfast went to Geo. Gray and had my hair combed,—returned and dressed myself, which when I had done, I saw my dear Hannah coming over. Went with her to Mrs. Blair's, where I staid all the day in company with her and the other ladies from Hayes.

Monday, 7th.—From breakfast went immediately to my office, where after having done what little business I had to do, went to Mrs. Blair's, and soon after accompanied them to the boat. Received an invitation to dine, which I gladly accepted. Returned to my office, and am now waiting for the boat, to be a few hours happy. Dined at Mr. Johnston's, and spent a most happy time there till seven o'clock, when I thought myself under a kind of necessity to come to town, and spend the evening with Mr. Buchanan, a gentleman from Philadelphia, who had asked me to dine with him after I was engaged over the creek. Could not find him, so came to Mr. Jones', and was drawn in to play cards, which I hate, and wish always to avoid. Lost nine shillings ; came home between ten and eleven, and soon after went to bed.

Tuesday, 8th Dec.—Most of the morning employed in my office. Went to Mr. Charlton's about twelve and staid an hour with him. Came home, and just as I was sitting down to dinner received an invitation to go over the creek. Went there soon after with Mr. Buchanan and Mr. Smith. As we were at tea, received an express from the Governor, which obliged me to come over to town for about two hours. Returned and spent a very happy evening at Mr. Johnston's, where we danced enough to tire me ; much less agreeable, as I could not have Miss Hannah for my partner. Came home between twelve and one, and went to bed very much out of order.

Wednesday.—Awoke in the morning and found myself incapable of doing business with any satisfaction. Walked about very dully till about eleven, when I went to Mrs. Blair's, where I staid above an hour. Came home,—felt very unwell,—ate little dinner. Just after it, was applied to by a sailor to recover his wages for him. This obliged me to be a little active, and I found myself greatly refreshed, as I always do after doing business. Drank tea at Mr. Jones'—walked home with Mrs. Wilson Blount and Polly Blount. On my return called at Mrs. Blair's, and staid very agreeably there till nine, when I came home and went to bed.

Thursday, 10th Dec.—Up a little after seven, reading Blackstone till breakfast and some time after. Almost all the morning in the office. After dinner read a little and went up town. Spent a very agreeable afternoon at Mrs. Blair's, where I found the Miss Johnstons and Miss Cathcart, with whom I went to see Mr. and Mrs. Pollock, who were just come from the northward ; found them very well.

Friday, 11th.—After breakfast met the ladies at Mrs. Blair's as I was going to Andrew Little's ; obliged very reluctantly to leave them, the rest of the morning employed in my office chiefly. Came home, and employed myself till dinner in copying part of my letter to my father on the subject of my connection with my dear Hannah. In the afternoon mostly loitering about, called at Geo. Gray's, and had my hair cut. Came home early and drank tea. Walked with Mrs. Hurst home, and immediately returned, and was reading Lawson's Oratory till I went to bed. Intended to have read Blackstone, but took the other book up by accident, and could not persuade myself to put it down. It is a book I must read attentively.

Saturday, 12th Dec.—Rose late. After breakfast, went up town and wrote constantly in my office till it was past one : passing by Horniblow's to go home, Mr. Charlton, who was there, tapped to me at the window, and very kindly told me when I went in, he only wanted to take me by the hand. These kind of attentions are pleasing, and make life pass more agreeably. He and I had some conversation about Blackstone, whom he greatly admires. No one can possibly read him without infinite pleasure and improvement. I was more pleased with the manner Mr. Charlton spoke of him, as upon a superficial view he had formerly mentioned him with indifference. I staid and dined with Mr. Buchanan at Horniblow's, with whom I after dinner went to Mr. Johnston's, whom I had the pleasure to see returned. All the family well, which made me happy. Mr. and Mrs. Pollock and Mrs. Hutton came over soon after, and obliged Mr. Buchanan and me, very reluctantly, to come over earlier than we otherwise should have done. Walked home with them, and on my return went to Mrs. Blair's and staid there till nine, when I came home and read Blackstone till between ten and eleven.

Sunday, 13th.—Awoke early, and soon after hearing Mr. Hardy was come, got up and went to his house ; found him very well and his family very happy. Just called to have my hair combed, came home and dressed myself, and afterwards went to see Mr. Hewes, who I had the concern to find very unwell. Came home and read about an hour in Mr. Burgh's Dignity of Human Nature, a book which does him much honor, and is finely calculated for the improvement and happiness of mankind. I was interrupted in reading it, by hearing the very mournful and affecting news of poor Milner's death, an event caused by a fall from a horse, which fractured his skull. His loss will be greatly lamented, and severely felt by all. I am much affected by it, for I loved the man. Of late we had grown intimate, and but for this unhappy circumstance, should have been perhaps much more so. He was a young man of many valuable qualities, and I believe had a very good heart. As a member of society he was really respectable. All who knew him liked him, and the love and respect which I believe will generally be shown to his memory will be a noble monument of his worth. We seldom properly estimate a blessing till we are deprived of it, and I now feel in greater force than I could have supposed possible, his untimely fate. May this be a caution to me how short, how uncertain the period of life is, and may I prepare in every respect as far as I can, for an event which may happen to-morrow for aught I know, the danger of which I am continually exposed to. Five weeks ago Mr. Granberry and Mr. Milner were here as well as I am. They now lie in the silent grave. In five weeks more I may be there too. To the good Providence of God I submit myself in every thing. Let it be my care to secure His favor hereafter, by an undeviating regard to his laws here. May I live to-day as cautiously as if I were sure of dying to-morrow. I need not repine at the thought. I should so live every day. I begin to consider that my principles and practice of religion grow rather more loose than formerly. Let me consider them attentively and abide by them firmly, under a confidence that if I can obtain the approbation and forgiveness of God, I have done my duty, whether I have the good fortune to be approved by men or not. A slavish acquiescence in any man's opinion in temporal things, is reckoned weak and unmanly. How much more is it so in the important point of religion, the best guard of virtue, and the best consolation in affliction. Let me adopt the noble sentiment I have somewhere read—I fear God and have no other fear. No pleasures do I feel more delightfully than when my attention is rationally employed upon religion. I am tempted to employ this attention often, from an interested desire of pleasure, and I know I am called to it by principles of duty. Natural and moral philosophy—a view such as imperfect beings like us can have of the government of God, in the natural and moral world—how infinitely superior in point of dignity, excellence, and as conferring pleasure, is the contemplation of these themes, to scenes of debauchery, and intemperance, the debaser of our nature, and the destruction of whatever is amiable and lovely, of that inward self-possession, and pleasing consciousness of doing well, which alone can make us truly happy. After dinner went to Mr. Jones' and spent the whole afternoon and evening with him.

Monday, 14th.—Rose late, having had a very uneasy night. After breakfast just called for three minutes at Mrs. Blair's, and left a note there from Mrs. Dawson. Went immediately to my office, whence I am but just come (near two), greatly pleased with having spent my morning so well, and determining to improve the habit of industry I have lately acquired, finding it not only very *useful*, but very agreeable. In the afternoon met with Dr. Cathcart and Mr. Johnston, drank tea with them at Mrs. Blair's, and in the evening came home, where I found myself unwell, which I at first supposed to arise from my disappointment in not seeing my dear Hannah ; but attempting to read, and not being able to do so, or to walk with the least satisfaction, I believed I must be sick, and soon after felt a very severe fever, which obliged me to go to bed at six o'clock, where I in a little time was very much refreshed, and got some very comfortable rest. Awoke in the morning perfectly well.

Tuesday, 15th.—After breakfast went up town, and while I thought a fire was making in my office called at rs. Blair's. Found Mrs. Clarke and the Miss Johnstons were going over to Pembroke. Obliged to return to my office—no fire yet made,—walked alternately to the court-house and the wharf, hoping to see the Miss Johnstons—was disappointed—went and staid about half an hour with Mr. Hewes. Did business in my office till near one—joined Mrs. Johnston and Miss Peggy, and went with them to Mrs. Blair's, where I had the happiness to see the Miss Johnstons. Some time after attended them and Mrs. Clarke to the boat, and was under the cruel necessity of declining to go over with them, having business to do in the afternoon which could not be neglected. A severe sigh at parting : went to my office, and was writing there till Mrs. Blair's girl came to call me to dinner, having promised to dine there. Soon after dinner was obliged to leave Mrs. Blair alone, which I greatly regretted. Went to my office, expecting Mr. Hardy and I were to examine the account. This business deferred till the next day, as that (which we did not know) would be time enough. Continued in the office till between four and five, when I went to drink tea with Mrs. Blair. Had some very agreeable conversation with her ; my mind a good deal dejected, not expecting the Miss Johnstons. But some time after sunset, had the happiness to hear they were come. Ran with rapture to meet them, and felt the most pleasing satisfaction. Staid and spent the evening there, together with Mr. Hewes, who came in. For some time we were all reading Shandy, the production of an author whose sensibility of heart and brilliancy of understanding are uncommonly entertaining and instructive. His Sentimental Journey I am delighted with, and know perfectly. His Shandy I must take some opportunity of reading, for the specimen I had of it gave me the most agreeable idea of it. In the course of the evening had occasion to admire the excellence of my dear girl's understanding, the uncommon justness of her sentiments, and her unequalled elegance of expression. Annie and she looked and spoke charmingly. Had a little private opportunity of conversation with Hannah, which I was obliged at last cruelly to snatch myself from. Between ten and eleven Mr. Hewes and I came away.

Wednesday, 16th Dec.—Up between eight and nine, reading Blackstone till breakfast. All this morning very busy in my office, except an interval of a quarter of an hour, during which I went to the court-house, and finding nothing doing there returned towards my office, when I met Mrs. Dawson and Miss Annie, with whom I walked to the wharf, and then went immediately to my office, after just calling to speak to Mr. Parson at Horniblow's. I feel unspeakable satisfaction in being able to reflect I have passed this morning well. The afternoon I hope to do so too, and in the evening to be rewarded for all with my dear Hannah's company at Mrs. Blair's.

Two o'clock.—All the afternoon busy in my office. Towards the evening Cumming and I got together at Horniblow's, and I staid with him about half an hour. Came home for two minutes and then went immediately to Mrs. Blair's, where I had the pleasure to find only herself, Mrs. Dawson and Hannah. Spent a very happy evening with them, in the course of which I had my dear Hannah's lovely and endearing company to myself for near an hour.

Thursday, 17th.—In the morning after breakfast went and staid at Mrs. Blair's about ten minutes. Returned into town and was all the morning in court. Dined with Mr. Hewes in company with Dr. Cathcart and Mr. Johnston. After dinner went to court, and was there alternately till six o'clock, when I came home, being somehow or other prevented from going to Mrs. Blair's, and took up Blackstone's Commentaries, intending to read in them all the evening, but an invitation came from Mrs. Jones to go and dance there. Mrs. Bondfield, Miss Nancy and I went, but found it was a trap to get us there. I was as much pleased with sitting still as with dancing, which I never much like without my dear Hannah. After supper though, we danced a little, Mrs. Jones joining us, and being very merry. Came home between eleven and twelve, and soon after went to bed.

Friday, 18th.—Not up till past nine, and since breakfast I have wrote my Journal from two o'clock Wednesday.

Two o'clock.—Just came from my office where I have been all the morning, entering eight New-England men, after doing other business. Greatly pleased with having been so busy, which has likewise given me a good appetite for my dinner. In the afternoon I propose putting the eight vessels on the Collector's and my books, and then going to Mrs. Blair's. Oh ! that Hannah may be there ! In the afternoon went to my office and staid there a little time, Cumming and Hardy being there. Could not refrain from going to Mrs. Blair's earlier than I intended. Staid there all the afternoon and evening. A most delightful tête-à-tête with Hannah. Came home about eleven and went immediately to bed.

Saturday, 19th.—Not up till breakfast. As soon as I could get a fire in my office went to it, and employed myself well. I have this morning had the happiness to receive a most pleasing, friendly letter from Sir N. D., wherein he discovers a most noble soul, generously extolling in terms of the highest admiration a conduct severely killing to his hopes, and congratulating me on a happiness raised on the ruin of his. Excellent young man ! may your lot still be a happy one, though indeed it will be very difficult to fix your affections on one so likely to insure it. He has the goodness too to offer himself as my valet on the dear occasion, wishing, as he expresses it, though he cannot be a principal, to be in some manner concerned. Oh ! how I long to see him, to thank, *thank* him kindly for it all. In the afternoon entered two vessels and then went to Mrs. Blair's, where I spent a most happy evening, indeed, till past ten ; my dear Hannah behaving like an angel.

Sunday, 20th Dec.—At home all the morning (except when I went to have my hair combed) writing a copy of my letter to my father about my dear Hannah. After dinner went to Mrs. Blair's, and spent a very happy afternoon and evening with Mrs. B., Mrs. Dawson, Mrs. Clarke, Miss Grace and Miss Hannah Johnston, with whom I had a little tender conversation for about five minutes, and to whom I gave my letter to my father.

Monday, 21st.—Busy in my office till near one, when, as I was crossing from Mr. Hardy's store with a book I wanted, I met the Miss Johnstons and Miss Cathcart, with whom and the Dr. I afterwards walked down town and saw them into the boat ; we having waited some time at our house and then at Mr. Jones' for Mr. Johnston. In the afternoon some time in my office, afterwards coming home with an intention to read Blackstone, met with Grainger, who wished to go to Mr. Jones', where I went with him and staid till about nine, when I came home, and meeting with a volume of Campbell's Lives of the Admirals, read in it till ten, and then went to bed.

Tuesday, 22d.—Not up till breakfast ; afterwards went up town,—could not get a fire made, Ned being out of the way, so loitered about a little, much contrary to my inclination. Heard from Littlejohn, of Mr. McCulloh, who was at the Marsh, just going into Suffolk, from whence he is to come immediately here. Asked to dine with Mr. Littlejohn, Buchanan going there too. Just come home for a moment, and now I go up town again. All the afternoon at Mr. Littlejohn's except a little while when we came into town, and I went to Mrs. Blair's The rest of the evening with Littlejohn.

Wednesday, 23d.—Not up till breakfast. Just after called in at Horniblow's to order a fire made in my office,—met with Cumming with whom I had some conversation. Afterwards I went to my office, and employed there chiefly in reading Blackstone till twelve, when I came home, finding myself rather unwell, at least not with my usual flow of spirits. After dinner purchasing two or three trifles, some cambric and handkerchiefs, which I took to Mrs. Allen. Talked a little with Cumming,—did some business in my office ; drank tea with Mrs. Blair ; came home, read an hour or two in Blackstone, and then went and danced a little with the children, who had a dance at the court-house, and went to bed very comfortably at ten.

Thursday, Dec. 24th.—Not up till breakfast, as usual, I may say, of late, though it is not very inexcusable, having for some time gone to bed very late ; the mornings now being short and cold. Very busy in my office from ten to two. Received an invitation from Horniblow to dine with him to-morrow, which I accepted, though I had hoped to have been asked to Mr. Johnston's, where, however, I intend going in the afternoon. This afternoon busy in my office till four, when I went to see Tommy Blount, whom I had the concern to find still very unwell. I greatly fear he is in a consumption. Came home, having received a letter from the Governor, and wrote an answer which I am not, however, sure that I shall send, as Mr. McCulloh will be here so soon, whose advice I shall abide by. Employed myself all the rest of the evening in reading Blackstone till I went to bed.

Friday, Dec. 25th.—Serenaded before I got up by a band of music, the sound of which soon raised me. Tom gave me an invitation from his master, which I was obliged to decline, being before engaged to Horniblow. Went up town, returned and drest myself. Having breakfasted, I repaired to my journal.

Let me for a moment address myself to my great Creator with humble adoration and gratitude for the blessings communicated to mankind on that heavenly day (such it most assuredly was) which this is designed to commemorate. May my mind ever be impressed with feelings suited to the grand and happy occasion, and may it be my constant endeavor so to discharge my duty, as hereafter to be entitled (by the mercy of God and my Redeemer) to the rewards which are promised to every one who, with sincerity and truth, shall to the best of his understanding and ability, practise the duties of morality—those laws of virtuous, or at least of innocent conduct which all ought to conform to, and which all who do conform to will certainly meet with the approbation of the Divine Being.

Went up town—staid some time with Mr. Cathcart, a gentleman of Jamaica, who is here on his way to the Northward, and is intimately acquainted with my uncle, who, I had the pleasure to hear by him, was well in Sept. last. Went to Mr. Hewes', thence to Mr. Hardy's, upon the subject of the Governor's letter. Afterwards to Mrs. Blair's, where I found Mrs. Dawson and Mrs. Clarke going to Church. Just as we set off from Mrs. Blair's, I had the unexpected happiness of seeing the Miss Johnstons, Miss Cathcart and Miss West coming up street. We waited for them, and all went together to Church. Walked with the Miss Johnstons thence to their sister's, where they waited some time for Mr. Dawson and Miss Cathcart, who had gone to Mr. Pollocks. After attending them to the boat, where I was under the cruel necessity of leaving them, went and dined at Horniblow's. Soon after I hastened over the creek, where I spent a very agreeable hour, when I was obliged to tear myself away, as Mrs. Dawson was going to town. My dear Hannah just gave me my father's letter, which I had lent her to read, and said something I did not distinctly hear. Wishing her to repeat it, I could not prevail on her. My heart has been a good deal depressed lest she may be somehow or other displeased with my letter. After staying some time with Mrs. Blair,* went and spent the evening at Horniblow's, and am just come home. It being near ten I will go to bed.

Saturday, Dec. 26*th.*—Not up till breakfast. From then till near two very busy in my office and Mr. Johnston's, who asked me to dine with him. Went over with him, Mr. Buchanan, and Mr. Smith. Just as we got on the other side had the cruel mortification of seeing the Miss Johnstons and Miss Cathcart coming down to go to Mr. Pollock's. For a moment, it being very late, entertained the flattering hope that they would wait till after dinner, which, however, was not the case. Came from Mr. Johnston's a little after sunset, and going up town met them coming down. No negroes being at the wharf, I proposed to Mr. Smith that we should row them over; hoping and intending then to have had an excuse from that cause for going to the house. But when I got over, Mr. Smith seeming to decline it, though I knew he wished to go, and I, fearing (though in that instance much too foolishly) that my motive might seem much too partial, too fond to myself, unhappily, miserably declined. I flatter myself Hannah looked kindly at me, and, I hope, had some reluctance at parting. Oh! how I curse my silly timidity. All the rest of the evening reading Blackstone.

Sunday, 27*th.*—Not up till breakfast, having slept very indifferently in the night, my mind being still very much dejected for having so foolishly given up four hours of delight. After breakfast went up town to be shaved and have my hair dressed, when I returned home, and soon after sat half an hour with Mr. Jones, whence I am just come. Going up town with an intention of visiting Mrs. Buncombe, I met Mr. B. and Pollock, with many other gentlemen at Horniblow's. The former soon left us, being to dine with Mr. Johnston. I staid with Mr. Cathcart and Corrie and Smith (who were to dine with me at Mr. Hardy's) till near two o'clock. Dined with Hardy and staid there till after sunset, when I went and spent the rest of the evening at Mrs. Blair's, where, though I was very happy, I every now and then was obliged to suppress a sigh for the absence of my dear Hannah.

Monday, December 28*th.*—From breakfast till dinner very busy. Had the happiness to receive a kind and affectionate letter from Mr. McCulloh. Dined with Mr. Pollock.* A little mortified, when dinner was upon the table, to find all of Mr. Johnston's family there except the young ladies. After dinner being obliged to return into town, I was called to by Mr. and Mrs. Pearson, with whom I walked to Mrs. Blair's, where I found all the young ladies, and in imitation of Mr. Pearson's pleasing example had a dear salute of them all in compliment of the season. Obliged to run from them and be busy, which I could not be in the degree I expected, as I wanted some papers which Mr. Little could not prepare till morning. Went in the evening to Mr. Pollock's, where we had a little dance, during the greater part of which my spirits were greatly depressed, as I thought myself obliged, out of a cursed complaisance, which sometimes thwarts our inclinations, to dance with Miss Julius, fearing if I did not, she might have been without a partner; and as all the world knows the nature of my connection with Miss Johnston, in a private little hop to have taken her to dance, and left a strange lady without a partner, would have seemed selfish. Came from Mr. Pollock's between ten and eleven to Mrs. Blair's, where we staid till between eleven and twelve, and then came home.

Tuesday, Dec. 29*th.*—This morning up at eight, being obliged to expedite my express to the Governor. My business

---

* Mrs. Blair's granddaughter, years afterwards, married Judge Iredell's only son.

* One of Mr. Pollock's ancestors had twice acted as Colonial Governor. He, himself, was a man of note and wealth. The last representative of the name was, at his death, the most opulent planter in North Carolina. His slaves exceeded 1000 in number. His large estate was inherited by the Devereuxes of Raleigh and the Burgwynns of New Berne.

---

all done, but I must wait a little longer for Andrew. Busy all the morning,—then I dined with Mrs. Blair.

Dec. 30*th.*—After breakfast, went up town and did a little business in my office till about eleven, when I went to Mrs. Blair's and saw all the ladies. Mrs. Pearson being expected to go over the Creek with them, I went to Mr. Charlton's for her. We called at Mr. Pollock's, and then came to Mrs. Blair's. About one I attended them all to the boat, and returned up town. Went for a short time to my office, when Mr. Johnston very kindly came and asked me to dine with him, which I did, and in the afternoon came over with Mrs. Blair and to her house, and staid there about half an hour. I then immediately came home and finished the second volume of Blackstone. Since then I have been reading till now, 10 o'clock, Fordyce's Sermons, which I admire and love above all things. How elegant, how just, how noble his sentiments! Excellent man! May your writings be productive of the universal good they are calculated to occasion; and oh! what rapture do I feel in reading him, when I compare my Hannah with his standard of female excellence.

Dec. 31*st.*—Busy in my office all the morning and part of the afternoon. Went and drank tea with Mrs. Blair, and staid there till about eight, when, hearing Mrs. Howe was come, I ran with pleasure to Mr. Jones's to see her—staid and spent the evening there."

The Journal seems an unstudied record, and was, clearly, never designed for publication. From this very cause it possesses a charming freshness of feeling, and "naiveté" of expression. Never was sketch drawn of a purer or more innocent individual life: or of a more social, genial community. Verily it might well have been said of the little city of Edenton, that if no God had descended into her lap in a shower of gold, the Deity she worshipped had transferred his laurel to her brow, and had caused her heart to reverberate, with perpetual iteration, the music of his cithern.

CHAPTER VI.

MR. IREDELL AT 21; JOURNAL; LETTER FROM MISS MACARTNEY; JOURNAL; LETTERS; MARRIAGE, &C. ÆT. 21-22.

At the period at which we have arrived, Mr. Iredell had attained the full stature of a man, physical and moral. His approaching marriage gave stability to his purpose, and determined that his future destiny was to be that of a citizen of North Carolina. If, as was natural, his thoughts sometimes reverted to England, and his heart yearned to the distant home of his childhood, the thoughts and yearnings were repressed. Soon, as young scions grow into verdure about a decaying trunk, new affections sprang up, and budded, and blossomed.

The society of Edenton, though refined, intelligent and hospitable, was not well calculated to strengthen or develope a young man's piety. Many of its most prominent citizens were professed Deists, while a sense of religion was vivid in but few.* There were not, at that day, many ministers of the Gospel in the province. The majority of them belonged to the jovial, fox-hunting race of English parsons; and were, probably, banished from home by the irregularities of their lives. If on Sunday they performed with decency the services of the Church, on festive occasions they participated, without scruple, in the dance, or took a seat at the card-table. So degraded were many of them become, that a drunken priest was sometimes sent for by the planter to make his guests merry.† The faith of Christendom had but recently been shaken by the wit and sarcasm of Voltaire; and Hume, Smith, Gibbon, D'Alembert, Diderot, and their disciples, constituted the most intellectual circle of the world. The intellectual, rather than the moral nature, was exalted and worshipped: and what should ever be united, were rudely severed. It was regarded as an honor to wear the badge of the school of the Philosophers, an evidence of independence and manliness,

---

* Hewes, Cummings, Charlton, &c.   † Avery's Diary.

The blameless lives and amiability of many of these skeptics, lent a witchery and charm to their persuasions. Mr. Iredell's religion was too deeply rooted to be torn up by the blast, too hardy to be killed by the frost: it was not simply one of faith, or one of passion: it was compounded of both. Approved by his judgment and his heart, it was ever present with him, an active principle. His was an impulsive nature; he ever had hope for this world as for the next. His emotions were easily susceptible of excitement. An exception to the general rule of men constituted like himself, he was not subject to violent reactions. He never desponded, he was always cheerful. When fatigued with study, or the labors of his office, he found a pleasant relaxation in conversation, and discussion with gentlemen; and a delightful recreation in the society of ladies: he could even condescend to the sports of children, and share in their mirth. He would sometimes stroll by the sparkling waters of the Albemarle; or where, through the wood, lazily floating upon the stagnant pool, the lily unmasked its beauty to the sun. The play of the clouds, the flash of the lightning, even the vine that clambered about his dwelling,—all taught him adoration of God; penetrated his bosom with a sense of gratitude, and exalted his imagination. He had fortitude to encounter, in his own person, toil and trials without repining or murmur; yet did not his manhood disdain the tribute of a tear to misery. He was guileless himself, yet no other had so tender a forbearance for a neighbor's errors. He was universally and deservedly popular. His practice increased. He was fast becoming a man of mark. It was already known that he wielded a ready pen; and could address himself to the most difficult task.

A gentleman of the bar, of whom it might have been literally said, that such law as he had, was "at his fingers' ends,' on a certain occasion exclaimed,—" Sir, I deny the statement, I have the law in my *hand* ;" the opposite counsel,* with impudent wit, promptly retorted,—" May it please the court, I have the law in my *head*—that is the difference between the gentleman and myself." The lawyers of the period of which I treat, were constrained to carry the law in their heads. Books multiply now with such rapidity as to induce the belief, that by the close of the present century, a lawyer's library must consist chiefly of digests. Not only does the American press produce original (?) treatises with marvellous fecundity, but every volume from the courts at Westminster is promptly seized by some briefless barrister, and reprinted with some few notes that authorize him to attach his name, and render it a species of business card. Then books were costly and rare. No libraries were to be found save in the towns, and these were limited to a few standard volumes.* Such books, however, as the lawyer had were read frequently and closely. As a lawyer, Mr. Iredell was indefatigable; none excelled him in the mastery of his cases. He was always thoroughly prepared. When engaged in a cause, his glance swept the field of debate, and seemed to fix, as by intuition, upon the key to his antagonist's position. Points of law were not, in his style, as pebbles borne along in the rush of a troubled stream; but, as gems set by a Benvenuto, they shone with such brilliancy as, by engrossing the attention, to hide the art of him who selected and combined. With unrivalled astuteness he examined conflicting decisions, and liberated from obscurity and embarrassment the current of the law. He never paused to glean straws—diverting the attention from the main points of his argument by trivial particularities. Disdaining meretricious ornament, he so condensed, that he generally said more in five minutes than others would in fifteen.

† Disputes peculiar to North Carolina, agitated the public mind. The new Assembly‡ convened on the 25th of January, attempted, unsuccessfully, to restrict the power of the Executive, who had the right of an absolute veto on their acts, as well as that of proroguing or dissolving them at pleasure; they also indignantly declined paying the claim presented by Thomas Polk for running the dividing line between North and South Carolina, assigning as a reason that they had hitherto refused their assent to the measure, believing the proposed line detrimental to the interest of their province.

The official term of the chief justice and his two associates expired at the close of the session, by limitation of the Act of creation. The Assembly promptly passed a new act for the organization of the courts; but added to it a clause insisting on the right of attaching the property of foreign debtors. Under express instructions from the British ministry the Governor refused his assent. The Assembly being soon dissolved, the province for a long period was in a most anomalous condition, only five provincial laws being in existence, and no courts other than those held by single magistrates. The Governor and his obsequious council endeavored to supply the place of the courts of justice by commissioners of Oyer and Terminer, but this step only strengthened

* Mr. Johnston's library was, probably, the most complete in the province.
† Williamson, Martin, Quincy, Wiley.
‡ The copy of Williamson, from which I quote, has the following inscription on one of the fly-leaves: "To James Iredell, Esq.: in pleasing remembrance of the friendship, and splendid virtues of his father, by the Author."

---

* Hon. Warren Winslow.

---

the opposition; and a subsequent Assembly peremptorily denied his right to issue commissions without their consent, and withheld the necessary appropriations. An unseen destiny was fast urging on the progress of events. The colonists recognized the signs of the coming storm, though they did not perceive the sun hid behind the clouds. The chords of private friendship were more closely drawn, and a common danger promoted a more intimate intercourse and correspondence, between the popular leaders, while the tie that bound them to England was becoming weaker, strand by strand fretted away and rudely snapped. A new-born thought stirred in the minds of men: vague and of indefinite form, at first,—it was with them by day and visited them in visions by night; and slowly but steadily grew to the form and substance of Independence. The English people could not understand that crossing the Atlantic could not change the essential relations of Englishmen to Government; and looked for a relief for themselves from onerous taxation to revenue from America. The Parliament, that, in 1667, had in its articles of impeachment against Lord Clarendon preferred, as a distinct charge, the introduction of arbitrary government into the American plantations, was now bent upon the exercise of despotic authority in America. The coming revolution cast its shadow before, but the Whig leaders in North Carolina, instead of withdrawing for shelter, looked forward to action for an increased circulation and more comfortable warmth. They were as obstinately determined upon the maintenance of their rights, as was the king upon sustaining his prerogative. Though the practice of the lawyers was sensibly affected by the non-existence of courts, still they were not entirely without professional income. An intelligent people soon devise a remedy for pressing ills. Points in dispute were referred to the gentlemen of the bar for adjudication; and many suits were thus cheaply and finally settled, the costs of the courts being saved.

JOURNAL.

Friday, Jan. 1st.—Went up town before breakfast, and drank a glass of raspberry with the doctor and some other gentlemen at the doctor's apartment. Met Hatch, who gave me some letters for Mr. Pearson and myself, and by a mistake (as I afterwards found) told me Sir Nathaniel would dine with me on Tuesday. Went immediately to give Mr. and Mrs. Pearson the pleasing intelligence. Came home to breakfast, and saw Hatch, who came to tell me it was Mr. McCulloh, and not Sir Nathaniel, he saw. Obliged to go and undeceive Mrs. Pearson, who was kind enough to excuse my having so much alarmed her. Some time after went to see a little race between a horse of Buchanan's, and a mare of Webb's—the latter beat. Had the happiness to see the young ladies from over the creek at Mr. Jones', and went to them, and afterwards accompanied them, Mrs. Dawson and some other ladies up town. After staying some time at Mrs. Blair's, went with Mrs. Buncombe, and to Mr. Pollock's, and immediately came back to Mrs. Blair's, where I staid some time, and then came home, finding myself very unwell. Afraid I could not go to the ball; but after dinner I found myself better, and went to Mrs. Blair's, where I found the Miss Johnstons waiting for Miss Cathcart, and attended them all to the boat. Came home, dressed myself about sunset, and went to Mrs. Blair's, and soon after went with them all to the ball. Obliged to return and get my hair dressed, and then went there again. Very happy all this evening, having my dear Hannah for a partner. This day received letters from my father and mother, and from Sir N. Dukinfield, dated in Sept., which made me very happy. I had also a letter from my brother Charles, which damped my spirits greatly.

Saturday, Jan. 2d.—Busy in my office till between twelve and one, and then went to Mrs. Blair's, and found the ladies all pretty well. Had the great pleasure of being alone with Hannah more than half an hour. They were all going to Mr. Jones' to dinner, where I might have expected to have been asked too, but it was not so. As I was engaged to dine with Mr. Hodgson, I, however, accompanied them there, and came away with a sigh. Went immediately to Mrs. Barker's, and spent an agreeable day there with Mrs. Clarke, and Mr. and Mrs. Pearson, who went away though early in the evening. About ten I attended Mrs. Clarke to Mrs. Blair's, where to my unspeakable and almost unexpected satisfaction, I found my dear Hannah, with whom, the greatest part of the time alone, I was unutterably happy till past one.

Sunday, 3d.—Nothing to remark this morning save that I went up town to Mrs. Blair's, whence I walked with the young ladies to the boat, which was lying at the wharf. Came home, spoke to Mr. Jones in his piazza, walked with him in his garden, *but was not asked into his house.* This is very different from former times, and I know I have done nothing to deserve this shyness. Him I do not *blame*, but *pity*; he is under a government that is very capricious, though it might be very good and agreeable, and some silly, supposed offence I take to be the cause of it. Oh! how pride and beggary are to be pitied. I feel with pain and commiseration what that passion with this situation will one day come to. Moderation, diffidence and reason are becoming in all,—of the best birth, and the greatest fortunes. But for all these to be absent, without either of these advantages, must be productive of distress (and my heart bleeds while I write it) to those who have such little prudence, where so much is wanting. Do I mean that poverty is a crime, or a reason why people should be slighted ? God forbid—I should be in that case badly off myself. But I must and do think that modesty ought ever to accompany it in an especial manner. And no sight can be more disagreeable to others, or more unhappy for the party, than the contrary appearance. After dinner went to Mr. Hewes' and staid, together with many other gentlemen, there, till towards evening, when we walked to Horniblow's, which I soon left, and went to Mrs. Blair's, whence I am but just come, near ten, and now to bed.

January 3d, 1773.

It's a long time, my dear Jemmy, since I had the pleasure of hearing from you ; perhaps you may say, that's my own fault ; but you should consider, that while I was in Ireland I had not such frequent opportunities of sending letters as you have, therefore you should not stand on the punctilio of waiting for answers to all your letters. By acquainting your friends of your health, and that you go on prosperously, will ever give them real satisfaction ; and you may be assured that no one has your interest more at heart than myself. In my last letter, I believe, I told you of the death of your friend Geo. Kerr ; and that his sister, who married Mr. Weld, had got a daughter, and was again in the increasing way. I have just received a letter that informs me she is safely delivered of another. Poor Mrs. Paumier continues very indifferent, and has lost the use of her limbs totally : it's really melancholy to see her carried up and down stairs, and in and out of the coach. She often inquires after you, as do all the Lang family, and the McCullohs. Willie, I hope, is a little better, but still continues under Dr. Clehghorne's care. He is to be entered this year into College. I spent a little time at Bath before I came here. Your father is grown very fat, but not much better in other respects. I received a letter from Charles the other day, in which he complains money runs short. I fear he is no economist. He says he has wrote twice to his uncle for clothes, and he has taken no notice of his letters. When you write to him it may not be improper to give him a caution, as from yourself, and to endeavor to make him sensible he should spend as little as he can help ; otherwise he will greatly distress his father and mother. I had a letter from Arthur the other day, in answer to a note I sent him to come and dine with me, which was forwarded to him at South Malling, where he was gone to spend Christmas. He seems quite happy, and in high spirits ; hopes to see me on his return to town. It gave me great pleasure to hear from my uncle McCulloh, that you were going on so well in your law practice. So I find I am to "wear the willow," as I hear you are going to be married. You might have had the civility to give me a little notice to have provided for myself ; but, seriously speaking, my dear Jemmy, I hope whenever you change your condition, you will do it prudently and happily. You have my best wishes for your success in whatever you undertake ; and I hope we shall some time or other meet, and talk over all the things that have befallen us in our excursions by sea and land ; the former indeed is an element I am not passionately fond of. I was fifteen days coming from Dublin to Bristol ; a most disagreeable time I spent—deadly sick. Mr. and Mrs. Spann were of the party. Nothing but the inducement of their company would have prevailed on me to go by Long Sea, and I think nothing ever will again. When I return to Ireland, which I purpose doing next May or June, I shall go by the Head. As to Bristol, it is so altered you would scarce know it again. They have thrown down narrow lanes, and are building fine streets. It is this winter, I hear, the gayest place in the world ; concerts twice a week, balls as usual, and plays three times. It is really astonishing the alteration a little time makes. I intend going down there in a few days, to see what they are about. Mrs. Rock has lost her husband, and Mr. Griffith his wife, and so the town, without further trouble, has given them to each other, but I apprehend there's no ground for such a report. Direct to the care of Mr. Maskelynn. I will write you a long letter by the first opportunity. Miss none of letting me hear from you.

My dear Jemmy, most affectionately yours,
M. MACARTNEY.

JOURNAL.

Monday, Jan. 4th.—Very busy in my office till dinner, which I ate at Mr Johnston's ; obliged to come over just after, expecting to clear a captain out, and when I was in town, he was not ready. This disappointment made me spend a very dull afternoon and evening, during which I staid at home, unable to apply myself to any thing, my uneasiness about Mr. Jones' family giving me great pain.

5th.—In my office till near one, soon after which Mr. McCulloh came, and we had a very happy, cordial meeting. Dined with him at Horniblow's, and spent the evening at Mr. Hewes'.

6th.—Breakfasted with Mr. McCulloh, and afterwards was busy with him in the office till dinner, chiefly in writing letters to Sir George Macartney and my uncle, relative to his change of office in my favor, for which I owe him all the gratitude and affection my heart can feel. In the afternoon and evening again mostly with Mr. Hewes, except for a little time I was at Mrs. Blair's.

7th.—Busy in the morning with Mr. M. till one, when we went over the Sound and slept at Halsey's that night, and breakfasted there, whence we went to Col. Buncombe's, where Mr. M. staid about an hour, and then set off, at which time I felt some pain at parting from so dear a friend.

9th.—With Col. B. all that day and till breakfast the next, when I came to town. In the afternoon, after despatching two or three little commissions, I went over to Mr. Johnston's with Miss Cathcart, and—in the evening came to town with Miss Hannah and her brother John, and staid very happily at Mrs. Blair's till near eleven.

10th.—Not going to church, the weather being rainy, and no ladies going from Mrs. Blair's, I went with Mr. Johnston whom I found there to Mr. Jones', and staid there with him till one, when I went to Mrs. Blair's, where I continued very happily till past eleven, my dear Hannah unspeakably kind.

11th.—Most of this morning in my office, the rest (occasioned by accident) at Mr. Hardy's, and at home reading newspapers. In the afternoon went to Mrs. Blair's, where I spent the rest of the evening.

12th.—Morning and afternoon busy in my office, and at home. Poor Tommy Blount died last night suddenly, after being in a weak, low way for nearly two years past. He died happy in the love and respect of all who knew him, and I doubt not is now in the mansions of the blest. This evening spent at Mrs. Blair's, where I had again the happiness of my dear Hannah's company, and sometimes hers only.

13th.—Went up town immediately after dinner, being engaged to go on board Capt. Barter with Mr. Johnston and Mr. Jones, and having beforehand to see that Eccleston mended one of my office windows. While I was in the piazza, had the happiness to see Hannah at her sister's, but my time was too limited to admit my going to her. Mr. Johnston and Mr. Jones came up soon after, and as I was talking with the former, her sister came down street with his little daughter, and being afraid she would see and cry for him, he walked on, and I met my dear Hannah, whom I was cruelly obliged to leave in the middle of the street. Spent the afternoon on board of Barter, and the evening at Mr. Jones' (a little unusual of late)—part of the time we had Mr. Johnston with us.

14th.—In the morning busy in the office. In the afternoon attending poor Tommy Blount's funeral, I had the mortification of seeing an unnatural father—a man unaffected with the loss of a most worthy son. Oh ! Nature ! Nature !

In the evening, after walking home with Mr. Johnston, I went and staid an hour or two with Mrs. Blair, and then returned home, and read in the London Magazine I lately had from my father, till ten, when I went to bed.

Friday, 15th.—Busy in my office in the morning. At dinner I heard my dear Hannah was come over to town. Went immediately to her, and, except the little interruption of about half an hour, that I was called out by an express from Faill and Jones' agent in Va., I was ineffably happy at Mrs. Blair's till the clock, striking twelve, warned me to depart.

16th.—This morning busy in my office and Mr. Johnston's till near two, when I came home to dinner. In the afternoon went to Mrs. Blair's, where I staid till between ten and twelve, greatly happy indeed.

Sunday, 17th.—In the morning after breakfast, went to Mr. Johnston's office about some business I had to do for him, expecting him over. We were there till one, when I came home to dinner, Corrie dining with us ; in the afternoon at Mr. Johnston's office again with him. I should not much approve of these transgressions, were they to be frequently repeated. One great end of the institution of the Sabbath was to remind us that there is a God who will one day call us to account, and this reflection, *properly entertained,* is a great guard to virtue ; *improperly neglected,* we grow less averse to the thoughts, and in time, to the practice of vice. But my heart does not much condemn me in the present instance. The business was necessary to be done ; and the gentleman with whom I did it an unerring observer of all the moral and social duties of life. Spent the evening at Mr. Jones'—the women foolishly shy, I think.

18th.—Morning in my office. At dinner was told that Hamlet, a negro I had sent to work in Col. Buncombe's garden, had been a few days ago where the small-pox was ; thought it my duty to acquaint him instantly with it, which I did by the opportunity of a little vessel of Mrs. Blair's, which was just going over. Then went to tell his mistress of it. On my return met Miss Annie and Miss Betsy West, going to Mrs. Blair's ; drank tea with them there. Walked with Miss Annie to the boat. Returned to Mrs. Blair's—in the course of the evening was desired to read in Sir Charles Grandison, which I did with the highest pleasure; for I admire that book as perfect in its kind. *There* is present to the imagination a living example of the dignity of human nature, and such an example as it is in the power of any with such accomplishments to exhibit; for herein consists the difference between a pleasing novel and a romance,—the latter is wholly out of nature, and is composed of fictions scarcely credible, or even scarcely possible; the former, if it does not show human nature as it is (which indeed would not be the most likely way to complete its view of *instruction*), yet shows it, as it *may* or *ought* to be; and in all Sir Charles Grandison, and indeed in all the works of that inimitable author, there is a *true*, a *possible* picture of virtue, and such as it is the duty of all to aspire to deserve at an humble distance, and of those possessed of such accomplishments and advantages as are there described, to deserve in all. And surely it is no objection to the excellence or propriety of the pattern that it is almost impossible for any to copy it perfectly. Is it any objection against moral or revealed religion, that we are directed to the practice of all virtues in a perfect degree, though we know human nature is not equal to it, free from foibles and faults, and faults without number? Mr. Richardson wrote to the heart and the understanding, and meant to show (as he has done with the most perfect beauty) by a series of adventures plain and practical, and such as happen often in the occurrences of life, what ought to be the conduct of a man in an exalted station, with an immense fortune and most elegant accomplishments, and who, having so largely the *power*, ought, therefore, to have the *will*, to do good. And I repeat, it is very possible for a man, such in accomplishments as Sir Charles Grandison, with a heart so good (and I trust there are many with the latter, if not the former) to do as he did in all the occurrences related of him. I only now speak from idea, for I have never had the honor of even seeing him, but I think (bating the elegance of his person, and for a private gentleman, the richness of his fortune) Lord Lyttleton comes very near that excellent standard. This nobleman's character (I know no more of him but from that, and what I can collect from his writings, which will do him immortal honor as a learned scholar, an accomplished nobleman, and a good man) I revere, I love, I almost *adore*. So indeed do all mankind. Long, long may he live, for the happiness of the world he is connected with; and God grant that his hours may be easy and happy. When I read a book that pleases me I do not inquire, is this what I *can* do, but is it what I *ought* to do? We can all do (no, I will not say *all*,—but we can most of us do) more than we are *willing* to do. Let it be our care to bring our conduct as nearly as possible to the highest standard, instead of wishing to level that with ours. The powers of the human mind are scarcely conceivable by the indolent and unthinking. One exertion prepares the way for another; and as this has frequently been known with respect to learning and the sciences, so I am convinced it may with respect to the moral virtues. These reflections I have been led to make from recollecting that I have often had with men more captious than wise—and who had neither strength of mind enough to aim at this admirable pattern, or candor enough to suppose a degree of virtue attainable above their own,—with such men I have had a contest of this nature. One young man of this kind I remember, who is now no more. He might have lived happier and more respected, had his education been superintended with greater care. We was warm on this subject, so was I; and it is not possible for me to forget how warmly my heart glowed, and was animated by the reflection that I spoke on the side of virtue, and the honor of human nature. God grant I may ever do so.

Tuesday, 19th.—Busy in my office till one; was asked to dine with Mr. Johnston; did so; came over in the evening, and being obliged to go up town to shut my windows, I was tempted to go and spend the evening with Mr. Hewes; repented it when I went, as they were playing cards all the time. Came home between ten and eleven.

20th.—Just up to breakfast. Since which I have wrote my journal since Saturday; now go up town. Very busy till two, when I came to dinner. In the afternoon about an hour in my office, when I went to Mr. Hewes', and staid another hour with him; thence to Mrs. Blair's, where I staid with her and Mrs. Clarke (though I had the concern to find them unwell) till nine, when I came home, and read in Blackstone till between eleven and twelve.

21st.—In the morning before breakfast reading one of my new magazines. Afterwards till dinner very busy in my office. In the afternoon there for about half an hour, and then I gave myself a kind of holiday, playing a game at billiards with Buchanan (the first for many months), walked with him and Worth, and on our return into town, we met all the ladies from Mr. Jones' whom we joined, and walked with round the town to their house, where we spent the evening.

Friday, 22d.—This morning before and after breakfast reading Blackstone. Received third volume from Mr. Johnston only two or three days ago. Very busy till dinner; after, reading Blackstone for half an hour, and then I went up town,—met Mrs. Barker walking to Mrs. Blair's, and went with her there; thence to Mr. Hewes', with whom I returned soon after and drank tea at Mrs. Blair's. Came home about sunset, and spent the evening with Mrs. Bondfield, most of the time reading Blackstone, and a little of the Annual Register for 1771; went to bed between ten and eleven.

23d.—Not up till breakfast. Very busy till past two, when I came to dinner. After dinner till sunset writing in my office, then came home and drank tea. Being by accident in the piazza I heard Mrs. Jones in hers, and called to her. She answered me very kindly, and I went over and staid an hour with them very agreeably. Oh! how I hate coldness, and love a cordiality of acquaintance. Returned and wrote a letter to Mr. McCulloh; afterwards read Blackstone till past ten.

Sunday, 24th.—Breakfasted with Mr. and Mrs. Hardy, and went with them afterwards to Mrs. Brownrigg's, a house as neat and elegant as ever. Oh! that the hospitable and friendly builder of it were alive! often did I think of him yesterday. Spent the day and evening there; during some part of which I fear I was a little rude, for happening to take up Clarissa Harlowe, I could not quit it; I read a little of the third volume, and a great deal of the seventh, which often obliged me to shed tears. The story itself so very moving, and the relation of it inimitable. No man surely was ever a greater master of the passions than Mr. Richardson, and none, in my opinion, ever knew better to describe his feelings. Nature indeed speaks so powerfully, and with such lively and affecting eloquence, I can hardly persuade myself it is a work of imagination only. Nor, I am told, is it altogether; although the real story had not quite so melancholy a catastrophe. I knew a gentleman, who said he had seen the lady, the original of Clarissa, but he could never be induced to mention her. And that gentleman's word I could in any thing rely on.

25th.—Being delayed for my horse some time, at Mrs. Brownrigg's, I did not get to town till past ten, when after getting a little breakfast, I went up town, and since have been mostly employed in my office till past one, when I came home to dinner. After dinner went over with Mr. Hewes to Mr. Johnston's, where I had the pleasure of seeing my dear Hannah (after near a week's painful absence) though no opportunity of saying much to her. Mrs. Johnston and the child tolerably well. We came over about sunset, and as I was coming up town met a girl of Mrs. Blair's with her fine little boy George, who asked me to go and drink tea there. Stept into my office and wrote a letter to Col. McCulloh, which I carried to Mr. Hewes, and then went to Mrs. Blair's, who, together with Mrs. Clarke, gave me a very kind reception, wondering, as they were obliging enough to say, what had become of me for two or three days past. Staid an hour or two with them, then came home, and alternately read in Blackstone and chatted with Mrs. Bondfield till bed-time—the former chiefly.

Tuesday, 26th.—After breakfast employed constantly in my office till dinner. Barter came and brought me the eight volumes of Clarissa, which I bought of him for 50s. If I read them as I ought and hope to do, they will be a very cheap purchase. After dinner doing business till sunset, and mostly in my office. The day before Mrs. Clarke had told me she should go at this day to Mr. Johnston's, and that Miss Hannah was then to come to her sister's. Now, though I am always extremely happy in Mrs. Blair's company, even without her sister, yet I confess I should not have gone this evening, but with the fond hope of seeing *her* (although I had little expectation of it, having seen Mrs. Clarke in the beginning of the afternoon at Mrs. Blair's), for Mrs. Bondfield was entirely alone, and I the rather wished to show her kindness and attention (such as it was) in giving her my company, as she was always so good as not to seem to expect it. And they were so kindly pressing at Mrs. Blair's for me to stay the evening, I could not decline it, and felt no other reluctance in so doing, but lest Mrs. B. should think herself slighted,—a circumstance which would give me much pain. At the desire of the ladies I read a good deal to them in Fielding's "Journey from this World to the Next," which is agreeably humorous and entertaining. There was one thing though in which he greatly displeased me, and that is where he casts a sneer at Mr. Addison and Sir Richard Steele, both confessedly his superiors, even in his own talent, humor. The former—a man who *unitedly* possessed all those elegant endowments which are thought *singly* to constitute a great character. His genius, his learning, the incomparable grandeur and sublimity of his sentiments on the highest subjects, and the most perfectly pleasing talent of delightful humor, with respect to the common affairs of life, added to an unerring attention to the interests of virtue, both in his writings and his conduct, certainly declare him to all unprejudiced minds, to have been one of the most respectable, amiable and endearing characters that ever lived. May all who have his talents imitate his example! and may all who have them *not*, at least imbibe his reverence for virtue and religion (a reverence formed on the most noble conviction), and, as far as they are able, carry these sacred and honorable principles into their practice. The other gentleman, Mr. Steele, though not Mr. Addison's equal, was far Mr. Fielding's superior, in *every thing*. Has the latter written any thing that can compare with many of the former's papers in the Spectator? At the same time, I have a great regard for Mr. Fielding's character, and some of his writings; but I cannot bear his presumption in censuring two gentlemen deserving so much praise and gratitude from *all*, and at least not persons proper objects of *his* satire.

Wednesday, 27th.—Not up till breakfast, being a good deal awake in the night. Till dinner very busy in my office, which I could not, however, go to till near eleven, for want of a fire; but I was not altogether idle till then, doing a little business at different places which I had to do. In the afternoon went early to my office, and could not resist the temptation of reading a little in Clarissa, having the first volume in my pocket; began it yesterday at home, and read a little in it this morning in my office. I greatly admire Mr. Richardson's excellent talent in this way. In my opinion it has not been *nearly* equalled by any other. To attempt to describe *one* or *many* beauties, when *all* is excellent, would be a difficult and unattainable task. I shall therefore only say, I am at a loss which most to admire,—the goodness of the author's heart, the fineness of his imagination, his elegant and admirable sentiments, or the uncommon strength and eloquence with which he expresses them,—and each character most excellently supported throughout. Met with Mr. Johnston, who I found was going over the Sound, though the weather was rainy. Went with him to his sister's, and sat some time with Mrs. Clarke. Had the pleasure to find Mrs. Blair was over the creek, so that I flattered myself her sister Hannah might possibly come over in the evening with her; indeed I greatly flattered myself with the hope. Staid with Mr. Johnston till he set off, which was about four o'clock. The Sound was quite calm, and as he had on his large cloak, I hoped he would not get cold, though it rained a little when he went, and a great deal some time afterwards. Went from the wharf to my office and read in Clarissa till sunset (with an interruption now and then to see if Mrs. Blair, and as I hoped, Hannah were coming up street.) Went to Mrs. Blair's, and finding her not come home, I walked to the water side to meet her. Saw Mr. J.'s boat returning from Mr. Jones' wharf, and met only Mrs. Blair and Dr. Cathcart. My heart much oppressed by this disappointment, though my dear girl might have, perhaps, caught cold. How selfish am I, that I only take this as a *consolatory* circumstance, now she *has* not come, and did not before think it a proper reason why she *should* not come. But I hope I shall certainly see her to-morrow. Mrs. Clarke says she will go over. Drank tea at Mrs. Blair's, then came home,—attempted to read in Blackstone, but the Dr. and Charles going to play cards, I came to my journal. Chatted the rest of the evening with Mr. and Mrs. Bondfield till I went to bed. Would have read Clarissa, but did not care to show the book lest it might have been borrowed from me, and I do not always get back the books I lend.

Thursday, 28th.—In the morning, before breakfast, reading Clarissa. Afterwards till dinner busy in my office. Till a fire was made, which was not till past ten, I held myself excused in reading that book, and parted from it with reluctance. Have the happiness to hear the Miss Johnstons are at Mrs. Blair's. I'll go by-and-by to see them. Busy in my office till after dinner. Afterwards, after doing a little business with John Hodgson, went to Mrs. Blair's, and staid very happily till near ten.

Saturday, 30th.—Up pretty early, and reading Blackstone till breakfast. Afterwards all day, except at dinner time, very busy in my office. In the evening attended a meeting of the gentlemen in town, on a rumor of the small-pox being here. They wishing a place to be looked for in the country, where they might be removed to, I agreed to go with Mich. Payne in the morning, though I had had thoughts of taking physic. But all the rest were silently reluctant. Went to Mrs. Blair's and drank tea; hoped to find Hannah there, but was mistaken, and this made me very low-spirited. Came home and read Clarissa till I went to bed.

31st.—After breakfast rode out with Mich. Payne, but we were unsuccessful. Returned and went to church, unexpectedly finding that Tommy Blount's pall-bearers (all but myself) were going to church. Drest as soon as I could and went there. Obliged to come home quickly and divest myself of my habiliments, so that I had not the happiness to speak to the Miss Johnstons. Buchanan and I were to dine at Mr. Pollock's, and went together there. Seeing, when I came in, two more plates than I could account for, I flattered myself with the hope that the Miss Johnstons dined there, but it was not so. All the afternoon there, and after tea just had time to catch the dear girls, and walked down to the boat with them, and when there, upon their kind invitation went over the creek. Mrs. Johnston was taken very ill while I staid. I had some happy minutes with the Miss Johnstons, whose company is inexpressibly dear to me. Came over between nine and ten, and wrote a letter to Mr. Johnston about the small-pox, which I was going to carry to the post-office, when luckily I met Mr. Jones, who told me, it was generally thought the public apprehension about that disorder was groundless.

Monday, 1st Feb.—Dr. Ferguson went to see the persons supposed to have the small-pox, and agreeably informed the town he did not think it that disorder. Busy in my office all the forenoon and most of the afternoon. In the evening went to Mrs. Blair's, where I had the happiness to find my dear Miss Hannah, and spent a very happy evening.

2d.—All the morning very busy. In the afternoon a little time in my office, and found a steady inclination to business, but having time enough before me, would not miss the opportunity of seeing my dear girl. Went to Mrs. Blair's and staid with them both till after tea, when I was obliged to go home, having promised Mrs. Bondfield to come to a little dance she was to have here. Met Mrs. Clarke; joined her and walked back again with Miss Hannah to the boat. Came home and spent a very *so so* evening with very *so so* company. Mrs. Bondfield the only one very agreeable.

3d.—Busy all the morning. Came home and found Mich. Payne here. Cards being proposed I unwillingly joined. When he went away I read in Clarissa till I went to bed.

4th.—This morning up before breakfast, not long enough though to read. Afterwards very busy in my office till one (I forget—only a little so). Went to Mrs. Blair's for a moment, and soon after had the happiness of seeing the Miss Johnstons come in. Betsey West being with them, and going to Mrs. Anderson's, I walked with her. Mrs. Blair kindly asked me to dine with her, but I was obliged reluctantly to decline. Soon after dinner went there, and came home about nine o'clock, having some little things to do, as I hoped to set off next day or Saturday at farthest.

Friday, 5th.—All the morning and most of the afternoon busy in my office. When I had done I went to Mrs. Blair's, but found the Miss Johnstons just gone. After calling at two or three places, as I had promised to go to Mr. Johnston's this afternoon or evening, I went to the wharf and staid some time, but had no opportunity of getting over. Came home in the evening and very uneasily waited in momentary expectation of Bob's coming from Virginia; reading Clarissa; at last went to bed, but could not sleep for a long time.

6th.—This morning going up town to prepare for my journey, expecting Bob every minute, I called to speak to Mr. Pearson, at Robert Blair's. Found there many gentlemen assembled, and had the melancholy intelligence that the disorder suspected to be the small-pox was certainly it. All day doing very little, being on the point, as I expected, of going to New Berne. In compliance with Dr. Lenox's[*] and Dr. Cathcart's desire I agreed to wait till Monday, that I might acquaint Mr. Johnston truly. I may not indeed be able to go there, for I must wait Bob's return. But he will certainly be here to-morrow, if not to-night. Just after dinner met Cumming and received from him a letter from Mr. Johnston and the Chief Justice. Went to carry a letter from the former to Dr. Cathcart. My dear Hannah came out to me, but seemed quite unwell. She complained of a headache, and had been lying down. Business I had to do for the Chief Justice obliged me to come away suddenly, and I am afraid my dear Hannah thought me cool. Oh! could she have seen my heart! Came over very sorrowfully, my heart greatly affected with the small-pox being here; and after loitering about at different places, went to Mrs. Blair's and staid, very agreeably, with her and Mrs. Clarke till nine. We had a good deal of conversation about the disorder in town. I see no other alternative for my near and dear friends but either to go to Mount Gallant with Mrs. Pearson, or be inoculated. The former will be a killing deprivation of their company to me; the other may produce dreadful consequences. But as I should abhor myself, did I think of my own situation, when they are in so much danger, I heartily wish the former scheme may be adopted; though at their return they may still be in danger. God grant a happy termination of this evil. I fear it will be a most unhappy one.

London, 20th January, 1773.

MY DEAR IREDELL:—On the 6th inst. I was very agreeably entertained with the reception of your favor of the 4th Sept. I am much surprised that you should not have received any letters from me at the time you wrote as I have written several, and some I thought must have arrived before the date of your letter. Some were forwarded to the care of Bolden and Lawrence in Norfolk by Mr. Alderman Sparling of Liverpool, others to Gilson, Granberry and Co. Since I came from Lancashire I have paid a visit to my relations in Bristol, and you will naturally conclude that I should not miss the opportunity of seeing Bath at such an agreeable season. I saw your father and mother several times, though I was not much in Bath, and one evening played a very agreeable Pool at Quadrille with them. Your father told me Mr. McCulloh had been lately at Bath, and informed him of

---

[*] Dr. Lenox was first cousin to Mr. Robert Lenox of New York. The Doctor's daughter Frances was the second wife of Mr. Samuel Tredwell of Edenton. She so well discharged the duties of a mother to his orphan children, as to merit and receive from them the fullest measure of grateful affection; she was intelligent, sprightly and amiable, and especially remarkable for her neatness. She retained her vivacity to the last, and died in 1848, at the advanced age of 85.

your matrimonial intentions. How he became acquainted with them is quite unknown to me. I am extremely glad that you have such a prospect of happiness. I don't know any couple so deserving of each other as yourselves, and as it was not my good fortune to be the happy possessor of Miss H. Johnston's affections, I rejoice exceedingly that such felicity was destined for you. Happy may you long continue to be together! I, perhaps, may never be an eye-witness of it. My intentions of settling in America are now at an end, and I am in hopes some time or other to acquaint you with the fulfilling of your wish that I may select some lady *here* for my own. I beg you will accept my thanks for your kindly communicating to my mother the account of my arrival here. She mentions the pains you took on a very rainy night to give her that satisfaction, in a very particular manner. My mother writes me that our friend Berry is addressing Miss Jones with a prospect of success, but Colonel Palmer (whom I sometimes see) tells me that, by a letter he has received from New York, he is informed that the Comptroller General is gone from Boston to visit her, with equal expectations. My mother has all the letters I informed you I had written to Miss Hannah, but I desired she would burn them. It was not a very easy matter to overcome my affection even after I was very well convinced that 'twould be in vain to cherish it; but with a good deal of the philosophy we have often joked at together, I did get the better of it. If I should again visit Carolina, I pledge you my assurance that the increase of happiness to yourself shall not, in the least, abate the ardor of my friendship for you and your partner. You will, I am sure, permit me to hold her in that virtuous esteem, which I can never remove,—though love farewell. That passion, though now disengaged, will not, I hope, continue so long. At present I think to amuse myself a little while in the army, and have a promise from Major Gen. Burgoyne of the next vacancy which shall happen in his Light Dragoons, if I shall not satisfy myself sooner. Willie Jones* I hear is desirous to marry Miss Sukey Cornell,† but whether he is likely to succeed, I'm not informed. If he does, I wish him happy. I beg you will present my compliments to my friends in Edenton. I am, my dear friend,

Your very affectionate
NAT. DUKINFIELD.

* Mr. Jones was distinguished as a patriot during the Revolution and subsequently as the leader of the anti-federal party.
† Mr. Cornell of New Berne was a merchant and member of the Council. He was a royalist during the war. His daughter married Mr. Le Roy of New York, and was the mother of the second wife of the Hon. Daniel Webster.

25th January.

I am just favored, my dear friend, with yours of 30th Nov. by Capt. Messenger. I'm very sorry to hear that my letters have not come to hand, as there are many matters which I wished to have been kept secret, and which may now be made public. I'm sorry for the situation you are now in, and notwithstanding the happiness which seems to surround you, yet you must be impressed with doubts and fears; but this winter, I hope, will dissipate them. Remember that delays are dangerous. I don't see the least reason why you should either of you defer the wished-for hour. I will endeavor to follow the example; I assure you, Iredell, this thought does not engage a little of my time. I shall be upon the watch, and intend to make sail upon some nice, well-laden frigate. I am not discouraged from the attempt, though I have met with more than one refusal; nor shall a hundred make me give up the pursuit, as I think it not the least dishonorable, but unfortunate. I'm much obliged by the compliment you pay my abilities, though if I was with you, I don't know what service I could be of to the province. *I'm very sorry that an embargo was laid on wheat.* I see no ill consequence that could arise if the whole was exported, save enough for seed. Who petitioned for it? You surprised me by mentioning Horniblow's being married, as I had never heard of his wife's death. I don't recollect Liddy Boyd—is it Boyd, the saw-miller's daughter? I wish the devil had the opening of every infamous scoundrel whose mean curiosity has induced him to open my letters. I wish you would acquaint me whether my addressing Miss Johnston was publicly known in North Carolina; and what she thought of my persisting to write to her. For the future I beg you will write by the post, and direct to me at Manchester; by this means I hope to get your letters safe. I shall not again write by any vessel.° &c.
NAT. DUKINFIELD.

LONDON, March 10th.

MY DEAR IREDELL:—Yours of the 2th January I received about four days ago by way of Scotland. I'm very sorry that Hatch should have been so great a fool as to make the mistake he did; it must, to be sure, have caused some uneasiness to my mother to be told so, and afterwards to have the report contradicted; but I'm sure she must easily pardon you, as your conduct was governed by sincerity and friendship. He merited a broken head. I am glad Miss Dawson's trial afforded you any amusement. I

* It is believed that Sir Nat. Dukinfield was a native of N. C. William Dukinfield, the friend of Gov. Sothel, was, probably, his grandfather.

am very glad that your happiness is so nearly completed, and I am very sorry it will not be in my power to be an eye-witness of it. But the particularity of my own situation obliges me to continue here, and I should think myself very happy if I could need a friend to execute for me the office I intended you. You will, my dear friend, before this time have received my letters acquainting you that my intentions of returning to Carolina were no more, or it would have given me great pleasure to have executed the part I proposed, and which I fully intended at the time I mentioned it. I have now the same reason to induce me to stay in England that I had to remain in Carolina, and which will, perhaps, be crowned with equal success. I am determined to marry as soon as I can meet with a lady whose person and fortune will be suitable, and who shall think me suitable for her; for without a unison of opinion in that point, I can never do it. You, my dear friend, are happy in the affectionate smiles of one to whom you are dearest, while I am obliged to be contented with the smiles of those who perhaps will curse me as soon as I leave them; but, notwithstanding, I sometimes flatter myself I have a great deal of pleasure even in those forced smiles. You know I can't live without them. But I'll change my way of life as soon as possible; and as the old saying is, live honestly. You may depend on my secresy in the matter you mention, and if I can, by any means, discover that the matter is finished, I will communicate it to you as soon as possible. I will very soon pay a visit to Mr. McCulloh; at present I have not time. I'm quite engaged in attending to French and fencing, both as an ornament, and a proper requisite. I hope soon to be "*en militaire*," but in what corps is yet uncertain. I think I shall see your father soon, as I purpose to visit Bristol in a few weeks. I hope Mrs. Johnston and her child will do well. I beg you to present my compliments to Mr. Hewes, and every body in Edenton and at Hayes. I am, my dear friend,

Your sincere
NAT. DUKINFIELD.

19th April, 1773.

I am now, my dear James, to acknowledge the receipt of your two last favors,—the first dated in January, the last, from New Berne, the 14th Feb. Be assured that each time I hear of your health and increasing prosperity, I feel an addition to my own happiness. Most sincerely do I congratulate you on the happy prospect you have before you. From the character I have heard of the lady, I honor your choice; and shall be well pleased to have a person introduced into our family who will do

so much credit to it. Had not that been the case, I should not have forgiven her for rivalling me. I am greatly pleased to find Mr. McCulloh has acted with so much friendship to you; but it's no more than I expected from the goodness of his heart. Long before this letter reaches you, I apprehend he will have left your part of the world. I, with you, admire the fidelity and attention of the old negro, and doubt not but his merit will meet with a reward. I have been at Bath, backward and forward, for near a month. I am at present with Mrs. Grayson (whom you may remember at the Hotwells, a little before you left England), your mother having no room for me. Thomas, who is at home for the holidays, went to the Rooms with me last night. He is really a lovely, fine boy.* I suppose you have had the particulars of the affair "de l'honneur," between Lord Bellamont and Lord Townshend. It's said that the *former* is coming here. I have the pleasure of being intimately acquainted with all his family. He is a sensible, agreeable young man, and quite the *man of fashion*. Lord Townshend, I hear, is soon to be married to Miss Anna Montgomery, who is a young lady possessed in the highest degree of every qualification except *fortune*: it therefore gives double pleasure to her friends, that, for once, merit has some chance of recommending its votaries. His lordship, though not much admired in his political character, merits applause in his domestic one, as a good husband, and tender father. Mrs. Humphreys, the housekeeper to the castle, died here recently, and, I hear, the competitors for her place are Mrs. Clements of the Park, Col. Cunningham's lady, and Mrs. Wayte, the Under Secretary's wife; but who will succeed is yet uncertain. You know, I suppose, that Sir George, in lieu of his place, has a pension of £1500 per annum.† Lord Clare, I hear, is quite out with Government. Mr. Hammond of Bristol has got the Comptroller's place, which has given great umbrage to old Mr. Jones, and he has resigned. Mr. Charles Harford (that you may remember went off with Mrs. Charles Vaughn) has got Mr. Hammond's place; most other things remain in "statu quo." Mr. Mallard, who married Miss Beaton, is in partnership with Mr. Cruger; and now, I think I've told you all the news I can recollect. Had I wrote as you do, this would have filled near two sheets; but I fancy when you are writing letters you sometimes mistake, and think you are engrossing parchment. You know how anxious I am to hear of your welfare, yet you neglect to tell me how your law-studies go on: but I must excuse, as, at present, you are allowed to be *absent;* and indeed, it's a bad time for any study at all. I must not,

* Thomas Iredell. † Sir George Macartney.

I suppose, finish my letter without telling you how our amusements go on. Last week, then, I went to one play and one ball—the former was the new comedy wrote by Dr, Goldsmith, "She Stoops to Conquer, or the Mistakes of a Night." Few pieces have occasioned more disputes : it was, however, received with great applause. I never, I think, laughed more. I have not read it, but I apprehend it will not afford so much entertainment in the perusal as in the performance. I had almost forgot to tell you Doctor Weld and his family are here. We are all to go to-night to the ball at the Upper Rooms. Miss Linley, I find, was married last Tuesday to Mr. Sheridan, the gentleman who fought Mr. Matthews. I suppose you had an account of that affair from your mother, so a repetition would be troublesome. I shall say nothing of your family, as your father and mother both write. Adieu ! therefore. I have to attend to my "frisure," and the *important* labors of the toilet. I am not sorry to resign my pen, as it is a very bad one ; and what is more, I have not a knife to mend it. God bless you, my dear Jemmy,—that health and uninterrupted happiness may crown your future days, is the sincere wish of

MARGARET MACARTNEY.

CAREY STREET, May 3d, 1773.

HONORED SIR :—After calling on Sir George Macartney several times, in obedience to your orders, without getting admission, I took the resolution to write him a letter, in which I acquainted him that you desired your best compliments, and would esteem it a favor if he would, through me, advise you, whether he had applied or intended to apply to Lord North, in my brother's favor, for the Collectorship. This morning I received a very obliging, though unfavorable, answer to it, from Sir George, which I shall transcribe, word for word. I make no doubt the unfavorable answer he received from Lord North was occasioned by his laying Mr. McCulloh's letter before him, without acquainting his lordship that he wished to procure it for my brother. I am heartily sorry for my brother, and the more so, because there seems to be such a flat refusal from the Premier as goes to all applications ; there has been a talk, for some time, I find, of Lord North's quitting the Treasury. I cannot close this opening of a correspondence, without expressing my grateful sense of the friendly regards you have always shown me, and my most ardent hopes of your receiving addition to your prospects of health from Bath ; and of my utmost readiness to fulfil any future commands you may please to lay upon me, either in respect of my brother's affairs, or any other.

Your most dutiful nephew, and obedient servant,
ARTHUR IREDELL.

Mr. HENRY McCULLOH.

CHARLES STREET, B. S. May 1st, 1773.

SIR :—I have received the favor of your letter, and am sorry that I had not the pleasure of seeing you, when you called at my house. If you had left your name, my servant would have admitted you immediately. He told me a young gentleman had called but would not leave his name, and till I received your letter, I did not know it was you. Be so good as to present my compliments to Mr. McCulloh, and tell him that I have applied to Lord North repeatedly, in order to get leave for his son to resign to your brother, and his lordship has refused it, peremptorily—it being a thing he says he never will allow, in any instance, except of a father to a son. I should be happy to get it done, but I think there are no hopes of obtaining it, whilst Lord North is at the Treasury.

I am, sir, your most obedient and most humble servant,
GEO. MACARTNEY.

Mr. ARTHUR IREDELL.

BRISTOL, 14th May, 1773.

I am happy in having received my dear friend's letters of the 21st Jan., from Edenton, and of the 20th Feb., from New Berne. In the first of these you mention to have written about a week before, via Virginia. That letter is not come to hand. These were received in London, on the 21st and 26th of last month, and I am ashamed that I did not buy the books you desired, before I left London ; but I had really mislaid your letter, and could not recollect the books. I had been reading in a French novel, and being called off, put your letter into the book, to discover where I left off, and did not look into the book, till last Saturday, when I left London, nor should I, perhaps, then, had I not been packing up all my things, and sending them down to Scotland.

You will, long before this time, have been acquainted with the plan of life I have entered into. You accuse me of not acquainting you with my intentions of settling. At the time I had then written, I intended to return to Carolina, though not without reluctance, as the little blind god had been at me : but not for Miss Jodrell ; as you hint, that matter is now at an end, though it was a chief inducement for my entering into the army, that I might have opportunities of seeing what I began to think (to borrow a phrase which I understand you make use of—my information was at Bath) a goddess. This, joined with my natural indolent disposition and inattention to business, the contrary of which is absolutely requisite for a planter, determined me to stay in England. I am now entirely free from the last tincture of that unhappy situation of being in love, but how long the warmth of my constitution will permit me to be thus cool, I will not venture to promise. I am, however, destined to a cold part of the Island, to join the Queen's (or 7th) Regiment of Dragoons, now quartered near Edinburgh, in which I have purchased a cornetcy. To marry in this country, there must be two considerations,—a lady and a fortune. But I must, as I have frequently said before, consider the lady first, and the fortune as a secondary (though a very necessary) recommendation. That is, I could marry a lady *with* a fortune, and not, as many do, *for* a fortune. I can, with great pleasure, look forward and perceive the happiness you are going to enjoy ; may it be long and perfect. When two such amiable persons meet together, 'tis, I think, impossible to avoid felicity, could you insure health, and I see nothing to prevent it. 'Tis a bliss which I fear I shall never know. The hopes which I once had were very distant, but from a certain behavior of the lady and her father, which I did not approve, I have totally obliterated all thoughts of taking any further notice of the affair. Indeed I never spoke but to the father of the demoiselle, and though he did not disapprove of it, entirely, yet he had reasons which would not let him think of it at the present, since which I know he has said that his daughter might marry whom she pleased, and he would give her £10,000 down, but would not oblige himself to do any thing more : but that would be too trifling for me to think of. I should be injuring myself, the lady, and my posterity. If I had either a large fortune myself, or had not a title, then £10,000 would be a snug thing ; but in my present situation, I cannot think of it ; besides I have not the least regard for the lady. I met her last week at Ranelagh, and walked with her round the room without the least emotion. I could not avoid speaking to her. I have too much pride to bear any thing which seems slighting or neglectful, without returning the compliment ; and I can now sing the old song with pleasure : " *Let her go, let her go, never mind, hearts alive, you're fairly quit.*" You see I am still the philosopher you knew me. I am warned to take care of the engaging Scotch lasses. The knowledge that they have no fortunes will, I hope, be sufficient to guard me from any imprudent behaviour, though I don't doubt but my heart will go pit a pat, before I return. I hope that I shall meet with some bonnie lassie to kiss and toy with, but no further. What is life without love ? I shall with more ease recover from a refusal than many, as I shall half expect it before I shall make an offer ; but I shall not be backward or ashamed to make my bad luck or good luck, or whatever luck it may be called, known to you.

Yesterday morning I went to Bath to breakfast with your father and mother ; they were very obliging and wished me to stay with them longer, but I was obliged to return to Bristol to dinner, and I must leave this place on Monday morning at the farthest and proceed to Manchester, where I must stay to finish some business before I go to my regiment,—where I am forced (though very desirous) to be in July—my cousins here will not let me be from them at all, while I am in this part, or I should have been glad to have spent more time with Mr. and Mrs. Iredell. Miss McCartney was of the tea-party—she seems a fine, and, from what I could discover, a very sensible woman. I have just sent down to the bookseller's for the religious books you desired, but fear they are not to be had in town. I shall not send you Blackstone's Comment. by this opportunity. There is an edition printed in Ireland, which is much cheaper, which I'll endeavor to get and send to you ; in the meantime I'm sure Mr. Pearson's are at your service. I shall forward this letter to Berry's care by a vessel which sails from hence for New Berne in a few days. You must excuse this scrawl, for I have not time to write well. I am much obliged by your communicating to me the state of politics—I think that before the jurisdiction of the county court was enlarged, a bill should have passed to have increased the capacity of the members,—as to your state of precedency in New Berne I don't know but you had better settle it by act of Assembly. I think you must be entertained by Mr. Cornell's jigging (as you call it) a minuet, and you must recollect having seen him hop a reel at the opening of the Palace, though at the closing of the evening. When is Berry to enter into the holy state of matrimony ? There is nothing going forward here ; but a late discovery is made between the Count de Guigne (" l'ambassadeur Francois ") and Lady Craven. 'Tis said Lord Craven will accompany his Excellency, when he returns to France, and settle this matter "en honneur." Her ladyship is sent into the country to do penance and fast. This discovery was made at a late masquerade. I was there, but was in no scrape of the kind. I don't think I should have had any objection to the matter ; but, as Paddy says, I should not be fond of the discovery at all.

A few weeks ago there was a little agitation in town on account of the expectation of war. Stocks fell; ships put in commission; and the king's proclamation issued, giving a bounty to seamen entering into his Majesty's service. I was in hopes to be in the way of promotion; but all is over now, which I'm sorry for, for I began to look for a troop or a company. The House of Commons is much busied about the East India affairs, but I can give you no account of politics; my time has been otherwise employed, and will be for some time to come. I must now busy myself in marching and counter-marching, as Major Sturgeon says. I am very glad you rode Primus to New Berne. I hope he behaved well. I bought a horse last week, which is very like him, but much larger; he is fifteen and a half hands. I intend him for a charger. He cost me 46 guineas, and is fallen lame, but I expect he will be well by Sunday. His shoes were too tight. Oblige me by making my respects to the family at Hayes and Edenhouse, and to my friends in and about Edenton and Halifax. Oh! what has become of Col. Eaton? The last thing I heard was that he was in prison for murder. Col. Palmer told me of poor Milner's death—he'll be a great loss.

P. S.—I might have told you that Sir H. Hoghton busied himself very much in the Dissenters' Bill, and got it through the House of Commons, but it was thrown out by the Lords; *one* bishop voted for it. 'Twas for Lady Hoghton that I addressed you in mourning. Since I wrote the above I have been able to get for you the books you wished, but I was obliged to Mr. Richards' library for one of them, as it could not be got in any of the shops. I can easily replace it. I think this is a pretty long letter for my stupid head to contrive. I'll write again when I get to Scotland or before.

15th. Saturday afternoon—Having my letters ready to seal up, I just walked with intent to call on Alderman Farr, and know from him the method to find the captain of the ship bound to New Berne, and accidentally tumbled upon Capt. Bog—not able to recollect his name, I enquired of him what it was and he told me. He is in a vessel of John Alexander's, called "The Christian," and he takes the care of this.

Adieu, my esteemed friend.

N. DUKINFIELD.

On the 18th of July, at Hayes, Mr. Iredell was married to Miss Hannah Johnston. Miss Hannah, born January 31st, 1747, was some few years his senior. His felicity being thus consummated and secured, after the usual time spent in receiving and returning the congratulatory visits of friends and relatives, and the wonted interchange of those elegant hospitalities that marked that era and locality, he removed to a residence recently purchased in the town of Edenton. The old mansion, restored by the hand of affection, still remains; it is now tenanted by Mr. Iredell's grand-nephew, the Rev. Samuel Iredell Johnston, of the Protestant Episcopal Church. Mrs. Iredell's character may well be regarded as complementary to her husband's. She supplie what he needed. She possessed, in an eminent degree, the practical talent that was characteristic of her race. Her sound sense and economical prudence were often to him useful counsellors, a shield against imposition, a check upon indiscretion, a gentle restraint ever felt, ever appreciated. He was confiding and unsuspicious, and his goodness was often abused. He listened readily to every tale of distress, and his credulity often rendered him the victim of knaves. He had no extravagant habits, yet he valued not money. " His generosity was indiscriminate—his heart too large."* She was his constant monitor, adviser, banker, and trusted friend. He communicated to her his every thought and act; he consulted her in matters of business; he had no secrets from her. When absent from her, he would write, at some periods, every day, occasionally two letters in the course of the same day. Their lives, united in one stream, flowed onward softly and gently; no petty quarrels rippled its surface; no deepseated griefs perturbed its calm; but as it approached nearer and nearer the great Ocean of Eternity, it became augmented in volume, and reflected the peaceful glories of an unclouded sky.

LINLITHGOW, NORTH BRITAIN, 9th Aug. 1773.

DEAR IREDELL:—I had the pleasure of receiving yours of the 22d April, when I was with my friend Mr. Bayley at Hope, and if I could have gone to Liverpool, should have written you sooner, but as I had not time to go there, and was coming to Scotland, I deferred it till I could tell you when I should be settled. I wrote to you in May, by Capt. Bog, who was bound to New Berne from Bristol, and by him I sent you, to the care of Mr. Berry,† two of the books which you desired, and gave you at the same time my reasons for not sending Blackstone's Commenta-

---

* Mr. James C. Johnston, of Edenton, a gentleman who vindicates the justice of Providence in bestowing upon him wealth, by the noble use he has ever made of his ample means. He is the sole survivor of those intimately and personally known to Mr. Iredell.

† Son of that amiable gentleman and upright judge, Charles Berry, Chief Justice of the province. Dr. Wm. A. Berry, of Wilmington, is his lineal descendant.

ries. The morning that I left Bristol, I received a letter from your mother, desiring to know what books I was to send to you, for I had told her what you desired, when I went over to see your family, and your father then thought that the Irish edition was equally good, and much cheaper, which made me think of getting a lot from thence I wrote to your mother immediately to acquaint her that Blackstone's Commentaries were the books which you wanted, and desired to know if she thought she could get them better than I could; if so that I would send her the price of them, or that I would endeavor to get them when I went to Liverpool; at the same time told her how long I intended to stay at Hope; but I have never received any letter from her since.

I am now with my regiment at this place, which is the Head Quarters; there are other troops here, two at Perth and one at Dundee. I have had surprising promotion, for though my commission is dated but the 30th of March last, I am already the third cornet. The officers seem to be an agreeable set of gentlemen. I came to them last Thursday se'nnight.

I shall be very happy to hear of your being established at Edenton in the situation you expect, and of your being in possession of the dear object of your wishes. I pity you sincerely for having been obliged to live in so disagreeable a state as that of expectation. I don't think I could have borne it so long. But I have not your prudence. My passions are violent, and I cannot govern them. Since my last to you, in which I told you of one disappointment which I had met with, I have had another with a young lady who, 'tis supposed, will be a fortune of near 100,000*l.*, and though I was much distressed at first, I got the better of it in a short time. I saw Capt. Messenger at Liverpool; he told me of my "penchant" for Miss Hannah, and I think said my mother mentioned it to him. I did not expect that it could be kept a secret. Will you tell Mr. Jones that I never received the letter you allude to? I have but one letter from him, which was with a barrel of hams for his uncle; in that he says,—"you shall hear from me in a few days, relative to affairs mentioned to you when here;" but I have received no other letter from him, and that was in September last, and the letter dated in March. I hear that you are in a very disagreeable situation in North Carolina, having no laws. Gov. Martin, I'm told, is out of favor, but from what I can collect, I don't think he deserves censure. He must follow his instructions and if they are peremptory that the Act with the Attachment clause shall not be passed, why should he be blamed? What are you lawyers to do in the mean time,—there can be no business done, but I think there will be a good deal brewing, against the time when the courts shall be estab-

lished. Does the Chief Justice look grave upon it? Dr. Cathcart's death must affect Mrs. Johnston very much. How does Miss Cathcart? is she under any matrimonial engagement yet? Berry's success with Miss Jones, you say, is doubtful. I'm quite out of conceit with matrimony at present, but I can't promise how long it will continue. There are some very pretty girls in this neighborhood. I called upon a pair of sisters, about nine miles from hence, yesterday morning (the daughters of a minister), charming girls indeed—and afterwards dined with a pair almost equal to them, and I'm told there are many others in this neighborhood whom I hope to see soon. They are excellent girls to flirt with, but nothing more,—they won't do for me. I expect to stay at Linlithgow till April next, when we hope to march to Manchester; this is 16 miles from Edinburgh, and about 30 from Glasgow. How does Mr. Hewes' and Mr. Jones' family? I hope Mr. Johnston's are perfectly recovered from their late indisposition. This is a disagreeable season with you, I suppose; for those who are not sick, are in fear of being so. I have not had any sickness since I came to England, except from inebriety. Make my respectful compliments to all my friends, and believe me, my dear Iredell,

Your sincere and affectionate friend,
NAT. DUKINFIELD.

In directing to me in future, always mention *Queen's Dragoons* after my name.

LONDON, 26 Aug., 1773.

DEAR JEMMY:—I wrote you the 18th and 22d, via Cape Fear and Bath, the Gov.—committee—and all friends, at large. This goes by way of Virginia, and if it arrives while the Assembly is sitting, I have directed it to be forwarded to you express, and am to desire you would immediately send it on to New Berne, as I think the good or bad issue of your next Assembly will depend on my letters coming in time. I have wrote triplicates, which has cost me infinite fatigue. My father has rendered essential service to the province; if continued, I make no doubt I shall be able to carry several very agreeable points for them, especially, a jurisdiction to their county courts of at least forty pounds. I wrote my friends to have the affair of the A—— determined one way or the other this session. My application in your favor is now before my Lord North,—time and patience are necessary in these matters,—he has not yet given any promise, but I flatter myself the event will be agreeable to our wishes. Sir

G. has not thought proper to stir in the matter; he is in Ireland. I remain, in haste, with great truth and affection,

Dear Jemmy,
Your assured
HENRY E. McCULLOH.

The following article, published in the North Carolina Gazette, Sept. 10th, 1773, number 236, was, probably, Mr. Iredell's first political essay.* An officer of the Crown, prudence dictated the disguise of a "nom de plume."

MR. DAVIS:—I have lately seen a letter in your paper from an anonymous correspondent, in support of the authority, and contending for the legality, of the constitution of the late Oyer and Terminer Courts, which contains a position equally new and alarming, though I flatter myself altogether unsupported by reason or authority, other than the *ipse dixit* of the writer, which he very modestly presumes no one will be hardy enough to impeach; but till I am better informed of the weight due to that authority, or hear some reason in support of the position, I can by no means agree that the Governor's commission and instructions are the foundation of our political constitution. That they are rules for the regulation of the Governor's conduct, and by which he ought to be bound, I readily admit; first, because he is privy to the import of them; and again, because the observance of them seems to be the condition upon which he is appointed to his government. Therefore any material deviation from them would be a breach of the confidence reposed in him by the ministry, to whom he is accountable for his conduct. But that the people are bound by a set of rules and instructions which are securely locked up in the Governor's strong box, and to which they have no means of access for information, is inconsistent with the very idea of civil liberty. "*Misera* est servitus ubi lex est vagavel incognita," is a motto prefixed to some of our law books, and is a self-evident truth; for it would be equally just to punish a man born blind for not being able to distinguish colors, as to suppose a man liable to censure or punishment for the breach of a constitution of which it is impossible he can be otherwise than ignorant.

I have always been taught, and, till I am better informed, must continue to believe, that the constitution of this country is founded on the provincial charter, which may well be considered

* The paper is 15 by 10 inches in dimensions—three parallel columns—its caption, "The North Carolina Gazette—with the latest Advices, Foreign and Domestick.—Semper Pro Libertate, Et Bono Publico."

as the original contract between the King and the inhabitants; and that the commission and the instructions mentioned by your correspondent, are in the nature of a special letter of attorney, impowering and directing the Governor in what manner to execute that contract on the part of the King. There is another fact which your correspondent takes for granted, in which he must not expect to meet with universal concurrence, that there is no act of Assembly now in force which establishes courts of justice; or, as he terms it, an exclusive rule for the trial of criminal offences. Had he looked for the constitution of this province in acts of Assembly, rather than the Governor's commission and instructions, he would have found, that in the year 1746 we were possessed of an establishment of courts of justice, with both civil and criminal jurisdictions, under several acts of Assembly, which were either virtually or expressly repealed by an act passed at Wilmington, Dec. 1746. This act established a new system of courts, and continued in force till 1754, when it was repealed by his Majesty in Council. The same year the act establishing Supreme Courts passed, in the beginning of Gov. Dobbs' administration. This act was likewise repealed by his Majesty in Council, in 1759. From that period our Court laws have been enacted, from time to time, with a clause limiting the term of their duration; the last of which the higher powers, by way of trying experiments, have in their great wisdom suffered to expire, at a time when they were hampered with a ministerial instruction, tying up their hands in such a manner that no act could be secured consistent with it. Now the lawyers inform me, and I think it not inconsistent with common sense, that when a repealing act is itself repealed, the first act revives, and is in force. As your correspondent seems conversant with acts of Parliament, and law books, he perhaps knows whether this opinion is law or not; if it is, our courts are now under the same establishment that they were before the passing the act in Dec., 1746.

I will not take it upon me to determine whether the commissions of Oyer and Terminer are legal or otherwise, but think they must be supported on other principles than those laid down by your correspondent.

I have often heard the lawyers say that the exercise of that branch of the prerogative under which these commissions issue is restrained and limited by divers acts of Parliament; others say that the King cannot delegate this part of his prerogative; but as nice points of law are above my capacity, I leave them to the discussion of those who have applied themselves to the study of that intricate science. Every one who is but a little acquainted with the English constitution, must know that prerogative is

a necessary part of it, and that its bounds and extent are as well marked as any other part of the constitution. It is by no means a discretionary power in the King and his ministers, to make ordinances to supply any defect which they may imagine in the constitution; this can only be done with the consent of the inhabitants, signified either by themselves or their deputies in some public act.

The law of discretion is the law of tyrants, and can never be admitted in any free State. How far the judges have acted under the influence of that law, in determining the challenges of jurors in the Courts of Oyer and Terminer, will appear from the apology your correspondent is pleased to make for their conduct in this particular. As they were by no means bound to govern themselves by the rules there laid down, they had it in their option to have laid down any others, and to have varied them occasionally, as the nature of the case might require.

I agree with your correspondent that our condition is indeed deplorable; not because "the right of punishing crimes is nowhere," but because criminals are tried by jurors whose qualifications are not consistent with the law of the land, but appointed at the discretion of judges acting under a commission of doubtful authority, and if supported by no other reasons than those offered by your correspondent, evidently illegal and void.

A PLANTER.

PASQUOTANK, Aug. 23d, 1773.

LINES IN MR. IREDELL'S HANDWRITING.

Almighty Love! who with resistless sway
Dost make thy vot'ries tremblingly obey,
And with a secret, fascinating charm,
Of all its force, the captive soul disarm:
If Innocence with thee cannot unite
T'impart the raptures of a pure delight,
Permit, at least, this consoling hope,
With which no guilty pleasures e'er can cope,
That though denied the happiest state on earth,
To which successful passion must give birth,
Yet conscious Virtue shall the mind sustain
Through all the thrilling agonies of pain
Which hapless Love must ever doom to feel
Those who have strongly proved his pointed steel.
And let this truth to noble hearts be known:
"Love yields to Virtue, though to her alone."

QUEEN SQUARE, Nov. 17, 1773.

DEAR BROTHER:—I return you many thanks for your kind favor of 12th June. You may be assured I will most punctually follow your advice in every thing; indeed, as it is always salutary, it is much my interest to do so. Nothing, formerly, gave me more satisfaction, than the repeated assurances you constantly gave me of your friendship, nor does the repetition of these assurances now afford me less pleasure. But, I must draw your attention to a more interesting subject; one that, as it has given me, so, I doubt not, it will give you, great uneasiness. My father departed this life the 24th ult., after an illness of about ten days, during which time it is imagined he received a second paralytic stroke. He had taken some of his powders (which, if you remember, he used constantly to take) in the morning, and found himself not quite so well after them, but thought he should be better when he had dined; during dinner time, he sunk gradually down till he almost fell into a lady's lap. He was then put to bed, but I believe after that time got up, and was able in a day or two, to walk across his room. It was on a Friday he was taken—the Sunday sevennight afterwards, about four o'clock in the morning, he grew worse, upon which Dr. Woodward was called in, who gave no hopes of him; and he died that day perfectly easy. These particulars I was acquainted with by some ladies who were at my mother's at the time; they added that she seemed pretty well reconciled to it before they came away, which was the day afterwards. Poor Frank's death had a much greater effect upon her, and this coming so suddenly upon that, was enough to make her very uneasy. Mr. Henry McCulloh sent a letter to the Sergt's, Queen Square, which upon our arrival I found, acquainting me with it, and desiring to see me immediately. I accordingly waited upon him, when he was so very obliging as to take me to his tailor's, where I was measured for a suit of mourning; he likewise furnished me with other necessaries. As soon as I heard this melancholy news, I wrote to my mother, condoling with, and at the same time endeavoring to console her upon so distressing an occasion. After living so long with a husband whom she tenderly, I may say passionately fond of, you may conceive how distressing a separation must be. I acquainted her with my intention of writing to you, and advised her not to exert herself in doing it, as I should advise you fully of this affair. As both your fortitude and good sense will point out its absurdness, I will not make a long harangue to mollify your grief. I shall leave so unpleasing a subject. I would willingly give you the outlines of a most extraordinary affair, now in litigation in the Common Pleas, concerning the powers of governors; but as a new trial is moved for, I shall leave it to my next letter, which will be shortly sent you— as soon, indeed, as I can find an opportunity. As I intend my next shall be a very long one, excuse me at present from making this a sermon. I have not yet had an opportunity of paying my duty to my uncle at Chelsea, so can only acquaint you that Mr. McCulloh, the last time I saw him, said he was tolerably well, but as I know he intends writing to you (my letter being enclosed by him), I shall say nothing concerning his health. I'm extremely obliged to him for his behavior to me in regard to mourning. I hope his endeavors to get you the Collectorship will be crowned with success. Mr. Mc. gave me assurances that I might by this time wish you joy; give me leave to do it heartily, as any thing that can afford you pleasure, must always meet with my approbation. I am satisfied from the letter you sent home, you will be very happy in the marriage state with a lady of so uncommon and amiable a disposition. If I did not believe that Goddesses do not frequent this sublunary world, I should conceive from the sketch you gave of Miss Johnston, she was a deity who, like Venus, honored you, her Anchises, with her embraces. I beg my best love to Mrs. Iredell,—that you may both long enjoy as great a share of health as I do, joined with prosperity and happiness, is the most ardent prayer and desire of, dear brother,

Yours affectionately,
A. IREDELL.

P. S.—I forgot to beg that you would excuse all blunders, as I have not been above ten minutes writing, and must make great haste to convey it to Mr. McCulloh, lest it should not be sent.

CHAPTER VII.

POLITICAL CONDITION OF THE PROVINCE; IREDELL A POLITICAL WRITER, COLLECTOR, DEPUTY FOR THE ATTORNEY-GENERAL; LETTERS FROM M'CULLOH, DUKINFIELD, BROTHER AND UNCLE; FIRST PROVINCIAL CONGRESS IN NORTH CAROLINA; WILLIAM HOOPER; SOCIETY AT WILMINGTON; A. NEILSON; ADDRESS; HEWES. ÆT. 22–23.

IN 1774 the Revolution was fairly inaugurated in North Carolina. Nowhere were the points in dispute between the colonies and Great Britain more clearly stated or more ably argued. The people were generally agreed. Even those who became known as Tories, when the sword was drawn, coincided with the Whigs in their political views. If dissenters were to be found, they existed only amongst the Regulators and the Highlanders about Cross Creeks. It is true that none meditated independence as an object of desire; but it was foreseen as a possible consequence. The contest, that was soon to be developed into flagrant war, was eminently, in North Carolina, based upon principle. The Whig leaders, ready with the pen, in the columns of the newspapers, and in pamphlets, discussed the tax on tea, and the vindictive measures that followed the prompt opposition of Boston, with a degree of learning and logic that was not surpassed by any of their cotemporaries in other provinces: those who possessed oratory gave full and frequent oral instructions to the masses. There was no array of class against class. The foremost in talent were foremost in all measures: they had the love and confidence of the people. The force of numbers was guided by genius with consummate skill. It is believed that the political questions of that day were as thoroughly comprehended by the people as those that now divide parties are by their descendants. The followers of such men as Harvey, Johnston, Ashe, Harnett, Hooper and Caswell, could not be otherwise than well-informed. Mr. Iredell was precluded by his office from public efforts. He could not share with John Ashe in the intoxication of successful oratory: he could not, as that great speaker, ex-

press the fire of his feelings in burning words that made the hearts of his hearers to beat as the drum that summons to battle: he had to curb the ardor of his nature, and forego the excitement of public discussion and the multitudinous shout that constitutes its triumph. In the quiet retreat of his study, with naught to stimulate but the prompting of his own honest heart, and, perchance, the smile of his noble wife, with patient toil, he forged and polished the weapons of debate: if they transfixed his mark, he recked not who claimed the honor of the cast. His recompense was found in the approval of his own conscience, and the generous praise of his most intimate friends, Johnston, Hewes and Hooper. His magnanimity was equal to the dignity of the occasion; thoughtless of self and the peril he saw of losing an office (collectorship), whose emoluments were probably the largest in the province, he maintained the rights of a Briton with such power and decorum and such superiority of prowess, as to merit and receive the utmost deference from even the polished Hooper. Iredell's influence, for a long time, was rather on the leaders, than exerted directly on the people. His pointed thoughts were the bolts whose peals were loudest, and whose force most stirred the upper air. All men looked to his brother-in-law, Mr. Johnston—"his actions were watched." If that strong man ever grew faint from the strife, it was upon the arm of Iredell that he leaned for support: it was to him that he confided his cares, and from him that he demanded counsel. Mr. Iredell always wrote anonymously; but so unrivalled was his ability, so peculiar his style, that his masks were soon penetrated, and the popular champion was exposed to popular admiration. His was especially the art of so conducting a discussion as to avoid unnecessary offence to opponents. The temper of his mind was calm and judicial. He never indulged in personalities; no acerbities poisoned his articles; and no virulence sullied his pages. He wrote no line that he could ever wish to blot. None but one whose character was balanced as his own could have escaped the misfortune of undisguised flattery. His correspondence was generally courted by the ablest men of the day. Young as he was, he became the companion and friend of sages. If my language seem eulogistic, a careful examination of his essays will rather condemn its want of warmth, than sustain the charge of undeserved praise. If any North Carolinian doubts the culture and merit of our Revolutionary Fathers, let him study my record for '74, '75, and '76, and if he blush at all, it will be for the degeneracy of their sons. The papers preserved by Judge Iredell are but a small part of the interesting and authentic illustrations of the history of the State still in existence—these are scattered here and there, or buried in private collections. There is a commendable activity now at work; and, I doubt not, "many a gem of purest ray" will be disinterred; and that our youth, hereafter, will find in the examples of our own progenitors every model of excellence, every incitement to virtue, every stimulus to patriotism.

Futile attempts were made by the Assembly of this year to establish Superior Courts, their bill being negatived by the governor, and their proposed substitute of Commissions of Oyer and Terminer being defeated by exceptions taken to informalities in the commissions by Maurice Moore and others. No courts existed, other than the inferior courts, until 1777.

Mr. Iredell's warrant as collector issued from the Treasury February 17th, 1774. In pursuance of this warrant, he received the appointment from Gov. Martin, 5th day of May, 1774, and a commission from Charles Paxton, Henry Hutton and William Burch, commissioners, dated Salem, 7th June, 1774. He gave bond in the sum of £1000. For this appointment he was indebted to Lord Macartney, who being in London but two days, devoted part of that time to the advancement of his young kinsman.*

On the 9th day of May, Mr. Iredell entered on the office; and immediately took upon himself the charge of receiving the Greenwich Hospital money, as the collector, by special appointment, had generally acted as receiver. On the 24th July following, he received a commission from Mr. Hutton.†

16th August, he was appointed by Thomas McGuire, attorney-general, his deputy for the counties of Hertford and Perquimans; and on October 3d, for the County of Tyrrel.‡

TEMPLE, 13 January, 1774.

DEAR JEMMY :—I have been now 5 months in England, without meeting a line from you. The books you sent to care of Mr. Elmsby have never come to hand—pray inquire and do the needful that they be not lost. "Apropos" of books, let me know what has become of those the Goths of N—k seized for me, and what I am likely to get. I hear of your marriage (from your mother) with

---
* Letter from Iredell to Macartney.
† The Hospital fees for one half year 1775, amounted to £20 3s. 9d.
‡ McGuire was the lineal descendant of the Lord McGuire of the Irish rebellion of 1641. He married the daughter of Col. William Dry, the great niece of Judge Maurice Moore, who died in 1766.—*Davis' Address at Chapel Hill*, 1855.
McGuire was a Tory; fled the State early in the war, and carried with him, to England, Nancy, a mulatto girl, who soon sickened and died. McGuire was inconsolable for a long time—" most terribly afflicted."—*Letter from Sir N. Dukinfield to Iredell, 4th February*, 1789.

Miss Johnston. I most affectionately wish it may prove a happy one, and have little doubt but that it will. I beg you will present me to her, and the family, as one who is happy in your connection, and who will ever endeavor to deserve their kind opinion. I am sorry that the affair of the collection remains still in suspense. I was in great hopes it would have been ordered before this busy season came on. I am assured there is no danger. Men in a Premier's situation are not to be precipitated. I have hardly any fear but it will go well, and hope very soon * * * Be guarded in your expressions when you write me, for fear your letters may meet a villain's intercepting hands, all whom may Heaven, in its justice, curse! I am somewhat surprised at not hearing from you. I am just returned from Bath, where I spent 6 weeks, and was immensely facetious, uttering "bon mots" in abundance, and playing whist without loss of either money or reputation, *dreaming life* away agreeably as I can. I left your mother well. My father adds his best wishes for you. My best compliments attend you and my new cousin; may every felicity I have dreamt of, in such a state, be realized by you! and that is not saying a little, for when awake I can dream very tolerably. My best respects to Mr. Johnston and family, and compliments to Col. Harvey, Mr. Hewes, &c. Write me often and fully.

I am ever
Your assured friend,
HENRY E. McCULLOH.

LINLITHGOW, 23d February, 1774.

I was favored with yours, my dear Iredell, dated in October, at Dukinfield, on the 23d ult. From the account you give of politics, your country must be in a very unenviable situation. And although you wish it, I am not at all sorry for being absent from your councils and assemblies. Nothing material happened while I was there to cause my character or abilities as a statesman to be called in question; but how long they might have stood unimpeached I don't presume to engage. Many persons with good intentions equal to my own, and with much superior abilities, have been drawn to the wrong side of a question, and then all their former good services have been entirely forgot.

You must have received letters from me since the one I wrote at Bristol, for I have written since I came here. Your letter, which now lies before me, is the only one unanswered, and which would not have been delayed so long, had I not been waiting for a letter from Mr. Almon, who was to have sent your books. I received a letter from him, dated 17th December, with the account of the books I had ordered. He told me they were packed up, and should be sent by the first ship upon receipt of a bill from me, and that I should receive advice of the ship's name by post. I sent him a draft on my agents on the 24th for the sum, and have not since that time had a line from him. The books ordered, with the prices, are as follows: Commons Debates, 9 vols., £2 14 0; Ainsworth's Dict., £1; Livy, £1; Horace and Virgil, 8s.;—in all, £5 2 0, for which sum I made the draft. I 'wrote to my brother, who is now in London, to desire he would call on Almon to know if he had received the bill and sent the books, and let me know the reason he had not written me.

I am glad you are so well pleased with our correspondence. I assure you it does not give me less satisfaction, nor can you have a greater wish for its continuance. Besides, the disagreeableness you mention of chance directions will now be obviated, for we shall always be quartered a year in one place. We shall remove from Scotland in about six weeks, and shall go to Manchester, where we stay till some time in March, 1775, and after taking the tour of England, we shall return to Scotland in 1779 or '80, if there should be no war in the mean time, and there is no prospect of it at present.

I congratulate you on your happy conjunction, and am glad you have had your health so well. July was a warm month—you would have no occasion for blankets. You have had a great many marriages very lately. I like Brimage's short courtship—'tis like running a hare with a greyhound. I don't think our friend Berry has played his cards well. How does he bear his disappointment? I'm told he was too inattentive, and thought her quite young enough; but my mother says, she supposes the lady thought herself old enough, and from what I can recollect of her, she was not a backward plant when I saw her. I suppose she has a fortune. How is Miss Sukey Cornell? I saw Mrs. T. Gilchrist when in Liverpool, who told me that her brother, Wiley Jones, had paid his addresses to her, but that her father had said he would never consent to his daughter's marriage with any person who would risk a fortune on a horse race—upon which he very properly and spiritedly declined any further solicitation, saying, that as it was his favorite amusement he would not be under any engagement to release it before marriage: but that if it had afterwards happened that his wife should solicit it as a favor, he would submit to any thing for her satisfaction. How does Col. Eaton? I have never heard mention of him since his confinement on account of the death of his sister's overseer. In a letter I lately received from Baldy Buchanan at Glasgow, he mentions the death of Mr. John Gilchrist, at Norfolk, and says that he shot himself in a fit of jealousy.

I went over in December last to see Buchanan, and to forward some letters to Mr. Pearson and you. Our surgeon, Mr. Thomson, was with me. We stayed five days there. The first day we dined alone, we drank more than we generally do when by ourselves, for the weather had been very stormy, and we were afraid of catching cold. We were very wet, and did not choose to stop and change clothes, on the way, but rode through without drawing bit---31 miles. We dined two days with a Regiment of Foot quartered there—one with Baldy, and another with one of his friends. I was very drunk each day, and never knew how I got to bed. Thomson was not quite so bad. They drink very hard at Glasgow, and indeed throughout the whole of Scotland. I told you in a former letter that we never drank much when alone. You desire I'll give you a sketch of our manner of living. In the first place, there is not a regiment in the service that lives more amicably together. There are few that have not some particular folly—some dress—some play—one is particular for each officer keeping his girl—others drink—and I believe we come in that set, and stand pretty high on the list. The inns in this town are so abominably dirty that we could not live in them, but took a house, and one of the dragoon's wives is our cook and himself is butler. The trumpets sound in the morning soon after 6 o'clock for the men to go to their horses; and again in about an hour afterwards, when it is the duty of the quarter-master and subaltern officers to visit the stables and see the men have taken proper care of the horses. The quarter-master goes round every morning, but 'tis not expected that the officers should do it more than two or three times a week, till we come to field days, and then every day: and they are not confined to that particular hour, but may order the men's attendance at the stable whenever they choose. I go this about three times a week, and generally in the morning, sometimes at three in the afternoon, for they go then, and at 8 at night. This is all our duty at present, except attending the parades every day, which we don't much attend to. Our men are very well behaved, and our superior officers not strict disciplinarians. When we get to Manchester I expect we shall have something more to do before the review. We expect to have three field days on horseback, and three on foot, every week, when the weather will permit, for the regiment has not been together these four years more than ten days at a time. I wrote to the governor while in London, and have received an answer from him. Is Mr. Palmer or Marmaduke Jones returned, and who succeeds me in the Council? What sort of a piece is Will Palmer's wife? I have neither thought, intention or wish for matrimony at present. I have got into a snug acquaintance which prevents my falling much in love. You must not let this letter be seen. I fear Mrs. Iredell would not entertain a very favorable opinion of me if she was to see it. I beg my respectful compliments to her, and wish her every happiness she can expect. Make my compliments to Mr. Hewes and all my friends. And believe me, my dear friend,

With great affection and esteem,
Yours sincerely,
NAT. DUKINFIELD.

TEMPLE, LONDON, 28th February, 1774.

DEAR JEMMY:—I have received but one letter from you since my return to England. I have wrote you several, and on very important business, and firmly rely that you have and will pay the most affectionate and proper attention to the several weighty concerns of property I have intrusted to your management. I have now the pleasure to inclose you the Treasury's Warrant (of the 17th) for your appointment as Collector of Port Roanoke, and wish you long and happily to enjoy it. It is to my father's exertions you are in the most especial manner obliged for this provision;—it was a favor asked, of a much more difficult nature than the obtaining of an office in the first instance, and granted on some very particular claims, and in consideration of our wishes to make a provision for so near a relation. I make no doubt but your conduct will deserve what we have endeavored to do for your service, and that you will approve yourself a faithful friend and agent to me in the several matters of property and interest I have intrusted to you. The governor, I presume, is to take your security,—should it be necessary. I will very readily become one of your bondsmen, and Mr. Thomas Frohock's signing for, shall be binding on me. Nothing has been said about the comptrollership, nor do I know in what channel it may go. I shall write the commissioners and Mr. Coffin on this event, and desire my accounts may be prepared for passing. Inclosed are a few lines for the governor. I suppose you will wait upon him,—and it may be right in you to cultivate his kindness. Make my best compliments to Col. Harvey, Mr. Johnston, Mr. Hewes, the chief justice, and other friends, not forgetting Mr. Cornell's family. Acquaint me of every circumstance that may interest me. Perhaps, hereafter, I shall wish you to take a trip westwardly. Remember the Indian land, and your correspondence with Mr. Harnett and Mr. McGuire as to bills of exchange. Mr. Howard can probably assist, and if so, I flatter myself he will. It is expected the Boston people will suffer for their late conduct as to their trade,—the southern colonies are out of the scrape. In every station, the rights and liberties of America shall ever be objects of my warmest wishes. All is peace. Administration as fixed as ever. Lord North very popular, and deservedly. Myself and my father tolerably well,—going to Bath. My affectionate service to my cousin Iredell and yourself, concludes me

Ever yours,
H. E. McCULLOH.

QUEEN SQUARE, March 2d, 1774.

DEAR BROTHER:—Inclosed I send you two letters from my mother, which were transmitted to me in a packet, that I was obliged to open, as it would otherwise have been too cumbersome when this letter was added. I should have sent them some time ago, but the Sergeant advised me not to do it, as he intended to have answered your letter early, and by that means have made only one packet. But as business obliterated those thoughts out of his mind, and as he is now gone the circuit, which will continue upwards of a month, I thought I should be inexcusable if I detained them any longer, which would deprive you of the pleasure you will doubtless receive from the agreeable account of my mother and Tommy's being perfectly well. The pleasing intelligence I learnt from a gentleman who called upon me to-day, and who is just come from Bath. I mean Mr. Crawford, who is lately from the East Indies. He acquainted me that you and he were very intimate when you were in Ireland, and desired his compliments. He was happy to hear you had been successful in being appointed Collector, which good news I learnt from Mr. McCulloh, whom I called upon to-day, and who told me he had sent over your commission. Give me leave to express those pleasing sensations I am now filled with, upon so fortunate an event, and accept my most unfeigned joy, as a token of my love and friendship. Be assured I could not be more happy, had I been the object on whom it was conferred. Mr. McCulloh seemed perfectly well—he told me his father was to set off for Bath, and that he himself intended going down, in a short time. But you will be surprised that I should dwell upon such trivial things, and quite forget the most material—I mean your marriage—for though in my last I wished you joy upon a supposition that you were married, yet now that I am assured of it, I should do it with more warmth. I have not words to express the great satisfaction I have received from the assurance of your being happy. The utmost I can say, to express what I feel, is to assure you nothing could afford me greater happiness than that did.

I am surprised you mentioned nothing in your letter in regard to Mrs. Iredell, not even that she was in good health. I attributed that to the hurry you were in when you wrote. I assure you that intelligence would not have been the least acceptable—for as I now look upon Mrs. I. as nearly connected to me, I interest myself materially in every thing that concerns her. Present my most affectionate love to her. I hope you are both well and happy. I confine myself to both, because I suppose your family is not yet enlarged. The Sergeant, I am sorry to acquaint you, has been lately very much indisposed, but, I doubt not, you will be happy, when I assure you that he is now perfectly well recovered. He intends writing a long letter to you in answer to yours. He is mightily pleased with your style, and recommends it to me, as a pattern for me to follow. I confess it is a field which inspires me with emulation, and I am so vain as not to doubt when the chasm which now lies between our ages is filled up, great revolutions will come to pass; and that though Arthur aged sixteen now writes in a slovenly, uncultivated, bewildered, ungrammatical style; yet, nevertheless, Arthur aged two and twenty may write, and I hope will write, in as neat, cultivated, polished, and grammatical a style as James Iredell, Esq., of Edenton, North Carolina, does. I am afraid you think me negligent in not writing to you oftener, but I doubt not you will readily excuse me, as Law and Parnassus are the cause of it. And I am satisfied you have too great a veneration for Blackstone and Virgil to accuse him of negligence who is busy in the pursuit of such captivating immortals. You will doubtless have a full account in the papers of the discussion of Literary Property, and therefore it will be absurd in me to endeavor to give you a sketch of the proceeding. I attended the House of Lords, during the time the opinion of the Judges was given, and the debate. Lord Clarendon shone with a peculiar lustre, and stood unequalled by any of the dignified orators. The Lord — Apsley, who never is very bright, as he spoke immediately after Lord Clarendon, was prolix, tiresome and insipid. But I refer you to the newspapers for particulars. I have wrote an Epithalamic Ode on your marriage (unworthy the subject) which I will transmit in the next. The manner in which I study and other particulars relative to myself, I shall advise you of at large in that letter from me, which will accompany the Sergeant's. At the present I have only time to assure you that hearing of your happiness will afford the most satisfactory and pleasing emotions to, dear brother,

Yours affectionately,
ARTHUR IREDELL.

P. S.—Excuse blots, blurs, &c.

DEAR NEPHEW:—I received your favor of the 10th of Nov. some considerable time ago, which should have been answered before, but I was expecting every day to hear of the arrival of your brother, of which your letter of the 9th of March informs me. I received an account of your father's death from my sister, and though I always considered his life in a most precarious state from the violent manner in which he was first attacked, yet the event, when I heard it, gave me a most severe shock. As regards himself, I consider his death as a happy escape from a world in which his portion was most severely bitter. I do not well know on what footing Arthur is with Sergeant Kempe. I think, in a letter I received from home, it was said he was to be entered in the Temple; but bringing up a lad a barrister, who has no fortune, and where the greatest abilities will hardly procure a support, appears to me a scheme too hazardous for prudence; but it may be the Counsellor has some dignity in the law, and in consequence thereof a place in his gift, which he proposes to qualify Arthur for—however it is, I should be glad you would explain it to me. I am most heartily concerned so great a mistake was made in embarking Charles; from the information received, I took it for granted he would have been with you in two or three days after landing. I have been inquiring for an opportunity of sending you three puncheons of rum, which a captain bound for your province, and known to you, offered to take, could he have procured twenty puncheons on freight; but as only twelve were offered him, it was not worth his while to go out of his way for them. You may depend on receiving the rum by the first safe hand. I think it will be in your power to be of great use to your brother in the way of instruction; but as that should be made subservient to his future destination, I will tell you what I hope to obtain for him, and it is the only eligible scheme I can devise. Ever since Mr. Lyttleton* left this country I have kept up a correspondence with him, and he has, in more letters than one, pressed me to point out something in which he could serve me. In a late letter he tells me he has declared himself a candidate for B——, and has secured his election. Now as he is a man of very extensive connections, and has great abilities as well as application for public business, I think he must, when a member of the House, attract the attention of the Ministry, and through his interest I have no doubt of getting Charles a commission in the army, and promotion afterwards, provided he renders himself worthy of it. I therefore think you should have this in your contemplation, and instil into him what

* Afterwards Lord Westcote.

knowledge you can relative to this intention. The turn he has for some parts of the mathematics may be of use, and enable him to acquire some knowledge of Fortification and Gunnery, by which, if he had taste for drawing, he might hope to make some figure as a soldier. It may be 18 months before this can be procured; but it matters not; he is young enough, and he will, in the meantime, under your prudent tuition, pick up some knowledge of men and things, without which a man has no business in the world. Great and unaffected politeness and civility of behavior, with some attention to dress, especially in neatness and cleanliness, well become a young man and an officer, and where these are wanting, respect seldom falls to their lot. You will say, and you will say what is true, that the emoluments of an ensign's pay will not support him; but assisted with clothes and exact economy, which it behooves him to acquire, he will be able to make a genteel appearance. You do not mention your wife, and therefore I believe and hope she is well. Pray make my most affectionate compliments to her.

I remain, dear nephew,
Your most affectionate uncle,
THOMAS IREDELL.

There were five men especially instrumental in projecting and promoting the first Provincial Congress in North Carolina. Of these Mr. Iredell was one. As early as April 5th, as appears from a letter written by Mr. Johnston to William Hooper, Harvey and Johnston and Col. Buncombe discussed and determined its propriety. "The proposition to organize a Continental, by the immediate agency of a Provincial, Congress, was first made to our committee of correspondence by the committee of Massachusetts, about the 1st of June;" but North Carolina needed no prompting, and had already boldly and wisely acted. The gentlemen of the bar were, then as now, very active members of society: if the uncharitable find a motive for their zeal in the Revolution, in their loss of business arising from the closing of the Courts, no such mercenary object can be imputed to Iredell. His office at that period was worth more than his practice, while he might well rely upon the favor of government for future promotion. Revolution appeared to be to him immediately distressing in a pecuniary point of view; its possible consequences to himself in the way of benefits too remote to affect his action. When Mr. Iredell first began to correspond with William Hooper is not certainly known. The earliest letter that I have seen is dated 26th April, 1774. Of this letter Jones remarks,—" I look upon this letter as not inferior to any event in the history of the country;

and in the boldness and originality of its views, I say that it is a document without a rival at the period of its date. It takes precedence of the Mecklenburg Declaration, as that does of the National Declaration of Independence." As the letter appears at large in Jones' volume,* I shall only make a few extracts, from which it will be seen that "Iredell had even anticipated Mr. Hooper in his patriotic reflections." I have Hooper's letters to Iredell, but not the other part of the correspondence; Iredell's letters to the former were, a few years ago, in possession of Hooper's granddaughter, the late Mrs. Watters of Hillsboro', but they have been sought by me in vain. I trust that they may yet be recovered, as their merit must be very great to have won such warm commendations as were bestowed upon them by Hooper. Mr. Hooper was nine years Mr. Iredell's senior, and already a man of mark at the bar, and in the Assembly. To estimate at its full value his deference to Iredell, these facts must be borne in mind. Mr. Hooper was a native of Boston, and a graduate of Cambridge, Mass. After studying law with James Otis, he removed to North Carolina in 1764. He became a citizen of Wilmington. That town and its vicinity was noted for its unbounded hospitality; and the elegance of its society. Men of rare talents, fortune and attainment, united to render it the home of politeness, and ease, and enjoyment. Though the footprint of the Indian had, as yet, scarcely been effaced, the higher civilization of the "Old World" had been transplanted there, and had taken vigorous root. There were Col. John Ashe (subsequently Gen. Ashe), the great popular leader, whose address was consummate, and whose quickness of apprehension seemed intuition, the very Rupert of debate; Samuel Ashe, of stalwart frame, endowed with practical good sense, a profound knowledge of human nature, and an energy that eventually raised him to the Bench and the post of Governor; † Harnett (afterwards President of the Provincial Council), "who could boast a genius for music and taste for letters," the representative man of the Cape Fear ——; Dr. John Eustace, the correspondent of Sterne, "who united wit, and genius, and learning, and science;" Col. Thomas Lloyd, "gifted with talents, and adorned with classical literature;" Howe (afterwards Gen. Howe), "whose imagination fascinated, whose repartee overpowered, and whose conversation was enlivened by strains of exquisite raillery;" Dr. John Fergus, of stately presence, with velvet coat, cocked hat and gold-headed cane, a graduate of Edinburgh, and an excellent Latin and Greek scholar; Wm. Pennington (Comptroller of the Customs, and afterwards Master of the Ceremonies at Bath), " an

* Jones' Defence of N. C., p. 312.
† Life of Wm. Hooper, by A. M. Hooper.

elegant writer, admired for his wit, and his highly polished urbanity;" Judge Maurice Moore, of "versatile talents, and possessed of extensive information, as a wit, always prompt in reply; as an orator, always daring the mercy of chance;" Maclaine, irascible, but intellectual, who trod the path of honor nearly "pari passu" with Iredell and Hooper and Johnston, and "whose criticisms on Shakspeare would, if they were published, give him fame and rank in the republic of letters;" William Hill, "a most sensible, polite gentleman, and though a crown officer, replete with sentiments of general liberty, and warmly attached to the cause of American Freedom;"* Lillington, destined soon to render, at Moore's Creek, his name historical; James Moore, whose subsequent appointment as Major General, and whose promise of a brilliant career were soon to be terminated by a premature death; Lewis Henry De Rosset, member of the Council, a cultivated and elegant gentleman; † Adam Boyd, editor of the Cape Fear Mercury (subsequently chaplain to the Cont. Line), "who, without pretensions to wit or humor, possessed the rare art of telling a story with spirit and grace, and whose elegiac numbers afforded a striking contrast to the vivid brilliancy of the scenes in which he figured;"‡ Alfred Moore, subsequently an associate justice of the Supreme Court of the United States; Timothy Bloodworth, stigmatized by his enemies as an impracticable radical; " every thing by turns;" but withal a true exponent of the instincts and prejudices, the finest feelings and the noblest impulses of the masses. These were no ordinary men. They were of the remarkable class that seem ever to be the product of crises in human affairs. Though inferior to many of them in the influence that attends years, opulence, and extensive connections, yet in scholarship and genius Mr. Hooper was pre-eminent. I use the word genius in contradistinction to talent. He had much nervous irritability, was imaginative and susceptible. With a well-disciplined mind, and of studious habits, he shone with lustre whenever he pleased to exert himself. He had generous impulses, and his intercourse with his family and friends was marked by a caressing tenderness. In the course of the Revolution he never wavered, though he often desponded. If hope seemed sometimes about to desert him for ever, and he felt in his heart the rustle of her wings as she prepared for flight, his deep-rooted principles were never shaken. He lived long enough to see the political edifice, to whose construction he had so largely contributed, completed, and its soaring dome to the nations of the earth

* De Rossett, being a Royalist, was, afterwards, expelled from the State.
† Josiah Quincey's Journal.
‡ A. M. Hooper.

as "a lamp unto *their* feet, and a light unto *their* path. As his fame is national, I need not dwell longer upon his career.

Wm. Hooper to James Iredell.

APRIL 26, 1774.

DEAR SIR :—You have great reason to reproach me that I have not long before this answered your most acceptable letter of the 30th of December last. Attribute my neglect to business which I might have postponed, to forgetfulness, to indolence; but by no means to want of respect, for be assured that this had not the smallest share in the omission. It is a crime, however, which, in some degree, has carried its punishment with it, as it has deprived me of a repetition of your epistolary favors hitherto, from which I might have derived ample instruction and amusement.

It has afforded me the utmost pleasure, that, notwithstanding the multiplicity of business in which you are engaged, you have found some leisure moments to dedicate to the investigation of those political subjects which have engaged the attention and hurt the peace of this province. Every man who thinks with candor is indebted to you for the share you have taken in this interesting controversy. You have discussed dry truths with the most pleasing language; and have not parted from the most refined delicacy of manners in the warmth of the contest. It is a circumstance which much enhances the merit of the performances written in opposition to the measures of government, that those who have attempted to answer them have for argument substituted personal invectives, and have lost sight of the measure to run foul of the man.

I am happy, dear sir, that my conduct in public life has met your approbation. It is a suffrage which makes me vain, as it flows from a man who has wisdom to distinguish, and too much virtue to flatter. * * * * While the scene of life in which I was engaged with them would have rendered any reserve on my part not only improper, but even culpable, you were destined for a more retired, but not less useful conduct; *and whilst I was active in contest, you forged the weapons which were to give success to the cause which I supported.** To your most trusted friends I am indebted for the discovery of you as a writer; and you will pardon them for the luxury they have furnished me in an opportunity of being grateful to an author who claims no reward for serving the public, but the pleasure of it, and deals out

* The italics are not in the original.

his bounty to them without suffering them to know the hand from which it flows. With you I anticipate the important share which the colonies must soon have in regulating the political balance. *They are striding fast to independence, and ere long will build an empire upon the ruin of Great Britain;* will adopt its constitution purged of its impurities, and from an experience of its defects will guard against those evils which have wasted its vigor and brought it to an untimely end. * * * *

Thus I have forced upon you my undigested thoughts upon a subject, which some hints in your letter have drawn me into the discussion of, with a prolixity that will require all your good nature to excuse.

I know too well your reverence for our Constitution not to forgive it in another, although it borders upon enthusiasm. There may be an excess even in virtue. Adieu, dear sir. I flatter myself that this may be introductory to a frequent and intimate correspondence between us, in which, though I am to be the only gainer in point of instruction or amusement, yet I shall in a manner thereby make you my debtor by furnishing you the highest entertainment,—the luxury of obliging a friend.

I am, dear sir,
With the most cordial esteem,
Your most obedient, humble servant,
WM. HOOPER.

WILMINGTON, June 21st, 1774.

DEAR SIR :—I was favored with yours by the express. Since my arrival in town I have been so totally occupied in the Boston affairs that I have had scarce time to run over Cato. I have had just taste enough of it, to give me higher "goût" for a more particular attention to it hereafter, when I shall give you my sentiments very candidly upon it.

I am absorbed in the distress of my native country. The inhumanity of Britain can be equalled by nothing but its mistaken policy. The only apology I can find for them, is to charge the depravity of their hearts upon the weakness of their heads. Infatuated people! Do they imagine that we will make a tame surrender of all that an honest man ought to hold dear without a struggle to preserve; and that our pretensions to freedom are chimerical—without being founded in Right and living only in empty profession? What will be the event of the controversy, I know not—I anticipate the melancholy circumstances which must pave the way—Nothing but a total interruption of trade with Great Britain can serve the purposes of the Colonies. Mankind feel most strongly when their interests are affected, and the present degeneracy of Britain calls for every supply for luxury, venality and corruption which they have hitherto derived from the industry of the inhabitants of this insulted country. They are too far advanced in the malady to admit a cure—Economy is a virtue that they have left too far behind to return to it.

Adieu, my dear sir. I have only time to assure you that, amidst the distresses of this country, nothing can tend more to lessen the melancholy share I take in them—than to hear frequently from you.

I am
Yours, with sincere esteem,
WM. HOOPER.

The following is the first of a series of letters, in my possession, to Miss Helen Blair. Nelly Blair, the niece of Mrs. Iredell, passed much of her time in her aunt's house. She had vivacity, quickness of apprehension, and brilliant beauty. Much petted and indulged, she was not without faults : was somewhat petulant, somewhat wayward. Weeds will grow apace in rich soils ; and if not sedulously exterminated by the hand of industry, will hinder the germination and growth of the seed sown by virtue. For many years childless, Mr. Iredell cherished for Nelly an attachment almost parental : she seems to have supplied to him a spiritual want, and he lavished upon her all the bounty of a father's love. He spared no pains in her culture ; and, though fond, corrected with firmness the errors of her education. He often had occasion for rebuke, yet the little girl so wound herself round his heart, that she received no little share of his care and attention. When away from home, in attendance upon legislative assemblies or upon courts, the man of business would ever contrive an opportunity to write his favorite. His letters were sometimes playful, and sometimes serious : at times, they possessed the finish of elaborate compositions. He was amply rewarded by Nelly's improvement, for she so ripened, that, in after years, it was no flattery to say of her,

"There dwells sweet love and constant chastity,
Unspotted faith, and comely womanhood,
Regard of honor, and mild modesty."

EDENTON, July 17th, 1774.

DEAR NELLY :—I had the pleasure to receive your letter this morning, and am much obliged to you for it. I hope you and Georgy will be now quite well : either of your indispositions I hope has been but slight. The reason the poor man's execution is delayed, is that the Governor may in the mean time inform himself of the Judge's sentiments, as he thinks it would be inconsistent with the deference due to them, to grant a pardon without their recommendation, and consulting them on the circumstances of the case. Be pleased to tell Mr. Pearson this particularly, and that I have heard nobody here find fault with it, and that the Governor's conduct on this occasion is such as in my opinion does him honor, and was most exactly proper. I send you some pens : you ought by no means to write with my hard-nibbed ones ; if you continue so to do, your handwriting will be good for nothing. You cannot conceive how happy your mamma's good report of you makes your aunt and me. Be assured, your conduct at all times will have great effect, one way or other, on the satisfaction of our minds. I forgot to tell you of a word that you spelt wrong in your other letter—*the* for *they*—and aint should not be used in a letter : *are not* is more proper. Adieu ! my dear Nelly ! God bless you ! Continue to be good, and consequently to be beloved, and to make us happy.

I am, ever,
Your most affectionate uncle,
JAMES IREDELL.

WILMINGTON, August 5th, 1774.

DEAR SIR :—I cannot better assure you of the pleasure I had from the receipt of your two letters by the express, than by taking up my pen to answer them by the return of it. I cannot, in justice to myself, omit any opportunity to promote a correspondence by which I am so much the gainer in intellectual improvement and amusement. As I know of no acquaintance which I began with more pleasure, so I shall endeavor earnestly to cultivate, and in some measure I hope to deserve it. My letters often will only be a dry detail of facts without embellishments, when you will be obliged to call forth all your strength of patience to wade through them, and all your charity to forgive the writer. You must seek part of my atonement in yourself, and skim lightly over my faults when you have in some degree tempted me to commit them. Had you not by your approbation sanctified my past scribbling, you had not been troubled again.

The share you take in the present distress of the town of Boston, bespeaks a heart that feels exquisitely for the calamities of your fellow-beings, and for the insulted rights of British subjects. It is an observation that has had the experience of ages to confirm the truth of it, that every human system degenerates, and that the political, like the natural body, is in a continual decay. The former has the advantage of the latter in this, that while the latter can only be patched and repaired, the other may become as pure and perfect as in its original. Government, by a variety of abuses, which insensibly introduce themselves into it, at length attains to the highest depravity that it can bear, and then a change necessarily ensues. I think it is Machiavel who says that no government can long enjoy liberty unless it be frequently brought back to its first principles. That *era* to me does not appear to be far remote. The independence of Parliament is now no more, and the constitution, of which that is a necessary basis, must fall with it. I can realize no distinction betwixt the subjects of a British sovereign on this or the other side of the Atlantic. Is the air of America less genial to freedom than that of Britain ? "Coelum non animum mutant qui trans mare currunt." Have the Colonies been a dead weight on the shoulders of Britain ? A drain for all its wealth without making any returns, or have the advantages been reciprocal ? if the latter, surely she acts with the severity of a step-mother. But if we view her conduct upon the scale of right, its injustice exceeds the powers of language. Condemnation without trial, taxation without representation, infringement of charters sanctified by age and the authority of kings, confiscation, or what amounts to the same thing, a denial of the use of a man's own property, without a conviction to incur a forfeiture—the spirit of a trial by jury sunk in the pitiful pretext, that a Middlesex freeholder is a peer of the vicinity, impartial and acquainted with an inhabitant of Boston, and competent for his trial, and add to all, that all this is the gift of his Majesty's most gracious bounty. 'Tis inhuman to add insult to injury.

A much greater man than I am once gloried that he was born a Briton ; with as much pride I boast myself an American. I cannot enough approve of your wishes to be perfectly independent of the smiles and frowns of Government,—like those of Fortune, they are always capricious, and often misplaced. Offices are not made the reward of merit, honorable distinctions for services that are meritorious ; but are made instruments to purchase integrity, and to reward the exertions of men who labor for the subversion of our blessed constitution. The removal of Governor Franklin for the offence of his father, will ever be recorded as a monument of the share which private prejudices have taken in the movement of the political springs of administration in the present reign, and transmit to an impartial posterity the authors of it with marks of the blackest infamy. I hope that there is a tribunal, where the present age will have an opportunity to resent such a prostitution of power, and do themselves justice. The people of Cape Fear have sent a vessel loaded with provisions for the support of Boston. The subscriptions in a few days amounted to £800, and in other respects they discover a very proper resentment for the injustice done to that people.

I thank you for your account of your Court of Oyer. Ours met an untimely end—four days had elapsed of the Court—several offenders been tried—one branded for larceny, and one convicted of murder. On the fifth day M. Moore excepted to the Commission for these reasons :—That the Province law which creates the Court gives to the Chief Justice the powers of Oyer and Terminer and General Gaol Delivery, but the clause which impowers the Associates to act in his absence, gives them only the powers of Judges of Oyer and Terminer (the words Gaol Delivery being omitted in the law), and therefore the Commission exceeded the Governor's power.

2d. The Commission was to try for the *District of Wilmington*, when no such district was made by the law ; but, that mention should have been made of all the counties.

M. Moore very indecently reflected upon the legislature, happy in the weakness of his Judge.

The Court took an *Adversari*, and adjourned.

Mr. Moore has furnished me with many materials for yourself and friends, which I shall communicate to you some day or other : they are truly picturesque of the man and highly laughable.[*]

Be that as it will, the Commission was so truly defective that it seemed to be so intentionally. The word *Felonies* omitted, and the jurisdiction given to *both Associates*, but not to *each* ; this I have observed without mentioning it but to you. It is replete with blunders of a smaller kind, and Atticus charges all on the Assembly. I have exhausted your patience. Forgive me only till I say that I am,

Dear Iredell, with sincere esteem,
Your friend and servant,
WILLIAM HOOPER.

Mention to my friend S. J. the state of our Court of Oyer. I have not yet received answers to your letters to the Attorney General. Should I, before I set off for Newbern, I will carry them with me. Yours, W. HOOPER.

The following letter is from the pen of Archibald Neilson.

[*] Maurice Moore, lately a judge.

He was the intimate and confidential friend of Governor Martin. On 7th Oct., 1775, he was appointed Naval Officer in the place of Samuel Johnston, superseded. He sailed from the Province in the Ship George, from Brunswick, in Nov., 1775, intending to return. The success of the Revolution prevented. He died some years after the war, in Dundee, Scotland. He never married. He was, undoubtedly, one of the most highly cultivated men of his day and region; and, though an adherent of Government, highly esteemed by Iredell and Johnston.

NEW BERN, 20th August, 1774.

DEAR SIR:—I esteem myself much favored by yours of the 15-20th ult., which I received on my arrival here two days ago.

I hope you did not seriously think that it was necessary to make any excuse to me, or to any one pretending to humanity and feelings, for the generous warmth of your application for the unfortunate convict. I thank my God, dear sir, that I have a heart, in so much like your own, as at once to have seized the worthiness of your motive; and well knew that both motive and manner would both do you honor with the Governor, in like manner as it endeared you to me. I thoroughly conceive and feel (I may say truly) from sore experience, the temper you mention, "tremblingly alive all o'er." Alas! it must be blunted, what perhaps is more to be desired than expected. I know that eight years' severe correction and resolutions forced by writhing agony, have not yet made a philosopher of me; the quivering heart-strings oft yet refusing to receive the tone of stoic reason. However, let us content us; the poet says, "The sweetest virtues from the passions flow."

I don't apprehend that I can write you any thing new of the political kind; as you have an opportunity of receiving the news from the northward, earlier than we receive any public intelligence.

The Council many of them are here, and I fancy their meeting will be full on the 25th. The Governor is gone down to the Bar with his family, on their way to New York; but is expected up to-day.

The political Phalanx at home seem to be changing ground, I mean the writers. You have no doubt seen Dr. Tucker's plan,—which has many advocates. Another gentleman comments upon it, wishing to retain the King's sovereignty, and put some few restraints on the American foreign trade, taken from the Act of Navigation. Others again contend that the King could grant no charters but as one of the members of the great whole of Government—Majesty holding no political authority but as head of the nation—that all acquisitions of new lands, though vested in the King, are belonging to the kingdom; that to suppose a charter granted by the King in his private capacity, is inconsistent and absurd; that, therefore, the colonists in holding their lands and civil government of the King by charters, hold both from the nation collectively in the supreme legislative body—and with regard to representation, that that want is more in words than idea; the subjects in the American part of the dominion, being as much represented in parliament as seven millions and a half or more of the subjects in Great Britain—the constituents there who send the members not exceeding 2 or 300,000.

Others again (whom I style latitudinarians in politics) take a larger range, talk of politics as a worldly science, in which prudence and expediency must have the same rule as in private life; that no great governments ever were or ever can be, in all circumstances, conducted after the restrictive idea of abstract and partial rights; that, so long as mankind are mankind, the particular interest of the parts must, in some instances, yield to the general advantage of the whole, whence what they lose for a time will flow back in multiplied value; that the protectors must always be superior to the protected, nor can colonists ever have a *political* right to all the advantages and immunities of the state emigrated from and holden of; that many regulations may appear wrong and unjust on a hasty view, in a partial light, which, when traced through political combinations and contemplated in the general and literal view, may appear perfectly right and just, &c., &c., &c.—for I am tired of it.

I take the liberty of sending for your perusal some plays, &c. The plays are new ones, and may perhaps amuse the ladies,—the Comedy is the performance of a Major Addington in Burgoyne's light-horse,—and the Prince of Tunis is the work of an old schoolfellow of mine, Mr. McKenzie, an attorney of Edinburgh. The magazine contains a remarkable account of the parliamentary representation. I also send Lord Egmont's *True History*; pray read it with due philosophy. You will please to observe, that I am by no means an enemy to Lord Chatham and his proper fame. I allow him great talents, which he has often exerted to the essential benefiting of his country; but he has been too passionate, too desultory, too vehement, too violently attached to popular fame, too impatient and overbearing, to attain the idea I have formed of a truly great man,—the "Semper Simplex, Fortis, Idem et Unus;"—I shall note to you a little anecdote of the D. of Ormond as a kind of commentary on my meaning.

The county meeting here is this day, and will be very much thronged; I hope to see Mr. Johnston, Mr. Hewes, and against the 25th I wish you may come with them, if you find it proper.

Present my respects if you please to Mrs. Blair, Mrs. Iredell, and the *family* over the creek—every occasion of hearing from you will give me pleasure.

I am with real esteem, dear sir,
Yours truly,
ARCHIBALD NEILSON.

P. S.—I have also sent you a magazine containing Lord Camden and Lord Mansfield's speeches, in the Douglas cause; which, when perused, I beg you will send, first opportunity, to Archie Corrie with my compliments. Before returning it, if you would get any young lad to copy them, I would willingly pay any expense. Your fast friend, A. N.

The first Provincial Congress assembled in North Carolina, at New Berne, August 25th, 1774, in despite of the threats and proclamation of the Royal Governor, and in illustration of its defiance, held its session almost in his very presence.* Of this body, Iredell's friends,—Johnston, Hewes, Thomas Jones and Hooper,—were conspicuous members. On the 27th, they passed resolutions claiming the rights of Englishmen without abridgment, and that no subject should be taxed without his consent, or that of his legal representative; they condemned the several acts of Parliament imposing duties on the Colonies; censured the Boston Port Bill, and approved the conduct of the people of Massachusetts; they insisted on the right of trial by juries of the vicinage, and denounced the sending of Americans, in certain criminal cases, to England for trial; they declared they would not, after January 1st, 1775, import any East India goods or British manufactures, and that, unless grievances were redressed before October 1st, 1775, they would not export any tobacco, pitch, tar, turpentine, or any other articles whatever, to Great Britain; they resolved not to use any East India tea after September 10th, and to hold no intercourse with any persons refusing to comply with such general plan as might be adopted by the Continental Congress; they approved of the proposed Continental Congress; appointed Hooper, Hewes and Caswell deputies, and invested them with the amplest powers. The execution of the Resolves of the Congress was intrusted to committees to be elected by the people in each county. These committees were soon formed, and proved most useful instruments. It was agreed that the Moderator, John Harvey, or in case of his death, Samuel Johnston, might at any time call them together, at such place as he might deem proper. The issue was thus fairly stated, and fairly joined. Iredell fought the battle on paper. The first of his political efforts preserved, on the subject, is the following Address. It is dated one month before the "universally admired" Address to the People of Great Britain, drafted by Iredell's future colleague on the Bench, John Jay, was adopted by the Continental Congress.*

TO THE INHABITANTS OF GREAT BRITAIN:

FRIENDS AND FELLOW-SUBJECTS:—United as we are by the strongest ties of affection and interest, descended from the same revered ancestors, and possessed equally of the blessings of a most happy Constitution, it is greatly to be lamented that differences should arise between us, which too fatally tend to disturb the harmony of a connection highly beneficial and honorable to both. Yet such, I have the concern to say, have heretofore arisen, and are now again occasioned, by an attempt in your Parliament to exercise a supreme authority over us, to which we cannot possibly conceive they are at all entitled upon any view of policy, justice, or the real nature of our Constitution. It has been our misfortune to suffer in this contest by the base misrepresentations of wicked and designing men, and to have the desperate doings of a factious and tumultuous mob, (from which your own country is not more free,) imputed to the turbulent and unruly dispositions of the inhabitants in general. How cruel and unjust such a construction is, your nation is an example—for none can deny that, at times, very dangerous and destructive mobs have done mischief among yourselves; and you would think it very hard that, for this reason, you should be considered in a state of rebellion, have the foundation of your civil liberties utterly destroyed, and be subject, not only to all the horrid expectations of a military government, but even immediately to some few of the effects of one. This, I take it, is exactly the case with America—Colonies planted originally by men emigrating from their own country, where they unhappily feared freedom was near losing its existence, in search of this desired blessing among woods and deserts, which they thought preferable to all kinds of ease and luxury enjoyed by a humiliating tenure; increased by the surprising industry of the first settlers, and by the blessing of Providence, to an amazing degree, and come at length to enjoy a pretty comfortable state of maintenance, secured to them, as they fondly hoped, by sanctions of a most sacred and inviolable nature. In these possessions they long lived easy and happy, flattering themselves that they should be permitted to enjoy freely property procured for them by the severe labor and virtue of their ancestors, and that the valuable blessings of the British

---

* Jones, Wheeler, Martin, Wiley.

* Hildreth.

Constitution, bestowed on them by their charters, would never be infringed. In this state of confidential security and hope, these Colonies continued at the commencement of the late war, when disputes arose between our sovereign and the French king about the limits of a part of this Continent. It was an object of great importance to both countries: yours had long discovered and felt the great advantages reaped from a connection with us, and was naturally jealous of having any part of so useful a country unjustly encroached upon;—ours was eminently endangered by so near and formidable an enemy being invested with the great power which so large an extent of territory as he claimed gave him. Thus situated, the war was on this account of great advantage to both; both engaged in it, therefore, with great cheerfulness and alacrity, and the success was answerable to our most sanguine wishes. America showed an uncommon ardor of exertion; the heart and hand of every man were at the public service, and no endeavors were spared on *our* part to co-operate in all *your* plans and regulations. Duty and affection prompted us with unsolicited zeal to prove ourselves worthy of a connection with the greatest (because the freest and most virtuous) state on earth; and to give unlimited proofs of attachment to that noble spirit which then delighted in seeing their friends as free and happy as themselves. At this time, I venture to say, America would voluntarily have gone any lengths to serve you, so much did she admire the generous turn of your minds, and your exemption from that arbitrary and capricious temper most free nations, arrived at happiness themselves, too often, unreasonably and unaccountably, discover towards others. You, yourselves, witnessed to the honorable exertion of our abilities; you thought we spent more than could be expected from us, or was properly our due proportion, and you ordered each of the Provinces to be refunded the surplus of its real share. Here was a period for good offices, and mutual obligations, to begin upon new terms of confidence, and to increase from year to year with added fervor and affection. Here was a glorious disposition to cultivate; and it might *easily* have been cultivated, to the mutual honor and happiness of us both. But, alas! this delightful prospect was but ideal: our happiness was soon to be blasted; Freedom was to be banished from our soil, endeared to us because it was laboriously tilled by our fathers; and we were cruelly and infamously told that we were, for the future, to be in absolute subjection to the British Parliament.

It is an obvious and sufficient answer to this extraordinary claim—of a sovereign dominion in your Parliament over us—that, if it in truth exists, we are possessed of no *liberty*; we have nothing we can call *our own*. The charters granted by our Sovereigns, instead of being considered as pledges of the honor and sacred faith of kings, were a mere snare and delusion to induce our forefathers to come abroad, with the utmost difficulty, expense, and hazard, and for many years almost entirely at their own risk, to make out of the wilderness, by their own and their children's labor, a fine country for you to spoil in. You are the *real proprietors*, we only the *tenants at will*, of these possessions. For this is exactly the case, if any part of our property is at your command. *What part* shall be received must be according to your judgment, if you can tax us *constitutionally*; for if we had a right to refuse any imposition, because *we* thought it was arbitrary and profuse, we could at any time defeat your power. You, therefore, (if your opinion be right,) can at any time require, *and be entitled to receive*, whatever part of our property you choose to order. Of course, that property we thought our own is not *ours* but *yours*, if the gracious, tender mercies you formerly showed us, should continue to be violated with as little scruple and decency as they have *lately* been. I mean, it would then be yours *in fact*; it is ours now only by *indulgence*. And upon your own principles, it was so at first. Our ancestors, therefore, had no *real security*; the charters conveyed only the temporary good-will of the Prince, and it was at any time in his and his Parliament's power to annihilate the rights which *they* guarantied, to destroy the property which *they* granted, and to deprive Englishmen of all those advantages, for the sake of which they left their native soil, and by the fond hopes of their securely enjoying which, they could only be induced to leave it. Our property at your disposal, our lives and liberties at your discretion, we subject at any time to whatever arbitrary laws your Parliament may think fit to send us; in the name of God, what is our condition? how are the hopes and expectations of our ancestors fulfilled? What becomes of confidence in Government, of reliance on the most sacred contracts of the state? But your Parliament, I suppose, can do no wrong: they are immaculate, and none of their proceedings can ever cause any real injury as to *us;* though you sometimes complain of them yourselves. Our complaints, you will say, are evidently founded in faction and injustice, in heated and erroneous ideas of the Constitution, and in endeavors to form a new system of government, destructive of that beautiful theory in political discourses—the necessity of an absolute power residing *somewhere* in every state.

As to *faction*, that has nothing to do with the speculative point in question. But you are much mistaken about the factions in America. They were originally caused by yourselves. Till you talked to us in arbitrary and haughty language, we loved, we revered, we did every thing in our power to assist you. We would voluntarily, so long as you treated us as *freemen*, have sustained any hardships, and, if necessary, laid down our lives in your support. This was, till the fatal period I have mentioned, the *general*, almost the *universal*, disposition of America. We looked up to you as our fathers and protectors, and we thought of the soil with reverence which had so long been the nurse of Freedom, Honor, Generosity, and Science. Things are indeed greatly changed. The same spirit of attachment which formerly devoted us to your service, now, upon a superior call, and as you have deserted your former noble principles, devotes us to the preservation of our country: for that word, that object, would be no longer dear to us, when liberty, its greatest and almost its only, certainly its *indispensable* ornament, was fled.

With respect to the *injustice* we are charged with,—by this I suppose is meant our unwillingness to contribute our proportion to the exigencies of the state. But if it be believed that our complaints are any way affected by this motive, it is a great misapprehension. We have hitherto been forward and zealous in the grant of our money, to a degree your Parliament thought to be extraordinary and profuse; and we should always, I am sure, be readier to give too much than too little, if you would allow us the merit of offering it ourselves. But we contend for an exclusive right of the disposal of our own property, because it is one of the most essential privileges of the British Constitution, and that which is the principal guard and protection of all the others. When the people have the grant of their own money, and a share in making the laws by which they are to be governed; unless they are either blind to their own interest, or wicked and despicable enough to betray it, they have every possible human tie for their own welfare and happiness. If they had the *latter*, without the *former*, and this resided in the Crown, their liberties might be easily taken from them; because the Crown, by raising money *ad libitum* upon the subject, could easily provide the means of effecting and maintaining encroachments upon the people's rights; and might also ruin them by wanton depredations on their property. But when the people have in *their* hands the only means of supporting Government, by the absolute disposition of their property, they can take care that the administration of their affairs is faithfully and wisely conducted; or, as an elegant writer of yours expresses it, by withholding supplies, peaceably admonish their Sovereign of his duty. It is needless to add, they have then something *they can call their own*.

These principles you like very well, when applied to yourselves, but you would willingly deprive us of the benefit of them. You think that your Parliament ought to have absolute authority over us, in order to secure our *dependence*, and to make the share we ought to take in your burdens *certain*, and not subject to our caprice. That harsh word, *dependence*, seems to me greatly to have misled your ideas. It is meant usually by it, I believe, that you should have an absolute security for our submission in all cases, and that we should have none at all for your faithful government of us. But this is not the condition of freemen, but of *slaves*. It is the very definition of slavery. That dependence, which is erected by affection and interest,—by a reverence for your and our common ancestors,—by an attachment to your excellent Constitution, and by gratitude for many past favors, and which may still, for a long time, be preserved by mutual good offices, and by a kind and generous conduct towards us,—has always been the delight of our hearts, and we used to think the highest honor of our condition. But if you mean that we are to be the subjects of *subjects*, and believe that we shall patiently bear whatever hardships you may choose to lay upon us, you will be fatally deceived: you will find that upon these terms *dependence* will be a hated word to us;—we shall scorn your impositions, we will defy your power. But suppose our assemblies should be refractory; should withhold supplies? I answer: Suppose your House of Commons should do so? Is there any remedy? I know of none. The danger is equal. No possible cause but two can be assigned for either. They must be tools, or they must be greatly oppressed. The first is an impossible supposition, and God grant that neither of us may ever lose this remedy for the latter.

A free government can only subsist by *the general confidence of the people*. Any other support is arbitrary and unreasonable because where the whole legislative power of the State abides in any particular man or set of men, independent of the rest of the community, there is no sufficient security that the ends of government will be properly answered: for the interests of the *few* (at least their *immediate* and *apparent* interests) may be formed on the destruction of those of the *many:* consequently, the public have not *that* security for the just administration of their affairs which a genuine share of freedom demands. Whether you at present enjoy *this* security is a question of some delicacy and importance. The principles of your Constitution, however, intended and at first provided, that you should. By giving the people a share of the legislative power, and allowing such of them as could be supposed exempt from influence, to choose persons to execute this trust on their behalf, it is evident that *their* interests were effectually secured, as far as human regulations could extend.

your representation is now extremely unequal (as it undoubtedly is), this is owing to the change in property, and in the scene of your transactions, that many ages have occasioned. It is a *necessary* evil that could not have been originally avoided. Its remedy, indeed, is a very desperate one, as none but the Parliament themselves can amend it, and there seems something unhallowed, as well as unsafe, in touching fundamentals. But what may best be conceived on this subject I leave to a fit time for a discussion of it. It has nothing to do with my present object—an endeavor to show the *unreasonableness* of your claim in taxing us, and to expose the futility of the suggestion that it is necessary you should hold it. For I hope it does not follow that if any of *your* rights are in danger, those of *all others* of the king's subjects must fall with them, and because you have not an entirely sufficient security for your Parliament's good conduct, therefore out of compliment to you we should reduce ourselves to a total dependence on *their honor and integrity;* and in proportion as the decrease of these, or of the security for them (which is nearly the same thing), brings us into more danger, so it should into a more humble submission. You ought rather, for your own interest, to reverse the desire; and, thank Heaven, there are a body of men in your empire who know no distinction between different parts of their duty, and are equally ready, upon the terms of their Constitution, to assist and protect the king, or to assist and protect each other from the hands of arbitrary violence, and the cruel exactions of usurped power.

You will observe, in your elections we have no interference; you have as much as the terms of a very free Constitution, and the great changes in your situation, can allow. Some think *every* man ought to have an individual vote for a representative. If every man was a good one, and had a tolerable understanding, this rule would be proper; but when poverty leads to temptation, and folly is ever capable of deceit, there must be some restriction as to the right of voting: otherwise the lowest and most ignorant of mankind must associate in this important business with those who it is to be presumed, from their property and other circumstances, are free from influence, and have some knowledge of the great consequence of their trust. It is, therefore, a capital object so to regulate the right of election, as that it may be presumed the choice of the voter is *free* and *able.* It is impossible that this care can always be successful: the provisions of State cannot reach the purposes of the human heart, nor guard against the continual fluctuation of all human affairs. But I doubt not the regulations which now govern you were wise *at the time they were established.* The corruption of national manners, and the causes I

before enumerated, render them very inadequate *now.* But, as the representation stands, if you would preserve your *virtue,* you could do great things for your country. It is not possible for *any* regulation to guard against the corruption both of the *electors* and the *elected.* You have another very strong security against very atrocious designs in your Parliament; *that their own freedom and happiness, and that of their posterity, are inseparably connected with yours, and that they can make no partial regulations from which themselves are exempted.* But how does the case stand as to us? We have no connection with them that secures their *affection;* we have no interest so attached to theirs as to secure their *caution;* they have no such merit as to obtain our *confidence;* and they may have an inseparably strong temptation to ease *their own* burdens by throwing them upon *us.* Let Reason and Justice attend to these things, and then let some narrow-minded advocate for Power and Oppression talk of *virtual representation.*

If the Equity and Justice of the British Parliament are mentioned, and that they are men of such discernment and wisdom, that, for their own sakes, they will not afflict us *unreasonably;* and that our first objections reached the *power* only, not the *expediency,* of their regulations; I answer, in the first place, that the fact is not so,—and, secondly, that if it was, it would be of no great moment. The Stamp Act was, I think, strongly proved to be as *burdensome* and oppressive in *fact,* as it was arbitrary and dangerous in *principle.* It would be tedious, as it is unnecessary, to mention all the regulations since that time we think grievous. It is sufficient, as a full and fatal proof of the wisdom and equity of Parliament, to refer only to the arbitrary laws of their last session;—laws which will stigmatize the British annals with a disgrace every honest subject will blush for. But had your Parliament to this day, in every instance, appeared the wisest and most virtuous body on earth, and had behaved with particular condescension to us, and they had passed a law enacting that every man in America should pay a shilling sterling per annum, in lieu of all other taxes, and that they would, in that case, be themselves at the expense of supporting our civil establishments; I would as strenuously have exerted myself against that small demand as I now do, and hope I ever shall do against the accumulated evils of taxes, arbitrary laws, and cruel orders of power, which we now feel, and which are but the natural consequence of the other. Your admired Junius, in his letter to Dr. Blackstone, has the following passage, which I may very well apply here:—"To say that they *will not* make use of this power, would be a language unfit for a man so learned in the law as you are. By your doctrine, they have the power, ,and laws, you know, are intend-

ed to guard against what men *may* do, not to trust to what they *will* do." The last-mentioned gentleman, Dr. Blackstone, (who, if I may judge of the *man* by the *author,* is the ornament of the age and country,) is remarkably careful that the distinction of the *possession* of a power and the *abuse* of it should not lead us into any fatal acquiescence, and in many admirable passage sstrongly urges and enforces a jealousy on this point. One I perfectly well remember. "Surely," says he, "the true liberty of the subject consists, not so much in the *gracious behavior,* as in the *limited power* of the Sovereign." In an excellent speech, ascribed to Sir William Meredith, it is said: "Not the man alone who *feels,* but he who is *exposed to* tyranny, is without freedom."* Again, then, let me repeat that it is the *principle* of your regulations more than the *matter* of them, against which we so strongly protest; though the latter, in many instances, we think is not altogether free from objection.

I think I have now sufficiently shown the unreasonableness of this claim in taxing us; inasmuch as we are *slaves,* if such a right truly exists: and also the futility of the plea of *necessity* that your Parliament should be possessed of it, for the sake of securing our dependence; because this *dependence* must be ultimately secured, as that of all free subjects, by their confidence in the good administration of Government, which in that case necessarily causes it; and also because we should, upon your terms, have no protection, nor any means of defending ourselves from an arbitrary and oppressive use of your power. I shall now proceed to examine this subject upon the principles of the Constitution, and the particular rights we derive under it.

You all know, and glory in it, that your Constitution is, and has been (in the opinion of your most approved authors) a free one from the earliest ages. You cannot also but know, (though I fear you do not sufficiently reflect on it,) that the chief essential of this freedom is, that share which the people have in the

* In the year 1771, a bill to regulate the prices of corn, &c., together with a bill inflicting penalties for killing game had been transmitted from the Commons to the Lords, and were returned by these with *some alterations.* The Commons were extremely offended that the Lords had *altered* these bills, because, in some degree, they were *money bills.* In the debate it was urged, that money levied by way of penalty could not be properly looked on in that light; to which the Solicitor General replied, it was not the sum to be levied, nor the manner of levying it, but *the precedent which it might establish, and the doctrines and principles it might hereafter maintain;* and concluded by remarking, that it was not for twenty shillings, the glorious Hampden contended, but for the properties, liberties, and privileges of his countrymen. The Speaker also, in the height of his zeal, threw both bills over the table. Since ideas of these gentlemen are so refined upon trifles, I should be glad to hear their opinions seriously delivered, upon principles of *law, reason,* and *political maxims,* whether in consistence with the British Parliament's claims (of which they are strong advocates), we are not *their slaves.* They cannot deny it, if truth and reason have the same effect, when applied to our case, as to others.

legislative power: for it would signify little to be possessed of an excellent code of laws, if there was an authority in the State, whose interest might be distinct from yours, that could at any time alter them. You are also justly jealous that the right of granting money shall not only be peculiarly your own, but the very proposal of it, and the manner in which it shall be levied: and the chief reason of this, the learned Blackstone tells you, is, not, as is commonly supposed, because the supplies are raised upon the body of the people (the Lords being taxed as well as them), but because the Lords being a permanent, hereditary body, created at pleasure by the King, are supposed to be more under the influence of the Crown, and when once influenced more apt to continue so, than the Commons, who are a temporary elective body, freely nominated by the people. (Thus admirably does this regulation guard against any invasion of the *principle,* as well as secure an observance of the *form.*) These are your great privileges, and they are certainly the cornerstone and prop of all the others. It only remains for me to show, what is the nature of our claim to the enjoyment of them, under the authority of our charters, independent of the rational claim which we otherwise make to them as men, as freemen, and as Britons.

It is a fact sufficient for our purpose, that at the time these charters were granted, it was universally acknowledged, that the king had a right to all uninhabited countries that should be discovered and possessed by any of his subjects, and also to all others that they should be able, by means of conquest or otherwise, to acquire. Of course he had a right to stipulate the conditions upon which his subjects might be encouraged to venture risks for the *purpose of such acquisition.* Had he not possessed this right, and possessed it *without limitation,* the other would have been of little consequence. No Sir Walter Raleighs would have been found to traverse unknown seas: no American empire would have been now the object of contention. Could our ancestors have foreseen the latent claims of a British Parliament lurking under all the fair promises and encouragements of a smiling king, would they have been deluded by the specious bait, to the destruction of their and their posterity's hopes? No. They would certainly have preferred a life of ease and security, though of indolence, at home: they would not have torn themselves from their friends and country to seek misery and slavery in a barbarous and hostile land.

King James, and King Charles the First, it is well known, both prohibited Parliament from interfering in our concerns, upon the express principle *that they had no business with them.* In any contract can the nature of it be better ascertained than by certainly discovering the sense of the parties? It may be said, those kings perhaps thought that *they*, in the plenitude of their power, had authority to revoke the charters, if necessary, or to make any other regulations for us they might think proper. They were indeed sufficiently arbitrary in their tempers to form an idea of that sort; but it does not appear that *they did*, and our ancestors were certainly not fools enough to consider the only foundation of their security as alterable at pleasure by one of the contracting parties.

It is said by some specious characters, that the king cannot be possessed of a right to allow his subjects to emigrate, because he might, by this means, depopulate the kingdom. Ridiculous reason! as if *any* laws could provide for every possible contingent evil, or as if, for fear of so imaginary, so improbable a circumstance, no useful projects of colonization ought ever to have been formed. For the same reason, the king should be denied the privilege of making war and peace, because he may make enemies of all mankind, or purchase peace by dismembering his principal dominions.

If they choose to deny the king the constitutional right over this country (for such I should apprehend to be the consequence of their opinion), who is to possess it? Are the Lords and Commons to share it between them? or the present possessors to hold it by *the right of possession?* or are we to seek for the descendants of the original proprietors and resign it to them? Let us hear no more of such paltry trifling. We respect and reverence the rights of the king; we owe, and we pay him allegiance, and we will sacredly abide by the terms of our charters. These were purchased by the hard and severe labor of our ancestors, which procured for our Sovereign this fine country. But we will not submit to any alteration of the *original terms* of the contract, because they were the price for which the service was engaged, and in the pleasing consideration of which it was alone performed. If Heaven has blessed the enterprise with greater success than could be hoped for, let not its favors be solely confined to the party who had so little a share in the exertions that were used to forward it. We mean not to depart from his rights; but we will sacredly preserve our own. If the British Parliament are not satisfied with the advantages which our situation *alone* affords (an exclusive regulation of a lucrative trade), they are welcome, if they please, to recur to their former prosperous condition, before these colonies were settled. But let them not churlishly refuse *some* advantages, because they cannot be allowed *all*. To put men upon a hazardous service, offer them wages; *accept the service, and refuse the wages.* Where, in the name of Heaven, is the justice, is the common decency, of such conduct? Be assured, we will not be deluded,—we will not be oppressed by it.

There are a few cases in the law books on the subject of the Plantations, but none of them, I think, rationally favor the arbitrary claim I am considering.

They all regard questions concerning the *incidental* operations of the laws of England in general, and principally refer to the effect of acts of Parliament passed *before the Conquest*. In none of them is particularly set forth *any settlement of the country after the Conquest, in consequence of charters from the Crown;* without which the Judges could not with propriety have determined on them. It is upon the authority of *these charters* that our liberties are chiefly founded. If, *in a conquered or ceded country*, the king has a right to make what laws he pleases, we contend that this right has been already exercised, by a compact that these countries shall be governed only after the particular mode mentioned in our charters. To conceive that no such establishment by the Sovereign, under whose auspices these countries were acquired, can be binding on his successors, but that the king for the time being may make in them any regulations he thinks proper, would be sporting with the happiness of mankind; and therefore I cannot believe such a notion was ever seriously entertained. Can it be conceived, for instance, that our present Sovereign has all Ireland at his mercy?

The points decided in the law books upon the different effect which would take place as to the laws of England, in case of the settlement of English subjects in an *uninhabited country*, or in one which they *conquered*, or obtained by *cession*, are now of no great moment. The laws of England, *as they stood at the time of our charters*, wherever they can be carried into execution, have been so generally received in America on some principle or other (either by adoption of their legislatures, or from a tacit reverence for their worth, and, as was conceived, their authority also,) that I believe, at present, either in England or America, the justice of such a practice would be little contested. And very probably had any of the charters been pleaded in some of the above cases they might have received a different adjudication. But, however, the circumstances to be considered in determining that question are far different from those which must influence the decision of the present one.

It certainly is an injury of which we have a right to complain, that maxims which are calculated only for a people *conquered*, should be applied to us, who are descendants of the *conquerors*, and who never intermixed with the original inhabitants. For the reasons I have given in the law cases spoken of, perhaps the Judges might not be at liberty to take notice of our particular situation in the *conquered countries*, and the rights under which we settled them: but I cannot but think it very extraordinary that the learned Judge, whose commentaries in general are so extremely accurate and do him so much honor, should fall into the error (if I may presume to call it one) of representing our legal condition to be that of *conquered subjects*, or subjects of a country *ceded* (whose rights, it is alleged, stand upon the same basis). It is evident that he has transcribed from the judicial decisions all that was said of *such subjects*, and applied it *in fact* to us. But if any man can make common sense of such an application, I confess he has more discernment than I have.

Some think that by the conquest of a country all its laws instantly cease; others, that only those in an infidel country do, if conquered by a Christian prince; others, again, that of these only such cease as are *contrary to the law of God*. The last opinion is the latest and seems the most favored. It is said, that the laws of the country from which the conquerors came cannot immediately take effect, because there would be wanted the necessary officers, &c. But I should be glad to know whether it is not easier to appoint officers than to learn a barbarous language, and a system of uncouth laws. In the mean time it would be very curious to see the victors soliciting the vanquished to appoint judges, and these latter perhaps immediately trying the former as robbers and murderers for the desolation they had brought upon their country. Do not these circumstances plainly prove, that all that is said about *conquered countries* in the law books can rationally have no other reference than to the *conquered people?* It is plainly from this title of conquest that in all the cases where the power of Parliament is extra-judicially recognized (as it is said that, though general laws do not take effect in the Plantations, because they are not supposed to be within the ordinary contemplation of the legislature, yet all wherein they are particularly named have authority there), that power is derived: of course, this source failing, it has from those cases no other support.

But another formidable (and, by many, thought unanswerable) one has been found, and to this source, rather than the other, I think, all our calamities may be traced. I shall endeavor to state the argument in as strong terms as I can use.

"The British empire consists of many distinct states. Each of these has a separate, as well as a joint interest, to pursue; and as present and immediate feelings are usually most powerful, it is probable that very often the former object may be preferred to the latter, if entire liberty of choice is left. These several states must, therefore, be subordinate to *some* power that shall superintend and regulate the whole, to make every thing conducive to the general good on the great imperial scale." Hence it is concluded that the British Parliament, being most ancient, and residing in the original kingdom, must be possessed of this *sovereign authority*.

With respect to this argument, it is first to be considered that the object of all government is, or ought to be, *the happiness of the people governed*. What is understood by policy, as I can conceive, is, the art of advancing their interest and welfare, considered as a *people*, not a *set of individuals*. Where an empire is divided into several *different* and *distinct* states, the aggregate good of all these ought to be consulted. For where would be the justice to regard only *one* or *two* of these as worthy of the care and tender provision of laws, and expose the rest to chance, or the very uncertain, whimsical caprice, or *mean rapacity* of the others? It is evident, therefore, that in such an empire, *that* cannot be just and true policy which provides for the happiness of *one* part of it, and neglects entirely that of *the others*. This truth neither admits, nor requires, any proof: the heart which is so callous and insensible as not to feel the force of it, would reject stubbornly every speculative proof that could ever be offered in its support.

Liberty, in some degree, is the right of every human creature. It is of infinitely more moment than the establishment of any speculative rule whatever; and no rule, in every possible application, can be a just one that is totally destructive of this universal right. God did not make men to be unhappy. Had he fitted any particular set of men to be the slaves of others, he would surely have distinguished them with some mark suited to the abject character. This mark we are not sensible we possess. We bless God, we are of the same make, and we flatter ourselves have souls equal to those who proudly think themselves the *lords of the creation*. We shall endeavor also to show, by our proper jealousy of *this liberty*, that we are not *unworthy*, because we are not *negligent*, of so great a blessing.

The rule whence the above argument is taken (the necessity of *one* supreme power residing *somewhere* in every state), applied universally, is a narrow and pedantic one. It is calculated to sacrifice to a *point of speculation* the happiness of millions. But that same rule, applied justly, and to the objects the authors had in contemplation, is right and proper. It is a long time since it was originally established, and at that time almost all the forms of government subsisting were *simple ones*. A monarchy, an aristocracy, a democracy, were the only common objects presented to the eyes of politicians. And though the British Government, *in its principles*, was extremely complicated, yet unquestionably, for many ages, those principles were so little attended to, that even that happy form of government, to persons at a distance from it, would scarcely seem an exception. For I do contend, upon the principles which now support it, that government is *an exception* to the very rule they lay hold of for our destruction. What is the chief object of this simplifying rule, as it affects us? Clearly, that there shall always be a power in motion to regulate the concerns of the commonwealth, that they may never suffer by inaction or delay. A monarch, an assembly of nobles, a collection of representatives, can determine instantly, when it is laid before them, upon any subject which it is necessary for them to consider. A result is formed; some scheme is executed for the public relief. But suppose some very trying exigence of affairs in the British state. It is submitted to Parliament. The House of Lords thinks one way, the Commons another, the king, perhaps, differs from both. Neither will accede to the other; each continues obstinate; the public suffers, and the grievance proceeds, even perhaps to the destruction of the kingdom. What becomes of the boasted rule? It will be said, this is not probable. I admit it. But it is *possible*, and this shows that rule has not *its effect* even in England, so necessary is it found to complicate the machine of a free government. *One exception*, once allowed, changes the controversy from the *point of strict adherence to the principle*, to the *propriety of forming limitations of it*.

I am aware of the objection that the British Parliament are, constitutionally, *one body*, though composed of different distinct members. But this removes not the difficulty. It is very possible that *those three members* may, separately, disagree upon any one plan of conduct that may be proposed. The public then suffers by a *collision of counsels*, which is the principal evil the rule in question is calculated to avoid. It may be said, indeed, that this will be attended with only a *negative disadvantage*, for they cannot, either of them, form any *distinct* plan. But there are many exigencies wherein this *negative disadvantage* may be equal to any *positive one*. Suppose, in the various circumstances of the late war, they could have come to no agreement: suppose they had differed upon their American policy. In the one case, a successful invasion might, perhaps, have been formed; in the other, we should not have been cursed with *so many fleets and armies*, to the great mortification of our haughty oppressors. Unless, therefore, *names*, not *things*, are regarded, this beautiful theory of *one supreme power*, applied to the British government, does not exist in such a manner as to answer the purposes with a view to which it was formed. Of course, they cannot, with a good grace, apply that rule for the accomplishment of our slavery, and absolute subjection to them.

It may be added, that as the king is supreme head of *every* legislature in the British dominions, his negative can prevent the actual injury to the whole of any *positive law* in any part of the empire.

I have hitherto considered the above rule upon the principles which generally support it in this controversy, though I am not ignorant that it has another basis, and that which I believe was the first suggestion of its political necessity;—I mean, the great solecism of an *imperium in imperio*. And this point being sometimes confounded with the other, has occasioned a good deal of plausible and perplexing sophistry.

The danger arising from this is, lest two independent legislatures should clash by different regulations about the *same objects*. Here neither can be executed, or distress and confusion must ensue. This is a real evil, certainly worth all the anxious care old authors have bestowed upon it. But what application does this make to the case of several *distinct and independent legislatures*, each engaged within a *separate* scale, and employed about *different* objects. The *imperium in imperio* argument is, therefore, not at all applicable to our case, though it has been so vainly and confidently relied on. The principal inconvenience attending our situation we readily admit; that it may not be always practicable to bring so many *different legislatures* to concur heartily in the prosecution and support of one common object. Judging of the future by the past, I do not think this would be found in practice so difficult as in speculation it may appear, but surely any remedy for the evil ought to be conducted on the basis of a general negotiation, and not violently sought by an unjust usurpation of power.

To conclude: If our charters had not been so express as they are, if there had been some clerical defect, or any jesuitical craft in the penning of them, the confessed intention of the parties, and the original rights of mankind, should correct and alter them. We would not be cheated out of our liberties by a few artful syllables. Our ancestors looked for freedom in this country, and thought they possessed it. They fondly flattered themselves that they had transmitted this blessing to their posterity, and they no doubt hoped that their posterity would not be base enough to resign it. God forbid we should disappoint this reasonable expectation. We desire to stand upon manly ground; not upon scholastic and trifling refinement. Such a power as you long continued to exercise, for your and our mutual benefit (though *our* particular interests were often made subservient to *yours*), we will cheerfully and readily submit to. Without critically inquiring whether you may not, *constitutionally*, be possessed of this power, as properly resulting from the relation between us, we are ready to offer our obedience to it as a proof of our regard and attachment, and our desire to cement a lasting union with you. This alone will put millions in your power. A power of taxing, and of harassing us with cruel, oppressive, and inconvenient laws, we will not give you; because it is a *novel* claim, and can never be exercised but to our destruction: any instance to the contrary, however, we think would only form exceptions to a general system of *weakness and injustice*. We cannot divest ourselves of every vestige of freedom to please you, nor even to remove some inconveniences with which the situation we contend for is certainly accompanied. But we are ready, at any time, to enter into a fair negotiation, by which means to concert a plan of cementing the general interest of the empire upon a broad basis, at once securing *a proper union of counsel and authority*, and the *individual freedom of each member of the empire*, so far as is consistent with the *general welfare*. But this object must not be secured by *any partial and contracted plan of ruining whole societies* to make the business of government go on more smoothly. This is *your* plan, which you are now proceeding to enforce with fire and sword. Which of the two is the most equitable, let Heaven and the world judge.

SEPTEMBER, 1774.

Letter from Archibald Neilson to Iredell.

NEWBERN, 14th, Oct., 1774.

DEAR SIR:—I am much indebted to you for yours of the 19th ult., and two of the 7th current, which I have never had an opportunity to answer since they were received.

Your interesting yourself so kindly and warmly in my welfare, and your punctuality in correspondence, are sincerely and feelingly agreeable to me, and bind my most grateful returns; I hope I may be able still to deserve the continuation of those marks of your regard. I yield in point of piety to you, perhaps I have too little of it; but in the matter you refer to, I believe we are agreed. I remember Hippocrates, in his Book de Aere locis et aquis, has this observation: It is true this disorder came from God, but it came in the same manner as all others do, no one more particularly from the Omnipotent than another; because, they are all a necessary sequel to the laws of nature which rule all things. I embrace with keen avidity the really friendly offer you make, of a liberal, flowing, unrestrained correspondence; it will be both infinitely pleasing to my heart, and improving to my mind, and, although, in the last instance, it may not produce an equal effect to you *directly* (I speak without affectation), yet the canvass of your own thoughts, in answering me, may produce it indirectly. I think well enough of both of us to dread not the usual interruptions of intercourse; we shall write always either for information or amusement, neither, I hope, to display our own parts or contend for victory; guarding always against misapprehensions, or taking any offence at such matters, as, although so despicably, yet too commonly corrode and eat away some of the purest friendships. Betwixt us nothing can be ill meant, so I am sure nothing will be ill taken. If haply, however, any thing should be misunderstood, or unkindly felt, let us attend to the advice of the preacher: "Admonish thy friend, perhaps he has not done it, and if he has done it, that he do it not again." Let us reciprocally give and take the license of an urbane friendship. Both of us, I dare say, lay our accounts with often differing in opinion; as that can be no surprise, neither must it give any offence; when an object may be seen from innumerable stations, it is natural that we should often contemplate them from different views and under varying appearances, nor is it reasonable that any sincere opinion should excite anger.

It is recorded of the Emperor Charles Fifth, that after he had retired to sigh down his days at St. Just, he sometimes amused himself in regulating and comparing watches and clocks, but finding, after repeated trials, that he could bring no two of them to go alike; he reflected, with astonishment and regret, how unfortunately and unprofitably *he* had been employed in vainly attempting to bring the more complicated mind of man to a similarity of thinking, notwithstanding the delicacy and intricacy of its movements, and subject as it is to be acted upon by so many various circumstances. I think that with respect to *certain* writings, your conduct has been praiseworthy; it instances a warmness of heart, and a regard for the interests of society which they would be unfeeling churls indeed who could blame. I think, however, you was prudent in dropping Atticus; he would have wrote till the day of judgment: the dispute was by degrees becoming warm and personal, and the authors were too well known. You were generally looked to here as being ——. People who read the letters, and many who did not, spoke as they were affected; in general, I think you was allowed to have the advantage. The old hackneyed politicians *sometimes* smiled at your solicitude and anxious warmth, and talked with an air of sagacious significancy of the easily agitated feelings of youth; which they allowed, however, were proper enough at a certain time of life, as age would mellow them down. As to myself, I did, from the beginning, think that these courts were unconstitutional, and, so far as I could judge from the authorities, illegal; but, politically considering the case, the necessity was urgent, and I could have wished that the discussion had been managed with a little more fineness and delicacy; (you will conceive that I mean only a certain prudence, not a disingenuous or culpable duplicity.)*

You remember the manner the Parliament acted with respect to the embargo on corn. Is it not somewhat remarkable, that several of the best lawyers in the other provinces have given their opinion *clearly* for the legality of those courts? four or five of them to *my* knowledge.

In the main, I am apprehensive that polemic political writings are, at certain times and in particular circumstances, rather a specious amusement than a solid advantage. It may not be so here, but at home I have remarked, that they very rarely convince any but those of the same principles and party with the authors. I observe what you say with regard to the principles of the constitution, and the probable want of support from the body of the people. Ay! there is the rub! All would be well, could they be preserved moral and public spirited. The connection of cause and effect is so complicated, and the action and reaction of cause so strong and overpowering, that it can hardly be expected; but, were it possible to preserve the great body of the people to a certain degree incorrupt, the constitution might survive for ages.

As things are at present, I feel inclined to the same apprehensions that you are; yet, perhaps, we are too much alarmed, much may arise from favorable and fortunate events. I see Dr. Campbell (whose character you know) in his Political Survey is of opinion, that the constitution is not only at present strong enough to resist all possible attacks, but, in all speculative probability, will continue invincible for many ages; that our measure of luxury is by no means full or overflowing, nor are we yet nearly arrived the ultimatum of national elegance, riches or strength; and, that our corruption is only the thermometer of our growing consequence, not the index of our decline.

What you mention as to the character of ministers, and the designs which actuate them, I believe in general to be very just, yet I cannot tell how it is, it may be simple, but I feel myself

---

* Was, not Atticus Maurice Moore? Moore lost his office as Judge by the action of the Legislature. Out of wounded pride did he wish to prevent the organization of any courts? Iredell, it seems, was anxious to preserve the province from the anarchy that must inevitably attend the want of courts; but, the whole matter is involved in such obscurity that I may not express a confident opinion. It is known that Moore on one occasion used the signature "Atticus."

biassed to think that Lord N——th rather labors under political error, than any consummate depravity of intention. The accident befallen Mr. Oliver he ought to have expected.* As I readily allow, and am pleased to find that the people have, in general, behaved more orderly than was to be dreaded; so I do think, the military have observed a propriety of conduct and strictness of discipline which does both them and their commander much honor.

I see you will make me sing my Palinode, with regard to Mr. Pitt: let me see after it then!

Think not, I beg you (and I know you will do me this justice), that I allow any nationality to influence me from his opposition to Lord B——te; or the remarkable distinction in comparing their administrations: the latter's character as a politician I heartily despise and disesteem.

I readily confess to you (candidly, but at the same time ashamed of it), that I have never given *due* serious attention to the examination of Mr. Pitt's character; nor am I sufficiently informed, of myself, to determine upon his merits. The truth is, my ideas have been biassed by habitudes with people indisposed to him, more than formed upon any regular and minute investigation. At the same time that I allow that *I* have been influenced by a Scott, a Smollet and a Gordon, permit me just to think it *possible* that your passions may have carried you a little into extremes.

Once thoroughly warmed with gratitude and admiration (in such case the prompt and generous propensities of a noble mind), you may, in some degree, have yielded to the general voice, without a thorough and cool examination; and, is not the name of Mr. Johnston's place Hayes? Eh!

I cannot help remarking that every sentiment of him, or every speech of his that consists with *your* idea of his character, you immediately conclude genuine; and every thing that is inconsistent with it is deemed false, forged and malicious. I won't say that the speech in the Carolina paper is certainly, or even probably, his: yet I think there is no exterior proof against it; the manner is well hit off, and the circumstance of the statue is so much one of his peculiarities (to my deeming), that it rather *makes for* its genuineness; besides, he has all along condemned the mode, though approved the principle of the present American opposition. The speech of Mr. P. which you have favored me with, is indeed a pretty rhetorical defence; how far a just one is a different question. It may, perhaps, be quite consistent that

---

* Peter Oliver, brother in-law to Governor Hutchinson—Chief Justice of Mass. Impeached by Assembly in 1774. He soon after went to England, were he died, 1791.

---

the same man should enter upon the guidance of measures essentially restricted in the modus operandi—in a manner the most contrary to his principles and the happiness of his country; that he should undertake the guidance of public measures, clogged with what he had so often harangued against; as the most absurd, depraved and impolitic principle; "a millstone which would sink whatever ventured, burdened with it into the ocean of affairs, &c.;" and that the same man should decline his office, because not implicitly obeyed, when demanding, with arbitrary hauteur, that his almost exhausted country should be *headlong* plunged into a new war with a powerful nation, and that that war should be begun by such a measure, an example of which would to God had never disgraced the British annals; the taking their ships before a declaration of war.

The review you mention, I have heard to be a panegyric wrote by a partisan; what the author gives as a character of Mr. Pitt, is only an eulogy, a kind of apotheosis.

Were I to enter into the investigation of this (Mr. P.'s) character, I would first consider his whole political conduct, in the extent of his career, and see if one *continued line* of well-marked, generous and constant patriotic virtue contoured the whole of it; and, then decomposing it, and viewing it in parts, I would examine if he has never exchanged parties but when parties changed principles; if his steps have been eagerly and devoutly directed after fame, or, if he has only endeavored so to act that fame might follow him. I would carefully distinguish his characteristic; if a great man as well as a great minister, or great politician only, or only a great rhetor of popular parts, successful rather from the fateful turn of events, than from the wisdom of his designs. I would particularly examine, if his plan were wise and probable, and the determinations proper deductions from the causes; how the means were proportioned to the end, and calculated for their expected effects; if the probability of gaining that end was, in general, greater than the risk of misfortune; if probabilities were properly balanced, and the advantages probably to be reaped proportional (in as far as prudence might judge) to the losses which might possibly accrue. To his colleagues, to the successful admirals, generals, &c., I would assign their parts of the fame, and attempt to discern how much was *solely* his own; and, if the most approved servants of their country, in his ministry, were the election of his penetrating genius, or owing their employments to the recommendation or protection of others; first discovered and called forth under him, or by former ministers. I shall weigh, also, if the advantages obtained, or possible (considering the political system of Europe), to have been ob-

tained by a peace, were, or could have been, any compensative retribution of the expenses and losses of the war. 100,000 citizens destroyed, and 70 millions of expense or debt incurred *mostly* under his ministry, was of high account.

It is said a man's real character is best learned from his private life; in *some* degree this may be applicable to the point in question; in so far, especially, as regards his title to be esteemed a *great* man; perhaps too in distinguishing the grand springs of his politics. I would not, therefore, entirely neglect examining into his private life, (through the conversation of those who have had best occasion to know it, and from such anecdotes as are well authenticated as the nature of the thing will permit,) if, on the one hand his deportment has been solid, equal, generous, prudent, cool, unambitious, and uniformly honest; or, on the contrary, superficial, inconsistent, interested, capricious, fiery, ambitious, or doubtful. I would strenuously endeavor to draw all my deductions and determinations from the simplest and plainest account of facts, and the most impartial history of his administration, not from impassioned and partial representations, and by *no means*, from party writings on either side.

Throughout the whole of the examination, I would sedulously guard against my passions, prejudices and prepossessions, and consider the matter naked and unadorned; reflecting that the best minds are often most subject to be biassed in *favor* of a character; our passions, particularly in youth, being warmly impelled from their own generous complexion, to the belief and admiration of virtue; and once favorably affected, our imagination tinges every thing with its own color, and bodies forth every action in its most virtuous appearance. This influence, though often unattended to or unperceived by ourselves, acts upon us in proportion to the warmth, openness, and good affection of our tempers.

Having by the above, or similar methods, (which your conception will readily point out,) and with such or such like caution, analyzed the whole, I would carefully combine the result, into one general character,—compare that with what I had before conceived, and, at length, finally *determine* upon the merit of it.

It is not to every one's judgment I would confide, even after all this has been done; but, I pay no other than a sincere compliment to yours, when I assure you, that if you have so deliberated to your own satisfaction, I will readily acquiesce in your determination.

I must repeat it again; what you signify to me as to an openness of communication, is perfectly agreeable and flattering to me. My silence on political matters has not proceeded from any close interested prudence; for where it could possibly offend or prejudice me, perhaps I have been more open than my friend might have wished, (but, therein I have only paid a just consideration to my own character, and that with which I was connected. Friendships which are not founded on reason, as well as affection, can never be steady or permanent,) but the cause has been, that, as my sentiments have all along coincided with the general voice, at first from the general constitution of my political principles and turn of mind, and *now* from the determination of cool, ample and deliberate inquiry, confirming and exalting the former conceptions, I was afraid that, in the circumstances I stand, unnecessarily exposing my sentiments might be deemed imprudent, and by the many who know me not, might be considered as an act of insinuation; an illiberal and ungenerous court paid to popularity. However, I have scribbled something on the great object of contest, which, if I remember, I will bring in with me. I have a good deal more to say, but I am tired, and—confess it, you are too. So, good night.

A. NEILSON.

The first Congress of delegates, chosen and appointed by the several colonies and provinces in North America,* to take into consideration the actual situation of the same, and the differences subsisting between them and Great Britain, was held at Carpenter's Hall, Philadelphia, Sept. 5th, 1774. The delegates from North Carolina, took their seats on the 14th. The following is so much of a letter from one of them, as is now legible. Mr. Iredell, during the whole course of his life, not only preserved copies of all letters, of any consequence, written by himself, but all that he received; these were assorted into various bundles, neatly made up and tied with red tape, each letter endorsed by him with the proper date and the name of the writer, so as to facilitate references. His son, the late Governor Iredell, permitted many persons, making historical or biographical researches, to examine the papers in his office. In this way, doubtless, many valuable documents have been purloined or mutilated. One individual so far abused his unsuspecting confidence, as to take a *great many* out of the State, even after an application to take a *few* from Raleigh had met with a decided denial. Among those thus taken were letters of a purely domestic interest, some of modern date, and others written by young ladies. A motive for their selection, other than the gratification of an impertinent curiosity, cannot be conceived; a gentleman would have respected them as sacred. Of the papers referred to, enough to fill a small trunk are now

* Elliott's Debates, Vol. I.

in my possession, through the courtesy of a friend, as a loan. They have never been restored to their rightful owners.

PHILADELPHIA, 31st Oct., 1774.

I had a very disagreeable time of it till I arrived here, since which, I have had but little health and less spirits.

The Congress broke, up on Thursday last, their proceedings are now in the press, part of which is published, and which I now send directed to myself as postmaster at Edenton. I have the pleasure to inform you that they are generally approved of here by all ranks of people; the Germans who compose a large part of the inhabitants of this province are all on our side; the sweets of liberty little known in their own country are here enjoyed by them in its utmost latitude. Our friends are under apprehension that administration will endeavor to lay hold of as many delegates as possible, and have them carried to England and tried as rebels; this induced the Congress to enter into a resolve in such cases to make a reprisal. I have no fears on that head, but should it be my lot, no man on earth could be better spared. Were I to suffer in the cause of American liberty, should I not be translated immediately to heaven as Enoch was of old?

I consider myself extremely happy in the good opinion my friends at Edenton have of me. I wish I had merit to entitle me to it. They have my grateful acknowledgment. I am much pleased with Miss Nelly's* letter, and am sorry I have trifled away so much time as not to be able to answer it by this post.

Dear sir,
Your obedient friend and servant,
JOSEPH HEWES.

* Miss Nelly Blair.

CHAPTER VIII.

LETTERS FROM T. IREDELL, NEILSON, A. IREDELL, SIR N. DUKINFIELD; IREDELL AND POLITICAL SUMMARY; LETTER FROM IREDELL; LAST SPEECH AND FLIGHT OF THE GOVERNOR; LETTER FROM A. IREDELL; "PRINCIPLES OF AN AMERICAN WHIG;" LETTERS FROM HEWES AND MRS. IREDELL; POLITICAL EVENTS; LETTERS FROM HEWES AND NEILSON; PROCLAMATION; LETTERS FROM JOHNSTON; CONGRESS AT HILLSBORO; LETTERS FROM JOHNSTON, NEILSON, AND HEWES. ÆT. 23–24.

ST. DOROTHY'S, 8th Jan., 1775.

DEAR NEPHEW:—I received your favors of the 31st Oct. and 17th Nov. by Capt. Dunlop, whom I will endeavor to see before he leaves the Island, and will be glad to have it in my power to be of use to him.

I am concerned to find you so full of politics. I am sure they can be of no use to you as a king's officer, at the head of the Customs in the province you live in. The people of America are certainly mad—do they expect protection from the monarchy of Great Britain, and will they not yield obedience? Must there not be a sovereign power lodged somewhere to make laws for the good of the whole, and would you have that power lodged with Great Britain or her Colonies? But the truth is, Liberty is only the pretence, and unlimited trade, though destructive to the Mother Country, is what the North Americans drive at. The manufacturers of France and Holland are to be supported, and not those of our own country—the former are also to be your grocers, &c., &c.—and why? because your merchants can make more by trafficking with them than with Great Britain. In short, the whole continent seems to me to be under the direction of mercenary men in trade,—and worse hands it cannot be in, for they judge of every measure by their account of profit and loss, and it matters not to them how destructive their schemes are to the general good, provided the balance is in their favor. I protest to God I would rather live in Turkey than in North America, where a man is obliged to give up his free agency—must think with the mob or have his person or property torn to pieces. The

Mother Country has hitherto treated the North Americans with lenient measures, considering they are in a state of absolute rebellion. She will never give up the Right of Taxing Trade—the ports and havens belong to the monarchy, and a British Act of Parliament will and must determine on what conditions imports and exports shall be permitted. The late Lord Littleton you speak so highly of was for enforcing the Stamp Act, and so were many of the most sensible men in England—not that they approved the measure, but they foresaw what has since happened. Let me desire you will keep yourself perfectly neuter in these disputes, both in words and actions, unless you choose to see yourself adrift with it—may be a family at your heels. I received from you some former letters relative to Charles which I answered. My last letter to you was dated Sept. 10th, by the Martin, Robt. Lennis, Master. I shipped two puncheons of rum, and inclosed you a bill of lading for them. A copy of that letter inclosing a second bill was sent by the Sch. Neptune, Capt. Hainey. The arrival of which letter I think I ought to have had an account of by this time, or indeed sooner, if the Captain is not turned patriot and gone a coloneling with your two puncheons of rum. I am glad to hear you and my niece are well; pray make her my most affectionate compliments. I had a letter from your mother some time ago. I observe with pleasure you allow her £40 a year. I will endeavor to send her something in the summer to enable her to live with decent frugality, which the situation of my own affairs has hitherto prevented. They are now something better than they were, and every year I think must mend. I am, with much truth, dear James,

Your most affectionate uncle,
THOMAS IREDELL.

NEW BERNE, 17th Jan., 1775.

DEAR SIR:—I have been obliged to write you very curt of late. Nash now only waits for the letter. The Governor arrived here last Sunday all in good health.* I suspect there will be an assembly, so you and Mr. Johnston may be greasing your boots by next month—however, mark, I speak with *caution* on state affairs, and pretend to no *particular information.* I hope that by this time I may give Mr. J. joy of a son and heir.

What shall I tell you! Lord Camden said on hearing of the American Congress, that he would have given half his fortune to

* Gov. Martin had gone on a visit to the North, Sept. 1774, perhaps, to confer with the late Gov. Tryon on public affairs—possibly to watch the Continental Congress.

have been a member of that which he believed to be the most virtuous public body of men which ever had or ever would meet together in this world. And so adieu, in haste, &c.,

A. NEILSON.

Mr. Jas. Iredell.

London, Queen Square, Jan. 31st, 1775.

Dear Brother:—Not having as yet heard that the American Congress have prohibited the correspondence of an Englishman, I am now sat down to extort from you, by a long letter, an acquittal from that opinion which, I doubt not, you have long since entertained of my remissness and negligence. Though unfortunately for me, at the time I wish to triumph over such an accusation, the inclosed letter bears evidence against me ; for by the date of that you will at first blush discover that it should by this time, that I am writing a cover for it, have been in your pocket at Edenton. Yet as I doubt not, though you are counsel against me, your candor will permit me to lay those facts before the court which will, I flatter myself, fully assert my innocence ; so I don't despair of proving myself undeserving of the appellation of negligent. Know then (and though what I am going to say has not undergone the solemnity of an affidavit, I trust you will believe it nevertheless) that the letter from my mother came to Malling whilst I was there during the holidays ; it was impossible for me to send it, till I came to town, and when I arrived in London I was willing to take the opportunity of a cover to ask you, my sister, and Charles how you all do. I have now taken the first opportunity, and to do you all the honor in my power, have taken a sheet of foolscap, a new pen, and (though I say it who should not say it) the ink is not much amiss. Gilt paper, perhaps you may exclaim, would have been more respectful ! Perhaps so, dear brother, but as it would not contain enough to tire you, and as it is not stout enough to travel a journey so long as that to you, I thought if I gave you my cap it would answer the purpose better. What do you think ? Pray are you become patriotic ? *I see by the newspapers the Edenton ladies have signalized themselves by their protest against tea-drinking.** The name of Johnston I see among others ; are any of my sister's relations patriotic heroines ? Is there a female Congress at Edenton too ? I hope not, for we Englishmen are afraid of the male Congress, but if the ladies, who have ever, since the Amazonian Era, been esteemed the most formidable enemies, if they, I say, should attack us, the most fatal consequence is to be dreaded. So dexterous in the handling of a dart, each wound they give is mortal ; whilst we, so unhappily formed by nature, the more we strive to conquer them, the more are conquered ! The Edenton ladies, conscious, I suppose, of this superiority on their side, by former experience, are willing, I imagine, to crush us into atoms, by their omnipotency ; the only security on our side, to prevent the impending ruin, that I can perceive, is the probability that there are but few places in America which possess so much female artillery as Edenton. Pray let me know all the particulars when you favor me with a letter. By a letter I received yesterday from my mother she informs me that she received a letter from you about three weeks ago, wrote the day after you returned from the county courts. How d'ye succeed as a counsellor ? I dare say extremely well. By your attending them, I suppose, the office of Collector requires but slight attendance. Pray inform me, when you are so good as to answer this, of every thing respecting Charles. Is he to settle in Carolina ? or what prospect has he of succeeding in life ? I am most materially interested in all his concerns, and feel myself anxiously solicitous of his being comfortably established in some employment. I am much indebted to him on the score of correspondence, and wish to pay him his demand upon me, but at present I am bankrupt in all epistolary subjects, and therefore unable to pay his debt, without which, I frankly confess, I have no right to expect a receipt in full of all demands. I sincerely hope my sister is as well as I wish her, which is that she enjoys her health as well as I do. From the lively picture you drew of her in one of your letters, I am often enabled to converse with her, and even the ideal conversations between her and me, have afforded me so much satisfaction that I can't help wishing it was in my power to enjoy real ones. Sometimes I make Charles and you of the party, and as I wish to do every thing completely, desire to know whether I may make more additions to the party. My mother informs me you and my sister have been kind enough to invite her to Carolina. You will receive her answer from herself. Though to be at such a distance from all those for whom I have so tender a regard, is not what I could wish, considering merely myself, yet as I am confident she would be considerably more happy and easy, in North Carolina, than she is in England ; sensible, too, of the mutual pleasure it would afford both you and her, I cannot but express my hopes that she will embrace the opportunity you have offered her. What will become of Tommy ? I don't know—my mother has not said any thing about him. My most ardent wishes are directed equally towards you all, and I enjoy as much satisfaction from the recollection of your happiness, as I should had it happened to me. You may perhaps wish to know what legal books I now study. I have read Blackstone's Commentaries over once, and then went over a little book, the title of which is Doctor and Student—a very old, but at the same time a very intelligent book ; and some of its doctrines are now exploded. Yet it is by no means even now out of repute, as it lays down with great judgment the principles of the Common Law. I am now reading Blackstone's Commentaries over again, and, by the Sergeant's direction, shall peruse as I proceed in him the authorities which he cites, so that in them I shall be informed at large of what he has only abridged. I am summoned by the little remains of paper now left, to conclude this tedious epistle. My most affectionate respects and love wait on my sister and Charles, both of whom, and also yourself, I hope enjoy a happy series of health. Beg you would excuse the many blunders and inaccuracies of this letter. I wrote it without care, and have therefore the more occasion to ask pardon. My mother and Tommy are well, as is also, dear brother,

Your most affectionate friend and brother,

ARTHUR IREDELL.

P. S.—You asked me in your last to acquaint you with my opinion of those who are now at the top of the profession. The first opportunity I shall do all in my power to satisfy you on that head. Till then adieu.

---

* On the 25th Feb., 1774, fifty-six ladies of Edenton subscribed a paper pledging themselves to sustain the resolves of the Provincial Congress, &c., &c. Am. Arch. 4th Series, Vol. 1, p. 891.—*Wheeler.* Many years ago there was found at Gibraltar, enamelled on glass, a picture representing the ladies of Edenton destroying their tea. The picture was sent to Edenton by an officer of the U. S. Navy ; its execution was so good that many portraits were recognized.—*Wheeler.*

New Bern, 4th February, 1775.

Dear Sir :—I have yours dated the 27th ult. I really could not say a word with the Chronicle, having happened just to stroll into Tomlinson's store, as the Postboy was going off. I am exceeding sorry to hear of Mrs. Iredell having been so much indisposed, and sympathize with your sufferings on that account. I flatter myself that by this time she is quite re-established in her usual health.

You ask me if I think Lord Camden did indeed say as I wrote. Upon my word I don't doubt it. The human mind strains to it every instance which can cherish a confidence of public and generous virtue in mankind, and finding few such at home it naturally seeks them from abroad—adopting and believing in them with a sort of energetic impassioned sentiment. You say nothing of the news from the northward—indeed you scarcely need. I fancy all liberal minds alike deplore the unhappy, the *impolitic*, the inhuman violences of the people. The ground is now entirely changed. From argument it is appealed to the most illegal and unconstitutional conduct—contrary to natural justice—the first great principle of all politics, and in the highest degree irritative of the essential characteristic national spirit of that people with whom it ought to be the general wish to be again cordially united. Such measures give great additional strength to the enemies and opponents of the real American cause ; it enables them to represent the Colonies as unjust, licentious and ungovernable—indisposes or even drives from among their advocates many good and moderate men as well as those who have keen and delicate sensations of political subordination and decorum, and those who are vehemently actuated by whatever seemeth to their high spirits affecting the national " Punto d'honore."

I need not mention to you the transactions from which I dissent ; you will have seen the grand articles in the newspapers—indeed I wish I could send you a *number* of New England papers which I have lately been reading, and which show a spirit to the northward I formerly had no belief in, and such as in my humble thought no true friend of liberty and just government professing allegiance to the sovereign and attachment to the mother country can vindicate on *principle.*

Such there are—and can it be believed—who seem to have naught but independency in view,—full natural freedom to form constitutions of their own—for which purpose and to serve private ambitious ends, discord, dissensions, every horror, civil war, are to be means. Good God ! is there not a political wisdom as necessary in the conduct of public life as prudence is in private manners ? Because it may not be consistent with the general combination of government to permit us that latitude which the few or even say the many think we should enjoy, shall we therefore reject the *essential* advantages we reap from such combination ? So long as America is in the situation of Colonies of Great Britain she to be sure will not enjoy all the advantages which *may* and will be enjoyed by her in a different and future situation ; but such considerations I apprehend to be disjoined from the present case. And that if Americans *cannot* have the first lot of political freedom and happiness, it notwithstanding would be foolish to reject the second and next best. And that because they cannot possibly have all they claim—that cannot militate against their taking what political necessity may allow and political prudence may prompt them for a period to bear with.

The Postboy is hurrying me, being in the room. I cannot have time to explain me. I throw myself on your liberal construction—indeed this is a subject on the principles of which I imagine all liberal minds think alike, and all prudent ones the same on the modes and circumstances of it.

Adieu, compliments, &c., &c.,
A. NEILSON.

MR. JAMES IREDELL.

N. B. Be careful. *People here talk of your being very warm.*

Though thus kindly warned from the Palace, where the Governor was already combining the means of suppressing by military force the rebellious spirit of the Province ; and though the voice of monition from that uncle from whom he might expect fortune, sounded in his ears, Mr. Iredell moved steadily onward in what he esteemed the path of duty—not rashly, but deliberately, and with a full knowledge of the probable consequences to himself. His personal sacrifices were destined in after times to add lustre to his patriotism : the gloom that soon darkened his path served as a background, to project more prominently his virtues. His course was well known to the Governor. Here, had he been timid, was cause for fear ; but his heart was already beating the march by which heroes rush to combat.

NEW BERN, February 18th, 1775.

DEAR SIR :—I am favored with yours of the 10th current—which pleases me infinitely ; the sentiments it contains are liberal and moderate, decent and truly spirited. You have done me the most candid and friendly justice and favor, in the construction you put on the expressions in my last. God forbid that I should think public wisdom or policy any more inconsistent with the most liberal and truest regard for liberty than private prudence is (in its proper nature) with the most liberal, ingenuous and ardent virtue. Though at the same time from the common abuse of both words they are both extremely liable to misconstruction. In short it appears to me that the most zealous friends to government—and such must be friends to liberty and the constitution—must approve of your political principles as contained in your last, and any difference that could arise behoved to respect the idea of the degree of provocation, the necessary combinations of government suitable to the gradation of empire, the infallible course of political things, and the fitness of measures not only to what should be, but also to what may be, or in the words of Aristotle, " Non enim solum Respublica, quæ optima sit, considerari debet, sediretiam quæ constitui posset, præterea quæ facilior, et cunctis Civitatibus communior habeatur. (Lib. 4 Pol.)

As to myself I deem it will be sufficient to say that the *great* part of the sentiments communicated to you at Edenton are (in so far as they are practicable) my *reasoned* principles.

You wish to attribute the errors of the popular leaders to the northward to other causes than wickedness. I am loth as you are, my dear sir, to putting the worst construction on motives, and to introducing the word wickedness into political discussions. But this much I believe, (that is so far as I can be convinced of such a matter on circumstantial evidence,) that many of them are independents in their wishes and republicans in their principles, and more so in their passions.

Hah! you think people at New Bern should not speak of you, and why the deuce should not they speak of the great men at Edenton with like freedom that the people at Edenton speak of our great men here ? Say ? *Why they say that you are hot as Tybalt in the play, and although some accuse your manner more than your mind, yet upon the whole they agree that you are to command the first troop of the Edenton Light Horse.* So your servant, Captain—a very pretty travelling name by my faith.

Your most obedient humble servant, Captain Iredell,
A. NEILSON.

P. S. Mr. Johnston will show you a pamphlet I send him. Compliments to the ladies. I am happy to hear of Mrs. Iredell's recovery, and thereupon congratulate you and her. B. will be with you in two or three days. I shall write Mr. J. by him. As the post calls cannot at present, but send you the pamphlet. It is the last come.

Sir N. Dukinfield to Iredell.

MANCHESTER, 26th March, 1775.

You must conclude, my dear Iredell, that I have been very long in answering yours of the 27th September, which I received in January. I have frequently intended, and as often been prevented doing it, and indeed till this morning, for some weeks, your letter has been lost, and I accidentally found it among some papers where I did not expect ; but now let me discharge this debt, though I fear not so satisfactorily as you may expect or I could wish, for there are few matters in my knowledge which can afford subject for a letter to you. I am not at all a ministerial man in this great dispute between England and America. Sometimes conciliatory measures seem to be uppermost and then forcible ones are resolved on. There is a regiment of Light Dragoons ordered to be ready for embarkation with some regiments of infantry. I sincerely wish some method to restore a reconciliation could be hit upon. I should be very sorry to have a commission in a regiment destined against the Americans. It would be to me the most disagreeable service I could be sent on.

I have for a long time past been endeavoring to make myself acquainted with the duty of a commission which I have been wishing for and have at last obtained—that of Adjutant to the regiment. 'Tis the busiest and most active in a regiment when properly attended to and executed, and I shall use my endeavors to go through it with satisfaction to my commanding officers and honor to myself ; how far I may succeed depends upon uncertainty. The time for our leaving Manchester draws near, though we are not yet ascertained of it, but do not expect to stay more than three weeks ; we shall then go to Worcester. The commission of Adjutant will confine me very much with the regiment—if not entirely so. I'm sure I can't recollect whether I wrote to Mr. Pearson when I did to you, but I think 'tis most likely that I did ; I keep not the least account of those matters, and trust a good deal to memory ; I seldom forget what business I write about. Upon what terms are the Governor and our friend Lancelot ? I expected he would have succeeded me in the council—nor have I had any account but from you respecting that matter ; but where are Palmer and Jones ? are they returned or have they likewise vacated ? I received a letter a few days ago from Mr. Pearson in which he tells me that Mr. Bodley is dead. I think that compliments of congratulation are more proper than those of condolence to be presented to Mrs. Bodley on the occasion. I have not heard a word in any letter about Mr. Pollock's family. How do they do ? Is Mrs. Hutton alive and unmarried still ? As you do not mention it, I conclude you have not yet any family. If I was married I should not wish to have children soon ; but 'tis all chance I believe. Are you employed by Mr. Dickenson, if so, you may perhaps be engaged against me very soon, for I returned a draft he made on me for £32 for two reasons ; the one because he charged me some years' interest on his account which he might have been paid when I left the province, if he would have complied with my request; and therefore I think it a very improper demand ; and the other reason because I could not spare the money. I wrote to Mr. Pearson to pay it, and if he was obliged to it, he must sell one of the negroes. I hope to hear no more of the matter, but that 'tis settled. I'm damned poor I assure you. I wish something could be done with my plantation to bring in some money. I hope Dickenson will not misunderstand the letter I wrote him and abuse me, if he does I wish you would endeavor to reconcile him, if you think I deserve to be defended. He can't think that I don't mean to pay him, but I must do it in a manner most convenient to myself ; if he had written me before, I should have given the same orders for the payment. I have, indeed, desired Mr. Pearson in several letters to settle the account, which he thought was overcharged ; but I would rather pay a little than have a dispute. You'll think I have no inclination to enrich you lawyers. I'm now in mourning for an uncle who died a fortnight ago. I beg my best respects to Mrs. Iredell, Mr. Johnston's, Mrs. Dawson's, Mr. Jones', Mr. Pollock's and Mr. Buncombe's families, and to my good friend Hewes. I wish I could say family to him. I am, my dear sir,

Your affectionate (though indolent with respect to letter-writing) and sincere friend,
N. DUKINFIELD.

Iredell to Mrs. Iredell.

NEW BERN, 31st March, 1775.

MY DEAR HANNAH :—I had the great pleasure of receiving your letter by your brother, and am extremely obliged to you for it. I hope, now you have begun so very kindly, you will not disappoint me by any discontinuation. Mr. Hewes and myself arrived here on Tuesday afternoon, after a very agreeable and fortunate journey, for we met with no difficulty at the ferries, though had we made any unncessary delay we certainly should. Your brother, Mr. Jones, &c., came here the next afternoon, perfectly well, as they still continue to be. Mr. John Johnston is not yet come, as indeed are very few members. It is thought Col. Harvey's proclamation will rally them by Monday. It is quite uncertain whether any thing, or what, will be done. If you should see any of our gentlemen, pray, let them know, they shall not go uninformed of any thing that is material. My eyes get better, and I am as well as I ever was in my life. I beg you will take very good care of yourself, and go abroad as soon as possible. You know what Dr. Lenox told you, and I hope, after escaping from so dangerous an illness, you will not risk the being ill again for want of following his advice. My happiness, I truly assure you, my dear Hannah, is entirely centered in yours, and if this is in any manner affected mine will be in a very great degree. I am much obliged to Nelly for her intention to write, and hope she will not always neglect it. I have not it in my power to write to her now, but propose it by Harry Montfort, who talks of going to Edenton, Monday or Tuesday next, so that you will probably receive that letter before this. But I was determined to avoid all accidents, and leave you in no kind of suspense. It is a mode in which I have most cruelly suffered myself. Mrs. Berry is extremely well. He looks worse than I have ever seen him, having been sick most of the winter. The boy is a charming one, and promises to be as big as Georgy, and he will certainly be much handsomer than his father. I have seen Miss Howard; she has not the least pretensions to *handsomeness*. She is the very picture of him and is very *chatty*, and I believe sensible.*

I must conclude for the present, my dear Hannah, with every tender wish for the continuance of your health, which I again repeat I beg you will take great care of, and with assuring you that almost every moment of my time is employed in anxiously thinking about you, being with unalterable truth, esteem and affection,

Ever, most tenderly yours,
JAMES IREDELL.

N. B. Tell Sappho, Andrew says his sister is well, and he is a very good boy.†

April of this year was full of stirring events: it witnessed the convocation and dissolution of the last Assembly under the Crown; the flight of the Governor; and the downfall of the royal authority in North Carolina. The Assembly convened on the 3d of the month at New Berne; and at the same time and place Col. Harvey's revolutionary Provincial Congress commenced its session. Mr. Iredell's brothers-in-law, Messrs. Samuel and John Johnston, were members of both bodies. Mr. Iredell was not a member, yet he promptly repaired to New Berne to watch the course of events; it was a period of intense excitement, and he was not the man to fold his arms when interests so grave were to be determined, and stakes so momentous were to be hazarded. That he was esteemed an useful coadjutor by the Whigs is apparent from the following letter: His Excellency if he had smiles for his adherents, had only frowns for those whom he regarded as arch-conspirators. In political contests as in actual warfare the hatred or fear a man inspires in his enemies is strong proof of fidelity to his friends, and zeal in the cause he espouses.

* Chief J. Howard. † Andrew—negro-boy in attendance on Mr. Iredell.

Iredell to Mrs. Iredell.

NEW BERN, 4th April, 1775.

MY DEAR HANNAH:—I was extremely disappointed just now in not hearing from you by Mr. Hearing. Mrs. Dawson wrote to your brother, and kept her letter for any chance opportunity. Why did not you, my dear girl, do the same? Information from a third person is very unsatisfactory. It does not entirely remove suspicion. I assure you at this moment I am uneasy about you. For heaven's sake do be watchful. If you will ask Mr. Smith to acquaint you of opportunities I am sure he readily will, and if you can only write me *one* line I beg you won't omit it. I did not know of Mr. Knox's express till after he was gone. He was coming himself to me, but met Jack and sent him, and by a cursed mistake I did not hear of it in time. I should have wrote by the post, but that I did by Mr. Brimage, who promised to send the letter to Dukinfield, and I knew of this opportunity. This made me more indifferent about the post, though I did write to go by it, that I might avoid all possible accident, but unluckily missed it. I wrote to you and your sister by Mr. Brimage, and inclosed the letters to Mr. Pearson, to whom Brimage promised immediately to send them. All is uncertain yet about politics. The Governor has just made a speech, a copy of which I will endeavor to get and send you. He is the same man as to *private shyness*, and has extended it to me. I have not yet had the honor of an invitation, nor expect it. If I was entirely at my liberty I would never more go near him. Mr. Hewes and Mr. Hooper went to see him, and have been served in the same manner. Your brother had not even the offer of his hand. The man that made the offers for your and your sister's land is a man of little property at present, and who lives at a great distance. Nothing can be done with him, but I mean to go in with your brother John to see about things, and to bear him company. You need not doubt that I shall return with all possible dispatch. It is really impossible to express my anxiety about you. I hope you are not without similar feelings. * * * * But this is the lot of human life. Every blessing has it attendant evil, and in proportion to the happiness of a matrimonial union is the distress even of a temporary separation. But, my dear Hannah, let me again beg, you will alleviate it as much as possible by inquiring, and employing others to look out for opportunities, and writing me by them. My eyes have been a little troublesome, but are almost entirely well. In other respects I have been as hearty as possible. I will not forget the land Betsy McCulloh spoke of. Mr. Kenan is not yet come to town, but is every mo-

ment expected. Poor Mr. Worth I am afraid is by this time gone. I can't help writing wide, but think notwithstanding I have wrote a good deal. Private news I have none of. Mr. Berry has been quite unwell last night and to-day, but we hope it is only owing to a cold. Everybody else is extremely well. I augur no good from the business of the Assembly, but am not warranted in any probable conjecture. I am ever, my dear Hannah,

Most truly and affectionately yours,
JAMES IREDELL.

On the 4th of April Gov. Martin addressed to the Assembly his last speech, to which the House replied with great dignity and firmness.* The proceedings of the Continental Congress were heartily approved, and the appointment for a second time of Hooper, Hewes and Caswell as delegates to that body by the Convention sanctioned. On the 8th the Assembly was finally dissolved by proclamation.

The Provincial Congress gave their assent to the association entered into at Philadelphia, Oct. 20th, 1774, their representatives being present to make a report to their constituents; and formally returned their thanks to their delegates for their services. The same delegates being reappointed, and a future meeting provided for, the Provincial Congress adjourned on the 7th. News of the blood shed at Lexington and Concord, on the 19th, added fuel to the popular excitement. Meanwhile the Governor, alarmed for his personal safety, busily endeavored to fortify his palace, and to raise a military force among the Cross Creek Highlanders, and the Regulators. On the 24th Alexander Gaston,† Richard Cogdell,‡ and other Whigs, while the Governor and Council were in session, surprised his artillery, and bore it off in triumph. The last act of the Council was one of piddling vengeance, striking out of a commission of peace for the County of Pitt the names of six obnoxious individuals. Governor Martin, apprehensive of further violence, attended by his Secretary, and a few of his councillors and friends, fled for refuge to Fort Johnston, at the mouth of the Cape Fear, where the guns of the fortress and the presence of the Cruiser sloop-of-war seemed to promise protection: the hope, however, was delusive, for in the subsequent July,§ the harassed and agitated official, hearing that

* Jones.
† The father of the late Judge Gaston, who, though retired somewhat from the public gaze, as an orator, scholar and jurist, was not surpassed by any of his contemporaries.
‡ Grandfather of Hon. George E. Badger, who since the death of Webster, has not his equal at the Bar of the Supreme Court of the United States.
§ July 17th.

" a certain John Ashe, who lately resigned to me his commission of colonel in the militia of the county of New Hanover, has presumed to influence and conduct a body of armed men of the said county, and of other adjacent counties, to the most daring and treasonable outrages," and that the said John was on the left bank of the river, in full march for the Fort, incontinently resolved on mischief, hastily removed his head-quarters on board the ship-of-war. While the valor of the Governor thus took counsel of prudence, Col. Ashe applied the torch to his Majesty's buildings.

ARTHUR IREDELL TO J. IREDELL.

April 25th, 1775.

DEAR BROTHER:—Your favor of 11th Feb., so justly reprimanding me for my negligence in not writing oftener, I received three or four days ago, and have made a resolution, as unalterable as the laws of the Medes and Persians, never more to offend in the like manner. And as the criminal when at the place of execution said,—" Well, whatever crimes I may have been guilty of, I have this consolation on my side, I never went into a church without pulling my hat off;" so I, whatever misdemeanors I may have committed, have this to console me, as soon as ever I have offended, I have always been sorry. Among many other circumstances that have concurred to effect this repentance, one, very cogent I'll assure you, I have just now perceived, and that is, my being prevented from interrogating you in the following manner, by being a culprit myself,—Pray why do you write so often? why are your letters so long? and many other pretty concise questions, which I am determined, by behaving as I should do, to have it in my power to ask you. But perhaps you'll say, I am a man of business. You know I can't spare my time as well as you. All that I'll allow, but I must insist on your acquiescence in one thing which I shall propose, and that is, that though you may have a better excuse to make than me, yet as I am as ardently eager to hear how you are, as you can possibly be to hear how I am, the disappointment is equal, though not the plea. I, about a fortnight ago, was at Bath, where I accompanied Mrs. Kempe, and where we stayed rather better than a fortnight. My mother, I am happy to inform you, is perfectly well, and assures me is always so. Tom is a charming boy; remarkably complaisant, and so obliging that every body is delighted with him. He too enjoys a fine cherubimical plumpness in the face, which distinguishes the youthful favorites of Hygea. Thus you see, every body I have seen, has been the picture of health. Be

VOL. I.—16

assured it gave me much concern to find that my sister has been an exception to that rule, which I was in hopes was not only universal on this, but also on your side of the water. I shall take the liberty therefore (as nobody is better pleased with things moving in unison with his own wishes than myself) to set Mrs. Iredell down by this time as perfectly recovered, which I hope you'll confirm in your next letter. Every obstruction to the universality of that rule being now removed, I may now contemplate in the manner I wish, the inexpressible happiness I feel at so flattering a circumstance. Long may you all continue so! Long may I be blessed at so flattering an idea! As I suppose my mother acquaints you with all her affairs, it will be needless for me to enter into a minute and tedious detail on that head. Mr. Pettigrew,* to whose care you some time ago consigned some letters to me, I had but once the pleasure of seeing in England, upon which account I am afraid he has conceived but a mean idea of my politeness. During the time I was at Bath he called at the Sergeant's chambers; but I, being absent, did not see him, he having, as I learned at his lodgings (where I called as soon as I was acquainted with the honor he had done me of a visit), left England. I understood from the porter of the lodge, who saw Mr. P., that he called upon me to know if I had any commands for you. Perhaps Mr. P. may not have heard that I was out of town, and consequently may have thought it odd my not taking the least notice of it. I beg if you see him, that you will be kind enough to give my compliments and thanks to him for the trouble he took, that he may not look upon me as totally divested of manners. I have made some inquiry, since I received yours concerning Capt. Scott, hitherto ineffectually, but by Mr. McCulloh's directions, I am in hopes my future search will be more successful. When I see him, you may depend upon it, I shall not let slip so good an opportunity. I yesterday dined at Chelsea with my uncle, who was then tolerably well, but had been complaining. He seems to take it ill that you don't write oftener to him, and thinks you neglect him. Pray don't be guilty of remissness; a fault of which I am sure you have great sensibility, by the feeling manner in which you chastised me. My cousin and a Mr. Boyd dined there likewise; the former of whom mentioned his having received a letter from you, of the same date with mine. That meeting was so fortunately contrived, that it furnished me with an opportunity to you—for Mr. McCulloh said he

---

* C. I. Pettigrew—subsequently a clergyman of the Prot. Epis. Church, equally distinguished for learning, ability and piety. At his death he was bishop elect of North Carolina, being the first ever chosen in that diocese. He was uncle to the eminent lawyer of the same name, who has so long stood at the head of the bar at Charleston, S. C.

---

was going to send a packet on Wednesday, and would convey a letter from me to you; so that within a short time (if Scott sails soon) you will receive two letters. In neither of them any thing, I can prophesy, interesting or entertaining. But however no evils are so justly showered upon mankind, as those which they themselves pray for. You will see by the enclosed papers I am willing at the same time to obliterate every trace of negligence from my character, by writing my sister (who you tell me thinks me negligent) a letter, and by gratifying her wishes with the fee simple of my ode. Though without conveyancing, yet with livery of seizin, which in this case I believe, there being a good consideration, will be effectually valid. At Bath, who should I see but your old school-fellow and acquaintance, Mr. Skeffington Thompson, whose person and address were not a little admired there. He has travelled a great deal, and acquired a very polite and pleasing behavior. Seeing the world, is surely the best kind of suds to wash away the barbarism a man naturally possesses: for though living in society he would not cut your throat; yet it by no means follows, as a consequence, that being trained in a civil state, he should not be rude and unpolished in the highest degree. Like steel, whose polish, when preserved, emulates the diamond, a man who has the happiness of a genteel and numerous acquaintance, contracts a bewitching politeness, which captivates, and must ever do so, all who converse with him, and is as superior, in every respect, to one whose behavior is tough, obstinate and stubborn, as that metal is in its artificial, to what it was in its natural state. But you will be looking about for Skeffington, and will suppose you have lost him. I beg your pardon for taking him away, but will call him back again. He has engaged me to correspond with him.* His eldest brother has, as I understand, lately got an estate—how I can't tell—I believe left him; but however that may be, he has it, and my mother acquainted me that Mr. S. T. was now adopted by the father, and will succeed to his estate, his brother being so amply provided for. He has some thoughts, nay, I think it absolutely determined on, of standing candidate for an Irish borough at the next general election—he expects great opposition. The current talk of Bath was (with some truth I fancy) that he and a Miss Osborn were to be joined in the holy bonds of matrimony. Whether or no any cold water has been thrown on the affair I can't tell, but I have not heard of the celebration, or of any preparation for that happy state. He is now gone over to Ireland to obtain, I suppose, his father's consent. Miss Osborn is extremely handsome, as report tells me, for I have never seen her. Can you require any proof of it, when I

---

* Mr. Thompson, it is thought, was probably related to the Earl of Massarene.

---

tell you such was the power of her charms over him, that he who came to stay two or three days, was chained there so many months. He surely has not made a bad choice, so fine a girl with several thousands portion. Now to be sure, by this time, you have perceived your error in supposing you had lost sight of Skeffington, and are so tired of him (under my influence at least) as to wish I had never recovered him again.

What are you Americans about? For God's sake, if you are determined to destroy your own peace, don't break in upon ours too. You may probably retort upon me my own argument, and exclaim, why do you Albions oblige us to proceed to these tumultuous proceedings? Nay, don't ask me! It is not in my power to resolve you. It is not for me to enter so deeply into the politics of these times as to be able to give you my sentiments: sentiments which will either be railed at by Sir Absolute Tory or Sir Oliver Whig—either of whose resentments I should wish to avoid. Perhaps you may expect me to deliver my opinions to you. You do; very well, then I have no objection. I profess myself absolutely, without equivocation or mental reservation, a downright honest whig, though I wear my own hair—that I hope you will not esteem an objection. I can assure you this, if it was one I would immediately cut it off, and not only be a whig in theory, but also in practice. Were you to hear me rail at the Jacobites, to Mr. Orton, who lives at the Sergeant's, and who is a most vehement one, you would require no farther proof. The most opprobrious terms my invention can select, I lard with the bitterest invectives. My principles being of this cast, coincide, I should suppose, in some respects, with your continental sentiments. It is well we agree in some particulars, for I can assure you, I differ in many with you Americans, and I do not wish to be a downright enemy. But enough of politics.

The most notorious and violent bribery has been proved in the House of Commons, since the last election, that was ever known. The committee appointed to examine the Hindon election, have rejected the sitting members upon evidence of the most flagrant violation of the laws against bribery,—as has also the one appointed to examine the Shaftsbury Petition. A bill is to pass the House against the former, incapacitating 188 voters—and in the latter it is said 140 odd are to be treated in the same exemplary manner. There is no mention about the candidates who procured their seats so scandalously. In my opinion they should have been the first scourged by the rod of Justice, but as the adage acutely tells us, "kissing goes by favor." The Shaftsbury committee showed the greatest perseverance imaginable, for they sat some weeks—a very considerable time, in the discharge of so disagreeable an office, as seeing the most notorious infringement of the laws, in the grossest perjury. My mother has as yet received no money from Africa. Poor Frank's effects, she was told, would be faithfully paid her, but she has never obtained a farthing. One cargo was sent over to Africa, and poor fellow! he was dead before it arrived. All these are great drawbacks upon her. One thing I am inexpressibly happy in, and that is, through all these misfortunes my mother preserves her spirits. I believe the exertion she is under a necessity of complying with, conduces in a great measure to effect this. And she seems as well, nay, I think better, than I remember, though she tells me, when she is by herself, a retrospect of past occurrences makes her sad. You never tell me how you are yourself—why don't you? Nor whether I may flatter myself with the appellation of uncle.

I am, dear brother,
Yours most affectionately,
ARTHUR IREDELL.

On the 20th of May, many citizens* of the county of Mecklenburg, in convention at Charlotte, made their famous Declaration of Independence, the boldest step as yet taken in the colonies. This, though the first public expression of opinion on the part of any considerable portion of the people of North Carolina, was not in advance of, but in true accordance with the general inclination. This was no idle bravado; it was made by men, who, subsequently, so maintained their words by deeds, as to win for their region the name of the "Hornet's Nest." The following imperfect article was written, I presume, about this period, though I cannot determine its date with certainty; it is fragmentary, mutilated—parts hopelessly lost. It is believed to be original for the same reason that other essays in this work are credited to Mr. Iredell—because in his handwriting; and because of the strong evidence furnished by interlineations and verbal alterations.

THE PRINCIPLES OF AN AMERICAN WHIG.

1. That mankind were intended to be happy, at least that God Almighty gave them power of being so, if they would properly exert the means He has bestowed upon them.

2. That the affections of the Deity are universally, not partially extended, and that the purposes of this Divine Providence

---

* Jones, Wheeler, Foote, Caruthers, &c.

are calculated for the happiness of the greater, rather than the smaller number.

3. That men united in society originally, or submitted to a continuance of any authority obtained over them, from a sense of the advantages derived from a regular government, where the joint force of individuals should be exerted to obtain right and justice for each, and punish the crimes and injuries which might be committed against the interest of the whole, or of any of the individuals who compose it.

5. That it is now a principle (to the honor of the present age) not to be questioned among Britons, that government being only the *means* of securing freedom and happiness to the people, whenever it deviates from this end, and their freedom and happiness are in great danger of being irrevocably lost, the government is no longer entitled to their allegiance, the only consideration for which it could be justly claimed or honorably pledged being basely and tyrannically withheld.

6. That in pursuance of this principle, in practice long known, though not in speculation so generally acknowledged, in most of the countries in the world there have been continual struggles either to reduce the power in being to a proper and secure boundary, or to oppose the uncovered and open attempts of tyranny.

7. That the true principle of resistance being, *that the public freedom and happiness are eminently endangered*, it is a point of little concern to the public, who feel grievous oppressions, whether they proceed from an enormous abuse of the powers in being, or a flagrant usurpation of new ones, either being contrary to the sacred trust reposed in the government, and if permitted, essentially destructive to the people.

8. That there is, however, a difference arising to the subjects' duty, from the nature of the two attempts, that always ought to be attended to, viz., that in the one case, many dutiful applications, and much forbearance on their part, ought to be shown before they arrive to the last stage of opposition, because it being an evil incident to the form of government they have acknowledged, they ought patiently to bear it, until it proceeds so far as to interfere with the great law of common happiness Nature has ordained for all mankind, and to which all men have a right ultimately to refer their political situation.

But in the other, it is the duty of the people not to submit a moment to any acknowledgment of the power; they must take no part actively or passively in its introduction; they ought indeed to try to convince the governors of their error (as possibly it may arise from their inattention), and not withhold their allegiance in other constitutional points, unless the one assumed is so pertinaciously retained, or its importance of so critical a nature, that the public welfare renders it indispensably necessary.

9. That the above principles seem not only rational in themselves, but have ever (in practice at least) appeared to influence the people of Britain, who on critical occasions have equally sacrificed any power admitted by the constitution to the masses of sufferers from its unjust exertion, and opposed by the most vigorous (and commonly by the most successful) efforts the introduction of new and unwarrantable authority.

10. That the ultimate principle of the people's obedience can be no other than mentioned above, arises from the imperfection of our nature, and the necessity of our situation. All power may be abused, and even perverted to ends quite contrary from those which were the purpose of its introduction, yet some power, and large discretion also, is necessary to be invested, for the public benefit, with persons partaking of all the infirmities, and who may be infected with all the vices of humanity. They are intrusted from a confidence *that they will do right ;* and in governments that are well modelled, other motives besides public virtue are afforded to them as an encouragement to do so: but the people may be deceived; men's real interest may be neglected, and the wild purposes of power and ambition sought to be gratified at any hazard. In this case the people are not to be ruined; they will not be so. They will say to their oppressors: " We employed you for our good; you conspire to our destruction. The object of this government is the happiness of the governed, not of those who govern merely. We will in no respect lose sight of this great object. God, nature, honor, duty, our and our children's happiness, all forbid it. Whatever may be the consequence, we will employ the—   *   *   *   *   *

In the case of several different countries, even headed by our common sovereign, it is far otherwise. The internal regulations of each may be so managed as not to interfere with the others (especially when the sovereign has a common control over all by his negative), and it is reasonable to suppose that in all *foreign affairs*, where there is a common interest, they will generally, if not always agree; and this is the more to be expected, when one country, in a great general system, such as commerce, has almost an absolute sway. It will at least be sufficient, in all probability, to guard against any other spirit, *than that of a just resentment against injuries*, and no country can be a moment free, where such a power is not ultimately to be dreaded. It is to be observed, the political maxim so strenuously urged is calculated to avoid *anarchy* and *confusion ;* as applied to us, it can have no other meaning than to cause a general active co-operation in all mutual concerns, beyond the internal government of each (for these, in other respects, have a separate scale to act in, co-ordinate with their power). It is therefore a matter of *convenience*, not of *necessity*. If the measure proposed should be good, and evidently useful, it would probably be assented to; if it should not, where is the justice, that *one* legislature out of *twenty* should say to the others: " You shall do as we please; we care not if it is disagreeable or prejudicial to you, it is agreeable to us. How dare you dispute the wishes of a people among whom your fathers once lived ? We will compel you to be more dutiful childen, and you shall be corrected for your past misbehavior." The people of Britain require that in order to make their government more easy, we should resign all our rights and powers of acting, to them, through the medium of their corrupt delegation. We have uniformly contended that there were some rights of *so sacred a nature*, we would resign them to no power on earth; that we were willing to perform *our* part of the contract, if they performed *theirs ;* we had experienced no unhappiness from it, but what probably was introduced by innovation, and we rather chose to refer our future prospects to the operation of principles which had already produced nothing but good, than submit every enjoyment of life to their humor and caprice, to guard them against imaginary dangers, and involve us in real ones. How have Ireland and Scotland lived, together with England, under one common sovereign, and with separate legislatures? The principle drawn from *necessity* is the same, whether the inhabitants of the two countries *were* originally, and at no great distance of time, connected with each other, or whether they had no common ancestors later than the sons of Noah. Ireland indeed is subject to the same haughty claims. But are they ever exercised ? A discourse upon the Unity of Empire there, would be burnt by the common hangman. We admit there were some inconveniences attending the situation we contended for, but they formed the alloy of infinitely greater advantages, and surely any remedy for them ought to have been conducted on the basis of a general negotiation, and not violently sought by an unjust usurpation of power.

18. To all the above principles the Americans could dare to add, that they and their ancestors had ever been *used* to be free; that custom and continual usage are of a much more unequivocal nature than speculation and refined principles, which are only known to men of superior understanding, and even these frequently differ about them; that the *views* and *intentions* of their ancestors were beyond all question, and during their lives, and the lives of many of their posterity, *in practice*, at least, honorably respected; that it was a debt of honor and gratitude they owed to *them*, to see that their *views* and *intentions* were not disappointed, and they were of such a nature, that their own *interest and security* were essentially concerned in maintaining them with the most sacred regard; and that, therefore, upon the land which their ancestors hardly earned for them, and *meant to make a Land of Freedom*, in support of *real* views, and to preserve themselves from misery and dishonor, they would, to the utmost, oppose the firm barrier of *Liberty* and *Virtue* against all the engines of arbitrary power, and all the subtlety of ministerial craft.

19. That, as in most other countries which have been cursed by the unfeeling rigor of despotism, insidious arts and plausible pretences have been the forerunners of its success, so in America such arts and pretences have been very liberally used. The pretence for the first great encroachment was to provide for *our defence*. Our defence was not so tender an object of Parliament, when we stood in more need of it. It was a long time, and not till the labor and sweat of the day was over, before England interfered with her powerful assistance. Till there was a prospect of being well paid for this defence, and of making it serve to very pretty purposes, we were suffered, in a great measure, to defend ourselves. I speak of our internal situation; for as to the other, Great Britain was equally, if not more interested than ourselves. She derived infinitely the greatest advantages from our commerce, and as she reserved the sole management of it to herself, and could make it flow into the channel most convenient for her, it was but reasonable that she should protect it. And the profits could well bear the expense. But her principal eye was on our situation within. The dangers of the war had made us better known. The Americans engaged in them with a courage and virtue that were universally admired; our loyalty to the king appeared to be of the most ardent kind; our affection to the parent country unsuspicious and unbounded; our minds endued with the most generous propension. A great people seemed rising from obscurity into dignity and reputation, and who, from the virtues they had already shown, were entitled to honor, respect, and every necessary indulgence. But these virtues excited the base passions of jealousy and envy.

At the time of the Stamp Act a difference had been taken between *internal* and *external taxation*. By the former were meant taxes out of the immediate power of commerce; by the latter such as were *within it*. The latter was more properly (when the subject was critically examined) called *duties ;* and it had ever been considered to have reference to *commercial* purposes. *Taxes* are the proper name for impositions, where *money* alone is the object. At the time of the Stamp Act this branch of the subject was not accurately canvassed ; the other was the great object of attention. Afterwards we were obliged to attend closely to it. A new and an artful mode was laid hold on to impose upon us, and it became necessary to dissect it into first principles. We did so. The result of our examination was, that this, in *principle*, in *substance*, and nearly in *danger*, was the same as the one we had been before cursed with. We had always conceded to Great Britain a right of regulating our trade, in order to make the commerce of the whole empire conduce to one great purpose, and as a kind of natural compensation for the advantage of her protection. In order to regulate our trade, the imposition of duties was on many occasions necessary ; otherwise, where *one* trade had interfered with another, the inconvenience must have continued, or been removed by (perhaps) the introduction of a greater, a total prohibition ; as for instance, in the case of our West India Islands. Duties were laid on some foreign commodities to give a superior advantage in these to the British (as it is stated by me before). But they were not totally prohibited, because our British Islands could not, it is supposed, have supplied the whole, or if they could, it would have been a means of hurting our trade to the foreign islands. At the same time had we once admitted, that the power of levying duties, *for the purposes of commerce, &c.*, is an incidental one to the right of directing that to flow in proper channels, and might at any time be converted into an indefinite power of laying taxes upon us, through the medium and under the shadow of commercial regulations, we should have been infallibly ruined. The repeal of the Stamp Act need not have been regretted. This mode would have equally answered the ends of that wise law. Our situation was such, that we could not subsist *without commerce*. The interest of England required that the commerce should be continued, and continued largely (so we were secure against an absolute want of it) ; but what security had we that all our own profits should not be exhausted by taxes, and we dependent on England even for actual subsistence ? The distinction pointed out by such a situation, however delicate or indefinable in express terms, however referring to circumstances of doubtful construction, and liable to cavil, in particular applications, is critical and essential. Our being, as freemen, was concerned in it. What other distinction could be thought of than this ? "We will not encroach upon any ancient or acknowledged power. We are sensible of the necessity of your regulating our trade ; we do not regret the vast advantages it gives you. We admit you may impose duties for this purpose ; it is in some instances necessary to do so ; we have been used to permit it. But, if you deviate from your duty—if you become ambitious or rapacious, and have no feeling for our rights, it may be grossly abused. You may pretend to lay duties *for this purpose ;* they may be really imposed for *another*. The duties may be so grievous as to make us miserable ; in all such instances, whether they are light or heavy, it will be a burthen we did not mean to be subjected to. Experience teaches us to distinguish between *objects*. We must do it ; however difficult the task, it is our duty to engage in it. So long as you confine these duties to *the purposes of commerce*, we will religiously obey them, however unreasonable they may appear : but if you impose duties on *this pretence*, when they are really calculated for *another* purpose, if we can detect the criminal intention (and in many instances it may be easily practicable), we will refuse obedience to so gross an abuse of power. Much more, when you dare to avow a purpose quite contrary to that for which alone so high a power is conceded. In cases that are at all doubtful, we shall think it our duty to submit, and this we apprehend is all the guard that can be reasonable in so dangerous and difficult a situation." Upon this principle duties, *for the express purpose of raising a revenue*, were objected to. After much solicitation all were taken off except the duty on tea. And this was retained as a badge of the *taxative power*, and in order to preserve some ground of contention. It afterwards proved a fruitful source of it. The East India Company were to be gratified in their desire of becoming mercantile engrossers of that commodity. Instead of relieving their distress by taking off this duty, before the exportations of the commodity (and no more favorable time, no more plausible pretence could possibly have ever offered for doing it, America being at that time in tolerable good humor with Great Britain, peaceably obeying every measure of government, and looking out with respect and without using any exceptionable measures, for the removal of this the only great remaining bar to their happiness), instead of doing this, I say, this new mode had every air of a governmental manœuvre to *give this taxation life*. The people were then convinced that this wretched, hankering thirst after power was again to torment them, and they were to prepare for new evils. The tea arrived first at Boston, that town so much hated for its unconquerable spirit, and early opposition to every arbitrary measure. Every body knows what was done there, and let people make the worst of that proceeding, it was an act of destruction committed *by a mob*. *Property*, not *Persons*, was destroyed. The exceptionable commodity alone was injured. Every thing else remained safe and untouched. The East India Company were injured, for their impertinent meddling, to the value of a few thousand pounds. The people concerned discovered their resentment for the perpetual attacks made upon their freedom. They destroyed *a means* that might have been fatal to it. They had been perpetually insulted for many years, by being peculiarly marked out with governmental rigor, and on all occasions treated with the most irritating opprobrium. They perhaps took this method to try what were the real views of administration, being impatient under the continual apprehensions they had of some lurking design, some wicked machinations being formed against them. They did indeed (if this is to be esteemed a crime) discover their rooted enmity to the whole schemes of ministerial artifice, and every species of unjust oppression. The consequences that followed these proceedings in England, were such as fully justified every apprehension that had been entertained of their dangerous designs. Millions of mobs have at different times done mischief in England and other parts of the British dominions ; many, much more mischief than this at Boston, and with equal defiance to government. Ireland is said to be indebted even for its famous Octennial law to a mob ; all these have, with little effort towards punishment, been submitted to as a kind of fine which the imperfection of human nature makes all free countries pay for their freedom. But this at Boston, because done *at Boston*, was much more criminal than all others. Its punishment can scarcely be told without horror. Though the act was committed by only 30 or 40, the whole town (consisting of 30,000 or 40,000) was immediately laid under a commercial interdict. No trade after a limited day (and that a very short one) of any kind, or in any degree, was permitted to the unfortunate inhabitants of that town. This was to continue till the East India demand (a sum not then noted) was satisfied, till compensation was granted to revenue officers and *others* who had *suffered* [the expression in the act] in particular riots specified, till the town should be adjudged to be in a state of peace, till the governor, &c., should certify these circumstances to the king in Council, and till his Majesty should be pleased in consequence to restore the town to its former privileges. This was the substance of the famous *Boston Port Act*. The particular provisions to effect these purposes were full of the arbitrary spirit of the principle, and this act is singularly marked by the condescending meanness of Parliament, in making an express clause for the malicious and unworthy purpose of injuring one obnoxious individual. This law, violent as it was, was followed by another still more so ; one calculated to obviate all future difficulties, and extending to the inhabitants of the whole province. This was by proceeding to the radical business of forming a *new constitution* for them. The old was thought to leave too much power in the people ; the new one was intended to turn the scale in favor of their prerogative. It was not in form very materially different from others on the continent (though there were some very exceptionable regulations in it), but it would do well to introduce the precedent till leisure could be found, and men prepared for the establishment of one more excellent. The same authority that now gave the prerogative *much* power, might by and by give it *all ;* Parliament kindly intending to take the trouble of judging always for themselves, and not being biassed by any tender connections with the people from making it severe enough to keep their unruly spirits in order. This was their preventive remedy against the necessity of new Boston Port Acts.

Next in order and dignity followed the law " for the impartial administration of justice in the province of the Massachusetts Bay," an act equally arbitrary with the foregoing ; framed upon a pretence that justice could not be impartially exercised on soldiers, by a people those soldiers were sent to humble, and yet transferring it to the persons by whom the soldiers were employed, and who certainly would be very little inclined to redress any sanguinary excesses in support of a power which blood alone could carry into execution : allowing complaints to be preferred by the obnoxious subjects of a country undergoing every stigma of infamy and persecution, against the favorite executors of the prevailing measures, in that country, which had unfeelingly and wantonly dictated them, and who were evidently, and would probably always be, inclined to consider any abuses of the power they granted, as proceeding rather from excess of zeal for their service, and as such deserving of reward, rather than as a brutal violation of duty, meriting the most exemplary punishment ; allowing indeed an alternative to the crown officers to send the accused persons either to Great Britain or one of the other colonies for trial, though no man living can believe this last would in any case have been chosen, unless some one colony had been found base enough to desert the interest and protection of the rest, and had carried its meanness so far as to be equal in fiery and unjust resentment against suffering virtue to the people of their *MotherCountry ;* leaving the accusers to depend for the transmission of evidence on the contingency of witnesses being persuaded to leave their country, their families, their friends, their business, to risk themselves on a great ocean (6000 miles going and returning), to support an accusation which they might be sure would be heard with prejudice, and stand very little chance of success; when they themselves would be pointed at, perhaps insulted by the populace, and at once suffer the excruciating torment of having their testimony questioned, their persons reviled, seeing cruelty and guilt triumph over innocence and virtue, and being themselves driven home to inform their countrymen, if they ever again chanced to see them, that they were a miserable, an injured, and a disgraced people. Upon this footing was left the chance of procuring justice against the worst actions of the soldiers to the people of the Massachusetts Bay. These were the restraints on the malicious and tyrannical conduct of the bloody instruments sent to execute the new laws. Thus, in the very instant of its formation, was their new constitution violated; that constitution whose lenity was so extolled, but whose favorers could not have the common decency to conceal, even for the useful purposes of deception, the infernal spirit of tyranny they possessed. But even here the vindictive spirits of administration could not rest. They dreaded the rising resentment of America; they feared the powerful efforts of virtue; they knew they could depend on nothing but meanness or want of power in America to give their acts success; and as they could not rely with confidence on the former, they hoped by a complete system of tyranny, to astonish and subdue us, without our finding any means of defence. The additional scheme was a little curious.

The arrival of all these thundering regulations (which very quickly succeeded one another) caused the greatest alarm in America. Here was a full avowal of tyranny in its most frightful form. We did not view the storm merely at a distance; it was almost at our very doors. These measures affecting one colony only, made no difference in the general indignation they caused. They all were interested in the *principle*. Their rights were nearly the same; an invasion of one was equivalent to a declaration of war against the rest. Heaven had placed them in the neighborhood of each other, as it were, for their mutual defence; such an union was absolutely necessary for their safety; *singly* they might be easily crushed; *united* * * * *

The Continental Congress reassembled in Philadelphia, May 10th.

HEWES TO IREDELL.

PHILADELPHIA, 23d May, 1775.

DEAR SIR:—I know your anxiety to be informed what is doing in Congress, and wish I was at liberty to gratify it, but the secrecy enjoined the members puts it out of my power to give you any information worth your attention. You will see by the papers which I send to Mr. Smith, the advice that is given to the people of New York relative to their city; to those papers I must beg leave to refer you for news; you will find by them the New Yorkers have taken an active share in the opposition; a tory dare not show his head amongst them; the cry of liberty is irresistible in most of the colonies; a military spirit has seized all orders of people; this city is full of armed men; they have now 28 companies of foot and two of horse; each company consists of 68 men including officers; they are called out twice every day to learn the military discipline, and I can assure you some of the companies perform it equal to any regular troops.

Capt. Gillis makes so short a stay here that I fear I shall not have it in my power to send any shoes by him. I have urged the shoemakers to get them done, but they had so many orders not completed when I applied, that I fear the ladies and yourself must wait till the next opportunity for them. I received the shell per Capt. Gillis, and shall get it made into a box for Miss Penny as soon as possible. The ladies have always my best wishes, make my compliments acceptable to them. I have wrote to Mr. Johnston, so has Mr. Hooper; if he is not at home when Gillis arrives, I desire you will open our letters to him, and read the contents before you send them.

I am, very respectfully, dear sir,
Your obliged and very humble servant,
JOSEPH HEWES.

I beg you will excuse haste. I now trespass on Congress hours.

On the 14th June, General Washington was appointed Commander in Chief of the Continental forces. The battle of Bunker's Hill occurred June 17th.*

Col. Harvey having died, Edenton, the residence of Samuel Johnston, became now the head-quarters of the Whig party.†

MRS. IREDELL TO ARTHUR IREDELL.

MY DEAR BROTHER:—You cannot imagine how much pleasure your agreeable letter gave me. I think myself much obliged to you for it. You delayed performing your promise so long that

* Marshall.   † Jones.

I was afraid you were so much of a courtier as never to have thought of it after it was made. All the amends I can make for a supposition so injurious to you, is an assurance that I will have more confidence in your word for the future. I thank you very much for the ode—I think it very pretty, and am highly pleased with it. I am as passionately fond of receiving long letters as you or any other Englishman can be, and would, with all my heart, write you one, if I could, on purpose to entitle myself to one in return, but I am such a dull mortal that I can find nothing to fill it up with that would be the least entertaining to you. The drum which is now beating while our soldiers exercise, drives every cheerful thought from my mind, and leaves it oppressed with melancholy reflections on the horrors of a civil war. However, do not be uneasy about your brother. He is too much respected and loved to be in any personal danger. Every body who is acquainted with him esteems him—his good sense and goodness of heart entitle him to it. Most of the king's other officers, through their own indiscretion, lead disagreeable lives here at present. I beg, my dear brother, you will write often to me, and with all the freedom of a brother, and then you can never be at a loss for a subject, and I promise to be pleased with any you shall choose. I will not trespass much longer on your time, which, I dare say, is seldom so triflingly employed as it will be in reading this. I must desire you to consider me as a sister who has a very great esteem and affection for you, and who would think herself very happy could she flatter herself that you thought but half as favorably of her as she does of you. I often please myself with the hope of one day seeing you and our dear revered mother, but I am afraid these unhappy differences will, for a much longer time than I could wish, suspend that pleasure.

Your affectionate sister,
HANNAH IREDELL.

During the whole of the spring and early part of the summer of this year, the Safety Committees for districts, counties and towns, were actively employed; they formed associations to sustain the Continental Congress, and by persuasion, or the constraint of public opinion, compelled a subscription almost universal; they collected powder and weapons, and enforced by word and example that retrenchment of expenses which was necessary for the crisis. The Committee of Wilmington, by their vigilance, confined the Governor closely to the decks of the Cruiser, stopped his supplies, and very effectually interrupted his communications with the interior. North Carolina was not a principal in the quarrel, but simply an accessory: high was the spirit of her people—ardent their enthusiasm. They could be only affected indirectly or remotely by the wrongs done Massachusetts. No selfishness actuated them. Their moral sense revolted at the injustice of the British Ministry. Their indignation was very audible at Mecklenburgh; very visible in the planting of flags, the roll of drums, and the rapid organization of military companies. So ready were her citizens to volunteer, so eager to master the drill and tactics of war, that without hesitation they gave permission to Capt. Charles C. Pinckney, and other officers from South Carolina, to engage recruits for the defence of that province.* It is believed that no people were more forward than those of North Carolina, in the cause of the revolution. If any thing could have added to their excitement, it was supplied about this time by a report, commonly accredited, that Gov. Martin contemplated an appeal to the slaves, and designed to glut his vengeance with the horrors of that most terrible of all calamities, a servile rebellion. There is no doubt that such was part of the Governor's projected plan for the subjugation of the province, but even he, subsequently, shrunk from the infamy of its execution. His friends spurned at the charge, and treated it as a calumny. Slaves were regarded by the British, during the whole course of the war in the South, as personal property, and constituted a part of the plunder which the retiring wave of invasion, eventually, bore from our shores. At this period what province had a council with greater wisdom to contrive, or more energy to execute, than North Carolina? Johnston was its undoubted head; Iredell and Hewes his brethren and constant advisers. Surely much of the success that smiled upon the province, the temper of the people raised just to the right pitch, and the triumph at Moore's Creek, must be ascribed to the three patriots who at one time met in Mr. Johnston's office in Edenton, and at another assembled in his parlor at Hayes. If either of these three gentlemen had his equal in purity and ability in other sections, what single point could boast a triad so cordially united, and possessed of such moral and intellectual power?

HEWES TO IREDELL.

PHILADELPHIA, 8th July, 1775.

DEAR SIR:—I have sent by Capt. Hatch's Sloop ten pairs of shoes for yourself, and six pairs for Mrs. Iredell and Mrs. Dawson. I did intend to have sent double the number for the ladies, but could not prevail with the workmen to get them ready in

* Vid. Proceedings of the Wilmington Safety Committee
VOL. I.—17

time; the demand for women's shoes is so great that the makers cannot complete half their orders; when a tradesman has made a thousand promises and broke them all, he has one answer ready for every charge: sir, I have been under arms in the field. I have sent to the Committee of Correspondence at Edenton a copy of a letter from General Gage to Governor Martin, also a copy of a letter from Governor Martin to Henry White, Esq., in New York; the first was sent to the Congress from the Provincial Convention of New York, the latter from the Committee of this city; by them you may see what part our Governor intends to take in the present unhappy dispute.

The Congress some days ago took into consideration the state of the trade of America; all the arguments that could be made for and against shutting up the ports on the 20th of July were duly attended to, and after mature deliberation they determined to let the matter rest on the Association Agreement entered into last Congress, so that the ports will remain open till the 10th of September next, unless shut sooner by the people themselves in their separate committees; a resolution was entered into against the two last restraining Acts of Parliament which you will see in the newspapers.

The humble Petition and Remonstrance from the New York Assembly has been treated by the King and Parliament with the same contempt and neglect as they treated that from the Congress, last winter. It is said the Ministry desired the Agent to inform the Petitioners that they might apply to the army and navy at Boston for an answer; this circumstance has induced many of the tories in that colony to renounce their principles.

It is certain that Administration have endeavored to prevail on the Canadians and Indians to fall upon our frontiers, and that they had in contemplation a scheme to set our slaves free, and arm them against us; by the fishing and restraining acts they meant to destroy our trade and starve us; they have made mean concessions to all the powers of Europe to prevent our getting a supply of arms and ammunition; they have sent a formidable fleet and army to seize our vessels and cut our throats; they then charge us with rebellion, because we will not believe that they have a right to make laws to bind us in all cases whatsoever. Strange that we should be deemed rebels for an article of faith,—after all this, they add insult to injury, and tell us we are all poltroons and cowards.

Close attention to business, bad health, and a weakness in my eyes, all contribute to prevent me from writing so much as I otherwise should do. I write in pain, and can scarcely see to read what I have written.

I have sent to Mr. Smith a number of newspapers, some magazines, sermons, articles of war for the Continental Army, and a declaration of war from the Representatives of the United Colonies of North America; they are all intended for the amusement of my friends. My warmest good wishes and best compliments attend you and the ladies of my acquaintance; desire them to pray for, dear sir,

Your most obt. humble servt.
JOSEPH HEWES.

JULY 8, 1775.

DEAR SIR:—I am indebted to you for sundry favors. I am sorry that you should make any excuse, and should be more sorry if I imagined you really thought that I could deem any thing a trouble which could serve you. On the present occasion, I am vexed extremely that I cannot return you what you want. When your first letter came, more than a fortnight ago, an express was sent to the Governor with a number of blank registers to be signed—Mr. B. having neglected to have any done before his Excellency's departure. In continual expectation of their being returned, to my utter disappointment and astonishment, they are never yet come to hand. Your express I detained until yesterday morning, as well from my expectation of these papers from the Governor as of Mr. Berry's arrival. Yesterday I detained him, hoping that the post or some other messenger might bring what was desired from the Governor. But all in vain. I can no other ways account for this than by supposing his Excellency unwell, or his despatches stopped by the way—as many letters to and from him have been lately. Even the mail, that arrived yesterday from the southward, had been broken open and searched. And I, myself, have received four letters opened, and miss others. I have twice wrote, lately, to the Governor about the registers, and send off another messenger to-morrow, by whom I shall also write on the same subject. So soon as they arrive, an express will be *sent you* with the number wanted. Berry has none, neither has Palmer any. You desire me to write you our town politics; they have been of too injurious and contemptible a nature. No gentleman can think of them for a moment but with the highest indignation. I cannot prevail with myself to dwell on them.

Now is the time for every man, with his hands upon his heart, to declare his sentiments and take side in the present unhappy war. All nice distinctions, minute objections, useless reflections on the past—all metaphysical wire-drawn theories—

vague general reasoning—must now give way to resolute, active determination on the immediate, real, simple, though essential, crisis of the dispute.

Born and educated a Briton, my soul is elated for the glory of my native country—ever honored, ever revered! For the just rights of that *dear* country, in support of her honor and constitutional power and splendid glory, and those of my respected sovereign, I will cheerfully risk every thing held dear by man, and with a generous and dutiful ardor, sacrifice life itself,—that life which has been lent me but for their service! Every advance to pacification, magnanimously and greatly made by B., has now been madly and contemptuously rejected by America. The designs of the demagogues now stand naked and disclosed in all their real deformity. A friend to liberty, I am also a friend to just authority; and an enemy to anarchy and all the scheme of unjust ambition. The dissolution of the connection between Britain and America, which is essential to the true interest of both, I think of with horror. After every patient, proper and possible determination, I am steadily determined. Firmly and resolutely attached to my sovereign, my country, and the true interest of America, I will, by every method honorable, dutiful and requisite, support the Constitution and supreme authority of England against, what appears to me, a violent attempt at independency, and a rebellious opposition in America. As I am sincere in my sentiments, and candid in my declaration, so may the Eternal Ruler requite and prosper me! I beg my thanks to Mr. Smith for his care of my letters, which I have received. To Mrs. Blair, Mr. Johnston, and their families, I request to be particularly remembered. *For Mr. Johnston, I have the truest esteem and regard. In these times, in spite of my opinion of his judgment—in spite of myself—I tremble for him. He is in an arduous situation: the eyes of all—more especially the friends of order—are anxiously fixed on him.*° I am honored and pleased by his letter. I shall answer him soon; in the mean time, assure him that, from my own knowledge, nothing is more infamously false than the aspersion some cast on the Governor, as hinted in his letter. If men of any character, who know him, so much as suspect him capable of harboring such an idea, they, in the party-man, forget the gentleman.† Adieu.

Yours, with real and unalterable regard,
A. NEILSON.

If the gentlemen of the committee at Bath stop this letter, they will please to forward it after perusal.

---

* This passage is not italicized in the original.
† The allusion is, I think, to the charge that the Governor intended an insurrection of the slaves.

The Provincial Congress had requested Mr. Johnston, in the event of Col. Harvey's death, to assemble a new convention.° On the 10th of July, a general order was issued by Mr. Johnston, summoning the freeholders of the different counties to elect delegates to a Congress to be held at Hillsborough, on the 20th day of August. On the 8th of August, from the Cruiser, Governor Martin issued a proclamation, termed by Jones his "dying effort." It was immediately provoked by Mr. Johnston's circular, and violently denounced the "traitorous contrivers and abettors" of the Congress.

JOHNSTON TO IREDELL.

HALIFAX, 14th August, 1775.

DEAR SIR:—I enclosed a line to Mrs. Johnston, under cover to you, this morning, but had not then time to write to you. Mr. Jones† and myself have had a very agreeable journey thus far, and propose leaving on Wednesday morning: he is much better than when he left home, and I keep my health very well. Andrew Miller and Col. Jones set off this morning, and have promised to procure us lodgings; so we shall be very snug there on this occasion. They have chosen a committee in Orange, and every thing is likely to go well, though a report prevails here that Hunter, the Regulator, threatens to bring a thousand men from Guilford to interrupt the Convention—but I do not apprehend any such thing, and should be perfectly happy could I know every body below was well. I have likewise heard, since I came here, that the Governor had sailed from Cape Fear. Remember me affectionately to your family, Mrs. Dawson and her children, and believe me always,

Dear sir,
Your affectionate brother,
SAM. JOHNSTON.

The Congress duly assembled at Hillsboro', on the 21st of August. On motion of Richard Caswell, Samuel Johnston was elected President.

JOHNSTON TO IREDELL.

HILLSBORO', August 22d, 1775.

DEAR SIR:—I thank you for your letter by Mr. Charlton, who never reached this place, and, I expect, is on his return

---

* Jones.   † Thomas Jones, of Edenton.

home. We have a very full meeting, some from every county in the province, all extremely well disposed to the common cause. They have done me the honor to appoint me their President—a very troublesome office, I assure you, and one that I would gladly have declined had it been practicable. We are under no apprehension from the Regulators, a committee is appointed to treat with them, and we have hopes of making them useful members of society by removing and obviating some scruples which, it is said, they have with regard to an extra-judicial oath imposed on them by Governor Tryon. Colson has surrendered himself, and has made his submission to this *Congress* (as we now style ourselves), with every appearance of humility and contrition—even to the shedding of tears, and has promised for the future to exert himself with as much assiduity in favor of our measures, as he has hitherto in opposition to them. Our principal debates will be about raising troops. I am afraid selfish motives influence some, but hope they will not prevail so as to disgrace our measures. I can take no share in the debates, though it will be difficult to contain myself. The delegates are all in good health, and we are tolerably provided with accommodations from the hospitality and obliging dispositions of the inhabitants of this town, and though I think the place for the town ill-chosen, yet I am delighted with the country about it—the face and appearance of it exhibit quite a new scene to me. Make my thankful acknowledgments to Mr. Smith for his obliging letter, and communicate the contents of this to him. I will write to him next opportunity, and then you must not expect a letter from me, for time and paper are too precious to write two letters on the same subject. Give my love to my sisters and the children, and to Mrs. Dawson and her children. Farewell, and believe me ever,

Dear Sir,
Your most affectionate brother,
SAM. JOHNSTON.

P. S. Booth and Duncan are still in South Carolina.*

JOHNSTON TO IREDELL.

HILLSBOROUGH, 5th September, 1775.

DEAR SIR :—I thank you for your letter of the 23d of last month, and wish I could gratify your expectations from this place, but though we have a great deal of business before us, there is very little accomplished. We have more orators than men of business among us, which occasions great delays. It is proposed to raise

* Tories.

a thousand minute men and to put the militia in training—this, it is thought, will be a sufficient defence. The ways and means of paying them and the time of their continuance are not yet determined on, neither is the plan of regulating our internal policy completed. I am, between ourselves, afraid there will be as much hurt as good done—we have not among us a sufficient quantity of virtue and public spirit; too many are actuated by little, mean, dirty and selfish motives. I have not been allowed to speak my sentiments, except on a paper, a copy of which I now send you. I was much afraid the plan contained in it would have been adopted, but in a Committee of the Whole House, though they at first seemed inclined to receive it, after hearing the reasons offered against it, it was almost unanimously rejected, and the delegates instructed not to consent to any thing of the kind in the Continental Congress till they had first submitted the plan to the Congress of this province and had their approbation. Mr. Jones mends slowly—many of the members have been and are now sick—one is dead—we buried him this evening. I hope my brother will be able to travel in a day or two. Please to make my compliments where due, and believe me always,

Dear Iredell,
Your most affectionate brother,
SAM. JOHNSTON.

This Congress placed the province in a state of military organization; provided a civil government; and issued bills of credit to defray the necessary charges of the same. Two regiments, of five hundred men each, were ordered; and, also, in each district a battalion of minute men was directed to be levied. The government was vested in a Council of Twelve, two from each district, at the head of which Mr. Johnston was placed for the province at large. Mr. Johnston seems to have acted in this capacity until October 18th, when Cornelius Harnett was elected. Mr. Johnston being appointed one of the two Treasurers of the Province, and the department of the finances needing, in a more especial degree than any other, the services of the most laborious and intelligent patriots, I suppose he resigned as President that he might the better co-operate with his colleague, Caswell, in restoring order, where order was so much needed; and in laying, with system and wisdom, the foundations of a treasury. On the 10th of September, according to Jones, (19th, according to Wheeler.) Congress adjourned.

NEILSON TO IREDELL.

Excepting, solely, Governor Martin and Judge Howard, Mr. Neilson was incomparably superior, in every respect, to any loyalist in North Carolina.

WILMINGTON, 20th October, 1775.

DEAR SIR :—I am to thank you for your last letter, which came safe to me through two committees : I have led somewhat of an unsettled life lately, which has prevented me from answering it sooner. In all the disturbances, amidst all the vehemence of party-outcry, I continued unthought-of and neglected, very properly safe in my insignificance, until an accident, of a nature so trivial, that I would never have thought it would have weighed with any other than the most contemptible, brought me forth at once, not only an object of popular indignation, but, as I have been informed, inveighed against by those who ought to judge better :—This was nothing else, than my being casually, subordinately, and, in a very slight degree, instrumental in forwarding a proclamation of government. Heavens! and this treatment from the same people whose delegate, a short time before, had recommended to them to pay all respect to civil government. At any other time, a distance betwixt me and my former well-wishers and acquaintances, in a country wherein I expect to pass many of my days, would sincerely affect me ; at present, I consider it a necessary consequence of the times. I am little uneasy at any mistaken opinion of the people : I am *intimately conscious* of having the highest sentiments of regard for their true interests, and the most inviolable attachment to the restrictions of the Constitution, and all the essentials of public liberty. But bounds must be set against that wild enthusiasm which the mind is apt to run into, in this respect ; for the Salus Populi depends, as effectually, in repressing licentiousness, as in fostering firm ideas of genuine freedom. What the thoughtless opine of my political character, I consider of little consequence. Nor, as it is the fateful, necessary course of things, is it much afflicting to me, that those who act from reflective and investigating principle, differ from me in the ideas of a complex form of government ; of the relation of its parts, their dependence, the necessary form of rule ; or in their opinion of public measures, right administration, or the due mode of subjection or opposition. All that can be expected of man, with respect to honor or dishonor, probity or depravity, is that, after making all possible use of every means of information, we should determine dispassionately, freely and disinterestedly. All this I am conscious I have done, to the utmost of my abilities : I long revolved the subject, before determining ; I allowed every due weight to every argument on every side ; I studied the theory of government in all its progress, especially that combination that exists in the British empire ; I endeavored particularly to fix what that has been from the beginning, is, and (so far as that could concern the discussion) might be, as relative to the mother country and her American colonies : On my ideas of this relation, I examined the conduct of administration in Great Britain and of opposition in this continent : Then weighing the aggregate attentively and deliberately, with all the collateral and consequent connections, I, in due time, made up the result in one precise, decisive judgment. What more can be expected of an *honest man*? Only, surely, that, from such judgment, he should act firmly, still paying strict regard to the grand principles of humanity, and distinguishing between spirited duty and illiberal violence. On occasion, I would draw my sword against the cause of men whose persons I would cherish ; whose friendship I value, and whose private character I highly esteem ! I have much more to write you, but should become prolix, and deviate into effusion ; I must prescribe myself bounds. I beg sincere compliments to Mrs. Iredell, Mr. and Mrs. Johnston and all the family, and to Mrs. Blair and her family : I remember all my friends in Edenton. The last letter I was favored with from Mr. Johnston was about four months ago, which I answered. I ardently wish for the time, when I may be, *properly*, indulged in a free intercourse with a gentleman whom I do, and have so much reason to, esteem and regard.

I am, with real affection and esteem,
Dear Sir,
Yours, A. NEILSON.

The Edenton district began soon to experience something of the consequences of war.* During the month of November, emissaries were discovered in the vicinity of the town, endeavoring to enlist slaves as auxiliaries for the royal governor of Virginia ; but the nefarious attempt was soon arrested by Col. Robert Howe, at the head of a detachment from his regiment.

HEWES TO IREDELL.

PHILADELPHIA, 9th November, 1775.

DEAR SIR :—When I came here and had conversed with the Massachusetts delegates, I found it a difficult matter to get a

* Jones.

letter sent to the Commissioners in Boston. I was informed no letter was suffered to go in till its contents had been examined by a committee, and that letters wrote by persons they thought disaffected, were sometimes stopped, though the contents were only business or compliments. Under the circumstances, I thought it prudent to open your letter, and put it under cover to Gen. Washington, at the same time requesting the favor of him, after he had read its contents, to send it into Boston, and to permit an answer to return the same way. I have not yet received an answer from him, but am in hopes it will not be long before I have that honor. I could think of no better way to get you an answer from the Commissioners. If I have done wrong I must rely on your goodness to excuse it. I can say but little on the score of politics—the present appearance is much against us and our cause. We have had no accounts from England later than the 26th of August. We are told our Petition will be disregarded; that we shall be declared rebels, and our estates confiscated; we are threatened with ships of war, troops, Russians, Hanoverians and Hessians. God knows how it will end. Some officers from Gen. Gage's army have been detected in enlisting men in the Province of New York to go to Boston; some of these recruits have been examined on oath, and declared that each of them was promised two hundred acres of land, not in the woods, but cleared cultivated land with houses thereon, that they were to be put in possession at the end of the war, when the rebels were subdued, which they were taught to believe would soon happen. We are in daily expectation of further intelligence from England, several vessels being expected here; the last ships that have arrived brought the king's proclamation. You will see it in the newspapers; it is remarkable those ships brought very few letters from private persons—it would seem as if the proclamation had deterred our friends from writing on the subject of politics. My best compliments to the ladies, and believe me to be, with much esteem,

Dear Sir,
Your most obedient humble servant,
JOSEPH HEWES.

The year closed, as regards events of importance in North Carolina, with the march of Col. Howe to Norfolk, to assist the Virginians in expelling Lord Dunmore from their territory.* Meanwhile, active agents were engaged in her own borders in preparing an explosion, whose flames could only be quenched in blood. The numerous emigrants from the Highlands of Scotland, with a terrible conviction of British power impressed upon their memories by the wholesale slaughter of battle-fields, and massacres such as attach for ever to Glencoe a tragic interest, were fit subjects to be tampered with by craft and fraud—to be moved by the hope of reward and the fear of punishment.

* Marshall.

CHAPTER IX.

LETTER FROM HOOPER; BATTLE OF MOORE'S CREEK; LETTERS FROM J. JOHNSTON AND HEWES; PROV. CONGRESS; LETTERS FROM JOHNSTON AND THOMAS JONES; CUSTOM HOUSE CLOSED; LETTERS FROM JOHNSTON AND THOMAS JONES; BRITISH RETREAT; IREDELL'S ESSAY; ATTACK ON FORT SULLIVAN; LETTERS FROM HEWES; THEFT OF UNPAID BILLS OF CREDIT; LETTERS FROM IREDELL, JONES, J. JOHNSTON, AND CHARLTON; DEFEAT OF MR. JOHNSTON; "CREED OF A RIOTER;" STATE CONSTITUTION; LETTERS FROM JOHNSTON. ÆT. 24—25.

Letter from Wm. Hooper.

PHILADELPHIA, January 6th, 1776.

MY DEAR FRIEND:—So great has been my proportion of scribbling public letters, that I have not had an opportunity to pay that respect to my private connections to which they have so just a claim—to you to whom I owe it as a duty, as well as a testimony of sincere reciprocal esteem. That day, I hope is not at a great distance, when retired from the bustle of public life, I shall enjoy all the sweets of domestic retirement and private friendship. I am weary of politics; it is a study that corrupts the human heart, degrades the idea of human nature, and drives men to expedients that morality must condemn; deep stratagems, dark disguise, fiction, falsehood, are but the fair side of the picture of a perfect politician—a Machiavel—a Hobbs—a Richelieu—a North. No, my friend; the science of politics is not to be learned in the principles of the laws of nature and nations; it is wrote only in the recesses of the minds of princes, and vice assumes another name, when it ministers to the strength and importance of the state. The black part of the character is ascribed to this, and virtues, if any there are, are the personal property of the prince.*

* This is so illegible as to admit of doubt as to the true word.

Hide the picture! 'tis a horrid one. We have met with nothing of much importance lately from the continental armies. A scarcity of gunpowder has for some time past kept them inactive; that want is now plentifully supplied, and I suppose ere long we shall hear of the happy effects. To what are we reduced that we can hear of bloodshed without remorse; and, amidst the horror of this unnatural war, derive consolation from a conquest sealed with the blood of our fellow subjects? Yes, Britain, it is the criterion of thy existence; thy greatness totters. Luxury and wealth, with every vice in their train, are hurrying thee down the precipice, and liberty shuddering at thy fate is seeking an asylum westward. Oh heaven! still check her approaching ruin; restore her to the affection of her American subjects. May she long flourish the guardian of freedom, and when that change comes, and come it must, that America must become the *seat* of empire, may Britain gently verge down the decline of life, and sink away in the arms of American sons. A fleet is begun here at the Continental expense. Should its success be great, it will much exceed my expectations. It has a formidable power to cope with; the luxury of Britain has not yet enervated its seamen. However, if this war continues, which God forbid, a navy we must have; that of the united provinces was trifling in the commencement; its increase and importance showed the propriety of it. Some small armed vessels about Boston have made some valuable acquisitions.

This city scarce feels the interruption of trade; the manufacturers, mechanics, and seamen find employment in the public works. And the merchants find means to dispose of their commodities, which are necessary to procure *the means of offence and defence*. The Eastern Colonies furnish soldiers and the necessaries for subsisting them, so that much of the Continental money will centre with them; their poor are employed and none left for clamor. The Southern Colonies will feel it first. The American army raised, and immediately to be raised, is as follows: In Massachusetts, twenty-seven battalions (i. e. New England). In New York, four. In Canada, one (Canadians). In Jersey, two. In Philadelphia, six. In Delaware Counties, one. In Virginia, six. In North Carolina, two. In South Carolina, three. In Georgia, one, besides the Provincial establishment in each province. Philadelphia is to be made the seat of action early in the Spring, so say private letters. I am extremely sorry that Pollock has been made the mark of public vengeance. I am told that he was examined and acquitted by the Committee of Safety; is it true? Oh the licentiousness of the times. Surely persecution never begot converts; such violence hurts the cause.

Remember me most respectfully to your lady and family. I

wrote Mr. Johnston, via Virginia, by an express. By a vessel which sails to-morrow for Wilmington, I wish to hear from him. Compliments to Mr. Smith, Mr. Jones, Mr. Charlton and all friends. I have only room to add, what I do with great truth and sincerity, that I am

Your sincere friend,
WILL. HOOPER.

On the 10th day of January, from on board his Majesty's Sloop Scorpion,* in Cape Fear River, Governor Martin issued a Proclamation, a copy of which is with Mr. Iredell's papers, declaring a state of rebellion; that he had erected the Royal Standard; and summoning all good subjects to rally to its support. From the 19th of July, 1775, "all our historians seem to lose sight of him." In Gov. Swain's lecture on the " British invasion in 1776," he very conclusively proves that not only the campaign of 1776 was suggested by him, "but that the entire system of operations for the reduction of North Carolina, until the retirement of Cornwallis, in May, 1781, was prosecuted to some extent under his immediate supervision." The Proclamation, of which the only copy I have ever seen is the one in my possession, is confirmatory of Gov. Swain's argument. On the 5th of February, Donald McDonald, " Brigadier General of his Majesty's forces for the time being in North Carolina," issued a manifesto, calling upon all loyal citizens forthwith to repair to the Royal Banner, in accordance with the Governor's proclamation.† McDonald's troops were to meet the Governor at Brunswick, on the 15th of February.‡ Sir Henry Clinton, destined for the chief command, was expected from New York, Lord Wm. Campbell from South Carolina, and Sir Peter Parker at the head of a squadron. The whole, united, were to advance into the interior, and crush the province of North Carolina; but, accidents beyond the ken of military forecast foiled the combinations of the campaign, and, for a time, saved the province from invasion. The Highlanders were soon assembled to the number of two or three thousand; they were animated with the hope of retrieving the past; but a remorseless fate was dogging the steps of these doomed men with a pertinacity surpassing that of their own " sleuth hound." One of their leaders was the husband of the celebrated Flora McDonald, whose services to their fallen prince invested her in their eyes with a sacred character; her presence in their camp, and her counsel, enforced by the charms of beauty and wit, exalted their courage

---

* Gov. Swain and others say from on board the Cruiser; doubtless an error
† A copy of this manifesto was also preserved by Judge Iredell.
‡ Swain.

into enthusiasm. Though ultimately trodden into the dust by the armed heel of the Briton, yet could they recall occasions, when their impetuous spirit had borne them, a resistless torrent, over the broken hosts of England. They, as soldiers, had been truly baptized in fire and blood; were renowned by their use of the claymore as the best swordsmen in the world, and now, certainly on the strong side, were flushed with the prestige of victory that attached to the meteor flag of St. George. They were marshalled by regular officers, and could not but feel some contempt for the raw, undisciplined militia of the Province. Evading the vigilance of General Moore, and crossing to the left bank of the Cape Fear, they moved rapidly down the road to Moore's Creek. About seventeen miles from Wilmington, Moore's Creek was, as now, spanned by a small bridge. The creek is narrow, but deep About one hundred and fifty yards from the bridge, on the afternoon of the 26th of February, Colonels Lillington and Ashe, at the head of a detachment of the Wilmington Minute Men and New Hanover Volunteer Rangers, had taken their post, determined to contest the passage of the Celts. They hastily threw up an entrenchment at right angles with the road: two small field-pieces were placed in the centre, so as to sweep the bridge; their flanks were protected by deflections of the swamp skirting the creek. Subsequently, Col. Caswell came up, and finding the front already occupied, drew up his forces in the rear, in a second line. The whole American force amounted to about one thousand men: they were not in military costume, but clad in simple homespun: in their hands were no muskets whose bayonets gleamed in the sunshine, but long, single-barrelled shot guns and rifles, whose range had been often proved in the deer hunt. About daybreak, on the 27th, the Highlanders came in sight of their antagonists. They rapidly formed into a storming column, with a forlorn hope of seventy-five picked men in front: their general being sick, Colonel Donald McLeod took the command. The planks of the bridge had been hastily removed. Their way was effectually barred. Fight they must. They were celebrated for their dashing onset. At the word of command, they passed the bridge; and rushed forward with the force of the hurricane. Though shattered by the fire of the cannon, they closed up their broken ranks and pressed onward, as if to assured victory, while loud cheers accompanied their advance: but now was heard the voice of Lillington, and a sheeted flame blazed along the American line, attended with a report as of thunder when it rattles amid the mountain crags. There was a moment of awful silence, in which the wind lifted the smoke, as a curtain, from that stage of death. Seldom has there been disclosed to

human eye a more appalling spectacle of carnage. In front were the dead, the dying, and the wounded—the background crowded with panic-stricken fugitives. Swift was the pursuit—the triumph was complete. Fifty were killed: among whom were Col. McLeod and Capt. Campbell. Fifteen hundred rifles; three hundred and fifty guns and shot bags; one hundred and fifty swords and dirks; two medicine chests, worth $1500; thirteen wagons with complete sets of horses, and $75,000 in cash constituted the booty. Eight hundred and fifty common soldiers, General McDonald, and many officers, were captured.* Thus was won in North Carolina, by North Carolina men, the first great, undoubted triumph of the American arms. This gallant achievement entirely disconcerted the well-organized plan of the intended campaign; and North Carolina had the honor to be the first of the provinces to repel the foe from her borders. Strange to say, these men of New Hanover, who so distinguished themselves, were content with the performance of their duty, and so indifferent to their renown that they took no measures to record their acts and assert their fame. Thanks were voted by the Provincial Congress to Colonel Caswell, who only participated in the pursuit.† The name of Lillington was omitted, who, modest as brave, submitted to the rape of his laurels. His true position, as the hero of Moore's Creek, was never assigned until, recently, at the first anniversary celebration of the battle (1856), by my accomplished friends, Hon. Wm. S. Ashe, Mr. Geo. Davis and Mr. James Banks: but meanwhile the tradition of the county took charge of his reputation, and the matrons and maidens of New Hanover would often beguile the winter nights by a popular song, whose burden was the field

" Where Lillington fought for Caswell's glory."

I trust my long digression may be pardoned. No son of New Hanover can allude to the event without kindling with honest pride, and charity, I know, will readily throw her mantle over the fault, pardoning garrulity prompted by reverence for the dead, and respect for historic truth.

February 28th.—The third Provincial Council,‡ assembled in New Berne, appointed Abner Nash and John Kinchen to meet at Charleston other delegates from the southern colonies; and to consult together as to the means of defence against invasion:

---

* Vide Swain's Lecture and the "Old North State" of the "judicious Caruthers"—Relation of the late John Larkins to Dr. James F. McRee, Senr. Mr. Larkins served under Lillington in the battle.—Statement of the late Col. Samuel Ashe.
† Caswell was a member of the Congress,—took his seat a short time after the battle.
‡ Jones.

at the same time, Mr. Johnston and Mr. Thomas Jones were designated as representatives of North Carolina to confer with the Committee of Safety of Virginia on matters of mutual interest.

JOHN JOHNSTON * TO JAMES IREDELL.

March 17th, 1776.

DEAR SIR:—I set out on Thursday after I left town last, to overtake our men on their march to Crane Creek, and overtook them near Neuse, at the house of one Sausers,† ready prepared for engagement, Col. Bryan having been robbed the night before by a party of one hundred and eighty Regulators—we were informed of this when the party of six that I was in company with was about two or three miles off from the main body, and we immediately charged and rode up full speed in order to have a share in the action, but just as we joined them an express arrived from Col. Long to inform them the matter was settled, and directed them to return; never were men more desirous to engage —when they found there was nothing to be done. However, on our return, to keep up their spirits, we raised a body of light-horse and scoured the country about Tarborough, where, we were informed, there were a great number of Tories, in particular on the Town Creek, where a body of twenty of them had assembled to defend themselves—twenty of us immediately marched in search of them, and, after going through almost impassable swamps, came upon them at a Pass where they might have defended themselves against two hundred, but the most of them, on our riding up full stride to them, quitted their arms and made the best heels they could—we, however, took twelve prisoners that night and next morning, whom we left under guard at Tarborough. I had marched that day twenty miles on foot, and was on horseback till eleven at night—the swamps were so deep that we all got wet—my horse, unluckily, fell into a hole and wet me up to the shoulders, and I remained in that condition till some time next day; till then I found myself grow, as to my health, better and better every day; I got a small cold by that night's expedition, but it is almost worn off. ∘ ∘ ∘ ∘ I should have wrote to my brother, but as I shall soon see him at Halifax, I make no doubt but he will excuse it—please to remember me to him and my sisters, and believe me to be,

Dear Sir, with the sincerest regard,
Your affectionate brother,
JOHN JOHNSTON.

---

* Mr. Iredell's brother-in-law. † Probably Sasser.
VOL. I.—17

HEWES TO IREDELL.

PHILADELPHIA, 26th March, 1776.

DEAR SIR:—By the return of our express, I have been favored with your letter of the 2d instant; I am much obliged to you for it. The letter you gave me for the Commissioners, and which I enclosed to General Washington, was by him sent into Boston, but no answer was ever returned. As I imagine you will be at Halifax, and will there see my friend Hooper, who will be able to give you all the news and politics, I shall not trouble you with any thing in that way; as to myself, I am ashamed to be always complaining, yet I must say I think myself declining fast; such close attention to business every day in Congress till three, four and sometimes five o'clock, and on committee almost every evening, and frequently in the morning before Congress meets, is too much for my constitution—however, my country is entitled to my services, and I shall not shrink from her cause, even though it should cost me my life. I send you enclosed the locket you desired me to get made for Mrs. Iredell; the jeweller was a long time about it, and has not pleased me in the execution; the letters are not plain enough. In these times, when every mechanic is employed in learning how to kill Englishmen, it is impossible to get any thing done right. I send you, also enclosed, a piece of hair-work in a bracelet for Mrs. Pollok—it is done with Mrs. Buncombe's hair, and, I think, pretty well executed. Will you do me the favor to deliver it to Mrs. Pollok, with my most respectful compliments? I have a favor to beg of Mrs. Iredell—a lock of Miss Annie's hair, if such can be had, and you will oblige me by sending it to me by the first opportunity; if enclosed in a letter by post, I believe it will come safe. My compliments to Miss Nelly—I am much indebted to her for her letter by the return express; tell her I cannot write; if she knew how much of my time was taken up on the public service and with how much pain I now write, she would excuse me for not doing it; tell her I am getting my picture drawn in miniature, and as she may never have an opportunity of seeing the original again, I shall send her the copy when it is finished.* My compliments to Mrs. Johnston, Mrs. Dawson, Mrs. Blair, Miss Peggy and all friends. Adieu, and believe me with great truth,

Dear Sir,
Your most obedient humble servant,
JOSEPH HEWES.

* The miniature, encased in gold and encircled with garnets, is now in the possession of Miss Helen Iredell, the grand-daughter of Miss Nelly Blair.

P. S. I said I had enclosed the locket, but I am so much displeased with it that I have retained it in hopes of getting it altered for the better; in the mean time, if Mrs. Iredell chooses to have hair put in it, and will send it me, with orders how it should be wrought in, I will have it done.
J. H.

At the summons of Mr. Johnston, the Provincial Congress assembled at Halifax, on the 4th day of April.* Mr. Johnston was immediately elected President.

HALIFAX, 5th April, 1776.

DEAR SIR:—I have the pleasure of yours by Capt. Hardy, and am very glad you are all well. We made a House only yesterday, and I am again placed in the chair, very much against my inclination, but there was no such thing as avoiding it. There is little done yet, except an order admitting General McDonald to go at large within the limits of the town of Halifax.† I am told he is much dissatisfied with being confined to this town, wishing rather to be at some gentleman's house in the country, and refuses to come out. Though I am told his situation is very far from being agreeable, he is very obnoxious to the people, and it was with difficulty that even this favor could be procured for him. Our wagons arrived yesterday with about 2500 pounds of powder, and drums, and colors, for the troops. I have likewise a letter from Hewes of the 20th of last month, but no news except what you have in the newspapers. He seems to despair of a reconciliation; no Commissioners were appointed the 25th of December, and the Parliament was then prorogued to the 20th of January. *All our people here are up for independence.* God knows when I shall have the pleasure of seeing you. There are very few among us capable of forwarding business—many of retarding it. I shall take care of your letters. I heard from Mrs. Johnston and the children to-day—they are well. Give my love to my sisters and the children, and believe me

Your affectionate brother,
SAMUEL JOHNSTON.

LETTER FROM JOHNSTON.

HALIFAX, 13th April, 1776.

DEAR SIR:—I have just received yours, and am very happy

* Jones.
† After the battle of Long Island, the British General proposed to exchange Generals Sullivans and Stirling for Generals Prescott and McDonald: Congress assented.—*Hildreth.*

to find you are all well. I heard from Mrs. Johnston this morning—she and the children are well.

The House, in consequence of some very important intelligence received last night, have agreed to impower their delegates at Philadelphia to concur with the other Colonies in entering into foreign alliances, and declaring an independence on Great Britain. I cannot be more particular—this is wrote in Congress. My love and compliments where due. Farewell.

SAM. JOHNSTON.

"This was the first open declaration for independence, by the proper authority, of any one of the Colonies, on record."*

EXTRACT FROM A LETTER FROM SAM. JOHNSTON.

"I must confess our prospects are, at this time, very gloomy. Our people are about forming a Constitution. From what I can at present collect of their plan, it will be impossible for me to take any part in the execution of it. Numbers have started in the race of popularity, and condescend to the usual means of success."

The attempt to form a Constitution soon developed radical differences in the political views of its members. The majority inclined to a pure democracy; the minority, under the lead of Johnston, leaned to representative republicanism, with constitutional guaranties to individuals as well as minorities against arbitrary legislation; and, in an especial degree, advocated the independence of the judiciary, secured by the only practicable mode—tenure of office, during good behavior, and election by a select body, rather than by the people directly.

LETTER FROM JOHNSTON.

HALIFAX, 20th April, 1776.

DEAR SIR:—We have not yet been able to agree on a Constitution. We have a meeting on it every evening, but can conclude on nothing—the great difficulty in our way is how to establish a check on the representatives of the people, to prevent their assuming more power than would be consistent with the liberties of the people—such as increasing the time of their duration, and such like. Many projects have been proposed, too tedious for a letter to communicate. Some have proposed that we should take up the plan of the Connecticut constitution, for a

* Jones.

ground-work, but with some amendments—such as that the great officers, instead of being appointed by the people at large, should be appointed by the Assembly—that the judges of our courts should hold their offices during good behavior, &c. After all, it appears to me, that there can be no check on the representatives of the people in a Democracy, but the people themselves; and, in order that the check may be the more efficient, I would have annual elections.

The Congress have raised four new regiments, making in the whole six; and three companies of light-horse. They are about to strike a large sum of money for paying them. General Lee promises us a visit soon; I want much to see that original. Mrs. Johnston and the children are well. I am far otherwise, but I make a shift to keep up, though with difficulty. Pray let my sister Blair know that I have not yet seen Mr. Patillo—as soon as I do she shall hear from me. Offer my love and compliments where due, and believe me,

Dear Sir,
Your affectionate brother,
SAM. JOHNSTON.

LETTER FROM THOMAS JONES TO IREDELL.

HALIFAX, *Sunday Morning*, 28th April, 1776.

MY WORTHY FRIEND:—You must pardon me for not giving you a line ere this, but if you really knew the amazing fatigue of business several of us have gone through, you would, I am fully assured, most readily forgive me. In my time I have been used to business, both public and private, but never yet experienced one-fourth part of what I now am necessarily obliged to undertake—we have no rest, either night or day. The first thing done in the morning is to prepare every matter necessary for the day—after breakfast, to Congress—there, generally, from 9 until 3 o'clock—no sitting a minute after dinner, but to the different committees; perhaps one person will be obliged to attend four of them between 4 o'clock and 9 at night—then to supper, and this generally brings us to 12 at night. This has been the life I have led since my arrival here—in short, I never was so hurried. I was in great expectation that it would have been in my power to have acquainted you with political affairs of moment, but nothing as yet has been digested, and the most material business secret—can only, therefore, acquaint you that the army affairs have taken up a fortnight of our time. The Constitution goes on but slowly. The outlines of it made their appearance in the House for the first time yesterday, and by the last of this week it, probably, may be finished. The plan, as it now stands, will be subject to many alterations; at present, it is in the following manner:—1st. A House of the representatives of the people—all free householders of one year standing to vote; and, 2d. A Legislative Council—to consist of one Member from each County in the Province—to sit as an Upper House, and these two Houses are to be a check on each other, as no law can be made without the consent of both, and none but freeholders will have a right to vote for the members of this council. Next, an Executive Council, to consist of a President and six Councillors; to be always sitting; to do all official business of Government—such as managing the army; issuing commissions, military and civil; filling up vacancies; calling the two branches of the legislature together; receiving foreign ambassadors, &c. &c. The President and Council to be elected annually, as also the Assembly and Legislative Council—but have some reason to believe the President will have a right to be chosen yearly for three years successively, and no more, until the expiration of three years thereafter. So much for the outlines of the Constitution. We expect Gen. Lee here every moment, on his way to the southward. He has two regiments in Virginia ready to assist this Province, as, we have reason to believe, North Carolina is their first object; thinking that we are the weakest of the thirteen—in this, perhaps, they may be mistaken. Gen. Lee holds these regiments in readiness at Suffolk to assist, as the case may be, either North Carolina or Virginia. Clinton is at Cape Fear, waiting for Lord Cornwallis and seven regiments—it's probable they may mean this as a feint to draw off forces from Virginia to Carolina, and then sail immediately and attack Virginia—as circumstances have materially changed since the date of Lord Germaine's letters to Gov. Eden, and Gen. Clinton having discretionary orders it's impossible to say what they will do; however, every necessary preparation is making for their reception both here and in Virginia. A Committee of Inquiry, or, in other words, an examining court was appointed by the Congress to inquire as to the conduct of the prisoners in the jail, on our arrival here; we have tried 102 of them —this was a troublesome job indeed—and sent off fifty-three of them, Gen. McDonald at their head, out of the country— the place of their destination I am not at liberty to tell you. General Armstrong went through this town the other day, on his way to South Carolina, to head the South Carolina forces. We have a printed copy of the South Carolina constitution, which is now in full force with the inhabitants of that country. A privateer from Philadelphia, of sixteen 4-pounders, actually engaged with and took an armed sloop, fitted out by Captain Bellew, and commanded by his lieutenant; the engagement lasted one hour and twenty minutes. The armed sloop is torn all to pieces, so that it was with difficulty she was carried up to Philadelphia— the lieutenant and thirty-five prisoners arrived safe at that city. Old Goodrich is here a close prisoner, with one Capt. Geo. Blair, and others. Since Goodrich was taken, the pilots and others at the bar have taken another tender by boarding, having on board 1000 pounds of gunpowder and sixteen men—the officers are in New Berne jail, and the men have cheerfully entered into the Continental service. The Province will instantly purchase the vessels of the pilots, and send them to the bar as tenders to the King Taminy and Pennsylvania Farmer. I do expect we shall vote 300,000, to be immediately emitted, for Continental purposes; and I have the pleasure to tell you that we have the greatest reason to believe that our last expedition against the insurgents will be paid by the united Colonies, and every other expense we may be at in future, as we are considered as an accessory and not a principal in the present disputes; in that case, our paper money will be upon a footing with the Continental. Mr. Johnston, Mrs. Johnston, and the children, are in high health. Mr. Johnston called at my lodgings this morning, and bid me tell you that he is so hurried he could not write to you by Vandewater—this I know to be the case. Mr. Charlton has been looked for here every day for these ten days past, or I should have wrote to him. My compliments to Mrs. Iredell, Mrs. Blair, Mrs. Dawson, and all the young ladies of both families.

I am, worthy sir,
Your friend and most obedient servant,
THOMAS JONES.

April 27th.—All transactions ceased in the Edenton Custom House; and Mr. Iredell finally closed his books and terminated his career as collector. His accounts were finally adjusted and settled with the Congress and the "Commissioners of Confiscated Property."

JOHNSTON TO IREDELL.

HALIFAX, 2d May, 1776.

"DEAR SIR:—Affairs have taken a turn within a few days past.* All ideas of forming a permanent Constitution are, at this time, laid aside. It is now proposed, for the present, to establish a Council to sit constantly, and county committees to sit at certain fixed periods, but nothing is concluded. We find it neces-

---

* Jones.

---

sary to emit a very large sum of paper money at the present emergency; a circumstance which gives me more concern than any thing else, and yet it seems unavoidable. You can easily see the evils attending this measure. I am pretty well this morning, and have leave to be absent from the service of the House in order to prepare my public accounts for a settlement. Allen Jones is Vice President."*

The President, Mr. Johnston, had leave of absence, for a few days, granted to enable him to prepare his accounts, as Treasurer, for examination.

T. JONES TO IREDELL.

HALIFAX, 7th May, 1776.

DEAR SIR:—I acknowledge, with great pleasure, the receipt of your very polite and sensible favor by Capt. Payne. We have not, at this time, a moment to spare—therefore you must pardon my not giving you at this time so long a letter as my last. I have only to tell you that the Constitution for the present is laid over and will be taken up again next October, at which time *you must be a judge—the matter is finally settled and determined upon—your amiable character and abilities are well known to many who never had the pleasure of seeing you.* Dr. Burke presents his best compliments to you—that gentleman and myself lodge in the same house together, and have frequent communion with each other on politics, defence of the country, &c.—our whole time has been taken up here in raising and arming men, and making every necessary military arrangement. The word is war, or, as Virgil expresses it, bella, horrida bella. 2000 Ministerial troops are in Cape Fear River—5000 more hourly expected— *to oppose the whole will require a large force, but large as it may be amply supplied from this province only*—though Gen. Lee has on the frontiers of this province 3000 brave men ready to assist us—we shall be under the necessity of striking half a million of money to carry on the war—this will perhaps strike you with astonishment, but when I see you, shall have it in my power to make you very easy on that head. I have a glorious magazine of matters of every sort for you—therefore prepare yourself to laugh abundantly. My best compliments to Mrs. Iredell, Mrs. Blair, Mrs. Dawson, and the young ladies—shall be at home some time next week. I am almost worn down with business, and my wish is that on my return I may enjoy one week's peace and quietness —longer I do not ask for. I am in great haste,

Dear sir,
Your friend and ob't humble serv't,
THOMAS JONES.

On the 14th of May Congress adjourned. Such was the exasperated state of party feeling that the Radicals had contrived to exclude Mr. Johnston* from the Council of Safety for the State: in his place Willie Jones was substituted, the most violent of his opponents; it might well have been supposed that they would have hesitated long before they would have incurred the hazard of alienating from the common cause its most powerful friend—such would have been their course with an ordinary man: but they well knew the temper of Mr. Johnston; that he was not the man to desert principle because of neglect or wrong; or to retire to his tent because denied the lead; that like the needle, however agitated, he would settle and point, as ever, true North in politics as in morals.†

JOHNSTON TO MRS. IREDELL.

HALIFAX, 31st May, 1776.

MY DEAR HANNAH:—I have often threatened to write you, and have taken my seat more than once for that purpose, but somehow or other I never could find matter for a letter—whether it was that I thought you expected something better from me than I was capable of executing, and that falling short of your expectations I should suffer something in your good opinion—and my vanity could not bear a shock of that kind—or what else might be the reason I can't tell, but I am now determined, at any rate, to entitle myself to a letter from you. I have seen you so seldom of late that we shall be as great strangers as if we lived an hundred miles apart, unless I can prevail on you to correspond with me.

I had a tolerably agreeable journey up, considering the heat of the weather. I keep my health pretty well, and have just business enough to confine me to the town. Instead of politics, the

---

* Jones.
† At its close Congress returned thanks to Mr. Johnston, as their president; "having in that, as in all other stations, approved himself the firm and liberal patron of liberty, and a wise and zealous friend and assertor of the rights of mankind."

---

* Allen Jones was a conservative leader—General of the Halifax District in '76 —Member of the Continental Congress in 1779-80—Senator in the Assembly, 1787. Though the brother of Willie Jones, he was a warm Federalist in 1788. His daughter, Sarah, married Gen. Wm. R. Davie: another daughter married Mr. Lunsford Long: from the latter union springs Mrs. Cadwalader Jones, of Hillsboro', who, with her husband, are the finest representatives, as a couple, that I know, of the virtue, dignity, grace and refinement of the "olden time."

general topic of conversation in this place is horses, a subject which, though apparently perfectly understood, and repeatedly talked over, seems never to be exhausted. When I first came up Gen. Lee * and his dogs had entirely supplanted the horses; a number of little anecdotes are told of them—among others, the general will not suffer Spado to eat bacon for breakfast (a practice very general both with gentlemen and ladies in this part of the country) lest it should make him stupid—this piece of satire, however, has not prejudiced him in their good opinion: he is considered as a very polite, well-bred, and sensible gentleman by every one I have heard speak of him, making allowances for a few oddities, which all great men are indulged in, and which were not so many as they had reason, from report, to expect. Give my love to Mr. Iredell, our sister and the children. I don't write him, but hope he will excuse it, and not neglect writing to me for that reason. It now grows late, and the bearer sets out early in the morning; I have therefore only to add that I am most truly, my dear Hannah,

Your most affectionate brother,
SAM. JOHNSTON.

In the latter part of May the British fleet, with Gen. Clinton's troops, withdrew from Cape Fear. Before they retired, their commander fulminated an idle proclamation, whose tone contrasted strikingly with the baffled expectations, the fears, and the disappointed hopes confessed by their retreat. They were gorged with no blood other than that of a few bullocks stolen from the plantation of Gen. Robert Howe; enriched with no plunder but a few slaves torn from the same gallant proprietor. What a commentary upon the chivalry of the English *Nobleman!* what a conclusion to an invasion to be made good by so powerful an armament! the shame of a dastardly act of revenge. Had he had the soul of a gentleman, he not only would have respected the property of the American General, but he would have placed a guard over his home to guarantee the safety, and calm the apprehensions of the ladies of his family.

I have claimed for North Carolina the honor of the first victory won by American arms; and the first authoritative instruction issued by any colony to its delegates, to declare Independence. I now claim for the same province an honor, equally signal,—a triumph won in the field of letters. It is true that many wished for independence as desirable in itself; but the great mass of the people were inclined to assent to it solely as a measure dictated by necessity. It was important that needless apprehensions should be allayed; that scruples should be quieted; and confidence, in the justice of their cause, inspired into the people. This work Mr. Iredell performed: and his essay, for simplicity of diction, comprehensiveness, order of arrangement, perspicuity, and force of argument, surpasses not only any similar production of the year, but of the Revolution. It is dated June, 1776.

This pamphlet was probably never published. Publication was then almost, if not entirely, impracticable in North Carolina. It is believed, however, that it had a very extended circulation among the prominent men of the province, passing in manuscript, from hand to hand.

" Having in the foregoing address slightly canvassed the subject of the American claims, and proved, as I conceive, to the satisfaction of every reasonable man, that they are founded in the highest justice, I shall now proceed to say something as to the *mode* which has been since pursued in the assertion of them, and to rescue us from the arbitrary dominion of an unlimited authority, not only speculatively claimed, but attempted to be carried into the severest and most cruel action.

" Much fault has been found with this. It has been represented as highly impolitic and unjust; not well calculated for the purpose we had in view, not to be justified in the abstract upon any footing of necessity. Equal, if not greater, clamor has been raised on this subject, than on the substance of our demands; and I am much mistaken if many well-meaning men have not been led away by flowery declamations on this point to take a bitter and severe part against us.

" It must, however, be admitted, that there is an essential and eternal difference between the *real nature of any claim that is in question*, and the *manner of resisting a violation of it*, and, that however mistaken men may be in *the means of redressing* an injury, the injury itself must be removed before justice can take place. All men are entitled to justice, but all are not possessed of wisdom; and, therefore, the means of defending a right can never come in competition with a title to the *right itself*.

" But I have the satisfaction to hope that I can make it appear, the steps which have been taken by America were just and necessary, and can be vindicated upon those great and honorable principles which have in a thousand instances prompted a defence of the rights of human nature against the attacks of tyrants; and can more especially be vindicated upon those principles which are the only real and solid basis of the very power which oppresses us.

---

* Gen. Charles Lee, in command of the Southern Department.

" It is difficult to unravel the complicated and perplexed accusations we are loaded with. They have been stated without any order, consistency or precision. Sometimes the whole of our claims are rejected; sometimes part only; a few think us right in *principle*, but reprehensible in *conduct*. There are still others who would grant our *present* demands, but apprehend *further*, and conceive we have been all along acting a base, disingenuous, and unnatural part. They will not, therefore, let us be on a *just* footing now, for fear we should afterwards aim at an *unjust* one. No professions contrary to this favorite epidemical creed; no past services; no endeavors (though they have been most earnest) to prove the calumny of the supposition, can have any effect upon a credulous (in this point), unhappy and misguided people. The assertions of many, whose whole conduct has been one scene of iniquity, are implicitly believed in preference to the solemn assurances of men, *who only can know the worst*, and who have never yet, considered as a people (notwithstanding every vile insinuation to the contrary), been guilty of any other crime than *an ardent love of liberty*.

" Different principles have certainly actuated our enemies. A variety of motives has arisen against us, and found advocates according to the humor, the understanding, and the hearts of men. Many, I doubt not, act from an honest prejudice; more, I am obliged to believe, from mean and wicked views. These unhappily have the direction, and conceal the truth from the former, giving them only partial and interested information. No pains have been spared to abuse us. Our intentions have been villainously traduced; our personal characters have been made to appear odious and contemptible, and the unfeeling moulders of every social virtue dare to represent themselves as wise and honest patriots.

" The *principle* of this controversy has undergone the most thorough discussion; and people who have not been convinced by the arguments already used, scarcely will by any other. In the preceding performance, I aim at little originality; I set down thoughts as they arose in my mind, without considering whence I first derived them. That is a point of little consequence to the public, provided they are just; and my motive of writing is not the hope of *fame*, but of *doing some good*; the only ground of that hope is, that the arguments are urged with great plainness, and in a manner easily comprehensible. My present subject has not been so fully discussed: it is not indeed of near so much importance, but yet it is of some. Men would wish to justify the *manner* of their conduct, as well as the *matter* of it; and are naturally ambitious to be thought to have some *understanding*, as well as *honesty*. I know many think the *latter* character is as much concerned in this question as the *former*; but then this can only be founded on a judgment of the *first* question. If our rights were *really* attacked, we were justified in making *some defence*; the nature of that defence our *opinion* of the necessity must determine; there can be no other arbiter, without placing the security of our liberties out of the hands of those who are alone capable and interested in defending them. If our pretensions were *unjust*, it is certain that every step taken in their vindication is *wrong*. Thus it is evident that as to our *integrity*, it has no immediate concernment with the present question; unless it will be pretended that we have *suggested fears*, where we really *entertained none*; but such an accusation affects our *moral* not our *political* conduct. This can only be judged of by *political maxims*, of which it is impossible there should be one which can have no adequate judgment to direct it.

" It will be impossible to treat this subject properly, without having some reference to its history,—but this need not be very minute: it will be sufficient to remark on a few leading circumstances.

" It is certain, that until the time of the Stamp Act there was no *public contest* between Great Britain and America. Whatever circumstances or causes of suspicion there might be (as I believe there were some) among individuals, there seemed to be a happy and harmonious connexion between the two countries. There were indeed some grievances beginning to operate about that time, that might afterwards (even if the Stamp Act had not intervened) have brought on dangerous controversies; but the magnitude of this swallowed them all up. The consequences of the Stamp Act are well known. It was considered in America with universal and just indignation. They would have been a troop of slaves if they had submitted to it; and must have been ruined in *fortune* as well as *liberty*; I mean *indulged* fortune; for as to *actual* they could have none without *liberty*. The resentment and resistance of a brave people had its effect. Moderate measures were pursued; the Stamp Act was repealed; and peace every where restored.

" It was considered by the then ministry, that though the Stamp Act was highly inexpedient, from many considerations, and would be in *fact* very grievous; yet that the *right* of Parliament to impose the tax was clear and indisputable. They believed that, from the principles of the Constitution, and from necessity, they possessed this right, and were, for all purposes, the superintending legislature of the whole empire. It appeared to them that, as in the delicate situation of such various and extended countries, a thousand unforeseen exigencies might arise to require an exertion of their *controlling power*, this power could not be limited in its objects without the utmost danger, and the hazard of general confusion. But at the same time they were of opinion, that the power ought never to be exercised in interference with subordinate privileges, while these privileges answered the end of their institution, and that nothing but *great and urgent necessity* would warrant the exertion of such extraordinary authority. That the people ought not to be alarmed, by seeing a power deemed necessary for *them* as well as the holders of it (and not justly allowable upon any other footing) abused to purposes *common and unnecessary ;* that this would lead them to suspect it would not be reserved for the ends only of a salus populi, but would be used occasionally and wantonly to their oppression. They thought, if the discretion of Parliament conducted them *wisely and moderately*, using the power only for evident ends of *public utility*, it would be submitted to always by a large majority from a sense of its necessity, and the great convenience *such a use* of the power would afford them. This, I have the charity to believe (and think the construction warranted not only by their *repeated professions*, but by the whole of their subsequent conduct) was all that the framers of the famous Declaratory Act intended by it ; and, if it had been possible or allowable to suppose that the Parliament could have preserved their virtue in so trying a situation, or even wisely and with deep foresight respected their own *real interest*, (which would have required a conformity to the above principles,) America might perhaps have remained satisfied with a *general exemption* from the authority of parliament, and silently submitted to such extraordinary exertions as might appear *absolutely necessary ;* reserving themselves (in practice) to approve and to submit to this authority, as the people of England occasionally submit to *stretches of the prerogative*, where the public good is the evident object of them : not, however, venturing to call in question so directly the *right of parliament*, but letting it remain in a discreet silence ; hoping that interest and affection, and mutual confidence, might long remove all occasions of distrust. Thus, perhaps, America might have been willing to compound the matter, if speculative questions had not been too nicely agitated, and if no good reasons of suspicion had been afforded. They did not, therefore, partly perhaps for this reason, but principally as parliament could not *assume* to themselves a power they did not *before possess*, publicly object to the Declaratory Act, but were willing to let it sleep till some future occasion of discussing it should be unhappily given to them. This was not long deferred. A new ministry (to the misfortune of the nation, and particularly of this country) took the reins of government, and a remnant of the Grenville faction being admitted among them, they were never at rest till they had introduced a new subject of controversy, and given America warning that she was to prepare for a *new system of government*, in demolition and contempt of that which had been the source of so much happiness and honor. Until a very late period, from their first establishment in the country, the Americans had provided, each province in its separate department, for the usual expenses of the government, and for such extraordinary exigencies as required provision. But the ordinary and extraordinary services had been faithfully performed, and there was no pretence for charging them with having neglected either. But Mr. Grenville, in the anxiety of his care for the British revenue, cast an eye towards these colonies, and felt himself strangely tempted to open a mine which all his predecessors had left to the care and management of the owners. This project he deliberately embraced, and with so much steadiness, that not all the unsuccess which attended it, not all the odium and unpopularity it occasioned, nor the most ruinous prospect of civil war, if it was persevered in, could shake him a moment from his purpose. It succeeded for a time but too fatally, until the happy event, the ever memorable repeal, gave us a temporary respite. A short time after, however, the event I mentioned above gave an opportunity once more to the *bigoted American taxers* to hazard a refined experiment. In the arguments occasioned by the Stamp Act, a distinction had been taken between *internal* and *external* taxes ; by the former were meant *taxes* on things out of the immediate power of commerce ; by the latter, *taxes* on such as were *within* it. These (being paid at the ports) were more generally called *duties*. The former had been denied upon the principle (among others) that such a power of taxing subjected the whole of every American's property to the power of Parliament ; by which means he could not be said to have any that was absolutely *his own*. The latter had been considered a necessary incident to the power exercised by Parliament of regulating our trade, and as such had been always submitted to by the Americans ; but as it was conceived that this power, from the nature of it, could not be limited, and the ministry were still hankering after a revenue from America, they laid hold of this expedient to answer their favorite purpose, without shocking (as they flattered themselves, *or seemed to do so*) the prejudices and principles that prevailed there. They imposed duties therefore on the importation of British commodities, and others, without even the suggestion of regulating our trade, (which indeed would in that case have been absurd,) but expressly for *purposes of revenue*, which they asserted in the most strong and unequivocal terms. They either hoped that the Americans would be more attentive to the *form* than the *spirit* of this new regulation, and therefore (to close with their distinction) made it a port duty ; or they determined at all hazards to enforce and to improve upon this *new method of taxation*, whether it should be pleasing to the Americans or not, whom indeed the preamble seemed little calculated to soothe. The act had a very motley aspect of *indulgence* and *defiance :* the *mode* was *condescending*, but the *matter*, if permitted, *ruinous*. It was become necessary now for the Americans to examine into their situation more closely and critically than they had ever done. The Government, instead of *protecting* them in their rights, seemed continually devising means to encroach upon them, and to abuse powers, vested in the parent state for their *mutual benefit*, to their *particular injury and oppression*. Such an abuse was discovered in the case before them, and this gave rise to a new distinction not apparently attended to before.

"It had always been admitted, that the British Parliament had a right to regulate the trade of the whole empire, in order that the united interests of the whole might be consulted, and they themselves derive that exclusive trade with their colonies which was thought essential to the nature of the connection between them. If this right was not conceded, twelve or thirteen different independent legislatures might form such a discordant set of regulations as to leave no connection between the *different* parts of the same *empire ;* not the general interest, but such as were local and partial, would be the object probably of their provision. This power therefore seemed necessary to preserve the whole in *due order*. Now there can scarcely be any other restrictive regulation of trade, than an absolute prohibition, or a slight restraint by means of duties. In the course of providing for commercial exigencies *both these* are necessary. The possession of the former without the latter must evidently appear incongruous, because it is a higher degree of the same power. It would be also in many instances injurious, because it would require, when any particular trade interfered with another, totally *to prohibit it*, when perhaps a small check might have removed the inconvenience, and the remedy not been pernicious. As, for instance, in many particulars of our trade with the West India Islands : duties are laid upon some foreign commodities, to give a superior advantage in these to the British ; but they are not totally prohibited, because our British Islands could not, I suppose, entirely supply the whole, or if they could it would be a means of hurting our export trade to the foreign Islands. Upon this reasonable footing stands, as I conceive, the point about duties. But then it is contended, the sole right of laying these consists in the power of regulating our trade ; if any imposition of them has not this circumstance for its object, it is an usurpation of our rights ; it is taking our money from us unconstitutionally. There is, I confess, a good deal of nicety in this matter, but it arises from the peculiar nature of our situation. It is necessary, for the reasons I have given, that the Parliament should have a power of regulating our trade by *duties*. But this power is liable to great abuses, if it is without restraint, as *under color of regulations of trade* may be collected the most heavy and dangerous impositions. Our property by trade would be altogether at their mercy,—and admitting their other claim to be just, of *restraining our manufactures*, by laying duties on the necessaries of life, which we were to receive only from *them*, every man in America might be dependent on them for actual subsistence. If that claim, however, was *not* gained the injury would be equally exceptionable ; the difference could only be in the *degree of hardship*. These considerations point out the necessity of considering this power to be merely incidental to the other of regulating, and that it no more implies a right of raising money *ad libitum*, in this manner, on the subject, than the incidental power which judges possess of imposing fines for particular offences would warrant a loose and arbitrary exercise of it, without regard to the objects for which it was established. The most that can be made of the argument for the right of laying duties *generally* is this, that none can certainly know the *intention* of the lawgivers (unless it is expressed, and this may be deceitfully) but themselves, and that consequently it being a matter which they can at any time disguise, under the pretence of *legal objects*, they may annihilate any objection at pleasure. To this it is replied, that as to the duties imposed as above (of which now remains that *on tea*), the intention is placed out of all doubt ; a regulation of trade is not pretended, *revenue* only is the confessed object. The power of regulating trade is not then here exercised, but plainly *another power*, and none else is conceded, or as it is supposed, can be alleged necessary ; or if it can be thought to answer any good purposes, it must be dangerous to our freedom ; if one penny can be raised a million may, and our liberties may be destroyed by the money extorted from us. But if it should be said, suppose it is called a *regulation of trade*, what then ? Will you establish a combat of opinions where there can be no fixed umpire ? To this the answer is, in whatever critical situation a free country stands, it is its duty to guard, by every means necessary, its freedom and its happiness, and it is as much its duty to resist the palpable abuse of an acknowledged power, as the arrogant usurpation of a new one. The public may be endangered either way. Suppose the king should pardon *every offence* committed; suppose he should establish 500 or 600 peers, or at any time when he was at a loss for a majority supply a sufficient number to make one ? This experiment, I think, was never hazarded but once. Suppose the House of Commons should grant a revenue of a million a year, for the expressed purpose of bribery ? All these, it will be said, are very extravagant suppositions, but they prove that no power can be granted which may not be abused,—that some kind of confidence must always be understood between the governors and the governed,—and that these last must ultimately judge whether powers, intrusted by the constitution for their benefit, are really so employed, or prostituted to wicked and concealed purposes. And in my opinion, as to the case in question, the real object of commercial regulations may be easily understood ; where they cannot, submission certainly is proper. Let it be added to all these considerations, the objects of these revenue laws were providing for our civil establishments, thus making them altogether independent of the people, and tending to render our assemblies useless.

In this light these laws were viewed soon after they were made, and were consequently complained of. In the course of a few years all were taken off but the duty on tea, and this was reserved as a badge of the taxative power. It was supposed to be somehow distinguished from the others by being a foreign commodity ; but this made no real difference in the case, as no commercial reason could be alleged for the restriction of the importation of tea, it being only receivable from Great Britain ; and the exportation of it so much an object of the encouragement of Parliament as to be allowed a large drawback. It is contemptible for the Ministry to say any thing about this drawback, for the very indulgence upon which they plume themselves proves the design of laying the duty on originally, and still retaining it.

This trifling article has been the cause of all our misery. Repeated applications for a repeal of this duty were repeatedly disregarded, and even treated with contempt. The most favorable occasions presented themselves of granting it without prejudice to *dignity*, but no argument could induce our wise rulers to embrace them. It was determined to hazard every thing in assertion of this *indiscriminate power of taxing*. There had been formal associations to defeat the purpose of it,—but they were languid, and by no means general. A kind of stagnating quiet prevailed. There were the seeds of much ill-humor prevailing, but *little shown*, and the peaceable exertion of every power of government left room for tenderness and discretion to operate. In this state of things the East India Company were in great distress, and stood in need of immediate and powerful assistance. They were taken under the care of Parliament, and one method of giving them relief was by enabling them to ship all their teas (immense quantities of which they had lying by them) to America on their own account ; whereas, formerly, they had sold all by auction, and it was shipped by private adventurers. It was well known at this time (or might have been) in England, that we were generally discontented on account of this duty, and that though no steps had been taken to enforce a general observance of the *non-importation of it ;* yet that such a step had by a kind of common consent taken place, and by the failure of imports occasioned by it had contributed in a great measure to the distress the Company then sustained. No mobs, no riots, *no resistance of its landing*, had, however, been attempted. The Americans had surely a right to determine whether they would *buy tea ;* they exercised no other right : and the exercise of that, though *pretty general*, was *not universal*. This condition of affairs proved sufficiently their *dislike of the duty*, to have given warning in time of the consequences of *enforcing it*, but no express resistance to it being formed, government was not *insulted*, nor its legislative power at stake upon any concession. Could there ever, then, have been a happier time for restoring peace, than that which this afforded ? How plausible would have been the motive of the *distress of the East India Company*, and the *necessity of their instant relief !* No revenue worth speaking of had been derived from the duty ; none could reasonably, at that time, be in contemplation. The theory of right had proved highly mischievous, and there was no immediate question about it, to render its assertion necessary. These circumstances, I think, might have greatly alleviated the pride of *our new legislators*. If any were still wanting to give their minds perfect content,—and to avoid all possible suspicion of undue motives, and not principle, actuating their conduct, they ought to have considered that they had brought themselves into such a situation, that there was no way of obviating this, but by exposing themselves to much greater danger. It was necessary to make a choice whether to return to the old and successful method of governing the colonies, or to persevere in the new, odious, and in all appearance, impracticable one. If men will hazard important interests to try dangerous experiments, they should be prepared for the consequences of a disappointment, and not calculate their measures so as to make a recession difficult or dishonorable.

The only real dishonor there could have been in the present case, was if they had acted from motives of fear alone, contrary to their notions of just and practicable policy : I say *practicable policy*, because no theory, however wise or right in the abstract, ought to be enforced at the utmost risk of a dreadful civil war, unless the political existence of a country is endangered by withholding it. Some, I know, will say this was the case in the present instance. Men of liberal and enlarged notions must, however, have been persuaded (and the event, if I am not mistaken, will plainly show) that three millions of free and high-spirited men are not to be governed by *force and terror*. The existence then of the connection between Great Britain and America, which formerly subsisted, so much to the happiness of both, it must have appeared, could only depend on a system of government which reconciled and healed the minds of men, and gave them no occasion of jealousy or alarm ; no fear that they were to be treated with ignominy and dishonor. Admitting, therefore, that the repeal had proceeded upon the motives alone of satisfying the Americans,—that this had been universally known, and even publicly avowed, I can see no dishonor that would have attended such a conduct. Let the language of the Repeal have been thus understood,—" A happy connection has long subsisted between this country and America. Both have flourished under the benign influence of liberty, and we have every reason to cherish and to bless that fortunate union of circumstances which have produced such happy effects. We were formerly betrayed into a mistaken measure that portended very dangerous consequences, but we stopt short the instant we found we had been mistaken in our policy, and that by persisting in it we should err against *better information, endanger the peace of our country*, and *miss our own essential interests*. It is singularly lamentable that we should have been mistaken on much the same occasion a *second time*, but there were circumstances attending this last affair which do not leave us altogether without excuse. We have misunderstood the condition of America ; we have not been properly sensible of her importance ; we were not well acquainted with the disposition of the people ; we did not think this last conduct would be generally offensive. However, we now find ourselves in a situation which makes it necessary to decide whether we will persevere in the *unnecessary* exercise of an *odious claim*, or by a prudent and political forbearance of it, bring us all back to our former prosperous circumstances. We cannot hesitate a moment on the choice. The happiness of millions is of too much consequence to be sported with, and we do not think it will be allowable to set our own *pride* and *reluctance to* make concessions in the opposite scale. Men are liable to mistakes. Public bodies are as much exposed to these, if not more so, than many individuals. Passion, prejudice, and inattention among such produce fatal effects. These are more likely to operate against a people at a distance, with whom they have no immediate connection. We do not deny but there may be some ground for a suspicion of such effects in the affairs of America. It is a natural infirmity ; and if there may seem any meanness in the confession, there would be much more in denying or concealing so important a truth. Our opinion of right, however, we cannot alter ; but we believe the exercise of it hitherto to have been *unnecessary* and *inexpedient*. In consideration of these circumstances we yield this unproductive tax, and we think we discharge our duty far better in relinquishing a *dangerous error*, than we could possibly do by enforcing what was originally *wrong in itself*, as well as *painfully afflicting to the parties.*"

This appears to me a language which comprehended no dishonor. And such a language must at one time or other have been adopted, or a determination formed to continue the duty, and preserve that occasion of discord. There could have been no time more proper for relaxation than this I speak of, which was so unhappily neglected. It must therefore have appeared to every one that the Ministry were obstinate in the *claim and exercise of taxing*. Indeed it was at the time so much credited that they were bent on violence, that it was generally believed, and not without some plausible reasons, that the provisions in regard to the East India Company had a particular aspect to the enforcement of the duty. In this situation surely the Americans had great cause of alarm. They had a prospect of such an inundation of tea, and of course of a large American revenue as the result, that they had every reason to fear, if free and unlimited importations of that commodity were admitted, that that revenue would have been unalterably fixed on them. The cargo for Boston arrived first. The minds of the people there had been long irritated by its having been a constant station, for some years, of a numerous body of soldiers, sent for the express purpose of subduing *their spirit*. This spirit, however, they believed, and many very worthy men in the other provinces believed, was only *a just and genuine spirit of liberty ;* carried perhaps, in some instances, too far, but in the main, highly laudable and virtuous. It had long (unhappily with too much reason) been supposed in that province that a formed scheme of subduing the Americans had been regularly concerted, and constantly pursued, and that the utmost vigilance was required on the part of America to prevent its imperceptibly and gradually taking effect. They thought that this specious East India business had for a very principal object the establishment of this tax, which they considered only as a precedent for innumerable burthensome impositions that would be the consequence of any mean submission to it. They dreaded the immediate receipt and sale of such an immense quantity of tea, which would produce so much money as to tempt a continuance of the favorite plan, and might perhaps be considered in general in a more innocent light than it deserved, and abstracted from the dangerous precedent it was meant to establish, and which justly made it so extremely obnoxious to them. These, I am persuaded, are the general sentiments of the people. Popular opinions are usually communicated with great fervor, and it is not wonderful if to men actuated by such nice and delicate feelings, the scheme appeared in the most odious light. The so much dreaded object at last arrived. The people assembled. They resolved to act with moderation, as well as firmness, and applied to the agents for the Company, to return the tea to Great Britain, without landing. These consented. The people were happy in the prospect of a peaceable riddance of it. But what was their astonishment when they were told that the governor had refused a "let pass," which was a mere official instrument necessary to be obtained before the tea could regularly depart out of the harbor. In this, he did not act from any necessity as governor, but officiously, as a friend to every irritating step against America. Government had no right to interfere with the conduct of the East India Company's servants, either in shipping or reshipping the tea. However respectable, or however numerous, the individuals of that Company may be, they are, in the eye of the constitution, *mere private adventurers*, and as such, entitled to the *general*, not the *particular* protection of government, unless where it is specially provided by law. But this was not in the nature of *protection*. Had it proceeded on this principle, it would have been his duty to have told the Agents that if they would retain the tea, he would *protect* it with all the powers of government; he might even (if he had conceived this property was refused a landing, merely *on account of a measure of government*) have recommended it to them not to reship it, lest it might seem an unworthy acquiescence to the *pretensions and violence* of the people. But it was to the last degree mean, first to encourage them to agree to reship it; then after that agreement (which must have been supposed their own choice, and on which they had a right to conclude *decisively*) to refuse a pass which was little more than a mere form, and by which he had no right to refuse a passage to merchandise, *exported with the consent of the owners*, and *rightfully exportable by law*, which this was; for though it could not legally be relanded in Great Britain, it might be carried to many other places, and the governor had no right *officially* to judge of the intention in this respect entertained by the reshippers. The governor's conduct on this occasion, therefore, naturally added to the jealousy and alarm of the people, and confirmed all the apprehensions which had been before suggested to them relative to the injurious and determined designs of administration. The consequence was, that seeing all hope of deliverance from this cursed article (with all its ruinous effects) was to be despaired of, the people being inflamed with resentment for past injuries, and dreading the still greater increase of them,—having before their eyes the most fatal consequences, and not knowing which way to avoid them; a few, more bold and desperate than the rest, determined to put the contest at once on an unequivocal footing, and to see the real extent of the indefinite claims our arbitrary rulers made on us. They put themselves in disguise, entered on board the ships and *destroyed the tea*. The motive I allege for this action may be questioned by those unfavorable to America, and I know a very base one has been assigned; but still I believe it to have been real, and am persuaded the action arose from a sincere (however extraordinary and mistaken) principle of patriotism. There can be no competent proof of the *intentions* of men, and in order to judge of these, in a rational light, a thousand circumstances are to be taken into consideration; and even these will not always enable men *very partial*, or *much prejudiced*, to judge properly. A great deal must be left to opinion at last. I have not time, and it is not necessary, to offer proofs in support of my favorable opinion of that much injured people. It will be sufficient just to say that I have long admired their *wisdom*, *steadiness* and *spirit*, and that with respect to most of the violences they are accused of, I believe them to have been the consequence of noble virtues carried to excess. A different opinion has unhappily too generally prevailed, and to this source, among others, perhaps, may many of our misfortunes be ascribed. But let us now attend the reception of this affair in England. It was there represented as a most criminal and daring outrage, which deserved, and called for, the most severe and exemplary punishment. It was said that that province had long been the firebrand of all North America, the leader in every opposition to the measures of Great Britain, and the promoter of every insult that had a tendency to bring that government into contempt; that this action evidently, and happily with too much plainness, discovered their extreme factious and seditious spirit, and put it in the power of government, with the clearest equity and justice, to provide curbs for its future insolence; that it must be apparent to all mankind, it was now become necessary to take such steps as should secure for the future some obedience to the *laws*, some respect to the *authority* of the parent State, in that turbulent and refractory province; that such a conduct, so evidently dictated by necessity, could not, it was supposed, be generally disapproved among wise and thinking men, even in America itself; if such an event, however, could be imagined, this still more evidently would justify measures that appeared not only immediately requisite in one colony, but which were required to give warning and serve for intimidation to the rest: and that, as these measures were thus immediately become necessary, every moment lost would be a moment of indignity and insecurity to the government, and even the Parliament of Great Britain, which had been so grossly insulted.

These were the general and prevailing arguments in defence of harsh measures. Unhappily they were too greedily received. Still, however, there were a wise and virtuous few who nobly stood forth on this occasion to check the headlong fury of their country, and to advise them in time of the fatal consequences of any exasperating conduct. They desired to recall their attention to the first rise of these unhappy troubles. They said that the circumstances of the two countries were by no means in so decided a situation, that they had an immediate right to consider themselves as persons injured, and *entitled to revenge*; that the claims of the Americans, if not absolutely just, were yet extremely plausible, and the arguments in refutation of them would not very well become the mouths of Englishmen; that these last had undergone a thousand struggles in defence of liberty, and had repeatedly declared that *life was a burthen without it*; that their American brethren (or *children* if they pleased) were derived from the same stock, and had imbibed a great deal of the same spirit, and could not easily be persuaded that liberty was a greater or more necessary blessing on the European than the American continent; that the ancestors of the Americans had left England with the hope, and in prospect of the enjoyment of this blessing among the deserts they were going to retire to, from the civilized advantages of a cultivated, but oppressed, and in danger of being an enslaved, people; that it was scarcely probable any other than such an exalted motive could have induced them to risk the great dangers they were preparing to encounter, and they accordingly took care to receive what at the time they deemed full security to this *happy purpose*; that in full confidence of this security for their *freedom*, they were animated to contend with innumerable hardships, and such as nothing but the hope of procuring a noble settlement for their posterity could have prevented their despairing subjection to; that during the course of these difficulties and dangers (which continued for a great number of years) they felt little of the kindness, and none of the *power* of Parliament, excepting the single instance of regulating their trade; that all their internal concerns were regulated with respect to their charter rights, and with reverence to the rights of freemen; that they looked up to the king of Great Britain as their sovereign, and paid him the most sincere and faithful allegiance; even at times when the other dominions of the crown were convulsed with plots and massacres and civil wars; that though they entertained a profound respect for Parliament, they never thought of acknowledging in them an indiscriminate power of legislation, which was a notion they had no encouragement to entertain, as until a very late period Parliament never interposed in their concerns, but where the interposition appeared necessary to the due maintenance of the connection between the two countries; the power that was judged necessary for which end they never had denied (considering them throughout), and all the colonies at the present still willingly submitted to; that in this pleasing situation, their minds attached and friendly to each other, no encroaching arts used, no usurping power thought of, and of course all cause of jealousy removed, these colonies flourished in a most astonishing degree, and, in the course of a few years, out of a mere wilderness raised cultivated and happy plantations—now the wonder, and which perhaps shortly will become the envy of the world: that when war became necessary for the preservation of both countries, both united with one soul and spirit, and the zeal and ardor of the plantations (though their danger or concern in the war was not so great as was generally apprehended) were the subject of continual praises, and were most strongly and gratefully acknowledged from the throne in repeated messages to Parliament for their compensation; that when peace was restored, the affectionate temper of the two countries might have admitted of many admirable plans for preserving the concord and happiness of the whole, but unfortunately *meanness* took place of *wisdom*, and the colonies had scarcely begun to breathe from the exhausting contributions they had made, before they were fined in a heavy tax to pay back some of the *very retributions* they had just before received (and which were far from being adequate to their due), and to give in return for the temporary loan of this little money, *large retributions of the expenses of Great Britain*;[*] that this really appeared a lit-

[*] The Stamp Act was indeed nominally calculated for revenue purposes of our own; but what security had we for the faithful application of the money? Who was to be judge of the particular purposes it was to serve? Bribes, and a large standing army might have been judged necessary for *our defence*.

tle whimsical, but so it was, and the colonies found themselves exposed to the danger of ruin in their fortunes by the operation of a grievous tax, as well as to the ignominious condition of a people who have *no freedom*; that though this tax was repealed, the policy of the repeal (which had had the most happy effects) could not be continued by men who were enemies to that just and necessary indulgence, and were more concerned to establish a favorite and destructive theory than to promote the true honor and interest of their country; that the same *little* policy had actuated their conduct since, and they had acted on all occasions upon mere *temporary* principles, not having the spirit to assert their own system with vigor, or the candor to correct an unfortunate and unhappy mistake; that this tea duty was a branch of the same system, established not from necessity (as nothing could be more evident), but to insult the colonies, and to awake their perpetual jealousy; if this last was not intended (though it might have been foreseen) it had, however, taken place, and the colonies had too much sagacity to be cheated out of an important privilege by the pilfering an unjust pretence, any more than they could be brought to submit to the daring assumption of an unconstitutional claim; that whatever might be the ideas in England, these were *theirs*; it was evident to all, who could see distinctly, that they were in earnest in their opinion, and would be ready to defend it to the last extremity; and no experience can justify governing a whole people contrary to *their determined principles*; that it was the duty of wise men to consider what was *practicable*, as well as what was *abstractly right*; and that to enforce the latter, with no hope or prospect of the former, was idle and ridiculous; that on the present occasion the people had had great provocation; they had repeatedly solicited a repeal of a trifling tax; a tax that produced nothing, that was established purposely to insult them (for more revenue was given up than established), which appeared only to be upheld as an occasion of discord, and which they had great reason to believe extraordinary measures had been taken to enforce; that the anxiety of the people in this situation ought to be considered; the fear of an unconstitutional power taking place, if the means concerted for effecting it were allowed freely to operate, and the resentment natural to men who see those who ought to be their protectors, take a pleasure in browbeating them; that if the injury was extraordinary, so was the provocation, and in all ages some indulgence was afforded to loose and disorderly men carrying the general principles of their country into too violent and precipitate action; that to punish a whole people for the faults of a few, was arbitrary and unjust, contrary to the fundamental principles of natural equity, and agreeable only to a spirit of the meanest despotism; that, admitting there were strong circumstances of suspicion against the body of the people, as indirectly concerned, or at least tacitly conniving at this outrage, surely proof should be required extremely explicit of this fact, in order to justify an enormous punishment on a whole people; men, women, and children should not thus be consigned, in the wholesale, to extreme and indiscriminate misery; that all *wise* people had ever been cautious of inflicting such *general* punishments; the humane sentiment that the innocent should not be confounded with the guilty, was deserving of the most sacred regard, and ought never to be violated but on the *greatest provocation*, and in the *extremest necessity*; and *such* a provocation, and *such* a necessity, could not decently be pretended in this case, by men who had been the too natural causes of the one, and deserved to feel some little punishment from the other; that the extraordinary measures proposed could not be taken against *one* colony, without irritating *all*; that they would not now, when Great Britain showed herself their enemy, listen to the ridiculous tale of their being only constitutionally connected with her; Nature would lead them to associate with their friends and fellow-sufferers against their common enemy, and form an union which was able to protect them, but without which they would singly fall a prey (and deserved to do so) to the dividing and destructive policy of their oppressors; that on this great occasion they would certainly join issue on the new question that would be introduced, not whether they had a power of *taxing*, but how far they had a right of *legislating*; and in judging of this, their sentiments would not be formed (as those in England were) by reasons of *policy*, but by motives of *safety*; and how far this would lead an enlightened and determined people was easily perceivable; that all measures of *force* against America would ever be found impracticable; that nothing could be done with that country but by *lenient measures* and *reconciling conduct*; and if this appeared in a mean light to government, they ought well to weigh their resources for any contrary plan; that the connection between England and America produced a new scene in the history of mankind, ought to be judged of by its own circumstances, and not by narrow pedantic rules which are by no means regularly observed in practice, and which a brave people will disdainfully reject, when they come in competition with *their liberty*.

The ardor of my feelings has drawn these reasons to a greater length than I intended. I by no means had in view to state all that might be said on this occasion, but to mention the princi-

pal arguments; and I am not sure that I have confined myself to those only that were actually used in England; for I suffered the impulse of my mind to carry me as it pleased. I thought it of little consequence whether I stated what *was* said, or what *might have been said*; for the arguments are all obvious, and ought to have been attended to. But the fatal haughty system prevailed. It was determined that Massachusetts Bay should feel all the rigor of Parliament, and that Boston should immediately be laid under a *commercial interdict*. No trade after a limited day (and that a very short one) of any kind, or in any degree, was to be permitted to the unfortunate inhabitants of that town. About 30,000 people were deprived of their support in a great measure for the riot of about 30 or 40. This was to continue till the East India demand (a sum not then stated) was satisfied; till compensation was made to all revenue officers, and others, who had *suffered* [the expression in the Act] in particular riots specified; till the governor, &c., should certify these circumstances to the king in council; till the town should be adjudged to be in a state of peace; and till his Majesty should be pleased in consequence to restore it to its former privileges. This was the substance of the famous Boston Port Act.

So extremely arbitrary was this Act in its nature, that it was not possible, if the people instantly on its arrival were willing to comply with its conditions, for them to avoid the harsh penalties it inflicted; an end to which depended on a thousand troublesome contingencies, that might postpone it (without any real disobedience to the act in the sufferers) to an indefinite period of time. Parliament even degraded itself so far as to place the private property of many individuals (the support of many industrious families) in the power of the crown, for the mean and unworthy purpose of injuring one obnoxious person. In short the particular provisions of the bill entirely partook of the arbitrary spirit of *its principle*.

But this bill, severe as it was, could by no means satisfy the vindictive spirit of the administration. This was considered only as a *temporary punishment* for a *temporary offence*. It was determined to inflict some heavy stigma upon them, that might sufficiently resent past disorders, and obviate future ones. There was conceived to be some permanent causes for so continued a refractory spirit, and it was thought necessary for Parliament to exert all its rigor to tame this colony into obedience. They therefore proceeded upon the radical business of forming a new constitution for them. The subsisting one, they thought, vested too much power in the people, and by this means contributed in a great measure to the usual turbulence of the State. The new constitution resembled in most respects some of the others on the continent, but there were in this some new and unusual regulations. I mean not to specify the particulars (I think that subject trifling), but to attack the *principle*. It may however be remarked, that such an unhappy fatality attended, at this time, all the public measures, that each was almost equally exceptionable for the *mode* of regulation as for the arbitrariness of the regulation itself. One instance of despotism in this bill deserves particular notice; that the sheriff was removable at any time at the pleasure of the governor, and that he had a power to make a new returning officer for every special cause. But these considerations (grievous as they might, and certainly would be in any other case) weighed not a feather in their present arguments. They thought the wisest and most equitable temporary regulation would be of little service, and could be of no *satisfaction* to them, so long as they held these benefits *at will*, were liable, at any instant, to be deprived of them, and subjected, if their sovereign and *remote fellow-subjects* saw proper, to the extremest severity of arbitrary power. The *same authority* upon the *same principle*, might have declared the king, by his representative, sole legislative as well as executive power, and thus have invested him with a right (so far as they could bestow it) to hold our lives, liberties, and properties at his mercy. I have considered in another place the arguments urged in support of the Parliament's unlimited power, and of course of their right to annul our charters, if they think necessary. But a particular argument is urged in defence (more particularly it seems to me) of this individual power. It is this: The crown, which granted the charters, is only *one* branch of the supreme power, and consequently his acts may be controlled by the whole. The *executive* power is inferior to the *legislative*, and of course the acts of the former must be subordinate, and subject to the superintendency of the latter. I shall make a very short reply to this. Was the crown *sole agent* in the business of these charters? Did not the people accept them as a condition for the great risk and innumerable hardships they were to be exposed to? Was it not, therefore, in the nature of a *mutual compact*, and of course not alterable but by the consent of *both* parties? In what manner did the people of England resent the repeated attempts to violate the *Great Charter*? Are these charters less precious to the Americans? Do they not form the only (or at least the *principal*) security for every thing they enjoy? Why then should a distinction be made between these two situations, apparently so exactly similar? Here, however, an answer is ready. The two parties concerned in the passing Magna Charta, that which conceded those privileges, and those to whom the concession was made, composed the *whole legislative power of the State*, and of course, this charter with respect to its provisions may be considered partly as a declaratory act (of rights before possessed, but which had been grossly infringed on), and partly as an enacting one (of such as were deemed still necessary for the full security of the kingdom). Admitting this account to be just (which it is in a great measure, though liable to some little objections), then it is to be enquired upon what footing our ancestors stood when they obtained *their* charters. That age, it is well known, was an age of great enterprise and adventure. Projects of settlement in the new world were zealously entertained, and attempted by many. At first the hope of plunder, and acquiring riches, was the principal inducement to adventurers, and these expeditions were chiefly made to the South Sea. At length, however, some bold and hazardous spirits found their way to North America, and by their representations encouraged numbers to attempt their fortune there. In the course of a few years a great many quitted England either from necessity, or discontent at the prevailing measures, and sought for a laborious, but more honorable situation in these then desert regions. As, however, multitudes of these people possessed a true genuine spirit of liberty, they were determined not to quit their friends, connections, and native soil, without some adequate equivalent. This equivalent they applied for to the crown, soliciting that they might be secure of enjoying *their freedom* in the land they *were going to conquer*. This was readily granted. The prospect of possessing these fine countries, and annexing them to the crown of England, and the hope that an honorable condition granted to the settlers would animate them to industry and perseverance, were sufficient motives, even to an *arbitrary prince*, to grant privileges, for the sake of acquiring territory, *which otherwise he could never have.* Let me now ask any man, whose soul is not of the most grovelling kind, could our ancestors, at this time, dream that their-fellow subjects whom they left wallowing in sloth and luxury at home, too many ready to bend their necks to the reigning despotism, would ever afterwards claim a right to *rob* them of acquisitions *their blood and treasure purchased,* and by this means derive to themselves the only essential benefits of countries they had *no share* in acquiring? I say *no share,* for as to the trifling assistance which these colonies originally received from their mother country (an assistance of such a kind as to make their *subsequent claims* most absurdly arrogant), this was merely the assistance of the crown, without any of her immediate participation, and which was sufficiently compensated by the important rights the *crown* acquired. Did the *crown* entertain any notion that Parliament had a right to interfere? On the contrary, there is evidence that James and Charles the First both forbade them intermeddling in our concerns, and *these orders were obeyed.* I have, in another place, remarked upon this circumstance. If it should be enquired what right had the crown to these, exclusively of the supreme power, I answer, that it was the general sentiment of that age, *the crown was so entitled,** and this is sufficient for our purpose. I do not know what extraordinary lights the present age has received to justify them in calling in question the most solemn opinions of their forefathers. The new opinion upon this subject, I conceive, is derived from the harmonious and convenient connection which of late years has taken place between his Majesty and his Parliament. This has introduced many pretty compliments, and handsome references from his Majesty to his *faithful subjects;* and these in their turn have been wonderfully condescending to him. This new system, as I take it, has occasioned this *new* and *mighty* opinion of all rights being ultimately consolidated in the supreme power. But in the age when these charters were granted, very different was the state of affairs. The crown and the Parliament had continual struggles for power, and it was understood they had *separate rights,* and different objects severally to act upon. All that the latter contended for was, that the laws in being of the kingdom should be observed, and no new ones enacted but with their consent. They thought themselves sufficiently fortunate if they could secure their own liberties from violation, without seeking for new subjects of their legislative power. Did the Parliament ever (even yet) form a declaration of war, or conclude a treaty of peace? These are prerogatives of the crown, ever deemed sacred, as many others are, and it may be said that the constitution would be subverted if the Parliament were *directly* to exercise them. The prerogative in question, as appears from remarkable instances cited, was deemed *equally sacred.* If this *supremacy* of Parliament (so loudly talked of) is well founded, how happens it that conquests belonging to the state (as the phrase is) should be altogether at the disposal of the crown in a *treaty of peace?* Is the settlement of a colony by useful subjects, for the purposes it has been found to answer, with such privileges as will make ex-

* With respect to the ordinance of 1650, quoted by Mr. Barrington, it is to be considered that at that time the *regal* powers were consolidated in the *democratical;* and that this ordinance was passed by the infamous Rump Parliament, 200 of whose members had been forcibly excluded by the army, who respected no rights that interfered with their own despotism; and who were guilty of such enormous iniquities that it is scandalous for any man to quote any part of their proceedings as a *precedent.* How many of these would Mr. Barrington wish to have followed in England?

istence tolerable to them, and give them some security that their labor and services shall not be converted to their injury and oppression, and to the *sole* benefit of those who participated in no part of them, a less useful, a less *necessary* object of an act of the prerogative to *promote such ends,* and consequently to *grant the only means of securing them?* The one is necessary to restore the country to a state of peace, the other (as is evident, considering modern situations) to raise it to a state of prosperity. In order to obtain the former, the *necessary means* are given; in order to secure the latter, *means adequate to the end* must be also given. And who would settle colonies, to depend on the caprice of their-fellow subjects they left lolling in indolence at home? But I refer for a more particular examination of this subject to what I have written in another place. I know not whether this discourse upon the *right* may be called a digression, but it offered itself naturally, and may be of use. I now resume the history.

It was naturally foreseen that these violent laws would produce the strongest opposition in the province they were doomed to subdue, and that nothing but a military force could carry them into execution. But as this state of things would of course cause an enmity between the executors of the scheme, and the sufferers from it, it was judged necessary to provide against any danger that might arise to the soldiers on this account. As juries were still indulged to the people (though under a partial nomination) by the *humane* law which violated their charter, it was thought not altogether proper to confide for a proper trial upon *their principles,* of those who might be accused of crimes, in enforcing the acts, even in juries which the sheriff (named and removable at pleasure by the governor) had it in his power to select. It was rightly judged, that *laws so grievous,* the exercise of a power *so arbitrary,* could not be enforced by any ordinary method of conducting business, even assisted by the most partial regulation of it. For this reason a law was prepared, which they entitled, "an act for the impartial administration of justice, &c." By this law a discretionary power was given to the governor, to remove, at his discretion, causes where any should be questioned, for supporting the crown in the execution of the laws, either to Great Britain, or (as I believe, for I do not remember this perfectly) to some other part of America, where an impartial trial might be had. The necessary concomitant power of transporting the criminal, witnesses, &c., was given of course. It was the favorite argument in support of this bill, that the criminal would not then be tried by *factious and rebellious subjects,* enemies from principle, or at least from passion, to the unhappy prisoner, and disaffected to the just authority he was called in question for supporting, but by an impartial jury of his fellow-subjects, who were in a state of peace, and had minds cool enough to listen to reason, and decide according to the laws. This reasoning would have been plausible if we could have been sure that the equitable consequences we were taught to expect from it would really have taken place, and if the admission of the *principle* of this bill had not had the strongest tendency to *endanger our liberties,* or I may say, to *destroy them.* For if we were once to admit an unlimited power in Parliament, or in the king, to establish such courts of justice, and such regulations for their proceedings as they pleased, we should not long have much reason to boast of *liberty.* Rights without remedies are a mere chimera. The governing power of every state is continually making encroachments. Ambition is natural to the mind of man, and too often unworthy means are made use of to gratify it. The very possession of *power* is intoxicating, and has been known to corrupt very good men; and many, without any ill intention, have been industrious to enlarge their own power, seduced by the prospect of some *temporary benefit,* and inattentive to the fatal consequences of such a precedent, when the ability *to do mischief,* without the *virtue to abstain from it,* is lodged in a worthless successor. The history of mankind unhappily justifies the strongest suspicion of men in authority, and proves that there can scarcely be any compensation for *powers dangerous to liberty.* The English, perhaps, of all nations that ever existed, if the principles of the constitution were in practice inviolably observed, and were it not for some ill effects that have flowed from a radical evil, would be the *most free.* Many causes, no doubt, have conspired to this honorable distinction, and it may be traced to a variety of sources, but it is universally agreed that no institution they have is more noble, or a stronger guardian of liberty, than the inestimable trial by jury. It is even believed by a celebrated author, that this institution alone may long protract the mournful period of her fall. The excellence of this trial consists in being judged by men who are equally interested with the prisoner in preserving the law from violation, may be placed in a situation to be affected by *their own precedents,* and at the same time that the principles of self-defence will urge them to condemn *the guilty,* the care of their own preservation (if no higher principle actuates them) will prompt them to acquit the *innocent.* This jury too, for their further security, must be composed of their *neighbors,* in order that they may be qualified to take into their consideration those important circumstances, the characters of the criminal and of the witnesses. It is obvious to every man, of how much consequence this regulation is. This last circumstance, I admit, the British legislature have sometimes found it necessary to withhold in particular instances, where similar effects were apprehended in *their country*, as in *ours*; but these are exceptions on *solemn* and *extraordinary* occasions to the usual excellent mode, (which is justly esteemed the birthright of an Englishman,) and they are exceptions found necessary by their own legislature. It is not my business here to write a full encomium on this admirable institution (which I could do with great pleasure), or I could mention a variety of considerations that press upon me in its favor. The above two grand and leading circumstances I mean to make use of in treating the subject of this *judicial act*.

With respect to the first, what benefit do we derive from it? The trial is to be either in Great Britain or one of the other colonies, (if this alternative be, as I think it is, provided.) Suppose it to be in the former, The prosecutor has the charge to transmit, or attend in person, three thousand miles, together with the witnesses to support it. These witnesses (I believe, indeed from the nature of the thing the contrary is not probable) he has no compulsive power over; they may therefore *refuse* to go. They may be *unable* to go. Their families probably subsist by their industry at home; perhaps by a business which no compensation for the temporary profits can indemnify their absence from. The dangers of the voyage would certainly require recompense beyond that afforded for the loss of time. They may lose their lives by being exposed to this danger; the witnesses, if they arrive safely, must be subsisted in England, and the same danger attends them on their return. They must go home under every painful apprehension, and the fear of brutal insult from mobs, who will be too ready to insult men of *another country*, and of a different faction, exposed to the hand of power. Under all these circumstances (and I am not conscious of any aggravation) what chance has any man of procuring witnesses? And is it just—can it be equitable—to let the event of a cause be guided by such hazardous contingencies? On the other hand, in what condition are the witnesses for the prisoner? He, from the tenor of the act, must be charged for some offence done in vindicating and assisting to carry into execution the high measures of the court. This act is held forth as an indemnity (I am loth to say an encouragement) to men who will afford that assistance. They are therefore to be tried in that country, which is *interested in acquitting them.* For the *principle* of their conduct must be maintained, at any rate, and when this is of such mighty consequence, we can never suppose they will be too scrutinous about the *mode*. The cause they are suffering for, is one that gratifies the *pride*, the *resentment*, the *ambition* of their country. They may therefore be assured, not only of the strongest support from the crown, but of the highest applause from the people. And in proportion as men's activity in an interesting cause is captivating to the people whom it favors, will be the *temptation* to bad men to distinguish themselves for that quality in its support. And we well know how little parties are apt to condemn too great an activity on *their side.* Let any man for a moment consider the great inequality with which the cause sets out, and what judgment will he form of the decision? Judges are but men, and though highly respectable have been for a great number of years the characters of the English judges, they have not all, not even the *present judges*, escaped censure. A bias (it may be said, I fear, with too much truth) has been seen to influence *some*. If such a bias can prevail in the affairs of *their own country*, to the prejudice of *their own real interest*, what may we not expect towards those of *another*, and where (if they have it at all in contemplation) their *interest* as well as *passion* will operate to our prejudice. Much, it is known, depends on the characters of the parties, as also of the witnesses. But neither judge nor jury know any thing of either, but what their conduct in the cause questioned can suggest to them. Will they not naturally, therefore, be inclined to think *favorably* of those of *their own side*, and *unfavorably* of *their unfortunate opponents?* If they should have received any *out-of-door* information, of what complexion might we suppose it to be? Thus far there is every danger to the prosecutor in point of *fact.* As to the *law*, he is under still greater disadvantages. This, wherever questions of right litigated between the two countries come into debate, will be decided instantly and indignantly against him. For their interpretation of our condition is, that we have *no rights*, we hold every thing at their mercy. What becomes now of the *impartial administration of justice?* If the supporters of the crown were in danger of suffering from unjust verdicts in the province of the Massachusetts Bay, what chance have the defenders of the people of procuring justice in England? It makes no difference, that, admitting the full latitude of my interpretation, there would only be sustained a *negative* and not a *positive* injury; that the only danger suggested is, that of an *acquittal*, and not of a *condemnation;* because the hopes of such an acquittal are held out to *authorize*, if not *encourage* murders, the unhappy objects of which might might have saved their lives, if *severe justice had been apprehended.* I shall say nothing on the supposition that any of the prisoners had been sent to one of the other colonies; because, as it is left at the discretion of the governor to send them either here or to Great Britain, there could be no doubt that he would always prefer the latter; at least he most assuredly would if there was not *one* colony at the absolute devotion of the mother country. I, therefore, can only believe, that this provision was held out as *a show of equity*, and to deceive the rest of the colonies (supposing them at the same time of very gross understandings) with *an appearance of confidence.* What now is the result of the whole matter? Odious acts are to be carried into execution by *one people* against another, in consequence of questions of right about which each party entertained different opinions. These acts are expected to be enforced by military power. Still, however, a regular government, equal to all the offices of law and justice, is permitted in the country; but this government, for fear of a passionate condemnation, is not to be trusted with the trial of *soldiers*, or other officious instruments of the new laws. These, for their more *impartial* trial, are to be tried by the people by whom they have been employed, and in judging of whose crime they, though parties, exercise the right of determination. On this side much stronger reasons are there (as may appear above) of suspecting a *partial acquittal*, than on ours of dreading an *unjust condemnation.* If there was a necessity to provide against *our* partiality, because we are *parties*, was it not humorous (if so unhappy a subject could be so contemplated) to see the remedy presented of an absolute reference to *them*, who are liable to the same objection, and with many aggravating circumstances? Upon these equitable and humane grounds stands the act of Parliament "for the impartial administration of justice in the cases of persons questioned, &c., in the province of the Massachusetts Bay." I am not in possession of the act, and remember it but imperfectly; but to the best of my recollection, I have mentioned its capital provisions. If it should be otherwise, I desire it may be understood that I mean not to deceive by any misrepresentation.

But the tower of despotism was not yet fully erected. In aid of the same violent system a farther measure was judged necessary. The ministry and their agents had affected to have been employed ever since the peace in the deepest meditation for a proper settlement of Canada. This was found almost insuperably difficult, on account of the rivalship of *interest* and of *wishes* between the old and the new settlers. The proper adjustment of this business had hitherto baffled men of the most enlightened genius, and the greatest political abilities. Success in this great point began to be despaired of, when intelligence arrived of the great commotions in America. They then applied to the subject with new ardor, and increased hopes. On a sudden they found themselves wonderfully illumined, and the divine rays of wisdom and policy immediately darted upon them. It was determined to *strike the iron while it was hot*, and not suffer the blaze of their genius to cool. They immediately formed a system suited to their new exalted conceptions. According to this system the old settlers were to be indulged in all their prejudices (admitting they entertained such, which is scarcely credible) in favor of *arbitrary power:* the French laws were to be continued; the poor Canadians were not barely allowed to enjoy their religion (persecuting in its *principle*, and horrid in its influence on the morals of mankind) free from molestation; but it was to be made the *established* religion of the country, and to be put in possession of all the ecclesiastical honors and immunities, thus affording the most tempting encouragement to the increase of this dangerous hierarchy. Thus far the old settlers were satisfied, (as the fact is asserted, though I cannot believe, however the great men may be interested, the people in general can be such idiots as to prefer an *arbitrary* to a *free* government; and I suspect this extraordinary exaltation of their religion was partly intended as a bribe to make them the more acquiescent in it.) What were the indulgences granted to the *new settlers?* Their religion was not worthy of a present provision, but left to the future mercy of the king; an assembly, or representative of the people, to give them some share in their own government, was denied them. Even a Habeas Corpus was refused; upon what principle no one can conceive, unless by supposing that even this arbitrary government intend sometimes to violate, in *individual instances*, their own *general provisions.* The trial by jury, so highly and so justly valued by Englishmen, that yet distinguishing privilege they possess, in all civil cases was denied to these unfortunate subjects of an English province. Is it possible for us to conceive, after such a detail, that this province is *English?* It is indeed so in name, but in *spirit*, in *principle*, in *dignity* (so far as its governors are concerned) it is still *French*,—and they ought well to be aware of the danger of assimilating the ancient inhabitants of a French colony, in *every* respect hurtful as well as beneficial, to the old manners of their former parent country; and of placing the English subjects there in such a situation as can give them no particular counterbalancing attachment to *their* native government. This act is the result of eleven years' close study, application and enquiry, made, as was pretended, in order, if possible, to reconcile the minds of both kinds of *subjects* to the new establishment; and ending in one which can entirely please *neither party;* is particularly odious to the English, and can possibly, in all reasonable construction, have no other tendency than to humor a few great lords in their *pride* and *dignity*, engage them by this bribe to favor the arbitrary designs of government towards us, effectuate these designs more completely by establishing a total contrariety between *our* religion and form of government and *theirs*, and by the extensive comprehending limits assigned to the territory (hemming us in on all sides) giving all possible scope to the propagation of the Romish faith, and of despotic principles.°

For the present, the rigor of power stopped here. In this manner did the auspicious system of subjugating America begin , aided by a large army to enforce it. The three first acts, indeed (the only ones whose *principle* we had any right to object to), only respected *one* province. Others, however, had been guilty of acts about the tea, in principle equally obnoxious, and in one a fact of the same kind had actually been committed. But it was deemed too dangerous to attack *all* or *many* of the colonies, and they hoped that the rest would be mean enough to enjoy an inglorious inactivity, while they should be at liberty to oppress and ruin the one they had devoted to destruction. But more virtuous and wiser principles actuated the Americans ; they now too plainly saw the plans of despotism making hasty strides upon them, and exerted in the highest instances of *absolute legislation*. Some of the regulations were not *temporary*, but intended to be *perpetual;* and it was evident to every man that had *common sense*, and *common feeling*, that an immediate and universal opposition was become necessary. What was the case of the Massachusets Bay to-day, might be that of New York, Pennsylvania, and any of the others to-morrow ; and they had no honorable security against such oppressions but in *their own resources*. Heaven had blessed them with a fine soil, with multitudes of people, with a patriot spirit, and placed them in the neighborhood of each other, nearly upon the same footing in point of *right*, and in point of *interest*. *United*, they could maintain a *vigorous defence;* were they to stand *single*, each might be made an immediate and disgraceful prey to an unmerciful and cruel tyranny. Providence had afforded them the means of this defence ; its exertion had become necessary for their safety ; a neglect or disregard of such fortunate circumstances

---

* In this act there was even so gross an absurdity as the following : It was enacted that the exercise of the Church of Rome should be subject to the king's supremacy, as established by the 1st Eliz. ; the oath however by which this supremacy was guarded, was dispensed with to the Canadians, (being Papists,) and a common oath of allegiance substituted in its stead; wherein is expressly renounced any *pardons, dispensations, &c.* By which the important purpose is answered of giving the priest a little more trouble in granting a more particular dispensation.

would justly expose them to eternal ignominy and dishonor, and entail upon their posterity a miserable subjection to a slavery their ancestors had it in their power to avert from them. These thoughts stimulated and fired the minds of the Americans ; they did not hesitate an instant upon the choice. They immediately concerted plans for forming a *general consultation*, and these were executed with dispatch. The people in the several colonies chose deputies to represent them in convention, and these sent delegates to meet in Congress in Philadelphia, and advise for their *common safety.*

A new and important scene of things was now opened ; the colonies had *constitutionally* no connexion with each other but through the medium of Great Britain. Such an union, as was now formed, had formerly been projected, but had come to nothing—the colonies finding the claims of their mother country more speculative than practical, and hoping, by a less obnoxious mode, to avoid any fatal effects from them. Now indeed the plans of despotism seemed to be regularly and fully concerted. It became necessary therefore to meet them on the part of America with becoming firmness, and every prudent exertion. Important rights were in danger of being lost, and they had only to determine whether they would submit in a *regular* manner to be made *slaves*, or *irregularly* nobly vindicate themselves from the imminent danger of so dishonorable a condition. Their liberties were at stake upon their determination. In competition with this superior object, petty constitutional regards they justly thought to be of little consideration. Their constitution was only valuable as the means of securing *freedom* and *happiness* ; when it no longer could serve to conduce to that end, it was their duty to select other means more *permanent* and more *effectual*.

These were the principles upon which this *honorable* (and I trust *lasting*) union was formed. The event of their councils was most anxiously waited for by their constituents. It being necessary that their consultations should be held in the closest secrecy, it is impossible for any person who was not on the spot, to conceive the extreme anxiety with which all men in America looked up to the decisions of this *great body* for their relief. Their virtue was not questioned, their abilities were greatly relied on ; but there was a difference of opinion every where prevailing as to the proper *mode* of discovering our resentment, and suing for redress. Some proposed the most moderate measures, a few very harsh ones ; the majority seemed inclined to a mixture of *lenity* and *severity; lenity* to give a fair opening to Great Britain to recede ; *severity* to convince her, we were earnest in *our demands*, and were determined to risk every thing in their

defence. It is not surprising, that there was such a difference of opinion. It was occasioned by the different sentiments men entertained of the disposition of our haughty rulers. In all other respects perhaps the sentiments of a great country upon so capital a question as then depended were never before so universal. Notwithstanding base and wicked assertions to the contrary, I am fully warranted in saying, that an honorable reconciliation with Great Britain was the first and most earnest object of every man's wish and attention. I do not mean to answer for *every individual,* (which would be ridiculous,) but for a *very large majority.* There was no other object in contemplation (I will even venture to say) so generally, as even to afford its partisans the title of a *faction.* The name of *independence* no man dared to mention but with horror and indignation. A declaration in its favor would have been then esteemed almost equally hostile to the honor and interests of America, as the proposal of absolute and unconditional submission. Then never, I will presume to say, was any opposition formed upon more *virtuous* or more *steady* principles. It proceeded upon the determination to insist on every thing necessary as a full security for our *liberty*, but the instant that was attained to return to the most entire and cordial connection with a country whose conduct might well nigh have driven us to despair. In order to form a judgment of the right measures to be pursued in the melancholy crisis America was reduced to, it was necessary previously to consider what might be supposed the sentiments and views of the administration of Great Britain, the fatal original authors of all these dire extremities. The espousers of moderate measures were inclined to think favorably of these. They said, that there was great reason, from every circumstance, to believe that Mr. Grenville, in the first capital error we complained of, had acted from *principle* and not from any *bad motive ;* his general character, in every other respect, the apparent earnestness with which he always conducted and supported this measure, and the plausibility of the motives suggested as the cause to a man inflamed with high ideas of his own country's power, and misconceiving (as was, and to our misfortune we may say, *still* is too general,) the true state of America ; these circumstances point out a presumption in his favor which men of candor cannot easily forego : that the ready and strong renunciation of this act, when it was discovered that America was likely to be kindled into a civil war, (though then little prepared to sustain it,) showed very general and very honorable principles to prevail in the nation in our favor, and in avoidance of any *fatal* discord ; that the subsequent establishment of duties was formed upon distinctions held out in that

famous controversy by *ourselves*, and it was some time before America itself could discern, and resolved to obviate, their fatal tendency ; that the factious and turbulent destruction of the tea must naturally have inflamed the resentment of the British nation to the highest pitch, and this would serve to account for, and greatly to alleviate, the passionate and vindictive acts they passed ; that it was scarcely to be conceived they would stand against the united sense, and steady opposition of the whole continent ; but, in order to avoid a civil war, (which otherwise must appear inevitable,) would relinquish laws that passion had excited, but cool reason (on a vigorous remonstrance) must certainly disapprove ; that in order to facilitate this desirable event, to place no obstructions in the way, to leave no pretence for the refusal of justice,—they apprehended the first application should be made free from *menaces,* or *restraint* of any kind ; if the application succeeded we should in all probability for the future be in a condition of greater *security* and *happiness* than any country the world had ever seen, (a blessing we ought not lightly to endanger ;) if it did *not* succeed, we should be justified by all mankind in every vigorous exertion we found it necessary to make, and should have the pleasing satisfaction to reflect that we had done all in our power to avoid the fatal extremities we were reduced to. These arguments were replied to by those who thought *other measures*, besides a remonstrance, immediately necessary, in a manner something like the following : They said, that it was an enquiry of very little consequence to America, whether the intentions of ministers were *good* or *bad* as to *themselves ;* but the proper enquiry was, how did these intentions affect *us ?* that the rectitude of Mr. Grenville's intentions in the first sense might readily be admitted, without prejudice to any argument they supported, but let any one consider what part he would probably take on the present occasion, (if he was alive,) and then consider the weight of any argument drawn from *good intentions* in a moral light, that the repeal of the Stamp Act was certainly conceded to *our resentment ;* for though the leaders of that measure might be men of honorable and enlarged views, and from a sense of its *inexpediency* and *injustice* (independent of the pressure of the *principle*) have been inclined to repeal it, yet so *favorite*, so *popular* an act could not easily have found a majority to destroy it, if the *interest of Great Britain* as well as that of *America,* had not been quickly touched ; that some apology for the subsequent duties might perhaps be found in the arguments at the time of the Stamp Act, but it was evident that *policy* had not been the object in their creation, (unless it can be political to establish duties as a bone of contention,) but a wanton desire of settling up an odious claim, and interfering in our internal concerns to have us more at their mercy; that this naturally and justly gave alarm to the Americans, and caused them to examine more minutely into the right of imposing such duties *at pleasure*; that the result they found was, if such a right was admitted, they must for ever be *poor dependent vassals*, and not *free subjects* of their mother country; that the right could only be pretended (upon constitutional principles) as a necessary consequence of *another* which had been always conceded to them, between which and the former, it was said *no boundary* could in the nature of things be set; but, however, it appeared that the exercise of the right in the present instance evidently transgressed those principles upon which it was pretended to be founded, and it was necessary to contend that *a boundary* should be generally established, and judged of at the time (as was in most cases practicable) from the nature of the imposition laid; that this could be productive of no more inconvenience than many other delicate limitations, by which a free people found it necessary to guard their liberty, were liable to; was *essential* to their freedom; and they admitted in all doubtful cases should be decided against the *limitation;* that these *sentiments* and *arguments* of the Americans were well known in England before they repealed any of these duties; and afterwards they excepted the article of *tea* from the deliverance they gave us of the others. That all petitions and remonstrances on account of this tax were repeatedly and contemptuously disregarded; and the conduct of Parliament towards the East India Company, as it respected the consumption of that article here, was either principally moved by the prospect of establishing the duty, or at least showed a determined spirit to enforce it; that the rigorous acts that followed the destruction of the tea at Boston (admitting that measure to be ever so heinous) by far exceeded the provocation; observed no manner of proportion between *offences* and *punishment;* violated all the laws of justice; and by being partially inflicted against *one* province, where *others* were equally guilty, discovered an evident intention to crush *that one* singly, and, as was conceived, by that means more effectually; that this attempt to *divide* the interest of the Americans, and to bribe the other colonies (many of whom were equally guilty with that devoted people) by an exemption from punishment, to suffer tamely its infliction upon *them*, ought to be instantly resented as an insidious and mean attack upon their virtue; that there was no ground to believe these late obnoxious acts were merely the effect of a *temporary passion;* they were evidently a branch of the great high-sounding system of compelling our submission; naturally followed the indignant rejection of every peaceable petition, and were passed in defiance of the most admirable arguments, and with the determined purpose of awing us into abject and disgraceful subjection; that a great and respectable province was now suffering "all the cruelties of ministerial vengeance" for their spirited defence of American liberties, and it would be infamous in the other colonies to consider, in the measures they adopted, only themselves at *ease*, and not their friends and countrymen in the most perilous and distressed condition; that such had been the tenor of the measures in Great Britain for some years past, so arbitrary were known to be *the principles of the ministers*, there was not the least probability of equity and justice alone having any influence upon them, and as America had long tried these in vain, and in the course of them had suffered the most grievous indignities, it was no longer consistent with her *prudence* or her *honor* to rely on those alone in the present exigency; that, however, a pleasing memory of the former happy connection with Great Britain, a desire of renewing it upon terms of *safety* and *reputation*, a great respect still entertained for the body of that people, a hope that a majority of them were *our friends*, and disdained the tyranny and selfishness of the prevailing party, a just dread of the horrors and uncertain calamities and event of a civil war,—all these considerations prompted us to act in such a manner as to leave room for a retreat with honor, and in the mean time to regard with all the tenderness our situation would admit of, those individuals of that kingdom who had long been intimately connected with America, and had property here upon which perhaps their existence and support depended; that the *detail* of these measures might admit of many questions, but the *principle* of them, it was conceived, for all these reasons, was apparently just and equitable, and suited to the dangerous and difficult situation in which we unhappily stood. These last arguments prevailed in the Congress, and the consequences are well known. They prohibited after a short day all imports from Great Britain or Ireland, and particular commodities specified from the West Indies; and after a distant day, if no redress of our grievances was obtained, all exports to Great Britain, Ireland, and the British West Indies were to cease. Notwithstanding all the clamor which has been raised against these resolutions, a very few words, I am sure, will be sufficient to vindicate them. The American trade, through the medium of Great Britain, considered in itself, was mutually beneficial to both countries. The immense advantage it was of to Great Britain, has been set forth in the most striking and powerful light by many able writers on the subject, and has been estimated many years ago by the great man to whom England and America owe so much, and who was Secretary of State during the greatest part of the last war, (which gave him the means of information,) at upwards of two millions annually. This trade was also of great advantage to America, as it furnished them with the means of making a natural and just compensation for the protection which was afforded them by a great and powerful nation, without whose assistance they could certainly have made but little improvement. This commercial monopoly they *willingly* afforded, and never called in question, notwithstanding it has been stated by many ingenious and worthy men, even in England, as extremely hard and rigorous; however, they cheerfully submitted to it; their ancestors had borne it from the beginning; it was esteemed the *proper* authority of a mother country over colonies; they felt themselves free in every internal concern, and particularly in the grand point of taxing; and they trusted to a delicate and just sense of interest as their ultimate resource against commercial oppressions. This trade had been carried on to an immense extent: America every year received still larger supplies than the foregoing; its necessary wants were many, its artificial ones more; and they were beginning to indulge themselves in luxury (*luxury* I mean for their *situation*) to such a degree, that in a few years half the property of America would perhaps have become that of British merchants, had this cause received no interruption. As it was, every ounce of gold or silver which America, by the most circuitous course of industry could collect, regularly found its way to Great Britain, besides vast imports of the most useful trading commodities. Such was our situation in this respect, that there were very few clear estates in America. This being the case, (as every man in America knows to be true,) a judgment may be formed how just was the inference which is said to have been made in favor of the Stamp Act from the great display of riches shown *by a few individuals*, and how contemptible that policy which was framed on such *trifling suggestions*.

Trade in its own nature is extremely free, and can only subsist by a *spirit of freedom*. The idea of obtaining a *direct* command of it by laws and regulations is idle and absurd. These may indeed *indirectly* possess a power over it, by confining it to particular channels; but this is all. It still must be left to the people from whom the advantages of trade are to be derived, whether they will submit to *these*, under every circumstance, or at any time they may think proper withhold the trade altogether. We cannot be ordered to import a certain quantity of goods. This can only be regulated by our occasions, and our wishes. We may require no goods, we may resolve to do without them. This was the case in the instance in question. We had for many years been importing ourselves out of almost all our property, our wealth was drained to the uttermost farthing for the emolument of Great Britain; the profits of all our trade centered there; we had the utmost difficulty of subsisting at home, under the heavy pressure of a debt we were continually seeking means to discharge; this monopoly, however, did not satisfy its engrossers; we were not only limited in the means of *getting*, but the little which with much labor and toil we *did get*, we were not suffered to enjoy; we were told, all this property should be held at the disposal of our monopolists; that what they did not take in the way of trade they might have occasion for in the way of *imposition;* and an earnest of a small sum was in the mean time required as a support of the principle; we were lately crushed with severe laws of *internal* regulation, such as grievously distressed one province, and threatened all. We saw no end to unreasonable demands, and tyrannous regulations. It was here necessary to make a stand. "We owe an immense debt already; a dreadful contest is arising, of which we know not the issue. No honest men can engage in debt they have no probable prospect of paying. We will therefore for the present import no more; we will endeavor to discharge former arrears as soon as possible, unfettered by *new engagements*. This is a debt we owe to our creditors. We also owe some to our country. Why should we run the risk of ruining ourselves to enrich a nation that is seeking to enslave us? They have considered our weight in the state as too little. Every instance of their late conduct has discovered marks of contempt, which no men of spirit could endure. It is time for us to convince them, that *they* have some dependence on *us* as well as *we* on *them*. A stoppage of the imports will enable them to look about them, and interest at least the manufacturers and the body of the people, (who will *feel* the impolicy of their rulers,) to remonstrate with vigor on our behalf. This has succeeded formerly; why should we despair of its success now? It is reasonable and just, that when every advantage which *power*, and *an unfeeling use of it*, can give to men is used against us, we should exert this natural, this peaceable power which the nature of things cannot deprive us of, and is our *principal resource*, short of a *civil war*. A war in the end may become inevitable, we should therefore contract our expenses, to enable us to maintain it the better; we ought also to show, by some little exertion of spirit, that we are not tamely disposed to submit to every act of violence; and by this means, much sooner than by pusillanimity, or marks of too great reluctance to close with them (if they shall render it unavoidable) in the last appeal, we may be able to avert its fatal necessity." These arguments are to my mind perfectly satisfactory in defence of the *non-importation*. The *non-exportation* is a more delicate matter. Private justice seemed here incompatible with public duty. The *American* merchants owed vast sums to the *British*, which they had no means to discharge but by way of trade. If this was prohibited, the source of payment was suspended. And yet this prohibition seemed necessary, for the great purpose of American opposition. How were these two points to be reconciled? The only way that could be thought of was this: "We will not immediately stop our exports: this we will reserve for the last extremity. If the ministry mean to persevere, an appeal must be made to arms; and then it will be ridiculous to think of trade: were this possible, it would be contemptible in us to think of it: we did not pledge our *freedom* for our *debts*: the little money we owe to Great Britain, would be a poor compensation for all the havoc of war, and the horrid desolation they would seek to expose us to; but however much, even in this situation, we might be inclined (as most, we are persuaded, would) to discharge our arrears to the merchants, can we be such fools as to attempt it by means that would serve to enable our enemies more effectually to crush us? If they mean not to come to these extremities, (of which, however, none can doubt, if they retain the acts,) this prohibition may be felt *severely enough* to awaken them to their senses: the withholding exports, such essentials in their commerce, may compel them to do us justice: all hope from reason and equity, and intreaty alone, every man of the least discernment must absolutely relinquish. What then can we do but immediately put a stop to that trade which is absolutely in our power, and solemnly resolve that after a few months, which may enable much of our debt to be paid off, and which will give time for Parliament by reconciling measures to prevent its ever taking place, we will suspend *every other commercial connection*, our only remaining peaceable resource when the operations of war are *not* concerned, and impracticable to be avoided when they *are?* This is our only resource, short of *an immediate commencement of civil war*. We lament the cruel necessity of our condition; we feel for our creditors; we shall be unhappy in not being able to discharge our debts: but these are considerations which affect individuals; and they must inevitably give way to those higher and more immediate considerations which concern the state. To the *constitution of our country*, to the means necessary for preserving *that constitution*, every other duty and demand is subordinate, and compared to these they are light as air, and to be sacrificed without a moment's hesitation." The same principles will vindicate us to Ireland and the West Indies. The common cant of their having done us no injury is scarcely worth notice. We never pretended they did. But those to whom those trades were of amazing advantage, had done us the greatest injuries. We ought to convince them they insulted people it was dangerous to provoke, and that their trade to America did not altogether depend on *acts of Parliament*, and *penal regulations*. If Great Britain had done us justice, *those trades would never have been injured*. She injured them by her *denial of justice*, not we by taking steps necessary to *enforce* it. Our exports to Great Britain, (whilst our debt subsisted,) if no invasion of our rights had been attempted, might have been considered as a matter of *duty*. But we owed no *duty* (speaking generally) to Ireland and the West Indies. We indeed owed them, and bore them affection, as fellow-subjects of the same empire. We were always disposed to support a friendly connection with them. But if such a connection is overborne by the grasping and violent hand of power, are the objects of *this oppression* to be blamed for it? Ireland should complain little. Her rights and ours stand upon much the same basis, with a little difference *in favor of America*. What would have been her conduct had she been so treated? How would she submit to a *single* regulation that did not affect *her trade?* Let her consider these things coolly, and then blame us if she can.

I mention these arguments with some confidence, because they have convinced *me*. I was formerly a great advocate for *moderation*. I could not bring myself to believe that the ministers would hazard their country's fate upon so delicate and critical a question. I thought they would have judged it necessary to concede to us the important and necessary claims we made, if they could have a fair opening to do it; at least that they would have relinquished their *practical, oppressive* laws. This was my sentiment of things. But I have unhappily found reason to alter it; and to applaud the deep sagacity, and clear penetration, of those whom I believed, at the time, to be in an erroneous opinion. The reception given by Parliament to the New York petitions, first opened my eyes on this subject. It had long been the favorite topic of ministerial advocates in America, that their claims were not so obnoxious to government, as their *mode* of asserting them; that if this had been more respectful and confiding, the other would have been easily adjusted. The New York Assembly adopted this way of thinking; their claim of rights was founded on the fullest American principles, except in one or two respects wherein I think, if they did not state them exactly as they *constitutionally* stood, they established useful practical distinctions. In the *mode* alone they materially differed from the rest of the continent. Here then was a fair opportunity to try the real views of administration. There being only *one* colony in this situation made no difference. They had always held it out as a maxim that the colonies ought to be considered as distinct, individual dependencies on the mother country, and by no means proper objects of a general and confederating union with each other. The policy had been in contemplation, and was believed to have been actually attempted, *to break this union*. No fairer occasion than this which New York presented could be hoped for. It professedly set on foot a separate interest from the rest of America, and had their demands been acceded to, a most important province would have been gained to government, and the assertions of all their retainers in America would have been verified. Instead of this, how were the petitions received? They were treated with the most *impudent* contempt and indignation. I hope the warmth of the expression will be excused from the atrocity of the conduct. A House of Commons that calls itself *our virtual representatives* to despise a petition couched in the most decent terms, and coming from a people who had had the signal merit (as it was deemed) to abstain from a general and prevailing violence through America! A petition that concerned their most sacred and important rights! that respected *freedom*, of which the British House of Commons used always to be esteemed the guardian! Blush, ye degenerate men, for this base and unworthy conduct. Was it not sufficient that you were determined to make us *slaves* in the end, but you must begin to insult us before your purpose was effected? Take care, ye mighty Dons, that this infamous behavior does not one day most bitterly and indignantly recoil upon you.

The establishment of committees to enforce these regulations has been the source of much pathetic declamation. Yet, abstracted from the other subject of the necessity we were under to form *such regulations*, it is an objection of no weight. No large body of men can act in a *common concert* without some rules to carry their proceedings into effect. Wicked and corrupt men are every where lurking to take advantage of the public distress, and a system would be very weakly formed that was not calculated to defeat them. There is not such a thing in the nature of human affairs possible as the *universal*, unanimous concurrence of a whole people in any *one* measure. The *majority* must govern the whole or there is an end to all society. This is not less necessary in the case of resistance to an oppressive government than in others. If the people have a right to *resist*, they have a right to take such measures as will give their resistance *efficacy*. It would be ridiculous to assent to the one, and withhold the other. Therefore this case, as all others, must partake of the usual infirmity of human nature, and *general* consent must supply the place of *universal*, which it is morally impossible to obtain. What would have been the present condition of England, had she waited for *such* a consent at the Revolution?

The events subsequent to those which I have related I shall not discourse of. They were, in substance, the natural consequence of the preceding ones; when each party obstinately maintained its ground, and no man can form any judgment of these but according to the sentiments he entertains of the foregoing circumstances. We are now, and have been for some months, in a state of hostility with our parent country, the most unhappy condition we could be exposed to. This has been endeavored to be aggravated by every possible injury the most brutal minds could conceive. Even the savage incitement of Indians to murder a few helpless people in the back country, and the more than diabolical purpose of exciting our own domestics (domestics they forced upon us) to cut our throats, and involve men, women and children, in one universal massacre,—these villainous attempts are to be numbered in the catalogue of our enemy's crimes. They have, however, thank God, failed of their desired effect. One danger may indeed still be apprehended; the other is less probable. Neither has, however, yet actually taken place. We have not been intimidated by this conduct from persevering in our duty, but on the contrary have been actuated by a more determined spirit. Resentment for such cruel usage has added spurs to our patriotism.

It will easily be observed that I have not noticed every grievance America has sustained, and that I have even omitted some very principal ones: my reason was, that they were not immediately necessary to illustrate my subject. The present *unbounded* claim swallows up all inferior ones; and I have confined myself only to a particular history of such measures as had some intricacy, or a superior importance in them. The reason for non-payment of the tea I have also omitted. It must be apparent to every one, that this could not be done without adopting the measure, sanctifying the unconstitutional acts passed to enforce payment, encouraging government to harass the public in the same manner for similar private injuries in future, and being mean enough to show no resentment for the arbitrary and unjust acts that accompanied it.

I avoid the unhappy subject of the day, *independency*. There was a time very lately, within my recollection, when neither myself nor any person I knew, could hear the name but with horror. I know it is a favorite argument against us, and that on which the proceedings of Parliament are most plausibly founded, that this has been our aim since the beginning, and all other attempts were a cloak and disguise to this principal one. If this supposition had been well founded, and a desire of redressing the grievances we complained of been entertained by government, they might immediately, by granting these, have detected and disappointed the other, or covered us with eternal disgrace, if we avowed it. But it is sufficient to say, our professions have been all solemnly to the contrary; we have never taken any one step which really indicated such a view; its suggestion has no better foundation than *mere suspicion*, which might countenance any falsehood whatever, and every man in America knows that this is one of the most egregious *falsehoods* ever any people were duped with. But so it was. This error they have been captivated with, and it has led them, as well as us, to the brink of destruction. Its consequences are now only to be deplored, not, I fear, to be remedied. I may venture to say, the dread, or the *pretended dread*, of this evil, has almost produced it. This suspicion, though so ill founded, has been, professedly, the parent of all the violent acts that now irritate the minds of the Americans. Some are inflamed enough to *wish* for independence, and all are reduced to so unhappy a condition as to dread at least that they shall be compelled in their own defence to embrace it. I profess myself of the latter number, in exclusion of the former. I am convinced America is not in such a situation as to entitle her to consider it as a just object of *ambition*, and I have no idea of people forming constitutions from *revenge*. A just and constitutional connection with Great Britain (if such could be obtained) I still think, in spite of every provocation, would be happier for America, for a considerable time to come, than *absolute independence*. No man can disdain, more than I do, the infamy and cruel violence of our oppressors' conduct. But I make a distinction between the ministry, and the Parliament, and the people of England. These last I do not consider as accessory in all the oppressions we have sustained. Many, I have no doubt, are great criminals; but more, I am persuaded, are deceived by *false* and *wicked* information. Great things have been attempted in our defence. But the misfortune is, the *inadequacy of the representation*, and the *corruption so universal*, leave little to the real voice of the people. If it is said that these causes may always give us such a Ministry and Parliament, I answer, that I form no idea of any reconciliation but where we shall have *full security* that even these can do us no essential injury, unless we conspire to it ourselves. In political affairs we are not always at liberty to choose what is best in the *abstract*, but what may be found so in *practice*. I can see no establishment in America, no turn to its affairs, that is likely to arise of a happier nature than such a *re-union*. But if a re-union is not practicable but upon terms of dishonor, if one essential point is required as a sacrifice to obtain it, I should spurn at the idea as scandalous and disgraceful; and in such an event, or on any occasion whatever, if *independency* should become necessary to our safety, I should not hesitate an instant in giving my assent to it.

June, 1776.

DUKINFIELD TO IREDELL.

LEWES IN SUSSEX, 10th June, 1776.

I received your letter of the 10th Jan. last (but not the one you had written a few days before), giving me an account of the death of Mr. Pearson. This morning I saw in the papers that a mail would be dispatched to-morrow night for New York, and I had just time to write to my mother under cover to Mr. Lowther, at New York, as you desired; but as another mail will be dispatched this week to the southern provinces, I hope you will receive this. A few days before I received your letter, Mr. Elmsly had acquainted me with the death of Mr. Pearson. I fear my mother will not have much to claim as legatee, though she may have a great deal of trouble as executrix. I assure you if he has been as incorrect in all his affairs as in those where I have been unluckily connected with him, I would not undertake to adjust them. I have long had a very mean opinion of his abilities, and am sorry to say that of late I have reason to doubt his principles; but perhaps he thought he might treat me, and take any liberties, as he pleased. It was more out of compliment to my mother, and my expecting to return soon, than from any expectation of his great management, that he was first intrusted with the management and direction of my affairs: and I thought they were so trifling, that I continued him. But I have long been so dissatisfied with him, that, had it been in my power, I should before now have been in Carolina, and endeavored to prevail upon other persons, whose judgment I have a greater opinion of, to undertake for me the direction of them.

I most sincerely hope that the present feuds will (as well for the general, as any private advantage) be honorably, steadfastly, and speedily settled, and then I hope once more to visit Carolina, though it can be but for a few months, as my military engagements will not permit me to require a longer absence. Mr. Pearson's conduct in regard to Dickenson has displeased me very much; and I am sorry if his account is not settled before this time, for Mr. Pearson must have received money on my account from David Turner—much more than was necessary to discharge all my debts; and in this expectation I refused to pay his account to Mr. Wilkinson; but if it should not yet be paid I hope Dickenson will not be uneasy about it, though I cannot acquiesce in his demand for interest before he sent me his bill. I told Mr. Wilkinson that as soon as I was ascertained that the account was not paid in Carolina, I would pay him the bill with interest from Jan., 1775. I received a letter from Mr. Pearson dated 10th Jan., 1775, wherein he says,—"Turner has not paid me one shilling;" but if Turner is to be credited, he paid him in May, 1774 (according to his letter to me dated 18th June, 1775), £44, though not the whole in money. I gave Mr. Pearson such positive directions (and since repeated them) for the payment of this account that I hope it is done. Mr. Pearson wrote me in Oct. last that my lands were to be leased out on the 25th of that month, and that I should see the terms in the packet sent me by the Commerce (Messenger's brig), but upon making every enquiry that I possibly could, from the master of that vessel, I never could discover that there had ever been any paper or letter put on board for me, though Mr. Pearson told me that all my papers and accounts were sent by her.

Mr. Pearson's brig has been very unlucky—she struck on the North Key of Cuba, and lay ashore about 52 hours, and in Jan. got to Kinsale in Ireland, where she put in to refit, and remains there now, but is expected in a very few days in Bristol. When she arrives there I shall go and meet Mr. Elmsly, under whose direction she is to be. I have desired my mother to take the care of my affairs at present, and to advise with you and Mr. Johnston. I hope to see you next year.

Most sincerely do I condole with you, my dear friend, on the loss of Miss Johnston. Each of that family is so estimable, that the loss is irreparable. Poor Berry will be a great loss to New Berne. Has he left any family? Knox I hardly knew. I should have told you I had been lieutenant four months.

I beg my best respects to Mrs. Iredell, Mrs. Blair, Mrs. Dawson, Mr. Johnston's family, and all my other friends, and believe me, my dear sir,

Yours most sincerely,
NAT. DUKINFIELD.

To JAS. IREDELL, Collector, Edenton, N. C.

The Council of Safety met at Wilmington, June 5th. Mr. Wilie Jones, designated as President by Congress, being appointed by the Continental Congress Superintendent of Indian Affairs for the Southern Department, Cornelius Harnett of Wilmington was chosen President. This officer was the virtual governor of the province.

On the 28th of June the British troops and fleet made their conjoint attack on Fort Sullivan, S. C. The two North Carolina Continental Battalions[*] under Cols. James Moore[†] and Alexander Martin, numbering about fifteen hundred men,—the whole under the command of Gen. Howe of North Carolina,—participated in the glory of the defence. In Gen. Lee's report of the action, to Mr. Pendleton, President of the Virginia Convention,[‡] he says,—"I know not which corps I have the greatest reason to be pleased with, Mughlenburgh's Virginians, or the North Carolina troops—they are both equally alert, zealous and spirited. I must now, sir, entreat that you will forward to Wilmington as much powder as can possibly be spared from your province, to supply the place of that which I shall draw from North Carolina." In addition to the forces already named, it may be mentioned that Capt. C. C. Pinckney's company consisted almost exclusively of North Carolinians.

Early in July, Gen. Rutherford, at the head of nineteen hundred men,[§] crossed the mountains, and so severely chastised the Cherokee Indians as to compel them to sue for peace. North Carolina not only maintained the integrity of her territory and enforced respect for her authority, by baffling the invader, and suppressing insurrection at home, but also aided, generously, South Carolina. Thus was the wisdom and vigor of her leaders illustrated! So ready were her sons to take the field, so many her soldiers, that large bodies were disbanded as useless.

HEWES TO IREDELL.

PHILADELPHIA, June 28th, 1776.

DEAR SIR:—I have to thank you for two letters, and believe me, I do it most heartily; you are almost the only correspondent I have in North Carolina, but more of this next opportunity; at present I would confine myself to news. Burgoyne, with a large force, is arrived in Canada. Gen. Sullivan sent 2000 men under Gen. Thompson to engage a party of the king's troops that were about forty miles below head-quarters, towards Quebec; but un-

---

[*] These were originally styled regiments, but their designation was changed to avoid a difficulty about the rank of colonel in effecting exchanges.—*Hildreth.*
[†] Subsequently Major General of the Southern Department.
[‡] Vid. Appendix to this volume for this report and another paper relative to the attack, preserved by Mr. Iredell.   [§] *Wheeler.*

luckily the evening before Thompson came up with them, they had been reinforced by Burgoyne with several regiments just arrived; notwithstanding the superior force, Thompson engaged them, was repulsed with the loss of 150 men, killed and taken prisoners. In the retreat, Thompson and five or six officers were taken prisoners by a party of Canadians, who, though they were supposed to be our friends, found this a lucky time to make their peace with the strongest party. Our whole army are retreated to the Isle a Noir a little on this side St. John's (1500 of them have the small pox; out of three regiments not more than fifty able to bear arms), in hopes to keep possession of the lakes. A damnable plot has been discovered in New York. The hellish tories had concerted a plan to murder General Washington and several other generals, blow up the magazine and spike up all the cannon. They waited only for the arrival of the king's troops, when this plan was to have been executed. The general has not yet got to the bottom of this affair; many persons are taken up and imprisoned, some persons of note among them: the mayor of the city, the famous Major Rogers, &c., &c.* It is said Gov. Tryon is concerned, but he is safe on board a king's ship at Sandy Hook. So much for the dark side. Things go a little better in another quarter. Our Continental vessels of war and some privateers have taken lately, at different times and places, six large transport ships from Scotland, having in all near 600 of Frasier's regiment of Highlanders on board, with their baggage, arms, provisions, &c. An express that came half an hour ago informs that he saw upward of 200 of these march out of Boston, in order to be confined in the jail in the country. He says they are fine men—have all new regimentals, scarlet faced with blue; he came out, he says, with them, and heard many of them curse most bitterly both king and Parliament for deceiving them. They had been told not a rebel would be found on the sea coast: that they had all fled fifty or sixty miles back in the country, and that they were sent here to enjoy the lands which the rebels had forsaken. They did not expect any thing else, and had brought their wives in order to set down quiet, &c. Gov. Franklyn is taken into custody, and sent prisoner to Connecticut.

On Monday the great question of independency and total separation from all political intercourse with Great Britain will come on. It will be carried, I expect, by a great majority, and then, I suppose we shall take upon us a new name. My compliments to Mr. Johnston; I received a line from him from Halifax, by the return wagons, also one from Edenton, by Williams, who is the

* Vid. Lossing's Field Book of the Revolution, Vol 1, p. 116.

bearer of this. I have not time to write him now; shall do it by post on Tuesday; he must consider this as written to him also. My compliments to the ladies.

I am, dear sir,
Your most obt. humble servt.,
JOSEPH HEWES.

JOHN JOHNSTON TO IREDELL.

July 4th, 1776.

DEAR SIR:—I wrote to you from home last Saturday, and as Mr. Buchanan is now going down, I take the opportunity of informing you that I am yet well. You have no doubt heard, by this time, of the English men-of-war's being cast away on Charleston Bar—a fifty-gun ship, a twenty-gun ship, and a sixteen gun sloop of war. They have made an attempt to land in the night, but were beaten off with considerable loss, by only one hundred men called the Raccoon Company (I suppose from their wearing the skin of that animal by way of caps). This news came so well authenticated to the Council, that I am informed they pay credit to it. It was brought here by Mr. Walter Gibson,* yesterday. We yesterday detected a parcel of fellows, and apprehended them, who had prevailed on a mulatto fellow that worked the press, to steal a quantity of unsigned bills for them, for which he was to have part—they had numbered and signed a great number, *but very luckily I detected one, and the first they had passed, with a woman,* and immediately had them taken up, and the house searched, and we got all the bills, save some that a butcher has gone off with to purchase stock with. We sent after him, and hope shall be able to give an account of him before night. I should write to my brother, but expect he will be off before this gets down. I delivered my sister's letters to Mr. Lindsay. I wrote her the same time I did to you, since which I received a quarrelling letter from her, by Mr. McNair. I should now write her, but have not one minute to spare, as the signers are now at my back hurrying me. Please to remember me affectionately to them all.

And I remain, dear sir,
Your most obedient servant,
JOHN JOHNSTON.†

* Gibson was from Bladen, member of the Prov. Congress, August, 1774.
† Mr. Johnston was one of a committee of four, appointed by Congress April 22d, to superintend the printing of bills of credit to the amount of $250,000.

IREDELL TO T. JONES.*

EDENTON, 15th July, 1776.

DEAR SIR:—I have nothing in particular to acquaint you with from here, but I cannot deny myself the pleasure of congratulating you on the glorious defeat at Charleston. It is one which will appear very illustrious in the annals of history, and is, in all its circumstances, very extraordinary. We had a most distinct and satisfactory account of it the day before your express arrived, from the mouth of Mr. Page, the Virginia express, who carried the account to his province from General Lee. A remarkable fatality attends all the measures of Great Britain (once so illustrious and so successful), now that they have converted the arms of free men into the instruments of tyranny. They appear no longer as the same people. Every measure of policy weak, impracticable, or ridiculous; every exertion of rigor against raw, undisciplined forces, ignorant of the military art, in almost every particular, and just from their plows to defend their country,—equal to their adversaries in nothing but *courage*,—every attack upon such men by disciplined and veteran forces, supported by every possible military assistance, fails of success, and is brought into contempt. Eight ships (several of them large) are not found equal to half the task assigned by one arrogant gentleman to two small ones. North Carolina with 1000 militia repulses 2000 Highlanders and Regulators, in whom the greatest confidence was placed. South Carolina with 350 repels 2000 British soldiers. These under the command of two generals, selected with particular choice for the business they have thus shamefully failed in. Where will Clinton *dodge* now, and what will become of Cornwallis? Wait, I presume, for a reinforcement, and try their luck once more; in the mean time perhaps losing half the men they were to conquer two provinces with, by natural causes incident to their climate. O Britain! miserable, unhappy country! losing half its dominions and greatly endangering the other half, by the mismanagement,

* There is a letter from Jasper Charlton to Mr. Jones, with Mr. Iredell's papers, dated July 8th, 1776, declining some appointment, the nature of which does not certainly appear, because of "the wound my feelings would receive at passing sentence against the properties of my fellow-subjects." He says further, "I am sensible by this resolution I may forego a lucrative employment." The Provincial Congress, May 11th, 1776, had empowered the Council of Safety to establish Courts of Admiralty at Edenton, Bath, New Berne, and Wilmington, and to appoint judges thereof. I suppose Mr. Charlton was tendered the post of Admiralty Judge for Edenton. When these courts went into actual operation, I do not know. In the fall of 1780 Martial Boitar, of the private ship of war, the Fortunate, was the appellant from a decree obtained in the Admiralty Court of Port Brunswick. Hezekiah Anthony and others were the respondents. Iredell for appellants.

villainy, and perfidious ambition of a set of rascals, destined, as it would appear by fate, to be the horrid instruments of destroying their country. Such are the blessed effects of a tyrannical temper, selfish infatuation, and weak, ungovernable pride.

The powder, I believe, will be forwarded with all expedition. But pray, my good friend, how came you to comprise a mighty secret in an open letter? This really would have become me much better than you.

Your children are all extremely well, both those in town and country. I heard of the last yesterday. I will keep my letter open to the last moment, that I may add any thing that may occur. I hope you will not neglect to write to me.*

On July 22d, the Continental Declaration of Independence reached Halifax, where the Council of Safety were in session:† they immediately ordered it to be proclaimed, in the most public manner, throughout the "State."

T. JONES (MEMBER OF THE COUNCIL OF SAFETY) TO IREDELL.

HALIFAX, 23d July, 1776.

DEAR SIR:—Your obliging favor, by Mr. Montfort, was delivered to me on my arrival here on Saturday morning last, for which I return you many thanks. You cannot imagine how much pleasure and satisfaction it gave me, and am extremely sorry it's not in my power, for the want of time, to give you in return for your politeness a long letter. And for public news, have nothing to mention but what you have heard long since from Charles Town, except the cruel Indian war brought about by the wicked and diabolical superintendent Cameron, who resides in the Over-Hill Cherokee towns. The Indians have already destroyed upwards of two hundred men, women and children. As this matter is perfectly ministerial, I hope a tory will never after this open his mouth in favor of the British government, which, of all governments on earth, I believe at this time is the most tyrannical and bloody. Do pray give me a line by the return of our express, and be kind enough to send a servant down to Mrs. Howe's, to enquire how my dear children are. If any thing of importance happens, an express will be immediately sent to Mr. Johnston, and you may depend upon hearing from me. My respectful compliments to Mrs. Iredell, Mrs. Blair, Mrs. Dawson, and all the young ladies. I am in the greatest haste,

With great regard, dear sir,
Your most devoted servant,
THOMAS JONES.

* The British forces in America, in 1776, amounted to fully 50,000 men.
† Jones, Wheeler.

P. S.—We have by this time a very large army on our western frontiers, so that the Indians will find, very shortly, business enough upon their hands. The Council have been on this Indian business near three weeks past, and in three weeks more I hope it will be in my power to give you an account of our success in that quarter. We have our hands full,—no sooner do we lay one devil, but up starts another ; but we shall prove too many for them all yet. I'll answer for it. My respects to Mr. Smith, I shall write to him to-morrow. I should have done it now, but the express waits.

JOHN JOHNSTON TO IREDELL.

July 11th, 1776.

DEAR SIR :—I have the pleasure, and just the time, to inform you that I still enjoy my health. I hope you and our friends do the same. Inclosed I have sent you a copy of Gen. Lee's letter to the President of the Virginia Convention, which I took from a certified copy that Mr. Hooper brought with him from the Council. My brother's stay from this place * longer than his appointed time, alarms me for fear he is unwell. Caswell† is here, and expected to meet him here. I expect my stay will be nearly one month longer. I am quite tired out, and long to see my friends at Edenton. Please to inform my sister that I really have not time to write by this opportunity, but will, if possible, by the next. Please to remember me to both.

I am, dear sir,
Your affectionate brother,
JOHN JOHNSTON.

On the 1st of August,‡ the day appointed by the Council, their President, Mr. Harnett, in front of the Court House, at Halifax, environed by the military, and in the midst of an immense concourse of people, read the Declaration of Independence. It was greeted with the firing of cannon ; and the assent and delight of the multitude were testified by clapping of hands, and joyous acclamations. So irrepressible was the enthusiasm, that the excited soldiers, breaking from their ranks, " seized Mr. Harnett, and bore him on their shoulders through the streets of the town, applauding him as their champion, and swearing allegiance to the instrument he had read."

* Halifax.
† Gen. Caswell, Mr. Johnston's colleague as Treasurer—subsequently first governor of the State of North Carolina.
‡ Jones.

T. JONES TO IREDELL.

HALIFAX, 17th Aug., 1776.

DEAR SIR :—Your very polite and obliging favor reached me here, on the 14th inst., for which you have my hearty and sincere thanks. The Council adjourned a few days ago to Wake Court House, and this evening Mr. Wilie Jones and myself set off to be there next Monday, the day on which the Council will meet. As to news from the North, the following is nearly the substance, and which may be depended upon, as I had it from Mr. Gwinet, a countryman of ours from Gloucestershire on his return from the Continental Congress, of which he is one of the delegates for the State of Georgia, viz.: That an elegant pamphlet written by the justly celebrated Dr. Price, on the present interesting and very important times, has had a very extraordinary effect on the minds of the people, industriously spread throughout the whole kingdom. The city of London, at a very full meeting, returned Dr. Price their thanks in great pomp and form, and the freedom of that city was presented him in Gold Box, much to the mortification of the ministry. As this piece is calculated to undeceive the ignorant, by the strength of its argument, and plainness of style, it had the desired effect—the whole was immediately in an uproar, and that it was generally believed no Hessian troops would be sent out, and that they are in daily expectation of a formidable army being landed from France, and that a revolution was expected. This may be depended upon, that there is not a complete regiment in the kingdom, and they have sent out to America the whole of their artillery. We have an army at Ticonderoga of 12,000 men, under the command of Gen. Gates to receive Master Burgoyne ; five armed schooners of ours are constantly cruising in the lake, and 300 men from New York and Philadelphia are building many galleys there ; General Lee has marched from Charles Town with 1500 men to join Col. Bull at Port Royal, 60 miles to the southward of Charles Town, then instantly to attack 1500 of Clinton's army, who are landed and intrenched near that place ; we expect to hear from that quarter. The Council have discharged the 1500 militia voted by the last Congress, as there is no business for them to do here. Our Indian affairs go on very well—the last 500 men from the Hillsborough, ordered by the Council, marched last Monday for Gen. Rutherford's head-quarters, near the mountains. I return you my thanks for your kind mention of my children. My compliments to Mrs. Iredell, Mrs. Blair, Mrs. Dawson, and all the young ladies. Pray let me hear from you.

Dear sir, yours ever,
THOMAS JONES.

JASPER CHARLTON TO IREDELL.

CUFFNELL'S, 24th of August, 1776.

DEAR SIR :—There was a happy time, when the duties of your office would illy admit of a more extensive correspondence than the one you had—that time is, alas ! no more, and I shall presume you can now and then find a vacant hour to commune with a solitary on paper. When I give myself that name, I would exclude every idea of melancholy attending that state ; no, on the contrary, I find blessings in retirement fancy never before suggested. How happily has the inimitable Dr. Goldsmith expressed them in his " Deserted Village."

" Blest retirement, friend to life's decline, &c., &c.*

How preferable, my dear sir, is such a state of existence, to the one our fraternity is fated to bear with ; how superior to the brawling and wrangling in an ignorant court. And how much more to be admired and courted, than the condition of a prostitute hireling to very often the most rascally part of God's creation. I will tell you plainly I am, and long have been, sick of my profession, and if the confusion of the times shall wear away, am determined to concenter the full value of my possessions in this spot, and here endeavor to attain to the greatest stage of felicity this life will admit of—i. e., —mens conscia recti. So much for my present state, and future views.

Although politics is a subject of conversation I would by choice decline, yet I cannot help giving you my sentiments respecting the most interesting event which as yet hath occurred, I mean independency. My idea of it is simply this, that America is as yet too young to effect her own salvation, more especially when respect is had to the tempers, complexions, and various conditions of its inhabitants. I think this business (if ever manageable) should have fallen into the hands of an united, robust and populous posterity ; and that at present she may be compared to a tender plant, by no means able to withstand the many rude shocks that a most inclement season will give it. God knows what the womb of time may produce. I will therefore quit a topic that awakens all my fears, and brings to my idea a train of melancholy events, and disastrous consequences. Let me then give a more pleasing direction to my thoughts, and they naturally lead me to cherish the wish of seeing you and Mrs. Iredell at Cuffnell's, the latter end of next month. I mention that time, because the weather I hope will be cooler, my house more airy,

* The quotation in the letter extends to sixteen lines.

and the nasty ticks, the great foe to walking [and beautiful walks have I to walk in] be gone. Moreover four stout horses will then be with an easy chariot in perfect readiness to attend you at Dukinfield, without the least inconvenience to myself. I want you to taste the Cuffnell's water, nor am I so poor yet but I can meliorate it. I can assure you, sir, that Mrs. Charlton joins me in my wish most cordially, and now I mention her, I will tell you she is in the blissful condition Yoric prays his dear Eliza may experience, in rest but unattended by Hygeia.

I am confident, sir, I need not request a communication of any important news from you ; you will be led to it by every consideration involving charity and a disposition to please. Consider the paucity of my connections—the unintelligency of them, and the few avenues I have for letting in news. And all these I am sure will conspire to let me know how the world passes. You will not, I am sure, be like a Romish priest—propagate a belief in things in which you have no faith yourself, nor like the pious St. Austin, who said he believed some things because they were absurd and impossible.

In most epistolatory productions I have observed the general conclusion of them to be,—I am afraid, sir, I have tired your patience. This conclusion, however modish or refined, I shall not imitate. There are times when congenial minds should give the most ample and unreserved participation of their sentiments to each other, without the supposal of tiresomeness, nor will I pay so ill a compliment to myself, as to believe I shall tire you, when I am not tired myself. But as all things must tend to an end, as well as my epistle, I with very great pleasure make an offering of Mrs. Charlton's and my best respects to Mrs. Iredell, yourself and all friends united in love or friendship to you, which will comprehend a great section of the community you live in. I am, dear sir,

Your sincere friend,
JASPER CHARLTON.

P. S.—I have this moment the honor of a visit from the present Duke of Bolton* and Lord Delawar.† When you come up I hope I shall introduce you to them. They seem to be plain affable men, no ways affecting pride or arrogance, and disposed to a civil acquaintanceship with their inferiors.

On the 9th of August ‡ the Council of Safety solemnly recommended to the people of North Carolina to pay the greatest

* Old Joe Knott.   † Boswell, the breeches-maker.   ‡ Wiley, Jones,

attention to the election of members of Congress on the 15th of October; and to have particularly in view the important consideration, that it would be the business of Congress not only to make laws, but also to *form a Constitution*. It appears from Jones' statement that the radical party of the State were bent upon the defeat of Mr. Johnston; and that the Council of State, misled by Wilie Jones, were privy to the conspiracy. The elections since 1774 had been conducted without opposition. Now it was pretended openly that the conservatives intended a government adverse to the liberties of the people; and covertly that they were in reality advocates of a monarchy. When danger was imminent, the public voice had demanded the services of Mr. Johnston; but now that comparative order reigned, and the arms and policy of the State were every where triumphant, the men who felt themselves overshadowed by the influence and power of the President of the Congress, and dwarfed in his presence, thought they could, temporarily at least, dispense with him. No means were spared to poison the minds of the people; to inflame their prejudices; excite alarm; and sow in them, by indefinite charges, and vague whispers, the seeds of distrust. Hot and spirited was the canvass in Chowan. It is not to be supposed that Mr. Iredell was an indifferent spectator of the struggle; as a lawyer, statesman, and politician, he had at heart Mr. Johnston's election; as a man, he could not but regard, with the deepest emotion, the attempts to undermine the well-earned fame of his most cherished friend, his most loved connection. In a blind hatred of England, the radicals were disposed to signalize their opposition by the distance placed between them and English laws, modes, and customs; and so far from comprehending the consummate wisdom of Mr. Johnston and his friends, who, while renouncing all that was evil in the English Constitution, desired to preserve all that was good, they were embittered by opposition, and exasperated into acts of folly and madness. It was useless to argue with such men, to urge great principles of freedom enunciated and guaranteed, the writ of habeas corpus, the trial by jury, the excellence of the Common Law: at the head were king and lords, and, guiltless of discrimination, all was condemned by them in one loud cry of execration. It were bootless now to inquire what base arts prevailed, or what calumnies were propagated. Mr. Johnston was defeated. The triumph was celebrated with riot and debauchery; and the orgies were concluded by burning Mr. Johnston in effigy. This was but one of the many instances, recorded in history, in which the people have wounded themselves through the bosoms of their best friends, acting often insanely in a moment of excitement, like the reptile that, when encircled with flame, stings itself to death.

Mr. Iredell's indignation was well expressed in the following paper, penned ere yet the passions had cooled, or the quickened pulse subsided to its wonted beat. It may be here remarked that though Mr. Johnston was beaten, his political and personal friends, Hewes and Jones, secured their elections, the former for the town of Edenton, and the latter for the county of Chowan.

CREED OF A RIOTER.

1. I am a sworn enemy to all gentlemen. I believe none in that station of life can possibly possess either honor or virtue.
2. I believe the best way to have a good understanding, is never to cultivate the mental powers, and that the most ignorant in appearance, are in fact the most knowing.
3. I impute to *gentlemen* all our present difficulties. If they had not been so cunning as to foresee distant evils, we never should have dreamt of them. We should then have been probably happy slaves, and the Parliament, finding no opposition from us, would, I doubt not, have treated us with no more rigor than was absolutely convenient for their own purposes.
4. I think the supreme felicity of life is to eat and drink, and as I cannot do that in my present situation quite as well as I used to do, I despise all the pretences of virtue which are urged to make me easy under it.
5. Let every man take care of himself is my maxim. The public interest is too troublesome to attend to. What care I who the devil is miserable, if I am not so?
6. I believe I have a right to take another man's property, if it will be useful to me. I surely am not to suffer, for fear of being called a robber. I think I have a right, if I can, to shift distresses from my own shoulders, and put them on those of my neighbors.
7. I am none of those over-wise and *irreligious* men, who are always thinking of the future. I devoutly obey that saying in Scripture,—"Let us eat and drink,—for to-morrow we die."
8. As I have the utmost confidence that all my own opinions are right, I despise every man who differs from me. I am sure he must be a tory.
9. I think a man more liable to be a tory, who has hitherto been most earnest in the cause, and sacrificed great interests to it; because I have no opinion of any man's acting from a principle of virtue alone, and therefore I can consider such a one in no other light than as a madman, who certainly will be as glad to lose his head as he has already been solicitous to forfeit his fortune.
10. I think that man alone a whig, who has sagacity enough to mind his own interest, resolution enough to plunder his neighbors, who views the storm coolly at a distance, and discovers his principles by getting honestly drunk and abusing *gentlemen*.

Lastly, I am of opinion that our affairs would prosper much better, if gentlemen who read and consider too deeply for us, were totally banished from all public business, and if those who neither read nor think at all (and consequently cannot injure us by the excess of those practices) were intrusted with the management of our present arduous concerns.

All the above I verily and truly believe, and G—d d—n all those who differ from me.

A RIOTER.

11. I believe it honorable and proper to persecute poor distressed individuals, when we have them *in our power*, provided we want courage to prove, in any other manner, the alacrity of our zeal against those we suppose enemies of our country.

With the formation of the Constitution, opposition to Mr. Johnston, in a measure, ceased. Not many months elapsed before reflection brought to his immediate constituents regret and contrition; and his ascendency was more firmly established than ever. In the stormy years that succeeded, when the loss of trade and the heavy taxation necessary to the support of armies, were as crushing weights upon people; when tory insurrections and hostile invasions ravaged the fields, fired the dwellings, obstructed the laws, and embarrassed the policy of the State; when Wilie Jones and his "clique" served, but as blinking tapers, to render more visible the darkness, then it was that men looked up to Edenton, where shone with calm and steady flame, a triple light,* whose rays, first concentrated into one burning focus, were so irradiated that they penetrated to the uttermost borders of the State—a light, uplifted high as that of Pharos, and supported by a structure of purity as spotless.

On the 12th day of November† Congress assembled at Halifax. Mr. Johnston was present on the business of the Treasury. The pressure of the conservative members, aided by the outside influence of Mr. Johnston, soon condensed and amalgamated conflicting opinions into an organic law of such excellence that it remained unaltered until 1835. So devoid of experience and learning were the radicals, that the Constitution was accepted from the hands of Thomas Jones, Mr. Johnston's devoted adherent. The Bill of Rights was ratified on the 17th day of December; and the Constitution on the 18th. Richard Caswell was elected governor. An ordinance was passed appointing Thomas Jones, Samuel Johnston, Archibald Maclaine, *James Iredell*, Abner Nash, Christopher Neale, Samuel Ashe, Waightstill Avery, Samuel Spencer, Jasper Charlton, and John Penn, Commissioners to review and consider all such statutes and acts of Assembly as had been, or were in force in the State, and "to prepare such bills to be passed into laws, as might be consistent with the genius of a free people," and to lay them before the next Assembly. "It is not now known how many of these Commissioners accepted this trust, or what share of its execution was borne by any one of them, but the fruits of their labors are manifest in the years immediately succeeding, laws which have received repeated encomiums for the ability and skill and accuracy with which they are drawn." Such is the language of the preface to the Revised Statutes of 1836–7. I shall, however, hereafter show that Iredell drafted the celebrated Act of 1777, known as the Court Law.* By the same Congress an ordinance was passed to establish "courts for the trial of criminals, in each district within the State, and for vesting, in the several sessions of the peace, the power of appointing jurymen for the said district courts, and constituting judges to preside therein." It does not appear that there were any judges, in the ordinary sense of the word, anterior to the 20th of December, 1777.

JOHNSTON TO IREDELL.

HALIFAX, 7th Dec., 1776.

DEAR SIR:—I got here this afternoon, and though I made short stages, find myself a good deal fatigued. My health is much the same as when I left home.

God knows when there will be an end of their trifling here. A draft of the Constitution was presented to the House yesterday, and lies over for consideration. The members are furnishing themselves with copies of it. I have had a glance of it, and could wish to have sent you a copy of it, but it was impossible—perhaps the bearer, Col. Dauge, may have one. As well as I can judge, from a cursory view of it, it may do as well as that adopted by any other colony. Nothing of the kind can be good. There is one thing in it, which I cannot bear, and yet I am in-

---

* Johnston, Hewes, and Iredell. † Jones, Wheeler, Statutes.

* Statutes.

clined to think it will stand. The inhabitants are empowered to elect the justices in their respective counties, who are to be judges of the county courts. Numberless inconveniences must arise from so absurd an institution.

You will hear, before this reaches you, of the surrender of Fort Washington. It is situated on the upper end of the island, on which New York stands. On the North River, directly opposite to it on the Jersey shore is Fort Lee, which I am afraid has, before this, shared the same fate. I have heard none of the particulars, but that the garrison, 2000 men, after a short but vigorous resistance, surrendered themselves prisoners of war, with all the artillery and stores of the garrison.

Much time is spent here in trifles. I will endeavor, as soon as possible, to get my business done, and leave them. I know you will write to me if any opportunity offers. Pray offer my love and compliments where due. Deliver the enclosed, and believe me always, with great esteem,
Dear sir,
Your affectionate brother,
SAM. JOHNSTON.

JOHNSTON TO IREDELL.

HALIFAX, Dec. 9th, 1776.

DEAR SIR:—I wrote to you the evening after I got here, since which I have been endeavoring to discover what will be done, but am as much at a loss as ever. The Constitution is to be debated to-day—some talk of finishing as soon as that is agreed on, others are for staying to appoint all the officers of the State, and establish courts of justice—which of these plans will take place is uncertain. No one appears to have sufficient spirit or authority to set them right. I am in great pain for the honor of the province; at the same time, when I consider only my own ease and peace, congratulate myself on being clear of any share of the trouble I must have had, if I had been a member. Every one who has the least pretensions to be a gentleman is suspected and borne down *per ignobile vulgus*—a set of men without reading, experience, or principle to govern them. I still have a fever every night, but am no worse than when I left you, and hope I shall be able to hold my own till I return. Mr. Penn * has just called upon me, and after an hour's conversation, leaves

* John Penn, signer of the Declaration of Independence.

me only time to request the favor of you to present my love and compliments where due, and that you will believe me,
Dear sir,
Your affectionate brother,
SAM. JOHNSTON.

P. S.—I found my brother much mended in his health. He went down yesterday to visit his family.

JOHNSTON TO MRS. IREDELL.

HALIFAX, 13th Dec., 1776.

MY DEAR HANNAH:—I don't know whether you will thank me for writing to you, as it will be a kind of demand for a letter from you. I was in hopes things here were drawing near a conclusion, and that I should get home in a few days, but unfortunately one of the members from the back country introduced a test, by which every person, before he should be admitted to a share in the Legislature, should swear that he believed in the Holy Trinity, and that the Scripture of the old Testament was written by divine inspiration.† This was carried after a very warm debate, and has blown up such a flame, that every thing is in danger of being thrown into confusion. They talk of having all the officers, even the judges and clerks, elected annually, with a number of other absurdities. It is very hard that nobody will write to me. Tell Mr. Iredell he owes me two letters, and he used to be a better paymaster. I have a good deal more news, but I won't write a word of it, unless I hear from him. Give my love to our sister and the children. John went down last Sunday, and is not yet returned. * Pray take care of yourself and establish your health. I don't expect to get quite well before spring, but I avoid exposing myself, and hope to return as well as when I left you. Farewell, and believe me,
My dear sister,
Your most affectionate
SAM. JOHNSTON.

* Rev. Dr. David Caldwell drafted the 32d article. The Episcopal Church was the established church before the war. The Dissenters regarded it with no love, and did not spare it in their denunciations; when they obtained power, with strange inconsistency and intolerance, they excluded from office all Roman Catholics, Jews, &c.—*Foote's Sketches of N. C.*
† Mr. John Johnston was a member of the Congress.

CHAPTER X.

NORTH CAROLINA ENJOYS PEACE; LETTER FROM MCCULLOH; 1ST SESSION OF THE ASSEMBLY; LETTERS FROM IREDELL AND MRS. BLAIR; LA NEUVILLE; LETTERS FROM IREDELL AND CHIEF JUSTICE HOWARD; LETTERS FROM IREDELL AND LA NEUVILLE; IREDELL A JUDGE; LETTERS FROM HOOPER AND MACLAINE. ÆT. 25–26.

DURING the year 1777, North Carolina enjoyed comparative tranquillity, and exemption from the evils of war. The State well employed the interval in consolidating its government, and organizing its militia. Occasionally the peace of particular neighborhoods was disturbed by tory outbreaks, but these outrages were promptly punished by forays into the tory districts, and the infliction of exemplary castigations. Every spark of rebellion was extinguished by the armed heel of power: the suspected were arrested, and the jails were crowded with those who were thought inimical to the liberties of the people. British operations being confined to the Northern Provinces, the North Carolina Continental Battalions were ordered to the seat of hostilities, and served under the commander-in-chief, in the battles of Princeton, Brandywine, and Germantown. In the latter combat their general, Francis Nash, was mortally wounded.

LETTER FROM H. E. MCCULLOH.

LONDON, 1st Jan., 1777.

DEAR SIR:—I recommend this, and three letters enclosed for Mr. W. Jones, Col. McCulloh and Thomas Frohock, to the care of our very worthy friend, Mr. Fanning, at New York, and entreat him, if possible, to find out some means of getting them conveyed to your hands. I leave the letters open for the inspection of those through whose hands they pass, and as they are entirely on private subjects, I hope they will be permitted to reach you,—and in that event, I make no doubt you will be able to obtain such further permissions as will enable you to forward

them as directed. Among the many unhappinesses of the present times, it is not the least, that we are in a manner cut off from all intelligence; however, as the post to New York is now again established, I shall try that conveyance, and hope it may be successful,—and I entreat you to make the same experiment, in writing me. You know how many weighty reasons, both of affection and interest, I have for wishing for a speedy, just, and honorable accommodation of all differences between Great Britain and America,—and I can now sincerely say that every heart and every tongue, here, joins in that wish. May God in his mercy grant it! I have obtained my father's consent, and wish and intend, if possible, to return to Carolina next summer. It has, in my humble and private station, been my constant care to avoid offence; and I hope I have been successful; and that no unkindness will be offered to my interests during my absence, nor to myself, should I return. Nobody can give me better information than *yourself;* and I ask it from your friendship to contrive some method of writing me, and giving me all the satisfaction in your power on these important points. I rely faithfully on your friendship and affection for me, and that you will do every thing your situation and *connections* can possibly enable you, to serve a man who, I think I may say, has ever wished and endeavored to promote your good,—and now you have the opportunities, I shall, and do, rely upon you to serve me, both by yourself and friends. I think it would give you pleasure to see me in Carolina this summer,—I wish it, but much, very much, must depend on what you inform me,—and I shall remain in anxious expectation of hearing from you, between this and May. Try every chance that offers.

I am informed that Mr. Montford * is dead, and that Mr. W. Jones married his daughter, and consequently has, I suppose, the management of his affairs. I refer you to my letters to that gentleman and cousin Alex. You know how I am connected with Mr. Montford's estate, and I must entreat you to take a journey to Halifax, or elsewhere, to meet his executors, and endeavor to get the security Messrs. A. M. & Co. are desirous of, and which I hope the executors will cheerfully come into, on the generous and fair offer made them,—and what they trust to you is that you will see the security is sufficient. I hope Col. McCulloh will, for his own sake, see we are properly secured in the other affair. If possible put every thing upon an amicable and safe footing, and I think what is now offered, there can be no objections to; and if the security is given, let that and the bill re-

* Montford was largely indebted to McCulloh.

main in Mr. Johnston's, or any proper third hand, till I either come out, or you have further directions given you.

Your mother is now in a new house at Bath, and your brother, and I believe all well. My father has his health as well as can be expected. It is needless to say what my mind suffers. You may easily conceive it. My constant prayer is for peace, and my earnest wish to return to Carolina. I hope Mrs. Iredell and you have your healths. Be assured of my constant and preferable regard and affection. I wish you to mention me kindly to all inquiring friends, particularly those your way. Be my friend in every thing you can; and fail not to write me. You must know how important it is for me to hear from you before I leave this. Direct to me as usual. I pray God to take us under His protection, and am always, dear James,

Your affectionate friend,
H. E. McCULLO

The following address to the king of Great Britain, bears date March, 1777. I learn from an endorsement, that it was never published. Two copies are extant. As the soiled garments of the veteran are eloquent of the hardships of the campaign, so do these discolored and well-thumbed pages furnish proof of service. In the same manner in which that admirable paper, the National Intelligencer, has for years supplied facts and arguments to the great mass of the whigs of our day, so, I presume, this, and similar products of Mr. Iredell's industry, afforded to the whigs of the Revolution weapons with which to maintain their position In lieu of an active press, they contributed the staple of most political discussions, and by informing the minds of the leaders, indirectly reached and enlightened the people.

To His Majesty, George the Third, King of Great Britain, &c.

Sir:—I once thought myself happy in my allegiance to your Majesty, and in my connection with the British Nation, and flattered myself that this honorable distinction would have continued, if not increase, at least without diminution. It has been my misfortune to have these expectations totally disappointed. I have been compelled to renounce my allegiance to your majesty, and to disown all connection with my native country.

Severe and painful indeed was this duty: I loved my country; I once loved my prince. It would have been the greatest blessing in life to me, had it been in my power to continue my attachment to both. This would have been the case, sir, if your majesty had not adopted measures of the most fatal tendency; measures insupportable to freemen, and which perhaps, in the end, may prove personally ruinous to yourself. I cannot yet, sir, without emotion, think of the complicated miseries yourself, as well as your subjects, may endure from your haughty and precipitate conduct.

I have been given to understand, and I believe it to be true, that your majesty has a personal, unrelenting inveteracy against the Americans; that you entertain the worst opinion of their principles; deride their conduct; and can bear to hear nothing in their defence. Your whole conduct has been a continued proof of the truth of this information.

I well know, sir, how much you will disdain, with this disposition, any thing that comes from an *American rebel*, and much more if he be a *British American*. I have not the least expectation that this address (should it chance to reach you) will have any influence upon your *principles*, or your *heart;* that it will change any of your opinions, or move your compassion. I have other views in writing it. I choose this as a channel of conveying some observations to the public, which may be of use, if not to you, to some well-meaning, but deluded persons, who with equal fondness and folly, revere all the shadows of authority, and submit to power without ever entertaining thoughts either of the source of its institution, or the end to which it should be directed.

It is at present, I fear, sir, of little consequence to your majesty, whether your opinions on this subject are altered or not. You have acted already with so fatal a precipitancy, that it scarcely seems probable you can gain any advantage from retreating. The melancholy, but necessary, expedient of a foreign alliance perhaps has been obtained, and your ruin too certainly projected. How much reason may you have to curse the day when you first sought to make yourself great by making America miserable!

Sir, you have either been grossly deceived, or you have basely imposed upon the public. You or your ministers (or perhaps both) have much to answer for to the people of England. The *throne* has uniformly deceived them. In every progression of this dreadful contest, the truth has been carefully concealed from them. In the beginning of this business they have been told that the Americans were far from being united; that their opposition and clamor were merely the bustle of a faction; and that time and reflection would cool the people's minds, remove their prejudices in favor of their present leaders, and make way for the influence of wiser and more moderate men. I need not say how this misrepresentation has been detected, or with what noble firmness the Americans have disproved so vile and atrocious a calumny.

When this misrepresentation was too glaring to be supported, and men yielded to shame what they had not the honor to sacrifice to truth, another courtly topic was suggested, and this has been propagated with all the malicious art and industry of a wretched and declining cause. It is, that the American leaders had, from the first, a secret view to *independence*, and that the hope of arriving to this state has been the ultimate principle of all their conduct.

Upon this subject, sir, I shall presume to speak seriously to your majesty. I do aver the charge to be *false*, and dare appeal to the great Searcher of all hearts for the truth of my present declaration. I have resided many years in America; I have had the honor of a personal intimacy with several of the most considerable characters, and firmest patriots in it; I have had many interesting and confidential conversations with them upon this great and affecting subject. I know well the general sentiments of the people at large. When this unhappy controversy first began, and until very near the time when the arbitrary obstinacy of your conduct left us no other alternative than indefinite submission to your will, or unreserved resistance to your power, I never heard a man speak on the subject of *independence*, who did not speak of it with abhorrence and indignation, and place the hope of all his felicity in a happy and honorable reconciliation with Great Britain. This was long the favorite topic of every conversation. The liberty of America seemed essentially connected with this object; nobody formed an idea (speaking generally, and within the sphere of my own knowledge) of forming a separation from it with the least prospect of success; we all hoped that you, sir, would at last act with wisdom and moderation, and again make your subjects happy. This was long the theme of all our thoughts, the ultimate object of all our endeavors. Men in America know this to be true. It was universally regretted, that it was not as well known, or affected to be disbelieved, in England. You perhaps received, sir (I doubt not that you did), other information. There are always, to the dishonor of human nature, sycophant parasites enough to flatter the opinions or wishes of men in power. Many such, Heaven knows, have been found in America. They, I doubt not, early trumpeted forth alarms about *independency*. They knew it was the favorite creed in England; it was a simple way of considering the subject; it saved the trouble of an accurate discussion of rights; it flattered the sagacity of its discoverers; it was a *plain* and *open* (though dirty) road to preferment. Some or all of these excellent motives co-operated to your deception, perhaps to your ruin. Your governors led the way to others. They had admirable opportunities of judging. They most of them took possession of their governments with high-flown ideas of *mother country* prerogatives, strong prejudices against the people, and a determined resolution to support the *dignity of their character*. In consequence of all this, they omitted no opportunity to treat the American principles with contempt; would hear nothing in their defence, either in public or private; and slighted in the most contemptuous manner every gentleman who was possessed of the confidence of the people, and attached to the liberties of his country. From these only they could obtain *full* and *certain* information; but these they disdained to consult. The information your majesty was to receive of the *general principles of your American subjects*, was to come from the few worthless and insignificant characters who had souls too grovelling to entertain such principles, or too mean and mercenary to adhere to them. These were in the bosom confidence of your governors. These were the little tell-tales of the peoples's *conduct*, without saying any thing (or saying *ill*) of their *motives*. They knew, from the general conversation on such subjects, that their motives, however mistaken they might be, were *good;* that they acted from *principle;* but they thought to make a merit of their sagacity by suggesting latent intentions, and great depth of wickedness; though many perhaps, judging from their own corrupt hearts, incapable of any real virtuous action, did sincerely believe there must be some foul design at bottom. Your ministers always encouraged such vermin; your governors encouraged them. You rejected every candid information; you despised every man whose good qualities made him generally respected; a man must be hated by *your subjects*, before he could be entitled to your or your ministers' favor. Was this, sir, the art of governing? this the way to secure a high-spirited, noble-minded people in their obedience? I confess when I reflect on these things, I am not surprised at the consequences which have followed. I am only surprised, and I confess grieved, when I reflect that it has been possible for your majesty to have continued so long the dupe of a most mean and contemptible policy.

Sir, at the beginning of this dispute, your majesty's governors, I am convinced, had it much in their power to moderate, perhaps entirely quiet our contentions. Had they taken pains (as was their duty) to gain information of the people's real sentiments; had they treated with respect the first characters in their country, without regard to their political principles, and selected some few for their particular and private confidence, and encouraged them freely to communicate their principles and the contents of them; had they represented these faithfully to your majesty, or your ministers, and averred (as they might then have known to be the fact) the pure integrity with which these sentiments were held; I can scarcely think that it would not have had some influence; happily perhaps it might have had a very considerable one; it must at least have raised your admiration for their character; you could not coolly, and with eagerness, have planned their destruction; you would have admitted of many amicable conferences; and been disposed to receive some plan that should effectually reconcile *power* and *liberty*.

Sir, your governors might have done us this good with truth and justice. Your majesty never had, and never will have, better subjects than the Americans. They were so upon terms of honor and reputation. They were attached to you as the king of a free people; not as the tyrant of a set of despicable slaves. They revered you as the guardian of their freedom. They considered this character as more honorable than any it was possible to sustain, and no consideration under heaven but your endeavor to degrade them, could have torn them from their allegiance. They had, it is true, great ardor of attachment to their own rights. They would have been criminal in the eyes of God and man, if they had not had. Those rights were intrusted with them as a deposit, not only for their own happiness and honor, but for the happiness and honor of their posterity. Even heaven itself was interested in the preservation of some part of the world from the infamous ravages and dishonorable condition to which the greatest part of the rest of it was exposed. Liberty seemed flying from every other quarter of the globe to take up her last, and perhaps her most exalted residence in America. We should have been little worthy the dignity of our birth, if we had not offered her a sacred and inviolable asylum. The fathers were running fast into idolatry; the sons saw, and lamented, their condition, but disdained to follow them.

Sir, the claim of the Americans was just and simple. They required only those liberties which were conceded to them in their charters, and which they had uniformly enjoyed, with very little exception, until the era of the encroachments which have so remarkably distinguished your majesty's reign. Those charters had some title to reverence, because they were the condition upon which our ancestors originally settled this country, and the means without which it never would have been annexed to the crown of England. Your predecessors had the prospect, with little difficulty and hazard, of greatly enlarging their dominion; our ancestors, at the expense of the greatest, were willing to live in any country *where liberty was to be found*, rather than continue in one which was already dishonored, and in danger of being enslaved. They accepted their powers with pleasure, almost entirely raised a fine country from an uncultivated desert, at their own expense, and flattered themselves each increasing year would add to their happiness, and improve their security; they long continued in a pleasing connection with their friends and countrymen, and whom they thought themselves honored in thinking their *protectors* also, and enjoyed in long succession before them the idea of an uninterrupted and continually improved union, highly redounding to the honor and happiness of both. Their attachment to the British crown was founded on those principles which your majesty has (from your own misconduct) so fatally experienced; they revered the *father*, they detested and renounced the *tyrant* of his people. The revolution, which rescued the throne from dishonor and bloodshed, was highly venerated, and ardently obeyed in America. The establishment of the crown in your majesty's family was a delightful object to them, and they fondly flattered themselves none of the Hanoverian princes ever could disown the principles which exalted them. Two desperate attempts have been made to wrest the sceptre from your ancestors' hands, which were supported but by too many (almost a fatal number) of your British subjects; America was free from the contagion; derided the claims of your antagonist; and considered him and his cause with as much contempt as indignation. Your royal grandfather, sir, was very sensible of their merits. He respected their rights, rejected with scorn tempting offers to invade them, and in the course of very critical times had the honor to receive from them the most liberal and cheerful aids, and the just consideration and gratitude, not only to acknowledge, but with strong expressions of esteem solicit an adequate compensation for them. The compensation was only granted in part, but it was thankfully received; the favorable regards of their sovereign, his honorable notice of their deserts, and the Parliament's confirmation of them, served as so many additional ties to the country they had always loved, and from which they were descended. This was the situation of things, under mutual gratuitous obligations, where generous minds are always striving to excel each other, and in comparison of which the dull, cold connection of *power* and *obedience* is odious and contemptible, when your majesty came to the crown, the inheritor of all this treasure, the possessor indeed not only of all your ancestors' dominions, but (a much more honorable title) the possessor of your *people's hearts*.

Unfortunately you were not long to enjoy them. Too soon it appeared that your majesty's education had been too *domestically* formed, and that the companion of your private hours must be the first minister of state. At that time your majesty had the singular happiness to have in that office the greatest and the best minister your dominions had ever known; a man revered abroad, beloved almost to adoration at home, the uncorrupt preserver of entire unanimity in your Parliament, the most illustrious and successful prosecutor of a foreign war, that perhaps had ever been seen in Europe. This was the man whose removal by little arts was to make way for your favorite's exaltation. I say nothing of the steps, sir, which brought about this affair; they are too well known to the world (though the ostensible cause was far from being the real, at least the only one), and belong not to my subject. It is sufficient to say, that the consequences which followed his removal have unanswerably proved the extreme value of the man. In what a continual state of distraction have your affairs been almost ever since? What a rotation of ministers, what jobbing, what discontent? Except in the little interval of a few months, when you really had a patriot ministry in your service (who could not, however, outlive the clamors of a mean and mercenary set), how much have your ministers been the contempt of the people? How many have they made justly discontented in your own kingdom? What will they have to say for the loss of your American territories?

This brings me to my present subject. Your ministers, who have involved you with America, seemed to have an idea that your majesty's *honor* and your subjects' *freedom* were incompatible. They have therefore taken much pains to promote the *former*, at the expense of the *latter*. America was saved from the enemy's sword, partly by England's assistance, partly by its own exertion. It is admitted, and there is the strongest proof (the acknowledgments of the late king and of Parliament) that the Americans did not only what was immediately incumbent on them, but *more*. They went *beyond their ability*. Great Britain, it is confessed, and gratefully acknowledged, did *her duty*. Is there any room for blame or recrimination of either side? Certainly not. Both were called upon by *ties of interest* to act the part they did. Indeed, if the subject be critically examined, Britain was perhaps *more nearly concerned* than America. The land in question which gave rise to the war, was *British*, not *American* property; the merchants whose commerce with the Indians was molested, were *British merchants*; the acquisition of such large additions of territory in America, very much lessened the value of our own lands; and it may be questioned whether the advantage accruing from our additional security, would not have been overbalanced by this circumstance, the scattered condition of our settlements, and the inactive, unwarlike situation a state of perfect repose would have left us in. I mention this, not with any view of detracting from any of the merits of the last war (which would be ungenerous and ungrateful), but merely to show that America does not stand in that condition of extreme obligation to Great Britain which has been so commonly supposed, and so arrogantly boasted of. No man of sense can doubt, none of candor will deny, even in England, that the policy of England in that war was directed *to her own advantage*, not ours, at least ours only *collaterally*. It is impertinent and absurd to pretend the contrary. Yet this was the shallow pretence upon which the Stamp Act was so violently defended. Sir, the Stamp Act was not opposed because we were *unwilling to contribute to our own defence*, or because we were *ungrateful*. It will be folly to assert the former. A whole people must have lost their senses before such can be the case in any country. We were *willing to contribute to our defence*, but we were willing to do it only in that way which is honorable and just, *by our own consent*. We knew, sir, that no people can be free who are absolutely dependent on another. We never had been so to England; no precedents (those resources of tyrants) could be produced against us; our charters, abstracted from other circumstances, exempted us from that indignity. We determined never to submit to it; we remonstrated; we withheld our trade; we plainly proved we were in earnest; the new ministry which had succeeded our taxing one, had more wisdom, and repealed the act.

The variety of ways in which we have been since harassed it would be equally irksome and unnecessary to relate. The facts are well known to the world. After a progression of preparatory strokes, we were at last astonished at the actual exercise of that stupendous claim, *a right to bind us in all cases whatsoever*. The sacred right of kings (which, sir, to your happiness heretofore, has been so justly ridiculed) of late years has been transferred to Parliament. Your majesty, rather than not have something divine about you, has condescended to participate it with your Parliament. Behold this venerable body, the monarch who owes his crown to the explosion of such impiety, the representatives of the British nation, who have in a thousand instances sacrificed their blood and treasure in contempt of it, together with the descendants of peers who have been such illustrious patrons of liberty and virtue, adhering to this claim, the most arrogant and presumptuous ever the pride of man formed, at the expense of the safety of their own kingdom, of the security of those subjects who are immediately placed under their protection, and to the hazard of the total destruction of those whose rights are thus daringly insulted! Behold this venerable body, the affected guardians of their people's liberty, seeking meanly and basely to deprive us of a freedom our ancestors hardly earned for us; those ancestors to whom this very country, now the plotter of our ruin, is almost entirely indebted for the territory in which she is aiming to enslave their posterity. Sir, you and your ministers, and your Parliament, may disguise this claim under what pretty colors you please; to us, in all shapes, it is odious and detestable. Do you speak of the unity of your empire? What signifies to us a unity, where, whoever are to be the masters, *we* are to be the slaves? There was nothing said about this unity when our ancestors came here. They expected to be governed by no laws but such as they gave their consent to. Custom reconciled us (however contrary to original stipulations) to your regulation of our trade. This, in respect to long usages, and from dislike of innovation, and a wish, if possible, to avoid contest, we were sincerely willing to continue. Further we could not grant without violating *the very guards of liberty*; further, neither law nor usage warranted us in granting. Any difficulties that might occur in interpreting your conduct justly, we were ready to adjust with candor, and required no limitation of your power in the article where we admitted its exercise, but what was indispensably necessary to our safety. We flattered ourselves a unity of interest would long preserve a unity of connection. This might, to our mutual happiness, long have been the case, if ambition had not swept every thing away with it. Ireland was our example. We saw no reason why we should not live with you upon as cordial terms as that kingdom. Heaven knows how infinite have been the oppressions inflicted by English power there. Yet how easily has its quiet been preserved since the revolution? The different circumstances of the two countries, taking them altogether, as to their capability of resistance, did not perhaps differ much. Ireland had a strong guard, America was naturally weak; Ireland had many disaffected subjects, America was universally, though upon liberal principles, loyal. The one country, if dangerously provoked, or powerfully invaded, had many bitter enemies to aid a revolution; the other could not be easily irritated, but when irritated, would probably persevere with spirit, and might be tempted to discover, and to carry to extreme length, the immense, but hidden and almost unknown resources Heaven had blessed her with. This condition of the two countries showed that they ought not, in policy, to be too haughtily treated. You well perceived this with regard to Ireland. You assumed great powers over her, but *you dare not exercise them*, and a discourse upon the *unity of the empire* to them would be burnt by the common hangman. Happy would it have been for you, sir, if you had used the same policy with the Americans. The consequences, I can venture to assure you, would have been equally prosperous. America has a generosity of soul equal to the greatness of her spirit.

Sir, the Americans considered themselves equally entitled to liberty with your British subjects, or any other subjects in your dominions. As men who had ever preserved their freedom, they had a right to continue free; as subjects of your crown, they were guaranteed by as strong, or if possible, stronger obligations. Our *original contract* is in being. That happy kind of monarchy which reserves just power enough to the crown to make it useful and respectable, but not enough to enable it to despise the people whom it governs, was instituted in America. We long were faithful subjects under it, until your majesty sought to overleap those bounds which the constitution, justice, and continual usage had prescribed. You were pleased to suggest a new system, and fearful of maintaining it upon the old beaten and worn-out topics of *prerogative and kingly power*; you solicited your Parliament to associate with you in the honor and the danger. These had no great difficulty in consenting. They had almost run themselves aground in their own kingdom, where their servility and corruption were in every body's mouth, and their disregard of the people's sentiments was, on all occasions, contemptuous and insulting. New and heavy impositions were to be laid; the funds of corruption began to be in danger; they began at last to fear the resentment of the people, and that these would require, when they were to be so heavily taxed, that they should be more moderately and equitably governed. America promised ample relief from all this danger. How easy would it be to suggest the obligation of the Americans for their protection in the last war, the great debt contracted *solely* on their account, and the clear equity and justice that they should pay for *their own defence?* These were fine popular topics that would do wonders with the people at large; besides giving them an object to inflame their pride and ambition: on the other hand, the great men who planned it, pleased themselves with the remote consequences of so bright a plan; the funds of corruption would not only be preserved untouched, but in a little time accumulate a tenfold addition; taxes and discontent could at any time be removed from Great Britain to America; the weakness of that country would compel them to submit for the present, and submission once obtained, it would be easy to provide sufficient curbs on them for the future, and hereafter, when the plan should be fully ripened, and the people's necks bowed low enough to despotism, then would be the time for the full harvest of courtly industry; oppressive laws, fines, exactions, hardships without number,—snares it would be almost impossible to break through, that confiscations might be more numerous and certain, and the descendants of the old, hardy race of the first American settlers give way to the parasites of a court, and the pimps of power. This was the brilliant prospect America had in view. You well know, sir, how much they disdained the thought of submission; how much they despised the mean pretences that were urged to justify it. They saw, sir, with what low artifice the popular topics above mentioned were babbled out on purpose to mislead the people from their true object, and to persuade them that America was senseless and ungrateful. They spurned at the imputation of ingratitude, so different from their general character, so contrary to that undistinguishing generosity of spirit which your ancestors, who treated us as freemen, had ever found. Admitting that they owed you even such immense obligations, you put it out of their power to prove whether they were grateful or not; you made no requisitions to try them; gratitude surely is not shown by obedience to acts of authority; it can only be expressed by voluntary and cheerful returns. Had you left the Americans to themselves, and it had appeared they were so highly indebted to you, they would, I am sure, have more than overpaid it. But this not being done, gratitude is out of the question, and can never be mentioned but to draw in some ignorant, unthinking fool to think worse of us than we deserve. With as little propriety is the other subject mentioned, of *providing for our own defence*. A free people will ever take proper measures for that purpose; they must be idiots to neglect it themselves; they will disdain to resign it to others. The Americans could not be charged with being remiss in this duty. They supported their civil establishments with honor and dignity. No inconveniences that they could ever feel had resulted from their regulation of them. Some persons indeed grumbled that they were so little dependent on the crown; but the Americans (who, as a free people, had a right to judge of this matter) had no desire to render them more so. They certainly did not mean to leave your majesty and your ministers without any control. But unless this could be effected, your scheme would be but imperfectly executed. You and your Parliament were therefore to be intrusted with *our defence*; you were to devise the means, and to judge of the extent of this service; we were to furnish the money, and to obey the regulations. We well knew of what nature these would be; armies would be kept in pay to support every new innovation; officers would be multiplied on us without number, solely dependent on the crown; every civil regulation would be made *ex prerogativa*; a few years would find us, if we were mean enough to crouch to these indignities, the most despicable slaves on earth. We were startled for a moment at the novelty of these encroachments, and had some curiosity to know the ostensible reasons upon which you pretended to justify them. These were at length unfolded. We discovered the mighty principle that was to do such mischief. It was a convenient one enough for your majesty and Parliament (between whom so friendly an alliance had been formed), but it was violative of every principle of the constitution, and every idea of justice. It was merely (to give it its due name) an impertinent confusion of two rights, in their nature totally distinct. Your Parliament had ever been considered the Parliament of *Great Britain*, only; the Peers were Peers only of Great Britain; the Commons representatives alone of that people. The Peers had no shadow of pretence for any authority out of the kingdom; the authority of the Commons, being only delegated, could not exceed the natural powers of the people at large; and what power could one set of *fellow-subjects* have over other *fellow-subjects?* Your majesty alone had any pretence, of the three branches, to any legislative authority over America, and this (as in other parts of your dominions) was shared with the people. Your arrogating a right to indiscriminate legislation, because usage had assented to it in a particular instance (for the mutual benefit of all, but principally for yours), was ungrateful and unjust. You rather ought to have been thankful that America had conceded so much, than resent her being discreet enough to withhold more. When these colonies were first settled, nobody dreamt of this triple prerogative of the king and Parliament over all the dominions of your crown. Ireland never consented to it; Scotland you never claimed it over. The condition of a conquered country, such as Ireland is, if we view the subject with an unfeeling coolness of argument that she little merits, stands upon much more unstable ground than we do. *We are descendants of the conquerors, and never intermixed with the original inhabitants.* Ireland and Scotland are examples, that in fact there may be a king over several different countries, without having one superintending legislature over all. This is a mere modern chimera, spun out of the cobwebs of the schools. I would undertake by the same means to prove that your majesty ought to be arbitrary in England, because a mixed monarchy is *a corrupt form of government*, and it is possible that a settled difference of opinion on important points between the different branches of the legislature, might be the ruin of the people. The truth is, there must necessarily be some supreme power in each individual country to regulate the concerns of the whole, or the society could not subsist, but it is not necessary that one and the same power should govern *different countries*. We lived happily enough, I think, a long time, to disprove this absurdity in fact: we never could be mean enough to assent to it in speculation. The substance of your demand is, that to make your government more easy, we should resign all our rights and powers of acting to you and a corrupt body you have at your devotion. We have, thank God, proved to you with sufficient clearness, that we understood the value of liberty better; it might have been happy for you, sir, if you had learnt to respect it more. Some inconveniences, indeed, we were sensible of, that formed a little alloy to the advantages of our unexpected and astonishing success; but surely any remedy for these ought to have been conducted on the basis of a general negotiation, and not violently sought by an unjust usurpation of power.

I fear, sir, I have already, on a subject that has been so much discussed, proceeded too far. I have been led away by the ardor of my feelings farther than I intended. Yet I flatter myself I have suggested some things that may not be unuseful. Notwithstanding the million of writings that have been published on this subject, many weak men are yet wavering, and some led astray by the delusive sophistry your majesty and your ministers (to say nothing of lesser characters) yet condescend to use. In spite of all these arts, truth, however, will at length, I trust, with its meridian lustre, enlighten the minds of the people. Indeed, your assertions begin already to grow a little stale. Men compare the facts that have already happened with former courtly assertions, and find the contrary event of almost every prediction. It is natural to judge of men's veracity and penetration by facts that are open. A man cannot long be hackneyed in a repetition of falsehoods without being detected, and once detected, his credit is for ever gone. Sir, your majesty must excuse me in saying, that *speeches from the British throne* seem nearly arrived to this disgraceful predicament. Your majesty has, without scruple, on many occasions, spoken with the most assured confidence, and the most violent malignity, of the intention of the American leaders. You have repeatedly declared they had, from the first, no other object than independency; in your last speech you seem to take it for granted, and as a point unquestionable, and expressly assert that *their object has always been dominion and power*. Sir, it is of little consequence to us whether you are personally answerable for this false and daring assertion, or whether, according to the usage of the times, it is to be ascribed to your minister. You have given it the sanction of your concurrence. The royal word is pledged for its truth. It is a point wherein your minister could not expressly deceive you, because it concerns a subject over which neither he nor your majesty, notwithstanding the plenitude of your power, is invested with a cognizance. Our hearts are known only to the Almighty. He, I am persuaded, well knows the utter untruth of so malignant and ill-founded a suggestion. Your majesty's piety may consider whether assertions so solemnly delivered, and which have already, at least, had a considerable influence in inflaming this unhappy contest, will not one day be examined into at a place where kings and subjects shall be equal, truth shall be laid open, and good and ill actions impartially meet with their recompense.

Sir, you say much on the subject of our independency, but not a word of the provocations that led to it. The indignant rejection of our petitions, the refusal to enter into any discussion of claims, the hire of foreign troops, besides employing numerous bodies of your own, the actual excitation of the Indian savages to destroy us, and that completion of all villainy, the endeavor to raise our domestics (domestics you forced on us) to involve us in one indiscriminate massacre;—these are the steps, sir, which irritated our minds, and compelled us to renounce you. We could frame an idea of no act of tyranny greater than these actions; we saw your determined purpose to ruin or enslave us; every shadow of hope of protection from your government was fled; you had indeed formally, as well as by a succession of cruel actions, abandoned us. It was not in men to submit to all these indignities. We renounced the tyranny of Great Britain, and bid defiance to all the power you and your Parliament could raise. We resigned ourselves to Heaven and our own resources.

Your majesty speaks of *means of conciliation* held out by your commissioners. To this hour no such means have been offered, but by a total submission of one party to the other. The commissioners declared they had no authority to treat with the Congress (the only manly and effectual means of doing any good), but they could converse with *private gentlemen* on the subject. That is, they had powers to draw off as many individuals from the confederacy as they could. Sir, the Congress, however (to avoid any blame to themselves, and in testimony of their sincere desire of peace), complied with these caprices; they furnished *private gentlemen* to hear and receive proposals. No proposals were made. Nothing but absolute submission would be accepted. The peace your commissioners were empowered to make, was *to secure the object of the war without bloodshed*. Can any thing be more ridiculous? Could any offers better deserve to be rejected, with *circumstances of indignity and insult?*

But your majesty, it seems, has yet graciously in reserve for us the blessings of *law* and *liberty*. What liberty does your majesty mean? It cannot be *that mild government under which we have been so happy*, because this is the only condition in which we have ever requested to be placed, and which you have stubbornly refused. If your majesty had disliked innovations as much as we did, this *mild government* would have still continued to make us happy. The liberty your majesty can only mean (consistent with the conduct and declaration of your servants) is the being governed by 700 or 800 tyrants, at the distance of 3000 miles from us, ignorant of our situation, unconnected with our interest, over whom it is impossible we should have the least influence, and who would find a thousand mean motives continually to oppress and injure us. For heaven's sake, sir, speak with common sense and decency, if not with truth.

Sir, these are facts which will, sooner or later, be known in England. The minds of that people perhaps are now a little inflamed by a continual recital of falsehoods, but they cannot always remain so. Insuccess, at least, will awake them from their delirium. Then they will see, in dreadful prospect, the miserable condition to which you have reduced them. Their resentment will first, as it ought, be directed against your ministers; perhaps it may spare your majesty. But if it does, you will find the remainder of your reign very different from the beginning. Instead of the continual blessings of your people, you will meet every where dismal groans, and the most affecting proofs of the misery you have created. America! America! where is America! will be the constant cry of your people. They will soon feel, I fear, the infinite loss they have sustained. Their commerce, which was once so brilliant, will gradually decay into nothing. The numerous individuals it supported will be every where clamoring for bread. The public taxes will sink; credit be exhausted; perhaps a national bankruptcy ensue; and in that case, too probably, the national ruin.

Sir, I am an Englishman myself, and am deeply affected with this prospect. I have in that kingdom many near and respectable connections, whose fate will be involved with the multitude. I have still a strong attachment to my native country. I am far from thinking the people in it universally corrupt, though too many, God knows, are, and this has been the cause of all our present calamity. I can truly say, sir, I have been greatly distressed at my critical situation, but I never hesitated a moment how to act. Becoming an American subject, it was my duty to support the rights of one, and exert myself to the utmost in defence of that political society of which I was a member. This I have ever yet done; this I ever shall do. The consequences I am not answerable for. If our salvation can be secured, without the ruin of Great Britain, I shall be inexpressibly happy: if it cannot, though I should feel the greatest distress for her fate, my attachment to America would remain unmoved: if we in the end should fail altogether, I should even then think we were greater and happier in our affliction, supported by a noble conscience, than our proud and unfeeling conquerors in all their prosperity.

These, sir, are the fervent sentiments of a man who was once your subject, but is now your enemy, though he wishes to be as little so as the indispensable safety of America (which it is his duty to support) will suffer him to be.

A BRITISH AMERICAN.

MARCH, 1777.

General Howe and his brother, Admiral Lord Howe, landed on Staten Island, June 28th, 1776.* By the late act of Parliament they were commissioned to receive the submission of such communities or persons as might throw themselves on the king's mercy. After the battle of Long Island they sent their prisoner, Gen. Sullivan, with a verbal message to Congress, desiring to confer with some members of that body, as *private gentlemen*. Congress appointed Franklin, Adams, and Rutledge, a committee to wait upon the English commanders. These, the Howes, were the commissioners referred to in the address of Mr. Iredell.

The Assembly convened at New Bern, April the 8th. Mr. Iredell, as one of the commissioners to prepare bills for the consideration of that body, arrived at that town on the 25th of the same month.

IREDELL TO MRS. IREDELL.

NEW BERN, 26th April, 1777.

MY DEAR HANNAH:—Mr. Johnston and myself gave a pretty good account of ourselves on the road; we arrived here yesterday morning, and are lodged tolerably well, considering, except that we have only one bed, which is disagreeable, but cannot at present be avoided. We have the satisfaction, however, of being quiet, and out of the noise of the politicians, few of whom are good for any thing. I am afraid things will not go on

* Hildreth.

very well here, and that we shall be obliged to wait a little longer for Court laws. The point is not yet finally determined, and there is room to hope a lucky stroke of fortune may yet give them to us. Your brother John is not yet come, which disconcerts me extremely. Mr. Williams and other gentlemen tell me too they expected him. I should be a good deal uneasy from his not coming, if he was remarkably punctual in these kind of engagements. How I shall dispose of myself in consequence I do not know. I must endeavor, at any rate, to see the plantations, at least one of them, but shall hasten home as soon as possible. I shall most anxiously hope to find you well on my return. I have been very well ever since I left home ; your brother has been a little indisposed, but is now pretty well. I shall expect you to go to Dukinfield with me at the time of Bertie Court, which I shall earnestly endeavor not to miss. May every happiness attend you! Mention me properly to your sister and Nelly, and believe me ever, my dear Hannah,

Most tenderly yours,
JAMES IREDELL.

NEW BERN, April 28th, 1777.

MY DEAR HANNAH:—Here I am, and very much disappointed and uneasy at not hearing from you by the post to-day. Your brother and I were both congratulating ourselves on its being the day of its arrival, and had no doubt of receiving some letter; but this unfortunately was not the case. How could you serve me so, when I was so good? Let me beg you not to repeat it. When I shall get away I don't know. Your brother is not yet arrived. I am heartily tired of this cursed place. Mr. Hewes was to-day left out of the nomination of delegates ; he had only 40 votes out of 90. The reasons alleged : his being so long at home, and his holding (as some wise men supposed) two offices under government, by being a member of Congress and a member of one of their committees. His friends exerted themselves, but ineffectually, against much underhand, contemptible dealing, and the last ridiculous objection I mentioned, which really possessed some well-meaning men, and they say, his well-wishers.* I shall think myself very happy when I get home again ; especially if we have laws enough to give me something to do. Politics I am really quite sick of. They have got into a most melancholy train. The best cause, and the most promising one, is grossly injured by many of its conductors in this country. Heaven grant us (I am sure it is most wanted) a speedy change for the better. Your brother is now quite well ; I have never been otherwise. God grant I may soon be happy enough to meet you so. Take the best care of yourself, if not for your sake, for mine. I shall indeed be inexpressibly happy to see you. I sincerely hope every body else will be well too. Pray mention me most affectionately to your sister and Nelly. You will also give my love to the children, and mention me, as I ought, to the gentlemen you have an opportunity to see. Adieu, my dear Hannah. Once more, take care of your health, and believe me, with the sincerest affection,

Most truly and unalterably yours,
JAMES IREDELL.

NEW BERN, April 29th, 1777.

DEAR HANNAH:—I have been a most punctual correspondent, and I hope you thank me for it. I wrote to you only last night by the post, but would not omit the present, though so early an opportunity after. I even put aside business of pressing importance, of a public nature, in which I am at last involved, to tell you how tenderly I love, how anxiously I wish to see you. My impatience indeed is great. When it can be gratified, is yet uncertain. Your brother's not coming has quite put me out of the course of my policy. *The houses are pressing forward fast now. To-morrow is the last day they will receive any bills. It is this makes me so busy.* I have one in my hands for establishing courts, that is to be presented to-morrow. Heaven grant it a favorable reception! A faint glimmering of hope yet remains.* They have resolved to-day on a general assessment of all property, that is to say, a tax of so much in the pound on the value of every man's property. This perhaps may lead to the desired object. Mr. Hooper to-day resigned his appointment to the Congress ; who may succeed him is uncertain ; probably Mr. Harnett. Mr. Hewes, I believe, might easily be chosen (it is said, *unanimously*), but his friends think it would be an indignity.

Though I have been here many days, I have paid very few visits. I have dined with Mr. Cook, Mrs. Gordon, Mrs. Edwards, been invited to Mr. Ellis's, and dine to-morrow with the Governor. I have yet to see Mrs. Cornell, Dr. Marslin, and the Chief Justice. Mrs. Allen Jones is here, and her two children : the

* The delegates appointed were Harnett, Penn, and Thomas Burke. Mr. Hooper declined.

* The italics are not in the original. I shall hereafter take the liberty, without note, of underscoring such passages in the letters transcribed, as I desire to direct particular attention to.

little boy has still got the ague and fever, but looks well, and all the rest of the family are in good health. Let me beg you once more to take care of yours. Don't fatigue yourself too much about my shirts, and walk sometimes in the garden. If I was not so much engaged, I would write a line or two to Nelly. I hope she will excuse me, for that reason. Pray mention me very affectionately to her, as well as to her mamma, and the children. Every body you will say, how d'ye to. Your brother is spending the evening abroad, as I should have been, *had not this bill been in my way. If it does not pass, I shall regret the time I spent upon it, and the pleasure it has deprived me of ;* not otherwise. Your brother, as he is not now at home, may possibly not write, but I assure you he is extremely well. Adieu ! my dear Hannah, I find it difficult to break from you,—but it must be. Take care of your health, and believe me ever,

Most tenderly and affectionately yours,
JAMES IREDELL.

Courts were not established at this session of the Assembly; the question was adjourned until its second session (Nov. 15th). Then the bill drafted by Iredell, revised, perhaps slightly altered by his friend Maclaine, was again introduced, and soon passed into a law. By North Carolina writers it is styled the "celebrated Court Law," and has been less altered than any act of any importance in the statute book. It has been often ascribed to Mr. Maclaine ; but I think there is no doubt that Iredell is entitled to the honor of its paternity.* At this period he began to be generally recognized as the ablest lawyer in the State.

LETTER FROM MRS. BLAIR.

1st May, 1777.

DEAR SIR :—Though my sister is writing you, yet I think gratitude for your so kindly remembering me when I am absent from home, ought, if I had no other motive, to prompt me to return the favor as well as I am able. Could I write half as well as you, my letter would be better worth your reading ; but such as it is, I have no doubt it will be agreeable to you. You cannot expect any news from me now, for when you are away none of our acquaintance think me worth calling on. Mr. Cabarrus and Mr. Pucheu come sometimes, and occasionally the doctor, but no others. You will hear of our being at a ball, from the gentlemen who gave it. My sister went, much against her inclination, and was a little unwell the next day, but she is quite recovered now. There were few gentlemen at it ; and the company not altogether pleased with each other, as I imagined, but perhaps I was mistaken. I believe our Edenton ladies are afraid of the Frenchmen. It is said our gentlemen intend returning the ball as soon as they (the French gentlemen) return from New Bern. Mr. Pucheu lamented much that you were not here, for he is sure you are fond of dancing ; however, he intends the pleasure of a dance with you at New Bern. They talk of giving a ball as soon as they arrive ; but I think (though you are a much better judge) if they could be persuaded to let it alone, unless there was one given to them first, it would be better. Mr. Pucheu seems to have a great regard for you ; and I am sure has the highest opinion of your goodness. Were you to tell him any thing he intended to do was improper, he would abandon it. They will, I dare say, mention their intention to you, as soon as they see you. I have wrote a good deal about what I have no business with ; but I have a regard for them, and I should be sorry that they exposed themselves to the ill-natured reflections of people, perhaps, not half so deserving. I do not think their ball has been any advantage to them here. Mrs. Johnston intends writing. I shall send over early in the morning for a letter. We anxiously expect to hear from you and my brother—pray do not let him see this unmeaning scrawl. Guns firing all day, and a grand supper in town to-night, in honor of St. Tammany. Excuse all mistakes—it is now after 12 o'clock at night.

I am, dear sir,
Your affectionate sister,
J. BLAIR.

During this year the Marquis de La Fayette, and many other foreign officers, visited America ; some in consequence of contracts entered into with Silas Deane, the American Commissioner to France—others as adventurers. It appears that a party of Frenchmen came to North Carolina, among whom the most intelligent were Pucheu, Noirmont de La Neuville, and La Tours.* Mr. Iredell both wrote and spoke French fluently, and these gentlemen soon conceived for him a friendship so strong that it survived their stay in America. Noirmont was the younger brother of the Chevalier de la Neuville, who was appointed an inspector in the army under Gates, and who was complimented when he

* Vid. Davis's Address at Chapel Hill, 1855, and Sketch of A. M. Hooper, N. C., Un. Mag., 1855.

* Washington and his Generals.—*Cary and Hart.* It is erroneously stated in this work that the La Neuvilles arrived in America in the autumn of '77.

retired, after six months' service, Dec. 4th, 1778, with a brevet commission of brigadier by Congress. Noirmont de la Neuville served two campaigns with credit; attained the rank of major, and colonel by brevet; and returned to France near the close of 1779. In 1782 he was "Capt. au Second de Chasseurs au Regt. Royal." They went to New Bern from Edenton, to solicit employment from the Assembly; but the tender of their swords was declined. Pucheu returned to France early in July, while La Neuville obtained rank in the Continental service.

IREDELL TO MRS. IREDELL.

NEW BERN, 2d May, 1777.

MY DEAR HANNAH :—I expected to have set off to-day for New River, but as Peter will not now go in, we have deferred going till to-morrow, as it will be then more convenient for your brother. I hope we shall have to stay but a short time there, and shall hasten home as soon as possible. I will mention no time, but strongly flatter myself it will be before Bertie Court. Prepare to go to Dukinfield with me then. I hope in God you continue to enjoy your health, and that you take the best care of yourself, for my sake, if not yours. I am indeed heartily tired, and sincerely homesick. My impatience to see you is inexpressible. It is more than probable your brother Sam will be home before me. He, I believe, anxiously wishes to leave this place. It is indeed melancholy to see the scenes going forward here: policy and reason neglected, mean and selfish purposes universally prevailing. He has enjoyed his health but indifferently here, as usual, though he is much better now. We have been inconveniently lodged; the whole time only one room and one bed between us. This would have done for you and me, but not for us. I have been perfectly well ever since I left you; so is your brother John. He was delayed coming in so long, on account of boils, that were very troublesome. I send by this vessel one pound of green, and three pounds of bohea tea; the last cost 16s., the other 48s. I have bought three yards of the cloth, which Mr. Corrie will be so obliging as to bring in for me. It is enormously dear, but my necessity was pressing.

I am very uneasy at never hearing from Edenton since I left it. I know not how to account for your neglecting the post, about which I entreated you so much. I can now expect to hear nothing till I get home. It would have made me very happy to hear you were well; but I must hope, and wait in patience. I have not time to add much more. You have no reason to complain of me on the score of writing. I wish you had given me no reason to complain of you. Heaven grant there was no unfortunate cause for it. You should have considered the extreme anxiety of friends at a distance, and how apt they are to suspect the worst. Pray mention me most affectionately to Nelly and *the other children*; make my best respects to your brother's family, and Mrs. Dawson; and ever think of me as

The most tender and affectionate of husbands,

JAMES IREDELL.

NEW BERN, 2d May, 1777.

MY DEAR HANNAH :—You owe me a thousand obligations. I have omitted no one opportunity of writing to you, when I could do it with any possible convenience. I have wrote to you already to-day, by an opportunity by water, by which I send your sister some tea: 3lbs. of bohea, one of green. I intend this shall go by your brother, who, I believe, will be at home before me, as he waits only the prorogation of the Assembly, and I the end of my jaunt to New River. I thank God I am perfectly well. I earnestly hope you are so too, and that I shall be blest in finding you so. Happy indeed shall I then be! I shall return, impoverished, by the want of court laws, but rich in every feeling of tenderness and affection for you. O, how does absence teach me how much I love you! I hope to be with you before Bertie Court, and shall expect your company to Dukinfield. O how I anticipate that happy time! It is not in my power to write much, but I could not omit it altogether. What would I give for so many lines from you. Take care of yourself, my dear Hannah; remember me to every body, and believe me,

Most affectionately yours,

JAS. IREDELL.

The Assembly adjourned on the 9th of May.

LETTER FROM MARTIN HOWARD.

Martin Howard, one of the royal judges in Rhode Island, 1765, being forced by popular indignation to fly that province, sought shelter in North Carolina, where, after the suicide of Judge Berry, he was made Chief Justice by Governor Tryon; he was also a member of Tryon's council.[*] His office as judge terminated with the expiration of the law creating the court in

[*] Howard had written in favor of the right of Parliament to tax America. For this offence, on the 28th August, 1765, a Rhode Island mob destroyed his house and furniture.—*Bancroft*.

1773. He is represented by Jones, Wheeler and others, as devoid of all the virtues of humanity, a ferocious despot, an execrable copy of the English Jeffreys. I cannot but suspect that the picture has been exaggerated; it has been blackened out of all resemblance to any being who ever sat upon the Bench within my knowledge in North Carolina. The Judge was certainly the ablest lawyer, and the most highly cultivated member of his court. The fact that he was permitted to reside quietly on his plantation until July, 1777, when he withdrew from the State; the further fact that he was kindly remembered by such a man as James Iredell, whose respect clung to him in his fallen fortunes, and the tone of the following letter, consist but badly with the moral deformity and atrocity attributed to him; and induce the belief that the removal of a little rhetorical lampblack will disclose a man, differing, it is true, politically, from the mass of the population, but in other respects, the peer of the proudest citizen of the realm. The letter of Howard to Iredell, dated 20th May, 1773, referred to by Jones as a confession of "malignity," has disappeared from Mr. Iredell's collection of papers.

RICHMOND,[*] May 15th, 1777.

SIR :—Your favor from New Bern gave me no small degree of pleasure. An instance of civility to an obscure man in the woods, is as flattering as a compliment to a worn-out beauty, and received with equal avidity and delight. I have lately been so little accustomed even to the common courtesies of life, that a sentiment of kindness comes upon me by surprise, and brings with it a double, because an unexpected, pleasure.

I sincerely thank you for your obliging expressions; they give me more than I have a right to claim, and greatly overpay any marks of consideration which I may at any time heretofore have shown to you, and which your merit entitled you to receive from me.

I wish you could have conveniently fulfilled your intentions of riding to Richmond. My little family would have been glad to see you, and you would have seen, I think, the best piece of meadow in Carolina, whence (when I leave this country) you might be able to add one to the few observations which may be made upon an unimportant character, viz., that I had made two blades of grass grow where only one grew before—a circumstance among some nations of no small honor and renown. I wish you all happiness, and am, with real esteem,

Sir, your most ob't serv't.

M. HOWARD.

Judge Howard died in exile, pending the war.

[*] Craven county.

IREDELL TO MRS. IREDELL.

EDENTON, 19th Aug., 1777.

DEAR HANNAH :—I have not, till now, had the least chance of writing you, and at present the probability of your receiving this letter, in any tolerable time, I think is very doubtful. When I came home, I found Peggy almost perfectly recovered, and your sister and the children well: your sister has been since a little sick, but is well again. Her sickness, and La Tours being here (of which your sister acquainted you), were excuses I readily took hold of, for not going to Tyrrel Court; so that I have been here ever since. I have had my health perfectly, but felt very uneasily ever since I came home. Indeed I can scarce think it my home. Your being absent makes my time dreadfully disagreeable. I have been able to apply to nothing. I can't read; I can't write. I do nothing but wish for you. I am disagreeably embarrassed by La Tours being here; I could easily be with you in two or three days, but I do not like to leave him behind me. And he has yet proposed nothing about going. What I shall do I don't know; I shall endeavor earnestly to get to you, but if I should not very soon, you must impute it to the above circumstance, and nothing else; for I assure you I never was better in my life. How happy it would make me to hear you were so. I hope you will send me a line by the Chair for Nelly. Your brother and his family are all extremely well. When I went over to his house the evening of my arrival, Penny met me with great pleasure, but when she heard you were not come, she cried bitterly for a good time. And she still expresses great anxiety to see you, and often inquires when you will be at home. Gaby seems to improve charmingly. I am much hurried. It is very late, and the doctor goes before sunrise in the morning. You must excuse all faults, and among the rest, the trouble I give you to find out my words. Your sister desires her best affection. Nelly knows nothing of my writing. How happy shall I be to assure you in a few days (if I possibly can) that I am

Your most affectionate

JAS. IREDELL.

IREDELL TO MISS BLAIR.

EDENTON, 3d Sept., 1777.

MY DEAR NELLY :—You must this time be content with a letter only from me, for it was late before any of us thought of writing by this opportunity (which is only a half way one), and your mamma and aunt are otherwise too importantly engaged, especially as it seems your mamma is not perfectly sure whether she rightly comprehends your letter; and your aunt is very doubtful whether you would not put her off in the same manner, by leaving yourself scarcely time to send an apology for scribbling in haste. I have the pleasure to assure you all in our family are extremely well; your uncle has been very unwell for two or three days, but is now much better; Miss Lenox has been so too, and is very little better (her eye being very much affected), and Miss Cathcart has been very violently afflicted with the toothache; the rest of that family are very well. So, in general, is Mrs. Dawson. We hope you keep yourself in health by gayety, exercise and good humor, and that before you return you will be able to manage a horse with tolerable dexterity. This exercise is both agreeable and useful, and it will be of much advantage to you to have it in your power to take it. I know you will have a violent passion to hear the little chit-chat news of the town, but I am a very bad hand to communicate it. Indeed I do not recollect any I have heard. There does not seem any thing at present going forward. All is stillness and dulness. Perhaps it may please you equally well to hear that letters have been received from Mr. Hewes since he arrived at Boston, that he was almost quite well, only complained a little of the rheumatism, that he is likely to have some success in his business, and that you may hope for the happy opportunity of admiring him once more some time next month. This gave me infinite satisfaction. What then must it do to his professed admirer?

Your mamma and aunt most earnestly request that your aunt Johnston will accompany your uncle down. It will make us all very happy. The compliment will be returned her next month, and it is hoped it may be done without much inconvenience. You must try what your persuasions can do, and they do not commonly fail for want of importunity.

Seriously speaking, your mamma bids me assure you, that she would certainly have wrote, but for the lateness of the evening. She has, however, some reason to complain of your negligence and indolence in writing, and she hopes you will take a good deal of pains to bring your volatility, at least sometimes, down to a reasonable standard. Her best affections and your aunt's and mine are ever yours, and we all think about you with more anxiety and tenderness than I believe you conceive. Your mamma's happiness you must know to be deeply interested, and I assure you your aunt's and mine is in a very considerable degree, in your entitling yourself to general esteem by a steady and uniform propriety of conduct. Adieu! my dear Nelly, and believe me ever,
Your most affectionate uncle,
JAS. IREDELL.

and his professional studies, interrupted by the agitations of the Revolution. He had been a member of the Committee of Safety for the Wilmington district in 1774, and subsequently a member of the Provincial Council. He had served at Halifax, in the State Congress, 1776, and, afterwards, in the Convention that adopted the Constitution; and at the time of his election was speaker of the Senate. He had much rugged energy of language, and was a man of strong will and violent prejudices. He was moderate in nothing:—he loved ardently; he hated intensely. His friends regarded him as eminently practical, and solid; his opponents denounced him as "stupid," obstinate, and impracticable. His patriotism was conceded. He was the brother of Gen. John Ashe. His influence, corroborated by that of his connections, was predominant in his county. In knowledge of human nature, and that rare talent that qualifies its possessor for the control of men, he had scarcely a rival. In after years, though many efforts were made to drive him from the bench, they were unsuccessful: the stability of his seat could not be shaken. So great was his popularity, that when his proud nature bent to the clamor of his enemies, and he proposed to abandon his office, the Assembly would not receive his resignation, and he retained his place until elevated, in 1795, to the higher post of governor. He had wealth. In politics was a leader of the radicals.°

Samuel Spencer had been clerk of the court for Anson county, under the Colonial government. In that office, by malfeasance, and the exaction of illegal fees, he had excited a tumult: five hundred men assembled together intent upon redress; and expelled the officers of the court from the court-house; ninety-nine signed an address and remonstrance to Gov. Tryon.† As a whig, he had been so active that he had been made member of Congress in 1775, and appointed Colonel for Anson county; he had also been of the Provincial Council. He certainly was not below mediocrity, even in his profession, but was not qualified by learning or dignity of manners for the office conferred upon him. He was as insensible to wit or sarcasm as a rhinoceros to the sting of a mosquito. He proved very unacceptable to the bar, but no indignity or neglect could ever tempt him to resign: to effect this end much inge-

* Three of his sons served in the army during the war: the eldest, John, was Lt.-Col. at Eutaw, a member of Congress, and governor elect when he died. Two of his grandsons had been members of Congress. In the year 1785 an act was passed, taking from all persons the right of suing for confiscated property. The judges declared the act invalid. One of the judges illustrated his opinion in this manner: "As God said to the waters, 'so far shalt ye go and no farther,' so said the people to the Legislature." That celebrated lawyer, John Haywood, in Moore vs. Bradley, in allusion to this decision, remarked—"Judge Ashe deserves for this the veneration of his country and posterity."—2d Haywood's Reports—N. C.
† Wheeler.

LA NEUVILLE TO IREDELL.

SIR:—If the war is indeed declared in France, we could stay but a very little while in the north; my books in this case become useless for me. This reflection, united to desire of leaving you a work when the reading appears to please you, engages me to pray you of keeping it till j come back.

I take upon myself to offer to your lovely niece another, entitled the Art of Loving, though written in french; j rely upon you about the translation of this witty poem. Besides you shall think as j, that it is convenient of presenting the art of loving to which possesses the art of pleasing. j am, with the sentiments of the most lively gratitude,
Your very humble servant,
NOIRMONT DE LA NEUVILLE.

The second session of the Assembly of 1777 was begun and held at New Bern, Nov. 15th. An act was soon passed for establishing courts of law, and regulating the proceedings therein. The State was laid off into six districts, i. e. the districts of Wilmington, New Bern, Edenton, Halifax and Salisbury.° Three judges were provided for. The courts were to have cognizance of all matters generally litigated and determined in courts of law; and all pleas of the State, and criminal matters. Equity jurisdiction was not conferred till 1782.† Any one judge might hold court in case of the death or absence of his colleagues, "provided always, that demurrers, cases agreed, special verdicts, bills of exception to evidence, and motions in arrest of judgment *should* not be argued but before two or more judges." To prevent irregularities in the records, the judges were wisely authorized to appoint "clerks of skill and probity," to hold office during good behavior.

On the 20th of December, Samuel Ashe, Samuel Spencer, and James Iredell were elected judges of the said court.

Samuel Ashe was a member of one of the most ancient and distinguished families of the State. His father had been speaker of the Assembly in 1727. He had read law with his uncle, Col. Sam. Swann; ‡ but his early education had been imperfect,

* Statutes.
† With Judge Iredell's papers, in Wm. Hooper's handwriting, are "Rules humbly submitted to the Court of Chancery, for the better order and government thereof," consisting of 85 sections, and almost identical with the established rules, as they appear in the "Revised Statutes," chapter 32.
‡ Attorney General; author of "Swann's Revisal."

nuity was exerted in vain: squibs and pasquinades rebounded from him as paper pellets from a wall of stone. Neither the avowed contempt of the most distinguished advocates, nor the sneer of the pettifogger, could penetrate his selfishness and avarice. In 1788, as a member of the convention at Hillsborough, he contributed largely to the rejection of the Constitution. Voluptuous, if not refined, in practice, if not in theory, it is said he was not averse to polygamy. In 1794, enfeebled by disease, as he was basking in the sunshine in his yard, a turkey, attracted by some part of his clothing which was red, attacked him with such fury, that he died of the wounds.

December 20th Waightstill Avery was elected Attorney General.

WM. HOOPER* TO JUDGE IREDELL.

NEW BERNE, 23d Dec, 1777.

DEAR SIR:—Before this reaches you, you will have received information of being promoted to the first honors the State can bestow. I sincerely congratulate you upon the favorable opinion which induced the people to this measure, and I confess I feel a sort of vanity in having borne testimony to the merit of him whom they have thus distinguished. You will be at a loss to conjecture how I could have been accessory to this step, after you had been so explicit to me on the subject. Be assured that I was not inattentive to your objections, nor did I fail to mention them and urge them with sincerity to every person who mentioned you for the office to which you are now designated. I urged the probability of your accepting the Attorney General's place, and proposed you for it with the fullest confidence of success. I considered that appointment genteel and the pay liberal, and that it would not interfere with your practice in civil suits, and was perfectly free from the objections which you made to the Judge's seat. A back-country interest and Avery's presence, gave him a prevailing influence, and your friends, finding that they must miscarry in this, resolved to make the effort in which they were successful, equal to their most sanguine expectations. I expostulated with them upon the impropriety of electing one who, in all probability, might decline, and leave one of the seats of justice vacant. They answered me by saying that you might possibly be prevailed upon to act for one circuit at least, that no material disadvantage could result to you from it,—that it would give you a weight and importance in those parts of the State where you

* Signer of the Declaration of Independence.
VOL. I.—24

had not had an opportunity to make yourself generally known, and prepare you for a more extensive and profitable practice, when you should think fit to descend again to the bar. That even if you declined the office altogether, that two would still remain, who for a while would be competent to the purposes of administering justice, and that they would hazard the experiment upon the bare possibility of filling the third seat with one of the respectable character you bore. Their reasoning prevailed, and you have now the satisfaction of an unrestrained choice. The appointment has been imposed upon you, and therefore you are at perfect liberty to act or not. I will not urge a circumstance to influence your determination. I have too much regard for you and yours to induce you to a resolution which might clash with your interest. As a member of the court—of the State—I am too much concerned to be an adviser. Should you acquiesce, even for a short period, in the intentions of the State, it will lessen, in my view, the fatigues which I must encounter in practice, and induce me again to open my law books.

Mr. Ashe desires me to inform you that he expects you here the 12th of January, when the governor will attend and take the qualification of himself and the other judges. My brother George is here, and begs me to mention to you that he is a candidate for the clerkship of Wilmington which he formerly had, and if you can, consistent with the duty you owe the public, give your vote in his favor—he solicits it.

I beg to be remembered in the most respectful manner to your good lady, Mrs. Blair and family, Mr. Johnston and his, and am,

Dear sir,
Yours affectionately,

WM. HOOPER.

ARCHIBALD MACLAINE TO JUDGE IREDELL.

Mr. Maclaine's family were from Loch Bowie, in the Highlands of Scotland. He was the near relation of that eminent divine, the Rev. A. Maclaine, pastor of the Protestant Church at the Hague, and translator of Mosheim's Ecclesiastical History. After serving an apprenticeship of three years to a merchant in Dublin, Mr. Maclaine came to Wilmington, where with his brother he established a mercantile house; failing in business he commenced the study of the law. His powerful frame and iron constitution fitted him to endure any amount of labor and fatigue. His indomitable will, and persistent industry were sure guarantees of success.* He not only mastered the subtleties of the law, but made vigorous forays into the fields of science and polite learning, from which he came laden with the richest plunder. A little awkward and ungainly, at first, his friends were despondent, and anticipated for him only disaster: to their delight and astonishment, however, he soon won his way to the front rank of his profession. Active, bold and intelligent, he was a prominent member of the Wilmington Safety Committee in 1774, and a member of the Congress at Hillsborough in August, 1775: he was often member of the Assembly, representing the county of Brunswick† in '77, '78, and '82, and subsequently the town of Wilmington, from 1783 to 1787.‡ When Judge Iredell resigned his office in August, 1778, Judge Henderson declining, Maclaine was elected (Feb. 1779), but would not accept. He was the intimate friend, personally and politically, of Judge Iredell, and one of his most frequent and accomplished correspondents. In the convention of 1788, he powerfully aided in the effort to induce the adoption of the Federal Constitution, and shared largely in the distress, the disappointment, and the gloom its rejection occasioned its partisans. In talent, learning and probity, he had few equals in the State. As a debater and writer, "he had no superior, except, perhaps, Davie, Iredell, and Johnston."§ He was of sanguine temperament, and irritable passions. The slightest spark sufficed to kindle into flame his combustible nature. The explosions of his wrath were sudden and terrific; and his fiery denunciations, and heated satire, seethed and scorched as burning lava. This infirmity of temper was his only fault: it was the source of much pain, mortification and regret to his friends; but as he was easily appeased, and prompt to atone for a fault, their attachment was never entirely alienated.

NEW BERNE, 25th Dec. 1777.

SIR:—I dare not venture to congratulate you on your promotion, because I am apprehensive that it is not suitable to your future prospects. I can only say that if it would answer your

---
* Wheeler, Davis's Address.
† Maclaine owned the Bluff plantation in Brunswick, where his grave may now be seen; the place is now the property of Col. Thomas D. Meares. His son Jerome was made a captain in the 4th Reg't., 1776, and served with credit in the war. Mr. Maclaine's daughter married Mr. George Hooper. Those fine scholars, George, and De Berniere Hooper, and that unrivalled "raconteur" of mirth-provoking stories, Johnston I. Hooper of Alabama, are his great-grandchildren.
‡ Sketch of A. M. Hooper, N. C. Un. Mag.
§ Wheeler.

---

purposes as fully as it has pleased your friends and the public, it would give me real satisfaction.

Mr. Hooper writes you that his brother George is a candidate for the Wilmington clerkship. The appointment of clerks is vested in the judges, or any two of them; but there is no room for solicitation, if the candidate is defective in qualifications, as the judges are bound by oath to nominate impartially, &c.—I have inclosed you a few of the heads of the court-bill, which may be useful if you are determined to practice; and before I conclude, give me leave to mention Mr. Gifford as a candidate for the Hillsborough clerkship. I think he must be tolerably well qualified to execute the office. Please to make my best compliments to Mr. Johnston, Mr. Hewes, and Mr. Smith.

I am, with real esteem, dear sir,
Your most obedient servant,

A. MACLAINE.

CHAPTER XI.

THE STATE; LETTER FROM MACLAINE; THE CIRCUIT; LETTERS FROM IREDELL, AND CHARGE TO THE GRAND JURY AT EDENTON; LETTERS FROM IREDELL; RESIGNATION AS JUDGE; LETTERS FROM CASWELL, NASH, IREDELL, AND HOOPER; NORTH CAROLINA SIGNS ARTICLES OF CONFEDERATION; LETTER TO BRITISH COMMISSIONERS; ASSEMBLY, LETTERS, &c. ÆT. 26–27.

NORTH CAROLINA continued to enjoy exemption from hostile invasion during the course of this year. The Continental battalions of the State continued at the North under Gen. Washington, shared in the glory of the well-fought field of Monmouth,* and remained until General Lincoln was ordered to the Southern Department in the fall,† when they accompanied him.‡ However united as regards the relations of the Colonies to Great Britain, the whigs were divided into two distinct parties on questions of internal polity. The ascendency of the radical or ultra-republican party was attested by the defeat of Johnston and Hewes, the elevation of Caswell, and the election of two of the three judges. Foreign trade scarcely subsisted at all; commercial intercourse with the North was environed with peril, and so attended with delays as to be almost impracticable.§ Charleston was the mart for supplies of groceries, and articles of exotic production. A considerable inland traffic sprang up, maintained by many hundred wagons; but as if to signalize their folly, the Legislature forbade the exportation of beef, pork, bacon and Indian corn, thus fettering the free spirit of commerce with restraints under which it ever languishes or dies, contributing to its own impoverishment, and deepening the distress of the people by clipping the wings of industry. Subsequently, when the State was invaded, and its

---
* June, 28th. † Sept. 25th.
‡ The Continental Regiments of North Carolina (two in 1775) were increased to six in 1776, by the N. C. Congress. Nine battalions were ordered by the Continental Congress in '76; but these were reduced to six in 1779, when Sumner and Hogan were added to the list of brigadiers. These battalions were surrendered by Lincoln at Charleston, May 12th, 1780. Vid. Hildreth, Journal N. C. Congress, Wheeler, Jones, &c.
§ Ramsay.

means of sustenance for armies nearly exhausted ; when its very salvation depended upon the success of its commissariat, and policy would have justified the measure, the embargo was removed.*

MACLAINE TO JUDGE IREDELL.

WILMINGTON, 8th Jan., 1778.

SIR :—Your acceptance of the office to which you were appointed by the *almost unanimous* vote of the General Assembly, gives me, as well as all others who either know you, or have heard of your character, entire satisfaction. We wish indeed, for your sake, and for the dignity of the station to which you are promoted, that the appointment had been such as it ought to have been ; but do not despair of making it better. However arduous the task you have undertaken, we have the most flattering hopes from your judgment and integrity, and these hopes are strengthened by your diffidence. In truth, sir, you lie under no obligations to the public (whatever may be the case as to your particular friends). The members of the Assembly in appointing you thought, with great reason, that they effectually served themselves and their constituents. As to myself, I confess I was actuated by duty to the public, having been taught that your promotion would more effectually serve them than you.

I return my best thanks for your attention to Mr. Gifford's interest ; as far as it can be shown consistent with your duty to yourself and to the public. When I mentioned that he was *tolerably* qualified, I meant it as a general expression ; but with respect to his competitors, perhaps I might venture to go farther. Mr. Hooper regretted that he had not mentioned that gentleman to you, as I believe he thinks him preferable to any that has offered for Hillsborough ; and I expect he will write you on the subject. As to Mr. G. Hooper, I am too much interested in his welfare to trust myself with saying any thing in my favor. I will only beg leave to observe that I hope his own merit will be his best recommendation. I wish your partiality for him may not induce you to overlook the merit of any other candidate. What I intended to send you from the court-law was upon a supposition that you might possibly resolve to practise. You will now have a better opportunity to inform yourself, as I imagine the laws will very soon be published.

I now venture to congratulate you on your appointment, being, with sincere esteem,

Sir,
Your most ob't serv't,
A. MACLAINE.

* Hubbard's Life of Davie.

JUDGE IREDELL TO MRS. IREDELL.

NEW BERNE, 14th Jan., 1778.

MY DEAR HANNAH :—The weather was so excessively bad that with all our efforts we could not get here till yesterday. We were obliged to ride a good deal in the rain, but notwithstanding that, my disorder continued better, and has now almost entirely left me. In every other respect I am as well as I could wish. We were qualified into our offices yesterday, and appointed clerks. Charles Bonfield was chosen for Edenton, without opposition—Mr. Eaton Haines for Halifax—J. Cooke for New Berne—G. Hooper for Wilmington—one Jos. Taylor for Hillsborough. The Salisbury clerkship is yet in suspense. We do not expect to leave this till Friday, and as we must go the upper road, I scarcely can expect the pleasure of seeing you till Monday or Tuesday. I am obliged to make haste not to lose this opportunity. Remember me to all as I ought to be, and believe me, my dear Hannah,

Most sincerely and affectionately yours,
JAS. IREDELL.

P. S.—The courts are to hold only 12 days ; *not* 15.

BOOTH, 25th Feb., 1788.

MY DEAR HANNAH :—We arrived here about eight this morning, perfectly well. Our journey hitherto has been, upon the whole, very agreeable, except that this morning, very unfortunately, the horse upon which Andrew rode appeared to be lame, and still continues so. The reason we can't easily suggest. We are at present a little embarrassed by this circumstance, but your brother is trying if another horse can be got here to his place.* It gives me great *concern* that I am obliged to trouble him so much. *If he was not the best and most generous of men*, he could not bear it with so much patience. I should promise myself great happiness in this little town with him, if I was not continually thinking of my absence from you, and feeling all that anxiety on your account which ever attends me when I am from you. But I hope, my dear Hannah, you will take the best care

* At this period double chairs or gigs were the vehicles generally in use, even with persons of condition : one horse drew, while a servant alongside, mounted on another, guided. There were probably fewer than one dozen chariots or carriages in the State: it is known that Dr. Cathcart possessed a four-horse chariot in Colonial times, and Mr. Charlton during the Revolution. The first four-horse chariot ever seen in Wilmington district was introduced by the Hon. Wm. H. Hill, in 1799.

of your health, and let me have the happiness of meeting you here as I expect, which time I assure you is continually in my thoughts.

You desire me to write you more particularly than I have been used to do, but it would not be very entertaining to give you many particulars at this time. How would you like to be told that we found half a dozen people drunk at Cumner's, the landlord at their head ; that in going thence, by my assuming the direction, we lost our way, and did not get to Mr. Baker's till 8 at night,—that we set off early the next morning and breakfasted at Wilton ; met Mr. Charlton soon after, and proceeded on to Colton's to dinner ? Here indeed was something worth telling you. We met your brother John, on his way to the court, perfectly well, as he said all his family were. We however were soon obliged to part with him, and came on in the evening to old Mrs. Bryan's, where we staid very comfortably all night, and came here to breakfast this morning. This is our little history ; I might, indeed, add, if it was possible for you to doubt it, that I have been very happy in your brother's company. *He has taken two or three lessons at his French, and is indeed a very apt scholar. I am afraid he will soon excel his master.* You must excuse the bad pen I write with, and the consequent scribbling I give you. If the pen had been better, I should have wrote better. Nelly must also excuse my writing to her now. *Your brother will very soon want the pen*, and we have no time to spare. Her 16th year I hope will not make her too proud to try to make up the vast quantity of time she has squandered. Adieu ! my dear Hannah. Give my love to your sister and 15, *and the other children*, and remember me to your brother's family and Mrs. Dawson, which compliments bring me to the great and sincere one of saying that I am, my dear Hannah,

Your entirely affectionate
JAS. IREDELL.

P. S.—My thin coat has done me no sort of prejudice, and I think I look very well and handsome.†

PUCHEU TO IREDELL.

[*The penmanship of this letter would do credit to a writing master.*]

MONSIEUR :—Je me suis comme vous trouvé bien privé, de n'avoir point eu le plaisir de vous voir avant votre départ, j'eusse

* The gravest statesman in North Carolina, at the age of 45, addressing himself to the mastery of French ! how characteristic of the man ! what a lesson for the young !
† A thin coat in February! It is, however, I believe, well settled, that the climate of North Carolina has greatly changed since its first settlement, and is gradually becoming colder.

eté charmé de vous temoigner combien je suis sensible á toutes les politesses que j'ai reçu dans votre maison. Si j'ai quelque regret, c'est sans doute celui de n'avoir point á ésperer de repondre á tant de bontés, mais je desire, et cela est en notre pouvoir, que vous me fournissiez des occasions á vous prouver qu'en effet j'y suis reconnoissant ; soyez bien persuadé que ce seroit veritablement m'obliger que de me le prouver. Madame Iredell m'a remise les lettres dont vous m'avez prié de prendre soin, vous pouvez être tranquille sur leur sort, et du moment que vous me sauriez arrivé, vous devez être persuadé qu'il n'aura pas dépendu de moi qu'elles ne soient parvenues exactement : ce dont je prendrai la liberté de vous informer moi-même. Je vous suis très obligé pour les souhaites gracieux que vous me faites, soyez convaincu que je n'en fais pas de moins sincéres tout ce qui peut contribuer á votre bonheur.

Veuilléz assurer Madame et Mademoiselle Blair, de même que Madame Iredell de mes très humbles respects, et croyez moi avec sinceritè et estime,

Monsieur, votre très humble et très obeissant serviteur,
PUCHEU.

I am very much obliged to Mistress Blair for the birds and butter.

IREDELL TO MRS. IREDELL.

SALISBURY, 12th March, 1778.

MY DEAREST HANNAH :—After so long an absence (for I really think it a very long one) it gives me great pleasure that I have an opportunity of writing to you, and thus enjoying, though at a great distance, some kind of communication with you. Until now, I have not known of any opportunity since I wrote you at Booth, so that I hope you will not charge me with remissness and neglect. Our journey up here was passed agreeably, on the whole, though not at all times equally so. If I can recollect a little detail, I will give it you. After finishing our letters at Booth, we proceeded towards Halifax, crossing the river at Booth, and went to Wilie Jones', who seemed glad to see us, and we staid with him all night, but had the mortification, as we left Booth too soon to dine, of fasting till near ten at night. We were obliged to wait to have our horses shod, and this was done in time for us to get to Col. McCulloh's about 12 next day. Here we were received with all the usual kindness, and staid the remainder of the day. Ben's boy is really a very fine one, and you may be assured gives a great deal of happiness. The next morning, after breakfast and receiving directions for our route, we proceeded on our journey, by a different way for about 25 miles than I had gone before, and a much finer one. The country is extremely beautiful, and Mr. Johnston and myself could not help continually admiring it. We began to ascend the hills after going about ten miles. They, most of them in Bute,* have a gradual ascent, and from the tops of them you have frequently a most extensive prospect, almost always a very fine one, and sometimes you have the view of a cultivated country; but in general, the richness of the soil, the extent of the prospect, and the pyramidical shape of the trees, form the beauty of the scene. We rode principally through such a scene as this, until we reached our first stage, about ten miles from the marsh, and where, had we not otherwise intended to stay, we should have been obliged to take shelter from a most heavy storm of rain, in which we had been under a necessity of riding for two or three miles. The house we came to was a poor miserable hovel, inhabited by a man and his wife and three or four very beautiful children. Here we staid four hours, and were once afraid we should be obliged to stay all night, which was a very uncomfortable prospect, but the weather clearing up a little, we determined to make a push in the evening, which we accordingly did, and reached Mr. Parke's about an hour in the night, after having got another wetting. Mr. Parke received us with extreme hospitality, and we staid with great satisfaction at his house that night. We did not see Mrs. Parke till supper time. I had never seen her before. She has a good deal of resemblance, I think, of her sister Mrs. Jones. She was obliging also. They appear to live in a plentiful manner, and have three very fine children. The next day we rode from his house after breakfast to a place called Harrisburg, about 27 miles, without stopping. We were excessively fatigued, but had the comfort to find an exceeding good house to rest in, and refresh ourselves for an hour or two. The country we passed this day, except about half a dozen miles, was nothing equal to what we had seen before, though here and there it is also very beautiful. Harrisburg contains half a dozen straggling houses, and is a burlesque upon a town. We travelled about nine miles farther that evening, and lodged tolerably. We were then within 12 or 13 miles of Mr. Bennyam's, who lives about two miles out of the way.† Here we had a great desire to go to breakfast, but were afraid of his hospitality. At last however we determined on it,

---

* Since divided into Warren and Franklin.
† Mr. Bennihan was an opulent farmer; his daughter married the late Judge Cameron, President of the Bank of the State of N. C. Mr. Bennihan's only son dying childless, his estate fell into the hands of the Camerons; under their thrifty management it has swelled until it has become one of the largest in the South.

and to leave it immediately after. When we came to the road, we again balanced; we however proceeded. He discovered great pleasure to see us, as did Mrs. Bennyam, who immediately went to provide breakfast for us, for we were disappointed in our expectation of finding them at theirs—they, though so young a married couple, being earlier risers than some I know. After breakfast was over, and we were talking of going, he immediately attacked us with such hospitable earnestness, that our resolution was almost overpowered. Your brother at last said to me,— "suppose we trust God Almighty for once." My piety and inclination induced me to consent, and thus we were doomed to spend the whole day there—and a very agreeable one it was. Mr. W. Johnston having lately come to reside at his place at Little River, about three miles distant, Mr. Bennyam sent for him, and we had a happy day in company with them and Mrs. Bennyam, whose amiableness of temper is extremely engaging.* Her life must be a very dull one. She has not a single woman she can associate with nearer than Hillsborough, which is at the distance of 18 miles. This is a circumstance she must feel very sensibly, and cannot be sufficiently compensated even by the great worthiness of her husband. The next morning, when your brother told her he would endeavor to bring Mrs. Johnston to see her, she could scarcely speak; tears flowed into her eyes, and it was with difficulty she could express the great pleasure it would give her, and ask me if I could not make her happy in your company also. 13th.—We went from here in company with Mr. Johnston and Mr. Bennyam to the former's house to breakfast, which is at the place where my cousin Ben McCulloh and myself happened fortunately to be at the time of the great disturbance at Hillsborough.† We arrived at Hillsborough about one, found a most elegant tavern, dined with great satisfaction, and proceeded in the evening to a place about 10 miles further. Hillsborough rather exceeded my expectations; it is far from being a disagreeable town, as to appearance, and there is a remarkable handsome church in it. Your brother and myself, before we came away, engaged a good room with two beds in it, for our use during the Court. It would be uninteresting and tedious to give you particulars of our march from Hillsborough to Salisbury. It was far the most disagreeable part of the journey. The country itself is not so pleasant, though there is a great deal of good land in it, the accommodations wretched, and we were forced to travel

---

* Member of Congress for Hillsborough, 1775–6—nephew to Mr. Sam. Johnston.
† 24th Sept., 1770, when the Regulators broke into the court-house, beat some of the gentlemen of the bar, and insulted others; and so riotously acted that Judge Henderson closed the court and fled by night.

in very bad weather. Your brother asked the woman of a very dirty Dutch house if there were any brooms in that part of the country. We, however, arrived here the evening of the court day. Mr. Spencer had been here a little before me, and we had the great pleasure of meeting with Mr. Hooper and Mr. Maclaine, with whom we board in the same house, and though in a tavern, have perfectly the command of a select company. I have been two or three nights at Mr. Frohock's, and we have all dined there. They are all very well, and seemed glad to see me. Mr. Frohock's obstinacy of conduct places me, however, in a very awkward and painful situation, and has prevented my going to his house so cordially and happily as I should otherwise have done, and as Mrs. Frohock's kindness would invite. For very frivolous reasons he refuses to deliver up the Records of the Court, notwithstanding he applied to your brother and Mr. Hooper for advice, and they in the strongest terms have urged it. I have myself, so far as is consistent with my situation. The affair is to be publicly determined this morning, and if he continues obstinate, he must be committed to gaol. You may easily conceive my feelings, but there is a necessity for its being done. The commitment will be till he delivers the Records.

14th March.—The affair of Frohock's is over. His obstinacy continuing unconquerable, he was committed to gaol, when after staying a few hours and distressing his wife in the most dreadful manner, who went to him, he thought proper to comply and to deliver the Records up. I shall leave this cursed place to-day together with your brother, Mr. Maclaine and Mr. Hooper. We take the Moravian town in our way, and shall endeavor to while away the time, till Hillsborough court, in as amusing a manner as possible. O! how long every hour seems to me. Never did I feel more anxiety to see you. God grant it may be in perfect health, and for heaven's sake do not disappoint me of seeing you at your brother's. I will apply day and night to the business at Hillsborough, in order to shorten the time of my further absence from you. I am not sure, but perhaps I may write a line to Nelly. My time has been much taken up. We have sat mostly seven or eight hours in a day, sometimes twelve. I have not been in the least sick, nor your brother either, though this place seems to me far from being a healthy one. I think you may permit me now, my dearest Hannah, to bid you adieu. It is with reluctance I do it even in writing. You will not fail to mention my most affectionate remembrance to your sister and Nelly and the children, and to your brother's family and Mrs. Dawson's, and believe me,

Most faithfully, most anxiously, and most affectionately yours,
JAS. IREDELL.

HILLSBOROUGH, 18th March, 1778.

MY DEAR HANNAH:—Having the satisfaction to overtake Mr. Fine here, I have it in my power to add another line by him, acquainting you of our arrival here, where we came about 5 o'clock this afternoon, heartily sick of our journey from Salisbury; for though we have travelled through a most delightful country, we have had the most wretched, dirty, and niggardly accommodations that can be conceived. We took the Moravian town in our way; the town in point of neatness, industry and ingenuity, far exceeded my expectations; in other respects, it came much below them; we met with a most dirty and rascally tavernkeeper who told us fifty lies about what he had in his house, until he was taken aside by one of their principals to whom we had a letter. But we could get none of their manufactures whatever. The outside of their houses is very neat; the inside of what we saw very dirty. Nothing could have made this ride supportable but the agreeable company we had. Mr. Maclaine and Mr. Hooper were with us the whole way. We have a tolerable, but not an extraordinary prospect of accommodation here. I regret exceedingly that the court will be so long in commencing. The first day is the 24th. I thank God I am perfectly well. Your brother has been a little indisposed since yesterday, though not so as to prevent his travelling, but he seems pretty well to-night. I have only to add to my fervent wishes and prayers for your health, and as much happiness as is consistent with my absence (for I flatter myself it cannot be complete with it), that I am, my dear Hannah,

Your most truly affectionate
JAS. IREDELL.

A letter from Mrs. Blair states the price of corn (March 27) at Edenton as being £5 per barrel, and flour £3 per hundred: she adds, "people talk much here of peace, and every thing mending in a few months."

The Assembly met at New Berne April 14th.

MISS HELEN BLAIR TO IREDELL.

EDENTON, April 14th, 1778.

MY DEAR UNCLE:—As Mr. Webb is going this evening, and I have not time to write to two, I think it my duty to write you, as you are always so good when you are from home. Your letter from Salisbury, I am sure, deserves a much better answer than I wrote by aunt. I should write you and all my acquaintance if I knew how to express my sentiments. I am certain I have as great a regard for you as you have for me ; and yet, to save my life, I could not tell you so handsomely. We dined yesterday with Mr. La Neuville, at his lodgings : it was very disagreeable to me, there were so many Frenchmen there, and you know they have not too much reserve. Please give my love to Aunt Iredell and uncle Sam. I would write you a longer letter, but my pen is so bad I have hardly patience to write with it at all. I am, my dear uncle,

Your dutiful and affectionate niece,
H. BLAIR.

At the court held at Edenton, May 1st, Mr. Iredell made the following address to the Grand Jury, to which their response is adjoined. It is memorable that so rare was the merit of Mr. Iredell's judicial addresses to grand juries, that they were commonly published at their request, and received the highest encomiums from the press. Such was the case when he was a Judge of the Supreme Court of the United States, at Boston, New York, Philadelphia, Richmond, Raleigh, Charleston and Savannah. This though the first, is not the least in excellence ; it is more political in character, and flushed by more warmth than the chastened judgment of soberer years permitted to similar efforts.

GENTLEMEN OF THE GRAND JURY :—In compliance with a custom which has long obtained, and is probably founded on very good reasons, it becomes our duty to address a few words to you, previous to your entrance on the discharge of the important office you are now called upon to exercise by your country, an office of great consequence to the community, and of which too awful ideas cannot well be entertained.

This court of justice opens at a most interesting period of the policy of this country. We have been long deprived of such from a variety of causes, in some of which we have shared with our brethren on the continent ; others were peculiar to ourselves.

The event, however, has been unhappy and distressing, and every well-wisher to his country must view with pleasure a scene of anarchy changed for that of law and order, and powers of government established capable of restraining or punishing dishonesty and vice.

Such powers have been established under circumstances which should induce to them peculiar reverence and regard. They have not been the effect of usurpation ; they have not proceeded from a wanton desire of change ; they have not been imposed upon you by the successful arms of a tyrant ; they have been peaceably established by the public at large, for the general happiness of the people, when they were reduced to the cruel necessity (a necessity they abhorred, and did all in their power to avoid) of renouncing a government which ceased to protect, and endeavored to enslave them, for one which enabled them with a proper share of courage and virtue to protect and defend themselves. You had not only for years been injured and insulted in the grossest manner ; you had not only felt innovations in your government, which were as repugnant to justice as they were unwarranted by precedent ; your petitions for redress, couched in the most humble and expressive (though not in the most servile) terms, had not only been rejected and spurned at, but when the crisis at last arrived for more vigorous exertions, or a mean and dastardly submission, and every hope of relaxation of the tyrannical system was fled, war was brought into your territories, and carried on with unusual circumstances of cruelty and rigor ; the British nation imposed upon by the vilest lies to exert every nerve in their power ; foreign troops were hired to slaughter a people who had never offended them ; the Indian scalping knife was employed ; and even that diabolical purpose of arming our domestics to involve us in one indiscriminate massacre, was openly and with triumph attempted. It was under these complicated circumstances of injustice, cruelty and insult, and with the just apprehension that these united efforts might overpower our own if our opposition continued to be languidly supported with the reserve of subjects ; that the once happy American colonies, whose loyalty had been unexampled, and had been exerted in the most conspicuous instances ; whose attachment to Great Britain was scarcely yet cooled by the numerous acts of oppression they had received from her ; reduced to the melancholy necessity of choosing their fellow-subjects for their masters ; or of exerting those latent powers of resistance, which heaven and favorable circumstances had blessed them with,—it was in this trying and painful situation, that they resolved to sacrifice all old connections, every favorite prepossession, and tear themselves from a country they would have bled to serve, but disdained to be enslaved by.—It is known to us all how reluctantly this measure was adopted, and how ardently until the moment when it appeared inevitable, we wished for a reconciliation with Great Britain, upon those principles on which our opposition had all along proceeded ; a wish that I can truly say, (notwithstanding the base reports to the contrary,) there is every reason to believe, was almost universal.

But every thing that could be urged in our favor was disregarded. Our enemies proceeded from one extreme to another, until they brought about an event which fatally, and I trust has finally severed this country from the dominion of Great Britain. Immense advantages have been lost in pursuit of a chimera, *for such must ever the government of this country be without the hearty support of the people.* The profits of our trade, an inexhaustible and increasing source of wealth, we freely bestowed. Our allegiance to our sovereign was perfect, on the conditions of our charter. He had a negative on our laws, and the whole executive department of the state. This was a power sufficient for every useful purpose ; we had no disposition to compliment him with any that was dangerous. We desired only the privileges of a free people, such as our ancestors had been, such as they expected we should be. We knew it was absurd to pretend we could be free, when laws might at pleasure be imposed on us by another people : a people who in many respects considered themselves our rivals, over whom we had no control, who were remarkably ignorant of our circumstances, who had strong (I had almost said, irresistible) temptations to lay burdens on us, in order to ease themselves. We knew of no right they could have to such a power. Our charters did not recognize it. It certainly was not in our ancestors' contemplation, who left that very country because freedom could not be enjoyed in it. Custom had given it no sanction, but on the contrary strongly discountenanced it. It was reconcilable to no principle of justice, or even common decency, that we could form to ourselves. We despised the miserable application of a few political maxims calculated for a single government, to the various and extended governments of the British Empire, and which to this hour is the basis upon which all the fraud, iniquity, injustice, cruelty and oppression which America has experienced from Great Britain, have been defended.

We may be thankful to Divine Providence, that we were called into this contest at a time when the principles of liberty were generally and thoroughly understood. The Divine Right of Kings was exploded with indignation in the last century. Men came at length to be persuaded, that they were created for a nobler purpose than to be the slaves of a single tyrant. They did not confine this idea to speculation ; they put to death one king, and expelled another. This was done in England, the seat of our haughty enemies, who seem to think the right of resistance is confined alone to their own kingdom. It is under this expulsion (for such it in fact was) that the present sovereign of that country holds his title to the throne. Whatever doubt there might have been entertained before, there could be none afterwards, that the family who were seated upon the vacant throne by the voice of the people, held it liable to the same resistance which had provided the vacancy for them. Accordingly, ever since this glorious revolution, it has been considered by the generality of the kingdom, and is now almost a settled axiom in their government, *that the government was instituted for the good of the people, and that when it no longer answers this end, and they are in danger of slavery, or a great oppression, they have a right to change it.* I lay it down thus generally, because the principle extends so far, and no man of reason and candor would attempt to narrow it. It is a principle founded in the clearest reason. It is applicable to all conditions and circumstances. It is not calculated for one party, or one set of men, or to color a particular job. It affords universal relief to all who groan under any species of tyranny, and have the virtue and opportunity of resisting it. I trust, as it has had its influence under one species of arbitrary power in England, it will not want its effect under one, if possible, still more severe and detestable attempted in America.

I confess, gentlemen, when I speak on this subject, I cannot avoid expressing myself with warmth. That such great, such real advantages should be lost, in pursuit of no essential object, is a consideration extremely affecting. We cannot help comparing, with a degree of regret and indignation, the former honorable and political conduct of the crown of Great Britain to the American Colonies with that which has been since pursued. Happy in the enjoyment of liberty, in the formation of our own laws, in the grant of our own money (subject only to a restriction we submitted to with pleasure, the negative of our Sovereign), we felt a felicity that could only be equalled by the hardships with which it was originally obtained, and the mixture of filial and social gratitude with which it was enjoyed. Great Britain was the constant centre of our thoughts ; her prosperity the most ardent desire of our affections. We contemplated with a pleasure which no scene of human life perhaps ever gave occasion for before, the entire and cordial union of many distant people, descended from the same ancestors, possessed nearly of the same rights, endowed with generous and noble minds, warm in their affection and zealous in their attachment to each other, under the influence of one common sovereign, and by the participation of a common interest, mutually contributing to the prosperity of the whole. The authority of the sovereign sufficient to preserve the whole in due order, but not to invade the liberties of any one. All the branches of the great stock willingly resigning to the parent kingdom the absolute management of the only concern that could probably interfere with the general happiness, unless the minds of the people should grow *irritated* and *discontented;* which their exemplary loyalty seemed a sufficient guard against, except in the case of a *just* and *severe* provocation. And though we viewed such a scene at a distance, and indeed as almost a thing impossible (at least to happen in our day, never dreaming of men sacrificing real advantages to vain and visionary expectations), yet we had been too well instructed in the principles of liberty, to view it with unconcern. We blessed heaven, that it had made us not only a *happy,* but a *free* people. Our ancestors came here to enjoy the blessings of liberty. They purchased it at an immense price. Their greatest glory was, that they had obtained it for themselves, and transmitted it to their posterity. God forbid that their posterity should be base or weak enough to resign it, or to let it appear that the true British spirit, which has done such wonders in England, has been lost or weakened by being transplanted to America. The very people who are now imbruing their hands in the blood of the Americans in support of the most arbitrary principles, have a thousand times bled in opposition to them themselves. Will you entertain so wretched an idea, that you are not as worthy of liberty as they are, and that merely because your ancestors quitted England, though with the public sanction, and guaranteed for the secure enjoyment of freedom, you are less deserving of human blessings than those who happen to reside in it, and not even entitled to the common benefits of what the worst of men have a right to claim, *the sacred observance of public faith?* But in this contest I will dare to affirm, the people of Britain sacrifice to their pride and ambition, not only the immense advantages I have already spoken of, but *the first principles of liberty which are the common right of all mankind, and the sacred ties of honor which even the worst people cannot violate without infamy.*

You will, I hope, excuse, gentlemen, the particularity, perhaps the too great particularity with which I have gone into this subject. Yet I thought it my duty to point out to you, some of the principles upon which the revolution in our government has taken place, and which, in my opinion, not only prove the propriety of its being effected, but the indispensable obligation we are under to maintain and support it. This can only be done by great public virtues and very spirited exertions. We have a great and exasperated people to contend against; a people, who, though they have wantonly thrown away many of their resources, have many still left, and are, no doubt, capable of powerful efforts. These must be withstood by great efforts on our part.

Let us not flatter ourselves that the war is nearly over, and that we are on the eve of enjoying the blessings of peace. Such ideas are pleasing, but at present they seem to be chimerical, and certainly they are dangerous. They tend to throw us too much off our guard, and to lay us open to the artful designs of our enemies. Review the great scenes of history, you will find mankind have always been obliged to pay dear for the blessings they enjoyed. This life may well be called a scene of trial, for vice has every where and long been seen to triumph over virtue. But though the trial be severe, thank God, we have no reason to believe it will be constantly unsuccessful. The struggles of a great people have almost always ended in the establishment of liberty. The enjoyment of it is an object worthy of the most vigilant application, and the most painful sacrifices. Is there any thing we read with more pleasure than the sufferings and contentions of a brave people, who resist oppression with firmness, are faithful to the interests of their country, and disdain every advantage that is incompatible with them? Such a people are spoken of with admiration by all future ages. Their history is put into the hands of youth, to form them by a spirit of emulation, if possible, to equal their greatness of mind. Their posterity for a long time (until the gradual corruption of all human affairs seizes upon them also), if they happen to be successful, which is generally the case, reap the benefit of their ancestors' virtue. Their souls glow with gratitude for the virtue and self-denial of their forefathers. They consider them as patterns for their own conduct on similar occasions, and are continually pointing them out to the reverence and imitation of their children. These are the glorious effects of patriotism and virtue. These are the rewards annexed to the faithful discharge of that great and honorable duty, *fidelity to our country.* On the contrary, what can we conceive more base and contemptible than a set of men, careless and negligent of their rights, regardless of their value, indifferent to their preservation, mean enough to crouch under the first insolent menace, without spirit to defend, without virtue to deserve them, at length easily deprived of advantages which they might, without much difficulty, have secured, and the loss of which they are forced every instant to regret, with curses on themselves as the authors of their own and their children's misery, under the gloomy tyranny of a proud and arbitrary despot. I pray to God, that the fair character I have described may be that of America to the latest ages, and that mankind never may be disgraced by the existence of so wretched and despicable a set of people as in the last.

Upon a subject so general, so warm, so animating as this, it would be easy to expatiate much farther; but the time, and even the occasion, will not properly permit it; and therefore I shall proceed to say something on the nature of the particular office you are at present called upon to perform. It is a glorious privilege by which the liberties of the people are secured, that no man can suffer in his reputation or his safety, by a public accusation, but after the solemn and impartial determination of a select number of his fellow-subjects, chosen to preside over his fate after every possible exception that can be made to any is removed. These men are no otherwise interested in the condemnation or acquittal of the suspected person, but that justice should be done to the public, and no oppression shown to the individual. Besides the common principles of decency and justice, they have also this farther guard on their conduct, that they may hereafter be affected by their own precedents, and that either as members of the community at large they may suffer by an undue relaxation of the powers of government, or as individuals—themselves accused, by any inequitable circumstances under which they have accused or convicted others. We are apt not sufficiently to value the blessings we enjoy, until we are deprived of them; but we may be in some measure sensible of this, by having recourse to the transactions of those countries, where juries are unknown, and where the torture prepares the charge, and an arbitrary, merciless judge decides it. The histories of all countries indeed show, that men, in fact, are more wicked than they could be supposed to be, and that there is no way to prevent an abuse of power but by not giving too much. I will venture to say, no man before its introduction would have had an idea that the practice of torturing people to make them confess suspected guilt could ever generally have obtained, and yet at this hour, to the disgrace of human nature, it subsists in some of what are called the most civilized parts of Europe. An infinity of other arbitrary actions have taken place, equally absurd and ill founded, and equally and strongly suggesting that great and necessary caution of *guarding our liberties with care.* Among which, this of a trial by jury must be deemed one of the principal.

You, gentlemen, are intrusted with the business of *accusation.* You form the grand inquest of crimes committed within this district. From the highest to the lowest, they being all cognizable by this court, come within your jurisdiction. You are not confined to present those only which may be transmitted to you by the Attorney-General. You may find of your own knowledge, in which case you present the charge in general terms, and the Attorney-General reduces it to form. I should be obliged to read a volume to you, if I were to attempt a complete catalogue of crimes. In all cases where you are in doubt you will apply to the court for information. There is one offence, however, upon which I think it my duty to say a little, because I hear it is unhappily too prevalent, and because it is particularly dangerous, and all, I fear, are not aware of its criminality. The offence I mean is, *depreciating the currency of this State.* This is a very serious and alarming evil. The profits of our trade having for a vast number of years centred in Great Britain, we were continually drained of all our gold and silver, and therefore a paper currency became necessary to be established to pass in payment among ourselves, and for which the public faith should be pledged. The unhappy exigencies of this war requiring very great expenses, and the people not being able, without the extremest distress, to raise the same annually by taxes (nor, perhaps, was the currency of the country sufficient for that purpose and private accommodation also), it became necessary to make more paper, as we had no gold or silver, or sink under the contest at once; for war cannot be maintained without money. The public faith is pledged for this, also. The necessities of the people require that its credit should be supported, for in proportion as this is impaired its use ceases, and all the evils attending the absolute want of money will attend a profusion of that which is universally disregarded. The very prosecution of the war, therefore, depends on the support of our currency. Yet I am told it is a common practice to make a difference between our own currency and the Continental, and also between the currency established since this contest began, and that which was in existence before. The difference that is made between any kind of paper and gold or silver is still more alarming. Every one of these practices is a great and dangerous misdemeanor against the State, punishable by this court, and therefore properly cognizable by you. And I hope, if you know of any instances of this kind, you will present them, though not laid in any formal manner before you.

I think of nothing material to add, gentlemen, but that it is necessary, at least twelve of your number should agree upon all questions.

Before I conclude, I cannot help expressing the very great pleasure I have felt in seeing so much peace and order subsist among the people, during the uncommonly long suspension of the courts of justice; an instance of regularity (with a few exceptions, not much to the honor of this part of the country) I believe not to be equalled, in similar circumstances, by any other people under heaven, and, I trust in God, a happy presage of that virtue which is to support our present government.*

* The author of the above charge, being an Englishman by birth, has reason to

To the Honorable James Iredell, Esq. one of the Judges of the Superior Court, held at Edenton, for the District of Edenton, on the first day of May, 1778.

We, the Grand Jury for the district of Edenton, return you our thanks for the charge which you were pleased to deliver to us at the opening of this court.

This charge vindicates the conduct of the American States in the establishment of independency, by arguments drawn from unalienable rights, and from real necessity, and grounded on incontestable facts. Every man who is not lost to the powers of reason and conviction, must feel their force and must bear a very active testimony in support of them.

It breathes a spirit of pure disinterested patriotism, and holds forth the most powerful incentives to persist in the opposition in which America has so successfully begun.

It points out persuasively the importance of a faithful observation of the various political and relative duties of society upon which the happiness of individuals, and of the whole depends, and which will tend to give stability to our present Constitution.

For these reasons, and as it may tend to invigorate the timid, rouse the indifferent, reclaim the disaffected, and call the united strength of the whole into exercise for the public good, we beg that your honor would favor us with a copy of it, that it may be transmitted to the press, and published for the information of those who did not hear it delivered. As we ask this not only for ourselves, but in behalf of the inhabitants of the district of Edenton, whom we represent, we flatter ourselves that you will give it to our solicitations, although you intended it merely as an exercise of official duty, and thought it not designed for a more extensive communication than to us, the Grand Jury.

CLEMENT COOKE, *Foreman,*
ANDREW LONG,
BENJAMIN BLOUNT,
SAMUEL FERRILL,
JAMES LONG,
JERE'H VAIL,
BARNABA WRIGHT,
THOMAS PRICE,
JOSIAH COLLINS,
A. TYMONS,
THOMAS LURRY,
TIMOTHY HIXSON.

apologize for some expressions which seem only proper for a person born in America. He confesses he was transported by the warmth and ardor of his feelings, into a manner of speaking, that he cannot strictly defend. Burke could not, upon so animating a subject, be cool and formal enough to make a discrimination between his own situation, and that of the public in general. In all essential points, he considers himself equally an American with any other; for, having become an American subject, he became entitled to all the rights of one, and, of course, interested in their origin and preservation.

Judge Iredell arrived at New Bern, May 3d. On the way, at Mr. MacKenzie's, his horses escaped from his custody, much to his annoyance; but the people residing in the vicinity, with much kindness, turned out in great numbers, and soon secured one, at a distance of twelve miles on the road to New Bern, the other was not recovered for some time afterward. Postscripts to his letter, detailing the accident to his wife, are as follows: "P. S. I must not omit telling you that Mr. Avery is elected a soldier, and is getting ready his camp equipage. I have extremely good lodgings at Mrs. Thomlinson's. I have received a very pressing invitation from W. Blount, but declined it on her account. You see I have almost as many postscripts as a woman."

NEWBERN, 23d May.

MY DEAR HANNAH:—I wrote you on Saturday, immediately on my arrival, giving you an account of my difficulties, and my recovery from them, which I sent by post; my history since that time is but short. I dined on that day with the Grand Jury yesterday with Mr. Ellis, this day with Mr. Cooke, and presently, by particular appointment, am to drink tea at Mrs. Vail's, the brilliancy of whose daughter is at present added to by the company of Mrs. Shaw. At six I am to attend a general rejoicing about the great news: the Governor received an express last night with very full and interesting particulars, entirely confirmatory of what we had heard before.* Some other particulars are added of less authenticity, such as that war is actually declared, and part of the British forces actually embarking, and the rest soon expected to follow their example, for the West Indies. I have been drinking a few glasses of claret, but not so much as to make me either drunk or sick. The Governor, a South Carolina gentleman, my brother Spencer and Mr. Leech formed the company at Mr. Cooke's. I receive as yet no proposals about the land. Mr. Nash can't purchase without the sale of his on Roanoke. I hope, however, to get a good price for ours. I shall wait for your brother till Thursday. If he is not then arrived, I will sell it alone if I can do it advantageously, not otherwise.

I had wrote thus far before I set off on my ramble. I went and sat half an hour at Mr. Vail's, and made an apology for no drinking tea there, and attended the grand celebration. Grand I can only call it on account of the occasion; the exhibition was poor and trifling. The discharge of a few trifling pieces, a wretched appearance of the Town Company, an huzza or two, and

* This was the first authentic news, in N. C., of the Treaty of Alliance with France, made Feb. 6th, 1778.

drinking *without toasts* formed the whole scene. There was a dry huzza to the King of France, and one to the United States, and this was all in that way. There was also an affecting prospect to a man who still feels for the condition of his native country, and laments the miserable but necessary disunion from her,—the British flag reversed, and the French and American meeting, and laid by the side of each other. The advantage of the connection, upon its present honorable principles, is undoubtedly great; but old attachments, and the possibility there once existed with prudent management of happier circumstances, will sometimes be unavoidably uppermost. I felt it this evening. Would to God, that in all cases it was possible to separate the bad from the good, the foolish from the wise; but human nature is too imperfect for this. You will excuse, I flatter myself, the hurrying and scribbling account I send you. I believe you are more anxious about the *matter* than the *manner* of information from me, though I should certainly think, if I could do it without abridging the former, that it was my duty to attend a little to the latter. * * * * * *

Most affectionately yours,
JAS. IREDELL.

NEWBERN, 28th May, 1778.*

MY DEAR HANNAH:—This is my third letter to you since I came to Newbern. The second was wrote two or three nights ago, when my head and hand were a little giddy, and intended to go by Mr. Nash, who I understood was to set off early next morning. This letter, together with one for your brother, is now in his hands; his journey to Edenton depends at present, I believe, on Dr. Savage's coming in, and you may probably receive this letter either from one or the other; I do not take it back, willing you should be convinced of my kindness and attention rather than of my formality. As I have hitherto given you an account of myself, I add that since I wrote that I have breakfasted with Mrs. Gordon, dined with Mr. Nash, and breakfasted with Mr. Ellis, from whose house I have just come. I have dined only once at home since I came, and not breakfasted more than two or three times. By the way, I think this breakfasting invitation very convenient: it has equal kindness in it, and is less troublesome and expensive. I have not done, nor am likely to do any thing about the land. The Governor has relinquished his

* Newbern, in consequence of the general politeness and cultivation of its population, from time immemorial, has been styled the Athens of North Carolina.

agreement with Heritage,* he being discontented with it, but has powers of negotiation. He proposed buying or selling, which at present was a proposal I could do nothing with. And for want of the Governor knowing the land, he could not determine whether the part we offered to lay off could be properly accepted. So this matter must be deferred. The sale would of course be put off, but I have received, which is much to my surprise, no offer of purchasing except from people on the spot, applying for small quantities, and from one man of the name of Brown, who lives on a detached plantation, which your brother John said might well be sold separately, and if I could do it to advantage, I believe I should sell it; but you may be assured I shall be on my guard against my total unacquaintance with these things.

If your brother does not come to-day I am not to expect him. I propose setting off to-morrow for Cape Fear, and going immediately to Mr. Hooper's, where I hope to spend the greater part of next week. I shall call on the Attorney-General and new soldier on my way, and see what kind of a habitation and lady he has got.† My brother Spencer goes with me. I hope, however, to drop him somewhere on the way before I get to Mr. Hooper's. Let me beg, my dear Hannah, you will write to me as I directed. I hope to have the pleasure of finding you perfectly well on my return. You must neglect no precaution to keep yourself so. You need not fear my attention. I shall fly to you with all imaginable expedition after Wilmington court. * * *

Yours most affectionately,
JAS. IREDELL.

P. S. I dined and spent the greatest part of the day yesterday with Wilson Blount. I have received great civilities from him and his wife, and am to stay with them when I come here for the future. They are soon going to Edenton, and I beg you will remember their kindness to me. Adieu! adieu!

MASON-BOROUGH, 4th June, 1778.‡

MY DEAR HANNAH:—I have the pleasure of writing to you from Mr. Hooper's, where I arrived about two o'clock on Tuesday

* Heritage was an attorney of some distinction, whose daughter Gov. Caswell married as his second wife.
† Mr. Avery had been appointed Colonel of the Jones County militia: he resided in that county at this time.
‡ Many of the Wilmington people possess now, as formerly, residences on the sea-shore ("Sound"), at distances varying from eight to fifteen miles from town to which they resort in the summer. Mason-Borough was so called, because number of zealous Masons built originally there, so closely together, as to create a straggling village, or hamlet.

he was not at home, having gone to town that morning about some business. You may believe, therefore, I was a little embarrassed, as I had not the least acquaintance with Mrs. Hooper. But she received me with such real politeness and cheerfulness, and in a manner so free from unmeaning ceremony and constraint, that my awkwardness soon wore off, and I entered into conversation with her with as much freedom as if I had been acquainted with her for years. Never was there in any woman more strongly exhibited the little power of beauty, opposed to the accomplishments of mind and behavior. Her appearance at first sight is very ordinary; though I had been prepared for it, I confess it struck me; but I defy any one to be long in her company, and still retain the same impression. Her mind appears to be highly cultivated; she has read much; her sentiments are just and noble; she speaks with great correctness and elegance, as well as with ease; her conversation is extremely interesting, and equal to high subjects. Her natural abilities appear to be very great; her distinctions are accurate and acute, and her knowledge of history, in particular, seems to be very extensive. I am really charmed with her. The idea I had formed of her, I find very far inferior to her real merit. Mr. Hooper, by bad weather or business, was detained in town till the next morning. But we were not at a loss for conversation the whole day; and though I was anxiously looking out for him till it was too late to expect him, I spent my time very agreeably. With how much happiness could I stay here for some time, if you were with me! You would be delighted too. They seem so happy in each other and their children; their deportment to me is so obliging and friendly, the situation is so agreeable (upon a Sound, in sight of the sea), that I want nothing at present to make me perfectly happy but our company. But alas! we live too far asunder for such happiness. The children are very fine ones, though none promise to be so handsome as himself; but they appear to be sensible, are extremely well behaved, and his little girl (about Peggy's age), I believe, will be pretty.* I live upon fish, crabs, &c., &c. Jem and Andrew provide them for us. Andrew seems to like the business very well. I thank God my health is perfectly good. I have not been a moment unwell since I saw you. The Court begins on Monday. I hear of no business but that of one man being tried for murder, but I fear the Court will be detained some days longer than I had flattered myself, for the Attorney-General is too busy preparing for the camp to come here, and I fear we shall be at a loss for somebody to prosecute. * * *

* Mrs. Hooper was Ann Clark, the sister of Col. Thomas Clark, of the 1st Regt. N. C. Cont. Line (1776). Col Clark subsequently became a general in the United States army.—*Life of Wm. Hooper by A. M. Hooper*

I cannot tell you particularly *when* I shall be at home; I can only say, that it shall be with as much expedition as possible after Wilmington Court. This place even shall not have charms to detain me one day. *I am fully determined on the point of my resignation;* this may perhaps occasion a little delay; for I am not absolutely determined whether I shall not send an express with it to the Governor, in order to receive his answer and return perfectly at liberty. I have it in contemplation, but *demur* a little. I have almost come to the end of my paper. You will please place to my credit the several letters I have wrote you, and though you seem very slow in payment, I shall expect it one day or other. Adieu, my dear Hannah. Heaven bless you till I see you. Love and compliments as proper, and believe me,

Yours most affectionately,
JAS. IREDELL.

Mr. Iredell attended Court on the 8th, and became the guest of Mr. G. Hooper. Mrs. Hooper, the daughter of Mr. Maclaine, he wrote, " is extremely genteel, has one of the finest persons I ever saw, and seems a most amiable woman." At the close of the Court Mr. Iredell tendered his resignation of his office to the Governor. Unable to determine the opinions of the Court, he was unwilling to share the discredit of ignorance, or participate in the odium of illegal decisions. There was no harmony on the bench; no cordiality between the judges and the attornies: and he could only anticipate collisions painful as disgraceful, and utterly inconsistent with his elevated standard of judicial decorum.

Gov. CASWELL to IREDELL.*
KINGSTON, 16th June, 1778.

SIR:—Your favor of yesterday was delivered me this day, when I immediately laid the same before the Council, who with reluctance have advised my acceptance of your resignation of the office of one of the Judges of the superior courts, which I also do with as much reluctance as you can well conceive, *well knowing your place cannot be supplied by a gentleman of equal abilities and inclinations to serve the State* in the important duties of that office.

I am, with very great esteem and respect,
Dear sir,
Your most obedt. servant,
R. CASWELL.

* For biographies of Caswell vid. N. C. Univ. Mag.—Lossing and Wheeler.

A. NASH TO IREDELL.

Abner Nash was a native of Virginia, and resident of New Berne.* He was elected the second Governor of the State in 1779. He was a lawyer by profession, and soon became enriched by marriage and the profits of his practice. His first wife was the widow of Gov. Dobbs. He was a man of fine natural parts, but lacked tenacity of purpose. Not very diligent as a student, he was what is known as a " case lawyer." He was not very assiduous to master law as a science—to grasp it in its integrity; but he attacked it in detail, as occasions arose, with great vigor, when his quickness of apprehension facilitated appropriation. At the bar he was " all vehemence and fire." When governor, the disordered state of the public finances, was, in a measure, attributed to his want of method and industry, and led to his defeat in 1781 by Dr. Burke. It is said, on the authority of his wife, that his salary while governor was scarcely sufficient to purchase her a calico gown, such was the depreciation of the currency. He served in the Assembly after the expiration of his gubernatorial term, and subsequently was elected to Congress. His patriotism and honor were universally recognized. He was the brother of General Francis Nash. In the public service he lost fortune and health, and when on his way to Philadelphia in 1786, to take his seat in Congress, fell victim to consumption.†

NEWBERN, 16th June, 1778.

DEAR SIR:—Your desire was that the enclosed letters should not be sent on to Edenton, unless a good opportunity by private hand offered, and, sir, having had no such opportunity, I now enclose them to you by Dr. Savage, and hope they will find you somewhat recovered from the fatigues of your late circuit. I assure you, sir, what you communicated to me last evening on the road, gave, and still gives me, uneasiness. I feel much for the honor of the bench; at the same time I must own that the duty of your late office was of such immense unreasonable fatigue and drew you necessarily so much from the comforts of domestic life, that it is by no means to be wondered at that you took the step you did. I certainly would in your case have done the same, and yet I cannot at the same time help *lamenting the loss this country has thereby sustained*—this, sir, I beg you will not consider as words of flattery—flattery is

* Un. Mag. Jones. Wheeler. A. M. Hooper.
† Gov. Nash was the father of the present chief justice of North Carolina, who not the equal, as a lawyer, of his eminent predecessor, Judge Ruffin, has a manifest superiority as a scholar.

a vice I despise, and what I say and think you may be assured is on this occasion the general voice and sentiment of the country. Mrs. Nash joins me in the kindest respects to your good lady.

I am, dear sir, most sincerely,
Your affectionate humble servant,
A. NASH.

The vacancy on the bench, after fruitless efforts to obtain the services of Judge Henderson and Mr. Maclaine, was filled by the election of John Williams, of Granville, May, 1779. Judge Williams was a native of Virginia, where " he was raised to the trade of a house carpenter." He was a worthy and patriotic citizen, but in an evil hour for his own fame and the profession, he turned his attention to law. In 1770 he was seized and beaten by the Regulators at Hillsborough Court; it had been well had he, then warned, abandoned a pursuit in which he was destined to attain office, but not honor. Accustomed, however, to climb, he was not to be deterred by one mischance, and persevered until his very " plain common sense," elevated him to a station in which his nakedness was sadly conspicuous.* He might have made a good farmer or respectable mechanic; he was but an indifferent judge, least in qualification, when equality would have conferred no distinction.

IREDELL to MRS. IREDELL.
CURRITUCK, 2d July, 1778.

MY DEAR HANNAH:—Mr. La Tour being obliged to go to Edenton about the troublesome business we have to do here, puts it in my power to give you some account of myself and your brother, and I beg you will not neglect to write by him. When it will be over I can't possibly say. I am in hopes, however, it will be on Tuesday or Wednesday. I have a hard fight before me, but have been prepared for it by two or three little skirmishes. I am in hopes not to be totally unsuccessful, though possibly I may not be so much as I expected. Your brother has been very well since we had time to rest here. We had a most cursed night at Relfe's; devoured by insects all night; not a wink of sleep, and scarcely alive in the morning. A few mosquitoes torment us still, but the salt air is lively and agreeable, and makes us bear it with more patience. After to-day we shall rest till Monday. Then and the next day the battle is to be fought. There are great odds against me, but I think I have justice to aid me. We shall have nothing to do in the mean time but to divert ourselves. I wish you were here to

* Wheeler.

bear a share in it. We have seen no fish yet, and but very few crabs, but I hope we shall have plenty of both before we return. Adieu! my dear Hannah. Be assured that I shall hasten home the first moment possible, with all the anxiety that on such an occasion always attends.

Your most truly affectionate,
JAS, IREDELL.

FINIAN, 15th July, 1778.*

MY DEAR IREDELL:—I thank you for your kind favor from Edenton, and congratulate you upon being again restored to the arms of your friends. No man ever descended from dignity with so much ease to himself; were it not that you have too great a share of virtue and wisdom you would make a tolerable figure in bearing all the vicissitudes of dignity and annihilation which mark the life of a courtier. How do you brook " May it please your worship," after having been exalted with " May it please your honor," Judge Iredell? Surely you feel very awkwardly. I thank you for the information of public matters which your letter so pleasingly afforded me. The character of Lord Abingdon is a singular one.† Such boldness and unaffected patriotism opposed to the court; to the source from which with his talents to serve it he might always command preferment and honor are truly extraordinary. I cannot believe him insincere, or that he is for sale; the breach he has made is so wide that the Court, base as it is, cannot condescend to hold an office forth to him; if they did he has put it out of his own power to accept it. I am anxious to know the progress of General Howe's army. I think their crossing into the Jerseys is a manœuvre to bring on an engagement to our disadvantage or to divide General Washington's army, that they may oppose effectually that division which is not under his own immediate command, *for believe me, I always fear when that man does not personally command*. Since you left us I have been somewhat indisposed; I owe my illness, I believe, to want of exercise, an inconvenience to which the extreme heat of the weather has subjected me. Our neighbor Derossett, the old lady whom you saw here, soon after you left us, was seized with the malignant

---

* Finian is now a pile of ruins; the lawn that ran down to the Sound invaded by wire-grass; the gardens desolate; there is nothing more attractive than the prickly pear, whose needles proclaim "Gare qui me touche" to him who is tempted by the beauty of its flower or fruit.

† Willoughby Bertie, 4th earl, was a very eccentric nobleman; he was once for an imprudence, imprisoned in the King's Bench; he assailed Mr. Fox, as a member of the Coalition by name in 1788, and with equal violence attacked the same statesman afterwards on the Regency question.—*Wraxall*.

---

fever which prevailed here, and in five days paid her debt to nature. Old Mr. Quince, from the same cause, but with shorter warning, soon followed. Some others, blacks and whites, have been seized since, but of the latter I hear of no deaths. It is most alarming illness.

The governor, I find, has called the Assembly at Hillsborough on the 3d day of August. I am at a loss for the especial occasion which prompted him to the measure; but I am well convinced that it affords an opportunity from which this State may profit greatly, if it should be steadily *confined to the purposes which you and I have in contemplation*, and which furnished us an hour's chat at my house. But I despair; the rage of locomotion which seizes every assembly of this State increased at this period by the busy crop season, will mar every good intention and every attempt to carry it into execution. shall attend, if God gives me health and strength, and the I flatter myself I shall meet *Mr. Hewes, who in his journey to Pennsylvania will probably take that in his way, as the route through the back country will most conduce to repair his shattered condition*. Thanks to Heaven! that he is better; I fore saw this; such intense application to business in such a country as this must gradually impair a more vigorous frame than Providence has allotted to his share. I am pleased to find that Mr. Johnston's family are all well. Oh! that Heaven had cast the common lot of three or four families with mine in the back country, or somewhere where health is not so dreadfully capricious as it is along the sea coast.* In fact, the Scripture expression was never more truly verified than in this part of Carolina in the summer and fall. We literally die daily. Bute is indeed my object, for I think that a few of you from the Edenton quarter must quit your "penchant" to that immense lake of standing water which surrounds you, and find some country which Providence intended for the habitation of man; and if we do not fly from this very soon, we shall find a habitation too permanent to be changed in this world, especially if this fever persists in his ravages. Bute—Bute is the word. Come along. You flatter us exceedingly by the very strong terms in which you speak of the hospitality you met with at the Sound. We can only regret that it was not equal to our wishes; an occasional habitation, devoid of any improvements but such as the la

---

* The healthiness of the N. C. seaboard has greatly improved since the revolution. Time was when no citizen of Wilmington, who could leave, would risk his life in town in the summer; now its per centage of death is less than that of any city to the North, and no citizen ever leaves but on business or in quest of pleasure.

---

of convenience requires, could not furnish a reception to Mr. Iredell which did not call for all his politeness to excuse. Such as it was, it was the offering of those who will be highly happy if Mr. Iredell will condescend to repeat the experiment of it. My little Betsy thanks you for your letter. She is, poor girl, a little indisposed at present, or would have answered it by this opportunity. I write under the influence of a fever at present and must therefore conclude, lest I should carry further proof of my disorder to paper, or leave no room to say, that I sincerely wish my kind compliments to Mrs. Iredell, Mrs. Blair, Miss Nelly and all Mr. Johnston's family, and Mr. Hewes. Mrs. Hooper begs to be remembered to you, and

I am, dear Iredell, with great regard,
Your affectionate friend,
WM. HOOPER.

July 21st.—John Penn, John Williams and Cornelius Harnett, ratified the Articles of Confederation in behalf of the State of North Carolina.

Soon after the treaty of alliance with France, the Earl of Carlisle, William Eden* and Governor Johnstone, were appointed by Great Britain to effect a reconciliation with America.† They arrived in the United States June 1st, but were too late to accomplish any good, for the national faith was already pledged to France. They offered terms that two years ago would have been gladly received; but now nothing less than independence would satisfy the wishes and demands of the Americans, whose affections had been completely estranged by the war. To their address Congress returned a very brief answer. It is said that one of their number afterwards made an insidious attempt to corrupt Reed, of Pennsylvania. Whereupon Congress passed resolutions of accusation against Johnstone, the party implicated, and declined any further correspondence with the commission. Thus baffled and angry, the Commissioners published a paper intended for the public at large, disrespectful to Congress and full of recriminations. They were answered promptly in publications by individual members of Congress. Participating in the general indignation, Mr. Iredell penned the following letter to the Commissioners, which ranks with the best produced by the occasion.

---

* Subsequently Lord Auckland:—he was a member of an ancient family in the north of England, raised to the baronetage under Charles 2d. It is believed that Charles Eden, governor of N. C. from 1712—1729, was a member of the same family. Penelope, the governor's daughter, after the death of her first husband, Governor Gabriel Johnstone, married John Rutherford, of New Hanover.—*Wraxall. Haywood's Reports*, 2d vol. † Hildreth.

To the Commissioners of the King of Great Britain for restoring Peace, &c.

GENTLEMEN:—You are continually boasting to us of the dignity and generosity of your nation, and the meanness and insincerity of the French, without appearing to attend to the following facts, which I hope you will animadvert upon in your next publication:

That the power claimed by Great Britain, and for years exercised and attempted to be carried into execution with all her might, was an unlimited authority over this country, to have no bounds but the moderation she pleased to prescribe.

That in forming and executing this plan, she trampled on and treated with contempt the charters under the faith of which this country was settled, and the almost continual and successful usage for more than a century of a mild and free government which made us prosperous and happy.

That this prosperity and happiness, with which we are so often *twitted* (if I may make use of the expression) was broke in upon by Great Britain's *cursed spirit of innovation*, and not by any discontent or ill conduct of us, unless it was ill conduct to say (and to act upon that principle), "*We disdain to be less free than our forefathers, and to become the despicable slaves of our fellow-subjects*."

That with a tameness almost unexampled, and which subsequent events have shown arose from nothing but an extreme affection for the Mother Country, and an unwillingness to enter into a contest with her, we confined ourselves for a long time only to the most respectful petitions and remonstrances, which were rejected with a degree of haughtiness and insult, that would deserve, if those only could suffer who were the authors of it, the severest ignominy it is possible to sustain.

That the only remission, even in show, of all these arrogant pretensions, was the ridiculous scheme of Lord North, by which if the Americans would collect all the money Parliament please to require, they were graciously to be allowed the privilege of raising it in their own way, and to have *nominally* the surplus of all the extravagant expenses that might be incurred under the auspices of a venal Parliament, applied to *their own account*.

That in the mean time every other plan of accommodation was rejected, particularly one presented by the great Earl of Chatham, which, though not fully equal to all our views, yet came so near them, that if it had taken place it would have be air to have promoted, at no great distance of time, a happy and solid ground of union.

That in the spirit of *absolute conquest*, and *unrestrained tyranny*, this war has been conducted on the part of Great Britain, with the utmost exertion of her own fleets and armies, the hire of mercenary forces, the employment of savages, the excitation and encouragement of an insurrection of our negroes, those very negroes the government of Great Britain refused the colony of Virginia the liberty of prohibiting, when they wanted to put a stop to an inhuman traffic Great Britain *found a profit in*.

That, contrary to the general character of the English, and the practice of all civilized nations, this war in many places has been carried on with a degree of cruelty that would make *savages blush*, and with a meanness and insolence in some of the commanders that will *damn their names to everlasting infamy*.

That America avoided, till the very last moment, a Declaration of Independence—the whole continent, almost to a man, reading it as an unhappy evil, which the necessity of their affairs compelled them to submit to, as a nominal dependence any longer would only serve to endanger their union, to hazard the peace of the community, to weaken their military preparations, and to make their enemies think, that they preferred the most ignominious dependence on them, to a *dangerous* but *honorable independence*.

That *since this declaration* (until the famous commission by which you are constituted), no plans have been offered of any accommodation, but *the pocket instructions of Lord and General Howe*; which, if pursuant to the act of Parliament, must have been of a most trifling kind, and were absurdly to be addressed to *non-existent Assemblies*, or to individuals that would be mean enough to betray the general interests of their country.

That as to your instructions, about which so much parade is made, one thing is very clear. The treaties are dated the 11th of February. Lord North's motion was made on the 17th. With respect to the secret negotiations, we are yet in the dark, or do believe you are fully informed. Lord North might talk in general, even before the holidays, of a *conciliation with America*, but I dare answer for it, he did not disclose the purpose of any so full as he afterwards offered, because it would have offended the pride of some of his warmest adherents, and he had no occasion to incur the *odium*, till he wanted the *vote*. From his former plans, and his despicable trifling conduct, it was more natural to think that he meant to raise fallacious hopes in the nation, without intending any solid reformation. And I believe it is certain, that until the 17th of February none but his confidential friends had the least suspicion that the man who was determined to have *us at his feet*, would ever be so humbly at *ours*. For what is the confession now? Either that an unjust war has been waged upon us for several years, or that our natural strength was too great to be subdued: or, that the powerful assistance of France made Great Britain tremble. Choose the alternative: for one it must be, otherwise no reason can be given why we had not long ago granted to us all we desired, which (before the Declaration of Independence) was much less than is now offered. It is, indeed, very farcical, that after you have been trying by force of arms, for several years, to make an absolute conquest of us—after you have repeatedly refused any terms of submission—after you have driven us (to what we most abhorred, except your tyranny) to declare ourselves entirely independent of you,—after we have been obliged to seek for foreign succors which we have obtained upon the most honorable and noble footing,—and you now find the whole efforts of your malice have been too weak for our destruction,—it is, I say, very farcical that after all this, you should expect, because it is now your interest to be quiet, that we should behave so villainously as to violate the faith of a most liberal treaty, to become tools to your repentance. You, no doubt, have your reasons for your resentment against the French; we have none. Their not interfering in a more effectual manner before, may have been owing to the state of weakness to which *Britain* and *America* in the last war reduced them, and which required a long time, and great efforts to recruit. Their interfering in so *noble* a manner now, gives them credit for the best intentions; for I am persuaded, notwithstanding your high opinion of your nation, *less generous terms* would have been accepted, rather than the least hazard incurred of any future dependence upon you. And, for my part, though no man in America hated the very idea of Independence more than myself, till it appeared to be inevitable, yet the moment it was adopted, I thought all dangers ought to be incurred in its support, and the most brilliant offers, if this was not conceded to us, rejected without hesitation. For it is a maxim, I believe, in general very just, *that when subjects have once drawn their sword against their Sovereign, it ought never to be sheathed*. There scarcely ever can be a cordial reconciliation afterwards, and it is more than probable, the temporary calm will serve only to lead them into more fatal dangers. This appeared very evidently in England, after the Restoration, for had Charles II. been a man of enterprise and ambition, he too surely could have effected (without leaving the task to his brother) the destruction of his kingdom.

I shall trouble you no more, gentlemen, than to lament, as a ever of virtue, the fall of such reputation as Mr. Johnstone's, a conduct, which perhaps his *master* may approve, but which, thank God, this rising and yet uncorrupted country holds in the highest detestation.

A MAN WHO DESPISES YOUR PARDONS.

On the 8th of August the 2d. Session of the Assembly was held at Hillsborough. They provided for the reinforcement of the Continental battalions of the State; and, with short-sighted policy, ordered an emission of £850,000, in bills of credit, without providing any adequate fund for its redemption. The members were unwilling to hazard their popularity by levying a sufficient tax to place the credit of the State on a sure foundation; and by their timidity increased and complicated the financial embarrassments of the future. To secure peace with the Indians they passed an act to restrain fraudulent traffic with the Cherokees, by "avaricious and ill-disposed persons;" and to prevent trespasses on their hunting-grounds. In December, Mr. Iredell was again at Currituck. In a letter to his wife, he says: "Mr. Cumming has been sometimes drunk, but much better tempered than usual. We have not had one quarrel, although sometimes I have made pretty free with him."*

HOOPER TO IREDELL.

WILMINGTON, Dec. 17th, 1778.

MY DEAR SIR:—Are we to ascribe it to a dearth of genius, or the restraint imposed upon the press, that no pen appears to lash the private and public vices of this licentious State? I never heard of a revolution brought about with such a succession of blunders in council, and errors in the field, as have marked the progress of America to Independency. They are not the follies of individuals or of separate States—the whole Continent seems to have run stark-staring mad, and to have a most full and equal representation in the Continental Congress of this assumed character. France, in possession of one of the British Islands, and meditating conquests of the rest, without any adversary force by land or sea in the West Indies to stay the progress of the united efforts of the French and Americans; thus circumstanced, I say, when General Clinton began a capital movement from New York, could the merest driveller in public affairs be one moment in suspense as to the true destination of the armament which he embarked. Yes, the Continental Congress were, or affected to be, and sagaciously concluded that General Clinton, to gratify a personal pique, to convince the world of his own prowess, to wipe away the stain which the British arms had suffered in a former attempt upon Charleston, was going pell-mell to run his head against the walls of Fort Moultrie, and possess himself of the all-important capital it led to,—" *cui bono!*" to pilfer a parcel of Jew merchants, burn their shops, and then, with his army, starve upon rice gruel, or perish with a putrid fever, for the honor of Great Britain. And that this truly farcical idea might not rest merely in speculation, this harassed broken-hearted country must be called in to play a part in this ridiculous expedition. That Author upon Stilts, Judge, General, Admiral, Counsellor,° is seized with a panic—intrudes his fears upon his fraternity, and the omnisapient edict which gave occasion to the repeated draughts we have had, issues forth, £150,000 is drawn into circulation to promote the depreciation of our currency,—our fields robbed of their husbandmen, our towns of our manufacturers,—husbands torn from their wives and children, who sought their daily bread from their personal labor and industry,—idleness and dissipation running riot in the land, the justice of the government called in question, with this as a consequence which must certainly result from it, that repeated calls into the field without occasion, will at length, like the cries of the boy in the fable, be disregarded when the danger becomes real, and her militia become necessary to oppose it. Our troops go to the southward never to return; a soldier made is a farmer lost; the South Carolinians will requite us as heretofore; they will take advantage of the necessities of our men when they get them amongst them, and by supplying wants which they can very *humanely* excite, they will entrap all our countrymen into their own regiments. Unless the councils of this country fall upon wiser men, the day of our perdition is not a great way off. With every thing in our power, we do nothing well. I hope in God that the next Assembly will redeem us from our present dangerous situation, or make some capital approaches to it.

It is with concern that I inform you that a man who was convicted of an atrocious murder at this Court, without a single circumstance to palliate his guilt or leave him open to mercy,—whose crime was perpetrated by secret stabbing; through the interposition of a certain Mr. Spillers (in whom, by the way, you have been dreadfully deceived), was reprieved by the Governor. Circumstances were such that the Judge had ordered an almost

---

* Mr. Cumming was a very small man, distinguished as much for the elegance and splendor of his dress, as for legal ability. His shoe-buckles, set with stones of Bristol Paste," are now in Mrs. Iredell's possession.

° Caswell?

immediate execution ; the Governor granted a respite to the 20th of January. The day after the reprieve, the culprit escaped. Tories make observations that are painful to men who love our cause. Our laws, they say, are a "*caput mortuum ;*" that they are such they cannot be executed, or that we are afraid to execute them. It becomes an encouragement to secret assassination, when aggressors thus escape with impunity. So much for hanging—now for matrimony. Thomas Hooper quitted his liberty on Thursday last, making a solemn resignation, then, to Miss Mary Heron, and begins to wear the phiz of Benedick, the married man : this traffic must thrive, let politics go as they will. He brought home with him from France a fine crop of health, and may take matrimony as philosophers do, to prevent the effects of repletion. Be that as it will, he is fast, one of us, and it is some comfort to have company—as Fitch says, "even in the rope." I fear that I shall have to be at Halifax during the latter part of the Assembly ; whether I shall or not, is problematical. I have no way to secure lodgings there, unless you can assist me by speaking to some of my Halifax friends, if at Edenton, or writing a line to one or more of them, to provide for me in season. I cannot get a line immediately from this, as there is not the least intercourse betwixt us. I must depend upon your interposition. Remember me most kindly and affectionately to Mrs. Iredell and Mrs. Blair. Mrs. Hooper begs leave to unite with me in compliments to you and them, and Miss Nelly. To the last I most especially request you to remember me, and thank her for the part she took in your last kind letter. That young lady honors me when she condescends to extend her attention to me, and I pay a debt of duty and inclination, when I assure her that I wish her every thing which can add to her happiness, and be a just tribute to the goodness of her heart, the improvement of her mind, and her personal accomplishments. I think kindly of the little branches of your worthy family, and am, my dear Iredell, with a warmth of friendship which I have pleasure to express,

Yours truly and affectionately,
WILL. HOOPER.

NOTE.—A vessel arrived from Cadiz in 1778: her cargo was sold to Webb, Littlejohn and Co., at the rate of 800 per cent. for dry goods: the purchasers were also to allow 400 per cent. for insurance: the invoices were made out in Spanish Rials. In consequence of a dispute the matter was referred to Mr. Iredell. It appears from his opinion, that a Spanish *Rial of Plate* was worth five pence sterling; that all mercantile business was transacted in pounds, shillings, and pence ; that a great deal of the old currency still remained all in pounds, shillings, and pence, and *was a legal tender at that day;* that the value of *North Carolina currency* could only be determined by reference to the old money ; that a dollar was estimated at eight shillings. Oct. 8th, 1778.

CHAPTER XII.

WAR IN THE SOUTH ; LETTERS FROM IREDELL ; CONFISCATION M'CULLOH ; LETTER FROM IREDELL ; SIR GEORGE COLLIER A NORFOLK ; LETTERS FROM MRS. BLAIR ; IREDELL ATTORNEY GENERAL ; LETTERS FROM IREDELL AND HOOPER ; SCHOOL IN N. C. ; THE CIRCUIT. ÆT. 27–28.

✻ ✻ ✻ ✻ ✻

IN consequence of an erroneous impression that South Carolin was to become the seat of war immediately in 1778, the militi of North Carolina had been called to arms.✻ A change too place in the plans of the British after the departure of the Commissioners, and they determined to direct their forces agains the Southern States. At the close of November Col. Campbell at the head of three thousand men, sailed from New York, com voyed by Commodore Parker. Thenceforth the southern department was destined to be the principal theatre of hostilities. O the 29th of December Col. Campbell routed the troops unde Gen. Howe, and captured the city of Savannah. Howe, th American commander, did all that courage and skill could effec to maintain his position in vain. His force was totally inade quate, and his measures had been embarrassed and thwarted b Houston, Governor of Georgia. Howe was removed by th exertions of the delegates from South Carolina and Georgia, an Lincoln substituted in his stead. From time immemorial Sout Carolina has manifested a singular jealousy of North Carolina affecting a contempt whose frequent expression affords a mos practical denial of its reality. In consequence of some offensiv remarks, Howe called Gadsden to account, and a duel was th consequence. Howe possessed, in a very especial manner, th confidence of Washington, yet was he destined again to expe rience the effect of South Carolina enmity ; the concurrence o the South Carolina delegates occasioned his subsequent remova from the important post of West Point, to make way for th traitor Arnold. No State, in a military point of view, was s weak as South Carolina ; she was often constrained to seek re cruits in North Carolina, and in the vicissitudes of the futur

* Hildreth. Marshall.

the latter State was a place of refuge to her citizens. Promptly in her hour of need, again and again did North Carolina send succor, but to meet with ingratitude. At the close of the year (1778) two thousand North Carolina militia had reached Charleston ; Lincoln had also with him the N. C. Continental battalions ; these constituted the major part of his forces. On the 3d of March General Ashe was surprised and defeated at Brier Creek ; his troops, chiefly militia, were badly armed, without cartouch boxes, wayworn and inexperienced. South Carolina, who had need of men, but boasted of wealth, had urged their advance from North Carolina, undertaking to furnish necessary equipments, but had failed to redeem the promise. When Ashe was ordered to the front he expostulated warmly with Lincoln ; he stated the true condition of his men, harassed by a long march, and insisted upon the propriety of forming the vanguard of the other troops, who had been some time in camp, were fresh, and prepared for action ; but a sinister influence was at work, the result of which was disaster.✻ When the British moved into South Carolina, North Carolina, become a frontier State, began to be disturbed by the loyalists.

The British successes in Georgia emboldened the Tories, and recovering their spirits, they rapidly formed themselves int organized parties. Afraid, however, to rouse the animosity o the Whigs, they stole out of the State to unite with the British A iterior to the defeat of Ashe, a large body of them, on thei march to Augusta, had been defeated by Pickens ; the survivor returned home to nurse their revenge and to await their oppor tunity. Active and watchful as they were they encountere equal energy and vigilance, were pursued to their secret hidin places, captured in the recesses of swamps, and arraigned befor the courts for *treason.*

IREDELL to MRS. IREDELL.

MRS. GRANBERI I'S, 10th January, 1779.

MY DEAR HANNAH :—I was regretting, as I rode along th road, that I had brought no book with me to solace me durin the dull hours of my journey, but soon after I came here had the pleasure to see Mr. Hewes's Jack arrive on his way t Edenton, which gives me the most agreeable employment I ca have in your absence—writing to you. I wrote to you a line o two this morning, to acquaint you of a most scandalous piec of negligence I had been guilty of in leaving behind Miss Cath cart's letter and Mr. Roulhac's to Savage. As I requested yo in that, pray be good enough to search carefully for them, en as Jack is to return immediately, do not fail either to give hi the letter for Savage, or let Mr. Roulhac know in time for hi to send another if he pleases. You will probably have tim enough to consult Miss Cathcart about hers, and I pray you t make excuses as little awkward as possible to her on the occa sion, though I really to-day could make none but very foo ish ones to Miss Mackenzie. All I could say was, pray forgi me, madam, a fault that is unpardonable. My neglect has be the more mortifying, as I took more than ordinary precaution avoid any bungling. But my distemper, I fear, is incurable.

I had a very good passage over the Sound, only an hour an a quarter, but I was detained at Mrs. Pearson's by one thing o another (you will not suppose it the charms of Miss N—) unt it was so late before I set off that I got to Mr. Charlton's tw hours in the night. I was received very kindly and cordiall but a slight indisposition of Mrs. Charlton's, or something els made the evening more dull than usual at that house. I wa very earnestly entreated to spend this day there, but resisted a importunities, notwithstanding Mrs. Charlton was so good as say she had had a turkey killed on purpose for me. Polly Payr was very affectionate, very engaging and very inquisitive abou

* The Continental Congress had requested Gov Caswell to command with a rank only second to Lincoln. As he was unable to comply he had pledged himself to the militia that Ashe should lead them. General Ashe, who was now advanced in years, reluctantly yielded to the urgent appeal of the governor.—*Vide Exec. Correspondence.*

Anecdote related to me by Thomas P. Hall, Esq., of Brunswick :—

Eaton (afterwards General) was at Brier Creek ; he had a very small foot and wore a boot of unusual finish and neatness ; in the haste of his flight he left his boots behind : they were recognized and purchased of a soldier by John Hamilton, who afterwards commanded a regiment of Loyalists in the British service. After the war, at a dinner party at Willie Jones's, Hamilton, with some good-humored raillery, produced the boots, and passed them to their former owner, who, greatly incensed, threw them across the table at Hamilton's head.

Hamilton was a short, stout, red-faced man : well bred, and well fed, he manifested by his generous enjoyment of life his gratitude to Providence. Originally he was a merchant at Halifax, N. C. At the close of the war he was British consul at Norfolk, Va. He so deported himself to such N. C. Whigs as by the fortune of war became subjects of charity, as to secure the cordial regard of the best men in the ranks of his enemies. He was the very crest of the Tory organization in the South.

At the siege of Savannah the North Carolina Loyalists, commanded by Col. John Hamilton, Gov. Sir James Wright, and Colonel Maitland, were in considerable force on the British right. Here the assault was pressed with the greatest vigor and fury, and the North Carolina Continentals met the North Carolina Loyalists in combat, and most gallantly did each maintain the reputation of the State for prowess.

Hamilton was captured by the Americans at the siege of Charleston, but regained his liberty when that city surrendered ; he was engaged in nearly all the actions in the South, and acquired great distinction as a soldier, and " was a gentleman of high tone and spirit."—*Governor Graham's Lecture at N. Y. Lee's Memoirs of the War in the South.*

you, and made me promise to call and carry a kiss to Gaby as I returned. Mrs. Charlton has promised me also abundance of seed on my return. I stopped only a few minutes in Windsor to leave my letter to you, and make my humble acknowledgment and condolence to Miss McKenzie. I had the pleasure to see her look extremely well, and her sister and family were so also, except one of the children. Poor Mrs. Granberry's daughter has been very unfortunate. She has not only lost her second husband, a young man of excellent character, but that fine little girl you and I admired so much and could not help wishing was ours. Her other children are also now very sick indeed. What poor miserable mortals we are! How little pleasure for how much pain! Born but to love, form connections, be happy in them, dread their loss, and part! Gracious God, may the misery you and I have felt of this kind long, very long indeed, be without renewal! I begin to grow grave and therefore must leave off. Jack will certainly bring me a letter from you, and I hope to receive one by all opportunities. On my part be assured I shall not fail, for it is not possible for me to express the anxiety and zeal with which I am

Your most faithful and affectionate
JAS. IREDELL.

P. S.—I trouble you with a letter for our little madcap niece, wrote with as little compliment as she generally speaks, &c. &c.

IREDELL TO MISS BLAIR.

MRS. GRANBERRY'S, 15th January, 1779.

MY DEAR NELLY:—As an Englishman is apt to undervalue the merit of the favors he bestows, I tell you very candidly that it is more than probable you would not have received this letter from me, but I neglected bringing any book from home, and I take up my pen to you for want of some more tolerable amusement. Does this gratify your vanity? No. Ought it to be gratified? No. God knows, there is enough already. Take therefore the plain truth as I give it; if it is unacceptable Jack will bring me no letter from you. If you have sense and address to be satisfied with it, he will bring a charming one; I mean, as charming a one as you can write. You still see I am determined to run no hazard of violating the truth.

But, say you, what news? News! what, after a day's absence from home, going through woods and swamps? Shall I tell you that Mrs. Pearson is well, that Miss Vail is well, that Mrs.

Charlton is not well, that Mr. Charlton *is*, that Miss Polly Payne is so-so, that Miss McKenzie is well, her sister also, one of the children sick, Mrs. McKenzie well, old Everett and his dame alive, Mrs. Granberry well, but her daughter miserably unfortunate. The particulars I have given to your aunt, and they are truly distressing.

I do not intend always to give you the triumph of a longer letter than your aunt. Remember you are already much in my debt. I expect very handsome letters, both in matter and form. I may perhaps, if you are a good girl, write you letters sometimes from other motives than those of amusement. You may be truly assured that nobody more ardently wishes your welfare, or will be more happy in endeavoring to contribute to it, than

Your very affectionate uncle,
JAS. IREDELL.

P. S.—You may think this compliment of some consequence, when my desire of making it has conquered my aversion to pale ink.

In August, 1778, Henry E. McCulloh arrived in New York. By an ordinance passed by Congress in 1776,* the Governor was empowered to issue a proclamation requiring all loyalists to take an oath of allegiance to the State within ninety days from the date of the proclamation; absentees were allowed the same time after their return, in which to make submission. Open enemies were excepted from the mercy of the Act; free pardon was offered to all who complied with its provisions; and the property of all recusants declared confiscated, &c. By an Act of the Assembly in the spring of 1777, the allegiance of all persons "now inhabiting or residing within the limits of the State," or "who shall hereafter come into the same to inhabit or reside," was claimed; treason was defined, and death declared as the penalty; and all late officers and agents of the King were required to take an oath of allegiance to the State or to depart the same. At a second session of the same Assembly, in November, a new Act was passed, amending and giving greater efficacy to the policy of the State as regards loyalists, and repealing "all former Acts within the purview of this Act." No person was to be excused for non-compliance, except for "sickness or unavoidable necessity, or other sufficient reason." Subsequently, the same Assembly passed an additional Act, directed against those who had withdrawn themselves from the State and attached themselves to its enemies; those who had left to avoid their proper and equal part in defence of freedom and independence;

* Vid. Statutes.

and also those who, living beyond the limits of the United States at the commencement of the war, had failed to return. McCulloh came within the latter class of persons and had incurred the penalties of the Act. In January, 1779,* a more stringent complementary act of confiscation was enacted; commissioners, three for each county, were appointed to take possession of the lands and movables, and to recover all sums due those who had incurred its penalties. With a commendable spirit of liberality, however, the legislature provided that indigent parents should be allowed necessary subsistence out of the estates of their "absentee" children. In October, 1779, by another Act the properties of seventy persons, named in the Act, were confiscated; of these McCulloh and his father were two. Other Acts were subsequently passed in reference to the same subject. By that of 1782, a generous allowance of one-third of the lands, or "so much thereof as will be sufficient for their support," and "share of the personal property," including all the "household goods," was made the wives and children, residents of the State, out of the confiscated estates. From the Act of pardon and oblivion of 1783, all were excepted who had been named in any of the Confiscation Acts. To conclude this succinct notice of this matter, it may as well be stated that, though by the treaty of peace with Great Britain Congress agreed to urge upon the States the repeal of their confiscating acts, the recommendation was disregarded by North Carolina.

Mr. McCulloh had intrusted his interest to Mr. Iredell's hands; at the same time he made a very touching appeal to his feelings. Charged with a petition from McCulloh, and actuated by a burning desire to serve his friend Dukinfield, for whose mother, Mrs. Pearson, he felt the most poignant distress, Mr. Iredell was on his way to attend the Assembly. The petition, drafted by him with much care and enlivened by occasional passages of much eloquence, may be seen in the appendix of this chapter. Mr. Iredell and Mr. Johnston, in consequence not only of legal preëminence, but of power with the Whigs of the State, were very frequently employed by wealthy and conspicuous Tories, to prepare petitions for them and to defend indictments against them; in this way, at times, the legitimate influence of these gentlemen was seriously affected and their popularity weakened, for the ignorant could not separate the counsel from the cause. The same reasons, however, that prevailed upon clients to tempt them with large retainers, operated to induce reluctance in their minds. They were unwilling to throw into the scales of justice the extrinsic weight of their own characters; often demurred; and often refused lucrative cases.

* Statutes.

IREDELL TO MRS. IREDELL.

MRS. GRANBERRY'S, Jan. 9th, 1779.

MY DEAR HANNAH:—Like people who are determined to be merry, or *loquacious* (which Nelly once, for a wonder, failed in), it seems as if when one was resolved to be careful *without possessing* the true spirit of it, we were liable to meet with an unusual share of disappointment and regret. I have already informed you of my sins towards Miss Cathcart and Mr. Roulhac (and which I yet blush at), and this morning I have discovered one to Mr. Knox, your brother, and myself, in omitting to send a letter similar to the enclosed. What will you think of all these things? I protest I am startled at them myself. I begin to doubt whether my head is not really turned, and fear soon being sent to a Bedlam. Possibly, however, this cool snow and a gloomy confinement, without any book but the Bible and a spelling-book, may bring me to a little, though if my disorder partook of a different kind of delirium instead of such a perturbation of spirits, it would certainly confirm it. I am particularly ashamed of appearing thus careless to your *brother, who is himself the most exact* man living. All I can say, with a very foolish face, is what the boys say at school, "I will endeavor to do so no more." * * * * *

Had I foreseen what has happened I might as well have been a few days longer with you, and saved Perquiman's Court. The Assembly, I am told, have not yet made a house. You will exult at this, and tell me you told me so. But how could it be supposed? Was it reasonable to think there would not be one in a fortnight? Was not a vast deal at stake, and where so much is depending, is it not better to be a *few* days too *early* than too late? Suppose (as it might have done) it had happened otherwise, and I had not gone till the business was nearly over, the patience of the members exhausted, their minds fretted, and perhaps a resolve passed (and such a one does pass almost every session) that after a particular day they would receive no business, and that day passed, what could I have said to Mr. McCulloh? What could I have said to my own consciencewhen he relied entirely on me in this momentous affair, and I certainly was in duty bound to make an application, which, however improbable the success of it may be, nobody with certainty could say, would have been unsuccessful if it had not been tried. I therefore acquit myself on this occasion, although I regret I could not have had a spark of that foresight which is denied to mortals.

Shall I read the Bible or spelling-book? I have tried the

latter, but cannot persuade myself to look into the former. You will tell me I ought not to lose this opportunity of perusing a book I know so little of, and perhaps my present situation is a punishment for so long a neglect which I ought to receive with humility and penitence. But my dear, as there are times for all things under the sun, there is a time for *spiritual things*, and my mind does not move me towards them at this present. So I will content myself with an old magazine which just now I happened accidentally to find, and defer devotional matters till I am more worthy of them. "*Apropos*," extreme sanctity has sustained a great blow in this neighborhood lately. A maiden about the age of 30, one of the sect called Quakers, a resident with the pious Mr. Peel, and herself remarkable for the most straitlaced affectation, lately afforded him the sight —— for which she was indebted to his son, and has since been expelled the father's house. They say it is only a repetition of an old disorder of which her conversion never thoroughly cured her. Adieu, my dear Hannah, and believe me

Most affectionately yours,
JAS. IREDELL.

The Assembly began its *third* session at Halifax, January 19th.*

HALIFAX, 22d Jan. 1779.

MY DEAREST HANNAH :—I should have had inexpressible pleasure in receiving your letter and hearing of your good health, if I had not at the same time heard of poor Corrie's death and of Gaby's danger.† These two events extremely distress me and have taken away all my spirits. I feel for the loss of a most worthy, benevolent man, and am deeply afflicted for your brother and Mrs. Johnston. Good God! are they never to enjoy a moment's peace? Is your brother doomed to be eternally miserable? Heaven avert the fatal stroke, and grant the poor lovely boy a long, long respite. I am here teazed and fretted to death. One minute hope, another despair. I am not without hopes, but I dread much. I wrote you more cheerfully to-day and with less despondence, but I have since had cause to be alarmed. At any event I *must* stay here some days longer or act a most unfriendly part. It is necessary to watch and be attentive to every circumstance. Were public councils always guided by wisdom and justice, so much trouble in applicants would not be necessary,

* Statutes.
† Archibald Corrie, of Tyrrel; he was a member of the Prov. Congress, April, 1776, and of the Assembly in 1777; the intimate friend of Iredell, Hewes, Johnston and Neilson.

but a great deal, I assure you, has been and is yet required here. Mr. Barker is perfectly well, but his wife has been sick ever since they came up. She stays at Mrs. Robt. Jones's, but principally at Mrs. Montfort's. I called at Mrs. Jones's as I came along; I found her very unwell, but was received with great kindness. Last night (as I wrote you) I went to Col. McCulloh's; it was a long time before I saw any of the family except B. McCulloh, unless when I went in. I met Mr. Frohock, who saluted me very coldly, and madam kept up a great deal of her stiffness. The rest were very kind, but I thought did not show quite so much cordiality as formerly. Mr. Hewes and Mr. Hooper are very well; Mrs. Hooper is not here, so (as I told you) my heart is quite safe, and I believe it will remain very secure in your possession unless any accident to him should tempt me to wish you had less health. As that however is no probable, I may with truth say (as I extremely feel) that upon your health principally and greatly depends my happiness. May Heaven (if you will forgive my wishing it) long spare us to each other!

The Assembly are likely to sit a long time. I hope at furthest to be at home Monday or Sunday se'ennight. Don't be angry with me for staying so long. Upon my soul nothing keeps me but a desire of doing my utmost in behalf of Mr. McCulloh, in order that whatever be the event I may have nothing to reproach myself with. I have a very comfortable room at Mrs. Elbreck's, and spend my time agreeably enough. I have dined with Wilie Jones, Mr. Gilchrist, and Mr. Webb twice at Mr. Gilchrist's, and was also invited twice to Mr. Jones's. I shall write a line to your brother. You will remember me kindly to all our family, and believe me ever

Your most affectionate
JAS. IREDELL.

HALIFAX, 26th Jan., 1779.

MY DEAR HANNAH :—As I am still doomed to wait here I can have no employment more agreeable to me than that of writing to you, and I embrace this new occasion of doing it with pleasure. I have not yet had the courage to present my memorial. I have been two or three times on the eve of doing it, but unexpected and threatening circumstances have deterred me. I have some faint hopes of the suspension of the evil day by general law, but hold myself prepared for a different event. The evidence of Mr. Harnett, Mr. Burgwynn and Mr. Hogg would

* Mr. Iredell, when judge, had committed him to jail at Salisbury.

weigh much if there was not such a great quantity of land in the opposite scale.

I receive here very great civilities.* I have only once dined in a tavern since I came here. I have dined at Mr. Gilchrist's four times, twice at Mr. Webb's, once at Mr. Jones's, and last Sunday at Mr. Montfort's; he has a very neat, comfortable house about half a mile from town, but there were about a dozen women there and very near as many men. This you may believe was not to my taste, and we passed the day very dully. I have not been out to Col. McCulloh's since I wrote you, and do not intend it but just to take leave. I am indeed obliged to be very attentive here; but besides, I will not voluntarily go anywhere where I am sure of being coolly received. This indeed is only from certain branches of the family, but I do not choose to be in the way of such treatment. Col. McCulloh has been excessively ill; very dangerously so, and Mr. and Mrs. Frohock were sent for on purpose. He is getting better, but very slowly, and is confined to his room. The colic, I believe, has been his principal complaint. I have had the distress to be certain of Miss Macartney's death. Mr. Burgwynn was a long time in Bristol, and lived with Mr. Maskelyn, who was, as I have told you, an intimate friend of hers; she died in August, 1775, of a consumption. I assure you it has most deeply affected me. This and my uncertainty about Gaby and pain about Mr. McCulloh, have taken away all my spirits, of which I had before a pretty good stock. I preserve however my health extremely well, and endeavor to console myself for my stay here in such disagreeable circumstances by reflecting that I am doing a necessary office of friendship at a most critical period, and discharging in part a debt of obligation much too heavy. My dear Hannah, when I am released with how much ardor shall I fly to you! Heaven grant that I may find my sweet little fellow out of all danger,† and the rest of you well. This will remove much of my unhappiness, but I shall long, very long regret the misery of losing so affectionate a friend, so agreeable a correspondent, so valuable a woman as Miss Macartney. I cannot bear to dwell upon it; my mind is too much distressed.

I don't believe I shall have either time or spirits to write to Miss Nelly, and I am sorry to send you so grave a letter. I wrote you I expected to be at home Sunday or Monday; it

* Halifax, on the Roanoke, is the centre of one of the most fertile regions in America; it was long noted for the opulence, hospitality, fashion and gaiety of its citizens; about 1805, when Gen. Davie and many others deserted it, decay began, and it was shorn of much of its consequence.
† Mr. Johnston's son, Gabriel.

seems now probable it may be a day or two later. You may be assured I will not delay a moment unnecessarily, but I cannot by too much precipitation or undue remissness, run the risk of ruining Mr. McCulloh, for it is in the power of this Assembly to do it if they please. Be good enough, &c. &c.

Unalterably and most affectionately yours,
JAS. IREDELL.

HALIFAX, 30th Jan., 1779.

MY DEAR HANNAH :—I had yesterday afternoon the pleasure of receiving two letters from you by Capt. Hardy, and was made very happy by hearing of your good health, and my dear little Gaby's recovery. I should have been in great pain for you if I had known you had suffered so great fatigue and want of rest, though I dare say it was necessary, and am very thankful it has done you no injury. I expected to have the satisfaction of setting off towards you this afternoon, but a most unfortunate and alarming report of a committee obliges me to stay. They talk of renting out the lands of all absentees, and taking immediate possession of their personal property. I must immediately now present my memorial, though I have no hopes of success for it. I am in great pain, as well about this affair as so long an absence from me. If these circumstances could well admit of consolation, I should not want it. I dine every day abroad somewhere or another, and last Thursday was at a very agreeable ball. I could not, however, though I had an exceeding good partner, be so cheerful as I generally am at such times. Mr. McCulloh's situation, Miss Macartney's death, and my uncertainty about poor Gaby, all conspired to make me dull. I bustled through the evening however tolerably well, and could not even help regretting that the ladies went away so soon. But intervals of reflection frequently occurred to make me low-spirited.

Mrs. Frohock has come to a great deal. We were very cordial at the ball, and she seemed to have a desire to make up for past improprieties. I went to the Marsh last night, expecting to go away to-day, but being disappointed, in complying with earnest importunity, I shall ride out there to-morrow, and shall have the pleasure of Mr. Hooper and Mr. Hewes's company. Tell Nelly she is an idle good-for-nothing girl. You refer me to her, but she has not wrote me a single word. I have no notion of keeping up a correspondent merely *to write to*, and therefore till she grows more industrious I must neglect her. When I shall see you, my dear Hannah, is really uncertain. I fret and strive to no purpose. I regret the delay the more, as

VOL. I.—27

Bertie Court will carry me from home the week after next. But when so much is at stake and my exertions are relied on, it would be criminal to be neglectful. How deeply is it to be regretted that such care and caution are necessary to obtain justice, and that *folly* and *private interest* bear so large a share in our public councils. Heaven grant an amendment of them! Of my health, my desire, my impatience to see you, be assured. I burn for it with the greatest ardor. May I enjoy that happiness soon, &c. &c. &c.

You never, I hope, doubt of my being most faithfully and unalterably, my dear Hannah,

Your entirely affectionate
JAS. IREDELL.

IREDELL TO MISS BLAIR.

HALIFAX, 31st January, 1779.

MY DEAR NELLY:—I am of a very candid and forgiving temper, and readily pardon an omission occasioned by such circumstances as you mention, though you ought not to be so particular with me. I do not expect you always to write me correct letters, but you will arrive at it in time by frequent use and proper attention. I shall be happy in contributing to it; and will sometimes take the liberty, after receiving letters from you, on my return, to point out any defects in them. By this method, with a little care on your part, you will soon acquire a greater ease and correctness of expression. I am still painfully detained here, and it is uncertain when I may return, though I am anxiously impatient to do it. You will expect me, I suppose, some news in return for yours. All I can tell you is, that I was last Thursday at a very agreeable ball, and danced with a genteel lady and an exceedingly good partner, Mrs. Willis, who formerly lived in Virginia, but at present in this county. A high freshet prevented many ladies from coming. There were, however, upwards of twenty dancers, and many awkward Members of Assembly. Two or three disagreeable circumstances oppressed my spirits a good deal, and prevented my enjoying the amusement as generally do. I had had the concern, a day or two before, to be made undoubtedly certain of Miss Macartney's death, which distressed and still does distress me, exceedingly. I had lived from my very childhood in intimacy with her; she was most nearly connected with me; had conferred on me many obligations; and was endeared to me by a thousand engaging ties. To lose such a relation, and such a friend, at so great a distance, without the opportunity of sharing any melancholy moments with her, or of convincing her of the extent and sincerity of my affection, is extremely painful. God in His mercy grant I may not experience many more of these calamities. I have sustained the deepest affliction of this kind since my arrival in this country, by the loss of the dearest connections both in England and here. Of all kinds of distress it is the most severe. But, my dear Nelly, I ask pardon for suddenly becoming so grave. It was unintentional and involuntary. Yet I know you have a feeling soul and will sympathize with me, &c. &c. &c.

Your very affectionate
JAS. IREDELL.

In February Mr. Iredell attended Bertie Court, and at its close, after visiting Edenton, he returned again to Halifax.

WINDSOR, 8th February, 1779.

MY DEAR HANNAH:—I have now the pleasure to congratulate you and myself on my arrival here, in perfect health, and possessing the greatest impatience to see you. When I can have that happiness depends on the duration of this court. It is a great misfortune, after so long an absence, to have such an obstacle in the way; but it must be submitted to. Every thing is going wrong at Halifax. That cursed Senate will not suffer any plan of moderation. The lands, I fear, will be sold as well as other things. The Commons passed the bill for hiring, but the Senate altered it, and I fear this will be acceded to. There is a humane clause in favor of wives and children, and I have hopes it will be extended to mothers, which will save Mrs. Pearson. I have not time to enlarge much. All you care for above are well, and *Mr. Hewes will be down soon, for he is thrown out of his seat by being elected a Delegate, and nothing now detains him, but his goodness in settling accounts he has no business with, and which no other man is equal to.* Adieu, &c. &c.*

Ever most affectionately yours,
JAS. IREDELL.

HALIFAX, April 19th, 1779.

MY DEAR HANNAH:—I have just received your last, with the greatest pleasure, by Mr. Payne. Notwithstanding the ——

* Mr. Hewes was elected Delegate to the Continental Congress.

---

of my horses, I got to Booth the first night, but found none of the family at home. They had gone to Mr. Jones's. I fared, however, very well; and the next day, after breakfasting with the General, called at Occoneechy and saw all your brother's family. I had the pleasure to find them all very well. * * * Mrs. Jones was very obliging and polite, and asked me to dinner that day and the next, but I have not had it in my power to go there since. Your brother is perfectly well, and stays constantly in town, and, as Mr. Hooper lodges with us, you may be assured I pass my time agreeably. An odd circumstance happened, however, to deprive us of a very pleasant evening last Sunday. We had got a room to ourselves at Martin's, a rousing fire (for it was very cold), and had ordered supper, expecting to spend two or three happy hours together. There is a negro who waits at Martin's, commonly called the *Parson*. Mr. Hooper desired his servant to call him, and he having made a mistake, ushered in Dr. Pasteur. We were cursed with his company all the evening, and I a thousand times wished he had been at the devil, or anywhere rather than with us. I went yesterday to the Marsh, and returned this evening; they were all *really kind*, and regretted you had not come up with me. Business goes on very slowly, notwithstanding there is very little, chiefly owing to the absence of the Attorney-General, who minds any thing rather than his business. I have but poor prospect of money; but if I get none, I shall have the consolation of knowing it is not my fault. It is certain that Congress have received *very great* and *very good news*, but it is yet a secret. Penn, Burke, and Whitmell Hill, all members, mention it. Peace also is suggested to be the object. * * * W. Blount and his wife are here on their way to Virginia to be inoculated. Mr. Nash and Mr. Ellis are expected here to-day, merely to be out of the way of it, I believe. Crowds are inoculating in Newbern. The Assembly are to meet at Johnston Court-house the 26th inst., and your brother will go to it immediately after our court, &c. &c. &c.

Very affectionately yours,
JAMES IREDELL.

May 3d, the Assembly met at Smithfield. They passed an Act for raising regular forces for the "defence of this and the neighboring States," and to pay the debt incurred in the support of their Continental Battalions ordered the emission of one half million of pounds, in bills of credit.

May 9th, Admiral Sir George Collier, with his fleet, entered Hampton Roads.* Aided by General Matthews, who commanded the land forces, he attacked Fort Nelson, which was immediately abandoned by its garrison, who retreated to the Dismal Swamp. Sir George subsequently took possession of Portsmouth, Norfolk, and Suffolk. After seizing much booty, destroying very valuable property, burning Suffolk and gutting Norfolk, the British returned to New York. The Dismal Swamp is partly in Virginia and partly in North Carolina. This irruption of the enemy created an intense state of alarm in Edenton. There were no troops there to repel a sudden invasion, while its wealth was a tempting bait to the marauder. The war was now assuming a character of greater ferocity; all hopes of reconciliation gone, it was waged with relentless fury. The most atrocious crimes were committed by the wretches, who hovered like vultures about the flanks or in the rear of the English forces. No house was secure against the burglar's torch; no man safe against the assassin's knife; females were outraged, and even children were, sometimes, the objects of wanton brutality.

MRS. BLAIR TO IREDELL.

EDENTON, 17th May, 1779.

DEAR SIR:—We have received all our things safe: I believe, with very little damage. Alarming accounts are continually brought to town, but nobody minds them now, except a few weak people. Some had their goods brought to town yesterday, and are sending them away to-day. Mrs. Barker and Mrs. Nash packed up every thing yesterday, even to the pictures and looking-glasses that were screwed to the wall; and intend leaving the town. They say the British troops will certainly be here by Wednesday night; whence they have their intelligence I do not know. Mr. Hewes and others were carried out late last night. The Dismal has been on fire for some days past; and the reeds make almost as loud a report as muskets. That foolish fellow, Badham, came to town last night, and said there were large fires kindled, and many guns fired out there; but I do not think it was any thing but his own fear. We are blamed for bringing our things back again; but for my part, I shall not be frightened again without more certain accounts of the danger being nearer. It is said they are fortifying Portsmouth, which I think the likeliest story. * * * Mr. Hewes had a warehouse broke open last night, and there have been some people taken up this morning. A

* Lossing.

negro of Mr. Rayner's, it is said, will be hanged. Two sailors were taken sleeping at the foot of my brother's garden; they were about the house all night. I do not know what they have done

Your affectionate Sister,
I. BLAIR.

May 26th, Gov. Caswell wrote Mr. Iredell, that if Mr. McGuire would not accept the appointment of Attorney-General, he would recommend him to the Council, and had no doubt his recommendation would meet with their approval.*

To the statesmen of North Carolina, the dawning future was ominously clouded. As peal answers to peal, so were the reports of the British guns in Virginia responded to by the thunders of British cannon in South Carolina, while the offer of Gov. Rutledge of South Carolina (May 11), to stipulate the neutrality of that State, flashed a vivid and fearful light upon the impending peril.† Georgia subdued! the spirit of South Carolina almost crushed! Yet, there was no wavering with the Whigs of North Carolina; there was no paling of cheeks—no trembling of nerves —no retreat of coward blood to the heart. Right gallantly did they gird about their loins, and prepare to meet, as men, the storm.

IREDELL TO MISS BLAIR.

This letter possesses unusual merit. Though capricious and wayward, there was such a charm about the petted Nelly, that I suspect Mr. Iredell was glad of an opportunity to *write* what he could not *say*. The time and care, evidently bestowed, evince the depth of his affection; while the sternness of his admonitions demonstrates how subordinate, in him, was feeling to duty. As a minister of grace, this letter exerted a salutary influence over the destiny of his niece, and I trust, it may benefit others of her sex.

CURRITUCK, June 11, 1779.

DEAR NELLY:—Being delayed setting off from here longer than I expected, and having a little leisure, I direct my attention to you, supposing that you would rather be attended to late than not at all, although I know that you passionately love to be of the first consequence. That you may ever deserve to be of very

* Col. Avery, diverted from his profession by military aspirations, I suppose, had resigned. McGuire soon afterwards withdrew from America, being a Tory at heart.
† Hildreth. Ramsay.

considerable consequence is my most sincere wish, but do you imagine that the *Desire* will constitute the *Desert*? Believe me no persons, let their natural qualifications be ever so great, or the adventitious circumstances of Beauty and Fortune ever so considerable, will acquire any great share of Respect or Esteem without much pains and trouble; because such is the imperfection of human nature, there is a necessity for continual self-denial to govern our temper, to regulate our passions, and to direct our conduct. Mankind (speaking of the greatest part) seem formed for difficulties and disappointments, and they who look forward to uninterrupted prospects of ease and satisfaction, will not only be chagrined by perpetual interruptions, but by having their minds indolent or relaxed, not be capable of enjoying the little good that is mixed with the greater portion of evil in the manner a firm, resigned and less confident mind would do. The latter, by receiving any considerable pleasure without any assured expectation of it, would feel it greatly heightened,—and the various distressing circumstances of life, which in some degree assail the happiest, would lose much of their poignancy by not coming by surprise. I lived long in the world without attending to this sentiment. Painful experience has, however, convinced me of its justice, and though I have not been able to adapt my conduct entirely to the precept, yet I am sure I have in many instances been benefited by it, and, according to my deliberate ideas, I think scarcely any may be applied to more real utility; for I am persuaded this ease and indolence of mind, and delusive prospects of imaginary future happiness, occasion more *misery*, more *repinings*, more *fretfulness*, and shameful inattention to serious and necessary occupations than any circumstance in life. Palpable and avowed vice, most people of any decency are free from, and it requires many seducing arts to corrupt a virtuous mind in those great points they have been always taught to reverence. But this is a fault almost every one will indulge in unless great pains are taken to correct it. It is natural to the human mind to think well of the future. It is pleasing to have in contemplation a happiness grateful to our minds, as a reward for present care and anxiety. Nothing in short can be more agreeable than those pleasing reveries people are so apt to delight in, but which are so seldom realized. But the misfortune is, by expecting *pleasure* we are not able to bear *pain*: by expecting *affluence*, we neglect a *necessary provision*; by flattering ourselves with constant health we become impatient in sickness. Whereas a contented and cheerful mind, which receives good without expecting it, evil without dreading it, is pleased and grateful for the former, resigned and submissive under the latter. Such a mind will doubly

relish all the blessings of life, feel less pain from the distresses of it; and at the same time that they sustain their part with dignity and reputation, they have an equal chance for happiness arising from adventitious circumstances with other people, and their mental enjoyment of those circumstances (no inconsiderable part of happiness) will be infinitely greater. Thus, my dear Nelly, I have preached you a sermon. I did it accidentally and unpremeditatedly, for it is a long time since I have written to you in such a style, as I thought it to no purpose to throw away time in instructions that were not regarded. The word instruction, I know, sounds harshly to a young ear, and permit me to add, a *vain* one,—but I have myself, I candidly confess it, suffered so much in a thousand circumstances from the uninstructed giddiness of youth, that I feel the most painful apprehensions for any young person I regard. Happy should I have been had I continued longer under some authoritative direction, whence I could have received friendly and severe admonition. But by being too soon (what you would think a great felicity) my own master, I lost many advantages, and suffered many inconveniences, which I frequently think of with regret. Be then, my dear Nelly, no longer that giddy, thoughtless, opinionative girl you have too long been. Make your mamma and all your friends happy by such an alteration of your conduct as is necessary for your own happiness. Consider a whole life is not to be passed in frolic and dissipation, and if it is attempted it will probably end in misery. God forbid I should wish to check that charming cheerfulness of disposition you possess, and which, if kept within proper bounds, would appear so amiable. May you enjoy every amusement suited to your age, and may you always have many light and gay hours mixed with serious ones. But, for God's sake, make not amusement the business of your life. Let not time you might so admirably improve, pass away in trifling insipidity. Let your mind sometimes receive useful and agreeable instruction, and your hands be employed in the pleasing task of not only serving yourself, but assisting your mamma, your brothers, and your sister. By such a conduct you will be more amiable, more happy, and all who know you will respect and love you. You will lose no satisfaction you at present possess, but have it infinitely heightened; you will lose many painful moments you must now feel, and many occasions of regret you cannot be insensible to. Will it be any addition to all these motives, that you will afford me the greatest satisfaction, whose desire of contributing to your happiness is extremely great, and who will ever promote it, whatever your situation or whatever your conduct may be, to the utmost of my power? Oh! my dear Nelly, attend to what I say to you. I

have been by degrees drawn to speak more affectingly on this subject than I had any expectations of when I began. And I believe I should not have wrote on the subject at all, if you had not lately intimated that you wished it from me. May you receive it kindly, and consider it with care! No time is to be lost. You are fast advancing into life, and the future fate of it will very much depend upon your present and almost your immediate conduct. Adieu! my dear Nelly. Nobody's heart beats with more warmth for your welfare than that of

Your truly affectionate uncle,
JAMES IREDELL.

Mr. Iredell was now at Currituck Court, where he made £160 inclusive of a fee raised by volunteers among the people, amounting to £100. It seems that a certain vessel and its cargo was in dispute. Mr. Iredell was employed to urge a claim in behalf of the State; he "really thought the State entitled;" and the "whole people were anxious for such an adjudication." Mr. Iredell's fees would have been more numerous, but he declined any new business."

IREDELL TO MRS. IREDELL.

CAMDEN, June 14th, 1779.

MY DEAR HANNAH:— * * * We came that evening to one Mr. Williams's about 10 miles from the court-house, who married a relation of Mr. Cumming's, that is really a very clever woman, after being hospitably entertained there, we dined the next day at Col. Lamb's* by invitation, in a very agreeable manner, and came in the evening to Gen. Gregory's,† where I still am. From all these, and from many more we have experienced every civility and the kindest endeavors to make our time pass away agreeably. It does in some measure, but I am constantly thinking of home, and wishing for the time that is to carry me there. I am still more impatient, because I don't expect to go home well loaded with money. Taverns are dreadfully expensive, and had it not been for some very unexpected business that arose, I should have

* Gideon Lamb of Currituck was a member of the Safety Committee for his District, 1775—of Prov. Congress, 1776, when he was appointed Major in 6th (Lillington's) Regt. He continued in service till the end of the war. He was promoted to be Colonel.—Vid. Wheeler, Niles' Register, v. 2, p. 292.
† Gen. Gregory, an active Whig, was appointed Colonel of 2d Regiment of Pasquotank, 1776, April 4th. He was also a member of the Convention that adopted the Constitution in 1776. He obtained the rank of General, I suppose, in 1779.

been badly off. Oh! what a curse is poverty! I feel mine still more severely because you must participate it with me. Could I charge myself with any criminal indolence, I should be doubly miserable, but I think I am only blameable for carelessness and profusion. They are, indeed, great faults, when they may occasion much unhappiness, but I know I am far less guilty now than I have been, and that I endeavor at all times to be as little so as possible. In this respect, I feel the ill consequence of being sent too young into life, under my own direction, without a kind friend who had authority to control me. Nevertheless, I must now remedy this disadvantage, and I am determined to use my utmost efforts. Reflections of this kind often distress me, but I must endeavor to bear them with fortitude, and act in the present situation of things the best part possible. I could be perfectly easy were I to suffer alone ; but I can't bear the thoughts of your suffering with me, and the knowledge of the generosity which will induce you to disregard it, makes the thought still more affecting. * * * * *

Pettigrew has been down here for near a fortnight, preaching to the people at many different places, and acquiring the character of an Apostle. The women admire him so much, that if he was not married, he might preach on the subject of *divine love* (with a glance at the *human*) to much more purpose than he did at Edenton, &c., &c., &c.

Most faithfully and affectionately yours,
JAS. IREDELL.

HOOPER TO IREDELL.

FINIAN, June 15th, 1779.

I know not, my dear Sir, whether this will find you in the state militant or civil, whether drawn up at Pasquotank County Court in single combat with the Currituck hero, or clothed with the rage of patriotic ardor, marching with the embattled squadrons of Chowan against the doughty Goodrich. Wheresoever it find you, All hail!

I have been very uneasy since I learnt that the landing of the British troops in Virginia had suggested the removal of the women and children from Edenton as a prudential precaution. It evinces the incapacity of the Virginians to make a stand against a very inferior force, and is an unfailing earnest of what may be expected from ourselves in the day of trial. How miserably have we been deceived in our own internal resources. Return to the continent the troops which the French have drawn from it

to the West Indies by their naval operations there, and our Independence would be of short duration. Fourteen hundred troops shaking the Dominion of Virginia to the centre,—they who boasted that they could singly maintain the contest with Great Britain; and that if the rest of the continent had not virtue and firmness to secure their freedom and independence, that they would conquer for them, and have the merit of becoming their benefactors.

I begin to think that the South Carolinians have more stuff in them than old Gen. Armstrong was willing to give them. They discover as yet no want of personal prowess ; like the animal spirits of a warm climate, I hope however that their heat may not exhaust their strength, and leave victory to be gathered by those who fit exertions to occasions and husband themselves for a distant day.*

I am convinced that the force which now opposes them might spread terror in Virginia, and deal out law from the very *capitol* of that *Dominion*. The petty Captain of a tender has exercised his private resentment to the prejudice of the subjects of that State, and has proved how little desirable that Government is which suffers itself to be insulted with perfect impunity by banditti.†

I am by no means apprehensive for the independence of America. The present conduct of Great Britain proves its despair ; these burnings and ravages are the convulsive agonies of expiring power; and as, in the natural body, they are more violent and continued in proportion to the former strength of the corporeal system, so we have reason to expect that the most important Kingdom upon earth will not be dismembered without giving a most violent shock to the limb which is to be severed from it ;

---

* Intimidated by the bold face presented by the American army, Gen. Prevost had retired from the lines before Charleston, May the 11th. At Stono, 20th June, the N. C. Continentals constituted the centre of Lincoln's front. Col. Davie, at the head of about 100 N. C. Cavalry, was wounded.

† Jefferson was elected Governor of Virginia, June 1st : he subsequently resigned, confessing his incapacity, and stating that the times required a man of military turn and countenance.

When Mr. Hooper * first addressed the Continental Congress, he was listened to in silence and with great attention. Such was the excellence of his speech, that some affected an impertinent astonishment at the display of such oratory by a North Carolinian. Was Jefferson jealous of Hooper? Was he impatient of what he did not himself possess—splendid elocution, as he was notoriously envious of military fame? Was there a feud between these two eminent men? An affirmative answer to these interrogatories will certainly throw much light upon the calumny of Jefferson, that "there was no greater Tory in Congress than Hooper," and explain Mr. Hooper's personal dislike to Jefferson and his followers, in the early days of the Republic. If Hooper's fame, so well defended by Jones, needed further vindication, his letters to Iredell place upon impregnable ground his virtue and patriotism.

* A. M. Hooper.—Wheeler.

---

leaving it in such a state of weakness, as will require a series of time to renovate and relieve the want of vigor it occasions. To hand us over to France in a situation that may make us a boon not worthy their acceptance ! Strange infatuation ! Is not this to alienate us for ever from any connection with themselves and wantonly to give away, what alone remained within their reach, a common share in our trade with the rest of mankind—but I drop the painful subject—it is painful to observe the dissolution of our friends, but inexpressibly so to find them surviving their reputation.

I hope Mrs. Iredell and your worthy sister, Miss Nelly, and the rest of the family, are perfectly relieved from any apprehensions of the approach of the Virginia Bloody-bones, Goodrich. You remember what you and Mr. Johnston have always said when I expressed my fears for Wilmington,—Cui bono ? What could the enemy get by it ? To rob the pine trees, and bear away the sandhills ? How ill we apply sayings when they show our own weak side and fit ourselves—but I forgive you, local prejudices are unaccountably strong, and I have heard of a man in New England, who in his prayers always thanked Heaven that he lived on Cape Cod (the desert of God's deserted work).

I must beg leave to refer you to a Mr. Henderson of your place, lately from South Carolina, and to a scrawl which accompanies this to Mr. Johnston for matters in that quarter, and must occupy the rest of my paper in soliciting you to present Mrs. Hooper's and my best respects to Mrs. Iredell, Mrs. Blair, Miss Nelly and Miss Peggy, and believe me ever,

Dear Iredell,
Yours faithfully,
WM. HOOPER.

IREDELL TO MISS BLAIR.

EDENTON, July 4th, 1779.

MY DEAR NELLY :—I should have received your letter with infinite pleasure, if I had not received it at a time when I was incapable of all pleasure. The poor little boy's life then hung suspended on a thread, and a short time after he expired. Never have I been witness to a more affecting or more unhappy instance of human mortality. So suddenly brought about ! So dreadful, so shocking in itself ! Your uncle and aunt are indeed deeply to be felt for. The loss of so lovely a child is one of the most calamitous that can be sustained. In vain may Fortitude and Philosophy exert themselves. The recollection of a thousand pleasing

actions (now never to be seen again) will imprint the bitterest sorrow and give rise to the most sensible grief. To dwell on the lovely object,—to talk of him,—to lament his loss,—now and then perhaps to intermix a thought about his own felicity,—these are the only alleviations they can be for a long time sensible of. And how dreadful must be that misfortune which can only admit of ease by preying on itself and continually recalling it to mind !

O! my dear Nelly, when life is so precarious, when we have scarcely a moment's security for any of our friends' stay with us, how much should we cherish the connection while it actually subsists, and endeavor by mutual good offices to make ourselves as useful and amiable as possible, by that means affording our condition all the advantages of which it is capable. The desire too of being remembered, when we are gone, by those we leave behind, with affection and esteem, ought surely with every generous mind to be a powerful inducement to such a tenor of conduct as is likely to insure it. Nothing can be more animating for such a purpose than a beautiful motto in Mrs. Dawson's Graveyard, with which I was very much pleased. " *Vivit post funera ille, quem Virtus non Marmor in œternum sacrat.*"

In English : " He lives after death, whom *virtue* not *marble* consecrates to eternal fame."

Your receiving so kindly admonitions friendly, but severe, gives me a most sincere satisfaction. It is more than I expected or hoped ; but feeling for you the most tender affection, and having extreme anxiety for your future welfare, I was prompted to express to you the strong feelings of a heart deeply apprehensive for it. Happy I indeed am, that you not only pardon my freedom, but are pleased with it, and assure me of its having had some good effects. Let me beg you, my dear Nelly, by every thing dear and sacred, to persevere in this charming disposition, by which you will not only secure your own felicity (as much at least as the general imperfection of human nature will admit of), but contribute greatly towards that of your friends : Of mine, I assure you, you will most essentially. And I promise you, after a short experience, you will look back with wonder and regret on the time you have imprudently dissipated and neglected. I am persuaded you must pass your time very agreeably with your cousin.* The near relation you bear to each other, and your equality of age, seem naturally to suggest it. You, I am sure, would be greatly benefited by it. The amiable gentleness of your cousin's disposition would tend to soften the ruggedness of yours (forgive the roughness of the expression), and perhaps she

---

* Miss Penelope Dawson, afterwards Mrs. Louther.

might be improved by losing a little of that softness which, though extremely amiable, is in her rather possessed in excess. May you both long live amiable, respected, and happy! beloved by your friends and each other, esteemed and admired by all! I have never doubted this happy consequence as to your cousin, and be assured, my dear Nelly, I am extremely happy in saying, that I can now entertain sanguine hopes for you. God grant you may not suffer me to be disappointed.

I cannot always write you sheets, and as I am going to Tyrrel to-morrow, and the unhappy funeral is to-day, I have no time to add more than to desire you will mention me in a very affectionate manner to Mrs. Dawson and your cousin, and present my compliments to Miss Gracey, believing me ever, and at present on account of your encouraging letter with additional satisfaction,
My dear Nelly,
Your most affectionate Uncle,
JAMES IREDELL.

On July 8th, Governor Caswell, by the advice and consent of his Council appointed Mr. Iredell Attorney-General; and, subsequently, November 20th, the appointment was confirmed by his election by the Assembly.

In a letter to Miss Blair, July 9th, Mr. Iredell remarks,—"Things of more consequence seem to hang in awful suspense. The operations of war are rather menacing than active, and the prospect of peace more gloomy than could be wished for, though it is not altogether out of sight. I do not despair, however, of one day seeing it, and upon terms honorable and satisfactory."

HOOPER TO IREDELL.

FINIAN, August 15th, 1779.

MY DEAR SIR:—Your kind favor announcing your intention to succeed to the honors and emoluments of the late Attorney-General, afforded me an unexpected pleasure. When at the last Assembly, I heard of Avery's resignation, I confess I thought there was a possibility of your being prevailed on to accept the appointment. I hinted my wishes to Mr. Johnston, who doubted as to the prudence of your accepting an employment when the pay depended upon the suffrages of a capricious Assembly, who exhibit upon every occasion such signal proofs of ingratitude to public merit. Since I came home, at the Wilmington Superior Court I proposed to Judge Ashe to mention you to Governor Caswell in case Mr. McGuyre declined. He doubted about it, not that he did not earnestly wish the event, but because he despaired of your encumbering yourself with an office, the duties of which were burdensome, and which would draw you from home half the year. These doubts are surmounted, and I have the happiness to assure you that the leading characters in this part of the country speak of you as a capital acquisition to our Courts, and exult that there is now a prospect of offenders being brought to due punishment, without the passions of party or the prejudices or passions of individuals swaying the prosecution. S. Ashe seems perfectly unaffected in his satisfaction, and I, my dear friend, if I have directly or indirectly influenced your determination, have much cause of triumph. I shall have one at least that I can humanize with, for I am an extravagant dog that asks more than one rational companion at a back country Court. But now for the *ardua officii*. S. Ashe says that the presence of an Attorney General will be absolutely necessary at Salisbury; and that many prosecutions hang suspended. I earnestly wish to meet you there, for I am under engagements that irresistibly draw me thither. The season will be pleasant, and it will I think operate so much to your advantage at a future Assembly, when it may be necessary to hold a candle to the great men of the West to show them the way to their Pure Springs—that I beg leave to hope it. Mrs. Iredell must forgive me; it is the last time I will thus trespass. It will probably save you from a severe drubbing from a detestable fever, the necessary and natural production of your execrable air at this season. Yes, my dear sir, sincerely do I sympathize in the afflictions of our worthy friend. If the undeserved misfortunes of this life are not to be compensated in another world, we have been created for a cruel purpose. If the thunders of heaven were always levelled at the rascally part of creation, I fancy we should have much less repining at the ways of Providence, and of course much less sin. But this is speculating in the dark. I adore in humble gratitude the dispensations of the God that made me, and whilst in a state of perfect composure from pain, when neither I nor my friends feel the lash of human woe, I can philosophize with as much pious firmness as ever animated St. Austin or any of the holy fraternity, and cry out, that all is for the best, and that whatever is is right. But bring it to myself. Let a brother leave his house early in the morning—his wife in bed, a sweet infant smiling at her breast with all the glow of health and innocence,—let him be alarmed in a few minutes with 'The child is dead—overlaid by his mother' —God! who can paint the agony when she awoke? She remembers the last kiss she gave it, the sweets of it still dwell upon her lips. She hugs a lifeless corse. This is the faithful recital of what lately happened in George Hooper's family. And how little does the calamity of our friend Johnston fall short of this? It was a heavenly babe. It had the whole force of parental affection poured upon it. Strength, health and beauty seemed to have been bestowed upon it in the greatest degree, that its death might be the less expected, and the disappointment the more pungent. These are the trying ordeals of human philosophy—here the pincer tears and blood must follow. For my own part I am a man, and feel like one. I despise the cant of divines, and the pride and hypocrisy of the schools. There is a luxury in woe, and I ever suspected a man's heart that was above indulging it. Would to heaven that I could minister to the consolation of my friend and his family, but the effort would be vain. He has all the philosophy that a good man ought to have, and as far as that ought to avail him he will draw it forth. He has all the religion that a wise man ought to have, and will lean upon it as far as it ought to support him. He has a large portion of human feeling, and happily for us, sorrow grows languid by exercise—time and change of objects are the only effectual cure. I shall write Mr. Johnston shortly—in the mean time remember me in the most affectionate manner to him, Mrs. Johnston, Miss Cathcart, and the remainder of his dear little family. I have scarce left room to assure your good family how gratefully and respectfully I hold them in remembrance. Pray offer my kind regards to Mrs. Blair, Mrs. Iredell and Miss Nelly—they must forgive me when I earnestly regret that the residence of so many amiable and worthy people has been pitched in so unhealthy a country. May you and they be sheltered from its effects, and be happy. Adieu!
Yours truly, WM. HOOPER.

NOTE.—Mrs. Hooper asks why she is forgot in her proper place. No one, she says, wishes more earnestly to be thought kindly of by you and your family, and hopes to be mentioned to them with regard. She flatters herself with another hop at the next Court with the new Attorney-General.

IREDELL TO MISS BLAIR.

EDENTON, August 29th, 1779.

MY DEAR NELLY:—Having been so long accustomed to my correspondence, I suppose you claim the continuance of it as a matter of right, and that whether I have any thing or nothing to say, I should with equal eagerness embrace all occasions of writing to you. You have indeed some reason for this, for as I feel great affection and anxiety about you, my own pleasure solicits this indulgence of secondary conversation, in absence of the principal, and I do it now with great additional satisfaction, as I form the most charming hopes of you. Suffer me to say, my dear Nelly, that you are really in general much altered for the better, that your Aunt perceives it, your Mamma acknowledges it, and we all, I was going to say, glory in it. It is however the source of many a heartfelt joy. God grant you may not check, but greatly cherish these delightful feelings. Your present situation is of great advantage to you. Not only health, but an additional strength of mind, I hope, will be the consequence of it. You now, I flatter myself, begin to perceive, that there are purer pleasures than those attending flutter and dissipation, and that in order to pass through life with ease, it is necessary to consult rather the general tenor of its satisfaction, than the loose and fluctuating enjoyment of one moment out of twenty. I have not time to add much. Your Mamma, I suppose, will write you all the news. Your Cousin Penny, as well as all Mrs. Dawson's family, except Billy, has been very sick, but is now a great deal better. Your Aunt Iredell desires to be most affectionately remembered to you, and I am, my dear Nelly, very truly,
Your affectionate Uncle,
JAS. IREDELL.

The first Academy established by legislative authority was that of New Berne, in 1767.* Martin says in his history, that there were but two Academies or schools, those of New Berne and Edenton, at the Declaration of Independence. I think this, clearly, a mistake. The legal maxim, "*de non apparentibus et non existentibus eadem est lex,*" is a very wise rule in determining facts in causes litigated in Courts; but not always a safe guide in other investigations, as one's ignorance may be the measure of truth. At a very early period, it is traditionally known that the Clergymen resident in the State eked out their small salaries by the emoluments arising from teaching schools. If Martin be correct, then, during the progress of the war schools multiplied—a singular fruit of troublous times.† There was a boarding-school in Granville in '78, where two of Mr. Iredell's nephews, the young Blairs, were matriculated. This school was discontinued in the autumn of 1779. January 1st, 1780, Mr. Springer established a school in Warren (old Bute), for 30 boys; the terms were £100

---

* Caruthers. † Letters from Mrs. Blair and Iredell.

a year, Virginia money, for tuition, £200 a year for board, and £14 6s. 0d. paid "towards the schoolhouse, firewood, &c." Boys from Edenton attended this school, not because there was none nearer home, but because it was in a healthy region. At this very time Parson Earl taught a private school in Edenton.

In a letter to Mrs. Iredell, dated Granville, September 9th, Mr. Iredell says: "Never scarcely in England have I seen more beautiful prospects than some I have passed through to-day."

Mr. Iredell was at Halifax, September 7th, on his way to attend Salisbury Court. In a letter to his wife, he writes, "the famous Mr. Somerville has ended his wandering at last, and is joined in the tender bands with Miss ——, I forget the name— W. Martin's niece, the girl I told you of. He brought her to town a few days ago. They stay at present at her Uncle's, but he has engaged for three years, Dr. Pasteur's house, where Mr. Nash used to live. They went out of town yesterday to see her grandmother, so that I missed the satisfaction of seeing him, which I greatly regretted, as we had a good deal of laugh together about his courtship."

Mr. Iredell was at Salisbury, September 20th. The criminal docket was unusually large, and he was greatly harassed with the State business, while the unexplained absence of his friend Hooper was to him a sad disappointment. "He was hurried to death." "Upwards of eighty persons were indicted, and mostly for capital crimes—the greatest number for high treason " (Toryism). "Notwithstanding the utmost diligence, no more than ten could be tried, every one of whom was convicted and condemned. Four the jury recommended to mercy," and several were young men "who possibly were artfully seduced."* Mr. Iredell was much gratified with the general opinion entertained of his conduct; and the many tokens of kindness he received from the citizens: he was retained in four or five civil suits, for which he received "only £206;" and felt himself constrained to refuse a very large fee, in a land case, as the State seemed *indirectly* concerned against the title. A modern officer, in such a dilemma, would not long be puzzled in discovering an expedient by which at the same time the pocket might be filled, and scruples of conscience quieted. At the close of the Court he had in ready money, inclusive of his salary, £456. He was disappointed in his official fees, for he had supposed that they had been raised; but ascertained, to his mortification, that no fees had been augmented, but those of the Attorneys in the county Courts. The reason for the distinction, assigned by Hooper, was "that they expected

* Letter to Mrs. Iredell.

that the office (Attorney-General) would be held by some booby." Mr. Iredell attended Hillsborough Court, October 1st, where he "was detained till the very last moment of the Court by the silly harangues of pettifogging practisers, rather than any degree of weighty business." From Hillsborough, he went to Halifax, where he arrived on the 15th October. Nobody attending, two days of the Court were lost. In a letter of the 17th, he says, referring to the family of Mr. Frohock, "the beginning of next month the grand removal is to take place, and the new quarters taken up at Hamilton's store."* "Miss Betsey Montfort was initiated into the rites of marriage, on the 7th, with the young gentleman she has been so long pining for." "I am extremely obliged to Mr. Allen for the paper, and beg you to return him my hearty thanks. I scarcely could have got a more valuable treasure, and the stock I brought with me is almost wholly exhausted. This was really kind in Nat., and I shall not forget it." While the Court was in session, the Assembly met on the 18th of October. A law promptly passed the latter body for sending aid to South Carolina and Georgia;† they also passed an act for punishing counterfeiting, which, it appears, had become common in the State.‡ Mr. Iredell was so engaged in business, that not a moment of his time was misemployed. One trial, of an interesting nature, lasted from 11 A. M. to 9 at night. A Colonel Walker from Virginia was arraigned for passing counterfeit money. "Public expectation was extremely raised, and he was with great difficulty acquitted." Though the circuit was only one half over, Mr. Iredell had received £700; less however, he says, than he expected.

NASH TO IREDELL.

HALIFAX, 26th Oct., 1779.

SIR:—I had the honor to receive yours of this date, and immediately communicated its contents to the House of Senators. And, Sir, it gives me very great pleasure to acquaint you that our House repeated on the occasion the entire confidence they had in your abilities and attachment, and that they think themselves happy in having the important office of Attorney-General

* Hamilton was with Prevost at Savannah. The assault upon the British lines, October 9th, was made by 4,500 men, of whom 3,500 were French; the remainder consisted of 600 Regulars (*chiefly North Carolina Continentals*), and Charleston Militia. Though ultimately beaten, the attack was made with much gallantry, the ditch leaped, and the standards of Carolina, for a time, floated above the parapet of the Spring Hill Redoubt. Lossing.
† Statutes.   ‡ Letter from Iredell.

filled by a gentleman of known and experienced ability.—I have the honor to be, with the highest respect, Sir, your most obedient servant,
A. NASH, S.S.

IREDELL TO MRS. IREDELL.

WILMINGTON, 8th Dec., 1779.

DEAR HANNAH:—I am still here, and as at most of the other courts, constantly teazed with vexatious prosecutions, most of which are personal and malicious. More business, much more, has happened than I expected, and we shall not close the court till the last moment of it, leaving then nearly every thing of a civil nature undone. * * * I am not without a little more than official business. Mr. and Mrs. Hooper's kindness grows upon me every hour, and I have experienced great civilities from many others. * * * Poor Mr. Hewes! * I have heard an account, I am afraid is too true, of his death. What wretched mortals we are, and what a world is this? The loss of such a man will long be severely felt, and his friends must ever remember him with the keenest and most distressing sensibility. Mr. Hooper and I have most painfully sympathized on it, and it has given us a shock we have not yet recovered. If this unhappy event should be true, I will be obliged to you if you will deliver his will, or if you are not in town, get your sister to do it, to your brother, or Mr. Smith or Mr. Allen. It is in my tin box. Good God! how little did I think I should so soon have occasion for it. * * Most affectionately and most anxiously yours,
JAS. IREDELL.

HOOPER TO IREDELL.†

MY DEAR SIR:—I have waited for more than a fortnight with extreme solicitude for an opportunity to answer your most obliging letter from Newbern. But no opportunity by a private hand has yet presented itself, and I am apprehensive that the post-riders, either from the extreme cold or the miserable support which the Congress afford them, have declined the office. When

* Mr. Hewes died Nov. 10th, in the 50th year of his age, at Philadelphia. His funeral was attended by Congress, the Assembly, and other authorities of Pennsylvania, the Minister of France, and a great assemblage of citizens. Congress resolved to wear mourning, crape on the left arm, for one month.
† The letter is without date.

I have finished this scrawl I will deposit it with some friend, and leave its further progress towards you to the chapter of accidents.

The strong sensibility which you express for the small attentions which my family had it in their power to show you while you were in this part of the country, gives us occasion to lament that they were not proportionate to your merit and our wishes. We have reflected with much concern since you left us, that you were exposed to the necessity of being at lodgings while at Wilmington, when, had we perfected the resolution which we had begun, we should have been inhabitants of the town, and had the happiness of having you altogether to ourselves. We, I say; for believe me you are the eternal subject of conversation with my wife and little ones, and the *dixit* of Mr. Iredell is a knock-down argument against any thing that I may happen to dissent from them in. Our pain at parting was reciprocal. Mrs. H. and myself moved on in solemn silence homewards, with a strange mixture of sorrow and congratulation—at once desirous to restore you to your amiable family, and lamenting that they could not be happy but at ours. The warmth of gratitude with which you are animated reminds me of an anecdote at John Cook's table; who, having set down McGuire and myself and others to a piece of roast beef, very devoutly cried out, "thank God for this"—to which McGuire replied, "Methinks you are very thankful for small matters." Would to God that souls that were made for each other, to give and to receive happiness, had not been made so much the sport of fortune as to be cast where they live to each other only upon paper, denied that fervor of sympathy which flows from personal intercourse and a communion of endearing offices.

I must again strike upon the melancholy string. It is eternally uppermost with me, and notwithstanding the wonted sprightliness of my disposition, the death of Hewes still preys upon my feelings. Little disposed heretofore to take the gloomy side of the picture, my imagination recoils from every thing that might tend to allay my present distress, and in spite of all my philosophy I am effeminately afflicted. He was my very intimate friend. I knew and had probed the secret recesses of his soul, and found it devoid of guilt and replete with benignity. I loved him, and I believe that I was very dear to him—but a long series of sickness had prepared his mind for the fatal stroke, and his body shattered with repeated violence could not, I was well assured, long brave his periodical complaints; the news of his dangerous antecedent illness was to me a harbinger of the worst. I anticipated it, and yet when the shock came I was unprepared for it. Happy apathy! How much to be envied are those who view the changes of human life as necessarily growing out of the eternal system of things, not to be lamented, because not——*

APPENDIX TO CHAPTER XII.

To the Honorable the General Assembly of the State of North Carolina.

The Memorial *of* James Iredell, *one of the subjects of the said State, on behalf of* Henry Eustace McCulloh, *Esquire, at present an absentee out of the same,*

Humbly showeth:—That Henry McCulloh, Esquire, father of the said Henry Eustace McCulloh, did many years past purchase and settle, at a very great expense, a large tract of land in the back parts of this State, to the extreme impoverishment and distress of his private fortune, and with the distant and precarious hope of its proving advantageous to his posterity, by means at the same time highly conducive to the well-being and prosperity of this country.

That the said Henry McCulloh did at various times, with great trouble and cost, procure numerous settlers to establish themselves on different parts of his said land; and your memorialist believes he effected this, not only without distressing, but greatly to the advantage of individuals, the posterity of many of whom feel the good effects of his care and attention at this very day.

That the said Henry McCulloh residing principally in England, his son Henry Eustace McCulloh came out to this country some time about the year 1761, and continued to reside constantly in it until the year 1767, during which time he was chiefly occupied, as agent for his father, in parcelling out the said lands, so as to afford convenient settlements for purchasers or lessees, many of whom by that means obtained comfortable possessions, and your memorialist has been informed, greatly to the improvement of that part of the country, and without any just ground for complaint of extortionate or unreasonable terms being imposed on them.

That the said Henry Eustace McCulloh having, during the course of so long a residence and so continued an attention to that business, settled the concerns of his lands upon a regular and satisfactory footing, went to England, partly to have the happiness of seeing his only surviving parent, and other near connexions in that country, and partly to solicit at the British Court some indulgencies concerning quitrents, to which he conceived his father was reasonably entitled, after the great care and pains that had been bestowed by him in the cultivation and improvement of so great an extent of country, which, though ultimately indeed calculated for his family's advantage, had been temporarily very distressing to himself, at

* The remainder of the letter is lost.

the same time that in its consequences it was highly beneficial to the public of the then Province of North Carolina.

That before the said Henry Eustace McCulloh left this country, he appointed proper agents to transact his business here, and during the whole time of his stay in England, was constantly attentive to their management of it; and your memorialist has reason to believe, not only attentive to his own immediate interest, but solicitous to take every step that might be conceived just and equitable, to make the individuals they had concern with as easy and contented as possible.

That in the month of October, 1772, the said Henry Eustace McCulloh returned from England (having before that time received a conveyance from his father of all his property here), and continued in this country many months, assiduously careful to effect the same purposes of promoting his own interest only by methods that made it perfectly consistent with the welfare and satisfaction of that part of the country where his estate lay, and enjoying the delightful prospect of seeing the increase of his private fortune, and the great public benefit derived from the improvement of a most valuable part of the country, going hand in hand together.

That during a considerable part of the above period, and for some time after, the said Henry Eustace McCulloh had the honor to act as agent for this country at the several Boards in England, which business his father attended to during his necessary absence here; and when he again went to England (which was in June, 1773), he was charged with public affairs of much consequence to solicit in his capacity of agent as aforesaid.

That at the time when the said Henry Eustace McCulloh thus took his departure for England, no great public dissension subsisted between Great Britain and America, the fury of British passion having long since subsided, and the principal ground of difference remaining, viz., the Tea Act, appearing to sleep under the unwillingness of both sides, as was then fondly hoped, to renew a contest likely to be productive of such calamitous consequences.

That the father of the said Henry Eustace McCulloh was then in a very advanced age, afflicted with many infirmities, and had had the misfortune to lose all the rest of his family, which made him extremely anxious to enjoy the comfort and satisfaction of his son's company, during the remainder of a life that in the course of nature promised to be very short, and which in so remarkable a manner had been devoted to procure the advancement and prosperity of his children, at the expense of his own.

That in January, 1774, the destruction of the tea at Boston furnished a pretence for the vindictive acts that followed, and which were of such a nature, as to make the great and dignified opposition which actuated all America indispensably necessary, and which every friend to both countries earnestly flattered himself would be attended with the desired success, when it was seen the good sense of America was not to be imposed upon by any *finesse*, nor its spirit and union to be awed by any desperate or partial measure of resentment.

That from this period until the fatal commencement of hostilities, and even until very near the time when a necessity which every well-wisher to his country deplored, urged an immediate and total separation between Great Britain and America, it was scarcely supposable that the mad career of conquest over a free country, by those whom Heaven had appointed as

its guardians, could possibly be suffered to proceed, when the union of America in its opposition was so powerful and strong, its resources so great, its spirit so determined, and when the nature of the country was such, that a conquest obtained over one part of it must be abandoned as soon as acquired, or its enemies remain satisfied with little nests for garrisons, leaving the open country in possession of those to whom fortune and their own industry had given it.

That in this situation, American gentlemen who happened to be at that time in England, might very reasonably and justly hope for a relinquishment of claims, which not only were highly unconstitutional and unjust, but thus promised not to be attended with even the shadow of success, without which the pursuit of the most favorite measures must be idle and ridiculous.

That the abovesaid Henry Eustace McCulloh did, however, from the very beginning of these disturbances, in the course of a long and frequent correspondence between him and your memorialist, which subsisted till an intercourse of private letters between the two countries was totally prohibited, express himself in terms highly friendly and affectionate to America, and repeatedly assured him, that nothing but the duty he owed his father detained him in England, and that whenever he should be unhappy enough to lose him, it was his fixed and determined purpose to come and settle in this country.

That for some time before, and constantly after the Declaration of Independence, the difficulty of coming from Great Britain to America, with an intention of residence, was very great; since, if coming either in British or foreign vessels, persons were liable to be taken and confined as prisoners by one party or the other; and prisoners taken by the British in particular, had been at times so cruelly treated, as well to deter a man in any but the most desperate case from exposing himself to the danger of so unhappy a calamity.

That these difficulties appeared to subsist in their full force until the memorable acts of the British Parliament at their last session, and which must amount, in the judgment of every reasonable man, to a full confession that their haughty claims were, even in their own opinion, absolutely insupportable, and that if they could not succeed in one more attack on the virtue and honor of this country, they must at length, with a good or a bad grace, recognize the dignity of its opposition, and grant such terms as in its present situation are only admissible.

That in this advanced period of the contest, when the weakness of Great Britain was acknowledged, and peace with all its blessings (it must have appeared) would in a short time most probably solely depend on the wisdom and moderation of the American counsels, there was no reason to suppose the enemy would have any desire to distress private gentlemen, by preventing their going to their estates; and therefore, in the month of August or September last, a great number of American gentlemen, among whom was the abovesaid Henry Eustace McCulloh, arrived in the packet from England at New York.

That since the arrival of the said Henry Eustace McCulloh at New York, your memorialist has received two letters from him, one of a more general kind, that your memorialist begs leave to submit to the inspection of your honorable body, at the same time with this memorial, and by which there seems reason to fear, he has met with unexpected detention;

the other concerning private business of much consequence, which he is also ready to produce, if it be desired, and the purport of which requiring papers of near concern to some relations in England, made it of extreme importance to Mr. McCulloh to receive them, if possible, before he left New York.

Your memorialist has thus taken the liberty, with a zeal and friendship which he believes the occasion justifies, and which he is persuaded the gentleman who is the subject of his application deserves, on a public as well as a private account, to lay his case before the Legislature of this country, for whom he is assured that gentleman, as well as himself, entertains the highest sense of duty and respect. Upon their mercy and justice he desires to throw himself, fully confident that the same dignity of sentiment, and pure attachment to liberty, which have hitherto carried them triumphantly through a most just and glorious opposition to measures of tyranny and oppression, will actuate them in their own conduct to persons within their power, and not suffer them to inflict punishment, where there has been no crime. The only crime that gentleman can be charged with, in your memorialist's opinion, is an innocent and unoffending absence from a country, which he left in a state of profound peace, to reside for some time in another, then in the closest connexion with it, and where circumstances even of public duty, as well as of the most tender concern, anxiously, and almost unavoidably called him; which, however, he has left, in spite of every endearing obstacle, as soon as it was in the least probable he could safely get here.

Your memorialist humbly begs leave to observe, that as the absentee law seems to have for its principle, the forfeiture of property which the owners criminally either refuse or neglect to bear their share in protecting (the justice of which your memorialist is far from wishing to deny), the spirit of that law cannot, in his apprehension, justly affect the case of a man who has been reluctantly absent from it, who has done every thing in his power to avail himself of the time allowed, and who is perhaps at this very moment arbitrarily, though unexpectedly, detained from hastening to become, as he wishes to be, a faithful and zealous subject of the State.

Your memorialist, therefore, with all the humility which becomes him, but at the same time with all the zeal and earnestness which can affect him, not only upon the motives of private friendship, but the higher and more important ones of public duty (which he never will, for any considerations, sacrifice to the former), submits to the deliberation of the Honorable the General Assembly of this State the case of the said Henry Eustace McCulloh, Esquire, and prays that they will be pleased to prolong the time for his personal appearance before them, and apply such further remedy to the difficulties he labors under as to their wisdom shall seem meet.

CHAPTER XIII.

LETTERS FROM IREDELL; ASSEMBLY; THE CIRCUIT; LETTERS FROM IREDELL; SOUTH CAROLINA SUBDUED; CONDITION OF NORTH CAROLINA; LETTERS FROM IREDELL; ROCKY MOUNT; HANGING ROCK; BATTLE OF CAMDEN; ASSEMBLY; LETTERS FROM IREDELL; SECOND BRITISH INVASION; BATTLE OF KING'S MOUNTAIN; CORNWALLIS RETREATS; LETTERS FROM IREDELL; ARRIVAL OF GREENE; ARMY; ADMIRALTY SUIT; LETTER FROM JOHNSTON, DELEGATE TO CONTINENTAL CONGRESS. ÆT. 28–29.

Abner Nash, elected at the last Session of the Assembly, succeeded Caswell as Governor, in December, 1779.

IREDELL TO MRS. IREDELL.

ELK MARSH, 13th April.

MY DEAR HANNAH:—Mr. Hooper is very well, and his company a great relief to me, otherwise my time at present would pass very disagreeably here; for that spunging creature Lathberry is shut up in the house with us, and so insolent with his tory conversation and sly slanders, that we have been obliged to handle him a little roughly, and should have done it much more if it had been in a different house. However, he seems a little sick of it, and much more humble for the reproof he has received. * * * Frohock is still severely confined, but in a fairer way of recovery than for a long time past * * Till within a few days, when a new Doctor from Halifax (one Dr. Love) came to attend him, his chance seemed very unpromising. * * * Your Brother, as I told you, got very little money at Hillsborough: Mr. Hooper, I believe, none but what was due him before; I only my salary. Strudwick has engaged me in his suits, upon a promise to pay me the value of £100, as money was at its best. This was what I asked upon consulting your Brother, who told me it ought to be £100 sterling, but he knew my modesty would not suffer me to ask it. I expect to receive between £500 and £1000 of this at Wilmington, which I think is a pretty good fee. Travelling has not been so expensive as I expected. * * Your Brother, in addition to his numberless acts of goodness, has conferred on me one which I value almost as much as any of the rest. He has had the kindness to give me advice, which I much wanted. He took occasion, in the most gentle and friendly manner, to speak to me about my intemperate manner of speaking, which, (if I did not get the better of it) he said, he feared would be a great prejudice to me. The confusion he was in, and the pain I am sure he felt, showed in the strongest light the extreme goodness of his heart, and his very flattering regard for me. I assure you, I am not only grateful for it, but proud of it. The few words he spoke have made the deepest impression on me. They are ever present to me. They frequently check rising passionate expressions, and if any escape me, I instantly reproach myself. I hope I shall be the better for them as long as I live, well knowing the happy advantage of having such a friend. How valuable are all his instructions, and how much I am concerned in observing them. I am well satisfied that it is in every body's power greatly to improve themselves, and that constant care, as it is requisite, so in all probability it will be successful. I view him, I view Mr. Hooper; I would wish to be like them. It would be my honor and happiness to be so, but that is impossible even in a very distant degree without extreme care and unremitting attention. * * The fate of Charleston is very doubtful, though it is extremely strong. Some intelligent people think the enemy have little chance but by water, and that there their operations will be extremely difficult. One passage to the country only is open to the town, by a ferry at a place called Haddrell's Point, on Cooper river, at the mouth of which several ships are sunk to obstruct the enemy. The town however are in the highest spirits, and even Ladies insist on staying to abide the fate of their husbands and relations. John Hamilton was lately taken a prisoner in a small party. I saw a letter from himself mentioning it. Give my love, &c., &c.

Your ever faithfully affectionate,
JAMES IREDELL.

On the 16th April Mr. Iredell and Mr. Hooper, after a short visit to Booth, one of Mr. Johnston's country seats, arrived at Halifax. The Assembly met at New Berne on the 17th: after levying a public tax, they provided for the emission of £240,000 in bills of credit.* There being great difficulty in obtaining salt and other commodities of foreign production, a Board of Commission-

* Statutes. Hubbard.

ers was established for carrying on trade for the benefit of the State: Ex-Governor Caswell, Benjamin Hawkins, and Robert Bignal, a merchant of Edenton, were appointed Commissioners, with authority to export and import. But little good was effected by this extraordinary expedient, and operations were soon discontinued. Acts were passed to check the circulation of counterfeit money; to protect Quakers, Moravians, Menonists, and Dunkards, against persons who had taken possession of their lands under the pretence that they had not "taken an affirmation to the State;" to prevent all armed or other vessels leaving the ports of the State; authorizing the Governor, with the advice of the Council, to send 8000 men to the relief of South Carolina; and providing for filling up the ranks of the Continental Battalions.*

In consequence of great freshets, Judge Williams, and the Attorney General, to reach New Berne from Edenton, were compelled to make a circuit by way of Halifax. Finding the way by Edwards's impracticable, in consequence of a "gut" surcharged with water, Iredell and Williams, leaving Judge Spencer behind "growling very ill-naturedly, and determined to get across *if he flew over it,*" went higher up, and crossed the swollen Roanoke at the town of Halifax.

IREDELL TO MRS. IREDELL.

NEWBERN, 18th May, 1780.

MY DEAR HANNAH:—At length, after an infinite deal of difficulty and trouble, we have arrived in Newbern. I wrote you from Halifax of the disagreeable Circuit we were obliged to make in consequence of a very high fresh, which made the road almost impassable. We staid only to dine in it, and proceeded on, little apprehensive of the further difficulties we had to encounter, and thinking only of the extraordinary distance. But this was nothing compared to other things. Besides Tar and Neuse Rivers, which were very high, and very difficult, we had to pass a great many deep water-courses, some where bridges were torn up, milldams broke, or the water from its natural depth at this remarkable season entirely unfordable. Notwithstanding all these things, we had, however, the good luck to avoid always swimming ourselves, though our horses were obliged to do it three or four times. Planks or canoes were fortunately at hand for us. The weather was excessively bad, and we got very wet several times. It has had however no ill-effect on Mr. Hooper or myself, who are quite well, but Mr. Williams has a most severe inflammation in his eyes, and pain in his head, and fever, which has confined him ever since he came to town. It was not in our power, with our utmost diligence, to get here sooner than last night, which completed the seventh since we left Edenton. We consoled ourselves very much with finding Mr. Spencer behind, for though he got over that Gut (at a higher part of it) I wrote to you about, yet he did not arrive here till this morning, having been carousing with perfect content for two or three days at Jacob Blount's, which we know was the only object that made him in a fever to leave us. I staid one night on the road with Dr. Ferguson. Mr. Hooper and Williams staid with Capt. Toole at about a quarter of a mile's distance. The Doctor received me very kindly, and his wife was extremely hospitable and obliging. She is one of the fattest women I ever saw, but has a likely face, and an agreeable manner. His son is a fine stout fellow. There is nothing to complain of but the house, only two small rooms under a very mean roof, but this is owing to the dwelling-house being some years ago burnt, and the present difficulty of building. The great toast, Mrs. Barron, is at last married, and *whom do you think to?* No other than the celebrated Mr. James Ellis. The ceremony was performed on Sunday last, in the presence of about fifty people. I saw them by accident at Cooke's this evening, having not had time to pay them a visit. Neither have I been able (which I much regret) to see Mrs. Gordon. Poor Peggy, from the accounts I hear, I fear is going. She is at present in the neighborhood of Bath. * * I have a great mind to ask her mother to send her for a while to Edenton. Possibly a little new society might revive her spirits. * * * Mrs. Vail died last Sunday.

The accounts are very distressing from the Southward. Charleston, without a most speedy and unexpected relief, must certainly fall, and the Continental troops with it. The town is entirely surrounded, many posts possessed by the enemy in the neighborhood, and some at a distance from it, and they have successfully surprised our people twice. Add to this melancholy account an intelligence that I am afraid is too certain, that the Garrison have only four weeks' provisions. They, however, support their spirits amazingly, and importunately urge, they say, to receive only a quarter allowance. It is said also, the enemy have been repulsed with considerable loss in his attacks. But notwithstanding these discouraging circumstances, it is a consolation that the Maryland troops, and perhaps more, are certainly advancing, and **that a large supply of muskets is arrived at Hali-**

* The act constituted Richard Caswell a Major-General, to command the "aid" ordered to be raised as well as *all the Militia belonging to the State now in service.* The Governor was by the constitution Commander-in-Chief; and this act, a clear violation of the powers vested in him, indicates that the confidence of the Legislature in the Executive was, if not lost, greatly shaken.

fax from Philadelphia. 8000 of our Militia are ordered, I am told, to be embodied : 4000 by the Assembly, and 4000 by the Governor, in consequence of a power given him. That number, I am sure, cannot possibly be raised, but it is certainly necessary to make very great exertions.

I have been skimming over the laws, so far as a very few minutes would permit me. They are certainly the vilest collection of trash ever formed by a legislative body. My salary, a court, is £500. I know not if they have done any thing about the fees. There seems very little business this Court, but of that little I have a share. *Though I say it who should not say it*, I appear to be of some consideration. This, you will say, will add to an intolerable stock of vanity. But I hope such a saying will have more smartness than truth in it. Expenses are monstrous. My jaunt has cost me about $600 on the road. *And the depreciation will certainly proceed most rapidly, for they are giving away the money at the printing office in so public and careless a manner as to make it quite contemptible.*

Wilson Blount pressed me very much to stay at his house, and when I declined that, to let him keep my horses, but I declined that also. ❦ ❦ ❦

I had the honor to dine to-day with his Excellency. I have not been able yet to mouth the word to him, but must learn it by degrees. The lady is highly pleased, and they are preparing to occupy the palace ✶ ✶ ✶ Direct your next letter to Wilmington, &c., &c.

Your most faithfully affectionate,
JAMES IREDELL.

NEWBERN, 21st May, 1780.

MY DEAR HANNAH:— ❦ ❦ I am now to give you very disagreeable news. Charleston, I believe, is certainly taken. It is said to have been on the 12th, and after two days' very severe attack, wherein the enemy, I believe, lost a great many men, and we, I am afraid, not a few. It is not certain whether the town was carried immediately by assault, or capitulation. The probability, from the best accounts we have, seems to be in favor of the latter, and we are told that the Garrison were allowed to march out of the town, and to have a truce for ten days, during which time they might carry out as many arms, &c., and as much provision as they could. These conditions, if true, will be favorable; but the account of them is clogged with this disagreeable appendage, that Lord Cornwallis had marched to Camden, where was the Governor and the whole strength of South Carolina. The people in this State are very much distressed, and every where flying from home. Wilmington is crowded with some of the first families. Fourteen ladies are said to have arrived there last Friday, and several were there before. They will be moving on, I suppose, some to Halifax, others here, and some, I am told, are going to Virginia. I wish I could offer a refuge among us. Such distress it is our duty to relieve. Many who have for years lived in opulence, will now, I suppose, have to seek for the common necessaries of life. Mr. Hooper intends bringing his family immediately here, and perhaps afterwards (which I strongly press for many reasons) going to Booth or the neighborhood of Halifax. Mr. Telfair and he understand each other about the former. Mr. Hooper will not interfere with the convenience of his family; but Mr. Telfair's being very large, he wishes, if possible, to get some other house, lest he should distress your brother by occupying the whole of his. George Hooper's family are coming along here, under the painful situation of her being ❦ ✶ ✶ But Wilmington is certainly no place of security, as the enemy may take it when they please. ✶ ✶ ✶ I shall stay here till near the time of Wilmington Court, and then go in, if there is no extraordinary alarm there, &c. &c.

Yours, most affectionately,
JAS. IREDELL.

With the surrender of Charleston, and the defeat of Col. Buford's detachment, on the 29th, the conquest of South Carolina was complete. North Carolina was now without regular troops—her Continental Battalions, with one thousand of her militia, were included in the capitulation of Charleston ; and it was long before new regiments could be established, or old ones reconstructed. I do not know when the troops were generally exchanged ; but in the Fall of this year and early in '81, a portion of the Continental officers were redeemed from captivity and restored to usefulness; these were immediately employed in training militia, or reforming, as far as practicable, by drafts from the militia, and stragglers picked up here and there, their broken battalions. North Carolina had been greatly impoverished by the war; besides the support of a domestic force, most of the supplies for the Southern Army were drawn from her granaries, while her fields were denuded by reinforcements from the Northward, who augmented the general distress; as, relying upon the harvest of this State, they came with but a slender commissariat.*
At the same time her population smarted under all the evils that

* Jefferson's Letters.

flow from an inflated, depreciated, and fluctuating currency; in apparent despair of any correction, the financial embarrassment was aggravated by the reckless disregard with which the circulation, already an object of contempt, was increased by the negligence of the public officers, by the spurious issues of knaves, and the forgeries of counterfeiters. Penal statutes could but partially check the evil, nor could the Assembly give vitality and value by enactment to what was almost worthless. What coin existed was in the hands of merchants, or secreted as a provision for extreme need. In defiance of law the mercantile community would discriminate between the different kinds of currency; some, simply for reasons of trade; others, hostile to the Government, to cripple its resources and expose it to contumely. Contemporaneously with the loss of Lincoln's army, the Tories began to manifest an unwonted activity. The expected advance of the British, so full of peril to the Whigs, was full of promise to them, and the blood danced in their veins, and their eyes gleamed with anticipated triumph. Emissaries soon penetrated in every direction, confirming their courage and stimulating their energies. As soon as the ripened grain should court the sickle, they said, Lord Cornwallis would advance, and they bade them be patient, but ready. The fire they kindled, however, could not be hid, but soon broke into blaze. The Tories were carried away by their ardor ; flew to arms, and by their precipitancy drew upon themselves the chastisement, swift and signal as their rashness and folly. The most manly and respectable part of the loyalists were well known, and had vindicated on the battlefield the sincerity of their convictions ; but there was a portion of them, traitors in disguise, especially dangerous because of their masks, their intelligence, and their command of money. These, generally Scotch and English merchants, by a confidence as unwise as generous, had been permitted, though suspected, to remain unmolested. Some who had even visited England during the war were suffered to return and "make their submission;" others were protected by influential connections in the patriot ranks ; many, conversant with refined life, had address, and had formed matrimonial alliances with the families of the most eminent men; they paid assiduous court to rank and riches, and obtained easy access to every circle. Traversing the State from east to west, they constituted to the British a means of communication with the disaffected; their wives were discreet counsellors, and often directed the course of events.* Was the husband watched, who would stain his gallantry by subjecting a lady to the rudeness of search? Some of these miscreants were

* Executive Correspondence.

even in lucrative offices. They soon became masters of every secret, and, assassin-like, the poniards concealed in their bosoms were never drawn, but stealthily, in the dark, to inflict mortal wounds. These were the only domestic foe, for the slaves were either so much attached to their owners, or, if you will, such was their habit of subjection, and consequent lack of enterprise, that they inspired no dread. Ordinarily they were identified in feeling with their proprietors; some few scamps, seduced and instigated by blacker scoundrels, perpetrated outrages on defenceless women and children, plundered a farm, or fired a dwelling; but these instances were rare. Doubtless at the period of which I treat, there were many villains for whose crimes neither party was strictly responsible : heretofore kept in awe by the strong arm of the law, the impending invasion enticed them from their coverts, as the first warm day of spring draws countless reptiles from their holes; and many a dark deed was done, at which humanity shudders, by those who at one time brought disgrace to the flag of Britain, at another, infamy to that of North Carolina. In the examination of the history of 1780, it is worthy of note, that though a large part of the white population of the State was inimical to its authorities, in despite or because of its slaves, yet was North Carolina able to cope with and defeat troops flushed with success, and to crown the campaign with victory. It is often asked by amiable Northern writers, "What if servile rebellion had been fomented ? " The query is designed to be minatory, and suggested by a thought, and hope of the future; but is easily answered :—As far as they could be used by the British and Tories advantageously, slaves were actually employed; that they did not play a more conspicuous part in the war, was not because of fastidious scruples of humanity, but solely because such as were obtained were utterly inefficient. Now, if North Carolina, under the most unfavorable circumstances, with a divided people and a powerful enemy within her borders, could keep her blacks in order, and make effectual her defence, why need the same State, with an united and homogeneous white race, ever entertain aught of fear on account of the machinations of incendiary Abolitionists? Though '80 and '81 were memorable years, and attended with much individual calamity and public disaster, yet I cannot but think the pictures we have of that era too sombre. Wreck enough there was—blackened ruins—unburied corpses; but yet North Carolina ever maintained its character as a secure refuge for exiles from the more Southern States. Regiments were shattered, dispersed, annihilated, but at no time was the State subdued or placed " hors du combat." If at particular periods there was no considerable organized force under the State "eo nomine," at such

VOL. I.—29

crises her citizens took charge of the war as volunteers; her sons, in the interior and on the seaboard, established a military police, and enforced order wherever the enemy was not in force; watched their posts, assailed their foraging parties, and captured their scouts; the ground won by the invader to-day was liberated by his march to-morrow. Meanwhile the men of the West, gathering as rapidly as their own mountain clouds, precipitated themselves, with a fury as sudden and remorseless, upon all who ventured beyond the Catawba. The correspondence of the period shows how high and indomitable was the spirit of the people; they never despaired, but as the plot thickened, became more and more ready to serve in the field. They needed no compulsion, for their spontaneous acts anticipated the "draft." The only difficulty was to find arms and equipments. Such was their zeal that they often went into action unable, from want of muskets and sabres, to attack or resist, but willing to interpose their bodies as a living screen between the Continentals and the British. The resources of the Confederacy had been expended chiefly at the North; such military munitions as were in North Carolina had been directed to the South. If the statements of the historians of other States be correct—" no magazine laid up; the commissaries without money or credit; soldiers living by impressment of lean cattle;" * the great array of troops by the State is almost incredible, and can only be referred to patriotism as conspicuous and dazzling as ever shone upon the combat or illumed the council of Greece or Rome.

IREDELL TO MRS. IREDELL.

NEWBERN, 22d May, 1780.

MY DEAR HANNAH :—I was most agreeably surprised this afternoon with your letter of the 18th, for I had no expectation of the post arriving till to-morrow, and should not perhaps have received your letter till then, if Mr. Cogdell, the postmaster, who is extremely obliging to me, had not been kind enough to send it. It makes me very happy to hear of you so lately, and I thank you for your punctuality in writing. I have felt deeply for the uneasiness I knew you would suffer in being so long without hearing from me. I think with great pain of the anxiety you would experience till to-morrow's post, which will contain a complete catalogue of our misfortunes and delays. We have been extremely fortunate, however, in preserving our health through all. Mr. Hooper and I are perfectly well, and Mr. Williams al-

* Hildreth.

most so. His company was a great relief to us, *for he is certainly one of the best-natured, and most cheerful men living.* I wrote you yesterday the melancholy intelligence we had received about Charleston. This letter I had intended, with some additions, sending by the post, but very accidentally this morning met with a private opportunity, and made use of it. It was so momentary, that I had it not in my power to write to your brother or any body else. I am sorry he complains so much of his shoulder. * * I think myself under infinite obligations to Mr. Smith. His goodness never deserts him, and while I live, I will endeavor to remember his attentions and real services with gratitude. ◦ ◦ I find Mr. Hooper, though he has engaged half a dozen houses here for himself and friends, does not intend to move his family till the enemy (if they come at all) arrive at Brunswick; and he insists, on pain of his utmost displeasure, on my going to his house immediately from here. So I have resolved to do it, and perhaps may be able to set off with him, for he is still detained here about some little matters of business. * ◦ The Governor has yet no official intelligence of the fate of Charleston. The fact of its being taken, I believe, is too true; but it is yet uncertain whether by assault or capitulation. This unhappy affair has put an end to a grand ball that was to have been given by the Governor to-morrow night, on occasion of his taking possession of the palace, which he did on Saturday, for his place of residence. ◦ ◦ We feast upon strawberries here. Don't fail to make my best compliments to all Mr. Cabarrus's family. I have great reason, considering every thing, to be satisfied with this Court. There has not been much business, but I have been applied to in almost every thing. I have already received in civil suits £1,240 in paper, besides 19 silver dollars; and I expect to receive to-morrow £500, and my salary for this and Edenton Courts, which will be £1000. I very much wish I could contrive you some of this, to pay for the rum and other things, but I can't devise any method of doing it. My fear is, that as usual the money will be much depreciated before I lay it out. I shall carefully preserve the little hard money to the last. Would you believe that I got my half Joe? The house was on our road here, and I found the woman had preserved it with great care. I regretted my not being able to afford her the whole, and paid her $50. You must not expect to hear with any regularity from me after this post, because Mr. Hooper lives seven miles from Wilmington, and the post is only there once a week. You may be assured, however, that I will be as diligent as possible in availing myself of it.

With respect to my heart, it is, my dear Hannah, entirely and wholly yours. I cherish the dear and agreeable persuasion, and will never part with it. My happiness, my thoughts, my every thing is centered in you. God grant you may be able to preserve your health. I shall chide every moment's delay, and when I am permitted to go, shall fly to you with all possible expedition. Let me again beg you to give my love to your sister, my dear Nelly in particular, and the other children, distinguishing also among these my young pupil, who I hope does something. Adieu! my dear Hannah. May heaven ever bless you!

Yours most faithfully and affectionately,
JAS. IREDELL.

NEWBERN, 24th May, 1780.

MY DEAR HANNAH :—◦ ◦ ◦ ◦ I am just setting off for the southward. Mr. Hooper went this morning. I wished, but was not able to go with him. I have received for fees here in all £2,340—besides nineteen silver dollars, and my salary money for Edenton and Newbern, and arrears of Halifax. But my expenses are very heavy. Thank God, there is no certain intelligence yet of the surrender of Charleston, which induces us to hope it is a Tory lie to discourage the people. There is much reason for this suspicion. The surrender is said to have been on the 12th. At Georgetown, only sixty miles distant, on the 19th, they had no certainty of it, and it began to be disbelieved. The account at first was only from a post-rider, and Charleston being blockaded, the enemy may fabricate what lies they please. Direct to me, as I before desired, in Newbern. I will give Cogdell directions. They have only one post a week from Cape Fear, so you must not after this expect regular intelligence of me. But I shall from you, there being no such reason to bar you. Tell the gentlemen all I wrote before is, as Mr. Penn would say, " in nubibus;" but I, to a lady who does not understand Latin, more politely say in plain English, it is *extremely uncertain,* &c., &c.

JAS. IREDELL.

MASON BOROUGH, 28th May, 1780.

DEAR HANNAH :—I have been at this agreeable place ever since Friday. I left Newbern so soon after Mr. Hooper, that, he being detained by indisposition and bad weather two or three hours on the road on Friday morning, I overtook him, and we came here together. The family are very well, and I, as usual, very happy; but not enough so to forget you, or to cease thinking continually of you. Charleston is certainly taken. I have seen a gentleman who heard the capitulation read. The garrison are made prisoners of war; the inhabitants, at least such as choose to stay, protected in their persons and property. The militia are allowed to go home on their parole; the continental troops, at least the officers, paroled to Hadrell's Point and the distance of ten miles about it. The surrender, it seems, was not from an immediate want of provisions, but in consequence of very near approaches of the British lines, which threatened in a short time certain success, perhaps on worse terms, and the inhabitants were extremely importunate, as we are told, for the surrender. This is the account as I heard it, and believe truly. I hope to be able to get a copy of the capitulation to send to your brother, but it is very uncertain if I can. We hear of nothing further of the British operations, although it is expected they will soon be about some mischief or other. Col. Washington's Light Horse have fled to Wilmington, and are now there, and will be, I suppose, joined to-day by a legion of about 200, partly horse, and part foot, commanded by one Col. Armand, who is on his way from the northward.◦ How either, or both intend to proceed, nobody I believe but themselves knows. Mr. Hooper talks of leaving this in a few days, and he most certainly ought to do it. I am to stay here till Tuesday, which is Court-day, and I believe *Post-day;* so, for fear of being too late, I shall endeavor to contrive this there sooner, and expect an opportunity to-day. ◦ ◦ ◦
Yours, &c., JAS. IREDELL.

P. S. I have had further particulars of the capitulation. Clinton first proposed it, representing his own strength and advanced works, and our weakness, with the improbability of relief. Lincoln desired time to consider. At length the terms were agreed on, when the garrison had been three days without meat (though they had plenty of rice, but not very good), and after sustaining a continual cannonade, some part of the town was in a manner open to them. L. desired leave to march out with the honors of war, drums beating, colors flying, &c. Clinton granted this, except that their colors should not be displayed, nor they play a British march. He marched out of town without any beat of drum, and with the colors cased. The British, with an uncommon and most pleasing delicacy, marched in exactly in the same manner. The officers are allowed their baggage, side-arms, &c., and Col. Clark is very safe and well.†

* Colonel Armand, Marquis de la Rouarie, appointed Col. '77. His corps was incorporated with Pulaski's in Feb. 1781. He received the rank of Brigadier-General in '83. He was active, intelligent, and brave.—LOSSING. A portion of Colonel Washington's command was destroyed at Buford's defeat.
† The brother-in-law of William Hooper.

WILMINGTON, 2d June, 1780.

MY DEAR HANNAH:—* * I thank God the business of this Court will be very much shortened, although the cause is not a very agreeable one—the universal alarm and anxiety of the people about the progress of the British army. We have heard no certain particulars of any thing since the surrender. * * The Judges came to town before us prodigiously frightened, and gave in a manner public notice that no business would be done, in consequence of which I fear we have lost some money. I have, however, received five guineas and £500, and am to have £500 or £600 on account of Strudwick. In the mean time I live very agreeably, at free cost, with Mr. Hogg, who is really a most valuable man. Mr. Hooper and I are together, &c., &c.

JAS. IREDELL.

MASON BOROUGH, 5th June, 1780.

DEAR HANNAH:—* * My horses, after staying a week here with perfect content, got away several days ago, and in spite of our utmost efforts and Mr. Hooper's most obliging attention, are not yet found. This now only detains me. * * * Our army in South Carolina are retreating before Lord Cornwallis, who is marching westward. Mr. Hooper talks of moving in a few days, and is doubtful whether he shall not first rendezvous at Edenton and look out for a settlement afterward. In this case, he says he has promised to stay at N. Allen's, &c., &c.

JAS. IREDELL.

Early in June, the militia of Mecklenburg and Rowan were ordered out to check the triumphant march of Lord Cornwallis.* Scarcely had they assembled, when they received intelligence of a body of Loyalists at Ramsour's Mill, near the present village of Lincolnton. Gen. Rutherford, unwilling that his force should be diverted from his primary object, despatched orders to Colonel Locke of Rowan to suppress the insurrection. In less than five days, Locke raised and united his levies. At sunrise on the morning of the 20th, at the head of three hundred and fifty men, he engaged the Loyalists, thirteen hundred in number, and after a well-sustained action of an hour drove them from their position. Seventy men were left dead upon the field, and more than two hundred wounded, the loss of each side being equal. "For daring courage on the part of the Whigs, considering that the enemy outnumbered them in the proportion of four to one, and had great advantage in position, it is surpassed by few events of the war."† It revived for a time the recollection of Moore's Creek, and created a salutary panic among the disaffected.

* Gov. Graham. † Ibid.

JOHN JOHNSTON TO IREDELL.

June 22d, 1780. (Bertie.)

DEAR SIR:—I wrote you once before I left Newbern, giving you an account of my proceedings respecting your lands; however, in case that may have miscarried, I have given my brother the same account, when he was last here. I had many offers for it, and some which might have been accepted, but as a division had not taken place between you and the Frankses and Heritage, I could not conclude any bargain. You may depend on it they will do every thing in their power to jockey you; this I am convinced of from their attempts upon me. Mr. Nash made large offers for it, but I found the tobacco which he offered was already partly disposed of, and the other part not yet made. In short, I found that none of the persons who offered could lay down. Young Izler's offer seemed the most calculated for your advantage, which was to give 35s. per annum, and pay down £600 of the hard money—the remainder to be paid next January either in the like money or in pork at the former cash price. This offer I should have taken, but not having time to run the line between these people and you, prevented.

I shall set off next Monday with about fifty or sixty Lighthorsemen, who have done me the honor to appoint me their Captain. As it is very possible some accident may happen which may prevent my return, I have made a will which is in the hands of Doctor Veher directed to my brother, who, with you, I have taken the liberty of appointing my executors and guardians to my three boys, Mrs. Iredell guardian to my little girl.

I am, dear Sir, with the sincerest regard, your affectionate brother-in-law,
JOHN JOHNSTON.

On the 20th of July that very enterprising partisan-officer, Major Davie, with a party of his dragoons and some volunteers, surprised and captured a convoy of provisions, spirits, and clothing, destined for the enemy's post at Hanging Rock. Towards the close of the same month, Col. Sumpter, with a number of South Carolina refugees, and Col. Irwin of N. C., with three hundred of the Mecklenburg militia, made a gallant attempt upon Rocky Mount, a fortified position; Davie, at the same time approaching Hanging Rock, encountered three companies of mounted infantry, halted at a farmer's house, after some excursion; and charged them with such fury that they were literally cut to pieces. All these corps uniting about the 5th of August made a formidable assault upon Hanging Rock, attended with much success, and rewarded with no small share of plunder.

* Hubbard.

The militia ordered by the Assembly in the Spring (8,000) were collected, and organized by General Caswell in the East, and General Rutherford in the West.* These forces were united the first of August at Thompson's Creek, S. C., three miles below the Cheraw Hill. Caswell had the chief command, and Rutherford, Gregory and Butler acted as Brigadiers.† The jail at Salisbury being insecure, they had taken away a considerable number of Tory prisoners, whom they had in camp under a guard. The militia were in fine spirits, awaiting the approach of Gates, and looking forward with eager hope to a conflict with the enemy. Moving cautiously on, they were by the 5th within 14 miles of Cornwallis. Gates, designated by Congress for the Southern Department, June 13th, reached De Kalb's camp upon Deep River, July 25th: here he found the Maryland and Delaware Continentals, Col. Armand's Legion, and three companies of Artillery. Giddy from success, and arrogant from flattery, the new General, despising counsel, determined upon a route through a barren and disaffected region. On the morning of the 27th he marched on the road to Camden, where the laurels won at Saratoga were destined to shrivel like parchment under the fire of a Southern sun. On the 28th he was joined by Lt. Col. Porterfield with 100 Virginians, and August the fifth, in the evening, he effected a junction with Caswell; the day after his arrival at Rugeley's, he was reinforced by Gen. Stevens, of Va., with 700 men. Militia are peculiarly liable to panics, hence the necessity of guarding them sedulously against a surprise. At 10 o'clock P. M., on the 15th, Gates pressed forward with so little prudence and so much fatuity, that Col. Armand, who was with the van, subsequently said, "that if he had desired to betray his army, he could not have chosen a more judicious course." The deep sand rendered footsteps inaudible. About 2 o'clock in the morning, the advanced guards of the adversaries came into collision: the shock was violent and sudden. Armand's troops recoiled upon the 1st Maryland Brigade; that gave way, and communicated its consternation to the whole line; the enemy's van, however, was soon arrested by Porterfield, and by Armstrong, with the North Carolina Light Infantry, who with equal spirit attacked them on the right and left. Both armies halted: the wounded were borne to the rear: each prepared for battle. A retreat was practicable and plainly dictated by prudence. Gates should have avoided an encounter until the "morale" of his undisciplined troops had been re-established. To fight now was to engage with forces already disorganized and beaten. Gates was most culpably ignorant of his real strength: he reckoned it at 7,000; the Dep. Adj. General, Williams, better informed, estimated it at 3,663 actually present. The effective force of the British was 2,500; but of these 1,600 were regulars.* At day dawn the British rushed with charged bayonets upon the American centre, and left, composed entirely of militia. A fatal mistake had been committed—the Continentals should have been here. That the raw militia fled before the charge of regulars is no matter of surprise. Caswell and Gates were borne away by the fugitives, while it is no extravagant figure of speech to say, that "Gates did not draw rein until he reached Hillsborough," accomplishing the distance of 230 miles in 75 hours.† Disdaining to fly, the Continentals on the right, with brilliant audacity, stood their ground: they numbered less than one thousand; but were gallantly supported by Col. Dixon's regiment of North Carolinians.‡ The flight of the militia was not universal, at one and the same time; a part of Gen. Gregory's N. C. Brigade fired one or two rounds before they imitated the shameful example of their comrades.§ Dixon, who had seen service in the Continental Line, was resolute to redeem the tarnished reputation of his State. "None, without violence to the claims of honor and justice, can withhold applause from Col. Dixon and his N. C. regiment of militia. ‖ Having their flank exposed by the flight of the other militia, they turned with disdain from the ignoble example; and fixing their eyes on the Marylanders, whose left they became, determined to vie in deeds of courage with their veteran comrades. Nor did they shrink from this daring resolve. In every vicissitude of the battle this regiment maintained its ground; and when the reserve under Smallwood relieved its naked flank, forced the enemy to fall back." ¶ Taken in flank, and De Kalb mortally wounded, the heroic Continentals, and their brethren by the best and proudest of all titles, the North Carolinians, who, with unequal numbers, had maintained so long the brunt of the contest, were finally broken and dispersed. The Americans lost 900 killed; and as many more, of whom many were wounded, were taken prisoners. The British lost 325 men. All the American artil-

* Hildreth. Iredell. † O. Davis to W. Jones.—Un. Mag.
‡ Lee. Ramsay. Lossing.
§ Governor Nash, in a letter from Hillsborough, September 10th, to Willie Jones, says, General Gregory's *brigade* bravely stood to the last, and pushed bayonets, after their ammunition was exhausted."—N. C. Un. Mag.
‖ Memoirs of the war.—Col. H Lee.
¶ Henry Dickson was appointed a Captain in Col. Moore's Regiment (1st), 1775.

* Griffith Rutherford was an Irishman, brave and enterprising, but uncultivated in mind or manners: he chastised the Cherokees in '76, being then Brigadier General. He was often in the Assembly. After serving as Senator, in the Assembly, for Rowan, in 1786, he removed to Tennessee, where in 1794 he was appointed President of the Legislative Council. Counties have been named after him in Tennessee and North Carolina.—Wheeler.
† Life of Caswell.—Un. Mag.

lery, baggage, stores, &c., fell into the enemy's hands. Gen. Rutherford, Col. Geddey, and Col. Lockhart, of N. C., were taken prisoners. Terrible was the disaster! For a time hope seemed crushed, and the way into the heart of North Carolina open to Cornwallis. But all was not lost: the energy of North Carolina, thus left, in a great degree, to her own resources, rose equal to the crisis. About the 19th of August, General Caswell, arrived at Charlotte, in a letter to the Governor stated that the regiments of Halifax under Seawell, Edenton under Jarvis, and New Berne under Pasteur, who were in the rear at the time of the defeat, had been ordered by him to Charlotte: he likewise had called out the militia of Rowan, Mecklenburg and Lincoln, to converge upon the same point, and was confident of a "formidable camp in a few days."*

The Assembly convened at Hillsborough, September 5th: they passed acts levying a specific provision tax for the support of the war;† for raising money on loan for immediate use; and for restraining any impressment or other interference with vehicles employed in the transportation of salt. They constituted a Board of War, consisting of " Martin, a *warrior of great fame*; Penn, fit only to amuse children; and O. Davis, who knew nothing but the game of whist."‡ Such was the opinion generally entertained by military men of the Board. The Board acted until January, 1781, when its authorities were restored to the Legislature:§ and, however inefficient their services, " they undertook the task devolved on them in the most devoted spirit of patriotism, and with a proper sense of its magnitude, and executed its duties with fearlessness." The measure was as extraordinary as unconstitutional, but adopted because of the critical condition of the State, and its imminent danger: it was manifestly disrespectful, and insulting to the Governor; but as he had no power of veto, he submitted in silence. By a resolution of the Assembly, General Smallwood of the Maryland line was requested to take the command of the North Carolina militia: he exercised the authority thus conferred until his departure North, December 3d.

In a letter from Dukinfield, 12th September, to Miss Blair, Mr. Iredell says: " I amuse myself here with my French History. You must not get before me in Robertson, for my only reason for

---

* September 10th, Governor Nash wrote Willie Jones, " our zeal and spirit rises with our difficulties, drafts are nearly at an end, our men yield to the necessity of the times, and turn out to service with willing hearts. We are blessed with plentiful crops, etc."—N. C. Un. Mag. 1855.
† Governor Johnston afterwards described it as the " most oppressive and least productive tax ever known in the State."—Life of Davie by Hubbard.
‡ General Davie. Hubbard. § Governor Graham.

---

not bringing him on here was that you might be a partaker. Let us enjoy the feast together, and not sit down to it churlishly alone." "I wish your Mamma had not served us with Mrs. Dawson's note as a careless gentleman did a fat Epicure, to whom he sent the compliment of some fine venison—in a letter only." He desired his shaving apparatus. This being neglected, on the 14th he wrote again: " I know you dined on venison over the Creek, I know you did not return till evening, I know you had two young gentlemen to gallant you; but all these, I think, are not sufficient for not stepping a moment into a room, or giving orders to somebody to do it, when you came home before Juba left. My excuse for you is, that you could not take time to read my letter, till those gentlemen were gone; and if that be the case, I send you my pardon under my hand, well imagining the little flutter there may be about a young Lady's heart on such occasions, and how uninteresting a formal Uncle's letter must be, that shall impertinently intrude." In her reply, Miss Nelly stated, " you will be surprised at my ill taste: I was over the Creek yesterday; there was a fine haunch of venison for dinner, tolerably good cheese and porter; and I never tasted either of them."

IREDELL TO MRS. IREDELL.

ELK MARSH, September 28th, 1780.

MY DEAR HANNAH:—I have now the pleasure to resume an account of my journey here, where I did not arrive till yesterday morning; for though I got to Colton's the second night, the weather was so extremely bad the next day, that I made free enough to put into Booth, which I did not leave till yesterday morning. I got a little wet, but not much; however, I exchanged my wet clothes there, and was very comfortable under the care and kindness of Sella, who was extremely obliging. My horses were swam over, and I came on directly here without stopping at Halifax. I found this family in an unexpected situation. Mrs. B. McCulloh had two days before made the family happy with two fine children at a birth, a boy and a girl. But their joy was much damped by the event of Mrs. Montfort's death, which happened last Sunday night, after an illness of three weeks, supposed to be a good deal aggravated by constant and alternate attendance on her two grandsons, I. Montfort and A. Jones. The latter I believe is got better, but the former died within a few hours of his grandmother, and they were both carried to the grave on the same bier. Sickness has been very general here. Mrs. McCulloh looks extremely ill, and prodigiously afflicted by the loss of her sister. They say she was getting better before. Mrs. Ash, who was here, and whom I saw at dinner, looks very ill also. B. McCulloh's eldest son has had the ague and fever a long time, but is at last getting better. Sally is very well, and they say their mother and the two young ones as much so as possible. Poor General Jones lost his fine boy the other day. He had been sickly for some time, but died in a very extraordinary and sudden manner at last—lay down in the porch, and kept screaming till he died. I hear of no other deaths of consequence, but these are melancholy enough.

By the last intelligence from the Army, a party of British, of about 1000 foot and 400 horse, who appeared to be advancing, had halted at the Waxaus* about 25 miles on this side of Camden, and were thrashing out wheat. It was supposed, by the smallness of the number, that they were only furnishing themselves with provisions, of which they had been in great want, so much so that they were at half a day's allowance before the action. It is imagined they had 2500 in the great engagement. Gen. Gates's conduct is much censured, and I am told by his officers in general, so that I fear there are too much grounds for it. The report is, that upon the militia giving way, he immediately fled without sending any orders to the Continental troops to retreat, some of whom were pushing the enemy before them, and afterwards, knowing nothing of the flight, were almost surrounded; whereas it is said that if he had given them timely orders to retreat, they could have done it in good order, and at least saved all the baggage and stores. But they would not retreat without orders until it appeared absolutely necessary, and even then they brought off 600 men (one half their number) entire. Armand's corps was almost cut to pieces, and he is gone to the northward, I am told, with violent exclamations against Gates. The Baron De Kalb was a quarter of a mile in advance of our army, when he was killed, pressing on with great success; and after he had received a musket shot, concealed it, and was animating his men in the most heroical manner, when a cannon ball gave him a mortal wound, of which he soon died. *Gen. Sumner has about* 2000 *men at Charlotte*, in Mecklenburg County, which I believe is about 70 miles on this side of the enemy. At Hillsborough there are about 800 of the old Continental troops (including 150 that were retaken on their way to Charleston), and a new regiment of 18 months' men brought from Virginia by Col. Blufort.† The horse, that have been so long at Halifax, set off about a week ago, completely equipped with every thing but bridles, which they expected to receive on their march. The number that went on was about 280, one-half of whom, it is said, are at present invalids, and to be left to recruit in Warren.

I have at length got a charming day, and intend setting off immediately after breakfast. After so much rain, and with the present temperature of the air, I have the prospect of a very pleasant journey the rest of the way. I intend calling on Col. Williams.* I was very glad to hear he had not gone to Salisbury, which left me perfectly excused. Poor Spencer trusted himself to the mercy of the tories with five or six men, which I think was much worse than going alone. I am afraid to hear of his being kidnapped. The language here is, that he has lost every thing, but his *two wives*. Surely his misfortunes might have tempered their animosity. I did not hear it from one of the family itself, but in the family, and suppose it to be originally theirs, &c., &c.
Yours, &c.
JAMES IREDELL.

About the 24th of September, the British began their second invasion of North Carolina. The State was not unprepared—had at least three or four thousand men under arms; and its most enterprising and effective officers, Sumner, Davidson and Davie, in front. On the 26th, the royal forces approached Charlotte.† The village is situate in an open plain, and was undefended by even the rudest field-works. Sumner and Davidson had retreated by the nearest route to Salisbury, leaving Charlotte considerably to the left.‡ Davie had been appointed, September 5th, Colonel of the Cavalry of the Western District: he was ordered to watch and annoy the enemy's advance: this service he performed with much gallantry. Though he had but two hundred men, one hundred and fifty of his own corps, and fifty volunteers under Graham,§ yet he determined to make a stand. Accustomed by his long proximity to the sight of scarlet uniform, familiarity, if it had not bred contempt, had confirmed his own courage, and that of his men. Though aware that his defence could not long be made good, he calculated wisely upon the effect of a chivalrous passage at arms upon the people of the vicinity; while by a lesson of brilliant audacity, he meant to impress on the enemy a proper caution, and a becoming respect. He judiciously posted

---

* About half a mile west of Waxhaw Creek, in Mecklenburg County, N. C., Andrew Jackson was born.
† Sept. 7th, O. Davis of the Board of War wrote Willie Jones,—" *We are again in a situation to make a stout defence.*"—N. C. Un. Mag. Mar. 1855.

---

* Judge Williams. † Foote.—Graham. ‡ Hubbard.
§ Gen. Joseph Graham. Father of the Hon. Wm. A. Graham, Whig candidate for Vice-President on the ticket with Scott. Gov. Graham amid cotemporary politicians, is as a classic statue—as calm, immovable, spotless, polished and as passionless.

his little band under cover of the buildings and enclosures of the town. The attack was commenced by the redoubted and sanguinary Tarleton. Twice charging at the head of his dragoons, he was twice repulsed: supported by a new regiment, again he assaulted, but to be again defeated, and to receive the reproof of his commander. A regiment of infantry now threatening his flanks, Col. Davie retired in order along the Salisbury road. The British loss consisted of twelve non-commissioned officers killed and wounded; Major Hanger and Captains Campbell and McDonald wounded, with about thirty privates. Cornwallis was now in possession of the Hornet's Nest; but found it no place of repose. To maintain his ground, though overwhelming his force, he must needs be vigilant and brave as he who would keep the Douglas Castle, in days of yore. His sentries were shot at their posts, his pickets disturbed;* and his wagons plundered within a few miles of his quarters. A foraging party of four hundred men was driven home with a loss of twenty-seven killed and wounded, by a party of seven individuals in ambush, who escaped unscathed.

About the 1st of September, Lord Cornwallis had detached Col. Ferguson to move on the west side of the Catawba, to rally the Tories, and intercept a party of Mountaineers, who had been harassing the upper settlement of Tories in South Carolina. Ferguson, his force increased to about one thousand men, penetrated as far west as Gilberstown,† when, becoming alarmed for his safety, he rapidly withdrew to King's Mountain.‡ There, on the 7th of October, he was assailed by Cols. Shelby, Sevier, McDowell, and Cleaveland of North Carolina, aided by Col. Williams§ of South Carolina, and Col. Campbell of Virginia. The whole American force amounted to 1,370, of whom 730, or more than one half, were North Carolinians.|| There, "each man upon his own horse, and furnished with his own arms," the temporary command bestowed by election, these volunteers from the valleys of the Blue Ridge won a victory decisive of the campaign. One hundred and fifty of the enemy, including their commander, were slain, and 810 captured, with 1,500 stands of arms. The *first British invasion* of North Carolina was defeated by the prowess of her sons at Moore's Creek, and now the *second invasion* was rolled back by the arms of the same race, aided by their neighbors of Virginia and South Carolina. In neither instance did the Confederacy contribute any thing to the result. King's Mountain crosses the line dividing the two Caro-

* Governor Graham. † Near Rutherfordton.—Gov. Swain. ‡ Foote.
§ Col. Williams was a native of Granville, N. C. Dr. Johnson's Reminiscences.
|| Graham.

linas. The battlefield is now in South Carolina: at the time of the action it was regarded by the people of both States as within the limits of North Carolina. Astounded by the news of this disaster, on the night of the 14th Lord Cornwallis began his retreat to Winnsboro', South Carolina. His march was precipitate his alarm evident. He was hotly pursued by Davidson and Davie who captured a portion of his baggage; and on the 19th evacuated the State, maddened as the bear in the fable, the hornet's buzz ringing in his ears, the hornet's sting in his body.

Whatever of gloom attended the inroad of Cornwallis, now gave way to animated exultation: hope lighted up every countenance, and cheering voices gladdened every household. Troops were rapidly assembling at every strategic point; and the hand of the clock already pointed to the end of the night. Since the rout at Camden, General Gates had been busily employed at Hillsborough in the reorganization of a new army for the next campaign. Thither also had repaired Governor Rutledge of South Carolina to consult with the authorities of North Carolina and to stimulate efforts for the relief of the South; a dictator in exile, without men or money, but still unsubdued; watching at a distance the fires he had kindled upon the altars of South Carolina, while his heart sank at one moment as they seemed to languish to extinction, at another blazed with patriotic ardor as the reddening glare gave token of a reviving flame. If he sometimes doubted the tenure of his own life, enfeebled by care and anxiety and suffering, often his glance, through the thickening mists of intervening years, penetrated to an enchanting future.

IREDELL TO MRS. IREDELL.

(Col. Williams's), Granville, 8th October, 1780.

My dear Hannah:—I have had no opportunity till the present of writing to you since I left Col. McCulloh's, which I have much regretted, as I know how anxious you would have the goodness to be about me in the present situation of affairs. I have been very unfortunate in weather. It was not only very bad for three or four days after I set off, but extremely disagreeable during the whole of my stay at Hillsborough, constantly cloudy and damp, and sometimes raining, and the town was so crowded that Col. Williams and myself were obliged to ride out to Dr. Burke's every evening, which is two or three miles, where we were treated with extreme kindness, and without this advan-

* Afterwards Mr. Iredell's friend and colleague on the bench of the Supreme Court.

tage I know not what we should have done. You may guess in what a situation the town is when we must have been deprived of this resource, if Governor Rutledge had not been so obliging as to stay in town, and take half of Penn's bed, in order to accommodate us. The rain I had coming up affected my health a good deal. I had a most violent lax here a day and a half. It very luckily left me just before I set off, but upon being again exposed I had a slight renewal of it, and should have been afterwards perfectly well; but upon being frequently in the night air and wet weather, I have got a sore throat, which is a little troublesome; but as I have nothing to do till Halifax Court but to take care of myself, and I have not the slightest complaint besides, I am sure I shall soon get rid of it. Col. Williams having been constantly with me is affected exactly in the same manner. We arrived here last night. A sufficient number of jurymen not being summoned, we did little or no business, and I got no money but my paltry salary. I expect to meet and receive money from Mr. Strudwick at Cape Fear.

Public affairs are not in so desperate a situation as perhaps at your distance may be conceived. The enemy have been a long time, without advancing, at Charlotte in Mecklenburg County, about 43 miles beyond Salisbury. Their numbers are not ascertained, but at most, I believe, do not exceed 2000 or 2500 men. A British officer of the name of Ferguson, who had marched at the head of about 1500 men (200 or 300 of whom alone were British) into Burke County, about 90 miles from Salisbury, was retreating. It is said that he told the South Carolina tories he should not want to carry them further than Burke Court House, relying upon the rascals in our country to join him there. In this, however, he has been much mistaken. A body of 1500 men under officers of the name of Selby and McDowell, another of 800 under Cleaveland, and a third of 450 horse under Col. Williams, were very near each other, and expected to join the day after the accounts came away, in pursuit of him. Upon intelligence of this the enemy detached 800 men, horse and foot, and two pieces of cannon, to attempt his relief. Whether they were able to effect it is not yet known. Ferguson's men, they say, deserted to about 500. On this side of the Yadkin (which is about 7 miles from Salisbury,) we have in all, on the banks of the river, and within a near distance of it, I suppose about 2000 or 3000 men under Generals Sumner and Butler. On the other side there is at least 400 or 500 horse under Col. Davie, a most active officer, within 20 miles of the enemy, at a flying camp at a place called Fifer's. These men have already much annoyed the enemy, killed many as they en-

tered the town of Charlotte, and have taken a good number of prisoners; 70 or 80 were brought to Hillsborough before I left it, 18 of whom were British, the others Tories. Two companies of Continental Troops, and one company of Col. Bufort's (nearly equal to the others), were to march from Hillsborough yesterday, under the command of General Smallwood and Col. Morgan (the famous Rifle officer), and Col. Washington with about 100 Horse (all who are well enough to go) is also to march immediately. We met them the night before last within 9 miles of Hillsborough. Col. Preston, a man of very great character in Montgomery County in Virginia, wrote to one of our Generals to the westward, that he and some other gentlemen in some of the neighboring counties, seeing the necessity of an instant relief, had raised a body of 1,000 men, 250 of whom were Horse, the others Riflemen, who were all nearly equipped, and that if they received the sanction of their Government, which they had applied for, and had no doubt of obtaining, they would rendezvous at the Moravian town on the 15th instant, and in the mean time he despatched two companies. There are at Hillsborough, besides those sent on, at least 800 men, 500 or 600 of whom are what they call the Maryland Troops, the rest Bufort's. These wait for clothing and other necessaries, of which most of them were in great want. While the enemy were thinking only of tormenting us, a Col. Clark with 100 Riflemen marched through the back parts of South Carolina, and collected on his route about 700 men more, with whom he marched into the town of Augusta, of which the enemy had possession, and brought away a vast quantity of Indian goods, which were stored there to be made use of to bribe the Indians against us. He was not strong enough to continue in the town, and retired with his booty to a district called Ninety-six in South Carolina, where he kept his men ready for any purpose that might offer, and intended to take care of his retreat if it should become necessary. Besides the above, Col. Marion has about 300 men at White Marsh in Bladen County, and General Harrington (a very fine fellow) had 450 (which by this time are supposed to be doubled, as the men were collecting fast) at Cross Creek. All this I give you from the best intelligence, official letters to General Gates and the Board of War. I have the pleasure to acquaint you, that upon conversing with many officers, General Gates's conduct appears in a much more favorable light than I had apprehended, and that the account gave of the action was in many particulars erroneous. I have not time to explain the matter now. I know not whether I shall have time to write to any body else, except a line to your brother, as this opportunity offers very unexpectedly, therefore must get you to distribute the news to my good friends, Mr. Barker, Mr. Johnson, Mr. Smith and Mr. Allen, &c., and I hope they will excuse my not writing to any of them, when it is not really in my power. Nelly must excuse me also, and I hope will be satisfied with receiving the news and assurances of my affection, from you. That she may not be too jealous, I do assure her, at any rate, if I know of an opportunity, I will send her a letter from Halifax. I hope upon my arrival at Col. McCulloh's to hear from you. I shall be extremely anxious to do so, and hope in God to hear of your perfect recovery. Oh! my dear Hannah, my thoughts are ever with you. I have been a thousand times distrest in thinking of the anxiety I am sure you would have about me. My principal uneasiness is ever in regard to you. *I thank God, things again wear a reviving aspect. There is a spirit rising not easily to be quelled.* Besides what I have wrote you, 4,000 troops will soon arrive from Virginia. Col. Morgan, who not long ago came from there, expects them with certainty. They are raised for 18 months, and to be under Continental officers. The British Army act most infamously. They have hanged 19 men, some who had taken protection for fighting against them, but others who had never joined them, and this only upon their being pointed out by some villainous Tories as bad men. This, I believe, is true. Adieu! my dear Hannah. I will hasten to you as soon as possible. Remember me most affectionately to your sister, Nelly and the rest, and in a particular manner to all my other friends. I am, my dear Hannah,

Yours, most affectionately,
JAS. IREDELL.*

IREDELL TO MISS BLAIR.

ELK MARSH, 12th Oct., 1780.

MY DEAR NELLY:— * * * * I can fix upon no time for being down, but I think Halifax Court will be short, and I shall not stay a moment after it. I hope to find you by that time improved by your copies. Let me entreat you not to neglect them, and be sure not to lose a day. If you lose one, you will many. A good hand is surely a very pretty thing, and worth taking some pains about, and I don't know how, but it seems a kind of prepossession in favor of a person's merit, although God

* According to Mr. Iredell's account, the troops assembled at this time, at his highest estimate, amounted to 5,350 men; at his lowest, to 4,100.
The Attorney-General in N. C. heretofore has been usually dubbed *General*, for life, by the people. It does not appear, however, that Iredell ever obtained this distinction.

knows it is no criterion of it. But every one ought to aim at as many agreeable accomplishments as they can acquire. I suppose you will have some news, and that of a public kind, to make you of consequence; therefore having given all the particulars to your aunt, I will tell you in gross, *that our public affairs do not seem in a very desperate situation, that they are retrieving fast,* that great numbers of men are collecting, the English seem afraid and in no condition to advance, some advantages have been gained over them since their possession of Charlotte, several prisoners taken, and that it is my firm opinion, if they attempt to advance much further in the country, *they will never be able to return.* I do not think this to be mere gasconade, but founded on fact and observation. So that your fears on this head may be quieted, as well as the hopes of any who had rather see red coats than blue ones. This letter will not be immediately closed, as I write without knowing of any opportunity, determining to keep my promise, not only *because it was a promise*, (which I hope you imagine I should deem fully sufficient,) but because I am happy in all occasions of giving you proofs of my affection, when I think you wish for and deserve it. God grant you may be ever that good girl I wish you. It will give me the most pleasing satisfaction. I consider you as in some respect belonging to me, and am proud as well as happy in instances of your merit, &c., &c.

Your most sincerely affectionate
JAS. IREDELL.

ELK MARSH, 12th Oct., 1780.

MY DEAR HANNAH:— * * * * Old Mrs. McCulloh was excessively ill, and still continued so, and I fear is in a great deal of danger, though she appears, I am told, rather better than she was. I was witness to a very affecting scene—a Parson Cupples in the presence of the family, and in her own bed-chamber, praying for her recovery. Col. McCulloh has been very sick, and is still extremely low, and appears much distressed by his wife's situation. Mrs. B. McCulloh not near so well as she was. Her mother had been here for a good while, and went away yesterday, and on that account the two young children were christened before she went. Capt. John Stokes* (one of

* John Stokes subsequently attained the rank of Colonel; and after the war, was made by Washington Judge of the United States for the District of North Carolina. He married a daughter of Col. Richmond Pearson; was brother to Governor Stokes, and died October, 1790. He resided in Stokes County, named in his honor. He was distinguished for bravery in battle, benevolence of character, and elevated mind.—Wheeler.

Bufort's officers, who had his right hand cut off, and received other bad wounds, a brother of Mrs. McCulloh's) and John Kinchen* were godfathers, and Mrs. Hewson and Miss Dolly Eelbrek, godmothers. The children's names, Samuel and Mary. A very crowded house all day—Mr. and Mrs. Ashe, Mr. and Mrs. Montfort, Miss Nancy Edwards, Mrs. Long, a young lady, daughter of Mrs. Hewson, and Somerville and your humble servant. Mrs. Montfort and Miss Edwards look dreadfully, particularly the former. Mrs. Ashe is much better, and *not extremely melancholy*. I hear terrible accounts of the people in town—one universal sickness. * * * * I am not so much pestered with politics as I used to be; I have avoided the subject all I could, but when forced upon it; have sometimes spoken a little firmly, which I find has not been without its effect. * * *

OCTOBER 17.

* * * But now for the news. My Granville letter must make this intelligible. The parties in pursuit of Ferguson all joined—1,000 Horse were selected out of the whole, to come up with him. They overtook him with about 1,400 men, 500 of whom were British, engaged, defeated the whole body, killed 150, (among whom was himself,) took 80 prisoners, (150 of whom were wounded,) and 1,500 stand of arms—our loss in killed said to be only 20, (in which number was a very brave, active officer, Col. Williams,)—wounded uncertain. This action happened in the afternoon of the 7th inst. at a place called King's Mountain, in what county I don't know. This intelligence comes from the very best authority, and is of extreme importance.

OCTOBER 20.

* * * Your brother looks perfectly well, and eats heartily, but has a little fever every night, after he goes to bed. We are in our old comfortable lodgings. I have received £2,700 here, which is all I expect, except my salary, £500, which perhaps I may receive, and perhaps not.

Your very affectionate
JAS. IREDELL.

Soon after the battle of Camden, General Leslie, with three thousand men, had sailed from New York, to co-operate with Cornwallis.† He had entered the Elizabeth River, and had

* John Kinchen, of Orange, member of Prov. Council '75, and of Prov. Congress '76.
† Hildreth.

fortified himself at Portsmouth; but upon hearing of the defeat of Ferguson he re-embarked his troops and proceeded to Charleston. In a letter from Mrs. Blair to Iredell, 22d October, she says: "Vessels cannot get out. There are two row galleys, with fifty men each, between this and the Bar. We are in daily expectation of them up here. If they come, I do not know what we shall do; we are unable to run away, and have hardly a negro well enough to dress us a little of any thing to eat." "We hear there is an English fleet in Virginia landing men at Kempes." Leslie was soon succeeded by Arnold in the same quarter. From this period the Albemarle was often infested with piratical craft of light draught, and the dwellings on its margin plundered by marauders.

IREDELL TO MRS. IREDELL.

NEWBERN, 16th Nov., 1780.

MY DEAR HANNAH:—I arrived here this morning, and with better luck than I expected, for after I left Mr. Charlton's I had not a drop of rain, and before what there was of little consequence, so that my health is entirely good. Mr. Ashe* came in the evening, and left Mr. Hooper and Mr. Maclaine on the road, who will be here, I suppose, to-morrow morning. Mr. Williams, I very unexpectedly found, had altered his intention, and came on here, fearing the Court might be lost, and in this he judged very prudently, for it otherwise would. Mrs. Gordon, I hear, is getting better; other people in general seem quite well. Oh! my dear Hannah, how happy should I be to know you were so. Believe me, I am most distrest about you. You are the constant subject of my most anxious thoughts. For Heaven's sake take all possible care of yourself. Let me entreat you, by every tender, by every generous motive, to do so. Your value to me is inexpressible, and seems to increase every moment. I dwell with misery on your situation, knowing how inattentive you are to your own ill health, and how bad you will suffer it to be before it may be discovered. * * * * (17th.) I wrote thus much yesterday, and have been since very much thronged with business. I am likely to get some money here, but the lawyers in this part of the country have smuggled up all the business of the prizes, so as to let Mr. Hooper, Mr. Maclaine and myself have no share in it, although both of them were wrote to, and promised to come in if it was put off a little. They did not come till to-day. Mr. Hooper's own family pretty well, but his

* Judge Ashe.

brothers have been very ill. Tom almost at the point of death, but he is now getting better. They have triumphed about his affair. The County Court discharged the arrest as illegal. I find the orders did not issue from the Governor, but on very unjustifiable pretences from General Lillington. Mr. Hooper was on his way to Edenton, and would have been there the first day, but both his horses failed on the road, and he was obliged to return. The French fleet has come to nothing. It was a fleet of transports with provisions from Cork.* It is reported here, but we know no authority for it, that Lord Cornwallis, with 300 Light Horse, had arrived at Charleston, leaving his army in jeopardy. 500 of the militia of this district, and a number from Wilmington, are embodying to go to our assistance if necessary, which I hope in God will not be the case. I shall be miserable till I hear about you, and of your being on this side the Sound. Mr. Hooper interests himself in it, and thinks by all means you ought to go there. Will not this have influence with you, joined to my earnest entreaties? Again let me conjure you to attend most carefully to your health, and advise me honestly how it is. I will drop you a line by the post to-morrow. Till then, my dearest Hannah, I bid you most affectionately adieu!

JAS. IREDELL.

IREDELL TO MISS BLAIR.

EDENTON, Nov. (date illegible).

MY DEAR NELLY:— * * * * Last Sunday was married here Mr. —— Green, about the age of 70, father of half-a-dozen men grown, and, I suppose, grandfather to a large brood of young ones, to Mrs. Hamiate, an antiquated widow of about the age of 45, old-fashioned, ugly, and horribly formal, but an excellent nurse; for which reason, they say, he with no less truth than candor honestly told her he wanted to make her his wife. The old fellow came to me about business, and looks like a hearty Methuselah, but more fitted for his grave than matrimony. However, they are yoked, and God bless them! You must remember me with affection to your mamma, and sister, and brother, and to your uncle and his family. Tell him the French fleet is turned into an English one of provision transports; that it is reported Lord Cornwallis with 300 Horse had got to Charleston; but there is no authority for this, and his army were certainly in jeopardy, parading with a trembling step Lord knows where. * * * Adieu, &c., &c.

Your extremely affectionate uncle,

JAS. IREDELL.

* In July, seven French ships, &c., with 6,000 men, arrived at New York.

NEWBERN, 18th Nov., 1780.

MY DEAR HANNAH:—I wrote to you yesterday and the day before by Captain Cotton, but am determined not to neglect one post, for fear of accidents; and to avail myself of it, I am obliged to steal a very early hour in the morning, for I am like the lawyer described by Horace, who is beset with clients almost at cock-crowing. Some of them are private, but more, I am afraid, will be public ones. Nevertheless, this Court will be far better than any yet. Mrs. Gordon is getting much better. Mr. Hooper came here only yesterday: his family are pretty well, but his brothers have been very severely sick, particularly Tom, who is, however, beginning to recover. He was only prevented by his horses giving out on the road from coming to Edenton, and since, he says, his brothers have been too sick for him to write. As to public news, the French fleet turns out to be an English one, with provisions; no troops, however, as the Governor tells me. Lord Cornwallis's army are still in jeopardy; but it is reported he himself, with 300 horse, had got into Charleston. This, however, is a mere report. * * * I am in great uneasiness and perplexity about the condition I left you in. The danger from the enemy, and your ill health, affects me very much. * * * I am perfectly well, and so is Sarah's husband,* &c., &c.

JAS. IREDELL.

NEWBERN, 26th Nov.

MY MOST DEAR HANNAH:—I had the pleasure to receive your letter about a week ago, by the post, but have since met with no opportunity of writing to you, nor, in spite of my efforts, have I been able to begin a letter to go by this post till this morning, so incessantly have I been harassed with business, chiefly of a criminal nature, but not entirely unmixed with civil, which is here much better than at any other Court; and Mr. Hooper, Mr. Maclaine, and myself, far distance all the rest in our share of it. I thank you most kindly, my dear Hannah, for the trouble you took in writing so much in your weak state of health. I fear it fatigued you extremely; but the goodness which prompted you to it, that I might have the satisfaction of hearing particularly from you, obliges me greatly. You comfort me very much in writing that you every day perceived some little amendment, and were beginning to take bitters. Heaven grant that I may have the happiness of hearing, to-day, you are still better. * * * * It distressed me greatly to hear of your brother

* His servant.

being so unwell. It happened at a most unlucky time; but I hope it did not long prevent him from availing himself of the remarkably mild and fine weather we have had.* I have already received at this Court £4,540 of this currency, £1,350 of Continental, and nine hard dollars. I expect to receive £1,500 for my salary at three Courts; *but my expenses here are monstrous*—£160 *a day for my board and lodgings only.*—I was just going to write on, when I had the inexpressible happiness to receive your letter of the 20th. Thank you, my dearest Hannah. Thank God you are so much better. I am glad to hear your brother is gone, as he will probably have fine weather all the way to Philadelphia. But I cannot bear to figure to myself the parting scene. I am glad the little fellow is called Sam. Kiss him for me, and Penny, and Gaby, whom I love in the most tender manner. Present my respects to Mrs. Johnston and her sister, Miss Lennox, Mrs. Pearson, Mrs. Dawson, &c. I am now all life and cheerfulness, hearing so happily of you. I will not fail to apply closely for the ginger. The story of the French conquest of Charleston is like all other stories about them, without any manner of foundation. I swear never to relate any other report upon them, *that I am not sure is true.*

I may luckily have an opportunity of writing to my mother and Arthur. A flag is going from here to Charleston, and an officer whom I have frequently mentioned to you, Captain James, goes in it.† I congratulate myself extremely on this favorable occasion, and entertain no doubt of the safety of the conveyance. I am perfectly well, and so is Peter. Business wherein I share as a man of consequence, and some which gives me profit and a little reputation, I rub through with cheerfulness, though very fatiguing. Adieu! my dear Hannah. I have only a moment to assure you that I am and ever shall be,

Your entirely, and most faithfully affectionate,

JAMES IREDELL.

NEWBERN, 26th Nov.

MY DEAR HANNAH:— * * * * I have not had scarcely a moment to spare till to-day (which I have been obliged unwillingly to make use of) to make purchases; for some, in spite of my poverty, I was determined to make, knowing the difficulty

* Mr. Johnston had been appointed a delegate to the Continental Congress, by the last Assembly.
† I suppose John James of the Wilmington district, appointed Captain 1776. His son, the late Hinton James, of Wilmington, was the first student of the University, 1795.

of getting any thing with us. I have bought four gauze handkerchiefs, six black silk ones, three small-tooth combs, and four common ones. After supplying your sister and Nelly, and perhaps with your leave reserving for myself one silk handkerchief, the rest are yours, to do as you please with. I wanted to have got some colored silk handkerchiefs for you, but they were all sold. There is a great quantity of shoes, and pretty good ones; and though they have very slippery heels, yet if I had yours, your sister's, and Nelly's measures, I would buy you some. Pray send me yours, and if you can, theirs, and I will endeavor to get you some on my return. I have tried to no purpose to get some ginger. Wilson Blount tells me, he has been long trying to get some, but without success, and that if he can procure me any in my absence he will. We leave this place to-morrow. Mr. Hooper, Mr. Maclaine, and myself, go together. I fear I shall not have it in my power to write you from Wilmington, as the post has been discontinued. By Mr. Hooper's extreme kindness, I find I am likely to fare very well there. He is to have very good rooms fitted up, and I believe I shall be at little or no expense. *Here my expenses are monstrous.* They will be, with my horses, £2,500 at least. I have made our tenants settle for their rents according to the depreciation. Some of the money I have received; the rest I have their notes for in hard money, and I have been promised that the greatest part shall be paid before Christmas. Their notes for this purpose I have left with Wilson Blount, having no other person to depend on. Many people think things will be cheaper on my return. At present they are very dear. * * * *

Yours, &c.,

JAS. IREDELL.

WILMINGTON, Dec. 8th, 1780.

MY DEAR HANNAH:—I have not known a single opportunity, till the present, of writing to you, since I left Newbern. I thank God I have been ever since, and am now, perfectly well. The business of this Court has been very troublesome, though not profitable; and possibly I may be detained a day or two beyond it, by an Admiralty suit in which I am engaged. I do not mean it shall be above a day or two at farthest, so that as the enemy are gone, and I hope not returned, I flatter myself Captain Johnston will excuse me, and that you will, as I mean to receive a pretty good fee. Mr. Hooper and I were obliged to take lodgings, in consequence of a very unexpected circumstance—Mr. Hogg and his daughter coming here from Hillsborough, and occupying his brother's house, where we were to have been; and though we receive all possible civilities from them, there is no room to accommodate us with a bed. This I am afraid will deduct largely from the little money I get here. I have kept so close to business, that I have not been at Mr. Hooper's house this week; nor was I there but one day before our Court began, which you may suppose has mortified me not a little, for the usual kindness and the usual happiness has now, as at all former times, captivated me. ✱ ✱ ✱ ✱

Yours, &c.,
JAS. IREDELL.

An inquiry having been ordered relative to Gates's conduct at Camden, General Greene was nominated by General Washington, to whom the selection was referred, as his successor.✱ Lee's corps of horse, and some companies of artillery, were ordered south, while Kosciusko was sent as engineer. Historians represent the three Southern States, during this year, and especially after the battle of Camden, as entirely prostrate, and "incapable of helping themselves."† This, certainly, was never true of North Carolina. When Greene came to this State, he found a numerous army in existence. According to the statement of Iredell, the Attorney-General, it numbered, east of the Catawba, from 4,750 to 5,850 men. After his defeat, General Gates repaired to Hillsborough, where, aided by Governor Nash, the Board of War, and Governor Rutledge, he addressed himself with great energy and zeal to the task of re-organizing a force to oppose the British. So successful were his efforts, that when Greene arrived at his head-quarters at Charlotte, December 2d, North Carolina was again "in a situation to make a stout defence." At Saratoga, Gates had reaped the harvest of glory, though Schuyler had made the combinations, and arrayed the force that secured success. Now, in turn, was Gates to see the fruits of his toil enure to a rival's fame. To the troops under Gates were soon added Lee's corps, consisting of 350 men, and the additional artillery companies. General Greene was warmly received in North Carolina, not only because of his own merit, but as the harbinger of substantial succor from the North. In the latter respect, however, the people of North Carolina were doomed to disappointment. The three Southern States were to realize the truth of the poet : "Who would be free, themselves must strike the blow." The General was now in the midst of a friendly region, whose population was probably the most spirited in America ; and in his ensuing campaign, though Tories were, undoubtedly, numerous, he could rely upon early and accurate information of every hostile movement. His policy with the militia seems to have been to use them as a cover for his regulars. Whether this was correct or not, I am too ignorant of the military art to hazard an opinion ; but the casualties of his battles induce a doubt. The militia soon suspected that they were lightly valued and heartlessly exposed ; and discontent spread among those, who ever claim social superiority to mercenaries, and expect some more tender consideration. Greene was cautious and prudent, and during his command the State was liberated. I would not tear one leaf from his brow ; but what would have been the result if the ardor of the troops had been indulged to the top of their bent, under leaders dashing and bold as Sumner or Davie, Marion or Sumter, Morgan or Washington ? Might not the campaign of '81 have been as memorable for a *masterly victory* as for a "masterly retreat ?" Would not action—constant action—in advance or assault, have rallied and supported the militia better than the continuous retreat ? "The mountainous region of North Carolina was inhabited by a race of hardy men, who were familiar with the use of the horse and rifle, were stout, active, patient under privation, and brave. Irregular in their movements, and unaccustomed to restraint, they delighted in the fury of action, but pined under the servitude and inactivity of camp."✱ The men of King's Mountain and Moore's Creek were of the same race ; the same blood flowed in their veins ; and they had the same fiery, impetuous temperament.

IREDELL TO MRS. IREDELL.

WILMINGTON, 13th Dec., 1780.

MY DEAR HANNAH :—I wrote you from here a few days ago, by an express going about the business of a vessel to Mr. Cabarrus. The Superior Court broke up on Saturday. I have since been detained about an Admiralty suit, which we ended about 11 o'clock last night.

This morning I set off on my way home immediately from here, having taken leave of Mr. Hooper yesterday. ✱ ✱ ✱

Yours, &c.,
JAS. IREDELL.

The following, which I transcribe from one of Judge Iredell's manuscript volumes, is, I suppose, the Admiralty suit referred to

---

* Hildreth. † Hildreth, vol. iii. p. 331.

* Lee's Memoirs.

---

in his last letter. As it is, as far as I know, the only report of any case of Prize extant, tried in the State during the Revolution, it will, I trust, prove interesting at least to the profession.

The following papers were prepared, in order to be transmitted to Philadelphia, concerning the subject-matter they refer to.✱

UPON AN APPEAL FROM A DECREE IN THE COURT OF ADMIRALTY FOR THE PORT OF BRUNSWICK, IN NORTH CAROLINA.

I.

Martial Boitar, Commander, and the Owners, other Officers, Mariners and Marines of the Private Ship of War the Fortunate, } *Appellants.*

Hezekiah Anthony, Commander of a Private Ship of War called the Hazard, and others, } *Respondents.*

CASE OF THE APPELLANTS.

A British schooner called the Adventurer, laden with turpentine and other articles, was taken at sea by the said Hezekiah Anthony, in the said private ship of war the Hazard, on the 17th day of November, 1780.

On the 22d day of November following, about 10 o'clock in the forenoon, she was retaken by the British frigate the Raleigh.

On the 24th day of the same month, at 12 o'clock at noon, she was taken from the Raleigh's people by Captain Boitar, in the said private ship of war the Fortunate.

Boitar's prize-master brings her and her cargo safely into the port of Brunswick, North Carolina, and there libels her in the Court of Admiralty.

Anthony puts in a claim as first captor, and prays that the schooner, and that part of her cargo which was on board of her at the time of her seizure by him, may be restored to him, for the benefit of him and his associates, on payment of salvage.

A jury having been summoned, according to law, to try the validity of the said claim, establish it by their verdict, finding that the property Anthony claimed should be restored to him on payment of one-third salvage.

Upon this verdict a decree accordingly is given for the claimants, from which the appellants appeal for the following among other

REASONS.

1. Because it is apprehended, that the property of a prize is not altered in consequence of a capture at sea, until condemnation. Whatever difference of opinion may have formerly subsisted among speculative writers on the subject, it appears to have been long the course of the Court of Admiralty in England not to adjudge the property altered until it is condemned. (See Burr. 4th part, vol. ii. p. 694.) And even so strong a case has happened as the following : A ship was taken in the year 1691 off Yarmouth, carried to North Bergen, then sold to A ; afterwards sold to B. B sends her to the West Indies, afterwards to France, and in the year 1695 to England, when, she being retaken, it was resolved that the property was not altered. (See Luc. 77, Hil. 11, Ann. B. R. Apievedo *vs.* Cambridge, Cunningh. Pol. of Ass. p. 236, c. 59.) There are other authorities to the same purpose (Burr. ibid. Whitehead *vs.* Bance, 1749. B. R. Cunn. Pol. of Ass. p. 266, c. 65), and reason seems in favor of the construction, because were condemnation held unnecessary, Courts of Admiralty could not have that check upon privateers at sea, which the public honor and interest, and the security of individuals require.

2. Because the Rules of Congress, upon which the Act of Assembly in the State of North Carolina is founded, appear to have adopted such a construction, since they seem to allow an owner to claim upon payment of salvage, without any limitation of *time.* If twenty-four hours' possession (that contended for on behalf of Captain Anthony in the present case) transferred the property to the enemy, our Act of Assembly could not divest the right out of the re-captor, for the owner is allowed to claim, upon a supposition that the *property is not altered.* The same reasoning may be extended to any other arbitrary period affixed ; for whenever the property has become absolutely the enemy's, no recapture can entitle an owner to claim.

3. Because, even admitting the possession of twenty-four hours to be the true criterion (contrary, as it is conceived, to public utility, to the opinion of many speculative writers of equal authority, and to a long uniform practice, adopted in a manner by our own Act of Assembly✱), yet the property in question

---

* For several years a standing committee of Congress heard appeals in prize cases from the States; but in May, 1780, an Admiralty Court of Appeals was established, with three judges.—Hild. Hist. U. S., vol. iii. p. 404.

* This parenthesis in the original transmitted stood thus: ("contrary, as it is conceived, to reason, to the opinion of many speculative writers of equal authority, and to a long, uniform practice"); which, upon reflection, I thought was not sufficiently accurate and comprehensive.

having been more than twenty-four hours in possession of the enemy, it upon this principle absolutely became the enemy's, and of course by the re-capture afterwards that of the appellants.

JAS. IREDELL,
Advocate for the Appellants in North Carolina.

UPON AN APPEAL FROM THE SAME DECREE.

II.

Martial Boitar, Commander, and the Owners, other Officers, Mariners and Marines of the Private Ship of War the Fortunate, } *Appellants.*

Thomas Young, *Respondent.*

CASE OF THE APPELLANTS.

This case arises from a claim for part of the property libelled in the British schooner mentioned in the former case.

Thirty-four negroes, and some other articles, were found on board the schooner at the time of her capture by Captain Boitar, which had belonged to the respondent, an inhabitant of Georgia, and had been taken from him on shore by Captain Anthony, who at the same time seized the respondent himself, and detained him as a prisoner.

These negroes, and the rest of the property in question, after the capture of the schooner by Captain Anthony, had been put on board of her, and remained there from that time until she was brought by Captain Boitar, as mentioned in the former case, into the port of Brunswick.

The respondent entered a claim for the said thirty-four negroes and other property, praying that the whole might be restored to him upon payment of salvage.

This claim was received, and a jury summoned, as in other cases, to decide upon it.

It appeared by strong implication from the respondent's own showing, and by express proof in the case, that he had taken an oath of allegiance to the British government, and was a voluntary and firm adherent to its interest.

Nevertheless, the jury by their verdict established his claim, and a decree was given accordingly; from which the appellants appeal for these, among other

REASONS.

1. Because it plainly appears from the allegations of the respondent himself, and the proofs in the cause, that he was a British subject, without any pretence of being so by compulsion, but voluntarily and heartily; and consequently he has no right to claim property in our courts.

2. Because it is supposed to be immaterial, and an improper subject of inquiry, *how property came on board a prize*, provided it appears to be the property of any of the *enemy's subjects.*

3. Because it is apprehended, that commanders of privateers are warranted, by an express power from Congress, to distress the enemy and seize property, as well by *land* as *sea*: a practice which their own example, if not the general law of nations, sufficiently justifies and requires.

JAS. IREDELL,
Advocate for the Appellants in North Carolina.

Dec., 1780.

JOHNSTON TO IREDELL.

PHILADELPHIA, 21st Dec., 1780.

DEAR SIR:—You will have heard, before this reaches you, the state of my health on my arrival at this place. I now begin to hope I may recover, though I am still confined to the house, and my cough, attended with fever, very troublesome; but I sometimes go down stairs and mix with the gentlemen who lodge in the house, and those who visit them, which I find of some service to me. I had the pleasure of hearing, by the last post, that Mrs. Iredell was getting better; I hope by the next to hear every body is well. Congress seem to be very busy; but as I have not yet taken my seat in it, I am acquainted with but few particulars, and if I was acquainted with any thing interesting, I should be afraid to write it by the post, as there is reason to apprehend that, before this reaches you, the enemy may be in possession of some of the towns in Virginia through which the post passes, as we have certain advices that 4,000 troops, under the command of General Kniphausen, have been some time past embarked, though we have not yet any advice of their having sailed, and their destination is kept a profound secret in New York. Congress have sent a Colonel Palfray, formerly paymaster of the army, to France, in the character of consul from the United States: Colonel Laurens, son of the late President, is appointed a minister for a particular purpose to the court of France. This last appointment is much disapproved of by some of the members, apprehensive of its disgusting Dr. Franklin, and by that means impeding rather than promoting our interest at that court. Mr. Dana, secretary to Mr. Adams, is appointed minister to the Empress of Russia: it is uncertain how he may be received, but the general opinion is, that the old lady will not be displeased with the compliment.

23d.—I have just heard of a brother of Mr. Granbury's, who sets out in the morning for Carolina; I will therefore close this letter, and endeavor to send it by him; and can now venture to mention the distresses of Congress in regard to money matters. Nothing can be more alarming. The treasury quite empty, and no means of filling it, to answer the pressing demands which are daily made upon it. What adds to their distress: the supplies for the army are not yet laid in, and they have been disappointed in getting over a quantity of clothing, promised for the use of the army, in France. Expenses here exceed all conception: from the great number of prizes brought in, and large importations from Europe to this place, the town is filled with all kinds of goods, and furnishes supplies to all the Southern States, and the State of New York; this draws all the circulating cash in these States to this town; this occasions such a profusion of money here, that every thing is most enormously dear. I had almost forgot to mention, that the British ministry have carried all before them in the late general elections. Most of the eminent characters in the opposition are left out—namely, Mr. Fox, Mr. Burke, Mr. Wilkes, with a number of others, whose names I do not recollect. An unsuccessful attempt was made to oust Sir George Saville. My best respects to Mr. Barker and all my other friends. You will observe there are some circumstances in this letter which should be communicated with caution. Tell Mr. Smith I will write to him soon; and let him see this. Present my love to my sister Iredell, my sister Blair, Nelly, and the children; tell them I think of them with all imaginable tenderness. Though I am now writing at two o'clock in the afternoon, it is so dark I can scarcely read what I write. Adieu! and believe me ever,

My dear Sir,
Your affectionate brother and most obedient servant,
SAM. JOHNSTON.

CHAPTER XIV.

COWPENS; LETTER FROM ROBERT SMITH; ASSEMBLY; C. JOHNSON TO IREDELL; S. JOHNSTON TO IREDELL; SPENCER TO IREDELL; HOOPER TO IREDELL; PIERCE BUTLER TO IREDELL; BATTLE OF GUILFORD; LETTERS; COUNCIL EXTRAORDINARY; LETTERS; PEOPLE OF EDENTON FLY; GREENE'S CAMPAIGN IN S. C.; LETTERS FROM BUTLER, JOHNSTON, MRS. BLAIR, &C.; TRICK PLAYED GEN. GREGORY; ASSEMBLY; GOV. BURKE; LETTERS; NEGRO INVASION; BATTLE OF EUTAW SPRINGS; CAPTURE OF GOV. BURKE; BATTLES OF ELIZABETHTOWN AND LINDLEY'S MILL; YORKTOWN; EVACUATION OF WILMINGTON; REJOICING. ÆT. 29–30.

THE year '81 was more full of stirring incidents, and momentous events than any other in the history of North Carolina. Centuries will probably elapse before her organism will be again subjected to shocks so rude, and trials so severe. Torn by domestic dissensions, her finances disordered, and invaded, yet was she ever true to herself, and equal to every emergency. Though the dye of her flag was deepened by the blood that streamed from her own bosom, yet was it ever uplifted high by the stout arms of her sons. Though her fields were ravaged, and her homes despoiled by friend and foe, wherever danger threatened, she promptly sent succor; while her ministers, save when interrupted for a time by the actual presence of the enemy, enforced her laws by the chastisement of criminals.

Either ignorantly or maliciously, the historians of the country have done much wrong to the State. Even so important a calamity as the capture and abduction of her chief magistrate has not been mentioned by any, save very recent writers.* No North Carolinian has as yet fairly addressed himself to the pious task of vindicating her fame. Dr. Hawks, Gov. Graham, President Swain and Dr. Carruthers have thrown brilliant flashes of light on the subject; but the skill of some industrious hand,

* Hildreth. Lossing. Wheeler.

enamored of the labor, is yet needed to remove the mould, and disclose to admiration the record engraven by the point of her sword in that dark hour when lightnings played about her brow, and the earth trembled beneath her feet.

Her fluctuating militia, assembled often at points widely apart, and varying in number from time to time; the appointment sometimes of officers from other States to lead her troops; the transfer of Continental officers to the militia; and the militia "aids" absorbed by the Continental lines, embarrass the inquirer, who endeavors to trace her military career. Each day, however, developes some new fact; the work grows by degrees to completion, and ere long the veil will be removed from the statue.*

The campaign of '81 opened with the victory of the Cowpens, won by Southern valor over superior numbers—a victory more resplendent in lustre, than that of Bennington, and attended by consequences as important.† The following paper, preserved by Judge Iredell, I transcribe from the original copy of Mr. Robert Smith, as it differs in some particulars from the relations of most writers.

"A particular account of the victory gained by Gen. Morgan over Lt. Col. Tarlton with 1,150 chosen British Troops with the Legion, and the first part of the 71st Regiment with two pieces of Artillery. Col. Tarlton with the above attacked Gen. Morgan at the Cowpens, near Cherokee Ford on the Broad River, on the 17th inst. (January). The battle lasted 50 minutes, when Gen. Morgan gained a complete victory. Took 502 Privates, 29 Commissioned officers prisoners, besides 200 wounded; 100 Privates and 10 Commissioned officers left dead on the field; 2 field-pieces taken, 35 baggage waggons taken, two standards and a travelling forge, 70 negroes and about 100 horses. Our light-horse pursued the enemy 24 miles. Gen. Morgan had little more than 800 men, 300 Regulars and 500 picked Militia Riflemen. About £20,000 sterling worth of drygoods is said to have fallen into our hands. The above is a copy of Gen. Morgan's return sent to Congress by his aide-de-camp to Congress. Whole of killed, wounded and taken, 841.

"Morgan's Militia were chiefly North Carolinians, the command of Major McDowell."

ROBERT SMITH TO IREDELL.*

HALIFAX, 30th January, 1781.

DEAR SIR:—We have this moment been favored with an authentic account of the glorious event of the 17th inst., on Broad River. I cannot inform you, or my other friends better than by inclosing a copy of the account from Gen. Morgan to Congress—it's rough but correct; this one blow secures us from the Southern quarter, and totally ruins this campaign to the enemy. I was under the severest doubts about Gen. Morgan's safety. I knew his number was far inferior to those against him after the reinforcement. Broad River was high; I was afraid he would be hem'd in, and cut off; pray show this letter with the inclosed to all my friends. I had sealed up all my letters, but luckily the boy had not gone. I wish our friend Gregory had this news—it will be a fine little pill to Arnold.† I hope in the goods taken we shall find sufficient to clothe our Troops, which will be of great importance.

I am, dear sir,
Your most obedient servant,
ROBT. SMITH.

Stung with rage at the defeat of the "élite" of his army, and abandoning all superfluous baggage, Lord Cornwallis immediately began an eager pursuit of the victors. Anticipating his Lordship's action, Morgan fled. Now commenced "that thrilling series of military movements, which was continued with the activity of a steeple-chase for quite two months."‡ Morgan had about twenty-five miles the start.§ The vanguard of the British

---

* The belief is generally cherished in N. C., that either Dr. Hawks or Governor Swain, or both, have been some time engaged in writing the history of the State.
In the battles of Rocky Mount and Hanging Rock, the North Carolinians under Irwin, Huggins and Davie, constituted the greater part of Sumter's command. In the following February, when Pickens was invested with the command of 600 or 700 men, in the rear of Lord Cornwallis, not more than 40 were from S. C., the remainder being North Carolinians. The brigade raised by S. C., in the Spring of '81, were mostly from N. C., under Col. Polk of the same State.—*General Joseph Graham.*
In the course of the war broken corps were often amalgamated together, under the command of the senior officer. Thus the lines of Maryland and Delaware were combined under Col. Williams; and Blands, Moylans and Baylor's under Washington. At the Cowpens, Washington's cavalry were reinforced by a company of mounted militia (Major McDowell's).—*Lee's Memoirs.*
It is believed that as fast as N. C. assembled Continentals, they were added to the lines North Carolina, until their numbers were sufficient to constitute full battalions. Under the general appellation of Continentals or Regulars their individuality was lost sight of.

† Lee.

* Smith was in the Assembly, from Edenton.
† General Gregory, with a body of troops, was watching the enemy in Virginia, and guarding the N. E. section of the State.
‡ Governor Graham says, "nec mora, nec requies"—which I beg leave to translate a *neck and neckrace.*
§ Governor Graham.

---

reached the Island Ford on the Catawba on the 29th; but found that Morgan had crossed two hours before. Here a providential flood detained them two days. With great gallantry General Davidson raised three hundred and fifty men; and with this small force resolved, as far as was practicable, to impede the passage of the enemy. Plunging into the river, the British (February 1st) waded across, but were received by a well directed fire from the militia, occasioning a loss of forty killed and wounded, including Col. Hall. Here Davidson received a ball in his breast—the second North Carolina General slain in the war. This sad accident more than counterbalanced the loss of the British. Davidson was one of those who long "*could* hold the combat doubtful:"* active, indefatigable, and of pleasing address, he was the chief instrument relied on by Greene for the assemblage of the militia: his career had been tracked with light: just as he attained the zenith, and while his countrymen looked upward with admiration and hope, he fell.

Effecting his retreat in safety, Greene crossed the Dan, Feb. 13th. Cornwallis, chagrined and baffled, soon afterwards occupied Hillsborough.

On the 18th of January, the Assembly met at Halifax.† Never before had they convened at a more critical juncture; never had the future worn so dark an aspect. Their attention was at once directed to the defence of the State. Bills were passed for giving greater efficiency to the militia, and for the reorganization of the Continental Battalions; the latter, nominally six, were reduced to four, and provision made for speedily filling up the ranks to the proper complement. The State had been constrained to resort in many instances to impressment to obtain supplies for the support of her troops. Even when paper money was given in exchange, the purchase had much of a compulsory character. With a hearty desire to maintain a reputation for fair dealing, auditors were appointed for each of the districts of the State to examine claims: when these were approved, the auditors were directed to issue certificates for the sums due; and all public officers were instructed to take them in the settlement of taxes, &c. The powers of the Quarter-master General were enlarged. The Board of War was discontinued. By an extraordinary stretch of authority, whose only palliations were the crisis and the purity of their motives, they established a "Council Extraordinary,"‡ to consist of "three persons of integrity and abilities, such as the General Assembly can have the greatest confidence in," and "invested the actual Governor (Nash) and this council, with the executive powers of government" after the expiration of his official term, provided the invasion of the enemy should prevent the holding of elections, and the meeting of the Assembly at the usual time. After thus guarding against the chances of war, the Assembly closed its session, February 14th. The Council of War consisted of Caswell, Col. Martin, and probably Bignal.*

CHARLES JOHNSON (SENATOR FROM CHOWAN) TO IREDELL.

HALIFAX, 8th February, 1781.

DEAR SIR:—Yours of the 5th I have this moment received. Private matters and considerations of every kind and thing are inadmissible, owing to the impatience of the members to get home. Finding no abler hand would undertake, I introduced a Bill for yours, and the Judges' Establishment, the salary to be fixed in a permanent manner out of the reach of depreciation. It has passed two readings—not without curtailments, which they call amendments. I hope, however, it will pass; even with the allowance it is reduced to, it will show a good intention, and a willingness to amendments, of which this may be considered as a beginning. I have likewise been the introducer of another Bill for encouraging the importation of Arms, and which passed unanimously—I think its principles are founded in justice—but am doubtful whether those of my own trade will think so—as it concerns them entirely; but one of the Legislature, I'm of opinion that private interest ought to give way to public utility —however, in this, I flatter myself, they are both happily blended. Col. Lee with his legion has surprised Georgetown, took the commanding officer and killed many of the enemy—this by express. It is too true the enemy are in possession of Wilmington and environs, and of poor Mr. Hooper and Maclaine's families; who are both here: their situation is truly lamentable, and I sincerely feel for them.† Boyd‡ is in such a dreadful hurry, I can only beg my compliments to your family, and am, dear sir,

Yours sincerely,
CHAS. JOHNSON.

---

* Lee. † Statutes. ‡ Gov. Graham.

* The Council Extraordinary was clothed with all the powers exercised by the Board of War and Council of State, and was required to keep a journal. Their salary £200 per day.
† Major Craig took possession of Wilmington, January 29th.
‡ Adam Boyd. One of the first acts of the Whig Magistrates in New Hanover County, after the Revolution began, was to turn out the old Clerk, Mr. John London, and to appoint Boyd in his stead. Boyd was Editor of the "Mercury:" he was afterwards made Chaplain to the Continental Troops, and after the war regularly ordained a Minister of the Episcopal Church. He was the second husband of the mother of the venerable Dr. A. De Rossett of Wilmington.

S. JOHNSTON TO IREDELL.

PHILADELPHIA, February 10th, 1781.

DEAR SIR:—As nothing new has happened since I wrote to my brother, which letter I desired him to communicate to you, and having wrote by this conveyance to R. Smith, I should not now have wrote to you, but having understood that my friends were alarmed on account of my health, this will enable you to assure them that I am now quite well, and attend Congress every day when the weather is good.

I congratulate you on Gen. Morgan's success; it is considered by the Military gentlemen here, as one of the most gallant and well conducted actions of this war. I have sent Wilie Jones the last papers, which I have desired him to forward to Mr. Smith. I would have sent duplicates, but it would have made my packet too large. Present my love to my sisters, Nelly, and the children. I congratulate my sister Blair on Billy's return. I hope the sea agrees with him. I wrote some time ago to Mrs. Dawson, and likewise to Mr. Pollock. I hope they received my letters —be pleased to present my proper respect to them. I long very much to be at home again. I have no relish for politics. Though the weather has been so remarkably temperate, that there has been no appearance of ice in the river, yet it has been very wet and disagreeable. I hope you will by some means let me hear from you; present my compliments to Mr. Barker in particular, and all my other friends, and believe me with every sentiment of affection and esteem,

Dear sir, yours,
SAM. JOHNSTON.

HOOPER TO IREDELL.

HALIFAX, Tuesday, February 13th, 1781.

MY DEAR IREDELL:—In the agony of my soul, I inform you that I am severed from my family—perhaps for ever!

The enemy landed at Wilmington on the 29th of last month, and took possession of the town without opposition. Well aware that the saltworks at and near my house might make it obnoxious to the enemy—I removed my family, and from the want of horses and carriages, and a thousand other circumstances, which I will mention to you as soon as I collect myself enough to think or write seriously upon the subject—I removed my family to Wilmington. Had I attempted to have carried them further, I apprehended that they must still have been subject to parties of the enemy, who would have been engaged in plundering without the restraint of any officer to check their depredations. In an enemy's country, at all events, I thought it best to trust them to the mercy of the principal officer who would be at Wilmington, and preserve some order there, rather than risk a perfect separation from Mrs. Hooper's friends. I have many friends in Wilmington who differ essentially from me in political opinions, but who, I think, would risk all to serve me and my family—to these and to God have I trusted almost every thing I hold dear in this world, and if He will preserve them in happiness, He may do with me as He thinks best.

The enemy are about 450 strong, commanded by Major Craig, late major and adjutant to General Burgoyne, escorted by a certain Dubois, and a Frenchman of the name of Treville, who left Wilmington and went to Charleston about three weeks ago. The troops are escorted by the Blonde of 36 guns, the Delight of 16 guns; Otter, 16 guns, and two or three gallies bearing some 18 pounders—12lb. and 16lb. The whole fleet makes about eighteen in number.

Their object, they say, is to unite themselves with the disaffected of Cumberland, and weaken the opposition to Cornwallis.

The enemy surprised the bridge called *Heron's* (you know it), the bridge at my brother's house (the Mulberry), and after burning all the public stores, they retired on the Wilmington side of the river again. They took possession of the Mulberry, and I fear my brother Thomas is ruined as well as his elder brother. Need I, my dear friend, add to the sympathetic emotions of your heart—that I left my wife in a very precarious state of health; my brother George upon his bed, where he has been for twenty-one days, ill of a putrid fever, his life despaired of by Cobham and all his physicians; his wife far from being healthy. The impress of horses and carriages has been so violent that a few, a very few, of the male inhabitants are out. I was obliged to rely on my legislative privileges and the secrecy of a cellar to conceal my horses from pursuit. Mr. Maclaine and I are together exiles—travelling as lightly as General Cornwallis does, and more so, with all our property on our backs. Perhaps we may see Edenton; perhaps shall advance to the Southward. Circumstances as they arise must determine our movements. We talk of being with you, but stand suspended. A country on the verge of ruin; a corrupt, or what is worse, an idiot Assembly; an indolent Executive; a Treasury without money; a Military without exertion; punctilios superseding duty;—in a word, upon the true test of patriotism, the approach of the enemy, the vociferation of persecution and confiscation being resolved into silence or ineffectual efforts in order to promote doubts and disputation, show what we have to expect from the opposition of this State. *Report* says, and *perhaps* it is true, that Cornwallis is at Magee's, forty miles from Salisbury, on this side; Greene, sixteen on this side of Cornwallis. Adieu, my ever dear friend. Remember me most affectionately to yours' and Mr. Johnston's family. Mr. Maclaine begs to be mentioned to you with much regard and esteem, and I am, my dear Iredell, ever yours; and may you never feel what does now for a separation from his family,

Yours,
WM. HOOPER.

Remember me most affectionately to Allen. I congratulate him on his happy change. May the connection be never interrupted by what I now feel. I will write him very shortly.

Yours affectionately,
W. H.

I can get no letter paper—pardon me.

JUDGE SPENCER TO IREDELL.

HALIFAX, 15th of Feby., 1781.

DEAR SIR:—The Assembly broke up yesterday, having, among other important matters, given the judges an order on the Treasurer for £20,000 a-piece, and the Attorney-General for £10,000, in pursuance of a resolve of last session for making up the depreciation of their allowance, and in full, as I take it, of all arrearages for past services. They have rejected a bill for giving them a decent salary without depreciation, have made them no further provision; but, as I am informed by some of the members, intend that civil business shall cease for a while. The Senate passed a resolve for making the further allowance of £20,000 a-piece to the judges, and £10,000 to the Attorney-General; but it was rejected in the House of Commons at the objection of Mr. T. Person,* who had like to have carried a rejection of the first resolve; but our friend M. Locke opposed him, and carried the important point in our favor. They have totally rejected Judge Ashe's claim for an allowance for courts; he was prevented from attending through sickness. We seem, therefore, to be left altogether in the lurch. I have put my office upon that footing that I shall never budge another foot in their service, at least as a civil officer, till they make proper provision for my support. I have no doubt but the other judges will do the same. No superior courts, I suppose, will therefore be held till after the next session of Assembly, let the event of our public concerns turn out as they will. They wear a very critical aspect at present; but I hope the cloud will soon be dispelled. You will have the news before this reaches you, more certain than any thing else I can at present relate to you.

I am, dear sir, with great respect and esteem,
Your most obedient humble servant,
SAMUEL SPENCER.

S. JOHNSTON TO IREDELL.

PHILADELPHIA, 15th February, 1781.

DEAR SIR:—I had the pleasure of receiving yours of the 5th inst., last night. I wrote a line by an express to the Governor, which I hope you will receive. I have very little hope that this will reach you. By a vessel, which arrived last Sunday from Cadiz, we have letters as late as the 19th December. The fleets at that time, as well of France and Spain as Great Britain, were in port; the Dutch had acceded to the armed Neutrality, notwithstanding which, the British continued to take their ships, and it was thought would make some attempts on their settlements in the East Indies. Mr. Cumberland is still permitted to continue at the Court of Madrid—*a very suspicious circumstance.* There is *great reason* to apprehend that the British mean to fortify and support their station at Portsmouth, or some other in that neighborhood, in order to shut up the navigation of the bay, and by making frequent incursions into the country, prevent the State of Virginia from sending aid to the Carolinas. Congress is every day engaged in a variety of matters, but under our present situation, it is probably best to say little as to the particulars. I hope to have some opportunity before long by which I may be more communicative. I have wrote a great number of letters to you and my other friends, particularly C. Johnson and R. Smith, which I fear have miscarried—having lately received a letter from Mr. Smith from Halifax, in which he complains of my not having wrote. I am now quite recovered, except a little remnant of my cold, which is attended with no other inconvenience, but that it makes me cautious of exposing myself. I am very happy to hear that my sister Iredell has quite recovered her health. I was long under very serious apprehensions for her

---

* Thomas Person of Granville; an eminent Whig leader, ultra-democratic in politics. He was made Brigadier-General in '76, and exercised in the legislative assemblies a very commanding influence. Person Hall at Chapel Hill was erected by means contributed by his liberality, and a county bears his name. He was a type of the class of politicians, of whom the late Mr. Macon was an illustrious representative.

safety; I shall be very happy if we should all once more meet in health. Present my compliments to Mr. Johnson, and all my other friends; pray don't forget Mr. Barker. My love to my sisters, Nelly and the children, and believe me with the most sincere esteem,

My dear sir,
Your affectionate brother, and obedient servant,
SAM. JOHNSTON.

After the death of General Davidson, General Pickens was elected to the command of his brigade.* In conjunction with Col. Lee, on the 25th February, he, at the head of these *North Carolinians*, surprised a body of 400 loyalists under Col. Pyles: ninety of the tories were slain, and the greater part of the remainder wounded; stratagem conspired with valor their destruction.

SAM. JOHNSTON TO IREDELL.

PHILADELPHIA, 27th February, 1781.

DEAR SIR:—Your letter giving an account of Morgan's victory, I had the pleasure to receive yesterday, but have heard nothing of those sent by the gentlemen to Virginia. Our accounts from General Cornwallis are very alarming, but we hope it will not be long before both he and Arnold will repent of their rashness. Congress are not inattentive to the state of the Southern States, but the unfortunate mutinies in the Army, and other unavoidable accidents have prevented them sending on more Troops, and put it out of their power to make such ample provision for those that were sent as would have been wished. Should the report, which from different quarters has arrived at different towns to the eastward, with regard to Count D'Estaing's having taken seven Ships of the Line, three Frigates and the greatest part of 90 sail of Transports of Sir Samuel Hood's Squadron off the Western Islands, be true, it will be a favorable presage of the success of the ensuing campaign. The French fleet hold the British ships blocked up in Gardiner's Bay, and only wait the arrival of the expected reinforcements to lay hands on. The safety or destruction of the British fleet, under Admiral Arbuthnot, depends entirely on this circumstance, whether a French or British reinforcement first arrives. The chances at present appear to me in favor of our Allies. General Washington will not neglect the relief of North Carolina, when circumstances will admit. I dare

* Gen. Joseph Graham.

not be more particular, but hope before this reaches you, Arnold's fate will be decided. I received Mr. Johnson's letter of the 6th January only yesterday. Be so good as to present my compliments to him, and let him know I wrote a long letter to him last week by the way of Halifax. Remember me to all our other friends. My love to my sisters, Nelly and the children: I long very much to see you and them, and am ever,

My dear sir,
Your affectionate and obedient servant,
SAM. JOHNSTON.

PIERCE BUTLER TO IREDELL.

Major Butler, was an Irishman:* a descendant of Ormond, the celebrated Jacobite Duke. He came to America as an officer in the British Army:† he soon resigned, married Miss Middleton, a lady of large estate; and settled in South Carolina. He was distinguished for his fine person, his elegant manners, his attainments, his talents, and his patriotism. After the fall of Charleston, he narrowly escaped capture, fleeing "literally barefooted." He sought shelter in North Carolina, where he was warmly received, and where his accomplishments and virtues soon won him friends. He was especially intimate with Iredell: their mutual attachment ripened with advancing years: their correspondence, cordial and unreserved, was frequent, and lasted during Iredell's life. Major Butler represented South Carolina in Congress in 1787, and in the Convention which framed the Constitution of the United States. His letters will show his views of Federal politics, and with what ardor and intelligence he watched and labored to advance the peculiar interests of the South. His grandchildren, by his daughter, who married Dr. Mease of Philadelphia, are his sole representatives: on succeeding to his fortune, they adopted his name.

NEWBERN, March 11th, 1781.

DEAR SIR:—I was just sitting down to write to you when Mr. Cogdell handed to me your truly acceptable favor of the 5th inst. I assure you, sir, the pleasure arising from the commencement of a correspondence, so desirable on my side, is reciprocal. I should do much violence to my own feelings, if I omitted the first opportunity of expressing the grateful sense I have of your

* Cyclop. Biog. Appleton.   † Johnson's Traditions, &c.

more than polite attention to me, during my stay at Edenton. I feel myself much obliged by it. However great my distress of mind may otherwise be, I shall, in prosperity or adversity, always reflect with a pleasing satisfaction, on the hours I passed in your company; and think some of my losses fully balanced by the acquisition of your acquaintance. To Mrs. Iredell, Mrs. and Miss Blair, I beg to present my thanks, for the obliging and truly flattering remembrance of me; and ardent good wishes for every event that can contribute to their happiness. I am additionally indebted to you, my dear sir, for the confidence you place in me by favoring me with extracts from Mr. Johnston's letter to you. The confidence I hope is not misplaced. A vessel just arrived here from Hispaniola brings information of Count D'Estaing's having taken six British Ships of the Line, two Frigates and forty-five Transports bound to America, via. South Carolina; if this be true, it is a respite to us. I agree with Mr. Johnston in opinion, that Mr. Cumberland's continuance at the Court of Madrid is a very suspicious circumstance. From their demands of certain territorial possessions in North America, and their general supineness in carrying on the war, I think there is too just cause for suspecting them of *duplicity*. The information I some time ago had, from men of abilities and discernment on the other side of the question, corroborates the suspicion. I have reflected on the consequences that might attend their withdrawing from the family compact. As far as I am capable of judging, I do not think that it can be attended with any fatal consequences to America. France finding herself deprived of her old friend, may be more desirous of securing a firm and lasting alliance with America, and of course be more decisive in her assistance, than she has yet been. If Britain can wean Spain from France, it will be a master-stroke in politics. Nothing less than the Sugar-Plum, Gibraltar, will catch Spain; which the present Ministry will hesitate to give up, if they find their situation critical, in order to save their own heads. Congress, and the affairs of America are brought to *that point* that, in my humble opinion, we are not to be saved or lost by any measures of that body. The imprudence and unbecoming haughtiness of the British Army will do more for us than Congress has yet, or now can do. Take an instance in point: The inhabitants of South Carolina, who had tamely, too tamely, at first submitted to the British Government, soon after the reduction of Charlestown, and to all appearances were perfectly reconciled to the change, find themselves now so disappointed, and greatly deceived, so ill treated by the officers, and despoiled in a wanton manner *in common with us rebels*, of their property, that a great many of them are actually at this time in arms

against the British Government. If Lord Cornwallis has ruined South Carolina in point of wealth, he has helped, though not intentionally, to preserve its freedom. The post calls for my letter, so must conclude. Pray, when you see my friends Mr. and Mrs. Pollock, present my best regards to them, and remember me in kind terms to Messrs. Johnson and Black.

I am, with great esteem and regard,
Dear sir,
Your affectionate humble servant,
P. BUTLER.

P. S.—Nothing doing at Wilmington. The Governor, though he *pledged* himself to the Speaker to spoil their mirth, has left them in full possession of it. General Lillington commands at Heron's Bridge, with about five hundred men. The British have made their post strong; so that it may be a Trojan Siege, unless some *abler* hands are sent against it.—I write in a hurry.

On the 15th of March, General Greene gave battle to Lord Cornwallis at Guilford Court-house.* So hotly contested was the field, that no action "in the course of the war reflects more honor on the British Troops than that of Guilford." It is generally charged that the North Carolina Militia under Generals Butler and Eaton, posted *three hundred yards in advance* of the remainder of Greene's Army, "fled in a dastardly manner." Our knowledge of the carelessness and ignorance of most writers in all that relates to North Carolina; and the vigorous logic of Dr. Carruthers, do more than create doubts of the justice of a general and indiscriminate censure. A part of the North Carolina line consisted of *volunteers* renowned for their skill as marksmen—the whole were partially sheltered by a fence. As the enemy advanced they took a deliberate aim, whose unerring accuracy was attested by the great number of the slain. Many of the North Carolinians were emigrants from the North of Ireland. Of the Scotch-Irish Presbyterians of America, I need not speak:† their record beggars the power of eulogy. Captain Stewart of the army of Cornwallis, in a letter to his relative, Donald Stewart, of Guilford County, N. C., says: "*In the advance we received a very deadly fire from the Irish line of the American Army, composed of their marksmen lying on the ground behind a rail fence. One half of the Highlanders dropt on that spot. There ought to be a pretty large tumulus where our men were buried.*" ‡ Davie, the Commissary General, an officer of approved gallantry, gave

* Marshall.   † Carruthers.   ‡ Carruthers.

to the North Carolina Militia, the support of his presence. Lee says: " the North Carolina Militia took to flight, *a few only of Eaton's brigade excepted, who clung to the Militia under Clarke; which with the Legion manfully maintained their ground.*" That the great body of the North Carolina Militia behaved badly, is admitted; but a general condemnation should be qualified by justice to the brave men, who uninfected by panic, executed with courage the command of patriotism. It will be seen hereafter that these very Militia, under the name of Continentals, at Eutaw, redeemed their fame by a discipline and valor that *extorted* the praise of Greene. It is not true that the whole body of the Militia dispersed to their homes. Immediately after the action three hundred of them were in camp under Col. Reade.*

Though Cornwallis was technically victor, yet was he substantially beaten. His heavy loss in killed and wounded, amounting to nearly one-third of his force, was decisive of the campaign. He soon began his retrograde march to Wilmington, by way of Cross Creeks, the most loyal settlement in the State.† About this time Governor Martin, who had accompanied his Lordship, deluded with the vain hope of regaining his lost authority, broken in spirit, and worn down by disease, finally left North Carolina, his departure for England being urged by his medical advisers. He had rendered very important services to Cornwallis; and had long flattered himself that his presence would entice large bodies of Tories to the English Standard, but so frequent, and severe had been the castigations administered by the Whigs to the loyalists, that he was constrained at last to the conviction that no very important aid could be received from this quarter. Lord Cornwallis arrived at Wilmington, April 7th, where his Troops, harassed by a long march, found shelter, rest, and abundant stores.‡ After a delay of three days at Troublesome Creek to restore order to his ranks, and to refresh his Troops, Greene began his pursuit of Cornwallis; but finding it difficult to procure subsistence, halted for a time on Deep River.

JOHNSTON TO IREDELL.

PHILADELPHIA, 20th March, 1781.

DEAR SIR :—Having received no letters by the two last posts, I suspect the course of it beyond James River must by some means be interrupted; this will therefore go under cover to Mr.

---

* Col. Reade of Wilmington, native of Ireland—grand-uncle of Bishop Davis of South Carolina, and Mr. George Davis of Wilmington.
† Wheeler. ‡ Governor Graham.

Neilson at Petersburgh. Before this reaches you, great events must have taken place in our country. God grant they may be favorable to our wishes. The paper which I have desired Mr. Neilson to forward to you with this letter contains all the news: whether good or bad for America, can only be known by the event. The immediate loss of property to the merchants of America in' Statia and other Dutch ports, will for some time have a very sensible effect on our commerce. Pray make all the interest in your power with your friends in the Assembly to have me relieved as speedily as possible—both my health and finances require it. Present my love to my sisters, Nelly and the children: I long much to see them. Remember me to all our friends, particularly Mr. Barker. And believe me ever,

Your affectionate and obedient servant,

SAM. JOHNSTON.

HOOPER TO IREDELL.

CUFFNELLS, March 22, 1781.

MY DEAR SIR :—At Balgray we experienced every satisfaction that could result from unbounded hospitality, politeness and good sense. It is indeed a happy house. Lord, what am I ! says a thankful sinner, that you are thus pouring your bounty upon us ! With equal gratitude and much more self-abasement do I exclaim, What is there in me that can entitle me to such expressions of generosity, politeness and attention, as I have experienced in Edenton and the neighborhood of it ! I shall never forget them while I have the faculty of recollection. I shall treasure them in my bosom as exceptions from the general depravity and narrowness of the times, and when I censure mankind at large, I shall give a large credit on the score of generous, hospitable Edenton. I had been too long in the experience of your friendship to suppose any thing that could add to my happiness, could be out of the reach of it, which you could command. I had been an uniform pensioner upon your benevolence and hospitality until you had made it a kind of habit necessary to my happiness. But from perfect strangers we received such unequivocal proofs of kindness, notice and distinction, as perfectly astonish me in the recollection. Think of me, my dear friend, as I hope you have always, that, although fortune may rob me of my property and separate me from my dear connections, that I can still defy her efforts, in the conscious satisfaction of having a grateful and honest heart.

I have wrote Smith all the news I can collect, and have inclosed the letter to you. Should he be in town, pray deliver it

to him, and he will impart the contents to you. But in case of his absence, open it, and reserve it for his return. The inner letter for him is on private business merely. We dine at Windsor with Stone to-day.* I will keep my letters unsealed till I return, that if any thing casts up I may add it. I am determined to go on to Halifax—thence to Greene's camp. I shall loiter a few days at Halifax, and then shall expect to hear from you and Mr. Smith under cover to Gilchrist. My companion† is not yet determined on his future operations, although he left Edenton much sooner than I wished, intending then for the southward. He is indeed a rigid non-conformist—but I must submit, he has striking virtues and his vices are only foibles. I beg you to offer my best respects to your good lady, Mrs. Blair, and the rest of the family. Do me the favor to make my compliments to the family at Hayes. Remember me to N. Allen, Collins. I cannot particularize further. To whom in Edenton do I not owe my kind wishes and regard ? Believe me ever, my dear Iredell,

Your affectionate friend,

WILL. HOOPER.

HOOPER TO IREDELL.

HALIFAX, 29th March, 1781.

MY DEAR IREDELL :—I inclose you a letter addressed to Mr. Smith in the first instance, but intended for both of you. Will you be pleased if he should not leave Edenton before it reaches you, to hand it to him, and share with him any intelligence it may afford ? Should he be absent, open it, give a sight of it to Allen, and any others of our choice friends who can make an allowance on the score of hurry and inattention with which I have wrote it, then give it a cover and forward it by a safe hand to Smith. *Col. Martin of the Council Extraordinary was here yesterday ; he tells me that the Council Extraordinary have passed an order that the Governor should give you a draft upon the Treasury for a further sum, not to exceed the full value of your salary with the depreciation, and that this draft would be granted you whenever you thought proper to apply, you to be accountable for the same.*

A partial exchange of prisoners has taken place to the southward ; 28 in the whole have been released from confinement, *Cosmo de Medici* amongst the rest. Col. Clark still there, and all the Colonels, with little hopes of exchange, as the British have no

---

* Father of Gov. Stone. † Mr. Maclaine.

full Colonels in their regiments, of course we have none such prisoners.

The Council have passed an order to take from every inhabitant a fifth part of his provision for the use of the army, and that every man who abandoned his post in the last action should be enrolled in the Continental Army for twelve months. Will not this produce great confusion ? Is not this tax of provisions very unequal ? Whilst one man gives a superfluous fifth, does not another give a fifth from his necessities ? He who has not enough for himself and family, can ill spare to the wants of others either a fifth or fiftieth. I reprobate the rest of the order. It is proposed with a good view, but they are miserably mistaken.

There will be no court here—from what I can learn, no jury has been appointed by the County Court. I shall go from this in a day or two. I wait with anxious suspense the event of Greene's approximation to his Lordship, as this will in a great measure decide whether I shall be permitted to visit Hillsborough or not before I go to Newbern.

I expected a line from Mr. Smith or you by Paddy Martin, and the more especially as you had obtained such interesting intelligence from the Capes of Virginia. Captain Jones, who arrived from Richmond the day Martin came home, informs me that 9 British ships of the line and 2 frigates are in the Chesapeake. If the Rhode Island Captain has not falsified, I fear the French ships had the worst of the contest. With my best and kindest regards to your lady and the family, and to the family at Hayes, I am, my dear Iredell,

Most affectionately yours,

WM. HOOPER.

The Extraordinary Council has so far escaped the research of American writers. Even Governor Graham, distinguished as he is for his knowledge of the history of his native State, in his Lecture at New York (1853), remarked, "I have seen no record of the organization of this Council, or any proceedings under these statutes. The result of the campaign probably rendered them unnecessary." Mr. Hooper's letter, and one from Thomas Gilchrist, April 6th, establish the fact of its organization, and of its vigorous action.*

---

* Governor Nash in a letter to Caswell, 23d Feb. 1781, says: "The General will also, upon his arrival at Halifax, call on the other members of the Council Extraordinary to meet, and he will pursue such further steps as may be concluded on by said Council for the further operations of the militia against the enemy." N. C., Un. Mag. March, 1855.

JOHNSTON TO IREDELL.

PHILADELPHIA, April 2nd, 1781.

DEAR SIR:—I have just had the pleasure of receiving your letters of the 11th and 17th, and one from Mr. Smith, and another from my brother. I wrote to them both last week. You will, before this reaches you, have received an account of the action between the two fleets off the Capes of Virginia. I have seen the New York account, which is rather more in favor of the French than their own. Upon the whole the French gained more honor than profit in that conflict, as they miscarried in their principal object, that of destroying the party at Portsmouth, who have since been reinforced, and I fear will be very troublesome. We have reason to expect essential reinforcement from our ally ; I am not at liberty to be more particular. There are many things I would wish to say as well regarding the public as my *private affairs,* but the fear of my letters miscarrying withholds me. I therefore submit every thing to your discretion. We have very speedy intelligence here of every interesting motion of the armies to the westward. I. Buchanan sent me the New York papers as late as the 29th ult. ; they contain nothing interesting, nor have we any late advices from Europe. My brother writes me of his indisposition, which gives me very great concern. I hope to be in as good health as ever in a few weeks of warm weather. Remember me affectionately to my sister, and the children, and in general to all our friends ; and believe me ever, with the most sincere friendship and esteem,

Dear sir,
Your affectionate brother,
SAM. JOHNSTON.

THOS. GILCHRIST TO IREDELL.

HALIFAX, April 6th, 1781.

DEAR SIR:—I had the pleasure to receive several of your favors by Mr. Bell, the latest of which is dated 1st inst., mentioning the arrival in Virginia of a British fleet, with land forces. We had heard of the fleet before, but not of the troops. Your letter likewise inclosed a packet for Mr. Hooper, which I shall forward to him at Newbern in a day or two by Mr. Bond. Ben McCulloh and he had left this the day before Mr. Bell got up. I am greatly obliged to you for the newspapers, which I will not fail to send Mr. Hooper by Mr. Bond. I am very sorry to inform you he appeared to be in very poor spirits when he left this. He had seen Major Butler here, which I thought contributed to it. Part of the scattered militia from the action at Guilford Court House were rendezvousing here at the time your letter came to hand, by one of them (a Captain). I sent Mr. Falcon's letter, being a neighbor of his, and previously made the pro tempore clerk, G. Davis, fill up the paper which I sent Mr. Falcon at same time. These militia are now marched under the command of Col. Linton, and are sentenced to do 12 months' duty as Continentals for their desertion. I fear our militia officers at the late action have not acquitted themselves with much more reputation than their men. I understand not enough of them remained in camp after the action to command the men that were left ; in consequence, W. Jones accepted the commission of Lieut. Col. in a regiment of 300, commanded by Col. Read, and Webb was appointed Major in the same regiment. By the last letter, they are stationed at Ramsay's Mills, having got there on the same day Lord Cornwallis left that ; but they had given over pursuit of the British for the present, as the time of the Virginia militia was nearly expired, and we had very few in camp ; besides, General Greene's cannon had not reached him —(got up). Wilie Jones wrote a very flattering account a day or two before the pursuit ended. He says Lord Cornwallis is retreating rapidly toward Cross Creek, but is greatly impeded by getting his baggage forward, with sick and wounded, &c. We expect to come up with them in a day or two, and to take part, if not the whole British army ; at least, we will recover our artillery. Mr. Bell will communicate any other occurrences here, to whom I beg leave to refer you. Mrs. Gilchrist begs her best respects may be presented to Mrs. Iredell and you, to which I desire to add my own. With the utmost respect and esteem,

Dear sir,
Your very obedient servant,
THOS. GILCHRIST.

At Ramsay's Mill, General Greene determined to march directly into South Carolina :* he calculated that either Cornwallis would, by a rapid pursuit, abandon North Carolina ; or that Lord Rawdon would fall an easy prey into his hands, and thus South Carolina and Georgia would be recovered. Accordingly, the vanguard under Lee being urged forward on the previous day, on the seventh of April, at the head of about 1,800 troops, Greene began his march. So great was his expedition, that in eight days Lee effected a junction with General Marion near the Santee, and the whole army encamped on the 19th

* Lee Ramsay. Hildreth.

before Camden. Cornwallis was completely surprised by the bold tactics of his antagonist, which he learned too late to succor Rawdon.

JOHNSTON TO IREDELL.

PHILADELPHIA, April 8th, 1781.

DEAR SIR:—I fear from our disappointment of succor from the fleet of our ally under the command of the Chevalier D'Estouches, that the enemy will be able to establish a strong post at Portsmouth, and maintain it during the summer, unless the arrival of the second division of the French, which we hourly expect, should give us the superiority at sea. In other respects our prospects are far from being flattering. You will easily judge that great delay in the deliberative councils of so numerous a body as Congress must necessarily take place ; add to this, that the frequent change of the members does in almost every instance break in upon the best digested systems, and renders inefficient the best concerted measures. *Much time is too often spent in debate, and there is no man of sufficient credit or influence to take the lead, or give a tone to the business.* Another circumstance which prevents Congress from taking its measures with a greater degree of confidence and decision is, the inattention which the States pay to the measures recommended by that body. I am fully satisfied that if the States would implicitly comply with every requisition of Congress, even when the propriety of the measure was not evidently apparent, it would be attended by the most salutary consequences, *as there is not the least reason to doubt but Congress, both as a body and individually, are disposed to do what is right, and appear to me in almost every instance that has fallen within my observation to be actuated by the most virtuous and disinterested motives.* In a few, very few instances, I have suspected individuals to be influenced by local or personal considerations, and this less often than might be naturally expected in so large a body.

Never was a poor fly more completely entangled in a cobweb than Congress in their paper currency. It is the daily subject of conversation in that body ; but our situation is so very intricate and delicate that I have as yet heard no proposal that is not subject to numberless objections. Dr. Burke, who is to be the bearer of this, has just called to tell me he is not to leave this for some days.

April 12th.

I was in hopes to have had some European intelligence before I closed this letter ; but Doctor Burke is to go in the morning, and there is nothing authentic from that quarter. A report prevails that the Dutch have declared war with Great Britain, which is not improbable. We have assurances that the aid to be furnished by our ally this campaign, will not be less than 12,000 land forces, and the same number of seamen, including those already in America. Should they arrive seasonably, I hope, with proper exertions on our part, the enemy may be driven from every part of the United States before Christmas ; but, should the ensuing campaign prove unfavorable to these States, our State must fall a sacrifice, and we shall be reduced to beggary. I have often attempted to form some plan of transferring some part of my property to a place of greater security, but can resolve on nothing, at the same time that I apprehend every thing.

Your own discretion will direct you not to make my sentiments on this subject public ; should you mention them to any of our particular confidential friends, I hope they will be cautious to keep it secret, as I would not wish that any thing which drops from me should occasion any degree of despondence. I am very sorry my sister finds so much difficulty in writing to me. She knows how much I love her, and how acceptable any thing that comes from her would be to me. I should have wrote to her, but consider my letters to you as if wrote to her. Present my love to her and my sister Blair and her children, &c., &c.

Your affectionate brother and obedient servant,
SAM. JOHNSTON.

MRS. BLAIR TO MRS. IREDELL.

EDENTON, 17th April, 1781.

MY DEAR SISTER:— * * * Jarvis has been in town : he says the enemy have not any boats ; nor are we in any danger here. Another man, come to town within this hour or two, says they have seven boats now at the North Landing, and more expected. Others say there are some at Knott's Island. The express is not yet come up from camp. Mr. Blair writes from South Quay, that there were twenty odd deserters just come in there : they say that the British troops at Portsmouth had mutinied, and that several were killed on both sides before they came off ; and they left them engaged. They say there is but one regiment in Portsmouth—the rest, people imagine, are at Suffolk, or near it. You may credit as much as you please of what I have wrote ; for my part, I know not what is true or what false. Mr. Johnson says he will attend the ladies on your side in a few days, out of downright pity and compassion ; and he is happy to have such an excuse; for though he wished to go over, he hated to go as a fugitive. * * * The man who carries our goods over, tells me that there is a certain account of the English setting off for this, both by land and water. The man who brought the account was sworn to it. He says Major Cooper and his brother were taken last night, or the night before, I do not know which. I assure you my hand begins to tremble, &c., &c., &c.   My dear sister,

Affectionately yours,
J. BLAIR.

As Edenton was much exposed, a very large portion of its population sought safety in flight. The village of Windsor, Bertie county, was crowded with fugitives, and its few houses literally swarmed with women and children: valuable furniture was thrust into barns, or slightly sheltered by open sheds; smoke-houses were converted into kitchens, and ladies, educated in luxurious habits, were fain to prepare their slender meals with their own hands. Midst all the confusion and bustle, however, good humor and old-fashioned hospitality prevailed; while the reports of the gentlemen, who were constantly passing and repassing the Sound, to and from Edenton, kept attention awake, and enlivened conversation.

IREDELL TO MRS. IREDELL.

EDENTON, 22d April, 1781.

MY DEAR HANNAH:—We set off without being plagued with breakfast, and soon got over. Your sister will carry all the private news to you. I am told all but one regiment have gone up James River; and it is reported that General Clinton has planned an expedition into the Delaware, &c., &c.

Yours, &c.,
JAS. IREDELL.

EDENTON, April 23d, 1781.

MY DEAR HANNAH:—General Gregory wrote to Mr. Smith by the express which returned last night, that the men at Kemp's landing had been drawn in, and that an embarkation of 2000 or 2500 men had taken place, the destination unknown. They gave out that they were bound up James River, but the wind for that purpose had continued fair for some days without their sailing, so that he conjectures they are bound to the southward. It is supposed they mean to leave only 5 or 600 men at Portsmouth and the Great Bridge. The flat-bottomed boats remained quiet, which he supposed they would do, unless Lord Cornwallis should intend coming to Newbern, when possibly they might be made use of. We have a report that General Clinton has arrived in Chesapeake, but we know not any good authority for it.

I have just received your very kind letter from Eden house. The alarm of yesterday proves to be nothing. It arose either from a mistake or a wilful lie. I am afraid it will not be in my power to come over to-day, much as I wish to comply with your entreaties. I have got to see some property of your sister's off—her negroes, her cows, &c., and her desk. Mr. Smith, too, being very sick, and Mr. Black out of town, I find I can be serviceable to Mrs. Johnston. She sent one boat off yesterday, and I hope to get another for her this morning. Then, I flatter myself, I can prevail on her to go immediately herself. I assure you, upon my honor, I will not delay a moment which I can avoid staying with propriety. It distresses me to refuse a request so tenderly urged. But, believe me, for some days there is not the least prospect of danger, for Gregory's letter was dated on Saturday, and the fleet had not then sailed, nor the boats been moved, &c., &c., &c.

JAS. IREDELL.

When Cornwallis heard of Greene's invasion of South Carolina, he was greatly perplexed, and hesitated long before he could resolve his doubts and settle his plan of action. Finally determining upon a rapid march upon Virginia, he crossed the northeast branch of the Cape Fear at the Oaks, on the 25th of April. Lillington commanded in the Wilmington district, but his force was too small to enable him to attempt any serious check to his Lordship's progress. "In high spirits from what had passed,"* the militia promptly turned out to cover military depots, and to capture unwary adventurers; if they dared not the hazard of an encounter, they literally trod upon the heels of the English, checked marauding, protected property, and recaptured much plunder from those who linger in the rear of armies for purposes of spoliation. The North Carolina cavalry, under the Baron de Glaubeck, armed with clubs in lieu of sabres, whenever chance invited, made a dash at the enemy, and used their hickories so effectually, that they took many prisoners. Before the British rear had evacuated Halifax, they had entered the town, and were engaged in quickening the flight of the enemy, and smoking out of chimneys tory miscreants, who had there sought concealment.†

* Lee.   † N. C. Un. Mag., p. 183, May, 1855.

On the 20th May, Lord Cornwallis effected a junction with the corps of General Arnold, in Virginia. It is foreign to my purpose to enter into any minute investigation of Greene's operations in South Carolina. North Carolina soldiers followed his flag to the close of the contest; and I believe that a careful examination will disclose the fact, that their number has been carelessly stated, and greatly underrated, by our historians. Colonel Reade's regiment of 300, under the command of Colonel Washington, greatly distinguished themselves at the battle of Hobkirk's Hill. A battalion from the same State, under Major Eaton, participated in the attack upon Augusta; that gallant officer, "who had served only a few weeks with the light corps, and in that short period endeared himself to his commandant and fellow-soldiers,"* falling, mortally wounded, in the moment of victory. Towards the close of April, a general exchange of prisoners was effected; and, after the junction of General Sumner's troops with those under Greene, the North Carolinians constituted more than one half his army.

MAJOR P. BUTLER TO IREDELL.

NEWBERN, April 27th, 1781.

DEAR SIR:—Your favor of the 14th inst. did not reach my hand till the 25th. I am not a little mortified at the first part of it. You say you have not received one letter since that dated the 17th ult., from me. I am satisfied you will believe me, when I assure you, that from the 17th to the 29th of March, the day I left this place for Virginia, I wrote three long letters to you; one of them was of such a length—three sheets of letter-paper—that I was almost fearful it might tire your patience, though I know you possess as large a stock as falls to the lot of most men. In order to be more certain, as I thought, of this same letter getting safe to hand, I sent it by a French doctor, bound to Edenton. He promised me faithfully to deliver it. I am hurt at the miscarriage of this letter, for many reasons. On my return from Virginia, I gave you a very full state of the situation of affairs there. If any circumstance that can well happen could discourage me from continuing a correspondence so desirable in itself, and from whence I derive so much heartfelt satisfaction, it would be the failure of so many of my letters. I have this day wrote to Philadelphia after that French doctor, to know what he did with the letter I entrusted to him. One went by Captain Botar; the remainder by post. There is no vice prevails more

* Lee.

at this time—when, God knows, vice of every kind is too prevalent—than an impertinent curiosity. I have sufficiently experienced it, even in South Carolina. My handwriting there was pretty well known. I could not write a letter, even of the most trivial nature, that escaped being opened; yet I could never trace it. To repeat now the information I gave, or rather, intended to give you, on my return from Virginia, would be to little purpose. I can't help repeating my concern at the loss of the letter I entrusted to the Frenchman, because it was wrote without reserve. I unbosomed myself to you; and in short, intended *that* letter as the corner-stone on which I hoped to erect a lasting friendship. The loss of the letter shall not, if I can prevent it, frustrate my hope. Let my ill fortune lead or drive me to what part of the world it may, I shall gladly embrace every possible means of maturing a friendship, the infancy of which affords me so much satisfaction.

To Mrs. Iredell, Mrs. Blair, and Miss Nelly, I beg to present my best respects and grateful thanks, for their kind remembrance of me.

The inhabitants of Newbern were alarmed yesterday at receiving an account from General Lillington that the British were advancing this way. I feel no uneasiness on that score, as I cannot see for what purpose they would march thus far. I think Edenton more liable to a visit from Phillips, though I do not by any means think you in immediate danger. If it is deferred a little longer, it may possibly be prevented altogether, by the arrival of a French fleet. A vessel just arrived here from Martinique brings *certain* intelligence that twenty-two sail of the line, with eight thousand land forces on board, had actually arrived there just before his departure. Surely they will visit America! But I am apprehensive, from the influence of the Northern States, that they may be drawn northwardly to accomplish that favorite plan, the reduction of New York.

By the measures and sentiments of some men in power, they appear to value New York more than the Southern States. Strange policy!

I am, with the greatest esteem and regard, my dear sir,

Your very affectionate friend,
P. BUTLER.

JOHNSTON TO IREDELL.

PHILADELPHIA, May 1st, 1781.

DEAR SIR:—Since my last we have had despatches from our Minister at the court of Madrid as late as the 22d February, which contain a minute detail of his negotiations at that court. They do him infinite honor. I wish it were proper for me to communicate them to you: I am sure the perusal of them would not only afford you great pleasure, but give you a very high opinion of his abilities. Our affairs at that court are in such a train as promises a favorable issue, and I have reason to believe, from the best authority, that none of the European powers discover a disposition to favor Great Britain, except the Emperor and Queen of Portugal. The former, I have reason to believe, made offers of his mediation to the court of Spain, which were not very favorably received. The Northern Powers will certainly support the Dutch. The two extracts of letters of the 22d February and 23d January, published in the paper of the 28th of April, under the Philadelphia head, are from the best authority, and the intelligence may be relied on. It is reported here that General Phillips has taken possession of Williamsburg, and that General Greene has turned off towards Camden. The first is what I have long expected; the latter, I must confess, appears extraordinary, and is what I cannot reconcile to any principle; and though I have the best opinion of his judgment and military skill, I cannot help thinking that Ramsay's Mill, on Deep River, is the most convenient position he could have taken to watch the motions of Lord Cornwallis. I am now very impatient of some one's coming on to relieve me, and am determined to wait no longer than the beginning of next month, and at all events will leave this before the middle of it. Present my love to my sisters, Nelly and the children. Remember me properly to all our friends, and believe me, with the most sincere affection,

Dear sir, your most obedient servant,
SAM. JOHNSTON.

P. S.—Let my brother see my letters and the newspapers.

MRS. BLAIR TO MRS. IREDELL.

BERTIE, 3d May, 1781.

DEAR SISTER:—I think we have jumped out of the frying-pan into the fire. Yesterday they brought the English within thirty miles of us, on their way to Halifax. We had heard before that eight of their boats were in Edenton Bay; and that the route marked out for Lord Cornwallis was from Halifax down this road, to join the troops in Edenton. These stories give me very little uneasiness, as I am sure they can never get very near us without our hearing of it beforehand. * * * I have been plagued, ever since I sat down to write, by two women who want to exchange home-spun for fine linen; they have made me make a hundred mistakes. * * I gave one yard for three. * * We have had Miss Cary's company to tea this evening. My brother found her at the back of the corn-field and brought her home. She behaved very well; seemed pleased at first, but while at tea groaned very much, and the tears stood in her eyes. I could not help thinking she recollected something of old times, and it affected me greatly. She remembered me, and gave me rational answers to my questions, &c., &c., &c.

Your affectionate sister,
J. BLAIR.

JOHN JOHNSTON TO IREDELL.

May 3d, 1781.

DEAR SIR:—Since writing the enclosed we have been alarmed by a report that the English army under Cornwallis were expected immediately at Tarborough, but upon further examination, we find the whole arose from a party of infantry and horse having marched to Kingston in order to take the magazine there, which being removed, they returned. However, it is said the Governor and Mr. Bignal are making great bustle, and preparing to receive them at Tarborough, where they have raised the Edgecombe militia, and four hundred of the Pitt militia, it is said, have joined them.* General Jones, it is said, has ordered every man in Northampton county, who is able to bear arms, to meet him this day.† The most of these reports seem to have too slender a foundation to be much depended on; however, the countenances of some of our leading men show that they believe the most of them.

I am, dear sir, your affectionate brother-in-law,
JOHN JOHNSTON.

ROBERT SMITH TO IREDELL.

EDENTON, 7th May, 1781.

DEAR SIR:—I received yours of yesterday; also that to Mr. Hooper fell into my hands, as the devil and old Barker drove him away from here yesterday morning; you will have met him before now, for he talked of going up Cashie. I expected the mighty matter

* April 17th, Nash the Governor wrote Caswell from Newbern: "As this place may shortly be an object, I think it prudent to move away."—N. C. Un. Mag., March, 1855.
† Gen. Allen Jones.

from Windsor would end in smoke. The letters you mention I shall reserve copies of for you. We had sent Horton to Hicksford; he returned last night, in the night, and brought a letter from Major Wall, which contains a good deal of intelligence. I will try to get it copied and enclose it for Mr. Hooper and you to amuse yourselves and your friends along shore with. I wish the damned dogs may not return to Portsmouth, and wreak their vengeance on this defenceless country. I cannot account for their destroying the tobacco at Petersburg and Osborne's, &c.; it does not look as if they expected to keep possession of Virginia. Something agitates their minds at present, and renders their councils fluctuating. May some good devil attend them as close as Arnold's monitor; and may he invent lies like a *Rice*, a *Savage*, or a Crook, and with the perseverance of a B—k—r, sound them into their ears till they become as stupid as an *Ashe*, and as ——— in their councils as a Cumming. In other words, ———. You may show *this innocent epistle* to Mr. Hooper. I will write him as soon as I can shake myself out of this serious philosophic mood, which unfits me for writing any thing suitable to his taste. This, I hope, will happen when the weather clears up and my spirits mend. Could I get clear of this side, I would go and see Wall, and go to Richmond, and all about that country. One would learn what is doing every where but about Edenton. I cannot be ready these two days at any rate. My compliments to the ladies. I anxiously wish myself with them; but it's my misfortune seldom ever to be where my heart is. Mr. Bennett will set out about Thursday or Friday. Both Mr. Hooper and you must have your letters ready. Mr. Hooper promised to inform Mrs. Johnston, and I took the liberty to write to Miss Cathcart. *I wish she may open the letter.* If she should take it into her head not to do it, she will lose the chance of writing, and I cannot help it. I could not get a girl of tolerable character to write for me: as Fort said, I was obliged to act the part myself.* I am, with unfeigned respect, dear sir,

Your obedient servant,
ROB. SMITH.

P.S.—I cannot now look over my letters, but I fancy my last from Mr. Johnston was 4th April; it enclosed one of the 7th. I am not alarmed at his finding he grows worse; as the spring advances, the impetuosity with which the blood circulates causes a tickling; but it generally wears off with the warm weather, and I shall expect to hear this is the case with him.

R. S.

* Mr. Smith had been an unsuccessful suitor for the hand of Miss Cathcart.

JOHNSTON TO GEN. ALLEN JONES.*

PHILADELPHIA, May 8th, 1781.

DEAR SIR:—I wrote you a few days since by an express to the Governor of Virginia, informing you of the downfall of the old continental dollars in this city. They still lie prostrate, nor is there the least probability of their ever rising. *I must repeat my request that you will either come or send some one to relieve me. I should have left the State unrepresented had not so many others been in that situation.* All the States to the Eastward of Jersey, and the State of Maryland, are without a vote in Congress, so that some of the most important business cannot be determined on agreeable to the Confederation. The scarcity of current cash makes it difficult to keep the several departments in motion. The pernicious practice of selling foreign bills at little more than half their value, is, for *very substantial reasons*, laid aside. My particular necessities must be too obvious; I therefore say nothing on that head. We had the misfortune to lose the Confederacy, with a very valuable cargo of clothing and other effects. Two ships, however, with about three thousand suits of clothes from Cadiz, are arrived at Boston. We have, by a great variety of untoward circumstances, been remarkably unfortunate in the transportation of supplies which have been procured in Europe. Mr. Jay has transmitted a full detail of his negotiations at the court of Madrid. They do great honor to his abilities, and promise a favorable issue; indeed, so far as I can collect from such intelligence as I have had access to, there are none of the courts in Europe who discover a disposition favorable to Great Britain, except the court of Vienna; and I think we and our friends have little to apprehend from that quarter. General Clinton's movements at New York still wear a mysterious appearance. They can only be explained by the event. Every circumstance concurs to confirm the opinion that their principal operations will be to the Southward; and appearances are not altogether against the probability of the total evacuation of New York, should our allies be superior in these sens. I think we shall soon do their business; if otherwise, we must be satisfied to stand on the defensive. There have been no official accounts from General Greene of late. I am very impatient to hear from

* This letter is somewhat out of place here, but preserved by Iredell, and illustrative of the patriotism of its writer, its introduction, I hope, will be pardoned. When the reader reflects upon the exposed condition of Johnston's family, and the delicate health of his wife, who was an invalid at this period, he will understand the sacrifice he made for the public good.

that quarter. Remember me to your brother, W. Hill, and all our other friends. Should you see Hooper, show him this letter; I would have wrote to him, but don't know where he is, for I have not heard a word from him. I am, with the most sincere respect and esteem,

Your most obedient servant,
SAM. JOHNSTON.

The following note and letter from Mr. Hooper are without date, but are introduced here, as about this time he was in the vicinity of Edenton.

Mr Hooper presents his very respectful compliments to Mrs. Blair, Mrs. Iredell, and Miss Blair, and thanks them for their very obliging inquiry concerning his health. He suffered less from his wetting yesterday than he had reason to expect, as he rode the whole of the way in the rain, and was wet to the skin. His fever generally visits him in the evening; but, like Dr. Fergus's, is complaisant enough not to rob him of a meal in the day.* Mr. H. would have been on his way to Dukinfield to-day, but Jim has taken his turn and is now down. Mr. H. will do himself the pleasure to dine with Mrs. Blair and the good family to-day.

Wednesday morning.

HOOPER TO MRS. IREDELL.

CUFFNELL'S, Friday.

DEAR MADAM :—I rode so briskly hither last evening that I suffered no inconvenience from the falling of the dews; but, alas! greater evils were reserved for me. A hot supper, backed with all the eloquence and importunity of a lady, was a temptation that set all my virtuous resolutions afloat. I saw, I tasted, I eat; a fever was the consequence, and I am not yet relieved from it. I do not, however, derive much consolation from the prop which Mr. Smith wishes to rest upon in sickness—that he *deserved it*. Like most modest sinners, however, I have vowed never to lapse again; and like them, whilst I am sick, I am very sincere. At all events, this shall be a day of fasting if not of prayer; and I will be penitent as long as any man with a good appetite can safely promise—as long as I can. I put the best foot foremost, and assure the good family that I am very well; but I have every now and then some sad remembrance of my in-

* Dr. John Fergus of Wilmington.

discretion. Oh gruel, how I reverence you! I found myself more fatigued with my short ride last evening than I apprehended would have been the case; I hope, however, that to-morrow, or next day, or whenever else you shall be disposed to set off for Dukinfield, I shall be in readiness to accompany you. I beg you to make my horses and servants convenient to you, and I shall think myself honored with being permitted to be your escort. I beg you to present my most respectful compliments to Mrs. Blair, and to assure her that her humane, kind, and polite attention to me during my late indisposition merits and has my warmest and most grateful acknowledgments, and has made an impression upon my mind that no change of time or circumstances can alter or efface. I want words, dear madam, to express what I owe to you and my dear friend your husband. May heaven shower its best blessings on you, and make you happy as my wishes! Pray make my compliments to Miss Nelly and Miss Peggy, and my good Cumming, &c., and believe me to be, dear madam, with the most sincere and grateful sense of your manifold acts of kindness to me,

Your most obliged and obedient humble servant,
WILL. HOOPER.

JOHNSTON TO IREDELL.

PHILADELPHIA, May 8th, 1781.

DEAR SIR :—I had the pleasure of receiving your letter of the 5th of last month yesterday, under cover from Mr. Neilson, who informs me that Edenton was abandoned by the inhabitants. I am much concerned for them on this occasion, as they must have sustained great loss and inconvenience in their flight, though I flatter myself their apprehensions were greater than their danger. I by no means blame them for taking early precautions for the security of their property, but I don't think any force could at that time have been employed against them which they might not have found means to repulse; they, however, must be the best judges of this matter, and I have no doubt but every thing was done that was proper on the occasion. Two ships have lately arrived at Boston from Cadiz with clothing for the army. The blockade of Gibraltar is still continued, covered by a fleet of thirty sail of the line. We every day expect the second division of the French fleet, though we have no certain advice of their having sailed. The Dutch are making very vigorous exertions in putting their marine on a respectable footing, and it is very generally thought that they will be effectually supported by the Northern Powers. None of the powers in Europe discover a friendly disposition to Great Britain, except the Emperor, who is kept in check by the King of Prussia. All Europe have their eyes on America, and particularly the Southern States. Much will depend on our exertions and success. The great and sudden fall of the old Continental money has occasioned very great convulsions and dissatisfaction in this city, and has reduced all paper currency to a very doubtful state, very many refusing to have any thing to do with it. We have no official accounts from General Greene or the Southern Army since the beginning of last month. Report says he has turned his face towards Camden—if so, I doubt not he had good reason for his conduct. Mr. Robert Morris is appointed to superintend the finances of the United States. Great matters are expected from this gentleman's abilities. The finances of no country were at any time more deranged or more in want of wisdom and political knowledge to make them effectual. Present my love, &c., &c., &c.

Your most obedient servant,
SAM. JOHNSTON.

MRS. BLAIR TO MRS. AND MR. IREDELL.

WINDSOR, May 10th, 1781.

MY DEAR SISTER :— ❀ ❀ ❀ The English are certainly at Halifax, but I will remain here as it is as safe as any where else, and I can be no longer tossed about. I have suffered a great deal of uneasiness within these few days. I should be glad to have Nelly and Peggy in a place of safety—if there is such a place to be found—but here I am determined to stay. You will think perhaps that one so young as Peggy might be safe any where; but children of her age were treated in a most shocking manner near about Hillsborough—their parents tied, and the girls abused in their sight. All my brother's negroes at Booth, except two fellows, are determined to go to them—even old Affra. W. Hill lost twenty in two nights. ❀ ❀ ❀

Affectionately yours, &c.,
J. BLAIR.

WINDSOR, May 11.

DEAR SIR :— ❀ ❀ ❀ Mr. Hooper will tell you that there was a certainty of the British light-horse being in Halifax; but I do not know if he had heard *that Lord Cornwallis had got there on Wednesday evening with the whole of his army*—about eight hundred men, besides the light-horse. Mr. K. McKenzie brought the account this afternoon. It is said that Arnold is on his march to join them at Halifax; but this is but a flying rumor. ❀ ❀ ❀ My brother has joined the militia, &c., &c.

Your affectionate sister,
J. BLAIR.

WINDSOR, May 15.

DEAR SIR :— ❀ ❀ ❀ When I first heard we were in danger here, I got the favor of Mrs. Clark, to let your desk be put in her house. Her brother told me he was sure any thing would be safe there as they knew her husband was in Wilmington. She offered to take any thing else I chose to put there. I placed the desk there, because I heard you express some concern about your papers. If your delicacy should be hurt by its being there, you may be assured none but Mrs. Clark and her brother know it to be yours, &c., &c.

Very affectionately, your sister,
J. BLAIR.

A. BLACK TO IREDELL.

EDENTON, 16th May.

DEAR SIR :—I thank you for your favor of the 12th, also yours of yesterday, which I received this morning. The former came very seasonably to amuse a few of our friends who were dining at Mr. Smith's, when I received it. Mr. Barker came in less than five minutes after I received the letter. He certainly keeps a good look-out for news: he must have known the negro had a letter for me before I received it. The expedition from Havana against Pensacola will be much in our favor. Two gentlemen came over from Mrs. Pearson's just now, that confirm your account of the enemies' movements, and the general opinion here is that we shall not be troubled with them in this quarter: it's much doubted whether they will even leave a post at Halifax. We shall send off an express this day by the way of Winton, to learn their route if possible. Should the French fleet and troops arrive that Congress expect, I hope we would be able to confound the schemes of our enemies—which I hope in God will be the case. It certainly is the next thing to H—ll to live in a country conquered by force of arms; and I am sorry to see some of my acquaintances who now and then stay in this town rejoice at our ruin. But I hope to live to see the Americans a free and happy people, and those who call themselves their friends at this time, dispersed; I mean friends to the English. I have enclosed two letters, and a newspaper for you enclosed in a letter to me from Mr. Johnston, dated April 8th, which Mr. Neilson assures me he forwarded from Petersburg some time ago. His letter was chiefly on private business. Charles Johnston came home yesterday from Pitch Landing on Meherrin River.* He brings no news. A gentleman came to town last night, says he left Philadelphia the 24th of April. He says they had received accounts of the French fleet sailing from Rhode Island before he left that place—if so, the second division must be on our coast. I will do myself the pleasure to inform you as soon as possible the news from Virginia, as we may expect a good deal from that quarter. Please present my respectful compliments to Mrs. Iredell, and am with great respect,

Dear sir,
Your most obedient and humble servant,
ALEX. BLACK.

P. S.—Pray sir, excuse this incorrect epistle, for so many come to inquire after news, it puts it out of my power to write.

Mrs. Blair to Mrs. Iredell.

Windsor, 19th May, 1781.

Dear Sister :— * * * Some say the English have left Halifax—others that only part of them are gone. General Wayne, it is said, is on Roanoke, and some of the Marquis's horse. Old Mr. W. Williams has been in, and taken a parole. The British have abused some women shamefully ; amongst them, my brother says, was H. Montfort's wife. John Right Langford's wife was served in the same manner ; and he stabbed several times in the thigh because he could not produce the horse Comus: they followed the fellow that had him to the ferry ; he had about half an hour's start of them. My brother has lost five or six negroes, and many other things, &c., &c., &c.†

Your affectionate sister,
J. BLAIR.

Charles Johnson to Iredell.

Edenton, 28th May, 1781.

Dear Sir :—I have only time to inform you that I last night received both your much esteemed favors. The letter for the

---

* Pitch Landing is in the south-east part of Hertford county, on the Mickason a creek that empties into the Meherrin.
† Stedman says: "Some enormities were committed at Halifax that were a disgrace to the name of man." Tarleton states that "a sergeant and a dragoon were executed for rape and robbery."—WHEELER.

General I shall take the first opportunity of forwarding. We last night returned from a cruise ; unfortunately not having taken the galley, our principal object ; but as we were so happy as to retake Mr. Smith's schooner, in which his whole property was embarked, it gives, as you may conceive, every person concerned in the expedition the most heartfelt satisfaction. Ten of her hands, the galley's, were taken by about the same number of ours in Mr. Johnston's canoe, after a smart fire on both sides, in which however nobody was wounded. We pushed them so close that they were obliged to set fire to Mr. Littlejohn's schooner, and under favor of the night, made their escape. We are now fully employed in fitting out three or four armed boats, to go in pursuit, Nelson's brig proving improper for the service. As the galley can always get in shoal water where a large vessel cannot follow her, if *she does not immediately leave the Sound or is not reinforced, which the prisoners seem to expect, I have not the least doubt of our people taking her. The inhabitants in general, and sailors have, and do, turn out unanimously. I never saw, nor could even hope to see, so much public spirit, personal courage, and intrepid resolution*—it would please you to see it. I am convinced, that was the measure adopted of fitting out one or two armed vessels, we might laugh at all attempts of the enemies' plundering Banditti. I feel for Mrs. Dawson's exposed and unprotected situation. I'm apprehensive this is but a prelude to what we must expect upon the return of the enemies' boats from the plunder of James River ; but thanks to Providence for the formation of our natural fortifications, which will hinder their small craft being supported by their large ships. I propose setting off for the Assembly about the 6th prox., as I think it essentially necessary that a house should be made at this critical juncture ; no other inducement could at this time draw me such a distance from my little affairs, which I shall be obliged to leave in great confusion. We have suffered severely at ——, and I suppose at Petersburg, as we had some effects there. A gentleman just from Philadelphia, in nineteen days, brings an account that the Dutch have declared war, and are joined by the Danes and Russians—the French squadron in Rhode Island at single anchor, expecting hourly to be joined by a large fleet with troops. Excuse my writing with red ink. Present my compliments to Mrs. Iredell, Mrs. and Miss Dawson and Miss Gracy, and believe me to be, with perfect esteem, dear sir,

Your most obedient,
CHAS. JOHNSON.

R. Smith to Iredell.

Eden House, Monday, 9 o'clock.

Dear Sir :—Mrs. Dawson writes you; to her I must refer you for the ill news this way. I am just going over to town to know the worst. They have given me a pretty little switching, but it might have been worse ; they have ruined poor Littlejohn, and would have left me nothing, had they not have taken fright. I shall let you know all the particulars from the other side, for I cannot even guess at my loss. Many of my papers are destroyed ; all my clothes, bed, table, and other linen squandered ; indeed, they must have done me more damage than I can name ; but it is useless to repine if even the rest should follow, which I expect will be the case ere long. It will be an easy matter now for Mrs. Johnston to determine what she will do. She should fix as well as she can up near Windsor ; at any rate, she need not think of Hayes for the present. I apprehend this visit is only a prelude to many such we are hereafter to expect. Give my compliments to Mrs. Johnston and Miss Peggy, and inform them I shall write up the situation I find matters at Hayes, and any other thing respects them that way, which I can learn. I have serious doubts some of these pirates may go up Cashy on information of vessels and goods being there. They went up to Stumpy-reach for my vessel, and must have had a pilot on board. But I shall know more about it in two hours more. So Adieu, my dear sir.

Yours ever,
ROBERT SMITH.

P. S.—I have no chance now but go a fortune hunting—what course am I to steer ?
R. S.

Mrs. Blair to Iredell.

Windsor, 29th May, 1781.

Dear Sir:—I think it will be very wrong for my sister to stay below any longer; for, though these boats come up to cut out vessels, it is, I think, more than probable they will call at plantations, and those in particular, where they see good houses, for there they will expect rich plunder. I believe they seldom want information where the most is to be had. I should think it would be better for Mrs. Dawson also to get out of the way, if it was only on account of the continual dread and uneasiness she will continue to be under. I would submit to many inconveniences, and live in a cabin, to have my mind at ease, and be able to sleep quietly in my bed. * * I must try to get sugar to exchange for chickens. I could get many for that. I am in hopes they will soon be glad to take money again. I heard something yesterday of a number of people somewhere about Newbern who had intended joining Lord Cornwallis ; some of them had been taken and nine executed. The man who brought the account said he saw one of them hanged. Captain Pasteur, one of the party who made the capture, while riding with a prisoner behind him, was fired at in passing through a swamp, and so badly wounded that he survived but three days. Dishon, who keeps the Ferry near Eden House, brought the news. He mentioned many circumstances, but some I have forgot, and others I did not rightly understand, &c., &c., &c.

Your affectionate sister,
J. BLAIR.

Iredell to Mrs. Iredell.

Edenton, 30th May, 1781.

My dear Hannah :—The boats went yesterday, four of them, under the respective commands of Captain Gale, Captain Bateman, Captain Addison, and Captain Finch, all together having about fifty men, or perhaps more. They are Mr. Johnston's canoe, Mr. Pollok's, the Caswells' barge, and Bonitz's boat, and each, I believe, has a swivel, besides muskets. The men are well chosen, and went with excellent spirits, without any kind of riot or disorder. The galley, when the last account came, was in the marshes. Two other boats were to go from Perquimons, and two, it was expected, would be fitted out by the Bankers below. Mr. Johnson, Mr. Allen, Mr. Black, Mr. Smith, Captain Collins, and, indeed, most of our acquaintances are in town, all well ; Mr. Smith, in particular, I think better than when we saw him. Mr. Smith has lost several of his papers, though not the most valuable, his table and other linen and clothes, and very near seven hds. of rum. Littlejohn has lost little, I am told, except his schooner. Two of his negroes are returned. The prisoners are gone on, under a guard, to Halifax. We have an account from Virginia that the British army have marched from Petersburg towards Richmond ; the main body, under Lord Cornwallis, crossed at Westover about fifteen miles below Richmond ; the horse, which is said to amount to a great number, about fifteen miles above. The Marquis was at Richmond, joined by General Wayne himself, but there is no account of his troops; I should suppose, however, they were at no great distance. We hear there are two or three privateers at the bar, but I suppose it was only to look for plunder, and finding none, they would probably leave it. I will be much obliged to Mrs. Dawson if she will be so kind as to send her canoe for me on Friday morning. I will endeavor to cross then, and should be glad if they would come very early. Pray remember me very affectionately to Mrs. Dawson and family. I wish you could contrive the news to Mr. Pollok, with my compliments to him and lady. I am ever, my dear Hannah,

Your very affectionate,
JAS. IREDELL.

JOHNSTON TO IREDELL.

PHILADELPHIA, May 30th, 1781.

MY DEAR SIR:—I thought about this time to be making preparations for leaving this place, but none of my colleagues appearing to relieve me, several States being unrepresented in Congress, and affairs of the first magnitude being now on the tapis, I thought it inconsistent with my honor to leave the State unrepresented at so interesting a period. Notwithstanding my anxious impatience to return to my family, I have determined to stay till I am relieved, or at least till the States are more fully represented in Congress. I don't doubt but you and my sister will offer such reasons to Mrs. Johnston as will reconcile her to this measure. I hope she will keep up her spirits, and if I should not return before the sickly season, I wish you would prevail on her to take the children down to the sea-side, if it can be done with safety; but as I have hopes of returning before that time, it will be unnecessary to say any thing on the subject till the season approaches. The uncertainty of a letter's getting safe to you, lays me under great restraints. I can only mention in general that the King of France has given us under his own hand very lately, the most unequivocal assurances of his friendship and support, and is at this time exerting his interest and influence at the different courts in Europe to bring our affairs to a happy and speedy conclusion; and I have in my own mind the most perfect confidence in these assurances. *We shall suffer much in this campaign; it will be very bloody, but I hope it will be the last. I may be disappointed, but was I at liberty to commit my reasons to writing, you would not hesitate to subscribe to my opinion.* Our prospects are very fair in Europe, but it is necessary we

should exert ourselves here, for every advantage we gain thi summer will count as so much solid coin. We are in daily ex pectation of hearing from the General, who has been lately a Connecticut to consult the officers of the French army and navy *My hopes and expectations of a favorable issue to our trouble are very sanguine;* but human affairs are governed by such variety of whimsical circumstances, that we should always b prepared to stand the shock of that disappointment which th best concerted measures are constantly subject to. Present my love to my sisters, the children, and all friends. Let my brothe see this and the newspapers, when you have an opportunity. present my best wishes to him and his family. I wish much t hear from you and him, and am, with the most sincere affectio and esteem,

Yours, &c., &c.*

About this time † a scandalous attempt was made to destroy the character of General Gregory, who, at the head of a portion of his brigade, was guarding the north-eastern frontier of the State against hostile incursions, and especially against predatory parties from Portsmouth. It was cunningly contrived that the following letters should fall into the hands of the Americans.‡

G. G.—Your well-formed plan of delivering those people now under your command into the hands of the British General a Portsmouth, gives me much pleasure. Your next I hope wil mention the place of ambuscade, and the manner you wish to fa into my hands, &c., &c., &c.

And am,
Dr. Gregory,
Yours with esteem.

GEN. GREGORY:—A Mr. Ventriss was last night made pris oner by three or four of your people. I only wish to inform you that Ventriss could not help doing what he did in helping to destroy the logs. I myself delivered him the orders from Col Simcoe. I have the honor of your acquaintance.

These notes produced a degree of excitement and alarm in the American camp nearly equal to what would have occurred had as many fire-balls exploded their magazines. For a time universal distrust prevailed. The General a *traitor!* Who then

---

* The letter is without signature.   † June.
‡ A copy is with Judge Iredell's papers, and endorsed by him June 5th.

---

could be trusted? The unfortunate victim of this foul conspiracy was arrested, and confined by his own men; and subjected to the degradation of a trial before a court-martial. The proofs of his innocence, soon collected, were overwhelming; and he was restored to his rank and the public confidence. His high spirit had been, however, incurably wounded, and the memory of the transaction cast a saddening shadow upon his after life. This was not of the nature of those stratagems that are sanctioned by military laws and countenanced by men of honor: a base and covert attempt to blast the fame of a patriot and soldier, it rivalled in infamy the turpitude of a blow dealt a woman by a coward. It is referred to by Simcoe in his volume recording the services of the Queen's Rangers.ᴳ

HOOPER TO IREDELL.

BALGRAY, June 14, 1781.

MY DEAR SIR:—I should have wrote you before this if any opportunity had presented to Windsor since you left this. I am under inexpressible obligations to you for your kind remembrance of me; our friendship formed in the happier days of life is knit together by the stronger ties of misfortune. I have bound you to my bosom like another self, and you have honored me by meeting my affections with increased tenderness. Yes, my dear friend, I shall embrace with a most sincere pleasure an opportunity to be near you and your family; and destined to be still a pensioner on the hospitality of the world, I shall soon avail myself of yours. In one word, I am under obligations that ages of endeavors, on my part, will never be able to repay to you, and your family, and your connections. My heart bleeds for the misfortunes of Mrs. Johnston's family. I can suffer my own with resignation, but cannot forbear to repine for those of my friends. I have letters from Mrs. Hooper since I saw you: they breathe a masculine patriotism and virtue that would do honor to stronger nerves and muscles. Give me leave to be a little vain on the occasion; to you I might be allowed even to praise myself, for you know my faults and would make a proportionable allowance for them. The conduct of my brothers and some others harrows up

---

* Some one has my copy of Simcoe, and, as I cannot make the reference myself, and my recollection of his relation of the occurrence is indistinct, I hope the reader will consult him.
A lady who remembers Gen. Gregory in his old age, says: "He was a large, fine-looking man,—had a very grand air,—was extremely polite,—in dress something of a fop." He lived, in his latter days, so secluded a life, and knew so little of events beyond his own familiar circle, that he addressed to a lady (the widow of Gov. Stone) a letter making a proposal of marriage full six months after her death.

---

my soul. What does not my dear Annie suffer? For what mis fortune is she yet reserved? I am much indisposed, but hop that in a day or two I shall be able to move southwardly. Re member me in a most respectful manner to Mrs. Iredell, Mr Blair and the family, Mrs. Dawson and hers; and if an opportu nity should open to speak my sympathetic woes to Mrs. Johnsto without increasing her own, you will embrace it. I do not know how it is; I find more milk about my heart since I saw Mr Dawson than I suspected I was constitutionally encumbered with Away with it; I will not give way to it. Mrs. Hooper's exampl shall place me above repining, and animate me to becoming resig nation. The loss of property I treat with contempt, and in thi the British have struck deeper than I suspected—but the drea of my family suffering from want—Oh, my God! Surely th British will indulge me with a flag to carry supplies. Adieu, th subject grows too tender in spite of all my resolution.

Ever yours most affectionately,
WM. HOOPER.

IREDELL TO MRS. IREDELL.

BALGRAY, June 26th.

MY DEAR HANNAH:— * * * * * I left Mr. Hoope worse than he had been, and am very anxious too see him agair Captain Hardy died yesterday afternoon. * * * * It believed, but not certain, that the brig called the Edenton come in, &c., &c., &c.

JAS. IREDELL.

JOHNSTON TO IREDELL.

PHILADELPHIA, June 27th, 1781.

DEAR SIR:—I was only yesterday favored with the letter which you were so obliging as to write me the 14th of April an 10th of May last. I have wrote to you frequently by casual op portunities, but cannot have any confidence of your having re ceived my letters. I write by this opportunity to my brothe and must refer you to his letter and the enclosed newspaper f news. I am sorry people were in such haste to remove themselve and property from Edenton I rather could have wished the had thought of defending it, which would have been attende with less risk and expense in my opinion, for till the conquest o Virginia is effected, which I flatter myself will not speedily tak place, I scarcely think you will be molested with any considerabl invasion, and if the plundering parties meet with opposition they will grow sick of the business. However, every one will and has a right to judge for himself on these occasions. So far as it respects me, I am perfectly satisfied, and shall ever consider myself under the highest obligations to you on this occasion for your friendly attention. I have been detained here longer than I expected from unavoidable circumstances, which I shall have the pleasure of communicating when I can see you. I hope to leave this place some day next week, but as it will be necessary for me to take a pretty extensive circuit to avoid the enemy's horse, and the weather being too warm for me to make long days' journeys at this season, I cannot form to myself any judgment respecting the time I shall arrive with you. I am truly sensible what anxiety and distress you must all have sustained in your alarming situation. I have often wished to have been with you on the occasion ; indeed my mind has been so much in that country, that it has rendered me almost incapable of attending to any thing elsewhere. This will probably be a very important, though perhaps not a decisive campaign. I am not perfectly informed of the plan on which it will be conducted on our part, nor is it proper that I should communicate so much as I do know to paper. Should a few fortunate events cast up in our favor, I hope there will be no more of it after this summer,—if otherwise, God knows where it will end, *for America can never submit.*

Pray remember me most affectionately to my sister and the children. I grow every day more impatient of being absent from my friends ; and had I not believed my services, or rather my vote, essentially necessary here for some time past, no importunity should have detained me. Present my compliments to such as you may think them acceptable, particularly my old friend Mr. Barker, and believe me with the greatest truth and sincerity,

Yours.

P. S.—Tell our friend Hooper I have just received his letter of the 16th of March last, but postpone writing to him till my return, not thinking it safe to be more particular than the above, which you will be so good as to communicate.

Some time in the latter part of June, the General Assembly met in Wake County. The day of meeting is not specified in my copies of the statutes of the State. It appears from a letter from Dr. Thomas Burke to Gov. Nash, dated June 28th, that Burke had just been elected Governor.* Nash had declared

* Vid. N. C. Un. Mag., May 1855, p. 147.

nis purpose to serve no more, because of ill health and his experience that "the Executive power had been so divided that it was impossible to govern with any advantage to the people." Burke, in the opinion of Nash, was a "gentleman of activity, experience, and ability, and public spirit." The Assembly passed acts "to raise troops out of the militia for the defence of the State ;" levy a money and specific provision tax ; for the relief of those who had inconsiderately taken British paroles ; to compel recusant counties to furnish their quotas of Continental troops ; prohibiting the exportation of provisions ; for the protection and security of Ocracock bar and the sounds and river scommunicating therewith ; drafting the militia to reinforce the Southern Army ; vesting the Continental Congress with power to levy a duty of 5 per cent. upon all foreign merchandise ; to enable the Governor to procure tobacco to exchange for arms ; compelling all fiscal agents of the State to account ; granting pensions to those who had been wounded in the service of the State ; and securing all articles left by the British in the State, whether taken from citizens or others. About the 14th July the Assembly adjourned. By the act of creation, the powers of the Extraordinary Council expired with the termination of this session of the Assembly, and were not again revived.

The people looked with great confidence and hope to Gov. Burke for reform, relief from onerous burdens, and a wise, prudent and vigorous administration : the Assembly shared, in a measure, in these sentiments ; but still, timid from past experience, and diffident of the future, were disposed to subject the Governor elect to a portion of the unconstitutional restraint they had thrown around his predecessor. The high-spirited Irishman revolted at the indignity, and informed the Assembly, before their adjournment, that if they persisted in their absurd purpose to divide the supreme military command between himself and the Council of State, as provided by one of their Acts, and involve him in the dilemma of disobeying either the Constitution or the law, he would surrender his office : he urged that he had not sought office, but office him ; and that their distrust and want of confidence implied dishonor, to which he had never stooped, and would not now submit.* How far the manly remonstrance of the Executive prevailed with the Legislature I do not know ; but he continued to discharge the functions of his eminent position until his career of usefulness was closed by the sad accident of his captivity.

* Un. Mag., May, 1856.—Life of Gov. Burke.

GEN. ALLEN JONES TO IREDELL.

WHEELER'S, July 2d, 1781.

DEAR SIR :—We have a report here that General Gregory, with all his party, is taken. I beg you to write me the particulars, if they have come to your knowledge, that I may lay them before the General Assembly, in order to induce them, if possible, to take decisive measures for the defence of our State. I had a letter dated the —— ultimo, from Mr. Johnston, in which he informs me Congress had received dispatches from Mr. Jay, in which he says the Court of Madrid are inclined to favor us in every respect ; also, that Sir H. Clinton's movements are very mysterious, and he does not seem to think the evacuation of New York, and a total transfer of the war to the Southern States improbable. This letter I would have sent for your perusal and Mr. Hooper's, but as he anxiously solicited that other delegates should go on, I thought best to lay it before the General Assembly, to whom I sent it by express. Gen. Greene has taken every post in the two Southern States but Charlestown, together with great quantities of military stores, spirits, dry goods, &c. Enclosed is a letter for Mrs. Johnston, which I beg you to send to her with my best respects. If the enemy have got possession below, I should think Booth a place of more safety than her present abode, and it would give me the greatest satisfaction to render her every service in my power. Pray write me if you have any late arrivals, with what news they may bring. I am, with great respect, dear sir,

Your most obedient servant,
ALLEN JONES.

CHARLTON TO IREDELL.

3d or 4th July, 1781.

DEAR SIR :—I am extremely obliged to you for the intelligence you have afforded me, and highly pleased that Gregory's situation is not so deplorable as from the first relation of it we had reason to apprehend. The recalling of the enemy, after their advantage over him, seems in some measure, in my humble apprehension, to fortify the account of a cessation of arms.*

My impatience for news hath for these few days strongly inclined me to write to my friends in Windsor ; but strong as the

* This, with a reference in a subsequent letter from Robert Smith, is the only notice of the attack on Gen. Gregory I have ever seen.

former desire was, and the pleasure of the latter would have been, I have been prevented by an innumerable set of blisters encompassing my poor contused breast, occasioned by the violent caustic applied to it. It was impossible for me to ride without exquisite pain, but I am quite fearless of danger. I wish in my soul poor Gregory's camp was as well secured by pickets and fortified by redoubts, abatis, &c., as my poor breast is circumvallated by ulcers. I am highly pleased to hear of the happy union between Mr. McKenzie and the late Miss Peggy.* I say a happy union, for kindred souls and congenial minds can never fail of affording it, and the more especially when the passions of each are founded in virtue ; and such theirs are, I am sure.

I shall be extremely glad to see you, and Mrs. Iredell, whenever convenience will admit of it, and with a very sincere offer of my best respects to you both,

I am, dear sir,
Your affectionate and obliged friend,
JASPER CHARLTON.

ROBERT SMITH TO IREDELL

WAKE COURT HOUSE, 3d July, 1781.

DEAR SIR :—I have not received a line from you, or any of you since I left Edenton. What is going on there God knows, I am very anxious to know. Some report from your quarter says Gen. Gregory has been forced from his post. I wish I could now and then receive a line, while I am consigned to this cursed place. We have no news from the Northward that is very late, or to be depended on ; to the South our affairs have taken an unfavorable turn. Gen. Greene has been under the necessity of raising the siege of Ninety-Six, after attempting to scale the walls, in which he sustained some loss. Rawdon with a strong party from Charlestown came up to its relief, and Gen. Greene was retreating before him to —— river. We are about reinforcing him, in order to keep the seat of war, if possible, out of this quarter of the State. We have not passed a single law as yet ; some are on their third reading ; and some I wish were at the devil. We might have done many good things at this time, but we have gone (as usual) the wrong track, nothing will set us right. We are a cowardly, revengeful set of wretches, too contemptible to merit a blessing or excite a damn ——. I have not time to write you particularly. A party of the English are out reaping wheat

* Miss Peggy Cathcart, sister-in-law of Mr. Sam. Johnston.

at Rutherford's plantations, and intend grinding it before their return at his mills.° I am, with compliments to the ladies,
Dear sir,
Your obedient servant,
ROBT. SMITH.

HOOPER TO IREDELL.

WAKE COURT HOUSE, July 13th, 1781.

MY DEAR SIR:—Mr. Charles Johnson will inform you that in addition to the other curses that have been allotted to my portion of late, an inflammation has taken place in my right arm, which swelled it to a size not much less than my leg. For several days it has been accompanied with very excruciating pain; I have been obliged to carry it in a sling, and this is the first moment I have been able to take pen in hand. I embrace it to make a very partial return for your manifold acts of kind remembrance of me. I write in so much pain that I must leave you to Messrs. Smith and Johnson for the news of the Assembly.

Major Craig is gathering strength every hour at Wilmington, and is making a strong post at Rutherford's Mills.† He obliges all his prisoners to enlist, or go on board a prison ship. The condition of enlistment is that they shall serve *for three months, or during the rebellion.* He has summoned all the loyal subjects of Wilmington to hold themselves in readiness to march the 10th day of August, as then the act of grace expires, and he proposes to carry havoc and devastation amongst the rebels.—There are 500 effectives at and near Wilmington.

I leave this day or to-morrow with a double flag for Wilmington, one of these to serve as introductory to the other, and at the same time to obtain a safe conduct for myself. Should I escape the many hazards I have to encounter on the road, and be suffered eventually to come out of Wilmington, I shall not fail immediately to write to you, perhaps see you. I yesterday availed myself of the right hand of another to assure Mr. Johnston at Philadelphia that I had no use of my own. I wrote a very few lines,

* With the exception of a small experiment by Dr. J. F. McRee on Rocky Point, wheat has not been cultivated in that region since the Revolution. Wheat grows well in our N. E. Counties. The Mills I presume were for corn, but made to do double duty on the occasion referred to.

† Rutherford's Mills (since called Ashe's Mills), were situated on Ashe's Mill Creek, a stream that empties into the N. E. Branch of Cape Fear River. The site of the Mills is on the Newbern road, 8 or 10 miles beyond Lane's Ferry, Rocky Point. Just beyond the site, the bank and ditch enclosing a regular field work constructed by the British, are still distinctly visible.

but Doctor Burke at my request wrote him very fully. I gave him perfect information as to the situation of Mrs. Johnston and the family, and the Governor insisted upon mentioning the death of Sammey, lest it should meet him on his road home. Adieu best of men. Every blessing attend you and yours.
Affectionately, and ever yours,
WILL. HOOPER.*

P. S.—I congratulate you and all friends to humanity upon the generous proclamation and cartel which has lately taken place between Gen. Greene and Cornwallis. I refer you to Mich. Payne for a sight of it. Show the enclosed to Mr. Pollok and Mr. Charlton when you have read it. I gave your letter for Mr. Samuel Johnston to Wilie Jones, who promised to forward them by the first safe opportunity. I hope you got my long letter from Col. McCulloh's, which I left in Kinchen's care.

MRS. BLAIR TO IREDELL.

WINDSOR, 21st July, 1781.

DEAR SIR:—Billy Blair came from Edenton yesterday *he says every body there was marching out to endeavor to surprise six hundred negroes, who were sent out by Lord Cornwallis to plunder and collect provisions. It is said they have no arms but what they have found in the houses they have robbed when they applied for arms, they were told they had no occasion for any, as they were not to go to any place where any number of rebels were collected. 'T is said there are two thousand of them out in different parties. Lord Cornwallis himself is at Suffolk with about nine hundred men, chiefly horse. They had an account of his having been defeated by the Marquis and that he (Cornwallis) had (whether before or after his own defeat I did not hear) beaten Gen. Wayne, who lost in the action two hundred men, and two field-pieces. South Quay is burnt and they were expected at the Pitch Landing. Every vessel that goes over the bar is immediately taken. Captain Martin, and the Irish Piper, are both taken, Capt. Gansel was taken : by the favor of some gentlemen in New Providence he got a new vessel, but was taken again in the same latitude : he has now got a large copper-bottomed brig, with which he is cruising against us. Our Edenton volunteers marched yesterday. The*

* Mr. Hooper, it appears, sat for Wilmington—as that town was in the possession of the British, no election could have been held—he must have been admitted a member because of the impossibility of an election, and because he had been a member of the last Assembly.

negroes were at the Folly, headed by some refugee officers. Billy says they had an account in Edenton that the English are going to embark. Mrs. Brimmage is in Virginia: she came in a Flag, and was very sick when she landed. There were no letters left for Dr. Williamson.
Dear sir,
Your affectionate sister,
J. BLAIR.*

WINDSOR, 23d July, 1781.

DEAR SIR:— ✧ ✧ ✧ Mrs. Nash came up from Edenton yesterday : she says they had an account from the northward, that Gen. Washington had possession of Long Island and King's Bridge, and was bombarding the city from the first of those places, and that the harbor was blocked up by the French fleet ; that Tobago and St. Lucie are taken in the West Indies, and the fleet had sailed against St. Kitts. ✧ ✧ ✧ They have had an account to-day from Winton, that Lord Cornwallis is throwing up works at Jericho ; and that the Marquis's whole army have crossed the river, &c., &c., &c.
J. BLAIR.

ROBERT SMITH TO IREDELL.

EDEN HOUSE.

DEAR SIR:—I am favored with yours by the Doctor, and I thank you for the extract. I heard from the town yesterday. They have no news there, only that the British army are all drawn to Portsmouth—some conjecture for immediate embarkation. I am not confident this conjecture is well founded—may it not be in order to oppose the French, should they send in troops into these capes ? or may it not be a deep manœuvre to draw the Marquis down, and with the assistance of their shipping, get to the northward and westward of him, and so cut him off from supplies ? But we will cease conjecture, a little time will determine. Mr. Black and Mr. Johnson write you all the news. To them and Mr. Johnston's letters I must refer you for the northern intelligence. Mr. Johnston has wrote to all at present within the pale of his friendship I fancy. I have not seen any more of his letters than the directions, which, from being once a little acquainted with his hand, I know it. I am informed, however,

* There is to me much novel information in this letter. Mrs. Blair's son William was at this time a man, just grown up.

he is soon expected home, which gives me great pleasure. I am sorry you should give yourself one moment's concern about our accounts—they do not trouble me the least ; at some convenient season, as St. Paul saith, we will have them all settled to your satisfaction ; I hope these times are near worn out, and that they will be succeeded by such as will make you ample amends for what you have suffered ; in the mean time I must insist you want for nothing I have the power of supplying, until these promised times shall arrive. I am still here in this hospitable house, having heard my home in town has been turned topsyturvy. I must take a turn over to-morrow or next day, and try to set matters a little to rights. I was down at Balgra yesterday ; they are all well there, and Mrs. Pearson is very hearty, and will soon be married, it's said ; but as Mrs. Jenkins says, it never shall be said of me that I tell *tails.* My compliments to Mrs. Johnston and family, Mrs. Blair and hers, and to Mrs. Iredell, whom I set last and next to yourself, wishing both to be assured you have and always will have my hearty wishes for your happiness. Being, dear sir,
Your very obedient servant,
ROBT. SMITH.
Hon. JAMES IREDELL, Attorney General, Windsor.

A. BLACK TO IREDELL.

EDEN HOUSE, 30th July.

DEAR SIR:—I saw Mr. Thomas Wynns at Winton, who went to sea last year in the brig Fair American, and was taken and carried to London, where he staid about six weeks, then was sent over to France, where he engaged a passage to Boston ; he brought the letters I have sent you from Mr. Johnston by him Mr. Johnston informs me he should leave Philadelphia in a short time ; Mr. Wynns will be at Edenton in a few days ; he has the London Magazine for the year 1780, which he promised to bring down with him. If possible, I will borrow, so as to enable me to send them up to you a few days ; I had the pleasure of receiving a letter from my brother in London by Mr. Wynns who was often in company with him while he staid there ; he likewise saw Dr. Lennox, who has been in a bad state of health but was getting better when he came away ; he did not write by Mr. Wynns, but told him he intended to take a passage to Bermudas, and requested of Mr. Wynns to wait on Miss Lennox and inform her that he was got almost well. Mr. Wynns promised me that he would come by your place. If so, you will be much pleased with him, as he is a very intelligent gentleman. He says Dr. Lennox and my brother treated him very kindly, which I am happy to hear. I am much obliged to you for your polite invitation to accompany Mr. Johnston to Windsor ○ ○ ○

Your obe't servant, &c.,
ALEX. BLACK.

P. S. Please inform Miss Lennox that the Doctor and Mr. John Lennox were both well last January. My brother writes me that Capt. Lennox was arrived from the East Indies.

R. SMITH TO IREDELL.

EDENTON, 3d Aug., 1781.

DEAR SIR:—We have various reports from Virginia, but so very vague I hardly think them worth mentioning; the last is that 27 sail of transports with 3,000 troops on board have sailed for Charleston, and the French fleet, consisting of 22 sail of the line, have blocked up New York. You may believe as much of this as you please. I, for my part, do not believe a word of it. I am trying to send an express to Virginia to know the certainty of the several circulating reports. You will be able to obtain much important knowledge from Mr. Johnston. My compliments to him and his family, if you please. Mr. Barker goes over to-morrow full tilt with such a political news thirst, that I question whether Mr. Johnston will be able to allay it; he panted about me since I came home, but alas! poor man, I could not furnish sufficient to cool his tongue; he haunts me like my evil genius, and still seems to think I have secrets which I ought to communicate, and hold in reserve; and assures me, that tho' I may be bound in honor to secrecy, I do not infringe by communicating to him, who is as close as ———. I have none, but had I any, I should not be of his opinion. Poor old gentleman, he's so connected with a group of rascals in this town, it would not be safe. You know something of this matter, and Mr. Johnston should have a hint of it. I am in a hurry,

Dear sir, yours ever,
ROB. SMITH.

After the march of Cornwallis to Virginia, Major Craig was by no means inactive in Wilmington; ○ he used every expedient to extend his influence, augment his forces and corroborate his strength. The people of the State suffered greatly for want of salt; he imported large quantities of that article, and thus was enabled by his command of this prime necessary of life, to draw not only Loyalists, but others within the influence of his seductions or intimidations. As occasion required he could increase his garrison (500 effectives) by summoning to his standard the Tories of the vicinage. Slingsby, Dubois, and others commissioned by him, traversed the country, enlisted men, and but awaited his signal for plunder and carnage. At different distances from town small parties of the militia, under Lillington, guarded all the avenues of communication; too weak to confine him to the limits of his post, they yet rendered important services to the State, not unattended with peril; the utmost vigilance was ever necessary to anticipate treachery, and baffle his untiring enterprise. Craig's men were mounted on the finest horses in the Cape Fear region, and his excursions, though on a smaller scale, rivalled those of Tarleton in celerity and dashing impetuosity; often before the astonished sentinel could give the alarm, the thunder of his cavalry was heard, and his sabres flashed over the heads of his victims. One of the bloody occurrences of the period still survives in the tradition of the county of New-Hanover, known among the people as the "massacre of the eight-mile house." I am unable to determine the date with precision. The scene of the tragedy is on the "Sound Road," leading from Wilmington to Newbern. A party of about twenty young men of the militia, chiefly officers, contrary to the advice of their seniors, had repaired to a tavern by the wayside to meet the maidens of the neighborhood at an entertainment they had ordered; they were betrayed by a merchant of Wilmington; and a party of dragoons were despatched for their capture; the revellers had imprudently laid aside their arms; excited by the animating notes of the fiddle, and intoxicated by the charms of their fair countrywomen, they disported themselves with as little thought as motes in a sunbeam; they had neglected every precaution; suddenly the sound of a bugle was heard in the yard—it was the knell of death; flight was the prompting of instinct, and egress was sought by every door and every window; as they emerged from the building they were butchered; but one escaped—Lt. Love, who, seizing upon a saddle, used it successfully as a shield. The traitor, disguised in British uniform, was recognized; he eluded the gallows and the whipping-post, but the general scorn and abhorrence that tracked him to his grave was punishment such as the brave would gladly seek shelter from in death.

President Swain says, Craig's "power was dominant from the

* Gov. Graham, Gov. Swain.

Cape Fear to the Neuse, from Brunswick to Orange."○ Though I dissent from any opinion of that learned gentleman with much diffidence, I cannot but think him inaccurate in this statement. Within a circle that might be described by a radius of ten miles, Wilmington the centre, Craig's power was dominant; in the country beyond this, the "possessio pedis,"† in a short and sudden incursion, was the frail foundation of his authority; no force, it is true, could arrest his forays, but as the waves of the sea close up again behind the leviathan, and sleep or bound as was their mood, so as soon as he retired Whig influence was again in the ascendant, the Cross Creek settlement being the solitary exception. Leonard and Moore in Brunswick; Starkey, Spicer, Cray, Rhodes, Doty, and Howard in Onslow; Brown, Robeson, Owen, Morehead, Gillespie, and Richardson in Bladen; and Kenan, Holmes, Rutledge, and Moore in Duplin, undoubtedly controlled the politics, and determined the destiny of their respective counties. New Hanover, whose very heart Craig may be said to have held in his hand, ever exhibited patriotic life at its extremities: Lillington, Bloodworth, Ashe, Devane, Walker, and Young were ever in motion, ever unsubdued, ever panting for revenge.

About the 10th of August Major Craig, at the head of all his available troops, set out on an expedition against New Berne, ravaging the farms adjacent to his line of march; on the 20th of the same month, he entered that ancient borough; he tarried long enough to fire some shipping, destroy some stores, and secure such booty as might be easily transported, and then directed his steps towards Tarborough; he had advanced some twenty-five or thirty miles, when he precipitately countermarched, alarmed, no doubt, at the report of Gen. Wayne's presence in Halifax County at the head of 1,100 Regulars; he returned to Wilmington in safety.

HOOPER TO IREDELL.

WINDSOR, 25th Aug., 1781.

MY DEAR FRIEND:—My fever continued after you left me with little or no intermission, night or day, until almost exhausted, I had recourse to my old friend, laudanum. Of this I took an overdose, which, instead of quieting the agitated state of my nerves and composing me to sleep, threw me into a delirium, and for a few hours I bore about me strong symptoms of frenzy. I did not sleep during the night, and the extravagances that

* Lecture on British Invasion, 1776.
† In the literal sense.

crowded my brain made my vigils ineffably distressing. The evil at length, however, produced its own cure, the fever rose to a crisis, broke, and an intermission was the consequence. Of this I have industriously availed myself, and ply the bark from the dread of a return. I am still very weak, but gather strength hourly.

Mrs. Iredell and Mrs. Blair have devoted themselves to bringing about my recovery, and to them, under God, do I ascribe it that it has been so soon effected. The business of the whole family seems to be to make me happy, and every other concern is postponed to the gratification of my wishes. My inclinations are all anticipated by the unbounded kindness of all about me. Mrs. Iredell prepares and administers my bark with such tenderness and address, that it loses all its bitterness. In a word, my dear friend, I am of twice the consequence I ever was, and a thousand times more than I ever deserved to be. Thank God, you keep no account but on the credit side of Benevolence. Were you to form a debit, what would become of me? an age of my endeavors would fall far short of discharging it. But I have still a charge against you that may help me out, which is the occasion I afford you of indulging the darling passion of your soul by relieving the wants of your friends and alleviating the distresses of humanity. Yes, Iredell, you have a conscience that will ever bear you up under the pressure of the most pungent calamity, and a heart like yours, all alive to the misfortunes of others, can never be wounded without the consolation of universal sympathy. May you never know real misfortune! is a wish that can scarcely be realized. May you never experience a calamity which you cannot find resources in yourself to brave and rise superior to, is the prayer of him who holds you dear to him as a brother, who has drawn your concerns near to himself, and will ever feel for them as his own. Adieu, my dear sir. I earnestly wish that you may escape a fever during your journey at this inclement season. Avoid the meridian sun, and evening air. For yourself—for your family—for my sake take care of your health.

With the most cordial affection and esteem
I am ever, dear Iredell, yours,
WILL HOOPER.

IREDELL TO MRS. IREDELL.

August 25th, 1781.*

MY DEAR HANNAH:—I got to court about 12, and have ever since been most busily employed. Contrary to my san-

* The place where the letter was written does not appear, because of an obliteration.

guine wishes and expectations, Linton I fear cannot be tried until some of those who actually shot are convicted, and there is none of them to be had but one, who has been made a witness of, and is necessary as such. I fear all the necessary witnesses will not be present to enable me to draw an indictment, though I have done all I could to procure them.

You will probably receive this by the Governor and Col. Davie. I wish you and your sister would be as attentive as possible to them. The worth of the latter rises every day in my estimation. He appears to me to possess uncommon abilities, and much goodness as well as greatness of soul. Craig is said to be 22 miles above Newbern, but the Governor is exerting himself to the utmost, and by an extraordinary instance of good fortune, Gen. Wayne with 1,100 regular troops is to be at Halifax on Wednesday.* I think there is great reason to believe *Craig will never return.* That Tory, Gordon of Wilmington, I believe is certainly shot. Mr. Sharpe writes that Congress had expectations of money from France, *and promise of a superior Naval force in this campaign.*†

I am absolutely obliged to write in this manner. Give my love to your sister, &c., and particularly to my dear Nelly. Remember me also with kindness to Mrs. Dawson's family, and respectfully to Mr. Charlton's, Mr. Gray's, &c. Hillsborough Court begins the 5th of September. Adieu! my dear Hannah. Take good care of yourself. I long most anxiously to hear of Mr. Hooper. I am ever most affectionately yours,

JAS. IREDELL.

BOOTH, Aug. 25th, 1781.

MY DEAR HANNAH:—I wrote you a letter this morning by the Governor. You will be disappointed in a sight of Col. Davie by his being detained to provide for Gen. Wayne's troops, and other reasons. I did not get here till an hour in the night, being kept at Court very busily all day. The bill is found against Linton and the others, there being a very full attendance of witnesses to-day in consequence of some measures I took yesterday. Whether he can be tried or not this time seems uncertain, though I find two of the men who were concerned in the shooting are still about Halifax, and have had proceedings taken to get them into custody. I thank you very kindly for your letter by Mr. McKenzie. Mr. Hooper still continuing so ill distresses me extremely. I wish to God your brother was with him. Pray assure him of my most affectionate thoughts of him, and that I regret infinitely the painful necessity of my separation. I wrote to him this morning by the Governor. We have since heard that the British were advancing a little further on. They were last Wednesday at a place called Shadrack Allen's, 32 miles from Newbern. It is supposed they are coming to Tarborough, but nobody knows; however, nothing could be more fortunate than Gen. Wayne's advance.

You may be assured, my dearest Hannah, I will run no unnecessary risks. I think Mr. Hooper's fears are without foundation, but Mr. Williams and myself will look to the right and left before we proceed. I apprehend now little from the British, and nothing at all from the parties westward. But be assured I will do nothing but what, in my opinion, my honor *really* and not fantastically requires. The Governor is to be at Gen. Jones' at furthest on Wednesday. Have a *long letter* ready for him. I will not fail to write you by all opportunities. My anxiety about you is ever most extreme and tender. Compliments as in my letter of this morning. Adieu! and believe me ever most fervently and affectionately yours,

JAS. IREDELL.

P. S. Tell Mr. Hooper Col. Clark is in Halifax now. I sent Alfred Moore his letter by Major Reed, whom I saw to-day, and gave him his own.

Mr. Sam Johnston in a letter, dated Balgray, Aug. 27th, mentions his purpose to return to Hayes with his family next day. So, I suppose, he no longer deemed Edenton insecure.

WHEELER'S,* Aug. 25th, 1781.

MY DEAR HANNAH:—Our Court ended to-day, but unhappily a day or two too late for me to have the pleasure of seeing you before I go to Hillsborough, which I had much wished, and firmly determined to do if I had had two days to spare. I am persuaded you need be under no apprehensions about my safety in proceeding to Hillsborough. The Governor has ordered out the militia of Orange, and Gen. Wayne's march through the country will intimidate the Tories, so that they dare attempt

---

* After Washington had decided upon a march to the South, Lafayette was requested by him to prevent Lord Cornwallis from saving himself by a sudden retreat to Charleston. Wayne was immediately despatched south of James River for this purpose.—*Marshall.*

† William Sharpe, of Iredell, a distinguished lawyer, soldier, and patriot—member of all the early revolutionary assemblies—aid-de-camp to Rutherford in '76—member of the Continental Congress in '79, '82; died in 1818. Ancestor of the Irwins, of Burke, and Judge Caldwell, and Hon. Joseph P. Caldwell.—*Wheeler.*

* Wheeler's, I suppose, was the residence of the grandfather of the Hon. Jno. H. Wheeler, minister to Nicaragua, author of a Hist. N. C., &c.: it is near the county seat of Northampton.

---

nothing. Whether we shall go to Salisbury is uncertain. If we do we shall have a strong guard thither, and when there, Col. Davie tells me we shall be perfectly safe, for all Rowan, (the county in which Salisbury stands,) and Mecklenburg which joins it, are extremely well affected, and *zealously so.*°

One of the men concerned in the actual shooting of Quinn was tried yesterday, but, in a great measure owing to the suppression of a most material part of the truth by a rascal, who was one of the accomplices, and swore differently to the grand jury and petit jury, he was not convicted. No other of the principals being now to be got, there was a necessity for admitting Linton to bail, which has been done.

The enemy burnt Gen. Bryan's mill, and afterwards one Longfield Cox's (*and I do not know but their houses*), *and then turned again towards Cape Fear. They destroyed salt, rum, rigging, &c., in Newbern, but did, I believe, no other mischief.* John Green, Cogdell, Ogden, and Harlin staid. I have heard of no other principal persons that staid. Mr. Nash, it is said, was confined there by sickness.

To-morrow is the day Gen. Wayne is expected, but it is doubtful if he can be here quite so soon. I hope to see him and his fine body of troops.

I keep my health perfectly well, and hope in God you do. My head-quarters have been here, where I have received all possible kindness and civility. This opportunity is quite an unexpected one. Mr. W. Jones came in this evening on his way to the Indian woods, and, as I dare say he intends going by daylight in the morning, I have no time to write to any but you and your brother John, to whom I shall enclose this letter. Pray mention this to my dear friend, Hooper, and beg him to excuse me. I shall certainly write him before I leave this part of the country. I am most anxious to hear about him, and pray to God it may be altogether favorable. Indeed I cannot prevail on myself to doubt it. It would make me too unhappy. Tell him Col. Clark is perfectly well, and still at Halifax, and likely to be so for some days. Remember me, also, very affectionately to Mr. Smith, and apologize for me. My affectionate compliments to your sister. Love to the children, and pray remember me particularly to Nelly and Mrs. Dawson's family. The only fault here is being sent to bed too early, which obliges me to finish my letter. Adieu! my dear Hannah. Heaven bless you!

I am most affectionately, and unalterably yours,

JAS. IREDELL.

P. S. The enemy certainly burnt Bryan's and Cox's houses.

* The underscoring is in the original.

HALIFAX, August 29th, 1781.

MY DEAR HANNAH:—I wrote you last night from General Jones' by his brother, who was going to the Indian woods. He came to town this morning, and soon after I had the pleasure to receive your letter by the governor, which made me very happy, for I was most anxious and uneasy about Mr. Hooper, and I longed most to hear from him and you. Colonel Clark is here at present, and as I find Mr. Hooper proposed coming up in a few days to see him, I pressed the former very strongly to go to our house, as I am sure it would be dangerous for Mr. Hooper to come out soon, and I knew you and your sister would be very glad of an opportunity to show kindness to a man every way worthy of being Mrs. Hooper's brother. His conduct, perseverance, and losses as an officer must highly endear him to every friend of *American liberty and virtue.* Nothing can ever be more painful to me than to do any thing disagreeable to your inclinations, but my honor compels me to attend as far as the judges do. *In times of tranquillity some liberties may be taken, but not in these.* I believe our guard and Gen. Wayne's march will make us perfectly safe. Be assured I will attend to my own security as much as I can with honor. It will be uncertain if we shall go to Salisbury.

As to the Governor and Mr. —— going by Mr. Pollok's, if there be any blame, I am not altogether or even principally answerable for it. Mr. Gilchrist mentioned it first, and asked me about it, and I said what surely I could not avoid, that I was persuaded it would give Mr. Pollok pleasure. I should be sorry if they thought me presuming enough to send any persons there upon my invitation. And Mr. Gilchrist's conduct I really think very extraordinary, for I understood he was to accompany them.

I did not know Nelly was to return so soon. Give my love to her most tenderly. I have her for her intention to write, and would write to her if I had time, but I really have not. Be pleased also to remember me most affectionately to your sister. She will forgive, I hope, the liberty I have taken in inviting Colonel Clark. *His worth is so great every body ought to be eager to testify their sense of it.* After all, I know not whether this will reach you immediately, for H. Bond who carries it is to follow the route of Dudley, which is uncertain. Adieu! my dear Hannah. Give my love and compliments at your discretion.

Most faithfully and affectionately yours,

JAS. IREDELL.

P. S.—Peter is well.

ELK MARSH, Aug. 30th, 1781.

MY DEAREST HANNAH:—The Governor coming rather sooner than we expected, we are thus far on our way to Hillsborough. I wrote you yesterday by H. Bond from Halifax in a great hurry, but it was uncertain whether he would go by Winton or Dukinfield. I have pressed Colonel Clark very much to go and see Mr. Hooper, and spend a few days with him at our house. I was sure I could take this liberty with propriety in respect to him, for he is one of the most valuable and respectable of men, and deserving of the highest attention for his uncommon personal merit and services to his country. I wrote a line of introduction to you and your sister by him if he should go. I retain my health perfectly well. Our danger, I believe, will be very little, as we shall be well guarded, and General Wayne's advance will intimidate the Tories. I wrote by Bond to your brother, Mr. Hooper, and C. Johnson. Mr. Hooper's letter I enclosed to you. As it is uncertain if Colonel Clark may not come down, I wish you would stay some short time in expectation of it—but not long, or so as to make it disagreeable to you. I enclose a letter for Mr. Hooper. I forgot to send sooner.

Pray let me hear from you if possible, and take the best care of your health. Of my own be assured. Give my love to your sister and the children. I will steal a bit of this paper to scribble a line to Nelly. Adieu! my dearest Hannah, and believe me in truth, with entire affection,

Ever yours,
JAMES IREDELL.

P. S.—An acquaintance of Mr. Hooper's, Mr. Craike, talked of going to see him. If he should, be civil to him. He is a very good sort of man.

To MISS BLAIR:

MY DEAR NELLY:—I have only time to tell you that I love you most tenderly, and am ever most anxious about you. I thank you for your intention to write to me, though you could not accomplish it. Be well and be happy till my return, when I shall have the greatest pleasure in letting you know how much I am

Your truly affectionate,
J. I.

IREDELL TO MRS. IREDELL.

COLONEL WILLIAMS'S, GRANVILLE, Sept. 3d, 1781.

MY DEAR HANNAH:—My last letter to you was from Colonel McCulloh's, which I wrote last Thursday. Judge Williams and myself left it that afternoon, and reached this his most hospitable and agreeable house the next evening. I regretted by my coming so soon, my having lost an opportunity of seeing General Wayne and his troops, but it seemed generally thought they would not be at Halifax for two or three days, and I hated upon such an uncertainty to quit agreeable company and impose upon myself a journey without rest to Hillsborough. We yesterday were most agreeably surprised at information that a French fleet, consisting of sixteen sail of the line, had arrived in Virginia, and that General Wayne had halted in order to co-operate with the Marquis against Lord Cornwallis, who was pushing to the southward. The Marquis has wrote to the Governor to have his passage opposed at Roanoke at all events; that he should keep upon his right flank, and hoped to bring him to action. He writes, I am told, in high spirits and with a good deal of sanguineness. The Governor is now at Halifax, so that I have this only at second-hand, but from persons I am sure I can rely upon.

Our affairs in South Carolina and Georgia are on a most agreeable footing. The enemy have no footing in those countries, but at Charleston and Savannah, and the spot which their main army occupies at Orangeburg and environs (about 70 or 80 miles above Charleston), where they get no rest night or day, Marion, Sumpter, and Lee, and occasionally Washington, continually hanging about them, and harassing them, for their cavalry is almost entirely destroyed. A short time ago, 30 of our horse attacked 50 of their dragoons, killed two or three and brought off the rest prisoners. Their infantry, I believe, is pretty strong, but they have met with so much difficulty in getting supplies, that they have already moved much lower down than they were, and it is expected they will soon go still nearer, if not entirely to Charleston.

Greene is encamped on a fine situation upon the high Hills of Santee, about 110 miles from Charleston. He very unfortunately is not very strong, or able to effect great things at present, but I am told he had a great scheme in agitation, which he hoped to be in a condition to execute soon. *The inhabitants in general are most friendly, and most cordially attached to his army.* General Leslie, it is said, has lately arrived at Charleston to take the command, but carried no troops with him.

The reign of the Tories, I believe, will soon be over. We hear there is a body of them about Cross Creek, but a much larger body of Whigs was advancing against them; *the Whigs in general were turning out with great spirit.* The governor also, whenever he is in a condition to act with all the vigor he wishes, will disconcert them very much by offering pardon to all who may be supposed to have adhered to them from fear and in consequence of the distraction of the times, merely in terror for their persons and property, and who shall within a limited time join our militia in arms. His intention has already spread ahead, and he has received applications and assurances in consequence, which promise him the happiest effects from such a measure. The leaders will then probably be left to suffer deservedly by themselves. We have little reason therefore to be afraid of any attempts from them, but shall, however, have an escort of 25 or 30 men to conduct us to Hillsborough (for which place we are to set off to-morrow), and when there shall have a formidable guard—at Salisbury, our danger will be still less. * * * * Pray mention me most affectionately to them, Mr. Johnston and the children, Mrs. Dawson's family, your sister, &c. I don't think I shall have time to scribble a line to Nelly, but beg her to be assured I hold her always most tenderly in my remembrance. If you see Mr. Hooper, desire him not to impute my not writing to him to neglect, and acquaint him and my other friends with the news, though most of it, I dare say, has reached them. If you have an opportunity, I entreat you to write to me. If you direct any early letter to the care of "Colonel Robert Burton, Granville,"* and get it safely conveyed to some careful person at Halifax, it will probably reach me. I intend to enclose this to Mr. McKenzie, to whom I have occasion to write, about some inquiries he asked me to make concerning Tory Kello, who last lived near Hillsborough, and is now deservedly a prisoner to the northward. Mr. M. is interested to know the condition of his property, about which I can now give him some, but not full information.

I shall not fail to write you from Hillsborough. Afterwards it may be difficult till my return. I shall be most anxious and uneasy about you for fear of your getting sick, so for God's sake take all possible care of yourself. As for myself, I hope to return as well and as hearty as I usually do, till which most desirable time believe me, my dear Hannah, with inexpressible tenderness and the greatest truth,

Most entirely and affectionately yours,
JAMES IREDELL.

P. S. Peter is well.

On the 8th September occurred the battle of Eutaw Springs. Full details will presently be given by a letter from Mr. Hooper. Much the larger part of Greene's troops were from North Carolina: of his front line of militia (4 battalions) one-half were North Carolinians, under Colonel Malmedy: three of the seven battalions of Continentals, who constituted his second line, were North Carolinians, commanded by General Sumner, Col. Ashe, Major Armstrong, Major Blount: of those who fought under the banner of South Carolina, "the greater part of the Regiments of Polk, Hampton, and Hill, were raised in the then counties of Mecklenburg and Rowan (N. C.), between the Yadkin and Catawba."*

IREDELL TO MRS. IREDELL.

GRANVILLE, Sept. 11th, 1781.

MY DEAR HANNAH:—I have the greatest pleasure in again taking up my pen to write to you. The day after I came here (which you must excuse my concealing in my last letter, thinking it would soon go off) I was attacked with a most severe fit of the ague and fever, which returned upon me, and almost each time with increased violence, every other day for a week. I was unfortunate enough not to have the proper remedies at hand, but Mr. Burke most obligingly furnished me with tartar, and prepared it for me. Three different days I took it, besides a purgative and three or four doses of bark, which was all I could at first command, and these shook the disorder almost entirely off. I have since completed my cure by means of some bark Mr. Adam Boyd (whom Mrs. Blair saw at Windsor) obligingly gave me. I don't remember my ever being worse. During the greatest part of the time my fever lasted, my head distressed me exceedingly, and I was a considerable part of the time delirious. My stomach also

---

* Colonel Robert Burton married the daughter of Judge Williams: he was a planter, officer in the army, and member of the Continental Congress, 1787–8. Hon. R. Burton and Mr. A. Burton, of Beattiesford, Lincoln Co., were his sons.—*Wheeler.* Colonel Burton's grandson, John Willis Burton, was with me at Princeton: he was the Bayard of the class that graduated in 1838. If ever there was a man ready at any moment, at the call of duty, calmly to lay down his life—he was that man. Of the social circle, of which he was a member, he was "dulce decus;" and by it he was cherished and loved. Too modest for that self-assertion, generally, exacted by the Bar as the price of distinction; and too proud to "elbow his way" amid clamorous applicants for his purity of heart, the soundness of his judgment, the variety and extent of his attainments were only known to his intimate friends. After residing some time in Tennessee, he removed to Louisiana, where he was, recently, borne to an untimely grave, before he had fulfilled the bright promise of his youth, or attained that rank to which his talents and industry entitled him.

* "Closing scenes of the Revolution in N. C., by General Joseph Graham, N. C., Un. Mag., June, 1852. Colonel Polk was from N. C.

continually sick. I was very fortunate however in my situation. Mr. and Mrs. Williams behaved to me with the utmost degree of tenderness and kindness, of which they could not have shown more had I been their own son. I wanted for nothing that could possibly be provided for me, and they took pains to borrow for my convenience. Mrs. Burke also was very kind and attentive as well as the governor during a little while he stayed, and he expressed (though not to me) his regret that necessary business called him away, and prevented his attention to my recovery, which otherwise he would most willingly have bestowed. My last severe fever was on Friday. Sunday I had a very little, but not enough to lie down. To-day (Tuesday) I have none at all. This disorder stopped my jaunt to Hillsborough, and I don't yet feel strong and hearty enough to go to Salisbury, so I have declined that disagreeable journey also. In the mean time, I am here in excellent quarters, wishing most earnestly to hear from you, even more (which is a great deal for a politician to say) than to know what General Washington is doing in Virginia, for it is certain from a letter from General Nelson to Governor Burke, that he was on his way there, and we are told an extraordinary cannonade that was heard distinctly, and almost shook the earth in this neighborhood last Wednesday (the 5th inst.),* was on account of his going on board the French fleet. What a sight! The French fleet, I believe, certainly consists of 27 ships of the line, and brought with them at least 3,000 land forces, and we are told also a great quantity of arms. The French troops from the northward and some Continentals were to come to the southward with General Washington. Cornwallis is fluttering about somewhere in Virginia, but we don't know exactly where, though people confidently say at York: *The Governor is at Hillsborough, so that the news flies by us without our catching any. He is meditating a grand scheme against the Tories, the particulars of which I don't know, and means, I believe, to head the militia in person.* His place of residence is in the town of Hillsborough, and Mrs. Burke is to go up there in a short time. It is my intention to stay here in this neighborhood till the time of Hillsborough Superior Court, which begins the 1st day of October. I heartily wish I could venture to go home first, but the sun is so extremely hot that I should endanger a relapse by it, and my stay at any rate must be very short, which would be greatly mortifying. I thank God, however, I am in a way of hearing frequently from you, if you will be kind enough to improve the oppor-

* Sept. 5th, there was an engagement between the French and English Fleets off the Capes of the Chesapeake.

tunity. *Enclose* your letters to "Robert Burton, Esq., Granville," and direct the outside cover to him "to the care of Colonel Nicholas Long, Halifax." They keep expresses continually passing to and fro, and Colonel Burton lives within *hollow* of his father-in-law.

You will please to remember me most affectionately to Mrs. Dawson, and family, and assure them how gratefully and kindly I ever think of them. Give my best respects to Mr. and Mrs. Pollok. Say every thing respectful and tender for me to your brother and his family, and tell him I shall have frequent opportunities from here and will write to him soon. You will not fail to give my love in the tenderest and strongest manner to my dear Penny and Gaby. I must desire also my very affectionate remembrance to Mr. Hooper, to whom I wish earnestly to write, but have it not in my power now, and beg him to excuse me. I have not heard from his son, but hope to do so soon. If you see Mr. Smith or Mr. C. Johnson, present them with my respects, and tell them I will write them soon.

Having despatched all these compliments, I now come to express the fervent sentiments of my soul, that I think of you, my dear Hannah, often and most anxiously, that I pray for the continuance of your health, which I earnestly entreat you to attend to, and that I am with unutterable tenderness, as well as the greatest truth,

Your most faithful and affectionate
JAMES IREDELL.

Sept. 12.—One-half of this letter I wrote to-day, and knowing how anxious you will be about me, I have the satisfaction to assure you, I feel myself grow stronger every day. Peter is very well, and attended me during my illness with the greatest tenderness and care.

J. I.

S. JOHNSTON TO MRS. IREDELL.

HAYES, Sept. 14th, 1781.

MY DEAR HANNAH:—I have had the pleasure of receiving your letter by J. Gray and likewise one by Mr. Allen, both of which gave me great pleasure, except that part where you suppose I might be offended with you; how could you suppose me so unreasonable. *I cannot charge my memory with a single action of your life that ever gave me a moment's uneasiness much less offence; it has always been my pride and chief pleasure to see and promote your happiness by every means in my power,*

and of late it has been no small addition to a number of other mortifications and misfortunes which have befallen me, that I have not had it in my power to do it more effectually. Mr. Hooper and Col. Clark have been so obliging as to spend a few days with us; they talk of going over to-morrow or next day. I write to-day that I may not lose the earliest opportunity of rectifying your error. We are all pretty well in health at present, so is every one in the town and neighborhood, except Charles Johnson, who has had a touch of the gout, but is recovering. Poor John Lowther died a few days ago after a very long illness. Billy Blair was here till yesterday. I missed him at dinner. I am afraid it will be some time before you see Mr. Iredell, as there is some talk of his going to Salisbury. If the success of the armies of America and France, now in Virginia, is in any measure adequate to our present prospects, I shall hope that the war will soon be removed at so great a distance from us that there will be no danger in your returning to your own house.

I am grown a very industrious planter. I go to bed very early, and am always up before the sun. I use a great deal of exercise all day, and avoid reading and thinking as much as possible, and hope soon to arrive to that degree of stupidity and insensibility which I begin to think can only make people happy, for I have long observed that the greatest fools, have not only the most pleasure in life, but are generally as much respected and have a greater share of good fortune than men of the best understanding. It will always give me great pleasure to hear from you, and though I should not write you as often as I ought, pray attribute it to any other reason than that of my being offended with you. Mrs. Johnston and the children desire their love to you. We should be all happy to see you here. I am ever with the most sincere esteem, my dear sister,

Your affectionate brother,
SAM. JOHNSTON.

While the patriot Burke was concerting measures for the subjugation of the Tories and the restoration of tranquillity to the State, David Fannen was contriving a counterplot. About 600 to 1,000 men recognized the authority of Fannen and Col. McNeil. Fannen had graduated in the school of villainy with the highest honors; a truculent, unscrupulous scamp, he was formidable for his craft, and his enterprise; his life could not be well said to have been *stained* with crimes, for it was one blood-red record; he inspired so much terror in the counties bordering on the Cape Fear, by the celerity of his movements and his atrocities, that mothers subdued with his name refractory urchins. Whether acting under instructions from Major Craig, or whether the scheme was the exclusive product of his own brain, does not appear: he designed the capture of the Governor, the Judges, and the Attorney-General: so well was he informed, and so ably had he devised his plans, that the providential sickness of Iredell (the Attorney-General) alone saved him and Judge Williams from the merciless grasp of the marauder. The following letter from Iredell to his wife contains the most complete and interesting account of this expedition, which robbed the State of its Chief Magistrate, that I have as yet seen. It has been generally supposed that the primary object of Fannen's advance was to assail the militia under Butler, some distance on the south side of Haw River; and that upon the escape of Butler, the surprise of the Governor was a conception as sudden as brilliant; but there are many reasons for a contrary belief:

GRANVILLE, Sept. 16th, 1781.

MY DEAR HANNAH:—I wrote you two or three days ago, acquainting you of my having been sick here, but then being recovered, and I thank God I still continue perfectly well. My sickness I at the time deemed a great misfortune, but I consider it far otherwise now, for in all human probability, nothing else prevented Col. Williams and myself sharing a very melancholy fate which now attends the Governor. On Wednesday morning last, about 7 o'clock, a large body of Tories, supposed to amount to 400, under Fanning and McNeil, entered Hillsborough, and with very little loss from the fire of an inconsiderable guard, got possession of the Governor, Col. Reade, Mr. Huske, Col. Lyttle, and a number of other persons. Lyttle, though a prisoner on parole, was hacked and cut by Fanning in a most cruel manner. The persons of the others do not appear to have been ill-used. They continued in town till two, rifling and plundering, and doing a good deal of mischief, and then carried off their prisoners and booty, making even the Governor walk on foot. During the time they were in town they released the prisoners that were in gaol, put arms in their hands, and turned the guard into their places. Some were killed in attempting to make their escape, and it is said three or four of the Tories were killed by the guards' fire. Two of the men at first came to Mr. Hogg's house, and insulted and abused him a good deal, and robbed him of his watch and buckles, and made him deliver up his keys; but he afterwards obtained a sentinel to be placed at his house, and he suffered on the whole little other loss than that of his watch. We have since had an imperfect account of the rear guard of hese rascals being attacked and routed with great loss by about 150 men under Col. Mebane (a most spirited continental officer). The Tories were far more numerous, but they nevertheless lost almost all their horses, guns, and the plunder they brought from Hillsborough. Seven of our men were killed, the number of wounded uncertain, but among these Col. Lutrell was shot through the body, though it is thought he may possibly recover. The rest of the Tories (supposed to amount to about 200) were with the prisoners two miles in front. Every effort was making to bring on a successful attack, and God grant such a one may have taken place ! The action was near Deep River, about forty miles from Hillsborough, a little above Ramsay's Mills. The weather has been excessively bad for some days, and still continues so, so that I could not have attempted travelling ; and Mr. Williams is now so ill that I cannot in common humanity leave him till I see him better. His disorder is much worse than mine, and rather of the remitting than the intermitting kind. Never shall I forget the kindness I have received here. Nothing could have exceeded it, unless it might be the readiness with which it was bestowed. As soon as possible I shall leave this, and go immediately in search of you. In the mean time, believe that I am here perfectly secure. I have not time to write to a single soul besides. Give my love and compliments where due, and be assured I am ever, my dear Hannah,

Yours most affectionately,
JAS. IREDELL.

In the attack the Governor's house was the principal object. Expecting from the savage appearance of the men nothing but massacre, the Governor, attended by his Aid, Capt. Read,* his Secretary, Mr. Huske, and an orderly Sergeant, resolved to die sword in hand. After sustaining for some time a close and hot fire, Capt. Read,† with great gallantry, penetrated the enemy's ranks, and returned with a gentleman in the uniform of a British officer, to whom, after repeated assurances of proper treatment, Gov. Burke surrendered. The captor had, afterward, much difficulty in preserving the Governor from the fury of the Tories, but succeeded in sheltering him from violence by the assistance of some Highlanders, who, as prisoners heretofore, had experienced humanity at the hands of the Executive. The Governor was taken to Wilmington, where he was put into close confinement as a *prisoner of State.*°

Thomas Burke was a native of Ireland, son of Ulick Burke, of the Tyaquin family of Galway, and nephew of Sir Fielding Ould. In 1772 he removed to North Carolina from Virginia, having emigrated to the latter State when but seventeen years old. He had been liberally educated, and had studied medicine and law ; he was of middle stature, well formed, and much marked by the small pox, which had occasioned the loss of his left eye. Though thus disfigured, his face was not without charm : his remaining eye, a fine expressive blue, now sparkled with wit, now blazed with passion, and, anon, in its merry twinkle was the very soul of humor. Such was the mobility of his features that in them might easily be recognized the shadow or the sunbeam of each thought, sad or gay. He was an admirable " raconteur" of mirth-provoking stories ; sang a good song ; and of " vers de societé," at the bidding of a fair friend, could dash off stanzas without apparent effort.† Few could resist the geniality of his manners : his frankness and cordiality warmed even the phlegmatic into unwonted life and action. Of ardent temperament, quick and impulsive, he was often betrayed into acts of rashness that reflection condemned. Prompt to resent an insult, he was equally ready to expiate a wrong. Certainly no cotemporary in North Carolina was so remarkable for versatility of talents. He soon established a brilliant reputation, and served in the Continental Congress from December, '76, till his election, by acclamation, as Governor in June, '81. In the battle of Brandywine, he had participated as an " amateur," deserting, for the nonce, his seat in Congress : the roll of the drum, and the thunder of the artillery, were more than his Irish blood could stand, " certamine gaudens." From Wilmington Gov. Burke was transferred to Charleston, where Gen. Leslie commanded. Leslie refused to regard him as a *prisoner of War*, though he was Commander-in-chief of North Carolina, and when captured was on the eve of taking the field in person ; he insisted he was a *prisoner of State*, and thus precluded all chance of release by exchange for an equivalent.‡ The Governor was paroled to James' Island, infested by large crowds of Tories of desperate character: there he was subject to constant insults, and his life was frequently imperilled : his remonstrances were unheeded by the

* Greene had threatened retaliation for the execution of Col. Hayne. Burke was highly valued by the British as a countercheck—a hostage for Greene's humanity.
† In the appendix to this chap. will be found some verses of the Governor, preserved by Judge Iredell.
‡ Gov. Graham.

* Burke's message to Assembly, April, '82.
† Capt. Reade and Col. Read, I suppose, were one and the same person.

British General ; and his applications for a guard contemptuously neglected. All law thus outraged in his person, and the British failing to protect him, the Governor determined to protect himself by flight, the only practicable mode. He embraced the first opportunity to escape, which he effected in the night, Jan. 16th, 1782. He promply proffered Leslie an equivalent in exchange for himself ; and in case of his failure, promised to return within his lines, provided that officer would pledge his honor that he should be treated as were continental officers, when prisoners of war. Leslie's neglect to reply seemed a studied contempt ; stung by the indignity, Gov. Burke proceeded to Salem, and resumed the government of the State : this step, though sanctioned by General Greene, was generally condemned by the American officers : their censure to one who, as Burke, cherished honor more than life, was an arrow dipped in poison ; his high spirit drooped ; his sensibility grew morbid. One delicately refined as he was, though he had courage to face any danger, started and trembled at the thought of disgrace. A sense of shame, however unmerited, pursued him by day, and pressed upon his slumbers by night. The gloom thickened about him, and as early as April, '82, he announced his determination to retire from office, a purpose finally executed in the subsequent December. He died on the 2d of December, 1783. Thus prematurely perished one eminently qualified to adorn and to elevate society. What North Carolinian can stand uncovered by his grave, what daughter of the State deny him the tribute of her tears ?*

During Gov. Burke's "inability and absence from the State," Alexander Martin, the Speaker of the Senate, about the first of October, assumed the powers of Governor, according to the provisions of the Constitution.

CHARLTON TO IREDELL.

CUFFNELS, Sept. 21st, 1781.

Your obliging favor this moment received hath made me exceedingly happy. I have long trembled for your fate, and my apprehensions on the score of your danger, were much multiplied when I heard the Governor's captivity. I confess I rejoice with yourself, Mrs. Iredell, and your worthy connections, at your very opportune sickness, which hath at least freed you from the insults of a capricious, if not a cruel enemy, and I sincerely hope that ease and a sight of your lady and friends will soon restore

* Vid. a most chaste and elegant sketch, contributed by Miss Phillips of Chapel Hill, to the Un. Mag., May, 1855.

you to perfect health. The loss of Governor Burke at this critical and momentous time I have truly deplored, from an idea that his head and heart have a very sincere attachment to this State. God grant that his escape may have been effected in the manner related by Tatem to Col. Burton. I could have wished you had afforded me your own private opinion in respect to the authenticity of that report, although upon reflection, as you say nothing in confutation of it, I take it for granted you believe it. I view with true anguish of mind, and every mark of pity, the deplorable condition of the southern and western parts of this State, but I hope the vigorous exertions of Gen. Butler and Col. Mebane will soon put an issue to their inhabitants' affliction. The prospect to the Northward brightens, as you will perceive by Mr. Payne's letter to me, received by Mr. Finds yesterday. Mrs. Charlton and myself will be made extremely happy, could you make your route to Edenton by the way of Cuffnels. I hope your desire of visiting that place will not deprive us of that pleasure, and that the law of convenience may yield to a superior one—that of friendship. Mrs. Charlton joins me in respectful compliments to you and Mrs. Iredell, and I assure you that I am most truly and affectionately, dear sir,

Your friend and obt. humble servant,
JASPER CHARLTON.

A. MACLAINE TO IREDELL.

SAMPSON HALL, 21st Sept., 1781.

DEAR SIR :—I have already made some attempts to convey you a letter, but from the public confusion have always been disappointed.

The present month seems big with events of importance. Cornwallis surrounded with powerful armies and a large fleet, and Washington, it is asserted, on his march to Virginia. I cannot conceive how the siege or even blockade of New York should be maintained if the General has in reality left it with 5,000 French troops ; what is left appears to me inadequate to any purpose of that kind, and I should think the fleet would not venture to encounter the equinoctial storms in a place so much exposed as that wherein it was stationed.

For want of the arms which have been so long expected, the Tories in this district, and the more western counties, have increased considerably. In truth, it is rather for want of good officers. Mr. Slingsby (Mr. Dubois' brother-in-law), who had accepted of the command of Bladen and Brunswick counties, and was at the head of a considerable number of Tories, was lately surprised and routed at Elizabethtown.* In this action we had only one man wounded, but it is thought dangerously. Killed, wounded and taken of the enemy, 19—Slingsby since dead of his wounds.† Several of another party have been since taken, but the intelligence which we have received of the Governor being taken at Hillsborough, may give a fatal turn to our affairs; as this is now the 10th day since it happened, you may probably have heard of it. The town of Hillsborough was plundered, and the Tories retreated with the Governor, and it is said about 100 Continental soldiers, and several officers, to some place near Lindley's mill. The paroled officers were taken, and Col. Lyttle much wounded, though he was unarmed. Whilst their horses were tied in a thicket, and their plunder displayed in an old field, two of the opposite parties met and engaged, which occasioned a smart action of the whole under Butler and Mabin; and though we wanted ammunition, they kept the field with clubbed muskets. The Tories fled, leaving their horses and plunder, but in the beginning of the action had sent off their prisoners under a guard through Guilford. McNeil killed and Fanning's left arm broken. Many of these particulars are from Abs. Tatum, who had been taken, and escaped in a dark night, and was got to Mr. Rand's. The prisoners are pursued by 200 of our horse, and expresses sent to waylay the passes; but Brown of Bladen has few men, and the Tories about him are numerous. Kenan does nothing in this county. As there is an opportunity to Newbern, I would not omit writing to you, though I want spirits even to move. *I have lost my only surviving son in Wilmington, and considering the situation of my daughter, may justly say I am bereft of all my children. But though all hopes of future happiness in this life are cut off, I still have a heart left for my suffering country.* The tyranny under which this part of the country groans, is to be attributed as much to the malice and self-interested views of the newly-converted *loyalists*, as to the avarice of the British officers. To such base motives I am indebted for my never-to-be-recovered losses. Though I have reason to believe Mr. Hooper is in your part of the country, I have not wrote to him. If he should be there, this will serve equally as well. Remember me affectionately to him, and present my compliments to Mr. Johnston and his family, Mr. and Mrs. Pollok, &c. I am, with best respect to Mrs. Iredell and your family,

Dear Sir, very sincerely yours,
A. MACLAINE.

* The Whigs were commanded by Brown, Owen, Robeson, Morehead, Irvine, Gillespie, Dickinson, and Wright. The Tories numbered about 300: the American force was much less. Caruthers, Wheeler.
† Slingsby was a merchant of Wilmington, an Englishman by birth.

JOHNSTON TO IREDELL.

HAYES, Sept. 24th, 1781.

DEAR SIR:—I received your letter of yesterday this evening, and am very sorry your indisposition continues so inveterate. I will pay particular attention to what you say respecting Gardiner's suit against Savage. We have an account in town to-day, which is said to come from Gen. Huger, of an action between Gen. Greene and the British, the event of which was favorable to the former, who routed the enemy and pursued them six miles, when they secured themselves from perfect ruin by entering and taking possession of a large brick house. They lost 250 killed on the field of battle, 450 wounded, and 150 taken prisoners. This victory was purchased at the expense of 250 killed and wounded, among whom are a number of valuable officers, a list of whom I have seen, but being a stranger to most of them, do not now recollect their names. Captains Goodman, Goodwin and Portersfield, of this State, are among the slain, and Col. Howard of Maryland among the wounded; it is said to have happened at the Congaree on the 8th inst. By Mr. Sharpe's letter, which you were so obliging as to forward, dated the 4th inst., I learn that the Commander-in-Chief had raised the siege of New York, and ordered all the French troops, and three thousand Continentals, under the command of Gen. Lincoln, to Virginia; these troops had actually passed through Philadelphia the 3d, and are undoubtedly arrived in Virginia. Col. Laurens had arrived at Philadelphia by the way of Boston, at which last place had likewise arrived a large supply of arms, stores, and clothing, and some cash, which has been obtained from our good friend and ally, the king of France. No foreign news, except that the British have suffered very greatly in the East Indies, and that ten sail of the line with eight thousand land forces had sailed from Cadiz on a secret expedition—supposed to have gone against Minorca. Reports of the day say, that Gen. Clinton has evacuated New York—that the British have left Wilmington, &c.

This is sent by a conveyance so very uncertain that I don't care to send my letters to the ladies by it, which I hope they will believe is a true reason, and not an evasion. Present my love, &c., &c., &c.

Your affectionate brother,
SAM. JOHNSTON.

HAYES, Oct. 1st, 1781.

DEAR SIR:—I had the pleasure of receiving your letter yesterday, and am very happy to hear that you have conquered your ague and fever, and that we shall soon see you and my sister here.

Reports from the camp are, that upon Gen. Washington's sending a summons to Gen. Lord Cornwallis to surrender, the latter demanded twenty days; the former agreed to ten, which was accepted; the term expired yesterday; that Gen. Clinton had embarked ten thousand men on board transports, but had not sailed—his destination uncertain. This intelligence comes by a stranger, a Frenchman, and of course but little credited; he adds further, that Gen. Washington had got possession of an advantageous eminence near the enemy's lines. Remember me, &c., &c.

Your affectionate brother,
SAM. JOHNSTON.

HOOPER TO IREDELL.

HALIFAX, Oct. 1st, 1781.

DEAR SIR:—Immediately upon my arrival at Gen. Jones', I devoted myself to an inquiry as to the particulars of the late engagement to the southward, and was fortunate enough to obtain from Col. Davie's recollection, who had seen a letter from Mr. Pendleton, aide-de-camp to Gen. Greene, wrote upon the field of battle after the engagement, information which at that time was satisfactory to me. *Since that, Col. Ashe, who was in the action, has arrived from camp, and has given me occasion in some circumstances to vary, and in many to add to the first representation.* It affords me the highest satisfaction that I can give you an account of this engagement, *the most bloody that has happened this war, to which you may almost in every particular give the most implicit credit.*

Greene had for some time before been encamped on the high hills of Santee, which are about thirty miles from Camden below it, and thirty miles above Nelson's Ferry—when he made a movement with his whole army to Maniguelt's Ferry, a few miles above Nelson's. The British, who were posted at Nelson's, in consequence of this movement fell down to Monk's Corner, but again returned to Nelson's Ferry, upon finding that Gen. Greene did not advance. This last movement of the British inducing a suspicion that they intended to make an attempt to cross at Nelson's, Gen. Greene ordered the legion to be thrown over, to be in readiness to obstruct their progress. But the militia assembling in great numbers on the opposite side, and having evinced their intention by taking prisoners twenty of the British who first landed on the opposite shore, the British declined the further prosecution of their design, and returned to the Eutaw Springs, six miles from Gen. Greene's encampment. On the morning of the 8th of September, Gen. Greene marched from his encampment, and very soon afterward the advance of his army were engaged with a foraging party of the British. The front line of our army was composed of Gen. Marion's Regiment, Gen. Sumpter's, (then commanded by Col. Henderson,*) the North Carolina Militia, the Legion, and Gen. Pickens' corps, and was engaged very generally about one and a half miles from the Eutaw Springs. The South Carolina troops on the left, commanded by Pickens, and *chiefly British parole men*, behaved well, broke and rallied often and formed again. The North Carolina Militia on the right behaved much better than usually, but the shameful conduct of Col. Farmer (Ruthy's husband), who headed them, damped their spirits and lessened the execution which might otherwise have been expected from them.

The second line, composed of the North Carolina Brigade on the right, Virginians on the left, and Marylanders in the centre, advanced into the action. Sumner's Brigade was first engaged; the Virginians on the left succeeded, and a most heavy firing continued for about two hours. The South Carolinians, ordered to form in the second line with the Virginians, kept up so heavy and well-directed a fire, that immediately upon the Virginians being ordered to charge with bayonets, the enemy entirely broke in that quarter. The Marylanders and North Carolinians at the same time pressed on to charge, the whole of the enemy then broke and retreated with the greatest precipitation. Our army pursued them through their encampment to a farm at some small distance, when the enemy possessing themselves of a strong brick house and some farm houses near it, again formed and put themselves in a posture of opposition. Gen. Greene did not think it prudent to attack them, thus advantageously posted, but returned to his encampment which he left in the morning. The enemy had seven hundred killed and wounded, and 527 were made prisoners, amongst whom (the last) sixteen are captains and subalterns. Our whole loss, in killed, wounded and missing, 523; seventy-two of whom only are missing. Col. Washington

* Pleasant Henderson, of Orange, N. C., the brother of R. Henderson the Colonial Judge, and the uncle of Chief Justice L. Henderson. The Henderson family is one remarkable for intellect—no other in the State has produced more distinguished men.

unfortunately is wounded, and is a prisoner. As it may be some satisfaction to you to know what gave occasion to this unfortunate event, I will mention to you the circumstances, as we have them from Col. Ashe : Col. Washington, in the beginning of the action, was ordered to take post on the right wing, to act as a corps of observation, and to act when and where occasion should prompt. Lee was ordered on the left to cover the militia and raw troops from the enemy's horse, and any close pressure from their veterans. Some time after the action, a prodigious clamor arose from that quarter where the militia were engaged, and an express reported to Gen. Greene that the enemy's horse had fallen upon them and were cutting them to pieces. He immediately detached an aid to the place where Lee was ordered to post himself, but he was not to be found—upon which the business allotted to Lee was transferred to the great Washington. He flew to the militia, but not finding the British in front, concluded they were urging the militia in the rear; he passed through these, and in a moment was encircled with the best troops of the British army; finding it impossible to retreat, he resolved to cut his way through the whole British army; his horse being shot, he fell under him, and as he fell received a slight wound from a bayonet. Thus encumbered with the weight of his horse, he was taken prisoner; one of his captains was killed and four of his lieutenants were wounded. It is with pleasure that I inform you that one only of his officers is dangerously wounded, and very few of his privates hurt. *Where Lee was upon this occasion may hereafter be decided, as it is a matter at present of the most interesting speculation ; his having varied the order of the day being the occasion of this very important disaster.*

We took on the field of battle 1,000 muskets, 700 of which are out of order, but may be easily repaired ; 300 fitted for immediate use ; 700 bayonets. The enemy, by fire and otherwise, destroyed their wagons and heavy equipage, so that no great part of this fell into our hands. Part of the Maryland troops, however, in pursuing found so much movable property, as tempted them to halt, at a time when if they had pressed on with the impetuosity with which they began, it is more than possible that the action had been much more decisive in our favor. What a misfortune that the bravest troops in the world are the greatest thieves ! Many officers who were at Camden observe that the enemy's camp on this occasion was a very lively representation of that of Gates, having the strongest marks of precipitation and disorder.

Gen. Greene lost his field-pieces, and had taken three pieces of the enemy's artillery ; *upon his ordering a retreat, some of his troops, impatient of this check to their ardor, disobeyed the orders, and brought up the pieces to play upon the brick house; but being weakly supported, the enemy sallied forth and regained them ;* and at the time Gen. Greene supposed that they were safely deposited in his camp, he was made acquainted with this act of disobedience, and its disagreeable consequence. Greene considers this day as the most glorious of his life, speaks in the highest terms of his troops, and declares that they are equal to the same number of troops, British or any other. Certain it is that the British on this occasion displayed masterly discipline and consummate courage, yet were overcome by a force, from the best accounts, little or nothing superior to their own. *The raw troops of the Continental line behaved like veterans, and* 100 of them who had reached camp only the day before under Captain Blount*, *maintained their post with the most obstinate bravery, until nearly two-thirds were cut to pieces.* Washington led about 83 horse against the whole British foot, and their horse nearly equal to his in number. I had almost forgot to mention to you that upon the enemy's taking post in the brick house, Gen. Greene ordered part of Marion's and Lee's legion to watch their movements, and give him the earliest intimation of their attempt to escape; but, alas ! they availed themselves of the night, and marched off in a single file, without a whisper to lead to a discovery, and were advanced three hours' march before the reconnoitring party knew that they had quitted the brick house. To overtake them then was impracticable. They were pursued below Monk's Corner, but in vain. What follows is copied from a return of killed and wounded furnished by Col. Ashe :

North Carolina:		North Carolina:		Maryland:	
3 Captains 1 Lieut.	killed.	1 Capt. 5 Lieuts.	wounded.	2 Capts. 2 Lieuts.	killed.
Virg. Brigade.		Virg. Brigade.		1 Colonel	
1 Lt. Col. 1 Capt. 1 Lieut.	killed.	1 Capt. 3 Lieuts.	wounded.	2 Capts. 4 Lieuts.	wounded.
Legion.		South Carolina:		Washington's Legion:	
2 Lieuts. wounded.		1 Major 2 Lieuts.	killed.	1 Capt. 4 Lieuts.	wounded.
S. Carolina Militia.		2 Colonels			
Gen. Pickens wounded.		3 Capts.	wounded.		
1 Capt. and 3 Lieuts. wounded.		1 Lieut.			

Amongst these are Col. Campbell of the Virginians killed ;

* Captain Reading Blount of N. Carolina : he acted as Major in the action. "The N. C. Brigade under Sumner was all new levies, and had been under discipline but little more than a month."—Greene's Official Report.

Major Rutherford (the General's son),* Captains Goodwin, Goodman, and Porterfield, Lieutenant Dillon, Lieutenant Polk, of North Carolina, killed. Ensign Lamb it is said is killed. Gen. Pickens and Col. Washington slightly wounded. Col. Henderson's leg fractured near the ancle, Col. Polk wounded ; Col. Howard of the Marylanders wounded ; Capt. Parsons, of Col. Washington's, is the only officer not killed or wounded.

Thus, my dear sir, I have given you a very full detail of this most interesting event, as far as I have been able to obtain it ; should any thing turn up before an opportunity offers to forward this to you, I shall not fail to give it to you by way of appendix.

From Virginia we have little new. Cook left camp 12 days ago, and McDowell 14. Gen. Washington was then on board the French Admiral, where he had been for some days. The Virginia surgeons are all employed in preparing bandages and dressings, from which it is concluded that an action is likely to take place in a short time. Gen. Washington's force consists of :

```
6000 French from New York,
6000   do.     West Indies,
3000 Continentals, Gen. Lincoln,
2500   do     Gen. La Fayette,
1000 Virg. 10 months' men, Marylanders, &c.
```
18,500. Militia more than wanted.

35 Ships of the Line, Frigates, &c.

I beg you to forward this to Mr. Johnston, who will consider it as addressed to you both. I cannot without much inconvenience copy it ; and were I to write particularly to him, I could add nothing to it. I beg you to accompany it with my best respects to him and his good family. By all means make my good friend at Cuffnels' acquainted with its contents, and assure him of my grateful sense of the many civilities I have received from him and his lady.

Ever affectionately yours,
WM. HOOPER.

If Greene had possessed more enterprise, or had shared more largely in the ardor of his troops, the battle of Eutaw would, probably, have closed the war in the Carolinas by the capture or extermination of the British. It is worthy of remark, that the men who bore themselves so bravely in this, "the bloodiest action" of the Revolution, with the single exception of the commander, (Greene,) were from the south side of "Mason's and Dixon's Line." Mr. Hooper's account of the action varies greatly from the Official Report of Gen. Greene, and the relation of Lee :* it agrees more closely with the statement of Dr. Ramsay : prepared after an interview with that accomplished soldier, Col. Davie, who had seen the despatch of Greene's aid, Capt. Pendleton ;† and after a consultation with Col. Ashe, who was second in command under Sumner, by one of the ablest lawyers and most intelligent gentlemen in America, it certainly is entitled to great weight and grave consideration.

PIERCE BUTLER TO IREDELL.

PHILADELPHIA, Oct. 6th.

MY DEAR SIR :—I have just heard of an opportunity of getting a letter to you ; and though the gentleman sets out in an hour, I will not omit writing, though I cannot be as full as I otherwise would, or as my inclination prompts me to be. It is indeed a long time, my dear friend, since I have heard from you. Though I am at all times very desirous and anxious to receive a letter from you, yet am I more so at this time, as the *last* informed me of your health not being good ; and, from the complexion of your letter, I learned that your spirits were not high. The former I sincerely hope is restored ere this ; and if the lowness of your spirits was occasioned by the then unpleasing prospect of our political affairs, the cause now ceases. I therefore indulge the belief that they will rise in the same proportion as our affairs improve ; and if they do, they will be as good as your best friends could wish them ; for surely the affairs of America, at no period of the contest, had so pleasing an aspect as at this day. Superior by sea and land to the enemy, we may justly, and on the best grounds, expect to put a happy issue to the contest, and very shortly be rewarded with the blessings of peace, sweet peace, freedom and security—those rich gifts of Heaven. If the army under Lord Cornwallis falls, and I see nothing to prevent it, surely the most obdurate and unfeeling in Britain must be compelled to think of peace, and give up the idle idea of subjugating America to British tyranny. The regular and well-appointed army now under Gen. Washington, must be equal to the whole force Britain has in

* Rutherford, Goodwin, Goodman, Porterfield, Henderson, Dillon, Polk, and Lamb, were all from North Carolina.

* Lee's Memoir of the War. † Ramsay's Hist. S. C.

New York, Virginia, and the Carolinas; these, with the assistance of the grand fleet under Compte De Grasse, and the great bodies of militia that can be brought into the field, must accomplish every thing we wish, and speedily give us security. You have, I suppose, before now, heard of the arrival of a large sum of money, five millions of florins, from France, a loan to the States, together with 13,000 stand of arms, and complete clothing for 20,000 men. It is almost incredible, though not less true, how little the loss of paper credit is felt or talked of this way. Here trade flourishes and plenty abounds; the war is scarcely felt here, while the Carolinas groan under the weight and miseries of it; but from which, I hope, they will very shortly be entirely relieved. There is a vast quantity of specie in circulation in this country; no other kind of payment is ever thought of; so that the husbandman and mechanic are sure of receiving the reward of their industry. Flour sells current here from 16s. to 17s., and in the greatest plenty; and the markets are well supplied with the best of meats. Shortly after my last letter to you, my family called for me at Beaufort; a pleasing meeting after so long and painful a separation. We got here in seven days, where we shall remain for the winter. Should any circumstance call you this way, we have a bed always ready for you; and, without compliment, no man could occupy it whose company would be more acceptable. Pray present my most respectful and best regards to Mrs. Iredell and the other ladies; and be assured, my dear sir, that

I am, with the highest esteem,
Your affectionate friend and servant,
P. BUTLER.

JUDGE WILLIAMS TO IREDELL.

GRANVILLE, Oct. 6th, 1781.

DEAR SIR:—Your favors of the 19th and 26th ultimo I with great pleasure received two days ago, and though sorry to hear that you have had a second attack of the ague and fever, happy to hear that you have got the better of it, and that you had got safe home, and had the pleasure of finding Mrs. Iredell, Mr. Hooper, and the rest of your friends well.

The report of Governor Burke having made his escape was without foundation; the Tories having, as we are told, got him safe to Wilmington. These banditti continue to collect themselves into considerable bodies between the Haw and Deep Rivers, and plunder the inhabitants of their household furniture, horses, &c. Gen. Butler, with most of the troops of this district, we are told, are somewhere about X Creek. Gen. Rutherford, with a pretty considerable force, was between that and Drowning Creek; his force was, about eight days ago, between five and six hundred, daily increasing, and he expected by the time he should have collected the several corps from his district, his force will be about 1,500: this I have from Col., alias Governor Martin, who is now here with his Council concerting measures for the operations of our State Army, &c., &c.

We have nothing new from Virginia. All we hear is, that Gen. Washington marched down to the enemy's lines about ten days ago, and that he intended to break ground yesterday was sennight: this is the report of some officers who left his camp about that time.

I suppose you have seen, before this, an account of the particulars of Gen. Greene's action with the British at the Eutaw Springs, on the 8th ultimo; if not, I can tell you that I have seen it from under his own hand, and describes it to be the most bloody action that has been this war, and indeed says it was the most bloody he ever saw; but that he gained a complete victory, took 527 prisoners, and killed and wounded a much greater number, and took 1,000 stand of arms, and that if it had not have been for one of those misfortunes incident to all military operations, he should have taken the whole British Army, the remains of which they secured by taking refuge in a large three-story brick house; he pursued them about thirty miles, and then returned to the Eutaw Springs. Gen. Greene's loss in killed and wounded was pretty considerable; he had fifteen commission officers killed, as many wounded, and Col. Washington and one other officer, a captain, taken prisoners.

Though I had no return of my fit after you left me, I continued exceedingly weak for about ten days, scarcely ever off the bed; however, thank God I am now getting tolerably well, and hope to have the pleasure of seeing you the 19th instant at Halifax, on which subject there was nothing said at our last parting. Mrs. Williams begs leave to join me in best respectful compliments to Mrs. Iredell, yourself, &c., and believe me to be, my dear sir, with the most sincere regard and esteem,

Your most obedient and very humble servant,
JNO. WILLIAMS.

October 19th, Lord Cornwallis surrendered at York Town.

IREDELL TO MRS. IREDELL.

EDENTON, Nov. 1st.

MY DEAR HANNAH:— * * * * Mr. Hooper sends to Mr. Pollok a copy of Gen. Washington's letter to Gen. Greene, which was enclosed open to Gen. Sumner, and thence by Davie sent down here (Col. Davie is not here himself). Mr. Hooper will desire Mr. Pollok to send it to Mrs. Dawson, otherwise I would have taken a copy of it. Adieu, &c., &c.

Most affectionately yours,
JAS. IREDELL.

PIERCE BUTLER TO IREDELL.

PHILADELPHIA, Nov. 16th, 1781.

MY DEAR SIR:—I wrote to you some weeks ago by a gentleman going southwardly. I hope that letter has got to hand ere this, and that I shall soon have the pleasure of hearing that you and Mrs. Iredell are in health and spirits; circumstances that must afford me real satisfaction. You can now occupy your own house in peace and security, and will remain undisturbed by the British for the remainder of the war. We are told here that the Tories are troublesome in some parts of your State. *I find you have passed an act giving to Congress five per cent. on imports, &c. This is really an extraordinary act of generosity and confidence, at a time, too, that you have no vote in the application of it, as you are not at this time represented in Congress. This is really neglecting your own interest, as it gives a balance to the Northern scale. Mr. Johnston, your brother, well knows the necessity of a full representation from the Southern States. You have no member here but Mr. Hawkins.*

We have little or no news of consequence stirring here at this time. I refer you to my letter to Mr. Black for the European news.

We hear nothing more of the Vienna Congress; yet I think when the news of the capture of Cornwallis's army reaches England, it will be again promoted. We can look and talk bolder at it than we could have done when it was first proposed. A peace must certainly, I think, take place in the course of next Spring. Britain has not any more troops to send to America, and this last stroke will, it is to be supposed, convince her at least of her folly, though perhaps not of her wickedness; for if we may judge by the conduct of her King, Ministers and Armies, we might well say that, as of old, the Lord suffered their hearts to be hardened.

Congress have appointed a variety of public officers, by which they have, in my humble opinion, given nearly all power out of their own hands, reducing themselves to a state of insignificance. The event must now prove the wisdom of the measure. Mr. R. Morrace, of this town, is appointed Financier General and Minister of Marine; a Mr. Livingston, Minister for Foreign Affairs, Gen. Lincoln, Minister of War. There are a variety of appointments of less note that I do not recollect.

Enclosed with this letter you will receive a number of newspapers, which will give you the little news stirring here. *In the Freeman's Journal of the 14th you will see two very extraordinary letters from Mr. Silas Dean. I took an opportunity of asking the gentlemen they are addressed to, being well acquainted with them, if they are genuine: they acknowledged to me they were—they received the duplicates by other vessels. What an unprincipled wretch must Dean be! He who puts his hand, as Minister from America, to the very Treaty he reprobates. From the whole tenor of his letters, I must think he has been bought—Money ill bestowed!*

I beg to present my best respects and good wishes to Mrs. Iredell and ladies with you, and to assure you that

I am with sincere esteem and regard, dear sir,
Affectionately your friend and servant,
P. BUTLER.

I beg leave to introduce to your notice the bearer of this letter, Major Parker. He is one of the suffering gentlemen of South Carolina."

As soon as the abduction of Governor Burke* became known, Gen. Rutherford, who had returned from his imprisonment in St. Augustine, raised a force in Mecklenburg, Rowan, and Guilford, for the purpose of liberating Wilmington. He moved in the direction of Fayetteville.

By the time he reached Drowning Creek, Robeson County,† his numbers had increased to fourteen hundred men, of whom three hundred and fifty were cavalry. After engagements with the Tories on the 15th October, near Rock Fish Creek, and at the Raft Swamp subsequently, the army arrived at the Brown Marsh, in Bladen County, where Gen. Butler had had an action with the Tories some weeks before: here Governor Martin reviewed and addressed the troops with words of encouragement and commendation. About the 25th of Oct., after a junction, as I suppose, with

---
* Governor Graham.
† Now known as Lumber River, the main branch of the little Pedee.
VOL. I.—36

the corps of Butler, Rutherford crossed the Cape Fear at Waddell's Ferry, intending to invest Wilmington on the north side: a body of men was detached under Col. Smith to proceed down the river, on the southern side, to a point opposite the town. Smith defeated a body of Tories at Moore's Plantation, but finding the brick house, about two miles from Wilmington,* garrisoned, protected by abattis, and the doors and windows barricaded, retired to Livingston Creek. Rutherford had a brisk skirmish with the British at the Big Bridge, 10 miles from town. Col. Lee, passing from head-quarters to South Carolina, brought the news of the surrender of Cornwallis, which was promptly celebrated by Rutherford with a general "feu de joie." Immediately after the fall of Yorktown, Gen. Washington despatched south the brigades of Wayne and Gist, under the command of Gen. St. Clair: these troops were now drawing near: hemmed in by the North Carolinians, and alarmed by the march of the Continentals, Major Craig evacuated Wilmington, sailing November 18th. Before the enemy were fairly out of sight, Rutherford entered the town. I am sorry to state that the militia did not deport themselves with much moderation and propriety; they seemed to regard the place as one carried by storm, a fair theatre for plunder and the display of the worst passions of our nature. Long crushed by the merciless exactions of Craig, the citizens now experienced brutality, outrage and spoliation at the hands of their own countrymen; all who had guilty consciences—all obnoxious as Tories had retired under the shelter of the British flag.† Much of the property in the town belonged to Whigs, who had fled upon its capture, or had been afterwards expelled or paroled. The streets, for days, were the scenes of riot and debauchery: highly respectable gentlemen were crowded into a pen coarsely constructed in the main thoroughfare, and subjected to jeers and contumelies, houses and stores were ravaged; the law-books of Maclaine stolen; and the beds of the patriot Hooper ripped open, the feathers scattered to the winds, and the ticking abstracted. (When Rutherford withdrew, his wagons left laden with salt, an article then of great value, taken from the "disaffected.") It is no matter of surprise that the choleric Maclaine denounced the General as a "petty scoundrel."‡

For a very interesting account of the "Closing Scenes of the Revolution," the reader is referred to the articles published in

* The brick house still exists, its walls indented by balls, within sight of the town, on the rise of the hill, just beyond Brunswick River, on the right of the Fayetteville road, leading over Eagles' Island from Wilmington.

† Life of Wm. Hill, by A. M. Hooper.

‡ Letter of Maclaine to Governor Burke.

the N. C. University Magazine (1856), from the pen of Gen. Joseph Graham, revised, I presume, by his son, Ex-Governor Graham.

Judge Williams to Iredell.

Granville, 16th Dec., 1781.

Dear Sir:—Governor Martin is now in this neighborhood; he tells me that he thinks it expedient to issue commissions of Oyer and Terminer, &c., for holding courts for the immediate trials of criminals now confined within the several public jails: whether one will be issued for the district of Halifax, depends on the contingency of there being any criminals in that jail or not when he gets there, to which place he is now going, and will, on his way to Edenton, give you notice, if he should find it necessary, to appoint a court to be held at Halifax. I purposed meeting them on the 10th of January next, and from thence to Hillsborough, or such place within the district as may be thought most proper for the holding a court, at which times and places I hope to have your assistance, and the pleasure of your good company.

One reason why I did not come to Edenton last term, as I promised, was, that, upon the confirmation of the news of the capture of Cornwallis, we were all so elated, that the time elapsed in frolicking, &c. This you will say is but a poor excuse for a man having neglected his duty; however, as Judge Spencer was there, no injury to the public could ensue; and myself the only loser by missing the agreeable company of so many of my friends, and partaking in the benevolent hospitality at all times so remarkable in your part of the country, but which, I am told, abounded more profusely on the above-mentioned happy occasion, on which, though late, I beg leave to congratulate you. Mrs. Williams joins in compliments to Mrs. Iredell and yourself.

I have the honor to be, dear sir, with great esteem,
Your most obedient and very humble servant,
JNO. WILLIAMS.

APPENDIX TO CHAP. XIV.

Song by Dr. (Gov.) Burke—Never before published.

Let bards who give voice to the clarion of Fame,
The worth of our Chief and our soldiers proclaim;
Such only can Washington's glory pursue,
Too sublime for our notes, and too bright for our view.

Let them paint our forces with France's conjoin'd,
Display'd before York, and *Cornwallis Burgoyned;*
Bid ‹ cean, asserted, triumphant display
The Navy that freed her from Britain's proud sway.

But let softer scenes, which we hope to enjoy,
Henceforth, gentle fair ones, our voices employ;
Our husbands, our lovers restored to our eyes,
Our cheeks know no tears, our bosoms no sighs.

No more shall the dread apprehensions affright
Of soldiers by day, and assassins by night;
Secure, bright, and cheerful our days shall now prove,
And our nights know no tumults, but transports of love.

To make home delightful henceforth be our care,
With delicate skill, the rich feast to prepare,
To converse with variety, freedom and ease,
And with elegant novelty always to please.

When mothers—to rear the young heroes to fame,
And infuse the true spaıks of the future bright-flame;
To deck the young virgins with graces refin'd,
And embellish with sense and good humor the mind.

APPENDIX.

EDENTON CUSTOM HOUSE.

Money received for "Country Duties" on Rum, wine and spirits, from May 20th, 1767, to Aug. 30th 1772. £3,867. 11. 2
Hospital money for same time, 123. 16. 8¼

A note in Mr. Iredell's handwriting says the following "account may be depended on as authentic, as I have extracted it carefully from the Custom House Books."

Principal articles exported from the port of Roanoke (Edenton), N. C., from 5th January, 1774, to January 5th, 1775, coastways, and to the Southern parts of Europe, Africa and the West Indies.

1,209 hogsheads and 4463 pounds of tobacco.
19,662 Barrels of Common Tar.
1,270 " Greene "
1,835 " Pitch
3,533 " Turpentine.
1,707,838 Staves and Heading.
57,868 feet pine plank and boards, and oak do.
648 feet pine and oak timber.
1,288 solid feet cedar timber, 100 pieces cedar, 909 cedar posts.
168,390½ feet scantling.
2,781 oars.
3,473,264 shingles.
3,271,268 lbs. 1 trs. and 4 hds. raw deer skins.
1,555 and one cask other skins.
5,660 lbs. bacon.
2,033 barrels of beef and pork.
130,704 bushels of Indian corn.
348½ barrels bread and flour.
16,922½ bushels pease and beans.
6,028½ " wheat.
6,325 barrels and two quintals herrings and oth er fish.
16 hhds., 14 tierces flax-seed.
441 pounds wax.
3½ barrels hogs' lard.
100 lbs. tallow.
1 bag cotton.
50 bls. rosin.
2 bls. spirits of turpentine.
10 bushels and 4 bls. rice.
30 bushels and 1 barrel of potatoes.
7 kegs of honey.
102 lbs. snake-root.
30 pieces of mahogany.
3,500 hoops.
Two bags of cotton were exported in 1772.

Vessels Entered and Cleared.

In 1771.

No. 85, Tonnage 2,731—men, 371.

In 1772.

No. 95, Tonnage, 3203—men, 458.

In 1773.

No. 99, Tonnage, 2,915—men, 424

NORTH CAROLINA.

By his Excellency Josiah Martin, Esq., his Majesty's Captain General, Governor and Commander-in-Chief in and over the said Province.

A PROCLAMATION.

Whereas a most daring, horrid and unnatural rebellion has been excited in the Province against his Majesty's Government by the base and assiduous Artifice of certain Traitorous, wicked and designing Men, and the same is now openly avow'd and declared, and actually threatens the sole subversion of the Laws and Constitutions of the said Province, and the Liberties and the Priviledges of his Majesty's Subjects Inhabitants thereof, I have thought fit to issue this Proclamation hereby to signify to all his Majesty's liege Subjects within this Province that I find it necessary for the safety and preservation of the rights, civil and religious, and for the maintenance of his Majesty's Government against the said desperate and unnatural rebellion to erect his Majesty's royal standard, and to collect and unite the force of his Majesty's people under the same for the purpose of resisting and subduing with the assistance of the Almighty the said impious and unnatural rebellion, and to restore the just rights of his Majesty's Crown and Government, and the Liberties of his People; and I hereby exhort, require, and command in the King's name all his Majesty's faithful subjects on their Duty and Allegiance, forthwith to repair to the royal Standard, hereby promising and assuring every Aid, Encouragement, and Support to all such as shall come to vindicate and support the violated Laws and Constitution of their Country, at the same time pronouncing all such Rebels as will not join the Royal Banner——Rebels and Traitors, their Lives and Properties to be forfeited: all such as will join shall be forgiven any past offences, even admitting they have taken up Arms, not doubting that every man, who knows the Value of Freedom, and the Blessings of British Subjects, will join his Heart and Hand to restore to his Country that most glorious, free, and happy Constitution and form of Government which the most desperate and abandoned Traitors only can wish to disturb or alter, or in time of danger, like the present, forbear to hazard every thing that is dear to support it.

Given under my Hand and Seal at arms on board his Majesty's Sloop Scorpion in Cape Fear River this Tenth day of January 1776, and in the sixteenth year of the Reign.
JO. MARTIN.
GOD SAVE THE KING.

(*Vera Copia.*)

By his Excellency Brigadier General Donald McDonald of his Majesty's Forces, for the time being in North Carolina.

A MANIFESTO.

Whereas Powers and Authority have been vested in me by His Exc. Governor Martin to array in Arms his Majesty's loyal Subjects in this Province, I hereby command and charge all his Majesty's loyal people to repair to the royal Banner, agreeable to the Governor's Royal Proclamation, of Date the 10th day of January last. I do hereby declare 'tis my Intention that no Violation whatever shall be offered to Women, Children, or private Property to sully the Arms of Brittons or Freemen, employed in the glorious and righteous Cause of rescuing and delivering their Country from the Usurpation of Rebellion, and that no Cruelty whatever be offered against the Laws of Humanity, but what Resistance shall make necessary; and that whatever Provisions and other necessaries be taken for the Troops shall be paid for immediately; and in case any Person or Persons shall offer the least Violence to the families of such as will join the Royal Standard, such Person or Persons may depend that Retaliation will be made. The Horrors of such Proceedings, 'tis hoped, will be avoided by all true Christians.—Given under my Hand and Seal this 5th Day of February 1776.
Sign'd DONALD McDONALD.

(*Vera Copia.*)

CHARLESTON, June 29th, 1776.

SIR:—

I took the liberty of detaining your Express, Mr. Page, concluding that something material must before this have arrived: but as I imagine you are extremely anxious for the fate of this important Capital, I think it my duty to dispatch him with a very compendious, or rather imperfect account of our present situation. Yesterday about eleven o'clock the Enemy's Squadron, consisting of one fifty, one forty, and six frigates came to anchor before Fort Sullivan, and began one of the most furious cannonades I ever heard or saw: their project was apparently at the same time to land their troops on the East end of the island; twice they attempted it, and twice were gallantly repulsed: the ships continued their fire over the fort till eleven at night. The behavior of the Garrison, both men and officers, with Colonel Moultree at their head, I confess, astonished me; it was brave to the last degree. I had no idea that so much coolness and intrepidity could be displayed by a collection of raw recruits, as I was witness of in this garrison. Had we been better supplied with ammunition, it is most probable their Squadron would have been utterly destroyed—however, they have no reason to triumph; one of their Frigates is now in flames, another lost its bowsprit, the Commodore and a forty gunship had their mizzens

shot away, and are otherwise much damaged—in short, they may be said in this their first essay on South Carolina to have been worsted, but presume they will make another attempt. Our loss is ten killed, twenty-two wounded, seven of whom have lost their legs or arms. The defences of the fort have received no injury, only one gun dismounted. I shall write, when the affair is finished, a more accurate relation to your Convention and to the Congress; in the mean time I think it but justice to publish the merits of Col. Moultree and his brave Garrison. Col. Thompson of the South Carolina Rangers acquitted himself most nobly in repulsing the troops who attempted to land at the other end of the Island. I know not which Corps I have the greatest reason to be pleased with, Mughlenberg's Virginians, or the North Carolina troops—they are both equally alert, zealous, and spirited. I must now, Sir, entreat that you will forward to Wilmington as much powder as can possibly be spared from your province, to supply the place of that which I shall draw from North Carolina; shoes, shirts, and blankets are likewise absolutely necessary for the North Carolinians, who are quite naked. I request, Sir, that you will order these necessaries with the greatest expedition. You will excuse the shortness of my letter, as you may easily conceive that I have a good deal of employment on my hands. I shall not write to the Congress, till the operations of the enemy are brought to something more like a decision. If you, Sir, think this short relation of importance sufficient, you will, of course, transmit it. I am, Sir, with the greatest respect,

Your most obedient, humble servant,
CHARLES LEE.

To the Honorable Edmond Pendleton,
President of the Convention,
Virginia.

NORTH CAROLINA. Whitfield Ferry on Neuse River, 7th July, 1776.

The foregoing contains a true copy of the original letter of General Lee, dated at Charleston, 29th June, 1776.
By Order of Council of Safety. JAS. GREEN, Secr.
Copyed from the copy in Mr. Hooper's hands by
JOHN JOHNSTON.

Narrative, by Thomas Burnitt, of Col. Davidson's Massachusetts Regiment, Daniel Hawkins of Boston, Robert Scott and Edmund Alston of New Hampshire, and James Scott of Virginia, deserters from the fleet which attacked and were beaten off by the Fort at Sullivan's Island, on Friday, the 28th, 1776. They are all Americans, and had been taken by the enemy at sea: Burnitt, Hawkins, and Scott in the Sloop Sally, Hawkins and Alston in the Brigantine Friendship.

The Bristol of 50 guns, commanded by Sir Peter Parker, greatly damaged in her hull, large kn—— and timber shot through and smashed: —if the water had not been very smooth, it would have been impossible to have kept her from sinking; all the carpenters in the fleet have been called to her assistance.

Main mast shot away, main mast badly wounded by 3 several shots, foremast by 2, rigging sails and yards much damaged.

The Captain of the Commodore lost his left arm above elbow; he was sent yesterday (30th June) to England in a brig. The Commodore breeches torn off—his backside laid bare, his thigh and knee wounded; he walks on when supported by two men. 44 men killed, and 30 wounded, among whom were many Midshipmen, and inferior Officers; 20 of the wounded dead since the action—talked in the fleet that the two large ships would go over the Bar again, and proceed to English harbour in Antigua to be repaired. The Bristol, when lightened as much as possible, draws 18 feet 7 inches water. Experiment of 50 guns on 2 decks, all 12 pounders; a slighter built vessel than the Bristol exceedingly damaged in her hull—several ports beat in, and her mizzenmast hurt, but uncertain of particulars. 57 killed, of the Captain and was over 30 wounded, several of whom since died; draws when lightened 17 feet water; the general opinion that neither of these large ships will go safely over the Bar again.

Solbay 28 guns, 2 men killed, and 4 wounded,
D'Active, 28 guns, Lieutenant killed, and 4 wounded,
Acteon, 28 guns,
Sphynx, 20 guns,
Syren, 28 guns,

all got aground, the first in coming up, the two latter in running away; the Sphynx cut away her bowsprit, the Syren got off, Acteon (by the assistance of 20 English seamen) remained fast, burnt and blown up by her own people (whilst she was on fire, Mr. Milligan, one of our Marine Officers, and a party of men boarded her, brought off her colors, the ship's bill, and as many sails and stores as three boats could contain).

The Thunderbomb lay at a considerable distance, throwing shells at the fort, and by overcharging had shattered her beds, and damaged the ship so much, as to render it necessary for her to go into dock before she can act again.—The Friendship, a hired armed vessel of 26 guns of various sizes, covered the Bomb, as did the Syren, who also fired briskly at the Fort Briocket shots; the whole fleet badly manned and sickly, particularly the Syren's men at two-thirds short allowance of provisions and water; they have had no fresh meat since their arrival, the 1st of June.

Lord Wm. Campbell had been very anxious for the attack, and proposed taking all the forts with only the Syren and Solbay. Lord Cornwallis has the chief command of the land force. He and Gen. Clinton are both on shore with the troops at Long Island. His Lordship had some time ago urged Sir Peter Parker to attack on the sea side, otherwise he would march up, attack, and take the Fort, and complain of Sir Peter's tardiness. The Commander replied: Cornwallis might march his troops when he pleased, but the fleet required a fair wind; the first that happened he would proceed against Fort. The General at that time believed we had no troops out of garrison, but he was soon better informed, being since repulsed and drove back with loss. He remained quiet, and left Commodore to enjoy the glory of being defeated alone. This must be a mistake, from Lord Cornwallis having the command when the fleet left Ireland.

A Negro Pilot was put down with the Doctor out of danger, when they sailed from Ireland the number of men 4000—11 transports parted from them had not been heard of since—which with desertions reduced them to 1500 or 2000 at most. They began to steal off between 9 and 10 of the clock, made no noise, nor waited to heave up, and not slipt cable. The Commodore only one anchor left 2 o'clock on Friday the Fort, waiting for a supply of powder. The men of wars men mistaking the unavoidable delay for surrender, cried "they have done fighting." "By God," says others, "we are glad of it; for we never had such a drubbing in our lives. We had been told the Yankees would not stand two fires, but we never saw better fellows."—All the common men in the fleet spoke loudly in praise of the garrison, brave, fine fellows; the men in general very desirous of getting on shore to join the Americans.

   Taken from a Copy, certified by JAMES GREEN, Clerk of the Council.

LIFE AND CORRESPONDENCE

OF

JAMES IREDELL,

ONE OF THE ASSOCIATE JUSTICES OF THE SUPREME COURT
OF THE UNITED STATES.

BY

GRIFFITH J. McREE.

"Hereditary honor is accounted the most worthy; but reason speaketh in the cause of him who hath acquired it."—*Dean Bolton.*

VOL. II.

NEW YORK
PETER SMITH
1949

ENTERED, according to Act of Congress, in the year 1857, by
D. APPLETON & COMPANY,
In the Clerk's Office of the District Court of the United States for the Southern District of New York.

Reprinted 1949

Lithographed In The United States of America
N. Y. LITHOGRAPHING CORP., NEW YORK 3, N. Y.

PREFACE.

I HAVE omitted much that I wished to say, and many papers, the publication of which was originally designed, that I might condense my work into two volumes. Whether a second edition, revised and enlarged, shall ever be published, or not, the public must decide.

Rev. Dr. Carruthers writes that Tarleton did not command at the attack upon Charlotte; but that, being sick, Major Hanger commanded his corps.

My connection, Dr. Goelet, states that the name of his grandfather, Col. Buncombe, was not Richard, but Edward. In both instances I was led into error by the authorities I consulted.

In the Appendix will be found some very interesting letters, just received, written by Iredell to Hewes. I am indebted for them to the kindness of Mr. Jas. C. Johnston, of Edenton.

To Messrs. H. L. Holmes and George Davis, of Wilmington, Mr. T. L. Skinner and Mr. Johnston, of Edenton, Mr. H. A. Gilliam, of Plymouth, and Mr. F. Kidder, of Boston, for very generous efforts to promote the success of my enterprise, I cannot well express my gratitude. Nor must I omit mention of my wife and her sisters, Mrs. Cad. Jones, Jr., and Mrs. Thos. D. Meares, whose delicate transcriptions redeem my manuscript from the sin of uniform ugliness.

PREFACE.

The DeRossett family, of North Carolina, are not descendants of the Loyalist of the same name, but of his brother, the patriotic Mayor of Wilmington during the Stamp Act troubles.

As the original address of Iredell to the people of Great Britain, in 1774, has been lost in the printer's office, N. Y., I give notice, if it be not destroyed, that I intend to reclaim it whenever and wherever found.

WILMINGTON, N. C., *December* 10*th*, 1857.

CONTENTS.

CHAPTER XV.

PAGE

Historical Summary.—Letters from P. Butler, Hooper, Iredell, and Governor Martin.—The Baron de Poelnitz, and Lady Anne Stuart.—Letters from Butler, Iredell, Dr. Hugh Williamson, and La Neuville... 1

CHAPTER XVI.

Historical References.—Letters from Gov. Nash, Sir N. Dukinfield, Dr. Williamson, A. Maclaine, Iredell, Pierce Butler, Jas. Hogg, Rev. A. Iredell, and Judge Henderson.—Public Meeting at Edenton.—Letters from Hooper, and Miss Macartney........................... 34

CHAPTER XVII.

Introductory Summary.—Letters from Hooper, Sir N. Dukinfield, Pierce Butler, Iredell, Rev. A. Iredell, S. Johnston, and H. E. M'Culloh... 81

CHAPTER XVIII.

Introduction.—Letters from Iredell, Hooper, Rev. A. Iredell, A. Maclaine, R. D. Spaight, H. E. M'Culloh, Sir N. Dukinfield, T. Lowther, Dr. Cutler, and Miss Blair................. 115

CHAPTER XIX.

Letters from Hogg, Hooper, Rev. A. Iredell, Iredell, and Maclaine.—Iredell's Address to the Public.—Assembly.—Alfred Moore.—Letter to Iredell.................................... 132

CHAPTER XX.

State Trials at Warrenton.—Strolling Players.—Letters from Hooper, Iredell, and Whitmell Hill.—Federal Convention at Philadelphia.—Letters from Davie, Spaight, and Williamson (Members of the Convention).—Federalist and Anti-Federalist.—Canvass at Edenton.—Letters from Cabarrus, Iredell, and Maclaine.—Constitution.—Meeting at Edenton, and Address of Grand Jury.—Assembly.—Iredell Councillor of State, and Commissioner to Revise the Laws.—Letter from Hooper.. 155

CHAPTER XXI.

Reply to Mr. Mason's Objections, by Iredell.—Letters from Davie, Maclaine, and Miss Williams.—Iredell to the Freemen of Edenton.—Letters from Witherspoon, Hooper, Dr. Williamson, and Swann.—The Convention at Hillsborough.—The Assembly.—Letters from Gov. Johnston.. 186

CONTENTS.

CHAPTER XXII.

Letters from Williamson, Iredell, Maclaine, Sir N. Dukinfield, Rutherford, A. Iredell, Davie, Pierce Butler, Judge Williams, John Steele, and Mr. Hogg.—The Assembly and Convention.—North Carolina Accedes to the Union.—Letters from Gov. Johnston, W. Dawson, C. Johnson, R. D. Spaight, and John Haywood.—The Revisal of the Laws.... 248

CHAPTER XXIII.

Letters from Hon. S. Johnston, and A. Iredell.—The Supreme Court.—Letters from A. Neilson, and P. Butler.—Iredell to the President.—Letters from Judge Ashe and Iredell.—The Spring Circuit.—Letters from C. Justice Jay.—Death of William Hooper.—The Fall Circuit.—Letters from Maclaine and Hay.............................. 278

CHAPTER XXIV.

Address to the People of the United States.—Difference among the Judges relative to Riding the Circuits.—Iredell's Defence of the North Carolina Senators.—Slavery Discussed by an English Divine.—Tom Paine.—The "Blind Philosopher."—Letter from Judge Sitgreaves.—Davie's Opinion of the Judiciary Act.—Duke de Liancourt.—Letter from A. Hodge.. 306

CHAPTER XXV.

Iredell to C. J. Jay, and to the President.—Letters from Rev. A. Iredell and Judge Pendleton.—Southern Circuit.—Supreme Court.—The Eastern Circuit.—"Marks of Aristocracy in Connecticut,".. 337

CHAPTER XXVI.

Chisholm vs. Georgia.—United States vs. Ravara.—Circuit Court at Annapolis.—Address to Grand Jury.—Circuit Court at Richmond.—Ware vs. Hylton.—Letter from Judge Bee.—The Yellow Fever in Philadelphia.—Letters from Dr. Duffield, Luther Martin, and Pierce Butler.. 379

CHAPTER XXVII.

Letters from Gov. Johnston, Rev. A. Iredell, and Pierce Butler.—Southern Circuit.—Charge to the Grand Jury in North Carolina.—Letters from Gov. Lee, Iredell, and Davie.. 405

CHAPTER XXVIII.

Party-Spirit.—Letter from Gov. Lee.—Supreme Court, February Term, and Letters from Iredell.—The Eastern Circuit.—Letters from Alex. Campbell, Simeon Baldwin, Gov. Johnston, and Dr. Wm. Samuel Johnson.—Supreme Court, August Term.—Letters from Wm. Dawson, Col. Davie, and Judge Blair.. 433

CHAPTER XXIX

"Treatise on the Law of Evidence."—Supreme Court, February Term.—Dr. Priestly.—Hamilton on the Carriage Tax.—Circuit Court, Spring Term.—Charge to Grand Jury.—Supreme Court, August Term.—Letters from Judge Patterson, Col. Davie, John Marshall, Gov. Johnston, &c.. 458

CHAPTER XXX.

Col. Davie to Iredell.—Supreme Court, February Term.—Closing Scenes of Washington's Administration.—Letter from Judge Patterson.—Middle Circuit.—Charge to Grand Jury at Philadelphia.—Charge at Richmond, and Presentment of Mr. Cabell.—Letters from Col. Davie, Gov. Johnston, Jno. Miller, T. Pickering, &c. 490

CONTENTS.

CHAPTER XXXI.

Supreme Court, February Term.—Southern Circuit, Spring Term.—Address to Grand Jury, at Charleston.—John Rutledge.—Supreme Court, August Term.—Death of Judge Wilson.—Letters from David Stone, Gov. Johnston, Judge Cushing, Bishop White, Charles Lee, William Rawle, Gen. Steele, and Judge Washington... 519

CHAPTER XXXII.

Supreme Court, February Term.—Middle Circuit, Spring Term.—Letters from Gov. Johnston, Rev. A. Boyd, Gen. Davie, Gen. Steele, Judge Chase, Jno. Miller, Judge Washington, Mrs. Wilson, &c.—Death.—Conclusion.. 543

APPENDIX to Volume II... 591

LIFE AND CORRESPONDENCE

OF

JAMES IREDELL,

ONE OF THE ASSOCIATE JUSTICES OF THE SUPREME COURT OF THE UNITED STATES.

CHAPTER XV.
Æt. 30—31.

HISTORICAL SUMMARY: LETTERS FROM P. BUTLER, HOOPER, IREDELL, AND GOVERNOR MARTIN: THE BARON DE POELNITZ, AND LADY ANNE STUART: LETTERS FROM BUTLER, IREDELL, DR. HUGH WILLIAMSON, AND LA NEUVILLE.

AFTER years of severe trial, destitution, and suffering, the people of North Carolina, during the year 1782, enjoyed a much needed repose. The exile again returned to his home; the fallen mansion was again upraised; and the field prepared for seed.

With the evacuation of Wilmington, the last of the invaders disappeared; and from that day to this, their red-coats have never been seen within the limits of the "Old North State." The war still subsisted in the South; but languished to its extinction: it had a technical, but scarcely a substantial existence. The enemy, vigilantly watched by Greene, were closely confined to the city of Charleston and its environs. North Carolina was still, however, burthened with the support of troops; and constrained by duty and policy to maintain, in camp, at its full numerical strength, her contingent. After the fall of the Continental money, Mr. Robert Morris had succeeded in procuring supplies for the troops at the North by contract; but was unable to effect a similar arrangement for the South, where the army was sustained by specific provision taxes, and the crushing system of impressments.* The strongest language cannot convey an adequate idea of the condition of the southern army; often without shoes; often without clothes; often without food; and driven by necessity to a frequent violation of the rights of those for whose protection they bore arms. All the most celebrated financier of the epoch could do to alleviate the distress of our people, was to order a secret agent to attend the movements of Greene, with instructions to maintain a masterly inactivity, unless *ruin* should impend. "Nec Deus intersit, nisi dignus vindice nodus." While the national currency had an appreciable value, the war raged at the North; and if that section sustained great losses, it was not without the compensating advantage of military disbursements, and the active trade created by military exigencies. When the South became the scene of hostilities, it was, in turn, despoiled by friend and foe: almost without currency or trade, it soon became covered with scars, and blackened with desolation.

Governor Burke, who had escaped from captivity, repaired to Salem towards the close of January, where it was anticipated that the Legislature, elected in '81, would hold its second session; but the expectation was disappointed. Whatever doubts the Governor may have had about the propriety of resuming his official rank, they were speedily resolved by Alexander Martin, who had acted as Governor during his disability.† By the expiration of the Assembly, Martin, Speaker of the Senate, became "functus officio;" and had Burke failed to grasp again the reins of government, the State would have been without a constitutional chief-magistrate.

A new Assembly convened April 13th, and remained in session till May 12th. Governor Burke declined a re-election, and Alexander Martin was made Governor. An act conferring equity jurisdiction on the courts of law, was passed; and a new circuit (Morganton) created. The number of circuits was now seven. In consequence "of great abuses" by making "unlawful impressments," &c., the commissariat and quarter-master's departments were abolished, and County-commissioners were restored. The Assembly sat only once, though former assemblies had generally held two, and sometimes three sessions, as the public necessities required. The criminal docket, in all the Courts, was large, the cases being mainly indictments for treason (Toryism); and Mr. Iredell, the Attorney General, of course, was actively employed as the chief prosecutor.

The Loyalists had now abandoned all hope of the success of the royal arms: they pondered subterfuge: they meditated submission: they fabricated masks: they contrived asylums. Singly, or in small parties,—furtively, or with ostentatious penitence, —they returned into the State. Some thought to elude notice by their obscurity; others, by servility and professions of remorse, sought impunity; and others, again, by services rendered Whig leaders in times of peril; for many of them had been double traitors. The mercantile class, subtle and avaricious, had reaped a golden harvest while Wilmington was held by Craig, and still drove a lucrative trade in Charleston: they trusted to the God they worshipped to deliver them. In many instances they were rudely repelled: some fled back to the British standard, terrified by threats; others, of guilty consciences, startled by their own shadows. The wisest and purest men in the State were eager to close gaping wounds as soon as possible; to throw over the past the veil of oblivion; to exercise mercy; to embellish the dawn of a new era by the delicate beauties of charity. That the mass of the people, they who had known every form of privation and abasement, and anguish—that they should cherish revenge for the mansion committed to the flames, the daughter violated, and the son left stiffening in his blood, a prey to the buzzards—need not be a matter of surprise: they clamored loudly for retribution; their hatred blazed at the sight of what they regarded as ill-gotten wealth; for words could not atone for priceless blood: they even doubted the virtue of the most trusted, when they urged extenuation, or plead for forbearance. It was extremely creditable to the Continental Line, that they, who in the field were most renowned for dauntless courage against the foe *in arms*, were most prompt to pardon, and to protect the same foe when *beaten* and *disarmed*. On the whole, though many were convicted, but few suffered the extreme penalty of the law; and the people who, though blind by passion, yet referred questions of guilt and expiation to the Courts, were entitled to great praise. During the year, a very considerable traffic was illicitly carried on with Charleston, the law being evaded by the abuse of *flags*, &c. The Tory refugees from the State, in this way not only found profit, but made new friends, or corroborated old attachments among the citizens of North Carolina, and paved the way for their own return.

The State, by an act of munificent bounty, conferred on

---

* Marshall.
† "Jack Falstaff to my familiars!" Among his friends, Governor Martin was known as *Paddy Martin*: he was a very active Whig, but not popular with the Continental Line: for England he had a genuine Irish hatred; but unlike the generality of his countrymen, seems to have entertained, so far as to influence his action, the creed,

"He that fights and *runs away*,
Shall live to fight another day."

General Greene 25,000 *acres of the most fertile land in Tennessee—wild land*, as Hildreth hath it.

PIERCE BUTLER TO IREDELL.

PHILADELPHIA, January 3d, 1782.

MY DEAR SIR:—My last letter to you was by a Major Parker. I have not had the satisfaction of hearing from you since my arrival here. I please myself with the hope that your silence is not owing to any other cause but want of a conveyance: thus we flatter ourselves through life, and construe things as we wish them to be.

I have but this moment heard of the bearer's intention of setting out this day. His chair is now at the door, so that I cannot detain him to write as fully as I wish and intended to do. I inclose the latest papers; they will give you the current news.

The last vessels from France bring accounts of ten sail of the line and twelve thousand troops, having sailed from France for the Islands; this addition to the force there, makes them truly formidable. We are told here, as a *half secret*, that this armament, in conjunction with a Spanish fleet, is going against Jamaica, to keep the Dons in temper; they must reduce it. Britain has nothing to oppose them. The Vermonters begin to be troublesome; they have lately confined a sheriff belonging to the State of New York for doing his duty; they refuse to release him. A Committee of Congress is now sitting on the affairs of Vermont. I am of opinion spirited measures will be adopted to bring these gentry to their senses. Their conduct gives too much reason for suspecting some of them to be under the influence of British gold. Congress have passed an act for establishing a Bank. People have suffered so much already by paper, that I should imagine it will not go down. I beg to present my best respects to Mrs. Iredell and the other ladies.

I am, Dear Sir,
Very sincerely yours,
P. BUTLER.

HOOPER TO IREDELL.

WILMINGTON, February 17, 1782.

MY DEAR IREDELL:—Since I left you and my other friends at Edenton, I have been involved in such a round of anxiety, bustle and fatigue, that I have had scarce a moment's leisure to devote to the duty which I owe to my absent connections. The particular attention paid me on all occasions by your most worthy family has raised me so much, in my own opinion, that I have the vanity to think that there is nothing very interesting to me, but what may in some degree affect them. I will therefore give you in detail the history of my movements since I left you, and their concomitant circumstances. From Edenton I proceeded to Newbern, and immediately upon my arrival heard that Mrs. Hooper, Mrs. Allen, Mrs. Drayton, Mrs. Ward, and others, had been expelled from Wilmington, and suffered to carry with them nothing but their wearing apparel;—that some of the ladies had sought shelter near Wilmington, but that Mrs. Hooper and Mrs. Allen had been seen with their families in wagons at Bryan's, in Johnston county, moving on towards Hillsboro'. I immediately made provision for following, but before I got off, the evacuation of Wilmington was announced to me. I then resolved to take that in my route, to secure, if possible, some of my negroes, and to collect what I could from the wreck of my property. I found that Mrs. Hooper had managed, with so much address, as to carry off all our household linen, blankets and all,—the wearing apparel of herself and children; but had been obliged to leave behind all her furniture, both standing and movable. This, as well as my books, the British pretended they had left in the situation it was when Mrs. Hooper went out of town. But this I found to be far from the truth. Except a few articles which Mrs. Hooper had secreted amongst the friends she parted from at Wilmington, the British had borne off every article of house and kitchen furniture, knives, forks, plates and spoons;—an almost general sweep; nor had they spared the beds to finish the business. Two nights before I arrived in Wilmington, Rutherford's militia had broken open my house, cut open the featherbeds that remained, plundered the tickings, and given the feathers to the wind. My library, except as to law books, is shamefully injured, and above 100 valuable volumes taken away. What vexes me most of all is, that they have broken several sets of books, where the volumes were so necessarily dependent on each other, as to make what remains useless lumber. You know my partiality to my books—of course my chagrin at the abuse of them. Three fellows of mine had gone off with the British;—one had been forced away by the militia, and I had lost five other negroes by the small-pox. After I had drawn together my few negroes that remained, and who were straggling in the town and its vicinity, and picked up the fragments of my property, I set off for Hillsboro'. I found my family there with Mrs. Allen, and hers under the roof of the house which Col. Clark had provided for them, and making an attempt at housekeeping with the few ticles they had brought, and the colonel's camp furniture. Mrs. Hooper had been ill for several months before she left Wilmington, and when she came out, was so much reduced by disease that there was very little reason to believe that she would have reached Hillsboro' alive. My son Tom was under the influence of a high fever. Craig, immediately upon issuing his edict of expulsion, had ordered a sergeant and a superior officer to take a list of my property, and Mrs. Hooper was enjoined to quit the town in a certain number of hours, under pain of the Provost. She was not allowed to carry out of it a riding carriage, though she had two, nor a horse, though Captain Leggatt and two others offered their horses to forward her on to the American camp. In this melancholy situation, Mr. James Walker offered a boat, and Mr. William Campbell's hands to row it up as high as Mr. Swann's, in the North-east. The ladies were seated in the boat, and passed through the painful scene of bidding adieu to their few friends, who were not permitted to accompany them, when Craig, who had not yet filled up the measure of cruelty allotted for these distressed women, forbade the boat to proceed. Again they came on shore—no house to shelter them, of their own—few that were hardy enough to receive them into theirs. They stood in the rain for several hours, when my daughter, overcome with the heat, called out, "Mamma, let us go home." Mrs. Hooper, whose firmness never forsook her in the severest moment of trial, answered—"My dear, we have no home." Betsy could not support it. She burst into tears. Several British officers publicly abused Craig's conduct, and said that such cruelty would disgrace a savage. Craig again shifted like the weathercock, and ordered the boat to go on, but would not suffer any gentleman to attend them, although James Walker requested it. A boy of about ten years old was sent up as their escort.

Rutherford was twelve miles from the North-east bridge. Mrs. Hooper, weak as she was, went in pursuit of him, and solicited two wagons to remove her family and friends. He granted her petition with the utmost readiness, and afforded her every assistance that could have been expected from the greatest humanity and most refined politeness. Mrs. Hooper was peculiarly happy in the superintendents of the wagons who accompanied them, as they did every thing in their power to make this new mode of travelling tolerable. I brought Mrs. Hooper from Hillsborough here about three weeks ago. Colonel Clark accompanied us. Mrs. Hooper has recovered surprisingly; and, upon the whole, the journey has been of no disadvantage to her health, or that of my children. I must not, after reciting so many trifles, fail to do just honor to my servant *John*. You remember him a boy about my house, to whom I was partial. He was not suffered to come out with his mistress; but after her departure, every thing was attempted to attach him to the service of the British. He was offered clothes, money, freedom—every thing that could captivate a youthful mind. He pretended to acquiesce, and affected a perfect satisfaction at this change of situation ; but in the evening of the day after Mrs. Hooper left the town, he stole through the British sentries, and without a pass, accompanied by a wench of Mrs. Allen's, he followed Mrs. Hooper seventy miles on foot, and overtook her, to the great joy of himself and my family. His sister, Lavinia, whom perhaps you remember, pursued a different conduct. She went on board the fleet after the evacuation of the town, and much against her will was forced ashore by some of my friends, and returned to me.

A flag arrived here from Charleston a few days ago, in which came passengers, Mr. James Walker, Peter Mallet and John Gilmore. Walker came with an intention to have settled in the country—to have surrendered himself to the public authority and take his trial; but hearing that some persons were very inveterate in their resentments to him, and that they were possessed of some facts which would press hard against him on a trial, he abandoned his project, and has gone back again. Mallett determines to stay and to hazard all consequences. He surrenders himself to Ashe, who, I suppose, will bail him. One Gilmore, brother to Charles, solicits to be a citizen; but having mistaken the manner of it, goes out in the flag, and returns by land. My brothers are both in Charleston—Tom carrying on an extensive trade, and making money rapidly. His wife goes to England in the spring, and he, I suppose, will soon follow her. George, at present in suspense what to do. Samuel Campbell, a militia colonel, and commands, on James' Island, a party of refugees. The enemy, in Charleston, about 3,000 strong, and expecting a siege. The bearer of this, Captain Waites, will give you a particular account of public matters to the southward. Before this I have exhausted your patience. I must still further trespass upon you, to request of you to offer my best respects to Mrs. Iredell and Mrs. Blair, my compliments to Miss Blair, Miss Peggy, and every other of your good family, to whom I am under obligations too great to express. Remember me to Mr. and Mrs. Johnston and the dear children at Hayes,—they are ever near my heart; and I can never forget their goodness while God gives me power to think.

To Mr. and Mrs. Pollok, what can I say expressive of what I feel, and of the multiplied acts of kindness which they extended to me in my exile. I think of them with the warmest gratitude and most cordial regard.

The family at Eden house have a claim to my most respectful acknowledgments for their thousand civilities. I hope to have it in my power to write Mr. Johnston, Mr. Pollok, and Mr. Smith; but perplexed as I am at this moment with the settlement of Mr. Hogg's estate—Mr. James Hogg and Burgess being now here purposely for that business, and busied in preparing despatches to go by flag—perhaps this will be the only letter I shall have opportunity to write. If so, pray show it to those gentlemen, and beg them to consider it as addressed to them as well as yourself.

Tender my kind service to my worthy friend, Mr. Smith. He is of the number of those whom no change of time or circumstances can ever induce me to think of, but as a warm friend and generous benefactor. Assure him that I shall not forget his commission about the house negro. I will write him very soon. My best compliments to my friend Allen and Mrs. Allen. Adieu, my dear Iredell, and believe me ever, with the highest esteem and heartfelt regard,

Your friend and obedient humble servant,
WILL. HOOPER.

IREDELL TO MRS. IREDELL.

WINDSOR, February 11, 1782.

MY DEAR HANNAH:—* * * * * *Will you believe me that the Governor has made his escape, and is now at Halifax?* It is undoubtedly true, and I suppose you have heard it before now, as General Jones was to be in Edenton to-day. He was guarded with great rigor, and in the midst of a number of refugee forces who had begun to massacre some persons, and had fired upon the house where the Governor stayed. He made his escape at first in a boat, and *passed some sentries unattended to, which induces a suspicion that his escape was connived at.* Upon the danger appearing imminent, he had solicited a life-guard from General Leslie, but received no answer. No assembly has been made. Turner, of this county, is returned. Colonel Thaxton, who is now here, saw Mr. Hooper's family quite well in Hillsboro'. They and Colonel Clark had left it before him. I have a prospect of some money here, but at present it is but a *prospect*. No people to-day. A great many are expected to-morrow, and I am told much business, &c., &c., &c.

Most faithfully and affectionately yours,
JAMES IREDELL.*

* A letter from Dr. Hugh Williamson, March 6th, announcing the death of Mr. Robert Smith, is the first of a considerable series. Williamson, who was a *Jack of all trades*, had drafted the will.

PIERCE BUTLER TO IREDELL.

PHILADELPHIA, April 5th, 1782.

MY DEAR SIR:—Mr. Black delivered to me on his arrival here your truly friendly and acceptable favor of January. As that gentleman speaks of returning to-morrow, I eagerly embrace so safe an opportunity of writing to you. Had any other conveyance, though not so certain or so safe, offered in the interim, I should have hazarded a letter. The very sensible satisfaction that I derive from the correspondence, will not let me lose the smallest opening. A friendly intercourse, even by letter, with a person who, either in the private line of friendship, or the more public walk of a patriot, justly merits, and deservedly merits the approbation and esteem of all ranks of men, is surely among the first enjoyments of life. An impertinent curiosity, or desire of reading letters, that seems to prevail a good deal at present, is a great drawback. I have great reason to think that several letters that I have wrote to you from hence, have never reached your hand; this obliges me often to write with a reserve that I otherwise should not adopt.

It gave me considerable satisfaction to learn from Mr. Black that you were once more settled in your own house; and that Mrs. Iredell and you were well. I think you must find a considerable relief in your release from the office of Attorney-General. *It was a post that ill suited a man of your feelings;* and in a pecuniary sense must, I should think, be attended with much disadvantage to you. *Your resignation of it was well timed. In this, as in every step you take, you consulted the nicest delicacy.** The letter you inclosed to me I had an opportunity of forwarding shortly after, by a very safe private conveyance to New York, to be sent from thence in a packet. We are here at present merely in a political calm—nothing doing as yet, on either side, in the field. General Washington has his head-quarters at Windsor, preparing, I doubt not, to assault the enemy in some place; but *when* he means to attack, I believe, *is not known to Congress.* So greatly altered is this *once august body,* that *as little as possible* is intrusted to them. And yet, among them are many

* Wheeler says that Iredell was succeeded by Alfred Moore, in 1790. This is an error. All the published lists of attorney-generals that I have seen are also wrong as to dates. Iredell was succeeded by Moore soon after his resignation. Moore prosecuted the tory colonel, Samuel Bryan, at Spring Term, 1782. In 1790, the office of solicitor-general was created. Mr. Moore, indignant at what he regarded as an unconstitutional interference with his rights, resigned, and the celebrated John Haywood succeeded him.—*Letter from the Hon. D. L. Swain, LL.D.*

individuals of the strictest honor, and great worth; but, *as a body, there is little dependence to be placed on them.* The *Northern interest* is all prevalent; their members are *firmly united,* and carry many measures disadvantageous to the *Southern interest.* They are laboring hard to *get Vermont established as an independent State,* which will give them *another vote,* by which the balance will be *quite destroyed.* In the midst of these great struggles between the Northern and Southern interests, *the issue of which is of such consequence to the Carolinas and Georgia,* your State remains *totally unrepresented. Unpardonable neglect!* We of the South, who consider ourselves as embarked in the same vessel with you, complain loudly of the desertion of our sister. *This Vermont business is a shameful and scandalous affair.* Governor Clinton, of the State of New York, by a *meritorious vigilance,* has intercepted letters and papers that reflect no credit on some individuals of Congress. *I believe it is beyond a doubt that Witherspoon and some others have received large tracts of land, at least grants of them, from the Vermonters, to support their claim in Congress.* Some inhabitants of this town, it is said, and generally believed, are concerned in encouraging the Vermonters to support their claim, *even by arms.* Where will villainy stop? *In my opinion, Congress are not authorised to admit them as an independent State. The Confederation expressly excludes every part of America, except Canada.* There are men in the world that care not what engagements or compacts they violate, if they can but accomplish their own ends.

We have some accounts in town of a late engagement in the West Indies, between Compte De Grasse and Sir Samuel Hood, in which the former gained a considerable advantage, having sunk one eighty-four gun ship, run one on shore, and taken two frigates. One British ship of the line blew up. This account comes in a letter to the French Minister's secretary, via Baltimore. It is also reported here that the Spanish and French fleets from Europe are arrived at the Cape, and that they are going against Jamaica with 35,000 men. How this account comes I know not. There are very few arrivals here. The British cruisers and privateers are so vigilant that they have taken almost every vessel coming here. There has not been six arrivals here, I believe, these three months. Into the port of New York *alone*, they have carried fifty-one prizes within the last six weeks. It is thought that the British will adopt the plan of distressing the trade of America by water, and confine their operations by land. They may distress the trade a good deal, unless our good ally, the king of France, keeps some ships on our coast.

General Washington narrowly escaped being taken, on h[is] way from hence to the North River: about 80 men from Ne[w] York lay in ambush on the road he intended to go; fo[r]tunately he changed his route. A small party of horse that [he] sent that way were attacked and defeated, with the loss of o[ne] man killed and one wounded. I am persuaded that the enem[y] know every thing that passes in Philadelphia. They must ha[ve] had notice of the General's leaving town.

Mr. Black informs me that he intends taking with him th[e] newspapers for some months back, otherwise I would have i[n]closed them to you. The inclosed Jersey paper has some debat[e] in the British Senate that I do not see in the Philadelph[ia] prints. Mrs. Butler joins me in best respects to Mrs. Iredell an[d] the ladies of your family, with many thanks for their obligin[g] remembrance of us.

Does this place afford any thing that you want; or can I b[e] in any way serviceable to you here? If I can, I beg you will b[e] assured that I shall find myself happy in the opportunity of te[s]tifying how sincerely

I am Mr. Iredell's
Affectionate friend,
P. BUTLER.

HOOPER TO IREDELL.

HILLSBORO', April (Monday) 8th, 1782.

Accept, my dear sir, my most unfeigned thanks for the in[stance] you have lately afforded me of your affectionate attentio[n] to the concerns of myself and family. Mrs. Hooper has great[ly] profited by her journey in point of health;—the back countr[y] air and exercise have repaired her shattered constitution, an[d] the fatigue of a few months is amply compensated by the acc[i]dental consequences of it.

I am here with a design to attend the courts, and if the As[sembly] had sat at the same time, to have contributed my mit[e] towards the relief of this wretched State from its present anarch[y] and gloomy expectations;—but was resolved to make no sacrific[e] of my private interest to the public concerns. My election wa[s] altogether unsolicited and unexpected, and it afforded me ver[y] small matter of triumph that my friends prevailed in a competi[tion] with John Walker, and that the Sheriff was so partial t[o] me as to give me the casting vote.* Of 25 votes I had 13 only

---

* John Walker, better known as Major Jack Walker, was born near Alnwic[k] Castle, England. After his emigration to America he became a merchant: shrew[d,]

Walker intends to contest the election. He will do so without an adversary, as I shall leave this on Friday next, not having the least expectation that a house will be made in less time than a fortnight. Ten members only attend, and this is the seventh day from that which was intended to be the first of the session. A report prevails that the back country members talk of not attending, being disgusted at the Assembly being called at this place.

I inclose you the King's speech, and addresses from both Houses. The remonstrance from the city of London, is, I think, spirited and elegant. It has led the way to one of a similar kind from Westminster, and I am told that the example will be followed by all the trading towns of Great Britain, Liverpool excepted. The King refused to receive the London address seated on the throne, but proposed receiving it at his levee. The Mayor &c. would not condescend to the latter, but published it in the newspapers.

My brother George, with Clayton*, Bryce, and a son of Gen-

eral James Moore, arrived at Wilmington a few days ago, in [a] flag from Charleston. George Hooper returns with his family and that of Samuel Campbell. Clayton stays, and intends t[o] hazard a trial. Thank ye a thousand times, my dear sir, fo[r] your kind invitation to me to spend the season of court at you[r] house. It affords me real concern that I cannot avail myself o[f] your very kind offer. When I was at Edenton last, Nat. Alle[n] exacted a promise from me that if from any circumstance I shoul[d] be prevented from fixing my quarters at poor Smith's, I shoul[d] take a room at his house. His invitation was so importunat[e] that I gave way to it, and my engagement is past recall. [I] shall, however, give a large portion of my time to your worth[y] family. I beg you to present my most respectful and kin[d] compliments to your worthy lady, Mrs. Blair, and the rest unde[r] your roof. Remember me, &c., &c.,

And believe me, with sincere affection,
Yours,
WILL. HOOPER.

REV. ARTHUR IREDELL TO IREDELL.

SOUTH MALLING, April 30th, 1782.

MY DEAR JAMES:—I shall not attempt to describe the emo[tions] with which I received your letter of the 20th of January or the joy which followed the perusal of it. You will, perhaps, be able to form a just estimate of both, if this shall ever be s[o] fortunate as to reach you. You are in the right. We have nothing to do with politics, and you did well to set me so fair a[n] example to follow. All I wished to hear from you, and all you assure me you desire in return, might *safely* be proclaimed a[t] Charing-Cross. It is not, however, the less valuable to us. N[o] Gazette has such value in my eyes, as a simple sheet of pape[r] which may satisfy me that you, my sister, and all your valuabl[e] connections are perfectly well, and as happy as people, whos[e] country is the seat of war, can be. This, it seems, was the cas[e] on the 20th of last January. May it continue to be so! I ha[ve] been ours since the commencement of the war, that is, since you had regular accounts from us. My mother resides almost con[stantly] in London; and is happier there in the midst of bustle and confusion, which engage her attention and tend to amuse

---

indefatigable, and frugal, he soon amassed a large fortune. Early in the Revolution he became prominent, and was elected in 1774 a member of the Wilmington Committee of Safety; in the course of the war he became Colonel of New Hanover County. As a Whig he was active, ardent, and uncompromising. He was distinguished for his prowess, not only in pugilistic encounters, but in almost every species of combat: he made no pretensions to refinement of manners; his uneared-for apparel, his broad Saxon, and his heartiness were no affectations, but expressions of a manly, earnest nature: he possessed a marvellous power of vituperation, and his maledictions inspired as much fear by their force, as they frequently astounded by their novelty. He was an unrelenting foe, and his intense hatred of the Tory was only extinguished with his life. He was fond of practical jests, and his performances in this way were often startling, and not always unpunished; but the good-humored fortitude with which he bore retaliation, secured pardon for his faults, and redeemed his character from the charge of brutality. When very much enraged, and successful in his fights, the revenge in which he took the greatest delight was to pull one of the teeth of his prostrate antagonist;—foreceps he generally carried in his pocket. With *one* or *two* friends he has been known, more than once, to place his back against the Court House, and whip the Sheriff and his whole "posse." A mad bull on one occasion rushed through the streets, to the great terror of the people: as he tore by, Major Walker seized him by the horn, threw himself on his back, and amid mingled exclamations of horror and astonishment, rode him in triumph round several squares. His disposition to avenge on the returning Loyalists, the wrongs of the war, brought him into collision with Hooper and Maclaine; but he was ever the cherished friend of the different members of the Ashe family, who valued his integrity, and had been cognizant of his zeal and intrepidity in the cause of the country. His ample estates he bequeathed to his nephew, the present Major John Walker—whose simplicity, spirit, benevolence, and integrity, have won for him an enviable popularity.

* Francis Clayton was a native of Scotland. He was a member of the Wilmington Safety Committee in 1774, and represented the borough in the Assembly the same year. In the course of the war he became a *pervert* to British arts; and betrayed at the same time his honor and his adopted country. He owned Clayton Hall (Rocky Point), a very fertile plantation. Before he finally left Scotland, he sent out an untutored countryman to manage his farm; and intrusted him at the same time with a stock of goods for a country store. When he arrived in Amer-

r, than she could be in any retired spot, where she would
ft too much to the melancholy of her own thoughts. Charles
in the East Indies, in the fleet under Sir Edward Hughes.
e is before this, without doubt, a Lieutenant. He went out
that station at the suggestion of Lord Macartney, who, you
ll have heard, has been appointed by our India Company Governor of Fort St. George. I had myself, at one moment, no very
mote prospect of accompanying his lordship thither. I had several interviews with him, but had been so very late in my application to him, that he could find no vacancy, and he did not
ink himself authorized to make one. He treated me, however,
so friendly a way, that I have not repented my introduction
him. Tom, after he quitted the militia, accepted a Lieutenancy of Marines (which, by the way, is a paltry provision for
m), and is now in that service. ❋ ❋ ❋ ❋
I left Cambridge last February, after I had taken my Degree. It may be necessary, perhaps, to tell you that I was of
rinity College. It is by no means clear to me that you have
eard of it. Before I left College, I took Deacon's Orders, and
n now, if not a main pillar, at least an humble support of the
hurch. I have, at present, no provision, nor have I any near,
even remote prospect of any; but, like all pious and unprovided sons of the Church, I live in hopes of some humble benefice. Nolo episcopari.
It is painful for me to bid you Adieu! but a thousand considerations force me. Assure my sister of my affection, and believe me, dear James, with every wish and prayer for the happiness of you both,
Your most faithful brother and friend,
A. IREDELL.

The Sergeant, I thank Heaven, is well. His wife has been
ad these six years. He is at present, for it is Term time, in
wn.

IREDELL TO MRS. IREDELL.
NEWBERN, May 17th, 1782.

MY DEAR HANNAH:—Mr. Hooper and myself, after a good
al of fatigue, reached this early yesterday. We had heard
eadful accounts of the small-pox as we came along, but upon
r approaching the town nearer, we found it much less alarming,
t that the small-pox was actually here; therefore thought it
udent to come in and reconnoitre, and leave Peter without the

town till I could determine how to act. Upon my finding that the disorder was of a favorable kind, and the inoculation extremely successful, I applied to a doctor, and had him sent for, and immediately inoculated. He was very willing, and there can be no doubt of his doing very well. ❋ ❋ ❋ ❋ We could not form a jury on account of the small-pox, and I expect the Court will rise to-morrow, much to our loss, I fear; for there was a prospect of a good deal of business: but I shall, nevertheless, not leave this without some money, for I have the satisfaction to find my name begins to be a little in vogue.

I believe I shall go hence on Sunday, and shall endeavor, if I can get along that road, to take Tuckahoe and New River in my way. I shall have a long time to stay at Wilmington. Mr. Hooper and I lodge and board at the same house. He had the goodness to press me when we understood the small-pox was unfavorable here, to send Peter immediately to Wilmington and have him inoculated under Mrs. Hooper's care, but I did not know whether inoculation might now be permitted there, and the very favorable condition of the disorder in this town rendered my availing myself of his kindness unnecessary. ❋ ❋ ❋ ❋
Your most faithful and affectionate
JAMES IREDELL.

NEWBERN, May 22, 1782.

MY DEAR HANNAH:—I wrote you a letter hence a few days ago, and therein told you I had had Peter inoculated. His arm shows that the inoculation has taken effect, and his fever is expected to-morrow or next day. He has been in high spirits almost ever since, and I believe is much pleased with the prospect of getting so well over so terrible a disorder. I shall leave him in the care of Mr. Thomlinson, who I am sure will be very attentive to him. He has hitherto been very exact in his regimen, and I flatter myself will continue so. Would to God you were in as favorable a way of conquering that disorder as he is! I have not been happy enough to hear a word from you since I left home. I am persuaded it has been for want of an opportunity, which makes me less uneasy about it. But it is really hard, that at such a little distance there should be so much difficulty in getting a letter. I am setting off this morning for Wilmington. Mr. Hooper went yesterday afternoon, being obliged to go the lower road, and I the upper, to try to get a little money from our plantation. Mr. Maclaine accompanies me. We have been detained here two or three days longer than we expected, principally owing to the admiralty cause I mentioned to you, which proved less important than it

ppeared at first. Mr. Hooper, Mr. Maclaine, and myself were
one side, and received altogether but £50, and lost the cause
to the principal subject, in my opinion, very deservedly. I
ave received as usual great civilities from every body here. On
onday night, Miss Betsey Nash was married at her uncle's, to
r. James Moore, a younger son of Maurice Moore's. Tuesday
ere was a grand ball, at which I had the honor of being present, and the greater of being selected a partner for Mrs. Frank
ash, who is infinitely agreeable, though full as ordinary as Mrs.
ooper, in which I was mistaken, as I had formerly understood
e was handsome. It is said with great confidence that she will
ry soon be married to Col. Clark, and I believe it is true.❋
I am abruptly called away by Mr. Maclaine. Adieu! my
earest Hannah, and believe me ever, most affectionately,
Yours,
JAMES IREDELL.

WILMINGTON, July 3, 1782.

MY DEAR HANNAH:—I have been here about ten days,
aving had a long interval before the court, which only began on
e 30th, and have been as usual very happy with my most excellent friends, Mr. and Mrs. Hooper, who now live in town, and
eat me rather with the goodness and affection of a brother than
e attention of a common friend. I have great pleasure in
quainting you they are all well. Col. Clark is with us too, and
assure you improves infinitely upon an acquaintance. His heart
eems replete with honor and generosity, and his understanding
rong and manly. The report I wrote you of the intended
atch between him and the widow Nash, I believe is well
ounded.
The court does not quite equal my expectations. There are
great number of persons to be prosecuted, but the three old
agers, Mr. Hooper, Mr. Maclaine, and Mr. Nash, in a great
easure eclipse my pretensions. I am, however, I am sure, highly
debted to the former upon this occasion, as upon so many others, and shall not go away without a moderate share of advange, but I am obliged to be content with notes payable at a
stant day, which are, however, I believe, very good. There is

❋ Sally Moore, sister of Judge Moore, widow of General Nash, slain at Germantown.
ne of her daughters married John Waddel; and is the ancestress of my estimable
end, Mr. Nash Waddell, of Wilmington; and that admirable specimen of refined
anners, unrivalled address, and nice sense of honor, Hon. Hugh Waddell, of Hillsrough—a gentleman distinguished as a politician and jurist; yet one who graces the
awing-room more than any other whom I have ever seen, by his amenity, his brilnt conversational powers, and a regard for the feelings of others as sleepless as delite.

not the least probability of the court finishing till the very last day, which will be the 11th, and as there then must remain a great many untried, it is not unlikely a court of oyer may be appointed for that purpose. If that should be the case, I have the prospect of an adequate recompense; I may perhaps await to attend it, though it will be with the greatest reluctance, as my impatience to see you, my dear Hannah, is really, without any affectation, very great. ❋ ❋ ❋ We have very great news from the southward. "That a change in the ministry had certainly taken place; that a vote had been passed, declaring any man shall be deemed an enemy who advises a further prosecution of the American War; that Dr. Franklin had been sent for, and was actually in London, and that General Leslie had received advice of a truce having been agreed upon to the northward." These accounts, in substance, have been brought from General Greene's camp, where they were said to have been communicated by an aid of General Leslie's, who said he was convinced a peace would very soon take place, when he hoped to have the pleasure of taking them by the hands as friends. Some Charlestown papers that he brought out confirmed the accounts he gave of what had passed in England. Happy, happy prospect! Devoutly grateful may we be for it, &c., &c., &c.

Your most faithful and affectionate,
JAMES IREDELL.

GOV. MARTIN TO IREDELL.
HALIFAX, June 24th, 1782.

SIR:—I am favored with two letters from you respecting a certain Middleton Maubly, under sentence of death in Wilmington jail, and am sorry to inform you, that having fully made myself acquainted with that criminal character, which did not appear at the trial, I, consistent with the great trust reposed in me, cannot extend mercy to him. Yet I wish that the prosecution had not been conducted for treason, for some of the reasons you mentioned, but for robbing and horse-stealing, or a less offence that might have been proved against him, and equally affected his life, that the example may deter others of those wretches from committing those common atrocious offences which they consider necessary in their military character against us. I am told other persons full as criminal, if not more so, have escaped justice, and it seems agreed that Maubly should be the only person reserved to expiate the offence of the Wilmington District, as an example is so necessary for that part of the State.

VOL. II—2

I should be sorry to deprive them of it, at this particular period of our affairs; at the same time every tender feeling I possess for humanity revolts at the idea, and I would gladly interpose, should I not perhaps commit a greater crime in being too lenient, when public justice calls for satisfaction.

I entertain the highest sense of your goodness and humanity, which, were I in a private station, I would gladly imitate, especially in the like particular; but, sir, you will pardon me, when I think, that the justice of this country, which has long been offended with impunity, should at this time receive some reparation, to convince our enemies we have a Government, and will support it against all opposers whatsoever, and that no British Commission shall give a sanction to the crimes of our citizens, or those living among us, when they fall into our power. The late cases of Bryant and others, at Salisbury, were different; their characters were generally good, and they had committed no offence, but in the military line only, which induced the Assembly to permit them to be the subjects of exchange.

I am, dear Sir,
With very great regard and respect,
Your most obedient humble servant,
ALEX. MARTIN.

On the 24th of July arrived at Edenton, Capt. Meredith, from Bourdeaux; with him came passengers, the Baron de Poelnitz and his wife, Lady Anne Stuart, daughter of Earl Bute. Lady Anne had been the wife of Hugh, Earl Percy, afterward Duke of Northumberland,* but had been divorced. One of her sisters was the wife of Earl Macartney; another of Earl Lonsdale; and a third, now deceased, of Gov. Lyttleton. On their arrival their pretensions were somewhat the subject of skepticism; but the Captain assured the good people of the little borough, that the merchant he dealt with knew her to be Lady Percy; and Mr. Cabarrus's uncle had mentioned him as a very distinguished gentleman, and that he had been chamberlain to the king of Prussia —in a letter to his nephew, a very respectable citizen. The Baron had long awaited in Europe for a passage to Philadelphia, but being disappointed, embraced the opportunity offered by Captain Meredith.

They remained some time at Edenton; and the propriety of their deportment soon procured them the esteem of its warm-

---

* The same who commanded at the North about the period of the battles of Concord and Lexington.

hearted people. Lady Anne claimed connection with Mr. Iredell through her sister, the wife of his kinsman, Lord Macartney. M[r] Iredell was much fascinated by the elegance of her manners, th[e] charms of her person, and the seductions of her conversation powers; for the Baron, also, he seems to have formed a stron[g] partiality, if not a durable friendship. The strangers remained North Carolina until September, when they left for the North commending their children to Mr. Iredell's care, who placed the under the tuition of the Rev. Mr. Earl, where they remained un[til] June, '83. As the Baron's history is curious, and his care[er] romantic, I trust I may be pardoned collating here the fac[ts] gleaned from his letters. He was intimate at Richmond, V[a] with Richard Gernon, and was sick there in June, '83. He settle[d] in the city of New York in '84, where he had a mansion Bowery Lane, and sported a chariot and horses; in '85 he an[d] Lady Anne visited England on business—her ladyship leavin[g] her children behind, and "every thing in hurry and confusion A certain Mr. Stephen Sayre, officious in the Baron's affairs, (t[o] that gentleman's great annoyance,) was instrumental in procu[r]ing a lease of the Baron's house for Gen. Knox.* How long th[e] Baron and his lady remained in Europe does not appear; b[ut] he in time returned to meet with blasted fortunes and withere[d] hopes; to atone by the desolation of his own heart for the wron[g] he had, perhaps, done another. Of his misfortune, the followin[g] letter gives a graphic picture:

NEW YORK, the 20th Feb'y, 1788.

DEAR SIR:—Your favour I received and its enclosed Acco[unt] I paid the 4th Dec'br to Messrs. Scott; but that I did n[ot] answer the former till now was Owing to Want of Health an[d] the Acc't I thought had been paid by L[y] Anne, because abou[t] Two days before my going to England I received One simila[r] Acc't which I gave to L[y] Anne To pay as well as Your Letter [to] answer. Tho She did not write to me that She had paid nev[er]theless I presumed it to be so as She had Cherfully Agreed to i[t] and Knowing that Ladies are Seldom exact in their Correspond[ence] I fancied her only in want of recording the Subject to me A Silence of above 4 years on Your part not repeating this De[bt] confirmed me in the Error, and I did cease to write to you Sir, b[e]cause I must of Course have ackwainted You of L[y] Annes behavio[r] who being as She told me a relation of Yours, I wished not [to]

---

* I am indebted to the politeness of Dr. Cogswell for the copy of a letter, label[led] in Gen. Knox's handwriting—"From the Baron de Poelnitz," "Nov. 5th, 1785," at Sir Robert Herries & Co., No. 16, St. James street, London.

---

bring without good reasons a heap of Schocking events to your notice but as to enter into This matter is now requisit I proceede to it.

The Duke of Northumberland had instigated the Creditors of L[y] Anne to Arrest my Property Consisting, in ready money (in hands of Joseph and Herman Berens Two Merchants in the City) for Debts She had made before her Devorce with the Duke, but as now Law could in my Absence from England enforce Such an Arrest (the Case not having been previously pleaded). The Duke persuaded my Correspondents Mess[rs] Berens to yield to the Arrest. This was the cause of my sudden Departure from America.

I wish not Extend in to remarks but must observe that out of the number of 15 Creditors only One attaquet me for £562:10 s stl and that was Andr[w] Corlet Esq[r] L[y] Annes Brother in Law, Tho others, (Tho powerfully invited by self intrest as the whole Sum of Debts was said to be £18,000 stl—by the Credit of the Duke, and by the connivance of Mess[rs] Berens) could not be persuaded that I was their Debtor, This Honesty I think worth recording, To Contrast this I must add, that Mess[rs] Berens were not so as the Creditors Strangers to me but friends full of Professions Transacting my Concerns this 20 years and (this case excepted) with integrity.

Those Debts became the Subject of a Letter intercourse between the Duke and me; and tho I was acquainted with the particulars of the Collusion in his Devorce, and that one Specific Term had been that he should pay the Debts, Tho also the Dukes conduct was Ungentlemanlike This notwithstanding I wrote to him politely but finally I was obliged to call Things by their True name and resuming All I made him known, That L[y] Anne and I would petition to Parliamen[t] for to Show that the Annuity of £1600 stl a year had been settled in the Act of Devorce as an Alimentary Pension for Life, This Devorce was a Collusion, promise had been made by the Husband to pay the Debts yet They were still unpaid therefore the petitioners prayer was that the House would explain his Sovrign intentions: To Know if the Annuity by them granted was Subject to The payment of Debts Contracted before the Devorce or not.

The Dukes Credit made the Contest pretty public in London There were Respectable Authorities of Opinion, that Such an Affair came into Evidence—Parliam[t] might perhaps revoque The Devorce as having been Obtained by fraude and Collusion. I only will mention this Single Opinion, because it would have Operated upon All parties in a most Extraordinary manner, if by chance Such had been the Issue of this Affair. Accordingly I

wrote to L[y] Anne to come to England but by all means in th[e] Brittish Paquet, Two such Paquets Arrived in England Sinc[e] I could Calculate that She had received this Letter of myne with out any news of her by the Thirde Mr Sayre Wrote giving m[e] Notice that L[y] Anne had quitted New York and ordered him [to] provide Boards for my children &c &c but of the Date of he[r] departure of the name of the Vessel and were it was bound to [no] mention was made of: This was perplexing News! but willin[g] to give the best Explanation to this Unsatisfactory Intelligenc[e] I fancied that L[y] Anne prompted by impatience had Slighted m[y] Advice and stept in some Marchand Vessel ready for sail as for [to] have put our Concerns in Such hands as those of Mr Sayre, Th[is] indeed it displeased me and that I had Cautioned her about h[is] Caracter, But as this Same Man had onse Allmost persuade[d] this State to put Money and Lands in Consequence of a Swindli[ng] Bank Scheme of his invention in his hands, I made Also Allow ance for this Step of L[y] Anne and put it to the Acct of hurrie an[d] imprudence, as I had no right to suspect foul play from he[r] because her hatered to the Northumberland Family was we[ll] Known, and all her Letters to me were full of friendship: B[ut] even had I been able to mistrust female Candour in those P[ro]fessions as Soon as borne: the Thought would have vanishe[d] Considering that recently She had Wrote to the Countess Bu[te] her Mother, to the Countess Lonsdale and L[y] Mcartney her s[i]ster in Terms of heigh regard for me, Enlarging on the Subject of h[er] happiness and of my Partiality, Who even she said had gone s[o] far, as to leave her full powers, and my All in her hand, Whe[n] lately I went to England. However Seeing that She did n[ot] arrive I Thought her shipwrekt and perished; in this Dilemm[a] I was Kept by the public Acct of Such Disasters who had hap[pened] pened about that time; Even her family was persuaded th[at] Such had been her Fate; but just when we were About to fi[x] the Day for Mourning we got some Intelligence of her Life b[y] means of the Enquiries made to know the Name and fate of s[ome] Vessels who since 6 months had been bound from New York English Ports a Gentleman charged with that Commission by th[e] Earl of Lonsdale spoke with Capt Coupar just Arrived from Ne[w] York who had seen L[y] Anne handed by Mr. Sayre on board of french Paket bound for L'Oriant, upon this Sir Robert Herries Banker in London wrote to france and received proofs that l[y] Anne had landed Several Months before at L'Oriant.

I must also mention that in his time I had been acquainte[d] that my Calling L[y] Anne to London had given great uneasiness t[o] the Duke, but that after the News of her Death had been sprea[d] the Seemed to be cured of his former Anxiety, But no Soon[er] ad I received the News of her Life, When I sent So as Usually my receipt for £400 stl due to me for a quarter of her Annuity, and as the rapport of her Death had been Circulated by myself I lined to it a Copy of the Letter received from France as a Testimony of her Life ; The Dukes answer was that when ever I did produce a receipt jointly Signed by her and me, that Then he would pay. In that moment I did not Understand the True Intend of this Answer, but after I had followed L^y Annes Track upon the Continant, I got proofs that when I asked pay^t of the £400 stl, that better than 2 months before my Application, the Duke had paid the Said Sum to L^y Anne, being than at Paris ; this made me Think that The Duke had taken an actif part in L^y Annes Expedition, and I found but too Soon my suspicions grounded.

However, to go into All the Windings of This Affair of Deceit exceeds the Bounds of a Letter. Thus I limmet myself to a few acts Sufficient to give (Though but a feeble Idea) of my Embarassments, of the Plan laid to my ruine, and of the Consequences the whole has had.

That The Duke had entered into a Correspondence with L^y Anne since I called her to come to England, the Concert of hers, and his Conduct, and my Ruine are proofs of ; But as a Woman will not Execute nor Undertake Such Violent Measures without the Speciale aid of a Man, So also She to be in Caracter, pitched upon Mr. Sayre, who was, So as I before have remarket, well fitted for any plan of Deceit : They Agreed Thus, L^y Anne was to remain 6 months incognito in france, Mr. Sayre had this Time to Settle his Affairs, and to Sell my Property in New York. To effect This Latter Object, he was Empowered by her ; in his Tour to Europe, he was to provide in Spain a retired place where they intended to Live, The Duke Agreed to pay the Annuity wherever he did choose to live, and to let her family and me in the Idea of her Death, further, as L^y Anne had found among my Peapers the proofs of our Marriage, it was resolved that in case that the place of her residence was by me Discovered, to deny Those Ties, and so she did til I was able to prove their reality.

Since This it is regulated that L Anne is nothing more to me in this world ; Mr. Sayre sits for debts in Kings Bench L Anne has voluntarily followed him to This Place, By ruining my fortune, The Duke is freed from what he Dreaded viz to account in Parliam^t for his Conduct of Deceiving the House, and as L^y Anne is now deserted by every one of her relations, The Duke has dropt her no longer useful ackwaintance.

In this my Situation, I intended to publish The proofs of Those Arts by which my ruine had been promoted ; this was near ready for the Press, when the following Considerations Occurred to me.

Of Several persons of L^y Annes family, and other People of Credit, I must of Cours, in a compleat narative, have laid open the behaviour, and Some of Those Caracters could not be shown in a favorable Light, it would have raised me a Host of enemies ; and it is an Axiome in Europe, that a ruined Man in oposition both to riches and Credit, can't but fare worse by an Apeal to the Public, whatsoever may be the justice of his Claimes : nay the Public Himself will Grant Oblivion to the Unjustice of the Powrefull, or at most give but a Momentary pitty to the unfortunate ! However, I would have scorned consequences, But The Duties I owed to my Children who were in America, and in Want of my Care, made me give up The Project of an Apeal. A Noble friend of myne, Lieut : Genl Clerk was of Opinion that I Should Publish my Case, but The Moment I left England, my Pride would not allow me (tho' I have both Respect, and Defference for his Person and Superior Abilities) to Stoop to this vengeance of the feeble, and to stand the Storm it would have probably raised, was Keeping myself in London (who could tell for how long) from every endearment, family, rest, and Liberty at home.

To enjoy those to nothing Comparable Blessings of liberty, Alone, had been from the year 1776 my chief Wish, Than allready I begun to range my Affairs in Europe, Though only in 1782 I could come out to America, Several and great Sacrifices I have made to gain that point, I was a Chamberlain of the King of Prusia, by Several Letters from him even to the last to in 1781, when he Granted me my Demission, I can Show that I was in favor, I had no Debts, and possessed a good fortune, who was Strengthened by my Marriage with L Anne, who did not take place til She Consented to go to America, no Compulsion, no Thought of Amelioration of fortune, but I say boldly, the Noble Ambition to be a citizen of Collumbia, was the only Motive of my Expatriation of This citizenship. I had formed (according to the Exertions of Spirit shown in the begin of The Revolution) a Grand Notion, and the federal Plan now likely to be Adopted leaves me no Room to repent of my Choice.

By the last Combination of Malevolence I have lost £2000 stl a year, besides movables of Worth, and in papers to an Amount I can not value, This I may Say with Francis the first, "Tout est perdu sauf l'honeur :" but as my Wealth was great, by Sweeping the Chips together, I have Secured enough for the necessities of Life. The Honble Alex^{dr} Hamilton a Gentleman of Shining habilities, in Law, in State business, and as

Soldier in the field, has Obliged me for ever by preserving for me in this Town, from The Devouring Feast of L^y Anne and Associates, a fine four Store Brick House, with 21 Acres of Ground which I thought lost.

But what so ever has been my Looses, I am Content with my present Situation and I leave the Destroyers of my former fortune ever to the Enjoyment of Their fellony, and to the Punishment of Their Concunces.

If Sir you Consent to renew our Correspondence it will be honoring me, and an Addition to the Contentment of
your most humble Servant,
POELLNITZ.*

To J. IREDEL Esq. Edenton, North Carolina.

Mr. Iredell sympathized with the Baron in his misfortune ; and wrote him a letter of condolence. In 1790 Poellnitz sent him an "Essay on Agriculture"—wrote in "confounded bad English;" but, because, though guiltless of the "impertinence to be an editor"—" I have been invited to do so, by patrons who have a better opinion of my abilities than I have myself :" in the same letter he says : " You will find in fenno's gazette of the united states, six letters signed Rusticus, on this subject which I have wrote.† The plates of the essay are drawn by my daughter." Subsequently the Baron desired to purchase the plantation of General Howe, on Cape Fear river, as he found the North too cold for him : whether his stormy fortunes were embellished in the end by rainbow, or gilded by a glorious sunset ; whether the darkness deepened slowly into night, or his career was terminated by sudden disaster, does not appear. Let him pass onward into the cloud that hides him from view, while I return to 1782 !

PIERCE BUTLER TO IREDELL.

Country near to FRANKFORT, July 31st, 1782.

MY DEAR SIR :—Your two very kind and acceptable favors of the 13th of May and 30th of June, found me yesterday at a place in the country five miles from Philadelphia, that I had retired to for the benefit of breathing purer air than the town affords at this season. These are the only letters that I have received from you for a long time past ; but that should not have prevented my writing to you oftener than I have done of late, had any means of forwarding my letters offered. We are here very barren of news. Trade that flourished so highly when I first arrived here, is very nearly, if not totally destroyed : insomuch that I believe there have not been six arrivals at Philadelphia for six months past. Scarce a vessel belonging to this port has escaped the vigilance of the British cruisers. Before this reaches you, doubtless you will have heard of the arrival of a French fleet on this coast. It is said that they are gone to Boston to refit ; some think they are destined to act against New York. I am not in the secret. Your acquaintance, Doctor Williamson, from his present situation, can give you better information on this head, as well as the state of our affairs, than I can.

Is it not astonishing that the present British Ministry should suffer themselves to be so blinded as to think of a reconciliation with America on any terms short of independence ? Yet are they deliberately passing what they term American Peace Bills through the different branches of their legislature. I do not find in any of their proceedings that I have seen, the Duke of Richmond giving into this idle notion of peace with America, on any terms short of a general one, with an open declaration of our independence. Next to Lord Abbington, the Duke appears to me the most candid and independent among the peers. I admire the character of Lord Abbington exceedingly : his bold, independent sentiments, are such as a peer of the realm should use, and give a dignity to the character. Have you seen his strictures on the conduct of Lord Cornwallis, and his plain opinion of Arnold ? They are worth your reading.

Mrs. Butler desires me to present her thanks to Mrs. Iredell and the ladies for their kind remembrance of her. She joins in best respects to them and you, with,
Dear Sir,
Your affect. friend and obed't serv't,
P. BUTLER.

I shall thank you for the news of your country, and your political situation.

IREDELL TO MRS. IREDELL.

ELK MARSH, Sept. 28th, 1782.

MY DEAR HANNAH :—My last letter was from Edward's Ferry, whence I reached Halifax before 12. I staid there to get my

---

* The initials of the Baron's first name defy any skill that I possess for deciphering eccentric letters.
† Application of the Quakers to Congress, relative to slaves.

horses shod, during which time I dined at a feast at Mr. Wilie Jones's, in company with the new bride and bridegroom, Captain and Mrs. Dawe (Davis that was), who were married on Wednesday night, and paid two or three visits. Mr. and Mrs. Hogg were married on Sunday, and set off on Tuesday to a horse-race at Warren. Upon coming here last night I met Mr. and Mrs. Pollok, and she requested that we might travel together, but we must manœuvre well if we do so, on account of the scarcity of corn. They are pressing to set off, so I can only assure you that I am ever

Most affectionately your
JAS. IREDELL.

In October, Mr. Iredell attended Court at Hillsborough, where he was pleasantly domiciled with his friend, Mr. Hooper: the business of the court was almost exclusively of a criminal nature; many were convicted—the greater part for horse-stealing: "the defences were committed chiefly to the most inconsiderable characters, who submitted to methods to obtain such cases, that men of honor and principle disdained." Still Mr. Iredell was so successful that he promised himself, with eager expectation, at the end of the Circuit, the purchase of a double gig, that would enable him to enjoy the companionship of his wife on subsequent journeys. He prosecuted his profession with great diligence. September 27th he wrote his wife that after intense labor, almost without remission, he had accomplished a "quantity of business;" "that he did not go to bed till between 11 and 12 last night, and was up in the morning between 3 and 4, waked Peter, was on horseback at 4, and here (Edward's Ferry, 15 miles distant) a little past 7."

October 16th, he arrived at Halifax: he and Mr. Hooper had not been in town much above an hour, before they were engaged for three dinners, after having received three or four invitations for the day of their arrival. At the Court Mr. Iredell received £60 in ready money: "he was plagued from morning till night with a variety of business, and repeated troublesome solicitations;" "Gray, one of the principals in the murder of Quinn, was convicted—the proof very strong, and almost irresistible:" Linton's trial was set for the next day.

From Eden House, November 15th, he wrote his wife—"Mr. Hooper and myself dined yesterday at Mr. Pollok's. Dr. Burke set off before dinner, intending to go to Mr. Gray's, being, as Mr. Pollok observed, *wife-hungry*." The Judge and the Attorney dine here to-day.

IREDELL TO MRS. IREDELL.

NEWBERN, Nov. 18th, 1782.

MY DEAR HANNAH:— ✻ ✻ ✻ Mr. Hooper and myself are extremely well lodged at Mrs. Carruthers', each having a separate room. ✻ ✻ ✻ I have little news to communicate, but have been told that an American captain, who came here about a week ago in a flag from Charleston, said that one-half the troops were embarked, and the rest preparing to embark, and that the evacuation of the town was considered as certain. I think, however, it would not be prudent to rely with too much confidence upon it. A flag went hence to Charleston a few days ago, in which among others went Wilson Blount, upon some frivolous pretext or other, but no doubt to purchase goods. Too much of this trade, I fear, is carrying on. ✻ ✻ ✻

NEWBERN, Nov. 20th, 1782.

✻ ✻ ✻ I have necessarily been engaged ever since I came to town, and had a considerable share of the business. ✻ ✻ Our lodgings, as I wrote you, are very good, and rendered more agreeable by the accession of Mr. Maclaine's and Mr. Hay's company. ✻ ✻ ✻ The Judges, I am sorry to say it, still preserve their animosity, and differ upon almost every disputable question, and with very near as much indecency as they did at Edenton: and Mr. Ashe has not come to incline the scale. Every thing here seems very dull. I see nothing lively or cheerful to atone for a dull, wrangling day, but our whole time is spent with importunate solicitation, idle debates, or during a moment's interval, insipid conversation. ✻ ✻ ✻ There is great reason to believe Charleston will be evacuated, every preparation having been made for that purpose, and General Leslie, in consequence of agreement with General Greene, has advertised that none of the negroes shall be carried off, and promised that they shall be restored upon their owner's application. This I am informed what I think good authority. In return, it is said, a number of British and refugee merchants are allowed to stay a few months longer in the town after the evacuation. Notwithstanding which, some persons still doubt whether the British will leave the town, supposing they will receive counter orders from England. I saw Dundee here the other day. He came in with a cart. I endeavored to prevail on him, if he could get his master's leave, to come and pay us a visit, assuring him of a safe conduct whenever he thought proper to return, and that if it were any loss to his master, I would deduct it out of his hire. He seemed inclined to come, and I will speak to his master also.

Tell Sarah, Peter is very well. ✻ ✻ A melancholy account has been received of the death of Mr. Lopez in Rhode Island, of whom you have frequently heard Mr. and Mrs. Pollok speak, and who was a very respectable man. He was riding into the country, in company with his whole family and others of his friends, and being foremost in a single chair, in attempting to pass a brook where the water was too high, or where there was a quicksand, was drowned in sight of his whole family. ✻ ✻ ✻

NEWBERN, Nov. 25th, 1782.

✻ ✻ ✻ Cooke is now a very happy fellow. Mr. Hooper and I with much trouble, though with the clear opinion of the Judges, have gained a very important cause for him upon which land of great value was depending. Every art of chicane was used to prevent its recovery, but all difficulties are now obviated. He has a brother here lately arrived from the West Indies, very like him but much soberer, to whom he has resigned his clerkship, which he was too indolent to keep in any decent order. His brother has a wife in Rhode Island, and means, of course, to settle here.

I have received at this court altogether upwards of £90 in ready money, besides which, I have owing to me, for business of the Superior Admiralty Courts, more than £110. Most, if not all of this, will remain on credit, I suppose, till next May; but the sum received, I think, is not a despicable one. Let me earnestly entreat you, on the strength of it, to supply yourself with things useful; and you will oblige me essentially in getting such things as you want, particularly for your own use.

Nothing further, with any certainty of Charleston, and there are various opinions as to the evacuation. ✻ ✻ ✻ ✻

Your ever and entirely affectionate
JAMES IREDELL.

DR. HUGH WILLIAMSON TO IREDELL.

Hugh Williamson* was born in 1735, in Pa., and educated at the college of Philadelphia; he was designed for the ministry by his relatives, but his own inclinations directed his attention first to mathematics, and then to medicine. After visiting Edinburgh and Leyden, at which latter university he received the degree of M. D., he returned and practised in Philadelphia; he was appointed in '69 by the American Philosophical Society one of the committee to observe the transit of Venus over the solar disc. In 1779, a draft of 5,000 men being ordered, under the command of Caswell, Williamson,✻ who had previously adopted Edenton as his home, was appointed at the head of the medical staff. In 1782 he represented Edenton in the Commons. In 17— he was sent to Congress for three years; and in 1787 was a delegate to the Convention which formed the Federal Constitution. Again in 1790, 1791 and 1792, he represented his District in Congress. He is well known by his publications, and his connection with the Literary and Philosophical Society of New York. His wife was the daughter of Hon. Charles Ward Apthorpe, New York. He died 1819. Dr. Williamson had talent, and much erudition, but the extraordinary character of his pretensions sometimes induced suspicion of their reality, and brought discredit on his actual attainments. He had much energy, or what is often mistaken for energy, a great flow of animal spirits. Modesty offered no obstacle to his advancement; ambitious of distinction, and an egotist, he never hesitated to blow his own trumpet, solicit friendship, or employ any other of the arts of advancement so well known to politicians. He was first appointed to Congress at a period when the eminent men of the State were constrained by the necessities of their condition, growing out of the casualties of the war, to decline public life. To dignify his story he, it is said, did not scruple to exaggerate; to embellish a or render attractive sober fact, he did not hesitate to heighten the color with carmine, or hide a defect by the flow of his drapery. He was an agreeable talker, though sometimes his incontinence of speech was a source of annoyance to others. As a member of Congress, Mr. Jefferson thought him "very useful, of an acute mind, and of a high degree of learning." No malice was attributed to him; but in his self-glorification, in his aspiration after promotion, he did not disdain efforts to exalt himself over the bodies of his rivals. He was the familiar acquaintance, a frequent correspondent of Mr. Iredell; but never commanded respect so far as to become entitled to the latter's *intimacy*. His history of North Carolina is more remarkable for redundancy of style, than patient investigation, accurate deduction, and reliable statement of facts.

PHILADELPHIA, Dec. 2, 1782.

DEAR SIR:—Your favor of the 13th ultimo came to hand by this day's post. The Secretary for Foreign Affairs had called on me some days ago to know what answer I had got on the subject of the memoir, and, supposing that it had missed its passage, I had made out another copy which would have been sent to-morrow. I had not recollected the circuit of courts.†

---
* Appleton's Cyclopædia of Biography.

† Memoir sent to Dr. Franklin by the Compte de Vergennes, at the instance

news, there is none in town, civil or military, foreign or domestic, since a foolish fellow, four months ago, blew out his brains, as a proof that he had none; or what is nearly the same thing, he killed himself, because a coquette proved to be nothing but a coquette. Since that event nobody has ever killed themselves for the amusement of the public, nor does this town produce any news!* To say that balls and dances are frequent is saying little, for we have them every night. Should I say that such are the late improvements in luxury, and the true style of living, that many of the citizens have found the means of spending more in one year than they make in two, you might be surprised, for "nemo dat quod non habet," but they contrive to spend what they have not. I hope the unsociable mode of making entertainments where the face of a lady does not appear, will not reach our country.

This body is torn to pieces with factions, not Whig and Tory, but Whig and better Whig. The Tory is a third party, and I think rather more numerous than either of the others. *I become daily more in love with our own State, and should I become more in love with the ladies of our State, you would readily believe me*, especially should I give you the description of a true city lady in full dress—head, hoop, and all, but I don't love caricature; to draw after the life might obtain that name. Now that I have naturally mentioned women, pray, how is your fair

---

the Ambassador in Switzerland, the Compte de Polignac, relative to the death of Jean Wallies, of the Canton of Soleure, &c., who died at Edenton, December 14, 1780, at the house of F. La Fond, of Bordeaux, just on the eve of his departure to Europe, by the ship "Vagington."

* MAJOR GALVAN TO MAJOR CLARKSON.

"Adieu, my dear friend! Life has become a burden to me; I shake it off. Men who don't reflect, will accuse me of weakness;—they will be mistaken. The same courage which enables me to face death, would have also supported me in bearing any degree of pain; but what end would have been answered by it? Love, in extinguishing in me every other passion, has disqualified me to follow any other pursuit from which my country, my friends, or my relations could receive any benefit. Why then should I preserve a life useless to them, and obnoxious to myself? I resign it coolly and deliberately. The only regret I carry with me, is that the sacrifice was made to my own ease, and not to some nobler or more disinterested motive.

Present my picture to Miss Sally Shippen; tell her my gratitude for her friendship will be one of the last sentiments that dies within me. Present also my compliments (let them be very affectionate) to all my friends, male and female—you know them.

The pistols are loaded—Adieu for the last time. Love me after I am no more, as you did when I was alive. Defend my memory against happy lovers, for I am sure unfortunate ones will not attack it. I march off as eagerly, and almost as gaily, as when our friend, General Wayne, sent me to attack Lord Cornwallis, and hope I shall be more successful in out-flanking love, than the British army.
GALVAN.

Vid. LOSSING, F. B. of the Revol. pp. 467—vol. 2d.

COL. LA NEUVILLE TO IREDELL.

ST. KITTS, Dec. 5th, 1782.

DEAR SIR :—Mr. Pembrune, a physician settled in your town, and whom I met yesterday at General's quarters, gave me the very agreeable information of your, and all your respectable family, being well. He has promised me to be the bearer of this letter; and I profit with the much more pleasure of this opportunity, that my everlasting gratitude for the civilities and kindness you have favored us with during our too short stay in your country, has always made me bitterly lament the want of a safe conveyance either to transmit my thanks, or to receive news from you.

Since I left your country, which happened in December, 1779, I passed near two years in France; at length, tired of being idle, I petitioned to join the 2d battalion of our regiment, then stationed in the West Indies; I obtained it, and arrived in the month of April last to Granada. Some weeks ago I was ordered to St. Christopher, and in this place I think I shall be confined till the war be over. I must confess that ten years of American war would be less tedious to me, than one single campaign in this cursed country. But I have nothing to reproach me on that head; I left your service but when my duty called me back to my regiment. 'Tis not necessary to tell you how pleasant a satisfaction it will be to me to correspond with you; what I regret is, that the news coming from so narrow a spot of land as this island, cannot bear the least proportion with those your interesting country brings forth every day; but, sir, you are used to lay the obligations on my side, and I never will cease to acknowledge it. Give me leave to present my respectful compliments to Mrs. Iredell and Mrs. Blair; I was in doubt whether, in recalling me to the remembrance of the charming Miss Blair, there was another name to join to her own; Mr. Pembrune has cleared my doubts, so I must reserve my congratulations for another letter.

My brother La Neuville* sailed from Ostend at the beginning of October; I expect him hourly; you may be persuaded he will share my satisfaction upon the news I will communicate to him about you and your family.

I am, with every sentiment dictated by the greatest consideration and warmest gratitude,
Dear sir,
Your most obedient servant,
Noirmont Capitaine en second de chasseurs au regiment Royal * * *†
a St. Christophe.

* Chevalier de la Neuville.   † Word illegible.

---

kinswoman on the other side of the Sound? Is she almost half French, half American? for as the wife is half, often the better half of her husband, I suppose the husband should be half of his wife. I wish I could think of this matter with a pulse perfectly regular. But a thousand things will happen not exactly as a lady could wish, and if we are not philosophers, we ought to be. I shall hardly hear whether dances or any other amusements help you in Edenton to pass the evenings, in fact I can hear of no domestic occurrences. Nobody has ever written me whether any vessel, prize, or merchant ship, has arrived at Edenton for the last six weeks.

Be assured that I am with the utmost esteem,
Your obedient servant,
H. WILLIAMSON.

IREDELL TO MRS. IREDELL.

WILMINGTON, N. C., Dec. 2d, 1782.

MY DEAR HANNAH :—* * * Mr. Hooper and I arrived here yesterday, and are both well, although not a little fatigued, in consequence of my bad accommodations on the road. The latest accounts from Charleston speak of the evacuation of it with great uncertainty. Mr. George Hooper very lately told a gentleman of this town, who saw him near Charleston, that he believed it would either be evacuated in ten days, or not till the spring. But there is already a very numerous garrison of the refugees at St. Augustine, commanded, as we are told, by Colonel John Hamilton, who has received what is called a *Letter of Service* for that purpose, though not regularly exchanged. This letter of service is explained to mean a permission to exercise any kind of authority short of actual military service,—which is a distinction that I confess I do not comprehend. * * * My life is indeed at present a very harassing one, and I am sure ought to be much more profitable than it generally is. But I think I see a very pleasing opening, and that we shall not be without some compensation for our long sufferings. If there be in Edenton any good superfine Ravens gray, I will be obliged to you if you will try to get me enough for a suit, for the coat I wear is really grown very dirty and shabby. But I am not very anxious to get a suit of any other color. * * *

Most faithfully yours,
JAS. IREDELL.

P. S. Mr. Pembrune has promised me to take care of a few bottles of old Rum, which I desire you to accept. But till now I could not send them to him, as he is seven miles distant from this place. I hope he will sail for Edenton from Sandy Point, so that will enable me to deliver them to him.

VOL. II.—3

CHAPTER XVI.

ÆT. 31–32.

HISTORICAL REFERENCES ; LETTERS FROM GOV. NASH, SIR N. DUKINFIELD, DR. WILLIAMSON, A. MACLAINE, IREDELL, PIERCE BUTLER, JAS. HOGG, REV. A. IREDELL, AND JUDGE HENDERSON ; PUBLIC MEETING AT EDENTON ; LETTERS FROM HOOPER, AND MISS MACARTNEY.

The preliminary treaty of peace arrived in America, March 12th, 1783 ; and the cessation of hostilities was published in the camp, at Newburgh, N. Y., April 19th.*

April 23d, General Greene was authorized to grant furloughs to the North Carolina troops, who, somewhat indignant at the maltreatment they had received, and the neglect of their claims upon the public, yet had manliness enough to attribute their wrongs to the true cause—an empty treasury—and to rely upon the gratitude and honesty of the Confederation for future compensation. Returning to the State in small parties, they quietly dispersed at convenient points : there were no riots, no tumults, no bloodshed : they were teachers of that great lesson, which, readily imbibed by their descendants, has won for North Carolina the reputation of a conservative, law-abiding, industrious community.

The Assembly met at Hillsborough, April 18th ; and closed its session May 17th.

The definitive articles of peace, signed at Paris, September 3d, and confirmed by Congress, January 14th, 1784, were not declared by the North Carolina Assembly " part of the law of the land," until the session begun at Tarborough, November 18th, '87.†

New York was evacuated Nov. 25th.

Of the general joy at the announcement of peace ; of the violent opposition to some of the articles of the treaty ; of the action of the legislature ; of the passions that agitated and divided the people, I need not speak here ; the letters of Mr. Iredell and his correspondents tell the story fully and perspicuously.

* Hildreth.   † Statutes.

Ex-Gov. Nash to Iredell.

PHILADELPHIA, January 18th, 1783.

DEAR SIR :—Our old acquaintance will very well warra[nt] the indulgence I allow myself of dropping you a few lines fro[m] this place ; at the same time I wish it were more in my pow[er] than I find it is, to enlighten you on the great topic of peace You, no doubt, see the gazettes of this place : I understan[d] Dr. Williamson sends them regularly to Edenton ;—these, si[nce] contain as much intelligence as a member of Congress can communicate ; at the same time an opinion may be ventured, an[d I] shall freely say to you, though I would not venture an opinio[n] to the public, that I hope and much believe the present ne gotiations for peace will have a happy termination. From th[e] facts you and the world know, I reason thus :—The belligeren[t] Powers must have known before commissions were exchanged the ultimate views of each party, respectively. With respect t[o] America, she demands only her independence ; this also is th[e] main object of the war on the part of France ; it effects, fully her views of diminishing the overgrown power of her natur[al] enemy and rival. As to Spain, her honor is satisfied in the con quest of Minorca. The Dutch have so little zeal for war, and s[o] much for trade and commerce, that a reasonable compensation or perhaps something less, for the outrages committed on th[e] property of her citizens, will satisfy her. Under this view o[f] interest, taking also into the account the humiliating concession of Britain, already made in granting a Commission to treat ex pressly with the thirteen United States, what less can be expecte[d] than the wished-for peace ? If Great Britain was not pretty su[re] that the ultimate concessions in the course of the treaty whic[h] she had determined to make, would ensure to her peace, woul[d] she be so weak as in effect to acknowledge American Independ ence ? Would she not rather, at least, affect to claim us as he[r] subjects, and keep this claim open for contingencies durin[g] the war ?—no doubt she would. Have not the British Counci[l] declared to the world, the impracticability of recovering the[ir] lost Colonies, and have they not now opened a treaty with the[m] as sovereign, independent States ?—yes ;—wherefore, then, carr[y] on the war ? Can we suppose that in her exhausted conditio[n] she is capable of forming projects of conquest against her othe[r] enemies, to make good what she has lost here ? The idea is to[o] chimerical. Therefore, on the whole, I conclude, and give it a[s] my chimney-corner opinion, that the parties are prepared fo[r] peace. Nothing, I do assure you, my dear sir, is more true tha[n]

that poor America is prepared for peace—indeed, it may be said she is prepared for nothing else. In the early periods of the war, Congress possessed powers very different from what they do now : they could order the raising of regiments ; organize armies ; and, what is of particular consequence, they held the purse-strings of America—that is, so long as paper could be found, they could find money ; possessed fully of the confidence of their country, they could turn even *rags* to *money*—Midas-like, whate'er they touched turned to gold ; but, alas ! this gold is all turned to rags again, and the art is lost, *lost* for ever : * they are able now only to apply to their constituents for money, who are either not able, or unwilling to pay. Perhaps you will say, let them exercise their power of borrowing, as other sovereigns do who enter into war ; but, I answer, if they will borrow as other nations do, they must provide and appropriate ample funds for payment of interest and principal, as other nations do. Promises won't do any longer ; and what funds, I ask you, have Congress in their power ? None. They made one attempt to bring the State into a consent that they might tax imports as far as five per cent.; and after advocating the propriety, nay, necessity of the measure, as a prop to credit for two years, they have at length the mortification to find it won't go down :—the little state of Rhode Island has had it in her power to blast the well-grounded hopes that were conceived of such a measure, and Virginia has since, on this head, gone retrograde. A deputation from the Northern army, is now before Congress, stating their distresses, and prophesying what will be the probable consequence of practising any longer on the patience of the soldiery. God grant us, you will say, a happy issue out of all our troubles ! So we all say, but this won't get the cart out of the mire. The truth is, the fault is in the constitution of Congress ; and if these distresses should happily point out a remedy, in the right place and way, we shall by and by say, as we have often had reason to say before, all is for the best. You will see to what my hopes glance —things will soon be better or worse. Our representation is now very full, all the delegates being here ; but as our finances are not calculated but for the support of a bare representation, Mr. Blount and myself will go home soon. The Doctor is satisfied to stay over his time, which is very agreeable to me.— Please present my best respects to Mr. Johnston and your lady, and believe me to be, with the sincerest regard,

Dear sir,
Your obed't, humble servant,
A. NASH.

* See McFingal.

In a letter from Dr. Williamson, on business, dated Januar[y] 20th, he says :—" I am not even a smatterer in the law. [I] hardly know in what Habeas Corpus differs from Hocus Pocu[s.] * * * I have taken the liberty to mention your name to M[r.] Mease, as a gentleman of the law, in whose integrity he migh[t] trust with the fullest confidence."

LETTER FROM SIR NAT. DUKENFIELD.

MARLBOROUGH, Feb. 13th, 1783.

DEAR IREDELL :—As a peace is at length established amon[g] the warring powers, I take the earliest opportunity to open [a] correspondence which has been a long while neglected. I re ceived your letter of May, 1779, but nothing from my mothe[r.] I now write to you both by Mr. Brimmage, who will shortly sa[il] to Carolina. In my military situation, I have been pretty fortu nate, having had a troop of Dragoons three years, and for th[e] last two years was aide de camp, first to General Style, and the[n] to General Warde—very quiet business, nothing to do. I hop[e] you and Mrs. Iredell have been well in general, though I doub[t] not the usual agues, &c., still remain in the country. Wha[t] family have you ? An engagement of this sort entirely puts [a] stop to my long intended plan of paying you a winter visit, upo[n] the conclusion of the war ; but in a fortnight's time I hope t[o] be married to Miss Warde (niece to the General) ; she is not o[f] a constitution to cross the sea, and it would not answer my pur pose to leave her behind ; therefore, my dear friend, we must b[e] content to converse by letter. I have been in general very we[ll] these many years, except what has happened from tumbles [in] hunting, &c., &c. From the many accounts I have received o[f] the losses caused in the circle of my acquaintance by death, [I] don't know who to inquire after, therefore must take the re maining ones in a lump, and hope they are well. Had the peac[e] been settled four months ago, I had, in all probability, paid yo[u] a visit next winter, as I had not at that time made Miss Ward[e] acquainted with my attachment to her, and probably shoul[d] have deferred it until my return from Carolina ; but now 'ti[s] not to be done. I wrote to you three years ago, when Docto[r] Lennox intended to return to Carolina ; but as he did not go a[t] that time the letter was returned to me, and I was not ac quainted when he did sail.

I trust in your friendship to my mother, whom I long to hea[r] from, as she has not wrote to me for several years. What to d[o] about my plantation puzzles me very much. I wish my mothe[r] would acquaint me what is done, and how it now is; and as I cannot come over, what is best to be done.

Brimmage says he is impatient to return; no wonder—his wife is there. I hope you will let me hear from you the first opportunity. I shall see Brimmage next week, as I am going to London in a day or two to be married, I hope, and will talk to and consult with him; though a man just going to be married is not in a very good condition to talk upon business. I feel it to be my case. My best respects to Mrs. Iredell, and all my remaining friends, and believe me,

Yours, most sincerely,
N. D.

DR. WILLIAMSON TO IREDELL.

DEAR SIR:—Have you fixed upon any place for our academy—are any subscriptions made for that institution? On the moment we have peace we should begin the building. Be so good as to inform me whether any steps are taken in that business. I have been importuned by the friends of sundry gentlemen to engage them as teachers; this I could not do for the want of a house to teach in. I observe what you say of Mrs. Dawson's proposing to send her son on in the spring. I fear her affections are not much weaned from him in the course of the last twelve months, and the former affection will operate. Is it not clear that virtue consists in a medium? You see that even maternal affection, which is so necessary, and in that lady so conspicuous, hardly escapes the suspicion of being a fault. I am glad that you can only say *you have been sick*. I have written to General Benbury a long letter, and to Mr. Allen a short one, respecting some improvements for the extension of our commerce on the Peace Establishment. I presume you will support those measures, provided you approve of them. By the education of our youth, and improvement of our commerce, and by these means alone, can we save our State from obscurity and debility.

For more than four weeks have we been constantly engaged in attempting to establish public funds, or fix a scale for settling the quotas of the different States. To-day we have agreed in one resolution, which the Southern States have carried with great difficulty; it is not so good as we wished, but the best we could get, for valuing the lands and their improvements, according to the Confederation. I believe we failed in twenty different plans before we fixed on one. I shall show you the Journal on the next month, which will explain some part of this business.

The framers of our Confederation, with reverence be it said, were not infallible. Congress have reserved the power of making treaties; those treaties include the relations of commerce, and yet Congress has not reserved any power over commerce. We borrow money, and have not the means of paying sixpence. There is no measure, however wise or necessary, that may not be defeated by any single State, however small or wrong-headed. The cloud of public creditors, including the army, are gathering about us; the prospect thickens. Believe me, that I would rather take the field in the hardest military service I ever saw, than face the difficulties that await us in Congress within a few months. I have fervently desired peace. Whoever my successor may be in the delegation, I shall not envy his station. I shall wish him as much diligence, a little more patience, and a great deal more political knowledge.

Be pleased to present my respects, &c., and believe me to be, with the utmost regard,

Dear Sir,
Your obedient humble servant,
H. W. WILLIAMSON.

A. MACLAINE TO IREDELL.

WILMINGTON, 21st of February, 1783.

MY DEAR SIR:—I had your letter from Newbern, but wrote with such villainous ink, that I could scarcely make it out with my bad eyes; but where it had lain, I do not know, as it came to town while I was absent at Hillsborough. You see how necessary it is to be explicit with ladies, and you must be convinced that a very modest fellow, like you, has no chance with them. I am glad you have secured the books for us; though if a true Hibernian had not interfered and led the way, a bastard of that country (as all Bristol men are) could never have expected to succeed.

You must have heard of the large Jamaica-man brought in about the latter end of last month, with 555 puncheons of rum, and 38 hogsheads of sugar. There is nothing else of consequence, but about half a ton of gunpowder. I expected we should have had a condemnation long before this time; but three or four days after the libel was prepared, our worthy Judge thought proper to resign. It seems he is concerned in a purchase of some shares, and probably might be apprehensive of Mr. Tisdale's fate. But I believe there was another reason. All the purchasers agreed to pay their money in a very short time after condemnation; otherwise the bargain to be void. It is impossible in this part of the country to raise money on short notice. The resignation will give time enough, if any is to be had.

In this prize, which was brought in by the crew, were passengers for New York, Lord Charles Montague, Captain Montague, his son, and four other officers. They wrote to the Governor, but I believe the messenger is not returned. One of the officers went to General Greene, and came back three or four days ago, with a letter to Lord Charles, couched in very polite terms, giving the officers permission to go on their paroles, by land or water, to any British post on the continent, or to Europe or the West Indies; only requiring that the paroles be inclosed to him. Lord Charles and most of the officers are now on their way to New York; and to avoid the fatigue of so long a journey, wish to go by water from Newbern to Edenton. You will be pleased with the plain and easy manners of this gentleman, and if he should go as far as Edenton, I know you will show him those civilities to which all gentlemen are entitled, and render him such services as his situation demands.

We are flattered from all quarters with a prospect of peace, and long for it so much, that we have lost all thoughts of war.

Please make my compliments, &c., &c.

I am very sincerely,
Dear Sir,
Entirely yours,
A. MACLAINE.

The next Assembly will be of so much future importance to the welfare of this country, and its proceedings will tend so much to our present happiness or misery, that I cannot think you and Mr. Johnston (to whom I have written) will be excusable if you should decline becoming members of it, should you sit only for a single session. But I think, with a little management, we may alter the annual meetings. When so much is at stake, it will not be much to sacrifice two or three courts if necessary, for a single term each. I can as ill afford to give up business as most practisers. Mr. Johnston is without apology, which I beg you will tell him. I question whether Mr. Hooper will be chosen for Hillsborough. The lower people will have one of their own order, and he has not been long enough resident.* It is said the Assembly of Georgia is remarkably moderate. That of South Carolina had not, when we heard, fully disclosed its sentiments. A new Governor, a Mr. Garratt, is chosen—a man of great moderation.

A. M.

* Mr. Hooper had but recently removed with his family, from Wilmington to Hillsborough:—the latter place became his permanent residence.

IREDELL TO MRS. IREDELL.

MR. BENNIHAN'S, April 1st, 1783.

MY DEAR HANNAH:—I think myself very fortunate in having met with Mr. Amis here last night, by whose return I can have the pleasure of writing to you. My last letter was a scrap from Halifax, which informed you of my having reached there on Saturday noon, and that I was immediately proceeding to Colonel McCulloh's, but with an intention to go further that night, which I accordingly did, though with some difficulty, having been much importuned to stay, and put up about thirteen miles from Halifax that night. Sunday evening I got to Colonel Williams's, and yesterday, in company with him and Mr. Henderson, got here. I have been lucky in having very little rain, and feel myself perfectly well, as you may tell Sarah for her comfort, Peter is.

You will hear with great astonishment, I imagine, that Mr. Hooper was not chosen for Hillsborough, though he was willing to serve. It was owing, I am told, to the imprudence of some of his friends, who said something that gave offence to the common people, such as that a drink of toddy would easily bring them over; and I understand this ill-timed sally was the sole cause of his not being chosen. Mr. Bennihan and his family are very well, and, as usual, he and his wife particularly obliging. You will not fail, I hope, to write me by some of the members of the Assembly, and as often as possible. I shall be most anxious and impatient to hear from you, and will not neglect any opportunity on my part. If it was not for the fine season of the year, I should be extremely uneasy at the state of health I left you in; but, thank God, that it is so favorable. I have every reason to flatter myself you will soon get well. Will you be pleased to present my best respects to your brother, and tell him I brought up the latest news with me: remember me also to Mrs. Johnston, and give a kiss for me to my dear little Jemmy.* Assure Pen and Gaby of my love, and constant remembrance of them. I enclose you a line to Nelly. Remember me particularly to your sister and James, Dr. Lennox and his nephew, Mr. Johnston, Mr. Black, Dr. Brewster, &c. You see my heart is in Edenton. God grant I may find you perfectly well! In the mean time, be assured that I am ever, my dearest Hannah,

Most affectionately yours,
JAS. IREDELL.

* Mr. Johnston's son, named after Judge Iredell.

HILLSBOROUGH, April 10th, 1783.

"* * * I have been, as I always am, very happy with Mr. and Mrs. Hooper, whose uniform kindness to me I can never sufficiently acknowledge; but I have had great concern in finding that almost the whole family have had very ill health here, and have experienced the most distressing scarcity of provisions. * * * I suppose you are all rejoicing about the peace, which I believe is now past doubt, though the Governor has not yet favored us with any information about it, and I do not know whether he has yet got out of *Hoop-hole bottom*. Very few members are arrived. There is likely to be much speculation about a Governor. Besides the present, Dr. Burke, Mr. Caswell, and the Judges, Ashe and Williams, are talked of. Dr. Burke talks of leaving the Assembly, but I much doubt it. Your brother would carry it from them all, if he would signify his acceptance of it. I know not how the other candidates are inclined—but I believe neither of the Judges would dislike the dignity." &c., &c.*

HALIFAX, April 16th, 1783.

* * * You greatly wrong my affection, in supposing that expressions of yours can ever be tiresome. Nothing can give me greater delight than such, and I could dwell with pleasure on the most diffusive expressions of it. I cannot readily forgive your insinuations to the contrary. In all other respects your letters charmed me, except as to your apologies, which were quite unnecessary, for nobody, in my opinion, writes more engagingly than yourself; indeed, my dear Hannah, whatever you may think of it, and however I may chat of other women, I can see none where I cannot make discriminations to your advantage. Such is sincerely my opinion—Mrs. Hooper comes the nearest—but she is not so young. * *

Wednesday night—11 o'clock.

I have not been able till now to renew this agreeable employment since I was so provokingly broke in upon. I dined with Colonel Ashe, who had prepared rooms in a very kind manner for Mr. Hooper and myself; but we contrived to parry his civility, as it would have much interfered with our business. I had again my bad success at Hillsborough. Not a farthing of money, and engaged in little more than one capital cause, for which I am to receive £100. Our client, Mr. Moore, did not meet us there

---

* Governor Martin served until the election of Caswell in 1784.

We hear he has got part of our money, but not the whole. I should have been much mortified had I been the only unsuccessful lawyer; but it was, I believe, a pretty general calamity, owing to the great scarcity of money. Here the prospect is indifferent also, for money is extremely scarce even here; and I fear until the peace makes it flow in, our profession will not be much benefited by it. Then I do not doubt it. This peace is really a most glorious affair. The Governor, just before I left Hillsborough, received an official account of Count D'Estaing's dispatches, but nothing further. Is it not wonderful? We heard of all that before he came to town, and informed him of it, when he had the King's speech in his hand to communicate as a matter of news. I left Hillsborough on Sunday. Then there were not, I believe, above a dozen members, but many came in afterwards that day, and I imagine they will soon make a house.
* * * I shall go by Winton, in order that I may see the Baron's children, as it may be the only opportunity I may have, &c., &c.

HALIFAX, April 16th, 1783.

* * Tom Buncombe's is really an extraordinary incident, and must, to be sure, greatly distress Mr. and Mrs. Pollok. I did not think the little dog had been so enterprising, and can scarcely think he met with provocation sufficient to cancel the obligations he owed them. There is another I am afraid will suffer for it. What a lesson to parents, so to live as to preserve their children from dependence. * *
Adieu! my dear Hannah, and be assured I am
Ever yours,
JAS. IREDELL.

PIERCE BUTLER, OF S. C., TO IREDELL.

CHARLESTON, May 5th, 1783.

MY DEAR SIR:—Your letter of the 23d of March, has just come to my hand. I participate, sincerely participate in your indisposition. If such great temperance as you observe will not preserve health, nothing can. Your bilious attack—for the jaundice is nothing more or less than a redundance of bile from relaxed habit, the consequence of impure air and great heat—confirms my opinion of Edenton being a most extreme unhealthy spot; trying beyond measure to the best constitution. The number of putrid fens interspersed in the town, added to the stagnant state of your bay, is enough to breathe the most pestilential disorders. I sincerely wish my friend could so arrange his affairs as to change his abode.

The interest you take, my dear sir, in my welfare and happiness, lays me under additional obligations to you; and creates feelings that can only be conceived by such a benevolent heart as yours; but not to be expressed by my pen.

I recovered more of my negroes than I expected, but I found every thing else as bad as possible. All my buildings burnt; and those settlements, that were accomplished by many years hard labor, laid entirely waste; but all this, and more, I could bear without a sigh, were it possible to have restored to me my favorite son, the promising prop of my latter days, that they wantonly robbed me of. But why pain my friend with such a subject? It is nearest my heart of all others; and from the fulness of the heart the mouth speaketh. But enough! I will try to forget as I forgive. Peace, as you justly observe, became essentially necessary to America—thank God, it is arrived. Not only the exhausted state of our finances, but the inquietude of our army, and distressed situation of all ranks, but *speculators*, called loudly for an honorable end to the war. Surely the British Cabinet is of all others the most inconsistent! At no time since the Convention of Saratoga were we less capable to make a formidable opposition, than at the very time the peace was concluded. But why should they not be consistent through the whole? They began in error, and ended with it. I was one of those sanguine people who never doubted of our securing independence; yet I confess to you, for these last twelve months I have thought it in a more precarious situation than it had been since Burgoyne's surrender; which, undoubtedly, laid the corner-stone of the edifice.

How will your legislature manage with respect to the British debts that they confiscated? By one of the Articles in the Treaty of Peace they are secured. Were not your law-makers a little hasty in this business? I am sorry your business would not admit of your serving in your Assembly; without compliment, they want you among them. Men of sterling virtue and real abilities, are very essential at this time in every State; and not less in yours than others.

Our Assembly sat for a considerable time, and on the whole behaved well. They showed more lenity and humanity to the families of the wretched refugees than I at first expected. Trade begins again to raise her head here; vessels from almost every quarter are daily dropping in, two or three a day. Goods of every kind are as cheap as they were ten years ago. If Mrs. Iredell, Mrs. or Miss Blair, or yourself want any thing this town affords, Mrs. Butler and myself will be happy in executing your commands. She joins me in best regards to the ladies.

Should your jaundice return, let me prevail on you to try the air of Charleston in the fall. We have a room at your service, and shall, *in sincerity*, be happy in your company. This town is certainly a healthy spot; infinitely more so than Philadelphia, of which there are incontestable proofs by the "bills of mortality." Indeed, the first physicians in Philadelphia acknowledged it to me. Let me prevail on you then, my friend, to try it. You shall be here as at home, free from all restraint, and by favoring us with your company, oblige,
Your affect. friend, and obed't servant,
P. BUTLER.

JAMES HOGG TO IREDELL.*

HILLSBOROUGH, May 17th, 1783.

DEAR SIR:—Your polite and friendly remembrance of us in your letter from Halifax, was truly agreeable. Nothing pleases me more than the regard of persons of worth whom I esteem and respect.

Soon after you left us, the Governor had official accounts of the preliminaries of peace, and a proclamation from Congress calling in all armed vessels, &c.; but I think he says he has had no accounts yet of the definitive treaty. No doubt you are a month, or two weeks at least, before us in public intelligence.

Mr. Maclaine before now will have given you a history of the proceedings of the Assembly. I have attempted to send you a list of the bills passed into laws, of which I am told there are about fifty, but I have got only the titles of thirty-six, a copy of which is inclosed. The taxable property is the same as last year; but the tax is 3d in the pound, two-thirds of which may be paid in specie certificates. The land office is opened at ten pounds per hundred, which may be paid in certificates: certain boundaries are laid off for the army, within which no persons but officers and soldiers can make entries before the expiration of three years, except the settlers, who are entitled to pre-emption rights.

Captain Gillespie of Duplin, and Colonel Geddy of Halifax,

---

* A relative of the late Gavin Hogg, of Raleigh, a gentleman distinguished at the bar for ability, as in social life for refinement and intelligence. Mr. Jas. Hogg was appointed by the proprietaries delegate to the Continental Congress, Sept. 25, 1775.—*Hildreth*, pp. 98, v. 3.
Mr. Hogg was the father of Mrs. Huske of Fayetteville, Mrs. Caldwell of Chapel Hill, first Mrs. Hooper, Mrs. Judge Norwood of Hillsborough, &c.

are appointed superintendents of the press for emitting £100,000, paper currency. Coor and Hunt are signers.

A suspension of suits for twelve months, after much debate, has also passed both houses—last evening.

An act of pardon and oblivion has now also passed, which excepts, I am told, all those that are named in any of the confiscation laws, and also Peter Mallett, David Fanning, and —— Andrews.

Also an act of indemnity—for pardoning all illegal impressments, and such like outrages committed by those well attached to the Revolution. I do not recollect, at present, any other public law; but I hope I shall have it in my power tomorrow to complete my list; and, perhaps, to get a copy of what is most material; and carry it to Wilmington, where I expect to have the pleasure of seeing you at court.

I will not venture to describe to you the temper of the Assembly—my style is too feeble for such a subject. I think you, and Mr. Hooper, and Mr. Johnston would have been of great service in this Assembly to the country, nor am I satisfied with your apologies;—if such men do not stand forth at this critical period, and lend their aid, this country won't be worth living in. A set of unprincipled men, who sacrifice every thing to their popularity and private views, seem to have acquired too much influence in all our Assemblies. Mrs. Hogg, and the girls, and Gavin, offer their compliments to you; and I am, with the most sincere esteem and respect,

Dear sir,
Your most faithful, humble servant,
JAMES HOGG.

IREDELL TO MRS. IREDELL.

NEWBERN, May 23d, 1783.

MY DEAR HANNAH :— * * * I assure you the going to Wilmington is very mortifying to me, but there are some reasons which now render it in a manner unavoidable. I received a summons, as well as Captain Collins, as executor of Mr. Smith, to render an account at Wilmington of what effects either of us has in our hands belonging to a company in England. The appearance must be in person, and the answer on oath, otherwise there may be a conditional judgment against us for the whole sum, which may be liable to be paid out of our private fortune, a loss I cannot think of resigning when I can so easily discharge myself, and the sum is near £10,000 stl. I think the proceedings are irregular and may be set aside, but *there is no risking*

the plainest thing with our Judges. I have some hopes, too, of getting a little money there out of what is due to me; and it is more necessary now to attempt this, as the Assembly have struck a fatal blow at our profession, as you will know before this. * * Mr. Maclaine, who was struggling there unsuccessfully the whole session, says, had we (Iredell, Hooper, and Johnston*) been there, he is sure we could have carried any thing. But the die is now cast, and a few months more ruin entailed on this unhappy country, &c., &c.

NEWBERN, May 24th, 1783.

* * * I have not attempted to buy any linen here. The merchants have scarcely fallen at all, and when I have mentioned the laudable example of our own, they say they cannot think of bringing themselves to that; so that they rather choose to keep up an air of importance a little longer, than wisely comply with a necessity they cannot avoid, &c., &c.†

NEWBERN, May 26th, 1783.

* * Mr. Williams and I are to go together this morning. Business prevented my being ready with Mr. Hooper. We are all very well. The Court has not been a bad one. If I get some money I expect this morning, I shall have received a good deal more than £100, &c., &c.

TWENTY MILES FROM NEWBERN,
on the road to Cape Fear, May 26th.

* * * I am in company with my friend, Judge Williams, who is one of the most agreeable men in the world, and we expect this evening, or in the morning, to overtake that indefatigable traveller, Mr. Hooper. I am quite well; but never was more fatigued with court business, and feel very much relieved now that I am out of the way of the importunity of clients, and the wrangling of the bar, &c., &c.

REV. A. IREDELL TO IREDELL.

CREWE HALL, CHESHIRE, May 30th, 1783.

For Heaven's sake, my dear brother, what are you about? Peace has been for months flapping her olive branch in your face,

* The parenthesis is not in the original.
† At this Court, Mr. Iredell wrote to Edenton to procure two umbrellas for a friend: either they were not to be had in Newbern, or the price was too exorbitant.

and you have not yet told me of it, or the wonders the placid maid has wrought in your affairs. I have sent more than one letter upon the subject of ours in England; but whether they will ever reach Carolina may be doubtful. Yours of the 11th of December, I received about a fortnight ago: it acknowledges only the receipt of *one* from me; and that, as it seems, by no means a satisfactory one. To say truth, I wonder that *one* has been so fortunate; for all have been exposed to the rude gripe of each party, without any other recommendation than that of being perfectly inoffensive. There were, doubtless, many better channels of conveyance than the British mails to garrison towns; but I could not hear of any, though I applied to Mr. McCulloh, and other people likely to possess the requisite information. Thank God! I can now do without their assistance. Apropos. I sent McCulloh, immediately upon the receipt of your letter, a copy of that part which respected him: it was not the most comfortable intelligence in the world. I really pity him, though I am convinced he deserves little favor from America, and not much commiseration from either me or my family; all of whom he has imperiously slighted, and some of whom, in particular my mother, he has materially injured. I really think him a very suspicious character. The interested manner in which he first sent you out to America—the hard bargain he extorted from you—his conduct as executor of Miss Macartney—and many other traits which I have marked in him, lead me to think very unfavorably of him. I have therefore been the less anxious to recover his good opinion, which I know, though I cannot conjecture why, I have long lost; it could only be from my spirited treatment of him in the way that became me, and was due to him. How he behaved in his political character, as agent to North Carolina, I well know—I mean after the commencement of the war. A particular friend of his, and an acquaintance of mine, though himself a Tory, declared to me he was shocked at the license he gave himself in talking on American topics. He is still, however, a relation; and I shall not think myself authorized to do him any injury, if I could, because he has been so uncurbed in his own conduct. I am persuaded your thoughts of him will be equally charitable; and your behavior, if you can do him a kindness, as humane as possible. At present, he has, I suppose, like other refugees, as they are considered, a pension from government; it is in agitation to grant permanent ones to the most material sufferers by the war. He, of course, will come under such a description. I should not have said thus much about him, if I did not believe that he had made complaints to you, as he has thought proper to do to others, of me.

He assured Tom I had used him *extremely* ill, and, to make him believe it, promised to make him his heir. He did not specify *how* I had ill-treated him, and he would have found it difficult, for I have never been in habits of intimacy, or even had more than the slightest acquaintance with him. Once indeed, many years ago, upon my own account; and once, a few months since, upon yours, I "checked his pride" in a way that it is most probable displeased him. But enough of McCulloh. To turn to another, a nearer relation, and, I am sure, a much better man, my uncle: you must know I regularly correspond with him; and his letters are full of expressions of kindness to all of us, though, I can tell you, he by no means approves of your conduct—the taking an oath of allegiance to the United States, in violation of your former one to Britain, he considers utterly indefensible. I have endeavored to defend it; but you had much better write to him yourself, and explain, which you may well do, your motives. He has of late made some very acceptable remittances to my mother; which, together with an annuity of £40 allowed her by Lord Macartney and Mrs. Catharine Macartney, have afforded her the necessaries of life, and but little more. She has notwithstanding been blessed with her usual share of good health, and a flow of spirits that have wonderfully buoyed her up in the most cruel, and the roughest storms of fortune; when almost every other person would have been overwhelmed by despair. You may be sure you are still in full possession of your share of her affections. Indeed, not one of us has any right to complain. Never did woman betray more maternal tenderness than she does upon every occasion; or would any one be more generous than she would, if she had the means of being so. Tom is still at Plymouth in the Marine service. I have of late given him so many home lectures upon his want of prudence, that I dare not as yet acquaint him with yours. I am afraid I colored his faults too highly when I wrote to you: he is certainly inconsiderate; but he has, which are the main points, a high sense of honor, and an excellent heart: his difficulties arise from the narrowness of his income, which, it must be confessed, calls for the wisest economy, and the most uncommon abstinence—prodigality and meanness are the Scylla and Charybdis every young man has to steer between; but how difficult a task is this when a person depends almost entirely upon his appearance in the world, and has little more than the means of procuring necessaries! For myself, you will probably have heard of my situation in Mr. Crewe's family. Nothing could possibly have happened more fortunately or critically. A very foolish connection which my friend, the Serjeant, had just before made with a woman who had lived with him some time in a very suspicious way, and who is every way unworthy of him, made it absolutely impossible for me to continue much longer in his house; and a Curacy was the only immediate good I hoped for. Conceive, then, with what readiness I accepted Mrs. Cath. Macartney's proposal to become tutor to Mr. Crewe's only son, who was to be under my care only two or three months in the year, the whole of which I might spend in Mr. Crewe's family. This I have actually done—at least, as long as I have chosen it, and I have been perfectly well off in every respect. They are the best kind of people in the world, and I am upon the best footing with them. Their style of living is very great, and the company they keep of the first kind. Mr. Crewe's estate is immense, though it is at present considerably encumbered. And, I *should* tell you, he is a very great patron—he has a living of £1100, two of £600, two of £300, besides lesser ones in his gift. Unfortunately for my prospects they have all very young incumbents. Charles is still in the East Indies, where he has seen a great deal of service, and many hard blows pass between our fleet and the French. Thank God! none have fallen upon him, though we have not received one letter from him since his arrival there. All we know of his safety we are indebted to the gazette, and admiralty books for. He is, I trust, in a fair way of rising, as Lord Macartney made many promises, all of which he may, if he pleases, fulfil. I cry your mercy. We have heard from Charles since his arrival in the East: his letter too was a very interesting one—it contained an account of two engagements, and of the very kind reception he met with from Lord Macartney at Madras. How could I, for a moment, lose sight of this? What a volume I have written! I shall expect in return a very long letter from you. All restraints are now removed, and I have no little share of curiosity to be gratified. Your whole history, from 1775 to the present moment, must be interesting—pray give at least the outline of it. Was it true that you accepted the appointment of a judge? If true, has it answered your expectations, and gratified your wishes? What change has it made in your affairs? Is Edenton still the place of your residence? And answers to a thousand other queries which I could put to you, and which you may easily conceive. Pray assure my sister of my unabated affection. The moment I am convinced that letters move in the ordinary channel, I will write, and very particularly, to her. I have not yet provided a female correspondent for her; but to make you my confidant, I have really one in view, whom, I think, you would not blush to acknowledge for a sister. One who, at the age of nineteen, with a fine person, with beauty, with good sense, and with many admirers, has yet more prudence than I ever met with in so young a person, and is already disgusted with the folly and dissipation of "the million." I have not known her long, but I am particularly intimate with her sister, who is her counterpart, and I may say, though I can as yet say no farther I am upon very good terms with herself. We seem to like each other's romantic notions very well. By the way, you must not hint a syllable of this to my mother, who is quite out of the secret, and who would pester me to death if she was let into it. For heaven's sake let me hear immediately from you—be particular about my sister, yourself, and your connections. Give my best love to her, and believe me ever, my dear brother, most cordially and most affectionately, yours,

ARTHUR IREDELL.

IREDELL TO MRS. IREDELL.

WILMINGTON, May 21st, 1783.

* * * On our way we staid the greatest part of a day at Mr. James Moore's, who married Miss Betsey Nash. She is now in pretty good health, and entertained us with great civility and kindness. I was sorry I had not called on Mrs. Nash before I left town, but the extreme hurry I was in, and my being in some measure uncertain whether I should come here, must apologize for me. Mrs. R. Moore lives in Wilmington; but I did not see her till this morning, as she had been very sick, and still is a good deal indisposed. Her sister told me she had talked of going into Edenton now, but I think she will scarcely be so imprudent in her present ill state of health. She has a great desire, I am told, to go to the Springs with Mrs. Pollok, but I suppose if Mrs. P. goes at all she will be too late for that. She says Mrs. P. is one of the most *amiable* women in the world. I told her she was certainly very *agreeable.* * * * I long greatly to be at home, where I should be very well satisfied, notwithstanding the pernicious and ridiculous laws that have been lately made. The event has justified my fears, and the strong conviction I had of the necessity of a more than ordinary exertion at the present period. Not only the most wanton injury has been done to individuals, but the national character disgraced, as more than one article of the Treaty of Peace has been expressly violated. If such things are much longer suffered, this will not be a country to live in, and in the mean time they must deeply wound the feelings of every man of sensibility and honor. I trust we are not without the means of redress, but God knows when there may be an opportunity, and it is painful to think of mischiefs that might have been avoided. As to the little spurt against the lawyers, I don't dread it, and I trust we shall find a way to live, &c., &c.

WILMINGTON, June 9th, 1783.

* * * I preserve my health perfectly well, though the weather is remarkably warm, notwithstanding which there was a very grand ball here the other night; the company was remarkably numerous and brilliant, and every thing extremely genteel, but the great warmth of the night and the smallness of the room for so large a company, very much abated the pleasure. There were obliged to be three successive sets of dancers, and I got only two dances the whole evening, my partner (a Mrs. Toomer) having been obliged to retire early. Mrs. Moore was well enough to be there, and to dance; and Mrs. Clarke was there also. The former I take it is on the brink of matrimony with a Continental officer of the name of McAllister, who came here lately from Charleston, and seems a genteel man, and acquired great reputation from the service. You may therefore suppose her jaunt to Edenton is over, though she expresses a great desire for it, and says nothing but the want of horses prevents her. * * * On Thursday (the day before the ball) the Proclamation of the cessation of hostilities was read in form by the sheriff, and the town was finely illuminated in the evening. Unluckily, though, upon the discharge of cannon a similar accident happened as at Edenton: a man who was drunk and careless was wounded in such a manner that he has ever since been in the most miserable condition, and his life is despaired of, though he still unfortunately lingers it out, for he is a most shocking object. His name is Player, and he has a wife and family in town, &c., &c.

Most entirely and affectionately, yours,
JAS. IREDELL.

In a letter to Mr. Robert Morris, dated July 12th, 1783, relative to a suit in which Mr. Morris was defendant, written by Mr. Iredell, for himself and Capt. Collins,* Mr. Iredell remarks: "We flatter ourselves, on account of the near approach of the Court, and the urgency of this particular case, you will be excused at our addressing you at this time personally to avoid any accidental delay, although we are fully sensible of the great importance to the public of your mind being as little as possible diverted from the arduous and most momentous duties of that employment,

---

* Captain Collins was the Rodolph of his race. Of Irish origin, his honesty, his enterprise, and his industry soon won for him station and wealth. His son, Mr. Josiah Collins, of Lake Phelps, is well known in the State for his hospitality, intelligence, and piety.

which you have hitherto exercised with a reputation and success that can never be too highly applauded, or too gratefully acknowledged."

IREDELL TO HENRY EUSTACE MCCULLOH.

* * I applied to Mr. B. McCulloh that I might know particularly what part of your property was sold; but he does not mention in his answer; he says all your bonds are yet safe where you had deposited them. I believe the greatest part, if not the whole of your property in the back country, was sold. The little tract in the Indian woods is not, in consequence of Mr. J. J. * interposing with a claim on account of the agreement he had partly concluded with you, and on which, but for Mr. Donaldson's sudden departure from the country, he thinks would have been perfected. There remained only the settlement of interest. He desires me to acquaint you of his having made this claim; that he never should have the least desire of preferring it to your prejudice, or of gaining any advantage over you by it, and wishes for nothing more than that through this means it may be saved, and he be able to account with you for the price. I had the pleasure to find Mr. Willie Jones, as well as B. McCulloh, had written you immediately on the reception of your letter. I am satisfied any claim on your behalf never can be preferred with the least prospect of success but upon this footing—that the execution of the Confiscation Act shall proceed no farther, and that you shall have restored what is yet in the hands of the public. For I find it to be the sentiment of the most moderate men, that those who have purchased under faith of Acts of the Assembly, cannot rightfully have their estates taken from them, and it is a melancholy consideration that the estates have sold for so little. The payment of the amount, I am afraid, would be an object scarce worth mention, and, I believe, there would be found very little disposition in the members to make up the difference. I am sorry to say that I am placing the case on the most favorable footing, and that there is such a disposition to violence, not yet cooled, all over the country, that it is indeed very doubtful whether our Assembly will go one step beyond what they are compelled to do by the Treaty. In regard however to the solicitation, B. McCulloh thinks, as well as myself, a personal one would have most chance of being successful; but, if that cannot be had in time, you may be assured of all possible exertions on my part to serve you. The Assembly are appointed to meet the 1st Monday in October next, at Hillsborough.

I wrote you in my other letters, or some of them, that I meant

---

* Mr. John Johnston, I conjecture.

o release to you Miss Macartney's legacy, in part of my debt of honor, and that so far from having any disposition to violate my engagement, which I consider of the most sacred kind, as there was nothing but my honor to bind it, I long ago made a provision in my will to secure it irrevocably to you in case of my death. You were in danger of losing it for some time, *for it was many years after Miss Macartney's death before I heard either of that event or of the legacy;* so that, had I died in the mean time, you might without any ill intention on my part have been a considerable sufferer, for I had otherwise no property but what I got by my wife, and which I did not think myself at liberty to dispose of from her. Your obedient servant,

JAS. IREDELL.

IREDELL TO REV. A. IREDELL.

EDENTON, July 30th, 1783.

MY DEAR BROTHER:—Though I have, ever since the peace, been anxiously looking out for letters from you, and my mother, I have been hitherto disappointed. I assure you the disappointment has been not a little severe, for the satisfaction of hearing frequently from you has been in my contemplation as one of the greatest blessings peace, with its other numerous and important ones, could bring me. If I do not soon hear, I shall be apprehensive of some misfortune: at present I am willing to account for the delay from the difficulty all at once of opening a new correspondence, and perhaps from your being in the country, out of the way of hearing of good opportunities. The present one I have of writing to you is as good as I could desire. It is by Mr. Alexander Black, a merchant in this town, who has long resided here, and been very particularly acquainted with me and my family. He is a brother to that Mr. Black who, I find, has been very obligingly attentive to my mother. He proposes to stay in England and Scotland till the spring, and then to return here. But do not, my dear Arthur, wait till his return to write me. Be so obliging as to write me frequently during his stay, and while he is in England commit your letters to his care. If you knew how very happy your letters made me, you would often favor me with them. The pleasing renewal of intercourse with England, and Mr. Black's going immediately hence, has tantalized me extremely with a desire it is unfortunately not in my power to gratify, of once more seeing my native country, and those relations who are dear to me in it. I believe I should have been tempted to go, narrow as my circumstances are, but that my profession requires my constant attendance here, and does not even permit me the hope of such an indulgence at any future time, while I am engaged in it, which may probably be my whole life; for though I flatter myself it will afford me a very competent support, yet this is not an Indies to raise a fortune in. Were it not, however, on yours and my mother's and my other brother's account, I could live very happily and contentedly in this country. I have the good fortune to have very respectable connections, some most valuable friends, and have experienced instances of general regard and esteem from the people, that have been highly flattering. You have heard, perhaps, of my being a zealous Whig. I am, indeed, but upon terms that I think have done me no dishonor. I took no active part, until after the Declaration of Independence, when no vestige of the British Government was left, and I thought every man had a liberty to choose his side. Even then I took care that no imputation of selfishness might rest on me, for I refused the office of Collector under the new Government, though my heart was devoted to it, and there was a certainty of the office in peace and independence being much more valuable than ever. In December, 1777, when our Courts under the new Constitution were first regularly established, I had the honor, not only without my concurrence, but after having been applied to and declined it, to be appointed one of the Judges of this State, which was owing to the particular partiality of some of my intimate friends, who thought my scruples might be overcome. My objection arose only from my inadequate knowledge of the law for so great an employment; and this I felt so powerfully, that nothing should have induced me to accept the office, but the consideration that I had never till then had a fair opportunity to avow my principles, and that after an actual appointment, my declining to serve might be imputed to unworthy motives. I therefore took it upon me, with a determined resolution to resign it after the first circuit, if our affairs were prosperous, otherwise to keep it, at all events, till I could part from it with honor. I was fortunate in the opportunity I wished. The French Alliance in 1778, enabled me, after the circuit ended in June, that year, to resign it with decency. I did so, assigning my motives fully, that I might not be misunderstood as unwilling to act in a high responsible station, for fear of marking myself to the enemy.

In the summer of 1779, I was appointed Attorney-General, and acted in that office, with very distressing service and very inadequate allowances (owing to the poverty of the public, and depreciation of our money), until November, 1781, when Lord Cornwallis's capture left me again at large to resign without censure, and to endeavor to repair the sufferings my poor circumstances had received in the public service. Since then, I have been only a private lawyer, but with a share of business very near equal to any lawyer's in the country. As I have given you a kind of history of my public life, will it be considered too ostentatious to tell you that in January, 1779, being accidentally without the bar of the Assembly, when they were about appointing delegates to Congress, I had the honor to be asked by the Speaker, at the desire of the House, if I would accept that appointment—an honor that surprised me, as it was without the least previous intimation; but my cursed poverty, and business in the country, obliged me, though not without some reluctance, to decline it.

In return for information, which your partiality for me may make you not displeased with, I wish you would send me a particular account of your own situation, and the manner in which you generally pass your time, an inquiry I would not presume to make of all clergymen, but which I think I may without offence of you. I shall not be satisfied unless I hear of great success in England compensating for the loss we have sustained of you here; for your coming to practise the law in this country was long a very favorite object of mine, as well as your sister's, and we had formed very pleasing ideas about it, which, but for these orders, might now have been realized. That obstacle, I suppose, is insurmountable. Were it not, what a delight would it not be for me to have you with me? I send, by Mr. Black, twenty guineas to my mother. I have been much concerned, I could not send more. But you may imagine that the practice of the law in a country, for a long time the seat of war, and where all the necessaries of life, particularly imported articles, have been exorbitantly high, could not be very profitable. Indeed, when I look back, I have been astonished how we have been supported. The difficulties, I assure you, have been distressing. However, I thank God, peace fully compensates for all. I must request of you a particular account of my mother's situation. I certainly shall be most happy in rendering her all the assistance in my power, and shall deem it at all times an indispensable duty to do so.

I have given Mr. Black three guineas to purchase for me the four last Annual Registers, and such other little things in the miscellaneous way, whether magazines, newspapers or pamphlets, as you may think proper to choose for me—remembering I have a great desire to see a good collection of late Parliamentary Debates, provided there be any honester account of them than is contained in that partial trash, the Political Magazine. You must know I am a great admirer of Mr. Burke, and I wish you could include in my little packet every thing of his that has been published, which he has *wrote* or *spoke*, since his two celebrated speeches of April, 1774, and March, 1775, which I have in good manuscripts of my own. Let me have, if you please, a Court Calendar, a Bibliotheca Legum, a Peerage, and a general Catalogue of Books, with their prices. In judging of what may please me, remember that I have not been lately in England, and therefore many things, within these two or three years past, would be very new and amusing to me, which perhaps have been long out of date there. For I assure you, during the war, all our intelligence from England has been very lame and defective. You will, I am sure, have the goodness to excuse this trouble, as I live in a retired place, where all such things are particularly agreeable and entertaining, and difficult to be had. I am very uneasy about Charles; I also learn there has been a great deal of fighting in the East Indies since the last intelligence I heard of him, and can scarcely flatter myself he has escaped safely through it all. But I will not indulge my fears too much, and will endeavor to preserve hope as long as possible. I always think of him very affectionately, as I hope he does of me, if, poor fellow, he is living! I wrote to you some time ago, and requested you to acquaint me what you thought Tom was qualified for. It will never do, I think, for him to continue in the Marines in time of peace. If I can in any way serve him, I will with the utmost pleasure, and request your opinion and advice.

It is uncertain whether Mrs. Iredell may now have it in her power to write you, though she much wishes it. She desires to renew her claim on you for a correspondence, and hopes you will not neglect it. She always joins me in the tenderest affection and anxiety for you. Though I have not the honor to be known to Mr. and Mrs. Crewe, I would wish to be considered by them as having so warm an interest in your concerns, as to feel very strong obligations for the kindness you experience from them. My heart, my dear brother, is indeed ever most strongly attached to you, and I can never think of you without the greatest sensibility. Pray, write to me often. Apprehend not any neglect of mine. I shall never wilfully be guilty of any, but at all times seize every possible occasion of assuring you how truly I am,

Your very affectionate brother, and faithful friend,

JAS. IREDELL.

P. S.—I take the liberty to inclose you a charge which I delivered to a grand jury while I was a judge, together with their address, which I had the honor to receive upon it; both which at their desire were published. I wish you would let me see some of your sermons and poems in exchange.

JUDGE HENDERSON TO MRS. IREDELL.

Richard Henderson was one of the colonial judges. Represented by North Carolina writers and tradition, as distinguished for industry, attainments and talents; he was regarded by the bar as an upright and faithful officer; yet, nevertheless, he was the subject of insult at Hillsborough, September 25th, 1770; and was constrained to seek safety from the violence of the Regulators, by a nocturnal flight. He was the leading member of a Company who, in 1774, purchased from the Cherokee Indians, "for a fair consideration," an immense tract of land south of the Kentucky River; though the purchase was declared fraudulent by North Carolina and Virginia, yet each of these States subsequently granted to the Company, in lieu of their claim, 200,000 acres—examples followed by the State of Tennessee.*

NUTBUSH, July, 1783.

The task of writing this, is to me very arduous. To dictate from a heart overflowing with gratitude, without incurring an imputation of flattery, is difficult; but confident of candor, I break through that barrier, and venture to make the united thanks of Mrs. Henderson and myself to a generous friend. Unwilling to cause embarrassment by a repetition or an attempt to describe my feelings on the subject in this letter, permit me shortly to say, that any kind and polite treatment of my daughter in your family, demands a better acknowledgment than I can write, or perhaps be well expressed. Mrs. Henderson and myself will, I hope, ever entertain a grateful sense of such essential favors, so generously afforded.

Please to acquaint Mr. Iredell, that from interruption of company I cannot, at this time, answer his letter by Judge Williams; but will by the first convenience after this, though, in the mean time, *he may be assured that the association of the western gentlemen of the bar has been dissolved.* I have the pleasure to be, Madam,

Your most obedient and much obliged humble servant,
RICHARD HENDERSON.

IREDELL TO MR. THOMAS IREDELL.

EDENTON, N. C., July 30th, 1783.

MY DEAR BROTHER:—I thank God that the happy peace which has at length arrived, hath put it in my power to write to you with perfect convenience, which I have long had the greatest desire to do, but was discouraged from it by the hazard attending any letters during the war, and especially a large packet, without which I could not well have wrote to you, as my mother and Arthur had claims upon me which I could not readily forego. It

* Wheeler.

has given me extreme pain to hear of your ill state of health, and that it continued so long. I hope in God it is now in a great measure removed, and that I shall soon have the pleasure to hear so. As I ever think of you, my dear brother, with the greatest tenderness, and the most faithful desire to serve you, I am anxious to know what situation in life is best adapted to your inclination, for I should think it would not be worth holding your station in the Marines during a peace—the pay being trifling, and nothing of consequence to be expected from it with regard to a solid provision for life. I will be obliged to you if you will write me fully, in order that I may judge whether it will be in my power to serve you. You will please tell me how far your education went, and if you should go into business, which you would prefer. I have ten thousand times regretted how the war, by depriving me of my office, defeated a favorite object I had in view,—the selecting an annual sum,—which in that case I could well have spared, to have procured you a liberal and enlarged education. But, alas! Fortune denied me so great a happiness, and you such an advantage. However, my dear Tom, let us do all we can to repair the loss. Though you have lost much time, you are still very young, and may do a great deal towards being well settled in life. In the mean time, it will be necessary to be as frugal as possible. A little self-denial at the beginning is often of the greatest moment in the progress of life, and without it, scarcely any are in circumstances sufficient to avoid distress and misery. I know, however, by my own experience, how difficult it is for a young man of your age to have a competent share of frugality; but I know, too, some of the inconveniences of a want of it, although few people, perhaps, of the same age, were more careful than myself in that respect, who were not naturally misers,—a character most odious and detestable. But having felt very severely the curses of poverty, I am most anxious to ward them off from any of my friends, and therefore most earnestly, my dear brother, convey the caution to you, whose youth makes it probable you may require it.

I shall certainly avail myself of the return of peace to write you often, and shall expect to hear frequently from you. Don't put it off until Mr. Black's return, but get instructions from him about opportunities during his stay, and oblige me as often as you can. Believe your interest and happiness are very dear to me, and consider me as your friend as well as brother; a friend faithful, affectionate and disinterested. Heaven knows how much I desire to serve you, and how earnestly I am solicitous for your being well established. Impart all your views and desires freely to me. Fear not a severity of judgment for any youth-

ful imprudence; I, who, with the best intentions, have been guilty of many, must certainly think with indulgence of others, but if any painful experience of my own can be of service to you, it will be better to avail of it, than to expose yourself to the same course of suffering and repentance. Your sister thinks of you with great affection, as she has the goodness to do of all my relatives. You are frequently in my thoughts and conversation. Nothing can be more tender than my affection, nor more lively than my anxiety for you. God grant you all happiness, my dear brother, a speedy restoration of health, if that blessing has not yet reached you, and every thing else which can give you solid satisfaction, and be productive of your real advantage. So prays, and so will ever most fervently pray, and do all he can to promote it,

Your truly affectionate brother,
JAS. IREDELL.

The following resolutions, and the instructions based upon them, were prepared by Mr. Iredell; they show the temper of the times, and the opinions and inclinations of conservative men,—those of constructive, organizing, creative talent:

STATE OF NORTH CAROLINA.

At a meeting of the inhabitants of the town of Edenton, on Friday, the first day of August, 1783, in order to deliberate on the present situation of public affairs, Samuel Johnston, Esq., in the chair, the sense of the meeting was taken, and ordered to be expressed as follows:

Whereas it is the undoubted right of the people at all times, either collectively or individually, to express their sentiments on the situation of public affairs; and from the various opinions expressed on certain important points throughout the United States, at this interesting crisis, they become proper objects of zeal and anxiety to us, as well as to others,

Resolved unanimously, That while we partake with the rest of our fellow-citizens in the United States, in the great and universal joy which a peace so glorious and advantageous has occasioned, we hope that the terms of it will be sacredly fulfilled, and that we may not be exhibited to the world as a people so mean as well as perfidious, as not only to be disposed to violate a most solemn engagement of our Government, but one which, by the blessing of God, has irrevocably established that Freedom and Independence to which we have been so long aspiring.

Resolved unanimously, That it is our earnest desire that effectual measures for the support of public order may be taken. No longer let Congress be distressed for the payment of even

common expenses. Let the public creditors at least inviolably receive payment of the interest, and have a fund provided for the gradual redemption of the principal of their debts. May those worthy officers and soldiers who have hitherto borne, with such unexampled patience, sufferings which perhaps no other army ever sustained, be delayed no longer of what they have so greatly earned than shall be absolutely unavoidable. On this occasion we have much to regret that the recommendation of Congress for the impost of 5 per cent. failed of its effect. It appears to us to have been a most wise and judicious measure, and as it was the result of the united councils of the whole continent, we think it ought not to have been lightly rejected. We observe with great pain the indecent license many people take in speaking of that august body. When we reflect upon the many and great difficulties with which America has had to contend in her late contest, and that the Congress of these United States, in spite of them all, by wisdom, virtue, and perseverance, hath at length obtained the great blessing we had in view, we feel a veneration and attachment to it which it gives us pleasure to express, sensible that without such an union, and a hearty support of it, we probably should now have been a miserable and disgraced people. We still see in a strong point of view the necessity of that union. In vain shall we hope to preserve the Freedom and Independence we have acquired, but by carefully cherishing those principles upon which it was formed. The power necessary for its support let us therefore cheerfully give. Let us have a proper degree of jealousy, but no unreasonable suspicion. The one is as wholesome as the other baneful. Whom can we trust if not our own Representatives, annually elected, and at any time liable to be displaced by ourselves?

Resolved unanimously, That we wish, so far as is consistent with the Treaty of Peace, proper measures may be taken to guard against the evils that might arise from a return of those persons who withdrew themselves from a defence of the country, and joined the British in the time of our distress. We scorn to triumph over enemies we have defeated, but considering those people in general, we are satisfied they never can make good subjects of these States, on account of their early prejudices against our government, their bigoted attachment to Great Britain, and the mortification they feel from their defeat, after the delusive hopes, and gasconading encouragements they held forth to induce a continuance of the war. Were they not now in distress, we could speak also of the cruelties of many of them, and the pleasure they used to take in every opportunity of insulting and speaking contemptuously of us. But their situation now forbids resentment. We only wish that the public in their conduct towards them may be guided by motives of policy, not of revenge, which we think is unbecoming a generous people. What step it may be proper to take, it is for the wisdom of the Legislature alone to decide, to whom we submit these sentiments with the utmost deference and respect.

Resolved unanimously, That in the mean time, it be earnestly recommended to the Magistrates of this town, to be vigilant in the execution of their duty against such persons as are above mentioned, who may attempt to return and render themselves obnoxious to the laws now in force against them.

It was then ordered that these Resolves be signed by the Chairman, and made public.

To Charles Johnson, Esq., Senator, and Thomas Benbury and Samuel Johnston, Esqs., Members of the House of Commons, for the County of Chowan, and William Cumming, Esq., Member for the town of Edenton.

GENTLEMEN:—We, your constituents, considering the present critical situation of public affairs, and the awful and important scene before us, as we are now, by the blessing of God, freed from the danger and uncertainty of arms in a doubtful and most momentous contest, and it will in a great measure depend upon ourselves, whether by our diligence and integrity we shall be a happy and respectable, or by our neglect or abuse of the great trust committed to us, a miserable and degenerate people, have thought this a crisis proper for the communication of our sentiments upon some subjects of public concern, that appear to us to be highly interesting, and worthy of the most careful attention; and we doubt not you will receive them with the regard always due to the voice of your constituents, and do every thing in your power to carry the purpose of them into full effect.

1. We consider it as indispensably necessary, that the requisition of Congress for the impost of certain duties as a fund for the payment of the public debts, should be complied with. Too long has such a measure been delayed for the honor and advantage of America. We are thankful that none of the ill consequences which may have resulted from it can be chargeable on us, as this State did not hesitate to comply with the very first requisition. Far from joining in indecent clamors against the proceedings of Congress, we entertain the highest reverence for that respectable body, and are thoroughly sensible of the necessity that its authority should be enlarged. We consider the union of the several States as the basis of the individual security and happiness of each. By our union alone have we been able to attain our present auspicious situation, and in vain shall we hope upon any other principles to preserve it. But this union cannot be expected to be lasting without an adequate degree of power as the cement of the whole. Are measures, upon which perhaps its very existence may depend, to be liable to be defeated by an accidental or capricious majority in any one out of thirteen independent Legislatures? Are the public honor and duty of our Federal Government to be committed upon a question, whether provision shall be made for the payment of its debts? And in the mean time, perhaps, while the different States are wrangling upon the subject with all the violence of party zeal, mixed probably with a great deal of weakness, and with some wickedness, the States become bankrupt, and their name and government contemptible? No idle suspicions shall ever induce us, in order to guard against imaginary and chimerical dangers, to be the instruments of such real and impending evils. We must have sufficient confidence in our Representatives to give them power equal to the ends of their institution, or our Government is an ideal one. Consistently with that let us be as jealous as we please, but at the same time that we distrust men who are of our own choice, and whom we may at any time remove, it may not be unuseful to entertain a little distrust of ourselves, and to suppose that sometimes our judgments may be perverted, our passions led astray, and we inadvertently, from a rash interference in subjects of great difficulty and moment, be the cause of evils we may long have reason to deplore, but can never remedy.

2. The subject of paper money is a matter of the utmost concern. We hear with pleasure that the last emission was made unwillingly by the Assembly, and solely for the relief of our officers and soldiers, who were suffering the most cruel distresses; distresses that were the consequence of long and arduous duty in the field, where they so nobly distinguished themselves in our defence. This consideration will induce us to do every thing in our power for its support; but we earnestly entreat for their sake, as well as our own, and that of the public at large, that no more, under any circumstances, may be made, and that as soon as possible the present emission may be redeemed and burnt, a measure necessary to gain the confidence of the people after such severe losses from former emissions, and which it appears to us the public interest will also require; for paper money being of no use but among ourselves, will enable us to discharge no part of the Continental debt, nor to answer any other exigencies out of the State itself, and in the mean time, we fear it will operate as a great discouragement upon our foreign trade.

3. As the act for suspending suits and executions, we presume, was intended merely as a temporary expedient, on account of the unusual scarcity of money, we hope it will now be repealed, as the circulation of the paper currency will remove that evil; and indeed its circulation will be greatly checked if that act should continue in force. The part of the law suspending suits we never could see any good reason for, since it created an unnecessary delay in ascertaining a debt, and rendered the creditor liable to the contingency of loss of proof which by the death of witnesses and other causes which might happen in the mean time, without any real service to the debtor there was the least pretence for, as he was effectually secured from injury by the suspension of execution; and it has created a difficulty which in some cases has been found insuperable, in regard to the security to be given under the direction of a Justice of the Peace; for the debtor must either give security for whatever sum the plaintiff demands, or the Justice try the cause in dispute, the first of which alternatives would be ridiculous, and the other unconstitutional, and unwarranted by the law itself.

4. We think it of very great importance that the finances of our country should be put into some more regular order. We are persuaded many thousands have been lost by the careless and improvident manner in which they have hitherto been attended to, and the public money being scattered in such a variety of hands. This now becomes of more consequence, as the taxes of an independent Government must necessarily be heavy, especially until the public debts are discharged, and many people in every part of the country have been greatly distressed to pay them. We hope proper care also will be taken to make all public accountants settle their accounts, and pay the balances in their hands.

5. As nothing can be of more consequence than to have the judiciary department of Government well filled, and rendered absolutely independent, we think liberal salaries should be provided for the Judges and Attorney General, and made equally permanent with their commissions, otherwise they cannot be truly independent, which is a point of the utmost moment in a Republic where the Law is superior to any or all the individuals, and the Constitution superior even to the Legislature, and of which the Judges are the guardians and protectors.

6. We consider it as an object of wise policy to encourage trade by every means in our power, for when it is free and liberal it quickens industry, provides a ready market for our commodities, and renders cheap all the necessaries of life. Above all should we desire to promote the settlement of merchants in our country, whose riches will then be added to the public stock, and whose services are often of the greatest moment in a crisis of public affairs, as we have frequently experienced from the generous exertions of many during the late war. No narrow and contracted system should therefore be pursued against such men, as is unfortunately the propensity of too many, who see not the evils of throwing the trade of our country altogether into the hands of foreigners, who will drain us of our cash, to the exclusion of our own citizens, who in the most useful manner will be continually adding to it. On the other hand, every inducement that our circumstances will admit of should be granted to the trade of foreigners also, because the more extensive our trade, of greater benefit is it to the public. Upon these principles each should be enabled to trade upon an equal footing. But you will permit us to observe, that there is a remnant of an old method of taxation still remaining, which seems to us greatly to injure our own merchants. At a time when money and money at interest were taxed, their stock in trade was taxed also. The former articles were withdrawn from taxation, the other preserved, whereas that certainly should have been withdrawn also, for no reason can be assigned why property of a particular species in their possession should be taxed, and not property of the same species in that of any other person. Their stock in trade even includes outstanding debts, and property at sea, objects certainly very unfit to pay taxes for, the one being an injury instead of a benefit, and the other not only liable to the danger of the sea, but subject to the restrictions of trade in every country it goes to. The taxing their stock in trade also gives foreigners the advantage of them, since with the double payment of duties and of taxes on their stock in trade, it is impossible they can sell for as low profits as strangers who pay the duties only. It is evident, too, that other people are taxed not in proportion to the value of their whole property, but upon particular parts of it, for which merchants of property pay in proportion with others, besides the duties they are liable to, which though ultimately perhaps resting on the consumer, are in the first instance a disadvantage to them, and lessen in some degree the consumption of their goods. Let justice and common policy attend to these considerations, and a restriction which operates partially to the oppression of many useful members of the community, besides being an injury to the public, be taken off.

7. We recommend it as a circumstance worthy of public attention to grant encouragement to the most useful manufactures; the more of which there are in any country the more independent it is of others, and in other respects they are of great advantage if they do not too much interfere with an attention to agriculture,

VOL. II.—5

which in a country like this ought as much as possible to be promoted.

8. We desire that you will exert yourselves to obtain an alteration of the time for the annual meeting of the General Assembly. No time can possibly be more inconvenient than that now appointed, since it is at a season when few planters without great distress to their private affairs can be absent from home, and when several of the Courts of Justice are held which necessarily require the attendance of many persons, either as lawyers, jurymen, witnesses, or parties, who might be capable of rendering great service to their country as members of the Legislature. And you are sensible, gentlemen, that we in particular suffer by this inconvenience, which we are extremely anxious should be removed.

Lastly, in general terms, we desire to express it as our wish, that every word in that great and good man General Washington's circular letter to the Governors, may be most zealously attended to, a letter which unfolds in the wisest manner the true principles of public policy, and by which, with a patriotic anxiety we cannot too gratefully acknowledge, he endeavors to perpetuate to his country the blessings of that freedom and independence he has been so glorious an instrument in procuring.

These sentiments, Gentlemen, we communicate to you, relying with the most pleasing confidence on the abilities and zeal by which your conduct, on many occasions, hath been distinguished.

IREDELL TO MRS. CATHARINE MACARTNEY.

MADAM:—I hope you will not think me impertinent in laying hold of the earliest conveyance after the peace, to make you my sincere and grateful acknowledgments, as one of a family you have unspeakably obliged, for the uniform and distinguished kindness you have for so many years shown them. Pardon me, madam, if I say, that I have felt the obligations, not merely for their own sake (though so valuable to the receiver), but as a man of humanity, pleased with every opportunity to admire virtue, and instances of benevolence proceeding from the most generous motives. Nothing can be more amiable than such a conduct, but how deeply must it impress those who receive the greatest benefits by it! What must my brother Arthur, what must those who love him feel, for the goodness with which you procured him his present happy situation! This, madam, is one great instance among many obligations you have conferred upon my family that can never be forgotten, or cease to be remembered with the utmost gratitude.

After suffering many of the distresses of war, I am fortunately in a situation which gives me hopes of being able hereafter to assist my mother effectually. My not being able to do it sooner has given me the greatest pain; but I do assure you, madam, has been absolutely unavoidable. I have ever, and shall always, I am sure, consider it as one of my first duties to render all possible assistance to her, and not among the least to take every occasion in my power of demonstrating my gratitude to her benefactors, and in particular, madam, to testify the sincere respect and grateful sensibility with which I have the honor to be,

Your most obedient, most humble servant,
JAMES IREDELL.

MACLAINE TO IREDELL.

WILMINGTON, August 4th, 1783.

DEAR SIR:—Had I not been much employed, and my mind constantly on the stretch, since I had your favor of the 14th past, I should have answered it sooner. It would be superfluous to give you any fresh assurances of my readiness to oblige you. You will certainly find me a cheerful assistant in your ejectment cause.

The paragraph in your letter relative to the meeting was very alarming indeed: but we have since been assured that all is now quiet, and that some officers who had privately promoted it are fled. I have, however, just seen a paragraph in a Maryland paper, which mentions that 1500 New England troops were at Frankfort, on their march to Philadelphia, under General Howe.* From this circumstance, I am apprehensive that a mob in Philadelphia are concocting measures to frustrate the articles of peace, so far as they are favorable to the Tories. In Charleston, Gillan and his first minister Fallon have actually begun that game, and several persons, to them obnoxious, were carried to the pump.† The executive power interfered, and the principal gentlemen convened the people in town, and put Gillan and his myrmidons to flight. In short, the people were convinced of the ruinous tendency of their conduct, and deserted their seditious leaders, who are now chewing the bitter cud of disappointment. The same scheme has been attempted here; but happily those among us who aspire to power by such means, want common understanding. Mr. G. Hooper had even been unmolested for a few weeks, when Brice, and James Cruden (a brother of the Commissioner) arrived from New York. These last were a few days in the place, when Mr. London arrived from Charlestown, accompanied by a Mr. Alexander from England, and Mr. Mackenzie (Mr. Camp-

* Of North Carolina.
† Commodore Alex. Gillan, vide Johnson's Traditions and Reminiscences.

bell's nephew). Mr. London was but a very short time ashore when two ruffians (secretly commissioned by Walker) paid him a very uncivil visit, and told him in express terms that if he did not return to the vessel, they would put him out of existence. After an ineffectual endeavor to soften Walker, Mr. London complied. Application was next day made to Judge Ashe, who had just then issued a precept to the sheriff to take up Brice, Cruden, Hooper, and one Smith. He then added London to his list. From what he wrote me, this appeared to have been intended to serve the parties, and I was the more convinced of it, as he purposed living in town himself. Before this warrant came to hand, Mr. Hooper was gone, having been ready to depart ten days before. Mr. Cruden, who was just ready to sail for Augustine, did not choose to lose his passage, and avoided the sheriff. Instead of the Judge's coming himself, the matter was referred to some Justices of the Peace—three met—Walker proposed sending the gentlemen off—the others insisted upon committing them, which was done. They are now in custody, and Mr. Ashe, who has been applied to, informs me that he is to be in town this day, or to-morrow, and from what he writes, *will* admit them to bail. I intend he shall bind over others to their good behavior. It is almost impossible to conceive what trouble and vexation is occasioned, by an intention to keep fair with the rabble—but I must conclude. Dear Sir, yours very sincerely,
A. MACLAINE.

DR. WILLIAMSON TO IREDELL.

PRINCETON, August 20th, 1783.

DEAR SIR:—It has been represented by some of the Trustees that Edenton appears to a majority of the Board to be the most proper place for erecting the seminary to be called Smith's Academy. * * * It will ever be in our power hereafter to remove our Academy to another place, should the people in and near Edenton become inattentive to the first command, and not have children to educate. * * * Within the last two months, five boys have come to this town from N. Carolina to a Grammar School. Much divination is not required to foretell that they must draw at least £400 per annum in hard money out of the State. The Grammar School here is taught by two lads who are themselves students in the College. By such industry they bear their own expenses. Is it not probable that our Academy would be at least equal to such a school? It is true the school is kept in one of the apartments of the College; and the boys have the advantage of all the inspiration that may be supposed to proceed from such walls. As the general observance of law, the peace of society, and the honor and prosperity of a State depend absolutely on the means that are used to instruct its inhabitants, I flatter myself the Trustees will consider what is best to be done on the subject, &c., &c.,

Dear Sir, your most obed't humble servant,
HUGH WILLIAMSON.

MACLAINE TO IREDELL.

WILMINGTON, N. C., August 25th, 1783.

DEAR SIR:—I am much obliged to you for the trouble you took in sending me the resolves of Edenton. They probably prevented, as you observe, some ridiculous measure taking place. Happily the attempt this way ended in smoke. There were two or three meetings of a few insignificant and worthless characters in town, and finding themselves too few, and too uninformed, they endeavored to effect their purpose by assembling the lower class of people at Bloodworth's in the country. About thirty met, and a considerable majority (Col. Bloodworth at the head of them) refused to come into the measure. John James and a few others are once more attempting to enforce their old accusations against me, and swear I shall not have a seat in the Assembly. But they go further. They are determined to turn out the judges and set aside the whole business of last Superior Court. This will be fine sport. I wish to God you were of the Assembly. With two or three men that I could name, we might set all matters right in a short time. I am certain the annual meeting might easily be altered, and that would make way for every thing else. I am glad my Acts of Assembly are safe; but how shall I get them?

General Greene has been here two nights, accompanied by Major Edwards and Major Hyrne. He is on his way to the Northern States.

Mr. Hill died the 22d of obstinate quackery. He called in the physicians about four days before his death, when his stomach would not retain medicines; nor indeed any thing.* A vesse-

* William Hill; a graduate of Cambridge, Mass. He was an opulent merchant remarkable for the liberality of his sentiments, and his enlightened attachment to the cause of the Colonies, though a Crown officer. Josiah Quincy, who visited Cape Fear anterior to the Revolution, speaks of him, in his journal, in terms of warm commendation. Regularly, every Sunday in the church at Brunswick (there was no pastor) Mr. Hill read the services of the church to congregations who, if not profoundly impressed with religious convictions, always manifested a decent respect for the house of God, and entertained for him a tender and affectionate regard. Early in the war, Mr. Hill removed to Wilmington, where he was captured by Craig. Though his losses had been very severe, at the restoration of peace, he was still worth £5,000. He married Margaret Moore, a member of an influential family: his descendants are numerous in North Carolina, and many of them have won distinction.

from Cork is lately arrived at Charlestown, by way of Madeira. The whole passage near four months. We have a new store here from Glasgow, and several vessels are expected from Ireland; one or two in particular from Newry. We have just received your association to support the paper money, and will immediately attempt the same thing here. I am with perfect esteem and regard,

Dear Sir, yours,
A. MACLAINE.

P. S. I have the pleasure to inform you that the Assembly of S. Carolina, who have been remarkably moderate, have complied with the requisition of Congress for the duties on imports; and until other States agree, they have laid a duty of 2½ per cent. for the use of the Union.

October 5th, 1783.

DEAR SIR:—You will receive by Captain Addison a small box, with Hawkins' edition of the statutes at large,—six volumes,—of which I request your acceptance.

I shall not set off for Hillsborough in less than six or seven days. What I shall be able to do there, God only knows. This I am well assured of; that if there is not a different temper in the majority of the members than what I experienced last session, and if I am not better supported than I was at that time, I had much better be attending to my own private business.

The mean arts used to promote private interest, and the low cunning practised to ensure the good opinion of violent men who appear to be popular, if not timely checked, must soon reduce us, as a nation, to insignificance, and even to contempt.

The latest accounts give us every reason to expect that the Definitive Treaty is signed; and my ardent wish is, that it may be laid officially before the Assembly.* Without it, I despair of doing any thing of immediate consequence. Should it be laid before us it will then be seen whether we will suffer anger and resentment so far to get the better of reason and sound policy, as to render us infamous over all Europe. If we do not, as far as lies with us, recognize the articles of peace, we are undone for ever. Yours very sincerely,

A. MACLAINE.

In October, Mr. Iredell, on his way to attend court at Halifax, was violently attacked by cholera morbus, and came near losing his life. Fortunately he succeeded in reaching Elk Marsh (the seat of Colonel McCulloh). To the utmost degree of kindness on the part of the family, and principally to the very generous and friendly assistance of Mr. B. McCulloh and Captain Stokes, with pious gratitude, "under God," he ascribed his recovery. While convalescent he wrote his wife, "My time passes along heavily, as I have read through Gil Blas, without being able to find any agreeable substitute, and my mind is not quite strong enough to digest harsh law compositions for any length of time. I wish you would send me some of my newspapers by your brother. I never see any here, nor know more of what is passing in the world scarcely than if I lived in a hermitage."

REV. A. IREDELL TO MRS. IREDELL.

CREWE HALL, Nov. 17th, 1783.

I have just written a long letter to my brother; but there are two subjects which I have kept sacred for one to you. You wish, it seems, to know how I spend my time, and you ask me, whether Love has never molested my quiet, or added to my happiness by success? I will give you full answers to both these points. When Mr. Crewe's family is here, I make for the most part one in it, as the acquaintance or friend, and not the tutor, a character I assume only a month or two in the year, when his son happens to be at home, which is never for a longer period. This is the more convenient for me, as I have a curacy in the neighborhood, which requires some, though not constant residence upon the spot. At other times, when Mr. and Mrs. Crewe are absent, I pay my visits in the country, and have always more invitations on my hands than I can attend to, at least *do* attend to, as there are few my inclination prompts me to accept. Crewe Hall is, of all others I ever knew, the most comfortable house to live in; it has all the grandeur and magnificence of a great, together with the comforts and convenience of a small one. Though Mr. Crewe is member for the county, and extremely popular in it, his retirement is seldom interrupted by much company. The neighborhood is not a large one; the roads in this part of England are very unfavorable for visiting, and Mrs. Crewe is very far from promoting what would not fail of breaking in upon her studies, which I can assure you she is far from neglecting. Note that for a great while together they have been here with me; and a straggler now and then dropping in upon them. The hours they keep are the most exceptionable points in the life they lead. We breakfast between ten and eleven; dine between five and six; sup at eleven, and go to bed, God knows when. Such an abuse

---

* For want of a quorum the Assembly failed to organize, and did not meet until the subsequent year.

---

of day and night is hardly tolerable in London, where every thing is irregular; it is absolutely intolerable for a long time together in the country, where time is so much at one's disposal, and depends so little upon accidents. Setting these aside, however, the life here, I think, is very rational. The morning, which is always a long one, is devoted either to exercise, study, or both; every one spends it as he likes best. At dinner all meet, and from that time do not separate. From the eating-room they adjourn into a very large withdrawing-room, in which you may form as many groups as you please. Cards, letter-writing, and reading, go on at the same time without interruption; and generally music, as an harpsichord and piano-forte, are placed invitingly for those who know how to play upon them. Conversation, and that seldom trifling, has its place among the amusements; and the evening generally concludes without fatigue, and always with good humor. After such a description of this place, and its enjoyments, will you not, my dear sister, be astonished to hear that I am heartily sick of such a life, and pant eagerly for another more humble, because I fancy more happy one? The discontent of man has been ever a very hackneyed, and is now, I think, an exhausted topic. It is certain that there is in all of us a restlessness of mind which palls our appetite for what we have, and quickens it for what we have not; but you must not lay my disgust solely to the account of this natural unsteadiness in me (for no doubt I have my share of natural infirmities); it proceeds from long experiment, and the most rooted conviction after it of the vanity of a luxurious life, and of the friendships which are grafted upon it. The one is excellently calculated for killing time; it soon passes in a succession of bewitching gratifications,—the others are clothed with that pleasing and delusive garb which answers all the purposes of such a life,—of a life that is made up of appearances. Thus I pass my time voluptuously at Crewe; not a moment in the day oppresses me; the night comes too soon. Time is charming in the prospect; but is it so in the retrospect? No. How have I passed the last month? Have I laughed with the gay? Yes; but have I wept with the unfortunate? Have I improved my old friendships? established new ones? I do not live for myself, and ought to be able to answer all these interrogatories in the affirmative; but I fear I cannot. It is for these reasons, then, my dear sister, that I wish to change my situation. * * * * My brother will tell you how my prospects have brightened in Jamaica, in consequence of the part he has taken on the continent; and yet I am afraid Hymen will not light his torch much the sooner upon that account. I have sounded my uncle on the topic of marriage; but he seems to expect a pedigree and rent-toll, neither of which I can send him. * * * Adieu! God bless you! I am ever most affectionately yours,

A. IREDELL.

REV. A. IREDELL TO IREDELL.

CREWE HALL, Nov. 17th, 1783.

I have at length, my dear brother, received the full and satisfactory account of you, which I have been so long waiting for; and trace with infinite pleasure through the whole of it, that pureness of intention, and assiduity in business, which must have done you infinite credit in your province, and are so highly grateful to those who have sensibly felt for you in situations peculiarly embarrassing to the honest and deserving. You have acquitted yourself, as might have been expected, with a firmness properly tempered with prudence; and as you seem to have satisfied your own conscience, so I think you may rely upon the approbation of your friends. I do not scruple to assure you of mine, though I agree with you in thinking that there are parts in your address to the grand jury, so very *animated* and *determined*, both in point of sentiment and language, as to require apology. But I can excuse even these. The people you lived with,—the cause you adopted,—the very air you breathed,—all conspired to heat your imagination, and inflame your zeal. Liberty is of all others the most bewitching cause to be engaged in; it is the cause of Nature; and in contending for it, we all feel as if we struggled for something inseparable from the good. To die or conquer is the only alternative proposed, the only end in view; and to be lukewarm or indifferent in such a contention would argue, in my opinion, a very loose and unworthy mind. Such are my sentiments, but they are not the sentiments of every man; and I am concerned to tell you they are not of one whose good opinion you would wish to conciliate, and whose favor you have the greatest claim to. My uncle, I have before hinted to you, has conceived the most rooted disapprobation of your public conduct, and seems determined not to change his sentiments upon it. He has written to me very unequivocally upon the subject, and in one of his letters says, that "he has *long* looked up to me for the support of our name and family," and that he shall make no division of his estate, but leave annuities, not large ones, to my mother and Tom. He had likewise remembered my poor Charles, who, alas, is out of the reach of his bounty! You see how much I am to profit by your disgrace; but you will, at the same time, I hope, judge of my feelings, by what would be your own, under similar circumstances, and suppose me to be as much chagrined upon your account, as I am grateful upon my own.

✱ ✱ ✱ ✱ Whatever his estate may be, should it ever devolve into my hands, I trust you are sufficiently confident in me to believe that you would want no assistance it might then be in my power to bestow. How happy I should be if it would enable us to live together in the same country, and almost under the same roof! But I must not augur such flattering events. A thousand cruel and unlooked-for circumstances may intervene to blast our projects in the very bud, or wither them before they arrive at maturity. "It is not for mortals to command success." Let us then follow Addison's excellent advice, and deserve it. You have long been treading the paths of public life, with reputation to yourself, and effect to your country. I have had as yet very little opportunity of doing the one or acquiring the other; for a university life, however useful to the individual, is not of much service to society; and since I quitted it for something more like action in the Church, I have been confined to the slender offices of a curacy. No preferment has as yet enlarged the sphere of my duty, and thrust me forward upon the canvass. God knows how long I may continue an insignificant figure in the background. I am very well disposed to become more conspicuous, and am not without a favorable prospect of rising to a certain height. You must not, therefore, be without hopes of me; and at the same time you must inclose them within narrow bounds. Both my pretensions and inclination are very confined. I cannot have much; and I have seen so much of the *world* as thoroughly to despise it, and to wish only for the "otium cum dignitate," which I translate into a respectable country life. I shall have great pleasure in collecting the books you have written for; shall, principally with that view, take a journey to London in about six weeks. ✱ ✱ ✱ I had almost forgotten to request that you will write my uncle; it is very proper, I think, you should do so. I may be a loser by such a step, but I care not, provided you are the gainer, &c., &c.

Believe me, my dearest James, ever
Most affectionately yours,
A. IREDELL.

WILLIAM HOOPER TO IREDELL.

NEWBERN, Nov. 23d, 1783.

MY DEAR SIR:—This is Sunday, the 23d day of November, and the tops of the houses covered with snow. As I am now free from interruption, and probably shall not find equal leisure before I necessarily leave this, I sit down to inform you that the long expected posthumous works of Mr. Blackstone have made their appearance. John Sitgreaves has got from New York, and they are now before me, two thick volumes in octavo, entitled, "Reports of cases determined in the several courts of Westminster, from 1746 to 1779, taken and compiled by the Hon. William Blackstone, Kn't, late one of the Justices of his Majesty's Court of Common Pleas. Published according to the directions in his will, by his executors, from his original manuscripts, with a preface, containing memoirs of his life." The publisher, Mr. James Clitherow, one of Mr. Blackstone's executors, informs the reader that "these reports begin with Michaelmas Term, 1746, when Mr. Blackstone was called to the bar, and there are some of every term, except two, to Michaelmas, 1750, from whence there is an interval to Michaelmas, 1756. The reason probably was, that during this period he was at Oxford, composing his lectures, which he began to read 1753. In the three following years, he attended the bar only in Michaelmas and Hillary terms, on account of his lectures, consequently there are among these reports none of the Easter and Trinity terms of those years," &c., &c. ✱ ✱ ✱ The edition before me is an Irish one, of *course you* will say incorrect. ✱ ✱ ✱ Thus having given you enough of this performance to excite your most sanguine wishes to be more intimately acquainted with it, I will only add that the cases appear, upon a cursory reading, to be much too short for entertainment. They are, like all that great man's, clear and perspicuous; but the arguments seem rather abstracts than otherwise. I conceived that he rather intended them as notes, to be the groundwork of a larger undertaking, if Heaven had spared him to us, with leisure to effect it.

Schulluck v. Rice is now before the Court, and to-morrow I expect their opinion. I have had the honor to participate in a political treat at which you were to have been a guest. It was given by Hay in the character of Tiberius Gracchus; and the feast was called an address to the Speakers of both Houses of Assembly containing observations moral and political upon the proceedings of the late Assembly. It is to be served up to the public in a sixpenny pamphlet, and will make its appearance as soon as the *Illumination* is over, which is now in its progress. I find that there is another in the State that has an equal rage with the *Illuminati* to become a scribbler; and I apprehend the world will profit about as much by his labors. I have seen also an advertisement for the information of the judges, stating the exorbitant fees charged on Mr. Hogg, which sets the affair in a more favorable view; and were it not for the personal rancor which runs through it, would I think be excusable at least in point of composition, and necessary in point of matter.

Alfred Moore is gone, having no business except a trial for murder to detain him, which he has shifted over to Maclaine & Hay.

Nov. 24th.—Since I began this letter I called upon Cooke. I found him by the fireside, thin and emaciated beyond any thing I have ever seen—the very figure of death itself. His legs are literally and truly not larger than a walking stick; his face wan; and his eyes, which contrasted with the hollowness of his cheeks appear larger than usual, stand forth like two globes of liquid fire. Near him stood a boy whose employment was to supply him with *toddy*. He has lost his memory to a great degree, and his understanding is much impaired. Upon my entering the room he must have mistaken me for you. He asked me whether I had just arrived from Edenton—whether I had come by way of Halifax—and said that my causes were all continued. His wife sat beside him, a mark for his continual cavil and reproach: and seems to be awaiting his dissolution with a becoming resignation to the will of Providence.

I have seen Silas's wife. She is not very handsome; but has something extremely engaging in her appearance and manners. She has had a genteel education: is free, social, and sensible; but extremely mortified at her situation—not a room to be had in town. She has taken up her residence at the palace, which, at present, has more the appearance of a neglected jail than any thing else.

Hay has had an explanation with the judges upon the subject of the report which has been circulated to his disadvantage. Ashe has shifted it to Williams; the latter has returned it upon him. This will be productive of a schism among the higher powers—this "entre nous."

We shall leave this on Wednesday, and move on as fast as we can to Wilmington—there I shall expect a line from you.

The girls unite with me in most affectionate regards to yourself and Mrs. Iredell, &c., &c.

Ever, my dear Sir, yours,
WILL. HOOPER.

P. S. *Oct. 28th.*—Judge Spencer sent Mr. Iredell a political piece, signed "Atticus," with a request that he would revise it, and procure it to be printed in Virginia.

MRS. MACARTNEY TO IREDELL.

RICHMOND (ENG.), Dec. 17th, 1783.

I return you a great many thanks for the favor of your obliging letter from Edenton, which Mrs. Iredell sent me: the affection you express for her she is very deserving of, I assure you. Your admiration and love would be considerably increased, could you (as I have) been the near witness of the amazing fortitude with which she has supported a weight of misery which threatened to overwhelm her. So large a portion of it should not have been hers had my power to support her been equal to my inclination but I am thankful to Heaven for having permitted me now and then to give her some assistance; and by making her virtues and suffering known to Lord Macartney, to interest him for her. Your best thanks are due to your uncle, who, upon my representing to him the distressed situation of his brother's widow and sons, very kindly and generously relieved them as soon as he could. Your brother Arthur does great credit to my recommendation of him to Mr. Crewe, whose favor, I flatter myself, will be of service to him. I am very glad that you are happily settled. You have my sincerest wishes for your long enjoyment of health and prosperity; and I must request that you will believe me, as I am, with regard, Sir,

Your obliged humble servant,
CATHARINE MACARTNEY.

IREDELL TO HIS MOTHER.

EDENTON, N. C., Dec. 31st, 1783.

MY DEAR MOTHER:—Since my last letter to you we have had the satisfaction to receive yours of the 2d of Oct., a letter of so late a date as quite surprised and pleased me, it being for so many years what I have been unfortunately deprived of. Neither had I much jealousy at its being wrote to Mrs. Iredell, and not to me, though I wished for a few lines to myself also; but Mrs. Iredell thought I had great reason to be satisfied, and as I could not well assign a cause for not being so, I pretty well reconciled myself to it.

We are very glad the hams pleased you, and only regret the quantity was not larger, which was owing to the opportunity not being foreseen: but as nothing can be more agreeable than making little presents to one's friends, we will endeavor another time to put it more in your power to enjoy that satisfaction.*

The circumstances that you and my brother Arthur mentioned of my dear brother Charles affected me extremely, and renewed in a most sensible manner all my grief for his loss. Thank God, that he was so worthy; a consolation, my dear mother, that you must continually think of, as suggesting the happy change for himself produced by the event so lamentable to us. And surely, for his sake, we cannot regret that he is removed from a

---

* An old North Carolina ham is the best in the world—far surpassing the more famous Westphalian.—"*Crede experto.*"

scene of so much care and trouble and misery as most people, and few more than our own unfortunate family, have found this world to be. This is the only alleviation I can think of for a calamity that is indeed very severe, and accompanied with circumstances that make it inexpressibly affecting. I hope in God, my dear mother, for the sake of those who survive, and to whom you are so dear, that you will suffer such consolatory reflections to move you, and restore you by degrees to as serene a state of mind as possible. Your dear daughter joins earnestly in this hope, cherishing her connection with you with the tenderest respect and affection, and anxiously solicitous for every thing that can contribute to the mutual happiness of us all. I enclose you a Power of Attorney to receive what I may be entitled to on my dear brother's account, and which I beg you to accept of for your own use. You will distress me if you attempt sending any present by way of return, either to Mrs. Iredell or me. For God's sake do not, except it be your picture, if you can afford it, which we greatly desire to have. We can get every thing we have occasion for here, and I had much rather, if you have any thing to spare, that you would let Tom have it than me, who have no want of it.

I have been extremely uneasy about my brother Tom. I know how ruinous his present situation is, and how paltry a prospect it offers of a solid provision hereafter, which a young man ought constantly to have in view. And I see nothing else that can be done for him in England, where money is indispensably necessary for every thing. In this country I have only one way of serving him, that of my own profession, if he can have steadiness and constancy to apply to it with the necessary assiduity; and it will require a great deal, and some years before it is possible he can be distinguished. If he thinks, however, he can submit to this, and is desirous to come to me, I will receive him with open arms, and can assure him of every thing he can expect from the most affectionate of brothers, and I may add of *sisters*, for it is my pride to say that Mrs. Iredell seems to love and interest herself in my relations as if they were her own. If he will apply to the study, his success in it in this country is certain, and he may promise himself hereafter a very genteel income. In the mean time he shall live with me, which will be very little additional expense, and that well repaid by the satisfaction I shall reap from it and the prospect of serving him: and it may be in his power to be serviceable also to me, as I very much want a young man whom I can rely upon to act occasionally as a clerk. I have been applied to to take several young gentlemen, but refused, and not altogether without a view to Tom, hoping that he might try this method if no other was likely to serve him. If you and he and Arthur approve of this scheme, he may come as soon as he pleases, but let him first resign his station in the army, and take care to bring no regimentals with him, which might occasion some little prejudice among a people whose minds are not yet entirely easy. If he should incline to come, he would be fortunate in being in time to accompany Mr. Black. If Mr. Black should have left England, I should wish him to come to James River, in Virginia; and land either at Norfolk or Portsmouth, whence it is only about 80 miles here. If he should go to Norfolk, let him apply to Mr. Alex. Diack, a merchant there, and who upon knowing him to be my brother would be very glad to assist him. If Mr. Black should have left England, and Tom not be able to take his passage in the month of April, he had better defer it till the Fall, as August and September are our principal sickly months here, although of late years they have not been so sickly as formerly: and in this case, let him be careful not to sail so as to be on the American coast sooner than the latter end of October, or beginning of November.

I inclose letters for Arthur and Tom. Let me hope you will have the goodness to write as often as possible, and be particular about every thing, especially yourself, and your means of support, which I am at a loss to conjecture. I look out from post to post with the greatest anxiety for letters from you, one as soon as I receive it making me earnestly wish for another, as my thoughts and attention are almost always present with you. Would to God it was in my power to go and see you; it would be the greatest happiness I could enjoy, and what I frequently wish it was in my power to accomplish; but it is impossible for me to quit my business here, which is indeed too valuable to be slighted, and will not permit even a short absence from the country. You are very good in having so earnest a desire to see your daughter. I wish you could; you would like her infinitely better than you can from any report or imagination. But how can I part with her across the seas! I should rejoice to attend her, but her going without me is impracticable. Would to God, however, we could meet! But I see, at present, only one way of effecting it, and that is, if, as you once flattered me, you could bless me with a sight of you in this country. This would make me happy indeed, but is, I fear too much to hope for

Many, many most happy years to you. Look forward, my dear mother, rather than to the past. Think of Arthur, who is such an ornament to us. Rely on every thing that is possible to be done by me. Reflect with pleasure and hope on the good qualities of Thomas, who is very near my heart, and shall ever experience from me the tenderest affection. I hope we shall all exert ourselves to render you in every respect easy and happy. Be assured, I shall never fail to do so, who am,

My dearest mother, with the greatest truth,
Your most dutiful and affectionate son,
JAMES IREDELL.

CHAPTER XVII.

ÆT. 32—33.

INTRODUCTORY SUMMARY. LETTERS FROM HOOPER, SIR N. DUKINFIELD, PIERCE BUTLER, IREDELL, REV. A. IREDELL, S. JOHNSTON, AND H. E. M'CULLOH.

MR. IREDELL continued during the year '84 actively engaged in his professional avocations.

At the close of the war commenced an animated struggle between military men and those who, amid the clash of arms, had been overshadowed. Upon the return of peace, those accustomed to command could not, without a sigh or effort, surrender their authority to others. Then began a contest, fierce enough, between *thought* and *action*: but, as must always necessarily happen where the press is unshackled and freedom of debate exists, mind soon established its ascendency. The return of the Tories, and their strenuous efforts to procure the restoration of their property; the activity of the lawyers, stimulated by the opening of a lucrative career; the commencement of new, the revival of long dormant suits—all conspired to foster exasperation, cupidity, avarice, revenge. It is never to be expected that *immediately* after a revolution effected by arms, the passions of the combatants will subside; and that trade and the currents of life will return to their wonted channels. The sea, disturbed to its depths, does not sleep quietly as soon as the storm is stilled; troubled dreams are, long afterward, attested by its heaving bosom.

A very violent prejudice, at this period, existed in narrow and vulgar minds against the legal profession: this antipathy was fomented by many persons of more talent and less principle, as a means of destroying those whom they feared as rivals, and as an instrument by which they might effect their political ends. The lawyers of the State were generally *conservatives*; hence it was that they excited, in addition to other causes, the animosity of the *radicals*; and in a signal degree the hatred of those who may be distinctively, and exclusively, characterized as demagogues, charlatans, and political tricksters.

VOL. II.—6

Though the weight of Mr. Iredell's business would have crushed one less resolute and vigorous, yet he was too good a citizen to fold his arms, in selfish apathy, to matters of public concern. With Hooper, Johnston, Maclaine, and others with whom he generally agreed politically, he labored to promote harmony, and induce wise legislation. Eager to sustain the honor of the Confederacy, they gallantly attempted to lift its banner while yet unsullied by the infamy of a refusal to comply with the terms of its virgin treaty, and to plant it in a rock. North Carolina was urged by every motive to a right discharge of duty, and appealed to by every art of rhetoric. In their honorable work they were not unaided by many of the purest and best of those from whom they generally, politically, dissented: of these the most prominent was Willie Jones, the "most adroit statesman," in the opinion of his party, in the State.

The augmentation of Mr. Iredell's practice, which now equalled that of any attorney in the State, enabled him to gratify a long-cherished wish of his heart by tendering his mother, and brother Thomas, a home in America : the latter arrived in the course of the year, and commenced under his auspices the study of the law.

I must now speak of the earliest and greatest sorrow of Mr. Iredell's manhood. His hopes had been greatly inflamed by the birth of a son, his *first-born ;* but even while the glow of exultation still dyed his cheek, and the tear of joy sparkled in the mother's eye, the bud, fresh with the dew of the morning, and almost before one ray of the sun had penetrated its heart, closed in death : it was a sad bereavement ! a terrible disappointment ! He often in his letters touchingly alludes to his loss, recurring again and again to the melancholy theme.

The General Assembly met at Hillsborough, April 17th, and adjourned June 2d : a second Assembly was "begun" at New Berne, Oct. 22d, and terminated its session Nov. 25th. The reader will find in the correspondence for the year set forth all their acts or omissions of general interest.*

HOOPER TO IREDELL.

HILLSBOROUGH, January 4th, 1784.

MY DEAR SIR :—Your very obliging letters which were handed to me when I was at Newbern, and announced your perfect recovery

---

* To the General Convention of the "Society of the Cincinnati," held in Philadelphia in May, '84, the State Society at their meeting in Hillsborough, April 18th, appointed as delegates Col. Lyttle, Major Reading Blount, and Major Griffith J. McRee. General Jethro Sumner was President, and Capt. Curtis Ivy, (of Sampson,) Secretary. The fact is mentioned, because I suppose a certificate in my possession to be the only documentary proof of the organization of a State Society extant in North Carolina.

---

from a dangerous and distressing malady, relieved me from the most painful suspense respecting your situation. The severe attack which you have had will render you more susceptible of similar disorders ; and the shock, which I fear your constitution has received from it, will excite what the physicians call a predisposition of habit to that particular species of complaint. Let me entreat of you to guard against it with particular caution ; and to avail yourself of the able advice of Dr. Ramké, to prevent a necessity of calling him again to your aid.

Our stay at Newbern was much more agreeable than I expected. Mrs. James Ellis, as well as himself, were singularly attentive to the girls. They saw the little variety that town afforded ; and the new faces and new fashions supplied them with subjects of new comment, and served them as matters of conversation here in discussing the comparative taste of the ladies of the different towns they passed through. Nothing, however, but suffers in the competition with Edenton. Their feelings are interested there and they have formed attachments which are very near their hearts. Your friends at Newbern inquired for you with real concern. Mrs. Gordon, poor woman, is hastening fast to a better world. She talks with great philosophy of her approaching dissolution, and seems to regret her separation from an existence which has been marked with such scenes of sorrow and affliction only because she leaves her son behind. Now and then her disorder presents a flattering appearance ; but the dangerous symptoms soon again recur, and blast every hope of the return of health. It was the wish of some one to die suddenly, and away from his friends. God send that I, and those I love, may not linger out life in the habit of seeing death constantly before our eyes, without availing ourselves of his fatal but friendly offices.

Dr. Burke died about a fortnight since, and fell, in some measure a sacrifice to the obstinacy which marked his character through life.* Had he declined his journey to Edenton, he might yet have been alive. It would, however, be a question with his friends whether life upon the terms he had it would not have been a curse in the extreme. Laboring under a complication of disorders ; oppressed with the most agonizing pains, which for months had deprived him of his natural rest ; his whole mass of blood dissolved ; his temper soured with disappointment ; and, to sum up his misery, no domestic prop to lean upon—no friend or companion, at his own home, to soothe the anguish of his mind, or mitigate his pain of body—was not death to him "a comforter, friend, and physician ?" He has carried his indifference to his wife to the grave with him. By his will he has left nothing ab-

---

* Gov. Burke.

---

solutely at her disposal. He has devised to her an estate for life—not half of his estate ; and, upon her marriage, has restrained, and curtailed that in some degree. Upon the death of his daughter, to whom he has given the whole upon the death of her mother, provided the daughter dies under 21, or without issue, the whole goes to the children of James Hogg and Willie Jones. These gentlemen are sole executors and guardians to his daughter:—no confidence reposed in the wife. Burke's debts, I fear, will swallow up the whole. Mr. Hogg, the executor, requests that you and Mr. Johnston, or Mr. Diack would, as soon as possible, inform him upon what terms or conditions Burke held the negroes that were purchased under Mrs. Aitcheson's execution. Did Burke purchase for himself, for her, or for whom ? Has he paid ? or what is his estate liable for ? Burke has denied all the negroes but one as his own property. Mr. Hogg is solicitous to know how this matter is circumstanced before he enters on the office of Executor.

Sincerely do I congratulate you upon the finishing stroke being put to the treaty of peace. I am yet, however, not without some apprehensions for the honor and faith of the United States, in carrying the articles of peace into strict and punctual execution. Col. Stephen Moore, who is here from New York immediately, informs us that the sending the negroes from New York to Port ****† is considered by Congress as an infraction of the peace, and will justify an infringement on the part of the States in another respect. The Virginians have seized (Mr. Moore informs us) the favorable occasion, and have passed a law to prevent carrying into execution the article for the payment of British debts. Is it so ? The example will soon pervade this State. Rivington holds his station in New York—Col. Moore assigns the cause of his security. It has come out, as there is now no longer any reason to conceal it, that Rivington has been very useful to Gen. Washington by furnishing him with intelligence. The unusual confidence which the British placed in him, owing in a great measure to his liberal abuse of the Americans, gave him ample opportunities to obtain information, which he has bountifully communicated to our friends. Several others, whom the British considered their devoted friends, have availed themselves of the same kind of merit. A certain *Black Sam* has been thanked for his services by a letter, wrote by Gen. Washington's order.

We have no domestic news here. My family enjoys their usual stock of health—Mr. Hogg's all well, except Mr. Hogg, who continues in the old state. "Entre nous," Betsey Hogg will

† Rominay ? the word is nearly illegible.

probably change her name before you see her—and, for the sake of a pun—and it is the first I ever made—will substitute the food for the animal.* The young gentleman is well known to, and beloved by us both.

I have seen Marmaduke Jones : he is the greatest coxcomb alive. Adieu, my dear Sir ! Pray make the compliments of Mrs. Hooper and her daughter, and mine, acceptable to Mrs. Iredell, and the others of your worthy family.—Accept them yourself, and believe me, Dear Sir,

Ever unalterably and affectionately yours,
WILL. HOOPER.

LETTER FROM SIR N. DUKINFIELD.

SULHAM NEAR READING, Jan. 11, 1784.

MY DEAR IREDELL—With great pleasure I received your letter of the 10th of August, and this pleasure was much enhanced by the friendship you continue for me. Your attention to my mother deserves my thanks much more than that to my interest; and I am very sensible of the part you and Mr. Johnston have taken in standing up as her protectors. Since my marriage I have not enjoyed the idea of Country Quarters, which I did formerly like very well ; but on considering the many inconveniences that might arise to a dear wife, by being worried at times when it might be most desirable to remain quiet, and then probably getting bad accommodations, I have quitted the Service in a manner, viz., have made an exchange with a Captain in the 82d regiment of Foot, which will be reduced as soon as it returns from Nova Scotia, and I shall be on half pay—and no more duty. I have taken a house in Berkshire about six miles from Reading, and am busy getting it furnished as I expect my Kitty will be brought to bed next month. Although you have no children, I hope you are not the less happy I assure you it would have given me no concern, if it had been my case, nor shall it affect my happiness tho' I have ; but I can't help wishing for a very few. As the pasture won't bear a great stock, two or three may live ; but if more, I must begin to look about. As my wife is past 28 and I'm near 38, I am in hopes I shall not have many. When I was last in London I met Mr. Dawson at Mr. Elmsley's twice ; the first time, he had a slight cold, but was better afterwards. I flatter myself with the hope of his company at Sulham, when he can make it convenient to relax from his studies.† I am greatly obliged to you for kindly informing me, by your brother, of my mother's

---

* Miss *Hogg* married Mr. *Huske.*
† W. Dawson of N. C., grandson of Gov. G. Johnston.

ealth. I have received two letters from him—one from Oxford n 1779, and the other in July last. I did not know his situaion in Mr. Crewe's family. I wish he was nearer than Cheshire, hat I might be acquainted with him. I shall write, and acquaint im with my habitation; and write him to see him whenever it nay suit him. I can't imagine how you think I shall come over o Carolina. I said, or meant to have said, that if I had *not* been narried I fully determined to do it; but I hope it will be quite nnecessary for me now, as it would be attended with not only great inconvenience, but distress. I could not leave my dear wife: she is not of the strongest constitution, and therefore I ould not think of resigning her; tho' I know she would venture very thing rather than be left behind—and what is to become of he Picininny? No, my dear friend, I give up all thoughts of isiting Carolina.

In consequence of the friendship I have received from you and Mr. Johnston, I have ordered a power of attorney to be made to ou, which I shall go to town to execute on Tuesday. I have irected it to give you the fullest power, as I have the greatest onfidence, to transact my affairs as you see proper. I wish in the irst case that my mother be taken care of °°° I enclose you wo copies of cases with Mr. Holliday's (a great conveyancer) pinions, which I took before I went to Carolina.°°° I'm setting ut upon a plan of strict economy, and hope to keep within ounds. I have an expectation of increase of my fortune; 'tis at great distance. An estate of near £300 a year is entailed upon e, by Sir Samuel, but there are five lives to depart before I ouch a farthing.°°° I'm most perfectly happy, and much onder of my wife than when I married, tho' married above ten nonths. She is not at all handsome, but what you may call a *devilish good one.* ° ° ° Let your first care be my dear nother, and her happiness your primary consideration. Whatver afterwards can be done for my interest I can have no objecion to. I give no directions, nor do I wish to be consulted upon ny point. My best respects to Mrs. Iredell, Mrs. and Miss Blair, and to Mrs. and Miss Dawson. I fear this destructive war as carried off many young men from the Province, who might ave made good husbands. I never heard whether Miss Peggy Cathcart was married or not.

Some time ago I met with a Captain Kinlock, who had served n Tarleton's Corps; he spoke with great respect of Willie Jones's enteel behavior. Kinlock had got possession of a famous mare f Willie's, which was some time afterward strained in the houlder, upon which Willie sent a card to Kinlock, wishing, as he mare was a favorite, and useless to him, he would return her, and any horse in his stable was at his service. Kinlock told me, he was so much pleased with him that he sent the mare back. Tarleton has, by his imprudent conduct here, lost all the laurels he got in America. His extravagance and folly have been beyond bounds, and his best friends condemn him. "Mais trève de la guerre et des guerriers." Adieu, my dear Iredell, and believe me,
Your much obliged and affectionate friend,
A. DUKINFIELD.

I see by the papers that the 82d is embarked for England, to be disbanded. I shall then have short pay, but no duty but family duty.

PIERCE BUTLER TO IREDELL.
CHARLESTON, February 4th, 1784.

MY DEAR SIR:—I was favored with your very acceptable and obliging letter of the 31st of December, some days ago; by it I learn with exceeding great concern of your indisposition. I ardently hope that the cool weather may have braced you up. I well know the strictest temperance cannot insure health in the sickly place you have fixed on for your residence, otherwise I am sure you would enjoy it. Edenton appeared to me, from its situation—the number of fens of stagnant water—the too little motion of the great body of water in front of the town,—to be more liable to putrid disorders than almost any other spot I ever saw. I often wished some circumstance might turn up to induce you to leave it.

Mrs. Butler and myself are much indebted to you for the warm interest you take in every thing that relates to our welfare and happiness. I thank God she is pretty well recovered. I am sometimes well, sometimes otherwise.

I rejoice, my dear sir, exceedingly, that our sentiments so entirely accord respecting the treatment of the wretched, deluded refugees. *Your sentiments paint in strong colors, that greatness of mind, generosity, and general philanthropy that so eminently distinguish you; and confirms me that I am not a bad reader of mankind. Such as I conceived you, you prove to be—the sincere and warm friend—the generous and forgiving enemy.* I have, for some time, had my apprehensions with you, that honesty and true greatness would have an ardent struggle in America; and much do I fear that the early pages of our history will be sullied by an unbecoming greediness for property,—that property that, as a great and generous people, we should disdain to touch. Here is lately arrived a Dr. Bancroft from France, whom you must have heard of as an appendage of Dr. Franklin.

He is an exceedingly sensible man. I had a visit from him yeserday. He took an early opportunity of assuring me that the haracter of America suffers much in Europe by the persecuting pirit manifested to the miserable refugees, and the too frequent nfringements of the definitive treaty. He says it is inconceivable o a person not present, the effect such conduct has on the differnt courts of Europe. How mortifying! how distressing to hear hat brilliancy of character with which we established our indeendence, so shamefully sullied! Our Legislature have been itting some time, and as yet have shown great liberality respectng those wretched people that went off with the enemy. Numers have already been taken off the confiscation list. *All* are llowed to return, to try to vindicate themselves if they can: so hat none may be condemned unheard. I hope we shall close the ession as we began, with acts of mercy and forgiveness. As an ndividual, I do all in my power to instil into the minds of the ack-country members, that mercy and forgiveness are Godlike irtues. I hope and think we shall restore and establish our creit. I have proposed to the Legislature to negotiate a loan in Europe, and establish a public bank. I think they will agree to my proposal; if they do, I will risk my reputation on it, that we will discharge our Continental and State debt in less than ten ears, and establish our bank on as good a footing as any on earth. A few of the adherents to Robert Morris are against the measure, ecause they think it will take us more out of his power, and essen his consequence here; but I think I shall carry it through. The propriety of the measure will speak for itself. The footing propose to put the bank on, is exactly the same as that of Venice; to keep constantly in bank a large sum in real specie. f your State does not shortly fall on some plan of finance to estore her lost credit, she must suffer much, and the citizens feel great distress.

Mrs. Butler joins in warm and sincere regards to Mrs. Iredell, and the ladies of your family.
Believe me to be, my dear Sir, very truly,
Your affectionate friend,
P. BUTLER.

HOOPER TO IREDELL.
HILLSBOROUGH, 7th February, 1784.

DEAR SIR:—I wrote you, some time ago, by a Mr. Bevan, a arpenter of your town, and inclosed you several letters for my ther friends, in and near Edenton. This I let off at a venture; t goes by way of Halifax, and if it ever hits you, it is to be oted in the chapter of accidents. Mr. Maclaine, in a letter, which I received from him a few days ago, informs me that you are well, and that he has Mr. Johnston's authority for saying so. I sincerely rejoice, as I have not heard a syllable since I left Newbern.

The weather has been severe beyond all experience. I have been so thoroughly frozen that it will require an extraordinary length of summer and sunshine to thaw me. While I now write before a good fire, the ink condenses in my pen, and my hand is so benumbed, that with difficulty I shape my letters. I have received the most extraordinary letter from our client Walker that was ever penned; it is addressed in the usual form, but begins thus: "David Walker to William Hooper;" and after a number of false, frivolous, disingenuous pretences for not sending us his notes according to his promise, he very generously promises not to avail himself of the late regulation made by our Assembly as to lawyers' fees; but will, when we have finished the business, pay according to his first engagement, and then most affectionately subscribe himself my friend. I keep the letter for your perusal, as a first-rate specimen of Virginia genius—formed at Williamsburgh-Alma Mater! and perfected under the auspices of a first-rate Virginia lawyer. I will not answer it until I see you.

Hay's Tiberius Gracchus is here: he has most liberally abused the Newbern Committee, who, in a body, called upon Keith for the author, and threatened that unless he gave him up, he must himself be considered as such, and punished accordingly. Keith's fear prevailed, and Hay was surrendered to their mercy.° Sitgreaves, James Ellis and Ogden, I hear, were delegated to perform this adventurous business. Great, I am told, are the menaces, and "scandalum magnatum" the sin to be atoned for.

"Entre nous," I think Hay's piece appears worse from the press than in manuscript. In the latter, perhaps, I viewed it as a production that was for the perusal only of his intimate friends; but when given to the world, I consider it as intended for an exhibition of parts that bids defiance to censure and criticism. The style is dull; and in many parts ungrammatical. I earnestly wish that for Hay's sake it had "prematur," not only "ad nonum," but "ad nonagesimum annum." Ashe and Hay had a terrible squabble at Wilmington. Ashe, from the Bench, told Hay that his conduct in the Admiralty to the Judge thereof ought to have been answered with a cane; and directed the Attorney General to indict him and Speller for "champerty." Judge how Hay felt: he behaved with becoming temper, and

---
* John Hay, of Fayetteville.

decency; but nourishes, I fancy, a flame in his bosom that will burn furiously when it vents itself.

I have not seen a paper or magazine since I came hither. We hold no more intercourse with the public and political world than if we were no part of it. When opportunity offers, pray send us all you can spare. Inclosed in my former letter were letters for Mr. Johnston, Mr. Dawson, Mr. Pollok, Mr. Allen, and, by accident, a letter for T. Gilchrist. Pray inform them of this, lest the letters should miscarry.

My wife, daughter, and myself, unite in our best acknowledgments and regards to Mrs. Iredell, Mrs. Blair, Miss Blair, Miss Peggy, and the young gentlemen. Accept them yourself, and believe me ever, under all possible circumstances,

Yours truly and affectionately.
WILL. HOOPER.

FEB. 12th, 1784.

MY DEAR SIR:—By accident I have heard that Skinner is in this town: at the same time, I learn that he leaves it immediately. I cannot, however, suffer him to escape without making him the bearer of my most sincere and ardent congratulations to you and Mrs. Iredell upon the happy addition to your family. Mrs. Hooper, and my daughters most cordially sympathize with you in the joyful event; and desire me to assure you of it. May it live to be a lasting blessing to its worthy parents! and be the forerunner, and harbinger of many such causes of rejoicing. Come hither with the dear babe to us. Snatch it from the air of your unhealthy climate; and give it in early life a vigor of constitution that may bear it up against accidents hereafter.

So Penny Dawson has changed her name. Mr. Johnston in his letter to me, says that Lowther would be unconscionable to refuse to be *hanged* ✩ ✩ ✩ Might he not have added damned too?—I mean a temporary damnation. If I had time I would rant a little upon the luscious subject: it sets my old blood afloat with youthful heat, and I find a glow about my heart that such a theme only could excite: but I was early taught, "Thou shalt not covet thy neighbor's—" you know the rest. ✩ ✩ ✩ Pray present my congratulations to the happy pair, and family.

Mr. Hogg's family dined with me yesterday, it being the anniversary of Washington's birth. You occupied much of Mrs. Hogg's thoughts: and, as it is customary among great people to register their toasts upon great occasions, Mrs. Iredell, and the little one, followed close at the heels of our Hero by order of Mrs. Hogg. ✩ ✩ ✩ Lytle has advertised the tract called Nugent's for sale: it holds about seventy families seated upon it: they menace loudly, and the event may, possibly, be another Regulation. In this case I may escape a whipping, as I am, very earnestly, on the side of the tenants, which fortunately is the strongest. Should Strudwick's men take the infection, you may perhaps get a scouring, &c., &c.

WILL. HOOPER.

IREDELL TO REV. A. IREDELL.

EDENTON, Feb. 16th, 1784.

MY DEAR BROTHER:—I had the inexpressible pleasure a few days ago to receive, all at once, three most charming letters from you, which gave me great satisfaction, though of such old date as May, June, and July. A letter of my mother's also, dated in July, accompanied them. They gave me the first intelligence I had received of the manner in which my mother had been supported during the war. How I admire and love the great goodness of my Lord, and Mrs. C. Macartney. God grant it may ever be in my power to express my gratitude to them. My Uncle's goodness also affected me very sensibly. I thank you for your particularity in acquainting me with the cause of his displeasure. *Never could I have dreamt that a man of such Whig family could have thought my conduct inexcusable for adopting principles of resistance, merely because I had taken an oath of allegiance.* Is this any other than the old, idle, exploded doctrine of *Passive Obedience;* and which I dare say my uncle would think very unjustifiably applied by a Jacobite against the Revolution of 1688? But it is not the first instance of the *same principles* serving one party, and not serving another, though there be no other difference but that the passions are "pro" on one side, and "contra" on the other. I have taken your kind advice, and wrote to my uncle on this subject; not, to be sure exactly in this style; but to the same purport, though in a more serious manner; and have assured him that however my *head* erred, my *heart* did not, and that I, in my conscience, thought I was acting right. I thank God, I am not apprehensive of, my dear Arthur, of your censure.

It is impossible for me to say how much I am obliged to you for the kind particularity with which you have wrote upon every subject; I thank you for it with my whole soul. Your situation and prospects (which I think are flattering) please me infinitely. That dear Lady you have been so good as to introduce to me, engages a great deal of my attention, and admiration. I rejoice in your having found such a one, and God grant you may not long be separated. Engage for me her affection as a sister. Your sister also bespeaks an interest in her favor, participating with me in all my anxiety for the happiness of you both. Would to God I could be blest with the sight of you; but cursed poverty and business confine me to this country, so as to deny me so great an indulgence. I wrote you the beginning of January, as also my mother and Tom. I therein proposed Tom's coming immediately to me, if it was approved of, and if he thought he could devote a few years' study to my profession under me; in which case, with proper application, he might be sure hereafter of a very comfortable and independent settlement. I mentioned, that in case this scheme should be approved of, he must entirely quit his station in the army; and that I would wish him, if possible, to sail in the month of April; but that if this was not practicable, that he should leave England so as to be on the American coast the latter end of October or beginning of November, and come to Norfolk in Va., which is about 80 miles hence, and when upon applying to Mr. Alex. Diack, a merchant there, he would meet with all possible assistance to get to me. He could live with me much to my satisfaction and Mrs. Iredell's, who would show him all possible affection, until he was in a way to provide for himself; and in the mean time might render me some useful services, which would more than compensate for the additional expense (which would not be much) of his support. But he must by no means come until he has entirely got rid of the army; and let him leave all his regimentals behind him, as it will require a good while to reconcile the people here to a British officer in uniform.

My letter by Mr. Black contained an epitome of my history during the war, and all at present worth imparting to you; it might be filled up with some episodes of private distress, but as my lot has been better than that of thousands, it would be ungrateful in me to dwell upon it. I have a curiosity to know, if it be not too troublesome, your conversations with Mr. McCulloh, both in regard to yourself and me. *I have long had reason to know him pretty well,* and am extremely concerned that his present unfortunate condition as to this country, obliges me to be upon terms with him, that I might not appear to be wanting in humanity. Except as to his debts, he is altogether at the mercy of this State, for the Treaty of Peace puts it fully in the power of the Assembly to be either rigorous or indulgent.

Let me request you, my dear brother, to write me at least once a month. I will observe the same rule, and have a letter ready, whether I know of an immediate opportunity or not. You can scarcely imagine what delight your letters give me, and it is impossible to express the extreme anxiety of my heart for your welfare. Be good enough to procure for me an interest with all your friends, who must ever be most dearly mine. Mr. Crewe's family, Mr. Kemp, and Mrs. Catharine Macartney have my constant and most anxious wishes for their welfare. I shall do myself the honor to write to Lord Macartney, when I hear of his arrival, and find a good opportunity to England. Mrs. Iredell desires her most affectionate remembrance, and joining in a request of the most respectful compliments to that lovely lad who, I doubt not, is deserving of your admiration, adds her tenderest wishes to those of, my dear brother,

Your extremely affectionate
JAS. IREDELL.

IREDELL TO PIERCE BUTLER.

EDENTON, March 14th, 1784.

MY DEAR SIR:—I received your most friendly and obliging letter of the 4th February a few days ago, with the greatest pleasure. Your kind and generous concerns for me, the recovery of Mrs. Butler, and a sympathy of sentiment which so highly and so strongly flatters me, made me read it with extreme emotion. My ambition has ever directed me, next to the approbation of my own heart, to wish for the esteem of men of sense and virtue. I thank God, I have hitherto been fortunate in that respect, and I am exceedingly happy that so respected and valued an approbation as yours is not withheld from me. *I have long learnt to despise that sort of popularity which is to be gained by flattering the passions of the multitude. It is not only dishonest, but it is weak and impolitic; for one kind of submission makes way for another, and a man must never stop, and so become despicable; or if he is disposed to recover his reputation, he has lost by unworthy sacrifices so much dignity of character, that it is ten to one if he is able to effect it.*

Mr. Johnston and myself have been almost the only persons here who have opposed outrages upon the refugees. The consequence of which conduct was, that we were looked upon by the patrons of violence with a hateful eye; and lately at an election of Assemblymen they openly opposed Mr. Johnston's re-election, although last year he had been courted to serve, and was then against his inclination chosen. His triumph, however, was complete. Though his name was not originally on the list of candidates; though he was absent the whole time, owing to sickness in his family; the utmost pains were taken to defeat him (even by setting up three candidates against him, most, if not all of them unwilling); and his intimate friends suffered all the efforts of his opponents to have vent, yet, when the Poll was closed, he had ery near double the number of votes of any of the others, and in spite of them is now Senator for the County. This, too, although the weather was so bad scarcely any could come in from the country, and the whole opposition came from our town. Other elections that I have heard of have proceeded in the same spirit, which gives me hopes that we may yet be a composed, and respectable, and happy people. Had one of the old members declined as was expected, and I been chosen in his room, I would have served, although it would have been extremely inconvenient to me ; but the circumstance did not take place, and I therefore did not propose myself.

I am very much obliged to you for your information as to Dr. Bancroft, and for your account of your Assembly's proceedings. They certainly do them honor ; and your proposal of the Bank I hope will take effect, being obviously most judicious and useful. I see nothing that can be objected to it in so rich a State as yours. You are fortunate in having a great number of gentlemen of fortune and education to conduct your affairs.

Your observations on the unhealthiness of this town are certainly just. Mr. Johnston and myself, and our families, suffered so severely last year, that we have at present serious thoughts of removing to Hillsborough, a very healthy town in this State in the back country, &c., &c., &c.

JAS. IREDELL.

HOOPER TO IREDELL.

HILLSBOROUGH, March 15th, 1784.

MY DEAR SIR :—With our friend, Capt. Stokes, I set off for Salisbury Court on Saturday last, and proceeded on my journey more than 20 miles, when, from a sudden and prodigious fall of water, the creeks and rivers became impassable. As I was not sanguine in my purpose of attending the Court, I returned ; but having a pressing call thither, upon some private business, thought proper to wait the fall of the waters, and was to proceed when that happened.

I regret this accident the less, as I now can avail myself of an opportunity to write you, which, otherwise, would have passed in my absence.

Our election, which was the most warmly contested of any which has ever happened in this county, has terminated in favor of Gen. Butler and your humble servant for Commoners ; and Major Macaulay for Senator. More than 650 persons voted. I had 100 votes more than Alex. Mebane, and 7 more than Butler. My friends exult at the success ; but I, who have been so

long hackneyed in public business, know too well the levity of the people, and the caprice of popularity to exult much in this momentary preference.

I am anxious to know what has been the event of the Chowan and Edenton elections. Nothing could have induced me to make the sacrifice, which I necessarily must, from the step I have taken, other than a confidence that I should be united with yourself and Mr. Johnston in the business of legislation. I shall very truly regret that I was ever a candidate for this laborious distinction, should I fall short in this expectation. Maclaine will be elected for Wilmington ; and, if he would bring a little temper with him, might be essentially serviceable. Tiberius Gracchus had hopes of being elected for Duplin.*

Judge of my mortification when I inform you that, although I have heard that *Cusatti*, and *Sully*, *The Citizen*, and *The True Citizen*, have stepped forth as combatants in the war, kindled by that redoubtable champion for the Constitution, Atticus ; yet I have seen none of them, except Sully, which Captain Stokes ascribes to Davie ; I believe it to be the performance of Maclaine ; but I judge only from the fire of the composition. Cusatti is said to be Martin, and I suspect it, from the quaintness of the signature. Is there such a name recorded in ancient or modern history ? I believe not. But observe that *Cusatti* is a transposition of all the letters which compose the word *Atticus*, and this may have given rise to the ingenious fiction.† The Citizen, it is said, is the production of a joint committee on Nutbush. All this, however, I have by vague report, and have nothing certain to ground my conjecture upon. I anxiously wish to get a sight of these political squibs ; and if by this, or any other opportunity, you could send me the papers which contain them, or any other papers, you would much oblige me, and your other friends, Hogg, Hall, &c.

Our spring scarcely begins to open upon us ; the extreme severity of the winter has destroyed, as it is apprehended, great part of the wheat in this part of the country, which has already had an effect upon the price of Indian corn, and the wheat of last year.

My family enjoy uninterrupted health. I have scarcely administered a dose of medicine for a twelvemonth past.

I hope in God that you, and yours are well. I have yet hopes that we shall, ere long, be nearer each other, and I shall

---

* Mr. Hay, I suppose.

† " I am longing to see Atticus again. When I was at Fayette, I saw a packet from him to Keith ; but I suspect he will assume a different signature. I was expecting from him some strictures on the Governor's Proclamation. I think the Citizen gives him room for a triumph."—*Letter from James Hogg to Iredell, March* 16, 1784.

---

then be very moderate in my further demands upon Providence. Adieu ! &c., &c.

WILL. HOOPER.

HILLSBOROUGH, March 18th, 1784.

MY DEAR SIR :—Your obliging favor by Cochrane, came to hand yesterday. Previous to the receipt of it I had wrote you, and had committed the letter to the bearer of this. I cannot suffer him to depart, without penning my most grateful acknowledgments to you for the newspapers. They are a feast of the most exquisite kind to us. What a whirlwind has the Judge raised about his ears. Where the devil is he, that the public do not hear again from him ? Never was a better opening than the Citizen has given him, both to support himself, and bestow abuse upon his adversaries.*

Judge Williams passed through this yesterday. Mr. Hogg charged him home with the *Citizen*. He sincerely disclaims, but do not believe him. I suspect that he furnished the materials ; Henderson connected them, and the Prince of Parnassus, Governor Martin, gave them the finishing polish.

I rejoice to hear you and Mr. Johnston talk seriously of coming among us. When I see you, we will cast about for houses to accommodate you.

I delivered your and Miss Nelly's letter to Miss Hogg ; but who will not long remain so. Such is the instinctive appetite of that said animal for *Huske*, that she has consented to sacrifice her very name for it. Alas ! I gave you this pun before ; but am so pleased with my first essay in that way, that I cannot forbear repeating it, &c., &c., &c.

WILL. HOOPER.

IREDELL TO MRS. IREDELL.

ELK-MARSH, March 28th, 1784.

MY DEAR HANNAH : * * * * Mr. Hooper is a member for Orange, and Colonel Ashe, from Cape Fear, says there is no doubt Mr. Maclaine would be chosen for Wilmington. They have begun to print a newspaper at Halifax, which is to be continued weekly. The only one of them I have seen contains instructions from the county of Northampton, in the highest style of moderation, and it seems to be the general sentiment this day, &c., &c.

JAS. IREDELL.

---

* I suppose the reference to be to Judge Ashe, between whom and the Bar existed, about this time, a violent feud. However deficient the Judge may have been in legal learning, the tradition of the profession is, that he got the better of his adversaries. Some very competent judges, who had seen his controversial efforts, have expressed to me great admiration of their vigor and sarcasm. The object of the Bar was to write Ashe off the Bench.

HILLSBOROUGH, April 8th, 1784.

MY DEAR HANNAH : * * * * Scarcely any members are yet arrived. Mr. Huske is not yet married, but expected in two or three days, when the wedding will certainly take place. Preparations are busily making. Your brother seems in earnest about a settlement here ; but there is a difficulty, owing to the want of houses, and of convenience, and workmen to build, &c., &c.

JAS. IREDELL.

REV. A. IREDELL TO MRS. IREDELL.

LONDON, April 9th, 1784.

MY DEAR SISTER : * * * * I have seen much of Mr. Black since my arrival in London ; and, as we have only one subject in conversation, you may, perhaps, give me credit for knowing a great deal about you all on the other side of the Atlantic, and for being, in short, every thing but an American myself. I am quite in love with the life you lead. I was before with the people ; and though the country about you be such a dead flat, as we should call it here, and at times not quite so healthy as might be wished, for the sake of the two first blessings, who would not brave an ague and shiver away a month or two in every year to be happy the rest of it ? No wise man, I am sure. I wish I had any thing to communicate that could possibly interest you ; but politics are the only things talked of here, and ours can no longer be interesting to an American lady, though your statesmen may pry with pleasure into what is " rotten in Denmark." They would find it easy enough. The English, who were always a silly people in politics, are more so than ever. They have been vilifying their best friends in addresses to the Crown ; and they are now as fast as they can returning the avowed advocates of prerogative to the new Parliament. The great contest is at Westminster, where Mr. Fox is a candidate ; it is now going on, and the result of it no one can say, but all are anxiously waiting for it. Will you believe that I am a very active partisan ? I am, I can assure you, and have actually canvassed, not without success. Mr. Black will tell you that he saw me with one of Charles Fox's favors in my hat. That is proof positive. Yet I will give you more. I dined yesterday with a select party of the leaders on that side,—Charles Fox, Sheridan, Hare, Mr. North (Lord North's son), Sir Godfrey Webster, Fitzpatrick, Pigot, one of the Commissioners of Accounts ; Mr. Gunning, a son of Sir Robert's, and a Mr. Dudley ; and I had the satisfaction of seeing Charles Fox scratch off an Address

VOL. II.—7

to the Electors, which will make a flaming appearance in to-day's papers. It is a most excellent one. I went from thence to Mr. Crewe's, where I met with the Duchess of Portland, and some other fine ladies, who were equally ardent, but not quite so able in the business as the party I have named to you, &c., &c.
Most truly and affectionately yours,
A. IREDELL.

SAMUEL JOHNSTON TO IREDELL.

HILLSBOROUGH, April 14th, 1784.

DEAR SIR:—The inclosed papers from Mr. Ruffin, I received after you left this. You will do what is proper with respect to them. I must request the favor of you to forward the inclosed letters to Messrs. Allen & Collins.

Very few of the members have yet come to town. God knows when we shall make a House. The Governor came to town on Monday, a few minutes after Atkins left it, as if by consent. I have seen him, but he has nothing new that I can learn. He had never seen the letter of our members, which accompanied the Treaty; and knows nothing of the copies that were intended for the members (*here*). My brother and his colleagues came in yesterday, and the members from Sullivan County. * * * I begin to be very impatient at being so long idle, though I would pass my time nowhere more agreeably under such circumstances, at so great a distance from my family. Mr. Hooper has carried me all over his plantations and improvements, the situation of which are very delightful, and the soil good, &c., &c.
Yours, affectionately,
SAM. JOHNSTON.

HILLSBOROUGH, April 21st, 1784.

DEAR SIR:—I have only a moment to inform you that the Assembly met on Monday. The Commons chose Mr. Benbury, the Senate, Mr. Caswell, Speaker. The Governor proposed making a speech to them; but they rather chose to receive his communications in a Message, alleging that it would save him trouble. Whenever any thing occurs of consequence to communicate, you may depend on hearing from me if opportunity offers, &c., &c.
SAM. JOHNSTON.

P. S.—Mr. Hooper and all friends here are well: he had all the wedding people, with the Governor, and other company, last night.

From Halifax, April 23d, Mr. Iredell wrote his wife: "My spirits have been a little revived by the sight of a little money, though it would do no great good to any but a very poor man. have received here about £70."

SAMUEL JOHNSTON TO IREDELL.

HILLSBOROUGH, May 1st, 1784.

DEAR SIR:—I have only a few minutes to inform you tha the inclosed should have gone by Gen. Skinner; but he did nc call on me.

The fifth Article of the Treaty has been under the considera tion of both Houses, where it has met with the most illibera reception. They have paid no regard to the recommendations c Congress; and there appears a settled resolution against the res toration of any part of the confiscated property. In arguing Gen. Rutherford denied that Governor Tryon, Governor Martin Mr. McCulloh, or Sir N. Dukinfield were British subjects. despair of doing any good, and heartily wish myself away fror this place. Mr. Hooper supported the recommendations c Congress in the House of Commons with the most masterh eloquence, though without support or success. Poor Maclaine . laid up with the gout. I said every thing that occurred to me Thursday, in the Senate, supported by Willie Jones, who spok very sensibly on the same side; but though there was not a wor of common sense spoken on the other side, they carried it agains us by a great majority. There is a strong party for fixing th seat of Government at Tarborough. They talk of great altera tions in the Court Law; also, of changing the time of holding th annual elections, and Assembly, &c., &c., &c.
SAM. JOHNSTON.

HOOPER TO IREDELL.

May 1st.

MY DEAR SIR:—I thank you a thousand times for your at tention to me and my wants since you left us. The tea cam safely by Mr. Davis: and Mr. Penn has since delivered m your letter inclosing the money. I had been happy to hav heard, with a full assurance of its being true, that your health wa confirmed.

I have waited with impatience for some time that somethin; might occur in our political operations decisive with respect t the temper of the Assembly, and which might be an earnest t you and every good man in the country, that they intended t avail themselves of the present great occasion to establish a na tional character, and to do justice to the treaty of peace. M hopes are at an end! This day has put the matter beyond

controversy: and there is not a phrenzy of misguided political zeal—avarice cloaked in the cover of patriotism—or private passion and prejudice, under the pretence of revenging the wrongs of the country—let these be carried to what excess they will —that can give me the least surprise hereafter.

The inclosed resolves, which (supposing they would afford you some satisfaction) I have had copied, are the result of the labors of a committee where Mr. Johnston, Maclaine, and myself, worked for many days. Every resolve but the 5th passed, almost "*nem. con.*" yesterday in the Commons; but that, in spite of every thing I could do—and alas! I labored without support—not a speaker with me but Cummings, *whose conduct does him honor,* (Mr. Maclaine being ill with the gout)—was rejected, scarce 20 of 80 for it. It fared worse in the Senate. *Mr. Johnston spoke longer, with less hesitation, more firmness; and as much sound solid reasoning as I ever heard him or any other man.* Willie Jones stept forward in a very becoming manner—their labor was lost! Griffith Rutherford called the objects of the recommendatory clause *Imps of Hell.* The vote was called, and not ten in favor of the clause of the report which applies to the recommendatory article of the treaty. We are here in the dumps—doubtful of doing any good.

Although the Quakers are at my elbow, urging me to finish; yet I must inform you that in a letter, which appears in the public collection, from Dr. Williamsom, there is a passage to this purpose, and nearly in these words. "On the last summer, Mr. Henry E. McCulloh wrote to us: he seemed to be pretty well satisfied that his property would be restored to him; we were, perhaps, pretty well satisfied before that it would not be restored to him." This, be assured, has had its effect.

Any thing in this letter that you may think proper to communicate to Mr. Barker, please inform him is at my desire. Remember me to Mr. Spencer; and do so to him also, assuring him at the same time that I will embrace the first opportunity to write. The Quakers had promised to wait until Monday: they disappoint us. I fear the session will hold till 1st of January. Expect a long letter from me by next opportunity. This family, my dear Iredell, hold you among their own first affections. Remember us to your worthy Mrs. Iredell, and the rest of the good family. I am ever yours, affectionately,
WILL. HOOPER.

SAMUEL JOHNSTON TO MRS. IREDELL.

HILLSBOROUGH, May 15th, 1784.

MY DEAR HANNAH:—* * * * I repent sincerely my having any thing to do with the Assembly. I lose much more to myself than I gain to the public. The most illiberal dispositions preva in most of the members: they seem determined to hold on upo the confiscated property. I don't believe McCulloh will get bac a single acre; *but of this say nothing,* &c., &c.
Yours, affectionately,
SAM. JOHNSTON.

In a letter from New Berne, dated May 20th, Mr. Irede wrote his wife—"I have my *landlady and her daughter,* all t myself; Hay having deserted for the present the Newbern re sentment (though I don't know that he did it designedly), by trip to the Assembly."

IREDELL TO THOMAS IREDELL, (his uncle.)

EDENTON, May 28, 1784.

MY DEAR AND HONORED SIR:—I have wrote you severa letters within these few months; but have not yet been happ enough to receive any from you, which I am very anxious to de remembering with great gratitude and pleasure the satisfaction derived from the correspondence you honored me with before th war; and earnestly wishing a renewal of it. I begin to receiv letters now and then from my mother and Arthur, though I fin many have miscarried; and I am willing to hope the sam cause may have prevented my having the pleasure to hear fror you. My situation in this country is almost as good as I could wisl my attention being entirely devoted to the profession of the law which is altogether suitable to my inclination, and my success i it equal to that of any lawyer here. It is, however, in this coun try a very laborious one; and has already so much affected my health, that I have been obliged to contract my circuit; bu thank God, if I have life and health, I have a very fair prospec of gaining an independent and genteel competency by it, thoug there is no such thing as a large fortune to be expected, or eve for a great number of years a cessation from severe business an fatigue. During the war my situation was distressing; but th effect it had on my circumstances, I hope now to get over; an have, indeed, little reason to complain, when my lot was so muc better than that of thousands. I was extremely glad to find, b a late letter from my brother, that in consequence of your advic he was likely to change his profession; and that you appeared t prefer that of the law for him. I had myself been persuaded that that in all probability would be a better one, as in his pres ent situation he is altogether dependent on others; and I ar satisfied he possesses abilities and application, accompanied wit an uncommon goodness of heart, that qualify him for any thing

Indeed I admire and love him with an extraordinary fervor of affection; and I see your kindness and attention to him, of which he speaks in high terms, with the greatest pleasure. I hope he will be enabled by it to chalk out a path of distinction and honor, in which, I flatter myself he will one day acquire fame, and reflect, as I am sure there is great reason to expect, lustre on a family of which he is so great an ornament.

I informed you, that upon reflection I had thought it best to give Tom an invitation to come and live with me, as the army was a dangerous situation for him, and he was a burthen to my mother. I do not find that he has any vices; but the gaiety of his disposition, indulged too much by a military life, has led him into imprudent expenses, which are too naturally to be expected from a young man in his situation, and who unfortunately has had a very slender education. If I can possibly induce him to apply to my profession he may do very well here: but I fear I shall be very much at a loss what to do with him. I have given my mother an invitation to come and live with me also, which I hope she will do, so that I flatter myself for the future the situation of our family will not be so marked with misfortunes as it has been for so many years. My resources I trust will be sufficient if my life and health be spared to me, the latter of which has for many months been extremely bad, but is now beginning to recover.

I hope I have sufficiently obviated in my former letter the cause of your displeasure against me, on account of my taking part with the Americans. Lest any of those letters should have miscarried, I will just again say, that I took no open part till long after the exercise of my office and all British power was impracticable; that however mistaken I might be, I really acted from *principle*, and conceived I had as good a right to vindicate American privileges, of which I was entitled to partake, as any man in the country; that the part I took being cordially *disinterested*, my sincerity is not reasonably to be doubted, and a man is only answerable for the errors of his heart, not of his understanding; and that the mere circumstance of my being an officer of the Crown, and having taken an oath of allegiance, when the office could not be exercised, and the claims of Great Britain appeared subversive of American rights (as I really thought them), no more precluded me from taking an active part, than such considerations prevented many of the greatest and best men at the Revolution in England taking a most decisive part against James the Second. You and I differ in the application; but I am persuaded we agree in the principles; and as in making the application I could only exercise my own judgment, so I can truly say I did it *deliberately, disinterestedly*, and *honestly:* and I hope I shall be excused for adding, that I have frequently rejoiced since I did not do as many others did, to be a despicable dependent upon a Court Pension, and to be disabled, perhaps, for any respectable, independent situation in life. As opportunities may offer very rarely here, I beg the favor of you at other times when you may have the goodness to write to me, to direct your letters to the care of Mr. Alex. Diack, merchant, in Norfolk; or Wm. Landing, merchant, in Charleston, &c., &c.

Your most dutiful and affectionate nephew,

JAS. IREDELL.

IREDELL TO H. E. McCULLOH.

EDENTON, June 15th, 1784.

DEAR SIR:— * * * I have the great concern to inform you that your petition has been presented, and rejected; and in such a manner, and by so great a majority that I am persuaded all further application would be fruitless: scarcely any persons of any consequence supported it, as I am informed, but Mr. Johnston, Mr. Hooper, Mr. Willie Jones, and B. McCulloh. The latter can give you more particular information as he was on the spot: mine principally respects the Senate where Mr. Johnston sat. He and Mr. Jones in that House, and Mr. Hooper in the other, supported your cause, and that of others in similar circumstances warmly; but without other effect than a great diminution of their influence and popularity. * * * Mr. Nash was at the head of the large majority who opposed any compliance with the Recommendatory Article; and he also opposed, and with success, the removal of obstacles to the bringing suits according to the fourth. The preamble, however, stated it as only doubtful whether such an act was necessary. I should hope the next session of Assembly would provide for this; but have already seen such a torrent of illiberality, and disregard of public faith prevail, that I think it is to be questioned. In the act proposed for selling confiscated estates, there was even included a provision for the recovery of the *debts* that had been confiscated, for the use of the public, though there can be little doubt I think, but that these, as well as other debts, come within the provision of the 4th article of the Treaty. * * * As to my appearing *professionally*, though that might have done in England where reason upon the subject of policy, in the midst of the most violent passions, can be heard, it would have been considered rather with ridicule here; for I conceive there was no point belonging peculiarly to my profession to speak to, as the subject of the Recommendatory Article appears to me to be altogether at the mercy of the different Assemblies; and any thing that could be said in favor of it from principles of policy, or natural or political justice, would come with much greater propriety and effect from disinterested Members of Assembly acting in the express line of their duty, than from an avowed advocate of a particular individual they were by no means inclined to favor, addressing prejudiced minds in an unusual manner. * * * A great object among my particular friends at the Assembly was such an alteration of the time of its annual meeting as would have enabled the lawyers who practise at the Superior Court to attend it. An alteration was made, but not so as to promote this purpose in any respect, for the only difference is that, instead of the first Monday in April, it is now to meet the first Monday in October, which interferes exactly in the same manner with the Courts as before, only at a different season. There is to be a new election in August, and I could easily be a member; but it is not in my power to be present under any circumstances at the time it would be held (the 1st Monday in Oct.) at Newbern, the place where it is next to sit, as I am under an indispensable necessity, which no consideration but absolute incapacity by ill health can change, of being employed the whole month of October, and till near the middle of November, at Halifax, Hillsborough and Edenton Courts, where there are such arrears of business as will not admit, without the greatest room for censure, and the most distressing inconvenience, and some injustice to individuals, of any further and voluntary delay, &c., &c.

JAS. IREDELL.

IREDELL TO A. NEILSON.*

EDENTON, N. C., June 15th, 1784.

DEAR SIR:—I had not the pleasure to receive your letter of the 6th October last, until long after the date; but should have acknowledged the kindness of it much sooner, if I had not been prevented by my ill health, and frequent absence from home upon an extensive circuit of courts, to which now I devote my whole attention. It gave me great satisfaction to hear of you after so long an interval, and I shall engage with much pleasure in a renewal of our correspondence. I flattered myself indeed, after the peace had taken place, there might have been an unreserved communication between old friends, however separated by the war or political sentiments; but the extreme violent spirit that has been excited against the Refugees indiscriminately, on account of the particular ill conduct of some, forbids, without great danger, the return of any who left the country after the war began. Some persons, who were not remarkably obnoxious, have tried it, and suffered by it, in spite of every effort of their friends; and Mr. Johnston and myself in particular, for discountenancing such violence have lost, in this part of the country at least, much of our weight and influence. It is to be hoped this intemperate spirit will subside by degrees; but I am persuaded it will be a long time before any persons, how respectable in private character soever, who are supposed to have taken any part in the war against America, can find that cordiality of reception among people in general in the country, without which, no gentleman, who valued his peace of mind, would wish to appear in it. This is very painful for me to feel or to write; but I think it my duty to be explicit on the subject, lest for want of knowing the temper of the people, you might be unexpectedly drawn into any disagreeable situation, as I have unavailingly had the misfortune to see others, for whom I had a very sincere regard.

My own sentiments upon the subject, I hope at the same time you will do me the justice to believe, remain unaltered; *that no man is either good or bad, merely for his opinions; that in political questions there is room for an almost infinite diversity of sentiment, among even the wise, as well as men of little understanding; and that no man in a civil war is justly censurable for any thing but insincerity in choosing his side, or infidelity in adhering to it, or in the course of his political conduct, deviating in any instance from principles of humanity and virtue.* And I heartily wish that the termination of the war could have been followed with an oblivion of its offences, though I cannot but observe, that it was conducted, in some respects, in such a manner as too naturally to cause a deep and lasting resentment in many who have particularly suffered by it.

This town flourished during the war, but has been very dull and inconsequential since. That amusing study, the Law, is my principal employment. I make a circuit twice a year, from Hillsborough, by way of Halifax and this town, to Newbern. A county court or two forms an episode, and this is my whole present history.

Are you a *Foxite* or a *Pittite?* for I suppose no man is allowed to remain neuter, nor is the thing possible. Scotland, we hear too, is putting in her claims for a little more liberty, so that I imagine very soon, the whole three kingdoms will be in a flame. Has not all this been kindled by the American spark, &c., &c.?

JAS. IREDELL.

HOOPER TO IREDELL.

HILLSBOROUGH, July 8th, 1784.

MY DEAR SIR:—Should this scrawl pursue the direction in which I let it off, it may possibly strike Edenton; but, like the

---

* A Refugee, the friend of the Royal Governor, Martin, &c.,—vid. vol. 1.

air-balloon, its progress, I fear, will be eccentric, so that it is in the chapter of contingencies when or whether ever it will reach you. Its manner of travelling is not very honorable, as it has taken its passage in a common cart to Halifax; but the scandal is much alleviated by its having the public records for its companions. I have consigned it to the care of Hans Bond, at Halifax. And now, having given you the history of its intended movements, it is necessary that I should come at the subject matter of it.

Know then, that the return of Mr. Alfred Moore has relieved us from much anxiety on the score of your health. When you left this, I considered it as by no means established against the influence of the air of the lower country; and I was too well acquainted with your devotion to study and business, to imagine that you would be disposed to give yourself the indulgence which your delicate habit of body so well deserves of you, and so pressingly demands, after the severe shock which it has so lately met with. Mr. Moore informs us, that though you were better than when you left this, yet, that you were not perfectly well. Let me entreat of you not to stop short of the latter; but with unremitting care and attention follow up the prescriptions which heretofore have proved so beneficial to you. Give me leave to hope that we may have the pleasure of seeing you and Mrs. Iredell with us in the course of the summer. Sure I am that the jaunt and change of air will do you both good, and you would make this family truly happy. You know our accommodations, and have experienced our homely fair; such as they are, they are yours, with a most hearty welcome;—to your horses, I will promise to send them back full and fat;—to yourself and Mrs. Iredell, what Edenton cannot give, an exemption from the fever and ague.

My family enjoys uninterrupted health. I had hopes from several conversations which I had with Mr. S. Johnston, upon his first arrival here, and while it was yet probable that Hillsborough might be the seat of government, that he would fix, at least, an occasional residence in or near this town. When the Assembly had resolved upon a flight to Newbern, I thought he became more indifferent about the change he had premeditated. Frequent indisposition, while here, arising from constant attention to business; the agitation of mind, and disappointment which accompanied it, and the want of the many conveniences which he left at home, have, I very much fear, banished every intention he had of becoming a citizen of this western world. I do not, however, yet despair; and have accordingly wrote to Pennsylvania concerning a tract of land, which Mr. Johnston has seen, and very much approves. Should the man close with the term I have offered, the land is mine—that is, Mr. Johnston's, if h chooses it upon the same terms. It will perfectly accommodat both you and him; and in the neighborhood may be had tw small pieces of land, with houses on them, which, with very littl attention, may answer the purpose of both families, until yo think proper to build upon a larger scale. The distance only thre miles from the town. What say you to this? Do not be per emptory in refusal. Let me at least enjoy the delusion for while, for it is essential to my happiness.

Mr. Johnston has given you the history of the session, whic will be a catalogue of blunders and disappointments. The poli tical phrenzy ran high, beyond any thing that I had foreseen Those obnoxious men, the lawyers, prevented some mischief bein done. But for them, we should have been saddled with som Acts of Assembly, that would have marked the annals of thi country with an infamy that no time or atonement could hav wiped away. A Court of Chancery, with ———— for a judge unlimited jurisdiction to County Courts; a law continuing con fiscation, and directly violating the treaty of peace. These ar a small part of the evils which died abortions, and owe their ex tinction to the men whom scoundrels reprobate.

I have absolutely refused to serve in the Assembly again Butler doubts. At the close of the session his and my conduc were severely animadverted upon by a few fools in the county for having patronized the cession bill,*—wretches, stimulated t it by that prince of fops and fools, A. M., whose conduct, M Johnston will inform you, was highly singular and unbecomin while the bill was in agitation.† To Mr. Johnston he wrote a apology, and called upon me before he left town, expressing grea contrition, declaring that his heat was aimed at N———h‡, an not at any of the company; and that he had played double,— promised him to vote for the bill, and then duped him. M Johnston will give you the particulars of this diverting "fracas. All clamor here is at an end, and Butler and I may go if w choose. *The people only want information to do right.*

Mr. Hogg has been at Fayetteville many weeks. I miss hi much, as I have not a single male in town with whom I ca converse. And the ladies, God bless them, like partridges an other very delicate food, one cannot feed upon them always— little bacon and greens now and then, by way of solids, makes pleasing variety. Huske left a few days ago. He and Bets

---
* Bill for the cession of Western lands to the United States.
† Alexander Mebane
‡ Nash.

---

were destined for each other, surely;—"Happy, if aught's happy here on earth." He returns this month to his better half. Mrs. Hogg is at the Springs, trying their influence. I have very little hopes from them.* Hope, however, is a sovereign balsam, and she has a large portion of it.

Let Mr. Johnston know that Mrs. McCarroll enjoys her usual health and spirits; and the widow B., like the sun, which for some time has been under a cloud, begins to beam forth in meridian lustre.† The small specks of black which appear upon her, like spots upon that luminary, serve to beautify what is uncovered. She looks as if she was disposed to make a second hazard, and trust to Providence for the event. Oh, the poor dear Doctor! But it is not in flesh and blood to weep for ever; and every one who has tried it, knows that a living husband is warmer than a dead one; and as the saying is, a live dog is better than a dead lion. If you have any thing about your town that could administer comfort to Mrs. McC., it would be charity to help her. She is, as our Haw-fielders here have it, *upon sufferance.*

We talk of a post from Halifax hither; as soon as it takes place, you cannot want opportunities to us. In the mean time, write as occasion offers to Hans Bond. We hear from Halifax, generally, once in a fortnight.

We are happily relieved from an insect which threatened destruction to all the grain in the country. The wheat and oats are greatly injured, but the Indian corn will escape them, &c., &c.

WILL. HOOPER.

Sir N. Dukinfield to Iredell.

Sulham, near Reading, Sept. 7, 1784.

Dear Sir :—A few days ago I was favored with a letter from your brother, with an account of your being well, and that Mrs. Iredell, in the gossiping style, was * * * . As this is a matter which will give you much happiness, I do with sincere pleasure congratulate you. If I go on as I have begun, this kingdom will soon recover the loss it has suffered by the late damned war, and will be in as great a state of population as at its commencement, for my wife is now * * * . My boy is a charming child, and I have no doubt you will soon have a like opinion of your own. 'Tis not known but to a parent, the pleasure there is in their little crows and attempts to talk and scold. I shall expect an early account of your produce. Lady D. joins in sincerest wishes for Mrs. Iredell.

---
* Mr. John Hogg, of Wilmington (the brother of Mr. James Hogg, of Hillsborough), inclosed with a ditch a tract of land adjoining Wilmington, on the north, intending to establish a market garden. The place has ever since been known as "Hogg's Folly."
† Mrs. Gov. Burke.

You will not be surprised at my being desirous that the plan tation should be sold, and the money secured for my use after m mother's death, as I have entirely given up all thoughts of set tling in Carolina; and should I have a large family it will b necessary, in order to keep the younger ones from being carpen ters and mantuamakers, &c., &c.

N. DUKINFIELD.

Rev. A. Iredell to Iredell.

Crewe Hall, Sept. 7th, 1784.

* * * We have lately had very fine folks indeed here,—th Duke and Duchess of Portland,* and Lord and Lady Clermont They left yesterday, and Crewe is now quiet and comfortable a ever. The Duke is a very good kind of man, well bred, and wit a reserve in his manner that, I think, becomes him, though i borders upon shyness. The Duchess, who, you know, is a Caven dish, has all the amiable qualities peculiar to that family, and is upon the whole, a charming woman. But I must not expatiate upon them, or say any thing of the rest, unless indeed to tel you that Lord Clermont, who is just come from Ireland, say the disturbances there are by no means so alarming as we ar taught to believe on this side of the channel, &c., &c.,

A. IREDELL.

Mr. Iredell had sent George McCulloh to London; he though the lad had talent and virtue, and trusted that his presence woul kindle a proper affection in the cold breast of his father, or a least induce a sense of shame for neglect, that would lead to th boy's education, and the promotion of his happiness. Henry E McCulloh, in a letter, dated September 10th, says: " I confes the sudden and unexpected arrival of George startled me a goo deal." He promised to send him to school for one year, and ther proposed that Mr. Iredell should take him as an articled clerk, proposal which was promptly declined. "Did he bear my nam in Carolina?"—is the inquiry, full of anxiety and alarm, of one who, however despotic, was not insensible to the opinion of th world. Verily "our vices come home to roost."

Iredell to Henry E. McCulloh.

Edenton, September 26th, 1784.

Dear Sir : * * * * Had my brother been fortunatel not too old, I certainly should have preferred placing him at som

---
* William Henry, third Duke, succeeded the Marquis of Rockingham as th acknowledged leader of the Whigs.—*Wraxal.*

school in England to having him with me, which is now his only resource,—the forbearance so long of the payment of any part of Miss Macartney's legacy to him * (contrary, as I am informed, to her intention expressed in her will), having made him lose, in a manner never to be atoned for, the best part of his youth. * * *

I formerly acquainted you, that there had been no laws passed here since the Peace in regard to *British Debts*, and that it was the opinion of many, and which had appeared to have the sanction of the Legislature, *that such Debts as were confiscated of Persons named*—so that no future process was necessary to ascertain them as objects of confiscation (which the Treaty would not allow)—stood upon the same footing as *other confiscated property;* that this construction was founded upon comparing the 4th and 5th Articles together, the latter appearing to consider all confiscated properties whatsoever as objects of recommendation only, and the 4th providing for such debts as either never had been confiscated at all, or belonged to British subjects unnamed, and of course protected from any future process. Though I doubt much if this be a just, and I am sure it is a very ungenerous construction of the Treaty ; yet great pains have been, and will be taken to inculcate it, and I fear greatly it will have a legislative sanction. Should this be the case, you may imagine the state of your debts, and in the mean time your chance of receiving payment of any.

My brother not being able to bring his trunk with him when he came, I have not yet received your power ; and permit me to say that it is not at all suitable to me to accept it ; for if your debts are to be collected, the principal scene will be the back-country, far out of my way ; I have long, a great deal too long, experienced the impossibility of satisfying you for any length of time. Your proneness to suspicion, which broke out on numberless occasions before the war, *and I find could not be restrained, in the midst of all my distress during the course of it,* makes it equally unworthy of me, and unavailing to you, to continue in a course which would subject me to indignity whenever you happened to be out of humor, and would be of little advantage to you when your business was conducted by a man irritated by a sense of ill-treatment, and therefore wanting that cordiality of attachment (I honestly confess it) which I once felt, and should have ever felt, had your conduct been as uniform as my own. What you said of me about your son has not been told me by my brother ; I have in vain applied to him for the particulars, which convinces me it must have been unpardonably offensive, though I had advanced money for him when I had scarcely enough to purchase myself bread, and put him in a way of life,

* McCulloh was Miss McCartney's executor.

from necessity, not choice, which was pursued by the sons of many gentlemen in this country full as good as yourself. You are, therefore, not to be surprised that this circumstance, in addition to many others which your recollection can save me the trouble of recapitulating (particularly your treatment of my mother, *which no length of time can efface from my memory*), has determined me to circumscribe my future connection with you within as short a compass as possible ; and that I will not, under any circumstances, agree to be your general agent, nor engage for any thing more than to render you what services I can (which in the present situation of things, God knows, promise to be very little) until another appointment can take place. If my opportunity of serving you has not been equal to my wishes, I can truly say my endeavors have been always faithful and sincere ; and so far from being directed by any interested views, that had your property in this country been equal to what it formerly was, I should have spoken in this language much sooner. The present occasion rendered explicitness unavoidable, and I heartily wish you may find in any future connection of the same kind more ability and success than you have found in me. My heart wishes you no ill ; but, I thank God, it is incapable of disguise, or pretending to an attachment which I do not feel.

You will oblige me in remembering me to George ; and acquainting him that I have received his kind letter, which I would have answered but for the increase of the postage.

Your obedient servant,
JAS. IREDELL.

IREDELL TO MRS. IREDELL.

EDEN HOUSE, Oct. 15th, 1784.

MY DEAREST HANNAH :—We got here a little after sunset yesterday evening, and had a very pleasant passage ; but I was much mortified after I left you in finding we had to cross the creek, and that the canoe was not immediately ready ; for had I known this, I could have staid with you at least a quarter of an hour longer, which, short as it would have been, would have been more satisfactory than being precipitated away in the abrupt and painful manner I was. Believe me, my dear Hannah, nothing can exceed the extreme anxiety I feel for you ; and think of me, though separated, as sympathizing every moment in the severity and hardship of your situation, though at the same time grateful, highly grateful indeed, for your own recovery. The enjoyments of life are fleeting and transitory ; so continually dashed with disappointment and distress, that, perhaps, upon our dear

little infant's own account, we have reason to be satisfied with so sudden and shocking a removal from us. He is gone to enjoy happiness without going through the usual gradations of misery ; and I trust, in the goodness of God, that though we were denied the blessing of his society in this world, we may be blest with it in another, and better. God grant, my dear Hannah, I may have the happiness to find you, on my return, a great deal better. I assure you I will take all possible care of myself, and endeavor by every means in my power to make the continuance of a life so valuable, and necessary to me, as agreeable as possible to yourself. I shall depend upon my brother writing by all opportunities. I will not fail on my part. Adieu ! my dear Hannah. God bless you and speedily restore your health.

With inexpressible anxiety and affection, ever yours,
JAS. IREDELL.

HALIFAX, Oct. 19th, 1784.

MY DEAREST HANNAH :—I wrote you a line last night by Medici. * * * Your brother and I both lodge very comfortably at Mr. Bond's. Mr. Hooper came two days before us and is quite well. * * * There has been the most shocking mortality among the children here ever known. Willie Jones has lost two, Dr. Pasteur one ; and Mr. Gilmore, W. Montford, and Col. Davie, their only ones. Most of them died suddenly, with fits. Geddy in the course of a fortnight lost his wife, two of his children, and a grandchild ; *and the day his wife was buried* (whose funeral he attended) dined abroad and invited company to sup with him. Did you ever hear of such a brute ? Willie Jones is very sick himself ; and almost distracted with the loss of his children. Good God ! my dear Hannah, how melancholy are these things, and how dreadful (for it is ever present to my memory) is our share in them ! To lose, too, our dear little creature in the manner we did. Do what I can, I cannot be sufficiently composed. A momentary gleam of cheerfulness is succeeded by the most bitter reflection. Oh ! how I shall ever cherish the two days when the dear little boy was spared to us ; at which I too little regarded at the time, being the most distant that any man could possibly be from the apprehension of what followed. But God grant ! my dearest Hannah, though you cannot forget it, and I cannot wish you to forget it, you may think of me, and how necessary your health and tolerable peace of mind are to me, who live now only in the hope of enjoying all possible satisfaction in your society, &c., &c.

I am ever your most affectionate,
JAS. IREDELL.

HALIFAX, Oct. 24th, 1784.*

MY DEAREST HANNAH :—I had once the fairest prospects of being now on my way to you, instead of writing you a letter ; *but the scandalous dilatoriness of the Judges, and their indifference about the trial of causes, has occasioned the necessity of our meeting again to-morrow, and possibly also on Tuesday.* My mind was greatly relieved, and indeed made very happy, by the receipt of your charming letter by Medici. Thank God ! for his goodness in restoring you so fast, a blessing I must continually think of when the memory of our dear little boy affects me, as it often does, very severely. The loss was dreadful in itself ; but the manner and circumstances of it such as I cannot bear to recollect. Good God ! what happiness this shocking incident has deprived us of ! I can too well sympathize with other melancholy sufferers in the same way ; and feel greatly for poor Silas Cooke, and his wife. The daughter they lost was a remarkably fine and healthy one. I am glad Mrs. Cabarrus bears her loss so well. Though now, undoubtedly, it must be very painful, her good sense must, every day, more and more reconcile her to it. I heartily rejoice in Mr. and Mrs. Pollok's good fortune, &c., &c.

JAS. IREDELL.

NEWBERN, Nov. 18th, 1784.

MY DEAR HANNAH :—We arrived here only yesterday morning, having proceeded along with great moderation, going no farther than Dr. Lenox's, on Sunday, for fear of the low grounds of Skewawky, and making very easy journeys afterwards. * * * We have very good accommodations, all three living in one large room at Mrs. Caruthers's, and a bed for each of us. * * * We are in the midst of politicians ; but find nothing is yet certainly concluded. The repeal of the Cession Bill to Congress, is likely to pass—I mean the Bill for the Cession of the Western lands. But there will be, I believe, no alteration about the Courts. Mr. Nash had a majority of 30 against him in the vote for Governor.†

I have scarcely had a minute to spare since I came here. As usual, a great deal of business, &c., &c. JAS. IREDELL.

* Newbern, Oct. 22d. "General Green has been here confoundedly frightened on account of Bank's death. The General has been security for that man to the amount of £60,000 st. : it was always suspected that the General was in partnership with that gentleman ; and that the money that was sent on to pay the Continental officers and soldiers, was given to Banks to pay for part of the purchase made at Charlestown. Should this appear to be true, as many think it will, the General will lose a great share of the good character he has maintained in the eyes of the world." Letter from Michael Payne, member of the Commons from Chowan, to Iredell.

† Caswell was elected for the second time.

VOL. II—8

NEWBERN, Nov. 20th, '84.

MY DEAR HANNAH:—I had great pleasure in receiving your kind letter by the Post; and having such favorable accounts of your, and the family's health; and the cheerfulness of the two eternal opponents, who seem always quarrelling, but when in a private "tête-à-tête." * * * My cold, which was really a bad one, is fast wearing away, owing to my prudence in abstaining from Court a whole day, in spite of a thousand teasing solicitations. The consequence is, I am now in a condition to bear, and comply with them.

This evening came on the election of public officers: they are as follows, (the number not yet being quite complete, 1 Delegate and 3 Councillors being still to be chosen):

Delegates—William Blount, John Sitgreaves, Timothy Bloodworth, Adlai Osborne, and Charles Johnson—their time to begin next November—Spaight left out, because after that time there was but a little while he could serve.

Councillors—Colonel Leach, Jonathan Hawks,—Armstrong and James Kenan.

Treasurer—Memucan Hunt, (for the whole State.)

Comptroller—Francis Child.

Mr. Nash was put in nomination for Delegate, and *not chosen*. The repeal of the law ceding Western lands, has passed. I think of no other of importance yet passed. The Assembly will certainly, I believe, break up next week; and to dispatch business disgracefully will meet to-morrow, &c., &c.

JAS. IREDELL.

REV. A. IREDELL TO IREDELL.

NOVEMBER 27th.

* * * * * I have neither time nor matter to amuse you with political information. A rupture between the Dutch and the Emperor is the grand, if not the only topic of the day; and of that you will hear fully from other, and better authority. Our domestic situation is just as it was. Pitt continues first Minister with the same Cabinet that he set out with; though arrangements are every day talked of, and must sooner or later take place, if he retains his post, as there is indubitably a want of harmony in the Cabinet. Lord Camden, your favorite, (though by the way a shabby *politician*,) and the Duke of Grafton, are persons talked of for office, &c., &c.

A. IREDELL.

CHAPTER XVIII.

ÆT. 33—34.

INTRODUCTION. LETTERS FROM IREDELL, HOOPER, REV. A. IREDELL, A. MACLAINE, R. D. SPAIGHT, H. E. M'CULLOH, SIR N. DUKINFIELD, T. LOWTHER, DR. CUTLER, AND MISS BLAIR.

THE years that intervened between the close of the war, and the Convention at Philadelphia, in May, 1787, have been hurriedly treated of by most American writers: they were marked by few striking incidents, that could be easily woven into stirring narratives: they possessed few salient features that could be wrought into glowing pictures. A period of transition, the early manhood of a nation, just emancipated from parental control, it is nevertheless fraught with profound interest to the historical student. Then it was that the organizations, heated and fused by the fires of the Revolution, began to crystallize into forms of utility and beauty. The brains of men, stimulated into abnormal activity teemed with theories, thick, and multiform as the vegetation of the tropics. In the speculations, the discussions the legislation, and the inchoate enterprises of that era, are to be traced the germs of national character, and national power; from the chaos of conflicting ideas good was educed; and progress without a parallel in the history of the world, became the law of the Union. As regards North Carolina, no adventurous pioneer has as yet attempted to trace the path of her history: the acts and journals of the Assembly afford but an imperfect light. I shall not essay with untutored step to thread the wilderness where the bark is rapidly closing over the incisions made by stalwart arms; but shall content myself with affording the reader such glimpses of political amities, and enmities, of social and domestic life, as the correspondence of Mr. Iredell supplies. From the letters I transcribe exhales the spirit of the age.

The Assembly convened at New Berne on the 19th day of November; and adjourned December the 29th. That our legislators had an enlightened sense of intellectual culture, and pur-

suits, is evinced by an act for securing literary property. The preamble is as follows:—" Whereas nothing is more strictly a man's own than the fruit of his study, and it is proper that men should be encouraged to pursue useful knowledge by the hope of reward; and as the security of literary property must greatly tend to encourage genius, to promote useful discoveries, and to the general extension of arts and commerce: Be it enacted, &c." The benefits of the act were generously extended to all the citizens of the confederated States. It was provided, in case the author should demand too high a sum for his work, that the Supreme Court, on complaint of two or more persons, should have authority to correct or settle the price. Contrary to the precepts of political economy, at war with the general tenor of the act, and sordidly mean, the clause can only be explained by the supposition that the Legislature participated in the, now obsolete, notions of those who advocated assizes of bread, and penalties for forestallers and regrators, &c.*

On the 22d of December, 1785, Mr. and Mrs. Iredell were blessed by the birth of a daughter, whom they named Annie Isabella.

IREDELL TO H. E. McCULLOH.

EDENTON, N. C., Jan. 6th, 1785.

DEAR SIR:—I have now the misfortune to acquaint you, that another petition for you has been presented, and rejected; and that a law has passed for the immediate sale of all the remaining confiscated property. The petition was in the name of B. McCulloh, and strongly supported by Mr. Nash, notwithstanding which, after some promising appearances of success, it was rejected by a considerable majority. Had it passed the House, it most probably would have been rejected in the Senate, where a clause that had been inserted and sent from the Commons in favor of Bridgen and Waller, at the express recommendation of Dr. Franklin, was thrown out, and, I believe, without a dissenting voice. Clauses concerning the collection of confiscated debts were proposed by persons not friendly to the Bill in general, with an equivocal exception "of those debts preserved by the treaty." The members could not agree upon the mode; and, it being at the very conclusion of a very long session, the clauses were at length rejected; not, however, from any dislike of the principle, for it is a prevailing opinion among many, who are at present the

* From an act of this session, it appears that during the war "a considerable number of heavy cannon" were thrown into a river near Edenton, to prevent their falling into the hands of the enemy.

most leading people in the country, that the debts of persons whose estates were confiscated by *name*, are not protected by the treaty, upon the principle I formerly wrote you.* * * *

JAS. IREDELL.

IREDELL TO SIR N. DUKINFIELD.

EDENTON, Jan. 7th, 1785.

DEAR SIR:— * * * I wish to God it was in my power to soften the melancholy account I must now give you of your own loss, and which it is unfortunate that you are obliged to receive without any preparation in a letter. I know, though it is no premature, it will affect you deeply; and I sincerely sympathize with you on so distressing an occasion. Your mother, after being a considerable time in a very ill state of health, died at Dukinfield on the 21st of December last. She had for a good while had a severe disorder in her bowels, and it at length terminated I believe, in a consumption of them. She was at our house great part of September and October: and had been very sick there but got much better; and then felt so great an anxiety to g home and attend to her affairs, that our most urgent solicitation could not prevail upon her to stay, a circumstance we regrette very much at the time, and still more when we had the misfor tune to hear of her illness at home, though this did not appea so dangerous till a very few days before her death. She ha made a will during the war. Some time ago Mr. Johnston ex pressed a desire that she should alter it; and she had intende doing so, but deferred it until a short time before she died. Sh sent for me, and I attended her on the 19th. A most melan choly affliction it was. The faculties of her mind were as stron and vigorous as ever; her affection and regard for her friends a lively; and her memory as perfect, I believe, as at any momen of her life; but her disorder had very much wasted her; and he looks too probably indicated the approach of death, though the I was far from supposing her fate so near at hand, nor, indeed that it was altogether impossible to save her. She dictated he will to me with great composure. Mr. Johnston will enclose yo a copy of it; but the substance was—a devise and bequest of he whole property, real and personal, to Mr. Pollok and Mr. John ston in trust to sell it, and pay the proceeds to you, after deduct ing a legacy of £300 stl. to Mr. Johnston (£150 of which sh kindly intended for me, and which I could not divert her from

* When McCulloh left America, the greater part of his bonds, &c., were le with Felix Kenan, for safe keeping.

though, as I was to draw the will, she directed me to express in that manner.) Your brother's legacy to her she gave to your son, her watch to Mrs. Iredell—and left Mrs. Pollock and Mrs. Johnston her rings. She particularly desired that I would in case of her death inform you of this melancholy event; and assure you and lady Dukinfield of her extreme affection, and her anxiety for your happiness; and let you know that her deferring to answer your and lady D.'s letters, and acknowledging the attention and tenderness of both, was not owing to any want of regard or respect, but that she was in hopes of being able to give you more agreeable accounts. After this she conversed with me on a great many indifferent topics, with as much ease and quickness of understanding as I ever knew her possess, and with no apparent difference but the want of that agreeable humor which in general mixed with all her conversation. After I had prepared her will, I read it to her; and asked her if that was conformable to her desire. She said perfectly; and conversed with me freely as before, though not quite so fully. I was most unfortunately at that time obliged to go instantly to Pasquotank, so that I could not stay longer. I expected she would have executed her will that day; but after waiting a considerable time for her to propose it, I at length asked her if she chose to execute it then, or at another time. She said another time, if it would do as well; and put to me the affecting question, whether, if she was not able to sign it, any body might do it for her. In this situation, with the utmost distress, I left her. The will was executed, and with sufficient form, the morning of the day she died. Her death was quite easy; and, what I hope will greatly soften your grief on this occasion, though Mrs. Pearson always before had expressed and discovered the greatest fear of death, she exhibited nothing of it in this last unfortunate illness; but bore, and spoke of the approach of it with extraordinary equanimity and composure. She was interred, at her desire, at Hayes.

I have thus gone through an undertaking which I dreaded, the recital of particulars that must ever pain and affect me in the recollection. My own regard for her was very great, and if it had proceeded from gratitude alone, and not from a respect for a most excellent mind that I sincerely entertained, it was justly merited, for almost ever since I have been in the country, she has uniformly shown me nearly as much attention and affection as if I had been her son. Mrs. Iredell, who equally loved and respected her, has been very deeply affected also, and had greatly to regret that her own state of health prevented her being with her till the very morning before she died, and when she was shocked beyond expression in finding her in a situation she at that time little expected. The Supreme Being certainly can never suffer such distresses to be without some compensation hereafter. Of all human evils, in my opinion, the loss of friends is the greatest, and would to me be insupportable, if I thought this life terminated our existence. * * * * Mrs. Iredell joins in respectful compliments to you and Lady Dukinfield, and in wishing you both, and your rising family, all manner of prosperity.

Adieu! my dear Sir, and believe me ever,
Faithfully and affectionately yours,
JAS. IREDELL.

A. MACLAINE TO IREDELL.

WILMINGTON, 7th March, 1785.

DEAR SIR:—I have just received yours of the 7th of last month. Where it has lain so long I cannot conceive, except for the last week, when there was no rider from Newbern. I have not yet fixed on persons for adjusting the accounts between Messrs. Spaight and Campbell—indeed it had escaped my memory. I was taken dangerously ill immediately after our Superior Court; and since I have recovered, I could not find leisure to think of any thing but what was before my eyes. Mr. Burgwyn is the surviving executor of Mr. Waddell.

We have been paid off here as in other places by the sickly season. The sore throat proved fatal to several. Dr. Claypoole says it is properly a scarlet fever, attended with sore throat; and we ought to conclude that he is no incompetent judge, as he has not lost a patient when he was called in the beginning of the disorder.* Mrs. Huske has got a chopping girl, and was perfectly well some time ago. Col. Clark is also well, and his wife much better—she has been lately thought past recovery in a consumptive complaint; but Fergus says she is recovering—I hope for the best. Mrs. Hooper and her daughter are now at Mr. Clark's, and we shall have them soon in town. Mr. Hooper is well. I heard from him a few days ago. Mr. Hay is now in Virginia, but expected home this month. Mr. G. W. Hooper and family were well a short time ago.

It gives me pleasure to hear that Mr. Johnston is so much better; and that Mrs. Dawson and all your friends are well. The last night of our Court Mr. B. Hoskins gave me some very extraordinary information. He had a conversation with Mr. Singleton about the suits commenced by the Cornell family. Sin-

---

* Dr. Claypoole was from Philadelphia, the son or brother of the well-known editor of that city. The family are descendants of Oliver Cromwell.

---

gleton appeared perfectly easy; said he depended upon Nash as his sheet anchor; and had nothing to fear, as he and his associates had *silenced* you, Mr. Hooper, and myself. He went, indeed, much further—he said that all the judges had been *sounded*, and were *favorable* to them. I wrote to Ogden, who appeared to be the agent of the gang, informing him that I would return the retainer, and looked upon myself as disengaged. I also wrote to Singleton, telling him that I had heard what he said, without naming my author, and assuring him that though he had deprived me of a fee, he should not seal up my lips. I acquainted Mr. Hooper of all this; but he seems to think we cannot appear against these scoundrels without injuring ourselves.* I think the best way will be to consult together when we meet. At present my own opinion is, that delicacy should prevent us from taking fees on the other side; but I do not see any reason why we should be altogether silent. If we at the trial should declare we are volunteers, and give the reasons for our conduct, I think I may venture to rely upon the facts for my justification, and this will probably receive some additional force from my usual disinterestedness. I suppose Mr. Johnston will laugh that we have been so damnably taken in. Among several others, Mrs. Derossett, Mr. J. Lillington, Col. Sampson, and Mr. Hasel, are dead.
Yours, with great sincerity,
A. MACLAINE.

RICHARD DOBBS SPAIGHT TO IREDELL.†

NEW YORK, 10th March, 1785.

DEAR SIR:—I did not receive your favor of the 7th of February until a few days ago, and have taken the first leisure moment to answer it. Upon reflection, I do not think it would be so proper to have applied to the Court to reinstate the report they had set aside; *it would at least have the appearance of their having acted inconsiderately, which the characters of the Judges in Equity ought not to admit of; and, therefore, it is better that the individual should suffer "pro tempore" than the least flaw be discovered in the Supreme Court*. As it is my disposition rather to make the best of the present, than to fret at what is past, I submit with patience to the delay, and must rest satisfied with the new Order of Reference. * * * *

The only European news we have here is the war between the Emperor and the Dutch. The season admits of nothing else but the various opinions of the politicians, whether the controversy will be put an end to by the negotiations of the winter, or decided by arms. For my part, from every account I have heard, I am induced to be of the last opinion. It is pretty certain that the only way of putting an end to it by negotiation is, either, that the Dutch must give up the free navigation of the Scheldt, or the Emperor desist from his demands. The former are decided in not granting the free navigation of that river; first, because it is contained in that treaty which confirmed their freedom and independence; and if they admit any of the articles of that treaty not to be valid, the others are equally so.—Secondly, they have kept the Scheldt shut up for more than one hundred and thirty years, without their right for so doing having been ever questioned. On the contrary, it cannot be supposed that the Emperor will recede from his demands: the ridicule it would throw on his character to have made such as he should be obliged to recede from, for want of a sufficient force (the only right he had to plead) to oblige them to comply, would be too great for a prince, of such abilities and ambition as he is supposed to possess, to submit to.

Congress have lately appointed Mr. John Adams Minister to the Court of London; it was a step absolutely necessary to be taken; and I think it has been delayed too long; and it's well for America if her saving policy don't cost her millions.

The holding of our Western Posts contrary to the treaty, her different arrangements in Canada, and the Lakes, added to the murmurs of the nation against America, and the restraints laid upon our commerce with them, show so hostile a disposition in the Court of Great Britain towards us, that I think we should at least be prepared for any thing that may happen. Yet the States seem to be lulled into perfect security: few of them have organized, and armed their militia: still fewer have taken any steps to procure a sufficient supply of military stores, without which no nation ought to be; and I think our situation at the beginning of the late war, for want of those articles, ought to be a warning to America, never to be unprovided. The want of money, and the unsettled state of Ireland, rather than the want of inclination, will prevent them from renewing the controversy.

Mrs. Montgomery, the widow of the late General of that

---

* The reader will please bear in mind that Mr. Maclaine's denunciations are often to be taken "cum grano salis;" he was an honest man, and very able lawyer: a fiery and uncontrollable temper was his great infirmity. When suffering under the torture of the gout, his wrath frequently exploded in acrimonious language, by no means the expression of deliberate opinion.

† Native of Ireland: grandson of the royal Governor Dobbs: graduate of the University of Glasgow; aid-de-camp to Caswell at Camden: Commoner from Newbern in '81, '82, and '83: member of the Continental Congress in '84: one of the delegates to form the Constitution of the United States in '87: Governor in '92: member of the House of Representatives in '98: slain in a duel with Hon. John Stanley, Sept. 1802.—*Vid.* Wheeler.

name, requested me to write to some of my acquaintance in Edenton, to know what had become of the statue (I believe it is) that was ordered by Congress to be erected to his memory: it was sent from France to Edenton; and lodged in the hands of Messrs. Hewes, Smith & Allen: an order of Congress passed at Annapolis for its being sent thence to this city. Shall I take the liberty of requesting you to make this inquiry, and to inform me of the result?

I have the honor to be with great regard and esteem,
Dear Sir,
Your most obedient and humble servant,
RICH^D. DOBBS SPAIGHT.

REV. A. IREDELL TO IREDELL.

CHESHIRE, April 30th, 1785.

DEAR BROTHER:— * * * I have lately been on a most delightful tour with Mr. Felton. He is intimately connected with the great Iron manufacturers in Shropshire; and I had anxiously wished for a sight of their works. He took me with him, and I saw them to the greatest advantage. They are situated in Coalbrook Dale, and the adjacent country; and you may have an imperfect idea of their magnitude, when you hear that in *one work only, they consume* 500 tons of coal every day! But I will give you in my next letter a very particular account of my tour. Coalbrook Dale is the most delightful situation I ever saw: it is just what a place, a fine place, should be, both beautiful and sublime. At Mr. Wilkinson's, one of the first manufacturers, *we met Silas Deane, your late Plenipotentiary to France. Is he a huge genius? He may be so; but he cannot talk English—though, perhaps, that is not necessary to an American statesman—or, your resentment against England may induce you to disgrace us by deforming our language, &c., &c.*

A. IREDELL.

McCULLOH TO IREDELL.

NO. 22 IRON-MONGER'S LANE, LONDON, 15th May, '85.

DEAR SIR:— * * * In case of the idea of an Act of Banishment being carried into execution, I beg my friends will not make any effort to take my name out of it; but "contra," I should wish it in: as things are, I consider myself as it relates to North Carolina, as a person, naturally as well as politically dead; and after all, my heart feels an additional pang, when it reflects that to the rest of my most unmerited and severe usage, I am obliged to add the painful thought, that shall now—probably never—see persons both most near an *dear* to me. Write me, I pray you, and send me the law soon as possible.

Affectionately and truly yours,
H. E. McCULLOH.

SIR N. DUKINFIELD TO IREDELL.

SULHAM, near Reading, 10th June, 1785.

DEAR IREDELL:—At the same time that I received your letter of the 9th of January, I was favored with one from Mr. Johnston enclosing a copy of my mother's will. I am sorry to hear of th loss you have sustained, but I flatter myself that may be retrieved. There are many persons who have been married as long a you have been without having a child, and afterwards have ha several. Lady D. brought me another son on the 3d Februar last, and his older brother was not a year old. They are bot very well at present. The young one I once expected would hav died; he was very bad, and even without hopes, which affecte his mother to so great a degree, that we both wished for his deat and release from pain—this has kept him rather backward. Th oldest is the finest boy *I* ever saw, and is every thing a fond pa rent can wish. Our fear is that we shall have more than we ca well provide for, and as Lady D * * * * * with great pain an distress, I hope we shall have no more: though I believe, if sh could be sure of one girl and no more children, she would rathe prefer that than stop here.

I am much pleased with my mother's will, (for I call her intentio to you a part of it,) though I was a good deal affected by the ac count of her death: yet I received much comfort in reflectin that though she had hitherto lived in peace and quiet, she woul probably have soon felt a different situation, by the Commissioner for the sales of confiscated property entering upon the executio of their trusts, and if she had not succeeded in making good he claims, it would have been distressing to her for her to have bee obliged to leave a place, which she had lived upon as her ow near 30 years. With this packet I send a letter to Mr. Joh ston, and a case on my father's and mother's wills, with M Madock's opinion, by which it clearly appears that my mothe has ever been entitled to the plantation and personal property I don't recollect any particular conversation with Captain We that can be drawn to my hurt; and if any word fell when w were talking in private and friendship, and he has used it to di

unfortunately, have been imbibed against me in this countr are confined to a very narrow circle.* Remember me in the mos affectionate and respectful manner to Mrs. Iredell, Miss Blair, an the rest of your amiable family; and give me leave, dear sir, t assure you that I shall ever consider your late goodness, and re flect upon it with a heart replete with the most grateful sensa tions, and that I shall remain while I live, with the greates sincerity and regard,

Your truly affectionate and much obliged,
T. LOWTHER.

HOOPER TO IREDELL.

HILLSBOROUGH, July 6th, 1785.

DEAR SIR:—This will be handed to you by a messenge whom we send to Mr. Pinto, to assist him with horses in his pr gress hither.† I have not heard of you, or any of my friends Edenton, since I parted with you at Newbern; and as your healt at that time was by no means confirmed, and the accounts fro Mrs. Johnston by no means favorable, I have been truly anxiou to learn how heaven has conducted itself to you, and your friend since your return to them. We here enjoy our usual good health not an individual of my family had been indisposed during m absence; I found them all in high health and spirits, enjoying a event, in common with the rest of the town, which had take place just before my return, of which, as I have given Mr. John ston an account, it will therefore be unnecessary to repeat it t you. Glorious example to all husbands in the like case offending

Our court at Wilmington went on in the old dilatory mode o doing business. Great threats of despatch accomplished in th usual way. Much conversation from Germanicus on the bench his vanity has become insufferable, and is accompanied with th most overbearing insolence. Maclaine and he had a terribl "fracas." Germanicus, with those strong intuitive powers wit which he is inspired, took up Maclaine's defence in an ejectmen and ran away with it before it was opened. Maclaine exposu lated, scolded, stormed, called names, abandoned the cause. prevailed. Spencer made condescensions; hostilities ceased, a peace was restored. It is a doubtful circumstance whether I sha be in the next Assembly. I have no desire to make any conces sions to men whom I heartily despise, to secure their votes or in terest. The courts must be altered; and most earnestly do hope that you and Mr. Johnston will have a principal share i

---

* Mr. Lowther was from England. † Isaac Pinto, a Portuguese economist.

---

serve me, he is a man to be scouted—as a friend and relation of Brimmage's I met him. I wished to have got the Attorney General's opinion. The case is before him, but my attorney says I shall not get it till the Parliament breaks up; he is so very busy in mending old acts and framing new ones—and I don't know if it will be of any use.

I am very glad that you and Mrs. Iredell were perfectly well: I hope you continue so. I am just recovering from a bilious fever which attacked me smartly for three or four days, and it was thought I would have the jaundice. I was most confoundedly low-spirited, with an universal languor, though I did not think I was immediately going "*au monde des taupes.*" It is the first of the sort I have felt since the year 1771 you will therefore think I have no great reason to complain. The beginning of this week I could not have touched a pen, but had as great an aversion to it as a mad dog has to water. But I can now say "a fig for the doctor." I have never had the pleasure of seeing your brother. He has promised me, by letter, that he will embrace the first opportunity; but I suppose his engagements confine him very much. If he should attend young Crewe to Oxford, my house is not above 22 miles distant.

My best compliments to Mrs. Iredell, Mrs. Blair, and my few (alas) remaining friends, and believe me ever
Yours, most sincerely,
N. DUKINFIELD.

T. LOWTHER TO IREDELL.

EDEN HOUSE, 4th July, 1785.

MY DEAR SIR:—I have the pleasure to inform you that I returned here yesterday in good health from Halifax; and that I have met with nothing to make me regret my journey; on the contrary, I have received the most flattering marks of attention and hospitality from all the inhabitants of that polite and agreeable place, of which I had formed a pleasing idea. I confess I found my expectations greatly exceeded. I consider myself under particular obligations to you for the letters of introduction you were so obliging as to favor me with to Col. McCulloh's family, and I have only to lament, that I had it not longer in my power to cultivate the acquaintance of a family whose manners, hospitality, and refinement cannot fail of attaching any person, very strongly, who has the happiness to know them. I have had the good fortune during my journey, considerably to extend my acquaintance among the inhabitants of this, Martin and Halifax Counties; and the pleasure to find that the prejudices, which, planning a new establishment. Against the present system the cries of the people are loud; they must be heard. But what affects me most is, that the censure is pointed at the Bar, when the occasion is seated much higher. It is a melancholy consideration that we have not proper materials in this country to form the officers which the constitution makes necessary. We must do the best we can with such stuff as we have, until our academies and colleges supply us with something that may be more equal to the purpose.

Our little town of Hillsborough begins to thrive; some new buildings are begun, and many more in contemplation. The Academy will give it a very considerable spring; and should the Assembly return hither, our importance is sealed—and then, Squehawky, what will become of thy healthy barrens? They will be, as they were intended by Providence, a desolate, uninhabited waste, to make poverty and wretchedness comforted in their condition, by showing them that, bad as the soil may be allotted to them, still there is a worse. The alteration of courts, I flatter myself, will again draw your attention this way, and give me what alone I want to make my situation here completely happy—your and Mr. Johnston's family.

I visited your old friend, Gen. Clarke, when I was at Cape Fear. A deep melancholy has fixed itself upon him; and he denies all comfort. His complexion is that of a deep jaundice: he has lost all his flesh; his conversation turns upon nothing but the occasion of his distress; and, when he is told that he cannot live long in that unhealthy place, he says, with the utmost earnestness, "I fear I shall." I fear a very few months will end him; and, alas! I tremble for the effects such an event would have on my wife. I earnestly wish that I could draw him hither; but of that I despair.

At Wilmington I saw Mrs. Thomas Hooper, who was there to attend the nuptials of her sister Betsey, who gave her hand to a Mr. McKenzie, (Billy Campbell's nephew,) while I was in town. Mrs. Hooper is a very fine woman, much polished by her tour through Britain; but alas! yet but a little while, and how useless all her accomplishments. She is in a consumption—my brother Tom in the same condition—both going to Rhode Island, flying from death, which, I fear, is at no great distance from them. George Hooper and his wife were also at Wilmington: he is much improved in his health and appearance. She had not her health in South Carolina; but is grown much more easy and affable than she was. Our meeting was awkward: distant and distressing to me.*

Your dunning letters were delivered; and the most solemn

* The brothers had adopted opposite sides in the Revolution.

promises made to deposit the money immediately with Mr. Thos. Maclaine; I had not entire faith in them.

I flatter myself I shall, by Pinto, get a long letter from you. Be not discouraged from any apprehension that I may in return distress you with another scrawl of equal length with this. There is no probability that I shall find another opportunity before I see you, as there is as little intercourse between this and Edenton, as between this and another world, &c., &c.

WILL. HOOPER.

P. S. Let me ask the favor of you to assist Mr. Pinto to come forward. Should he meet any obstructions, be pleased to obviate them.

A. IREDELL TO IREDELL.

GUILFORD, August 5th, 1785.

DEAR BROTHER:—Since I last wrote you I have undertaken the curacy of this place, which is very laborious; and occupies far the greater part of my time, for I write my own sermons. Tom's old friend, Lord Onslow, is the great man of the town, and has been very civil to me; but my greatest comfort, and the chief inducement I had for coming here, is my good friend, Captain Wilson, whom Tom likewise knows. I live almost entirely in his family; and am more obliged to him than I can tell you. * * * McCulloh, I imagine, has got something from Government, for I saw his name, together with that of the other agents, to an address of thanks to the King. * * * There is no very material news circulating at home,—I mean in this island. A very violent contest for Westminster has just terminated in favor of Lord John Townshend, the popular candidate. The King is drinking the Cheltenham waters. The Russians have just obtained a signal naval victory over the Turks. The French still at loggerheads among themselves. Your American General, the Marquis de La Fayette, is cooped up for taking too forward a part. These are all the topics I can think of—for my being lately elected, with the Duke of Richmond's nephew, and some others, a freeman of Seaford, though it did get into the papers, has not, I think, made such a noise over the island as might reasonably have been expected, &c., &c.

A. IREDELL.

DR. SAMUEL CUTLER (a Loyalist) TO IREDELL.

HARTFORD, Conn., August 7th, 1785.

DEAR SIR:—Your very obliging letter of the 20th of March, I received by Mr. Lowther, since which I have had no opportu-

nity of writing you. As I am now going to New York, I hope to find some conveyance thence.

Mr. Webster last spring set off for the Southern States, and did me the honor to take charge of a letter for you. But as it is very uncertain if he took Edenton in his way, or whether you have received it, I will now tell you that I have formed a connection with an English gentleman in a little business in Connecticut, by which I hope to live comfortably the remainder of my days. I have here received every civility I could wish; yet this forming new connections at my time of life, among a people, in their genius and manners totally different from those I have lived among for near twenty years past, to me is truly disagreeable. But the most unpleasing circumstance of all, is my separation from my friends in every quarter, for whom I have the most tender regard. This State is remarkable for having the first Bishop settled in it: Dr. Seabury has arrived within these few weeks, with powers of ordination. Four gentlemen have already received holy orders; and his coming, I believe, meets the approbation of the Legislature, and of the generality of the people. One unfavorable circumstance, however, attends it: this is, the society withdrawing the salaries from the clergy they have kept upon their books till very lately, they having discovered that it is inconsistent with their charter to continue their missionaries in the United States: they have given assurances, however, that they will provide for those that will remove to any of the British settlements.

Notwithstanding our distance from each other, the many pleasing hours I have spent in your family, and the most agreeable conversation I have enjoyed, often occur to my mind, and make the subject of my most delightful reflections in my solitary hours; and when I consider the great improbability of ever participating again of those enjoyments, (melancholy thought!) I feel the obligations I am under to your goodness with double force. Be assured, my dear sir, my best wishes are, and ever will be, for your and your family's welfare. You will know who my friends are; will you, *in your manner*, make my compliments to them, particularly to Mrs. Iredell. Believe me, dear sir,

Yours, most sincerely,
SAM'L CUTLER.

MISS HELEN BLAIR TO IREDELL.

EDENTON, October 14th, 1785.

You see, my dear uncle, notwithstanding your efforts to the contrary, I am determined to continue a correspondence, which

has ever been to me the source of so much pleasure. It is very selfish in me to insist upon it; but I will be doubly disinterested on some other occasion to make amends.

Mrs. Dawson has been over the creek now a fortnight. It is impossible for me to express how dull the house has been since you and she left it. I assure you we pray for your safe, and *speedy* return. We have lost all our visitors, too. Mr. Black is in Virginia; Dr. Ramké has so much business he scarcely ever has time to call; and poor Mr. Borneike has been at the point of death, and is hardly able now to go about. All these things were not mortifying enough; but you must write to Aunt Iredell, and your brother, without even an apology for neglecting me. Dr. Williamson and I have become great friends. He has sent me translations of the plays of Sophocles, and Euripides; and spoke as if he had other books to lend me when I have done with them. This, I fear, will not be shortly, for though I read the plays with eagerness, yet there are long comparisons between the plays—the ancient and modern theatre—and an account of the rise of the Greek theatre, which I suppose the Doctor thought the most useful part, but which, somehow or other, I never can find time to read.

Your ever affectionate,
H. BLAIR.

IREDELL TO MISS BLAIR.

HALIFAX, October 18th, 1785.

MY DEAR NELLY:—You did great wrong to my gratitude, and taste, in supposing I meant to discourage so valuable a correspondence as yours, for such it has ever been to me, and I hope will long continue so. Far from slighting it, I received your agreeable favor by your uncle with very great satisfaction. I relied on your candor to excuse me without a formal apology, not suspecting the inference you have drawn from the want of one, for my affection would of itself have prompted a letter, had I had time to write it; and I am sure for the future my vanity will be an additional incentive, since I am flattered with finding it of consequence. It gives me concern to hear you have been a little indisposed, though upon the whole I have great reason, as I truly am, to be thankful for the accounts I have received. I am sure you must miss Mrs. Dawson, and her charming daughter, very much. Happy shall I again be in mixing with our agreeable circle. I am glad to hear of Dr. Williamson's attention; and that it displays itself in a manner that may be useful to you. My books have come by mistake here, but no letters for me, at

VOL. II.—9

which I am really surprised; but I really am more grieved at Mrs. Dawson's disappointment than my own, thinking it peculiarly severe, and provoking. I hope, however, she is well satisfied of her son's health, since it is so well vouched by that precise man, Mr. Elmsley. I am quite vexed (between ourselves) at the levity, and indifference of Sir N. Dukinfield's letter, wrote in answer to mine giving a very particular, and to me very affecting, account of his mother's death. He bears it with all the cursed stoicism of a philosopher; and is still afraid that his wife will ruin him with a great number of children. He well deserves a Xantippe for his next wife, and a double set of children into the bargain. It is intolerable to see a young man so insensible, and so avaricious.

I have a letter for you from Mrs. Huske, but I don't know whether I shall inclose it now. Your friend Mrs. M'Coy and her gentleman are well. I inclosed your letter under a cover to him, and put it in the care of Governor Martin.

Contrary to a custom you have complained of, I have wrote this letter first, determined you should not be without one. You will be so good as to remember me affectionately to your mamma and sister. Adieu! my dear Nelly, and believe me ever, whether I do or do not write, most sincerely and affectionately yours,

JAS. IREDELL.

SAMUEL CUTLER TO IREDELL.

NEW LONDON, CONN., Dec. 13th, 1785.

DEAR SIR:—Although business at the approach of winter is pressing, I cannot neglect so good an opportunity as the sloop Friendship, now going to Carolina, to write you. It is now a long time since I have had the pleasure to hear from you—not since you wrote by Mr. Lowther, when I find you did not enjoy so good health as for some time before. *I have, my dear sir, often remonstrated against your too close application to study, and want of exercise. I now tell you, that I fear your perseverance will deprive you of your health, and me, and thousands, of your friendship. The very means you take to render yourself useful to your friends, will disappoint them.* You know very well, when I was at Edenton, I was at best but a convalescent, which I have not the vanity to charge to books, but rather a shameful inactivity. I am now engaged in business that calls me up before the sun. I am on foot the whole day, and often by night, very much fatigued; yet I never enjoyed so good health, which I attribute as much to change of manner of life as of place; and was it not for my separation from a few for whom I entertain a most tender regard, I should bless God for the cause that removed me. Medicine may, my dear sir, for a time relieve you; but it must be change in your manner of life that will keep you in health. You will excuse my freedom in writing, when I assure you that it is your life and health, and the happiness of your friends, that dictate it. When you have one half hour of leisure, lend it me in telling me how you are, and of the welfare of my friends. Where is Lenox? Has he left you for Charleston, the West Indies, or the other world? I hear nothing of him. Remember me with tender regards to Mrs. Iredell and family, and believe me, dear sir, yours most sincerely,

SAM'L CUTLER.

CHAPTER XIX.

ÆT 34—35.

LETTERS FROM HOGG, HOOPER, REV. A. IREDELL, IREDELL, AND MACLAINE; IREDELL'S ADDRESS TO THE PUBLIC; ASSEMBLY; ALFRED MOORE; LETTER TO IREDELL.

JAMES HOGG TO IREDELL.

HILLSBOROUGH, January 19th, 1786.

DEAR SIR:—* * * * I have written a long letter to Mr. Johnston on this subject, and have sent him a copy of the wonderful law by which the Assembly have arrogated to themselves the judicial power in all suits regarding confiscated property. How the people at large will like the innovation, I know not, &c., &c.

Although the Southern and Western people have prevailed, and fixed next meeting of Assembly at Fayette, Mr. Hooper says it will never sit there again; but I must differ with him. To me it appears that the interest of that place will yearly increase, though I suspect the duty laid on British goods will give a great check to their trade for a time; and I am afraid the new emission of paper money will be of no service.

The laws of this State seem very favorable to knavish debtors, &c., &c.

JAS. HOGG.

HOOPER TO IREDELL.

HILLSBOROUGH, 22d January, 1786.

MY DEAR SIR:—Mr. Moore forwarded me, from Wilmington, your very affectionate letter, dated at Newbern. I also received a few lines from you, acknowledging that my scrawl by the Quakers had reached you.

I would have availed myself of some one of the many opportunities which offered to Edenton, at the close of the session, to inform you of what had been done in the Assembly, but I found myself so crowded with business in the moment of departure—my passions so agitated with the unbecoming means which had been used to cast a stigma upon the Bar; and, upon the whole, so large a portion of our time had been occupied to accomplish purposes, either nugatory or disgraceful, that I forbore to give you a detail of our proceedings. It now becomes unnecessary; you have had frequent opportunities, I doubt not, to mix with your legislators; and, were it only to give you proper ideas of your own parliamentary consequence, they would not fail to inform you of all that had passed in the Assembly, and the distinguished share which they had taken in it. In the new Court law, if it merits the name, for it had been much better christened, as I proposed, a bill inflicting pains and penalties on attorneys, Edenton district conducted themselves, with a very few exceptions, very differently from what I expected. Cabarrus, Sawyer, Eurigen, acquitted themselves honorably. Cabarrus' conduct through the whole session was upright, sensible, and independent; and, in the investigation of public frauds, he proved himself a very useful and industrious committee-man.*

I inclose you, without a comment, certain papers, which made their appearance in the course of the investigation of the conduct of the Judges. This ridiculous pursuit of Hay's ended as we expected. It was conceived in spleen, and conducted with such headstrong passion, that, after the charges were made, evidence was wanting to support them.

You have inclosed a letter (a copy) of Mr. Ashe's; it carries its own commentary with it. I leave you to judge how far we have merited the charges it alleges against us. I will not spin this scrawl to a greater length, and will only add, that no time of my life has been so decidedly misspent as that which passed in the last session of the Assembly. God forgive me this public political sin! and I will do so no more, &c., &c.

WILL. HOOPER.

In a letter to Hooper, January 29th, Mr. Iredell wrote, in reference to the Confiscation law, "no consideration under Heaven shall induce me, directly or indirectly, to support, countenance, or have *act* or *part*, in carrying so infamous a law into execution." In the same epistle he said, "I admire Alfred Moore's conduct beyond expression. God grant he may continue in office. He may in time put even one J— to the blush!"

* Stephen Cabarrus was a native of Bayonne, France. From the same town, in the year —, emigrated one of the same name to Spain, who there established the first Bank of Spain, and was created a Marquis, —. *Vid. Young's Travels in Spain.*
The second husband of the celebrated Madame Tallien was a Marquis de Cabarrus. I suppose our North Carolinian was a member of the same family.—*History of France.*

In a letter to Mr. Hogg, of the same date, he again denounces the same act. "It is a melancholy thing, that in support of a favorite system, every principle of decency and justice should be so wantonly sacrificed, as it has been in the last act concerning confiscation; and barefaced as it is, the conduct of the Court at Wilmington gives very little prospect of relief from them."

REV. A. IREDELL TO IREDELL.

LONDON, February 21st, 1786.

MY DEAR BROTHER :— * * * * My friend, Mr. Kempe, has lost, or rather got rid of, his wife,—a most fortunate event, for he may now live comfortably if he will—he has had no option before. I have already passed some time with him in Sussex; and he has desired me to consider Malling as my home, when I have no better place to go to. So you see my stars do now and then twinkle kindly upon me.

There is nothing momentous upon the political carpet at present, but an impeachment against Mr. Hastings, initiated by our friend, Mr. Burke, and now in its infancy. I hardly think it will attain to manhood, notwithstanding the apparent impartiality, and candor of the Minister. Burke will certainly not relax, or flinch from the business; but there are few in either House, or out of them, so zealous or hearty in the cause as himself. I was yesterday morning with Mr. Crewe, and he fairly confessed that he thought the only point that would be gained by the attack would be that of exposing Dundas, whose character was never specious, in my opinion to be mistaken. * * * I have been fortunate enough to procure the papers from Woodfall; and I have ordered the Morning Chronicle to be sent, &c., &c.
A. IREDELL.

The following manly, and admirable letter from Mr. Iredell to his uncle, in Jamaica, is the last he ever addressed to that obstinate and implacable gentleman.

EDENTON, N. C., Feb. 23d, 1786.

HONORED SIR :—I confess a letter which my brother yesterday received from you has given me very great pain, not from a consciousness that I deserve in any degree the reflections you think proper to bestow upon me, but that the manner in which these reflections are made implies an inveterate prejudice against me I can entertain little hope of removing. It is not my intention, sir, to force upon you a correspondence which has become disgusting. This letter is the last probably you will ever receive from me, unless you shall condescend to desire otherwise; and being so, I trust you will forgive an attempt, which, if troublesome, will not be renewed, to convince you I have neither been that bad man you have figured to your imagination, nor do my letters, if expressive of my present sentiments, as I believe they are, merit the reproach of *disingenuousness* and *prostitution of good sense*, which are the severe characteristics you fix upon them. As I may, perhaps, have suffered before from too little accuracy of expression, I beg leave now, though at the risk of being thought pedantic, to take slight notice of your objections to my particular conduct in order, carefully avoiding, however, any thing on the great subjects of controversy, which it would be equally improper, as it is unnecessary to discuss.

The objections, as I understand them, are, 1. My having taken an oath of allegiance. 2. My holding an official character. 3. My being an Englishman by birth.

To the first I say, that admitting the resistance of the subject is allowable in any case, the circumstance of an oath of allegiance is of no weight, since allegiance is as much due without an oath as with it; and if all who had taken such an oath were debarred from resistance, no effectual one could be formed. This every Whig must agree in as a *principle*. The Revolution in 1688 clearly proves so much; though it does not indeed ascertain, nor is it possible for any single case ever to do so, the particular instances in which this principle may be applied. This must be left to every man's conscience and judgment, taking due care to be well informed of all circumstances; and being as much aware on the one hand of the great duty, and indispensable obligation of allegiance till forfeited, as of the clear right to resistance when it is.

In regard to my official character, I was scrupulously careful so long as the least vestige of a British Government remained, to do nothing inconsistent with it. But afterwards, I thought myself as much at liberty to choose my side as any man. I should have disdained any office which was to be purchased by a sacrifice of public duty, nor could I conceive any such abject condition annexed to it, when the King himself is merely a trustee for his people, and certainly, in the distribution of public offices, to be considered rather in that light than as a distributor of private favors. This I do not say with any view to detract from the obligations conferred upon me. I admit them fully; but they were in my opinion always subordinate to public motives; and, if instances were wanting in so plain a point, I recur to the many great examples at the time of the Revolution you so justly call a glorious one. Permit me to say, that I was not altogether fed by the bounty of England. The offices I held had severe duties annexed to them, which I performed faithfully. The first was a mere pittance; and the latter I had for little more than twelve months.

The remaining objection against me, is that I am an Englishman by birth. I glory in being so: I glory that I was in truth brought up in that country in the bosom of liberty; and in principles which I have never departed from. I left England, as I had a right to do, to become an inhabitant of an American Province: I then belonged to a new society, whose welfare by all possible means it became my indispensable duty to promote. Nothing could be more painful to me than a conflict between the country of my birth, and the society of which I was an actual member long before the war broke out. It imposed a distressing alternative upon me. But I never doubted, whether or not it was not my duty to defend my own rights as well as those of the society I belonged to. I never considered myself as a spy, placed in America to promote the views of England upon it. Thus circumstanced, therefore, *I had only to fix my principles*, and doing so, to choose my side. I did so, to the best of my judgment, and have acted accordingly; but with so little bigotry of mind, that I do assure you, in the very heat of the contest, I held in equal respect, so far as personal character was concerned, men of principle on both sides, for such there are, and will be in every civil war. The very nature of one supposes something difficult in the question. And I cannot but think myself peculiarly unfortunate, that, entertaining such sentiments even in regard to strangers, some of my own nearest relations should be unwilling to exercise the same candor towards me.

I never meant in respect to the two Revolutions, (as you will find if you will condescend to look at my letters, in case you have preserved them,) a comparison between the personal or political characters of the two Kings. God knows nothing was farther from my heart; and in respect to the American Revolution, I look upon it to have been much more brought about by the intemperate violence of the people of England themselves, than from any other cause. The effect, however, as to us was the same, and it would have been a poor consolation in viewing the miseries of our country, to have said, "The people of England are much more to blame for this than the King."

You will observe, I waive any particular questions of the controversy, as those perhaps we should never agree in. I contend only, and have a right to contend with warmth against any construction of *immorality* in my conduct, since I was obliged to act according to my own judgment, and I call God to witness I did so honestly, sincerely, and voluntarily. If it shall, nevertheless, in spite of any thing I can say, continue to preserve your strong prejudices against me, though I shall lament this as one of my greatest misfortunes, I shall never repent of obeying the dictates of an honest mind.

I have troubled you with this long letter, for no other purpose but to clear myself of misrepresentations which I think nothing but the strongest prepossessions against me, and a want of a little attention to my letters, have occasioned. Your favors are at your own disposal, and God knows, I had never any selfish, presumptuous views upon them. But my character I hold sacred, and as your estimation of it is a matter of great moment, I hope you will have the goodness to consider again whether you are warranted in renouncing me as unworthy of your name and blood, a sentence of too awful a nature to be pronounced by a man of principle without very good reason.

I should some time ago have had hope, that it would have given you pleasure to hear I had a fine daughter born on the 22d of December, and that both mother and child have been since in remarkable good health.

I have now only to add (which I cannot but do with particular earnestness), that whatever may be your sentiments towards me, I shall never cease to pray for your prosperity and welfare, and that I ever am,

With the greatest respect,
Dear and honored sir,
Your sincerely affectionate nephew,
JAS. IREDELL.

A. MACLAINE TO IREDELL.

WILMINGTON, March 6th, 1786.

DEAR SIR :— * * * * * The Assembly and the Judges have indeed found an easy way to evade the treaty. The former refuse to point out any method to ascertain what is confiscated, (for they know they cannot,) and the Judges refuse to let any person, whose property may be taken by a rapacious Commissioner, maintain a suit; so that we seem to be at the mercy of a set of needy adventurers, whose interest it is to pillage us; and that no loophole may be left unguarded, an act was passed last session, intended to give a sanction to every thing that has been done, and may be done for the future.*

---

* The Commissioners appointed by the Assembly in 1784, to sell confiscated lands, had all been officers of the Continental line. They might well have

The Commissioner in this district has, I believe, so far relaxed as to consent that only part of Burgwyn's property shall be sold, in such manner as that he may have the legality of the sale tried. I wish that you could do something more than give advice, as I am persuaded that if the Judges are beset by the principal gentlemen of the bar in a proper manner, they will not venture to go any great lengths.

I believe indeed that Williams was long since determined; and I know that Spencer is a man of firmness; but I know also that he is an apostate from his principles. The conduct of all these worthies at last Wilmington Court, shows what we have to expect from them. You know the sneaking part they acted, in order to avoid determining against popular prejudices. They found that the Assembly would not interfere, and they learned that there was a clamor against them for the little good which they attempted. They therefore determined to plunge through thick and thin, and now they rise like the diver in the Dunciad,

"Shaking the horrors of their sable brows,
And each ferocious feature grim with ooze."

They believe that the Assembly will not censure them for misbehavior in office, when their vengeance is aimed at a defenceless Tory, and as they are not under the impulse of fear, they, luckily for themselves, have no principle to restrain them.

How it happened I know not, but notwithstanding the intentions of so many of the gentlemen to get into the Assembly last year, they almost all failed. To this we owe the want of a reform in our court system; and possibly to this we owe a fresh influx of paper money. To this it is owing that we have so many wicked, and scandalous acts of last session; and it is certainly owing to this, that the bills which I introduced, and which were recommended by Mr. Johnston and you, fell to the ground in the Senate. Want of principle, and want of knowledge have occasioned these evils. I am sick of legislating. There is no dealing with fools and knaves, unless they are powerfully opposed. There will be no living in the country without a reform, and in truth it will be a disgrace to live in it. If there are no hopes of having a better Legislature, I shall bid adieu to public business for ever. What effect has the approaching paper money on you

been styled "needy adventurers" in a very different sense from that intended by Mr. Maclaine. They had been *adventurers* in the cause of their country; and at the close of the war, after wasting the prime of their manhood in the army, they were *needy* enough. Their appointment was an expression of gratitude on the part of the Legislature; and designed to afford them an opportunity of honest pecuniary gain for patriotic sacrifices, and arduous services. Major Griffith J. McRee was the Commissioner for the Wilmington district.

at Edenton? Nobody gets tobacco in this quarter but the Commissioner, though many thousands of pounds were to be discharged in that article; but the merchants will not take it at the public price. This is a new way of monopolizing the staple commodities of the country; but the monopoly will not last long. I believe those who have sold their property for paper, will be good boys, and never do so again.*

Mr. Hay is lately married to Col. Rowan's daughter, who is I am told, a very fine girl, for I have not seen her for upwards of three years. I expect to see him in about a month, and will then deliver your compliments. Mr. Huske, and a number of Commissioners of Pilotage, are now at Baldhead, with Gen. Howe, Mr. B. Smith, &c., fixing the place for a light-house, and expect to begin it very shortly, &c., &c.

A. MACLAINE.

The Assembly of South Carolina have continued their valuation-law for a year, so that there will be no collection of debts. Mr. G. Hooper is now there, and will come back with his finger in his mouth.

REV. A. IREDELL TO IREDELL.

SOUTH MALLING, May 1st, 1786.

MY DEAR JAMES:—Yours of the 2d of January arrived here yesterday, and very satisfactorily *confirmed* what I had been told two months ago; but pray remember, I have an invincible aversion to old dates, and that the speediest conveyance (cite as many proverbs in point against me as you may) is with *me* the best. If a balloon, therefore, should leave Edenton for Europe, write by that, and direct "to the care of Francis Vincent, Esq., Threadneedle Street, London," per favor Mon. Blanchard or Dr. Franklin, who, I suppose, reviews your continent in an airy car, and seldom creeps (for an ordinary man may do that even better than the doctor) upon the surface of this vile globe. He has already mastered *one* element, you know; and since he has lost his *fire*, it is natural enough that he should have to contend with *wind*. You will pity me for writing such trash, to a man of business too, whose circuit continued from September to January (I want *faith*, James); but what can I do, who am neither a man of sense, nor a man of business? Why, I must write stuff, and nonsensical

* In 1785 the Assembly appropriated £36,000 for the purpose of purchasing tobacco on account of the State. The Commissioners were restricted in buying, to fifty shillings per 100 pounds. The tobacco was ordered to be shipped to the West Indies, that bills of exchange or money might be obtained to pay the State's portion of the debt due from the United States.

stuff, for there are good stuffs as well as bad ones. * * * We are not so inclined to croak as you are; for it is part of our creed, that in some future happy day we shall meet either in Europe or America, in your house or mine, and examine the lines of each other's countenances, which shall be frequently discomposed by loud laughs (yes, my Lord Chesterfield, loud laughs), and every species of hilarity. * * * * I was so much in the *great world*, when in London, that I often met Lord Macartney, who was very civil to me. Just before I quitted it, Mrs. Crewe invited me to meet a party at her house, consisting of the Duchess of Portland, and your favorite Mr. Burke and his wife. He is really a wonderful man. I will get the printed accounts of his impeachment of Hastings, and send them to you. Adieu! &c., &c.

A. IREDELL.

HOOPER TO IREDELL.

August 1st, 1786.

MY DEAR SIR:—Your very kind favor, by Mr. Johnston, has relieved me from much concern upon account of yourself and family. I have with much anxiety, since my return home, sought an opportunity to get a letter to your hand; and I flattered myself I had succeeded. I inclosed one to Davie by a very special messenger, and urged his utmost care and assiduity to forward it to you. What has become of it, he best knows.

We are all mortified that you are determined to balk the flattering expectations we had of having Mrs. Iredell, and others of your family, under our roof this fall. I was the more encouraged to hope this, as Miss Nelly, in a letter to Mrs. Huske, at Wilmington, mentions that, after your return home from Newbern, you talked as if your purpose was serious. My letter to you, via Halifax, was to press the propriety of this journey upon you, not only as your own, and the health of Mrs. Iredell, might profit by it, but to awaken your apprehensions on the score of that dear, lovely infant, with whose health your own happiness (I might say, perhaps, your life) is inseparably united. I wish that you may yet have occasion to alter your resolution, provided the want of health has no share in it. I confess I should be gratified at your feeling a few fears, if they should induce you to fly to us for allaying them. My Betsy had anticipated some pleasing rural scenes, to the enjoyment of which Miss Nelly's humor, vivacity, and good sense would have greatly contributed.

All of Mr. Hogg's family are here, except himself; he is busied in preparing the Capitol for the reception of the Assembly at Fayette. A thousand obstacles are cast in his way, and I am

somewhat doubtful if he will surmount them all. Our election will present a very busy scene of tumult and altercation. A vast variety of candidates, amongst whom I am not. I have received three deputations from the Hawfields. All they have drawn from me is, *that I shall think it my duty to serve, if elected; but that I am not a candidate, and shall bestow no pains to secure a seat in the Assembly.* What will be the event, is in the book of contingencies. The present competitors for the county are, Butler, two Mebanes, Carrington, M'Cauley, Cain, and some others of more ignoble note. For the town—Lytle, Taylor, Watters,*—the latter has some chance of success, though I think it rather doubtful.

I shall be happy to hear that the people of your county are restored to a lucid interval, and that they have given an earnest of their future sanity, by electing Mr. Johnston and yourself. Much good you may do them. You may temper the ardor of Maclaine, and keep under you the combustible stuff, which is so ready to burst and blaze forth, in our friend Hay, though, perhaps, the latter may fall short in his election, of which he is indecently sanguine in his expectations. He boils with as much fury against the judges, as Saul did against the Christians.

Perhaps you have not heard of the adventure in court at Wilmington, the last hour of the last term. Williams expressing his opinion upon the treaty of peace to Hay, and craving his attention to him. "So this is your opinion, Judge Williams—your servant, sir—I wish you a good night;" and, waving his hands and hat, and dodging his elegant bow, he marched out of the court-house. Williams, highly incensed, in strong terms proclaimed the insult to the Bench, and himself personally. He proposed that Hay should be struck off the roll of attorneys. Ashe acquiesced. Spencer sat silent. Huske was ordered to make the entry. It was partly finished. Ashe desired time to cool; stopped Huske's hands; the court adjourned without any thing more decisive. This was part only of the disgraceful business of the day. From the beginning to the close of it, Spencer and Williams were engaged in the most bitter altercation—nothing was wanting but blows to complete the farce. Thrice Williams furiously descended from the bench; and fifty times Spencer interrupted him attempting to speak. "Suffer me to do justice,—if you will not, I wash my hands clean—I wish others could." This becoming quarrel took place upon the question of Mallett's suits being suspended. Mallett prevailed.

* William Watters, of Cape Fear, represented Brunswick County in the Commons in '82 and '83; and in the Senate in '84 and '85. He removed subsequently to Hillsborough, where he wedded Mr. Hooper's daughter, Elizabeth. He was an amiable and estimable gentleman.

B⁕⁕⁕⁕⁕'s business is as it should be. Upon my arrival at Wilmington, I discouraged Marmaduke's action for slandering [t]le, and proposed that the whole merits of the question should be [d]iscussed in a suit in ejectment, to be brought by B—— against [t]he commissioner. It was agreed to, and stands for hearing.

I moved for a new trial in the pitiful suit that has given s[o] [m]uch uneasiness. I prevailed with the opinion of the thr[ee] [j]udges. I think him now in a favorable way, if he does not m[ar] very thing by his mean, low, servile condescensions. I would [n]ot for the best estate in this country stoop to such indignities as witnessed in his behavior at Wilmington. He talks of seeing [y]ou here at September Court. I have taken the liberty to hint [t]o him, that, if he expects your services, he must talk of sterling money, and something considerable. He professes great promptitude. "Caveto, hic niger est." I regret that our press here [h]as stopped. Davis has failed to supply us with paper. I am [s]omewhat at a loss how to act. I would certainly forward the [in]closure, with which I am highly pleased, to Newbern; but my [p]ower is circumvented by your letter; and, perhaps, you can [f]ind a more direct and immediate conveyance from Edenton.

I will no longer trespass upon you. I am highly favored [w]ith a letter from Mr. S. Johnston. I will answer it as soon as [I] have a belief that he is returned from Roanoke. Make the cor[d]ial regards, &c., &c.

WILL. HOOPER.

NOTE.—We have had our annual commencement or examination. The boys exceeded our most earnest expectations. They were examined in Latin, English, Natural Philosophy, Geography, Geometry, and Euclid: spoke a little in Latin and English; and diversified the scene by some ludicrous, well-chosen dialogues —to the high satisfaction of a vast concourse of people. Believe me, my dear Sir, my heart expanded with joy at this promising appearance of a school, which is a child of my own, and which I shall continue to rear with unremitting care. Pardon this effusion of *vanity* in an overweening parent. Tell Miss Nelly she [l]oses a Play by not spending the summer with us. ⁕ ⁕ ⁕ ⁕ ⁕

I had almost forgot to tell you, that a letter from Hay to a [f]riend of his has this passage: "I had wrote you before, but [h]ave been busily employed in collecting materials for a history of [t]he last Wilmington Superior Court, which I shall shortly entertain the public with."

What a feast have Johnston, you, and I, preparing for us!

MACLAINE TO IREDELL.

WILMINGTON, August 3d, 1786.

MY DEAR SIR :—Since our Superior Court, I have frequently determined to write to you; but at the close of the term, and several days before, I was greatly indisposed, and continued so almost the whole month, so that I was utterly unable to attend to any thing. At the County Court in the beginning of last month, I was seized with a slight fit of the gout, which confined me in no small pain for about ten days. Since that I have been constantly engaged. I am sorry the paper which you inclosed me, and which I received this day, did not come to my hands sooner. It is forwarded with this; but I am afraid will not get abroad as soon as might be wished.

At Superior Court we did business as usual—Tried about half-a-dozen jury causes; wrangled with the Judges, and they with each other; at least Spencer and Williams. The latter has sworn solemnly and openly, never to sit with the former again. The most shameful partiality disgraced the Bench; but the most curious case was that of Mallett. It cost the Court nearly three days, though the judgment of May 1783, on his acquittal, restored him to all the rights and privileges of a citizen, and ordered his causes, which had been suspended, to be put in their proper places on the docket. When their own judgment was produced against them, Williams boldly questioned the authenticity of it, though in the handwriting of Lillington, and prior to the answers of Nat. Allen & Collins, on Brailford's attachment. Ashe disavowed all knowledge of it. We suspected this, and were prepared for it. Luckily for the memory of poor Lillington, and as luckily for the reputation of Mallett's counsel, the entry was drawn up by Spencer, under one that Hay had offered, and which was thought not full enough. This paper had been with other loose ones carefully preserved in the office. Spencer, when called upon, acknowledged that the entry was word for word with his paper; which, however, I believe was pocketed by him or Williams; for it is not now to be found. The Court took till next day to deliver their opinion; and then, very wisely, determined that the question had been decided before: when Mr. Ashe declared that he did not recollect any thing of it, Mr. Moore pertinently remarked, that he was not surprised at it, for he remembered that his Honor had carried a recognizance to the ⁕ ⁕ ⁕ ⁕ ⁕

Our friend Hay is in disgrace with Ashe and Williams. The latter at the last hour of the Court (8 or 9 o'clock), began to preach with his usual effrontery, in order to convince Mr. Hay, that the Treaty of Peace, the Constitution, and the Articles of Confederation, had nothing to do in a question in which Mr. Hay had made a motion, and which was decided against him. Mr. Hay made a low bow, and wished his Honor a good night, leaving there *their Honors*, their Honors' clerk, Spiller, and a constable. Williams still proceeded, till Ashe asked him, to whom he was speaking? for that Mr. Hay was gone. Williams replied that Mr. Spiller was present, and willing that somebody should have the benefit of his sermon, continued as follows : " I say, I will convince *you, Mr. Spiller,*" &c. Ashe, not willing to lose an opportunity of striking at Hay, observed that he thought the latter did not use them well. Williams assented, and replied, that he should be struck off the list of attorneys. To this, Ashe said that *he* had no objections. Spencer was silent. The clerk was directed to make the entry; but before it was finished, Mr. Ashe observed that they might be too fast, and that it would be better to cool upon it. It seems, however, that the virtuous tumvirate have determined that Hay "shall apologize before he will be admitted to practise before their Honors."

I believe that Mr. B. is now perfectly safe, as the Commissioner has been prevailed upon to institute two suits against him. I am happy to hear that Mr. Johnston may be one of the Assembly. I shall be doubly so, if you will consent to be chosen. I have no idea of attending Newbern, though I have some business there, which should not be neglected. I have reason to believe I shall be chosen in preference to any who may offer; and, though my old friend walker has been long doing his best for others, as well as himself, not a man in the place thinks he can succeed. *Gen. Howe will, I believe, be returned from Brunswick, though opposed with great assiduity. He openly avows the most liberal principles,* and execrates the judges and other officers. If Mr. Hooper should be returned, as I expect will be the case, I believe he does not intend to be at Newbern, nor do I imagine that Col. Davie will be there. Every thing depends upon mustering all our forces, attending early, maturing our plans, and engaging auxiliaries. It will be easy for the lawyers to inform their Honors the judges, that the importance of the approaching session prevents their attendance at court; and with respect to our clients, they had better wait a term (and as business has been conducted, many of them will be obliged to wait), than have their cases continued for ever. Consider how much depends upon a reform, and how few men of business we have among us, &c., &c.

A. MACLAINE.

The letters I have transcribed are expositions of the opinions and prejudices of but one party; the views of the other side have either not survived the grave, or are still imprisoned in old desks, musty trunks, or in the crannies of crazy tumble-down dwellings. It is but right and proper that a fair allowance should be made for the flush of passion, and the exaggeration of political hatred. The judges, if imbued with prejudices originating in the war, had the countenance of the Assembly, and reflected truly the sentiments of the mass of the people. This powerful support alone enabled them successfully to resist the assaults of the best writers, the ablest advocates, and most erudite lawyers of the State. It is not fair to determine their merits, by referring to the standard of a more modern and cultivated period, though there is much in their career to kindle an ingenuous blush. Yet, even later, if Lord Cockburn is to be believed, scenes occurred frequently in the courts of Scotland, far transcending in infamy any that ever were enacted in North Carolina. In the Newbern paper, August 17th, appeared the following address from Mr. Iredell. It is an able examination of questions, then, it seems, much mooted, though now determined—the subordination of the Legislature to the authority of the Constitution, and the duty and right of the courts to pronounce null and void Acts of the Assembly inconsistent with that instrument, the supreme law. It is calm and judicial in its tone, compact and perspicuous, its argument cogent and direct, and its conclusions irresistible. I doubt if any superior contemporary effort on the same subjects is in existence.*

TO THE PUBLIC.

As the question concerning the power of the Assembly deeply concerns every man in the State, I shall make no apology for delivering my sentiments upon it. They are indeed only the sentiments of an obscure elector, but one who, he trusts, has rights that he as much values, though with less ability to defend them, as the proudest member of Assembly whatever.

I have not lived so short a time in the State, nor with so little interest in its concerns, as to forget the extreme anxiety with which all of us were agitated in forming the constitution, a constitution which we considered as the fundamental basis of our government, unalterable, but by the same high power which established it, and therefore to be deliberated on with the greatest caution, because if it contained any evil principle, the government formed under it must be annihilated before the evil could be corrected. It was, of course, to be considered how to impose restric-

---

* This was the earliest discussion of the doctrine in the United States; and was mainly instrumental in causing the decision in Den on the dem. of Bayard and wife *vs.* Singleton, Nov. 1787,—*vid.* Martin's Rep. vol. 1, p. 42,—ed. by Battle. This decision in N. C. was the first upon the point in the American States.

tions on the legislature, that might still leave it free to all useful purposes, but at the same time guard against the abuse of unlimited power, which was not to be trusted, without the most imminent danger, to any man or body of men on earth. We had not only been sickened and disgusted for years with the high and almost impious language from Great Britain, of the omnipotent power of the British Parliament, but had severely smarted under its effects. We felt in all its rigor the mischiefs of an absolute and unbounded authority, claimed by so weak a creature as man, and should have been guilty of the basest breach of trust, as well as the grossest folly, if in the same moment when we spurned at the *insolent despotism* of Great Britain, we had established a *despotic* power among ourselves. Theories were nothing to us, opposed to our own severe experience. We were not ignorant of the theory *of the necessity of the legislature being absolute in all cases*, because it was the great ground of the British pretensions. But this was a mere speculative principle, which men at ease and leisure thought proper to assume. When we were at liberty to form a government as we thought best, without regard to that or any theoretical principle we did not approve of, we decisively gave our sentiments against it, being willing to run all the risks of a government to be conducted on the principles then laid as the basis of it. The instance was new in the annals of mankind. No people had ever before deliberately met for so great a purpose. Other governments have been established by chance, caprice, or mere brutal force. Ours, thank God, sprang from the deliberate voice of the people. We provided, or meant to provide (God grant our purpose may not be defeated), for the security of every individual, as well as a fluctuating majority of the people. We knew the value of liberty too well, to suffer it to depend on the capricious voice of popular favor, easily led astray by designing men, and courted for insidious purposes. Nor could we regard, without contempt, a theory which required a greater authority in man than (with reverence be it spoken) exists even in the Supreme Being. For His power is not altogether absolute—His *infinite power* is limited by His *infinite wisdom*.

I have therefore no doubt, but that the power of the Assembly is limited and defined by the constitution. It is a *creature* of the constitution. (I hope this is an expression not prosecutable.) The people have chosen to be governed under such and such principles. They have not chosen to be governed, or promised to submit upon any other; and the Assembly have no more right to obedience on other terms, than any different power on earth has a right to govern us; for we have as much agreed to be governed by the Turkish Divan as by our own General Assembly, otherwise than on the express terms prescribed.

These are consequences that seem so natural, and indeed s irresistible, that I do not observe they have been much conteste The great argument is, that though the Assembly have not *right* to violate the constitution, yet if they *in fact* do so, the onl remedy is, either by a humble petition that the law may be re pealed, or a universal resistance of the people. But that in th mean time, their act, whatever it is, is to be obeyed as a law; fo the judicial power is not to presume to question the power of a act of Assembly.

To these positions, not unconfidently urged, I answer :—

1. That the remedy by petition implies a supposition, that th electors hold their rights by the *favor of their representative* The mere stating of this is surely sufficient to excite any man indignation. What! if the Assembly say, we shall elect onl once in two years, instead of electing annually, are we to petitio them to repeal this law? to request that they will be gracious pleased not to be our tyrants, but to allow us the benefit of th government we ourselves have chosen, and under which they alon derive all their authority?

But 2. The whole people may resist. A dreadful expedient i deed. We well know how difficult it is to excite the resistanc of a whole people, and what a calamitous contingency, at bes this is to be reduced to. But it is a sufficient answer, that noth ing can be powerful enough to effect such a purpose in a govern ment like ours, but *universal oppression*. A thousand injurie may be suffered, and many hundreds ruined, before this can b brought about. A majority may see A. B., C. D., and E. F., an hundreds of others quietly injured one after another, and not st a step towards a civil war. Let any man then ask himself, Sup pose a law is passed by which I am ruined! Have I interes enough to overturn the government of my country? If I have we still may be a ruined people, and myself ruined among th rest. If I have not, upon what footing do my liberties depend The pleasure of a majority of the Assembly? God forbid! Ho many things have been done by majorities of a large body in hea and *passion*, that they themselves afterwards have repented of Besides, would the *minority* choose to put themselves in th power of a majority? Few men, I presume, are always in *majority*. None, therefore, could have even a chance of bein secure, but sycophants that will for ever sacrifice reason, con science, and duty, to the preservation of a temporary popula favor. Will this not put an end to all freedom of deliberatio to all manly spirit, and prove the utter extinction of all rea liberty?

But this resource is evidently derived from the principle o *unbounded legislative power*, that I have noticed before, and tha

our constitution reprobates. In England they are in this condition. In England, therefore, they are less free than we are. Every parliament in that country chosen for *three* years, continued itself for seven. This is an absolute fact, that happened long within the present century. Would this be a fit precedent for us? May our Assembly do so, because their Parliament did? May our governor have a negative on the laws, because he has a faint image of monarchical power? As little, I trust, is the government of Great Britain to influence in other things, equally inconsistent with our condition, and equally preposterous as these.

These two remedies then being rejected, it remains to be inquired whether the judicial power hath any authority to interfere in such a case. The duty of that power, I conceive, in all cases, is to decide according to the *laws of the State*. It will not be denied, I suppose, that the constitution is a *law of the State*, as well as an act of Assembly, with this difference only, that it is the *fundamental* law, and unalterable by the legislature, which derives all its power from it. One act of Assembly may repeal another act of Assembly. For this reason, the latter act is to be obeyed, and not the former. An act of Assembly cannot repeal the constitution, or any part of it. For that reason, an act of Assembly, inconsistent with the constitution, is *void*, and cannot be obeyed, without disobeying the superior law to which we were previously and irrevocably bound. The judges, therefore, must take care at their peril, that every act of Assembly they presume to enforce is warranted by the constitution, since if it is not, they act without lawful authority. This is not a usurped or a discretionary power, but one inevitably resulting from the constitution of their office, they being judges *for the benefit of the whole people*, not *mere servants of the Assembly*. And the danger, about which there is so much alarm, attending the exercise of this power is, in my opinion, the least that can be imagined to attend the exercise of any important power whatever. For the judges, besides the natural desire which must be entertained by every man living in a popular government, of securing the favor of the people, are in fact dependent on the Assembly; for though their duration in office is permanent, at least as long as the act is in being which establishes their court, *their salaries are precarious;* and in fact are they only nominally independent in point of station, when the Assembly may every session determine how much they shall have to subsist upon. Did any man in England, previous to the Revolution, apprehend any injury to the prerogative from the judges of those days? They depended indeed, both for salary and place, on the breath of the crown. But the dependence here, I am persuaded, will in general be found equally effectual, at least to prevent a wanton abuse of power, and, it is much to be feared, may

in some instances produce an actual bias the other way, which, i my humble opinion, is the great danger to be apprehended. may also be observed, that if the judges should be disposed to abus their power, merely for the sake of the abuse, they have mean enough of doing so, for every act of Assembly may occasional come under their judgment in one shape or other, and *those ac may be wilfully misconstrued, as well as the constitution.*

But it is said, if the judges have this power, so have th county courts. I admit it. The county courts, in the exercis of equal judicial power, must have equal authority. But ever argument in respect to the judges (except their dependence fo salary), and other obvious ones, occur in great force against thi danger, besides the liberty of appeal, which ultimately rest every thing, almost, with the superior courts. The objection, how ever, urged by some persons, that sheriffs and other *ministeria* officers must exercise their judgment too, does not apply. Fo *if the power of judging rests with the courts*, their decision is fina as to the subject matter. Did ever a sheriff refuse to hang a man because he thought he was unjustly convicted of murder?

These are a few observations that have occurred to me on thi subject. They are given by a plain man, unambitious of powe but sincerely and warmly interested in the prosperity of his coun try; feeling every respect for the constitutional authority of th legislature, which, in his opinion, is great enough to satisfy a ambitious, as well as to support the efforts of a public-spirite mind, but a determined enemy on all occasions to arbitrary powe in every shape whatsoever; and reverencing, beyond expressio that constitution by which he holds all that is dear to hi in life.

AN ELECTOR.*

MACLAINE TO IREDELL.

WILMINGTON, N. C., August 24th, 1786.

DEAR SIR :—We have had the heaviest and most constan rains in this part of the country which I have known for year They began the 17th, and continued, almost without ceasing, fo

---

* The doctrine maintained by Mr. Iredell in this address, and in his letter to D. Spaight (August 26th, 1787), in its application to acts of Congress, inconsiste with the Federal Constitution, was long a matter of dispute among lawyers, a only authoritatively settled by Chief Justice Marshall, in the noted case of Marbur *vs* Madison (1 Cranch's Reps.), 1803. The principle was asserted by Judge Patte son in the earlier case of Van Horne's Lessees *vs*. Dorrance (2 Dallas), 1795, an by Judge Iredell, in Calder et ux *vs*. Bull (3 Dallas).

Long before the final adjudication by the Supreme Court, Iredell seems almo to have exhausted the argument.

two days and nights. I am afraid we shall have no corn on the low lands; and if the waters have been as high in Roanoke, I do not know what will become of us.

I should have wrote you sooner, but I wished to inform you of the elections in this neighborhood; and though I have waited so long, I have heard very little; for this country is yet afloat. Gen. Howe is returned for Brunswick. For New Hanover and Wilmington the old members. Duplin nearly the same. From the other counties in this district, I have not had any certain news. I am particularly anxious to hear from Bladen and Cumberland; from the former, in hopes that they have exchanged a very bad man for a very good one; and from the latter, in hopes that Mr. Hay and Mr. Winslow are chosen. When I learn I shall acquaint you, in hopes that you will communicate the names of those elected in your district, especially those for Chowan and Edenton. About these two places and Orange I am more solicitous than any others; if I do not think of them in my prayers, which are generally very short, I make it up in dreaming of them. Next to the places I have mentioned, I wish to know the fate of Craven and Newbern, as that arch-scoundrel, Coor, has been doing every thing that cunning and malice could suggest, to keep Spaight and Sitgreaves out.* Yesterday came to my hands the New Bern paper of the 17th, in which I observe a piece signed "An Elector," which I wish had been sooner published, as in the light reading which my time permitted me to give it, it appears to me to contain true constitutional principles. It is however to be lamented, that those who may be esteemed tolerably qualified for giving information on subjects of so much importance to the people, are so widely scattered over an extensive country, and the greatest part of them so distant from the press, that it is extremely difficult to discuss such subjects so as to have the intended effect. Very extraordinary exertions are necessary to arouse the people to a sense of their danger; for notwithstanding the plain principles of the constitution, they seem to think themselves safe from every species of internal tyranny, having succeeded so well in freeing themselves from a foreign yoke—a palpable proof of their ignorance, or want of virtue. Pray let me hear from you, &c., &c.,

A. MACLAINE.†

* James Coor, member of the "General Meeting of Deputies," Aug. 15th, 1774, of the Assembly, April, 1775, and also 21st of August, and again in 1776; in 1775 of the "Provincial Council of Safety;" he served in the Senate 1777–'87; in 1786 this "arch-scoundrel" was elected Speaker of the Senate. His record seems an honorable one. Of his private character I know nothing.

† Maclaine's friends, Hooper, Hay, Col. Davie, Sitgreaves, Spaight, and General Allen Jones, were all elected. These, with himself, formed a very formidable array, possessing talents, learning, and experience. General Rutherford, Jesse Franklin, and Col. Jno. B. Ashe were also of the same Assembly—the two latter were subsequently elected Governors, and belonged, I suppose, to the opposition, of which the former was a conspicuous leader. Mr. Cabarrus represented Edenton, vide Wheeler.

IREDELL TO MRS. IREDELL.

HALIFAX, September 30th.

* * * * "It is reported that Captain Fenner is to be married to Miss Houson. Tell my niece that that Porpoise, Capt. P******, is so much in love with Miss Lucas, that he would fan her the other evening, though the weather was extremely cold to everybody but himself. I came here to dinner, and had the luxury to dine with her. She and Miss Cooke were both at Bond's, where I was pressed to dine."

The Assembly met at Fayetteville, the 18th of November. As frequent acts of hostility had been committed by the Indians on the inhabitants of Davidson county, for a considerable time past, two hundred and one soldiers were promptly ordered to be raised, and marched into the Cumberland settlements.* Five Commissioners were appointed to the Convention proposed to be held in Philadelphia, in May, 1787, to revise the Federal Constitution. The preamble to the act embodies the sentiments of Mr. Iredell's friends, and its passage was due in a great degree to their exertions. Of the five Commissioners appointed three were of the opposition. Dr. Williamson was afterwards appointed in the place of Wilie Jones, who declined. His colleagues were Gov. Caswell, Col. Davie, A. Martin, and R. D. Spaight. The Assembly adjourned January 6th.

REV. A. IREDELL TO IREDELL.

REIGATE, Surrey, Dec. 5th, 1785.

MY DEAR BROTHER:— * * * * I passed indeed a most delicious month; and at the same time contrived to pay a visit at Crewe Hall, where I stumbled upon Lord Macartney. They were all vastly civil to me; but in my then temper of mind, the very sight of a *great house*, a large establishment, fine folks, and, above all, the glittering of a star, was hateful to me. I pined (as you did some ten years ago) for shady walks, and purling streams; the breathing zephyrs, and the cooling groves. Without burlesque, I was miserable till I returned to my small, but infinitely rich circle at Doddlespool—where you, I do assure you, and your friends, were a very frequent topic. The little Annie was often dandled on the knee; and sometimes her awkward uncle, in the riot of his imagination, would caricature the atti-

* Davidson county and the Cumberland settlements were in what is now Tennessee.

tudes of a nurse. And by the way, sir, when I get a house of my own, and you have more children, I shall lay a very serious claim to the possession of the *aforesaid* Annie, that I may realize the *above-mentioned* ideal happiness. * * * * These are troublesome times, I fear, in America; and from what I could learn from Mr. Traill, the situation of North Carolina is not so enviable a one as I could wish it to be. However, that gentleman (whom I had the pleasure to see on my return from Cheshire, and who is a very agreeable man) gave me the last accounts of your family, and with them I will be for the present content. I mean to call on him whenever I go to York, where he resides, I find, during the winter; but that will be very seldom, as "*entre nous*," my finances are at this time, like the national, not in the most flourishing condition. I have a curacy near this place, to which I stick remarkably close. * * * I will stretch a point to allay, if possible, your political thirst. A commercial treaty with France has been concluded; and will be ratified by Parliament the moment it meets after Christmas. You will have seen the articles long before this reaches you. One of them greatly affects the West Indies, that relative to brandy, which is to be imported at the reduced duty of seven shillings per gallon. What will become of the rum trade I know not; but a meeting of the West India proprietors, merchants, &c., has been held, and a committee has waited upon Mr. Pitt, who has refused, I hear, to lower the duties on rum in a proportionate degree, which was the proposition they submitted to him. Mr. Eden is about to return to conclude another commercial arrangement, by which the English and French islands are to be suffered to trade with each other. How will that affect the United States? All the papers and conversation here are engrossed by Mr. Bowes, who had forcibly taken away Lady Strathmore, his wife, and confined her in the country: a "habeas corpus" issued: he paid no obedience; and an "attachment" followed, under which she is now in the King's Bench. The fact is, Lady S. is, and ever was, a strange woman. She was an immense heiress: a poor Scotch Lord married her: she broke his heart. Bate (the famous fighting parson, and editor of the Morning Post at that time), put some paragraphs against her in his paper. Captain Stoney, who wanted her *fortune*, fought him, and was wounded: she married him, having lain the night before with *another* man. Since that time it has been a constant struggle which should behave the worse, and no one can say which has succeeded,* &c., &c.

A. IREDELL.

* Mary Eleanor, daughter of George Bowes, of Gilside, county of Durham, married John 9th, Earl of Strathmore; after his death she married Robinson Stoney, who assumed the name of Bowes.

ALFRED MOORE TO IREDELL.

Mr. Moore was born in Brunswick county, May 21st, 1755: he was the son of Maurice Moore, one of the royal judges, and member of a family otherwise distinguished in the annals of Carolina, for opulence, talents, and the dignity of the positions it had held. After receiving an imperfect education at Boston, he entered the army as captain of the first regiment of the North Carolina Continental line in 1775. At the close of the war he commenced the study of the law, and succeeded Mr. Iredell as Attorney-General in 1782? In 1798 he was called to the Bench of the State; and was appointed December 10th, 1799, one of the "Associate Justices of the Supreme Court of the United States," to fill the place made vacant by the death of Judge Iredell. "He was a small man, neat in his dress, and graceful in his manners; his voice was clear and sonorous, his perceptions quick, and his judgment almost instinctive; his style was chaste, and his manner of speaking animated. His language was always plain. The clearness and energy of his mind enabled him, almost without an effort, to disentangle the most intricate subject, and expose it in all its parts to the simplest understanding. He spoke with ease and force, enlivened his discourses with flashes of wit, and when the speech required it, with all the bitterness of sarcasm. His speeches were short and impressive: when he sat down, every one thought he had said every thing he ought to have said."* A parallel has often been run between him and General Davie; as a lawyer he bore the same relation to Davie that, at the New York bar, Col. Burr did to Gen. Hamilton. A participation in the conviviality that characterized the profession, and the politicians of that era, induced an indolent habit, and led to his resignation in 1804. Retiring to his plantation, upon the Cape Fear, he devoted the remainder of his life to the care and augmentation of his estate. In his latter days he spent much time in the instruction of his grandchildren. His temper, acidulated by the infirmities of age, sometimes broke out in sallies of passion; but the untiring care, with which he watched and stimulated the intellectual and moral culture of his little ones, attested his profound interest, and redeemed from censure the frailty of his humanity. He died October 15th, 1810.

WILMINGTON, Dec. 14th, 1786.

DEAR SIR:—The Court has risen; and the Judges have notice of charges against them before the Assembly; that they *may* attend if they *please*. We have very little news of impor-

* Judge Murphy's address at Chapel Hill, 1827.

tance from the Assembly, except the above : I believe, indeed, that little has been done, if we except the zealous measures that are pursued against the forgers of military claims : many of these are in close confinement, and their money seized as we hear : this iniquity does not seem to be confined to Dobbs county, which can only claim the *greatest* rogues.——Judge Spencer showed me to-day an abstract from a letter of Mr. Hay, containing the charges against the Judges—some of them are quite new to me.

"High fines, and a shameful appropriation of them.
"Admitting new, and illegal prosecutions (depreciation, &c.)
"The banishment of Brice and McNeil.
"Dispensing with laws (the Newbern case).
"Negligence of their duty, and delay of business.
"Ill behavior to Mr. Hay at Wilmington."

These, and a few other charges which I did not understand when I read them, nor can remember now, are urged against their Honors with great violence. Mr. Ashe says, he has clean hands, and a pure heart; and disregards the clamor : he stays at home ; but Mr. Spencer, and Mr. Williams will set off with me to-morrow for Fayette. The Assembly have resolved that I shall attend them ; but do not say for what purpose : a day or two ago this resolve was handed to me by the express who brought the notice to the Judges.

It is supposed that our present Courts will be continued ; *because they cannot agree on* a plan to succeed, of which, however, they have a multitude. The line between this State and South Carolina is to be run, to the great delight of Dr. Williamson, who, I learn, is to be the Palinurus to guide them through darkness and difficulties.

There have been three grand balls, and two horse races at this place within a week : and at this moment five fiddles are playing a lively tune, and the whole town are dancing to it. I am struck with a vain conceit of my superiority over you, being able to write, when you could do nothing but dance. I hope, however, if you are not dancing, that you are well enough to do so; and that your whole family are in perfect health.—Be pleased to give them my best respects, and believe me, dear Sir,
Very sincerely yours,
A. MOORE.

Gen. Howe is at the verge of the grave : it is supposed he will die in a few days : he has only got as far as Gen. Clark's.

CHAPTER XX.

ÆT. 35–36.

STATE TRIALS AT WARRENTON, STROLLING PLAYERS, LETTERS FROM HOOPER, IREDELL, AND WHITMELL HILL ; FEDERAL CONVENTION AT PHILADELPHIA, LETTERS FROM DAVIE, SPAIGHT, AND WILLIAMSON (MEMBERS OF THE CONVENTION) ; FEDERALIST AND ANTI-FEDERALIST, CANVASS AT EDENTON, LETTERS FROM CABARRUS, IREDELL, AND MACLAINE ; CONSTITUTION, MEETING AT EDENTON, AND ADDRESS OF GRAND JURY ; ASSEMBLY, IREDELL COUNCILLOR OF STATE, AND COMMISSIONER TO REVISE THE LAWS ; LETTER FROM HOOPER.

THE most striking incidents of the early part of the year 1787 were the State trials at Warrenton. In '85 Ben. McCulloh, John Macon, and Henry Montfort, had been appointed commissioners to liquidate the accounts of the officers and soldiers of the Continental Line. Not long afterwards rumors, exaggerated by a thousand echoes, spread abroad, that two of the commissioners, and other persons, had contrived and carried on many notorious, fraudulent, and indecent practices, to the public detriment, and to the injury of many of the citizens ; that the said commissioners, with a view to their own exorbitant profit, had dishonestly confederated, in violation of the trust confided to them ; and that they had been guilty of pernicious and infamous corruptions, to the ruin of the public credit.* Great was the popular indignation ! The attention of the Assembly was soon directed to the investigation of the alleged frauds. Satisfied of their reality, they ordered a special court of Oyer and Terminer, to be held at Warrenton on the last Monday in January. Indictments were speedily found against McCulloh and Montfort, and others of less note. The military and legislative services, the wealth, the social

* Vide Statutes.

rank, the influential connections of the commissioners, the array of attorneys, renowned for eloquence and learning—all conspired to raise public expectation to the highest pitch. Alfred Moore was prosecutor ; Iredell and Davie appeared for the defendants. The profound interest of the public in the success of the prosecution, and the heavy stakes of the defendants—their fortunes, and, more than all, their characters, stimulated the efforts of counsel to the greatest degree; and seldom in North Carolina has a more brilliant display of forensic power been witnessed. Montfort was acquitted ; but McCulloh was convicted, sentenced to pay a fine of £4,000, and to be imprisoned twelve months in Halifax jail. His advocates thought that " through his whole trial he met with the greatest tyranny and injustice from two of the court ; that he was charged beyond his real offence ;" that " he had strong prejudices, both of the people and court, to encounter, and had been convicted of more than he had done, or been capable of doing—taking accounts to pass them, *right or wrong.*" The people of Warren spoke " with the utmost horror and resentment of his sentence." The white hairs of his venerable father (Hon. Alex. Mc. Culloh, member of the royal council, &c.), now trembling upon the verge of the grave, the distress of his wife, and the tears of his children, soon awakened for him the sympathy of the compassionate, and touching appeals were made, though in vain, to the clemency of the governor and council. Mr. McCulloh protested against his complicity in any fraud ; but privately confessed that he had become voluntarily interested in accounts that were to be examined by a Board, of which he was a member. This disabled him from performing his trust impartially, and certainly was sufficient to justify the suspicions of men experienced in the ways of the world ; and, if established at the trial, excused, if it did not justify, the verdict of the jury. At the same court, Price, Butcher, and Reid were convicted—the two former of presenting fictitious accounts, and the latter of signing blank accounts for pay. The moral result of the trial was most salutary; it vindicated the supremacy of the law, and the confinement of Mr. McCulloh in a rude and noisome cell, " whose stench was intolerable ;" proclaimed to the world, that in North Carolina neither wealth nor influence could shelter any man from the penalties of crime.*

The following letter from that mutilated veteran, John Stokes, shows how sensibly that high-spirited gentleman was affected by the disgrace of his brother-in-law.†

* Letters from Iredell to Mrs. Iredell.
† Subsequently Judge of the Court of the U. S. for the district of North Carolina.

SALISBURY, 1787.
MY DEAR SIR :—I have received your very obliging favor by the hands of Col. Davie. I am singularly happy to learn that you are (after so many severe attacks of illness) now in good health.

It was unnecessary for you to have mentioned to me the extreme pain which the situation of B. McCulloh gave you. My knowledge of your goodness had informed me as much long before I received your letter. It is needless to add more on that subject. You can readily imagine how I feel on the occasion. The subject is too disagreeable to dwell on. I wish I was ignorant of it. I think of it by day. It is represented to me in my dreams, which are wont to make it nothing but a phantom. The blushing morn establishes the reality, and renews my grief. Believe me, my dear sir, there is not a man in the world more happy to hear from you, or more solicitous for your happiness, than
JNO. STOKES.

For the first time in many years, a company of strolling players visited North Crrolina, and performed in all the chief towns. It appears that they kindled quite a spirit of emulation in the breasts of the young, that led to many associations for gratuitous exhibitions. Miss Blair wrote Mr. Iredell, from Edenton, " Folly, you will hear, has not altogether taken her departure from this town with the actors ; our young gentlemen are going to distinguish themselves." At Halifax the " Spanish Friar " was advertised, but as there were only five tickets sold at sunset, the doors remained closed. " I am told the indelicacy of it was the cause, and if so, I suppose it is very indelicate indeed "* At New Bern, Mr. Iredell and Mr. Johnston attended the play (the Miser). The former wrote his wife: " I never was so disgusted in my life. They are a most execrable set, infinitely worse than ours ; and the great Mr. Smith appeared to me the greatest blockhead I ever saw. This opinion was pretty general. The place was a most abominable one, and one.half the audience could neither hear nor see. When the Spanish Friar was performed, two of the actors (Kidd and McGrath) fought behind the scenes ; the stage was soon invaded by a crowd of people ; the curtain was down at the time. When they arrived at Wilmington, Mr. Robinson, manager of the " American Company of Comedians," inserted a notice in the State Gazette,† that he had fitted up an " elegant theatre," that he intended to stay one month, and would give Mr. Solomon, comedian, a " cordial reception,' if he would come on.

* Letter from Mr. Iredell.
† Published at Newberne, by Hodge and Blanchard. See No. 107.

HOOPER TO IREDELL.

HILLSBOROUGH, March 1st, 1787.

DEAR SIR:—Your kind favor by Mr. Moore, together with a letter of a later date, came safe to hand. Accept my grateful acknowledgments for your kind remembrance of me.

I have just now returned from the most painful visit that I ever paid in my life. Your old friend, Gen. Clarke, is struck with blindness. He went to bed in perfect good health; rose at the accustomed hour; opened his window shutters; the view of the house appeared to be in an undulating motion; black and yellow spots floating upon the surface of the earth; the floor of his chamber covered with dry brush, which he attempted to kick away; complained to his servants that the day was dark and cloudy, who informed him that the sun shone with remarkable brightness; bound up his eyes, and the next morning awakened stone blind. My hand was in his without his knowing me; my voice helped him to the discovery. His firmness is beyond all description. Thus, he tells me, he reasoned when he was first attacked: "Shall I blow my brains out? It will be pusillanimity. I can do it. But to dare to be blind for life, will be an effort that will discover real resolution." Not a single complaint, no repining. He is now on his plantation, without a single white person. It is a school to which I would recommend youth, to learn philosophy, and to bear misfortune. I always loved the man; I reverence him blind; he is something more than man. I shall carry a statement of his case to Dr. Lennox, when I visit Edenton, that we may avail ourselves of his advice.

I rejoice that your dear little girl is well—that you are all well. God bless you all! May you never feel the affliction with which Providence has wounded us! Love to Mr. Johnston and family.

Bring your *gown* with you. The judges have issued their edict, that we shall wear gowns, or not have the supreme honor to appear in their presence, &c., &c.*

WILL. HOOPER.

IREDELL TO MRS. IREDELL.

MY DEAR HANNAH:— * * * The Court have done an amazing quantity of business both here and at Salisbury. They be-

* The Judges so rigidly enforced the rule, that only one counsel should be heard in any cause, that Mr. Iredell felt himself constrained to refund his fee in a case, wherein he was retained with Mr. Hooper.

gin punctually at ten, and continue sitting until near sunset every day. I am heartily glad of it. The people about Salisbury say, they are convinced the fault before was in the Judges, not in the lawyers, the latter discovering no kind of reluctance at the present amendment, &c., &c.

JAS. IREDELL.

WHITMELL HILL TO IREDELL.*

DEAR SIR:— * * * If they (*the Judges*) are disposed to afford me another hearing, I shall suppress the article for the press of course; but, if not, I shall feel a great propensity to expose them to the world; and am in earnest to endeavor their removal at the ensuing Assembly. I wish you could be elected. Surely your enemies are a blind, stupid set, that wish *damnation* to their country: I wish I knew who were most pointedly against you: I would take some pains to set them right: I expect it is within your own town, &c., &c.

WHITMELL HILL.

From New Berne, May 25th, '87, Mr. Iredell wrote his wife:—" We are doing an immense deal of business here, which is signified to the world in a very ridiculous puff in favor of the Judges in one of the newspapers."

The 1st of May was the day designated for the meeting, at Philadelphia, of the Convention to revise the Articles of Confederation. It was not, however, until the 25th, that the Convention organized by the election of Washington as President.

COL. DAVIE TO IREDELL.

William R. Davie was a native of England. As a partisan officer, during the war, he was greatly distinguished for his enterprise and gallantry. As Commissary-General of the Southern army, he became familiarized with accounts; and acquired mercantile precision, and accuracy in business. In '83 he settled at Halifax, and commenced his first circuit in February. In '86 and '87, he represented Halifax in the Commons: and in the latter year was also a member of the Federal Convention at Philadelphia. He was again in the Assembly in '89, '91, '93, '94, '96, and '98. He was appointed by the President a Briga-

* Whitmell Hill of Martin—member of popular Assemblies in '75 and '76—member of the Continental Congress, 1778-81. Wheeler says: "He was a man of fine literary attainments, a devoted patriot, and useful citizen."

dier General in the army of the United States in '98; and on the 4th of December of the same year, was elected Governor of the State. In '99 he went to France, with Ellsworth and Murray, as American ambassadors. He filled, also, at different times, various other important offices. He was tall, well made, and remarkable for his manly beauty, and the dignity of his manners. If he had superiors in legal learning, and close reasoning, he as an orator was inferior to none in the State. His diction was copious; his illustrations opulent, and varied; and his periods well balanced, and ornate. If he had faults as a speaker, they were—that he spoke too much "ore rotundo;" that he sacrificed simplicity and perspicuity, to pomp, and majesty; that he thought more of what it became him to say, than of producing conviction. Thus it was, that though he ever charmed his auditories, he often failed to change a vote in legislative assemblies. His arrows, though pointed with wit, frequently flashed above the heads, instead of reaching the hearts, of those he designed as victims. In physical attributes he was highly endowed: his voice, though sonorous, was yet mellifluous, and capable of infinite intonations; and, at times, its melody had all the fascination of music. Select and cultivated audiences, such as listen to the efforts of Everett, and Choate, in the great cities of the Union, he would have startled by his brilliancy, and excited to rapturous applause.

His fortune grew rapidly; and, in his mode of life, perhaps, he was luxurious: his habits were studious: his tastes refined; and his intimate companions carefully chosen. He seemed ignorant of the fact that the populace are ever won by the condescensions of the great; or his pride would not stoop to low arts for the sake of popularity. To the establishment of republican principles he had eminently contributed; and among them he cherished none more than those which secured to the individual his independence: he would never admit the right of a mob to invade the sanctity of his privacy; to proscribe his pictures, or comment upon the extravagance of his equipage. For the good of the state, he bore himself too loftily; and thus forfeited the love of the people. In 1803 he was beaten for Congress by Willis Alston. The charge of aristocracy, fatal in America! was pressed against him, and the radicalism of the people caused a revolt against their ancient leader. The disappointment and the mortification consequent upon it, drove him from the State. He retired in 1805 to Tivoli, near Landsford, S. Carolina, where he died in 1820.*

* Vid. Wheeler; and the admirable memoir contributed by Prof. Hubbard to Sparks' American Biography, vol. 15.

PHILADELPHIA, May 30th, 1787.

DEAR SIR:—After a very fatiguing and rapid journey I arrived here on the 22d. The gentlemen of the Convention had been waiting from day to day for the presence of seven States; on the 25th the members from Jersey attended, and Gen. Washington was chosen President. Yesterday nine States were represented, and the great business of the meeting was brought forward by Virginia, with whom the proposition for a Convention had originated.

As no progress can yet be expected in a business so weighty, and, at the same time, so complicated, you will not look for any news now from this quarter.

Be so good as to favor me, by the next post, with your opinion how far the introduction of judicial and executive powers, derived from Congress, would be politic or practicable in the States. And whether *absolute* or *limited* powers for the regulation of trade, both as to *exports*, and *imports*, &c.

I shall trouble you frequently; and I shall expect your opinion without reserve, &c., &c.

W. R. DAVIE.

PHILADELPHIA, June 19th, 1787.

MY DEAR SIR:—I am under great obligations to you for your letter of the 4th inst. I was agreeably surprised at the unexpected firmness and independence of Judge Williams: he has deceived the whole party: they counted on him as "*dead sure.*" How mysterious are the ways of Providence! This is the effect of the Fayetteville business. Mr. Blount's case is a remarkable instance of the deep political sagacity of our Judges, and the high and delicate sense they have of their duty. What a blessed trio for the reformation of morals! and to preserve and promote the happiness of a community. So all *actions* are to be deemed laudable or criminal by their consequences to society, without any respect to the cause or motive!

Among the late publications of particular merit, a performance of Mr. J. Adams, the American Minister at the British Court, now signally engages the attention of the public: this book, which he calls a defence of the Constitution of the United States against the opinions of Mons. Turgot, is one continued encomium on the British Constitution, and that unequalled balance and security produced by the admirable mixture of democracy, aristocracy, and monarchy in that Government.

I have nothing worth inclosing you, but a paper containing a list of members, &c., &c.

W. R. DAVIE.

VOL. II.—11

Spaight to Iredell.

PHILADELPHIA, 3d July, 1787.

DEAR SIR:—* * * The Convention has made, as yet, but little progress in the business they have met on; and it is a matter of uncertainty when they will finish. Secrecy being enjoined I can make no communications on that head.

By advices from France we are informed that great confusion prevails there on account of the total derangement of their finances. Mons. De Calonne is removed from office; and is impeached by the Marquis De LaFayette, for malpractice and embezzlement, &c. Its consequences have had a disagreeable effect upon mercantile transactions here: it is said to have occasioned a number of Mr. Morris's bills to be protested, to a very considerable amount—the particular sum I don't know—report says from 50 to £150,000 sterling. What effect it will have I know not: a number of persons are interested in the event.

The General Court of Massachusetts have lately passed an act for raising a body of regular troops for the *support of Government*, not to exceed 800 men, nor less than 500. This is strictly within the Articles of Confederation. The General Assembly of Connecticut have reprobated, in very severe terms, in the course of their debates and proceedings, the conduct of the State of Rhode Island: and have ultimately come to a determination to remonstrate to Congress, against the injustice of the proceedings of Rhode Island. I should not be surprised if they were to compel them by force to do justice to their citizens (citizens of Connecticut). It seems their laws enable them to pay the citizens of any other State off with their paper money which is depreciated to eight or nine for one; but do not allow the citizens of any other State to pay them off with it. Their mode of process is, that any citizen of Rhode Island who is indebted to the citizen of any other State, or a foreigner, may go and lodge the debt in paper money, in the hands of any magistrate, who gives him a discharge for the same, and advertises the payment that the creditor may come in and take his money, which, if he does not do in a certain limited time, the law requires that it shall be paid into the public treasury for the benefit of the State.

I am sorry to find by letters from the Governor, that the conduct of the Franklinites is likely to involve the Western country in a civil war,* &c., &c.

RICH'D DOBBS SPAIGHT.

* The inhabitants of Western Carolina (Tennessee), alarmed at the act ceding their territory to the United States, revolted against the State of North Carolina,

under the lead of Col. Sevier (of King's Mountain), and formed an independent constitution. North Carolina proceeded vigorously to enforce her authority; and after great tumults and much civil commotion, the rebellion was crushed. The last Assembly of Frankland met September 17, 1787. The Act of Cession, passed April, 1784, was repealed in October of the same year. This territory was finally conveyed to the United States, February, 1790.

Dr. Williamson to Iredell.

PHILADELPHIA, July 8th, 1787.

DEAR SIR:—I received your favor by which you were so good as to inform me of the issue of my suits. I was by no means surprised that all your endeavors proved fruitless to obtain the proper value of tobacco. When it becomes a man's interest to do wrong, Judges themselves may try to pervert justice. I hope the necessary steps have been taken to recover the adjudicated balance from Montford, for it would be grievous "*post omnia perdere naulum.*" In this State, the season, which has been rather wet, is becoming dry. I have wished very much to hear what prospects there are for crops of corn in North Carolina, but nobody thinks it worth while to mention such a subject. Our accounts from Virginia are that great complaints of drouth prevail. I think it more than likely that we shall not leave this place before the middle of August. The diverse and almost opposite interests that are to be reconciled, occasion us to progress very slowly. I fear that Davie will be obliged to leave us before our business is finished, which will be a heavy stroke to the delegation. We have occasion for his judgment, for I am inclined to think that the great exertions of political wisdom in our late Governor,* while he sat at the helm of our State, have so exhausted his fund, that time must be required to enable him again to exert his abilities to the advantage of the nation.

If the good citizens of Chowan should think fit on the present year to dispense with the abilities and labor of Squire Jordin and should submit to such services as, Mr. Samuel Johnston can render, I hope that he will not refuse to serve. My reason, as you may readily believe, is that some men of understanding may be in the House who are capable of explaining and promoting such measures as may be recommended by the Convention, &c.

HU. WILIAMSON.

Maclaine to Iredell.

WILMINGTON, July 11th, 1787.

DEAR SIR:—Mr. Rutherford sending to Edenton upon business, affords me an opportunity of writing to you, and sincerely

* Governor Martin.

expressing my hope that you have recovered from your late indisposition.

Constantly as my time was employed in Newbern, it was nothing to what I have had to do here. Numbers of plaintiffs were nonsuited, some of them whose witnesses were not above thirty or forty steps from the Court: if my clients were known by the Judges (for some of them were favored), they had no quarter. My whole time has been employed in, and out of Court, in drawing declarations whenever there was a leisure moment. The equity business, except a very few causes (one of which was determined most iniquitously), all lie over, and in such confusion that it is impossible they should ever be decided properly, but by chance. The criminal business has been trifling, and no otherwise remarkable than for trifling fines for atrocious trespasses, when the favorites of the Court were defendants; and heavy fines, when the malice of the Judges was to be gratified. In one of those against the Commissioners of the town, for pulling down the old Court-house, Ashe reflected upon me with his usual rancor, and I returned it with my usual warmth, to the great satisfaction of the bystanders. Upon the new trial upon Burgwin's disability to sue, he was triumphant, the Judges, in particular, being strongly in his favor. The confiscation suits lie over, and we may be assured will end in smoke. I have, in addition to other torments, been tormented with the rheumatism. Out of two hundred and thirty causes on our last County Court docket we did not get over thirty tried. The Rocky Point Justices and their adherents are numerous; and they kept possession of the Bench the whole term. I am told they alleged that the judgments given in the Superior Court last Circuit amount to more than all the money in the country would pay, and that the people ought to have a respite. The truth is, they and their friends were all sued.*

Mr. Jones continues still in a very debilitated state, and has not been able to attend the Courts; but he eats like a dragon. The lawyers' letter to Judge Ashe is now ready, and will be delivered immediately. Spiller put his hand to it last Saturday. I shall give his honor a week or two to answer; and then send

* Soon after the war, commenced a feud between the town of Wilmington and the county of New Hanover. The leading men "upon 'Change" were either Tories or those whose lukewarmness had provoked suspicion: the agrestic population could but illy brook their prosperity. From that day to the present the polities of the burgess have been antagonistical to those of the farmer. The merchants have ever been the predominant class in the borough: daily intercourse has enabled them with facility to form combinations that have given them the control of the moneyed institutions; while their patronage has added a potent influence with the press. A majority of the merchants have, generally, as now, been from the North.

it to the press, that it may be printed with his curious address to the Assembly, and such justification and apology (if any) as he may think proper to make, &c., &c.

A. MACLAINE.

12th July.—Yesterday afternoon Mr. S. Swann was killed in a duel by Mr. John Bradley. Mr. Rutherford will give you the particulars.* On Monday was lost in the river a Mr. Marley and a Capt. Low, with a negro. The boat filled and sunk in a thunder storm. A sailor made the shore with difficulty.

Davie to Iredell.

PHILADELPHIA, July 17th, 1787.

MY DEAR SIR:—I have the pleasure of acknowledging your letter of the 3d. I am obliged to you for the information relative to our "vindicatory letter," a circumstance my feelings were much interested in; and which, I really was afraid, would be neglected until the length of time would have formed an objection against the measure.

The two great characters you inquire after move with inconceivable circumspection. This hint will satisfy you. Their situations, though dissimilar, are both peculiar and delicate.

I shall not stay until the business is finished. I am sorry it will be out of my power. As soon as the general principles are established I shall set out, &c., &c.

WILLIAM R. DAVIE.

Iredell to Davie.

EDENTON, July 19th, 1787.

DEAR SIR:—I have had the pleasure of receiving your favor of the 27th of June, for which I thank you, also for the pamphlet

* Mr. Swann was a man of wealth, and distinguished provincial descent; his amiability won him friends, while his high and chivalrous qualities, those that mark the finest specimens of the Southern gentleman, excited a general admiration. An English officer, who had suffered disaster by sea, was brought to Wilmington in a state of great destitution. Moved to pity, and attracted by his intelligence Mr. Swann made him his guest. While the officer was one day in Mr. Bradley's store, a number of rings that were on the counter disappeared. The popular hatred and suspicion of Englishmen had not yet cooled. Mr. Bradley charged the soldier with the larceny. Mr. Swann was indignant: he said an insult to one under his roof was an indignity to him. The unprotected position of the foreigner forbade a resort to the duel on his part; for, if successful, he could scarcely expect to escape the popular vengeance. Swann challenged: Bradley accepted. The ground selected for the combat was immediately in the rear of the Episcopal church. Mr. Swann, who was the most expert shot in the district, before he

nclosed. What blockhead is it who supposed it was written by Junius? for I have, somewhere or other, seen it ascribed to him. Though it is certainly well written, yet, in my opinion, the author, whoever he may be, has evidently affected the style of Junius (at becoming distance, however), and by his three or four times nauseously mentioning him, wanted to make the resemblance catch. I take it the pamphlet was written on purpose to serve Rodney and Hastings, both of whom seem in a fair way of meeting their deserts, for whatever may have been their successes, they certainly have been guilty of the basest barbarities; and England would be as infamous as Algiers if it was to suffer the excess of plunder to be a cover for its villainy. I am glad to see that country still has so much virtue left as to hold forth such examples of punishment. It may be the means of redeeming its character, and preserving much longer its Constitution and Government. A few more Hastingses to pass with impunity would transmit the name of Englishmen with detestation to all future ages, and make the government the most odious and corrupt that ever yet existed. You may suppose this writer's supercilious treatment of Mr. Burke has kindled my indignation a little, and I assure you it has. The manner in which he speaks of him is so detractive from his acknowledged character, that nothing but the utmost rancor of party could have produced it. But the cause is evident—the *prosecution of his great favorite* (perhaps *paymaster*) *Hastings*. This is the flight of imagination, *unregulated by temper or judgment*, which has drawn down the reviewer's resentment upon him. This is not a means of giving that kind of strength most pleasing to the reviewer, a strength derived from enormity of villainy, and satiety of cruelty and plunder. It is indeed astonishing, and a thing greatly to be lamented, to see men of parts prostituting themselves to purposes so notoriously base. But it is perhaps equally so, to find a pamphlet, consisting, indeed, for the most part, of very good words (though in many places, in my opinion, they are by far too gaudy and affected), but containing matter so destructive of every principle of public justice and humanity, greedily caught up as a thing highly deserving of admiration. I am persuaded you think of it just as I do; a temporary *catch-penny* to subserve a vile purpose, and as little fit to go down to posterity, which the writer has the effrontery to speak of, as the late proceedings of Rhode Island, if it was possible to bury them in oblivion.

reached the ground, told his second that he only intended to inflict a flesh wound upon Mr. Bradley. At the "word" Swann lodged his ball " *dans les flancs* " of his adversary. Mr. Bradley fired when in the act of falling, and his ball penetrated the brain of Swann, who fell dead upon the field.

I am extremely obliged to you for the kindness of your attention to me, and wish I could repay it with any thing interesting from this region. But ours is a dead, dull calm, unanimated with any thing but now and then a few fevers and agues, &c., from which I hope you are exempt. Your family was very well when I heard last (which was very lately) from Halifax. Col. Ashe intends going by water to New York from this town. I have not a word about our election, so that I imagine there is some such manœuvring going on as formerly. I flatter myself there will be no doubt of your being elected. I heartily wish success to the great business you are engaged in, and should not doubt it if less than an *entire unanimity* would do. But when that is the case it is difficult to carry any thing, &c., &c.

JAS. IREDELL.

DR. WILLIAMSON TO IREDELL.

PHILADELPHIA, July 22d, 1787.

DEAR SIR:—After much labor the Convention have nearly agreed on the principles and outlines of a system, which we hope may fairly be called an *amendment* of the Federal Government. This system we expect will, in three or four days, be referred to a small committee, to be properly dressed; and if we like it when clothed and equipped, we shall submit it to Congress; and advise them to recommend it to the hospitable reception of the States. I expect that some time in September we may put the last hand to this work. And as Congress can have nothing to do with it but put the question—pass or not pass,—I am in hopes that the subject may be matured in such time as to be laid before our Assembly at its next session. This being my expectation, I hope that our friend, S. Johnston, if asked, may not refuse to succeed Mr. Jordin, for surely there will be much need of abilities in the Senate as well as in the Commons. I also think that if he shall be in the Assembly he will, in all probability, be our next Governor, which certainly is a particular object to the town of Edenton, as well as a general one to the State. Two delegates from New Hampshire arrived yesterday, so that we have every State except Rhode Island, &c., &c.

HU. WILLIAMSON.

DAVIE TO IREDELL.

PHILADELPHIA, August 6th, 1787.

DEAR SIR:—I have the pleasure of acknowledging your letter of the 17th ult. The author of the political review has, *poor dog*, suffered what I expected, a most merciless criticism. His partiality, servility, and prostitution, indeed, merited no quarter. The temper, dignity, and judgment, with which Mr. Burke has conducted the prosecution against Hastings, even to the last parliamentary stage of the business, notwithstanding the influence of wealth, and the favor of the court, do not seem to be the effect of an "eccentric, ill-regulated imagination;" but the result of experience and abilities, which reflect a dignity ever on national measures. This writer is often happy in his expressions; but so frequent an affectation of elegant ornament, has rendered his style extremely unequal, and far inferior to the graceful and venerable solemnity of Junius.

I wish it was in my power to forward to you Mr. Adams's celebrated "Defence of the American Constitution." I think you would be pleased with it, although it is rather an encomium on the British Constitution than a defence of American systems.

I shall leave this place on Monday next; and, probably, be in Halifax by the time you receive this, as the great outlines are now marked, and have been detailed by a committee: the residue of the work will rather be tedious than difficult, &c., &c.

WILLIAM R. DAVIE.

SPAIGHT TO IREDELL.

PHILADELPHIA, August 12th, 1787.

DEAR SIR:—* * * * * The Convention having agreed upon the outlines of a plan of government for the United States, referred it to a small committee to detail: that committee have reported, and the plan is now under consideration. I am in hopes we shall be able to get through it by the 1st or 15th of September.

It is not probable that the United States will in future be so ideal as to risk their happiness upon the unanimity of the whole; and thereby put it in the power of one or two States to defeat the most salutary propositions, and prevent the Union from rising out of that contemptible situation to which it is at present reduced. There is no man of reflection, who has maturely considered what must and will result from the weakness of our present Federal Government, and the tyrannical and unjust proceedings of most of the State governments, if longer persevered in, but must sincerely wish for a strong and efficient National Government. We may naturally suppose that all those persons who are possessed of popularity in the different States, and which they make use of, not for the public benefit, but for their private emolument, will oppose any system of this kind.

The late determination of our judges at Newbern, must, in my opinion, produce the most serious reflections in the breast of every thinking man, and of every well-wisher to his country. It cannot be denied, but that the Assembly have passed laws unjust in themselves, and militating in their principles against the Constitution, in more instances than one, and in my opinion of a more alarming and destructive nature than the one which the judges, by their own authority, thought proper to set aside and declare void. The laws I allude to are the *tender laws*, and the laws for increasing the jurisdiction of the justices of the peace out of court: the latter they have allowed to operate without censure or opposition; the former they have openly and avowedly supported, to the great disgrace of their characters. I do not pretend to vindicate the law, which has been the subject of controversy: it is immaterial what law they have declared void; it is their usurpation of the authority to do it, that I complain of, as I do most positively deny that they have any such power; nor can they find any thing in the Constitution, either directly or impliedly, that will support them, or give them any color of right to exercise that authority. Besides, it would have been absurd, and contrary to the practice of all the world, had the Constitution vested such powers in them, as they would have operated as an absolute negative on the proceedings of the Legislature, which no judiciary ought ever to possess: and the State, instead of being governed by the representatives in general Assembly, would be subject to the will of three individuals, who united in their own persons the legislative and judiciary powers, which no monarch in Europe enjoys, and which would be more despotic than the Roman Decemvirate, and equally as insufferable. If they possessed the power, what check or control would there be to their proceedings? or who is there to take the same liberty with them, that they have taken with the Legislature, and declare their opinions to be erroneous? none that I know of. In consequence of which, whenever the judges should become corrupt, they might at pleasure set aside every law, however just or consistent with the Constitution, to answer their designs; and the persons and property of every individual would be completely at their disposal. Many instances might be brought to show the absurdity and impropriety of such a power being lodged with the judges.

It must be acknowledged that our Constitution, unfortunately, has not provided a sufficient check, to prevent the intemperate and unjust proceedings of our Legislature, though such a check would be very beneficial, and, I think, absolutely necessary to our well-being: the only one that I know of, is the annual election, which, by leaving out such members as have supported improper measures, will in some degree remedy, though it cannot prevent, such evils as may arise. I should not have intruded this subject upon you, but as it must certainly undergo a public discussion, I wish to know what is the general opinion on that transaction.

Since I wrote you Mr. Morris has had the satisfaction of receiving accounts that his bills that had been protested for non-acceptance, have been paid, &c., &c.

RICH'D DOBBS SPAIGHT.

It seems that the judges, to the great amazement and chagrin of their partisans, had given a reluctant assent to the doctrines maintained by Mr. Iredell in his "Address to the People," Aug. 17th, 1786. Their action illustrated a general moral law, that *radicals* out of power are wont to become *conservatives* in power.

Dissenting widely from the opinions advanced in the ingenious argument of Mr. Spaight, Mr. Iredell in his reply to that gentleman, (August 26th,) made a careful and powerful exposition of the views entertained by himself, and his friends—views that have become *settled law*.

Cotemporaneously with the meeting of the Convention at Philadelphia, the two great parties into which the people were divided, began to be known as "Federalist," and "Anti-Federalist," or "Republican." The former in favor of a more *intimate* union of the States; and fully prepared to receive a *new* plan of government; the latter, either content with the Confederation, or willing to submit to slight or partial amendments alone. The election for members of the Assembly excited an unusual degree of interest, and was fiercely contested. It was known that the Federal Convention had agreed upon a Constitution; and that, in relation to it, the new Assembly would be called upon to act. Those who wielded the greatest amount of popular influence in North Carolina talked of the folly of hazarding positive in quest of possible good; and were violently opposed to any change that might cause them loss of authority and diminution of personal consequence. The Federalists, if animated by patriotism, doubtless looked to the future with the hope of their own elevation, and of a triumph over their adversaries: very generally their most popular men were proposed. Great bitterness was infused into the canvass; and at many points tumults and assaults occurred; in Orange, "Mr. Hooper had an engagement with McCauley, in which he came off second best, with his eyes blacked."* On the day before the

* Letter from Mr. S. Johnston, August 22.

election Mr. Iredell, without his knowledge or assent, was nominated as candidate for the town of Edenton, by his friends Messrs. Cotton and Littlejohn: it was too late for success; and he was beaten by Mr. Cabarrus.

STEPHEN CABARRUS TO IREDELL.

EDENTON, August the 18th, 1787.

DEAR SIR:—I received your kind favor Before dinner, and most Sincerely thank you for the very obliging manner in Which you are pleased to Express yourself about the present Election Give me leave to inform you, of my Conduct in the business, I owe it to your Character I owe it to myself. Before I left this place Some weeks ago, I declared in a large Company, that if you proposed yourself as a Candidate for the Town of Edenton at the Ensuing Election, I would decline that honour; but that on the Contrary and my friends were desirous I Should represent them once more, I would accept of it. I returned to this place the day before the poll was opened and not hearing that you had any intention to Stand as a Candidate for the Town, I most Chearfully offered myself. But Judge of my Surprise, When yesterday in the afternoon I was informed of the greatest Exertions been made to overset my election. The manner in which it was Carried was more than a Sufficient proof that you was Entirely unacquainted With it and when some of my friends informed me of a Tavern been open for all friends that would vote for you, I declared publickly that I was certain of your not having been consulted or even asked wether you would offer as a Candidate—this gave me much uneasiness I thought I discovered A disposition in Some of your friends rather to turn me out than to accept of my resignation. I thought it ungenerous, it Would be a Triumph over me, I did not merit, after the Concisions I had made you, my Dear Sir, that I was Sensible of your total ignorance of this matter and felt in my own heart that I had never merited the ungenerous treatment of Some of your friends.

I am as ever Dear Sir, With very great Respect
Your most faithful and Obedient Servant,
S. CABARRUS.

IREDELL TO CABARRUS.

AUGUST 21st, 1787.

DEAR SIR:—I had the pleasure of receiving your letter on Saturday, which I should immediately have acknowledged, in order to have expressed my thanks for the liberality of your con-

duct in respect to me, but that I thought you would probably be at that time a good deal engaged. The very polite *declaration* you mention I casually heard of; but it was not mentioned to me with the particular circumstances you relate, and which certainly made it of much more importance than it otherwise would have been. I have long resolved, and hitherto uniformly adhered to the resolution, never to offer myself; but never to refuse serving, so far as I could, if I had the honor of being applied to. A friend of mine spoke to me a considerable time ago to know if I would suffer my name to be put in nomination, and I expressly declined it, assigning my reasons particularly. It was introduced, as I informed you before, without my knowledge; and I have had no other concern in the election than in saying (which I thought my duty indispensably required) that I would serve, if chosen, to the utmost of my power; I took care to explain how far that might be, stating that I could not attend the Assembly until after the court at Newbern. I have the pleasure of thinking the report of an open house being kept on my account was founded in a mistake. Common as that practice is, I should have been sorry if the zeal of any of my friends had induced such a step. Feeling the greatest satisfaction in thinking that the accidental conflict of our names will cause no change in our sentiments of each other, I subscribe myself,

With great truth and respect, dear sir,
Your most faithful, humble servant,
JAS. IREDELL.

IREDELL TO SPAIGHT.

August 26th, 1787.

* * * In regard to the late decision at Newbern, I confess it has ever been my opinion, that an act inconsistent with the Constitution was void; and that the judges, consistently with their duties, could not carry it into effect. The Constitution appears to me to be a fundamental law, limiting the powers of the Legislature, and with which every exercise of those powers must, necessarily, be compared. Without an express Constitution the powers of the Legislature would undoubtedly have been absolute (as the Parliament in Great Britain is held to be), and any act passed, *not inconsistent with natural justice* (for that curb is avowed by the judges even in England), would have been binding on the people. The experience of the evils which the American war fully disclosed, attending an absolute power in a legislative body, suggested the propriety of a real, original contract between the people and their future Government, such, perhaps,

as there has been no instance of in the world but in America. Had not this been the case, bills of attainder, and other acts of party violence, might have ruined many worthy individuals here, as they have frequently done in England, where such things are much oftener the acts of a party than the result of a fair judicial enquiry. In a republican Government (as I conceive) *individual liberty* is a matter of the utmost moment, as, if there be no check upon the public passions, it is in the greatest danger. The majority having the rule in their own hands, may take care of themselves; but in what condition are the minority, if the power of the other is without limit? These considerations, I suppose, or similar ones, occasioned such express provisions for the personal liberty of each citizen, which the citizens, when they formed the Constitution, chose to reserve as an unalienated right, and not to leave at the mercy of any Assembly whatever. The restriction might be attended with inconvenience; but they chose to risk the inconvenience, for the sake of the advantage; and in every transaction we must act in the same manner: we must choose between evils of some sort or other: the imperfection of man can never keep entirely clear of all. The Constitution, therefore, *being a fundamental law*, and a law *in writing* of the solemn nature I have mentioned (which is the light in which it strikes me), the judicial power, in the exercise of their authority, must take notice of it as the groundwork of that as well as of all other authority; and as no article of the Constitution can be repealed by a Legislature, which derives its whole power from it, it follows either that the *fundamental unrepealable* law must be obeyed, by the rejection of an act unwarranted by and inconsistent with it, or you must obey an act founded on an authority not given by the people, and to which, therefore, the people owe no obedience. It is not that the judges are appointed arbiters, and to determine as it were upon any application, whether the Assembly have or have not violated the Constitution; but when an act is necessarily brought in judgment before them, they must, unavoidably, determine one way or another. If it is doubted whether a subsequent law repeals a former one, in a case judicially in question, the judges must decide this; and yet it might be said, if the Legislature meant it a repeal, and the judges determined it otherwise, they exercised a *negative* on the Legislature in resolving to keep a law in force which the Assembly had annihilated. This kind of objection, if applicable at all, will reach all judicial power whatever, since upon every abuse of it (and there is no power but what is liable to abuse) a similar inference may be drawn; but *when once you establish the necessary existence of any power*, the argument as to abuse ceases to destroy its validity, though in doubtful matter it may be of great weight. Suppose, therefore, the Assembly should pass an act, declaring that in future in all criminal trials the trial by jury should be abolished, and the court alone should determine. The Attorney-General indicts; the indictment is found; the criminal is arraigned, and the Attorney-General requires his trial to come on. The criminal objects, alleging that by the Constitution all the citizens in such cases are entitled to a trial by jury; and that the Assembly have no right to alter any part of the Constitution; and that therefore the act appointing the trial by the court is void. Must not the court determine some way or other, whether the man shall be tried or not? Must not they say whether they will obey the Constitution or an act inconsistent with it? So—suppose a still stronger case, that the Assembly should repeal the law naming the day of election, (for that is not named in the Constitution,) and adjourn to a day beyond it, and pass acts, and these acts be attempted to be enforced in the courts. Must not the court decide whether they will obey such acts or no? And would it be approved of (except by a majority of the *de facto* Assembly) if they should say, " We cannot presume to declare that the Assembly, who were chosen for one year, have exceeded their authority by acting after the year expired." It really appears to me, the exercise of the power is unavoidable, the Constitution not being a mere imaginary thing, about which ten thousand different opinions may be formed, but a written document to which all may have recourse, and to which, therefore, the judges cannot wilfully blind themselves. This seems also to have been the idea of some of the early Assemblies under the Constitution, since, in the oath of allegiance are these expressions: " I, A. B. do sincerely promise and swear, that I will be faithful and bear true allegiance to the State of North Carolina, and to the powers and authorities which are or may be established for the government thereof, *not inconsistent with the Constitution*. (Act of Nov. 1777.) In any other light than as I have stated it, the greater part of the provisions of the Constitution would appear to me to be ridiculous, since in my opinion nothing could be more so than for the representatives of a people solemnly assembled to form a Constitution, to set down a number of political dogmas, which might or might not be regarded; whereas it must have been intended, as I conceive, that it should be a system of authority, not depending on the casual whim or accidental ideas of a majority either in or out of doors for the time being; but to remain in force until by a similar appointment of deputies specially appointed for the same important purpose; and alterations should be with equal solemnity and deliberation made.

And this, I apprehend, must be the necessary consequence, since surely equal authority is required to repeal as to enact. That such a power in the Judge may be abused is very certain; that it *will* be, is not very probable. In the first place, in a democratical government like ours, it is the interest of every man ambitious of public distinction to make himself pleasing to the people. This is so much the case, that there is great danger of men sacrificing their honor to their popularity, if their principles and firmness of mind are not of a texture to keep them steady in an honorable course. It can be no man's interest certainly to make himself *odious* to the people by giving unnecessary and wanton offence. It is also to be considered, that though the Judges are permanent in station (at least as long as the Act of their appointment is in force*), yet, as their salaries are during pleasure, they are in fact dependent on the Assembly, few men likely to be Judges being rich enough to consider them as a trifle. Besides, if they are disposed by a gross abuse of power (for the mere pleasure of abusing it) to put their *negatives* on our laws by giving them a false construction, cannot they do this every day with other Acts of Assembly (few of which I believe are more exempt from cavil than any article of the Constitution)? So that it really seems to me, the danger is the most chimerical that can be supposed of this power being abused; and if you had seen as I did, with what infinite reluctance the judges came to this decision, what pains they took by proposing expedients to obviate its necessity, you would have seen in a strong light how little probable it is a judge would ever give such a judgment, where he thought he could possibly avoid it. But whatever may be the consequences, formed as our Constitution is, I cannot help thinking they are not at liberty to choose, but must in all questionable instances decide upon it. It is a subject indeed of great magnitude, and I heartily lament the occasion for its discussion. In all doubtful cases, to be sure, the Act ought to be supported: it should be unconstitutional beyond dispute before it is pronounced such. I conceive the remedy by a new election to be of very little consequence, because this would only secure the views of a majority; whereas every citizen in my opinion should have a surer pledge for his constitutional rights than the wisdom and activity of any occasional majority of his fellow-citizens, who, if their own rights are in fact unmolested, may care very little for his.—I believe many think as you do upon this subject, though I have not heard much said about it, and I only speak on the general question, independent of an application to any case what-

* I mean the Act constituting their courts.

ever. Most of the lawyers, I believe, are of my opinion in regard to that. The power of the judges, take it altogether, is indeed alarming, as there is no appeal from their jurisdiction, and I don't think any country can be safe without some Court of Appeal that has no original jurisdiction at all, since men are commonly careful enough to correct the errors of others, though seldom sufficiently watchful of their own, especially if they have no check upon them.

JAS. IREDELL.

The acerbity, engendered by the election in Chowan, led to some rather personal articles in the newspapers. The following communication, in the handwriting of Mr. Iredell's niece, I suppose, was written or dictated by that gentleman:

" Hic murus aeneus esto:
Nil conscire sibi; nulla pallescere culpa."—HORAT.

SIR:—You have shown an impartiality becoming the editor of a paper, in the publication of the two pieces under the signatures of B. and C., which appeared in your last Gazette. It is to be lamented that the prevalence of party spirit is so great as to render such impartiality a subject of praise. To a benevolent mind there cannot be a more distressing prospect than that which our country presents, distracted as it is, and threatened with ruin, by the violence of this fatal spirit of party. Addison observes that, " There cannot a greater judgment befall a country than such a dreadful spirit of division as rends a government into two distinct people; and makes them greater strangers, and more averse to one another, than if they were actually two different nations." This picture is, unfortunately, too applicable to the present state of our own country. In such a condition of things, the only check which is left to this spirit, and the only remaining support of the peace of society, is to be found in that system of politeness and urbanity, which characterizes modern manners. This system forbids all exterior signs of angry and turbulent emotions; and prevents the expression of any sentiments which may disturb the peace and security of society. And surely some degree of the same temper should preside over the productions of the press. No gentleman, in a publication designed for general circulation, should allow himself to be so far hurried away by the violence of passion, as to use expressions which would not be allowed in general society; or to indulge in personal reflections, which would be equally inadmissible.

I have been led to these remarks by the perusal of the piece under the signature of C., the latter of the two to which I alluded in the beginning of this address. This production appears to me to be written with a violent rancor, and a grossness of personal invective altogether unbecoming any man pretending to the character of a gentleman. In addition to these capital faults, it is not only a most wretched composition; but, notwithstanding the rudeness of the author, written in a most dastardly and pusillanimous spirit. As to the facts alleged by the two writers, I shall enter into no examination of them: they were public transactions, and are only to be proved by public testimony. I can only express my own belief that the former writer was perfectly correct in his statement; and that the latter has been guilty of a most monstrous perversion of truth. Indeed the author's own violence is a strong argument against him: rage and passion seldom produce conviction; and we are strongly tempted to suspect the merits of a cause are insufficient to support it, when we see such auxiliaries called in to its aid. As to the composition of this essay, it is by no means worthy of a minute criticism; and would have passed altogether unnoticed, had not the author provoked some attention to it by his attempted witticisms on the expressions used by the former writer; though, so wretched are these efforts that they recall to mind the satiric poet's charge to dulness—

" If e'er to wit a coxcomb makes pretence—
Mark the sure barrier between that and sense."

Diffuseness and obscurity are the prevailing characteristics of his style. The writer, either from inability to express himself in clearer terms, or purposely with a view to afford himself subterfuges beneath which he might escape responsibility for any of his assertions, has written in so confused and perplexed a manner, that it is extremely difficult to sift a meaning from many of his phrases. But as this writer professes to have taken his pen in defence of truth and virtue, in so noble a cause we might overlook the comparatively trivial faults of composition. Let us see then how he supports his boast. He begins with asserting that the publication under the signature of B., " is the undoubted offspring of mortified pride and disappointed ambition: the sullen bantling of a vindictive, unforgiving temper." What does he mean by this sentence? What can he mean, but that he is certain, the piece in question was written by the Federal candidate, on whom he is pleased to confer these amiable qualities. An assertion so positive he ought to be prepared to support by proof: yet, a few sentences after, shrinking even in his anonymous character from any responsibility, he explicitly declares that he is " unable to point a suspicion." And thus sheltered himself, he ventures to assert, that "a more gross and detestable misrepresentation never saw the light." So much for the consistency of this pretended champion of virtue and truth. I do not mean to undertake the defence of the gentleman against whom his attacks are aimed. His character cannot be injured, though it should be assailed by an abler pen, guided by a cooler mind. For its worth and excellence, private friendship might appeal to public opinion, and to the suffrage of all who are acquainted with it. But it is unnecessary. To malevolence and aspersions such as these

"Let his only answer be his life."

There is some doubt whether the above was a reply to an attack on Mr. Iredell, or on Mr. Charles Johnson: the latter had been, at the election, defeated for the county of Chowan.

MACLAINE TO IREDELL.

Wilmington, August 29th, 1787.

DEAR SIR:—I am much obliged to you for your election intelligence; and am not surprised at any part of it, but that which relates to C. Johnson, who, I thought, was so popular that e would have been chosen at an hour's notice. But the truth is, that we have a set of fools and knaves in every part of the State, who seem to act as by concert; and are uniformly against any man of abilities and virtue. Lawyers of character are particularly obnoxious to them; but if they can find a profligate character at the bar, they caress him as one of themselves.

I am clearly of opinion that it is for the interest of the State, that certain lawyers should (for some time at least) decline all public business. Possibly they might indeed be of some service at the next Assembly, when the Convention business will probably be considered. I hope we shall have some men of understanding, who will endeavor to do what is necessary. Happily our Assembly, except when particular interests interfere, have generally appeared well disposed to coincide with the proposals of Congress. Possibly, indeed, apprehensions may arise from the expectation of heavy taxes when the Federal Government have sufficient power to compel payment. In that case we shall be opposed by a nest of hornets, with Tom Person at their head. I had long been thinking of withdrawing myself from public business; and the conduct of last Assembly determined me. I am now no longer a legislator—and feel myself happy in having thrown off the load, which so long oppressed me. Before I declared my intentions, I had, with the concurrence of a few friends and the principal mechanics, fixed upon a successor—Joshua Potts, the partner of Boritz.* Several undertook to secure his election, which would have been easily effected; but secure in their own opinion, they neglected any exertions; and Jack Walker, who had been aiming at the county, the moment he was acquainted with my intentions, went secretly to work among the lowest of the people, and what with misrepresentations on one hand, and a number of illegal votes, who were admitted when the poll first opened, he had almost succeeded. Potts carried it by a single vote.

J. A. Campbell is Senator, Tim. Bloodworth and Devane in the Commons. In Brunswick, where Ben Smith was an unsuccessful candidate, one Foster is Senator, and Col. Leonard and L. Du Pré in the Commons. Col. Owen, Senator for Bladen;—a brother of Brown's, and Sam Cain, Commoners. Cumberland has sent to the Senate old Macalister; and Col. Thackston and Mr. Grove (Mr. Rowan's son-in-law) to the House. These are all I have heard of.

This day week we buried Mr. M. Jones; and yesterday, Mrs Shaw—she had been long declining, and did not confine herself to a proper regimen. I do not recollect any other news, except that we have recommended your old acquaintance, the Rev. Dr. (*Adam*) Boyd, to the American Bishops for ordination. He has been some time in Georgia, whence, I suppose, he will go to Philadelphia for holy orders, &c., &c.

A. MACLAINE.

The Federal Convention, at Philadelphia, agreed to the Constitution, September 17th: and forthwith transmitted it to the United States in Congress assembled; whereupon Congress ordered the report, resolutions, &c., of the Convention to be laid before the several Legislatures, in order to be submitted to a Convention of Delegates chosen in each State by the people thereof.

MACLAINE TO IREDELL.

Wilmington, October 10th, 1787.

DEAR SIR:—✻ ✻ ✻ ✻ You will have seen at Hillsborough Judge Ashe's letter to the Bar. In this quarter, where we are not famed for any intimacy with Scripture, we were for some time at a loss to know who Gallio was; but a New England man, one George Hooper, found it in the eighteenth chapter of the Acts of the Apostles, that Gallio, before whom the Jews brought Paul, was deputy of Achaia. The application would have better suited his purpose, had the Judge substituted the Assembly in place of Judge Gallio, himself for the Apostle, and the lawyers for the Jews; but the fool had not understanding sufficient to apply the text, so as to prove from Scripture his own righteousness. Having taken the name of Judge Gallio upon himself, it may very properly be applied to him for the future. His Scripture would have been very expressive of his own feelings, had he compared the lawyers to Sosthenes, whom all the Greeks (the Assembly) beat before the judgment; for, undoubtedly, *he cared not for any of those things*, &c., &c.

A. MACLAINE.

---

* Joshua Potts was a very shrewd, but illiterate Yankee; after residing some few years in Wilmington, he returned to New England.

Of all those who were most active in pressing upon the people the adoption of the Constitution, Mr. Iredell was, undoubtedly, the ablest and most energetic, in North Carolina: he urged them by voice and pen; and gave to the cause all he had of personal influence. Though the question was, in his opinion, of vital importance, yet his passions were ever under the control of his judgment. With one great object constantly in view, he was never diverted from his purpose by side issues, nor did he ever imperil the result by harsh expressions, either oral or written. His equanimity was of such a nature, that no provocation disturbed it; he defended, he explained, he simplified; he was far above the petty ambition that delights to dazzle by its brilliancy, or astound by its learning.

The Assembly met at Fayetteville, November 18th; and adjourned December 22d. Mr. Samuel Johnston was made Governor, and Mr. Iredell a member of the Council. Mr. Iredell was also appointed sole Commissioner to revise and collect the Acts of the Assemblies; and authorized and directed to leave out all laws repealed or obsolete, all private acts, and *all acts in which no question of property could arise*, &c.

The first public movement in the State, in favor of the Constitution, was inaugurated, it is believed, by Mr. Iredell. A public meeting of the citizens of Chowan convened at Edenton on the 8th day of November, and Mr. T. Benbury was placed in the chair. They passed resolutions instructing their members to use their utmost efforts to obtain the sanction of the Assembly, pursuant to the recommendation of the Federal Convention, for the choice, and meeting of representatives of the people in a Convention on as early a day as possible; and expressed their hearty approbation of the new Constitution. The preamble and resolutions were drawn by Mr. Iredell. Subsequently, November 12th, the Grand Jury for the Edenton District, William Bennet, Foreman, presented to the Court the following address, written by the same pen.

Edenton, November 12th, 1787.

We, the Grand Jury for the district of Edenton, considering the present as a very important crisis in the affairs of America, and being deeply sensible of the necessity of a firm and lasting union among the American States, to ensure the common safety and liberty of all, hope it will not be deemed presuming in us, that we take this occasion to express our sentiments on the subject of the new Constitution, proposed by the late respectable Convention. We believe none can be so ignorant as not to know, and we hope few are so unfeeling as not to regret, the disordered and distracted state in which the affairs of the Union have been for a long time past. No sooner was the danger of a common enemy removed, than the States immediately detached themselves from the general concerns of the whole, as if our future fate was out of the power of fortune. The consequence has been, our public debts unpaid, the treaty of peace unfulfilled on both sides, our commerce at the very verge of ruin, and all private industry at a stand, for want of a united, vigorous government. Quotas demanded which we can never pay, and Congress preserving merely the shadow of authority, without possessing one substantial property of power. These evils dictated the necessity of a change, and the same happy expedient of an union of counsels which formed the confederation, was adopted to remedy its defects. Experience had pointed these out, and we believe it would be difficult to draw together in any country, a body of abler men than the persons appointed on this important occasion. They were not only able men, but entitled to the highest confidence which can be bestowed by any people from illustrious and successful leaders; and the same patriotism of character which formerly distinguished so many of them in the most trying scenes, was visible in the anxious and deep attention they employed on this momentous subject. A work coming from such men, after such long deliberation, is entitled to the utmost respect, especially as all the States assembled were unanimous, a circumstance that strongly shows the purity of their intentions, their sense of the absolute necessity that a new constitution should be immediately formed, and that little subordinate attentions to local interests ought to give way to the great object of the general good. There is nothing we hold in greater disdain, nor is there any thing more inconsistent with common prudence, as well as the most ordinary share of public spirit, than that we should cavil about trifles when our all is at stake; that we should slight the present favorable opportunity, which may be the only one we may ever enjoy, to establish a free and energetic government, when we now lie at the mercy of the most inconsiderable enemy, and have an union in nothing but in name. We admire in the new Constitution a proper jealousy of liberty mixed with a due regard to the necessity of a strong authoritative government. Such a one is as requisite for a confederated, as for a single government, since it would not be more ridiculous or futile for our own Assembly to depend for a sanction to its laws on a unanimous concurrence of all the counties in the State, than for Congress to depend for any necessary exertion of power on the unanimous concurrence of all the States in the Union. One weak, corrupted, or unprincipled State might in such a case destroy the whole. This evil, the effect of which we have already felt, is, in our opinion, happily remedied by the constitution proposed, with an advantageous addition of a popular representative of the people at large, accompanied with useful checks to guard against possible abuses. It is also a part of the constitution, that we observe with particular pleasure, that nine States may at any time make alterations, so that any changes which experience may point out can be made without the danger of such calamities as are incident upon changes of government in all other countries, where they can be only brought about by a civil war. Nor can we avoid dwelling with delight upon those many provisions, calculated to make us as much one people as possible, and to impress upon the minds of all that useful and important truth, that our strength consists in union, and nothing can hurt us but division. May this great truth, so important for us, so formidable to our enemies, rest upon the minds of all well-wishers to their country, as the watch-word of American liberty and safety! The various attempts that were made to divide us during the war, and the danger of similar efforts being used on the present occasion to make us distrust our best and ablest characters, ought to put us upon our guard, that we may not suffer ourselves to be the dupes of an insidious policy, working for our destruction. But we trust in God, that the same all-powerful Providence, which has hitherto so wonderfully preserved us, will still continue to protect us from the machinations of all our enemies, internal and external, and that by a wise use of the vast advantages in our possession, this country may become, as it seems destined to be, an asylum for all the oppressed upon the globe.

Entertaining these sentiments, which the warmth of our feelings hath carried to a greater length than we intended, we most earnestly wish that the General Assembly may appoint the meeting of a Convention on as early a day as possible, that no reproach of unnecessary delay may lie on us, when, in all human probability, upon our speedy adoption or rejection of this constitution it may depend, whether we shall be truly a nation, happy in ourselves, and respected by the rest of mankind; or an inconsiderable scattered people, perpetually driving to and fro, in search of a perfection which never can be found, amusing ourselves with visionary ideas, when we might be enjoying real blessings, and at length doomed to feel the curse of all human discontent, the consciousness that, by rejecting the means Providence had put into our power, we had become both wretched and contemptible.

COL. DAVIE TO IREDELL.

December 13th.

MY DEAR SIR:— * * * Judge Spencer's bill has, in his own language, been *damned*, in spite of every thing I could do for it in the Senate; and their memorial has been treated with the most contemptuous neglect, &c. &c.

WM. R. DAVIE.

MACLAINE TO IREDELL.

WILMINGTON, 25th Dec., '87.

DEAR SIR:—You will probably have heard before this time that we are to have a Convention at Hillsborough, in July. As any freeholder can be chosen to represent any county, Mr. Moore, some time ago, upon that supposition, proposed to set you up for Brunswick County; doubting, I conceive, whether you would be chosen in your own town or county. If you are of the same opinion I will certainly give in aid what little influence I have, not only from my own knowledge of your general principles; but because I wish to have as many of the friends of the new constitution as possible in the convention. There are a set of interested people, and petty tyrants, (among whom are the Judges,) that are and will be exerting all their influence, and straining every nerve, to prevent the new government taking place.

From the presentment of the Edenton Grand Jury, and the instructions of the town, I should conclude that you would be one of the members chosen; and in that case, if you should be at the same time elected here, we might lose a good vote. This is a matter of some consequence, and I wish to hear from you on the subject.

I hope Mr. Johnston will be chosen, which is in no way incompatible with his new dignity. I am indeed concerned that his promotion has been attended with a diminution of salary, which, if we did not know our Assemblymen so well, might be interpreted into an insult. No people ever more fully made good the old saying of "penny-wise and pound-foolish." I hope, however, this will not occasion him to decline the government, to which, in my opinion, he will give a dignity which it has generally wanted.

It is some comfort to me, under the abuse of "A Farmer," that the profession of the law, as well as myself, lie under his tremendous lash; and that your observations on Judge Ashe's letter, have the honor to be placed beside that elegant performance in the same paper. I have been too much engaged to give it more than a light reading. I would readily submit my conduct to men of sense and candor, without taking notice of the numerous falsities which that paltry scribbler has asserted; but unfortunately, many of those who read have neither understanding nor honesty, or at best have but one of them. The difficulty with me is, how to disprove the assertions, without discovering a resentment, of which the writer is unworthy. I must endeavor to tone myself to a proper temper to turn him into ridicule. You will hear more of him soon, relative to an affair that will place him in a still more contemptible and detestable point of view, &c. &c.

A. MACLAINE.

HOOPER TO IREDELL.

POINT REPOSE, 31st Dec., '87.

MY DEAR IREDELL:—Immediately upon my arrival at Wilmington, it was announced to me that my son William, at midnight, had left his uncle George Hooper's house, to visit Gen. Clarke, who had been attacked with a violent disorder in his head, which had utterly deprived him of his senses, and left him (stone-blind) to the care or inattention of nearly 40 slaves, without a white person on his plantation to attend to his distresses.

Judge of my feelings from your own, such as they would have been on such an occasion. I sought an early opportunity to come hither; it happened in the most busy and interesting part of the court; I lost two days of it, but to the friendly offices of Mr. Moore and Mr. Maclaine I am indebted that my clients did not suffer. I found the general ill indeed; he consented that I should send for his sister, proof positive that he thought himself near his dissolution. With poor Drinker, and another horse which bore Spencer to Portsmouth, Jem left this; and, with an aid of two plow-horses, delivered Mrs. Hooper and Tom here the fifth day, before noon, after they left this—going and returning 348 miles, with scarce as much flesh on my horses as would protect them from the depredation of the buzzards before they died.

Mr. Clarke is in a recovering state of health; his sight is, however, very bad, and I suppose will never be better. Mrs. Hooper and I are here; she waiting his consent to return, I preparing to leave this to-morrow or next day.

Thus have I troubled you with a detail of my private family affairs. I shall not attempt an apology. I know too well the share you take in my family feelings to conceive it necessary.

I am happy to hear that the Convention is so appointed that you can take your seat in it without interfering with your law engagements. Mr. Moore has thought of proposing you for Brunswick, lest by any possibility you should not be elected for Chowan or Edenton. Your election for Chowan, I think (if the Devil has not made himself an uniform inmate of the souls of the voters for your county), must be certain. Make it so there, or somewhere, for in the Convention you must be. I shall exert my powers to be there, but I conceive the chances very much against me. Watters proposes for the town; if I divide against him Taylor goes in, and Watters surely is to be preferred to him. The county members are opposed to me—some from interest—and from ignorance oppose the new constitution—and I have been explicit and decided in my approbation of it.

During the court nothing happened to the disadvantage of Maclaine. The Judges and he kept up a kind of *apparent* respect for each other. If there was any deficiency, Maclaine was the *aggressor*. He talked loud, laughed in court, carried on business in a kind of conversation, attended with much delinquency, yet never met with a reproof.

Geo. Hooper, after court, called Spencer, with due spirit and decency, to account for expressions which he had made use of respecting himself and Maclaine in Burgynn's business. Spencer degraded himself. Of this when I see you, &c. &c.

WILL. HOOPER.

CHAPTER XXI.

Æt. 36—37.

REPLY TO MR. MASON'S OBJECTIONS, BY IREDELL. LETTERS FROM DAVIE, MACLAINE, AND MISS WILLIAMS. IREDELL TO THE FREEMEN OF EDENTON. LETTERS FROM WITHERSPOON, HOOPER, DR. WILLIAMSON, AND SWANN. THE CONVENTION AT HILLSBOROUGH. THE ASSEMBLY. LETTERS FROM GOV. JOHNSTON.

The following admirable pamphlet bears date January 8th, 1788; it was first forwarded to Hodge & Wills at Newbern, and printed by them in their *State Gazette* in fragments, and, subsequently issued as a pamphlet accompanied by an "Address" to the people by "Publicola," Mr. Archibald Maclaine. It attracted much attention, and no doubt effected no little good. It is greatly superior to any defence of the Constitution published in North Carolina anterior to its adoption. The author was immediately recognized by his vigor, as a giant by the imprint of his foot. *This publication preceded all of the "Federalist," but the earliest numbers.*

Answers to Mr. Mason's Objections to the New Constitution recommended by the late Convention at Philadelphia. By Marcus. (James Iredell.)

I. Objection.

"There is no declaration of rights, and the laws of the general government being paramount to the laws and constitutions of the several States, the declarations of rights in the separate States are no security. Nor are the people secured even in the enjoyment of the benefit of the common law, which stands here upon no other foundation than its having been adopted by the respective acts forming the Constitutions of the several States."

Answer.

I. As to the want of a declaration of rights. The introduction of these in England, from which the idea was originally taken, was in consequence of usurpations of the Crown, contrary as was conceived, to the principles of their government. But there no original constitution is to be found, and the only meaning of a declaration of rights in that country is, that in certain particulars specified, the Crown had no authority to act. Could this have been necessary had there been a constitution in being by which it could have been clearly discerned whether the Crown had such authority or not? Had the people, by a solemn instrument, delegated particular powers to the Crown at the formation of their government, surely the Crown, which in that case could claim under that instrument only, could not have contended for more power than was conveyed by it. So it is in regard to the new Constitution here: the future government which may be formed under that authority certainly cannot act beyond the warrant of that authority. As well might they attempt to impose a King upon America, as go one step in any other respect beyond the terms of their institution. The question then only is, whether more power will be vested in the future government than is necessary for the general purposes of the union. This may occasion a ground of dispute—but after expressly defining the powers that are to be exercised, to say that they shall exercise no other powers (either by a general or particular enumeration) would seem to me both nugatory and ridiculous. As well might a Judge when he condemns a man to be hanged, give strong injunctions to the Sheriff that he should not be beheaded.*

2. As to the common law, it is difficult to know what is meant by that part of the objection. So far as the people are now entitled to the benefit of the common law, they certainly will have a right to enjoy it under the new Constitution until altered by the general legislature, which even in this point has some cardinal limits assigned to it. What are most acts of Assembly but a deviation in some degree from the principles of the common law? The people are expressly secured (contrary to Mr Mason's wishes) against *ex post facto* laws; so that the tenure of any property at any time held under the principles of the common law, cannot be altered by any future act of the general

---

* It appears to me a very just remark of Mr. Wilson's, in his celebrated speech, that a bill of rights would have been dangerous, as implying that without such a reservation the Congress would have had authority in the cases enumerated, so that if any had been omitted (and who would undertake to recite all the State and individual rights not relinquished by the new Constitution?) they might have been considered at the mercy of the general legislature.

---

legislature. The principles of the common law, as they now apply, must surely always hereafter apply, except in those particulars in which express authority is given by this constitution; in no other particulars can the Congress have authority to change it, and I believe it cannot be shown that any one power of this kind given is unnecessarily given, or that the power would answer its proper purpose if the legislature was restricted from any innovations on the principles of the common law, which would not in all cases suit the vast variety of incidents that might arise out of it.

II. Objection.

"In the House of Representatives there is not the substance, but the shadow only of representation; which can never produce proper information in the legislature, or inspire confidence in the people; the laws will therefore generally be made by men little concerned in, and unacquainted with their effects and consequences."

Answer.

This is a mere matter of calculation. It is said the weight of this objection was in a great measure removed by altering the number of 40,000 to 30,000 constituents. To show the discontented nature of man, some have objected to the number of representatives as being too large. I leave to every man's judgment whether the number is not sufficiently respectable, and whether, if that number be sufficient, it would have been right, in the very infancy of this government, to burthen the people with a great additional expense to answer no good purpose.*

III. Objection.

"The Senate have the power of altering all money bills, and of originating appropriations of money, and the salaries of the officers of their own appointment, in conjunction with the President of the United States; although they are not the representatives of the people or amenable to them.—These, with their other great powers (viz. their powers in the appointment of Ambassadors, and all public officers, in making treaties and trying all impeachments) their influence upon and connection with the supreme Executive, from these causes, their duration of office,

---

* I have understood it was considered at the Convention, that the proportion of one Representative to 30,000 constituents, would produce at the very first nearly the number that would be satisfactory to Mr. Mason. So that I presume this reason was wrote before the material alteration was made from 40,000 to 30,000, which is said to have taken place the very last day just before the signature.

---

and their being a constant existing body almost continually sitting, joined with their being one complete branch of the legislature, will destroy any balance in the government, and enable them to accomplish what usurpations they please upon the rights and liberties of the people."

Answer.

This objection, respecting the dangerous power of the Senate, is one of that kind which may give rise to a great deal of gloomy prediction, without any solid foundation: An imagination indulging itself in chimerical fears, upon the disappointment of a favorite plan, may point out danger arising from any system of government whatever, even if angels were to have the administration of it; since I presume none but the Supreme Being himself is altogether perfect, and of course every other species of beings may abuse any delegated portion of power. This sort of visionary scepticism therefore will lead us to this alternative, either to have no government at all, or to form the best system we can, making allowance for human imperfection. In my opinion the fears as to the power of the Senate are altogether groundless, as to any probability of their being either able or willing to do any important mischief. My reasons are,

1. Because, though they are not immediately to represent the people, yet they are to represent the representatives of the people who are annually chosen, and it is therefore probable the most popular, or confidential, persons in each State, will be elected members of the Senate.

2. Because one-third of the Senate are to be chosen as often as the immediate representatives of the people, and as the President can act in no case from which any great danger can be apprehended without the concurrence of two-thirds, let us think ever so ill of the designs of the President, and the danger of a combination of power among a standing body generally associated with him, unless we suppose every one of them to be base and infamous (a supposition, thank God, bad as human nature is, not within the verge of the slightest probability), we have reason to believe that the one-third newly introduced every second year, will bring with them from the immediate body of the people, a sufficient portion of patriotism and independence to check any exorbitant designs of the rest.

3. Because in their legislative capacity they can do nothing without the concurrence of the House of Representatives, and we need look no farther than England for a clear proof of the amazing consequence which representatives of the people bear in a free government. There the King (who is hereditary, and therefore

not so immediately interested, according to narrow views of interest which commonly govern Kings, to consult the welfare of his people) has the appointment to almost every office in the government, many of which are of high dignity and great pecuniary value, has the creation of as many Peers as he pleases, is not restricted from bestowing places on the members of both Houses of Parliament, and has a direct negative on all bills, besides the power of dissolving the Parliament at his pleasure. In theory would not any one say this power was enormous enough to destroy any balance in the constitution? Yet what does the history of that country tell us?—That so great is the natural power of the House of Commons (though a very imperfect representation of the people, and a large proportion of them actually purchasing their seats) that ever since the revolution the Crown has continually aimed to corrupt them by the disposal of places and pensions; that without their hearty concurrence it found all the wheels of government perpetually clogged; and that notwithstanding this, in great critical emergencies, the members have broke through the trammels of power and interest, and by speaking the sense of the people (though so imperfectly representing them) either forced an alteration of measures, or made it necessary for the Crown to dissolve them. If their power, under these circumstances, is so great, what would it be if their representation was perfect, and their members could hold no appointments, and at the same time had a security for their seats? The danger of a destruction of the balance would be perhaps on the popular side, notwithstanding the hereditary tenure and weighty prerogatives of the Crown, and the permanent station and great wealth and consequence of the Lords. Our representatives therefore being an adequate and fair representation of the people, and they being expressly excluded from the possession of any places, and not holding their existence upon any precarious tenure, must have vast influence, and considering that in every popular government the danger of faction is often very serious and alarming, if such a danger could not be checked in its instant operation by some other power more independent of the immediate passions of the people, and capable therefore of thinking with more coolness, the government might be destroyed by a momentary impulse of passion, which the very members who indulged it might for ever afterwards in vain deplore. The institution of the Senate seems well calculated to answer this salutary purpose. Excluded as they are from places themselves, they appear to be as much above the danger of personal temptation as men can be. They have no permanent interest as a body to detach them from the general welfare, since six years is the utmost period of their existence, unless their respective legislatures are sufficiently pleased with their conduct to re-elect them. This power of re-election is itself a great check upon abuse, because if they have ambition to continue members of the Senate they can only gratify this ambition by acting agreeably to the opinion of their constituents. The House of Representatives, as immediately representing the people, are to *originate* all money bills. This I think extremely right, and it is certainly a very capital acquisition to the popular representative. But what harm can arise from the Senate, who are nearly a popular representative also, proposing amendments, when those amendments must be concurred with by the original proposers? The wisdom of the Senate may sometimes point out amendments, the propriety of which the other House may be very sensible of, though they had not occurred to themselves. There is no great danger of any body of men suffering by too eager an adoption of any amendment proposed to any system of their own. The probability is stronger of their being too tenacious of their original opinion, however erroneous, than of their profiting by the wise information of any other persons whatever. Human nature is so constituted, and therefore I think we may safely confide in the free admission of an intercourse of opinion on the detail of business, as well as to taxation as to other points. Our House of Representatives surely could not have such reason to dread the power of a Senate circumstanced as ours must be, as the House of Commons in England the permanent authority of the Peers, and therefore a jealousy, which may be well grounded in the one case would be entirely ill directed in the other. For similar reasons I dread not any power of originating appropriations of money as mentioned in the objection. While the concurrence of the other House must be had, and as that must necessarily be the most weighty in the government, I think no danger is to be apprehended. The Senate has no such authority as to awe or influence the House of Representatives, and it will be as necessary for the one as for the other that proper active measures should be pursued: And in regard to appropriations of money, occasions for such appropriations may, on account of their concurrence with the executive power, occur to the Senate, which would not to the House of Representatives, and therefore if the Senate were precluded from laying any such proposals before the House of Representatives, the government might be embarrassed; and it ought ever to be remembered, that in our views of distant and chimerical dangers we ought not to hazard our very existence as a people, by proposing such restrictions as may prevent the exertion of any necessary power. The power of the Senate in the appointment of Ambassadors, &c., is designed as a check upon the President. They must be appointed in some manner. If the appointment was by the President alone, or by the President and a *Privy* Council (Mr. Mason's favorite plan), an objection to such a system would have appeared much more plausible. It would have been said that this was approaching too much towards monarchical power, and if this new Privy Council had been like all I have ever heard of, it would have afforded little security against an abuse of power in the President. It ought to be shown by reason and probability (not bold assertion) how this concurrence of power with the President can make the Senate so dangerous. It is as good an argument to say that it will not as that it will.* The power of making treaties is so important, that it would have been highly dangerous to vest it in the Executive alone, and would have been the subject of much greater clamor. From the nature of the thing, it could not be vested in the popular representative. It must therefore have been provided for with the Senate's concurrence, or the concurrence of a Privy Council (a thing which I believe nobody has been mad enough to propose), or the power, the greatest monarchical power that can be exercised, must have been vested in a manner that would have excited universal indignation in the President alone.—As to the power of trying impeachments:—Let Mr. Mason show where this power could more properly have been placed. It is a necessary power in every free government, since even the Judges of the Supreme Court of Judicature themselves may require a trial, and other public officers might have too much influence before an ordinary and common court. And what probability is there that such a court, acting in so solemn a manner, should abuse its power (especially as it is wisely provided that the sentences shall extend only to removal from office and incapacitation) more than any other court? The argument as to the possible abuse of power, as I have before suggested, will reach all delegation of power, since all power may be abused when fallible beings are to execute it; but we must take as much caution as we can, being careful at the same time not to be too wise to do any thing at all.—The bold assertions at the end of this objection are mere declamation, and till some reason is assigned for them, I shall take the liberty to rely upon the reasons I have stated above, as affording a belief that the popular repesentative must for ever be the most weighty in this government, and of course that apprehensions of danger from such a Senate are altogether ill-founded.

IV. Objection.

"The judiciary of the United States is so constructed and extended, as to absorb and destroy the judiciaries of the several States; thereby rendering law as tedious, intricate and expensive and justice as unattainable by a great part of the community, as in England; and enabling the rich to oppress and ruin the poor."

Answer.

Mr. Mason has here asserted, "That the judiciary of the United States is so constructed and extended, as to absorb and destroy the judiciaries of the several States." How is this the case? Are not the State judiciaries left uncontrolled as to the affairs of that *State* only? In this, as in all other cases, where there is a wise distribution, power is commensurate to its object. With the mere internal concerns of a State Congress are to have nothing to do: In no case but where the Union is in some measure concerned, are the federal courts to have any jurisdiction. The State judiciary will be a satellite waiting upon its proper planet: That of the Union, like the sun, cherishing and preserving a whole planetary system.

In regard to a possible ill construction of this authority, we must depend upon our future legislature in this case as well as others, in respect to which it is impracticable to define every thing, that it will be provided for so as to occasion as little expense and distress to individuals as can be. *In parting with the coercive authority over the States as States, there must be a coercion allowed as to individuals. The former power no man of common sense can any longer seriously contend for; the latter is the only alternative.* Suppose an objection should be made that the future legislature should not ascertain salaries, because they might divide among themselves and their officers all the revenue of the Union. * Will not every man see how

---

* It seems by the letter which has been published of Mr. Elsworth and Mr. Sherman, as if one reason of giving a share in these appointments to the Senate was, that persons in what are called the lesser States might have an equal chance for such appointments, in proportion to their merit, with those in the larger, an advantage that could only be expected from a body in which the States were equally represented.

* When I wrote the above, I had not seen Governor Randolph's letter. Otherwise, I have so great a respect for that gentleman's character I should have treated with more deference an idea in some measure countenanced by him. One of his objections relates to the Congress fixing their own salaries. I am persuaded, upon a little reflection, that gentleman must think this is one of those cases where a trust must unavoidably be reposed. No salaries could certainly be fixed now so as to answer the various changes in the value of money that in the course of time must take place. And in what condition would the supreme authority be if their very subsistence depended on an inferior power! An abuse in this case too would be so gross that it is very unlikely to happen, but if it should it would probably prove much more fatal to the authors than injurious to the people.

irrational it is to expect that any government can exist which is to be fettered in its most necessary operations for fear of abuse?

V. OBJECTION.

"The President of the United States has no constitutional Council (a thing unknown in any safe and regular government), he will therefore be unsupported by proper information and advice, and will generally be directed by minions and favorites—or he will become a tool to the Senate—or a Council of State will grow out of the principal officers of the great departments; the worst and most dangerous of all ingredients for such a Council in a free country, for they may be induced to join in any dangerous or oppressive measures, to shelter themselves, and prevent an inquiry into their own misconduct in office: Whereas, had a constitutional Council been formed (as was proposed) of six members, viz., two from the eastern, two from the middle, and two from the southern States, to be appointed by vote of the States in the House of Representatives, with the same duration and rotation of office as the Senate, the Executive would always have had safe and proper information and advice: The President of such a Council might have acted as Vice-President of the United States, *pro tempore*, upon any vacancy or disability of the Chief Magistrate, and long-continued sessions of the Senate would in a great measure have been prevented. From this fatal defect of a constitutional Council has arisen the improper power of the Senate, in the appointment of public officers, and the alarming dependence and connection between that branch of the legislature and the Supreme Executive. Hence also sprung that unnecessary and dangerous officer, the Vice-President, who for want of other employment, is made President of the Senate; thereby dangerously blending the Executive and Legislative powers; besides always giving to some one of the States an unnecessary and unjust pre-eminence over the others."

ANSWER.

Mr. Mason here reprobates the omission of a particular Council for the President, as a thing contrary to the example of all safe and regular governments. Perhaps there are very few governments now in being deserving of that character, if under the idea of safety he means to include safety for a proper share of personal freedom, without which their safety and regularity in other respects would be of little consequence to a people so justly jealous of liberty as I hope the people in America ever will be. Since however Mr. Mason refers us to such authority, I think I cannot do better than to select for the subject of our inquiry in this particular, a government which must be universally acknowledged to be the most safe and regular of any considerable government now in being (though I hope America will soon be able to dispute that pre-eminence). Every body must know I speak of Great Britain, and in this I think I give Mr. Mason all possible advantage, since in my opinion it is most probable he had Great Britain principally in his eye when he made this remark, and in the very height of our quarrel with that country, so wedded were our ideas to the institution of a Council, that the practice was generally if not universally followed at the formation of our governments, though we instituted Councils of a quite different nature, and so far as the little experience of the writer goes, have very little benefited by it. My inquiry into this subject shall not be confined to the actual present practice of Great Britain; I shall take the liberty to state the constitutional ideas of Councils in England, as derived from their ancient law subsisting long before the Union, not omitting however to show what the present practice really is. By the laws of England °the King is said to have four Councils,—1. The Hight Court of Parliament; 2. The Peers of the realm; 3. His Judges; 4. His Privy Council. By the first, I presume is meant, in regard to the making of laws; because the usual introductory expressions in most acts of Parliament, viz., "By the King's most excellent Majesty, by and with the advice and consent of the Lords spiritual and temporal, and Commons," &c., show that in a constitutional sense, they are deemed the King's laws, after a ratification in Parliament. The Peers of the realm are by their birth hereditary Counsellors of the Crown, and may be called upon for their advice, either in time of Parliament, or when no Parliament is in being: They are called in some law books *Magnum Concilium Regis* (the King's Great Council). It is also considered the privilege of every particular Peer to demand an audience of the King, and to lay before him any thing he may deem of public importance. The Judges, I presume, are called "a Council of the King," upon the same principle that the Parliament is, because the administration of justice is in his name, and the Judges are considered as his instruments in the distribution of it. We come now to the Privy Council, which I imagine, if Mr. Mason had any particular view towards England when he made this objection, was the one he intended as an example of a *Constitutional Council* in that kingdom. The Privy Council in that

---

* See Coke's Commentary upon Littleton, 110. 1. Blackstone's Commentaries 227 and seq.

---

country is undoubtedly of very ancient institution, but it has one fixed property invariably annexed to it, that it is a mere creature of the Crown, dependent on its will both for number and duration, since the King may, whenever he thinks proper, discharge any particular member, or the whole of it, and appoint another. ° If this precedent is of moment to us, merely as a precedent, it should be followed in all its parts, and then what would there be in the regulation to prevent the President being governed by "minions and favorites?" It would only be the means of riveting them on constitutional ground. So far as precedents in England apply, the Peers being constitutionally the *Great Council* of the King, though also a part of the legislature, we have reason to hope that there is by no means such a gross impropriety as has been suggested in giving the Senate, though a branch of the legislature, a strong control over the Executive. The only difference in the two cases is, that the Crown in England may or may not give this consequence to the Peers at its own pleasure, and accordingly we find that for a long time past this great Council has been very seldom consulted; under our constitution the President is allowed no option in respect to certain points wherein he cannot act without the Senate's concurrence. But we cannot infer from any example in England, that a concurrence between the Executive and a part of the legislative is contrary to the maxims of their government, since their government allows of such a concurrence whenever the Executive pleases. The rule, therefore, from the example of the freest government in Europe, that the Legislative and Executive powers must be altogether distinct, is liable to exceptions; it does not mean that the Executive shall not form a part of the Legislative (for the King, who has the whole Executive authority, is one entire branch of the legislature, and this Montesquieu, who recognizes the general principle, declares is necessary); neither can it mean (as the example above evinces) that the Crown must consult neither House as to any exercise of the Executive power. But its meaning must be, that one power shall not include *both authorities*. The King, for instance, shall not have the sole Executive and sole Legislative authority also. He may have the former, but must participate the latter with the two Houses of Parliament. The rule also would be infringed were the three branches of the legislature to share jointly the Executive power. But so long as the people's representatives are altogether distinct from the Executive authority, the liberties of the people may be deemed secure. And in this point surely there can be no manner of comparison between the provisions by which the independence of our House of Representatives is guarded, and the condition in which the British House of Commons is left exposed to every species of corruption. But Mr. Mason says, for want of a Council, the President may become "a tool of the Senate." Why? Because he cannot act without their concurrence. Would not the same reason hold for his being "a tool to the Council," if he could not act without their concurrence, supposing a Council was to be imposed upon him without his own nomination (according to Mr. Mason's plan)? As great care is taken to make him independent of the Senate as I believe human precaution can provide. Whether the President will be a tool to any persons will depend upon the man, and the same weakness of mind which would make him pliable to one body of control, would certainly attend him with another. But Mr. Mason objects, if he is not directed by minions and favorites, nor becomes a tool of the Senate, "a Council of State will grow out of the principal officers of the great departments; the worst and most dangerous of all ingredients for such a Council in a free country; for they may be induced to join in any dangerous or oppressive measures, to shelter themselves, and prevent an inquiry into their own misconduct in office." I beg leave to carry him again to my old authority, England, and ask him, what efficient Council they have there but one formed of their great officers. Notwithstanding their important *Constitutional Council*, every body knows that the whole movements of their government, where a Council is consulted at all, are directed by their *Cabinet Council*, composed entirely of the principal officers of the great departments; that when a Privy Council is called, it is scarcely ever for any other purpose than to give a formal sanction to the previous determinations of the other, so much so that it is notorious that not one time in a thousand one member of the Privy Council, except a known adherent of administration, is summoned to it. But though the President under our constitution may have the aid of the "principal officers of the great departments," he is to have this aid, I think, in the most unexceptionable manner possible. He is not to be assisted by a Council summoned to a jovial dinner perhaps, and giving their opinions according to the nod of the President; but the opinion is to be given with the utmost solemnity, *in writing*. No after-equivocation can explain it away. It must for ever afterwards speak for itself, and commit the character of the writer, in lasting colors, either of fame or infamy, or neutral insignificance, to future ages, as well as the present. From those *written reasons*, weighed with care, surely the President can form as good a judgment, as if they had been

---

* 1. Blackstone's Commentaries, 232.

given by a dozen formal characters, carelessly met together on a slight appointment; and this further advantage would be derived from the proposed system (which would be wanting if he had constitutional advice to screen him), that the President must be *personally responsible* for every thing—for though an ingenious gentleman has proposed, that a Council should be formed who should be responsible for *their opinions*, and the same sentiment of justice might be applied to these opinions of the great officers, I am persuaded it will in general be thought infinitely more *safe*, as well as more *just*, that the President who *acts* should be responsible for his *conduct*, following advice at his peril, than that there should be a danger of punishing any man for an erroneous opinion which might possibly be sincere. Besides the morality of this scheme, which may well be questioned, its inexpediency is glaring, since it would be so plausible an excuse, and the insincerity of it so difficult to detect, the hopes of impunity this avenue to escape would afford would nearly take away all dread of punishment. As to the temptation mentioned to the officers joining in dangerous or oppressive measures to shelter themselves, and prevent an inquiry into their own misconduct in office, this proceeds upon a supposition that the President and the great officers may form a very wicked combination to injure their country, a combination that in the first place it is utterly improbable, in a strong respectable government should be formed for that purpose, and in the next, with such a government as this constitution would give us, could have little chance of being successful, on account of the great superior strength and natural and jealous vigilance of one at least, if not both the two weighty branches of legislation. This evil, however, of the possible depravity of *all public officers*, is one that can admit of no cure, since in every institution of government the same danger in some degree or other must be risked; it can only be guarded against by strong checks, and I believe it would be difficult for the objectors to our new Constitution, to provide stronger ones against any abuse of the Executive authority than will exist in that. As to the Vice President, it appears to me very proper he should be chosen much in the same manner as the President, in order that the States may be secure, upon any accidental loss by death or otherwise of the President's service, of the services in the same important station of the man in whom they repose their second confidence. The complicated manner of election wisely prescribed would necessarily occasion a considerable delay in the choice of another, and in the mean time the President of the Council, though very fit for the purpose of advising, might be very ill qualified, especially in a critical period, for an active Executive department. I am concerned to see, among Mr. Mason's other reasons, so trivial a one as the little advantage one State might accidentally gain by a Vice President of their country having a seat, with merely a casting vote, in the Senate. Such a reason is utterly unworthy of that spirit of amity, and rejection of local views, which can alone save us from destruction. It was the glory of the late Convention, that by discarding such they formed a general government upon principles that did as much honor to their hearts as to their understandings. God grant, that in all our deliberations, we may consider America as *one* body, and not divert our attention from so noble a prospect to small considerations of partial jealousy and distrust. It is in vain to expect upon any system to secure an exact equilibrium of power for all the States. Some will occasionally have an advantage from the superior abilities of its members; the field of emulation is however open to all. Suppose any one should now object to the superior influence of Virginia (and the writer of this is not a citizen of that State), on account of the high character of General Washington, confessedly the greatest man of the present age, and perhaps equal to any that has existed in any period of time; would this be a reason for refusing a union with her, though the other States can scarcely hope for the consolation of ever producing his equal?

VI. OBJECTION.

"The President of the United States has the unrestrained power of granting pardons for treason; which may be sometimes exercised to screen from punishment those whom he had secretly instigated to commit the crime, and thereby prevent a discovery of his own guilt."

ANSWER.

Nobody can contend upon any rational principles, that a power of pardoning should not exist somewhere in every government, because it will often happen in every country that men are obnoxious to a lawful conviction, who yet are entitled, from some favorable circumstances in their case, to a merciful interposition in their favor. The advocates of monarchy have accordingly boasted of this, as one of the advantages of that form of government, in preference to a republican; nevertheless this authority is vested in the Stadtholder in Holland, and I believe is vested in every Executive power in America. It seems to have been wisely the aim of the late Convention, in forming a general government for America, to combine the acknowledged advantages of the British constitution with proper republican checks to guard as much as possible against abuses, and it would have been very strange if they had omitted this, which has the sanction of such great antiquity in that country, and if I am not mistaken, a universal adoption in America.* Those gentlemen who object to other parts of the constitution as introducing innovations, contrary to long experience, with a very ill grace attempt to reject an experience so unexceptionable as this, to introduce an innovation (perhaps the first ever suggested) of their own. When a power is acknowledged to be necessary, it is a very dangerous thing to prescribe limits to it, for men must have a greater confidence in their own wisdom than I think any men are entitled to, who imagine they can form such exact ideas of all possible contingencies as to be sure that the restriction they propose will not do more harm than good. The probability of the President of the United States committing an act of treason against his country is very slight; he is so well guarded by the other powers of government, and the natural strength of the people at large must be so weighty, that in my opinion it is the most chimerical apprehension that can be entertained. Such a thing is however possible, and accordingly he is not exempt from a trial, if he should be guilty or supposed guilty, of that or any other offence. I entirely lay out of the consideration the probability of a man honored in such a manner by his country, risking, like General Arnold, the damnation of his fame to all future ages, though it is a circumstance of some weight in considering whether for the sake of such a remote and improbable danger as this, it would be prudent to abridge this power of pardoning in a manner altogether unexampled, and which might produce mischiefs the full extent of which it is not perhaps easy at present to foresee. In estimating the value of any power it is possible to bestow, we have to choose between inconveniences of some sort or other, since no institution of man can be entirely free from all. Let us now therefore consider some of the actual inconveniences which would attend an abridgment of the power of the President in this respect. One of the great advantages attending a single Executive power is the degree of secrecy and dispatch with which on critical occasions such a power can act. In war this advantage will often counterbalance the want of many others. Now suppose, in the very midst of a war of extreme consequence to our safety or prosperity, the President could prevail on a gentleman of abilities to go into the enemy's country, to serve in the useful, but dishonorable character of a spy. Such are certainly maintained by all vigilant governments, and in proportion to the ignominy of the character, and the danger sustained in the enemy's country, ought to be his protection and security in his own. This man renders very useful services; perhaps by timely information, prevents the destruction of his country. Nobody knows of these secret services but the President himself; his adherence however to the enemy is notorious: he is afterwards intercepted in endeavoring to return to his own country, and having been perhaps a man of distinction before, he is proportionably obnoxious to his country at large for his supposed treason. Would it not be monstrous that the President should not have it in his power to pardon this man? or that it should depend upon mere solicitation and favor, and perhaps, though the President should state the fact as it really was, some zealous partisan, with his jealousy constantly fixed upon the President, might insinuate that in fact the President and he were secret traitors together, and thus obtain a rejection of the President's application. It is a consideration also of some moment, that there is scarcely any accusation more apt to excite popular prejudice than the charge of treason. There is perhaps no country in the world where justice is in general more impartially administered than in England, yet let any man read some of the trials for treason in that country even since the revolution: he will see sometimes a fury influencing the judges, as well as the jury, that is extremely disgraceful. There may happen a case in our country where a man in reality innocent, but with strong plausible circumstances against him, would be so obnoxious to popular resentment, that he might be convicted upon very slight and insufficient proof. In such a case it would certainly be very proper for a cool temperate man of high authority, and who might be supposed uninfluenced by private motives, to interfere and prevent the popular current proving an innocent man's ruin. I know men who write with a view to flatter the people, and not to give them honest information, may

---

* I have since found that in the constitutions of some of the States there are much stronger restrictions on the Executive authority in this particular than I was aware of. In others the restriction only extends to prosecutions carried on by the General Assembly, or the most numerous branch of legislature, or a contrary provision by law; Virginia is in the latter class. But when we consider how necessary it is in many cases to make use of accomplices to convict their associates, and what little regard ought in general to be paid to a guilty man swearing to save his own life, we shall probably think that the jealousies which (by prohibiting pardons before convictions) even disabled the Executive authority from procuring unexceptionable testimony of this sort, may more fairly be ascribed to the natural irritation of the public mind at the time when the constitutions were formed, than to an enlarged and full consideration of the whole subject. Indeed, it could scarcely be avoided, that when arms were first taken up in the cause of liberty, to save us from the immediate crush of arbitrary power, we should lean too much rather to the extreme of weakening than of strengthening the Executive power in our own government. In England, the only restriction upon this power in the King, in case of Crown prosecutions (one or two slight cases excepted) is, that his pardon is not pleadable in bar of an impeachment. But he may pardon after conviction, even on an impeachment; which is an authority not given to our President, who in case of impeachments has no power either of pardoning or reprieving.

misrepresent this account as an invidious imputation on the usual impartiality of juries. God knows no man more highly reverences that blessed institution than I do; I consider them the natural safeguard of the personal liberties of a free people, and I believe they would much seldomer err in the administration of justice than any other tribunal whatever. But no man of experience and candor will deny the probability of such a case as I have supposed sometimes, though rarely, happening; and whenever it did happen, surely so safe a remedy as a prerogative of mercy in the Chief Magistrate of a great country ought to be at hand. There is little danger of an abuse of such a power, when we know how apt most men are in a republican government to court popularity at too great an expense, rather than do a just and beneficent action in opposition to strong prevailing prejudices among the people. But says Mr. Mason, "The President may sometimes exercise this power to screen from punishment those whom he had secretly instigated to commit the crime, and thereby prevent a discovery of his own guilt." This is possible, but the probability of it is surely too slight to endanger the consequences of abridging a power which seems so generally to have been deemed necessary in every well regulated government. It may also be questioned, whether supposing such a participation of guilt, the President would not expose himself to greater danger by pardoning, than by suffering the law to have its course. Was it not supposed, by a great number of intelligent men, that Admiral Byng's execution was urged on to satisfy a discontented populace, when the administration, by the weakness of the force he was intrusted with, were perhaps the real cause of the miscarriage before Minorca? Had he been acquitted, or pardoned, he could perhaps have exposed the real fault: as a prisoner under so heavy a charge his recrimination would have been discredited, as merely the effort of a man in despair to save himself from an ignominious punishment. If a President should pardon an accomplice, that accomplice then would be an unexceptionable witness. Before, he would be a witness with a rope about his own neck, struggling, to get clear of it at all events. Would any men of understanding, or at least ought they to credit an accusation from a person under such circumstances?*

VII. OBJECTION.

"By declaring all treaties the supreme law of the land, the Executive and the Senate have, in many cases, an exclusive power of legislation; which might have been avoided by proper distinctions with respect to treaties, and requiring the assent of the House of Representatives, where it could be done with safety."

ANSWER.

Did not Congress very lately unanimously resolve, in adopting the very sensible letter of Mr. Jay, that a treaty when once made pursuant to the sovereign authority, *ex vi termini* became immediately the law of the land? It seems to result unavoidably from the nature of the thing, that when the constitutional right to make treaties is exercised, the treaty so made should be binding upon those who delegated authority for that purpose. If it was not, what foreign power would trust us? And if this right was restricted by any such fine checks as Mr. Mason has in his imagination, but has not thought proper to disclose, a critical occasion might arise, when for want of a little rational confidence in our own government we might be obliged to submit to a master in an enemy. Mr. Mason wishes the House of Representatives to have some share in this business, but he is immediately sensible of the impropriety of it, and adds "where it can be done with safety." And how is it to be known whether it can be done with safety or not, but during the pendency of a negotiation? Must not the President and Senate judge whether it can be done with safety or not? If they are of opinion it is unsafe, and the House of Representatives of course not consulted, what becomes of this boasted check, since, if it amounts to no more than that the President and Senate may consult the House of Representatives if they please, they may do this as well without such a provision as with it. Nothing would be more easy than to assign plausible reasons, after the negotiation was over, to show that a communication was unsafe, and therefore surely a precaution that could be so easily eluded, if it was not impolitic to the greatest degree, must be thought trifling indeed. It is also to be observed, that this authority, so obnoxious in the new Constitution (which is unfortunate in having little power to please some persons, either as containing new things or old), is vested indefinitely and without restriction in our present Congress, who are a body constituted in the same manner as the Senate is to be, but there is this material difference in the two cases, that we shall have an additional check, under the new system of a President of high personal character chosen by the immediate body of the people.

---

* The evidence of a man confessing himself guilty of the same crime is undoubtedly admissible, but it is generally, and ought to be always received with great suspicion, and other circumstances should be required to corroborate it.

VIII. OBJECTION.

"Under their own construction of the general clause at the end of the enumerated powers, the Congress may grant monopolies in trade and commerce, constitute new crimes, inflict unusual and severe punishment, and extend their power as far as they shall think proper; so that the State Legislatures have no security for the powers now presumed to remain to them: or the people for their rights. There is no declaration of any kind for preserving the liberty of the press, the trial by jury in civil causes, nor against the danger of standing armies in time of peace."

ANSWER.

The general clause at the end of the enumerated powers is as follows:—

"To make all laws which shall be necessary and proper for carrying into execution the *foregoing powers, and all other powers vested by this constitution in the United States, or in any department or office thereof.*"

Those powers would be useless, except acts of legislation could be exercised upon them. It was not possible for the Convention, nor is it for any human body, to foresee and provide for all contingent cases that may arise. Such cases must therefore be left to be provided for by the general Legislature as they shall happen to come into existence. If Congress, under pretence of exercising the power delegated to them, should in fact, by the exercise of any other power, usurp upon the rights of the different Legislatures, or of any private citizens, the people will be exactly in the same situation as if there had been an express provision against such power in particular, and yet they had presumed to exercise it. It would be an act of tyranny, against which no parchment stipulations can guard; and the Convention surely can be only answerable for the propriety of the powers given, not for the future virtues of all with whom those powers may be intrusted. It does not therefore appear to me that there is any weight in this objection more than in others. But that I may give it every fair advantage, I will take notice of every particular injurious act of power which Mr. Mason points out as exercisable by the authority of Congress under this general clause.

The first mentioned is, "That the Congress may grant monopolies in trade and commerce." Upon examining the constitution I find it expressly provided, "That no preference shall be given to the ports of one State over those of another;" and that "citizens of each State shall be entitled to all privileges and immunities of citizens in the several States." These provisions appear to me to be calculated for the very purpose Mr. Mason wishes to secure. Can they be consistent with any monopoly in trade and commerce?* I apprehend therefore, under this expression must be intended more than is expressed, and if I may conjecture from another publication of a gentleman of the same State and in the same party of opposition, I should suppose it arose from a jealousy of the eastern States very well known to be often expressed by some gentlemen of Virginia. They fear, that a majority of the States may establish regulations of commerce which will give great advantage to the carrying trade of America, and be a means of encouraging New England vessels rather than Old England. Be it so. No regulations can give such advantage to New England vessels, which will not be enjoyed by all other American vessels, and many States can build as well as New England, though not at present perhaps in equal proportion.† And what could conduce more to the preservation of the Union than allowing to every kind of industry in America a peculiar preference! Each State exerting itself in its own way, but the exertions of all contributing to the common security, and increasing the rising greatness of our country! Is it not the aim of every wise country to be as much the carriers of their own produce as they can be? And would not this be the means in our own of producing a new source of activity among the people, giving to our own fellow-citizens what otherwise must be given to strangers, and laying the foundation of an independent trade among ourselves, and of gradually raising a navy in America which, however distant the prospect, ought certainly not to be out of our sight. There is no great probability however that our country is likely soon to enjoy so glorious an advantage. We must have treaties of commerce, because without them we cannot trade to other countries. We already have such with some nations; we have none with Great Britain, which can be imputed to no other cause but our not having a strong respectable government to bring that haughty nation to terms. And surely no

---

* One of the powers given to Congress is, "To promote the progress of science and useful arts, by securing for limited times to authors and inventors the exclusive right to their respective writings and discoveries." I am convinced Mr. Mason did not mean to refer to this clause. He is a gentleman of too much taste and knowledge himself to wish to have our government established upon such principles of barbarism as to be able to afford no encouragement to genius.

† Some might apprehend, that in this case as New England would at first have the greatest share of the carrying trade, the vessels of that country might demand an unreasonable freight. But no attempt could be more injurious to them as it would immediately set the Southern States to building, which they could easily do, and thus a temporary loss would be compensated with a lasting advantage to us; the very reverse would be the case with them. Besides, that from that country try alone there would probably be competition enough for freight to keep it on reasonable terms.

man, who feels for the honor of his country, but must view our present degrading commerce with that country with the highest indignation, and the most ardent wish to extricate ourselves from so disgraceful a situation. This only can be done by a powerful government which can dictate conditions of advantage to ourselves, as an equivalent for advantages to them ; and this could undoubtedly be easily done by such a government, without diminishing the value of any articles of our own produce ; or if there was any diminution it would be too slight to be felt by any patriot in competition with the honor and interest of his country.

As to the constituting of new crimes, and inflicting unusual and severe punishment, certainly the cases enumerated wherein the Congress are empowered either to define offences, or prescribe punishments, are such as are proper for the exercise of such authority in the general Legislature of the Union. They only relate to "counterfeiting the securities and current coin of the United States," to "piracies and felonies committed on the high seas, and offences against the law of nations," and to "treason against the United States." These are offences immediately affecting the security, the honor or the interest of the United States at large, and of course must come within the sphere of the Legislative authority which is intrusted with their protection. Beyond these authorities, Congress can exercise no other power of this kind, except in the enacting of penalties to enforce their acts of legislation in the cases where express authority is delegated to them, and if they could not enforce such acts by the enacting of penalties those powers would be altogether useless, since a legislative regulation without some sanction would be an absurd thing indeed. The Congress having, for these reasons, a just right to authority in the above particulars, the question is, whether it is practicable and proper to prescribe limits to its exercise, for fear that they should inflict punishments unusual and severe. It may be observed, in the first place, that a declaration against "cruel and unusual punishments" formed part of an article in the Bill of Rights at the revolution in England in 1688. The prerogative of the Crown having been grossly abused in some preceding reigns, it was thought proper to notice every grievance they had endured, and those declarations went to an abuse of power in the Crown only, but were never intended to limit the authority of Parliament. Many of these articles of the Bill of Rights in England, without a due attention to the difference of the cases, were eagerly adopted when our constitutions were formed, the minds of men then being so warmed with their exertions in the cause of liberty as to lean too much perhaps towards a jealousy of power to repose a proper confidence in their own government. From these articles in the State constitutions many things were attempted to be transplanted into our new Constitution, which would either have been nugatory or improper. This is one of them. The expressions "unusual and severe" or "cruel and unusual" surely would have been too vague to have been of any consequence, since they admit of no clear and precise signification. If to guard against punishments being too severe, the Convention had enumerated a vast variety of cruel punishments, and prohibited the use of any of them, let the number have been ever so great, an inexhaustible fund must have been unmentioned, and if our government had been disposed to be cruel their invention would only have been put to a little more trouble. If to avoid this difficulty, they had determined, not negatively what punishments should not be exercised, but positively what punishments should, this must have led them into a labyrinth of detail which in the original constitution of a government would have appeared perfectly ridiculous, and not left a room for such changes, according to circumstances, as must be in the power of every Legislature that is rationally formed. Thus when we enter into particulars, we must be convinced that the proposition of such a restriction would have led to nothing useful, or to something dangerous, and therefore that its omission is not chargeable as a fault in the new Constitution. Let us also remember, that as those who are to make those laws must themselves be subject to them, their own interest and feelings will dictate to them not to make them unnecessarily severe ; and that in the case of treason, which usually in every country exposes men most to the avarice and rapacity of government, care is taken that the innocent family of the offender shall not suffer for the treason of their relation. This is the crime with respect to which a jealousy is of the most importance, and accordingly it is defined with great plainness and accuracy, and the temptations to abusive prosecutions guarded against as much as possible. I now proceed to the three great cases : The liberty of the press, the trial by jury in civil cases, and a standing army in time of peace.

The liberty of the press is always a grand topic for declamation, but the future Congress will have no other authority over this than to secure to authors for a limited time an exclusive privilege of publishing their works.—This authority has been long exercised in England, where the press is as free as among ourselves or in any country in the world ; and surely such an encouragement to genius is no restraint on the liberty of the press, since men are allowed to publish what they please of their own, and so far as this may be deemed a restraint upon others it is certainly a reasonable one, and can be attended with no danger of copies not being sufficiently multiplied, because the interest of the proprietor will always induce him to publish a quantity fully equal to the demand. Besides, that such encouragement may give birth to many excellent writings which would otherwise have never appeared.* If the Congress should exercise any other power over the press than this, they will do it without any warrant from this constitution, and must answer for it as for any other act of tyranny.

In respect to the trial by jury in civil cases, it must be observed it is a mistake to suppose that such a trial takes place in all civil cases now. Even in the common law courts, such a trial is only had where facts are disputed between the parties, and there are even some facts triable by other methods. In the Chancery and Admiralty Courts, in many of the States, I am told they have no juries at all. The States in these particulars differ very much in their practice from each other. A general declaration therefore to preserve the trial by jury in all civil cases would only have produced confusion, so that the courts afterwards in a thousand instances would not have known how to have proceeded.—If they had added, "as heretofore accustomed," that would not have answered the purpose, because there has been no uniform custom about it.—If therefore the Convention had interfered, it must have been by entering into a detail highly unsuitable to a fundamental constitution of government ; if they had pleased some States they must have displeased others by innovating upon the modes of administering justice perhaps endeared to them by habit, and agreeable to their settled conviction of propriety. As this was the case it appears to me it was infinitely better, rather than endanger every thing by attempting too much, to leave this complicated business of detail to the regulation of the future Legislature, where it can be adjusted coolly and at ease, and upon full and exact information. There is no danger of the trial by jury being rejected, when so justly a favorite of the whole people. The representatives of the people surely can have no interest in making themselves odious, for the mere pleasure of being hated, and when a member of the House of Representatives is only sure of being so for two years, but must continue a citizen all his life, his interest as a citizen, if he is a man of common sense, to say nothing of his being a man of common honesty, must ever be uppermost in his mind. We know the great influence of the monarchy in the British government, and upon what a different tenure the Commons there have their seats in Parliament from that prescribed to our representatives. We know also they have a large standing army. It is in the power of the Parliament, if they dare to exercise it, to abolish the trial by jury altogether. But woe be to the man who should dare to attempt it. It would undoubtedly produce an insurrection, that would hurl every tyrant to the ground who attempted to destroy that great and just favorite of the English nation. We certainly shall be always sure of this guard at least upon any such act of folly or insanity in our representatives. They soon would be taught the consequence of sporting with the feelings of a free people. But when it is evident that such an attempt cannot be rationally apprehended, we have no reason to anticipate unpleasing emotions of that nature. There is indeed little probability that any degree of tyranny which can be figured to the most discolored imagination as likely to arise out of our government, could find an interest in attacking the trial by jury in civil cases;— and in criminal ones, where no such difficulties intervene as in the other, and where there might be supposed temptations to violate the personal security of a citizen, it is sacredly preserved.

The subject of a standing army has been exhausted in so masterly a manner in two or three numbers of the Federalist (a work which I hope will soon be in every body's hands), that but for the sake of regularity in answering Mr. Mason's objections, I should not venture upon the same topic, and shall only presume to do so, with a reference for fuller satisfaction to that able performance. It is certainly one of the most delicate and proper cases for the consideration of a free people, and so far as a jealousy of this kind leads to any degree of caution not incompatible with the public safety, it is undoubtedly to be commended. Our jealousy of this danger has descended to us from our British ancestors ; in that country they have a Monarch, whose power being limited, and at the same time his prerogatives very considerable, a constant jealousy of him is both natural and proper. The two last of the Stuarts having kept up a considerable body of standing forces in time of peace for the clear and almost avowed purpose of subduing the liberties of the people, it was made an article of the bill of rights at the revolution, "That the raising or keeping a standing army within the kingdom in time of peace, unless it be with consent of Parliament, is against law ;" but no attempt was made, or I dare say ever thought of, to restrain the Parliament from the exercise of that right. An army has been kept on foot annually by authority of Parliament, and I believe ever since the revolution they have had some standing troops ; disputes have frequently happened about the number, but I don't recollect any

---

* If this provision had not been made in the new constitution no author could have enjoyed such an advantage in all the United States, unless a similar law had constantly subsisted in each of the States separately.

objection by the most zealous patriot, to the keeping up of any at all. At the same time, notwithstanding the above practice of an annual vote (arising from a very judicious caution), it is still in the power of Parliament to authorize the keeping up of any number of troops for any indefinite time, and to provide for their subsistence for any number of years. Considerations of prudence, not constitutional limits to their authority, alone restrain such an exercise of it—our Legislature however will be strongly guarded, though that of Great Britain is without any check at all. No appropriations of money for military services can continue longer than two years. Considering the extensive services the general government may have to provide for upon this vast continent, no forces with any serious prospect of success could be attempted to be raised for a shorter time. Its being done for so short a period, if there were any appearances of ill designs in the government, would afford time enough for the real friends of their country to sound an alarm, and when we know how easy it is to excite jealousy of any government, how difficult for the people to distinguish from their real friends, those factious men who in every country are ready to disturb its peace for personal gratifications of their own, and those desperate ones to whom every change is welcome, we shall have much more reason to fear that the government may be overawed by groundless discontents, than that it should be able, if contrary to every probability such a government could be supposed willing, to effect any designs for the destruction of their own liberties as well as those of their constituents; for surely we ought ever to remember, that there will not be a man in the government but who has been either mediately or immediately recently chosen by the people, and that for too limited a time to make any arbitrary designs consistent with common sense, when every two years a new body of representatives with all the energy of popular feelings will come, to carry the strong force of a severe national control into every department of government. To say nothing of the one-third to compose the Senate coming at the same time, warm with popular sentiments, from their respective assemblies. Men may to be sure suggest dangers from any thing, but it may truly be said that those who can seriously suggest the danger of a premeditated attack on the liberties of the people from such a government as this, could with ease assign reasons equally plausible for distrusting the integrity of any government formed in any manner whatever; and really it does seem to me, that all their reasons may be fairly carried to this position, that inasmuch as any confidence in any men would be unwise, as we can give no power but what may be grossly abused, we had better give none at all, but continue as we are,

or resolve into total anarchy at once, of which indeed our present condition falls very little short. What sort of a government would that be, which, upon the most certain intelligence that hostilities were meditated against it, could take no method for its defence till after a formal declaration of war, or the enemy's standard was actually fixed upon the shore? The first has for some time been out of fashion, but if it had not, the restraint these gentlemen recommend, would certainly have brought it into disuse with every power who meant to make war upon America. They would not be such fools as to give us the only warning we had informed them we would accept of, before we would take any steps to counteract their designs. The absurdity of our being prohibited from preparing to resist an invasion till after it had actually taken place* is so glaring, that no man can consider it for a moment without being struck with astonishment to see how rashly, and with how little consideration gentlemen, whose characters are certainly respectable, have suffered themselves to be led away by so delusive an idea. The example of other countries, so far from warranting any such limitation of power, is directly against it. That of England has already been particularly noticed. In our present articles of confederation there is no such restriction. It has been observed by the Federalist, that Pennsylvania and North Carolina appear to be the only States in the Union which have attempted any restraint of the Legislative authority in this particular, and that their restraint appears rather in the light of a caution than a prohibition; but that notwithstanding that, Pennsylvania had been obliged to raise forces in the very face of that article of her bill of rights. That great writer from the remoteness of his situation, did not know that North Carolina had equally violated her bill of rights in a similar manner. The Legislature of that State in November, 1785, passed an act for raising 200 men for the protection of a county called Davidson county against hostilities from the Indians; they were to continue for *two years* from the time of their first rendezvous unless sooner disbanded by the Assembly, and were to be subject to the same "rules with respect to their government as were established in the time of the late war by the Congress of the

* Those gentlemen who gravely tell us that the militia will be sufficient for this purpose, do not recollect that they themselves do not desire we should rely solely on a militia in case of actual war, and therefore in the case I have supposed the cannot be deemed sufficient even by themselves, for when the enemy landed it would undoubtedly be a time of war, but the misfortune would be, that they would be prepared; we not. Certainly all possible encouragement should be given to the training of our militia, but no man can really believe that they will be sufficient, without the aid of any regular troops, in a time of foreign hostility. A powerful militia may make fewer regulars necessary, but will not make it safe to dispense with them altogether.

United States, for the government of the continental army." These are the very words of the act. Thus, from the example of the only two countries in the world that I believe ever attempted such a restriction, it appears to be a thing incompatible with the safety of government. Whether their restriction is to be considered as a caution or a prohibition, in less than five years after peace the caution has been disregarded, or the prohibition disobeyed.* Can the most credulous or suspicious men require stronger proof of the weakness and impolicy of such restraints?

IX. OBJECTION.

"The State Legislatures are restrained from laying export duties on their own produce."

ANSWER.

Duties upon exports, though they may answer in some particulars a convenience to the country which imposes them, are certainly not things to be contended for, as if the very being of a State was interested in preserving them. Where there is a kind of monopoly they may sometimes be ventured upon, but even there perhaps more is lost by imposing such duties, than is compensated for by any advantage. Where there is not a species of monopoly, no policy can be more absurd. The American States are so circumstanced that some of the States necessarily export part of the produce of neighboring ones. Every duty laid upon such exported produce operates in fact as a tax by the exporting State upon the non-exporting State. In a system expressly formed to produce concord among all, it would have been very unwise to have left such a source of discord open; and upon the same principle, and to remove as much as possible every ground of discontent, Congress itself are prohibited from laying duties on exports, because by that means those States which have a great deal of produce to export would be taxed much more heavily than those which had little or none for exportation.

X. OBJECTION.

"The general Legislature is restrained from prohibiting the further importation of slaves for twenty odd years, though such importations render the United States weaker, more vulnerable, and less capable of defence."

* I presume we are not to be deemed in a state of war whenever any Indian hostilities are committed on our frontiers. If that is the case, I don't suppose we have had six years of peace since the first settlement of the country, or shall have for fifty years to come. A distinction between peace and war would be idle indeed, if it can be frittered away by such pretences as those.

ANSWER.

If all the States had been willing to adopt this regulation, I should as an individual most heartily have approved of it, because even if the importation of slaves in fact rendered us stronger, less vulnerable and more capable of defence, I should rejoice in the prohibition of it, as putting an end to a trade which has already continued too long for the honor and humanity of those concerned in it. But as it was well known that South Carolina and Georgia thought a further continuance of such importation useful to them, and would not perhaps otherwise have agreed to the new constitution, those States which had been importing till they were satisfied, could not with decency have insisted upon their relinquishing advantages themselves had already enjoyed. Our situation makes it necessary to bear the evil as it is. It will be left to the future legislatures to allow such importations or not. If any, in violation of their clear conviction of the injustice of this trade, persist in pursuing it, this is a matter between God and their own consciences. The interests of humanity will, however, have gained something by the prohibition of this inhuman trade, though at the distance of twenty odd years.

XI. OBJECTION.

"Both the general Legislature and the State Legislatures are expressly prohibited making *ex post facto* laws, though there never was, nor can be, a legislature but must and will make such laws, when necessity and the public safety require them; which will hereafter be a breach of all the constitutions in the Union, and afford precedents for other innovations."

ANSWER.

My ideas of liberty are so different from those of Mr. Mason that in my opinion this very prohibition is one of the most valuable parts of the new constitution. *Ex post facto* laws may sometimes be convenient, but that they are ever absolutely necessary I shall take the liberty to doubt, till that necessity can be made apparent. Sure I am, they have been the instruments of some of the grossest acts of tyranny that were ever exercised, and have this never failing consequence, to put the minority in the power of a passionate and unprincipled majority, as to the most sacred things, and the plea of necessity is never wanting where it can be of any avail. This very clause, I think, is worth ten thousand declarations of rights, if this, the most essential right of all, was omitted in them. A man may feel some pride in his security, when he knows that what he does innocently and safely to-day, according to the laws of his country, cannot be tortured into guilt and danger to-morrow. But if it should happen, that a great and overruling necessity, acknowledged and felt by all, should make a deviation from this prohibition excusable, shall we not be more safe in leaving the excuse for an extraordinary exercise of power to rest upon the apparent equity of it alone, than to leave the door open to a tyranny it would be intolerable to bear? In the one case, every one must be sensible of its justice, and therefore excuse it; in the other, whether its exercise was just or unjust, its being lawful would be sufficient to command obedience. Nor would a case like that, resting entirely on its own bottom, from a conviction of invincible necessity, warrant an avowed abuse of another authority, where no such necessity existed or could be pretended.

I have now gone through Mr. Mason's objections; one thing still remains to be taken notice of; his prediction, which he is pleased to express in these words: "This government will commence in a moderate aristocracy; it is at present impossible to foresee, whether it will in its operation produce a monarchy, or a corrupt, oppressive aristocracy; it will most probably vibrate some years between the two, and then terminate in the one or the other." From the uncertainty of this prediction, we may hope that Mr. Mason was not divinely inspired when he made it, and of course that it may as fairly be questioned as any of his particular objections. If my answers to his objections are, in general, solid, a very different government will arise from the new constitution, if the several States should adopt it, as I hope they will. It will not probably be too much to flatter ourselves with, that it may present a spectacle of combined strength in government, and genuine liberty in the people, the world has never yet beheld. In the mean time, our situation is critical to the greatest degree. Those gentlemen who think we may at our ease go on from one convention to another, to try if all objections cannot be conquered by perseverance, have much more sanguine expectations than I can presume to form. There are critical periods in the fate of nations, as well as in the life of man, which are not to be neglected with impunity. I am much mistaken if this is not such a one with us. When we were at the very brink of despair, the late excellent Convention, with a unanimity that none could have hoped for, generously discarding all little considerations, formed a system of government which I am convinced can stand the nicest examination, if reason and not prejudice is employed in viewing it. With a happiness of thought, which in our present awful situation ought to silence much more powerful objections than any I have heard, they have provided in the very frame of government a safe, easy and unexceptionable method of correcting any errors it may be thought to contain. Those errors may be corrected at leisure; in the mean time the acknowledged advantages likely to flow from this constitution may be enjoyed. We may venture to hold up our head among the other powers of the world. We may talk to them with the confidence of an independent people, having strength to resent insults; and avail ourselves of all our natural advantages. We may be assured of once more beholding justice, order and dignity taking place of the present anarchical confusion prevailing almost every where, and drawing upon us universal disgrace. We may hope, by proper exertions of industry, to recover thoroughly from the shock of the late war, and truly to become an independent, great and prosperous people. But if we continue as we now are, wrangling about every trifle, listening to the opinion of a small minority, in preference to a large and most respectable majority of the first men in our country, and among them some of the first in the world, if our minds in short are bent rather on indulging a captious discontent, than bestowing a generous and well-placed confidence in those who we have every reason to believe are entirely worthy of it, we shall too probably present a spectacle for malicious exultation to our enemies, and melancholy dejection to our friends; and the honor, glory and prosperity which were just within our reach, will perhaps be snatched from us for ever. MARCUS.
January, 1788.

DAVIE TO IREDELL.

Halifax, January 11th, 1788.

MY DEAR SIR:—I am happy to find your election was secured at all events. I am very sure there will be no danger, either in the town or county for you; and I hope Mr. Johnston will not think himself at liberty to refuse, should his country call upon him at this important crisis.

Mr. Jones continues perfectly anti-federal; and is inducing the people here to doubt, very generally, of its adoption in the present form.

I am much obliged to you for the inclosures; the letters for Hillsborough shall be forwarded by the first opportunity. You have seen the "Freeman;" this piece exceeds in meanness any thing I ever saw; but, I believe, is a true picture of the person whose image it really bears. These fellows must be extinguished. I hope you will do your share of this business. You observe it is a part of a fixed design to raise a general jealousy and distrust against every member of the profession.

I am very happy the Governor was received in a proper manner. At the Assembly, a number of gentlemen were to meet him on his coming to town; *and Caswell must have felt some mortification at this attention to Mr. Johnston, as no notice had been taken of him.* I was happy in having the opportunity of showing *them* what homage freemen would bring to a *virtuous man* in office, &c., &c.

WILLIAM R. DAVIE.

MACLAINE TO IREDELL.

Wilmington, 15th January, '88.

DEAR SIR:—I had the pleasure of receiving yours of the 3d inst. this day, covering a letter for Mr. Moore, whom I expect to see to-morrow, as he is yet in this neighborhood. From the purport of yours, I find you had not received mine on the same subject. Mr. Moore had recollected the objection you make with respect to the seat of government, and consequently had abandoned the idea of proposing you for Brunswick.* He has, however, offered his own services, and I make no doubt will be elected.

I am happy to hear that Mr. Johnston's elevation has been received in a manner suitable to his merit. I had no doubt that this would be acknowledged at a future day, whether he was living or dead. I shall always endeavor to pay a proper deference to every man in office; but I request you will present to Mr. Johnston my sincere respects as a man.

The new constitution, we are informed, has been received and ratified in three States; and I have no doubt it will be received by nine, exclusive of our own. Once the new government is set agoing, I am convinced that any State that may be refractory, will be obliged to comply. Indeed, from all the information I have had, there is little or no doubt of our State. In New Hanover county, the people, if left to themselves, are in favor of a change. Some demagogues, a few persons who are in debt, and every public officer, except the Clerk of the County Court, are decidedly against any change; at least against any that will answer the purpose. Our friend Huske is the loudest man in Wilmington against the new constitution. Whether ambition, or avarice, or a compound of both, actuates him, I leave you to judge.

Parson Tate has picked up all the arguments, good or bad, that have been published against the new form of government.* The only original objection he had, was the want of a mint in each State; this he alleges is a never-failing mark of sovereignty, and is to keep the money with us; he appears to be greatly distressed that we shall be obliged to send our *bullion* to the seat of government. It is indeed truly distressing.

Why do you pay the postage of your private correspondence? When the expense is chargeable to others in the way of business, it is well enough—otherwise I expect you will not do so in future, &c., &c.

A. MACLAINE.

DAVIE TO IREDELL.

Halifax, January 22d, '88.

MY DEAR SIR:—We have nothing worth remarking here, but the dissemination of anti-federal principles. Mr. Jones continues to assail the constitution, and the Virginia communications have strengthened his party. You know his opinion has great weight here, and that it is much easier to alarm people than to inform them.

Col. Geddy, who is a late convert, has announced himself a candidate for the convention; and is a most furious zealot for what he calls *W. Jones's system*, which is indeed all he knows about it; but he has raised the old cant that "the poor were to be ruined by taxes, and no security for freedom of conscience, &c."

I have not yet heard what the New Jersey convention have done; however, I think that there is little doubt but they will adopt the government proposed, as its consequences are so highly favorable to the non-importing States. The great deference this State has been accustomed to pay to the political opinions of the Old Dominion, will, I believe, have a very bad effect on the determination of this great question: this circumstance, added to

---

* The Cape Fear interest was in favor of Fayetteville as the capital of the State; the Eastern and Middle sections for a more central location. The question was virtually determined by the defection of Mr. Bloodworth, member from New Hanover. The change was, I believe, a fatal blow to the interests of the State, and the development of its resources—a change from a town in " esse " to one in " posse." Fayetteville would soon have become a flourishing city; Raleigh can never have any other consequence than what attaches to a mere seat of government.

* Rev. James Tate, a Presbyterian minister, came from Ireland in 1760, and for his support opened a classical school in Wilmington. During the Revolution, being a stanch Whig, he found it prudent to remove into the "up-country;" he was courteous, neat in his dress, and winning in his conversation; his company was prized by young people, and his influence over them was highly improving to their morals, manners, and culture.—*Foote's Sketches N. C.*
Many of the Tate family still reside in New Hanover. The Rev. Robt. Tate, from 1798 until very recently, officiated in the Welsh district, near South Washington; the Hon. T. Bloodworth was of his congregation.

the opposition already formed, in my opinion, renders its adoption in this State extremely doubtful.

The Governor writes me there have been twenty-five numbers of the Federalist printed; I will be obliged to you to forward me as many as you can, as we are in greater want of its assistance here than you are in Edenton, &c.

WILLIAM R. DAVIE.

Mrs. Iredell, in a letter to her mother-in-law, January 31st, said—"Your sons, you may well believe, are in good health, as they are now at a ball; they are both fond of dancing, the eldest full as much so as the youngest, though were you to see the gravity of his countenance, when he sits biting his nails over a law book, you would hardly think it possible he could be so delighted with a country-dance." "Have you seen Mr. Trail, a gentleman who went hence about eighteen months ago? He was very intimate in our family, and carried a letter from Mr. Iredell to his brother. You will find him a very entertaining acquaintance. Ask him for the history of his own and Mr. T. Iredell's passion for Miss Dawson; he will relate it to you with great humor."

Miss Williams to Iredell.

Edenton, Feb. 9th, '88.

Sir:—Being unable in your presence to unburthen my mind by acknowledging the great obligations I am under to you, I take this method of relieving myself, unwilling (though out of my power ever to return them) that you should think me insensible. At first your kindness flattered my vanity, till I looked around and found you the common friend of humanity. May a kind Providence reward you for all the favors you have conferred upon me! may you ever be a stranger to affliction! may peace and concord reign throughout your family! and may your little Annie live to be the pride and comfort of your life! These lines will be delivered to you by my aunt, as I feared your benevolence of heart might dictate such things as would be extremely painful to me, because of my unworthiness; they require no answer. If they have conveyed to you in an inoffensive manner the sensations of gratitude which fill my breast, the end I proposed will be fully answered, and I will have secured the only thread of happiness which is not out of my reach. That you may be blessed with every happiness which this life can afford, is the sincere wish of your

Greatly obliged

ELIZABETH WILLIAMS.

In truth his objections are a disgrace to his understanding as well as his principles, &c., &c.
A. MACLAINE.

Iredell to the Freemen of the Town of Edenton.

Gentlemen:—The distinguished honor of having been unanimously elected your Representative in the ensuing convention, without the least solicitation on my part, has made an impression on my heart which no time or circumstances can efface. My gratitude for it is inexpressible, but I am sensible will be shown in the most proper manner, by the zeal and fidelity with which it will be equally my duty and pleasure to execute this important trust. I shall have nothing to lament, but that my abilities will fall so far short of my ardent ambition to serve you. Under the conviction of my present sentiments, that the security of every thing dear to us depends on our adoption of the proposed constitution, I consider it one of the most awful subjects that was ever proposed for the consideration of a free people, and in giving it my utmost support (as I probably shall do), I shall have occasion for all the strength I can derive from the pleasing consciousness that in so doing I shall truly speak the respectable sense of my constituents. This will animate me beyond every thing in what I conceive the cause of Truth and Liberty. God forbid, indeed, that I should, by a blind admiration, imitate the conduct of those who indulge themselves in a blind rejection of it. The one would be as unworthy of the dignity of a free people, as the other is derogatory of those sentiments of respect and deference which we owe the great characters who formed it; and owe certainly as much for our own sakes, whose welfare they took so much pains to consult, as from the sentiments of gratitude with which every mind of sensibility must remember their former eminent services to their country. But I am convinced the more narrowly the constitution is examined by impartial minds, the more highly it must be approved; and from the consideration of our present critical situation, it will, perhaps, be deemed the only probable means of safety we have left.

I am, gentlemen, with the greatest respect and attachment,

Your faithful and obedient servant,

JAS. IREDELL.

Maclaine to Iredell.

Wilmington, April 2d, 1788.

Dear Sir:—I deferred answering your favor of the 11th past until the election should determine who were to become members.

A letter from John McLean, printer at Norfolk, Virginia, dated February 15th, '88, communicating his purpose to publish Mr. Iredell's "Answers to Mr. Mason's Objections," states—"Several political pieces have been sent for appearance in my next, but, defective of Marcus' merit and argument, I shall take the liberty of laying them on the shelf of old maids."

Maclaine to Iredell.

Wilmington, March 4th, 1788.

Dear Sir:— * * * You have no doubt seen that in New York there was very nearly one half of the Assembly against calling a convention; yet I am informed by a letter from that place, it is the general opinion that the new constitution will be adopted. This opinion is probably founded on the belief that it will be ratified by nine States, in which case, it will be certainly embraced by the remaining four. That this is the idea of those in the opposition, I have no doubt, for a number of their emissaries were at Boston, during the deliberation of the convention, endeavoring to scatter their poison among the members. It is, however, extraordinary, that though there were in the convention a majority, and that considerable, against the proposed government, it should have been ratified by a majority of nineteen. This is attributed to the Good Genius of America. A rejection in Massachusetts would probably have proved fatal. As the convention of New Hampshire have been sitting now near three weeks, and are said to be unanimous, we may conclude that seven States have come into the measure; South Carolina is certain. Among the other four we shall probably have a ninth. My principal reliance is on Maryland.

I expect in a few weeks the Federalist in a volume. He is certainly a judicious and ingenious writer, though not well calculated for the common people.

Your old friend Huske, and Col. Read, have joined all the low scoundrels in the county, and by every underhand means, are prejudicing the common people against the new constitution.* The former is a candidate for the county; but although in the beginning he was ridiculously loud, and even clamorous, he has been taught prudence by his associates. As a proof that he is not actuated by principle, he condemned the whole, after having a slight view of one half only over the shoulders of another person

---

* Major Walker, Major Sam. Ashe and Col. Read (officers of the Revolution) Judge Ashe and Mr. Bloodworth, though denounced by Mr. Maclaine, were all gentlemen of rank and influence.

---

bers. Below you will find a list of them in such counties as we have heard from.

Our old friend Huske, who very early set his face against the new constitution, has discovered an inordinate ambition, which his friends for some time past have observed to be growing very rapidly. When I mention this, you will not be surprised to hear that he descends to such humiliating methods of attaining his purpose, as you could not formerly have believed. The sheriff has declared him duly elected with 97 votes against T. Devane who had 172.* There are three men of the same name, the two youngest of them magistrates. The eldest of these two was the candidate, and in above 80 of the tickets was distinguished as T. Devane senior—the other was simply T. Devane; but it is known that every vote meant the same person. It is remarkable that Mr. Huske not only depended upon the interest of this man; but that in all his own tickets, many of them written by himself, the name T. Devane is mentioned without any additions. Mr. Wright sent to request my advice, and whether he should not make a special return: and though I advised him to this, as the safest method, he thought proper to decide in favor of Mr. Huske. The jest is, that this gentleman dares not avow his motives; for his opponent is as much determined as himself in favor of the seat of government at Fayetteville, and against the new constitution. Ambition frequently is blind to its own interest; for it is not impossible that a vote may be lost for Fayetteville; and Mr. Hogg's family are deeply interested in the fate of that place, &c., &c.

A. MACLAINE.

Dr. Witherspoon† to Iredell.

New Bern, 3d April, 1788.

Dear Sir:—I have read with very great pleasure your answer to Mr. Mason's objections; and surely every man who reads them, and on whom Mr. Mason's observations, or indeed the arguments of those in opposition in general have had any effect,

---

* The Devanes are an ancient and numerous family long settled in the upper part of New Hanover. They claim to be of the royal family of Stuarts. The head has always exercised a kind of patriarchal influence over the rest of the name. Very lately Stuart Devane was called by the neighbors, "the bell-wether of the flock." John Devane was appointed Major of his county in '76, and was afterwards, as previously, an active patriot; he served in the Senate in '79, '80 and '81; and many of the family have since held seats in the Assembly. The name is pronounced Devorn.

† The son of Dr. Witherspoon, signer of the Declaration of Independence.

must be convinced that the objections to the constitution are without foundation.

If we expect a constitution the principles of which *cannot* be violated, we had better, instead of amending that proposed, amend the hearts of men.

I am afraid there will be a powerful opposition in this State; but am happy in observing that the proportion of well-informed men on that side will be very small.

In Dobbs county, the federal-men, finding that they were in danger of losing their election, raised a riot, put out the candles, knocked to pieces the boxes which contained the votes, and destroyed the books.

From this county and town we have four federal men.

Your publication has been made, I believe very correctly by Hodge. I was sorry that my business called me out of town while it was in hand. You were very soon known to be the author—by what means I do not know, &c., &c.

D. WITHERSPOON.

HOOPER TO IREDELL.

HILLSBOROUGH, April 15th, 1788.

MY DEAR SIR:—Very much do I thank you for your kind letter by Mr. Hunt, and the papers which accompanied it. I have read the letter with the greatest pleasure, and flatter myself that they will not fail to work conversions among the many political infidels who have hitherto shut their eyes to the means of salvation held forth to them by the convention. I am heartily in sentiment with you, but alas! I fear those who favor the new constitution will be far outnumbered by their adversaries. The Western country in general is decidedly opposed to it. Mr. Moore, and myself, essayed in vain for a seat in the convention: our sentiments had transpired before the election.* ° * * We have had a very severe winter; but are now blessed with a most delightful spring, &c., &c.

WILL. HOOPER.

MACLAINE TO IREDELL.

WILMINGTON, April 29th, '88.

DEAR SIR:—I cannot suffer Mr. John Hogg to leave this without dropping you a line. I believe his business at Edenton is to know whether Mr. T. Davis is to have the appointment of Master in Chancery at Wilmington, as in that case, he is to be the deputy. My own opinion is, that he is, of the two, much more proper for the principal, though he has no hopes of succeeding against a man who is connected with one of their Honors (*Judge Ashe*). Not being restricted in the appointments by the letter of the act, these very honorable gentlemen look upon it that they are at liberty to bestow sinecures upon their friends, who will be obliged to employ others to do the business.°

Martin's paper, which teems with anti-federalism, made Gen. Washington lose his election for Fairfax county; but we since hear that he declined being a member, that federalists are chosen, and that Mr. Mason was rejected. We have also heard that many of the people in that State are changing in favor of the new constitution. This is said to be the case with several in this part of the country. It is, however, no very good sign, that in some counties so many have been left out for their attachment to a form of government so well calculated to make the people happy. Gen. Jones, W. Blount, Mr. Hooper, Mr. Moore, Governor Martin, and even Judge Williams (who was mistakenly supposed to conceal his sentiments), have been rejected. I suppose you have heard of the doings in Dobbs. Thank God, we have had nothing like it in any other county. It is said several of both parties were killed.

We learn that Spencer is returned, so that we shall have the honor of *one* of the Judges among us. His honor Judge Ashe, who had by his friends as well as himself announced his inclination to serve the people on this important occasion, and who seemed so secure of being chosen, that he told one of his friends to whom it was inconvenient to attend the election, that he need not go, as he, the Judge, was certain of succeeding—had only *eight* votes. This was the more remarkable, as the bulk of the people were, like himself, anti-federalists, &c., &c.

A. MACLAINE.

DAVIE TO IREDELL.

HALIFAX, May 1st, '88.

MY DEAR SIR:—Yesterday I got home from Tarborough, where I have been this week past, and have to-day finished twenty-five pages of our little collection on the subject of the Federal Government. I was so constantly interrupted by people on business last week, that I am sure what is done is extremely imperfect; you will, therefore, have much to add, if, on examination, you find room in the compass of such a pamphlet as we propose.

On the subject of a religious test, I have struck out a part of what we had written. You can, however, reinstate it if you think proper.

The judiciary I have left entirely to *you*, as you have already wrote on that subject, and are possessed of all the objections against it.

You will find many of the popular objections still omitted, which should be answered, if it can be done without swelling the publication to too great a size. I do not know whether the order and manner we have adopted will meet your approbation; if it should not, I hope you will make no scruple to alter it in any manner you think proper.

In the hurry this business has been done, I am apprehensive it may want considerable correction. I must, therefore, beg you and Mr. Moore to attend to this matter.

Mr. Sitgreaves, who will hand you this with the papers, will also assist in attending and correcting the press, &c., and is extremely anxious for the success of our little publication. He brings with him Mr. Hawkins' subscription, and his own; and has promised me to have it considerably enlarged, so that I am in hopes five or six reams may be printed.

I congratulate you on the adoption of the constitution in Maryland, by so respectable and decided a majority. I have some hopes, I think well-grounded, that South Carolina and Virginia will put the government in motion before we meet in convention.

It will be necessary to preface our pamphlet with a note, that it is not offered as an original production, but as a compilation from several fugitive pieces, &c., which will excuse us to the author of Marcus and others for the liberties we have taken with them.

The Address, and *title-page*, you will observe, I have left altogether to you, &c., &c.

WM. R. DAVIE.

THOS. IREDELL TO IREDELL.

EDENTON, May 22d, '88.

MY DEAR BROTHER:— ° ° ° ° Mr. Allen this morning read to me part of a letter he received from a gentleman of his acquaintance, who mentions a conversation he had with General Parsons, (*S. Person*,) the substance of which was, "*that General Washington was a damned rascal, and traitor to his country,* for putting his hand to such an infamous paper as the new Constitution*." Mr. Allen's correspondent desires him to have it published; and, at the same time, to have it inserted "that any person who may be desirous to know his name, may be informed of it by the printer," &c.

T. IREDELL.

IREDELL TO MRS. IREDELL.

NEWBERN, May 23d, '88.

MY DEAR HANNAH:—I have the satisfaction to tell you I am quite well, and lodged in the same house with Mr. Hooper, at your brother's old lodgings, Mrs. Marshall's. He was first with Mrs. I°°°°°°°, but she gave him so much of her story about Mr. Spaight, (to whom she fancied she was to be married,) that he was very glad to withdraw.

I am truly concerned to communicate the melancholy catastrophe of Mrs. Huske. She is unfortunately no more, and there is reason to fear, owing to a mistake of her case. Her father was with her. You may imagine the dreadful condition of him, and her husband. Poor Huske is in very great distress. She is universally lamented, and none certainly ever better deserved it, &c.

JAS. IREDELL.

THOS. IREDELL TO IREDELL.

EDENTON, May 27th, '88.

DEAR BROTHER:— ° ° ° ° The Players approached as near us as Windsor. I have the satisfaction to inform you they have wheeled about to take a view of Hillsborough and its environs, to fix upon some spot so enliven and cheer the vacant hours of the Conventional Heroes. Mrs. Parsons has again assumed her old line of life, and is head cook to Mr. Stone at Windsor, &c.

T. IREDELL.

MACLAINE TO IREDELL.

WILMINGTON, 4th June, '88.

DEAR SIR:—I had scarcely reached this before I received the pleasing intelligence that South Carolina had adopted the new Constitution, by a majority of seventy-seven. Though I have not seen a line on the subject, it is past all doubt, as there is a handbill in town, directing the procession which is to take place at the celebration of the happy event. It is said to exceed that

VOL. II.—15

of Massachusetts; and was ordered by the Convention, being drawn up by a committee appointed for the purpose. I understand it is to be in a very few days,—I suppose on the anniversary of a fortunate one.

By a letter which I found on my return, dated the day after the Convention met, it was expected that the majority would be small, as great pains had been taken in the back-country to poison the minds of the people; yet it was carried by above two to one. Though I could not be more particular in my information, I would not omit communicating what I know will give you heartfelt satisfaction.

Yankee doodle, keep it up! &c.

A. MACLAINE.

Dr. Williamson to Iredell.

New York, 11th June, '88.

Dear Sir:—The public papers have not for many days afforded us any news. All expectation is turned towards Virginia. We take it for granted, I do at least, that North Carolina will follow Virginia in adopting or rejecting. I confess that my hopes are not sanguine; but of this I do not consider myself bound to say all I think.

Congress have before them sundry matters of considerable import, which have been depending some months, for there have been nine States on the floor for a few days last past only. Having come on here with a resolution to indulge myself in as much leisure as any others of my fellow-laborers, the start I have been somehow constrained to take has not fully accorded with my plan; but I shall try to mend after a few land questions are determined. These questions are extremely weighty, as the national funds are concerned. At present I have not leisure even to return visits.

Will you be pleased to forward a line to Mrs. Templeman, who is probably anxious to hear the fate of her son. You may inform her that he was inoculated on Thursday week. ° ° ° He would now attend in Congress was it not that the place on his arm is not quite free from inflammation, and renders it inconvenient to put on a coat with tight sleeves. ° * ° °

I was yesterday surprised by a message of the Spanish Minister, who sent one of his family to our lodging to apologize for his not visiting us in person, for *he has not had the small pox:* he had left his card at the door without coming in, &c.

HUGH WILLIAMSON.

New York, July 7th, '88.

Dear Sir:—Virginia having confederated, North Carolina in opposition, should she be disposed to stand out, can only expect countenance from Rhode Island or New York. Let me state in a few words the politics of Rhode Island. You have heard of the effect of the Know Ye Law by which every debtor is enabled to wipe off a debt by paying 2s. 6d. in the pound, for their paper is now at 8 for 1; the money being paid into the hands of a magistrate remains there for some time for the use of the creditor, and if he neglects taking it the State Treasury becomes heir general. Their private debts by this time are nearly discharged in that State. The State Certificate debt is nearly paid off by similar means. The domestic or private debts of the State were, to the best of my recollection, about $556,000. A law was made for paying one-fourth of this debt; and all holders of securities were called to bring in their claims and receive one-fourth of the amount. Every one who neglected tendering his claims forfeited the amount that was offered. The creditors, in general, neglected. A second and a third payment was offered in the same manner; and now they have advertised for paying the last portion of the debt. Thus the whole State debt is soon to be expunged by a kind of legerdemain, for little or no money has issued, during the process, out of the Treasury. It is thought that Rhode Island will pretty soon be ready to confederate; but I was told a few days since, by a leader of the Know Ye men, that the good people in that State have two capital objections against the new constitution: first, they think that every slave should be taxed as a white man, and not represented; second, they think that the ratio for taxing is not proper; and that the States should not be taxed according to the number of inhabitants, but according to the amount of produce exported from each State, or grown in it and exported from any other State. I asked him what Rhode Island grew and exported; he answered nothing except a little cheese and potash. You see how reasonable a plan his would be; Maryland, Virginia, and North Carolina would be delighted with it.

The politics of New York are not so villainous in their face, but not much more honorable, considering them as part of one nation. They, during the war, agreed to give Congress power to collect the 5 per cent. impost; as soon as they got possession of the city they refused to let Congress have such power, because they found the selfish advantage of imposing a duty on imports for their own use. Half the goods consumed in Connecticut, or rather three-fourths of them; the goods consumed in New Jersey, or three-fourths of them; all the goods consumed in Ver-

mont; and no small part of those consumed in the western parts of Massachusetts are bought in New York, and pay an impost of 5 per cent. for the use of this State. I say nothing of what the good citizens of North Carolina import from New York, wherein they pay part of the New Yorkers' taxes. 'Tis easy to discover why New York does not like the new government. But this very argument must be a very good one with the citizens of North Carolina why they should like that government. Consequently, it is to be hoped they will neither copy New York, nor Rhode Island, &c.

HUGH WILLIAMSON.

John Swann to Iredell.

"John Swann was the son of Samuel Swann of Pasquotank. He received his preparatory education under the auspices of the Rev. Charles Earll, a minister of the Church of England, who was a missionary at Edenton, of the 'Society for the Propagation of the Gospel,' and of estimable character as a man and a Christian. Mr. Swann afterwards graduated at William and Mary College, Va., and was at an early age appointed a Member of Congress (1787); he died in '92 or '3, at the age of 32 or 33. He was greatly beloved and esteemed by all who knew him; and from the few remnants of his literary productions which I have seen, must have been a man of excellent judgment, and an enlightened patriot. He married Penelope, daughter of Gov. Samuel Johnston, by whom he had one child, which died in infancy after the death of the father, and gave rise to the celebrated case of Doe dem. Shepard *vs.* Shepard, 3 Murphy's Report, which continued in the Courts some twenty years."°

New York, July 7, '88.

Dear Sir:—I received your favor some time since, and should have acknowledged it some time before this, but was at that time in the height of the small-pox. You will give me leave now, sir, to thank you for your polite engagement in the business on which I wrote you.

From the slow and irregular conveyance which sometimes attends letters, you may possibly hear of the decision of this State on the new constitution before this reaches you; however, as there are chances against it, I shall take the liberty to mention

---

* Letter from Hon. John Bryan. Mr. Swann was the half-brother of the venerable Mrs. Shepard of Raleigh, the mother of the Hons. Charles, William, and James B. Shepard; all men of mark in the history of the State. The Rev. Mr. Earll was the grandfather of Dr. C. E. Johnson, of Raleigh.

their extreme indecision on that subject—an indecision the more astonishing since they are apprised of its ratification by ten States. The constitution is ably supported by gentlemen of great literary merit; but the opposition, who are by no means contemptible, seem determined to dispute the ground inch by inch. What they propose to themselves from their inflexibility is hard to discover; since it is certain, if we are to judge from their situation, and the disposition of a great part of the State, that they will find their concurrence sooner or later not only expedient but unavoidable. However, should their determination be contrary to the general sense of the Union, I hope it will not be made an example to influence the deliberations and conduct of our State. We are, sir, in the most painful suspense for Carolina. I confess I should be most sensibly mortified were Carolina to reject the constitution, however unavailing her dissent might be with regard to its establishment; and doubly so when I reflect that in such a determination she would have the *countenance of Rhode Island alone*, who in all probability may veer about when a certain State system of business is gone through with.

The arrangements for putting the new Government in action have been committed for some days, and will in all probability be reported this week.

I should, sir, most certainly beg the favor of a line now and then, but knowing you are so variously employed, you are seldom allowed leisure.

I am, dear sir, with great respect,

Your obedient servant,

J. SWANN.

Hooper to Iredell.

Hillsboro', July 8th, '88.

My dear Sir:—We are kept in a state of anxious ignorance as to what may be the final result of the Virginia deliberations upon the new constitution. To-day we are flattered with a report of its being embraced by a large majority, to-morrow we may possibly be mortified with accounts of its fate being in doubt, or that it is utterly rejected. People in this Western country have become more moderate, and many who were zealously opposed to it have changed their tone. It is said that the Mebanes advocate it unreservedly, and endeavor to make converts. The Quakers are for it, and O'Neall's brother-bullies in its favor. I have not a tittle of doubt but that our Convention will have a favorable issue.

Mr. Moore and I, after attending the Court at Fayette three days, and being two days thence on our way thither, found our families in good health and spirits. Not so Mr. Hogg's family. The shock of Mrs. Huske's death has been almost too much for them all. He bears it with much seeming firmness when in company; but, when surprised, in his retirement, the big tear steals from his eye. Mrs. Hogg is reduced to a skeleton: worn down with anxiety and deep distress. Poor Nelly has almost wept herself blind. A family most deeply to be commiserated! Huske is a walking ghost.

While we were at Wilmington, and soon after Mrs. Huske died, Mrs. Lyon, Mrs. Fowke, and Mrs. Wilkinson were buried: the latter a very fine young woman, the wife of Jack Wilkinson. The town was generally healthy when we left it.

I hope in God that your dear little girl is perfectly recovered; and that Mr. Johnston's family are restored to health. Pray present him and them with my most affectionate regard.

Remember me kindly to Mrs. Iredell, and the rest of your worthy family: and if Helen the fair, who sojourneth within thine house, should have taken unto herself a helpmate, pray salute her in my behalf with a holy kiss of congratulation, &c., &c.

WILL. HOOPER.

DAVIE TO IREDELL.

HALIFAX, 9th July, '88.

MY DEAR SIR :—I have the pleasure of acknowledging your letter of the 30th of last month with the Pennsylvania debates, and the second balance of the Federalist, for which you will be pleased to accept my thanks.

The decision of Virginia has altered the tone of the Anties here very much. Mr. Jones says his object will now be to get the Constitution rejected in order to give weight to the proposed amendments, and talks in high commendation of those made by Virginia—they have reached you, no doubt, before this time. Those that were of any consequence by affecting the operation of the principles of the Constitution are, in my opinion, quite inadmissible, particularly the 3d, and the amendment to the Judiciary.

Yesterday I saw a Mr. Lambert from Richmond, who said Gov. Randolph informed him the day before he left, that New Hampshire had ratified the Constitution.

We spent the 4th of July here in good humor, notwithstanding our differences about the new Government.

Please to have the inclosed inserted in your Gazette, and make my request to your brother to correct the press for us, or your Printer will make an entirely different story of it.*

Mr. Lamb as Chairman of a Committee in New York, which he styles the "Federal Committee," has written to Mr. Jones, T. Person, and Tim Bloodworth, recommending them to be steadfast in opposition, and inclosing a large packet of anti-federal pamphlets to each of them. It is astonishing the pains these people have taken!

Wilie Jones felt some mortification in finding himself in the company of Bloodworth and Persons, &c., &c.

W. R. DAVIE.

McCULLOH TO IREDELL.

NEWMAN-STREET, London, July 16th, '88.

DEAR SIR :—* * * This is a great, noble, a generous country, and America (North Carolina most especially, *witness her naval stores, &c.*) may, must, and will, from day to day, rue her separation from it. Did North Carolina deserve any thing at my hands, connected as I am, here, *I might do her great service.* Apply to the State for the debt they owe me as their agent. For shame sake they will not refuse payment, &c.

H. E. McCULLOH.

THE CONVENTION.

The Convention to consider the propriety of adopting or rejecting the Federal Constitution met in the Presbyterian Church at Hillsborough, July 21st, 1788; and consisted of two hundred and eighty members.

The most prominent Federalists were Iredell, Davie, Gov. Johnston, Spaight, Maclaine, and Steele. "Foremost in their number, and the leading spirit in the whole body, was the late Judge Iredell, conspicuous for his graceful elocution, for the apt application of his varied learning, his intimate knowledge of the working of schemes of government, and his manly and generous temper."†

Davie, with spotless plume, towering in intellect as in stature above the majority of the members, stood like a knight of the olden-time, lance in hand: the lustre of his military services

---

* Mr. Iredell had contracted with Hodge and Wills to print his Revisal of the Statutes; and had induced them to transfer their Press from New Berne to Edenton.

† Vide Hubbard's Life of Davie.

---

played about him, and was reflected in flashing light from hauberk, morion, and polished shield.

Governor Johnston, the President of the Convention, "calm, lucid, and convincing," seldom participated in the debate; it was only when, in Committee of the Whole, he saw his friends hard pressed by their adversaries, that he spurred into the "melée," then his blows were always delivered with stunning effect.

Maclaine, "sensible, pointed, and vigorous," was the Hotspur of his party: choleric, and defiant, his iron-heel, instead of extinguishing, kindled animosity into flame.

Steele was "laborious, clear-sighted, and serviceable by his knowledge of men."

The other side was led by Wilie Jones, Caldwell, T. Bloodworth, Judge Spencer, and McDowell.

Wilie Jones, of Halifax, was the most influential politician in the State: ultra-democratic in theory, he was aristocratic in habits, tastes, pursuits and prejudices: he lived sumptuously, and wore fine linen; he raced, hunted, and played cards; he was proud of his wealth, and social position; and fastidious in the selection of associates for his family. A patriot in the Revolution, he was now the acknowledged head of a great party. He was jealous of his authority, and prompt to meet any attempt to undermine his power. His knowledge of human nature was consummate; and in the arts of insinuation he was unrivalled. He had the powers of forecast, and combination, in an eminent degree; and his plans, if sometimes intricate, were always ingeniously constructed. As a spider in its web, speedily apprised of any disturbance at its extremities by the vibration of its thread, is alert to repel assault or secure a victim, so ever on the "qui vive" he was resolute and efficient in his defence, and the assailant often became the assailed. Though generally relentless, and uncompromising as a partisan, he had a generous heart, and on more than one interesting occasion, had given signal proof that he could soar above the murky atmosphere of party. He was a loving, and cherished disciple of Jefferson, and was often taunted with his subserviency to Virginia "abstractions." He seldom shared in the discussions. His time of action was, chiefly, during the hours of adjournment: then it was that he stimulated the passions, aroused the suspicions, or moderated the ardor of his followers; then it was that, smoking his pipe, and chatting of crops, ploughs, stock, dogs, &c., he stole his way into the hearts of honest farmers, and erected there thrones for himself.

Judge Spencer, "candid and temperate," was far superior to his associates as a debater.

David Caldwell, a Presbyterian divine, was learned and intelligent. Residing in a region but sparsely populated, and whose necessities were great, he had for years discharged the triple functions of preacher, physician, and teacher; and for all these various offices his industry and sagacity had so qualified him, that he had no rival. The love and confidence of the people to whom he ministered, were as unbounded as his own charity. His isolation from the great world, and the relations he had so long occupied to others, had rendered him somewhat pedantic, and dogmatic: "a man of the closet, and theories, he was impracticable," and tenacious. Thoroughly conversant with the most difficult questions of polemical theology, when he entered the political arena he was as a rash adventurer at sea, ignorant of the distinction between "main-sheet" and "main-sail," and without the necessary instruments, or the requisite knowledge, to effect his voyage in safety.

McDowell, the rival of Davie in military renown, was a man of action rather than words.

Timothy Bloodworth, by no means the least among them, was one of the most remarkable men of that era, distinguished for the versatility of his talents, and his practical knowledge of men, trades, arts, and sciences. The child of poverty, diligence and ambition had supplied the place of patronage and wealth. Preacher, smith, farmer, doctor, watchmaker, wheelwright and politician; if his brain was a receptacle of ideas somewhat ill-assorted, and his learning so ill-digested as sometimes to excite ridicule, and expose him to the charge of quackery, his manifold services, his unheralded charities, his gentle offices, had been received by his neighbors as testimonials of a mission almost divine. In the social circle, good-humored, gay, and full of his anecdotes, as a politician "he was resolute almost to fierceness, and almost radical in his democracy."

Immediately upon the report of the Committee to prepare rules for the government of the Convention, Mr Jones moved that the question upon the Constitution should be put, alleging that every man's mind was made up. This was promptly opposed by Mr. Iredell, and "so much against the sense of the house," though a large majority was with Jones on the main question, that it was defeated.

Mr. Caldwell then submitted some abstract propositions, which he styled "maxims"—"fundamental principles of every safe and free government :" they were six in number; and he insisted that they should be regarded as a standard by which to estimate the Constitution. He was resisted by Iredell, who demonstrated in a very few words the absurdity of one of his propositions. After some little altercation, the previous question was put, and resulted in a vote of 90 for the maxims—169 against them. Encouraged by these preliminary successes, Mr. Iredell wrote his wife, on the 25th, " the prospect at present is rather against us, but I do not despair. The opposition attempt to disconcert us by entering into no debate. However, we notice all material objections which we know have been made, and answer them." Conscious that they were greatly overmatched in ability by their antagonists, the anti-federalists seemed resolute to avoid discussion. Jones remarked that " he could put the friends of the Constitution in a way of discussing it. Let one of them make objections, and another answer them." Gradually, however, the followers of Jones were seduced into the debate.

The burden of the argument appears to have been thrown upon Mr. Iredell by his party. He spoke more frequently, and at greater length than any other on the floor. His object was to conciliate ; of this he never lost sight. No impertinence tempted him to angry retort. Under temptations and provocations, such as often drove his friends to invective and personalities, he preserved the equanimity of his temper. He defended, he removed objections ; he persuaded, he appealed to interest ; and awakened into life the spark of national pride. His vigor, and the extent and variety of his attainments, excited the admiration of his adversaries. His words were neither too few, nor too many, but such as were in common use, and conveyed his ideas clearly and distinctly, to the simplest understanding ; his style was terse and condensed ; his arguments, direct and solid, struck their mark with the force of cannon balls. But genius and eloquence, and learning and patience, were exhausted in vain. Jones's forces were too numerous and too well disciplined to be beaten. With them, his nod was approval of the highest authority ; his sneer the refutation of the most perfect logic ; the scrape of his foot the signal for attack ; his uplifted finger the token of caution or silence.

The Federalists manœuvred for a direct vote—aye or nay—upon the Constitution, but were foiled. The Convention determined neither to ratify nor to reject ; but to recommend a declaration of rights and twenty-six amendments ; and, meanwhile, to await the action of the confederated States. The amendments were, in the main, those proposed by Virginia. Mr. Jones quoted a letter from Mr. Jefferson, in which he stated that he wished nine States to adopt, to preserve the Union ; but that the other four would reject, that there might be a certainty of amendment ; this was conclusive with his party. On the final vote they had a majority of 100.

The Convention being also commissioned to fix a seat of government, determined that the plantation of Isaac Hunter, in Wake county, or such spot, within ten miles of said plantation, as the Assembly might select, should be the future capital of the State.

Though Mr. Iredell, in the Convention, made few or no converts to his cause, he gained many friends for himself. The Western members in particular were so won by his amiability, that at the ensuing session of the Legislature, when Rowan was divided, the new county was named, in his honor, Iredell.

A Mr. Robinson attended the Convention as stenographer. The Federalists were desirous that the debates should be published, trusting that their dissemination would produce a salutary change in the opinions of the people ; at their instance Iredell and Davie assumed the responsibility and care of the publication. Neat copies were made in Edenton by Mr. Lorimer (an Englishman), from the notes of the reporter ; and as far as practicable, the speeches were submitted to their authors for correction. This enterprise involved Iredell and Davie in some pecuniary loss. The debates are to be seen in Elliott's collection, and do so much honor to the State, and compare so well with the debates on the same subject in other States, that no North Carolinian can fail in grateful recollection of the energy and industry of the two eminent men to whom he is indebted for their preservation.*

After spending a day with Mr. Hooper, who " swore he would have him at least one day to himself," Mr. Iredell, on the 4th of August, commenced his journey home, leaving Governor Johnston to " finish copies of the business " transacted by the Convention.

DR. WILLIAMSON TO IREDELL.

NEW YORK, July 26th, '88.

DEAR SIR :—You may be assured that the delegates from North Carolina have not been inattentive to the respect they owe the State, whatever may be their private sentiments respecting the new Constitution. When a committee had reported, and the question was taken up for putting the new government into motion, and a time was proposed for choosing electors and representatives, and for the members entering on business, we stated fully the situation of our State, and it was immediately agreed that the time should be put off as far as we should allege was absolutely necessary. But no final question is yet taken ; and we believe we shall be able to obtain such delay, that North Carolina may in the " interim " take her measures. Every thing on this head is at present stationary.

* The debates were printed at Edenton by Hodge & Wills, and made their appearance about the last of June, '89. 1000 copies were published.

Some days ago there was a large procession here on ten States having confederated. Congress were invited to dine with the company, some thousands, under a particular pavilion in the fields. The other States attended, but the North Carolina delegates stayed at home. We conceived it was a respect we owed the State, not to celebrate an event in our public characters, which the State we represent has not hitherto sanctioned by her approbation.

Hitherto the State of New York in Convention has not taken its measures ; it is thought they will be curious, and a species of Delphic Oracles, neither an adoption nor rejection, or both, as parties may be disposed to esteem it, &c.

HUGH WILLIAMSON.

NEW YORK, July 26th, '88.

DEAR SIR :—We give bad proofs of our knowledge, whatever we may give of our candor, while we go on making mistakes, and confessing that we have made them. After the inclosed was written, the information in the inclosed paper came to hand, by which it would seem that the New York ratification is not like to prove a Hermaphrodite, as had been apprehended. Such have been the effects of the mighty reasoning of the minority, and other very *mighty* considerations. By the way, the anti-feds were conscious that they have, in many cases, carried their elections by imposing false representations on their constituents, and propagating impudent lies. We take it for granted that North Carolina will not be the only associate of Rhode Island, &c.

HUGH WILLIAMSON.

Mr. Iredell, having been solicited by many gentlemen to become a candidate for the Assembly, on the 15th of August addressed them a letter declining, as his attendance would conflict with his business.

DR. WILLIAMSON TO IREDELL.

NEW YORK, August 23d, '88.

DEAR SIR :—By letters from sundry correspondents, it appears that North Carolina has at length thrown herself out of the Union, but she happily is not alone ; the large, upright, and respectable State of Rhode Island is her associate. This circumstance, however, does not, I hope, render it necessary that the delegates from North Carolina should profess a particular affection for the delegates from Rhode Island. That State was some days ago represented by a Mr. Arnold, who keeps a little tavern ten miles out of Providence ; and a Mr. Hazard, the illiterate " quondam " skipper of a small coasting vessel, who now, the very leader of Know Ye justices, officiates at county courts, and receives small fees, not as a lawyer, but *agent for suitors*. These two respectable delegates, with the innate desire of promoting a bad measure, lately voted on several questions respecting the organization of the new government, in order to fix it in New York, a corner of the Union ; but before the final question was taken on the ordinance, they caused a member to move in Congress for a vote " that nothing which the delegates from Rhode Island or North Carolina had done, or might do in voting on the subject, should be construed as in any measure affecting the rights of their constituents." On the motion, the delegates from North Carolina moved that the word North Carolina should be struck out of the vote of *absolution*, and thereon called for the yeas and nays, to prove that we did not wish to have North Carolina associated in any vote with Rhode Island ; that we did not wish for *absolution*, being conscious of having pursued our duty ; that, with respect to the final vote which was to be taken on the ordinance, we proposed never to assist in such vote unless North Carolina should confederate, for we would not be guilty of parricide, by throwing our State out of the Union. On this the motion was withdrawn ; and the Rhode Island gentlemen missed the promised pleasure of doing wrong, and on the next morning they returned home.

I wrote the Governor a letter concerning the conduct of some members, when the business referred to was first moved in Congress ; and, with my usual want of prudent dissimulation, I expressed an honest indignation by calling Spade a *spade*. The letter, it seems, has been read in Convention ; and a correspondent, up the country, writes me that he fears it has hurt me greatly. As I did not consider that letter as official, and one that should be communicated to a public assembly, I took no copy of it, and do not know what it contained ; but as I am conscious that I never write, in the most careless mood, any thing but what I think, and as I am also conscious that, since I have been honored with a commission from the State, I have not in a single instance preferred my private interest to the benefit of the State ; that I never have, through private indulgence, omitted a single opportunity of serving the State ; and, conscious of no corrupt motive, my zeal on a late occasion to serve the State has not been abated at an hour when I had reason to suppose that my action would not be popular. Had I supported what I conceive to be a dishonest measure, in pursuit of popularity, I should, for the first time as a public man, have had occasion to condemn myself. Doing what I conceive to be the true dictate of honesty and patriotism, I mean to abide consequences. My friends know that I do not depend for support on public favor.

The 22d Amendment, so called, was certainly a very important one for North Carolina. If an East India Company or a Mediterranean Company should be created, it would greatly interfere with her trade to those regions. What could have put foreign troops into their heads? They should have excepted particularly against the Japanese, who are *heathen*. The 12th Amendment I take for an *original*. Others have talked about *a rebellion in a State*, but the North Carolina Convention speaks of the *State being in rebellion*. Are these the same things, according to the conceptions of Tom Person, and Tim Bloodworth, not forgetting the learned Judge Spencer? It is like the various expressions of *an old turned hat, and a turned old hat*. Perhaps you conceived that the Federal Congress might undertake to declare that a State out of the Union was in rebellion. To obviate this, it would have been safer to have required thirteen-elevenths. The other amendments, or Pejorations, I fully understand; but this I do not, &c., &c.

HUGH WILLIAMSON.

HOOPER TO IREDELL.

HILLSBOROUGH, Sept. 2d, '88.

MY DEAR SIR:—I render you many thanks for your kind favor from Halifax, and sincerely congratulate you upon the authentic accounts which we have had from New York, of the new Constitution having been adopted in that State. North Carolina will become a by-word among the nations. We have been amused here with a story that Wilie and Person have been burnt in effigy. Is it true?

The elections to the westward are almost all in favor of Federalism. The Surry members, who were all Anties, after experiencing much abuse, are all left out, and three Federalists elected. Locke and Rutherford left out; Feds in their stead. A. Martin is elected.

This will be handed to you by a Mr. Hunter, who drives a wagon. I must request the favor of you to apply to Edmund Blunt in my behalf for a barrel of clover-seed. If you could find us two pounds of tolerable tea you would much oblige us, and I will reimburse with thanks when we meet.

If you or the Governor should have any papers which you could spare, they would be very acceptable to us, &c.

WILL. HOOPER.

DAVIE TO IREDELL.

Sept. 8th, HALIFAX.

MY DEAR SIR:—As the publication came by some unknown hand in my absence, I had no opportunity of returning it to the printer, as you requested; it is very well received here, and I shall disperse it all the way to Salisbury; and cannot help hoping that it will give a determination to the public mind, at present strangely unsettled and wavering.

Persons and Mr. Jones were both holding out the doctrine of opposition for five or six years at least.* Mr. Jones says we must have that time at least, before their Judiciary are let in upon us; he is continually haranguing the people on the terrors of the Judicial power, and the certainty of their ruin if they are *obliged now* to pay their debts; we are almost led to believe there is something more than a mere mistake in point of principle in his conduct. * * * *

I think the Governor is right with respect to the *uniformity* of petitions; the measure, however, must be promoted. I wish you would correspond with the gentlemen at Newbern on this subject; I will take care of this business to the westward, &c.†

WM. R. DAVIE.

MACLAINE TO IREDELL.

WILMINGTON, 13th Sept., '88.

DEAR SIR:—I thank you for the Address, which however I had from Hodge the post before I received yours. I had no doubt of the author the moment I had given it a reading. I wish you could get the printer to forward a few of them here. Papers of that kind come by the post without charge, and he is to send forward proposals for the laws. Let him know, if you please, that I have received his letter, &c., and that I and my friends in this quarter will procure him subscriptions.

I expect to see part of the Address in our next paper. Some of the subscribers will make a point of having it inserted. Howard is a rank anti-federalist; and what is, if possible, much worse for himself, a fool. On my return, I found that he had published a very stupid and scurrilous piece, by way of answer to my Ad-

---
* The name of Gen. T. Person was indifferently written and pronounced in North Carolina Persons, Parsons, and Passons.
† Petitions to the Assembly for a new Convention.

dress (which you saw at Hillsborough) to the electors of Wilmington. This publication had the signature of William Fabkam, who had left the place on his way to Europe. I expostulated with Howard, not without bitterness, and sent him an apology, requiring him to insert either that or my letter. After promising, on his honor, to insert the apology *as his own*, he altered his mind, wrote to me, and wanted some alteration in it respecting Mr. Jones. I wrote him again, desiring him to return the apology, if he did not choose to adopt it; when he informed me that he should publish in his next paper, not only the apology, but our correspondence; and they appeared accordingly, but the former as what I dictated, not as his own. I have, with a few others, withdrawn my subscription, and intend to procure another printer, as this man is certainly under the influence of Walker, and two other fools and scoundrels; and Bowen, his partner, the man whom we engaged, is, God knows where, having purchased some wax-work figures, with which he is going about as an exhibitor of shows.

We have in this quarter a very indifferent representation in every respect. Yet I think we shall have another Convention called. The people in general cannot bear the idea of living out of the Union. Mr. Jones's opponents declined the poll, but a new one started up without effect.* He had a majority of 50 votes, &c., &c.

A. MACLAINE.

JOHN SWANN TO IREDELL.

NEW YORK, Sept. 21st, '88.

DEAR SIR:—I received your favor of the 27th of August, inclosing a copy of an Address to the good people of North Carolina. You will give me leave to thank you for that inclosure. I do hope and flatter myself that there is too much good sense, candor, and personal independence among the majority of that State, not to do justice to the merit of that publication. I mean that they will, at least, allow it a cool, liberal, and dispassionate reading; a claim which the author has an undoubted right to expect.

North Carolina, you know, sir, has been generally considered to depend, in some measure, on her neighbors for her politics; at

---
* Edward Jones, the brother of the celebrated Wm. Todd Jones of Ireland, and a descendant of the more celebrated Jeremy Taylor. Mr. Jones, after representing Wilmington four years in the Commons, removed to Chatham County: he was for many years Solicitor-General of the State. He was the intimate friend of Peter S. Duponceau, of Philadelphia; the patron of Capt. Johnston Blakely, U. S. N. His manner was courteous, his courage indomitable, and his talents of a high order. Vid. sketch by Prof. Hooper.

least it is affirmed that she discovers on all occasions an attentive disposition: an opinion which has been so unexpectedly contravened by her late conduct, that you will find no difficulty in figuring to yourself the extreme astonishment manifested on all hands at the news of her rejecting the Constitution. The thorough investigation which that subject has undergone, the late period at which it was taken up by our State, added to the example of so many respectable States, had induced a kind of repose in the public mind with regard to the event of her deliberations, from which the transition was not very difficult to censure and crimination. Hence the reason, probably, that all were so ready to impute her conduct to the *very virtuous motive* of preserving paper money and tender laws; indeed, some, taking a retrospective view of her conduct since the Revolution, and finding her delinquent in complying with requisitions, &c., have not hesitated to pronounce her of little importance to the Union. However, this, like all other violent gusts, was too impetuous to last long; and I now have the pleasure to assure you that her conduct is considered in a much less censorious light. The resolutions passed by the Convention were too evincive of a federal disposition at least, not to have had considerable influence in changing the public opinion.

Congress have at length finished the preparations necessary to give the new Government effect, after a great deal of debate, and perhaps some warmth, occasioned by the indecision, or rather decision of the members, about a place the most proper for the first meeting, &c. This question, sir, had the power to collect all the delegations from the different parts of the Union, so that there has not been a fuller Congress since the declaration of independence. However, this business being settled, Congress, I fear, like all other bodies about to expire, will scarcely have a witness of its dissolution, &c., &c.

JNO. SWANN.

DR. WILLIAMSON TO IREDELL.

NEW YORK, 22d Sept., '88.

DEAR SIR:—Before this time you must have heard that the new Government is to originate in March next, before which time Virginia could not have made all her elections, with time for the Kentucky members to attend. The new Congress is to meet in New York, a place very eccentric. Eastern members will be able to attend with too much ease; this will give them a legislative advantage, an improper one. Had North Carolina been in the Union, her five members in the House of Representatives could have easily turned the scale in favor of a more southern position. My patience and temper have been tried by this question; and the more so, perhaps, because for some time past I have not considered it proper to vote on the subject. I think that all attempts to induce our Assembly to call another Convention immediately will be to little purpose, for, whatever we may publicly say, I do privately think that a want of honesty is at the bottom with many of our oppositionists. If they seriously have alterations at heart, I think they had best adopt, in order to secure them by legal compulsion. Be pleased to calculate—New Hampshire, Massachusetts, New York, Virginia, North Carolina, and South Carolina, call for amendments, and a strong body in Maryland and Pennsylvania. The representatives from the six States requiring amendments will be 37, while those from the other seven States are only 28, to say nothing of the help the amending corps may get from Pennsylvania and Maryland. They may compel amendments by refusing to vote supplies except for a very limited time.

That our State might not be universally abused abroad, I have written the best apology I could make for it, which you will see in the New York Daily Advertiser for 17th inst., a copy of which I have inclosed to Mr. Collins, &c.

HU. WILLIAMSON.

A certain Wm. Falkner, a man of evident cultivation, being charged with being a spy in British pay, wrote Mr. Iredell a very touching letter, dated Warrenton, October 5th, praying his interposition and protection; and laying his claim upon his own destitution of friends, being a stranger in North Carolina. Falkner alleged that the sole foundation of the charge was a notice in a British newspaper that a Mr. Falkner had been promoted to some appointment in the Post Office; and inclosed a letter from Dr. John Jebb, of Parliament Street, Westminster, bearing honorable testimony to his character, and stating that he was "one of the first, at great risk and hazard to set on foot and carry into effect a subscription for the relief of American prisoners confined in the different gaols of England during the war."*

A Mr. Robert Lemen, or Leeming, a merchant in Edenton,

---

* "John Jebb, a steady and consistent asserter of the rights of mankind; the firm opposer of Ministerial tyranny, and arbitrary power; and a warm advocate for the American cause during the late controversy; and a cheerful contributor towards the maintenance of their officers and men whilst in confinement. To whose memory greater attention was paid by the citizens of London and Westminster than upon any other similar occasion except the interment of the late illustrious Earl of Chatham."—*Falkner.*

had received a letter from England, describing the character and person of Falkner, and it was notorious that British emissaries were at this time tampering with the Western Indians: Mr. Iredell, however, replied to Mr. Falkner that he thought the charge against him not only false but preposterous.

MACLAINE TO IREDELL.

WILMINGTON, October 27th, 1788.

DEAR SIR:— * * * * It would be vain to attempt petitions in this, and the neighboring counties, unless persons of some degree of popularity would undertake to forward the business. In most of them there are none who will stir a foot, and I have no communication with the press. Bowen, indeed, is at last returned, after an absence of several months, and appears very unhappy at the disputes with his partner, who has been dangerously ill as well as their journeyman. He has been told by myself and my friends (who not only patronized, but presented him with a liberal donation to defray the expense of removing here) that we would not have any thing to say to a press conducted by Mr. Howard without an explicit and satisfactory apology for his conduct. Bowen agrees that he shall either do this or relinquish the business; but nothing is yet done.

There has been a County meeting of Onslow, and a petition agreed on. On Saturday evening we had one for this town. It had been proposed for the preceding Tuesday, when the meeting was too small. At that time, however, Read and Huske attended, and endeavored to throw cold water on the business. The former with much cunning: the latter with barefaced impudence. He went so far as to reprobate meetings of that kind, for this memorable reason,—that something might be proposed, which if adopted, would disgrace the town. When it was shown that this argument proved too much, and would operate as forcibly against all assemblies, of whatever kind, he still pertinaciously maintained his proposition, until I told him it was stupid nonsense, and an insult to the understanding of every man to whom it was addressed. On Saturday Read absented himself altogether; and Huske, after informing the chairman, with as much importance as he could assume, that he did not think any instructions were necessary, sneaked off, without hearing any thing that might be offered.

An instruction to our member to promote the recommendations of the Convention for sinking the paper-money, and the passing a law for ascertaining the value of contracts, passed unan-

imously. That for calling a new convention, was carried against one dissenting voice. This will be further supported by the signatures of most of those who were absent. As you did not in your letter of the 8th say any thing of a publication, I thought myself indebted to the printer for half a dozen copies. Pray who is the author of this curious performance? Is he in earnest in his proposed separation? or is it held out only as a scarecrow? I take it to be a young lawyer in your town, with a dash of the Edenton member. I understand W. Jones has published an answer; but I have not seen it, &c.

A. MACLAINE.

On the 2d of November Mr. Iredell's son James was born. Losing his father when but a lad, his uncle, Governor Johnston, supplied to him a father's place. After graduating at Princeton, in 1806, he studied law; and consecutively filled, to the public advantage, and with credit to himself, many distinguished offices. In the war of 1812, at the head of a company of volunteers, he marched to the assistance of Norfolk. He represented Edenton for ten years in the Commons, and was speaker of that body in 1817, and 1818. In 1819, he was made Judge of the Superior Court; Governor in 1827; and a Senator of the United States in 1828. He was, subsequently, for many years reporter of the Supreme Court of North Carolina. Just before his death, in 1853, he published a treatise on "Executors and Administrators."*

The Assembly met at Fayetteville, November 3d, and adjourned December 6th.

GOV. JOHNSTON TO IREDELL.

FAYETTE-VILLE, 8th November, 1788.

DEAR SIR:—The Assembly met here the first day, and chose their speaker. Since that I cannot hear that any material busi-

---

* The following extracts, from a very just and chaste tribute to his memory by the Hon. George E. Badger, are taken from the Raleigh Register—"Born in the County of Chowan, of parents distinguished for eminent worth and mental endowment, he was raised in a polished and refined society, and he profited by the examples which were thus afforded.

"The lamented deceased, though distinguished for talents of the highest grade, was yet more distinguished for his excellent judgment and kindness of heart. To his younger brethren of the legal profession he was ever considerate, indulgent, and eminently fair: instead of seeking to take advantage of any error or oversight in their practice, he was ever ready to extend to them the most liberal forbearance, and was always content to try causes fairly upon their merits.

"His house was the delightful abode of old-fashioned hospitality, and long will his memory be gratefully cherished by those whom his kindness has encouraged and cherished in the rugged pathway of life."

ness has been agitated in either House. At first a great number of our friends were very warm for a new Convention; and were very sanguine in their expectations. Within these few days, they begin to have apprehensions that they are at present too weak, especially in the Senate—many of the members who are in favor of that measure being absent.

I understand that there will be a strong opposition to the appointment of Commissioners to fix the seat of Government.

The Western Affairs, and disputes with the Indians seem more particularly to occupy the attention of the members at present.

An Indian War seems almost inevitable, and never were a people worse prepared than we are for a thing of that kind, while the Indians are supplied and supported with every thing necessary for their purpose by the British on one hand, and the Spaniards on the other. There appears to be a general Confederacy of all the Indian nations between the river St. Lawrence and Mexico: the Western inhabitants appear very much alarmed; and some of the members from Cumberland, have very strongly expressed their wishes to me to be under the protection of Congress, and that the Act repealing the Law ceding that country to Congress might be repealed. I encouraged them with hopes that it might possibly be brought about; but don't know whether the Assembly will take it up, &c., &c.

SAM. JOHNSTON.

MACLAINE TO IREDELL.

WILMINGTON, 17th November, 1788.

DEAR SIR:—* * * * Mr. Hogg also mentions, first that there is no prospect of a Convention, and finally that there will not be one. He adds, by private information from Virginia, which it is expected will be authenticated, that the Assembly of that State have been prevailed upon by Mr. Henry to refuse doing any thing towards the organization of the new government.

Though a man of sense, Mr. Hogg is, I think, a very bad politician, and so credulous that he is as ready to swallow what he fears as what he hopes. I have had no letter from Jones by the boat which brought Mr. Hogg's (perhaps he did not know of it), but there was, I am told by Mr. G. Hooper, a sensible man, a passenger, who knows nothing of Mr. Hogg's news, but the election of a Governor, and yet seems well acquainted with what is doing, as well as what is said at Fayetteville. I should have told you that in Jones's last letter of the 9th, he says that there had, on the preceding evening, been a secret meeting of Federalists, in consequence of previous notice, when it appeared that they had a majority, though a small one.

I have had a letter from Mr. Hay, dated Belfast, August 6th, wherein he mentions "the many kind inquiries after Mr. Iredell; although when here but a boy of fourteen, he is remembered with pleasure." * * *

Since I wrote the above, I have had a letter from Mr. Jones of the 13th, wherein he mentions his doubts of a Convention, which was to be tried the next day; that there would not be more than four or five either way; that some are for again ceding the back country; and that others, who are against it, wish to send troops, to support the inhabitants against the Indians. Amazing great quantities of tobacco—now at 40s.

Mr. Jones makes no mention of Mr. Hogg's news from Virginia. I lose my ideas as fast as they rise, and my memory is good for nothing—I should have told you, that a scale of depreciation is much talked of, and that Wilie Jones has promised to bring it forward; and it is said that T. Person concurs in this, and even says, that he intends the paper-money not to be any longer a tender; but, with this condition, that £70,000 more be emitted. I have as small an opinion of one of these gentlemen as I have of the other; and therefore would not trust either of them. W. Jones would, in my opinion, sacrifice any thing rather than give up the party which he has so scandalously patronized. The inflexibility of his pride will soar above every other consideration, &c., &c.

A. MACLAINE.

IREDELL TO MRS. IREDELL.
SKEWAWKY, November 19th, 1788.

MY DEAR HANNAH:— * * * * Your brother has been re-elected Governor; and the Council are W. Hill, John Skinner, Jo. Collins, D. Connor, Armstrong of Pitt, and myself. Poor Martin, I dare say, will be much mortified. He should be very welcome to my place if I could give it to him, &c.

JAS. IREDELL.

GOV. JOHNSTON TO IREDELL.
FAYETTEVILLE, 20th November, 1788.

DEAR SIR:— * * * There is no probability of a Convention until about the time of the next Assembly in the Fall. There is no bill completed except the division of Rowan County. * * * Commissioners are appointed to attend the General Convention, whenever appointed by Congress. The Western people are very pressing for an Indian War, which is strongly opposed by the Eastern members, who have introduced a Bill to cede all the country West of the mountains to Congress. T. Person had Judge Spencer's Court Bill taken up, which, after one or two readings was laid aside. The Bill for compelling debtors to pay agreeably to their contract is lost. Upon the whole I fear the code of laws for this State will receive very little additional honor from the acts of this Assembly. Judge Spencer is spoke of as a Commissioner to attend the General Convention. * * *

I am uncertain when I shall be able to leave this place: indeed, were I not very anxious to be at home and my presence very necessary there, I should be altogether indifferent about the matter, as in every respect I am perfectly at my ease here, &c.

SAM. JOHNSTON.

CHAPTER XXII.

ÆT. 37–38.

LETTERS FROM WILLIAMSON, IREDELL, MACLAINE, SIR N. DUKINFIELD, RUTHERFORD, A. IREDELL, DAVIE, PIERCE BUTLER, JUDGE WILLIAMS, JOHN STEELE, AND MR. HOGG. THE ASSEMBLY AND CONVENTION. NORTH CAROLINA ACCEDES TO THE UNION. LETTERS FROM GOV. JOHNSTON, W. DAWSON, C. JOHNSON, R. D. SPAIGHT, AND JOHN HAYWOOD. THE REVISAL OF THE LAWS.

DR. WILLIAMSON TO IREDELL.
NEW YORK, 5th January, '89.

DEAR SIR:—Your favor of the 11th ult. came to hand three days ago. The post in cold weather seems to move slowly. I am very glad that the subject of the new Constitution is to be again before the citizens of North Carolina. Presuming that the same cause that prevented your attendance at the last meeting of the Assembly will prevent you from attending at the next Convention and Assembly, I shall, in such case only, assure the inhabitants of Edenton of my readiness to serve them; but if you can make it convenient to attend as the representative of that town, which I heartily wish, I shall offer to serve some of the counties as delegate in the Convention only. I have, as you may believe, the business much at heart, and wish to add my small mite to the endeavors of our friends.

Mrs. Williamson, who has at this instant been inquiring to whom I am writing, and been informed that I am writing to an inhabitant of Edenton, who is a particular friend, and one of the best men, as well as best lawyers in America, says that either of these circumstances would induce her to present you with her compliments, but all of them united engage her to request that I would present you with a tender of her esteem, &c.*

HU. WILLIAMSON.

*Mrs. Williamson was the daughter of the Hon. Charles Ward Apthorpe, of New York.

IREDELL TO THE HON. WM. CUMMING.
Jan. 6th, '89.

DEAR SIR:—I return you the bills you were pleased to leave with me. I suppose, with regard to that concerning executions, you will think it proper to wait to see the Maryland act. But I have great doubts about its propriety in many respects. I think it would militate with the principles of the new constitution, and I am so sure of this being adopted in November next that I don't think it worth while to prepare a bill which would be useless if it is, or immediately cause a quarrel between our Legislature and the General Government. I think, however, there are objections still more formidable. It may operate in many instances very injuriously; as, for example, A. obtains a judgment against B. for £100; B. obtains a judgment at the same court against C. for the same sum; C. is a man of consequence, and can obtain security; B. is poor, and can obtain none. B.'s goods must be immediately sold, whereas if he could levy immediately on C., he could get the money without this necessity. This reason alone would be with me a decisive one, since it proves that the poorer sort of people, who are in general the greatest objects of compassion, upon execution would scarcely ever be protected, and would be placed on a worse footing than they are now. I could enumerate other objections that occur to me, but really I have not leisure sufficient, and it is unnecessary.

In regard to your bill concerning promissory notes, I confess myself very reluctant to innovate upon a law that, by great experience, has been found very beneficial in England, and given rise to a series of excellent decisions calculated to avoid injustice as much as possible. I think your proposition of a protest unnecessary; and that it would create a great many difficulties in practice without doing any good, *since now the law is clear that if an indorsee of a promissory note does not give due notice of non-payment, &c., the indorser is not liable.* What due notice is must depend upon the circumstances of the case; and I am satisfied in this country no one uniform rule could properly be laid down. If all parties, for instance, lived in Edenton, earlier notice would be required than if one lived in Edenton, another in Hillsborough, and the third in Wilmington. I thought a regulation might be useful in regard to *sealed notes,* but that can't be done properly without altering the whole law as to single bills; and for my part that is an undertaking I should by no means venture to engage in. I think it would be very dangerous to mention a particular form in the act, since an innocent man, unacquainted with or not remembering it, might lose a debt by an immaterial variation. Neither should I approve of the method of proposing questions to a plaintiff on oath, since the blending of common law and equity proceedings together would, I am persuaded, in practice produce great confusion ; and if an example was once set, it would probably be followed in other cases, to the entire destruction possibly in the end of the regular principles of both systems. In one respect I agree with you in opinion, and that is, that bonds ought not to be assignable upon the same principles as promissory notes ; and though the legal interest might be permitted to be in the assignee, yet it should be subject to every kind of *defence** which the obligor might have had against the original obligee.

I make no apology for the freedom of my remarks. I know you love sincerity more than flattery. I cannot help saying that many of your propositions appear to me very ingenious, though they do not altogether suit my notions of public policy. And I beg leave to add that I should not choose to have any share in forming a law which I could not be present to support. I well know how bills are garbled after they are introduced, and all the blame of the whole is laid on the persons originally concerned in drawing them. *I have frequently felt this in regard to the law giving the equity jurisdiction, and do not choose to expose myself to the same mortification again.*†

Yours very sincerely,
JAS. IREDELL.

MACLAINE TO IREDELL.

WILMINGTON, 20th Jan., '89.

DEAR SIR :—I was but just beginning to recover when the Superior Court commenced here, and so weak that I could not attend till the last three or four days. Mr. Hooper, who was apparently well when he arrived, was taken ill, and kept his chamber during the whole term ; so that we had only two inquiries executed, two or three appeals from the Court Merchant tried, and a few of the injunctions dissolved. * * *

What has become of the delegates of our Convention ? Mr. Hooper was so much indisposed, and when he was able to see company, had so many people about him, that I forgot to mention the subject.

* This word doubtful.
† The Equity Law has been heretofore ascribed by me to Mr. Hooper, erroneously as it now appears.

I suppose with you, that we shall have a hard struggle for the seat of government, notwithstanding the new counties, from which I am doubtful whether we shall derive any strength. Those over the mountains will not vote from any local views, for they cannot have any ; but unfortunately for us, their private interest is somehow connected with that of a set of people who are strongly opposed to us. Upon the whole, however, I believe we shall succeed. There are a considerable number of people who are not materially interested in the dispute, who cannot shut their eyes to the manifest advantages which will accrue to the public at large from the encouragement which the seat of government will give to a great commercial town, merely because that town is a few miles distant from the centre of the State. As for you, I know you are an obstinate infidel, and argument would only tend to confirm you in error. *You would maintain your opinion at the stake.* But I will appeal to Gov. Johnston, who I know is opposed to Fayetteville, whether it does not in every respect come up to the representations given of it.

Judge Spencer neither read his argument from print nor from manuscript. He gave us something to the same purpose, but much worse. Judge Ashe, notwithstanding he had declined interfering, was obliged to decide. He, however, took time to *consider ;* that was to rake up all the mouldy authorities which he could collect, or rather to have it believed that he had been searching for law, for I am persuaded he had prepared them in vacation. He even cited Junius ;—very little, as I thought, to the purpose. As a favor, Bradley was admitted to bail till next Court. He struggled hard to put off the trial till December, that he might go to England, or to come to trial immediately ; but the Attorney-General wanted Tabb as a witness. This Tabb is the person between whom and Bradley the dispute originally was, and knows no more of the deed and the circumstances attending it than you do. He was, however, privy to the paper which Bradley signed and published, in which Mr. Swann's name was not mentioned, nor even alluded to. It contained a contradiction in very offensive terms of an assertion, which it seems Mr. Swann was the author of ; but of that circumstance Bradley was ignorant, &c.*

A. MACLAINE.

* Bradley was indicted for the murder of Swann, slain by him in a duel. Swann was the near kinsman of Judge Ashe ; the shooting was a clear case of murder in the eye of the law, though not so regarded by society ; that Ashe admitted Bradley to bail is conclusive proof that he was actuated by no undue bias.

DR. WILLIAMSON TO IREDELL.

NEW YORK, Jan. 24th, '89.

DEAR SIR :— * * * * The General Assembly of this State, after spending two months in pure wrangling, during which time many of them have had the felicity to make a clear saving of one dollar per day, have at length agreed to divide the State into six election districts for the choice of the representatives in the new Congress. They cannot yet agree about the mode of choosing Senators. The Commons wish to have all Anties, and the Senate wish to have at least one Congress Senator a federal-man, &c.

HU. WILLIAMSON.

SIR N. DUKINFIELD TO IREDELL.

SULHAM, 4th Feb., '89.

DEAR IREDELL :— * * * * Mr. Johnston's last letter gives me sad accounts of the universal sickness that had prevailed among you ; and that Mr. Pollok had prudently withdrawn to the Westward, possessing the great advantage of no business to confine him, and finances to defray the expense of rambling. I hope both he and Mrs. Pollok, by so doing, avoided the sickness they might have expected by remaining at Edenton.

Mr. Johnston's appointment to the Government is more honorary than otherwise advantageous, I fear. I flatter myself, however, that it has enabled him to give you some good appointment, and yet allow you to pursue your profession. If you have written to me since Sept., 1787, your letter has miscarried.

We have lately been in a pitiable state by the indisposition of our King, whose mental faculties have been these three months so entirely deranged as to deprive him of every power of business, and God only knows when his senses will be restored. Some of his physicians are more and others less sanguine in their expectations of his recovery. But I fear even in this situation their judgments may, in some degree, be biassed by party politics. O tempora, O mores ! but such is the land I live in. The Prince of Wales will be appointed Regent, during his father's indisposition, under some restrictions. The ministry will be changed, and Mr. Fox at the head of the new one. Mr. Pitt's resignation I regret.

The commissioners of American claims have allowed me £3,000 for my confiscated property, which will be paid by half yearly instalments in eight years, with interest at 3½ per cent.

'Tis lucky, as you observed in one of your letters, that the confiscation did not lay hold of my negroes, which I had lent to my mother. I think I wrote to you last year soon after the death of my youngest son—Mr. Johnston does not mention any increase to your family—I am in daily expectation of an addition to mine. I was introduced to Mr. Crewe last spring in London, and inquired after your brother. He told me he had left his family some time, and was settled in Suffolk, but he could not give me the least information further about him. I have long wished to see him, but do not at present think there is any probable chance of such an event.

Mr. Lowther is now in London, and I hope to see him, as I must go there as soon as Lady D. is safe in her bed and I can leave her.

I don't know at all what allowances have been made to Mr. McCulloch, but have been told they are very considerable : though (by what I've heard him say) I conclude much short of his expectations. I saw Palmer in November last, and he told me the commissioners had allowed him an annuity of £300 ; whether this allowance or any part of it is to be continued to his wife in case of widowhood, I don't know. Brimmage I fear has not been very greatly considered ; I'm sorry for him. I think I never saw a man more dotingly fond of a child than he is of his son, and very much does he lament his unfortunate separation from his family. McGuire seems very happy, though I'm told he was most terribly afflicted when *his Nancy* (the mulatto girl he brought over) died last year, and was quite inconsolable for a long time. Colonel Hamilton I have seen sometimes but know little of him. I do not immediately recollect any other Carolinians of your acquaintance.

Lady D. is as well as her situation will admit, my two boys and I perfectly well, and I hope you are all long ago recovered.

I beg my best respects to Mrs. Iredell, Mrs. Dawson, Mrs. Blair, Mr. and Mrs. Pollok, and am yours,

Very sincerely,
N. DUKINFIELD.

P. S. Feb. 7th. Lady D. was safely delivered of a daughter, about four o'clock this morning.

21st. As I mentioned the King's illness with little prospect of recovery, I am happy to tell you that the accounts we now receive of him are very favorable, and we are in hopes of an immediate and perfect recovery.

IREDELL TO STEELE.

EDENTON, Feb. 17th, 1789.

DEAR SIR:—Few things that ever happened to me in my life affected me with greater surprise and pleasure, than the distinguished and, I am sure, most unexpected honor of having the new county that has been formed out of Rowan called by my name. I have reason to believe, sir, that this has been in a great measure owing to your kind partiality; and I feel not a little pride in thinking that I have been able to recommend myself so strongly to your esteem. Permit me to return you my sincere thanks for so flattering a proof of it, and to request that you will be pleased to express my acknowledgments in the warmest manner to the other gentlemen from your part of the country who concurred in conferring upon me so great a distinction. My opportunities of rendering any public service have been very few; but no man's heart is more warmly disposed to the public interest than mine. I think neither you nor myself could give stronger proofs of it, than in supporting with all the earnestness in our power a Constitution which, in my opinion, gave us the only chance of being rescued from the dreadful evil of universal anarchy, which is as far removed from true liberty as despotism itself. But unfortunately few can be sufficiently sensible of this danger, though all are deeply impressed with the other, &c., &c.

JAS. IREDELL.

MACLAINE TO IREDELL.

WILMINGTON, Feb. 22d, 1789.

DEAR SIR:—* * * * I hope you will be a member (*of the next Convention*); and that you will be able so to dispose of your business at Newbern as to attend. Notwithstanding I am of opinion that a great majority are already prepared to adopt the new government *next fall*, it will be proper that there should be in the Convention a few men who may have it in their power to prevent the majority from running into absurdity.

British politics seem to engage our attention here as much as the new government, in which we have no immediate interest. The indisposition of the sovereign of that country appears from the papers to be very extraordinary. It is not simply mental, for frequent mention is made of his fever, and in one place of a discharge from his leg; but it does not appear whether this may have not been procured by the advice of his physicians. The system of government will probably undergo some alteration, or at least some of the opposition be called to office. If what is mentioned in Martin's paper be true, that Mr. Fox is a member of the upper house by the death of his nephew, Lord Holland, a title and a great estate, added to such abilities, must give great weight to the party. Many people here appear to be pleased that confusion is likely to be introduced into a government, which is not friendly to us; others from curiosity are anxious to know the event; and I suppose some of the British merchants sympathize with their fellow-subjects. It is not a little strange (if true) that a King who has foolishly and wickedly thrown away thirteen Provinces, should be so much beloved: no reason can be assigned for this infatuation, but that he has, by chance, appointed a Minister of abilities, who has made a reform in the commerce and finances of the nation. History will speak more impartially of him than his subjects do at present.

We have had more vessels here this fall and winter than have been known at any one time since 1775, the greatest part of them for West India cargoes; so that saw-mill lumber, staves, and shingles are in great demand, &c.

A. MACLAINE.

DR. WILLIAMSON TO IREDELL.

NEW YORK, March 2d, 1789.

DEAR SIR:—It has not been because I have any thing to write that I have taken up my pen; but to tell you, that my not writing frequently in future must be passed to account of not having the privilege of franking letters, after the 4th instant: and I am conscious that very few of them are worth the trouble of reading, much less the expense of postage.

There has been a considerable debate among the citizens of New York whether a Lawyer or Merchant, both Federalists, shall represent this District in the new Congress. The election comes on soon: it seems to be at length agreed to support the Lawyer. Gov. Clinton will be hard run: a moderate Antifed is started against him, &c.

HUGH WILLIAMSON.

IREDELL TO THE MISSES BLAIR.

March 15th, 1789.

MY DEAR GIRLS:—It is with the greatest concern and reluctance that I find myself obliged to leave home at this affecting period; but I can truly assure you that I shall sympathize with you every moment during my absence on the dreadful loss you have sustained. We have great reason to regret it, for certainly never was there a more affectionate friend as well as tender mother. Would to God it had been possible to preserve her! But, since Heaven has been pleased to decree otherwise, our greatest consolation must be in cherishing her dear memory by the fondest recollections, and endeavoring to imitate her virtues. Long, long will they be remembered by all who knew her. My heart bleeds at the recollection of many happy hours, now for ever past. I beg of you, my dear girls, to consider me as one of your sincerest commiserators, one of your tenderest friends, whose whole life will be employed, as opportunity shall be afforded, in rendering yours as easy and comfortable as possible. Your poor aunt feels exquisitely for you as well as herself. She longs, yet dreads, to meet you again. Regard us, so far as we can become so, as your Father and Mother. We shall anxiously endeavor, by every means in our power, to evince the tenderness and reality of the strongest attachment. Adieu! for the present, my dear girls, and believe me ever,

Your most affectionate Uncle,

JAS. IREDELL.

JOHN RUTHERFORD TO IREDELL.

WILMINGTON, 22d April, '89.

SIR:—I take the liberty, upon the acquaintance you have honored me with, to beg the favor of you to use your interest in a business which will probably come before the Governor in Council. The case is that of Mr. John Bradley, who unfortunately killed Mr. Swann. He means to make application to the Governor for a pardon. Though I esteemed Mr. Swann, yet I cannot help feeling for the distressed situation of this young man, who is not only a peaceable and well disposed citizen, but has really had a great deal of merit in supporting a mother, brother, and several sisters, in ease and comfort, by his industry. Mr. Bradley has sent testimonials of his conduct in that affair to his Excellency, which you will no doubt see. I sincerely hope the case may appear to you such as will merit the clemency of Government, and that you will use that confidence, which you so justly possess, to relieve a distressed family.

I am sensible the liberty I have taken, in obtruding myself upon you in this business, is beyond what I have any right to. But as your opinion may materially effect Mr. Bradley, and as the private traits in a man's character in a case of this kind should, I suppose, in a great measure guide the decision, the circumstances, which appear to me to do honor to the unfortunate party, may have some weight with you.

I must beg the favor of you not to let this go any further, as it may procure me enemies in this quarter, who may very materially injure me.

Your obedient servant, &c.,

JOHN RUTHERFURD.*

INAUGURATION OF THE GOVERNMENT OF THE UNITED STATES.

The 4th of March was the time appointed for the meeting of Congress; but on that day only eight senators and thirteen representatives made their appearance. A quorum of the representatives was not made until March 30th, and of the Senate until April 6th. Mr. Adams was installed as Vice President, April 21st. The oath of office was administered to General Washington, as President, by Chancellor Livingston, of New York, April 30th.

REV. A. IREDELL TO IREDELL.

GUILFORD, May 30th, '89.

MY DEAR JAMES:— * * * * The accounts you had of our King were well-founded. His death was reported and believed within an inch of the palace where he was confined, and his insanity was at last avowed. He has had, however, a most surprising escape, and is now, as to his mind, as well as he ever was in his life. Lord Onslow told me yesterday he thought it in a better state than he ever knew it; for that before his indisposition he was too much agitated in his manner, and used to speak in a very hurrying way, for ever repeating "what, what, what, &c;" but that, since that time he has been perfectly calm and collected. He was with him two days ago; and he then talked both in a jocose and serious way, and with the strictest propriety. However, he says his health is by no means so strong as he could wish it to be; which he attributes to the anxiety he has for ever on his mind on account of his son's opposition to him in politics. You will hear a thousand reports about his going to Hanover this summer, but not one of them will be true, though they are generally believed here. Lord Onslow assured me that it was quite certain that he would not go this year.

Your friend Burke has been getting into another of his

---

* At the session in November '89, Mr. Bradley was pardoned by Act of Assembly.

VOL. II.—17

scrapes. His imagination for ever gets the better of his judgment, or rather he has no judgment at all, *out of his closet.* In one of his late speeches to the House of Lords, as leading manager of Hastings' prosecution, he ran riot in abuse. Hastings petitioned the House, and Pitt, with the Indian squad (which he dare not disoblige), is now pursuing him to censure. Some people think they will succeed; and if they should, that the managers will throw up their *briefs* in disgust, and the prosecution terminate prematurely. In that case, I for one shall know what to think of Mr. Hastings.

I laughed immoderately at the expense of *Iredell-shire,* and I beg you will send me a very particular account of that respectable district, to which I feel nearly allied. To be serious, it was a most flattering testimony of public regard to you, my dear brother, and it gives me (who have not the meanest opinion of you) a very high one indeed of the people who have conferred it. For my part, I feel grateful to you for giving an "eclat" to our name, &c.

A. IREDELL.

T. LOWTHER TO IREDELL.

NEW YORK, 9th May, 1789.

DEAR SIR:—I arrived here on Saturday last, after a very tedious and disagreeable passage of fourteen days, which was so contrary to my expectation, that it required some exertion of patience, and was the more particularly to be regretted, as it deprived me of an opportunity of seeing the ceremony of administering the oath to the President of the United States, which took place amid the acclamations of thousands the day before my arrival. Since then I have constantly attended the debates of the House of Representatives, and have received great pleasure from observing the liberality and spirit of mutual concession which appear to actuate every member of the House. I have not observed the least attempt to create a party, or to divide the House by setting up the Southern in opposition to the Eastern interest, except in Mr. Jackson, from Georgia, the violence of whose passions sometimes hurries him into expressions which have, or appear to have, such a tendency. The members all appear to be very able men, particularly a Mr. Ames, from Massachusetts, who, notwithstanding he is a very young man, delivers his sentiments with the greatest ease and propriety, and in the most elegant language of any man in the House. As for Madison, of whom I had formed the highest expectations, I have had very little opportunity of forming an opinion, for whenever he has spoke, while I have been attending, it has been in so low a tone of voice, that I could not well distinguish what he said; his voice appears to defective for so large a man; however, I shall be better able t judge when he brings forward his motion for considering th article of the constitution respecting amendments, which he in tends on the 4th Monday of this month. This has excited genera expectation, though it appears to be the general opinion of peopl out of doors that nothing will be done; and is the more probabl from the debates which took place when Col. Bland presented th application of the Virginia Legislature, when it was strongly con tended by Mr. Boudinot, supported by a number of members that the application should be laid on the table, and that Con gress ought not to take notice of any such applications until the were made by the number of States required by the constitution It is still uncertain, and will remain so until the 17th, who wil be Governor of this State; but it is imagined that the presen one will be continued, for his friends have found means to per suade the people of the Southern district that he was always op posed to the confiscation laws, and to the partial tax, which ha procured for him a number of partisans; and the popularity o Col. Hamilton has been hurt by his declining to represent thi district in Congress; it is supposed he looks up to be Financier General, for which he has been preparing himself, or to be ap pointed a foreign ambassador, for either of which he is extremel well qualified. He is said and believed to be a man of suc extraordinary powers as to be able to render himself master o any subject in a week, &c., &c.

T. LOWTHER.

MRS. HOOPER (WIFE OF WM. HOOPER) TO IREDELL.

HILLSBOROUGH, June 2d, '89.

DEAR SIR:—With your usual humanity and goodness, which interest you in the distresses of your friends, you communicated t us in the tenderest manner Mr. Hooper's indisposition. I dreaded it when he left us; but he gave us such flattering accounts from Edenton that we began to be quite easy. I sent Billy to assis his father in his return, which, by this time we hope, he will b enabled to effect. How shall I express my gratitude to you, sir for your assiduous attention to him, and your tenderness t the whole family? Be assured we all feel it in the most sen sible manner; and pray that you and yours may find at all times but particularly in the hour of distress, so cordial, benevolent and disinterested a friend, whose heart entering into your suffer ing, will mitigate it with so lenient a hand. I rely upon you information, convinced that as you are aware that a deception in so interesting a situation as ours would be only increasing our affliction at a future period, you would not beguile us. I hope for the best; and that his present illness may make him more attentive to his health, as well in consideration to his friends as on his own account, in which case, sir, I will still flatter myself that some event will enable us to spend many more agreeable and happy hours in your society and that of your virtuous and amiable family. My best respects wait on Mrs. Iredell. Believe me ever, dear sir, with the greatest esteem and respect,

Your obliged and grateful servant,
ANNE HOOPER.

DAVIE TO IREDELL.

HALIFAX, June 4th, '89.

DEAR SIR:— * * * * The Anties here were remarking with great triumph, the fulfilment of their prophecies with respect to Congress never taking up the subject of amendments; when we, critically, received an account of Mr. Madison's notification that he would move this subject; nothing ever gave me so much pleasure, and this, coming from a Federalist, has confounded the Anties exceedingly, &c.

WM. R. DAVIE.

LOWTHER TO IREDELL.

NEW YORK, July 1st, '89.

DEAR SIR:— * * * * I had the pleasure of receiving your favor by Capt. Swift, and the debates by Mr. Black, who arrived here three days ago. I beg to return you my acknowledgments. It gives me great satisfaction to hear that the judges are becoming more liberal in their determinations, as, I am well convinced, it will have the most beneficial effect on our trade. A few more such judgments would tend to re-establish the credit of our country, for merchants would not be averse to giving the same credit to Carolinians, which they give to the other States, if they were assured of recovering their debts in our courts. * * * * Inclosed is a bill for the establishment of the Judicial System, it was principally drawn up by a Mr. Elsworth of Connecticut; but, it is supposed, considerable alterations will be made before it passes both Houses. There are not many lawyers in the Senate, but they compose three-fourths of the Representatives, &c.

T. LOWTHER.

IREDELL TO LORD MACARTNEY.

July 15th, '89.

MY LORD:—Since your lordship's arrival in England, o which I heard with very great pleasure, I have several times had an inclination to take the liberty of writing you, being persuaded that the same goodness which formerly induced such extrem kindness to me, would still influence you to hear with some sat isfaction of my present situation, which, though not free from some embarrassments, is on the whole respectable and happy. was the more desirous of acquainting you of this, because it wa owing to your generous influence that I was originally fixed here and I can assure your lordship that the uncommon obligations owe you, not only for your frequent and kind applications in my behalf, but more particularly for your obliging personal attention to myself, have never been absent from my memory. Never shal I forget the readiness with which your lordship, though only ir London to stay two days, took the trouble to devote a considerable part of that valuable time to me and my concerns! and ever to call upon me personally on the subject! But, my lord, great as these obligations were, and little as I thought they could b enhanced, how much have they been increased by your nobl bounty to my mother, and kindness to my brother since. Permit me to assure you that I never have regretted my poverty on my own account so much as that I could not devote annually a sufficient sum for the support of my excellent mother, or ever offer her any occasional relief, but such as must have appeared paltry indeed. God, who sees my heart, knows with what cheerfulness I would have done more, had it been in my power. Unhappy in being able to do so little! accustomed to find littl more in my power than to sympathize, with the strongest feelings of my soul, in every emotion of gratitude to you and other generous friends, for every assistance she received. Among these with what sincerity, what gratitude, and what respect, shall not ever remember your truly noble relation, Miss Catharine Macartney, of whose death I heard with the most poignant grief And permit me, my lord, to say that I feel infinitely more strongly than I can express, that greatness and goodness of mind with which Lady Macartney has seconded your generous and extraordinary exertions in my mother's favor. May Heaven for ever bless you both! and long preserve you for the mutual comfort of each other! Rejoiced I indeed am, that, amidst the great honors and universal applause you so deservedly have acquired, you have been so happy as to be allied to a lady whose soul seems so well fitted to your own.

Before I conclude, I think it my duty to mention one thing your lordship, lest you should suppose I had acted in any manner unworthy of the recommendation your lordship was pleased to give me. In the course of the American war, I took the American side of the question, and I confess, warmly; but I took no active part until long after all exercise of my office was rendered absolutely impracticable, and independence had been in fact declared. Being then at liberty, I chose my side according to the best of my judgment, and I certainly did so very disinterestedly, as no man could suffer more by the war than I did. I knew your lordship's sentiments on the subject and mine totally differed; but I am also assured your lordship has too much dignity of mind to condemn any man for the part he takes in a civil war, if he selects his side honestly, and upon due deliberation; and in no instance of his conduct afterwards violates those principles of honor and humanity, which are indispensable in every situation in life.

I shall esteem it as a particular favor if you will do me the honor to present me to Lady Macartney, as a man who feels the utmost gratitude for her extreme goodness to my mother, and who will be ever deeply interested in hers, as well as your lordship's happiness.

I am, &c.,
JAS. IREDELL.

MACLAINE TO IREDELL.
WILMINGTON, 1th August, '89.

DEAR SIR :— * * * I have heard nothing of the Debates since I received yours with seven copies. This is the more mortifying, as I believe some of them would sell here, and at Fayetteville. Exclusive of some palpable errors, they are in many places defective. No notice is taken of my calling upon Spencer to declare whether the Judges had enforced the Treaty of Peace. This must have been *intentional*, and is the more provoking, as in some places I have no reason to be pleased with the figure I make in the group. * * * I perceive that McCallister, who is now in New York, has been offering Gen. Howe's plantation for sale. He purchased from the heir at law, upon credit, for some trifle above $1200, then as I recollect at 16 shillings. But a small part of the purchase money has been paid, and no title made, and young Howe is still in possession. I do not know whether there are more than 300 acres; but with a privilege of cutting wood and fencing-timber on Mr. T. Hooper's land adjoining. There is a pretty good house, though I believe the inside will want some repairs; and there *were* convenient offices. The valuable part of the land is about 180 acres of very excellent marsh, about half of which was once well banked, and Gen. Howe did a good deal towards the repairs; but I do not know that they are complete, and I believe not. The buildings and other improvements are worth more than McCallister was to give. * * * If the Baron (*Poelnitz*) wishes to become a Carolina planter, he cannot purchase in a better time; nor can he have a better bargain, if he has it on the terms of McCallister's purchase. * * * I am very much pleased with the Address of the Governor and Council, and the President's answer. Among such as mean well, it must have a powerful effect; but we have a set of mean, swindling scoundrels, who, with all their bellowing for liberty, are fit only to be the slaves of a tyrant. Jones will be opposed in his election by W. Hill, whose merit (from a foolish publication which I have not seen) consists in being a *native*, &c.* He is supported by some of the Scotch merchants, by Major Walker, and by Mr. Jno. Huske, who, though upon terms of intimacy with Jones, declared openly that he would vote for any one who opposed him. Huske is again a candidate in the county for the Convention, &c.

A. MACLAINE.

PIERCE BUTLER (Senator from South Carolina) TO IREDELL.
NEW YORK, August 11, 1789.

MY DEAR SIR :—I was on Friday last honored with your very kind and very acceptable letter of the 25th of July. I am indeed much gratified by your friendly remembrance of me. I do with truth assure you, that neither time nor a long separation have weakened those strong impressions that the goodness of your heart and the fineness of your feelings made on me in our early acquaintance; but on the contrary, convince me daily of your inestimable worth. I have long considered North Carolina fortunate in claiming you to aid in her councils, and promote her wel-

* Wm. H. Hill: appointed by Washington District Attorney for North Carolina, 1790; member of Congress, 1799–1803; "he had a fine voice, and was a fluent, eloquent, and impressive speaker."—*A. M Hooper*, (*Maclaine's grandson*.)
Mr. Hill married the daughter of Gen. Jno. Ashe. His son, the late Joseph Alston Hill, was distinguished in N. C. for his amiability, and transcendent talents; equally unrivalled as a writer and orator. In the Assembly, as a debater, it is said, he never had but one equal, the Hon. Jno. Stanley; as an advocate at the bar, he was pre-eminent. He died at the early age of 35, but yet had lived long enough to establish a brilliant reputation. Such were his readiness and logical power, that it was common with his friends to compare him with the celebrated Charles Fox.

fare. I am sure, if she is sensible of the justness of your opinions, she will be led to true honor and substantial happiness.

I am unfortunate in the miscarriage of your letters, as the one above referred to is the only one I have received since last February twelve-months. I wrote you then a pretty long letter from Charleston, which I hope got to your hand—I wish to know if it did.

I am truly concerned at the loss your family have sustained in the death of Mrs. Blair and her son. "In every friend we lose, we die." How just the observation! You inform me that your two dear children have been at the point of death. I am only surprised that they have lived so long; and still more so, that you, so attached to a domestic scene, can think of keeping your children in Edenton, where, if I do not greatly mistake, I was assured scarce ever a child was raised to manhood. Why not retire to a more healthy situation? Assuredly Edenton has all seeds of putrefaction in her river and many stagnate ponds. Am I to hope for the satisfaction of seeing my friend on the floor of the Senate? *The Southern interest calls aloud for some such men as Mr. Iredell to represent it—to do it justice.* I am almost afraid to enter on the subject of the Constitution, yet I will confess to you, from whom I can conceal nothing, that I am materially disappointed. I find locality and partiality reign as much in our Supreme Legislature as they could in a county court or State legislature. Never was man more egregiously disappointed than I am. I came here full of hopes that the greatest liberality would be exercised; that the consideration of the *whole*, and the general good, would take place of every other object; but here I find men scrambling for partial advantages, State interests, and in short, a train of those narrow, impolitic measures that must, after a while, shake the Union to its very foundation. I once fondly thought that we should by our example contradict the assertion of Mr. Gillies, the Grecian historian, and evince to the monarchies of the East, and mankind in general, that there can exist such a thing as a free, tranquil, and happy Republic, securing to the individual his dearest rights. But, indeed, I am more than short-sighted if we shall do so, unless we very soon turn from the recent error of our ways, and determine to feel for all alike. I write freely to you, but my opinions are only for you. Perhaps I am something like the fox in the fable, having lost my own tail, I wish North Carolina to do likewise. I confess I wish you to come into the confederacy, as the only chance the Southern interest has to preserve a balance of power. Col. Davie and Mr. Williamson can witness for me that I was strongly federal; and that I conceded many points for the pur-

pose of bringing about the Union, and a form of government less exceptionable than that of the old Confederation, where every power was centred in one set of men; but I could not suppose that those *concessions* would be so abused and taken advantage of. Yet so it is; the acts of Congress will speak for themselves. I inclose you some of them. Pray give me your opinion of the Judiciary, Tonnage, and Impost bills. Some *gentry* proposed in the Impost and Tonnage bills some regulations with a view of forcing North Carolina into the Confederacy; I opposed it; I told the House you might be led, but not forced. If you wait for substantial amendments, you will wait longer than I wish you to do, speaking *interestedly*. A few *milk-and-water* amendments have been proposed by Mr. M., such as liberty of conscience, a free press, and one or two general things already well secured. I suppose it was done to keep his promise with his constituents, to move for alterations; but, if I am not greatly mistaken, he is not hearty in the cause of amendments.

It is at the moment I write as warm as I have felt it in South Carolina. Will you be able to decipher this? I write in much hurry, without being able to look over what I have wrote. You will be pleased to recollect it is for *yourself*, and not the public. With best respects, &c., I beg to subscribe myself, as in truth I am, Your affectionate friend,
P. BUTLER.

DR. WILLIAMSON TO IREDELL.
NEW YORK, 12th August, '89.

DEAR SIR :—Major Butler has just sent me two packages to be forwarded by the first vessel; and those contain all articles of public note so fully, that I shall not send a single paper. The North Carolina Debates are considerably read in this place, especially by Congress members; some of whom, who formerly had little knowledge of the citizens of North Carolina, have lately been *very minute in their inquiries concerning Mr. Iredell. By the way, I have lately been asked by a Senator, whether I thought you would accept a Judge's place under the new Government, if it required your moving out of the State, as we are not in the Union.* To this, as you may suppose, I replied that I was not prepared to answer, the question being so complicated—as how far the removal, what the allowance, &c.

I am so often asked what I think our State will do, that I have left off answering, except that we will probably do right, if Congress set us the example. The Board of Commissioners is now filled up by a Mr. Kean, from South Carolina; and we shall presently see where is the weak place in our code of accounts, &c.

HU. WILLIAMSON.

JUDGE WILLIAMS TO IREDELL.

MONTPELIER, 11th Sept., '89.

DEAR SIR :— * * * * I thank you for the few copies of the Address of the Governor and Council, and the Answer. I wish there had have been more of them, as I intend to take them to the back-country, and to dispose of them in a manner in which I doubt not but they will have the desired effect. Col. Davie had, a short time before, favored me with about the same number, which I had disposed of up and down my county; and which had been particularly pleasing, and met the approbation of all I heard speak of them, except our friend (who is within your number) Gen. Person. You say you think that I should be pleased with the answer; but I assure you, sir, not more than I was with the address itself, which in my opinion was a well-advised thing at a proper time; and will, I am persuaded, answer very salutary purposes, as well with the President and Congress of the United States, as with the citizens of this State.

I am also much pleased with what, you inform me, Mr. Madison wrote the Governor, and shall make use of that paragraph in your letter to evince to those to whom I show it the probable effect the address may have, &c.

JNO. WILLIAMS.

MACLAINE TO IREDELL.

WILMINGTON, 15th Sept., '89.

DEAR SIR :— * * * That fool, Spencer, is again chosen for Anson. * * * Clinton, who is returned again (*from Sampson*), is a convert to Federalism. I am persuaded we might have carried our point last year, but for Willie Jones; and therefore I am anxious to know whether he is a member. As I do not, however, believe he acted from principle; and as he was convinced last session of the Assembly, that he had not acquired popularity sufficient to insure the passing of a single bill into a law, I am in hopes he will now take the other side, for which the amendments will furnish him a sufficient justification. Should I be mistaken, however, there is one thing pretty certain, that he will find a great number of well-meaning members who, ashamed of being led by the nose last year, will prove very restive. Upon the whole, I think we shall succeed; but I am apprehensive that our success will be accompanied with an evil of very pernicious tendency,—namely, paper money. Those who wish to defraud the creditors, and those (a still greater number) who think we can not pay taxes without bills of credit, will be clamorous for an other emission of paper.

To whom was Payne's expression, "the mechanics must do as the gentlemen bid them," applied? I thought Hamilton was the first gentleman among you; I am sure Cumming frequently boasted of his *noble birth*. Strudwick, a strong Anti, was a candidate for the Convention, and within three votes of Col. Campbell. I see his son is chosen for Orange. Strudwick had a Judge Ashe's family and connections. The Judges not only wish to keep their seats, but to keep them uncontrolled. * * * question whether I shall ever be well, though I have been taking guiacum near three months, and mean to continue it. I do not know what effect it has had upon others; but I am persuaded from two trials, that with me it has increased the pain to a great degree for some time. Had it any thing like that effect upon the Governor? Yours, &c.,

A. MACLAINE.

JOHN STEELE TO IREDELL.

SALISBURY, September 26th, '89.

MY DEAR SIR :— * * * * We regret extremely that you are not of the ensuing Assembly or Convention—because no man has done more for our common cause on a former occasion, and there is no man from whom we might expect so much at the ensuing *struggle*. A *struggle* I fear it will be, because the State, except your District, seems much divided. If an adoption should take place, we will rejoice; but if it should be rejected, we must, like *good Christians*, mourn for the sins of our countrymen.

Yours, &c.
JOHN STEELE.

REV. A. IREDELL TO IREDELL.

GUILFORD, ENGLAND, Oct. 6th, '89.

DEAR BROTHER.* * * * Baffled as you were in the Convention by a majority, whose heads were no otherwise of value than as they might be counted; and whose hearts were, in general, fancy, of no value whatever; the struggles made by you and your party reflect the brightest lustre upon your character. Your abilities and patriotism have been fully established; and in the event I doubt not they will be crowned with the success they deserve.

I could say much of the part *you* took on that memorable occasion, if I did not fear to offend your delicacy. Allow, me, however, to say this much, that I feel a considerable degree of pride in being so nearly related to a man whose eloquence is only exceeded by the unvarying rectitude of his public and private conduct. It was impossible that you could add any thing to my affection; but you have taught me to respect your talents, and to venerate your principles, even more than I have been accustomed to do. The country and the times you live in open a fine field for the exertion of both; and I anticipate with no inconsiderable delight the good it is likely you will do, and the rewards you are likely to receive. Such talents as yours, my dear Brother, are rarely to be met with, and there is no object of laudable ambition to which you may not reasonably aspire. I perceive you are now at the Head of the Council. When did that event take place? and by whose appointment? You cannot do me a greater favor than by communicating to me as much information about yourself and the State you live in as possible. I am at present as ignorant about your government as the face of your country, and a pamphlet from the Journals of a Convention down to a Provincial Calendar, must have its charms for me, &c.

A. IREDELL.

MRS. HOGG TO IREDELL.

HILLSBOROUGH, 11th October, '89.

SIR :—By favor of Mr. Pollok, I give you the trouble of this line to acknowledge the receipt of your valuable and very kind present delivered me by Mr. Hooper, for which I return you my sincere and hearty thanks.

You and the Governor have furnished me with ample evidence of the innocence of the much and long injured Mary. Truth must prevail when attended to. Even Mr. Hogg seems to place his greatest confidence, not in the truth of the facts set forth by his favorite authors, but in their superior style, which he says will cause them to be read when Tytlor and Stuart are forgotten. It is a pity a bad cause should ever have a good advocate. Mr. Hogg, and all the family join me in respectful compliments to you and Mrs. Iredell. We are happy to hear your little ones are well again : long may they continue so! and that they may be spared to answer your most sanguine expectations is the sincere wish, sir, of

Your obliged and very humble servant,
McDOUAL HOGG.

IREDELL TO MRS. IREDELL.

HALIFAX, October 27th, '89.

MY DEAR HANNAH : * * * I had the pleasure on Sunday of seeing General Lincoln, and Col. Humphreys, two of the commissioners for making a treaty with the Indians. They came to town on Saturday evening, but none of us knew of it. On Sunday morning they called on Col. Davie, who did not know before that they were in town, and I luckily happened to call at his house while they were there. They said they had had a great mind to have called on him the evening before, but the weather was bad. We greatly regretted they did not, as we could have spent an agreeable evening with them, the Judges, Mr. Moore and myself having that day dined with him. They went out of town almost immediately. General Lincoln seems a very plain man, but Humphreys is a lively, agreeable fellow. They made no treaty, but concluded a truce, &c., &c.

JAS. IREDELL.

REV. A. IREDELL TO IREDELL

GUILFORD, November 3d, '89.

DEAR BROTHER :—I wrote you by the last New York packet and I believe promised to write by this; but to avoid repetition and to be as malicious as possible, I will do more now. I will engage to write you a few lines, at least, by every packet ; *provided*, you will on your part agree to follow my example. If you shall do so, in *any* degree, I shall think myself a great gainer by the compact ; probably in the same proportion that you have convinced me North Carolina would gain by acceding to the Federal Union. The privilege of comparing great things with small, and "vice versa," is you know of great antiquity; and therefore you will not wonder at the effect of your eloquence upon me, though you little dreamt, when you were making your fine speeches, of the comparison they have thus provoked. I have read them over and over, and "decies repetita placebunt." would say more if I did not fear to offend the modesty of a transatlantic lawyer. Did you practise in Westminster Hall, I should have much less reserve. Bashfulness is with us a tender plant that will not *thrive ;* and they do not cultivate it therefore in our Courts of Justice. But I must venture to compliment you upon one talent, which I wish, in your charity, you could communicate to me. *There is no waste of language in your speeches. You say more in five words than is commonly expressed in fifty.* don't know whether you meant to feed the appetite your pamphlet has given me for American politics ; but I must tell you that expect you to do so, by continuing to transmit every thing of the

nd in which *you* are at all interested, and as many others as
ou shall think proper to add : remembering always to give the
earer a hint of the *broadest* kind that we have such things as
age coaches in England, which have the art of conveying a parcel
well as the Post. Our politics are at this time very uninter-
ting. We are, I thank God, idle spectators of intestine wars
on the Continent, which every day spread wider and wider ;
d will, probably, deluge it with blood. The last accounts from
rabant inform us that the insurgents in that country had possess-
 themselves of Antwerp and Lille. One report is that the King
 Prussia is to join them ; and that the Prince of Orange is to
 declared Duke of Brabant. The Emperor has taken Belgrade ;
t he would like to keep Brabant for all that, &c.
A. IREDELL.

The Assembly met at Fayetteville November the 2d, and
ganized by the election of Mr. Cabarrus Speaker of the Com-
ons, and Charles Johnson Speaker of the Senate. At the same
me and place a second Convention on the Federal Constitution
nvened. Over the deliberations of the latter Governor Johnston
esided. Chowan occupied a most conspicuous position amid
ster-counties. The Governor and both the Speakers were from
at county, while another citizen was revising the statutes of the
ate. At this juncture, Governor Johnston's influence was
obably greater than it had ever been. He was unanimously
-elected Governor ; and the Convention having adopted the Con-
itution, was by a similar vote chosen the first United States
nator from North Carolina. He was succeeded as Governor by
lexander Martin. The Assembly passed an act establishing a
niversity, now located at Chapel Hill : this wise, and beneficent
easure was chiefly due to the exertions of Col. Davie, aided by
e exterior influence of the Executive. At the head of his list
 Trustees, Davie placed the names of Samuel Johnston, and
mes Iredell. The Legislature seems to have been actuated by
spirit of unusual liberality : they passed an act to encourage
e manufacture of potash ; and also, another act prohibiting
e exportation of hides, skins and furs, as a means of encourag-
g domestic manufactures : if they violated in the latter act a
inciple of political economy now well understood, their motive
as laudable. The Assembly adjourned Dec. 22d.
It is worthy of remark that while North Carolina was out of
e Union, her government was prudently administered ; her com-
erce revived ; and a general repose prevailed from the seaboard
 the mountains : nor was her capacity for aggression in war con-
mptible : she had raised troops, in '86, in defiance of an article
 the confederation, to protect her frontier settlements ; in '88 a
body of her militia, under Gen. Joseph Martin, had made an ex-
pedtion against the Chicamaga Indians ; and such was the
ardor and eager desire of her Western borderers for an Indian
war in the present year, that it could only be counteracted by
the influence of the East. The Western men proposed to levy
fifteen thousand volunteers ; had the Legislature assented, the
force would have been raised immediately.

Mr. Iredell's correspondence will furnish a more interesting
insight into the action of the Assembly, and the motives of its
members, than can be gleaned from the Statute-book and
Journals.

GOV. JOHNSTON TO IREDELL.
FAYETTEVILLE, 13th November, '89.

MY DEAR SIR :—I am here among a great number of busy
people, without being able to form a conjecture with respect to
what will be the result of the mighty bustle. The principal
business, which I have heard mentioned, relates to an alteration
in the Court System ; some mode of calling in the specie certificates, incorporating the towns of Newbern, Halifax, Edenton,
and Wilmington ; altering the land tax so as to make it more
equal. A great variety of other matter is talked of, but very
little brought forward in form.

There is still a violent and virulent opposition kept up to
the new Constitution, but the friends of that measure count upon
its adoption by a considerable majority. My particular situation
prevents my mixing much among the people : indeed were it
otherwise my health would not admit of it, &c.
SAM. JOHNSTON.

COL. DAVIE TO IREDELL.
FAYETTEVILLE, November 16th, '89.

MY DEAR SIR :—We have gone on smoothly as yet. The
Superior Court Bill seems to meet the general approbation. The
University Bill will certainly pass. Gov. Johnston has been
unanimously re-elected. He was also elected President of the
Convention to day, though too unwell to attend the House.
Charles Johnson Vice President. The Anties attempted to put
Spencer upon us, but the business was better managed.

The calculations are greatly in favor of the Constitution : its
friends say there is no doubt : of this, however, I am not so confident, &c.
WM. R. DAVIE.

DAWSON TO IREDELL.
FAYETTEVILLE, November 22d, '89.

DEAR SIR :—Permit me to congratulate you on the happy
ecision of the important question which has so long, and so vio-
ntly agitated the State. The business has been conducted
roughout with great moderation. Some of the gentlemen of
he opposition, to be sure, have been unreasonably tedious, trifling,
nd, I might add, absurd in their objections, which was all sub-
itted to by the majority with a degree of patience that aston-
hed every body. On taking the question for its adoption, there
ppeared Yeas 193—Nays 75. The minority seem to be per-
ectly satisfied since the decision, not because their doubts and
ears have been fully removed, but because they have determined
 acquiesce cheerfully in every measure which meets the appro-
ation of a majority of their countrymen. ° ° ° The Conven-
ion meet on Monday to consider of the amendments necessary
 be adopted. Yours, &c.
WM. J. DAWSON.°

GOV. JOHNSTON TO IREDELL.
FAYETTEVILLE, November 23d, '89.

DEAR SIR :— ° ° ° I congratulate you on the adoption of
he new Constitution by a majority of 118. The Anties behave
ith great good humor on the occasion. A few amendments
ill be recommended, which I expect will finish the business
his day. Fayetteville is to have a member.

I have been very earnestly solicited by a number of members,
nd particularly by the anti-Federal party, to take a seat in the
U. S.) Senate, which I have agreed to. Charles Johnson is
alked of as Governor : Billy Blount will be opposed to him.

I was not able to attend the Convention till the two last days
f last week. ° ° ° °

There has been very little done in the Assembly hitherto, so
hat it is probable that they will continue at this place some time
onger. I will leave them as soon as I can with decency.
2 o'clock in the afternoon,
The Convention has adjourned, "sine die."
Yours, &c.
SAM. JOHNSTON.

* Member from Bertie: Member of Congress 1793–'95: Grandson of Gov.
abriel Johnston : educated in England.

CHAS. JOHNSON (Speaker of the Senate) TO IREDELL.
FAYETTEVILLE, November 23d, '89.

DEAR SIR :—Your much esteemed favor of the 8th, I received by Mr. Mare ; and, agreeable to your request, I have the
pleasure of informing you that on Saturday the Constitution was
finally adopted, and ratified. ° ° ° Permit me to congratulate
you upon this glorious event, which I know will give you the most
singular satisfaction, as I believe nobody had it more at heart
than you ; nor has any person contributed more to bring about
the amazing change in the sentiments of the people, that is
evident from the great majority in favor of the Constitution,
even exceeding that at Hillsborough against it.

We have lost General Caswell, who died the 10th. ° ° °
Several gentlemen are mentioned and are candidates for the other
Senator—viz. : Mr. W. Blount, Hawkins, Williamson, Parsons,
D. White, Bloodworth, Stokes, Osborn, McDowell, Lenoir, B.
Smith, Galloway, &c. It seems to be settled that one is to go
from the Western country,° &c.
CHAS. JOHNSON.

R. D. SPAIGHT TO IREDELL.
CLERMONT, November 26th, '89.

DEAR SIR :—I return you my thanks for the agreeable information you sent me yesterday, "the adoption of the Constitution by our Convention." I am very happy to hear that wisdom
has at last presided in our councils, and enabled the Convention
to break through that cloud of ignorance, and villainy, which has
so long obscured our political horizon. I am much obliged to
you for sympathizing with me in my sore afflictions : I have,
indeed, suffered severely. Since the Convention at Hillsborough
in July '88, I have never enjoyed one day's perfect health ; and,
except two or three months last summer, which enabled me to
crawl about a little, I have been very ill, and at present see very
little prospect of a speedy recovery, &c.
R. D. SPAIGHT.

MACLAINE TO IREDELL.
WILMINGTON, November 26th, '89.

DEAR SIR :—° ° ° We are told that Mr. Huske, to appear the more conspicuous, walked out at the head of the minori-

* Ben. Hawkins was subsequently elected.

ty (*in the Convention*). I suppose Judge Spencer was too much mortified to push himself forward. From the various intelligence we have received, I am very apprehensive of an instalment or valuation law; but as the Assembly are determined to have all the money out of the treasury, even if they purchase certificates with it, I am not altogether without hopes that the evil may be avoided. It seems to be the general opinion of the members that there is no danger of a new emission, though Person, the Blounts, &c., are very earnest for it. These last are, however, unpopular; and, we are told, have been petitioned against as holders of public money. They have besides lost a principal prop, by the death of Caswell.

Your representative, Mr. Hamilton, distinguished himself by supporting Jones's election against Hill's petition. On the question of concurrence with the report of the Committee, which was in favor of the election, the vote was unanimous.

I should not omit to mention, that this Assembly is said to be the most moderate one that we have had since the Revolution, and that there are nearly one-half new members, &c.

A. MACLAINE.

REV. A. IREDELL TO IREDELL.

GUILFORD, December 1st, '89.

MY DEAR JAMES:— * * * * You are all doubtless interested about these continental disturbances. You will hear of the Duke of Orleans coming over to this country, and many curious conjectures about the cause. The fact is this: he was sent over to be out the way of mischief. He is an ambitious fool, and has paid for all the horrors you have read of, with a view of being seated upon the throne, or becoming regent. De Lafayette told him so in *express* terms before the king: he did not deny it; but agreed to come over here, where he could do no harm. I was told this by a lord of the bed-chamber, and I tell it to you, because it is only privately known as yet, &c.

A. IREDELL.

HON. S. JOHNSTON TO IREDELL.

FAYETTE, 1st Dec. '89.

DEAR SIR:— * * * * I had a considerable conversation yesterday evening with Col. Davie, who seems to think that, on account of some difficulties, no change will be made in the court system this session.

Spencer is here soliciting some further compensation to himself and brethren for their faithful service; but is not like succeed; and so dissatisfied with the conduct of the Assembl that he has expressed a wish to offer his services to the Unite States, and would condescend to accept an appointment in the courts, whether as a judge of the Supreme Court, or of the Di trict Court, I have not heard. It is said that neither Cushin nor Rutledge will accept their appointments; and he has n doubt of his being equal to either of them in point of abiliti and reputation. He has asked Col. Davie to recommend him Mr. Ellsworth, and Dr. Johnson: he is to apply to me on t same subject, but has not yet done it, &c., &c.

SAM. JOHNSTON.

MACLAINE TO IREDELL.

WILMINGTON, 9th Dec., '89.

DEAR SIR:— * * * * I suppose you will have Mr. Johnst with you before this gets to your hands. I find he will ha numberless applications for the few offices to be distributed North Carolina. Present my compliments to him, and let hi know that I have nothing to ask for myself, unless he could pr cure for me a rich sinecure, for I am not fit for any thing el I despair, however, of any such being established in my tim though I believe the Anties, with all their patriotism, would li their lips, if such a prospect should be held out to them. Wh would you think of being the District Judge? or could you mal more by practising in the federal courts? We have a great la of men to fill law departments. As Mr. Hay is a young ma and capable of great application, I have thought it might be f his advantage, if he could procure the appointment, to be t attorney of the district; though I do not find that there is an salary annexed to the office. What I am particularly anxio about is the judge, and I wish to hear from you on the subject.

I have seen the *Cherie*, which I have read over very light! The hero of the piece is represented in a detestable as well as a ludicrous light. The allusions are sometimes happy, and t author has in a few instances expressed himself in a pleasir manner. In one or two places he is disgusting, and the lines not deserve the name of poetry. It is upon the whole a miser ble hotch-pot, and has nothing to support it but the contempt ble character of ———, &c., &c.

A. MACLAINE.

WILMINGTON, 22d December, '89.

DEAR SIR:— * * * * The cession of the Western Territo is at last completed, so that we are rid of a people who were

pest and burthen to us. The election for representatives, it is said, will be some time next month; and over the mountains in February. The five districts are, Newbern and Edenton, Halifax and Hillsborough, Salisbury and Morgan, Fayetteville and Wilmington, and the two districts west of the mountains. Mr. B. Smith and Bloodworth are candidates here. The former has no popularity, and the latter very little out of N. Hanover. Perhaps some other will start up.

We do not know here what is done about sinking the certificates; but we hope some method will be fallen upon to set the money now in the treasury into circulation. Never was such a scarcity known, and the paper is now in an actual state of appreciation; but whether that will continue is questionable. * * * At our court, we tried exactly ten jury causes, dissolved four injunctions, and left near four times that number where we found them, &c., &c.

A. MACLAINE.

JOHN HAYWOOD TO IREDELL.

FAYETTEVILLE, Dec. 22d, '89.

DEAR SIR:—From being much busied, it has too long been my custom to defer almost every thing, although ever so agreeable in itself, to the last moment: this custom, from being very imprudently indulged, has grown into habit, and it is to that cause I attribute my very unjustifiable and impolite behavior, in failing hitherto to acknowledge the receipt of your highly esteemed and truly friendly letters of June last: I beg you to be assured, my conduct in that particular has not by any means comported with my feelings; and that, even at this moment, the reflection on your goodness in writing them, and on the obligations they laid me under, affects me not only with the most tender and lively sentiments of gratitude, but calls into action every better sensation of my soul.

The Assembly have this evening closed their session: I intended to write you of their acts, but it is all hurry and bustle here, and my office is filled with men who are importunate for their money: Mr. Cabarrus, too, who obligingly takes charge of this, leaves town early on the morrow, so that of necessity I am compelled to forego the pleasure; however, you will permit me to send you here inclosed, such of the laws of this session as have been printed. * * * Suffer me to request that you will be pleased to offer, in the most acceptable manner, my best respects to your lady, and to the Miss Blairs: enhance the obliga tion by accepting them yourself, and believe me, with eve friendly and respectful sentiment,

Very much and very truly yours,
JOHN HAYWOOD.*

Mr. Iredell, having performed his duty as commissioner revise, the laws were printed, under his inspection, during t year '89, by Hodge & Wills, at Edenton. The laws so revis included the acts of 1788. The work was approved in every r spect by an act passed in 1791, and has since been common known as "Iredell's Revisal."

Pending his labor, Mr. Iredell addressed a letter to the Legi lature, in which he stated, "I take the liberty to suggest that the original Act there is an expression which appears to me, wi great deference, to admit of too great a latitude. I am direct to leave out "all acts on which no question of property ca arise." I apprehend it to be extremely difficult, if not imposs ble, to foresee in almost any case of an existing Act, whether question of property upon it may arise or not. If, therefore, am not too presuming, I beg leave to say, that I think this pa of the Act, if not thought proper to be entirely repealed, migh at least, admit of an amendment." The Assembly gave him signal proof of their confidence by leaving the whole matter his discretion. Such modesty and caution if not rare then, co trast admirably with the audacity too characteristic of many the legal fraternity in our own day. Now impudence, a sonoro voice, and incontinence of speech, are often the counterfeits the just confidence, and energy, that are the fruits of abiliti study, and reflection: rash presumption illustrates the li "Fools rush in where angels fear to tread;" and the verie tyros, like Trapbois for a "con-sid-e-ra-tion," will readily unde take, not only the most difficult legal questions, but even to e plode the Baconian Philosophy, square the circle, or establi perpetual motion.†

---

* Treasurer of the State 1787-1827. Haywood County was called after hi he was the father of Hon. Washington Haywood of Raleigh, and uncle of the la senator, Wm. H. Haywood.

† The Revisal, printed and bound, was announced by Mr. Iredell to the Ass bly, Nov. 21st, 1791, as ready for delivery.

CHAPTER XXIII.
ÆT. 38—39.

LETTERS FROM HON. S. JOHNSTON, AND A. IREDELL. THE SUPREME COURT. LETTERS FROM A. NEILSON, AND P. BUTLER. IREDELL TO THE PRESIDENT. LETTERS FROM JUDGE ASHE AND IREDELL. THE SPRING CIRCUIT. LETTERS FROM C. JUSTICE JAY. DEATH OF WILLIAM HOOPER. THE FALL CIRCUIT. LETTERS FROM MACLAINE AND HAY.

HON. S. JOHNSTON TO IREDELL.
NEW YORK, January 30th, 1790.

DEAR SIR :—I got to this place the 28th, and yesterday took my seat in Congress. I found the act for regulating the Ports in our State, and enforcing the payment of Duties and Tonnage, had already passed the House of Representatives, and was before a committee of the Senate. This business, which I did not expect would come forward before the arrival of our Representatives, engaged my immediate attention. Though I find myself not so well prepared as I could wish, yet there is no preventing its going on. They say we are now enjoying the benefit of the revenue of the United States, without contributing any thing on our part ; and that, when our Representatives come forward, they will agree to any amendments that may be thought necessary. Our people are obliged to pay the Tonnage Duty, &c., all owing to the folly of our Assembly in not directing the regulations of Congress to be enforced immediately in our Ports.

I waited on the President the day after I came to town, but he was abroad. I visited the Vice-President to day at his seat in the country : among other things I asked him what he thought of the affairs of France : he thought they would end in a civil war, which would, probably, be of long continuance : though he gave some reasons in support of his opinion, which appeared plausible, I hope he is mistaken.

I have not yet had time to look much about me, my time being very much engaged in getting myself settled, and in paying and receiving visits of *ceremony*, which begin in my opinion to be carried to a ridiculous height, but those who are better informed think otherwise.

My nerves have not yet quite recovered the shock of the *wagon*, though I came through in very good health, and less fatigued than I expected after riding from Baltimore to this place in less than four days. The roads were very bad, and we rode much at night. Once it was near twelve at night before we arrived at our inn, &c., &c.

SAM. JOHNSTON.

REV. A. IREDELL TO IREDELL.
GUILFORD, February 2d, 1790.

DEAR JAMES :— ° ° ° I lent the Debates in your Convention to Lord Macartney, and he returned them to me yesterday, the whole of which I passed with him at his seat in this neighborhood, with many encomiastic remarks upon the part *you* bore in them. He promised me likewise that he would write to you, and for that purpose took your address. ° ° ° We have no public or domestic news, at least that I know of, to communicate. The most important is a question that respects the abolition of the Slave-trade ; but I have *very good authority* for believing that it will end only in *regulation*. Hastings' trial has outlived human patience. I meet with no one who does not yawn while he talks of it, &c.

A. IREDELL.

The first term of the Supreme Court of the United States was held in New York, in February 1790. Chief Justice Jay, and Cushing, Wilson, and Blair, Associate Justices, attended. No business was done except the adoption of a few rules. Judge Rutledge was absent. Robert H. Harrison, of Md., having declined, Mr. Iredell was appointed in his stead, and *unanimously* confirmed by the Senate, February 10th, 1790. The appointment was made without any solicitation on the part of Mr. Iredell. He had been induced to think that he would be made District Judge for North Carlina : when the higher dignity was tendered, it was to him a matter of agreeable surprise. Washington, it is said, derived his conviction of Mr. Iredell's merit from a perusal of the debates in the North Carolina Convention. When Mr. Iredell's name was sent in to the Senate, Major Butler, of South Carolina, bore honorable testimony to the merit of his friend. A member, from New Hampshire, said that though he had the highest confidence in the gentleman from South Carolina, he wished to hear the sentiments of the gentleman from the State where Mr. Iredell resided : whereupon Mr. Hawkins of North Carolina confirmed all that Butler had stated, and added something of his own : the Senate was then perfectly satisfied. Before Mr. Iredell's name was sent in to the Senate, the Eastern members had opposed to him some one from their own region.°

HON. PIERCE BUTLER TO IREDELL.
NEW YORK, February 10th, 1790.

DEAR SIR :—I was favored with your letter by Gov. Johnston. I thank you for making me acquainted with so amiable a man. It gave me much satisfaction to see him on the floor of the Senate. Indeed the Southern interest needs some such characters to take care of it. I should have been happy to have had you in Congress. The Union will no longer be deprived of your aid, and the benefit of your abilities. You have this day been nominated by the President, and unanimously appointed by the Senate to a seat on the Supreme Federal Bench. I congratulate the States on the appointment, and you on this mark of their well-merited opinion of you. I please myself with the expectation of seeing you soon here. I think you will save the lives of your children by bringing them here. Provisions, and every thing, but house rent, is cheaper here than with you. It is probable you will find it more convenient and eligible to settle your family somewhere to the North than keep them at Edenton. The House of Representatives are busily employed in doing something with the public debt. I think it will be provided for, &c., &c.

P. BUTLER.

HON. S. JOHNSTON TO IREDELL.
NEW YORK, February 13th, '90.

DEAR SIR :— ° ° ° The Secretary of the Treasury's Report still occupies the principal attention of Congress. There is nothing yet concluded on that subject. A proposal of Mr. Madison, supported by a very elegant speech of considerable length, has greatly alarmed the holders of Certificates or those who have been purchasers. It was to this purpose—that all those who had purchased should be allowed to fund them at the highest market price, about 10s. in the pound, and that the persons to whom they were originally granted should be entitled to the balance from the public. This proposition was opposed by Mr. Boudinot and others, by a variety of plausible arguments, but there was no decision, &c., &c.

SAM. JOHNSTON.

NEW YORK, February 18th, '90.

DEAR SIR :— * * * * After the adjournment of the Senate this morning I attended the debates in the House of Representatives. I was very much pleased with part (for he had been some time up before I came in) of a speech from my friend Madison. The subject was a proposition of his own to make a discrimination between the *original* holders of Certificates and *purchasers*. ° ° ° The debates on this subject will yet continue for some time. When they are closed I will send them forward to you. If justice is done to the speakers in taking down what fell from them correctly, you will be greatly entertained, &c., &c.

SAM. JOHNSTON.

NEW YORK, February 25th, '90.

DEAR SIR :— ° ° ° ° The House of Representatives have come to a resolution to fund the foreign and domestic debts ; and are now debating on the propriety of funding all the State debts. This last measure meets with considerable opposition ; but I am inclined to believe, as far as I am at present capable of judging, that it will be ultimately adopted. The great difficulty seems to rest on the ways and means ; but, your favorite, the Secretary of the Treasury, whose application is as indefatigable as his genius is extensive, encourages us to hope that they may be found.

I wish to God he may not be too sanguine. We cannot be too cautious of any future breach of faith, &c.°

SAM. JOHNSTON.

NEW YORK, February 1st, 1790.

DEAR SIR :—I have just returned from dining at the President's with a very respectable company, the Vice-President, the Judges of the Supreme Court and Attorney General, the Secretary at War, and a number of others. *The President inquired particularly after you, and spoke of you in a manner that gave me great pleasure.* ° ° °

° Letter from Gov. Johnston.

° Colonel Davie, in reference to the assumption of State debts, wrote Mr. Iredell in April—"I am tremblingly alive to every thing that may threaten the prosperity of the government ; and such bold politics are rather unfitted to its infant resources."

The Act for enforcing the collection of the Impost in our State has passed the House of Representatives, and was on the third reading in the Senate before I got to this place, so that I had only an opportunity of getting a few alterations inserted in it. The President will, probably, give his assent to it to-morrow. As soon as it is printed I will send forward a copy to you, &c.

SAM. JOHNSTON.

A. NEILSON TO IREDELL.

DUNDEE, (Scotland,) February 28th, 1790.

MY DEAR SIR :—Nothing can be kinder and more friendly than your letter: and the sentiments contained in the one of which you send me a copy accord most perfectly with those of my own breast. Your letter has indeed relieved me from a very poignant regret, which often crossed my mind ;—for I could not form any guess that pleased myself of the cause of your silence. I was, however, certain that you were above withdrawing private friendship on account of any political situation I happened to find myself engaged in.

It would have been the more pity had I been unlucky enough to have made no friends in America, for I certainly made nothing else, unless, to speak "à l'Irlandoise," a loss of constitution and years—which, and perhaps from my own fault, I have not been lucky enough to have compensated by Government, though others, in my opinion as little entitled to it, have had that good fortune.

Indeed I doubt I may be called a "devilish unlucky fellow." From one romantic notion or another I have neglected the happiness of matrimonial connection ; and I begin now to recollect that I may get old. Neither have I paid my proper court to Fortune: nor do I suppose that she, unlike other Goddesses, will be more propitious to me when old, than I have found her in youth. I can live with decorum—and for the rest it depends much on our estimation of it.

I congratulate you, my dear sir, most affectionately, on the health and happiness which I flatter myself you enjoy. Long may you enjoy them with that calm sunshine of mind which is the emanation of a good heart and a good head !

I see your Province has joined the General Constitution, which as far as I understand American politics, I think a most proper measure ; nor can I imagine what Rhode Island means by holding out.

The letter from the Governor and Council of your State to Mr.

Washington I thought excellent. His will be a great name—that is certain—and deservedly. What an era we live in ! "Patriots to act, and Emperors to behold the swelling scene !"

Of the French and Brabant Revolution you have so full accounts, both from France and Britain, that I cannot hope anything I might say could be new to you : the first, though by means perfect, is much more complete than the other, for the Brabanters have yet to reform.

You have, I dare say, seen a speech of Mons. Garat in the French Assembly. If I thought it probable that you had not I would send it to you, for it gives the completest idea of well-regulated free Constitution that I have ever read.

I beg my best compliments to Mr. Johnston : he will, I hope have received mine in reply to his last. I have orders lodged with a friend in London to send him Mr. Verrier's books on Portugal, to the care of either of the gentlemen he mentioned. Pray inform him that Tealing has been lately very badly, but surprisingly recovered, though at the age of 84.*

I am very keen just now on the idea that *flax* and *hemp* may be raised in America so as to supply this country. I wish you were a merchant or a planter, that you might assist me in this plan. I wrote to Mr. Johnston fully of it. I wish he would write to Mr. Morris of Philadelphia about it (for that is the place), and say I mean to correspond with him on the subject. I knew Mr. Morris formerly ; but so long ago he must have forgot me, and my approach will be easier through Mr. Johnston's introduction.

I left a negro lad in Mrs. Gordon's care at New Bern ; but think Mr. Johnston wrote me it was useless to think of recovering him. And there are other losses I might recapitulate, but it would be idle at this distance of time. One of them I regret perhaps more than all others—the loss of *a last* letter paternal affection and admonition from my father, written at his death when I was only 4 years old : it had accompanied me in all my travels, and was in my trunks at Halifax under Andrew Miller's care, which I hear were pillaged.

You ask me whether I am a Pittite or Foxite. I am considered as the latter, for I am a member of our Association of Reform in this country—associated to procure some enlargement of *liberty* in our municipal government : nor am I certain but that an apprehension of my political sentiments, arising hence, have caused me some little disasters of late.

My best wishes, &c., &c.

A. NEILSON.

* Mr. Scrymsour, of Tealing or Zealing, Scotland. The word is indistinct.

IREDELL TO THE PRESIDENT OF THE UNITED STATES.

EDENTON, North Carolina, March 3d, 1790.

SIR :—I had this day the distinguished honor to receive the letter you were pleased to write me on the 13th inst., accompanying a Commission by which I am appointed to the high and important office of one of the Associate Justices of the Supreme Court of the United States. In accepting this dignified trust, I do it with all the diffidence becoming the humble abilities I possess ; but at the same time with the most earnest resolution to endeavor by unremitting application, and a faithful discharge of all its duties in the best manner in my power, to evince the awful sense I entertain of its importance, and prove myself not entirely unworthy of a confidence which is so very flattering and pleasing to me. I hope you will accept, Sir, my warmest thanks for the great honor you have conferred upon me, and believe that I shall constantly feel the weight and dignity of the duties incumbent upon me, as requiring every effort of my mind to execute them as I ought and hope to be able to do.

I have the honor to be, with the greatest respect,
Sir, your most obedient and
Most faithful servant,
JAMES IREDELL.

HON. S. JOHNSTON TO IREDELL.

NEW YORK, March 4th, '90.

DEAR SIR :— * * * * I received a letter from Col. Ashe, informing me that he and the Doctor (*Williamson*) were elected.

A bill has this day been read a second time, and passed unanimously in the Senate, for accepting the cession of our Western Territory. As soon as this Bill becomes a law, the Act for extending the Judiciary of the United States to North Carolina will be brought forward. The House of Representatives are still deliberating on the Report of the Secretary of the Treasury.

A general inspection of commodities under the laws and officers of the United States is talked of ; and a Committee of the Senate, a member from each State, appointed to consider this subject under an idea of regulating Exports. I have just left the President's, where I had the pleasure of dining with almost every member of the Senate. We had some excellent champagne ; and, after it, I had the honor of drinking coffee with his Lady, a most amiable woman. If I live much longer I believe I shall at last be reconciled to the company of old women for her sake, a circumstance which I once thought impossible. I have found them generally so censorious, and envious, that I could never bear their company. This, among other reasons, made me marry a woman much younger than myself, lest I should hate her when she grew old ; but I now really believe that there are some good old women, &c.

SAM. JOHNSTON.

NEW YORK, March 11th, '90.

DEAR SIR :— * * * * The Committee of the Whole in the House of Representatives have voted the assumption of the State Debts by a majority of five. This was strongly opposed.

The House of Representatives having taken up most of the business recommended by the President, there has not yet been much debating in the Senate. In some few instances where there has, *it would appear that the sentiments of the Northern or Eastern, and Southern members constantly clash, even where local interests are out of the question. This is a thing I cannot account for ; even the lawyers from these different quarters cannot agree on the principles and construction of law, though they agree among themselves, &c.*

March 18.

The Southern Circuit is assigned to you and Mr. Rutledge for this time : *it is expected that the Judges will take it in rotation, &c., &c.*

SAM. JOHNSTON.

MACLAINE TO IREDELL.

WILMINGTON, 31st of March, 1790.

DEAR SIR :— * * * * Mr. Blount informs me that your route from Edenton to Fayetteville will be through Washington or Greenville, as you may choose. If it is convenient for you, would recommend Greenville, as you will probably find Mr. Blount at home, who can give you every stage, and all the distances, from his own door to Augusta. He said, indeed, that he would make out the route for you, which notwithstanding his unvaried attention to twopenny matters, he might possibly have done, had he not promised to wait on me about some business of importance which, I have reason to believe, he has long studied to avoid, as it might have ended, either in an obligation to pay a considerable sum of money, or an avowal that he did not intend to pay it. The latter, I have long known, he wishes to postpone by general and indefinite expressions. After waiting for him about four hours

I was obliged to leave town, which he perfectly well knew must be the case; for he was apprised of my business. You, however, he will readily oblige, which in truth he is disposed to in general when it costs him nothing; and in the present instance, perhaps he will do it the more willingly, as he probably looks upon himself as already an officer of distinction under the federal government, being *assured* (as he says) that he will be appointed Governor of the Western Territory ceded by this State last session,* &c., &c.

A. MACLAINE.

HON. S. JOHNSTON TO IREDELL.

NEW YORK, April 6th, 1790.

DEAR SIR:— * * * The great object of funding the public debts is still before the House of Representatives. If our members come forward in time, I have hopes that the assumption of the State debts will not take place. I am still of opinion that if Congress adopts that measure one of two evils will necessarily ensue, either they will not be able to comply with their engagements, or in order to enable them to comply they will be reduced to the necessity of laying taxes which will be oppressive to the people and injure the Government in their opinion. The House, at this time, is very nearly divided on the question. Bloodworth came to town to-day, which I hope will add one vote to the opposition. Our friend Williamson has taken a conspicuous part in the debate. We perfectly concur in sentiment, &c., &c.

April 27th, '90.

* * * The gentlemen who are in favor of the assumption (*of State debts*) are very sore and impatient under their defeat: they will, probably, endeavor to bring the matter forward again. I scarcely think they will succeed this session. If they do, it

---

* Hon. Wm. Blount, of Craven; member of Cont. Congress '82-3 and 86-7: delegated to the Convention that formed the Constitution U. S. in '87: Governor of the "Territory South of the Ohio" in 1790: Senator from Tennessee 1796. In '97, fearing that Louisiana would be transferred by the Spaniards to the French, and believing it to be to his interest, as he was largely concerned in land speculations in that region, he engaged in an intrigue for placing New Orleans and the neighboring districts in the hands of the British, relying upon his influence with the Indians and backwoods men, who cherished an intense hatred against the Spaniards. He was impeached and expelled from the Senate, July 8th, '97. On his return home, he was received with great ceremony, presently elected to the Legislature, and made Speaker of the Senate. The Spanish authorities had opposed obstacles to the survey of the Southern boundary of the United States, and hesitated to deliver up the ports north of the 31st degree of north latitude, in accordance with their treaty. Blount, undoubtedly, had with him the sympathies of his people. He married Mary Grainger of Wilmington.—*Hildreth. Wheeler.*

---

will be with so small a majority, that, in my opinion, if the measure was even less exceptionable than this appears to be in the estimation of many, it had better be laid over to another session than be now adopted, contrary to the judgment of so respectable a minority, &c., &c.

SAM. JOHNSTON.

JUDGE ASHE TO IREDELL.

HILLSBOROUGH, April 10th, 1790.

DEAR SIR:—Your polite favor, of the 31st March, informing us (the Judges) of your late appointment, was handed to me by Mr. Blair. I am at once affected with different sensations upon the occasion: in the same instant I rejoice, and am sad: in the moment that I regret your leaving us, and am sensible of the loss we shall sustain, I am pleased that you are appointed to an office of such dignity and importance, which I am sure you will fill with reputation to yourself and the fullest satisfaction to the public.

While you sit every jealousy and fear will subside; and every apprehension of encroachment from the newly erected jurisdiction will cease.

From Mr. Blair, I understand that you set off immediately upon your Southern Circuit, and that, at your return you mean to embark with Mrs. Iredell and family for New York—there to reside. In that case I despair of the pleasure of seeing you again, for my glass is nearly run out, and before your second circuit this way, probably, will be entirely exhausted; but, however that may be, be assured, my dear sir, that while I have the power, I shall not cease to put up my fervent and best wishes for you. Adieu, my dear sir, I had almost said for ever. May God have you in his favor and protection, and every felicity attend you, is the sincere wish of,

Your obedient humble servant,
SAM. ASHE.*

April 3d, Washington addressed to the Judges of the Supreme Court a letter, expressing his desire that the judiciary system should not only be independent in its operations, but as perfect as possible in its formation; and inviting communications upon the subject, and such remarks as might be suggested, during their first Circuit, by occurrences in an "unexplored field."

At this period the State of North Carolina was visited by

---

* Judge Spencer, the Court of Chowan, and a multitude of friends, about the same time, addressed to Judge Iredell very flattering congratulations upon his appointment.

---

many "speculators from the North for the purpose of purchasing Certificates, acting on a presumption that they would be funded; they at first purchased army certificates only; but afterwards, all kinds were brought up with avidity."

"Late frosts had done much injury, and the fruit crop had been generally cut off."*

Judge Iredell commenced his first Circuit in May.

IREDELL TO MRS. IREDELL.†

CAMDEN, SOUTH CAROLINA, May 10th, '90.

MY DEAR HANNAH:—I am thus far on my way to Columbia, which is only about 35 miles hence. I have been so fortunate as to have had company the whole way from Fayetteville till within 10 miles of this place, and expect to go in company with some of the Members to-morrow. My journey has been a thousand times more agreeable than I had expected—the road in general a very fine one, and the accommodations rather more than passable. This really is a very pretty town—a fine, high, healthy situation—and many very handsome houses in it. As I go forward I expect the country will improve. I scarcely thought there had been so much barren land in all America as I have passed through. * * * I met with the greatest civilities at Fayetteville from Mr. and Mrs. Hay; and Dr. Ingram, whom you will see in New York, was also very attentive and obliging to me. Be you so therefore to him. Mr. Hooper, I am told, talks of going to New York if his health does not improve. I have pressed him (as surely I could do no less) to make our house his home there in case of this event; to enlarge his plan by carrying his wife and daughter. Without some extraordinary change, poor fellow! I fear a few months will finish him. Good God! what an awful example! &c., &c.

GRANBY, May 12th.

I arrived in Columbia yesterday, and found Mr. Rutledge had been so obliging as to direct lodgings to be procured, at this place, for himself and me. Granby is about 3 miles distant from Columbia. I came here yesterday afternoon, hoping he would arrive

---

* Letter from John Haywood.
† Just before Judge Iredell started on his Circuit, Mr. Cullen Pollok wrote him that he had £175 sterling in hard money, for which he had no present use; that there would be difficulty in procuring coin for a long and expensive journey; and that, if the Judge should need it, the money was at his disposal, to be repaid *whenever convenient.*

---

in the evening. But he has not yet come. I don't think the Court will last more than this week, so that I shall probably see Charleston. Mr. Rutledge has resigned his place in the Convention, on account of the Court. I hope to have the pleasure of his company to Savannah, so that I consider I have pleasure rather than trouble before me.

CHARLESTON, May 23d, 1790.

I arrived here last night in company with Mr. Rutledge, from whom I have received the greatest and kindest civilities, and at whose house I now have the pleasure of staying. He is one of the most agreeable men I was ever acquainted with; and his wife seems a truly respectable and amiable woman, who has received me in the most obliging manner: I am already almost on the same footing with them as with Mr. and Mrs. Hooper. They have a remarkably fine family of eight children; the eldest married to a Mr. Kinlock, a very agreeable young gentleman, of large fortune, whom I saw at Columbia. The next is a son, who I believe is a very promising one indeed, who has been travelling in Europe for near three years, and whom his father and mother expect to meet this Summer at New York, for both intend to be there, together with a younger daughter than Mrs. Kinlock, about sixteen, whom I have not yet had the pleasure to see, she being with her sister. I am to see them both to-morrow. The other five are sons now at home, receiving education under an excellent private tutor. I saw and became acquainted with most of the principal characters of this country at Columbia, who all behaved to me with extreme kindness, and I am very much pleased with them indeed. This city far exceeds my expectations; and to-day I had the pleasure of attending a very handsome church, hearing as good a sermon as ever Crutchley preached, and I believe as well delivered; and also a very fine organ, which was extremely agreeable. This was in the forenoon, and in the afternoon Mr. and Mrs. Rutledge ordered their coach, and did me the honor to attend me on purpose to show me the different parts of the town. I called on Mr. Lindsay this morning. He looks as well as he did eighteen years ago, but is rather stouter. Thompson was there. He is better, but still an invalid. I am to dine with Mr. Lindsay to-morrow. He wanted me to take a bed with him, but I was previously engaged. On Friday we are to set off for Savannah, &c.

SAVANNAH, May 29th.

I arrived here yesterday in company with Mr. Rutledge, from whom I continue to receive the greatest attention. I never was more disappointed in my life than in the road from Charleston to this place, for until we came within twenty-five miles of Savannah I found it one of the finest roads I ever saw in my life. It was sometimes perfectly straight, and shady for five or six miles together. The last part of the way we came down by water, chiefly on Savannah River, in a canoe with four of Mr. Rutledge's hands, as he has a plantation in the way. Mr. R. carried me to some excellent private houses on the road, and we lay by as much as we could in the heat of the day, so that the journey has been upon the whole agreeable, &c.

JAS. IREDELL.

As it was *generally expected* that the Judges would ride the different Circuits in rotation, Judge Iredell had determined to remove his residence to the seat of Government. It will be seen hereafter that his removal subjected him to great loss, and inconvenience in consequence of a species of "Snap-Judgment," taken by the C. Justice. Towards the close of May Mrs. Iredell and her family proceeded to New York, where a house had been engaged for them by Gov. Johnston.

IREDELL TO MRS. IREDELL.

CHARLESTON, June 7th, 1790.

MY DEAREST HANNAH:—Mr. Rutledge and myself returned here from Savannah on Friday last. * * * Nothing can exceed the universal kindness I have experienced. Mr. and Mrs. Rutledge's has been beyond acknowledgments, and I have had the honor of several visits, particularly in a high style from the British Consul in his chariot. He is Mr. George Miller, a gentleman of an excellent character who formerly lived in North Carolina, where I did not know him. His manners are very plain and agreeable. The Convention has just broke up, so that several of my acquaintances at Columbia will be in town to-day. I have met with such extreme attention and politeness in this country, that I cannot avoid feeling some degree of pain in parting from it, notwithstanding the delightful prospect I have in view. Mr. and Mrs. Rutledge, with their youngest daughter and a fine boy seven years old, will probably sail hence for New York about the last of this month. Let me entreat that you will pay them the utmost attention you can. Mrs. Rutledge, though very agreeable, is a very plain woman in her manners, with genuine and *heartfelt* politeness and ease. Her heart and disposition appear to me most excellent and friendly, and I am sure you will be greatly pleased with her, &c., &c.

WILMINGTON, N. C., June 18th.

I arrived here on the evening of the 15th, and received immediately the delightful intelligence of your safe arrival at New York, for which I am devoutly thankful to that good Providence to which we owe so many blessings. I came this way because I was induced to believe a Court would be held at Newbern. * * * Had the weather not been so hot, my circuit would have been quite a jaunt of pleasure, for I have been everywhere received, by everybody, with the utmost kindness and distinction, and by many of the first families in South Carolina with a degree of unaffected politeness which was gratifying indeed. I spent one day at a place called Hadrell's Point with Mr. Francis Kinlock. There we had a fine view not only of the whole harbor, but of the sea on one side, and Charleston on the other; and while I was there I saw, several miles at sea, over the bar, three vessels coming in full sail, with a fair wind; one of them a large ship from Bourdeaux. In the afternoon we took a little excursion in the harbor in a boat of Mr. K's, which he keeps for the purpose. I spent a most agreeable day with them, and we were upon as social a footing as if we had been acquainted for years. I had also the pleasure of hearing Mrs. Kinlock play extremely well upon a piano-forte. Her harpsichord was in Charleston. This is a little rural retirement, at which they stay on account of the small-pox being in the city, &c., &c.

JAS. IREDELL.

From Charleston Judge Iredell had proceeded to North Carolina, under the impression that the Judiciary Act had been extended to that State. As this was doubtful, Judge Rutledge remained at home. After a delay at New-Berne of three days without receiving a copy of the Act, establishing Federal Courts in North Carolina, the Judge continued his journey northward.

HON. P. BUTLER TO IREDELL.

NEW YORK, July 5th, '90.

DEAR SIR:—If my little interest has been instrumental in placing you where you will do honor to the recommendation, and render so essential service to the country, my feelings are more highly gratified than I will venture to express. In paying a tribute to sincere friendship, I have at the same time not only discharged my public duty, but served the United States.

May you live long, my dear Sir, to enjoy the honorable station,
where the unanimous voice of such of your fellow-citizens as had a right to a voice on the occasion has placed you, is my ardent wish.

I am very glad that my country, South Carolina, and countrymen meet with your approbation. I thank you for the copy of our constitution. I hope it will answer the purpose for which the Convention were called. I have seen systems that I like as well. It is not for me though to say any thing against it. I can live under it as well as others. Congress are still sitting: if I did not hope to have the pleasure of seeing you soon here I would tell you what we have been doing. The House of Representatives are now debating the questions of Permanent and Temporary Residence. * * * Mr. Johnston was really dangerously indisposed with (*the influenza*): in this situation, contrary to my pressing recommendation, he suffered himself to be brought in a chair to the House to vote on the question of Temporary Residence. He is now recovered, &c.

P. BUTLER.

Judge Iredell arrived late in July at his residence, number 63 Wall Street, New York.

C. JUSTICE JAY TO IREDELL.

NEW YORK, September 15th, 1790.

DEAR SIR:—I have the honor of transmitting to you herewith inclosed the Draft I have prepared of the proposed Letter to the President. Be pleased to return it with such alterations and corrections as you may think it requires.

I shall send copies to the other Judges, with the like request; and on receiving them again will incorporate such additions and make such other alterations as all may agree in.

With sentiments of esteem and regard,
I have the honor to be, dear Sir,
Your most obt. and humble servt.

JOHN JAY.

As the draft inclosed by the Chief Justice is unsigned by Judge Iredell, I infer that the latter did not concur in opinion with his colleague. It is certainly well settled now, that the constitutional point, chiefly urged by Judge Jay, has no valid foundation.

SIR:—We, the Chief Justice and Associate Justices of the Supreme Court of the United States, in Pursuance of the Letter which you did us the Honor to write on the 3rd of April last, take the liberty of submitting to your consideration the following remarks on the "Act to establish the Judicial Courts of the United States."

It would doubtless have been singular, if a system so new and untried, and which was necessarily formed more on principles of Theory and probable Expediency, than former experience, had in practice, been found entirely free from defects.

The particular and continued attention which our official duties called upon us to pay to this Act, has produced reflections, which, at the time it was made and passed, did not, probably, occur in their full extent either to us or others.

On comparing this Act with the Constitution, we perceive deviations, which in our opinions are important.

The 1st Section of the 3rd Article of the Constitution declares that "the Judicial Power of the United States shall be vested in one *Supreme* Court, and in such inferior Courts, as the Congress may from time to time ordain and establish."

The 2d Section enumerates the cases to which the Judicial Power shall extend. It gives to the Supreme Court original jurisdiction in only *two* cases, but in all others vests it with *appellate* jurisdiction, and that with such exceptions, and under such regulations as the Congress shall make.

It has long and very universally been deemed essential to the due administration of Justice, that some national Court or Council should be instituted or authorized to examine the acts of the ordinary tribunals, and, ultimately, to affirm or reverse their judgments and decrees: it being important that these tribunals should be confined to the limits of their respective Jurisdictions, and that they should uniformly interpret and apply the Law in the same sense and manner.

The appellate Jurisdiction of the Supreme Court enables it to confine inferior Courts to their proper limits, to correct their involuntary errors, and, in general, to provide that Justice be administered accurately, impartially, and uniformly.

These controlling Powers were unavoidably great and extensive; and of such a nature as to render their being combined with other Judicial Powers, in the same persons, unadvisable.

To the natural as well as legal incompatibility of *ultimate* appellate jurisdiction, with original jurisdiction, we ascribe the exclusion of the Supreme Court from the latter, except in two cases.

Had it not been for this exclusion, the unalterable ever-bind ing decisions of this important Court, would not have been secured against the influence of those predilections for individual opinions, and of those reluctances to relinquish sentiments publicly, though, perhaps, too hastily given, which insensibly and not unfrequently infuse into the minds of the most upright men some degree of partiality for their official and public acts.

Without such exclusion no Court, possessing the *last* resort of justice, would have acquired and preserved that public confidence which is really necessary to render the wisest institutions useful. A celebrated writer justly observes that " next to doing right, the great object in the administration of public justice should be to give public satisfaction."

Had the Constitution permitted the Supreme Court to sit in judgment, and finally to decide on the acts and errors, done and committed by its own members, as judges of inferior and subordinate Courts, much room would have been left for men, on certain occasions, to suspect, that an unwillingness to be thought and found in the wrong had produced an improper adherence to it ; or that mutual interest had generated mutual civilities and tendernesses injurious to right.

If room had been left for such suspicions, there would have been reason to apprehend, that the public confidence would diminish almost in proportion to the number of cases in which the Supreme Court might *affirm* the acts of any of its members.

Appeals are seldom made but in doubtful cases, and in which there is, at least, much appearance of reason on both sides : in such cases, therefore, not only the losing party, but others, not immediately interested, would, sometimes, be led to doubt whether the affirmance was entirely owing to the mere preponderance of right.

These, we presume, were among the reasons which induced the Convention to confine the Supreme Court, and consequently its judges, to appellate Jurisdiction. We say, " consequently its judges," because the reasons for the one apply to the other.

We are aware of the distinction between a Court and its Judges, and are far from thinking it illegal or unconstitutional, however it may be inexpedient, to employ them for other purposes, provided the latter purposes be consistent and compatible with the former. But from this distinction it cannot, in our opinion, be inferred, that the Judges of the Supreme Court may also be Judges of inferior and *subordinate* Courts, and be at the same time both the *controllers* and the *controlled*.

The application of these remarks is obvious. The Circuit Courts established by the act are Courts inferior and subordinate to the Supreme Court. They are vested with original jurisdiction in the cases from which the Supreme Court is excluded, and, to us, it would appear very singular, if the Constitution was capable of being so construed, as to exclude the Court, but yet admit the Judges of the Court. We, for our parts, consider the Constitution as plainly opposed to the appointment of the same persons to both offices, nor have we any doubts of their legal incompatibility.

Bacon in his abridgment says, that " offices are said to be incompatible and inconsistent, so as to be executed by one person, when, from the multiplicity of business in them, they cannot be executed with care and ability, or when, their being *subordinate* and interfering with each other, it induces a presumption they cannot be executed with impartiality and honesty—and this my Lord Coke says is of that importance, that if all offices, civil, ecclesiastical, &c., were only executed each by a different person, it would be for the good of the Commonwealth, and advancement of justice, and preferment of serving men."—" If a Forester by patent *for his life*, is made Justice in Eyre of the same Forest, *hac vice* the Forestership is become *void* ; for these offices are incompatible, because the Forester is *under the correction of* the Justice in Eyre, and he cannot *judge himself*. Upon a mandamus to restore one to the place of Town Clerk ; it was returned, that he was elected Mayor and sworn, and therefore they chose another Town Clerk, and the Court were strong of opinion that the offices were incompatible, because of the *subordination*—a Coroner made a Sheriff, ceases to be a Coroner—so a Parson made a Bishop, and a Judge of the Common Pleas made a Judge of the King's Bench, &c."

Other authorities on this point might be added, but the reasons on which they rest seem to us to require little elucidation or support.

There is in the Act another deviation from the Constitution, which we think it incumbent on us to mention.

The 2d Section of the 2d Article of the Constitution declares that the President " shall nominate, and by and with the advice and consent of the Senate shall appoint Judges of the Supreme Court, and *all* other officers of the United States, whose appointments are not *therein* otherwise provided for."

The Constitution not having otherwise provided for the appointment of the Judges of the Inferior Courts, we conceive that the appointment of some of them, viz., of the Circuit Courts, by an Act of the Legislature, is a departure from the Constitution and an exercise of Powers, which constitutionally and exclusively belong to the President and Senate.

We should proceed, Sir, to take notice of certain defects in the Act relative to Expediency, which we think merit the consideration of the Congress ; but, as these are doubtless among the objects of the late reference made by the House of Representatives to the Attorney-General, we think it most proper to forbear making any remarks on the subject at present.

We have the Honor to be, most respectfully,
    Sir, your most obedient, and
        most humble servants.

The President of the United States.

At the August Term of the Supreme Court, the Commission of Judge Iredell being read, he was qualified according to law. Thereupon the Court adjourned "sine die."[*] In due time Judge Iredell left New York to hold the Fall Term of the Circuit Courts in the South : before he departed he made arrangements to remove to Philadelphia, Congress having passed an Act, July 10, fixing the seat of Government permanently on the Potomac, directing that the Government should remove to the new city in December, 1800, and that meanwhile the seat of Government should be at Philadelphia.

IREDELL TO MRS. IREDELL.

PRINCETON, September 14th, '90.

MY DEAR HANNAH :—We have had a very agreeable ride thus far through a charming country, and I am extremely pleased with the company. Gen. Mifflin, whom we took in at Elizabeth Town, is a very agreeable man indeed. We breakfasted at Elizabeth Town, about 14 miles from Powles Hook ; dined at Brunswick, a pretty little town on the Raritan, which is about 20 miles further ; and arrived here some time before dark, which is about 17 miles from Brunswick. This is a very pretty place indeed. Though the situation is high the town seems quite level, a good deal in the manner of Flatbush, &c.

                  JAS. IREDELL.

MRS. IREDELL TO IREDELL.

NEW YORK, September 15th, '90.

Could you wish a more obedient wife, my dear Mr. Iredell ? I wrote you last night, and am now attempting another letter.

[*] 2 Dallas's Reports.

Indeed writing to you and attending to my children will be the most pleasing amusement I shall have in your absence. * * * * There came a very polite note for you to-day from Gen. Knox, in which he says " he looks forward with pleasure to the Judge's residence in Philadelphia, when he hopes a more intimate connection may take place." Mrs. Dawson spent the day with me : Mrs. Romain and Mrs. Williamson drank tea with me ; and Mrs. Jay did me the honor to call for half an hour. I wish you had been here. When shall I get spirits to pay all the social debts I owe, now that I have not you to go with me ? Our sweet children are both asleep. I put off writing until they were in bed, that I might give you the latest account of them, &c., &c.

                  H. IREDELL.

IREDELL TO MRS. IREDELL.

PHILADELPHIA, September 15th, 1790.

MY DEAR HANNAH :—We arrived here to-day, after a very pleasant journey, about 2 o'clock. * * * I have since dined with President Mifflin, our most agreeable fellow-traveller, whose wine was so good and importunity so pressing that I could do nothing more since dinner but engage places in the Baltimore stage for Friday, &c.

BALTIMORE, September 19th.

We arrived here yesterday about 4 o'clock, after a very agreeable time from Philadelphia. I had taken my passage, without knowing there were two stages, in one by mistake by the Eastern Branch of the Chesapeake, so that we had to cross a ferry of 15 miles, but the wind was favorable, and upon the whole my time passed pleasantly. My company consisted of a Mr. Sharpe, a wine-merchant of Philadelphia, a cheerful clever man, with a modest engaging young lady of Baltimore, who had been at a boarding-school in Philadelphia, and a very decent seafaring man. Baltimore is a prettier place and more regularly built than I expected to find it. There is a beautiful view from some parts of the town. But the finest country I have yet seen is Pennsylvania, &c., &c.

                  JAS. IREDELL.

On the 20th of September, after a passage of eight weeks, Judge Iredell's mother arrived at his house in New York. She had come, at the invitation of her first-born, to pass the remainder of a life, many of whose days had been sadly clouded, under the shelter of his roof.

IREDELL TO MRS. IREDELL.

FAYETTEVILLE, October 8th, 1790.

MY DEAR HANNAH:—I arrived here in very good health before sunset yesterday evening, and am staying here to-day to rest, have my horses shod, &c., intending to proceed forward early in the morning. Having heard Mr. Hay was at Hillsborough I went to a tavern; at which Mrs. Hay has obligingly expressed great regret, but I shall be as attentive as possible to show her all the respect I can, which she well deserves of me. Poor Hooper has been at times, and is now part of every day a raving madman, but fortunately his health declines so fast that he cannot probably last much longer, and in his present situation the best thing that can be wished him is death. My God, what a shocking fatality! His family, I am told, is pretty well, though his miserable condition has affected his wife's health lately. The 15th October is really fixed on for Betsey's wedding (to Mr. Harry Watters,) but the family doubt if he can be present at it, and have some thoughts of having it over without him. If they do, it will make him ten times worse. His situation is now known to everybody. Your brother mentioned our having the largest house, as we have the largest family: pray let him have a real preference of which he pleases, and not yield the least out of kindness to us, &c., &c.

JAS. IREDELL.

MACLAINE TO IREDELL.

WILMINGTON, Oct. 18th, 1790.

DEAR SIR:—* * * * Mr. Stokes (*Dist. Judge**), whom I find you left indisposed at Fayetteville, on Saturday the 9th, had that morning a violent fever, which did not intermit, and died on the Tuesday following. * * * He (*Mr. Hay*) now says, "he would willingly accept a station independent of our Judges." He must have made this determination since Mr. Stokes's appointment, as he all along believed that Mr. Davie would decline acceptance if he were appointed, and never intimated the least inclination for the office. I hope, however, for the credit of the State, that he may be approved, and I have informed Mr. Johnston of his willingness to serve. I do not know who is to oppose him except Spencer. * * * The account you give me of my grandson (*A. M. Hooper*) is indeed very acceptable to me; and the more so, as it corresponds with the partiality I entertained for him, as well as with Major Rutledge's representation. I will indulge the hope that he will turn out a respectable as well as useful character,* &c. &c.

A. MACLAINE.

* The appointment of District Judge was first tendered to Col. Davie, who wrote Judge Iredell, that, though he was anxious to escape from "our d—d Judges," the salary was so paltry that he was constrained to decline.

MRS. IREDELL TO IREDELL.

NEW YORK, Oct. 21st, 1790.

MY DEAR MR. IREDELL:—* * * * I have paid very few visits, notwithstanding your injunction. Had you been here, I could have gone anywhere with you with pleasure; but how could I find spirits to go alone? At a distance from all my friends, what satisfaction could I find in visiting strangers? I never was intended to move out of the circle of my own family; it is only there that I can either give or receive pleasure. I called on Mrs. Buchanan, and she returned my visit; she has promised to introduce me to her mother, and she appears to be a very genteel woman. James Buchanan is still the same I fancy. The Bishop's lady has done us the honor to drink tea with us; her brother is married to the lady you were so fond of in Bristol, &c.

H. IREDELL.

IREDELL TO MRS. IREDELL.

CHARLESTON, Oct. 30th, '90.

MY DEAR HANNAH:—I arrived here on the 23d in perfect health, which thank God I possess at this moment; and it is most extraordinary that I should have escaped so well, as unfortunately there has been a great deal of sickness everywhere around me, ever since I came into the lower parts of Virginia. Neither Mr. Rutledge nor Mr. Pendleton was at Augusta, though I kept the Court open there five days. Mr. Rutledge arrived on the 20th; the latter at Savannah on the 16th. * * * I have passed my time here in the usual, agreeable manner. I stay at a boarding-house, but have never once dined at home. Mr. Rutledge, whom I waited upon after I had taken my lodgings, expressed great concern that he could not offer me a room, as his mother was with him, but their civilities have been very great indeed. Poor Stokes is dead, and Mr. Rutledge not going to Newbern, which, indeed, after so severe an attack, might be very dan-

* Mr. Hooper became a graceful and pungent writer; an Attorney; Editor of the Cape Fear Recorder; Cashier of the State Bank, &c. J. J. Hooper, of Ala., author of Simon Suggs, &c., is his son.

gerous to him, so that I expect to do the business. * * * I had last night the pleasure of dancing with Mrs. Kinlock at a ball, and was not in bed till 2 o'clock; nevertheless I got up at sunrise, and am perfectly well, &c. &c.

JAS. IREDELL.

IREDELL TO MRS. HOOPER.

Nov. 6th, '90.

DEAR MADAM:—I was so unhappy as to hear on my arrival here of the late dreadful loss you have sustained—a loss in which none can sympathize more truly than myself. I well know, my dear Madam, how much you must have felt on this trying occasion, and with what anxiety you must ever cherish the memory of a man whose talents and virtues were so many and respectable; although unhappily they at last yielded to an unfortunate weakness, which sometimes has been the fate of the best of men. I have for some time dreaded this melancholy event, and have constantly sympathized with you in the distressing circumstances which have preceded it. There are few virtues for which exercises are not provided. Your fortitude and magnanimity have had a severe trial. I have frequently feared they must at last yield to a sensibility fully equal to them. God grant you may yet be spared for a blessing to your dear children, and that they may prove constantly worthy of you, and equal to your fondest expectations! Nothing I am sure could have supported you hitherto but the consciousness of having in every situation acted with a degree of exemplariness almost beyond human attainment. Pardon me, my dear Madam, for saying this. It is the only possible consolation your unfortunate situation can admit of. All are subject to misfortunes. How few can have any right to think they did not deserve them by the slightest failure of duty!

Affecting as this subject is, I could not bear to go along without assuring you of my participation in your sorrows in this melancholy situation. An attachment founded on the most perfect esteem, and upon a gratitude excited by repeated and most flattering obligations, ought not, and in me I trust is not capable of being weakened by any change of place, time, or circumstance. Wherever I am it will be one of the warmest wishes of my heart, that you and yours may enjoy every relief and comfort that can remain to you. I heartily hope my dear Miss Betsey's marriage may prove a happy one. Poor girl! what must she have suffered under the attendant circumstances of it!

Be so good as to remember me affectionately to her, and your sons. I lament that my chance of seeing any of you is now rendered so precarious; but hope that you will believe me, dear Madam, constantly interested in you and your friends' welfare, and that I sincerely am, with the utmost respect,

Your faithful and obedient servant,

JAS. IREDELL.*

REV. A. IREDELL TO IREDELL.

GUILFORD, Nov. 30th, 1790.

MY DEAR BROTHER:—* * * * Burke has been publishing a pamphlet, that has made a great noise all over Europe, upon the French Revolution. It is a masterly performance, and betrays profound erudition, and the deepest reflection; and yet, after all, he has not satisfied my mind that the French have not been perfectly right in demolishing their old form of government. As to the conduct of the *reformers*, it ought not to be weighed in golden scales.

No revolution can be looked for in which great blunders may not be detected. We look for heroes, not legislators—patriots, not statesmen. I wish I could send you the book, however you will see it in fifty places. There are answers without end to it. All people are employed, either in praising or decrying it. The King, it is said, has bought him an annuity of £1000 out of his privy purse, &c. &c.

A. IREDELL.

MACLAINE TO IREDELL.

WILMINGTON, 18th Nov., 1790.

DEAR SIR:—* * * * Our Assembly are again running riot. A great majority of them are highly exasperated with Congress for the assumption of the State debts, and they are now actually laying their heads together to defeat that measure, so far as it regards this State.† The project is to subscribe, in Mr. Skinner's office, all our paper credits, now in the hands of the Treasurer and Comptroller, and which have been not actually charged to the United States. How this is to be effected I do not know; for no State can be a creditor to itself, nor can any State have a

* Mr. Wm. Hooper died at Hillsborough, Oct. 14th, at night, aged 48.

† Jno. Hay, of Fayetteville, wrote Judge Iredell—"Unless the Commissioner of Loans be most guarded and circumspect, as large an amount as our proportion of the fund will consist of fraudulent certificates, which the rage of speculation on our low credits has given birth to in every corner of the State. The purchasers of certificates, whether real or false, are, almost to a man, of the State of New York or Pennsylvania."

demand against the United States, so as to be entitled to fund that demand, until after a final settlement. The Commissioner cannot, therefore, in my opinion, receive any such subscription; but I suspect that in order to effect the intended purpose, the paper may be vested in the hands of some persons *in secret trust* for the use of the State, and if they are presented in this manner, perhaps, they cannot well be refused. I do not certainly recollect, but I believe all the paper received for taxes, lands, &c., has been directed to be funded, through an anxious desire to prevent its going again into circulation. If that is the case it will show in whom the property is. Would it not be proper that Mr. Skinner should be informed of the intentions of the Assembly, that he may in time consult his principal, and receive the necessary instructions? It is past all doubt, that if the Assembly can effect their purpose, they will, so far as the amount of the paper proposed to be subscribed, defeat the intention of funding the State debts.

Mr. Hawkins, I am informed, is wholly out of favor with the Assembly. They have not the least confidence in him. How he comes to be in a worse plight than Mr. Johnston, I do not know, unless more pliancy was expected from him, than from the integrity of the other.

Williamson is at Fayetteville, and it is alleged is at the bottom of the project to defeat the Assumption Act. He and the other Representatives (Sevier excepted) are waiting with impatience for a new division of the State, that they may secure their elections, before their return to Congress, &c. &c.

A. MACLAINE.

JNO. HAY TO IREDELL.

FAYETTEVILLE, Dec. 16th, 1790.

DEAR SIR:— * * * Late in the evening, Nov. 1st, a House of Assembly was made. In the absence of Mr. Charles Johnson, detained by indisposition, Col. Lenoir was chosen Speaker of the Senate, and Mr. Cabarrus reappointed for the Commons. Col. Polk had intended a strenuous opposition to the latter, as I conceive, in order to raise himself to a dignified station, that a grade to congressional appointment might be obtained; however, the propriety of Mr. Cabarrus's former conduct, added to the indelicacy of a rejection (without his declining to accept the Chair), prevailed.

Much discontent obtained as to our Federal Senator, which, by the ambitious and the disappointed, will be fostered. I am extremely sorry Gov. Johnston did not attend. I trust, however, a well founded confidence in the integrity and ability of our friend will prevail, beyond the idle clamor of the vain and interested. * * * After a session of 45 days, the Assembly arose, late ast night. From so long a "sederunt," it may be expected much business has been done. But the fact is, the whole time has been consumed in grumbling at the Assumption Law of Congress, and in private jobs. Of all the numerous laws, in the catalogue inclosed, only two can be said to be of a public and interesting nature. The alteration in the Court-law is certainly material, as far as it divides the ridings and extends the terms, and places the judges on the civil list, instead of giving, as heretofore, so much by the court at which they might attend or not at their pleasure, and for their appearance at which, for a single hour, they drew as if they had attended throughout the term. The new bill for electing Representatives to Congress will make an essential difference in the next return from this State. Steele's election is very doubtful, the opposition of Col. McDowell growing formidable—Macon's and Ashe's elections ascertained for Hillsborough and Halifax—no possibility for Williamson, who will be succeeded by Chas. Johnson—Bloodworth will be ousted by Billy Grove. Many ill-natured remarks were passed on our Senators. They have not written long letters to the Governor and Assembly, and they did not send on their Journals. There has been no consideration for Mr. Johnston's indisposition. To him, in common with Hawkins, has been contrasted the vigilance of our Representatives, who have appeared merely to solicit an interest for the coming election. Steele and Williamson, who are eminent in the display of their own peculiar brilliancy, have contributed not a little, by express charges or secret innuendoes, to fan the flame; and a set of resolutions have gone forward which would disgrace a pettish school-boy of thirteen, instead of a sober public body—or one that should be so. Our Judges were applauded for refusing a return to a "certiorari" in a cause pending in Edenton court;* and by a public law, all persons holding, under the United States, are disqualified for offices of trust, profit, or honor, for the great State of North Carolina. * * * We have strenuously endeavored to procure a recommendation to Congress, asking a federal court at this place alternately with Newbern, and subordinate courts in the

---

* Judge Iredell and Mr. J. Collins were executors to the will of Mr. R. Smith; both qualified, but Mr. Collins alone assumed the management of the estate. Smith's representatives brought suit; they were British subjects. A certiorari issued from the Circuit Court of North Carolina, by direction of Judges Wilson, Blair and Rutledge, to the Judges of the N. C. Court of Equity, to bring up the cause. The State Judges refused obedience.

Mr. Iredell's co-executor had pleaded the "Confiscation Act," but he refused to join in the plea.

---

seaports for the despatch of maritime affairs. * * * The merchants of Wilmington and this town have sent on petitions to Congress, requesting attention to the importance of this place, from its commerce, situation, and intercourse with the more internal and most distant parts of this State, which if duly weighed and considered must have their effect, Williamson and Steele to the contrary notwithstanding. Under Mr. Steele's insinuation that he is at Congress all-powerful, a route of posts has been *most wisely* designed by way of Halifax, Hillsborough, and Salisbury. * * * Mr. McCoy has been appointed additional Judge, to the great satisfaction of all men; and the reading-clerk of the House of Commons, Solicitor General to succeed Mr. Moore in the circuit he could not ride as Attorney General.*

In our Treasury and Comptroller's office are certificates to a very considerable amount. * * * The Assembly, with its contingent charges, have drawn from it £12,000, and not performed any useful service. The Treasury, however, could well spare it, as £50,000 is left behind; and a public debt to the State of £90,000, which will be collected the ensuing year. The surplus in the Treasury might well be employed in purchasing, at market rates, our certificates; but the knowing ones thought it better to let it lie snug, and to reduce our public tax so low as not to be worth collecting. * * * Mrs. Hay is learning to play on the guitar; and will be happy, when she sees you next at Haymount, to render her singing more agreeable to you, by that pleasing accompaniment, &c. &c.

JNO. HAY.

NOTES TO CHAPTER XXIII.

Mr. Thomas Iredell visited Halifax in July or August, '90. A letter from him gives a very characteristic account of that gay and opulent Borough. "The divine Miss Polly Long" had just been married to Mr. Bassett Stith, "a Virginia beau." The nuptials were celebrated by twenty-two consecutive dinner-parties, in as many different houses, the dinners being regularly succeeded by dances, and all terminating with a general ball. Miss Wallace, an heiress, Miss Pasteur, Miss Hooper, and Miss Lucas, were the belles of the occasion.

In 1780 a judgment was obtained in Bladen Court, "by surprise and fraud," by Col. Richardson, against certain Tories. The defendants had

---

* Hon. Spencer McCoy: educated by Rev. Dr. Caldwell: married the daughter of G. R. Henderson: died 1808.—*Wheeler*.

---

attacked and beaten Richardson at the head of a body of militia, and deprived him of his horse and arms. R. sued for and recovered damages; but suffered the judgment to sleep until 1790, when a motion was made to revive it; this was resisted by Mr. Hay for the defendants. "Judge Ashe, in a *most pathetic* display of patriotism, observed that such men as the defendants were not designed to be protected by the treaty; and that if they were the Commissioners for treating of peace, had no right to interfere with the allegiance of the citizens of North Carolina to her laws. When Mr. Spencer doubted, Ashe *wondered at his stupidity*; and expressed much concern that the judgment of a *good citizen* should be objected to against a *fellow*, who had been a *traitor* and a *rebel*."—*Letter from Mr. Hay.*

VOL. II.—20

CHAPTER XXIV.

ÆT. 39—40.

ADDRESS TO THE PEOPLE OF THE UNITED STATES. DIFFERENCE AMONG THE JUDGES RELATIVE TO RIDING THE CIRCUITS. IREDELL'S DEFENCE OF THE NORTH CAROLINA SENATORS. SLAVERY DISCUSSED BY AN ENGLISH DIVINE. TOM PAINE. THE "BLIND PHILOSOPHER." LETTER FROM JUDGE SITGREAVES. DAVIE'S OPINION OF THE JUDICIARY ACT. DUKE DE LIANCOURT. LETTER FROM A. HODGE.

Though Judge Iredell resided but a short time in New York, he yet made many warm and valued friends in that city. Upon the removal of his family to Philadelphia, Mr. Robert Lenox, a distinguished merchant of New York, who had acted as his agent, wrote him: "It was never my intention to make charge for any service I have been so fortunate as to render you. I am sufficiently repaid in the acquaintance of a gentleman for whom I have so much respect; and if I have been so fortunate as to have laid a foundation for your friendship also, I am repaid indeed."

REV. A. IREDELL TO IREDELL.

GUILFORD, February 1st, 1791.

MY DEAR JAMES:— * * * * * I read with surprise of the extent of your Circuit. I had before formed an estimate of it, not from the Home Circuit with us, but proportional to my ideas of America, a vast Continent over which a Junior Judge must lead the life of a Postboy. Besides in an infantine Empire, every man toils: he can relax, and be luxurious only after the sinews of Government have been relaxed, and the State itself is dissolved in effeminacy. There was a time when even Bishops ("incredibile dictu") were frugal, laborious, unaspiring men: and there is, I find, in America a Judge who can ride 1900 miles upon a Circuit. It is too true that we belong to countries very differently circumstanced. When I think of America, I am lost in admiration! When I think of England, I could weep over her degeneracy! With you a Washington presides, and every man is a patriot. I see no Washington here, but I see a Machiavel, followed by a servile train, as profligate though not as polite as himself. Your hemisphere is illuminated by the sun of prosperity, opening with uncommon splendor the morning of social life! Every head is clear—every heart is warmed—the whole man is agile, indefatigable, and virtuous. Your advance to wealth and *glory* (Circean good) is rapid. England and Britain have trod these paths before you! They have attained the summit of human grandeur: they are now proudly preëminent; but their sun is sinking in the West—his beams are refracted by intermediate clouds; and the timid mariner marks in the sky the fearful symptoms of a gathering storm. But I cannot support this exuberance of imagery into which an enthusiastic fervor of the moment has betrayed me, and will felicitate you in plainer language upon the exalted station you hold in the most enviable government on earth, &c., &c.

A. IREDELL.

The following anonymous address to the citizens of the United States was contributed by Judge Iredell to the columns of the Federal Gazette, a paper published in Philadelphia, and appeared in print, February 1st.

For the Federal Gazette.

To the Citizens of the United States.

You are frequently addressed in the language of flattery and violence: I mean now to address you in that of truth and moderation: a language more deserving of your attention, though perhaps not so likely to excite it. The subject is one in which you are deeply interested, and upon which I think much misrepresentation hath been employed—*the conduct of your Representatives in Congress*, whose existence is now drawing to a close, and who ought to be judged of from a true estimate of their proceedings, upon the large scale of the real interests of the Union, not from a partial or prejudiced state of them as they respect merely local or private considerations. By that test, which I take to be a fair one, I wish you to decide the merit or demerit of their conduct.

The true sense of the people, as it is an awful so I believe it is almost always a just one, when they are rightly informed of the facts upon which their judgments are to be founded. But dispersed as their situation is, confined as the members of Congress are during their attendance on their duty to a particular spot, the objects of jealousy to some, of envy to others, of proper consideration to few, and vigilant as the great body of the people always are and ought to be to the most distant alarm of danger to those liberties which so justly make an American proud, under these circumstances it is not to be wondered at, that misrepresentations should take place, and that therefore many of the people being deceived should feel uneasiness or express resentment at what they suppose had been done to their prejudice, and with respect to which, if it had been really done, such uneasiness would be naturally felt, and such resentment properly expressed.

This is one cause of public discontent. There is another not quite so easy to be removed: *The consequences of a real difference of opinion as to the propriety of public measures.* The heat of party will sometimes honestly misinterpret the motives of its opposers. They will be designedly misinterpreted by others. If a decision is thought to be even remotely injurious to liberty, those who entertain such an opinion will be apt to express themselves in warm terms, suited to the strong attachment they have to the liberty they think in danger. Language of this kind, though sincerely delivered, may do mischief, because though those who use it really think it is justified by the existence of such danger in their own imagination, it will frequently be found, upon a cool and impartial examination, that such a danger does not in reality exist, and yet the alarm may have upon many for a time the same effect as if it did. Besides the temporary mischief such a groundless alarm may occasion, it may produce this permanent one, that the cry of liberty having often been raised when it was not in any danger, the alarm may be disregarded when it is really necessary, than which a more serious evil never can happen to a country of freemen.

When the affairs of a great empire, in a situation new and unexampled, where there is a variety of opposing local interests, all to be consulted if possible but all to be subordinate to the general good, amidst not only the passions of private individuals, but the more formidable ones of large collective bodies acting on a contracted but more immediate scale of public confidence,—when the affairs of such an empire so circumstanced are to be discussed, the discussion certainly requires not only the joint aid of the most enlarged and comprehensive minds, but the utmost moderation and candor to make allowances for those unavoidable differences of opinion which on such momentous and difficult subjects will arise among men of the greatest abilities and the purest and most candid intentions. Such a disposition is no less necessary to secure the lasting welfare and benefit of that country in whose service such abilities are employed, than it is due in justice to the characters of the public servants exerting themselves with a laudable and an honest zeal, in the midst of contending difficulties, for the security and prosperity of the community at large.

Having made these preliminary observations, I now proceed to consider with you those particular parts of the proceedings of your representatives which have been most objected to. These are, I think,—1. Allowances to the members of Congress. 2. Salaries to their public officers. 3. The establishment of a funding system. 4. Their not making a discrimination between original holders and assignees of the public securities. 5. The assumption of the State Debts. 6. Their making a part of the debt irredeemable, but in certain specified proportions in a given time. 7. The proposition of an excise now under consideration.

1. *Allowances to the Members of Congress.* It is certainly a very invidious situation, and to men of delicacy a very painful one, when they are under the necessity of providing for allowances in which they are for a time personally interested. The members of Congress were placed in this situation by the Constitution, and I believe unavoidably, for if a provision for them had been left to the State legislatures, the general government would have existed at their mercy; and from the nature of the thing, a permanent provision in the Constitution would have been very improper, owing to the fluctuating value of money, and the variation in the prices of the necessaries of life. The allowances are, to each Senator and Representative six dollars a day for each day's attendance, and a proportionate sum for travelling; provided that after the 4th of March, 1795, a Senator is to be allowed seven dollars a day: and the Speaker of the House of Representatives has six additional dollars a day for his services and incidental expenses as Speaker. In regard to the allowance to the Representatives it is said to be, and I believe it is so, less upon an average than was allowed to the former members of Congress, although their allowance, as the Congress was almost constantly sitting, amounted in effect to an annual salary, whereas after the various powers of the present general government are once executed, by a provision of laws in such cases as the Constitution requires, it is probable a session will not usually last above three or four months in the year, which, together with the time allotted for travelling, will be the only time for which a member of Congress will be paid, as the allowance is *so much a day*. Compute

therefore the amount of that, and consider if it is an object to induce a man to come from the extremities of the Union, leaving all his private affairs unattended to, a family to be provided for at home, unless he brings his family with him, which must occasion a great additional expense, and himself placed in so precarious a situation, as to his public duty, that it must be impracticable to pursue any profession, or almost any other kind of business, by which he may have formerly subsisted. We have few men even of large fortunes in America who can be long absent from their estates, without their suffering much by it; and if we had, God forbid that the allowances to members of Congress should be such, that no men but men of fortune could be induced to represent us. That might indeed lead to an aristocracy so justly execrated. I hope always to see that the allowance to a member of Congress is such, that a favorite of the people, if he is the poorest man in the country, may be able to step forward and render the services they hope for from him. What trifling it is to compare, as some have very gravely done, the allowance to a member of Assembly in his own State with that to a member of Congress! Members of Assembly seldom sit above a month, or at most six weeks in the year; they appoint the most convenient time; and there is not one in an hundred who cannot spare such an absence from his family with little or no inconvenience to himself. This surely is a very different situation from that of members of Congress, as I have above without exaggeration stated it. One writer, I think, undertook to say, that in England the allowance to members of Parliament was four shillings a day for a knight of a shire, and two shillings for a citizen or burgess. He forgot however to tell us, that this was the rate of wages established in the reign of Edward III. (as appears in 1 Black. Comm. 174,) and that the value of money at that time, compared to what it is at present, was at least ten for one. (I state it so from Mr. Hume, 2 Hist. 496, 8vo Edit. 1782—and the value of money is, I believe, lower since he wrote.) Taking the wages therefore at that standard, a knight of a shire had the value of forty shillings sterling a day, and a citizen and a burgess had each twenty shillings sterling a day. I suppose however, if wages were now to be received by members of Parliament, instead of seats being most corruptly purchased, a member for a city or borough would be allowed at least equal to a knight of a shire, to whom no insolent superiority would be conceded. But average the two, and you will find the allowance to our Representatives less—It was attempted from the first to make the allowance to Senators one dollar more than to the Representatives, because in common with the legislative duty which devolves on the other House, they have a very important and troublesome share in some of the executive branches, are of course liable to be employed longer and to be called upon oftener, and it was also supposed that the House might be generally composed of men more advanced in years than the other, and whose attendance would be of course more particularly inconvenient to them. It ended however in a compromise as it now stands. The additional allowance to the Speaker is not only because his duty is of great importance, and his station of high dignity, which he ought to be able to support in a proper manner, but because it is an office which requires much greater application and closer attendance than that of any other member. Compare the probable amount of his salary with that of the Speaker of the House of Commons of Great Britain, which has lately been raised to £6000 sterling a year.

2. *Salaries to their Public Officers.* Upon subjects of this kind differences of opinion will always be entertained. There is a presumption, however, in favor of the integrity of the members upon this subject, because by an express article of the constitution none of themselves could, during the time for which they were elected, be appointed to any office whose salary they fixed. Let it be considered, that in this government we have not, and I hope we never shall have, any sinecures,—that most of the officers, particularly in the higher departments, have severe and laborious duties to fulfil, such as will usually require the greatest part of the officer's time,—that therefore the persons filling them can for the most part engage in no other pursuits, but must devote themselves to their offices solely,—that several of the offices are not only offices of high trust and confidence, and which therefore ought to command the best services that can be engaged, but that they require superior and uncommon abilities, and constant application to preserve and improve the knowledge and capacity of service already acquired. Let it also be considered, that in whatever station a man is employed, whether a private or a public one, it is a natural aim, and is to a certain degree his duty, not only to secure a temporary support for himself and his family, but to enable himself to lay up something out of his income, that his family may not be a burthen on the community after his decease, or in case of any accident to himself by which he is unable to exercise his office, and therefore from that cause or any other loses it, that they may have some little temporary subsistence at least, and not be instantly driven upon the charity and the compassion of others, already perhaps overburthened themselves. We have, as I observed before, few men of large independent estates. If we had such, and they were able to fill the offices, surely we ought not to rely on the *rich* alone for the support of the government. We commonly find most application and industry among those who have nothing to depend on but the constant application of the talents which nature has given them. To be sure this is not always the case—there are some brilliant exceptions to it—but it is so commonly the case, that in fixing upon a salary for any office, we ought not to make it necessary that a man of fortune should be appointed to it. And in my opinion it is a most desirable thing, that those offices of the government which require a constant succession of able men, should have such appointments annexed to them as to make them objects of ambition to all, by which means a constant succession of able and respectable candidates may be expected. But if they are made *honorable* only, and with salaries too incompetent for a prudent man to rely upon, an opportunity may be lost of employing many worthy characters from whose abilities and integrity the public might derive the highest benefit.

3. *The establishment of a Funding System.* Though this is a measure which I believe may be attended with some political advantages, I cannot say that I should have approved of it if it had not appeared to me to be *necessary.* America had an immense debt to discharge,—I mean immense for her immediate resources, though to a remarkable degree less than that of Great Britain contracted in the same contest, with an entire loss of the object, whereas we, by the blessing of Providence, most gloriously gained ours. If ever a debt required an honorable discharge, that certainly did which was due to those who had upheld America in a conflict upon which her *all* depended, and who had the more merit in their confidence as the chance of repayment upon any terms was so precarious. What then was to be done, but either to pay the principal, or provide upon effectual funds for the constant payment of the interest? No one will pretend we could do the former. We were therefore indispensably obliged to do the latter, or provide a satisfactory substitute. Funds were accordingly provided upon terms, though not exactly agreeable to the literal terms of all the contracts America had engaged in, yet upon such as were deemed a fair equivalent at least, and which it was supposed the good sense, moderation and patriotism of those of the public creditors to whom such an equivalent was offered, would induce them to accept of, in the present situation of their country, rather than distress it by a rigorous exaction of a literal compliance.

4. *Their not making a discrimination between original holders and assignees of the public securities.* You all know such a discrimination was proposed, and the propriety of it supported by a gentleman, who is deservedly held in the highest respect, who hath long, with uncommon abilities, distinguished himself in the public service, and whose honor is I believe as pure as any man's on earth. This gentleman, actuated by a warm zeal for the interests of many unfortunate men, who after having served their country essentially in the army, were compelled to receive certificates instead of money, and afterwards, from distress, not from views of speculation, were under the necessity of parting with their certificates for a very small consideration, proposed that the present holders who were assignees should be allowed to fund it at the highest price that had been known to have been given in the market, and that the balance should be allowed to the original holders. This was in substance his proposition, and he supported it with great ability, and a degree of eloquence which none could hear without being warmed by it. He contended, that the original holders had never been fairly paid—that a certificate was not *payment,* only *evidence of the debt really due*—that if the original holders could be indemnified, and the present holders of the securities literally paid, this might be more desirable than an encroachment on the strict claim of either; but as this was evidently impracticable, a composition was the only expedient, and this he thought upon a great scale of national equity, under such extraordinary circumstances, it was competent and desirable in Congress to provide for; especially as it would be particularly hard that the original holders should not only be sufferers by an actual loss, but made to bear their share in making good the deficiency to persons who had merely speculated for profit. To this it was answered, 1. That though the securities were at first only *evidence* of a debt, yet by an act of Congress, expressly passed for the relief of the original holders, and which was the only relief Congress could at that time afford, the securities were made *assignable,* and the solemn faith of the United States, after liquidation and after paper money was at an end, pledged for payment to the *assignees,* in consequence of which the securities were advanced in credit, and money (though far less than the nominal sum) was obtained upon them. 2. That those who assigned their securities, under these circumstances, knew that they assigned the *debt* as well as the *evidence* of it, the risk of which the assignee took upon himself, and which risk at the time of such contract, was a very hazardous one indeed, and was deemed so by the best friends of their country, so that a very imminent risk was incurred of nearly the entire loss of the debt. 3. That this therefore constituted a *contract,* which if unaffected by fraud or imposition was binding and conclusive upon both parties. 4. That as the purchaser could not have applied for a

reimbursement from the original holder, had the debt been entirely lost, so on the other hand it was not just that when, in consequence of an extraordinary resolution in the government, and such as no man living at the time of the contract had any reason to expect, the securities were risen in value, the purchaser should refund the profit he had thus fairly acquired. 5. That all species of speculation was not unfair, but on the contrary, when honestly conducted it was highly useful to the public, by promoting its credit, and a free circulation of its paper, and many assignees had purchased their securities in a fair and honorable manner, though it was to be lamented that others had practised the basest and most fraudulent impositions. 6. That it would have been very desirable if Congress, consistently with public faith and the constitution under which they acted, could have made a discrimination, and been able to effect it, between *fair* and *fraudulent* assignees, but this was the province of courts of justice alone, and however difficult or impracticable it might be for them to do it, yet this was no reason why it should be assumed by Congress, who were not trusted with any arbitrary authority over private rights, which were protected by the constitution in the most sacred manner, as well against legislative violations, as any other, and it was conceived wisely; for if a majority of the legislature could be warranted to interfere directly or indirectly with any private rights under the pretence of an equitable adjustment of them, no rights within the sphere of their authority could be considered as properly secure, no opposition of individuals having ever been found more outrageous than those committed by legislatures whose powers over private as well as public rights were unbounded. 7. In addition to all these reasons, it was shown, I think clearly, that the proposition, had it been ever so unexceptionable in its principle, was impracticable in the execution of it. And therefore, though no man who had a spark of sentiment or gratitude could avoid feeling greatly for the distresses that many of the original holders had sustained, it was considered by a large majority that the proposition for their relief was neither practicable nor such a one as Congress had constitutionally a right to enforce.

5. *The assumption of the State Debts.* This measure has occasioned perhaps more discontent than any of the other measures which Congress has adopted. It may still remain a questionable point of policy. But I hope to show you that if the reasons for it are not perfectly convincing to you all, they are at least very weighty ones, well deserving of your consideration, and which may exempt your members from the charge, in this instance, of having wantonly taken upon themselves a business they had no concern in. The principal objections to this measure, I think are, 1. That it is unconstitutional. 2. That it is particularly injurious to some States, which having already been heavily taxed to pay a part of their own State debts, will now be taxed to pay those of other States which have been more deficient.—First objection, *Its being unconstitutional.* Answer. 1. The Congress have authority "To lay and collect taxes, duties, imposts and excises, *to pay the debts and provide for the common defence and general welfare of the United States.*" 2. The State debts, *as such,* are not assumed ; none are assumed but those contracted for the general defence of the Union, which debts are certainly all fairly chargeable against the United States, since it was the duty of the whole to provide for the defence of each particular part, and not leave the whole burthen of the defence upon that part only. This principle is so obvious and just, that the most violent opposer of this assumption in any part of the Union will insist on charging to the United States *every shilling of such debt so contracted by his State.* What therefore has this assumption done, but undertaken to pay to the individual creditor a debt due upon every principle of honor and honesty by the United States, instead of leaving such creditor to be paid by a particular State, which though the *nominal* is not the *real* debtor (in point of conscience, I mean), and must be reimbursed by the United States again ? 3. Is not a provision for the payment of debts so circumstanced, a provision for the *general welfare* (at least may it not be fairly supposed so ?) of the United States ? and this the Congress are constitutionally to judge of.—Second objection : *Its being particularly injurious to some States, in the situation above stated.* Such a case is certainly a hardship, but the circumstances of the several States were so different during the war, some being much more pressed by the enemy than others, and of course the exertions of the various parts of the Union were so unequal, that they could not all be in a condition to start upon an equal footing at the peace. A State in proportion to what it suffered during the war was commonly more or less able to revive after the peace. Think for instance, of the deplorable condition of South Carolina and Georgia, which were so long in possession of the enemy, and which made such wonderful and great exertions, that the people of those States ever since have suffered very great private distress, and do to this hour—*on account of their sufferings in the common cause*—the cause as well of *Massachusetts, Connecticut, Pennsylvania,* and *Virginia,* as their own. The State of South Carolina is now burthened with an immense debt, most honorably contracted in the course of a very brave defence against the common enemy for several years. There is no doubt but that the whole amount of her *nominal* debt, contracted for the purposes of the war only, is far greater than her fair proportion of the unsettled expense of all the States can be. I am not qualified even to conjecture the amount. I state, therefore, sums merely for illustration. Suppose her nominal debt, such as she undertook, but which the United States ought in duty to pay, amounts to 500,000 dollars, but that her real proportion of all the debts the several States owe on account of the war, and of those that have been discharged, is 100,000 dollars. Would it not be a very great hardship indeed, that in addition to all those private distresses they must long feel, not only in consequence of the war, but of the heavy burthen of their debt since the peace, they should now, under a system calculated expressly for the equalizing of all the public burthens, continue to provide for 400,000 dollars more than was their real proportion of the debt ? Surely it is proper in considering questions of this kind, not to consider the condition of one or two States only to which we are particularly attached, but to take a general survey of the whole, and I believe we shall find that those States which most anxiously wished for the assumption, have been full as heavily taxed as those that were against it. What occasioned those taxes to so great an amount, but either a provision for their share of the foreign debt, or the domestic debt of the Union, or that part of the domestic debt which, though nominally theirs, I consider to be as justly a part of the debt of the Union as any other part of it, so far as it was fairly contracted for the common defence ? Comparisons are invidious, and I forbear them by avoiding particulars, which would easily show that no exertions by any one of the States averse to the assumption have exceeded those of some of the States that are in favor of it. And will not all be benefited by its being rendered unnecessary to any one of the States to continue a provision (which must be by excise or direct taxation) for that part of the debt which the United States have assumed ? This benefit will probably, upon the whole, be equal, or nearly so, to the disadvantage any State may sustain by its additional share of duties or other species of taxation, which the assumption may give rise to, until the final settlement of accounts with all the States, when there is reason to believe complete justice will be done to all, so far as it can be affected, in the adjustment of such complicated and difficult claims, which from the very nature of them require great mutual indulgence. And I beg leave to add, that one good has resulted from the assumption, which I believe will be felt more particularly in the dissatisfied States, that a degree of liberality is directed to be observed in the settlement of the public accounts, far superior to what was practised some years ago—since the commissioners are to allow all claims for general or particular defence, *whether sanctioned by the resolves of Congress or regular vouchers, or otherwise,* upon an enlarged system of general equity, in order to make the reimbursement as full and as exact as possible.

6. *Their making a part of the debt irredeemable, but in certain specified proportions, in a given time.* If the government could, consistently with the convenience of the United States, and with good policy, have provided for the full payment of 6 per cent. interest to all the public creditors, there probably would have been no occasion for this proposition, and in that case I think it ought not to have been made, for I heartily agree with all who are of opinion that we ought to get clear of the principal of our debt as soon as we can. But it was considered, that a provision to the full amount of the interest of the whole debt could not be made, without proceeding to a degree of taxation beyond either the actual convenience of the people, or that boundary which it would be for the present imprudent to exceed, lest unexpected contingencies should arise which it would be difficult to provide for. Equivalents were therefore to be offered to the public creditors sufficient to induce them to dispense with a literal compliance with their contract (which extended to a reimbursement of principal as well as interest), and among other equivalents that occurred was that of making the debt irredeemable but in certain specified proportions in a given time, as may be particularly seen in the act of Congress on the subject ; by which provision a creditor was not liable to be injured by an abrupt and unexpected payment of the whole of his principal in case of a reduction of interest, which it was deemed probable would take place in a few years : On the other hand, the public gain this advantage at least, that no creditor could, after he had subscribed upon the terms offered, ask for his principal, but only for his interest (because it is expressly said in the act, "That it shall not be understood that the United States shall be bound or obliged to redeem in the proportion" mentioned, "but it shall be understood only that they have a right so to do"), wherefore it would be no longer in the power of the subscribing public creditors to harass the United States by a demand of their principal, whether it was possible or convenient for the United States to pay it or not. It is also to be observed, that Congress have directed that the surplus revenue may be applied to a purchase of the debt of the United States, at its market price, if not exceeding *par* or its true value ; which method of redemption will probably answer for some years to come every good purpose that could be

fected by an unlimited right of redemption in form, without the consent of the creditor, and in every instance of a purchase under *par* it is clear that an advantage is gained by it. For further satisfaction and illustration on this important subject, I take the liberty to refer you to the report of the Secretary of the Treasury, dated the 9th of January, 1790; a report that does him the highest honor, and which will be admired for genius, accuracy, and able information on a most intricate and difficult subject, as long as the language in which it is written shall remain in being.

7. *The proposition of an Excise now under consideration.* It is difficult to speak of a bill which is yet on its passage, which has already undergone some amendments, and may perhaps receive others before it finally passes into a law. I have not indeed had an opportunity of seeing it, so that I can only speak in regard to any particular in the bill from mere report. It is undoubtedly to be lamented, that a necessity should at any time exist for passing a law, which is disagreeable to a great body of the people, nor do I believe that Congress would pass a bill creating any excise, if they could possibly avoid it. But the public credit must at all events be supported, or we must relapse into that state of weakness and disgrace from which the people have had the good sense and fortitude to emancipate themselves. The Secretary of the Treasury has reported a deficiency to be provided for, and recommended additional duties on imported spirits, and also an inland duty on spirits distilled in the country, which commonly goes by the name of an excise. The duties upon imported articles, with the increase thus proposed, will go to as great an extent as is deemed advisable, for the present at least, and in addition to other reasons which recommend the inland duty is this strong one, that unless such a duty be imposed, the advantage will be so much in favor of the home distilleries, that sufficient reliance cannot be placed upon the duty laid on the same article imported; and although at some future period a decided preference may be wisely given in favor of every branch of American manufacture, yet when we rely upon imported articles for the chief part of our revenue, it would be madness to discourage the importation so as to destroy it. We must be content, as other nations are obliged to be, without enjoying contradictory advantages. If this inland duty be not laid, not only the additional duty on imported spirits may be defeated, but, recourse must be had to direct taxation, if such can be now constitutionally imposed, which many very sensible men doubt, because a *census* has not yet been completed, so as to ascertain the proper relative proportion of each State; but at any rate, surely, a *direct tax* (which must be paid whether convenient or not, even if it ruins an individual) would be much more obnoxious, and in many instances much more oppressive, than a moderate duty on distilled spirits, which no one will pretend to be a necessary of life, and any reasonable consumption of which cannot be materially lessened by the present bill. Does not every man who drinks *imported* spirits pay in proportion much more? It is not therefore, I apprehend, because this duty will in fact create any sensible inconvenience, if it is fairly and unoppressively collected, that it is so warmly opposed, but because strong prejudices prevail against it, and in some of the States it will be altogether a novelty, as they have never been used to excises of any kind. And this to be sure is a very serious consideration, and therefore for one I should have been heartily glad, if an excise could have been dispensed with, but I am sensible it cannot, and accordingly in this instance, as I hope I shall in every other, I acquiesce in the consequences of a necessity I cannot control. The principal reasons however why excises have been so particularly obnoxious to those States, I presume were, because in *England* (from which we used to take our examples) an *excise* extends to a vast variety of objects, including many of the absolute necessaries of life; a trial by jury is not allowed in disputed cases; and the powers of the officers, all absolutely dependent on the crown, are enormously great. The present *excise* scheme, as I understand it, is liable to none of these objections. It extends only to *distilled spirits*: a trial by jury is provided for; the powers of the officers, I believe, are not only guarded with jealous caution, and much more restricted than those of excise officers in *England*, but this great additional check (which is certainly a very formidable one) is provided against an abuse, that if an officer shall be convicted of oppression or extortion in the execution of his office, he shall, besides being liable to fine and imprisonment, *forfeit his office*: thus making the very existence of his office to depend upon his good behavior in the opinion of a jury of his country, as well as on an unlimited power of removal by the President. There are not only these striking differences in the two cases of an *excise* in *England*, and of the excise thus proposed in *America*, in the provisions of the respective legislatures, but surely there is an immense difference in the situation of the respective countries. Would any *excise* officer dare, in *America*, to be guilty of wanton oppression? I will venture to say, under such a Constitution as we have now the happiness to live under, no man will ever do so with impunity. *Excises*, though not practised in some States, have long been familiar to others, particularly the States of New England, where the pulse of liberty has beat as high as in any country in the world. These States now advocate this tax, though to be sure they will pay a very large proportion of it. They have long experienced that an *excise* and *freedom* can exist together, when the former is under proper regulations, and the latter in the possession of a sensible, a vigilant, and well disposed people. I trust in God, how long soever the former may last, the latter will exist in *America* to the latest period of time.

I have now gone through the task I proposed to myself. I was urged to it by seeing with regret strong prejudices indulged, for which it appeared to me there was no foundation. I have always considered a union of the American States absolutely necessary to their prosperity and their safety. I well knew how such a union was liable to be endangered by mutual jealousies and ill-founded suspicions, and therefore I rejoiced when a government was formed, calculated upon the noblest and most enlarged principles of freedom and justice, to keep together the several parts which composed it from clashing with the common interest of all. So far from believing that the present Congress have in any number disregarded the great duty it was incumbent upon them to perform, I believe they have wisely and conscientiously executed it, though they have had such difficulties to encounter, and such prejudices to overcome, that they have been for a time subjected to much misrepresentation and calumny. This is unfortunately the lot of almost all who are in public stations, but it is seldom that the public confidence is long withdrawn when it is deserved, and therefore it is to be hoped that the present unpopularity attending some of their measures in some parts of the Union, will disappear in proportion as they are better understood. Every man should constantly bear in mind that the interest of every State, and of every individual in every State, is inseparably interwoven with that of the whole Union, of which they constitute parts: that that Union cannot be preserved without reposing a proper degree of confidence in those to whom the care of the general government is intrusted: and that it is as great a crime to our common country which we are all bound to serve, to withhold confidence when it is merited, as it is to bestow it with an implicit and slavish submission.

A CITIZEN OF PENNSYLVANIA.

January 27th, 1791.

Contrary to general expectation, at the 2d term of the Supreme Court, Judges Jay, Cushing, Wilson, Blair, and Iredell being present; it was determined that thereafter the Judges should be divided into pairs, and each pair confined to one Circuit permanently. Judge Iredell was taken by surprise, and Judge Blair voted under a misconception, or was designedly misled. Judge Rutledge was in the city of New York, but indisposed. Had all the Judges been present, and the question been fairly put, the Court would have been equally divided. The Southern was of the three Circuits much the most arduous. As the Court was first constituted, before the resignation of Mr. Harrison, but one of the Judges resided in what, subsequently, formed the Southern Circuit. When Judge Rutledge resigned, in August '91, Mr. Johnson, a resident not of the Southern but the middle Circuit, was appointed. The law directed that each Circuit Court should be holden by two Judges of the Supreme Court in conjunction with the District Judge. In consequence of the rule established by the Supreme Court, the difficulty of travel, the peril of life in the sickly season, and the business of the Southern Circuit fell chiefly to the share of Judge Iredell. His brethren admitted the hardship of his case, but still adhered to their resolution.* To say the least, their conduct was extremely selfish, and illiberal. Mr. Jay was inclined to constrain Congress to relieve the Judges of the Supreme Court from the duty of the Circuit, by the appointment of Circuit Judges. Judge Iredell was not a man tamely to submit to wrong: finding his colleagues impracticable he appealed to his friends in Congress. As Congress for some time failed to act, he proposed to the Judges that each should surrender $500 of his salary as an inducement to the appointment of Circuit Judges. All promptly assented but Judges Jay and Cushing, who seemed reluctant. The disputed point was finally adjusted by the interposition of Congress.† The whole matter is fully argued in the letter of Judge Iredell to the Judges of the Supreme Court. In confirmation of the position assumed by Judge Iredell, Judge Blair wrote him—"I confess, that I did not understand that the question of rotation was *decided* at New York: some arguments were urged against the rotatory duty which, it must be admitted, had considerable force; but the great inequality of the Circuits, respecting both the labor and expense of service, was a striking argument against fixing any pair of Judges to the Southern Circuit, and had so great weight with me, that if I had supposed what we were doing at New York was to have that effect, I probably should have voted against it. I perfectly recollect that in giving my opinion on that occasion, I expressed my sense of the hardship of such a determination, conceiving at the time the question to be

---

* "The Circuits press hard upon us all; and your share of the task has hitherto been more than in due proportion."—Jay to Iredell. March 16th.

† Act of April 13th, 1792.

whether we should then make an appointment once for all; but was corrected by the information of the other Judges, (some of them at least,) that they did not mean to go so far."*

COPY OF A LETTER FROM JAMES IREDELL.

To the Honorable John Jay, Esq., Chief Justice, and William Cushing and James Wilson, Esquires, Associate Justices of the Supreme Court of the United States.

GENTLEMEN:—When I had the honor of meeting you and Mr. Blair at New York, in order to deliberate on the ensuing Circuits, I was entirely unapprised that any general question was to be put, whether there should be a rotation at all, until the moment when it was proposed, and I confess it was so unexpected by me, and I saw it lead to such distressing consequences to myself, that I had it not in my power to state such reasons on the subject as occurred to me afterwards. I hope therefore to be now permitted to state them.

The first allotment of Circuits was made, not only when I was not present, but before I knew of the great honor which had been done me in my being appointed one of the Judges. The reason assigned in a letter of the Chief Justice to Mr. Rutledge, an extract of which he was pleased to enclose to me, was a temporary one, viz., that the Judges could with most propriety determine on the applications for the admission of lawyers in the Districts wherein they respectively lived.

If afterwards a permanent establishment was in contemplation, in my opinion all the Judges ought to have had notice, that they might all have had an opportunity of voting when so important a question was to be put. At the time of the above decision, Mr. Rutledge was in New York, and though confined with the gout was in general as capable of conversing about business as he ever was in his life. He had no notice that such a question was to be put at all till after it was decided. To my knowledge he only considered we were to meet on a temporary appointment, as he desired me to request that he might for that time be placed on the Southern Circuit. I have reason to believe, had he been present, the Judges would have been equally divided.

If, however, notwithstanding this circumstance, it was right to take that general question at that time, I submit to you, Gentlemen, that some more equitable rule in the allotment of Circuits so unequal in point of duty ought to take place, than that they should be for ever fixed in the same manner in which they were for a temporary reason at first. A fixed duty is not annexed to any of the Judges by the law. It was not, I am persuaded contemplated by the President, for originally one Judge only (Mr. Rutledge) was appointed, who lived in the Southern Circuit. The gentleman whom I had the honor to succeed lived in the middle Circuit, where I now do. Had I continued to live to the Southward, and constantly attended that Circuit, I must have travelled the same distance in a year, as my duty requires me to be twice in a year at the Seat of Government.

These reasons, I apprehend, are entitled to some consideration, as to the propriety of fixing the Circuits in the manner and at the time it was done. I now with great deference submit to you an answer to the only argument that I recollect was offered against a rotation. That was, that two Judges might hear a case, and take time to consider of it, and if they did not go again to decide it, it might occasion an inconvenient delay. This is indeed an argument of some weight against the system as it now stands, but I cannot think it is of sufficient weight, for the purpose to which it was applied, opposed to considerations on the other side. I will venture to say no Judge can conscientiously undertake to ride the Southern Circuit constantly, and perform the other parts of his duty. Besides the danger his health must be exposed to, it is not conceivable that accidents will not often happen to occasion a disappointment of attendance at the Courts. I rode upon the last Circuit 1900 miles: the distance from here and back again is 1800. Can any man have a probable chance of going that distance twice a year, and attending at particular places punctually on particular days? Surely delays from this cause are much more to be apprehended than from the other. This, that I know of, (if the Circuit is constantly fixed), admits of no remedy, from the nature of the thing. The other does. If two Judges hear a case argued, they of course take down the case, the substance of the arguments and authorities on both sides, and such being given to the two succeeding Judges, they will be, I believe, at least 19 times out of 20, as well instructed and prepared to hear another argument if necessary, and finally decide on that case, as the Judges who first heard it. In regard to an appeal, if that should be objected, the two first Judges having heard but not decided, *their opinions are not committed.* They cannot surely be disqualified as Judges of Appeal merely from having a knowledge of the case as it was impartially heard on both sides. This I admit is not in general so desirable a way as that of the same Judges hearing

---

* Letter from Williamsburg, July 25th.

---

a case throughout. But I should consider, that besides that cases of this kind will not probably happen very often, this single inconvenience cannot be alone sufficient for imposing upon two Judges, equally possessed of every power and privilege with the rest, so much greater a proportion of duty (if it can be executed at all) than the others will have to perform, besides a considerable additional expense which must unavoidably take place.

There are however to be sure strong reasons in itself in favor of a Rotation, since some countries not only permit, but absolutely require it. I am told that is the case in Virginia, where within two or three years they have had Circuit Courts erected. It has been lately so regulated in North Carolina. And I believe the decision at New York is the first instance of a contrary rule being established in the case of Circuits with no particular allotment of duty. The instances in Virginia and North Carolina apply to the very case, if I am not mistaken in supposing that in Virginia, as in North Carolina, the Circuit Courts have complete authority extending to judgment and execution, and are not merely established for the purpose of trying issues, which I admit is the case of the Courts of *Nisi Prius* in England, and therefore the example in that country, where a rotation also takes place, is not so immediately in point as the examples I have above stated. In that country, however, so far from confining a Judge constantly to the Circuit wherein he happens to reside, it is expressly directed "that no man shall be a Judge of Assize in the country wherein he was born, or wherein he is resident." And this *Blackstone* calls a *prudent jealousy.* I presume, therefore, there is some reason for doubting the propriety of a fixed establishment on contrary principles to any of these.

In addition to all these reasons of a general nature, I now beg leave to state to you one, why I apprehend it would be peculiarly improper that I should for some time go the Southern Circuit. A Writ of *Certiorari* issued from the Circuit Court of North Carolina, by the direction of Mr. Wilson, Mr. Blair, and Mr. Rutledge, directed to the Judges of the Court of Equity in North Carolina, for bringing up a cause in which (as an Executor) I am one of the Defendants. The State Judges have refused obedience to the Writ, expressly denying its authority in that instance. This is a case which will require the fullest consideration that can be bestowed upon it, and I presume if ever a full Court is to be wished for in any instance it must be on an occasion like this. There ought, however, to be *some* decision upon it, and I leave you to imagine the consequences, if by any accident occasioning the failure of attendance of either of two Judges, (if they only should be relied upon,) so that no decision at all could take place, the delay should put it in the power of the State Court to give a Decree, and proceed in consequence of it in such a manner as to defeat the object of the *Certiorari* altogether.

I hope you will excuse, gentlemen, the liberty I take in this representation. My situation is a very hard one. I had no reason to suppose any thing but a rotation would take place, and accordingly when I had the honor to be appointed one of the Judges of the Supreme Court, I resolved to remove my family to the seat of Government, in order that I might be enabled to perform the duty of my office more faithfully than I thought I could possibly do in so remote a situation. I submitted to your decision at New York, hoping it would be the last sacrifice necessary, under circumstances of private inconvenience and distress almost too much for me to bear. It is not possible for me to undertake to perform the same tour of duty constantly. I am persuaded it is impracticable for any man. It is absolutely incumbent upon me therefore to state the case as it really is, lest the public interest should suffer by my presumption in undertaking what I could not execute. This representation I thought it proper for me to make in the first instance to you, gentlemen, hoping that I might by that means obtain the relief which I am entitled to, and wishing in every part of my conduct to demonstrate the sincere respect my heart constantly feels for you. But I must take the liberty to add, that if contrary to my wishes and expectation you should still continue to be of opinion that as the law stands at present it must receive the construction you gave it at New York, and therefore that decision is to remain unaltered, I shall be under the painful necessity of trying in some manner whether an alteration of the law in that particular cannot be obtained, so as to leave me at least a practicable share of duty, and the public unexposed to the danger of suffering by their business being unavoidably undone.

I have the honor to be, with very great respect,
Gentlemen,
Your most obedient and most humble servt.,
JAS. IREDELL.

Philadelphia, February 11th, 1791.

N. B.—The above is nearly, but I believe not exactly, a literal copy.

Judge Iredell attended the February and August terms of the Supreme Court. By the kindness of Judge Blair, who rode the Southern, he held with Judge Wilson the Courts of the Middle Circuit in the Spring. In the Fall, I presume, he rode the Southern Circuit.

IREDELL TO JOHN HAY.

PHILADELPHIA, April 14th, 1791.

MY DEAR SIR:—I was preparing to write to you long ago, as well as to my excellent friend Mr. Maclaine, when a report of his death reached us, but in such a manner that I was in hopes it was not true. I then resolved to wait for a confirmation or contradiction of this melancholy information;—it was at length unhappily confirmed. You may easily conceive my heart was deeply affected by it, and that it would be some time before I could bring myself to write in a channel of correspondence which would revive so many painful ideas to me. I had, however, summoned resolution to do so, when I received another most unfortunate and unexpected shock—the death of my near friend and very near connection, Mr. John Johnston, for which we were entirely unprepared, and which has thrown a gloom over my family that will long remain there. My God! how many awful trials of this kind are we doomed to sustain only in the course of a very short life! and what would be human existence but for the hope of a better and happier futurity! I found your letter of the 1st August, on my arrival here. I have since had the pleasure to receive those of the 1st November and 16th December, and am extremely obliged to you for them all. The acts of the 2d Session of Congress have not yet been printed in 8vo; but I have reason to hope they will be, as also those of the succeeding Sessions, and in that case I shall not fail to transmit to you copies as they come out. I well know the value of such an edition. I have not heard of any causes in this part of the country being removed from a State into a Federal Court, and therefore know not any practice concerning it. The Circuit Courts establish their own mode of admitting lawyers. The general rule has been, an authority to practise two years in the highest State Court, and a fair personal and professional character, and in the Circuit Courts of South Carolina and Georgia, any two Judges of the Court were authorized to admit in the vacation, upon the oath of office and that to support the Constitution being taken. I presume the same rule will be adopted in North Carolina. It gave me great concern that so much ill-humor prevailed in the Assembly against our Senators. It certainly was very ill-grounded. Had they had any private *jobs* to carry they would not have failed to write. They attended to their duty most punctually, Mr. Johnston sometimes at the hazard of his life. He was two or three times in most imminent danger. It was the business of the Secretary of State to transmit all the public acts. An accident alone prevented. The Journals of the Senate as well as of the House of Representatives are regularly printed, and these as I am informed, it is the duty of the Clerks to transmit to the several Executives. Formerly it was necessary to correspond frequently with the Executive and Legislature of each State, because their co-operation was constantly wanting to carry into effect almost any public measure. Congress have now authority to execute their own acts. I presume this distinction of the cases has not been sufficiently attended to. If they have no *official* communications to make, with what propriety can they write *officially?* A letter to an Assembly detailing Newspapers or Debates, or speaking of unfinished business, would in my opinion appear highly ridiculous. A correspondence therefore could answer no purpose but to transmit the public acts, &c.,—*but that is the proper business of others.* Why therefore should the Senators be required to do what is within the particular department of other men? They have, I assure you, sufficient to do if they execute their own. As to their not attending at the Assembly, which seems to have been expected—The Assembly met at Fayetteville the first Monday in November: Congress were to meet at Philadelphia the first Monday in December. The interval of time was too short to make it prudent for a Member of Congress to attend at that time at Fayetteville without real necessity, because he must endanger being at Philadelphia at the time when his duty required him to be there. Our Senators, as it was, barely arrived in time—Williamson and Bloodworth did but just do so—Ashe, Steele, and Sevier long after—and all had travelling inconceivably bad. Mr. Johnston had to carry his wife and a young child with him, who for three months almost had appeared to be at the point of death. Besides, I suppose it is not yet *treason* against the State for a Member of Congress to attend a little to his private concerns. In regard to the public matter of the resolutions, the Assembly saw their way much clearer before them than many very sensible and impartial men do. I did indeed conceive myself that not the slightest color of a reason could be assigned for not opening the doors of the Senate. But I have lately heard reasons assigned for it which deserve, I think, a very candid consideration. If the doors were open, one consequence would undoubtedly ensue. Many of the members (I beg pardon, perhaps I ought to say some) instead of confining themselves strictly to the discussion of business, would frequently make oratorical speeches to display their eloquence to the gallery, which is every day done in the other House. The desire of applause is so natural to the human mind, that few men have fortitude enough, merely from abstract notions of public utility, to resist opportunities to acquire it, when they think it within their reach. This would occasion of course some addition to the expense already so *enormous.* The audience would undoubtedly on some occasions influence the opinions of members. That audience will almost always be composed of *Philadelphians.* Has not Pennsylvania sufficient influence in the scale already? Would the Southern States be benefited by such an increase of it? The object to be obtained by the opening of the doors, I suppose, is by the watchfulness of the people to prevent improper measures taking place. But what may appear improper to Pennsylvania may be in fact highly pleasing to North Carolina. The influence on such an occasion, if any, would surely be disagreeable to the latter State. If it is supposed that the admission of an audience would check any improper designs on the liberties of the people, should the Senators contrary to common sense and their own interest attempt such, how futile the precaution. North Carolina indeed imposes no restriction. But this Session the House of Representatives, whose doors are in general open, have found it necessary to shut them on particular occasions which in their judgment required secrecy. Could not the Senate, if their doors were in general open, and they had formed a tremendous scheme to betray their country, concert the scheme in private, pretend that certain measures absolutely required secrecy, and *shut their doors while it was concocting?* To remedy this danger must the doors be open without any restriction? Abuse the Representatives then for setting the example, provided North Carolina seriously supposes that a Legislature in this respect is to exercise no discretion at all. Let her consider the case of her own secrecy about the Warrenton business, and perhaps she will at length be convinced that no Government on earth can subsist on principles destructive of all confidence, and which admit nothing but a peevish and perpetual jealousy.

As to the economy recommended, I am authorized to say, the Senate, by various amendments, have saved *many thousands* to the United States. The *monstrous salaries*, which I suppose are alluded to, were all provided before our Senators took their seats. I believe our Senators, however, would not approve of starving men out who are rendering great services to their country in confidence of receiving salaries which were fixed before their appointment. I assure you none of the Departments are idle, or are *sine-cures.* The Secretary of the Treasury, the Secretary of State, and the Secretary of War, have most laborious duties to perform. The two former have already had infinite trouble, and Congress every day experience the benefit of their uncommon abilities. Unfortunately the state of the Western country is likely to give his share of trouble to the latter, who is also excellently qualified for his office. Does any reasonable man suppose that men in such offices will serve the public for their daily bread, so as to expose their families to the danger of wanting the common necessaries of life after their decease, which might be the unfortunate case of many a man qualified for such departments, if he was enabled to lay up nothing out of his income. The Senators are directed, without any restriction, to oppose any excise or direct tax. The Assembly do not say, as they might truly have done (and in which their Senators would most heartily have concurred), that either tax would be particularly obnoxious to North Carolina, and therefore they ought not to consent to it, but in a case of *absolute necessity.* But they are to oppose it at all events, whether necessary or not. For what purpose then was that power given in the constitution? Does North Carolina trifle in such a manner with the other States, as to say a power they have solemnly consented to shall never be exercised? What! is the safety of our country to be endangered—the honor of it to be sullied—its public faith broken—and the Government of the United States to become a mere mockery, merely to gratify the wishes of North Carolina, in opposition to strong and irresistible necessity? All prudent men agree the impost will be carried far enough by the present bill. A necessity remains to be provided for, not only to maintain the public credit as to its revenue, *but to defend the Western country, now in a state of serious hostility.* An excise or direct tax is the only alternative. But the Senators of North Carolina must not agree to either. What then becomes of their oath, of their duty to the Union whose interests they are appointed to guard, of their honor as public men to support the public faith inviolate, of their pride as individuals to save their country from disgrace, of their attachment to North Carolina, to shield her from a share she cannot avoid in the common calamity and wretchedness of the whole?

A minority in the House of Representatives (I believe it was a small one) were not convinced that the necessity did really exist for either provision at the present session, and some of them thought if it did, other means might be pursued. Those who entertained this opinion, therefore, properly voted against the Excise Bill. But a great majority were fully convinced of the necessity—thought the system of imposts could not be safely extended—that an excise on spirituous liquors was far preferable to any direct tax, even had the right to impose such, before the completion of the census, not been, as it really is, doubtful—and therefore the bill passed, containing an additional duty on imported spirits, and a small one on spirits distilled in the country. Our Senators agreed in opinion with the majority in the other House, as to the absolute necessity of the case, and therefore, from motives of duty, they voted for the bill. But I must tell you that this Senate, *who are to swallow up all the liberties, &c.*, took uncommon pains to amend the bill, amended it in a great many particulars, and *every amendment*, as I am told, *is in favor of the convenience of the people.* As to your instructions about the Post, when you can agree among yourselves as to the route, it will be time enough to throw an implied censure on your members. At the session in New York, however, our Senators proposed continuing the route on the sea-coast, and to give a post from Petersburgh, *the very route the Assembly have now recommended*, having the presumption to suppose that a cross-post from Wilmington would do for Fayetteville ; they perhaps, however, were wrong in overlooking the convenience of the intermediate, fine, and well-inhabited country through which the post would have had to pass on the way therefrom to Halifax. They also proposed, and so sent the bill to the other House, two places for the Circuit Court. But here again they committed a great offence. It was Newbern and Hillsborough, not Newbern and Fayette, nor Newbern and Salisbury, and because it was finally decreed to stand at *Newbern* only. * * * The President will certainly visit the Southern States soon after the expiration of the session, but he has not yet absolutely concluded on his route, &c. &c.

JAS. IREDELL.

T. IREDELL TO IREDELL.

March 4th, 1791.

DEAR BROTHER : * * * So poor Bloodworth's political career is at present terminated ; Grove had a majority of 800. You have seen I suppose the change in our court system, since which Mr. Moore has resigned his place as Attorney-General—a prelude, I suppose, to his leaving the bar.

We have been a good deal alarmed with a report in circulation here respecting the forgeries committed in South Carolina, by a Major Washington and some others. The reports varied so that we knew not whether it was Col. Washington, the General's nephew, or a noted villain of that name in South Carolina ; it now seems pretty evident, however, it must be the latter, &c.

T. IREDELL.

GOV. JOHNSTON TO IREDELL.

HAYES, 15th April, '91.

DEAR SIR :—I arrived at this place on the 12th, and found the court sitting, Ashe and Williams Judges. Davie is here, but Moore was obliged to attend at Hillsborough. A young gentleman of the name of Sampson takes charge of his business, and acts as Attorney-General "pro-tem.," by order of the Court. The Governor has not thought proper to make any appointment. I find that Davie and Moore are not pleased with the present court system ; and that they both propose to serve in the next Assembly, in order to put it on a better footing. The Judges look as if they would never die. * * * The revenue act has been very much misrepresented to the westward, which has occasioned great ferments and murmurings. When it is properly explained, I hope they will be satisfied, &c. &c.

S. JOHNSTON.

REV. A. IREDELL TO IREDELL.

GUILFORD, May 3d, '91.

DEAR BROTHER:— * * * * I had entertained a serious alarm for the property, to which you will perceive I look forward, for I imagined that Wilberforce's motion for an *immediate* abolition of the slave-trade would have passed the House of Commons, the two great leaders having exerted themselves to the utmost, but it was lost by a majority of nearly two to one. The Islands may therefore escape the ruin that threatened them. You must have heard of the insurrection in Dominica. A similar one may, for aught we know, *have* taken place in Jamaica ; it is probable it would have broken out, if a seeming victory over the planters had reached the ears of their slaves. The people here discriminated between slavery and the slave-trade. Would the blacks have done so ? Would not that which told them that one was iniquitous, have established the iniquity of the other ? As it is, much light has been thrown on all sides of the subject ; regulations will in consequence take place ; the *rational purpose* of humanity will be answered ; and injury will, in no material degree, be done to any description of men. But do you not, a a philosopher, mark the folly of those philanthropists who look only to one point ? They would unsettle an immense property ; they would provoke the passions of many thousand people, by an innovation upon old laws the most daring that ever was attempted. It might be proved (not in this letter) that slavery has existed at all times, and in all countries ; and that, in many cases, an hereditary slave is better off than the peasant who has a choice

* Michael Sampson, of Sampson county : first cousin to the celebrated Counsellor Sampson, of New York: noted for his practical jokes, and as the most incorrigible quiz in the State: he was much esteemed by Mr. Gaston, Mr. Jocelynn, and his professional brethren.

of masters, but who may be abandoned by all his species. Who is the worst of slaves ? Is not the soldier ? How is he entrapped into his slavery ? What are press warrants ? The simple man, who knows so little of the *detail* of human life as to suppose that *any* class of men, however lofty or protected their station, can be happy, may indeed bestride the hobby-horse of humanity, and set forward in search of adventures ; but will he not be like the hero of Cervantes, and see frowning castles in very good-humored and useful wind-mills ? I see much of common people in this country, and I declare that comparing what I know of them, with what I hear of negroes in the Islands, I am satisfied the latter, upon the whole *do*, and assuredly *might*, lead much happier lives. However, I will give no more of my paper to the slave-trade.

Your famous Mr. Paine runs as madly into the extremes of liberty as our Wilberforce. Paine's liberty is licentiousness. By the by, I can tell you an anecdote of that gentleman. He was an Exciseman at Lewes, where he married, and though a man of gallantry, gave his wife reasons, after a considerable time, to prefer a complaint which, in consequence of a *professional* scrutiny, was proved to have been ill-founded. His defence was that, being already married to another woman, by whom he had children, *he had some scruples of conscience.* A Lewes gentleman called on me, a few days ago, and told me this story, &c. &c.

A. IREDELL.

Washington, having previously made a tour through the Northern States, in the Fall of 1790, in the Spring of this year visited the South. Of his reception at Halifax, North Carolina, Gov. Johnston wrote Judge Iredell (May 23d)—"It was not such as we could have wished, though in every other part of the country he was treated with proper attention." Upon this excursion the President tarried long enough upon the Potomac to select the site of the National Capital, since known by his name.

A. NEILSON TO IREDELL.

DUNDEE (Scotland), June 25th, '91.

DEAR SIR :— * * * I must request a favor for a particular friend of mine, Dr. Moyes, the Blind Philosopher, who travelled in America some years ago. The case, as well as I can narrate it, is as follows : When in the Jerseys the doctor was induced by friendship to lend Col. Geo. Morgan £1000 currency, secured by a mortgage on his estate adjacent to Princeton ; the money to be repaid in London, principal and interest ; the bond was recorded in the State Registry. Morgan afterwards sold the property to Harman & Co., of Philadelphia. He has since removed to a Spanish settlement on the Mississippi, but after the first year has never paid any interest. It is true Harman & Co. advised him of their purchase, and that they meant to sell a last November, when they would remit the amount of his preferable debt. He has, however, never heard again from them. * * * If you knew the doctor you would be strongly inclined to serve him. Though blind since he was 18 months old, he knows more of both abstract science and practical arts than most seeing men, and his manners and eloquence are quite captivating. I would be a shame to America should such a man have to complain, in travelling through the world, that he could not command so large a part of his little modicum of fortune, from want of friends in America.

I hope I am not the first to inform Mr. Johnston of the death of Mr. Scrimseour, of Tealing, about five or six months ago, in his eighty-sixth year, regretted by all who ever knew him. He died most easily, and had a true euthanasia. He was playing a hand at ombre, when he suddenly laid himself back in his chair, and with a sigh expired.* His son now lives on the estate ; he tells me he means to write Mr. J. soon, &c. &c.

A. NEILSON.

SITGREAVES TO IREDELL.

In '76, John Sitgreaves was appointed a Lieutenant, and afterwards served as Aid to General Caswell, at Camden. He represented New Berne in the Assembly from 1786-89. He was a member of the Continental Congress in '84, and again in '87, '8 and '9. He succeeded John Stokes as District Judge of North Carolina. He was a clever gentleman, and esteemed a good lawyer. His wife was the sister of Mrs. Davie.†

NEW BERN, 2d Aug., '91.

DEAR SIR :—I am extremely glad to hear from you, that Mr. Spaight will probably regain his health. I think much may be expected from the Bristol waters.

Mr. James Davis, the brother of Tom, to whom I showed your letter, is very thankful for your friendly intimation of his brother's conduct and situation, and says he will endeavor to procure his discharge, but despairs of his reform.

* Mr. S. was a near relative of the Johnstons. † Wheeler.

With respect to the certiorari, Mr. Hamilton informed Judge Blair and myself that Mr. Morris has desired him not to urge it further, that as he was a member of the Legislature of the United States, from motives of delicacy he would rather the cause should be proceeded on in the State courts; if this should be done I suppose the question, so far as it relates to the authority of the courts, will be suffered to sleep.

I had heard that Mr. S. Cooke, as attorney for some British merchants, had been served with an injunction from the State Judges to restrain him from commencing suit in the Circuit Court. Although the thing appeared too absurd to be believed, yet as I knew he had the care of a suit of consequence which had been some short time since commenced in the Superior Court of the State, and which he had lately dismissed in order to sue in the Circuit Court, I thought there might be something in it, and mentioned the report to Judge Blair. Col. Davie has since told me that the apparent object of the bill was to restrain him from proceeding further at common law (supposing the suit to be still existing in the State court), and to answer touching some fraud or hardship attending the contract which had created the debt; but that doubtless it was intended to operate indirectly as a restraint from suing in the Circuit Court. I have troubled you with the circumstance in order that you may correct the mistake to Judge Blair, if you should hear him mention it while at Philadelphia, which I will thank you to do.

A suit has been commenced in the District Court by a citizen of another State against a citizen of this State, for a sum under $500, and the defendant has pleaded to the jurisdiction of the Court. The judicial law is to me in many instances very ambiguous, and, although a cognizance of cases of this description is not expressly given to the District Court, it appears from many parts of the law to be strongly implied. The constitution has made no distinction of cases by their importance, and the law having excluded these from the Supreme and Circuit Courts, and not expressly admitted them in the District Court, it would seem they were left with the State courts, where the plaintiff may suffer one of the great evils the constitution meant to protect him against, a depreciated paper money. I should be very glad to hear whether this question has been decided by any other of the federal courts. Will you be pleased to inform me if you have heard of any such decision.

I have just heard that the Governor and Council, at a late meeting at Hillsborough, have directed the Comptroller to find all the certificates belonging to the State. This information comes from the Treasurer, and of course may be depended on, &c. &c.   JNO. SITGREAVES.

COL. DAVIE TO IREDELL.

HALIFAX, Aug. 2d, '91.

MY DEAR SIR:— * * * * I am sorry the letter you mention in yours of March was mislaid. You knew I should expect your remarks on this performance of a man we both admire. Although Mr. Burke may have carried his veneration for old establishments too far, and may not have made sufficient allowance for the imperfections of human nature in the conduct of the French Revolution, yet I think his letter contains a sufficient degree of excellence to have rescued him from the undistinguishing abuse of Paine, or even the more decent insinuations of Dr. Priestly. Mankind naturally feel an interest in a character, whose enlightened mind and superior talents have reflected honor upon human nature; and I should be exceedingly afflicted to see that man decline, either in intellect or principle.

I am happy to assure you that the alterations the Excise Law received in the Senate have almost perfectly reconciled the people of this country to that measure; and I hope that a judicious appointment of officers will now ensure tranquillity in that quarter.

I sincerely hope something will be done at the next session of Congress with the Judiciary Act; *it is so defective in point of arrangement, and so obscurely drawn or expressed, that, in my opinion, it would disgrace the composition of the meanest legislature of the States.** The Attorney-General's report is a type of it—an elegant piece of unmeaning obscurity. I was indeed greatly disappointed when I read it, &c. &c.

WM. R. DAVIE.

The Duke "de Liancourt" travelled in America during the present year, and, from a letter to Judge Iredell asking information relative to the government, laws, productions, trade and agriculture of North Carolina, appears to have been a shrewd and intelligent observer. He had made Judge Iredell's acquaintance at Richmond, and the inference from his inquiries is, that he was collecting statistical information for a projected publication.†

GOV. JOHNSTON TO IREDELL.

PHILADELPHIA, 13th Nov., '91.

DEAR SIR:— * * * * The House have not given up the idea of a reform of the Judicial system; I do every thing in my

---

* The Judiciary Act was drawn by Ellsworth, of Ct.
† Rochefoucauld—Liancourt—vid. "Voyage dans les Etats Unis d'Amerique."

---

power to keep it up. The Southern members complain loudly of their being so much neglected by the Judges. I hope every thing will go right, &c. &c.

SAM. JOHNSTON.

A. HODGE (Printer and Editor) TO IREDELL.

EDENTON, Dec. 1st, '91.

DEAR SIR:— * * * * You may remember that I mentioned to you when you was last here, that a young gentleman of the name of Richards, of Washington, who was an officer in the late American Army, and who has resided in this State for these eight years past, was desirous of being appointed an Inspector for this State, should such an office be established. He has pressed me to write to you on the subject, saying "that he has understood from his friends at the North, that your interest with the President is such as would leave him little doubt of success, in case you spoke in his behalf." He would have wrote to you himself on the subject, but the want of a personal acquaintance prevented. He, however, desired that you might be referred for his character to the Secretary of War. Should it be such as is agreeable to you, and should you be under no other engagement, I really think the appointment would be well bestowed, as the unfortunate young man spent the prime of life in the service of his country, has since met with losses in trade, and is left without means of support. I beg you will pardon the liberty I now take; and should it appear presumptuous, I flatter myself you will ascribe it to the right motive—the desire to serve a friend, &c. &c.   A. HODGE.

CHAPTER XXV.
ÆT. 40—41.

IREDELL TO C. J. JAY, AND TO THE PRESIDENT. LETTERS FROM REV. A. IREDELL AND JUDGE PENDLETON. SOUTHERN CIRCUIT. SUPREME COURT. THE EASTERN CIRCUIT. "MARKS OF ARISTOCRACY IN CONNECTICUT."

IREDELL TO CH. JUSTICE JAY.

PHILADELPHIA, January 17th, 1792.

DEAR SIR:—I had not the honor to receive your letter of the 7th instant, inclosing the extraordinary paper from North Carolina, till yesterday afternoon. The writer's intellects are certainly deranged, though I hope not in consequence of the beating he complains of. I have heard of his name, and know several of the persons mentioned.

I presume, whatever else may be decided as to the Circuits, that upon consideration it will not be expected I shall go the Southern Circuit soon again, because setting aside the circumstances of private hardship, and danger to the public by relying on the performance of an impracticable duty, which I fully stated last year as reasons against a permanent allotment, particular circumstances make it, I apprehend, highly improper that it should be required of me for the present. One or two suits were returned to the last Circuit Court of North Carolina, to which I am a party as an Executor. Process had been served on my Co-Executor. I was applied to afterwards to know if I would dispense with a formal service of process as to myself, and I agreed to do so upon being furnished with proper copies to enable me to plead. The Certiorari suit that I mentioned before is also depending. It was not dismissed as Mr. Blair expected it would be, nor could I find that any declaration in court had been made to that effect, but what passed which induced Mr. Blair to expect it was in private conversation only. It now stands on this critical footing. You may remember, sir, it was a Certiorari at the instance of Plaintiffs in Equity in an injunction suit, in one of the

Courts of Equity of the State. That Court at the last Term, in October, divided about dismissing the Bill. One of the Judges, two only being present, was strenuous for it. To be sure the honor of the United States is deeply concerned in their courts deciding solemnly whether the writ issued erroneously, or ought to be enforced. It is of more importance that it should not go off by an act of defiance of the State Court, because the General Assembly of North Carolina in their session last Winter *thanked the State Judges for their conduct in disobeying the Writ.*

Whatever weight these circumstances may have, I must take the liberty to say that I can no longer undertake voluntarily so very unequal a proportion of duty, &c., &c.

JAS. IREDELL.

The Chief Justice, in reply, could see no remedy but by act of Congress revising the judicial department : and Judge Iredell was constrained, after attending the February Term of the Supreme Court, to ride again the Southern Circuit. Judge Johnson was allotted as his colleague, but was prevented by sickness from attending.

The Hon. Charles Johnson, Representative from North Carolina, in the following letter to Judge Iredell, expressed in strong terms the indignation of the Southern Members at the conduct of the Bench.

"I enclose the copy of the letter which you were so obliging as to leave with me ; and I cannot help expressing my astonishment that a representation so modest and respectful, yet so strong and firm, of your distressing situation, and intention of attempting a remedy, did not from mere feelings of generosity, without regard to more weighty considerations, induce the gentlemen to whom it was addressed, to lighten some part of that excessive duty with which you have been so unequally overburthened. You must pardon me for adding that their preferring their own ease and convenience to every generous feeling, principle of justice, or regard to public duty, very much lessens their character in my estimation. In short their conduct appears to me—little, unjust, ungenerous, and unpatriotic."

On the 19th of January, Judge Iredell's third, and last child, Helen Scrimseoure, was born.

IREDELL TO THE PRESIDENT.

PHILADELPHIA, January 23d, '92.

SIR :—In consequence of the letter you did the Judges of the Supreme Court the honor to write to them on the 3d April, 1790, I presume it is not only proper for a single Judge, but his express duty, when he deems it of importance to the public service, to state any particular circumstances that occur to him in the course of his personal experience which occasion unexpected difficulties or inconveniences in the execution of a system so new and in many respects unaided by any former examples. I therefore, sir, take the liberty to state some circumstances of great moment that occurred in the last Southern Circuit, which was attended by no other Judge of the Supreme Court but myself.

A decision extremely interesting to many suits in the Circuit Courts, took place in the Supreme Court in the term in August last. It was, that a writ of error to remove any proceeding out of a Circuit Court to the Supreme Court, must be taken out of the clerk's office of the latter. By the act of Congress that alone concerns that subject, a writ of error can only operate as a *Supersedeas*, and stay executions in cases where a copy of it is lodged for the adverse party in the clerk's office, where the record remains within *ten* days after the Judgment complained of is given. The above decision therefore made it appear, that after a Judgment was given against a defendant in the Circuit Court, if the Circuit Court was at such a distance from the clerk's office of the Supreme Court that it was impracticable to obtain a writ of error from that office, and send a copy as directed by the act within the time limited, which was so short that it could avail in very few instances, the defendant, if desirous to prosecute a writ of error, might, without any fault of his own, be subjected to an immediate execution, though he still might prosecute such a writ, and Judgment be eventually given in his favor. This consequence the Judges of the Supreme Court were aware of when they gave the above decision, and they were persuaded that if the mischief had been foreseen as resulting from the law in question, it would never have existed. But they conceived the principles upon which they were bound to determine, rendered such a decision unavoidable, and they were unanimous in the determination that was given. The mischief however was so palpable, that there was no doubt but that the Legislature, upon its being made known to them, would provide an early remedy. In the mean time it became a subject of very great concern to parties in causes then ready for trial in the Circuit Courts. The Courts upon the Southern Circuit, which I had the honor to attend, and where this evil might have existed in every case that was tried in which a writ of error could be brought, felt it accordingly, and the Court in each District stated the circumstances to the Bar, hoping that some measure would be adopted by consent, to prevent any defendant from suffering by such an unforeseen consequence of a law under which it was intended both parties might have complete relief. But though the Bar seemed generally to acquiesce in the propriety of a continuance of such causes when a writ of error might really be desired if Judgment went against a defendant, yet some gentlemen wished to make distinctions which others would not agree to, and the interposition of the Court, if such interposition was proper, became unavoidable. The Court, upon reflection, although they were fully sensible that in general it was their duty to administer the law as it was, regardless of its policy or consequences, thought that this was so extraordinary a case, the unequal condition of the parties was so glaring, the intention of the Legislature if it could have been expressed must have been so utterly contrary to any design of making an injurious discrimination between citizens of the same government in a point where no locality as to right could at all come in competition with the equal principles of impartial Justice,—that as they did not entertain the smallest doubt but that the Legislature would provide an early remedy for the evil, so it was their duty, by the exercise in this instance of a discretionary power as to the time of trying causes, which they conceived to be vested in them for the purposes of public justice, to prevent any immediate injury by ordering a continuance of all such causes in which the evil I have stated could arise, unless they were brought on by consent. And the Courts accordingly did so in each of the three Southern Districts, in the fullest confidence that a remedy would be provided during the present session ; after which undoubtedly no such reason for a continuance could have any effect.

Another circumstance of great importance, though perhaps not admitting of so easy a remedy, arose in the Circuit Court of Georgia. There were depending there some suits for the recovery of debts, to which pleas were put in by the defendants, not denying the existence of the debts, but showing (as they conceived) a right in the State of Georgia to recover them under certain acts of Assembly of that State passed previous to the Treaty of Peace. The Attorney, and Solicitor-General of the State were directed to interfere in the defence, but the counsel for the defendants refused to permit them. The Attorney and the Solicitor being dissatisfied with the Pleas, applied to the Court for leave to interplead on behalf of the State. The propriety of this application, if the law had admitted of its being granted, and it could have been done with proper effect, the Court were very sensible of, because it was evident on the face of the pleadings, from the statement of the defendants themselves, that the State was materially interested in the most effectual defence being made that the nature of the cases would admit of ; and nothing was more desirable than that in all cases, but particularly in cases of such high importance, all parties concerned, so far as it was practicable, should have their pretensions fully examined. However, we could find no instance where an Interpleader in a Court of Law was directed, but on an application of a defendant, much less against his consent ; and therefore were under the necessity of rejecting the motion. It was also questionable, if that difficulty had not intervened, whether, inasmuch as by such a proceeding a State would become a party, though collaterally to the principal action, it was not a case which ought to be tried in the Supreme Court. It did indeed occur, that the State perhaps had a remedy by a Bill of Interpleader in Equity—but no such bill had been brought nor, in all probability, if such a bill was proper, could it be brought in the Circuit Court, the reasons against this method of proceeding being competent in any but the Supreme Court operating, I apprehend, more strongly than in the other case suggested above. I have been thus particular in stating this interesting subject, because it appears to me of the highest moment, although I believe it would be difficult to devise an unexceptionable remedy. But the discussion of questions wherein are involved the most sacred and awful principles of public justice, under a system without precedent in the history of mankind, necessarily must occasion many embarrassments which can be more readily suggested than removed.

I should have taken the liberty to make this representation sooner, but that I thought it probable that, before this time, a Bill which has long been in contemplation by the House of Representatives for amending the Judicial system, would have been brought in, in which a provision might have been made for the peculiar cases I have mentioned ; but as other important business has hitherto delayed this, and the time of the Circuits is approaching, it appeared to me that I could not justify any further delay in communicating the important information which is the subject of the present letter.

I have the honor to be,
With the greatest respect, sir,
Your most obedient and faithful servant,

JAS. IREDELL.

THOS. IREDELL TO IREDELL.

February 10th, '92.

DEAR BROTHER :— * * * * Davie and Hamilton, it seems had high words in the House. Davie after answering some of ervations of Hamilton, which he conceived necessary to comment upon, remarked that some personal reflections had been made by Mr. Hamilton, which he should make a point of procuring private satisfaction for. H. immediately answered across the House—"any time and place" he thought proper. To every person's astonishment, however, nothing further has transpired. Some of the gentlemen from the Assembly say that Davie became very unpopular during the session, &c., &c.

T. IREDELL.

REV. ADAM BOYD TO IREDELL.*

AUGUSTA, GA., February 15th, '92.

DEAR SIR:—I was unfortunately deprived of the pleasure of waiting upon you, as I intended, the morning of your departure hence. The cold weather had affected my old knees in such a manner, that they did not recover their usual, necessary flexibility till near noon; and then I supposed you had been twenty miles off, as you mentioned an early hour.

I am truly sorry for this, because I wished to have some conversation with you, that would have been of use to me, and in which I persuaded myself you would have indulged me. My situation here is not pleasant, because I cannot receive as much from the parish as will support me, and a very little would do that. So that I shall decamp once more, unless they make some provision for me by the middle of next month.

If I thought I could make any interest, I would visit Philadelphia in April; but I am not a man of address, and a series of disappointments and afflictions has made me perhaps less so than I originally was, or might have been.

I did wish to return to Carolina, but can get no letter of encouragement. Parishes there are like those here, I believe, in great confusion. Wilmington is not suited to my constitution: but I might as well encounter climate as want. I have solicited a chaplainship, if any troops are to be stationed here: but this is from necessity. The pay is low, and yet I would rather have half the sum from some little appointment that I might attend to "day school at home." I beg leave to add that I flatter myself if you can with propriety favor my interest, you will embrace the opportunity. Poverty, old age, and sickness, anticipating time, are too powerful assailants long to be withstood. The first and last are the reward of my public services.

* A Revolutionary patriot: Editor of the Cape Fear Mercury, 1775: Chaplain in the Cont. Line, &c.

Please to remember me to Mr. Johnston. Wishing you and Mrs. Iredell the enjoyment of life, and favor of Heaven, I am with the most perfect respect and esteem,

Your most obedient servant,
A. BOYD.

REV. A. IREDELL TO IREDELL.

NEW HAVEN, SUSSEX, March 5th.

Although, my dear Brother, I write to you from a Rectory of my own, a small one it is true, but not the *smallest* or *least* desirable in the Kingdom; I have another much less within eight miles of me—that Parish is a suburb of Lewes, and in it formerly stood a proud Abbey, where voracious Monks swallowed up almost all my tithes. My good friend the Sergeant (*Kempe*) procured me both offices by means of the Duke of Richmond, who recommended me to the Chancellor my patron. There is a house and very good Glebe here, but the former is in so wretched a state that I shall be obliged to rebuild it. I am now endeavoring to get money for dilapidations from the last Incumbent's Executor, who has driven me, much against my will, to sue for it in our Ecclesiastical Court. With that (if I can get it), and two years' income, which I am enabled to borrow by an act of Parliament in this King's reign (and, I fear with the addition of some of my own money), I shall some time or other, it is likely, have a snug Parsonage most delightfully situated, with a small Bay at a mile's distance, on one side, the town of Lewes terminating a valley, on the other—in front, the village descending to the harbor, and at my back a range of downs. Will not all these objects tempt you and my sister to take a peep at us? or at least to trust one or two of your children to us? * * * * Are you not in America extremely anxious about the fate of France? She is in a more critical situation than ever, according to the newspapers. The Northern powers are all on the point of invading that devoted country, which is, beside, on the eve of a civil war. For my own part, I cannot help wishing success to their new Government, and, though I dare not enter the lists with a newspaper, I shall be much surprised if the people of so large an Empire, once freed from oppression, should bend their necks again to the yoke of a very few compared with their own number. La Fayette, who carried the epidemic ardor of your Continent to his own, has lately been honored with a Maréchal's staff. Will such a man be defeated? No—that country, like yours and like mine, is free, and will continue so, perhaps, longer than the last which

gave liberty to both the others. That a wiser Code than that which the National Assembly has digested might have been formed, you know much better than I do; but any body of laws inspired with the just principles that gave birth to theirs, must be infinitely preferable to those they have destroyed. I could have wished indeed the French Revolution had not crossed the Channel, and raved, like a Bedlamite, in this Island, which had nothing to do with it. And I could also have wished it had not taken a longer voyage across the Atlantic, and acted the same frantic part in the West Indies. May these mischiefs be soon done away! That must now be the prayer of the friends of human kind, and its enemies alone will then deplore the Revolution in France.

Our Parliament is now sitting. Mr. Pitt has been roughly handled by the opposition on the Russian Armament, and most justly, for in manœuvring to keep his place, he has put it out of his power to justify his conduct. It is lucky for him that his popularity could bear so violent a shock. A common share of it would not have kept him in his place. * * * * My uncle is, no wonder at it, quite disgusted with the prevailing humor of the times. His island (*Jamaica*) was in great danger, and I still apprehend much future mischief will arise there, in consequence of the blind zeal with which people of this country, bad as well as good, interest themselves against the slave-trade, as if humanity was not at all concerned in the means made use of to work good. You would hardly credit what I know to be true, and that probably falls short of what my uncle is told. All this, at the close of a long life spent in the acquisition of that which may be at one moment lost, is it not enough to sour any temper? I have shown your charge to my friend the Sergeant, who is in the habit of making very good ones (he is Chairman of our Quarter Sessions), and he *highly* approved of it.

Pray would it be worth while to lay out a little money in the purchase of lands in America? I hear they are sold remarkably cheap, and that a little English cash goes a great way in such bargains, &c.

A. IREDELL.

JUDGE PENDLETON TO IREDELL.

SANS SOUCI, (GA.) March, 19th, '92.

MY DEAR SIR:—Having been on the Circuit the last time, I do not imagine we shall have the pleasure of seeing you at the ensuing one. The fatigue of so long a journey twice a year is more than the strength of any man can bear. I have been expecting every day to hear that Congress have taken up the subject of the judiciary; but it appears to me as if the public mind was not sufficiently impressed with the importance of a steady, uniform, and prompt administration of justice; or what would be worse, that money matters have so strong a hold on the thoughts and personal feelings of men, that every thing else seems little in comparison. When the inhabitants of a town were consulted on the manner of fortifying it, every tradesman was for making the fortifications of the materials of his particular trade —the tanner with leather, the blacksmith with iron, &c. I may perhaps be governed by the same partiality in attributing so much importance to the judicial part in any system of government. In my mind, neither public nor private credit can be supported; nor will commerce, agriculture, or mechanic trades flourish, without an effectual administration of the laws.

I have been hopeful the hint given in the report of the Attorney-General about collecting and revising the laws, would have been taken up, and Commissioners appointed; but it is now so late in the session, I suppose nothing will be done.

We have been somewhat alarmed by the hostile appearance in the Creek Nation, but I have hopes no mischief will ensue. I am particularly interested in this subject, as there are not more than two or three families between my estate and that Nation, &c. &c.

NATHL. PENDLETON.*

IREDELL TO MRS. IREDELL.

CHARLESTON, April 8th, '92.

MY DEAR HANNAH:— * * * * I have bought a pair of horses, and, agreeably to your wishes, not showy (for they are confoundedly ugly). The price is $172. I may, perhaps, sell them for plough-horses in North Carolina.

I dined with Lindsay and Thompson yesterday, and am to do so again to-day; at Major Butler's lodgings to-morrow, and with Mr. Gilchrist on Tuesday. Mr. Rutledge is not in town, but I have experienced the kindest attention from Mrs. R. and the family. Two of the sons waited on me very soon after my arrival, but I happened to be out; and an invitation to dinner came in my absence. They are all well. I saw young Miss Rutledge last night, who is a very pretty young lady. Lindsay is extremely well, and has a very excellent house indeed, too handsome for a bachelor. My passage was upon the whole very agreeable, though we had very rough weather. Neither Major Butler nor myself had any sickness of consequence. The young ladies had a great deal. They improve extremely upon acquaintance.

* U. S. District Judge for Georgia.

Their father, I am persuaded, has taken uncommon pains with them, &c. &c.

April 19th.

I feel inexpressible anxiety for the arrival of Burroughs from Philadelphia, whom I expect now every day. I don't think I shall go hence till Thursday. I receive such great civilities that I have been engaged to dinner every day since I came, and shall till I go. Mr. Lindsay and an eminent lawyer here (Mr. Dessasaure) both pressed me to stay with them, but I declined. The change of climate, and going about a great deal, gave me a little fever one evening. Major Butler was very sick indeed one night; his daughters have gone into the country. ° ° ° I this day heard an excellent sermon from a Mr. Jenkins, a Tory Parson who was banished, and has no regular parish, and I believe preached to-day for the first time since his return. I dined on Friday with young Mr. Rutledge, where there was a very large and genteel company, and very elegant dinner. His wife is not only very handsome, but appears to me very accomplished and agreeable. ° ° ° Major Pinckney (the Minister to Britain) and his family sail to-morrow. I have received a renewal of such uncommon courtesies from him, and his connections, that I must again earnestly entreat you to wait on Mrs. Pinckney soon after her arrival. The only fault imputed to her is the very same to which you are liable, her too great fondness for retirement, and an exclusive attachment to domestic life. She is a most amiable woman, and none can be more perfectly free from any kind of pride or affectation. I am told that she has been in tears almost ever since her husband's appointment. She has very near connections and many friends to leave, who are extremely attached to her; and to add to her distresses, she has had a child lately inoculated, whose situation is still critical, &c. &c.

Savannah, (Geo.) April 25th.

° ° ° ° I still continue perfectly well, and receive most agreeable courtesies here, from very genteel people. I have dined abroad every day since I came, and am engaged every day that I expect to remain. The weather is most delightful. The Grand Jury have not only thanked me for my charge, and the punctuality of my attendance, but *presented the neglect of the other Judges.* Judge Johnson has not arrived, nor have I heard from him on the road. There have been such violent freshets that it is not unlikely they may have obstructed him.

April 26th.

° ° ° We have a great deal of very important business to do here. My horses turn out very well, but owing to my carelessness in driving, I had liked to have suffered a good deal. Having understood that the horse in the chair was very gentle and the road being a remarkably fine one, I was going on at my ease, when part of the rein getting under his tail, he ran away the chair struck against a tree, and overset, throwing me out, and one of the wheels went over my leg. I was able to proceed however (as the chair was not broken) about ten miles, but then was in so much pain, I was under the necessity of staying very inconveniently at a house on the road. Fortunately, however the hurt was only a swelling in my ancle, that subsided next day I afterwards overtook a very respectable, agreeable old gentleman (Mr. Brailsford) at Judge Bee's, where I had appointed to meet him, and by his means got the greatest part of the way to genteel houses, where we lived as elegantly, and were treated with as much kindness, as we could have experienced in Charleston, &c. &c.

JAS. IREDELL.

A CHARGE

Delivered to the Grand Jury for the District of Georgia, in the Circuit Court of the United States for the said District, held in the City of Savannah, on the 26th day of April, 1792, by JAMES IREDELL, *one of the Associate Justices of the Supreme Court of the United States.*

[Published at the Grand Jury's Request.]

GENTLEMEN OF THE GRAND JURY :—

Among the various duties which the citizens of the United States are occasionally called upon to exercise, none is of greater importance, or of higher dignity, than that now required of you A government, founded on proper principles of freedom, will take equal care to detect the guilty, and secure the innocent. It will consider, on the one hand, that the safety of the good depends on the punishment of bad members of society; and, on the other, how much men's actions are liable to be misrepresented, and how necessary therefore it is to investigate every charge in the fullest, the most attentive, and most impartial manner. This duty, if vested in fixed magistrates, might frequently be converted (as it has been in other countries) to purposes of the grossest oppression; the guilty might be screened, through favor or corruption, the innocent might be made the sacrifice of malice or ill-will. But, by vesting this awful and important power in citizens occasionally drawn forth from the body of their fellow-citizens, in the most unexceptionable manner that circumstances will admit of, and who are to execute the trust for a single time only, there is the best reason to hope that the power will be as little susceptible of abuse as such a one in the nature of things can be. A free and enlightened people will for their own sake not overlook the necessity of securing an observance of those laws framed by the common consent and for the common welfare of the whole; and they will at the same time know and feel the importance of rejecting unsubstantial accusations, whether proceeding from ignorance or malevolence, being impressed strongly with this interesting sentiment, that not only the life, liberty, and property, of each citizen, are entitled to the most sacred protection, when unforfeited to the laws of his country, but that his reputation also, so far as he is deserving of it, ought as much as possible to be preserved inviolate.

The crimes cognizable by you, gentlemen, are crimes committed against the *United States.* We ought never to forget that there are two Governments to which we owe obedience; each limited, but each perfect in its kind: the State Governments, in all instances of authority under their own constitutions, not relinquished to the United States; the Government of the United States, in all instances of authority so relinquished, and of which the Constitution of the United States forms the evidence and the barrier. If this complication of authority requires greater care and attention than formerly, let us remember that we are amply recompensed for it by the greater blessings we enjoy. The happiness of our country certainly depends, not only on the preservation of the State Governments in their due sphere of authority, but on the firm union of the whole for the great purposes of the common welfare of the whole, which fatal experience hath long since told us cannot be secured without an energetic government to effect it.

The crimes against the United States of which you have cognizance are declared by certain acts of Congress, in virtue of the authority vested in them by the constitution.

An exact enumeration does not appear now to be material, as I flatter myself there are few, if any, crimes you will have occasion to present. I shall therefore confine myself to such as are of the most importance, and the most general in their nature (contained in the principal act relating to this subject), taking occasion at the same time to point out some improvements that have been introduced, which every friend to justice and liberality must, I think, observe with pleasure.

The principal crimes are:

1. Treason. 2. Murder. 3. Piracy. 4. Forgery. 5. Being accessory to certain Capital Felonies before the fact.

1. Treason. Treason consists in two articles only : " Levying war against the United States," or " adhering to their enemies, giving them aid and comfort." The plain definition of this crime was justly deemed of such moment to the liberties of the people that it was made a part of the constitution itself. And the constitution further, with a caution equally wise, expressly directs, " That no person shall be convicted of treason, unless on the testimony of two witnesses to the same overt act, or on confession in open court." None can so highly prize the importance of these provisions as those who are best acquainted with the abuses which have been practised in other countries in prosecutions for this offence. No man of humanity can read them without the highest indignation, nor, in particular, can they be read by any citizen of America without emotions of gratitude for the much happier situation of his own country, in which guilt alone, and not innocence, need dread a conviction. The humanity of the present system is also conspicuous over former ones, in declaring (as the constitution does), " That no attainder of treason shall work corruption of blood, or forfeiture, except during the life of the person attainted." The act of Congress on the subject is still more indulgent, and contains such a provision without the exception. This provision not only saves from ruin the innocent family of the offender, but it removes an execrable temptation, which has not been without its effect in former times, of prosecuting for the offence with a view to obtain the benefits of the forfeiture. We now may hope that the page of American history will never be stained with prosecutions for treason, begun without cause, conducted without decency, and ending in iniquitous convictions, without the slightest feelings of remorse.

2. Murder. This may be committed, either " within any fort, arsenal, dock-yard, magazine, or in any other place or district of country, *under the sole and exclusive jurisdiction of the United States;*" or, " upon the high seas, or in any river, haven, basin, or bay, out of the jurisdiction of any particular State."

This crime, therefore, must be committed in some place out of the ordinary jurisdiction of the State courts, otherwise the courts of the United States have no cognizance of it.

If committed in any of the places first mentioned *on shore,* the common distinction applies of homicide that is felonious, and such as is not so. Felonious homicide is distinguished into murder and manslaughter; the former being a felonious killing with malice aforethought, the latter a felonious killing without malice express or implied. Homicide that is not felonious is what the law terms either *justifiable* homicide, in which case the party killing is deemed perfectly innocent of any crime; or *excusable* homicide, wherein some little blame is supposed to be imputable, but, according to modern practice, when the homicide appears to have been of that nature, the party is usually acquitted generally. The distinctions between these various species of homicide are in many cases nice and complicated, and frequently require great care and consideration. It is therefore usually thought best, that, where a *killing* is clearly proved, if the case be not very plain indeed, the Grand Jury should find the indictment for murder, and leave the consideration as to the species of homicide to the court and jury on the trial. I say the *court and jury*—for though it is held to be the province of the court to decide what species of homicide the offence belongs to, and that the province of the jury is merely to be confined *to the facts*, yet, in my opinion, this can mean nothing more, according to the true principles of law, than that, if a jury find a special verdict stating the facts, the court may pronounce the law upon it, and give judgment as effectually as they could have done on a general verdict. But as it is in the option of the jury to give a special verdict or not, and as they unquestionably may find a general verdict, I conceive they must find that verdict conscientiously, on the best of their judgment, after receiving all such assistance as the court may think proper to give them; which assistance, where points of law are complicated with facts, will often be found very useful, and in some instances absolutely necessary. But as they, in the case of a general verdict, are by the law *judges in the last resort* (so far at least as the giving of that verdict is concerned), they have, I think, clearly a *right* as well as *power*, to determine as shall appear to them to be just; *since it seems to me absurd to say, that where there is a lawful authority to determine, that determination must be made, not according to the judgment of those who have such authority, but according to the judgment of those who have it not*. I know no trammels of precedent in this country to overrule a principle which appears to me so plain, and which is so well calculated to guard against indecent altercations between a court and jury, as well as, in my opinion, to prevent any of the rights or liberties of the citizens being overborne (as might otherwise sometimes be the case) by violent exertions of power. In very flagrant cases indeed the same law which vests this authority in juries, permits the court to grant a new trial *in favor of the prisoner*. But it allows no such authority (and God forbid it ever should) to his prejudice; so that a new trial may in some cases be granted after a conviction, but never after an acquittal.

The importance of this subject has drawn me to say rather more than I intended, but I flatter myself not more than its high consequence, and the long controversy which has subsisted on the subject, merited.

I am next to speak of murder committed " upon the high seas, or in any river, haven, basin, or bay, out of the jurisdiction of any particular State."

Murder thus committed is not to be decided on the authority of Common Law principles, which can only apply to cases happening within the bounds of some particular State; in which cases we have seen, if the person be killed in any particular place *under the sole and exclusive cognizance of the United States*, the courts of the United States have jurisdiction; otherwise the State courts have exclusive cognizance of it. But if the person be killed upon the high seas, or in any river, haven, basin, or bay, out of the jurisdiction of any particular State (which are the cases now under consideration), the decision must take place upon the principles of the Law of Nature and of Nations, as enforced by the Legislature of the United States, to whom such authority is expressly delegated. Cases of this kind, I believe, in England are determined according to the principles of the Civil Law, though the mode of investigation and trial is, by a particular act of Parliament, conformable to the mode of proceeding at Common Law. And by the Civil Law, so far as I have been capable of discovering, there is no distinction of various species of homicide, so that if a killing be clearly proved, the person charged must be either found guilty of murder or acquitted altogether. This method, however, may frequently be productive of too rigorous a conviction, or too favorable an acquittal, varying perhaps too much according to the more or less operating influence of collateral circumstances; and therefore I think the law of the United States has more wisely provided, that in this case, as well as others similarly circumstanced in all essential points, a distinction shall be observed between obvious differences of guilt. It accordingly branches homicide into the two great and principal species of murder and manslaughter; a division which (as I have before stated) in effect comprehends all the cases of homicide, wherein punishment is now inflicted in cases triable at Common Law.

The clauses within which the remaining capital crimes I have enumerated are comprehended, are as follows. [He here read the sections 8, 9, 14, and 10, of the act entitled, " An act for the punishment of certain crimes against the United States."]

In addition to these, another capital offence is declared in these words: " That if an person or persons shall by force set at liberty or rescue any person who shall be found guilty of treason, murder, or any other capital crime, or rescue any person convicted of any of the said crimes going to execution, or during execution, every person so offending, and being thereof convicted, shall suffer death."

The principal crimes not capital, and the punishments to be inflicted on them, are ascertained as follows. [He here read the sections 2, 6, 11, 12, 13, 15, 16, 17, 18, 21, 22, 23, of the act before referred to.]

It having been thought proper, in order to deter more effectually from the horrid crime of murder, that the court before whom such a conviction took place should have authority at their discretion (in case of very aggravating circumstances) to add to the judgment, that the body of the offender, after the execution done, should be delivered to a surgeon for dissection, it became necessary to guard against a rescue of such body before such part of the judgment could be complied with, if any should dare to attempt it. This is accordingly done by the following provision. [He here read the 5th section of the same act.]

The remaining offences which I shall notice are such as concern a violation of the Law of Nations, and are defined, and the punishments described, as follows. [He here read the 25th, 26th and 27th sections of the act.]

These are the principal offences, and all of them, you will observe, are relative to the great objects of the General Government only. I omit others, interspersed in various acts, which either are on the same principle with similar ones in this leading act, or arise from the exercise of particular authorities vested in public officers, whose duty it will be, upon the knowledge of the commission of any such crimes, to give regular information of them.

I now beg leave to point out to you some interesting particulars in regard to the mode of prosecution and trial.

It is enacted, " That no person or persons shall be prosecuted, tried, or punished, for treason, or other capital offence aforesaid, wilful murder or forgery excepted, unless the indictment for the same shall be found by a Grand Jury within three years next after the treason or capital offence aforesaid shall be done or committed; nor shall any person be prosecuted, tried, or punished, for any offence not capital, nor for any fine or forfeiture under any penal statute, unless the indictment or information for the same shall be found or instituted within two years from the time of committing the offence, or incurring the fine or forfeiture aforesaid: *Provided*, that nothing herein contained shall extend to any person or persons fleeing from justice."

At Common Law there was no limitation of time for the prosecution of any offence. Limitations however have been prescribed in England by some acts of Parliament; but they extend only, I believe, to cases of treason and misprision of treason, with certain exceptions; to appeals for murder, which are in the nature of a private prosecution; and to informations for the breaches of penal statutes.

The extension of this principle to all offences whatsoever (with the exception only of murder and forgery), appears to me a very considerable improvement, alike founded on justice and humanity.

The manner of trial is guarded with great caution. The following excellent provision is made concerning it :

It is enacted, " That any person who shall be accused and indicted of treason shall have a copy of the indictment, and a list of the jury and witnesses to be produced on the trial for proving the said indictment, mentioning the names and places of abode of such witnesses and jurors, delivered unto him at least three entire days before he shall be tried for the same ; and in other capital offences shall have such copy of the indictment, and list of the jury, two entire days at least before the trial : And that every person so accused and indicted for any of the crimes aforesaid shall also be allowed and admitted to make his full defence by counsel learned in the law, and the court before whom such person shall be tried, or some Judge thereof, shall, and they are hereby authorized and required, immediately upon his request, to assign to such person such counsel, not exceeding two, as such person shall desire, to whom such counsel shall have free access at all seasonable hours ; and every such person or persons accused or indicted of the crimes aforesaid, shall be allowed and admitted in his said defence to make any proof that he or they can produce, by lawful witness or witnesses, and shall have the like process of the court where he or they shall be tried to compel his or their witnesses to appear at his or their trial as is usually granted to compel witnesses to appear on the prosecution against them."

The importance of these provisions will justify me, I hope, in detaining you a short time with some observations upon them.

The provisions in regard to treason are nearly similar to provisions, by different acts of Parliament in Great Britain, in regard to most cases of treason and misprision of treason. The principal difference consists in the interval allowed between the time of delivering the copy of the indictment, and a list of the jury and witnesses, and the time of the trial. It was formerly in that country three days ; it is now ten days, which some men

VOL. II—23

of great discernment and humanity, and much experience in the Crown Law, have considered as too long. Possibly however in Great Britain, where the Crown is so powerful, and prosecutions for treason have been in former times at least conducted in a very sanguinary manner, it might not be an unnecessary provision. Thank God there is no reason to fear in our own country the influence of such prosecutions to any dangerous extent.

But it is an improvement which I hope we shall know how to value, that in other capital offences a copy of the indictment, and list of the jury, is to be allowed two entire days at least before the trial. This I believe is wholly unknown to the law of England even at present.

So also is the allowance in all cases of a full defence by counsel. A very great Crown writer says, "At Common Law no counsel was allowed upon the issue of guilty or not guilty, in any capital cases whatsoever, except upon questions of law, and then only in doubtful, not in plain cases." What a barbarous principle! and how unsuitable to the usual justice of Common Law principles! Accordingly the learned, I had almost said the immortal author of the Commentaries, after expressing in pointed terms his opinion of its injustice, shows that it was not a part of the ancient law of England, which certainly in its groundwork was highly favorable to the liberties of the people. Yet such is the force of custom that the eminent Crown writer I before alluded to (Mr. Justice *Foster*), who was in general a man of high respectability, and whose name was almost proverbial for a sacred regard to justice, hesitated at the condemnation of this detestable practice. And the only alteration that has been introduced in England at this enlightened period is, I believe, in the principal cases of treason and misprision of treason. It is material to observe, that the person indicted is not only entitled to employ counsel, but to have assigned to him such, not exceeding two, as he shall desire; so that if he should happen to be a poor man, and unable to make a reasonable compensation for the trouble of defending him, he yet shall not suffer upon that account.

It is a thing perhaps that will scarcely be believed, that, according to the practice of the Common Law of England, a prisoner in capital cases was not only not allowed a process to compel the attendance of his witnesses, but not even to have any examined on his behalf—a gross defiance of common sense as well as common justice! and said by a very great lawyer to have been introduced (as I am persuaded it was) without any color of law. This led to a practice, if less unjust, yet perhaps nearly as dangerous as the other, to examine the witnesses for the prisoner without oath. At length acts of Parliament (though not completely till so late as Queen Anne) abolished this abominable remnant of the tyranny of courts over the personal rights and safety of the people.

I trust, gentlemen, this view of the general code of the Criminal Law of the United States, though it has occupied a good deal of your time, will not be deemed uninteresting. It is pleasing to see the progress of reason and humanity, that seems to be still daily increasing, and it must afford the highest gratification to every citizen of America to reflect, that the noblest path to liberty was first explored in the happy country that he lives in. May we be all sensible of the grandeur and importance of this awful station! and, at the same time that we cherish with the fondest attachment those principles of freedom, which are likely to prove a blessing to other parts of the world, as well as to ourselves, remember that true freedom cannot exist without a regular government to support it, and that as union alone enabled us to reach our present envied situation, so, under the blessing of God, nothing but disunion can in all human probability deprive us of it!

SAVANNAH, STATE OF GEORGIA. We, the Grand Jury of the Circuit Court, present our thanks to his Honor Judge Iredell for his constant and uniform attendance to the duties of his office in this State, and are sorry to observe that other Judges do not give the same attendance, by which means the business of the Court is obliged to be postponed, to the great injury of individuals, and more particularly so at this time, when questions of such magnitude are to be decided upon, in which the State is also deeply interested.

We join the Court in our congratulations on the wise and humane amendments made by Congress in the criminal laws of the land, as stated to us in the charge, and are happy to inform the Court, that no criminal business or informations have come before us.

We recommend to Congress a total repeal of the Excise Laws, conceiving them oppressive and dangerous in a free country, and the worst mode of taxation that can possibly be devised by any Government.

We lament the want of a Seaman's Hospital in the port of Savannah, in consequence of which great distress arises to mariners, and much inconvenience to navigation, and recommend that adequate provision be made out of the general tonnage for that purpose.

We return our thanks to his Honor the Judge for his charge, and request that it may be printed in the Gazette.

GEO. HOUSTOUN, *Foreman*, (L. S.)	ALEXR. WATT,	(L. S.)
WM. EWING, (L. S.)	EBENR. HILLS,	(L. S.)
WM. LAMB, (L. S.)	NICHOLAS MILLER,	(L. S.)
J. HALL, (L. S.)	JAMES GIGNILLIAT,	(L. S.)
JOHN PRAY, (L. S.)	JOHN Y. WHITE,	(L. S.)
JOHN HAMILTON, (L. S.)	R. WOODHOUSE,	(L. S.)
WM. PINDER, (L. S.)	J. WHITE,	(L. S.)
JAMES HOUSTOUN, (L. S.)	ROBERT BOLTON,	(L. S.)
MATTW. JOHNSTON, (L. S.)	DAVID ROBINSON,	(L. S.)

GOV. JOHNSTON TO IREDELL.

PHILADELPHIA, 10th May, '92.

DEAR SIR:— * * * The papers are filled with abusive publications against Government: most of them very ill-founded, as far as I am capable of judging, but are written so as to captivate, and deceive the multitude: aided by some inflammatory harangues in the House, I fear they will have an unfavorable effect on the minds of the people in prejudice of a Government, which, I really think, has done more good than any other so circumstanced ever did in the same space of time:—the interest of the public debt regularly paid, and nearly or quite two and a half millions of dollars of the principal paid off: add to this all the contingent charges of Government paid; and all this without oppressing any branch of useful industry, with an increase of commerce, manufactures, agriculture, and arts, in a degree unknown in any country in so short a space as three years. Should these wise *patriots* by their exertions so sever the hearts of the people from their Government as to throw us back into the deplorable and helpless situation from which we have just emerged, God knows what may be the event, &c., &c.

SAM. JOHNSTON.

IREDELL TO MRS. IREDELL.

AUGUSTA, GA., May 10th.

MY DEAR HANNAH:—I left Savannah on Sunday last, and travelled up in a very delightful manner in company with Major Forsyth (the Marshal) in his caravan—something like a stagewagon. We arrived Tuesday evening, and I shall set off for Columbia to-morrow. In the mean time I am resting myself and horses very pleasantly at his house. His family are very genteel, and obliging to me. The weather is uncommonly agreeable, the nights cool enough for blankets. This town is now one of the most beautiful in America, &c.

COLUMBIA, South Carolina, May 15th, '92.

I arrived here very early yesterday morning, and, contrary to my expectation, we finished the whole business of the Court in the course of the day. * * * I everywhere meet with great distinction and kindness, and have great reason to rejoice I came southward; for otherwise the Judiciary of the United States would have been greatly disgraced, &c.

JAS. IREDELL.

Mr. John Haywood wrote Mr. Iredell, June 18th: "Brandies almost without measure will be made in Carolina this summer but bad crops of corn." "The Trustees of the University have fixed upon Ceputt's Bridge, in Chatham county, as the given point which shall govern the Commissioners in fixing on the ground in which buildings are to be erected: in making choice they are only allowed a latitude of 15 miles. Other orders were made at the meeting, where every thing was conducted with unanimity and good humor, and much to the satisfaction of the Trustees from the Western parts of the State."

CIRCUIT COURT OF NORTH CAROLINA.

Congress had lately passed a law providing for the claims of widows and orphans, and regulating claims to invalid pensions. The act directed that claims should be exhibited to the Circuit Courts; and that all to whom the Courts granted certificates should be placed on the pension list by the Secretary of War, unless he had cause to suspect imposition or fraud, &c. Conceiving that the Legislature had encroached upon the independence, and invaded the rights of the Judiciary, Judges Iredell and Sitgreaves then holding the Circuit Courts of North Carolina, on the 8th of June, addressed an able remonstrance to the President of the United States. The letter, drawn by Judge Iredell, appears in Dallas's Reports, Vol. 2, p. 412. C. Justice Jay and Judge Duane in a decision in New York, April 5th; and Blair and Wilson, of the Circuit Court of Pennsylvania, in a similar letter, April 18th, had taken the same ground: that Congress had no right to impose upon them any but purely judicial duties, or to subject them to the revisory power of the Secretary or any one else; and that the act was unconstitutional, and void so far as it related to them. Judges Jay, Duane, Iredell, and Sitgreaves, expressed however their readiness, not *judicially* but as *Commissioners*, to make the required investigations. Judge Iredell acted in this manner upon the Eastern Circuit, in the Fall: Judge Wilson absolutely refused to have any thing to do with the business. To test the validity of the act, at the next session of the Supreme Court (in the case of Hayburn), Mr. Randolph, the Attorney-General of the United States, moved for a mandamus, premising that his motion was "ex-officio," without an application from any particular person. The Court being divided, the motion was not allowed. The Attorney-General then changed his ground, and moved in behalf of Hayburn. The Court took an "advisari" till the next term; but no decision was ever pronounced, as in the mean time the act was repealed.

SUPREME COURT. AUGUST TERM.

At the August term of the Supreme Court the first motion was made in the important case of the State of Georgia *vs.* Brailsford et al. Several novel questions connected with the constitutional jurisprudence of the country were presented by this case; and, in its later stages, it is remarkable as the only case in which a special trial by jury has ever been had before the Supreme Court. By an act of confiscation, a bond made by Kelsall & Spalding to Brailsford and others, alleged aliens, had been sequestrated to the State of Georgia. Brailsford and his co-partners had brought suit on the bond. The State of Georgia had unsuccessfully applied for permission to assert her claim in the Circuit Court, where judgment had been entered for the plaintiffs. The State now filed a Bill in Equity for an injunction to stay proceedings in the Circuit Court, and praying an order to the Marshal to pay over to the State all moneys in his hands, or that might at any time come, &c. The Chief Justice, Iredell, Blair, and Wilson granted the injunction, Johnson and Cushing dissenting.

This cause was brought up again at the February Term, 1793, upon a motion to dissolve the injunction. The Court ruled that the injunction should continue until the next term; when, however, if Georgia had not instituted her action at common law it should be dismissed. Jay, Cushing, Wilson, and Johnson, thought the State had a "plain, adequate, and complete remedy at common law;" and yet, strange to say, with the exception of Johnson, sustained the injunction. Iredell was in favor of the injunction, because he thought the State had *no complete and adequate remedy at common law*: he had rejected the application of the State in the Circuit Court, because the Supreme Court had exclusive jurisdiction of a suit whenever a State was a party: he replied to the suggestion of a Writ of Error, that it could only affect the original parties to the suit; remarked that an action of Assumpsit, "the legal panacea of modern times," could not be brought by the State before the plaintiff had received the money; and considered it useless for the Court to grant an injunction, if they could not devise a mode for a fair determination of the claim, but expressed his own conviction that a mode might easily be prescribed, in strict conformity with the principles and practice of equity.

At the February Term, 1794, the right of the State to the bond was tried upon an amicable issue, by a special jury, and a verdict found against the State, the Court having charged that the act of Georgia did not vest the debt in the State at the time of its passage, that it was subjected to *sequestration* only, and the owner's right to recover it revived at the peace.*

THE EASTERN CIRCUIT.

Judge Iredell rode the Eastern Circuit, for the first time, in the Fall, with Judge Wilson.

IREDELL TO MRS. IREDELL.

NEW HAVEN, September 23d, 1792.

MY DEAR HANNAH:—We left New York between three and four o'clock on Friday morning, but there were such a number of passengers that Mr. and Miss Wilson and myself were in an extra stage, Peter and our baggage in the other. We had not proceeded many miles before we perceived that some of the baggage was gone, and on examination found that it was Mr. Wilson's trunk, and mine. We sent back instantly for it, and we ourselves squeezed into the other stage—to Kingsbridge, where we waited in very painful suspense upwards of two hours. At length all returned safe, though they had been obliged to proceed as far as the Fly-market, where by accident they met a boy who had driven a wagon to town, had picked the trunks up, and very honestly deposited them near the city, in safety. This delay forcing us to rely on the extra-stage, which had only two horses, we got no further than this last night. Hartford is forty-

* Dallas's Reports. Lives of the Chief Justices, by Van Santvoord.

two miles further, for which we shall set off in a very short time. We wished to have staid here and gone on to-morrow, partly in conformity to the law, and as we wished to see a little of this town. But we can be provided for to-day, and it is uncertain to-morrow; therefore hope to be forgiven for the sin, especially as we intend to be present at a meeting in our way about thirteen miles off. The country has not disappointed my expectations. It is most beautiful. The land is continually broken. There are the most stones in it I ever saw. The roads in many places are execrable: the worst Maryland roads are a bowling-green to them. But the prospects are in numberless places very extensive and delightful. The country is all cleared. You are scarcely ever out of a sight of a house; and frequently pass little towns in charming situations, with a number of very neat, and some elegant houses—mostly laid out like villages, with a great plenty of ground about each house. We never have stopped in one town where there were not at least two elegant Churches, with handsome steeples—one Episcopalian, one Presbyterian. The whole country, I believe, is laid out into townships; but I imagine in each there is a part which is more immediately called the town. I heard more particularly about the township of Norwalk: that was 8 miles east and west, and 10 miles north and south, and contained 1000 heads of families. In Fairfield, which is a remarkably pretty place (I think it must be meant of the township), they have two Episcopal Churches and four Meeting-houses with steeples, and one without. This seems to be a very large and handsome town, though I have not been able to see much of it, &c., &c.

HARTFORD, Sept. 25th, '92.

* * * On our way Judge Wilson and myself stopped at a meeting-house, where we heard a very dull minister, and found not a genteel congregation. It was at a place called Wallingford. One part of his prayer was, that they might come better prepared in *body* and mind for public worship in the afternoon. We dined at Durham, a very small place but with beautiful views from it. We passed through Middletown, a delightful town or city, and a pretty little place called Wethersfield before we got here, which we did in good time. This place in point of beauty is far inferior to almost any I have seen in the State, though the Capital. Had we seen it first it might have passed tolerably well. It is said to be far less agreeable (which I believe) in all respects than New Haven. It has the most trade of any in the State. We are very well accommodated, though Mr. Wilson and myself have only one room between us. In New York I called at Mr. Maxwell's, Dr. Romayne's, Dr. Bard's, Mrs. Edwards's, Mr. Jay's, Lenox's, Ramsay's. I saw only Mr. Maxwell, and met him in the street. None of the family were at home. Mrs. Romayne seemed very glad to see me, and expressed a very great desire to meet you again: she greatly regretted your departure from New York: she talked better than I expected. He had called on me at the City Tavern, but I was not at home. I saw Mrs. Edwards only of her family: the most of them were in the country: they now live in a very elegant house in Wall street. Mr. Jay was not at home; but we drank tea very agreeably with Mrs. Jay, who looked extremely well. I intended to have called at Leroy's, but the family were out of town: they were in danger of losing their only son. I dined in New York with a Mr. Hammond, a very genteel man, and possessed of a large fortune, who married a Miss Ogden of Newark, whose father I know. Miss Wilson staid with them: she is a very agreeable girl indeed, and her health is already much improved. So is mine, &c., &c.

September 30th, '92.

* * * We have had a great deal of business to do here, particularly as I have reconciled myself to the propriety of doing the Invalid-business out of Court. *Judge Wilson altogether declines it.* I think we shall set off on Wednesday for Boston. We have no extraordinary inducement to stay in this town. Colonel Wadsworth is very obliging to us, but his and one more are the only private houses in which we have been. I am told many other towns in Connecticut are much more agreeable. A great deal of the ancient simplicity of manners your brother so much admired still remains here. For instance, all their elections are conducted with so much order and decorum, that I am told it would be fatal to the interest of the most popular man to offer himself as a candidate, or solicit one vote: and many thousand votes were lately given in, without the slightest confusion, in an hour and a half, &c.

September 30th.

* * * Wilson has resolved to return on very urgent business to Philadelphia, though with an intention still to meet me at Boston, as it is absolutely necessary both of us should be at New Hampshire, the D. Judge being there incapable to act. * * * I have been twice to meeting to-day, and heard most delightful vocal music, which I was very much tempted to "encore," &c.

October 4th.

The Invalid-business has scarcely allowed me one moment's time, and now I am engaged in it by candle-light, though to go at three in the morning. I was at a ball the night before last, and staid until one. I danced a little, but it was not a remarkably agreeable one, &c., &c.
JAS. IREDELL.

DR. DUFFIELD TO IREDELL.

PHILADELPHIA, October 5th, '92.

DEAR SIR:— * * * Miss Anne has, within these few days, been roughly treated by a severe sore throat and fever, of the kind we Pedants call "Angina Scarlatina." She was yesterday able to walk from one room to another. * * * * I thought it my duty to inform you particularly myself, as the anxious mind of a mother does not always find itself sufficiently easy under the pressure of distress, to present an accurate history of disease.

From late arrivals from England and France, we find strange foundation for conjecture. The riots in Birmingham, Sheffield, and London; the continuance of the *bounties* for seamen, as well as of the *press*; the spark of commotion which seems spreading throughout the Kingdom; the strict attention paid to the naval force, seem to denote (at least) apprehensions of war and tumult. On the Continent, by the Dutch and French papers, another scene, of a more purple coloring, seems to be drawing in perspective at the bottom of the horrific stage. Germany is drawing forth her Houlans and Hussars, as well as all the infantry she can spare, to spread on the borders of Flanders. In the bosom of France, discontent has lighted up a flame, which the death of some more of her citizens, even within the walls of Paris, has not been able to extinguish. It is said, that if the Empress survives, Russia also will lead a few of her savages to enjoy the sanguinary pleasure. And all this terrible preparation, this din of arms, this destruction of the human race, to gratify the ambition of *a man*.

Our State will lose one representative in the Senate this year, because the etiquette of its election could not be fixed between *our* Senate and the House of Representatives. However these two have voted 20,000 for buildings for the President and Legislature of the United States to be commenced as soon as possible. Their situation is to be just above where Mr. Randolph lived, up Market street, and the buildings to be afterwards rented by the State, &c., &c.
B. DUFFIELD.

IREDELL TO MRS. IREDELL.

BOSTON, Oct. 7th, 1792.

MY DEAR HANNAH:—I arrived here yesterday evening before sunset, and soon after had the great satisfaction to receive your letters of the 27th and 30th September. Was it not a little hard that I should travel in company with them all the way from Hartford, and not receive them sooner! * * * * I have seen in many places since I left Hartford a very fine country (in some parts remarkably romantic) and passed through some pretty towns. But in general it was by no means equal to Connecticut. But I am told the part I passed through is the worst part of Massachusetts. I persuaded our driver to go a little out of his usual route, that I might see Cambridge, the seat of the University of this State, and about 3¼ miles from town across the famous Charlestown Bridge. I had great reason to be satisfied, for it is a most beautiful place, and contains many very elegant houses. Mr. Gerry, among others, has a delightful one in a most beautiful situation. I saw him and Mrs. Gerry at a little town on the road about sixty miles hence. He seemed extremely glad to see me and regretted he was not at Cambridge to receive me, and both he and Mrs. Gerry were so obliging as to request that you and I might make a visit into this country and stay some time with them. He gave me a letter of introduction to one of the first gentlemen here, and promised of his own accord to wait on you soon after his arrival to let you know he had met me. Mrs. Gerry is much improved. They will travel slowly. After what I have mentioned, I am sure you will think them entitled to particular attention. He is certainly a very agreeable man, and I am persuaded from every thing I have heard and observed a very worthy one.* The bridge fully equalled my expectations: it is indeed a very noble one. I was so fortunate as to get into an excellent house immediately, a Mr. Cotton's, where I am indeed *quite comfortable*, &c., &c.

October 11th.

Since I last wrote you I have met with the most distinguished civilities not only from gentlemen to whom I had letters, but from many others, and very soon found myself engaged for every day in the week—sometimes different invitations for the same day. The society here is in my opinion extremely agreeable, although every body tells me I see the town to great disadvantage, as so many families are scarcely yet recovered from the small-pox, and

* Elbridge Gerry, Signer of the Declaration of Independence: Vice-President of the U. S.

many in deep affliction for melancholy losses. According to an authentic return lately made, the numbers are as follows—Whites inoculated 8804, of which 158 have died: Taken naturally 214, of which 27 have died. Blacks inoculated 348, died 7. Taken naturally 18, died 6. Number from the country, &c., 1038. Do. removed out of town 262. Subject to the infection 221. Now sick 181.

I am going this evening to the first Assembly. My health is now very good. Our Court begins to-morrow. The weather is extremely fine: this day is like Spring. I must endeavor to bring you here: you would, I am sure, be pleased with the society of both ladies and gentlemen. Their hospitality and manner are very frank and engaging. I have not yet seen Mrs. Howard, but intend waiting on her. Judge Lowell has been particularly kind to me: I have not yet seen his family as they live out of town.* Some time ago they had the misfortune to be overturned in their carriage, and Mrs. Lowell was very much hurt, but has now quite recovered. Be so good when you see Mr. Anthony to give my best respects to him, and tell him I am extremely obliged for the letters he gave me. The gentlemen to whom they were addressed have been very attentive to me. One of them, Mr. Branch, who has had 17 children, 7 of whom are living, lately had a very critical escape with a fine son about eight years old. He was under the small-pox, and a sudden change induced his parents to send for the Doctor, who was not at home, but afterwards passing the house thought he would call in, though he did not know there was any particular occasion for him. The moment he saw the boy he seemed greatly shocked, and said he was gone. He, however, ordered as much wine and cordials as could be administered, and the little fellow happily recovered. The Doctor said six minutes longer would have been too late. Unfortunately at this very time a child in the Doctor's own house was taken in the very same manner, and died because he was not on the spot. It was a singular fate, &c., &c.
JAS. IREDELL.

On the 12th, assisted by Judge Lowell, Judge Iredell opened the Circuit Court. His charge was generally applauded, and appeared in the Columbian Centinel, Oct. 20. With the accompanying editorial encomium, it is here reprinted from that paper.

* John Lowell, a distinguished Federalist.—Vid. Sullivan's Letters.

[As uniting elegance with extensive knowledge and liberality, the CHARGE of the Hon. JUDGE IREDELL has been universally spoken of.—The *Editor* is therefore happy in having it in his power to communicate it to the public this day.]

A CHARGE

Delivered to the Grand Jury for the District of Massachusetts in the Circuit Court of the United States, for the said District, held in the Town of Boston, on the 12th of October, 1792, by the Hon. JAMES IREDELL, *Esq., one of the Associate Justices of the Supreme Court of the United States.*

GENTLEMEN OF THE GRAND JURY:—

In having the honor to address you for the first time in my judicial capacity, I do it with particular satisfaction at a period of so much dignity and prosperity to the United States. Perhaps in no country in the world have been within so few years exemplified such awful and important lessons. We have been taught, not only the value of Liberty, but what it was much more difficult to learn, that liberty itself, in order to be truly enjoyed, must submit to reasonable and considerate restraints. The unbounded liberty of the strongest man is tyranny to the weakest: The unlimited sway of a majority is oppression to the minority: Unlicensed indulgence to all the passions of men is an impious rejection of the control of reason which Providence has given for their government and direction.

True liberty certainly consists in such restraints, and no greater, on the actions of each particular individual as the common good of the whole requires. The exact medium it may be difficult to find, but we have reason to hope it is most likely to be found in that country which can draw forth, by the choice either direct or indirect of the people themselves, those characters for the immediate exercise of public trusts in whose abilities and integrity they can place the greatest confidence. The modifications under which this important good can be effected, we have the most reason to respect, when they have been deliberately formed, and solemnly ratified by a fair and adequate representation of that people for whose welfare they are, and ought alone to be intended. Such have been these governments, as well of the States separately, as of the United States, under which we have the happiness to live.

Many nations, both ancient and modern, have had the glory of acquiring and for some time of preserving liberty by the most noble and virtuous exertions. But *America*, I believe, furnished the first instance of a number of powerful and respectable States, impressed with the highest sense of liberty, voluntarily relinquishing large portions of power which they separately enjoyed, for the sake of forming a more perfect union for their future welfare. The success hath hitherto exceeded the most sanguine expectations. God grant, that no subsequent disappointment may weaken the effect of so magnanimous an example.

In consequence of this great revolution, more wonderful and not less glorious than the first, we have now two governments to which we owe obedience: The respective State Governments in all instances which concern the interests of each State singly: The Government of the United States in all instances which concern the interests of the Union at large. Each of these governments is sovereign and supreme, within the appropriated sphere of its authority. The common object of both is the happiness of all the citizens equally and without distinction, so far as it is possible for systems of government to secure it. The peculiar object of the government of the United States is to cement by an effective, not a nominal authority, that union to which, under divine Providence, we unquestionably owe all the blessings we now enjoy, and without a preservation of which we should too probably become a prey to intestine discord, and find ourselves the miserable victims of local and conflicting pursuits.

To consult the welfare of each citizen individually; the welfare of each State separately; the common welfare of the whole jointly; so far as they can all be rendered compatible; are great and noble objects, worthy of our most zealous care, and most unremitted attention. The task is certainly not easy, but we have no reason to fear it is altogether impracticable. Moderation and good sense, however, are necessary to perpetuate, as they were at first to assent to measures calculated to secure perhaps the greatest blessings ever devised by any human systems. Let each man consider, that his liberty and property cannot be secured without forming a common interest with all the other members of the society to which he belongs; that this common interest can only be protected by the co-operation of common councils, and a submission to laws framed to give them effect; and that as each State naturally and properly is the guardian of its own separate and individual interests, so the United States can alone rightfully determine in cases in which not one State singly, but all the States have a common and united concern. Providence has designed man for society, and those who either from pride or vanity, or any worse motive, refuse to yield to the conditions it indispensably requires, counteract so far as in them lies, the provisions of divine wisdom for the good order and government of mankind.

These principles should be ever present to our minds, and to a large majority I flatter myself they constantly will be, for I am persuaded the more they are attended to, the stronger will be their impression. An enlightened sense of the true interest of each individual will naturally lead him to a proper estimation of those principles best calculated to secure it. But it is in vain to expect, let us have what form of government we will, that the laws enacted under it, however wise and patriotic, will meet with universal, much less with respectful obedience. In all societies there will be bad men, whom no laws nor any principle can restrain; there will be weak men, easily misled by artful and imposing misrepresentations. Attempts may therefore be expected to undermine, if not to destroy the best constructed government which it is possible for human wisdom to form. When therefore a government is formed, one of the first duties incumbent upon it is to provide for its own preservation, by guarding against the machinations of evil men, either for its total destruction, or for any material injury to it in any of its operations.—This gives rise to what is usually termed *the Criminal Law;* a law which has for its object the punishment of bad actions, by which the security or welfare of the community is in any essential degree endangered.

This being the true and only proper object of the Criminal Law, it should be calculated to meet this danger, and this alone. At the same time that it is efficacious, it should be as mild as the nature of the case will admit of. In providing for the detection and punishment of the guilty, it should be careful to secure the safety, and guard the reputation of the innocent. It being one of the most awful concerns of human legislation, and that in which personal liberty and safety are more immediately interested than any other, the utmost attention ought in a very especial manner to be paid in this case, in order to prevent an abuse of authority entrusted for the most sacred purpose for which any authority can be. Every law on such a subject ought to be passed with the most trembling solicitude, lest any unfortunate individual should become the object of injustice or oppression.

The Constitution of the United States, distinguished as it is in all its parts for an invariable attention to a true and rational spirit of freedom, has not been inattentive to it in this its most important concern. It is not trusted solely to legislative discretion. Restrictions are imposed, in order to render secure, beyond the possibility of attack, the personal safety of the people in cases where it might otherwise be sometimes exposed to no small danger. A latitude of discretion, I believe, has been left in no instance where it could be safely avoided.

There is one crime in particular, which it was justly thought proper the constitution itself should define. That is, the crime of treason. This undoubtedly is the highest crime known in the law, because it aims at the subversion of the Government, and of course at the destruction of all the private happiness and public security derived from it. But at the same time, it is a crime in the prosecution of which great abuses are liable to be committed, if the government is left altogether without restraint, because usually the whole arm of power is exerted against the person accused, and therefore resentment may be apt to have too powerful an operation. In monarchies, where the person of the monarch is apparently if not directly the sole object of attack, a man under trial for this offence may frequently expect the sympathy of the people, who in such countries often suppose (and sometimes with great truth) that their interest and that of the monarch are far from being the same. But in a republic, where the government, the subversion of which is aimed at, is truly the government of the people, there may be great danger of the person accused being the object of a strong popular prejudice, as well as of a legal prosecution. If therefore there be at such a period any ambiguity in the definition of the crime, or the mode of trial be unfavorable to the security of the person exposed to it, there can be no reason to expect a fair and impartial trial. The constitution has guarded against the first danger, by a plain and express definition, clearly comprehending real, and not constructive acts of treason. Against the latter, it has not only used the precaution of particularly specifying the evidence which shall alone be sufficient for a conviction; but there is in common with all other crimes, the great and inestimable security of a trial by jury.

This excellent method of trial may, in respect to criminal cases, be considered as divided into two branches: 1. For the purpose of accusation. 2. For the final decision. The first, gentlemen, is the high and important character now devolved on you. No person is to be held to answer any capital or other infamous crime of a civil nature, committed within this district against the laws of the United States, except upon your presentment or indictment. Any person, without distinction, may, upon your authority, be put upon his trial for such. From your impartiality there is the utmost reason to expect that no prosecution will be commenced without grounds, or forborne from any undue motive. As members of the society yourselves, you will not fail to consider the necessity of a due maintenance of the laws of it. As men who may be affected by your own precedents, you will feel the importance of establishing none that may be applied to an oppressive purpose. These circumstances, in themselves so favorable to impartiality, added to the solemn obligation of duty, will naturally inspire the public with confidence, the guilty with terror, and save the innocent from alarm.

But, gentlemen, how noble is the thought, how consolatory the reflection, that after you have deliberately weighed, and solemnly presented, an accusation against any man, another trial yet remains, a public one, in the face of the accused; a trial by another jury of his fellow-citizens, with the full assistance of counsel, with the right and the opportunity of summoning witnesses for his defence, with the right also, in capital cases, of peremptorily challenging a large number of the jurors, called upon his trial (in treason thirty-five, in other capital offences, twenty), accompanied also with other privileges, I believe never granted in the same extent in any other laws, the having delivered not only a copy of the indictment and a list of the jury and witnesses in prosecution for treason, but a copy of the indictment and a list of the jury in other capital prosecutions, a certain time before the trial. In most cases of treason and misprision of treason, all these advantages exist in *England,* in their fullest extent. But in all other capital cases (astonishing as it is), at this very day, in that enlightened country, counsel are not allowed to speak to any but questions of law, and it is considered a matter of favor in the court, to permit them even to ask questions for the prisoner. It is indeed a most melancholy consideration, that long after liberty had been contended for, and to a great degree obtained, as to other objects, the personal safety of individuals should have been so little regarded. It was thought to require laws in *England,* some years after the revolution, in 1688 (one indeed even so late as Queen Anne), to entitle a prisoner to have witnesses examined on oath, in his defence. According to an iniquitous practice originally introduced, as there is great reason to believe, without any color of law, prisoners had not only been excluded from this privilege, but also from being allowed a full defence by counsel; and this unprincipled practice had so long prevailed, that it at length acquired the pretext of an unsurmountable prescription. Happy are that people whose liberties depend, not on the mercy or discretion of courts, but upon written provisions, too plain to be misunderstood, and protected in the most sacred manner, by guardians, too watchful and too powerful to be overcome!

The constitution itself, together with amendments to it, which have received the requisite consent, secures the invaluable benefits I have mentioned, of a trial by jury, of a public trial in the face of the accused, of having processes for witnesses, and the assistance of counsel. The other advantages enumerated, form part of the criminal code, derived from the Legislature alone, and partake of that discerning zeal, for the real security and true happiness of all the citizens, which so eminently distinguishes a government, founded on the very basis of freedom and justice.

Another protection, gentlemen, in laws whose spirit of mildness and liberality we cannot too much admire, is a limitation of time for the prosecution of offences. No capital offence (murder or forgery excepted) is to be prosecuted but within three years after the commission of it, nor any prosecution for any offence not capital, or for any fine or forfeiture under any penal statute, but within two years after the commission of the offence, or the incurring of the forfeiture. There is an exception, however, in both instances, of persons fleeing from justice. This also, in its extent, is an improvement, I believe, on former systems.

The crimes, gentlemen, of which you are to inquire, are crimes committed against the United States within this district. These are defined, and the punishments prescribed, in certain acts of Congress, passed in virtue of powers contained in the Constitution of the United States. They will be found, I trust, all of them congenial to the spirit of a free people, the principle of whose aim it invariably is, and ought to be, to unite all the energy necessary for the support of government, with an inflexible attention to the proper security and protection of individuals. It does not appear to me material now to point them out particularly to you, not only because I presume you are well acquainted with most if not all of them, and can have easy access to them, but because I have reason to hope you have no occasion at this time to present many, if any particular offences. The very favorable accounts I have every where heard, since I have had the pleasure of being on this circuit, of the good order and respectful submission to the laws which universally prevail in it, have given me the utmost satisfaction. In addition to my own personal observations, they have impressed me with the highest respect for a people who have had the good sense so happily to combine an invincible spirit of freedom, with an enlightened regard for such a government and such laws as can alone be adequate to secure it. May this excellent disposition for ever prevail! May it be rewarded with as much happiness as it is possible for men to enjoy! And may the true spirit of freedom and order united, actuate all virtuous citizens of the Union, to the end of time!!

IREDELL TO MRS. IREDELL.
BOSTON, Oct. 13th, '92.

MY DEAR HANNAH:—I would rather have deferred writing until to-morrow, but Judge Lowell has pressed me to go to his house in the country, and probably I may do so, though I shall endeavor to await the arrival of the post. * * * I went to the ball Thursday evening. Very few ladies (only about 24), which was partly owing to many families having sickness or being in distress, and partly to a kind of etiquette many ladies have here of not going the first night. There were many more gentlemen, but scarcely any lady or gentleman of my acquaintance. I danced down two dances, and that was all. All the ladies were handsomely dressed, and there were at least six beauties out of the small number present, and several more that were nearly such, &c.

Oct. 14th.

I went out with Judge Lowell, and have just returned from his house. Mrs. Lowell seemed very glad to see me, and expressed a great desire to see you there. I write this by Mr. John Coffin Jones, one of the gentlemen Mr. Anthony introduced me to, and who has been particularly kind indeed. I hope you will see him, and if you do, be as civil to him as you can. He is a man you will be much pleased with, &c., &c.

Oct. 21st.

Judge Wilson arrived here yesterday evening. * * * I have been excessively fatigued the last week. One cause alone lasted almost the whole of it, and we did not break up yesterday till in the night. I have constantly received the utmost distinction and courtesy here, and like Boston more and more. One practice is very pleasing. One or more of the clergy are constantly invited to all entertainments, and when too many gentlemen are not unavoidably invited, there is a mixture of ladies and gentlemen. It is scarcely possible to meet with a gentleman who is not a man of education. Such are the advantages of schools by public authority! Every township is obliged to maintain one or more, to which poor children can have access without any pay. A very pleasing instance happened here lately. A poor man's son, who had been at school, discovering an uncommon genius and propensity to learning, a number of gentlemen subscribed and sent him to the University, where he now is. From every account I can collect, there is almost as much order and complete obedience among the people, as to all public concerns, as there usually is in other countries in private families. I am satisfied so much regularity and decency do not exist in any other country in the world, as in Connecticut and Massachusetts; and I suppose it is much the same in New Hampshire. Rhode Island, I believe, is not on a par, but much improving. The clergy here, whom I have seen, are in general sensible, well-bred, and agreeable men, &c., &c.

EXETER, NEW HAMPSHIRE, Oct. 25th, '92.

We left Boston on Monday morning, and after spending Tuesday at a very agreeable and considerable town, Newbury Port, about 45 miles from Boston, came on here yesterday. I met in Boston with a gentleman who lives in Newbury Port, of the name of Parsons, *who appears to me to be the first lawyer I have met with in America, and is a remarkably agreeable man.** He insisted on my visiting him, and on our arrival invited Judge Wilson also, and we received great civilities from him and Mrs. Parsons, who seems a very amiable woman. There was also another gentleman there, an agreeable man, of the name of Jackson, and to whom we had a letter from Judge Lowell, who was particularly obliging to us; we spent an evening with him. Mr. Parsons came on with us here, and we shall probably return with him. I don't think I should have left this country so soon, as I was desirous of seeing more of it, but Judge Wilson wishes to press on immediately to Newport, as he has some important business, which makes him anxious to be as near Philadelphia as possible. I think I shall spend most of my leisure in Boston, till near the time of going to Providence. I am in a manner domesticated there in several families. Many parts of this country are pleasing, but still not equal to Connecticut. Newbury Port is a pleasant situation, very near the sea. Salem (about 15 miles from Boston) is a much prettier place than I expected. Peter is well, &c. &c.

BOSTON, Oct. 25th.

Judge Wilson and myself returned here yesterday evening from New Hampshire. * * * I do indeed find every part of this country highly agreeable, and it would be perfectly so were you and my children with me. As it is, I assure you, Philadelphia would be much more so. Judge Wilson talks of going to Rhode Island on Tuesday. But I don't think I can leave Boston so soon. * * * I refused a seat in a coach with a very fine young lady, to come home and write this letter. However I must go and drink tea with her, &c., &c.

BOSTON, November 1st.

I like Boston so well that I shall stay till Monday next. I went on Tuesday to Cambridge to see a quarterly exhibition, and was much pleased. One or two of the young gentlemen distinguished themselves very much, and I liked extremely well all I saw of the College. I had the honor of dining with the Committee and Corporation of the College, and being seated next to the Lieutenant Governor, the famous Samuel Adams, who though an old man has a great deal of fire yet. He is polite and agreeable. *I think he is the very image of the pictures I have seen of Oliver Cromwell.* I am to dine with a very agreeable family to-day, where I dined once before—with the Governor to-morrow, and at Cambridge on Saturday. I spent yesterday evening at a gentleman's house, where there were a number of ladies and gentlemen, among others Mrs. Hancock, the Governor's wife, whom I had not seen before. She is rather handsome, and uncommonly pleasing; her manners altogether untinctured with any pride or affectation. Mr. Jones arrived the evening before last; but, as I was that night at Judge Lowell's and we missed each other on reciprocal visits yesterday, I did not see him till this evening. * * * * James's being at the head of his class greatly delighted me. I have been very near telling it to several, &c.

PROVIDENCE, November 5th, '92.

I arrived here this evening extremely well. This Court does not begin until Wednesday, and I find there is a great deal of business to do. Judge Wilson is at Newport, but I expect to see him here to-morrow night. I continued to the last moment to receive the greatest courtesies in Boston, and was not a little affected in parting from it. The Governor (*Hancock*) insisted on my naming a day to dine, and spend the evening with him. I named Friday, and he invited a very numerous and genteel company of ladies and gentlemen, and some of them danced. Though so infirm as to be carried by his servants from room to room he was in high spirits; and, at parting, as he did yesterday again when I waited on him, not only expressed a great desire to see me again, but requested me to recommend any of my friends, I might please, to his attention. So did many others, &c., &c.

JAS. IREDELL.*

IREDELL TO REV. A. IREDELL.
PHILADELPHIA, November 30th, 1792.

MY DEAR BROTHER:—Upon my return here from the Eastern Circuit on Friday last I had the pleasure to find your letter of the 31st of July. I passed my time in my absence very agreeably indeed. Sickness prevented my attendance at New York, but I was at the Courts in Connecticut, Massachusetts, New Hampshire and Rhode Island. The country in general is a very fine one: the habits of the people, particularly in the three

---

* Theophilus Parsons, afterwards Chief Justice of Massachusetts.

* With Judge Iredell's papers is a list, in his handwriting, "of families in Boston and vicinity to whom I am under great obligations for civilities."

former States, industrious and virtuous in a very great degree, and nearly as much order prevails as I believe the condition of human nature will admit of. The gentlemen generally have an extraordinary degree of liberality, even on religious subjects; and at the same time, they are perhaps more untinged with infidelity or an indifference about religion altogether, than any other set of men of condition in any other country. The people are strongly and zealously attached to the Government of the United States: even Rhode Island itself, which State I am told has been principally brought over to a degree of content by the decisions and manner of doing business of the Courts of the United States, is in every respect infinitely better than it was. The principal men, who were borne down in *paper-money* times, are beginning to recover their influence; a strong proof of which is, that all the members of Congress in both Houses are now what we call Federalists. More discontent prevails in the Southern States, but I think it is every day lessening; and, very possibly, the horrid confusions in France will bring many to their senses who now seem to be out of them. I spent near three weeks altogether in Boston, where I met with the most distinguished attention. They absolutely made me sick with too great a profusion of good things, the only circumstance I had to complain of. But their hospitality was truly genuine, mixed with a cordiality and kindness that could not be mistaken. In other places, also, we met with the greatest politeness. There is no country in the world where education is so general. * * * *

Instead of the narrow and illiberal spirit, which formerly prevailed so much in Boston, all the Clergy (except a Roman Catholic priest, a convert from *Protestantism*) have generous and enlarged minds, mix on a sociable footing with each other, and have as noble sentiments of indulgence to a real difference in religious opinions as can be expected from any men sincerely attached to a religion they cherish. They are also treated with high respect by the inhabitants. I scarcely dined at any table upon invitation without one or more of the Clergy—a circumstance, I think, of reciprocal advantage to them and their associates, &c., &c.
JAS. IREDELL.

REV. A. IREDELL TO IREDELL.

No. 11 QUEEN'S BUILDINGS, BROMPTON, December 4th.

DEAR BROTHER:— * * * * * You know in this country how much we are the slaves of ceremony. How long we shall continue so I know not. All slavery, it seems, is to be crushed "a la mode de Paris." God forbid it! that we should ape such examples! And yet some Englishmen certainly do. You will hear, I cannot report, a thousand strange stories. Our Ministry have at length been roused into action. The Tower of London is strengthened: many of its so long vacant apartments are now tenanted. The King has dismissed from the Army Lord Temple and Lord Edward Fitzgerald, who had shown violent symptoms of disaffection to his government. Troops are collecting round the Metropolis. A Fleet is equipping. Some of the militia are called out; and Parliament is to meet next week. Besides these precautions, people friendly to the present state of things are associating in many places, and will probably in all. May their cause prosper! I approved in its birth, and continue to admire, *your* Republic. The French one is a monster—"informe, ingens, cui lumen ademptum." I too am grown enthusiastic about Burke. He had disgusted me by matters that cannot have reached you; but I forget them all when I read one page of his late writings. By the bye, I am told, your Charge has been in the Papers, but there is no buying an old Paper, nor can I get at the title of the one or more in which it was printed, &c., &c.
A. IREDELL.

In this year the people were much agitated by alarming reports of a nefarious design to subvert the Government, and to establish a monarchy upon its ruins. The Federalists charged that the sole foundation for the rumors were Mr. Jefferson's letter to Washington urging him to consent to a re-election, and certain articles in Frenau's Paper; and that they were the offspring of an imagination heated by party fury, or the spectres of a troubled dream. The undisguised fears of many of the Federalists that the Government could not last, and that it carried in its bosom the seed of its own dissolution; and the avowed opinion of some of their leaders that it was not strong enough, though accompanied with the declaration that they would give it a fair trial, and honest support, constituted for the suspicious a reasonable basis for uneasy apprehension.

The Revolution had liberated men from political dependence upon Great Britain tbut as regards a considerable and cultivated portion of the citizens of the North, it had not emancipated them morally from English influence. They doubted the capacity of the people for self-government; and holding up the light of history, when they would penetrate the future, could only see by its flickering rays, the monstrous form of anarchy, or the sword of a military despot. As a matter of speculation, in such a case, they would take refuge under the shadow of a throne. It cannot, however, be credited that any respectable number of the people regarded the establishment of a monarchy as an object of immediate desire, or looked to its future erection with any settled, practical view.

The following ironical essay of Judge Iredell, though without date, I refer to this period.

MARKS OF ARISTOCRACY IN CONNECTICUT.

1. All the men in that State, almost, are land-holders, as they have never chosen in that country to have a few aristocratical characters, but a great many. This spirit their laws have carefully preserved, making their lands inheritable by all the children, and not by him who happens to be eldest only.

2. Education is provided, at the public expense, for all the children in the State, the *poor* as well as the *rich*, by which means many of these *poor* have a chance of becoming rich, and of course the aristocratical interest is increased.

3. Their lands, as well as personal property, are liable to the payment of debts. This very much tends to keep up the aristocratical spirit in the country, because as it enables creditors to receive their debts fully there is no danger of the creditor being diminished by the dishonesty of the debtor.

4. Except at the beginning of the American War, when they ran mad as well as the rest of their countrymen, they have always been lovers of good order, as well as liberty. Thus every man being secure in his estate, he had a great encouragement to make it better, and of course himself richer; which all tended to the same point: *the establishment of a general and formidable aristocratical interest.*

5. They have always been remarkable for quiet and regularity at their elections. They never would suffer any man to offer himself as a candidate, or make interest for any place. Owing to this cause, they have generally chosen the most experienced men of the most distinguished families, to the great discouragement of promising young men of genius, who with more fire and patriotic ardor might have infused a stronger portion of *Radical Assafœtida* into the political cup.

6. They are almost to a man attached to the present General Government. They have been weak enough to re-elect every one of their own Members who was willing to serve. They foolishly take it for granted, that all men, though entitled to *equal protection*, are not in all other respects equal; they believe in the exploded doctrine that men are born with different capacities and different dispositions, that their conduct is generally very much influenced by the education they receive, the company they keep, and the habits they are accustomed to: that there are, therefore, bad men as well as good, and some neutral characters, scarcely one or the other; and consequently, that laws are necessary to prevent or punish mischief which may arise to the public from the ill conduct of any individuals. They believe that the General Government can do no good without some efficient powers; that debts cannot be paid without revenue; nor laws be of any efficacy unless they are obeyed. They thus entirely disregard the modern doctrine, that liberty is no liberty unless it is altogether without restraint; that man is too noble an animal to be meddled with; and that, as it has been often supposed, if there were no physicians there would be no diseases, so (improving upon all ancient maxims) *if there was no restraint at law* (the very idea of which is so revolting) *every citizen of America would be a virtuous and inflexible patriot, neither do any private or any public mischief, and would voluntarily contribute his full proportion of the necessary revenue of his country.*

7. Every one of their Electors has lately voted for the present Vice-President, a man generally considered at the head of the *aristocratical interest.* They are attached to him principally on this account, not having had the sagacity to see through the deepest hypocrisy of which we have yet had an example in America. This gentleman from his very infancy has been remarkable for a studious, contemplative, and orderly disposition: was an eminent lawyer, in good practice, when the American War began, esteemed highly for his professional abilities, and for his private virtues, and was apparently in a happy and enviable situation. Nevertheless, when it was necessary to quarrel with Great Britain he was among the most active in the most dangerous scenes, in his own State and in the United States, and served abroad with great acceptation in different Courts in Europe, and is supposed to have had no small share in procuring the late Peace, and particularly in securing an important article (the Fisheries) to this country. Accordingly no man was more highly respected in his country than himself. But, behold! such is the weakness, such the vice of man! The secret at length came out, and what was still more wonderful, with a kind of *Irish folly* it was told by *himself.* He wrote a book on the American Constitutions, of which the principal tendency appeared to be, to show the danger of having Republican Constitutions too much of the Democratical form, and the advantage of having *different Bodies of Legislation,* an *Executive* not entirely dependent on the *Legislature,* and a *Judiciary* independent of both. To show this general position he ransacked with the most wicked industry all histories ancient and modern, and must have pored over others

which no man with a good design in view would have ever looked into. He did not directly say, that we must have a King, Lords and Commons, but he praised very much the theory of a government in Europe of that kind; and he insinuated, that if we had not a much greater portion of good sense and virtue than other countries *those Conventions which hitherto had formed must alter our Constitutions*, or they would not be found sufficient to guard against anarchy and confusion. This we have indeed already done. The present General Government has been since formed : so have some State Constitutions; and all made *stronger*. Thus far Mr. A. has proved a true prophet, if he only *predicted*, and did not *secretly occasion*, these changes. There are still, however, symptoms of weakness in the General Government, and some shrewdly suspect that Mr. A. has furtively fomented the present discontent against the Government, and even against his own re-election, on purpose that it may be found no other expedient will answer than by other Conventions of the 13 States to abolish Republicanism altogether in America, and elect him King, in which no doubt all the discontented party will join, although they would not have him for Vice-President. This is a scheme deeper than I am afraid the Connecticut patriots have genius to comprehend; otherwise, I am sure, they never would have voted for him as Vice-President, they being, I am persuaded, as averse to monarchy as they are friendly to aristocracy; but I hope, as the matter is now made public, that previous to their voting for him at the next election, they will require him to give security that if he should be elected King he will not accept.

CHAPTER XXVI.

Æt. 41—42.

CHISHOLM VS. GEORGIA. UNITED STATES VS. RAVARA. CIRCUIT COURT AT ANNAPOLIS. ADDRESS TO GRAND JURY. CIRCUIT COURT AT RICHMOND. WARE VS. HYLTON. LETTER FROM JUDGE BEE. THE YELLOW FEVER IN PHILADELPHIA. LETTERS FROM DR. DUFFIELD, LUTHER MARTIN, AND PIERCE BUTLER.

SUPREME COURT. February Term.
CHISHOLM, Executor, vs. GEORGIA.

At the February Term, 1793, this case was brought on for argument. "This great case excited an unusual degree of attention, both on account of the novelty of the questions raised and the important political consequences that were supposed to be involved in the decision. The doctrine of State Sovereignty and State Rights was for the first time brought before the Court for discussion. The question was, whether a State was amenable to the jurisdiction of the Supreme Court, at the suit of a citizen of another State—a question which might resolve itself into another no less radical than this: 'Do the United States constitute a nation?' Chisholm, a citizen of South Carolina, had brought an action against the State of Georgia, by service of process upon the Governor and Attorney General of that State. Georgia refused to appear, and now Randolph, the Attorney General of the United States, moved that unless Georgia caused her appearance to be entered by the next term, judgment should be rendered against her by default, and a writ of inquiry issue. No case of a similar kind had yet been brought before the Court for adjudication. The State of Georgia refused to recognize the jurisdiction even so far as to appear upon the argument, but presented by Dallas and Ingersoll a written remonstrance and protestation." The motion was granted by the Court. The views of his colleagues were not concurred in by Judge Iredell. "That able jurist considered the question also in a constitutional point of view, and

as a question of strict construction. With great force of reasoning, and admirable precision and clearness of illustration, he analyzed the argument of the Attorney General, and arrived at exactly the opposite conclusion. His opinion was that no part of the existing law applied to this case; and even if the Constitution would admit of the exercise of such a power, a new law was necessary to carry the power into effect, and that assumpsit at the suit of a citizen would not lie against a State. One can scarcely arise from a careful perusal of this able opinion without being sensibly impressed with the force of the reasoning of the learned Judge, and the accuracy of his deductions;—lucid, logical, compact, comprehensive, it certainly compares very favorably with that of the Chief Justice, in every respect, and *as a mere legal argument must be admitted to be far superior.*"*

Hildreth, the historian, says: "The case seems to be plain enough, since, by the terms of the Constitution, the jurisdiction was given in so many express words:" again, "Judge Iredell, who *seemed* to lean against the jurisdiction, wished to *escape* a decision on an objection to the form of the action." Such statements are, hardly, fair and ingenuous. The authors of the Federalist had, a few years before, declared such a jurisdiction to be without *a color of foundation.*† In the Virginia Convention, June 2d, 1788, John Marshall, afterwards so justly celebrated, had said: "I hope that no gentleman will think *that a State will be called at the Bar of the Federal Court.*" "It is not rational to suppose, *that the Sovereign power shall be dragged before a Court.*"‡ That Judge Iredell had a very clear and decided opinion against the jurisdiction of the Court is not to be doubted. In his "Answers to Mr. Mason's Objections," January, 1788, page 3, are these words: "*In parting with the coercive authority over the States as States there must be a coercion as to individuals. The former power no man of common sense can any longer seriously contend for.*" Almost to the same effect, in his opinion pronounced in this cause, he remarked: "The powers of the General Government, either of a Legislative or Executive nature, or which particularly concern treaties with Foreign Powers, do for the most part (if not wholly) affect individuals, and not States:" "this is the great leading distinction between the old articles of confederation, and the present constitution."§ In addition, his opinion, certainly a masterpiece of judicial reason-

* Van Santvoord's Lives of the Chief Justices. Judge Jay's opinion is the most elaborate ever delivered by him.
† Federalist. Kent's Commentaries.
‡ Elliott's Debates, Vol. 3, p. 505.
§ 2d Dallas.

ing, was in accord with the views, generally, if not universally, held at the South by Federalists as well as Antifederalists: in that section it met with the warmest commendation, the most generous applause.

The decision of the Court "created much excitement in the public mind at the time. The subject was at once brought before several of the State Legislatures, and an amendment of the Constitution proposed. The advocates of State rights viewed the decision as a direct attack upon the sovereignty of the States. Georgia openly defied the federal authority, and refused to enter her appearance. The Supreme Court however stood firm. At the February Term, 1794, judgment was rendered against the State by default, and a writ of inquiry awarded. Where the controversy would have ended, it is impossible to conjecture, had not the question been put at rest by a speedy amendment of the Constitution, which declared that the jurisdiction of the Supreme Court should not extend to suits against a State by citizens of another State, or subjects of a foreign State."*

The opinion of Judge Iredell enunciates either directly or by implication the leading principles of what has been since known as the "State Rights Doctrine." Extreme federalists, in determining the character of State Sovereignty, look chiefly to the Constitution itself, and resting upon the declaration of its preamble, "We the people of the United States," &c., "do ordain and establish this Constitution," regard it somewhat in the light of a mere *abstraction*. The application of force to refractory *Southern* States has been a cherished idea of prominent New England politicians; and a threat has been made by their ablest representative, in a certain contingency, to test by experiment "whether the Union be a mere rope of sand," losing sight of the great fact that a violent remedy would be the death of the patient, and that subjection by force of arms would be in itself the subversion of republicanism. In consequence of some essential differences in their mental and moral constitutions, the men of the Eastern States are wont to regard the Constitution as an instrument, not to be construed strictly as a penal statute, but liberally because beneficent in its nature; and in their desire to promote the good of majorities, to neglect the interests, happiness, and independence of individuals: on the contrary, the men of the South, in measuring the Sovereignty of the States, do not simply look to the Constitution, because, in the language of Judge Iredell, "A State does not owe its origin to the Government of the United States: it was in existence before it," but regard the records of the past as establishing as a great *historical fact* that

* Van Santvoord.

the Government is *a confederacy of sovereign States*, and not a Government of one, undivided people ; they insist upon a *strict* construction of the Constitution ; are jealous of the rights of minorities ; and inclined to expect the greatest general good from the action of many individuals, each seeking his individual good in proper subordination to law, rather than by the efforts of associated power, either numerical or pecuniary. The tendency of the masses at the North is towards an *unmixed democracy :* the conservatism of the South, in its attachment *to representative republicanism*, is more manifest and confirmed every day.

Colonel Davie, one of the framers of the Constitution, and one of the most eminent Federalists in the South, in a letter to Judge Iredell, made the following comments upon the decision of the Supreme Court :—

"I confess I read some of these arguments and particularly that by Mr. Wilson with astonishment : however, the scope and propriety of this elaborate production called an argument, were expressly reserved for the contemplation of 'a *few*, a *very few* comprehensive minds ;' and, perhaps, notwithstanding the tawdry ornament and poetical imagery with which it is loaded and bedizened, it may still be very ' profound.' On this I shall give no opinion ; but as a law argument it has certainly the merit of being truly '*original*.' His definition of the American States as sovereignties is more like an epic poem than a Judge's argument, and we look in vain for legal principles or logical conclusions.

"The illustration which he has drawn from the relation of the word subject to the word sovereign, as contradistinguished from the appellation of *citizen*, as the correlative of the American Government, is no better than a contemptible play upon words, like his 'collection of original sovereigns :' indeed, speaking professionally, or as he says '*politically* and *classically*,' this whole argument of his seems to be the rhapsody of some visionary theorist, and entirely unworthy of my former idea of that man.

"Mr. Jay, whose talents appear to be of a superior cast, and whose argument is undoubtedly more solid and ingenious, appears to be also taken by the novelty of this idea, and gravely gives his sanction to the solecism of 'sovereigns without subjects'— that is, without sovereignty. To use the style of Mr. Wilson, ' this transcendentally sublime' antithesis seems to be transplanted from some speech in the Jacobin Club, or the satire of Peter Pindar, and looks quite like an exotic in his Honor's argument.

"The supposed spirit or design of the Constitution is a dangerous guide in a case of this sort, where mere general principles or objects are expressed in general terms : there is no doubt but the contract of a State may raise a *moral* obligation ; but it does not follow, that although it would be '*honest*' to comply voluntarily with such contract, that it would be *wise* or *useful* for the Federal Government to enforce it. The policy of no nation has gone so far as to enforce every *moral* obligation ; and the instances where matters of mere *moral right* have submitted to the policy of institutions, or the general interests of the community, are numerous even in the municipal laws of our own country ; and with respect to maintaining suits of this kind against a State, I am not only clear there is no authority beyond the opinion of the Court for such a doctrine, but that it is neither warranted by necessity nor policy."*

Rev. A. Iredell to Iredell.

London, March 5th, 1793.

My dear Brother :— * * * * These are pleasant subjects to sport with. Would I met with no other ! but in this horrid age how scarcely is domestic happiness the lot of any description of men ! In France—alas ! what humiliation, persecution, tortures, and finally death ! to the most elevated, yet most virtuous—and so downwards through all ranks. In that immense Kingdom, has *one* adult out of twenty-four millions of people known domestic peace during the last six months ? What an idea of extended misery does this present ! for the fact is not *one* sound mind has been at rest : it has been employed in machinating mischief or avoiding it, in ruining his countrymen or in flying from ruin and assassination himself, or in a defence of others, or in a more dreadful solicitude and uncertainty about them. The world is at war with them. Is not Heaven at war with them ? Most assuredly it is. The measure of their crimes is full ; and the wisdom of Providence will soon be conspicuous in the restoration of order, and peace ; resting, probably, upon a more sure foundation than the old state of things could possibly have afforded under any *modification*. The convulsion of all Europe may have been therefore necessary ; but the Eye that saw, and the strong Arm that brought it about, will see and will bring about only what is desirable and best. The passions of men are ready means by which great events may be matured : when matured, they cease to have any avail. However, I must not attempt profound subjects, and especially as I now do "stans pede in uno." I will only rejoice that the conduct of

* Letter dated June 12th.

America at this time is so strictly neutral. But it is high time I should change my posture, &c. A. IREDELL.

At the April Term of the Circuit Court for Pennsylvania, Wilson, Iredell, and Peters, present, the case of the United States *vs.* Ravara came on for argument. The defendant, a Consul from Genoa, was indicted for sending threatening letters to Hammond, the British Minister, &c. A motion was made by the defendant to quash the indictment, on the ground that the Supreme Court of the United States had exclusive cognizance of the case, on account of his official character. The majority of the Court rejected the motion. Judge Iredell dissented, because it appeared to him, "that, for obvious reasons of public policy, the Constitution intended to vest an exclusive jurisdiction in the Supreme Court, upon all questions relating to the public agents of foreign nations ;" and because "the context of the judiciary article of the constitution seemed fairly to justify the interpretation, that the word *original* meant *exclusive* jurisdiction."*

Rev. A. Iredell to Iredell.

Brighthelmstone, April 29.

Dear Brother :— * * * * The wretched country, beyond the channel that rolls under my window, is every new day more distracted than before. Dumouriez, who was the life of her bad cause, has deserted. She is shedding the blood of her citizens, without law, or the semblance of it, to protect any one life among so many millions. Such a state of anarchy is unprecedented, and must have tremendous consequences. Our condition has of late been made very distressing in every part of the kingdom by a sudden check to the immense paper credit, which had, I believe, been carried much too far ; but should have been, if possible, gradually discountenanced. The Bank effected it in a moment by refusing to discount as it had been accustomed to do. Judge how this must have operated in a capital, where it formerly discounted, I am told, three hours in the day, and each hour, upon an average, to the amount of £500,000. Bankruptcies innumerable have followed this check in the necessary supply of cash, which had been made to flow only through that channel. One of our frigates, however, has lately retaken a register ship, and the French privateer which captured her, both of which, they say, are worth a million of money. So who's afraid ? &c., &c. A. IREDELL.

* 2 Dallas.

Iredell to Mrs. Iredell.*

Baltimore, May 5th, '93.

My dear Hannah :—I arrived here very well yesterday afternoon, after passing most execrable roads. This morning I had the honor to breakfast with the famous Antifederalist, Luther Martin, the Attorney-General of this State, and am to go in company with him to-morrow to Annapolis.† I have just come from church, where I heard Mr. Bond preach, with his usual excellence. I find he is a very great and general favorite here. I am to dine with Buchanan. * * * Give my respects to Mrs. Bond and her amiable daughter. It is a great consolation to me that you live so near those kind and charming ladies. I hear lottery-tickets have gone up to ten dollars, &c.

JAS. IREDELL.

Gov. Johnston to Iredell.

Williamston, 9th May, '93.

Dear Sir :—I wrote you a few days since from Hayes. I am now at my little "Hermitage," in the neighborhood of this town. I cannot say I am settled : I yet want many things to make it comfortable. We are, however, all well ; and the solitude and tranquillity which exist on all sides are very grateful to me, after the scenes of hurry and business upon which I have turned my back. I shall have sufficient to engage my attention the remainder of my days in improving this little spot, and adding every year something, either of beauty or convenience, to it. I have an opinion that nothing in life gives a man more satisfaction than improvements, planned and executed by himself. The more rude and uncultivated a situation is, the greater the scope for the play of the imagination in schemes of improvement, which, if never carried fully into effect, will answer the purpose of keeping the mind in action. My health improves surprisingly, the effect of much exercise, &c. SAM. JOHNSTON.

Iredell to Mrs. Iredell.

Baltimore, May 16th, '93.

My dear Hannah :—Mr. Jay arrived here the day before yesterday, and we are to set off in the stage to-morrow together.

* Judge Iredell resided, at this time, at 189 South Third Street, Philadelphia.
† Though Mr. Martin had opposed the adoption of the United States Constitution, he subsequently became so noted as a *Federalist* as to be styled by Mr. Jefferson, "the federal bull-dog." If character can be inferred from letters to Judge Iredell would seem to corroborate Judge Story's opinion of "that compound of strange qualities."

vol. ii—25

I am glad the time is so near, for I am heartily tired of the idle life I have led here, and my time has passed for the most part very dully, though I have experienced a good deal of civility. I drank tea one afternoon with Mr. and Mrs. Bond. They have a most delightful situation, and an excellent house. They both look well, and seem very happy. Mrs. B. says she likes Baltimore better than Philadelphia. Mr. Bond last Sunday preached a charity sermon for the benefit of the widows and orphans of clergymen; it was an admirable one, and produced $200. His church, every Sunday morning, is crowded. Bishop Carroll carried me to the Roman Catholic church to see an exceedingly fine picture, just come from Rome. It is a copy of one of Raphael's, and represents our Saviour appearing to the Apostles after the Resurrection. All the figures are very striking; and when I saw it, I could not help lamenting that the great zeal against the Roman religion should have occasioned so much indifference about fine paintings on religious subjects, for certainly they are great helps to devotion, and are very useful in impressing more strongly the great events they are calculated to represent. Bishop Carroll lives next door to Mr. Bond, and, I am told, they are on very friendly terms.

I waited on the new French Minister here, in company with many other gentlemen, and was very much pleased with him, as were, I believe, all the rest. He is a very handsome man, with a fine open countenance, and pleasing, unaffected manners. He spoke highly of the courtesies he had received on his journey,* &c.
JAS. IREDELL.

The Circuit Court was opened at Annapolis by the Chief Justice and Judge Iredell, when the latter delivered the following charge to the Grand Jury:

GENTLEMEN OF THE GRAND JURY :—

It is a custom, I believe, founded in great utility, that before you enter on the performance of your duty, after being sworn to the faithful discharge of it, you should meditate for a few moments at least on its high importance. In a country which happily is governed by law, and by that alone, and in which no distinction as to rights is made between one individual and another, no trust can be of more consequence to the community than that which holds in an impartial balance the scale of justice between the public on the one hand, and individuals on the other. The security of each individual consists in a due obedience being either voluntarily paid, or properly enforced, to the laws framed

* Mons. Genêt.

by common consent for the common welfare of the whole, and in those laws being administered in such a manner as to be a terror only to the guilty, and a protection to the innocent. This impartiality, which ought in all countries to prevail in the administration of public justice, ought to be attended to with the utmost possible strictness in a republic, the very basis of whose government it is that no one man is superior to another, but the law is superior to all. She is the depository of the common happiness and security of all the citizens. Without her voice none ought to be condemned. From her awful censure none ought to be exempted.

The peculiarity of our political situation, which requires essential duties to be performed, not only as citizens of a single State, but as citizens of the United States, should be frequently revolved in our minds, in order that we may comprehend its true nature and importance. It has arisen from a necessity we have all felt, and from an anxiety, in which I trust we all participate, the necessity of maintaining a strong and cordial union with each other, and an anxiety to promote the real and effective purposes of that union by the best means calculated to secure it. However we may have differed in opinion as to the means, the end has certainly been long the object of the most anxious solicitude in every part of the United States. It has been, I believe, as generally as justly thought, that the mischiefs of disunion, however lightly contemplated at a distance, would upon an unhappy experience be felt in a manner we should have eternal reason to regret. To prevent so great a calamity, rendered too probable by former examples, and of which we had in some degree felt the symptoms among ourselves, the present Constitution of the United States was formed.

The objects of this constitution being solely the preservation and security of the Union, it in no instance interferes with the internal regulations of any State, in cases which concern the interests of such State only. There are therefore two governments to which we owe obedience: the State government to which we particularly belong, in all instances which concern the interests of the State alone; the government of the United States in all instances which concern the interests of the Union at large. Each of these governments deserves our equal confidence and respect. Each is calculated to promote, though in different ways, the security of those blessings we have here the happiness to enjoy. Both are restricted within those bounds which the people have thought proper to prescribe, and neither can violate, without violating a most sacred duty, the peculiar province of the other.

The formation of the Criminal Law of the United States, as distinguished from that of each State in particular, would naturally have devolved (as it must do in every government where power is unrestricted) upon the Legislature alone, if the constitution had not imposed restrictions on this authority, calculated to prevent its possible abuse. It may be interesting to inquire into the nature of these restrictions, and to see upon what footing the Legislative authority of the United States is placed.

The following are the restrictions which the constitution (including amendments to it which have received the requisite consent) has provided.

1. "The privilege of the writ of *habeas corpus* shall not be suspended, unless when in cases of rebellion or invasion the public safety may require it."

The nature of a *habeas corpus*, so far as concerns our present subject, is well known. It is a writ which upon an application of a prisoner he is entitled to, in order that he may be brought before some legal authority, and the cause of his commitment examined, in consequence of which, if entitled to a discharge or to bail, he is to be discharged or bailed as the case requires, otherwise to be remanded, to be proceeded against further as the law directs. The many thousand instances which have taken place at one time or other in every country in Europe, of arbitrary and unjust imprisonment, by which innocence has been basely sacrificed, sometimes to motives of unprincipled policy, and not unfrequently to the gratification of mere private malice, or for the purpose even of family or personal convenience, might well excite the vigilant precaution of a free and enlightened people, although they had been uniformly distinguished in their own country by a happy exemption from such tyranny and oppression. A practice of this kind, indeed, would be at this time so abhorrent to the feelings of the most callous mind, that it certainly could not be indulged without meeting universal resentment and indignation. But what precaution can be too great, where personal liberty is concerned, the natural and just claim of every honest man, unoffending against the laws of his country? There may, however, be occasions where the public danger is so imminent, that a power of discretionary imprisonment may for a time be necessary to save the public from destruction. Such critical emergencies have been in all countries. We well recollect periods of the late war when this authority was indispensable. The occasions named in the exception must be admitted to be such where a discretionary power may be necessary to be lodged. It can, however, I apprehend, even then be alone authorized by an express act of the legislative body, who for their own sakes as well as the safety of their constituents, will take good care that the authority never shall be allowed but where the danger shall be imminent, and the necessity real indeed; and a severe responsibility will be annexed to the exercise of it, proportionate to the detestation in which an abuse of so formidable a power would be held by every virtuous mind.

2. "No bill of attainder or *ex post facto* act shall be passed."

An act of attainder may be defined to be, an act of a legislative body deciding in a single case, upon mere arbitrary discretion, on the life or fortune of an individual. The very definition of the power shows of what an outrageous nature it is. No trial by jury, no certainty of defence, no security in innocence. All those guards against injustice which have been wisely established in all other cases, are taken away in this, the most dangerous of any, in which a bare majority of a legislative body, governing themselves by no rule, and under the influence of violent party prejudices, too apt to sway even virtuous minds, may rashly take away the life of the most innocent man. Justly has so despotic a power been rejected by our constitution, which takes care not only of whole classes of men, but also of each individual, whose rights are deemed too sacred to be left to the mercy of any party upon pretexts easily assumed, and naturally susceptible of abuse, and which have in fact been productive of the grossest abuses in countries where such a power was possessed.

An act of attainder is in some degree, and that indeed very essentially, an *ex post facto* law, since it subjects a man accused of a crime, not to an ordinary trial, and a fixed punishment, but to a legislative condemnation, which may be without a trial at all, and to a punishment altogether discretionary. But as it usually, if not always, proceeds upon the presumption of the commission of a capital crime, which the ordinary proceedings at law for some cause or other are not competent to reach, it may naturally enough stand as a case upon its own footing, and as some respectable law books tell us, may rather be regarded as a sentence than a law. An *ex post facto* law, so far as it respects crimes (its only meaning we have now occasion to consider), means, as I understand it, a law that in any manner alters the consequences of an act from what they were at the time when the act was done, whether the action at the time was wholly innocent and afterwards made criminal, or was at the time criminal in a less degree than it was made by the legislative act afterwards passed. The same principles of regard to private rights which occasioned the rejection of acts of attainder, naturally dictated a rejection of every species of *ex post facto* acts, as grounded on no better foundation, and equally violative of that security of individuals, which it was an invariable object of the constitution to protect.

3. "The trial of all crimes, except in cases of Impeachment, shall be by jury, and such trial shall be held in the State where the said crimes shall have been committed; but where not committed within any State, the trial shall be at such place or places as the Congress may by law have directed."

This was the original provision in the constitution, but as a great many respectable persons, and even some of the conventions that ratified the constitution, did not think it particular enough, the amendments contained in the following articles were proposed by Congress at their first session, and have since been ratified, and now form a part of the constitution.

"No person shall be held to answer for a capital or otherwise infamous crime, unless on a presentment or indictment of a Grand Jury, except in cases arising in the land or naval forces, or in the militia when in actual service in time of war or public danger; nor shall any person be subject for the same offence to be twice put in jeopardy of life or limb; nor shall be compelled in any criminal case to be a witness against himself, nor deprived of life, liberty, or property, without due process of law; nor shall private property be taken for public use without just compensation."

"In all criminal prosecutions the accused shall enjoy the right to a speedy and public trial, by an impartial jury of the State and district wherein the crime shall have been committed, which district shall have been previously ascertained by law, and to be informed of the nature and cause of the accusation; to be confronted with the witnesses against him; to have compulsory process for obtaining witnesses in his favor, and to have the assistance of counsel for his defence."

The most innocent man, I apprehend, cannot wish for better securities than these. But how happy is that country where protections like these are no novelties, but have long been so familiar, that a sense of the value of them perhaps is not sufficiently shown! If we desire, however, to be truly sensible of their value, let us turn over a few pages of any ancient or almost of any modern history, and we shall be devoutly thankful for the uncommon share of personal as well as political liberty, these States are blessed with.

4. "Treason against the United States, shall consist only in levying war against them, or in adhering to their enemies, giving them aid and comfort. No person shall be convicted of treason unless on the testimony of two witnesses to the same overt act, or on confession in open Court.

"The Congress shall have power to declare the punishment of treason, but no attainder of treason shall work corruption of blood, or forfeiture, except during the life of the person attainted."

The crime of treason in all countries where arbitrary power has prevailed, or personal freedom has been too little regarded, has either been so indefinite in its nature, or such latitude has been taken in its construction, that perhaps it has occasioned more victims than any other instrument of tyranny. Resentment, full as often as justice, has whetted the sword of State, and caused many an innocent man to fall, and many a worthy family to perish. The mischiefs indeed that under a color, and sometimes barely a color of justice, have been wantonly occasioned to mankind by prosecutions for this offence, cannot be contemplated without horror and indignation. Justly therefore have precautions been taken against such abuses here. The crime itself, it is true, when real is of deep malignity. An attempt to throw a free government, and a happy people, into disorder and confusion, to dissolve all social ties, and risk the security and happiness of every private family, is certainly the highest offence which can be committed against society. Such a crime must be of peculiar aggravation when committed against a government deliberately established by the people themselves, and susceptible in itself of regular and peaceable alterations. But in proportion to the interest which every man feels in the preservation of a government, will be the warmth of his passions in its defence, and consequently it is of extreme moment that he should be upon his guard to prevent their misleading him, which all violent passions are apt to do, and none so much as those which have the public, as well as private interest, for their object. The law, therefore, in such cases ought to be peculiarly circumspect, in order to secure by every possible means a fair and impartial trial; and this appears to have been anxiously aimed at, not only by the provisions in the constitution I have read to you, but by every material legislative provision which concerns this important subject. The declaration as to corruption of blood and forfeiture (formerly no slight objects of rapacity to abandoned men), is an additional proof of the liberal and manly spirit with which the whole of these excellent constitutional provisions were framed.

Besides the restrictions in the constitution I have already noticed, there are other provisions in it calculated to secure still further the invaluable possession of personal liberty, so that it may not be unjustly sacrificed to any arbitrary measures. They are as follows:

"The right of the people to be secure in their persons, houses, papers, and effects, against unreasonable searches and seizures,

shall not be violated, and no warrants shall issue, but upon probable cause, supported by oath or affirmation, and particularly describing the place to be searched, and the persons or things to be seized."

"Excessive bail shall not be required, nor excessive fines imposed, nor cruel and unusual punishments inflicted."

The above contain all the restrictions on the criminal law I proposed to enumerate. Subject to these, the authority of the Legislature in that respect seems to be as follows:

1. They have express authority given in the constitution to define and punish piracies and felonies committed on the high seas, and offences against the Law of Nations.

Crimes that are committed upon the high seas, are not the objects of any law merely territorial, that is, a law resting entirely on the discretion of the Legislature of the country, but being crimes equally against all the nations in the world, are equally punishable in any, and therefore must have some common principle. For this reason laws concerning crimes of this nature ought to be materially the same in every country. But in every country there must be some authority which has a right to expound and enforce this law, so that every violation of it may be properly punished. In our country this authority naturally devolves on the Government of the United States, as having alone the care of the public interest with foreign nations; and it is peculiarly proper that the right of defining, and prescribing the punishment of such crimes should be vested in the Legislature, with whom the important power of declaring war, or authorizing any inferior species of hostility, is intrusted, otherwise they might be accountable for breaches of the Law of Nations committed without their sanction. The same observations apply to other violations of the Law of Nations as well as the particular instances of piracies and felonies committed on the high seas: such, for instance, as any violation of the privileges of an Ambassador or other public Minister, or of any safe conduct or passport under the authority of the United States. All which cases are provided for in the Laws of the United States.

2. The Legislature has authority given in the constitution, "To exercise exclusive legislation in all cases whatsoever over such district (not exceeding ten miles square) as may, by cession of particular States, and the acceptance of Congress, become the seat of the Government of the United States, and to exercise like authority over all places purchased by the consent of the Legislature of the State in which the same shall be, for the erection of forts, magazines, arsenals, dock-yards, and other needful buildings."

The necessity, as well as propriety, of this authority, is obvious. Provision has accordingly been made in an Act of Congress for this object, but it is liable to this exception, that by an express proviso contained in the Act accepting the cession of the District of ten miles square which has been ceded to the United States, it is declared, "That the operation of the laws of the State within said District shall not be affected by that acceptance, until the time fixed for the removal of the Government thereto, and until Congress shall otherwise by law provide."

3. As incidental to the power of legislation over the great objects of the General Government, the Legislature has authority to enforce its laws by proper sanctions, without which laws would be useless.

Thus, for instance, if any public security of the United States should be forged, this forgery may be tried under the laws of the United States, by whose authority the security issued, and whose protection therefore the possessor has a right to claim.

So if a record or process of any Court of the United States should be stolen or falsified, this is an offence against the United States, and of course triable in some of its Courts.

In like manner, if perjury should be committed in any of the Courts of the United States, this must be admitted as a proper instance of the jurisdiction of the United States.

Authority for these purposes, and others of a similar kind, is expressly given in the following words, which are contained at the end of the special enumerated powers of Congress, viz.:

"To make all laws which shall be necessary and proper for carrying into execution the foregoing powers, and all other powers vested by this constitution in the Government of the United States, or in any Department or officer thereof."

Though these words do not perhaps convey more real authority than would have been conveyed by fair implication, arising from the special powers of legislation before expressed, yet in an instrument of this high importance it was certainly wise and safe to leave as little room as possible for any doubt in its construction.

These, gentlemen, are the grounds upon which the legislative authority of the United States as to this interesting subject is placed. We find no power conveyed that does not appear to be necessary, nor I believe are any restrictions wanting that the general safety would admit. If it was material now to enter into a detail of all the legislative provisions on this subject, which I do not think it is, I trust you would find them congenial with the same high spirit of freedom and liberality which dictated the constitution itself. Most of them have been formerly explained from this Bench, and their superior excellence pointed out, in a manner I should in vain attempt to equal.* In many other countries the criminal law is the dread and terror of the people, and they are afraid to look at it. Ours, thank God, courts the light instead of shunning it, and never can suffer but by being defectively seen. If ever any people indeed had reason to repose confidence in their governments, the people of these States surely have. The people in each State, solemnly and deliberately, by Representatives fully authorized, have chosen their forms of government for themselves. They have chosen their own State constitutions. They have agreed to and ratified the Constitution of the United States. A higher degree of freedom, consistent with any government at all, is not exerciseable by human nature. So high a degree perhaps never was exercised until America tried the noble experiment. May she prove, by the support of her own work, that she has not been in search of an unattainable good! and that after passionately following that Liberty which she has constantly adored, she has at length succeeded in fixing her, by bringing to her her best beloved and only safe companions, Order and Justice!

[CIRCUIT COURT AT RICHMOND, VA.

IREDELL TO MRS. IREDELL.
RICHMOND, May 20.

MY DEAR HANNAH:—We have just arrived perfectly well, but extremely fatigued. We have each of us got an excellent room in the same house. *Mr. Jay improves infinitely upon intimacy*, &c.

May, 27th.

I am perpectly well; so is Mr. Jay, with whom I am more and more pleased. We began on the great British causes, the second day of the Court, and are now in the midst of them. *The great Patrick Henry is to speak to-day. I never was more agreeably disappointed than in my acquaintance with him. I have been much in his company, and his manners are very pleasing, and his mind, I am persuaded, highly liberal.* It is a strong additional reason I have, added to many others, to hold in

---

* A detail of all the legislative provisions on this subject I consider to be unnecessary; neither do I deem it material to point out the particular authority of this Court in respect to it, it being so general that it comprehends almost all the principal offences cognizable under the United States. The exceptions are few, and easily discoverable, though I am sensible of some important differences of opinion in regard to some of them, and therefore ought not to anticipate a decision of the Court if such should come in question.

---

high detestation violent *party prejudice*. It will be some time before we shall get away, for we are resolved, cost what time it will, to finish the business, &c.

June 7th.

We have this day given judgment on the great question as to British causes which has been depending so long. The judgment was in favor of the plaintiff, but with the exception of certain sums paid into the Treasury. Mr. Griffin and myself concurred. Mr. Jay was for overruling it, &c., &c.

JAS. IREDELL.

The great case of Ware *vs.* Hilton was tried at this Term. "The question was one of the highest interest to the people of Virginia, involving as it did the honor of the State, and the fortunes of many of her citizens." Henry, Marshall, Innis, and Campbell appeared for the defendants; and Wickham, Ronald, Baker, and Starke for the plaintiff. The magnitude of the cause justified such an array of counsel. "The discussion was one of the most brilliant exhibitions ever witnessed at the Bar of Virginia," then the first in the Union. Mr. Henry spoke for three consecutive days. It is said that his eloquence extorted from Judge Iredell the exclamation, "Gracious God! he is an orator indeed." In pronouncing his opinion, Judge Iredell remarked, "The cause has been spoken to, at the bar, with a degree of ability equal to any occasion. However painfully I may reflect at any time on the inadequacy of my own talents, I shall as long as I live, remember with pleasure and respect the arguments which I have heard in this case. They have discovered an ingenuity, a depth of investigation, and a power of reasoning fully equal to any thing I have ever witnessed, and some of them have been adorned with a splendor of eloquence surpassing what I have ever felt before. Fatigue has given way under its influence, and the heart has been warmed, while the understanding has been instructed." The Judge's notes of the trial are still in existence: the late Governor Iredell told me, that upon an examination of them, he inferred that, however much his father may have been impressed by Mr. Henry's oratory, his arguments did not strike him with any extraordinary force.* An appeal was taken to the Supreme Court.

GOV. JOHNSTON TO IREDELL.
June 10th.

DEAR SIR:— * * * * I have been altogether out of the way of news and politics. Wherever I have been people seem

---

* Vid. Van Santvoord, and Wirt's Life of Henry.

---

perfectly quiet and satisfied. Tell Fenno if he will forward me a form of subscription to his paper, I will endeavor to procure him some subscribers. * * * * When I laid aside my public character, I flattered myself that I had nothing to do but to attend to my own business; but I fear it is my fate to end my life as I set out in it, without any prospect of rest, until I am laid in the resting-place appointed for all mortals. * * * I sincerely lament the loss which Colonel Wadsworth has sustained in his daughter. Colonel Coxe's death is a favor both to him, and his family: it has put an end to his sufferings, and time will alleviate theirs. * * * Be so good as to procure a copy of Addison's Cato, and send it to James: I know no book more proper to infuse an exalted love of virtue into a young mind, &c.

SAM. JOHNSTON.

COL. DAVIE TO IREDELL.
HALIFAX, June 12.

DEAR SIR:— * * * * * In your letter of the 14th of February you mention a Bill in Equity being filed by the Indiana Company to *recover damages*, &c. This is surely of the first impression, and has excited my curiosity very much. Pray what rules are you guided by in the Supreme Court, for this is not the first novelty your practice there has produced? I left Judge Patterson at Newbern, detained by criminal business: his deportment as a Judge was highly approved: his fine understanding, affable manner, and social temper, make him a most agreeable man: you will be greatly pleased with him, &c.

WM. R. DAVIE.

GOV. JOHNSTON TO IREDELL.
WILLIAMSTON, July 22d.

MY DEAR SIR:—I am this day favored with your letters of the 29th of May and 7th of June. I am very much obliged to you for the particular account of the proceedings at Richmond. I am very sorry that the Appeal cannot be immediately taken up to the Supreme Court for a final decision. As far as I am capable of judging, the reasons on which you found your opinion are unanswerable, and will stand the test of the strictest criticism, whatever the final decision may be. * * * *

SAM. JOHNSTON.

IREDELL TO MRS. TREDWELL.
PHILADELPHIA, July 30th.

MY DEAR NELLY:— * * * We have lately had a very affecting death in this city. Mrs. Lear, the wife of Mr. Lear the

President's Secretary, died on Sunday last, after a short but very severe illness. She was only 23, and beloved and respected by all who knew her, and she and her husband had been fond of each other from infancy. He attended the funeral himself, and so did the President and Mrs. Washington. Mr. Hamilton, Mr. Jefferson, General Knox, Judge Wilson, Judge Peters, and myself were pall-bearers, &c.

JAS. IREDELL.

The prevalence of the yellow fever not only dispersed the great body of the inhabitants of Philadelphia, but interrupted the business of the Supreme Court at its August Term. Judge Patterson appeared and qualified. The Court adjourned, it seems, without the trial of any cause of importance.

HON. THOMAS BEE (Judge of the District Court of South Carolina)
TO IREDELL.
CHARLESTON, August 9th.

DEAR SIR:—I return you many thanks for your favor of the 19th of June, with the copy of the arguments in the Supreme Court upon the Georgia cause. Mr. Rutledge has promised me the perusal of the statement you sent him of the late decision in Virginia respecting the British debts.

The case then did not turn on the same points with the one argued before Judge Patterson, and myself: in this cause there was no State law that intervened, but a special agreement between the parties, prior to the contracting of the debt, and an acknowledgment of a balance, *after the Peace*, by the surviving co-partner, which he suggested was obtained by duress. The arguments of the Counsel were ingenious and diffuse. I wished the cause to have gone to a Jury, which you will recollect was my opinion at the first argument on the Plea and Demurrer to the Bill: at this last sitting the Court was divided on that point, it therefore came on for hearing on Bill and Answer in Equity. Mr. Patterson and myself agreed in some points, for a variety were brought forward; but, with respect to the interest, I was decidedly of opinion that it should cease during the war. From Vattel, Grotius, Bynkershoek, &c., it seems to be a clear principle with civilians, that if a party is prevented by the act of God or the law of the land, from fulfilling a contract, he shall be excused from the penalty.

The prohibitory acts of Great Britain prevented a remittance in produce, the acts of Congress forbade the purchase of

British bills of exchange. It appeared in evidence that a cargo of produce shipped by the house here to a neutral port as a remittance to the complainants, was captured at sea by British cruisers: under all these hard restrictions is it reasonable that interest should accrue ? I have long been of opinion that the fourth clause of the Treaty with Great Britain was solely intended to prevent a payment of debts in paper money, or any thing but gold or silver ; and that the matter of interest was not in contemplation at the making of the Treaty, otherwise it would have been fully expressed, and inserted of course. But the case in 1st Brown's Parl. Reports, 256, had great weight with me also. This cause was determined in the House of Lords upon an appeal from Ireland; and although it is expressly said to have been decided according to the "lex loci" of Ireland, "that in great national calamities, when the profits of an estate cease, these rents or *interest* shall cease also," yet, as the question was still unsettled in America, the Courts have a power to fix a precedent. The "lex loci" of Ireland in this instance appeared to me to be a very good law for us ; and, therefore, I was for the adoption of it, and thus far fixing a precedent in America. This cause will, of course, come forward again at the next Circuit Court for this District, and from thence be removed to the Supreme Tribunal, both parties being determined to appeal.

We are at present without intelligence of any kind from abroad. I sincerely hope that the stand the French are making against their numerous foes will be the means of detaching a part of them from this unnatural Alliance ; and, in the event, bring about peace ; or otherwise, I fear, we shall be dragged into the contest by the ill-behavior of a few, although I am convinced the great body of the Union are for a strict neutrality. Mrs. Bee is much mended in her health. My son and all the family desire their best compliments to be presented to you. The recollection of the satisfaction we experienced whilst you were amongst us, always affords pleasure, and we look forward to similar sensations at no distant period.

I am, my dear Sir,
With very sincere respect and esteem,
Your most obt. servant,
THOMAS BEE.

Alarmed for the safety of his family, and expelled from his home in Philadelphia by the yellow fever, the thoughts of Judge Iredell reverted to Carolina. His affection for his old home had never been estranged : a wider experience of men, and localities, had but deepened and corroborated his attachment. True, in despite of its sparkling waters and luxuriant vegetation, the "malaria" of Edenton, more or less, every year, generated fever and agues ; but then it was exempt from the terrible scourges that so frequently afflicted the Northern cities, while its society, if more limited, was preferred by him, certainly a most competent judge, to the more brilliant circles of the metropolis. In the following letter to his niece, he announced his intention to return, a purpose that he executed about the indicated time.

IREDELL TO MRS. TREDWELL.
PHILADELPHIA, August 12th, 1793.

MY DEAR NELLY :—I assure you I sincerely rejoice in the probable prospect which I now have of going with my family to Carolina in October or November next ; about the middle of the former month is the time I now fix upon, and hope then to accomplish it. The sacrifice I must personally make in being so much more absent from my family, I flatter myself, will be compensated by the greater satisfaction they will enjoy, and the money I may be enabled to save by it. With regard to the difference of society, considering how many dear friends I have in Carolina, I prefer it infinitely, &c., &c.
JAS. IREDELL.

REV. A. IREDELL TO IREDELL.
RINGMER PARK (near Lewes), September 3d, '93.

DEAR BROTHER :— * * * * You favored me with an interesting account of the great question that had, but unsatisfactorily, been reported in our papers. You will laugh at my presumption in having any opinion upon such high matters, but it will be ungrateful enough in you, for I approve entirely of yours on each point of difficulty. I met the other day with a *good* lawyer, to whom I read your statement, and he was decidedly with you. He thought a similar case had been determined in our Chancery upon the very grounds that guided yours, and promised to send me the *chapter* and *verse* of it out of a modern Report (for cases do not now long sleep in manuscript) ; but he has not found it, or at least he has not sent me any account of it. Pray favor me often with such delicate "morceaux."—It is strange a French word has escaped me, for I have forsworn every thing that belongs to that contemptible people ; and I hope you, and every good American, have done the same. *Our* Jacobins will have it otherwise. They say you were all in love with prin-

ciples, if they may be called such, that set religion and morality at defiance ; and, according to them, you have laid an embargo on our shipping, and are at war with us ! Then Washington is dead, the liberty transplanted in America is dead too ! No, my dear brother, I know that the land of *atheists* and *assassins*, called the Convention, is nowhere more reprobated than in the United States—I mean by those who have respectability enough among you to have weight. The French political creed never renders your persons and property as insecure as ours ; indeed it is a creed that can only suit such miscreants as they are who framed it. Humanity, and reason, both disclaim it. But my patience will not brook this hateful subject, &c., &c.
A. IREDELL.

THE YELLOW FEVER.
DR. B. DUFFIELD TO IREDELL.
PHILADELPHIA, September 5th.

DEAR SIR :—I have snatched a moment to request that you will not think of returning here. It is really hazardous, although the alarm has been too much spread by timidity, ignorance, or avarice. But at our end of the city, the disease is likely to continue, and increase, from the Naval Hospital being crowded with 200 diseased Irish, who, before a guard was planted to prevent their crossing the Schuylkill, were endeavoring to slide into the city through its lower avenues, in spite of all the vigilance of the Mayor and Corporation. I have yet lost but two patients by actual disease ; but if a tooth aches, such is the general trepidation, that "*it is this Fever*" certainly, &c., &c.
B. DUFFIELD.

HON. P. BUTLER TO IREDELL.
ONE MILE FROM JENKINSTOWN, IN THE OLD YORK ROAD, September 9th.

MY DEAR SIR :—I have this moment heard that the fever becomes serious. I am uneasy for you, Mrs. Iredell, and the children. If you incline, which I think you must, to leave town, I think I can get you accommodated near us. Suppose, my friend, you ride up and see the place yourself ; and if you like it, you shall take down my caravan for Mrs. Iredell. The solicitation for lodgings in this neighborhood exceeds credibility. I cannot keep the preference longer than to-morrow. If you come you must have your own servants. Provisions are plentiful. You can't miss the road to Jenkinstown, by the Rising Sun on the German- town road. The road forks at the Rising Sun : take the right. When you get to the tavern at J. ask for Jesse Roberts's, one mile off : there you will find us. If Mrs. Iredell will not leave town, suppose you send your two elder children to us. Believe me, they shall be treated as if they were my own. Let me prevail on you, my friend, to quit town. At all events come up, and see the accommodations ; and if you like them, take down my caravan. Need I assure you that you may command the best services of me and mine—Being with real regard,
Your affectionate friend,
P. BUTLER.

Mary Dusenbury, a servant in Judge Iredell's family, wrote his wife, September 18th, "The fever is all around us, and one calamity seldom comes alone ; there is a set of villains that feel not for the distressed citizens, but take this opportunity of plundering the houses of those that are absent. Mr. Megans has been attacked three times. Mr. Franklin's sons are gone to York, and Mr. Cuthbert's family to the country. * * * Business of every kind is stopt, and provisions double price. I have had the furniture in the tea-room packed, but Mr. Eldridge will not take it for fear of carrying the fever with it. * * * I have tried every means to get to you, but can't. Give my thanks to Mr. Iredell for his kind letter."

DR. DUFFIELD TO IREDELL.
September 21st.

DEAR SIR :—The immense labor I undergo leaves me scarcely a moment to think, much less to write. Our mortality here is deplorable indeed ! and so acrid, so fierce a contagion, I believe, never before visited North America. As soon as you may venture with safety I will write you. I really know of no place where you can retire to. If Bethlehem is disagreeable, Reading is as pleasant, as healthy, and much cheaper to live at, &c.
D. DUFFIELD.

GOV. JOHNSTON TO IREDELL.
WILLIAMSTON, 10th October.

DEAR SIR :—I have had the great pleasure of receiving your two letters of the 8th and 15th of September. I hope this will find you in Philadelphia, if not on your journey to this country where your friends anxiously expect you. Your letters contain the latest accounts we have from Philadelphia. The recovery of

VOL. II.—26

the Secretary of the Treasury is a circumstance which gives very general satisfaction. For my own part I consider him the second hope of the United States. I sincerely congratulate him on his recovery. I am much pleased to hear of Dr. Duffield's success. I have a great partiality for him; and, indeed, for all of his father's family with whom I was acquainted, as much for the old gentleman as for himself, &c.

SAM. JOHNSTON.

DR. DUFFIELD TO IREDELL.

November 2d, 1793.

DEAR SIR :—Not knowing you were at Wilmington, until yesterday, I wrote to Bethlehem, to acquaint you of the situation of poor Polly. She has been as ill as any body I ever saw in the prevailing fever, even in the Hospital. Blood flowed from every aperture in her body, and her gums and eyes. She had black evacuations upward, and downward; but last night I found her so much on the recovery, that I flatter myself she is nearly out of danger.

The rain has given the disease a mortal blow: it was quite time, for destruction seemed to wanton in the ravages it occasioned. For a few days there were but two physicians on foot; and with all my strength and spirits, I was obliged (as Dr. Johnson would say) to succumb under the pressure of fatigue, and the languid lassitude of corporal imbecility, &c.

B. DUFFIELD.

LUTHER MARTIN TO IREDELL.

BALTIMORE, December 18th.

MY DEAR SIR :—It is with real pleasure I received the information of the safe arrival of yourself and family at Edenton, after so tedious a journey, and under circumstances so disagreeable: and we sincerely participate in the happiness you enjoy from the restoration of health to your lovely children.

If it was in any degree in our power to render the situation of your lady more satisfactory than it would have otherwise been, we are more than compensated by the satisfaction we experienced; at the same time we regret that our mutual situations were such as prevented a more intimate intercourse and interchange of civilities.

Mrs. Martin has for some time enjoyed an astonishing degree of general health, notwithstanding which she is at present increased so much in size as to give room for apprehension that she must soon undergo another operation.

Should we ever from the vicissitudes of fortune, find ourselves near Edenton, we shall embrace with great satisfaction the opportunity of visiting friends we shall ever esteem, and for whose felicity feel an interest. At the same [time] we rely that when you pass through Baltimore we shall have the pleasure of seeing you; and, if accompanied with your family, it will be an additional pleasure.

Our little girls are in perfect health, and thank their young friends for their affectionate remembrance; and on their parts present them with their best respects, and an assurance that they shall not be forgotten.

Be pleased to make our very respectful compliments to your lady, and family; and accept our best wishes for your and their happiness. Believe me to be, with every sentiment of esteem,

Dear Sir, your very obedient servant,

LUTHER MARTIN.

HON. P. BUTLER TO IREDELL.

PHILADELPHIA, Dec. 19th.

I was much gratified, my dear sir, to be informed from your acceptable favor of the 4th inst., which I have just received, that Mrs. Iredell, yourself, and children were well, after, I have no doubt, a fatiguing journey. I sincerely wish that the air of Edenton may have all the good effects you expect. My daughters are well, and much obliged by your remembrance of them. They and their father will always be happy to see you.

The too few opportunities I have had of trying to prove my friendship are infinitely overrated by your all-feeling and benevolent breast: they have been abundantly repaid in the pleasure, and, indeed, pride, I take in an acquaintance and friendship that I am persuaded will be continued through life. It is one of the few I have aimed at, and it has more than met my expectations.

Notwithstanding that the apprehension of infection pressed on the minds of some of the members, we made a Congress the first day, which I think reflects credit on the members. We have been occupied heretofore in reading reports from the Secretaries of State and War; and, which I should have mentioned first, communications from the President. By these we learn of the entire indisposition of Britain and Spain to enter into any treaty with the United States; and of the conduct of the British ministry in increasing our savage enemies, by letting loose the Algerines on our trade. This step reflects no credit on Britain: it has made a strong impression on the minds of most men here, in or out of Congress; and may check the machinations of some to dissolve the ties between America and France. You will see all the publications from and to Messrs. Jay and King. I need not then mention them. I think they must wish themselves well out of it. Nothing of late date from Europe, &c.

P. BUTLER.

CHAPTER XXVII.

ÆT. 42–43.

LETTERS FROM GOV. JOHNSTON, REV. A. IREDELL, AND PIERCE BUTLER. SOUTHERN CIRCUIT: CHARGE TO THE GRAND JURY IN NORTH CAROLINA. LETTERS FROM GOV. LEE, IREDELL, AND DAVIE.

JUDGE IREDELL was extremely anxious to attend the February Term of the Supreme Court, on account of the variety of important business depending. He left home on the 14th of January; but when advanced about 40 miles on his journey, was taken sick, and constrained to return. In a letter to Mr. Jay he proposed to attend the ensuing Southern Circuit; and recommended that the time of future meetings of the Supreme Court in the winter should be the 1st Monday in January, instead of February. In conclusion, he remarked, "I don't believe we have many Genet men in this State."

GOV. JOHNSTON TO IREDELL.

HERMITAGE, January 27th.

DEAR SIR :— * * * Yesterday finished my sixty-first year; and, I thank God, I find myself in as good health as I ever was in my life. On looking back, what I have the most to regret is the loss of many valuable friends whom I had reason to esteem; those who are left are now reduced to so small a number that I shall consider myself unfortunate indeed if I should survive any more of them. I am not tired of life as long as I can live with them; but without them it would be intolerable, &c.

SAM. JOHNSTON.

In a letter to Mr. Randolph, Secretary of State, February 13th, requesting, to be apprised as fully as possible of the proceedings of Congress in the course of his Circuit, and copies of such acts as might be passed, Judge Iredell remarked—" Permit me to say, sir, that though I could not but regret Mr. Jefferson's resignation at so critical a period of public affairs, especially as I had recently read his masterly correspondence, which certainly does him great honor, yet your appointment to succeed him gave me very high satisfaction, and I am persuaded will be more generally acceptable than perhaps any other that could have been made."

Rev. A. Iredell to Iredell.
Lewes, March 31st.

My dear Brother:— * * * * I am alarmed at the accounts that are circulated respecting your Government. The diabolical notions that have been diffused among you, as with us, seem to threaten even your democratic form ; and, indeed, they are as destructive of well-regulated republics, as of the most odious monarchies. God grant you may not experience any of their horrid effects ! The fate of France will, I trust, preserve this country ; but we have means of defence, and a power over the disaffected which you want. It is not *liberty*, but an *equal partition of all things*, that is aimed at ; this our "noblesse," gentry, clergy, yeomanry, and traders, see, and make it a common cause. Their combined strength in this opulent kingdom is prodigious. Hence our security. Our insular situation ; our dense population ; an inveterate dislike of other people, proper to islanders ; and many other great advantages which we have, but which North America has not, may guard us at the very door of *contagion*, as it were, which may be wafted across the Atlantic, and infect you, who have not such preservatives, most fatally. I wish I could reason myself out of this opinion, but I really cannot ; and I am, therefore, more than usually impatient to hear from you. You have hitherto carefully avoided every political subject, and will, perhaps, continue to do so. Nor would I have you deviate from that apparent rule, if there be any impropriety or danger in broaching your sentiments (I mean any chance of your letters being opened), because in the public character you bear, what you write may justly be considered as of the greatest weight. If your letters be written in good spirits, and contain no bad news, I shall be satisfied, &c.

A. IREDELL.

Hon. P. Butler to Iredell.
April 3d, Phila.

My dear Sir :—I hope you received a letter that my daughter had the honor of writing to you in my name some time ago. I was at the time confined to my bed. It will afford me and my children much satisfaction to know that you, Mrs. Iredell and children, and Mr. Johnston and family, are well.

If you get the newspapers, you will know all the public news stirring here. We have had a strange, lingering, inactive session. One minute feeling bold, the next apprehensive lest we should draw on us the displeasure of Britain. At this moment all legislation is at a stop, in consequence of a publication of a paragraph of a letter said to be received at Boston, from Bird, Savage & Bird, of London, which you will see in the public prints. Before the receipt of that letter, the House of Representatives were making some arrangements for placing the States in a situation to do justice to the citizens. The general conduct of Britain—the violation of the laws of nations in the depredations on our trade—the speech of Lord Dorchester, aided by a combination of circumstances, leave little room to doubt that war against the States was intended ; but the success of the French at Wysemburg, the recapture of Toulon, the disappointment of Lord Myra, aided by some jealousies among the combined powers, may have induced a sudden change. It is whispered here that the President proposes to send a Special Minister to Britain for a full explanation.

You will see by the debates in the House that the Republican party gain ground. What shall I say of the Senate ? I will say that we are looking to North Carolina for a *good Republican* Senator when Mr. H. (*Hawkins*) may be disposed to retire to private life. I know, my dear sir, it is much in your power to promote this much desired object. I wish you would throw your well-merited influence into the scale of a Republican candidate. We are told that Mr. S. (*Steele ?*) means to try to get into the Senate. I question his steady Republicanism. I judge from events—from part of his conduct in the other House. Gov. M. (*Martin*) behaves steadily well, and with credit to his State, &c., &c.

P. BUTLER.

Gov. Johnston to Iredell.
Hermitage, 2d June, '94.

My dear Sir :— ***** In what you say of our Philadelphia account, I am sure you must be mistaken. If you have kept an account, which I hope you have, of the money you must necessarily have expended for Fanny, there must be a considerable balance due in your favor.

I flatter myself that our affairs with Great Britain will be amicably adjusted to the satisfaction of all parties, I mean all such of them as are friendly to order and good government. The Democrats will be satisfied with nothing less than the abolition of the present Government.

Mr. A. Elmsley's letter is dated 30th March. He mentions nothing of public news which I have seen in the papers, except that Lord Hawkesbury had moved that the House of Lords should be summoned some day soon, to take under consideration what new regulations might be proper respecting their commerce with America, &c.

SAM. JOHNSTON.

Judge Iredell held, at the appointed times, the Courts in Georgia and South Carolina. At the opening of the Circuit Court for North Carolina, he delivered the following charge, which was published, in accordance with the request of the Grand Jury, contained in the annexed letter.*

[COPY.]

To the Hon. James Iredell, Esquire, one of the Judges of the Federal Court.

The Address of the Grand Jury of the Federal Court for the Circuit of North Carolina, held at the city of Raleigh, on the 2d of June, 1794.

We, the Jury aforesaid, impressed with a lively sense of the exemplary pains which you have taken in your charge to point out to us our duty as Grand Jurors of this Court, consider ourselves bound in gratitude to return you our sincere and ardent thanks : The strong and lively colors in which you have painted our situation with the belligerent powers, and the advantages we derive from a state of neutrality, must convey conviction to the mind of every person who wishes the welfare of his country. We are happy to observe that the President's Proclamation has met with the general approbation of the citizens of this State ; had it not been consonant with the general opinion, we are apt to believe some part of the attention of this Court would have been occupied in trials of that description.

As your charge was particularly addressed to us, and but a few of the inhabitants were present, we request it as a favor, that you would grant us a copy thereof, with permission to have it published ; that the comprehensive view which you have taken of the subject may be generally disseminated. That you may enjoy a long succession of years, with the blessings of health and prosperity added thereto, are the sincere wishes of this Jury.

Signed for the whole,

AMBROSE RAMSAY, *Foreman*.

ANSWER.
To Ambrose Ramsay, Esquire.
Wake Court House, June 5th, 1794.

Sir :—The business of the Court put it out of my power, before the Grand Jury had dispersed, to express in the manner I wished, the high sense I entertain of the honor of their address. Their approbation of my sentiments on so interesting a subject, accompanied with the pleasing information they convey, convinces me of what I had before every reason to believe, that whatever may be the sentiments of a few individuals, the great body of the citizens of this State consider the peace and reputation of their country of no common value, and that it is their indispensable duty to obey the constitutional authorities, which they as well as the citizens of the other States have concurred in establishing—authorities formed on the strongest basis of freedom, and calculated without the slightest distinction for the equal security and happiness of all.

Whatever may be our future state, either as to peace or war, such a disposition can alone preserve us a united people, give dignity and energy to our government, maintain the character of a respected nation, and convince the world that the same sense of duty which dictated the preservation of peace, when peace was the object of our common councils, will equally lead to a vigorous support of any war into which the aggressions of any other nation may force us.

You will oblige me in communicating this letter as you have opportunity, to the several gentlemen who composed the Grand Jury, assuring them at the same time, that I shall retain through life the most grateful sense of their personal kindness, and that I reciprocate in the warmest manner the same wishes for their health and prosperity which they are so good as to express for mine.

Such, sir, I shall ever entertain for yourself personally, being, with great regard,

Your faithful and obedient servant,

JA. IREDELL.

---

* Judge Iredell was requested by Mr. T. G. Guignard, in a very well-written letter, at the instance of the Grand Jury, to publish his Charge, delivered at Columbia in May.

A CHARGE

Delivered to the Grand Jury for the District of North Carolina, in the Circuit Court of the United States, held for the said District, at Wake Court House, June 2d, 1794, by JAMES IREDELL, one of the Associate Justices of the Supreme Court of the United States.

[Published at the Grand Jury's Request.]

GENTLEMEN OF THE GRAND JURY:—

The war which unfortunately has been for some time raging in Europe, placed this country in a new and critical situation, which required the utmost attention of those concerned in the government, and the exercise of important duties by the citizens of the United States. With all the powers engaged in the war we were at peace: with most of them we had treaties, either of a mere friendly or of a commercial nature: with one we had connections more intimate than with either of the others, and particularly endeared by the recollection of the signal benefits we had derived from its exertions in the time of our distress. The danger that we might, in the course of so extensive an hostility, be drawn again into a state of war from which we had so recently, and after experiencing so many evils, emerged, was alarming to every considerate mind. But we had the consolation to reflect, that no authority of our own but that of the Legislature of the United States could deliberately bring such a calamity upon us; and we were well assured, from their patriotism and integrity, that nothing but the necessity of self-defence, or the duty of a public obligation (if that unhappily should be found to require it), would induce them to risk the growing prosperity, and almost unexampled free condition of our country.

As the Constitution of the United States intrusted the Congress alone with the authority of declaring war, or permitting any inferior species of hostility, it was evident that until they exercised such an authority, it was the duty of all the citizens of the United States to remain in a state of peace and neutrality with all the hostile powers. It is a principle of common sense, as well as a very clear one of the law of nations, and is for the most part expressly stipulated in those treaties where the preservation of peace is mentioned, that it shall be maintained as well by the individuals of each nation as by the respective governments. A distinction between the two cases, in any instance, would be trifling to the utmost possible degree, and in the instance in question would involve such absurd consequences as to make the futility of it obvious to the least discerning mind. None can deny that if one citizen could take a part in the war, all might. Suppose such an event. We should then present the ridiculous and contemptible spectacle to the world, of the officers of our government, in their official transactions, bound to the observance of a strict neutrality, and the people themselves, by whose authority and on whose behalf they act, individually engaged on one side or the other. The mischiefs of such a distinction (if we can for a moment lose sight of its absurdity) would be pernicious beyond all estimation. The great excellence of every government must be, when those who have the direction of public affairs, and those for whose benefit they are directed, coöperate in one uniform conduct. But what must be their situation, when not only no such coöperation exists, but when one-half of the people take up arms in support of one foreign power, and the other half in support of another, and for a foreign quarrel, in which their government has no concern, and in which it can honestly take no part, are thus cutting one another's throats? Such absurdities, such mischiefs, are not deducible from any rational principle; accordingly the distinction animadverted upon cannot be maintained by any abstract reasoning. A few words will be sufficient to show this. When a treaty is entered into between two powers, it is not a treaty between government and government, but between nation and nation. The government is only the trustee for its nation, in this respect as well as in every other exercise of its power. It is so with regard to all the countries in the world, whether the government be monarchical or republican. For which reason, though our treaties with France were on the part of France entered into by the King then Sovereign of that country, yet they are obligatory now on both countries, though France has since become a republic, and the government of the United States is materially changed. I said, government was a trustee in every other exercise of its power as well as this, and the exposition of this sentiment may serve to illustrate still more fully the position it is now my purpose to establish. When any act of the government is performed, it is not an act of the government merely, but in reality an act of the people whose trustee the government is. The people not being able to exercise the various departments of government in person, they necessarily must be devolved on others. Upon whom they are to be devolved, depends on the particular constitution of each country. Whatever dispute may arise as to the constitutions of other countries, there can be none as to the various constitutions of the United States. Their origin is as well known as it is respectable. Their powers are all defined in writing. The various legislative, executive and judicial powers of the United States, all originate from a system the people themselves have agreed to be governed by, and derive the whole of their validity from such system voluntarily established. The different branches of government are therefore expressly trustees for all the people of the United States, and accordingly every act of the Legislature of the United States, is an act of the people of the United States, in their legislative capacity, every act of the executive in their executive capacity, every act of the judiciary in their judicial, and not merely an act of so many individuals exercising independently either legislative, executive, or judicial authority. In respect, therefore, to every act of government, either within our own country, or as to foreign nations, it is an act, in a constitutional point of view, of all the people of the United States, it being altogether grounded on their authority, and exercised for their benefit, and in no instance upon any pretended authority, or for the least exclusive benefit of the persons with whom such particular delegation of power is intrusted.

If any addition was wanting to reasons which seem so complete and satisfactory, I might say that it is in the nature of things unavoidable that all the citizens of a country must be personally affected by the good or bad government of it. Through their government alone can they speak or be spoken to by foreign nations, which in itself implies the notion of a united and inseparable interest. If war be declared by that branch of the government intrusted to declare it, all the citizens must be immediately liable to all the consequences of that declaration, however calamitous or however fortunate they may prove. Government ships, and government property of any other kind, will not alone be the objects of hostility, but the property of every kind belonging to any citizen coming within reach of the enemy. The laws of war impose duties to which the citizens will be unquestionably liable; they in a few instances give individual rights, though these are usually inconsiderable, compared to the others, so certain are the mischiefs, so comparatively light are the advantages to be derived from so unhappy a condition. In peace we all know the blessings individuals are entitled to—life, liberty, and property, secured from any hostile invasion. If a country is thus happily circumstanced, when a war breaks out between other powers, and its situation will admit of a neutrality between them, new duties are essential to this condition, which must be faithfully performed, or the rights of such neutrality will not nor ought to be respected. As these rights imply all the security incident to profound peace, so far as the persons and property of the neutral nations are concerned, upon the principle of observing perfect neutrality as to the objects of the war between the belligerent powers, it is surely evident that, as this principle alone gives rise to the neutrality, and it can have no other basis, those who personally enjoy the benefits of such neutrality must personally respect and obey the principle from which all their rights are derived. Every right, either private or public, implies a correspondent duty. To claim the right and withhold the duty, is a daring violation of all morality, if grounded upon power; if attempted to be maintained on principle, a defiance of the common sense of mankind.

Upon so plain a foundation stand the duties of neutrality to which the present unfortunate war gave rise, as to the citizens of the United States. But as the occasion was of great importance, and there was reason to fear that a number of individuals, either from unguarded zeal, or some other motive less excusable, if unchecked by timely interposition, might precipitately take a part in the war no less dangerous to the peace than injurious to the honor of their country, then bound to the observance of a real, and disdaining the subterfuges of a fraudulent neutrality, the President of the United States thought it expedient to issue a proclamation to the following effect, viz.: To declare the disposition of the United States to observe a neutrality between the belligerent powers, to exhort and warn all the citizens against any acts contravening such disposition; to inform them that if by any violation of the neutrality, any citizen should render himself liable to any punishment or forfeiture under the law of nations, the United States would afford him no protection against such punishment or forfeiture; and that instructions had been given to the proper officers to cause prosecutions to be instituted against all persons who should, within the cognizance of the courts of the United States, violate the law of nations with respect to the powers at war, or any of them. This proclamation has received the most general and warm approbation, which has been expressed in the fullest manner, not only by individuals, but by the highest public authorities in our country. It has nevertheless been the subject of animadversion by some persons, who appear to have paid very little regard to the principles upon which it was founded, and the necessity which at that time I conceive rendered it indispensable. It is the duty of the President, as the Supreme Executive of the United States, to do every thing in his power to support the execution of the laws, and to maintain peace until Congress think proper to declare war. No one needs to be informed that a proclamation cannot change the law; the days of such folly are past; but every one knows that in all countries there are critical occasions when it is material for individuals to be reminded of their duty, and that special directions should be given for carrying on prosecutions in which the public prosperity is more than ordinarily interested. No occasion for such interference ever existed more critical than that in question. The situation in which we were placed was new, and required perhaps some reflection even in the best informed minds, before it was thoroughly understood. There was every appearance of its strongly engaging the passions, not only of a few, but of a great number of individuals. Some violations of neutrality had actually been committed; more alarming ones were in contemplation. Had the President, under these circumstances, been silent, our whole country would soon have been set into a flame, and foreign powers would have suspected that government were either indifferent about preserving a neutrality, or under the pretence of it meant to countenance partial hostilities, which would be one of the most justifiable, though on the part of the aggressor, one of the most dishonorable causes of war. Happily for the public safety, neither negligence nor a want of the purest integrity was ever imputable to the high character invested with this important trust; and he has accordingly conducted himself, in one of the most critical situations in which any man was ever placed, in a manner calculated, not only to secure an addition, if possible, to his former fame, but to support with new lustre the dignity and independence of his country.

Notwithstanding any defensive measures which Congress may think proper to adopt in consequence of aggressions we had little reason to expect, after the uniform integrity which our government hath so strongly and unequivocally shown, yet until the contrary is clearly warranted by the same high authority, it is the duty of each individual to conform his conduct to the same principles of neutrality as before, since the fatal die of war or peace is not yet irrevocably cast; and God forbid that the rashness of any individual should in any manner aggravate the subsisting difficulties of his country. Let us therefore consider, as well for the sake of the future as the past, in what those duties consist, which can only be ascertained by consulting the law of nations, a law of so much moment to the peace and happiness of mankind, if sacredly regarded, but which too frequently is made the sport of the worst passions of human nature. The nature of this law (it appearing to me in general not to be well understood) I beg leave to state to you, before I point out the duties of neutrality which it inculcates.

In all cases which affect the rights of independent sovereignties, who have no common superior, the only way to ascertain the duties which one nation owes to another, is to inquire what reason dictates, that attribute which the Almighty has bestowed upon all mankind for the ultimate guide and director of their conduct. As among individuals in a rude state of society, before any form of government is established, there are certain rational principles by which each man is bound to regulate his conduct to his fellow-creature man, so among different nations, which have no superior human authority to decide their differences, they can only be determined by the principles of reason, in which all mankind, when their minds are not debased by ignorance, or corrupted by vices, generally agree. In this, however, as in all other cases, mankind acquire not information without an effort. Providence has given us faculties of mind to acquire knowledge, as well as faculties of body to undergo the necessary labor for the purposes of human life; but intending man for an active being, and to attain all human advantages by means of his own industry, some degree of application is necessary to discover the dictates of reason, even in the commonest instances which lie within her province, until habit has rendered them familiar. It is the more necessary, because as man has a variety of duties to perform, it is requisite in order to discover them in all their relations, to examine and compare one duty with another, and see, in case of a competition, which is the superior and which the subordinate duty, that we may make the latter give way to the former. Thus there is a duty to a man's self, which in case of a competition ought to give way to the duty which he owes to his family; and his duty to his family, in all instances where they are incompatible, to give way to the higher ones he owes to his country. But though the discovery of these duties, in all their perfection, may be a work which requires great thought and sagacity, the ordinary duties of human life are sufficiently obvious, and even those, the occasions for which are more rare, may easily be comprehended when the reasons of them are clearly stated and defined. To discover the elementary principles of arithmetic required a great genius; but to understand them when proposed and explained, the dullest mind, if capable of comprehension at all, is perfectly equal. We have the happiness to live in an age when human knowledge in all its branches has been carried to a great perfection. The law of nations, by which alone all controversies between nation and nation can be determined, has been cultivated with extraordinary success. In its main principles, as stated by many able writers, all civilized nations concur. Those that are really questionable are neither many nor importan Within these few years this law has not only been stated with peculiar accuracy and conciseness, but all its principles have been traced to their source, with a power of reasoning which has commanded universal assent, and with a spirit of freedom and an enlarged liberality of mind entirely suited to the high improvements the present age has made in all kinds of political reasoning.

The general duties of neutrality, under the guidance of the respectable and approved authorities I have alluded to, may be thus briefly comprehended—Voluntarily to furnish neither party with troops, arms, ammunition, or any thing of direct use in war; nor indirectly to favor one party to the prejudice of the other, if done for the express purpose of assisting one party in its contest with the other, since this would be taking a side, which the strict laws of neutrality forbid. But the exercise of independent rights, with no view to favor one party to the prejudice of the other merely on account of the war, such (for example) as the carrying on any accustomed trade only from commercial motives, in any article whatsoever, is no breach of neutrality, though the particular instance specified is liable to this restriction, that all commodities which are usually termed contraband, and by which are understood all articles peculiarly subservient to war, though the particularrs are not perfectly agreed upon, if bound to any port of one of the belligerent powers, or articles of any kind, whether such as are usually termed contraband or otherwise, bound to a place actually besieged or blockaded, are liable to seizure and condemnation.

These appear to me to be the general principles as to the conduct of a neutral power; but there are special exceptions in particular instances, where in virtue of previous treaties the engagements of the neutral power contain stipulations more in favor of one of the parties than the other. In respect to the present war, the United States are a neutral power of this description, they being expressly bound by their commercial treaty with France, to grant certain privileges to French vessels of war and privateers, which they are not at liberty to grant to any other. So far, however, as they confine themselves to a perfect performance of this treaty upon its true construction, and are in all other respects neutral, they are undoubtedly entitled to all the privileges and benefits of a neutral nation.

With regard to all the questions which may arise either on the duties of neutrality abstractly considered, or the particular construction of the treaty constituting certain exceptions to the general principles of it, the limits of a discourse proper for this occasion, will by no means admit of a full discussion of them. But I deem it my indispensable duty to give you my opinion upon two pretensions which have been very confidently urged, and have been attempted to be supported in such a manner as tended, in an alarming degree, to disturb the good order of our country, and produce the greatest mischief, as well as greatest disgrace that can ever happen to any, the introduction of foreign influence to counteract the execution of the laws by that authority intrusted by the people with this portion of their power, and in every instance responsible for the due exercise of it. Happily, however, all danger of this kind has been honorably removed by an additional proof of national attention and respect, which must be highly grateful to every friend of his country.

The two pretensions upon which I have to remark are these:
1. A claim on behalf of the French, to fit out privateers in the ports of the United States.
2. A right in the French nation to enlist any of the citizens of the United States, either on board their armed vessels, or even on shore, and in the very bosom of our territory, without the consent of the government, upon the principle that any citizen has a right to expatriate himself at his pleasure.

The first claim is founded upon the 22d article of the treaty of amity and commerce, which is in these words:

"It shall not be lawful for any foreign privateers, not belonging to subjects of the most Christian king, nor citizens of the United States, who have commissions from any other prince or state in enmity with either nation, to fit their ships in the ports of either the one or the other of the aforesaid parties; to sell what they have taken, or in any other manner whatsoever to exchange their ships, merchandise, or any other lading; neither shall they be allowed even to purchase victuals, except such as shall be necessary for their going to the next port of that prince or state from which they have commissions."

The true construction of this article is of the highest importance, because if the French derive under it the right which has been insisted on (though I flatter myself it is now relinquished), it is undoubtedly a breach of faith in the United States to deny them the exercise of it; if, on the other hand, the treaty confers no such right, it will be a violation of the neutrality to permit it; and if supposed to be done deliberately and partially, and not merely from a mistaken construction, would be a justifiable cause of war.—Fortunately the construction is not so difficult as it is important.

If words alone are to be regarded, they contain nothing more (so far as they affect the present question) than a stipulation that an enemy of either party shall not be permitted to fit out privateers in the other's ports. Whether the citizens of the United States shall be permitted to fit out privateers in the ports of France, or the French in the ports of the United States, the article does not say.

The usual way to ascertain the meaning of parties is to consider the words they use, by which their meaning is or ought to be expressed. It must, however, be admitted, that a meaning is sometimes to be collected by implication; and it may be alleged in support of this claim, that the implication in this case is sufficient to convey the right contended for.

To such an allegation the following objections occur:

1. That a construction by implication is never to be received but where such construction is necessary and unavoidable, or the meaning of the parties can be collected either from the context or concurring circumstances. If such a construction was admitted upon any other principle, no man in any contract could be safe, unless he excluded every possible implication by direct negative expressions, a thing impossible to be practised, and highly irrational to be required.

2. There is not the least necessity for such a construction, the meaning being very sensible and complete without it. Was it not important to stipulate for the exclusion of an enemy of either from the ports of the other, without at the same time agreeing to permit either of the contracting parties to arm in the other's ports? Do not the two cases stand on a very different footing, and have we not a right to say, that as the one is stipulated for and the other not, the former must be granted, but the latter may be refused? The article being silent on the subject is easily to be accounted for. An express grant of the right would have imminently hazarded the peace of either country, in case the other was engaged in a war in which they had no common concern. An express negation of it would very idly have excluded voluntary favors, altogether in the power of either party to grant or to refuse; and would have been a stipulation (the first perhaps of the kind) for the benefit of other countries, without the least possible utility to either of the contracting parties. I might add, if the same provision was not to be found in other treaties where the circumstances were different, that the situation of the two countries at the time, naturally dictated the silence observed upon this subject. The treaty of commerce was signed on the same day with the treaty of alliance. The former was permanent; the latter, as to its principal object, temporary. While the war subsisted, in which both parties were fully engaged as allies on one side, the ports of either would of course be open to the vessels of war and privateers of the other. When peace took place, and the principal object of the alliance was thereby obtained, it became of moment to both that neither should be endangered, without a new engagement, by hostilities which the subsisting one had not contemplated. The case therefore was properly left at large to the discretion of either party, as future contingencies and the honor and interest of their respective countries might require.

3. There not only is nothing in the context or any concurrent circumstances requiring the construction contended for; but there are very material circumstances to evince that such could not have been the intention of the parties. I might instance its inconsistency with the famous family compact entered into between France and Spain and the King of the two Sicilies (a treaty universally known long before our connection with France) but as that stands on peculiar grounds of its own, I choose to confine myself to some striking circumstances of inconsistency where the cases are exactly parallel, in relation to the respective commercial connections of Great Britain (before the present war) and the United States with France. At the time of the signature of our treaties with France, a commercial treaty between Great Britain and France was in full force, containing substantially if not in the very same words, an article like that of the 22d in ours. The treaty (if I recollect right, for I have not now the book by me, though I am certain of the fact in substance, because I have compared the treaties) was the commercial treaty of Utrecht, of 1712-13, renewed as to this point from time to time, and finally by the treaty of Paris of 1763. In the commercial treaty between Great Britain and France in 1786, there is also an article to the very same import. It is therefore apparent, in case the construction which was claimed against us be right, that under the joint operation of either of the treaties between France and Great Britain, and that between France and the United States, if we had been at war with Great Britain, and France neutral, France would have been bound by her treaty with Great Britain to admit her privateers to arm, and exclude ours; by her treaties with us, to admit ours, and exclude theirs. A consequence so absurd or so iniquitous, we surely have no right to fix on any engagement, without the least color of evidence, and most ungrateful as well as weak should we be to attempt it in regard to a treaty which we have uniformly acknowledged and sincerely believe was conducted, together with that which accompanied it, on the part of the French government towards us, with singular magnanimity and candor, and on the part of our own with extraordinary ability, vigilance, and precaution. It is highly probable that the American negotiators who signed, and the Congress of the United States who ratified the treaty, were well acquainted with the contents of the commercial treaty of Utrecht, which was executed so many years before, and I doubt not had been repeatedly published, with its several confirmations;

and it is certain that Great Britain, when she executed the treaty in 1786, well knew all the particulars of ours of 1778, a complete copy of it having been published in England (as I have lately had an opportunity to know) soon after its execution. She therefore could not have been deceived, if we were, had there been any real perfidy in the case, a supposition which, unsupported as it is by either evidence or probability, we reject with disdain.

Objections like these would, in my opinion, be sufficient to destroy any construction, even if the words were doubtful, but in the face of such objections to contend for such a construction by implication, is paying very little deference to the understandings, or relying very much on the passions of those who are expected to acquiesce in it.

I therefore have not the smallest doubt that the pretension I have been considering is utterly groundless.

The second pretension involves the very important question as to the right of the French, or any other foreign nation (for in this respect they are all on the same footing) to enlist citizens of the United States, either for their naval or land service, within the territory of the United States, without the consent of the government. This is so palpably contrary to the law of nations, that it has scarcely been attempted to be supported upon its own ground; but a color has been devised for it, one of the most extraordinary which to be sure ever was attempted in a country where common reason had any sway. When a citizen of the United States is charged with this offence against his country, he very gravely defends himself by saying, that he has a right to quit his country when he pleases; that no country has a right to confine him as a prisoner for life; that it is at his option when he thinks proper to cease to become a citizen of the United States, and become a citizen of another country; that he did so in the present instance, and therefore his conduct was innocent. All this time, however, he forgets that it is material to prove the fact, or expects that we will take his word for it. Gentlemen, nothing but the prevalence of high passions, in disregard or contempt of the duty incumbent on all to respect and maintain the laws of their country, could among men of sense give currency to an absurdity like this. Let this right of expatriation be admitted, in the language of its warmest advocates, to be a natural and unalienable right, incapable of any modification, even by legislative authority, to guard against injuries to the rights of others by an abuse of the exercise of this—yet common sense must inform every man that this important, and perhaps irrecoverable act, ought to be done with some degree of deliberation and solemnity—that it should take place before any act inconsistent with the duty of a citizen is committed; and that in case of the fact being drawn in question, it should be capable of proof; juries in all cases being to be guided by proofs, and not by the allegations of any parties whatever. No person will be so absurd as to say, that a citizen of the United States may not, if he pleases, without abandoning his country, or intending to abandon it, enlist himself on board a foreign vessel, or in a foreign regiment, running the risk of detection and punishment for this breach of a citizen's duties. What would have been thought of one of your citizens, when he was on his trial for treason in the late war, if he had alleged in his defence that the mere act of joining the enemy of his country constituted him a British subject, and of course he was entitled to be deemed a prisoner of war, and not liable to be tried for treason? The difference of joining a friend or enemy is nothing as to the question of expatriation. Joining the former in hostilities contrary to law, is equally an offence, though not in the same degree as the latter; and when once a man is really expatriated, he has certainly a right to choose his future country, whether it be that of a friend or an enemy, if he can get admitted by either. The fact, therefore, which is to constitute the vindication, must in all instances be satisfactorily proved. What may amount to a real expatriation, as it is a point much questioned among able men, had better be reserved for discussion when a case of the kind shall arrive. I doubt much whether in all the instances which have occurred, of citizens of the United States enlisting themselves in a foreign service, any case has happened where there was a previous deliberate attempt at expatriation upon any principle. So far as I have observed or heard, the crime itself has been alleged to form its justification. It would give me pleasure, however, to find in any instance a more favorable case than that which I have supposed. But expatriation alone does not immediately entitle a man to be a citizen of any other country he chooses to adopt. It will therefore be necessary always to inquire further, whether the laws of his new favorite country have really recognized him as such, before we admit him to the privileges of that character. The imminent danger, gentlemen, to which some neighboring States have been particularly exposed by secret and unauthorized endeavors to raise troops among them, for the purpose (as it is alleged) of acting against some of the enemies of France, has naturally excited great anxiety and alarm in all. No power on earth but the Congress of the United States can authorize such a measure. Every step, out of the usual course, by which a neutral nation extends a favor to one of the belligerent powers to the injury another, has a direct tendency to produce, if it does not in itself justify, a war against such a neutral nation by the party injured. If a war takes place against the United States, all the citizens of the United States must be involved in it. It is therefore as just as it is constitutional, that their representatives alone should give authority to any hostilities which may occasion it. It certainly ought not to depend on a few unauthorized individuals, whether we are to enjoy the blessings of peace, or be exposed to all the calamities of war. The danger too of such a practice to the internal peace of our country, is a consideration of no small moment. The power of raising troops, even by regular authority, is a very formidable one. There can be no security that when raised for one purpose they will not be employed for another, unless they are under the vigilant eye of men fully responsible for their conduct, and within the reach of being called to a strict account for it. The prevention of mischief by them, is often found difficult under the best regulations—but what security can we have against foreign officers, and men who, pretending to have abandoned their country, may be expected to pay very little deference to its interests? The weight of these considerations every reflecting man must be sensible of, and they have already appeared to have had their proper influence upon a people who value liberty. and naturally jealous even of armies raised by their own authority, feel proportionable indignation at an attempt to raise one in defiance of it.

It thus appearing, that the second pretension is as groundless as the first, and still more dangerous in its nature and tendency, it follows that neither can constitute any exception to the general duties which a state of neutrality requires. Those duties, so far as an actual observance of the laws is concerned, are equally incumbent upon persons who are resident in our country, though not citizens, during their stay in it, as upon citizens themselves. They have not indeed equal motives to attach themselves to its honor and interest; but they receive the protection of the government; they partake of its benefits; and of course must be subject to its laws. That order and tranquillity which every citizen is bound sacredly to support, ought not to be disturbed with impunity by any foreigners whatever. They, therefore, excepting those only who may be exempted by peculiar privileges, are equally amenable to the justice of this court as citizens.

There still, however, remains a very important inquiry, whether a right of prosecution exists in cases where the legislature of the United States has made no special provision, most, if not all of the cases I have been considering (unblended with other circumstances), coming within that description. I shall give you my opinion, gentlemen, upon this subject, with all the clearness and distinctness of which I am capable, and this I think it is more particularly proper for me to do, because I confess I had at one time considerable doubts in regard to it, though subsequent reflection and attention to very able arguments in an important case entirely removed them.* The reasons upon which my present opinion is founded, that a prosecution is maintainable for such offences as I have been considering, though no act of Congress expressly prescribes it, are as follow :

1. The common law of England, from which our own is derived, fully recognizes the principles of the law of nations, and applies them in all cases falling under its jurisdiction, where the nature of the subject requires it. Even the Legislature cannot rightfully control them, but if it passes any law on such subjects, is bound by the dictates of moral duty to the rest of the world, in no instance to transgress them, although if it in fact doth so, it is entitled to actual obedience within the sphere of its authority. In whatever manner the law of nations is violated, it is a subject of national, and not personal complaint. The nation injured, whether the injury be in fact committed by any branch of the government, or by any individual, is to apply to that nation from whose government the injury proceeds, or in which it is committed ; and if due redress be not given, it is a cause of reprisals, and under some circumstances may even justify war. Since, therefore, the nation to which any individual belongs, is accountable for his personal observance of the law of nations, in all instances where his conduct may affect it, at the hazard of hostilities to the whole government, and every person belonging to it, there can be no case in which it is more sacredly the duty of any individual to conform his conduct to those principles which ought to direct it, nor can a violation of any duty of an individual be attended with greater danger to the community. Consequently, if there be a principle in the common law (as there unquestionably is) which subjects a man to a public prosecution for a contempt of his duty to the community, this must be understood as one of those cases comprehended within that class of public offences, and may be proceeded against accordingly. These principles are now so familiar, that I believe it will scarcely be questioned (whatever doubt might formerly have been entertained), that upon the genuine principles of the common law, where they are permitted to operate, a prosecution for an offence of this nature would be held maintainable. The act of Parlia-

* The point has since been settled otherwise. Iredell, it seems, at first had "considerable doubts." I am inclined to think he was betrayed into error by his characteristic modesty, yielding too readily to the authority of his colleagues.

ment passed on the complaint of the Czar of Muscovy, has been clearly considered by very high authorities to be in affirmance of the common law, which it is presumed would have afforded redress in that case if political considerations had not induced a different kind of satisfaction.

2. It will not be denied that this part of the common law subsisted in full force in this State previous to the Revolution, it being in no respect inconsistent with the peculiar circumstances of the country (which in case of an interference must necessarily control the general operation of the common law), nor superseded by any special act of legislation. An offence against the law of nations might have been equally injurious to the public welfare, and to individuals, if committed by an inhabitant of this country, as if committed in England ; and therefore there was the same reason for the application of the common law principle to it.

3. The change in the government could not do away the common law in this particular, that continuing (according to acknowledged principles universally received in America) upon the same footing as before, except in cases where its operation was absolutely inconsistent with the change in our situation, until altered by some act of the people, or of the legislature of the State ; and no one will pretend there was the slightest inconsistency in this principle of the common law with the change in our government, because under the present, as under the former, the same injury would expose the State and all that belonged to it to the like danger, arising from the misconduct of any individual, and of course the same security was required against it.

4. The only two acts, either of the legislature or the people, affecting this subject, were the articles of confederation, and the present Constitution of the United States. I shall give these, for the greater perspicuity, a distinct consideration.

1. The articles of confederation gave all external authority as to peace and war to the Congress of the United States, but left full, complete legislative authority as to all internal concerns in the several States, and except in very special cases, no way relative to our present subject, the whole judicial authority was likewise in the several States. The public faith could be pledged by Congress, and each State upon a principle of duty was bound to fulfil it, but if they omitted to do any thing on their part which a constitutional act of Congress required, though this might be deemed a breach of faith in the Union, the law subsisted as before. These articles, therefore, in themselves, effected no change, for if they had still continued, the only remedy of Congress on an occasion like the present, would have been by causing an application to be made to a competent State court, acting under the laws of the State and the control of their public duty, as bound to regard all the constitutional measures of Congress as to peace or war, which fixed the relative situation of the United States as to other powers accordingly.

2. The effect of the present Constitution of the United States, in my opinion, was not to vacate all State laws concerning subjects in respect to which judicial authority was given, but to authorize Congress to establish courts for the trial of such cases, and, also, to make any alteration in the laws concerning such particulars as the nature of the new situation of the United States, under a proper construction of their legislative authority, might require. This view of the subject, if it be not strictly just, yet is certainly conformable to the actual situation in which we are placed, because the Congress in their judicial act passed at their first session, have provided as follows, viz. :

"That the laws of the several States, except where the constitution, treaties, or statutes of the United States, shall otherwise require or provide, shall be regarded as rules of decision in trials at common law in the courts of the United States in cases where they apply."

There is a statute particularly providing for the punishment of crimes against the United States, passed at the second session of Congress, and there are some other statutory provisions on the same subject interspersed in other acts. So far as these make provision they supersede all principles of common law in regard to them. But where they are silent, for the reasons I have stated, the common law which existed before (so far as it is applicable to our present situation) must still operate. They are silent in respect to most if not all offences for breaches of neutrality, merely as such ; the common law therefore as to such offences is still in force, the prosecutions it authorizes for such offences being so far from any inconsistency with the constitution or treaties of the United States, that they tend in the most effectual manner to protect the former, and give due efficacy to the latter.

Having had occasion, gentlemen, to take up so much of your time on a subject which naturally and properly, at the present momentous period, engages so strongly the attention of us all, I shall not trouble you on any other. I doubt not your strictest attention to the whole of your duty ; but I thought it of the highest importance on the present occasion, to rectify many misrepresentations which had taken place, and to point out in the clearest manner I was able, that duty of individuals in support of the government of their country, which I fear is too little understood, and too slightly regarded. Such a support is necessary for all governments, but is the natural protection of a free one, which glories in having no other object than the true liberty and genuine happiness of that people by whom it was formed, for whose welfare it was intended, and whose prosperity, I trust, by an invariable adherence to the principles which produced it, will be perpetuated, with increasing splendor and renown, to the latest period of time.

Gov. Lee of Va. to Iredell.

July 22d, '94.

"Gov. Lee is much obliged by Mr. Iredell's attention to his wishes, and will take pleasure in procuring publicity to sentiments which do the highest honor to the author, and cannot but essentially promote a right understanding on subjects in which are involved some of the best interests of our common country."

To a friend who applied at this time for his aid in procuring a public office, Judge Iredell replied, that though it would give him great pleasure to serve him in any instance in his power, he had, ever since his elevation to the bench, deemed it improper for him to solicit advancement for others, and had rigidly adhered to the rule.

Judge Iredell attended the August Term of the Supreme Court, but as there are no reports of cases in Mr. Dallas's volumes, I presume little or no business was transacted.

Iredell to Mrs. Iredell.

Philadelphia, August 3d, 1794.

"My dear Hannah:—I arrived here yesterday, extremely well, though greatly fatigued, and am very comfortably lodged at Mrs. York's. She and Miss York seemed very glad to see me. Molly Sprogel had the disorder very badly last year, and was in danger of losing her arm. She is at present in the country, and quite well. The city was never known to be healthier. I have seen Mr. Mease's, Mrs. Stocker's, Mr. Bond's, and Mr. Anthony's families. Miss Mease has been very ill with an intermitting fever, but is quite recovered. I saw Mrs. Bond, Miss Fanny, and Mrs. Cadwallader. Mr. Bond, and Miss Beckey, were at Germantown with Mrs. Travis, who has been very ill, and is still a good deal so. Mrs. Anthony has gone with her son Tom to Rhode Island. All appeared glad to see me. Fanny Bond says she shall be much mortified if Helen forgets her. All of your friends express a great desire to see you back again. I will see Polly as soon as I can. I sent to Peter, and he came to me last night. He will wait on me while I am in town. Poor fellow! he looks very thin, and gets his living by cutting wood every day. Edy never rested till she got Dundee from Mr. Mease's, and I believe he is bound to Levy, the lawyer. I shall however make inquiry about it.*

I am going to take a family dinner with Judge Wilson. There is a report that Mr. Jay's arrival in England has been heard from, but there is no such authentic account. The President and his family are at Germantown. He is, however frequently in Philadelphia. The papers will give an account of a very melancholy resistance to the Excise-law in this State, which has already cost some lives. The Governor is to march to-morrow from this place with some troops, part of the militia of this State, and is resolved to support the execution of the laws by all the means in his power. As worthy a man as any in the State a General Neville, after defending himself with great bravery was overpowered by great numbers, and had his house, &c., burnt. His only offence that we hear of was, his being an Excise officer Mr. A. says no vessel has as yet sailed large enough to carry your carriage, but one will soon be ready. I went to Chris Church this morning, but unfortunately Blackwell preached This was additionally provoking, as Mr. Bond preached at St Peters, &c., &c.

JAS. IREDELL.

In a letter to Judge Wilson, declining to ride the Southern Circuit in his stead, August 5th, Judge Iredell remarked that he had rode that Circuit *five* times in *four* years.†

Gov. Johnston to Iredell.

Williamston, 14th August.

My dear Sir:— * * * * I have perused Mr. Necker's remarks on the French Constitution with that attention which it merits: it contains much good matter; and afforded me both information, and entertainment. The style is Mr. Burke's, who I shall presume, was the translator, till I am otherwise informed

Our election commences this day. The candidates are very numerous. Some of the principal inhabitants solicited me to represent them in the Senate, but I was afraid to hazard my constitution at the *inclement* season when the Assembly is to sit Lodgings will necessarily be scarce, and bad, &c.

---

* Peter, Edy, and Dundee were negroes whom Judge Iredell had taken to the North when appointed to the Bench.

† By an Act of Congress, supplementary to the Judiciary Act, the Judges have been directed to ride by turns the Circuit most distant from the seat of Government.

Hermitage, September 10th.

* * * * I am very much obliged to you for the newspapers. I about the same time received a Petersburg paper with intelligence of a later date, tending to confirm the idea that matters were in a fair way of being accommodated with the rioters in Pennsylvania. I hope, however, a few examples will be made, to discourage such doings in future. Though I am by no means pleased with the temper, and manners of the French, as they at this time exist, the accounts of their repeated victories and success in Flanders give me great pleasure. The English, who of late years have had little cause for exultation for success, either at sea or on land, would have been too highly elated with their late naval victory, and their achievements in the West Indies. Were not our "quondam" countrymen now and then to meet with a pretty severe check, that national pride and haughtiness, which they possess in so eminent a degree, would be intolerable to the rest of the world, &c.

October 1st.

* * * * I have seen a detail of the proceedings of the Commissioners, and the Committee of the Pennsylvania Insurgents: the folly of their leaders, and their own temerity, have drawn them into a dilemma painful to contemplate. A little wholesome severity will bring them to a proper sense of their duty. I am glad to hear that Mr. Mifflin takes so active a part, that it may not appear altogether an affair of the General Government, &c.

October 15th.

* * * * I am very much concerned to understand that the President has been under the degrading necessity of taking the command against the Insurgents. The necessity, it seems, arose from a point of etiquette between the Governors of Virginia and Pennsylvania: neither would submit to the command of the other, &c.*

SAM. JOHNSTON.

Iredell to John Hay.

Edenton, November 24th.

Dear Sir:— * * * * I hear Judge Wilson was so pleased with Fayetteville, that if he had a vote for our seat of government poor Wake would stand no chance with him.

I thank you kindly for your letter of the 8th, which I received a day or two after I wrote you by Mr. Jones. I give you no news, as you will have later at Court. I pray sincerely in the usual form—"*Counsel our Counsellors, and give our Senators wisdom,*" &c.

JAS. IREDELL.

Iredell to Judge Wilson.

Edenton, November 24th.

Dear Sir:—It was a great satisfaction to me to hear that you and Mrs. Wilson had got safe so far on your journey as Fayetteville. I anxiously hope this letter will find you both perfectly well at Wake, and less dissatisfied with your journey, troublesome as I know it must have been, than perhaps you expected. I have suffered, almost ever since my return home, from a continual scene of distress, and anxiety. *All* of my family have been sick; some of them repeatedly. I thank God, however, they have all been preserved, and are now in good health.

I wrote a letter to you immediately upon my return home, but I fear you did not receive it. It was my intention to have spoken to you on the subject of the allowance belonging to the Southern Circuit, but was so very much indisposed a day or two before I left Philadelphia, and had so many things to do, that I omitted it. I know not whether there was any particular agreement among the Judges who were together in February, as to the time when the allowance should begin, but as I assented to the proposal immediately on its being made (which I did in a letter to the Chief Justice), and was the first Judge who went the Southern Circuit afterwards, I considered myself entitled to receive the money agreed upon: this I thought of when we met together in August, but, as it would have seemed like an indirect demand on the other Judges, I could not bear to do so. I shall be perfectly satisfied if I am permitted to give myself credit for it against a similar charge upon me. If my idea be just, your account, and mine, are balanced. If not, I will with pleasure pay the $100 for which I am indebted. This was the particular subject of the letter I mention above.

You will have later intelligence from the Northward at Wake than any I can give you. I warmly congratulate you on the great success of the Western expedition. I am persuaded it has added strength and dignity to the Government. We have many discontented people among us, but I think Federalism is in a state of convalescence; and if Mr. Jay's mission should be successful, it will keep under the little barkings of ill-humor which are now perpetually assailing our ears.

---

* Gov. Lee of Virginia had the chief command. The President inspected the two divisions of the troops, but did not accompany them into the seat of the "Whiskey Insurrection."

It would give Mrs. I. and myself great pleasure, if you and Mrs. Wilson could spare the time to see this part of the country before you return. In that case we hope you would be so good as to accept during your stay here an apartment under our humble roof, where, with no elegance, you would meet with a most sincere welcome.

This letter will be handed to you by Mr. Collins, who has for a great many years been a very respectable and eminent merchant of this place, with a degree of industry equal to any in a Northern climate. I beg leave to introduce him to the honor of your acquaintance. He can give you a great deal of valuable information as to the state of this country, particularly its commercial concerns, &c.

JAS. IREDELL.

Gov. Johnston to Iredell.
November 26th.

Dear Sir :— * * * * From what appears in Hodge's last paper, I flatter myself that the Pennsylvania Insurrection is entirely suppressed by this time, in a manner highly honorable to Government. Even the great Brackenridge cries "*peccavi*," or rather seems to wish to be thought innocent. I hope Government will treat him with contempt by taking no notice of him, unless there is such proof against him as cannot be controverted: in that case he would be a very proper subject for an example. He puts me in mind of those *snarling curs* who have not spirit enough to bite, but excite others to bite—a perfect *Thersites*.

The Duke has had another *drubbing*. If his great grandfather was now living, he could explain the meaning of that word to him as well as the Duke of Bedford could have done, to whom it is said the late Earl of Chesterfield referred him for an explanation of it.

I am glad to see the Convention putting off that sanguinary spirit, which has so long disgraced them, and assuming a more humane disposition since the fall of that monster Robespierre; but am much concerned to hear that Tallien was assassinated—I hope that it is not the case.

I see that Taylor has resigned his seat in the Senate; and that a Mr. Mason and a Mr. Tazewell, succeed him and Monroe. As I am a stranger to these gentlemen, I cannot decide whether the change is for the better.

December 10th.

* * * * I am very glad to see so good an understanding between the President and the Senate; and that the latter have denounced the *Jacobin Clubs*. I wish they may be joined in this particular by the House, but I understand the opponents of the administration muster a strong party there.

I hope that this will be a less turbulent session than the last; and that the successful measures against the Western Insurgents will confirm the friends, and overawe the enemies of Government.

I am very much pleased with the President's Address, in particular with his animated manner when he speaks of the Constitution, &c., &c.

SAM. JOHNSTON.

Col. Davie to Iredell.*
Halifax, December 15th.

My dear Sir :— * * * * * I have felt considerable anxiety respecting the choice of a Senator. You know how much I have our reputation at heart, and what mortification I have suffered on this head. The gentleman you mention has good dispositions; and I believe is strongly attached to the interests of his country; and is not deficient in integrity and independence: these virtues may render a man harmless, but with these qualifications alone he would be useless. Excuse me—he is perhaps the best who has been mentioned. Our whole representation is but a type of Shakspeare's old man—" sans teeth, sans eyes, sans every thing."

I congratulate you on the happy termination of the Whiskey business. For a time that affair wore an ugly aspect. All the bad consequences, however, of that project have been baffled by the decision and energy of the President. How great, and how fortunate is that man!

Jude Wilson's affability and politeness gave great satisfaction to both the bar and the people; a circumstance I mention with pleasure, because I have observed its conciliatory effect with respect to the Government, &c.

W. R. DAVIE.

Iredell to Gov. Lee of Va.
Edenton, December 26th.

Sir :—I have never been unmindful of the great honor you did me in wishing that I would write to you; and had you continued in Virginia, I should certainly have done so long ago. * * * *

I congratulate you, sir, with my whole soul, on the glorious success you have achieved with a *Patriot Army*, which has exhibited such interesting and affecting marks of genuine republican virtue; cheerfully sacrificing all private convenience; and, what was yet more difficult, all party prejudices to the great object of their country's good; and discovering with a unanimity, I believe unexampled among any militia, and scarcely to be exceeded by Regulars, a degree of moderation, order, and obedience, when they were entire masters, that are the themes of general gratitude and admiration in their own country, and will scarcely be credited in any other. It will, I doubt not, have the happy effect, not only to keep under a spirit of discontent which really was proceeding to a very alarming height, but to impress foreign nations with a greater respect for a Government, capable, with so much dignity and moderation, of suppressing in so short a time so formidable an insurrection.

My confined situation since my return to this State, has disabled me from forming any very accurate opinion of its general disposition. I think, however, a better test could scarcely be had than the proceedings under the late draft of militia. Very uncommon pains were taken to make the people discontented. The complaint of the smallness of the pay was universal, and every art used to inflame the minds of the people on this topic. A ridiculous notion was generally diffused, and credited in a manner almost beyond belief, that the drafted men were to be sent immediately to France. Notwithstanding these circumstances, I have not heard of more than two or three counties where the draft was altogether obstructed: in some, where difficulties were found early in the day, they were removed by reasoning in time to effect the purpose: in one county in particular, near us, there appeared no prospect of effecting a draft at all until near sunset, when volunteers offered nearly to the amount of the whole number required, and it was supposed more than enough would have offered had the day not been too far spent: in some more than sufficient, and the contest was who should be accepted. These things, and many others, satisfy me that the conduct of our members is little affected by any general discontent here, and that the disposition of this State is good. Our members who vote almost constantly in opposition, out of deference for *your members*, would, if a majority of them took a different turn, join them with cordiality. I am as certain as I am of my existence, that the discontent of Virginia has been the principal cause of ours, which is a strong proof how important it is to gentlemen of character, to consider well the grounds upon which they encourage any, &c., &c.

JAS. IREDELL.

---

* It is worthy of note, as illustrative of character, that all Davie's letters are written on gilt-edged paper.

CHAPTER XXVIII.

Æt. 43—44.

PARTY-SPIRIT. LETTER FROM GOV. LEE. SUPREME COURT, FEB. TERM, AND LETTERS FROM IREDELL. THE EASTERN CIRCUIT. LETTERS FROM ALEX. CAMPBELL, SIMEON BALDWIN, GOV. JOHNSTON, AND DR. WM. SAMUEL JOHNSON. SUPREME COURT, AUG. TERM. LETTERS FROM WM. DAWSON, COL. DAVIE, AND JUDGE BLAIR.

We are apt to suppose that the party-spirit that now rages with indecent excess, and disturbs with its criminations, its passions, and its tumults, is without a parallel in our history; but a retrospect of the past is instructive, and consolatory. "The thing that hath been, it is that which shall be; and that which is done is that which shall be done: and there is no new thing under the sun." However dreamers may speculate about the progress, and perfectibility of the human race; and predict an era of unbroken peace and happiness, unmolested by strife, and unperplexed by even "rumors of oppression and deceit," history confirms the declaration of the Bible. The relations of man to the Almighty remain the same in all ages; and life, with its temptations, its pleasures, its pains, its success, its adversities, and its trials, teaches all the same lesson, that this world is but an arena in which we are placed to qualify ourselves for immortality. As long as God's scheme for the government and redemption of his creatures remains unaltered—and who shall dare infer change without a revelation!—like events will continue to flow from like causes. The play of the passions centuries ago, will find its reproduction in the exhibition of to-day; *perfect happiness here* is an airy fabric, unsubstantial as the golden cloud that decks the dying day; "Jam redit et virgo, redeunt Saturnia regna," an expression of joy that must be reserved for the millennium.

During the latter term of General Washington's administra-

vol. ii.—28

tion violent was the temper of opposing factions, impassioned their language, and loud their clamor. Malice was active, and attained the climax of audacity by assaults upon the exalted character of the President. The Federal and anti-Federal parties each charged its antagonist with treason—a design to subvert the Government. The anti-Federalists alleged that the Federalists intended a monarchy. The Federalists retorted with the accusation, that their enemies designed a democracy with an agrarian code. Though the roar of the waters seemed to indicate a cataract, and the timid startled at the thought of impending destruction, yet the bark, freighted with the hopes of liberty, found, provided by the wisdom of the Executive and the good sense of the people, a channel avoiding peril, wide, deep, and secure. When the French Revolution occurred, it was but natural that the hearts of the Americans should beat responsive to those of their recent allies ; and that they should gaze with exultation upon the flame kindled at their own altar. When, however, carnage became a law, and revolted humanity could only perceive in France objects stained with an ensanguined hue, a large portion of the people turned away in sorrow or disgust from a cause so disgraced as to appear accursed of God. Many still cherished hope ; regarded the horrors of a few years as but a reasonable expiation for the tyranny of centuries ; and looked to the future as a period when, striking the balance, the gain would be found to be on the side of humanity. The monarchs of Europe, agitated by the smoke and cinders, and terrified by the explosions of the volcano whose burning lava spread over so many smiling plains, determined to encircle and confine the danger by a barrier of armed men. The war between England and France, the news of which preceded by a few days the arrival of the French Minister, aroused to the highest pitch the sympathy and enthusiasm of the partisans of France. Received with distinction, and accompanied with plaudits to the Federal capital, Genet was but badly prepared to encounter or submit to the wise policy of the President, who, a pillar of fire in the darkness, pointed out to the people the path of safety. Many, in a spirit of generous devotion, were deaf to the voice of prudence, and scorned the calculations of interest : their warrior blood leaped at the thought of exchanging blows again with Great Britain ; and sentiment sanctified the impulse to succor an ally : if their conduct was not wise, it was at least honorable. The neutrality laws of the Union were openly violated. Finding the Executive resolute to maintain the law, Genet, with the characteristic ardor of his countrymen, lost his cause by his indiscretion in offering insult to Washington, and his threatened appeal from him to the nation. Had the Union been strong enough to wage an effectual war against France and England at the same time, it would have been well for the world ; for both France and England, by restrictions, and decrees in violation of the law of nations and the rights of neutrals, essayed to constrain the United States to become a party to their feud.

The Federal Judges, in their addresses to the grand juries, labored earnestly to commend the Constitution and the Government to the affection of the people. Their charges have more of a party character than is reconcilable with modern notions of strict judicial propriety, but then they should be judged by the standard of their contemporaries ; and the patriotism of their motives, and the exigencies of the times be permitted to hallow the error. A closer intimacy subsisted between the Judiciary and the Executive, than obtains now ; and the charges of the Judges were printed, and circulated by his friends as means of defence and popularity.

The gross accusations, and the intemperate denunciations of political opponents, whose memories we all now revere, to be found in the letters of Judge Iredell's Federal correspondents, should teach us moderation ; and impress upon us the beauty of that charity which "beareth all things, believeth all things, hopeth all things, endureth all things."

GOV. LEE TO IREDELL.

RICHMOND, VA., January 21st, 1795.

SIR :—Yesterday Mr. Campbell presented to me your letter of the 26th ult.

With very great pleasure I perceive, from its contents, your determination to carry into effect my proposition of a regular exchange of sentiments, and information on public matters ; for while I cannot fail to receive therefrom personal gratification, I have some hopes to be enabled thereby occasionally to benefit our common country. Your remarks concerning the temper of North Carolina are perfectly just, and I have not the smallest doubt if Virginia could be rectified in her politics, the happy event would embrace your State in its benign effects—" Hoc opus, hic labor est."

The impressions which many artful, designing individuals have made by their representations on the mind of the people of this State could readily be removed, were they not confirmed in a manner by the part which Mr. Madison takes. The virtue and ability of this gentleman, deservedly give to him the confidence of his countrymen ; and, with respect to political affairs, this confidence derives additional influence from the zeal and decision with which he supported the adoption of the Constitution. It is not possible, they suppose, so good and so enlight-

ened a citizen could be brought to act with the known enemies of the Constitution, as to its administration, without positive, and ample cause ; therefore they credit the aspersions with which the measures of Government, and the plans of ministers, are charged ; and, crediting the allegations, it is not surprising they should act with jealousy, distrust, and occasional enmity towards Government.

Better would it have been for the harmony and happiness of the United States if Mr. Madison, governed as he is at present, had originally been an opposer of the Constitution. Less weight and influence would have attached itself to his character ; and, consequently, the power he deservedly enjoys in the public opinion, would be less operative in their decision on public questions.

I had reckoned on very auspicious effects to the general good, from the wise and vigorous measures adopted by the President in crushing the late wicked insurrection ; and as that event may be fairly traced to the principles and sentiments delivered by members of Congress, I had also presumed that the experience of the case would have rendered good men more prudent, and bad men less daring.

But it seems, from some untoward accidents, little or no good has been derived therefrom so far as respects Congress.

The dilatory meeting of the Senate had malign effects. The public mind was big with gratitude ; and had the two Houses assembled with punctuality, the President's speech would have been received with due respect and affection ; and would have laid the foundation for the full accomplishment of his enlightened policy, by producing a harmonious coincidence of sentiment in every branch of Government.

The Senate's delay gave time for the wicked to agitate their schemes, and to correspond with each other in different parts of the United States. The emotions of gratitude so general, and so sincere, in which even the vicious participated in appearance, began to subside, and a certain party reassumed confidence. On the meeting of the two Houses, the temper of the members, in consequence of the delay, was not so prone to the promotion of right as it had been when they left their homes ; and the disgraceful debates about the article "a" and the possessive "you," with the vicious opposition to the President's censure of certain self-created societies, ensued.

The baneful effects were immediately felt everywhere, and discord with all its evils prevailed, where every circumstance seemed to have invited full and perfect harmony.

It is the lot of mortals to be disturbed nationally, and individually. One comfort solaces me in my reflections on our situation, that we continue to be happy, more happy than other nations, in spite of these rude blasts that chill us.

For my own part I shall not seek, nor avoid, public life. I shall confine myself to my own State. In every character to which it may be my lot to be carried, I shall with frankness and firmness oppose those measures which are so zealously supported by many, virtuous citizens, for some of whom I have a real regard in a high degree, because I do believe our common peace and prosperity involved in the timely check to their politics and influence.

Truth must at last prevail, and the enlightened freemen of America, though slow to discover the real views of the different parties, will in time perceive with accuracy the distinction which marks them, and will be sure to encircle with their best affections the steady and determined friends to order and good government.

In Kentucky the people are beginning to act after some years' credulous submission ; and, from the last accounts from that quarter, the friends to law and the constitution as administered, begin to lead in the public councils. So it must be here, and with you in a few years.

Your commendation of the manly and patriotic exertions of my late companions in arms is very grateful to me ; and I can with truth assure you that they merit the applause their countrymen honor them with.

Wishing that the restoration of the health of your family may be complete, and you with them may long enjoy the best gratifications in the reach of mortals,

I have the honor to be with great respect,
Your most obedient servant,
HENRY LEE.

IREDELL TO MRS. IREDELL.

BLADENSBURG, MD., January 28th, 1795.

MY DEAR HANNAH :—I wrote you from Petersburg and Richmond ; and, without a moment's delay, came on here, expecting to be in Baltimore to-night ; but upon my arrival here yesterday, in the midst of a torrent of rain, I found it was a general opinion that it would be impossible to cross the Patuxent river, which is usually fordable about fifteen miles from this place ; and another gentleman and myself resolved to stay for the next stage. The stage having the mail was obliged to proceed as far as the river at least ; but, as we afterwards heard, it was swimming water, and the stage must have returned nine miles back, where the accommodations are very indifferent. Our landlord and landlady, returning from Baltimore, came very near being drowned. My determination to stay was very fortunate. I have a good room to myself, with a fireplace, and am perfectly at my ease. Though I have come through exceedingly bad roads, and some very bad weather towards the last, yet my health is much better than when I left home, and I can eat heartily three times a day. The weather has cleared up delightfully, and I hope to be in Baltimore to-morrow. I have heard nothing of Mrs. Wilson, and the Judge's son. She must have had a most disagreeable time, and been much exposed. A gentleman here has been so obliging as to lend me Mr. Hamilton's and Mr. Monroe's pamphlets. The latter appears to no advantage in either. It was principally owing to him that Mr. Hamilton thought himself obliged to disclose circumstances which must have been so painful to himself and Mrs. Hamilton. But it appears probable, that Mr. Hamilton rather yielded to temptation than was guilty of any seduction; and the most villainous artifices were afterwards practised to extort money, both by the husband and the wife. The former actually compromised the injury for $1000, but afterwards extorted more under a menace of revealing the matter to Mrs. Hamilton. However unwilling the lady may have been at first, she was very importunate for his visits afterwards: and it seems after all, that though she passed for Reynolds's wife, she had been married to one Clingman, who was a confederate in the plot. My respects to Judge Wilson, &c., &c.

PHILADELPHIA, February 3d.

I have the satisfaction to acquaint you, that I arrived here safe and perfectly well on Saturday afternoon. ✽ ✽ ✽ ✽ Mr. Dawson has been very sick indeed, and was for some time confined to his bed: he is still confined to his room, but is much better. His eyesight appears to me to be very bad, but he tells me it is better than when I saw him last, though he fears he has lost the sight of one entirely. It greatly affected me to see his situation. A new Doctor, whom he has consulted, whose name I don't recollect, thinks he has discovered the cause of his disorder, and is to perform an operation which Mr. Dawson is told will not be very painful. ✽ ✽ ✽ ✽ Your old friends in general are very well, except Helen's friend Miss Fanny Bond, who has suffered a good deal during the winter, and is still very much confined. I did not see her, though I did the rest of the family. It is certain that Mr. Jay has signed a Treaty with Great Britain, though the official dispatches have not arrived. It was signed on the 19th November, and is said to have adjusted all the subjects in dispute. God grant it may prove satisfactory, and permanent.

February 5th.

Mr. Dawson is much better, and able to attend Congress. ✽ ✽ ✽ Miss Anthony is certainly going to be married, and soon, to a Mr. Pollock, a merchant of New York. I went last evening with Governor Mifflin and family, and my brothers Blair and Patterson, to see the "Clandestine Marriage," but was much disappointed, for it was wretchedly acted. Mr. Whitlock did not perform. Mr. Wolcott is Secretary of the Treasury, &c., &c.

JAS. IREDELL.

SUPREME COURT.

At the February Term the important cases of Bingham *vs.* Cabot, and Penhallow *vs.* Doane, came up for argument and the Judges delivered their opinions "seriatim."✽

IREDELL TO MRS. IREDELL.

PHILADELPHIA, February 13th.

MY DEAR HANNAH:—I thank you for your punctuality in writing, and am happy to find that you and the children continue well; but was extremely shocked at the death of Mr. Lowther, an event which I am afraid will occasion great distress to that unfortunate family, especially perhaps as he left no will, which was an instance of unpardonable neglect. Poor Mrs. Page was particularly unfortunate in the manner of receiving the account. The letter came when Mr. Page was shaving, and she opened it with great gayety, though he insisted she should not, as it was directed to him, and, poor woman! she soon fell senseless on the floor. She speedily however recovered, but her sensations must be terrible indeed. ✽ ✽ ✽ ✽ Our Court is yet sitting, and probably will till some time next week. The Circuits are not yet assigned, but it is understood I am to go the Eastern Circuit, though it is in contemplation at present that I shall only go part of it, and Judge Cushing the remainder, that I may return here to assist Judge Patterson in trying the insurgents. If this be so, Judge Wilson will attend the remainder of the Middle Circuit, and Judge Blair the Southern. ✽ ✽ ✽ I am so much engaged with Court business, that I cannot possibly write now to any body else. Tell James his favorite Miss Betsey Cox is well. I drank tea with one of her sisters at Mr. Rutherford's. I sent Peter yesterday to Woodbury.† The following is an extract

* Vid. 3 Dallas.
† Andrew Hunter taught a school at Woodbury. Governor Johnston's son James is the pupil referred to. Mr. Hunter was in 1804 appointed Professor of Mathematics and Astronomy at Princeton College.

from Mr. Hunter's letter: "Since he has been with me he has not had an hour's illness. He grows finely, and improves very well in his studies. His conduct in every respect is amiable and respectable, and I think at some future day he will be among the first men of the country."

The beautiful Mrs. Anthony was married last night to Mr. Ewing, a respectable merchant in this town, a widower, with two or three children, &c., &c.✽

PHILADELPHIA, Feb. 20th.

✽ ✽ ✽ ✽ Our Court is yet sitting, and probably will for three or four days longer, and the business before us is of such great importance as to require almost our constant attention. ✽ ✽ ✽ I was at a dinner the day before yesterday, where there were about 150, given by the merchants of this city in honor of Mr. Hamilton and General Knox, on account of their public services. The highest testimonies of approbation were shown, particularly in respect to the former. The thanksgiving day yesterday was observed here in the most becoming manner, &c.

February 26th.

✽ ✽ ✽ ✽ It is expected that the insurgents will have their trial at the Circuit Court here; and therefore that Judge Patterson will not be able to attend any other Court in the Middle Circuit, in which case (if the C. Justice does not come in time) Mr. Wilson has promised to attend the other Courts. There was no offer to exchange with me, or I should have liked it very much. Agreeable as the Eastern Circuit would be to me in all other respects, it distresses me beyond measure to think of the painful situation in which it places me with regard to you, and my dear children. The last Court will be held in Rhode Island the 19th of June, and probably continue until the latter end of the month, if not till some time in July, for there is always a good deal of business there, so that I have no expectation that I can get home until after the Supreme Court in August, which will probably have a very long session, as perhaps the great Virginia cause and some others will then come on. ✽ ✽ ✽ ✽ The President's birthday was celebrated with uncommon zeal and attachment, and I never saw him in better health and spirits. The crowds of gentlemen that waited on him in the day were innumerable, and in the Assembly at night it was scarcely possible to move. I came off a little after eight, having business of great importance to attend to, and indeed the room was much too crowded to be comfortable. Mrs. Cabot among others was there.

* February 14th Governor Johnston wrote Judge Iredell, "Bloodworth beat Alfred Moore one vote for Senator (U. S.). O tempora! O mores!"

She is in much better health than she was, and always inquires very kindly about you. She, and Mrs. Cushing, and many others desired their respects to you. Among the rest, *Caradine*, our acquaintance at Bethlehem, who is idling away his time here as agreeably as he can. I have seen Miss Anthony's husband elect, Mr. Pollock. He is a very likely, genteel man; and, from his appearance, I should judge about 35. Much to our surprise and concern the Treaty has not yet arrived. Mr. Dawson is in very good health, except as to his eyesight; the New England gentlemen speak respectfully of him. Mrs. Blackbourne desires to be presented to you. I never was better in my life, not having even a cold, in which respect I am unfashionable, &c., &c.

March 6th.

✽ ✽ ✽ ✽ Our Court did not break up till Tuesday; and, though we were all very much fatigued, we should probably have sat several days longer but for Judge Cushing's indisposition, who suffers severely by a cancer on his lip. ✽ ✽ ✽ There was a very severe fire about 2 or 3 this morning, that broke out in the coachmaker's shop opposite Mr. Ross's; and two dwelling-houses (Mr. Allibone's one) were burnt, and others saved with difficulty. I never saw fiercer flames in my life. Immediately after leaving Mrs. York's, the flames, and instantly conjectured they were near the New Market. ✽ ✽ ✽ ✽ The Treaty has not yet arrived. The Senate is summoned specially to meet on the 8th of June, it being hoped that it will arrive in the mean time, &c., &c.

March 30th.

✽ ✽ ✽ James Johnston is now with me at Mrs. York's. He is extremely well, and a very fine boy indeed. I took him on Wednesday night to the play, to see the "School for Wives," and the "Children in the Wood," both very interesting, and very well performed. A little girl and boy, about six years of age, performed wonderfully. James was highly pleased, and I could not help wishing our dear children had been present. I dined yesterday with the President. He was in fine health and spirits, and so were Mrs. Washington and the whole family. There is now there an elder sister of Miss Custis's, not so handsome as herself, but she seems to be very agreeable, &c., &c.

JAS. IREDELL.

THE EASTERN CIRCUIT.

Judge Iredell opened the Court at New York, April 6th, with a charge, which soon made its appearance in the papers of the city.

IREDELL TO MRS. IREDELL.

NEW YORK, April 7th, 1795.

MY DEAR HANNAH :—I left Philadelphia on Friday morning, but the roads were so bad that we did not get further than Newark on Saturday night, and here on Sunday forenoon. I have very good lodgings in Wall street, have my health perfectly well, and pass my time agreeably. * * * ° I have engaged a new servant, who was very well recommended to me. He is a young mulatto, who had been set free under his master's will in Maryland, has since lived in Delaware, and was working day by day when I heard of him in Philadelphia. His name is David, he seems very good-tempered, and has hitherto behaved remarkably well. I am to find him in every thing, and pay him four dollars a month: he asked more, but agreed to take this, and though it appears to be high wages, it is comparatively low according to the rate of wages in Philadelphia.

8th.

Our Court ended yesterday, having sat but two days. I dined with Judge Lawrence. His wife is a very agreeable woman. To-day I am to dine with Mr. McCormick, and three more invitations ahead, so that I am likely to experience a good deal of the New York hospitality. Gen. Schuyler came, and sat with me two or three hours last night. I never saw him look better, and he was in high spirits. Mr. and Mrs. Hamilton are in Albany, having now no house here, but are expected in May. It is said he has already received more than a year's salary in retaining fees. At the dinner given to him here, all parties attended, and shared in the hilarity of the day. A number of mechanics here have declared they will build him a house at their own expense. Mr. Jay is expected. It is thought he will certainly be elected Governor if he returns soon: some think he will at all events. C. J. Yates is the other candidate. You will have heard of the entire conquest of Holland by the French. Private letters from Amsterdam speak in high terms of the moderation and humanity of their conduct. Their whole conduct indeed, since the fall of that villain Robespierre, seems to have done them the highest honor. There appears a terrible commotion in England: the King and Ministry bent on prosecuting the war at all events: the nation generally, and warmly against it; and feeling the highest resentment for being drawn into such difficulties by the scandalous obstinacy of the Government bent in not endeavoring to make peace. No spring ship has yet arrived here.

Poor Mrs. Romaine died here about six weeks ago; she had been long in ill health, and out of her senses for many days, though she recovered them before she died: she declared she had seen her Maker; was sure of happiness, and eager to meet it. I have not yet seen the Doctor, &c., &c.

April 15th.

° ° ° As the Court at New Haven does not begin till the 25th, I expect to be here a week longer. I receive very great civilities indeed, but nevertheless my time drags on heavily, as none of my intimate friends are near me; and, whatever you may think of it, I prefer them to the most agreeable strangers. I am almost opposite to Mr. Bayard's family, with whom Mrs. Edwards lives, and have dined with them, and been there three or four times besides. Mrs. Jay I think looks younger than ever. She is in high spirits, in expectation of Mr. Jay's arrival, though she has had no letter of a later date than the 11th December. He had gone down to Bath, and there has been no vessel this spring from England except one from Liverpool. You remember Warrand said *Mrs. Jay had her night*. She has still so far, that she is always at home every Thursday evening. She inquired very kindly after you and Mrs. Johnston, and I have taken tea with her on a special invitation. I have not seen Miss Marshall that was, though she is in town. Neither have I seen Dr. Romaine. He lives somewhere now about Cuyler's Hook. I called at his house, but found it full of Frenchmen who had lately rented it. Mrs. King has lately brought her husband another son. I dined with him soon after I came, but she was not then visible. This city is increasing and beautifying very fast. The walk at the Battery I am persuaded is one of the finest in the world. They have planted some young trees, which when grown up must add greatly to it. The Governor's house appears to great advantage. There are many more elegant houses in Broadway than formerly, and several more building. There are also some very elegant ones towards the lower end of Broad street. Property is even dearer here than in Philadelphia, &c., &c.

SPRINGFIELD, Mass, May 7th.

I left New Haven yesterday, and arrived here this morning (distance 70 miles), after travelling through a delightful country, passing several pretty towns, and enjoying (almost for the first time this spring) most charming weather. I was certainly intended for a New England man. I admire the people, and the country, as much as many of our Southern people affect to despise them. I preserve my health, and am to set off in the stage for Windsor, Vermont, to-morrow. I am told the road is a very fine one, &c., &c.

WINDSOR, VERMONT, May 18th.

I have been here about a week, and am to set off to-morrow for Portsmouth. My health, thank God, is perfectly good; and I have passed my time very agreeably in this place, where there is a small but genteel society, who have shown me many pleasing civilities. They gave a ball one night in a very elegant room, and where there was so agreeable a company that I danced with pleasure till after two in the morning. The country in general is very rough and mountainous, not only in this neighborhood but almost all the way up the Connecticut River from Springfield, in Massachusetts (about 115 miles below), but it is relieved in many places with fine fertile valleys, and some of the mountains are cultivated almost to the summit. In many places on the road the prospects are more extensive, variegated and romantic than any I have seen in any inland part of America. You see not only a great many distant waving mountains, but very large plains below dotted with houses, detached from each other, and here and there pretty little towns ornamented with handsome steeples. These are chiefly on the New Hampshire side of the river, for about 60 miles below this the Massachusetts line ends, and New Hampshire and Vermont are divided by the river. I am now sitting in a room with the river close by me in front, and on the other side a lofty mountain. This town is indeed surrounded with mountains. In Charlestown, New Hampshire, about eighteen miles hence, a very pretty place, there are two more elegant houses than any I saw in Connecticut. Having occasion to stay one day on the road, at a little town called Walpole, in New Hampshire (27 miles from this place), I heard Dr. Cutler lived at Rockingham in this State (about 6 miles distant). I accordingly went and spent the day with him. I met him within a little distance of his house, as he was coming in search of me, having heard a day or two before of my being expected up. His wife and daughter are at Hartford in Connecticut. He has only that daughter and two sons, who are both fine boys. I was very much affected to find that he had called his youngest (about three years old) after me—James Iredell. He looked very well, and I am told is rather in an easy situation in his circumstances. He does not practise physic professionally, though he is occasionally consulted. He tells me he has a little store, is a farmer, a miller, and a distiller, and much more industrious than he ever was before. But he has no society where he lives, and has some intention of removing to Charlestown. He has been a Member of Assembly in this State, was lately highest on the list in this part of the country as a Member of Council, and it is expected will be elected. Many have told me he is highly respected in this State; and that he would be, probably, very popular but for the little cloud on his political character during the war. He desired to be very respectfully remembered to you, and all his old friends, &c.

GREENFIELD, Mass., May 20th (at night).

I am now about seventy miles below Windsor, on my way to Boston, by which I am obliged to go to get to Portsmouth, though a great way round, there being no stage across the mountains above, nor scarcely a practicability of travelling on horseback, &c.

PORTSMOUTH, N. H., May 27th.

I arrived here the day before yesterday, and never was in better health in my life than I am at this moment, though I had to travel almost the whole way in the rain from Windsor, Vt., to Boston, we having had the latest, wettest, and most disagreeable spring that, I am told, can be remembered in this country. Yesterday and to-day the weather has assumed something like a summer appearance. I was received with the greatest cordiality and politeness by all my old friends, in Boston, whom I had an opportunity of seeing. I found Mrs. Hancock just going to comfort herself for a slavish confinement for many years to a goutified, ill-tempered husband, by marrying a Captain Scott, an old captain in Gov. Hancock's employ, who sails in the London trade, and who arrived much to her satisfaction on Sunday last. I had not time to call on Mrs. Howard, but heard she was well. She lately lost her father, who was upwards of ninety. Mr. Guier and his wife inquired very kindly after you. Their daughter, who was in Philadelphia, is well married to a Mr. Amory, who lives in Boston. Mr. Gerry has been in ill health, and is travelling with his wife and children to recruit it. He went from the house in which I am the morning of the day I arrived, and obligingly left his compliments for me. Her eyesight, I am told, is better, but her health otherwise not good. They have the misfortune of having nothing to do but to enjoy life, and accordingly, it is said, feel the "ennui" of the French, though I believe it is only what they know by name. I wish we had the trial of such a disadvantage. This town is in a very pretty situation near the sea, but it is laid off in a very irregular, and disagreeable manner, with narrow streets, but, here and there interspersed, very handsome houses. The road from Boston to it (65 miles) is a remarkably fine one, but the country does not look at all like Connecticut, nor have the little towns the same neat appearance as even in Vermont. ° ° ° The improvements in almost every part of America are wonderful. The bridge between Boston and Cambridge far exceeded my expectations. The causeway leading to it from Cambridge, which is now as good a road as the road by Roberts's, and railed in like the bridge, is a mile and a quarter long; and the bridge itself three-quarters of a mile, the whole as straight as an arrow; the carriage way very wide, with passages on each side for foot passengers, beautifully painted, and with an astonishing number of fine lamps all along on each side. The river is very deep and very rapid, notwithstanding which the whole of this bridge was completed, so as to be passable at least, in about six months. We passed an excellent and beautiful bridge over the Merrimac River, near Newbury Port, which was building when I was there before; and they have a very fine one, I am told, over the Piscataqua River, which runs by this town, a few miles above, &c., &c.

Boston, June 5th.

* * * Though there have been two plays performed here since I came, I have been at neither; but as the weather is very fine at present, I believe I shall go to-night. I continue to receive the greatest attention. I met Mrs. Cabot in town one day. She looked very well, and inquired kindly after you. Mr. Cabot was just then setting off for Philadelphia. He sent me a very obliging message, not being able to come himself. Mrs. Cabot invited me to go and see her, which I intend to do. She lives only about four or five miles from town, just beyond Judge Lowell's, with whom I shall spend next Sunday. I have received several invitations into the country, which my time will not admit of accepting. Mrs. Langdon desired her compliments to you. I received great courtesies from Mr. Langdon and her. They gave me a very polite invitation to their house, but I declined. I staid two days with Mr. Parsons on my way here, and was obliged to force myself away at last, so importunate was he with me that I should stay longer. Mrs. Parsons, though unknown, desired to be mentioned to you. She is an amiable woman, and they have five lovely children—four daughters and a son. They have lost three sons, though Newbury Port is generally reckoned a very healthy place. Last year they had a fatal dysentery among them. Mr. Parsons' family then escaped. The loss of his children was before, &c., &c.

June 12th.

* * * General Knox and his family came to town a few days ago, all very well. A subscription is going about for a public dinner to the General, which undoubtedly will be given him. Here where he is known so well he is universally beloved and respected. I believe the Court will end to-morrow, and that I shall go to Rhode Island on Monday. We yesterday tried a man for manslaughter on the high seas, and he was convicted on the most satisfactory though affecting evidence. The circumstances were so aggravated, that the Court deliberated whether they should not direct an acquittal on that indictment on purpose that he might be found guilty of murder. But, finding that it had been under consideration of the grand jury, we did not think ourselves at liberty to do so. I went on Saturday evening to Judge Lowell's (three miles from town), and staid at his house, which is delightfully situated, till Monday morning. He has a very agreeable family, and I always pass my time very agreeably with them. His third daughter, who is a charming girl, is shortly to be married, with the approbation of the whole family, to a young gentleman, who lodges in the same house with me, of the name of Gardiner, with whom I am much pleased, and who is a merchant of a very respectable and amiable character. On Sunday evening we went and drank tea with Mrs. Cabot, at a beautiful place Mr. Cabot has lately bought. She looks much better than I ever saw her. She and Mrs. Lowell expressed a great desire to see you in this country, &c., &c.

New Port, R. I. June 20.

* * * I left Boston, and not without considerable pain in parting with the many respectable people who had shown me the greatest kindness, on Wednesday last. I had dined the day before at a very superb public dinner given to General Knox, and received marks of the personal regard of the company to myself which were extremely affecting. I arrived here the evening before last, &c.

June 22d.

* * * I find an infinite difference between this place and Boston, though we have very agreeable company in the house where I lodge, and I dined yesterday with a very genteel South Carolina family with whom I was well acquainted, and for whom I had a great regard, &c., &c.

New York, July 2d.

* * * I am extremely mortified to find the Senate have adjourned without the appointment of a Chief Justice, as I have much reason to fear that, owing to that circumstance, it will be unavoidable for me to have some circuit duty to perform this fall. Four Judges out of five were upon duty the last time, and there is some business which will make it indispensably necessary that two Judges shall be on the Eastern Circuit. Judge Blair (on account of the Chief Justice's absence) went upon the Southern Circuit this last spring, when he was entitled to stay at home if possible, and Judge Wilson had also several courts to attend, though it was his turn to stay; and they had additional duty on the same account twelve months before. At least four Judges must be on the Circuit this fall, and I hear with great concern that Judge Blair was so sick in South Carolina, that he was not able to do any business there. If I have to attend any, I presume it will be the Middle Circuit, which begins at Trenton on the 2d October. Should I be so unfortunate as to find this inevitable, I will, at all events, go home from the Supreme Court, if I can stay but a fortnight—but how distressing is this situation? It almost distracts me. * * * Though I receive the greatest possible distinction and kindness everywhere, and experience marks of approbation of my public conduct very flattering, yet I constantly tremble at the danger you and my children may be in, without my knowledge, in a climate I have so much reason to dread. My anxiety embitters every enjoyment. May God Almighty in his goodness preserve you! I must either resign, or we must have in view some residence near Philadelphia. Mr. Jay was sworn in as Governor yesterday. He was in danger of dying on his passage, and does not look well now. *I am told, which has greatly astonished me, that he did not send his resignation of Chief Justice till two or three days ago, since the Senate broke up. Whatever were his reasons, I am persuaded it was utterly unjustifiable.* The President may himself make a temporary appointment, but it is not much to be expected, I fear, as few gentlemen would accept under the circumstances, &c.

July 3d.

* * * I supped with a very agreeable company last evening, of which Mr. and Mrs. Hamilton formed a part. They both looked extremely well. She inquired very particularly about you. The other day a very fine boy of theirs, about two and one-half years old, got away, and was missing for an hour, but was at length found, and brought home safe. The same accident happened to another family the same day. I have seen Mr. Jay several times since my arrival here, but Mrs. Jay has been so unwell as to be confined to her room, and I have not seen her. She is now much better, &c., &c.

JAS. IREDELL.

A. Campbell to Iredell.

Richmond, Va., July 16th.

Dear Sir:—Permit me to introduce to your acquaintance the Marquis de Clugny, who is going with his daughter into your State. The interest which I take in the fortunes of this respectable gentleman, and his amiable daughter, makes me very solicitous to render their time agreeable to them as they pass through our country. To this I am sure no one can or will contribute more cheerfully than yourself. The high respect I entertain for the Marquis thus affords me an opportunity of expressing that with which I have the honor to be, dear sir,

Your most obt. and most humble servant,

ALEX. CAMPBELL.*

The Marquis de Clugny remained some time in Edenton, North Carolina. He taught there a dancing-school, and gave private lessons in French to Judge Iredell's children.

Iredell to Mrs. Iredell.
Philadelphia, July 24th.

My dear Hannah:— * * * * It gave me extreme concern to hear of Mrs. Hooper's death, though it was an event I had too much reason to apprehend. Poor woman! I am convinced it was her distress of mind, * * * * which originally threw her into such ill health, and probably broke her heart. Charlotte Mackey is again in a very dangerous state. She some time ago had a relapse, and has been to Bristol, but returned rather worse than before, to the great concern of all her friends. * * * No Chief Justice yet appointed, that I know of. I suppose brother Cushing does not augur well from the delay,† &c.

JAS. IREDELL.

Simeon Baldwin to Iredell.
New Haven, July 28th.

Sir:—I duly received yours of the 20th of May, inclosing several papers by Mr. Buck—am much obliged to you for introducing him to me, although he could allow me but little time to form an acquaintance or show him attention.

I have also the pleasure to acknowledge the receipt of yours of the 15th inst., inclosing a copy of your Charge to the Grand Jury. I have handed it to the printer, who will gratify the Jury and the public by the publication of it in his paper of this week.

---

* United States Attorney for Virginia: cousin-german to Thos. Campbell, the poet.
† Judge Cushing was afterwards tendered the appointment, and declined.

I am happy to hear that your circuit has been agreeable to you. New England has heretofore prided itself on being friendly to government and good order, and it gives me pain that the intemperate conduct of several towns, in so hastily condemning the Treaty, the merits of which they could not then understand, should in this crisis tarnish that character. The people in Connecticut, though materially interested in the West India trade, I am confident are fully disposed to leave the discussion of that question to the powers constituted for that purpose; and from what I have seen, it appears that the more they reflect, and are informed upon the subject, the better they like the instrument.

Mrs. Baldwin joins me in respectful compliments and sincere wishes, &c., &c.
SIMEON BALDWIN.

GOV. JOHNSTON TO IREDELL.

WILLIAMSTON, Aug. 1st, '95.

MY DEAR SIR:— ✕ ✕ ✕ ✕ I am very thankful to you for your letter by Capt. Yellowly, and the copy of the Treaty; it appears to be a *hasty* performance; the stipulations in the 12th article, restraining the exportation of certain enumerated articles, are highly exceptionable; some mention certainly ought to have been made of the negroes which were carried off, in my judgment naturally connected with the debts due to British merchants, and a claim that might have been properly submitted to the same commissioners who were to take cognizance of the claims of the British merchants; the owners of these slaves had certainly a legal and equitable claim, under the Treaty of Peace; the passing it over in silence on this occasion will have too much the appearance of abandoning it. Though these are the only striking objections which occur to me on a perusal of the Treaty, without any conversation on the subject with others, yet I must confess that *they have greatly lessened my opinion of Mr. Jay's abilities as a negotiator;* at the same time, I think it most wicked and illiberal in those who charge him with perfidy and corruption. Time I hope will do justice to his character, and confound those bad men who are endeavoring to blacken it. I cannot easily prevail on myself to believe that the man who was incorruptibly steady to his trust when our affairs were doubtful, if not desperate, should turn apostate at a time when a benevolent Providence and good fortune are smiling on every part of our country,✕ &c., &c.
SAM. JOHNSTON.

* Gov. Johnston's opinion was undoubtedly that entertained by nearly every man south of the Potomac. The *public* expression of similar views caused Mr. Rut-

---

DR. WM. S. JOHNSON TO IREDELL.✕

NEW YORK, August 5th.

DEAR SIR:—It gives me great pleasure to find, by your agreeable favor of the 30th ultimo, that our brethren in North Carolina are seriously determined to establish a University, and I shall be happy if I can give you any facilities to the establishment of it. Science is the truest security of liberty.

The two inclosed pamphlets will give you, I imagine, all the information you wish relative to Columbia College. Some changes have indeed been made since these publications, with regard to Professors, &c., but none of any importance to your views. If you wish any further intelligence with respect to us, I will give it with pleasure.

Let me request that when you have opportunity, you will be so good as to present my best respects to Gov. Johnston, for whom I retain the highest esteem, and the most affectionate regards. Mrs. Johnson joins me in respectful compliments to Mrs. Iredell, and I remain, with sincere respect and esteem, dear sir,

Your most faithful and obedient servant,
WM. SAML. JOHNSON.

SUPREME COURT.—AUGUST TERM.

At this term Chief Justice Rutledge presided. The most interesting case that came up for trial was that of Talbot *vs.* Jansen. "A question of the gravest character was raised and discussed for the first time in the Federal courts—a question upon which the judicial mind remained unsettled for years subsequently—and which in some respects may be considered a *questio vexata*—namely, whether the common law doctrine as to allegiance and expatriation was to be regarded in America as a rule of municipal law."† The question was considered by Judge Iredell, in a very able and carefully written opinion. He said that it was not necessary that it should be explicitly decided in this cause, but that he would freely express his sentiments on the subject—" That a man ought not to be a slave; that he should not be confined against his will to a particular spot, because he

ledge's rejection by the Senate as Chief Justice. Personally friendly to Mr. Jay, and a staunch Federalist, the disapproval of such a man as Gov. Johnston is the strongest condemnation of the Treaty.
* Wm. Samuel Johnson—member of Congress in New York, 1765—Judge of the Supreme Court of Connecticut—one of the framers of the Federal Constitution—President of Columbia College, N. Y.
† Van Santvoord's Lives of the Chief Justices.

---

happened to draw his breath upon it; that he should not be compelled to continue in a society to which he is accidentally attached, when he can better his situation elsewhere, much less when he must starve in one country, and may live comfortably in another; are positions which I hold as strongly as any man, and they are such as most nations in the world appear clearly to recognize." The Judge thought that other rights, however, besides those of the party seeking expatriation, were to be considered; the rights of the community, for instance, to which he belonged, rights that might be imperilled by his action in cases of war; that the rights of the individual should be subordinate to the general good, and only exercised in conformity with the mode established by the legislature, "the constant guardian of the public interest;" that a "legislature would be weak to the extremest verge of folly, to wish to retain any man as a citizen, whose heart and affections are fixed on a foreign country;" and that it was the duty of the legislature to make the necessary provision for expatriation. Upon the whole, he inclined to the opinion that a citizen does not possess the right of voluntary expatriation, without the permission of his own government.✕

Were a soldier, during war, upon the expiration of his term of enlistment, to enter the ranks of the enemy, and be taken prisoner in battle, I presume the most ardent advocate of the right of expatriation would scarcely condemn a swift and capital punishment.

IREDELL TO MRS. IREDELL.

PHILADELPHIA, August 13th.

MY DEAR HANNAH:— ✕ ✕ ✕ ✕ I greatly flattered myself I could have fixed to-morrow a day for my departure, but it is impossible, we have so much business to do, and the lawyers so scandalously long in arguing the causes. We have one cause now depending that began on Thursday of last week, and probably will not end till Saturday. Mr. Rutledge (my old friend) has arrived, and yesterday took his seat as Chief Justice of the United States. Though I very much lament his intemperate expressions with regard to the Treaty, yet altogether no man would have been personally more agreeable to me. I have now great hopes of resting entirely this fall, &c., &c.

August 14th.

✕ ✕ ✕ ✕ When I wrote yesterday I was afraid poor Miss Mease was at the point of death. There are now great hopes of

* 3d Dallas.

---

her recovery. She returned in the highest health from Maryland, but was soon after taken with a most violent inflammatory fever. Dr. Rush is treating her on the bleeding system. He has already taken 80 ounces of blood, and says he will bleed her three or four times more rather than lose her, &c.
JAS. IREDELL.

GOV. JOHNSTON TO IREDELL.

Aug. 15th.

DEAR SIR:— ✕ ✕ ✕ The whole continent appears to be highly enraged against Mr. Jay and his Treaty. 'Tis a pity that there is seldom so much pains taken to conciliate the minds of the multitude as is taken to inflame them. Unfortunately it is much easier to fire a town than to extinguish the flames. Nothing seems so much to contribute to the happiness of some people as to see every one distressed and discontented with the state of public affairs, &c.
SAM. JOHNSTON.

HON. WILLIAM I. DAWSON TO IREDELL.

Friday, Sunrise.

DEAR SIR:—I thank you for your favor of yesterday, and most sincerely congratulate you upon your safe return, and the health of your family—so much better than general experience, and the particular unhealthiness of this season, had left room to hope for. I feel the more pleasure in this, when I recollect your melancholy anticipations on the subject, when I had last the pleasure of seeing you; and which, at that time, I apprehended to be too well founded.

I very much regret the death of Mr. Bradford, which may justly be regarded as a public loss—a remark that does not in my opinion apply with so much propriety to the resignation of the Secretary of State, at least, in his late capacity.✕

I wish to God the report of a truce between France and England may be true; but I have seen nothing yet that would warrant such a hope.

Our family are much distressed now by the indisposition of poor little Will, which, though nothing but ague and fever, is very severe. On Sunday or Monday I hope to have the pleasure of

* Wm. Bradford, of Pa., Attorney General U. States. Edmund Randolph, Secretary of State, had resigned in consequence of extraordinary disclosures in the intercepted correspondence of the French Minister.

seeing you. In the mean time accept our united good wishes, and believe me, very respectfully and affectionately,

Your obedient servant,
W. I. DAWSON.

Col. Davie to Iredell.

HALIFAX, Sept. 4th.

MY DEAR SIR:—I have been flattering myself with the expectation of receiving a letter from you on your return, anxious to know in what health you found your family, and how you had finished the circuit. As to myself, I have been unfortunate. My family have been more sickly than usual, and my youngest son was the first victim to the season in this part of the country. This is one of those dreadful strokes in human life that I sincerely hope you will never feel.

The present crisis appears to me to be the most delicate and important since the organization of the Government. The Anti-Federalists, and the personal enemies of the Administration, have rallied with astonishing activity. The circumstances of the Treaty has ranged a variety of parties on their side, and given an imposing appearance to their numbers; and I believe they will now make their last effort to shake the Government.

The treatment of Mr. Jay is a satire upon humanity; no calculation on the baseness of human nature could have produced so shameless a degree of ingratitude.

Pray what has been the cause of Mr. Randolph's resignation? Nothing in this way has astonished me more. I cannot conceive what are his prospects.

I will be obliged to you to let me know what Judge rides the Southern Circuit. If your Chief Justice raves on the bench as he does at a town meeting, we shall be highly edified. Adieu! &c.

WM. R. DAVIE.

Judge Blair (U. S. Sup. Court) to Iredell.

RICHMOND, Sept. 14th.

DEAR SIR:—Mr. Blair, of this place, informed me that he received from you, in your way to Edenton, a letter for me, which he had forwarded to Col. Bell, of Charlottesville, where he expected I should get it earlier than if he had kept it till my return. Unfortunately, however, I have never yet seen the letter. Yet I must endeavor to answer it from the information of Mr. B. with regard to the probable subject. Col. Carrington, it seems, had had some conversation with you; and conceives that the design of it was to propose to me, if not too inconvenient, to ride the Middle Circuit, otherwise that you would do it yourself. This makes it proper that I should inform you that my trip up the country has not brought me any relief from the strange disorder, which for a considerable time past has afflicted my head, and renders me incapable of business, which I have been obliged to neglect, in a degree very painful to me. Sensible of the advantages of my official character, I have not been in haste to resign. I have been willing to take every chance for a removal of the complaint, consistent with a resolution I have taken, in case an unexpected recovery should not prevent it, to resign so long before the court in February next, as to give the President sufficient time to supply the vacancy against that court. The time I had limited for that purpose will shortly expire, and then I shall not think of any further experiment. As the performing the duty of the Middle Circuit, would in other respects be less inconvenient to me than to yourself, as it would not take me quite so far from home, I would most freely assume it, if I had not ample proofs that I am utterly unfit for it. But I am utterly at a loss to conceive why that course of duty should have been assigned to either of us, when both of us had taken a tour in the spring, you in the Eastern Circuit, myself in the Southern, besides having had the Middle Circuit in the fall. When I last had the pleasure of seeing Mr. Cushing, he expected to have the Middle Circuit at this time. My best respects to Mrs. Iredell. I hope that she and all your family enjoy good health. My infirmity will, I fear, deprive me of the pleasure of ever seeing you again. God bless you, &c.

WILLIAMSBURG, Oct. 10th.

Your favor of the 24th ult. reached me yesterday. I feel much gratitude for the concern which you and Mrs. Iredell take at my loss of health, for your anxiety that I should not resign, and for your obliging readiness to assume for my accommodation still further fatigue of duty than is properly your own. You may, probably, be right also in the confidence you express, that in this the rest of the Judges would willingly concur with you; but this appears to me so unreasonable an imposition that I cannot think of it. * * * * *

My complaint is nothing but an overbearing noise in my head, which distracts my attention; but which, from experience, seems to be consistent with good health in other respects, &c., &c.

Your faithfully affectionate friend,
JOHN BLAIR.

Iredell to Mrs. Iredell.

RICHMOND, VA., Nov. 27th.

MY DEAR HANNAH:—I arrived here on Sunday evening. * * * There is so much business here, that I don't think we shall finish till the latter end of next week. I receive great civilities and distinction here. I dined the other day with Mr. Hylton, and in the evening went with his wife and daughter to the play ("As you like it"), which was very indifferently performed, except by a Mrs. West, formerly Mrs. Bignall, who is really a pleasing actress.* In the farce (Le Foret Noir) a little boy of five or six performed admirably. They have a neat little theatre. * * * * Mr. and Mrs. Randolph have arrived. He was so obliging as to call on me yesterday, and had begun to enter into a very interesting conversation concerning the circumstances of his resignation, when we were interrupted. The town was so full that for three or four nights I was obliged to lodge in a room where there were three other beds, but my landlady was so obliging as to engage another room immediately opposite her house, where I lodge very comfortably, and am entirely alone. Though the General Government here has many opposers, it has no small number of very powerful and respectable friends. In the late debate about the Treaty, I am told there were few members who were not convinced by Mr. Marshall's argument as to its being constitutional, which few members thought it was before the debate began, and some of the speakers on the other side had the candor to acknowledge their conviction, though not in the House. He and others were prepared to speak to the policy of it, but the majority, without considering that at all, or suffering it to be fully debated, proceeded to an immediate vote of thanks to their Senators, which they carried by 100 to 150, and it has since passed by a large majority in the Senate, &c., &c.

JAS. IREDELL.

The following letter to Thomas Martin, of Portsmouth, New Hampshire, conveys a mild and dignified rebuke.

EDENTON, Nov. 12th, 1795.

SIR:—I received by post, a day or two ago, your letter of the 30th Sept., with a pamphlet inclosed. I am persuaded you were not sensible of any impropriety in the proceeding; but it is my duty to tell you, that I think it extremely improper that a Judge should have the slightest private communication with any party in regard to a suit, either before it is depending, during the time, or after its determination, for he cannot be in all cases certain whether the same case or the same question may not come before him in some other shape, and his mind ought to be perfectly unbiased, which it may not be (notwithstanding all his precaution), if he listens to any thing but what he hears judicially in court. As an individual not so particularly circumstanced, I should pay proper respect to any communication of yours, and take care that it was not altogether unavailing; but in the present instance I shall not think it right even to read the pamphlet, and I regret that I cannot immediately return it without putting you to a heavy expense of postage, which I am very unwilling to do. At the same time, sir, I hope you will believe, that I am not influenced on this occasion by any want of regard for you personally, but entirely by a sense of duty, which, in a situation of so much trust and public importance as that I have the honor to hold, I cannot too sacredly regard.

I am, sir, your obt. servant,
JAS. IREDELL.

---

* Wm. Hylton, a West India planter. From a letter to Judge Iredell on the process of sugar making, and reviewing a pamphlet of Dr. Rush's, he appears to have been a man of science.

CHAPTER XXIX.
ÆT. 44—45.

"TREATISE ON THE LAW OF EVIDENCE." SUPREME COURT, FEBRUARY TERM. DR. PRIESTLY. HAMILTON ON THE CARRIAGE TAX. CIRCUIT COURT, SPRING TERM. CHARGE TO GRAND JURY. SUPREME COURT, AUGUST TERM. LETTERS FROM JUDGE PATTERSON, COL. DAVIE, JOHN MARSHALL, GOV. JOHNSTON, &C.

WITH Judge Iredell's papers is an original "Treatise on Evidence:" it is divided into twelve chapters; and consists of two hundred and seventy-five pages. A memorandum states—"this is intended as an Appendix to the Law of Evidence originally published in 1777 (by an anonymous author), and particularly the third edition of it, published in 17—." It does not appear when the work was completed; but it must have been either anterior to, or about this time, as other works—"An essay on the Law of Pleading;" and "The Doctrine of the Laws of England concerning Real Property, so far as it is in use or force in the State of North Carolina,"—left unfinished at his death, must have engaged all his leisure in the interval between '96 and '99. He was deterred from publication, I presume, by his narrow means. The manuscript is more than neat; it is elegant, and ready for the printer's hands; but its value is doubtlessly impaired, if not destroyed, by more recent books. With him labor was so ceaseless as to seem to have been beloved for its own sake. He took copious notes of all the cases tried before him: they now exist in many volumes, bound strongly in calfskin. One can scarcely reflect without amazement upon his severe and unremitted toil. That he should have travelled so much, performed so much judicial service, composed so much, and conducted so extensive a correspondence, teaches what wonderful results flow from systematized industry, and is at the same time a lesson to the sluggard, and an encouragement to the diffident.

GOV. JOHNSTON TO IREDELL.

HERMITAGE, 9th January, 1796.

MY DEAR SIR:— * * * * I neither regret nor wonder that the Senate should have refused their assent to Mr. Rutledge's appointment; it would have been unfortunate, after what has appeared, if they had concurred. The only disagreeable circumstance is, that the enemies of good order will endeavor to impress it on the minds of the people that the majority were influenced by improper motives. I most sincerely lament with you the melancholy cause of Mr. R.'s disgrace.

The replies of the Senate and House of Representatives to the President are tolerably decent. Your friend, Major Butler, took care not to let that of the Senate pass in silence, &c., &c.

SAM. JOHNSTON.

SUPREME COURT.—FEBRUARY TERM.

At this term Oliver Ellsworth took his seat as Chief Justice. The first case that came up was that of Hylton *vs.* the United States. This was a very important cause, as it involved a question of constitutional law. The point was the constitutionality of the law of Congress of 1794, laying *duties* upon carriages. If a *direct tax*, it could only be laid in proportion to the census, which had not as yet been taken. The counsel of Hylton, Campbell and Ingersoll, contended that the tax was a *direct tax*; and were opposed by Lee and Hamilton. The Court unanimously agreed that the tax was constitutional, and delivered their opinions "seriatim."

The celebrated cause of Ware *vs.* Hylton succeeded. Marshall was of counsel for the defendant. The case had been originally tried before Judge Iredell at Richmond. Pending the Revolution the Virginia Assembly had passed a law confiscating the debts of British subjects, and directing that all payments on such debts should be made to the Loan Office of the State. The defendants, who owed a bond to the plaintiff, a British subject, had made a partial payment on said bond in accordance with the Statute. The majority of the Court held that the Act of Virginia was annulled by the Treaty of Peace, and that the foreign creditor should recover his debt, even though such debt had been paid under the authority of the State. Judge Iredell dissented in a very elaborate, and carefully written opinion: he thought that the plaintiff should not recover the sum actually paid into the Loan Office; but agreed with his brethren on the other points. His opinion "as a legal argument may be regarded as one of the best specimens that have been preserved of the old Supreme Court." *

Judge Chase took his seat for the first time, at this Term of the Court. John Marshall, also, made his first appearance, as an advocate; and at once achieved a distinction nearly equal to that he subsequently gained as Chief Justice of the same tribunal.

IREDELL TO MRS. IREDELL.

PHILADELPHIA, Feb. 19th.

MY DEAR HANNAH:— * * * * The Treaty with Algiers has arrived, and the other day was laid before the Senate. No authentic copy either of that with Great Britain or Spain has arrived. It is supposed that the British Treaty will undergo great debate in the House of Representatives, but that a majority will be for carrying it into effect. Judge Cushing has been sick for almost a week, and is still so. Judge Patterson was for two days, and Wilson a little (which was a great wonder), so that I began to think an influenza was going to seize the whole Court; but, thank God, I have been perfectly well, and Mr. Chase as much so as usual. No Chief Justice has been yet appointed on Mr. Cushing's resignation. We have had an account that seems not improbable of a total defeat of the Austrians by the French, but it is not absolutely certain. It is undoubtedly true that there are great commotions in England. It is the opinion of many that a peace in Europe is not at a great distance; but this is merely a conjecture arising from the general aspect of affairs, &c.

February 20th.

* * * Miss Hewes, who was to leave town for Pottsgrove this morning, particularly desired her love to you. Mrs. Phillips is much better. We are now deeply engaged on the subject of the British debts. There is absolutely nothing new in the political world: no late accounts from Europe that seem authentic, and no important business in Congress but in the several Committees. We have some faint hopes of an alteration in the Judiciary System; but I don't sanguinely rely upon it. Mr. Cushing, with an extraordinary degree of moderation, has declined the office of Chief Justice on account of his age and infirm state of health, but retains his seat on the Bench. The President and Mrs. Washington both look extremely well, and inquired kindly after you and Mr. and Mrs. Johnston, &c., &c.

* Van Santvoord's Lives of the Chief Justices.

February 25th.

* * * * I forgot, I believe, to mention to you that I heard Dr. Priestly preach the two last Sundays. His first was an introductory discourse to a series of discourses on the evidences of the Christian Religion. He had at each time as crowded an audience as could attend. He preached in the Universal Church, the only one the orthodox in Philadelphia would allow him. He is an ordinary man, marked with the small-pox, about the middle size, and has not a good voice, nor a graceful manner; but speaks with great distinctness, and so much plainness, perspicuity, and such an extraordinary degree of candor and good sense, that I heard him the whole time with the highest pleasure and admiration; and in his last sermon when he said—"To conclude"—I felt almost as painful a sensation as if I was going to part with a most intimate friend. The Vice President and many members of both Houses went both Sundays, and when the service was over, there seemed a universal eagerness in the whole congregation to express their admiration to one another. Though so highly distinguished in life, and possessing such transcendent abilities and universal learning, his manner is altogether modest and unassuming; and, through the whole service, he never seemed to think of himself. He delivered written prayers of his own composition, of an uncommon and very superior cast, almost every line insensibly conveying some useful instruction. There was nothing in either of his sermons conveying his peculiar tenets. Yet this man, who has written more and with greater ability than any man in America in defence of the Christian Religion, is excluded from all the Pulpits in this city, but the above, because he has had the manliness to express a different opinion from many prevailing ones, in regard to some unessential doctrines, which may either be believed or disbelieved without prejudice to a sincere faith in the divine authority of the Christian Religion. I have been anxious to wait upon him, and shall as soon as I can, but our Court has been so constantly engaged that it has not yet been in my power.

February 26th.

The day before yesterday Mr. Hamilton spoke in our Court, attended by the most crowded audience I ever saw there, both Houses of Congress being almost deserted on the occasion. Though he was in very ill health, he spoke with astonishing ability, and in a most pleasing manner, and was listened to with the profoundest attention. His speech lasted about three hours. It was on the question whether the carriage tax, as laid, was a constitutional one. In one part of it he affected me extremely. Having occasion to observe, how proper a subject it was for taxation, since it was a mere article of *luxury*, which a man might either use, or not, as was convenient to him, he added, "It so happens, that I once had a carriage myself, and found it convenient to dispense with it. But my happiness is not in the least diminished."

I dined in company with him yesterday. He was still very unwell, but better, and he told me he believed it was a good deal occasioned by his having left his youngest son ill with the measles, and hearing since that he was much better. I saw Fanny Bond last night. She is very thin indeed, but looks much better than I expected. She spoke of you and our dear children in the most affectionate manner, and seemed very much pleased to hear so good an account of Helen, whom she said she loved better than any child she had ever known. Not then having heard of my dear Mrs. Swann's misfortune, I went to the Amphitheatre the President's birthnight. It is a building erected between Congress Hall and Deller's, and is the place where Ricketts usually performs, and was fitted up at great expense on the occasion. It is supposed that there were about 400 ladies present, and 600 gentlemen, and the sight was a very splendid one, &c., &c.

JAS. IREDELL.

GOV. JOHNSTON TO IREDELL.

February 27th.

DEAR SIR :— * * * * I am sorry that Mr. Cushing refused the office of Chief Justice, as I don't know whether a less exceptionable character can be obtained without passing over Mr. Wilson, which would perhaps be a measure that could not be easily reconciled to strict propriety. I have no personal acquaintance with Mr. Chase, but am not impressed with a very favorable opinion of his moral character, whatever his professional abilities may be. I am glad that the Senate have again taken up the Judiciary System ; and hope they will at last see the necessity of having a separate set of District Judges, leaving the Judges of the Supreme Court to hold that Court only, reducing the number to one half as the present Judges resign or die. The expense can be the only objection to the plan, which in so important a business should not be an object, &c., &c.

SAM. JOHNSTON.

IREDELL TO MRS. IREDELL.

PHILADELPHIA, March 3d.

MY DEAR HANNAH :— * * * * Mr. Chase is laid up with the gout. A member of the Senate, usually in opposition to the Government, told me the Spanish Treaty was so favorable, that if the Spanish Government had asked the American Minister to dictate his own terms, he could scarcely have asked for better. * * * * I had a very kind invitation from Mr. Breck to his Sunday evening parties at his house (they being every Sunday), and have been there twice. His whole family are extremely amiable and agreeable indeed.

I have quite done with Priestly. I went there again last Sunday, in company with Mrs. Cushing, and there was collected a most genteel assembly, consisting, among others, of a great number of the most respectable ladies and gentlemen in town, and the house was so crowded that many were obliged to go away. In pursuing his subject, in regard to the Christian religion, he undertook to show the necessity of it from the great prevalence of vice and debauchery in the heathen world, and gave many instances of it in such shocking terms of indecency, as not only must have deeply affected every lady of common sensibility present, but excited the highest indignation in every gentleman who knew how to respect the honor and delicacy of the sex.* He was rising highly in the public estimation. This has completely sunk him ; and next Sunday he will speak, perhaps, to little more than bare walls. How astonishing such conduct was in a man, who has long been accustomed to the first company in England ! What is most extraordinary, he suppressed some accounts because he said they were too indecent to be mentioned there ; and for my part, I can scarcely conceive what could be much more so than many descriptions he did give, &c.

March 4th.

I dined at Mr. Mease's yesterday with a very genteel company, of which Dr. Rush was one. Mrs. Mease and Miss Mease desire their love to you and the children. The latter I think is much improved in all respects. I wish you would sometimes write to one of them, as I believe your omission to do so gives them concern. * * * * I have this moment read in a newspaper, that Mr. Ellsworth is nominated our Chief Justice, in consequence of which I think it not unlikely that *Wilson* will resign. But this is only my own conjecture, and therefore I wish you not to mention it, &c.

March 11th.

* * * * Chief Justice Ellsworth goes to the Southward : Mr. Chase to the Eastward : and I am to attend the Middle

---

* In a letter to one of his correspondents, the Judge says, "He spoke in plain terms of Priests castrated, and men and women being put to death in the very act of fornication—the altars being scenes of lust, &c.

Circuit, all but Delaware, which is after Virginia ; and Judge Wilson or Patterson has promised to take that in my room. Though the Circuit is by far the easiest and most convenient for me, yet I don't expect I can be at home till the middle of June, and I must leave it the middle of July to return here again. It is impossible I can lead this life much longer, and I see no prospect of any material change. To lead a life of perpetual travelling, and almost continual absence from home, is a very severe lot to be doomed to in the decline of life, after incessant attention to business the preceding part of it. * * * * The Supreme Court is yet sitting, and we shall not be able to finish half the business, so that I expect we shall be here three or four weeks in August. The other Judges all differed from me in regard to the British debts, but my opinion remains unaltered. We were unanimous in support of the Carriage Tax. The House of Representatives are in high debate upon a motion for papers concerning the British Treaty, &c., &c.

March 18th.

* * * * Our Court broke up on Monday last, but unavoidably left much business unfinished.* * * The House of Representatives are still debating upon the call for papers concerning the Treaty. I have attended the debates regularly since our Court broke up, and heard many able speeches on both sides. The papers in some mode or other will be undoubtedly called for, but I believe on the final question a majority will be for carrying the Treaty into effect. The uncommonly warm and animated terms in which some of the gentlemen unfavorable to the Treaty have spoken of the President personally, have done them honor, and must have gladdened the hearts of every person present, whose feelings were not totally dead to all sensibility. There are no late accounts from Europe, but some accounts have just arrived from the West Indies of very villainous treatment by some captains of men-of-war to American seamen. Mr. Ellsworth is to sail in a few days for Charleston. * * * * I drank tea the other evening with Mrs. Cox. She and her daughters Mary and Theodosia (both of whom are very fine girls) inquired most kindly about you. James's favorite Betsey is still very small of her age, but a sprightly, engaging girl, and plays remarkably well on the *piano-forte*. The Stocker family, Mr. Phillips's, and Mr. Mease's, all desire to be kindly remembered to you. I have not yet been at Mrs. Barclay's, as the family have been in such distress ; but I saw Miss Barclay the other evening at Mrs. Cox's, and attended her home. Upon my alluding to the occasion of my not calling there, she was greatly affected, and could not for some time speak. She said they all remembered you with the utmost regard, and frequently regretted the loss of your society. She obligingly pressed me to visit them frequently, &c.

March 25th.

* * * * The kind expectations of my friends that I might be appointed Chief Justice were too flattering. Whatever other chance I might have had, there could have been no propriety in passing by Judge Wilson to come at me. The gentleman appointed I believe will fill the office extremely well. He is a man of an excellent understanding, and a man of business, &c., &c.

JAS. IREDELL.

THE CIRCUIT.

IREDELL TO MRS. IREDELL.

PHILADELPHIA, March 31st.

MY DEAR HANNAH :—I am perfectly well, and am going to Trenton to-morrow. The Court here will be held on the 11th. * * * * The House of Representatives have asked for the papers concerning the British Treaty, which the President has thought it his duty to refuse. I sincerely lament what I conceive is a real difference of opinion, and not an affected one on either side. God forbid it should affect the final question as to the Treaty, but I have some fears about it. Some gentlemen by too much warmth on both sides have occasioned an irritation which might well have been avoided, and happy would it have been had it been so. * * * * The judicial committee, after a great parade, have made no report, and I expect no alterations of moment, after the fairest prospects. We are still doomed, I fear, to be wretched *Drudges*, &c.

JAS. IREDELL.

REV. A. IREDELL TO IREDELL.

NEAR LEWES, April 5th, '96.

MY DEAR BROTHER :—I had the satisfaction of receiving a few days ago your letter from Virginia, dated January 21st. It is many years since I saw Mr. Dawson, and I saw but little of him ; enough, however, to believe that his death must have been truly afflictive to his relations and to those who had the pleasure of a more intimate acquaintance.* Such trials are indeed severe ! how exquisitely so under certain circumstances ! You have a book to read (which, judging by your partiality for the author, as

---

* Hon. Wm. Dawson of the Edenton District.

well as its own intrinsic merit, you will, I am persuaded, devour with inexpressible delight,) in which there are one or two passages on this subject that will affect you most sensibly. It is Burke's last publication, a "Letter to a noble Lord." I shall send it to you with the papers, and I shall expect in return your "critique" or rather eulogy; for, though weak and bad people here criticise Mr. Burke, I do not think you are weak or bad enough to do it. Pray tell me something of Peter Porcupine. I am one of his admirers, of whom there are many in England. I think America ought to be vain of him. I had heard of Mr. Rutledge's appointment and rejection; but things are so badly stated in newspapers that I fancied the speech, which displaced him, had operated with Mr. Washington in his favor. Such *anodynes* are very common in Europe; but I find you trust more to nature, &c., &c.

A. IREDELL.

GOV. JOHNSTON TO IREDELL.

April 9th.

MY DEAR SIR:—✱ ✱ ✱ ✱ The change of sentiment which does justice to the President's merits, must afford a sensible pleasure to every lover of virtue and patriotism, which are so conspicuously united in the mind and actions of that great man. Were his virtues less conspicuous, he would be less envied, and of course have fewer enemies.✱ ✱ ✱ I received your letter of the 18th of March. Nothing appears to me more glaringly absurd than the doctrine of Judge C.: that a duty once executed under the sanction of a legal authority can be regenerated, and created anew so as to subject the debtor to a second recovery, is so opposite to every idea I am capable of forming of equal law and equal justice, that it would require the most powerful arguments to reconcile it to any rational or legal principles. I am sorry to find the debate on the motion for the production of papers, and *agree with you*, that it had far better have been acceded to with a good grace under the restriction you mentioned, than to have given an opening to the opposition to show their virulence, and excite jealousy and uneasiness abroad, &c., &c.

SAM. JOHNSTON.

The Circuit Court opened in Philadelphia with the following charge, delivered by Judge Iredell April 12th.

A CHARGE

Delivered to the Grand Jury for the District of Pennsylvania, in the Circuit Court of the United States for the said District, at Philadelphia, April 12, 1796, by JAMES IREDELL, *one of the Associate Justices of the Supreme Court of the United States.*

[Published at the Request of the Grand Jury.]

GENTLEMEN OF THE GRAND JURY:

The business for which you are now assembled is of no small consequence to the peace and happiness of the community. The people of the United States having thought proper to establish a Government, for the management of all its general concerns, in which not one State only, but all the States are equally interested, it is necessary to take care that their intentions may not be defeated by the misconduct of any individuals. All who love their country may be expected to obey its laws; those who have right notions of a republican government, and possess a proper degree of zeal and virtue to support it, will cheerfully submit to the only terms upon which it can be enjoyed—a deference of private sentiment to that of the public, constitutionally expressed; men of morality will in all instances abstain from any criminal conduct which may injure any individual, or community, or mankind at large. Were all men of these happy dispositions, criminal laws would be useless, and we should in fact see something like that *millennium* which has been so sanguinely the theme not only of heated divines, but of some enthusiastic politicians. Experience too forcibly teaches us, that in all countries, even in those most happily situated, even in our own, enjoying every political blessing to which the mind of man can aspire, there are bad men incapable of being restrained by any moral or political tie, from devising the most nefarious schemes and perpetrating the most wicked actions. The instances, I trust, are rare, but we are well convinced of the reality of some.

The general objects of the criminal law of the United States are the following:

1. Offences against the United States, considered in their national character, for the internal purposes of union, and wherein their own government is alone concerned.

2. Offences against the United States, considered in their national character as one among the nations of the earth, holding a common cognizance of offences against the universal law of society, committed out of the limits of any particular territory.

3. Offences against the United States, considered in their national character as connected with other nations, either by the common tie of the laws of nature, or by any particular treaty or compact.

A full discussion of each of these branches of jurisdiction would take up your time in a manner equally tedious and unuseful. I shall therefore only observe upon such detached parts of the subject as may appear most interesting in a discourse of a general nature, on the present occasion.

Under the first head I shall mention only one offence, but that of the greatest importance, and which cannot be too frequently the object of consideration. The offence I speak of is that of *treason*.

As it is not only natural, but the duty of every government to take care of its own preservation, this crime in all countries is considered of the highest rank; the object of it being the total destruction of the government itself, and of course of all the order, peace, security, and happiness connected with it, thus involving (where the government is a good one) the greatest accumulation of public and private misery which any crime can possibly occasion. But where so much is at stake an extraordinary degree of jealousy is usually proportioned to it, which jealousy will be entertained by a bad government as well as a good one, and always in a greater degree from a consciousness of deserving ill. Accordingly it has in fact happened, that in most countries, in all ages, and under all forms of government, the abuses which have been committed in prosecutions for this offence have been among the most atrocious ever perpetrated to the injury of mankind. Suspicion has supplied the place of evidence, the most distant approaches of danger have armed the hand of power against the greatest of men, and not unfrequently the highest instances of public virtue have been doomed to the punishment of the highest public offences. Happily for the United States, such scenes have been known to them only by the history of other nations. The mildness of their own governments has long been one of the most distinguished, as well as one of the most honorable characteristics of their country. But the framers of the present Constitution of the United States were too wise to depend for permanent security on occasional temper, or even the strong and tried basis of a national character. Knowing well the mischiefs which prosecutions for this offence had occasioned, glowing with proper indignation at the tyrannies of other countries, and thinking no precaution too great to exclude them from their own, they took especial care to guard against the danger of such, by provisions in the constitution anxiously adapted to that end. Every person conversant in such subjects knows, that the great engines of this species of judicial tyranny have been these: 1. So loose a definition of the crime that it was easy, by means of plausible subterfuges, to charge that as an act of treason which was never intended to be deemed such. 2. The admission of such slender proof that an unprincipled government in tempestuous times, taking advantage of favorable conjunctures, could often find means to obtain the conviction of an obnoxious though innocent man. 3. (And which is scarcely credible, if the proofs if it were not too numerous and too plain to be questioned) A spirit of rapacity, which dictated accusations of treason upon insufficient grounds, in order to obtain the benefit of the forfeiture of property, annexed to the crime. Thus infamously taking away a man's life to rob himself and his family of his estate! Such have been the methods by which man has preyed on his fellow-man, and inhuman tyrants, without one spark of feeling, have sported with the happiness, the peace, the security, of the human race! The provisions in our constitution meet each of these causes of so many evils, and I trust will for ever prove a sufficient barrier against them, should it be the fate of this country, at any future unhappy period, to have to dread a tyrannical disposition it has never yet experienced.

Before I dismiss this subject, I cannot avoid recalling to your recollection with emotion and gratitude the memorable events of a very recent period, a period which will form as bright a page as any in the American annals. A large and considerable part of this important State appeared in open insurrection against the government, after having been gradually seduced to it by the basest artifices, and the grossest misrepresentations of a few designing men, whose views in all probability were much deeper and more malignant than they were avowed to be. The executive branch of the government, in duty bound to suppress this insurrection by every constitutional means in its power, but willing before the exertion of force to try the effect of lenient measures, although justly irritated by some very exasperating instances of private injury, in defiance of public authority, sent, in concurrence with the executive of the State, a respectable delegation of men standing high in the public estimation, to state to the insurgents the criminality and danger of their conduct, and to try every pacific means of rendering a recourse to arms unnecessary, even offering a general pardon on condition of general submission. But this humane effort failed of its effect; though it conciliated many, the conduct of others too plainly showed that nothing but arms could restore the law to its wonted energy. This means was then employed, in a manner worthy of the government of a free people, by a militia of different States cheerfully obeying the orders they received, among whom were found many who, sacrificing all private considerations, engaged voluntarily in the service, with a disinterestedness, alacrity and zeal which I believe have seldom been equalled, and never exceeded on any similar occasion. Nor was this merit altogether confined to those who were personally partial to the government, and supported it with warmth from affection and sympathy. Several who had strong prejudices against some of its most important measures, even those which afforded the pretext if not the ground of the insurrection, readily engaged with them in support of the common cause of their country, of republicanism whose principles were so daringly attacked, of order in danger of being immediately subverted, of justice which was set at defiance, of those social ties without which liberty is a name, and existence of no value. Success beyond the most sanguine expectations followed measures so honorably begun, and so nobly conducted. In three months the insurrection was suppressed. The principal fomenters of it either fled from the danger as it approached, or by disgraceful means sheltered themselves from the punishment of their crimes. Many who had been more deluded than criminal were probably seriously convinced of their errors, and disposed to repair them. Not a drop of blood was hostilely shed in the field. Vast numbers partook of an amnesty freely offered; a few only, comparatively, were reserved for trial; two alone have been convicted, to whom has since been extended the sceptre of mercy. The whole scene has exhibited a lesson for governments and people, which never before was displayed on the theatre of the world. God grant it may not be without its effect on other times and other countries, nor ever be obliterated from the memory of our own.

2. The second class of offences I proposed to speak of, was, such as are committed against the United States, considered in their national character as one among the nations of the earth, holding a common cognizance of offences against the universal law of society, committed out of the limits of any particular territory.

Crimes of this description, among others, are piracy and murder committed on the high seas. These being committed out of the particular territory of any State, must either go without any punishment at all, or be equally punishable by any nation into whose country the criminals may afterwards arrive. They being unquestionably a violation of that law of nature by which man is bound to abstain from injuring a fellow-creature, wherever he meet with him, and more especially from robbing or murdering him; all civilized nations concur in the punishment of such offences, each nation proceeding to enforce the law of nature in such instances, in the manner which it conceives most conducive to justice. The laws of the United States have made special provisions on this important subject.

3. The remaining class of offences I stated is, such as are committed against the United States, considered in their national character as connected with other nations, either by the common tie of the law of nature, or by some particular treaty or compact.

The principles which regard the former class of offences are principles, in general much better understood than the principles of this class. But yet this in itself is of great importance, and ever since the present unfortunate war has prevailed in Europe, it has been of the greatest. I hope, therefore, you will not think your time misspent, while we employ a little consideration upon it.

Though particular incidental duties may be incumbent upon individuals, when their own nation is engaged either wholly or partially in a war, yet as in such a case it is most probable they will receive express injunctions from the legislature, and there is no present appearance of such an event, I shall confine my attention under this head, to those which result from a state of general peace, as to the world in general, or a state of neutrality in respect to other nations at war when our own is at peace.

The first, though it gives occasion to the exercise of many humane and benevolent virtues, seldom can occasion offences of a kind peculiar to itself. It will therefore be sufficient, to observe generally, that no nation, when in a state of peace with another nation, can justify doing it any injury whatever; that if any injury is committed by authority of the government itself, the government is immediately answerable for it, and if due satisfaction be not given, it is a justifiable cause of war, or of any lesser species of hostility which may be deemed adequate to the object; that if any injury is committed, though without the authority of government, by a citizen of one nation against another nation, or any individual of it, when no redress can be otherwise obtained, it is a cause of complaint which may be presented by the one nation against the other, in consequence of which it becomes the immediate duty of the government of the aggressor to inquire into the complaint, and upon satisfactory proof to afford all the redress it is susceptible of; and if this be not done, it may be considered as an indication of a hostile disposition in the government, and the nation injured may proceed to such vindicatory measures as upon a fair construction of all the circumstances of the case it shall deem most advisable. Since, therefore, a whole nation may be answerable, even at the hazard of a war, for any violation of the law of nations which its citizens may commit, and since each citizen is entitled to the full protection of his own government, upon the principles I have stated, it follows that each citizen must be answerable to his own government for a disregard of his duty in this particular, he being indispensably bound to serve his country by every means in his power, and not to injure, much less disgrace it by any. This being a result of natural reason and propriety, it forms a part of what is called *the common law*, though statutes, to give it greater force and efficacy, frequently make express provisions on the subject, as has been done by the Congress of the United States. But as it is altogether a subject of national concern, as those intrusted with the national authority in this particular must be responsible for the rules of action observed in relation to it within their own territory, as various unforeseen deviations from general principles, not capable in their nature of reaching every possible case, may be rendered justifiable by extraordinary exigencies, of which alone each nation must judge for itself, each nation has the power of prescribing rules for the observation of its own citizens in this particular, and in our nation this power is expressly delegated to the Congress of the United States. If therefore they should prescribe different rules on this subject for the observation of their own citizens, than those which theoretical writers on the law of nations teach, I apprehend the citizens of the United States must obey that rule prescribed by the competent authority of their own government, which in the exercise of this, as well as every other species of constitutional authority, binds the whole, because it is appointed a trustee for the whole, to whose wisdom and discretion the subject is submitted. Consequently, when an individual is guilty of a violation of what is usually termed the law of nations in our own territory, he is not chargeable with this in our courts merely as a violation of the law of nations, but as a violation of the law of his own country, of which the law of nations is a part, and of which Congress is the sole expositor as to us, when it takes that duty upon it. When no act of Congress interferes, it is an offence at common law, in the same manner and upon the same principle as any other offence committed against the common law, and in respect to which no particular statute had passed. Where there is any special act on the subject, it is an offence against that act in the same manner and upon the same principle as an offence against any other act would be. In short, my idea is, that in all such instances each citizen is answerable to his own nation, and the nation itself answerable to other nations, for the proper conduct of its own citizens, over whose actions the nation necessarily must have control, so far as they affect the interests of other nations, otherwise upon no principle of justice could each nation be fully responsible for the conduct of its own citizens in such instances, which all the writers on the law of nations agree they are. The same observations as to citizens will almost in every case equally apply to others residing in the country and amenable to its laws, as to citizens themselves.

2. Those general duties incumbent upon the government and its citizens, as to mankind at large, when in a state of universal peace, cannot be changed merely by the event of two other nations being at war, with which the United States have no connection. In regard to them, however, certain new duties arise superadded to the former, which being relative to the peculiar nature of the case, may be called duties of neutrality, it being inconsistent with the pacific conduct due to both to favor the hostile purposes of either. What may be construed to do so would open a large field of inquiry, with which I shall not now trouble you, but of which, within these few years, you have heard a great deal. If one of the hostile powers should even be an ally, which the United States are bound, by an antecedent treaty, either generally or partially to assist, I apprehend no individual citizen could be justified in actually affording assistance, unless the Congress of the United States, with whom the power of declaring war or authorizing any actual hostilities is invested, should direct or authorize such assistance to be given, they being to judge in relation to those objects, in all cases of that description, of the nature of the obligation, as it originally existed, whether any change of circumstances has since intervened to do away or weaken its force; or if assistance is to be afforded, at what time and in what manner, and also to what extent it shall be afforded; since in all these respects the nation, whom Congress represent on this occasion, is accountable on the one hand to the other contracting power for a proper observance of the public faith pledged by such treaty; and on the other hand the Congress are responsible to their own country, that any reciprocal rights of the United States are duly protected and secured, and their real interest and safety not disregarded. Until, therefore, some active measure of this kind be taken, each individual is undoubtedly bound to act according to the existing situation of his country, which is a state of peace, until a state of war, or any inferior state of actual hostility, is created by the authority constituted for that purpose. In this situation the United States were, at the commencement of the present European war, and have uniformly remained since. Upon these principles was grounded that

proclamation of the President, the propriety and utility of which have become more apparent under every discussion. The Congress, though so often in session since the war began, never have decided that any obligation of duty required, or any motive of policy induced the United States to take a part in the war, either wholly or partially. Much less have they by any act authorized any hostilities whatever. On the contrary, they have passed laws more strictly to enforce those duties of neutrality, which, upon general principles, it is conceived were incumbent upon all before, though certainly it was a desirable thing on so important an occasion to obviate all possible doubts by express provisions of the legislature itself, which none could mistake, and accompanied with sanctions less indefinite than those which existed before.

Independently of what I have already said, the subject under discussion, if fully investigated, would naturally lead me to a consideration, under many aspects, of the nature and effect of treaties; those solemn national compacts, in which the peace and happiness of mankind are so deeply interested, and which acquire a peculiar sanctity from the good faith they indispensably demand. But though no topic can be more interesting to us as individuals, especially at the present momentous crisis, yet as I know no case likely to arise upon which a judicial consideration of it will be requisite for any official business before you, I forbear any particular observations upon it.

I shall now, gentlemen, only add, that the government we enjoy can alone be supported by a due mixture of vigilance and moderation; by inviolably adhering to the principles of the constitution, but at the same time making reasonable allowances for real differences of opinion, whenever they occur, and the various difficulties to which the affairs of a great country will always be subjected; by paying proper obedience to the constituted authorities of our country, relying upon those guards against abuse which the constitution has not only carefully, but I am persuaded efficaciously provided; and by constantly bearing in mind, that that law which protects others protects ourselves, and therefore that we shall arrogate what no true friend to liberty can consistently claim, if we fail in that measure of obedience to the government of our country in cases that are not perfectly agreeable to us, which we expect from all others in those that are.

IREDELL TO MRS. IREDELL.

PHILADELPHIA, April 15th.

MY DEAR HANNAH:— * * * * The friends of the Government are now universally in great alarm. A proposition came forward yesterday on the part of those who lead the House, ending with a declaration that it is not now expedient to carry the British Treaty into effect. It being of high importance I shall inclose a newspaper containing it. The shock it has given to the trade of this city is beyond all conception. A meeting of the merchants and traders is to be held to-day, to consider the propriety of addressing the House, and a meeting of the Insurance Company to consider the propriety of carrying on the business. There is too much reason to fear every one of our members (except Mr. Grove) will vote for it, including Mr. Blair's favorite Mr. Burgess, who on all occasions has shown himself a thorough-paced Virginian. He has been, too insignificant to attempt speaking. * * * * Priestly has preached not only remarkably well, but *unexceptionably*, since the day I was out of humor with him. *The next Sunday some ladies went who had gone before, but not many.* One or two that day vindicated every thing he said—I thank God they were none of my acquaintances, &c.°

May 3d.

I am to-morrow to set off for Annapolis. * * * Table-China is now about $70. * * * Last Saturday the House of Representatives, by a majority of three, agreed to give effect to the British Treaty—a resolution which caused more joy in this city than, perhaps, any event remembered, the Declaration of Independence and the Treaty of Peace excepted. Mr. Grove was the only one of our members who voted for it. More of them, I believe, would have done so but from an apprehension (altogether groundless) that Lord Granville's right to his former estate in North Carolina would be revived by the 9th Article of the Treaty. Only one member from Virginia (Mr. Hancock) voted for it. Findley, a member from this State, who has been constantly puffed as a great patriot, to his eternal disgrace, withdrew, after the call of the House, and before the question was put. Thus evading, as he thought, a responsibility which every other member met in a manly manner. It is to be hoped that no man of any honor will ever countenance by a future vote such scandalous conduct, &c., &c.

JAS. IREDELL.

* April 28th Mr. Ames made his great speech on the Treaty. Vice President Adams wrote his wife, "Judge Iredell and I happened to sit together. Our feelings beat in unison. 'My God! how great he is,' says Iredell; 'how great he has been!' 'Noble!' said I. After some time, Iredell breaks out, 'Bless my stars! I never heard any thing so great since I was born.' 'Divine,' said I; and thus we went on with our interjections, not to say tears, to the end. Tears enough were shed."

IREDELL TO MISS GRAY.*

RICHMOND, June, '96.

DEAR MADAM:—You really conferred upon me a very great and pleasing obligation by attending so kindly to my anxiety for the fate of your sister as to inform me of the birth of her son, and that they were in such good health. I sincerely rejoice in an event, which must make the whole family and all her friends so happy. I offer my warmest congratulations. The only abatement of satisfaction I felt in reading the letter you did me the honor to write arose from the information that you were so soon to go to Boston, so that I fear it may be a long time before I shall again have the pleasure of seeing you. It is one of the painful circumstances attending the life I lead that I form many agreeable acquaintances whose society is dear to me, and from whom I part with an uncertainty of ever seeing them again. My disposition is not such that I can feel such a situation with indifference.

I endeavored, with as much justice as I could consistently with some envy of his good fortune, to represent your and Miss Wilson's favorable sentiments to Judge Griffin. He is not only highly sensible of the honor you both do him, but if I may judge from his expressions, as well as the pleasure with which he seems to recollect May, 1795, there is a perfect reciprocity on the occasion. He joins me in sincere congratulations on the birth of your nephew, and in hoping that in due time he may have a cousin and nephew as charming as himself. My wishes extend further as I don't forget any of my friends in Boston.

Your obliging expressions in regard to my being there hereafter flatter me extremely. I never go to that agreeable place without pleasure, nor leave it without pain. Either will be increased in no inconsiderable degree if I should be so fortunate as to find you among a set of acquaintance to whom I owe so many obligations, and whose society has afforded me so many happy hours. They are frequently in my recollection, and must be so through life. But if I should ever be there again there will be one very melancholy drawback on the satisfaction I should otherwise feel. Every hour I should miss that excellent man Mr. *Russell*, who from the first moment of our acquaintance showed me such uniform and distinguished kindness as, added to his numerous virtues and agreeable qualities, impressed upon me the highest sense of attachment and respect.† As long as I live I shall venerate, and love his memory, and feel anxiety for the happiness of all his family. If you should have an opportunity you would confer upon me a great favor by presenting my most respectful compliments to Mrs. Russell, Miss Talbot and Miss Russell.

I take it for granted you will have left Philadelphia before this letter can arrive there, and therefore shall commit it to the care of my friend Judge Wilson. You will be so good as to assure your mamma and sister of my remembrance. I hope the health of the former will be better; and that of the latter as good as it was. You have all my constant and warmest wishes for your happiness.

I am, dear Madam, with great respect,
Your obliged and obedient servant,
JAS. IREDELL.

IREDELL TO MRS. IREDELL.

HEAD OF ELK, July 29th, 1796.

MY DEAR HANNAH:—I have this moment arrived here perfectly well, but extremely fatigued. Our stage broke down yesterday, but did no damage to any of us, except our arrival so late in Baltimore, that it was impossible for me to call on Polly.° Judge Chase is with me, having relied so much on my punctuality as to take a place for me in the stage. We are also in company with Mr. De Nar, and Mr. Bouquet, &c., &c.

SUPREME COURT.—AUGUST TERM.

PHILADELPHIA, August 1st.

I arrived here on Saturday last. I was very much shocked to hear of the death of Miss Bunner at Alexandria, and immediately on my arrival here of the death of our worthy friend Mrs. Mease, which happened on the 25th instant. * * * * Miss Mease, owing to extreme anxiety and fatigue, has been very unwell herself, but is now in much better health, though she looks ill, and her melancholy is very affecting. She aims at all the composure she can, but every now and then bursts into tears. The poor old father and mother are in the deepest distress, and can't avoid frequently talking of their daughter.

August 3d.

* * * * We have a vast deal of business to do, but as the Court meets punctually at 9 every morning, I hope we shall dis-

* Sister to Mrs. Judge Wilson.
† Probably Ben. Russell, Editor of the "Centinel." Vid. "Sullivan's Familiar Letters."

* A former servant.

patch more in proportion than usual. I am afraid, however, it will take us at least three or four weeks. Every one of the Judges was here on Saturday. * * * Though a few people have lately died here after a short illness, Dr. Rush says the town is healthier than he ever knew it, &c.

JAS. IREDELL.

At this Term the United Sates vs. La Vengeance was decided, which has always been regarded as a leading case upon the important question of the nature and extent of the Admiralty jurisdiction of the Federal tribunals. The precedent was then established, and has never since been shaken, that the admiralty and maritime jurisdiction of the Federal Courts extends as far as the ebb and flow of the tide.

In Wiscart vs. Dauchey, the Court "laid down a principle of vast importance to the profession, so much so indeed, as to lead in a short time to a change in the Judiciary Act." The Court held "that in causes of equity or admiralty jurisdiction, removed to this Court, accompanied with a statement of facts, but without the evidence, the statement is conclusive as to all the facts which it contains. If such causes are removed with a statement of facts and also with the evidence, still the statement is conclusive as to all the facts it contains."

Another interesting Admiralty case was that of Moodie vs. the Phœbe Ann. "One thing was clearly established by the decision—namely, that the Judges of the Federal Courts, notwithstanding any political prejudices they might have been supposed to entertain against the 'regicide republic,' were determined to carry out in good faith the provisions of existing treaties with France."*

IREDELL TO MRS. IREDELL.

PHILADELPHIA, August 12th.

MY DEAR HANNAH:—I have now every reason to think that our Court will end to-day or to-morrow. * * * Judge Cushing goes to the Eastward, Judge Wilson the Middle Circuit, and Judge Patterson the Southern, &c.

JAS. IREDELL.

IREDELL TO JUDGE WILSON.

RICHMOND, August 20th.

DEAR SIR:—I arrived here last night extremely fatigued for want of sleep, but my last night's rest has completely recruited me. I intended going down the bay, had there been an immediate opportunity, but finding only an uncertain one could not bear to stay. Reflecting upon what you said to me concerning my eventual attendance at this Court next November, I think it proper to state more particularly circumstances which have occurred to me than I could then. A suit in Equity of great importance, and upon which a large sum in money is depending, came on last November before Judge Blair and myself. An issue had been directed by Judge Blair and Judge Griffin, which was tried before us last November, and a verdict found in it to a large amount. Upon the trial of the issue, it occurred to me for reasons that I stated that it was an issue which could not be made up at law. Judge Griffin was of a different opinion,—so that there could be no decree. The difference of opinion continued at last Term,—which necessarily occasioned another continuance. There is no prospect of our ever agreeing, and another delay to the same cause might occasion great injury, and certainly would much discontent. In addition to this reason of a public nature, let me add—that I have not been at home six weeks since the 18th of January,—that being now to return in the midst of our sickly season, I expect not to enjoy one hour of unmixed satisfaction till it is over, which can't be counted on until the beginning of November,—that to attend this Court, at the distance of 160 miles, which I should have to travel back again before I set off to Philadelphia, would break in upon almost the only remnant of truly valuable time in point of happiness, should my family's escape from the season be ever so fortunate, which I could rely upon during the interval allowed me; and, preceding a new absence of five or six months at least, not only my personal enjoyments would thus be distressingly interrupted, but a considerable additional expense incurred, and all attention to my little property, which requires some consideration, rendered in a manner impossible. I state these circumstances thus particularly, as I am anxious to show you how unwilling I am to decline any request of yours without the strongest reasons.

I never expect to hear in a letter from you how you and your family are. But I assure you I shall always be solicitous to know, and shall feel real satisfaction in hearing favorable accounts, whenever opportunities offer. You will oblige me in presenting my very respectful compliments to Mrs. Wilson, Miss Emily, and your sons, who are capable of receiving them. The youngest has my wishes equally for his happiness, as he has no small share of my admiration, &c., &c.

JAS. IREDELL.

* Vid. the admirable volume, "Lives of the Chief Justices" by Van Santvoord, and 3d Dallas.

COL. DAVIE TO IREDELL.

HALIFAX, November 11th.

MY DEAR SIR:—I received your letter by Mr. Sitgreaves; the actual result of the election here is still in doubt. Mr. W. Jones has certainly failed without the appearance of means to defeat his election. * * * Spaight will be elected in Newbern, and John G. Blount at Washington: both these gentlemen were stanch friends of the present President, but they will be both opposed to Mr. Adams. I had a long conversation with Mr. Blount at Newbern on the subject, but a promise not to decide till we met again was all I could obtain from him. I sincerely hope John Skinner may be elected. Several of the candidates westward of this are decidedly in favor of the present Administration: with these men something I expect may be done; and as I owe nothing to any man or party in or belonging to the Federal Government, I shall feel myself entirely at liberty to act without reserve in any direction the public good may require, and any little influence I have shall be exerted, provided I find it can be with effect. Uncommon pains have indeed been taken by the Jacobin party to insure the election of Jefferson, particularly in the Southern States, and considerable hopes are entertained by them of Pennsylvania, where neither activity nor expense have been spared, &c., &c.

WM. R. DAVIE.

JUDGE PATTERSON (SUP. COURT, U. S.) TO IREDELL.

RALEIGH, December 1st.

DEAR SIR:—I received your obliging favor by Mr. Collins, who delivered me a packet of newspapers, which I read with much avidity. The contest between Mr. Adams and Mr. Jefferson will be severe; but I am of opinion, that it will terminate in favor of the former. I will give you my calculation. The whole number of votes will be 138; of course 70 will be the majority. From New Jersey to New Hampshire inclusive the votes, being 58, will be for Mr. Adams; then say—

3 from Pennsylvania.
3 " Delaware.
5 " Maryland.
3 " Virginia.
1 " North Carolina.
—
73

I do not reckon on South Carolina. The Legislature of that State met on Monday last, and, I suppose, have by this time appointed the electors. Some suppose that the electors of that State will be entirely in favor of Mr. Jefferson; others suppose they will be divided, and that Mr. Adams will have a moiety of them. I believe, however, that the estimate above-mentioned is moderate, and that Mr. Adams will run higher than what is there stated.

It would give me much pleasure to pay a visit to my friends at Edenton, but this I cannot conveniently do, as the winter is coming fast upon me. Make my best respects to Mrs. Iredell; and remember me in the best terms to Gov. Johnston and Mr. Skinner. It is necessary that wise and good men should exert themselves in every State in the Union; and therefore I regret that Mr. Skinner has been so inert on a late occasion. With respect, believe me to be,

Yours sincerely,
WM. PATTERSON.

Judge Iredell's family have preserved many letters addressed to him by his colleagues; but, as the majority of them possess no public interest, a number have been, and will be omitted. In neatness and legibility they rank in the following order of merit. —Iredell, Jay, Patterson, Blair, Chase, Cushing. Judge Chase's have this peculiarity—the lines do not cross the page in the usual manner, at right angles, but diagonally. Judge Cushing's performances are execrable scrawls. The manuscripts of Chase, Blair, and Cushing, do little credit to the chirographic skill of the Bench. These remarks are for the benefit of those curious in autographs.

GOV. JOHNSTON TO IREDELL.

HERMITAGE, Dec. 12th.

MY DEAR SIR:— * * * I have not yet heard for whom our electors have voted, but have understood from a gentleman from Raleigh, that there would be at least three votes in favor of Mr. Adams—some thought four. I am not acquainted with any of the Virginia electors except Josiah Riddick, and he, I think, will vote for Mr. Jefferson, as he is one of the family of the *Wrong-heads*. * * * The weather has been colder than I have ever known it at this season, and the frost of longer continuance. The mercury in the thermometer was at one time eleven degrees below the freezing point: a few days after, it was as high as 75.

VOL. II.—31

This sudden change gave me a cough, that will probably stick by me until Spring, though I am no way confined by it. I am constantly busy about my little farm, which turns to very little other account than to afford me exercise, and to secure me effectually against hypochondria, vapors, and melancholy: attention to it gives me a good appetite for my food, and disposes me to sleep soundly at night, without any other medicine, *my cough notwithstanding*, &c., &c.

SAM. JOHNSTON.

When the electors assembled at Raleigh to vote for President and Vice President, Judge Iredell received three votes. Gov. Johnston was similarly complimented by Massachusetts with two votes.

JOHN MARSHALL (subsequently, C. Justice U. S.) TO IREDELL.

RICHMOND, Dec. 15th, '96.

DEAR SIR:—I had not the pleasure of receiving till yesterday your favor of the 3d instant. Since then, I have seen the votes of North Carolina, and you, I presume, those of Virginia. Mr. Adams would have received one other vote had Mr. Eyre really been elected, but he was left out by accident. There was supposed to be no opposition to him, and in consequence of that opinion the people in one county, on the eastern shore, did not vote at all, and in the other a very few assembled. On the day of election the people of Princess Ann, whose Court day it happened to be, assembled in numbers, and elected Mr.———, who voted for Mr. Jefferson. From that gentleman you will have heard there were twenty votes for Mr. Samuel Adams, fifteen for Mr. Clinton, three for Burr, Gen. Washington one, Mr. Pinckney one, and Mr. John Adams one. I received a letter from Philadelphia, stating that five votes south of the Potomac would be necessary to secure the election of Mr. Adams. It is then certain that he cannot be elected. Our Assembly, which you know is in session, displays its former hostility to federalism. They have once more denied *wisdom* to the administration of the President, and have gone so far as to say in argument, that we ought not by any declarations to commit ourselves, so as to be bound to support his measures as they respect France. To what has America fallen! Is it to be hoped that North Carolina will, in this particular, rather adopt such measures as have been pursued by other States, than tread the crooked paths of Virginia?

I have received a letter from Mr. Dallas, and will furnish him with my argument in the case of the British debts. I expect to be under the necessity of getting the opinions of the Judges, except yours, from Mr. Dallas, whose report of the case will be published before mine. With very much respect and esteem, I am, dear sir,

Your obed't
JOHN MARSHALL.

GOV. JOHNSTON TO IREDELL.

December 25th.

MY DEAR SIR:— * * * * Nothing can be more insolent than Adet's Appeal to the people of the United States against their Government, in his note to the Secretary of State; and nothing more extraordinary than the conclusion, where he informs them that, though the Directory have determined to act in direct violation of an express article of the Treaty, that no *rupture* is contemplated with the United States. If Congress do not exert themselves with spirit in support of the honor and authority of Government, I shall tremble for the event, and I am not without very painful apprehensions in that respect. * * * * Since the commencement of this severe season, several weddings have been consummated in this neighborhood—Mr. Keys of Washington to Miss Sally Bryan, Dr. Picott of Plymouth to Miss Hannah Bogg, and last night Thomas Hunter, Esqr., to the *amiable* Miss Betsey House; and it is thought that if the mercury continues below the freezing point a few days longer, there will be several others, &c., &c.

SAM. JOHNSTON.

APPENDIX TO CHAPTER XXIX.

A CHARGE,

Delivered to the Grand Jury for the District of Virginia, in the Circuit Court of the United States for the said District, at the city of Richmond, May 23, 1796, by JAMES IREDELL, *one of the Associate Justices of the Supreme Court of the United States.*

[Published at the request of the Grand Jury.]

GENTLEMEN OF THE GRAND JURY:

Among the numerous means put into our power for preserving the public blessings these States so remarkably enjoy, perhaps none are of greater importance, certainly none deserve a more sacred regard, than those that relate to the administration of justice. Liberty without law is anarchy; law without liberty is oppression. A due mixture of both, can alone make any people at once prosperous and happy.

What may constitute the proper union of both, it is difficult to say in regard to any people until experience has given some sanction to theory. The habits, manners, principles and propensities differ so much in different nations, that it is impossible that the same kind of system can suit them all. No people, however, can rationally desire more than that they should themselves choose the government under which they are to live. There is no alternative between this, but no government at all, or one which owes its birth to usurpation or accident.

The people of the United States not only were the first who enjoyed the high distinction of choosing a government of their own, but in the course of many years' experience of war and peace, they have had opportunities to put many principles to the test, and to appreciate their value accordingly. Thus it was found, that in time of war, when a vast majority of the people concurred in one common object, being actuated by a common danger, and having one great end only in view, the feeble articles of confederation were sufficient to keep them together, to conduct them gloriously through the trying conflict in which they were engaged, and at length terminate it with equal honor and advantage. But when this common object was obtained, when the danger of a foreign enemy was removed, then soon appeared the influence of selfish and contending interests, too many forgetting how necessary union was to preserve what had been with so much difficulty acquired. The consequences we well know. The voice of the Union disregarded—public debts not only unpaid, but unprovided for; private, as well as public credit, at a very low ebb; commerce languishing; agriculture discouraged; measures of disunion every day adopting; an illiberal and malignant jealousy taking place of a rational and manly confidence, and the most melancholy symptoms prevailing of a speedy dissolution of the Union, or a disgraceful and ungovernable anarchy. The magnitude of the danger alarmed all considerate men, and by one of the greatest and most disinterested efforts ever made by public bodies, each making voluntary sacrifices to accomplish a magnanimous reformation, the present Constitution of the United States was formed and adopted. The consequences which have happened, I need not depict. They are felt, if not acknowledged, by all. They have advanced the United States to a degree of prosperity and glory to which no imagination reached before the experiment was made. They have scarcely any thing to wish, but that rashness may not throw away what wisdom has so nobly procured.

All governments depend more or less upon the confidence and support of the people for whose benefit they do, or ought, to subsist. But a free government more especially does so, and the freer the government the greater such dependence must be. Every citizen, therefore, of the United States, whatever may be his station or situation, has an important responsibility attached to himself. He owes to his country, by all possible and honorable means, to promote its prosperity, and to do nothing either negligently or with design to counteract it. Considering himself as a member of a single community, which is itself a member of another in a larger sphere, he should reflect that he is only one individual connected with a great number of others, whose authority separately is equal, and each of whose sentiments are entitled to equal deference with his own: That his individual interest, when it comes into competition, must yield to that of the State in which he resides; and that the interest of the State itself, when it stands in competition with that of the United States, must yield to this as a superior interest also, since a real and effective union can be founded upon no other basis. At the same time that he exercises with zeal, and maintains with firmness, the right of each individual to express his sentiments on all public concerns, he should endeavor, as well as his opportunities will admit, to understand them thoroughly, that he may neither be unwarily misled himself, nor unwarily mislead others. He should seriously meditate on the awful stake which not only himself, but millions of others have in the public prosperity, and make reasonable allowances for the difficulties which will perpetually occur in the management of the concerns of so great a number, so as to combine as nearly as possible the interests of the few with the interests of the many, and render the whole subservient to the exalted principles of honor and justice. To effect these great objects is indeed no easy task, and he who thinks it so, shows either an extreme ignorance of the subject, or a vain presumption in his own powers, for which no judicious man will give him any credit. As long as governments shall subsist, under any form or of any description, various opinions will be entertained upon the subject of political regulations. They embrace a variety of interests, all of which cannot be equally promoted, though all ought to be consulted, and as much as possible to be reconciled. They respect future contingencies, upon which the limited foresight of man can enable him to form at best but probable conjectures. Cases of extraordinary exigency sometimes present themselves, which confound the clearest understandings, and in which no steps however cautious can be sure to tread with safety. The ablest men in investigating a subject to which so many intricacies belong, will often differ about the proper means of effecting the same common object. These difficulties occur even if the best dispositions should universally prevail. But that never can be the case in an extensive country. However numerous the well disposed may be, there will be always ill disposed men, ready to take advantage of opportunities to do mischief. They will neglect no means of doing it, where they have any chance of success. Misrepresentations may be easily made which for a time will impose on many who possess the purest intentions, since no man can judge but according to the information he receives, and if that be erroneous, an opinion grounded on it must necessarily be so too. Plausible reports will be raised to catch the credulous; unwarrantable apprehensions will be suggested to alarm the timid; arrogant pretensions to patriotism will be employed to seduce those who revere and practise it. By arts like these much mischief may be effected before the public mind can be thoroughly informed, and the true grounds of public measures rightly understood. It is in this interval alone that a free government, conscious of its integrity, has any thing to fear. The government of the United States has passed through several of these trials. Through them all time has removed prejudices which successively had great sway. Reason, when it was allowed a fair scope, has had its full effect on an enlightened, justice on a virtuous, candor on a generous people. They have never yet failed, and I trust never will, to bestow their confidence when convinced it has been really deserved. They well know how much is in their power if in any instance it be abused, but they will not suffer men to be condemned unheard, because they have been thought worthy of their highest confidence, nor will they be prevailed upon, under any temporary delusion, to abandon a government of their own choice, and which has constantly risen in their estimation after every attempt to discredit it.

I make these observations, gentlemen, because it is the glory of a free government, and I doubt not the first wish of our own, to rely upon the good opinion and affections of the people as the firmest basis of its power: Because ill-grounded discontent not only preys upon the mind, and diminishes its usefulness in society, but has too natural a tendency to create an indifference, if not an aversion to government, and from either of these the gradation to actual disobedience is less than seems commonly to be considered: Because though Courts of Justice have authority to punish disobedience, yet if they can be in any manner instrumental in rendering the exercise of such authority unnecessary, they may perform more real services to their country (and certainly such as are more pleasing to themselves), than by appearing only in the stern character of power; and a humane precaution to prevent crime can never be deemed an improper attribute of justice.—I may add, perhaps without impropriety, Because I am persuaded that the better the measures of the government are understood, the more they will be approved, and whatever differences of opinion may still remain as to the policy of some of them, there will be found upon the most scrutinizing research, no reason for supposing that they have not originated in the most upright intentions to promote the welfare of our common country.

I have heard, gentlemen, of no offences likely to come before you but such as are unquestionably of a very immoral and dangerous nature, and altogether unconnected with political dissensions. No particulars have come officially to my knowledge, but I have understood that very serious prosecutions are depending for some species of frauds committed upon the public mail, which by a special act of the Congress of the United States are made highly penal, in some instances punishable with death. It would be improper for me to enter into a detail concerning transactions of which I have received no official information, but I think it proper to read to you such parts of the act as may concern the prosecutions in question, not doubting that you will proceed in the investigation of the charges with all the attention and care suited to their solemnity and importance.

[Here he read the 16th and 17th Sect. 3 Vol. p. 48-49.]

If in the course of your inquiry upon these prosecutions, or any other, you should require any assistance from the Court which can be properly afforded, it shall be most readily given.

The Grand Jury returned the following answer:

To the Honorable Judge Iredell and Judge Griffin:

Gentlemen:—We are convinced of the importance of the observations delivered in your charge, to men who have the happiness to live under a government of their choice. It can subsist only in the confidence of the people; and any attempt to destroy this support, leads directly to its subversion. But we can with pleasure declare, that the government of the Union, which was called into existence by the voice of the people, is still the object of their warmest attachment; that they are sufficiently enlightened to appreciate justly, as well the blessings it has bestowed, as the calamities it has averted; and clearly to perceive that their very liberty, peace, and prosperity, can rest on no other secure foundation.

If various interests agitate the different parts of the Union, as their various sentiments might lead us to fancy, it is fortunate that their government compels them at last to harmonize; that dissension evaporates in debate, instead of engendering hostile feuds; and that while the Senate is convulsed, the people are tranquil. But instead of deriving this difference of opinion from opposite and irreconcilable interests, which only our enemies would delight to mark, we may fairly trace it to local and temporary circumstances which the hand of time is gently removing, and anticipate a period, when the national character, as well as national government, shall be the pride and boast of every American.

It is to be expected, that the people will watch the conduct of a government, in which are deposited their hopes of happiness, with a jealous attention. And this irritable state of the public mind, may sometimes receive, too favorably, the seeds of distrust and suspicion, which are every where scattered by industrious malice; a temporary delusion may succeed, which soon, however, will yield to the genuine good sense of the people operating upon fuller and more accurate information.

Our government, as you observe, has more than once experienced these crises of public opinion; and we trust that instead of suffering by the shock, it has grown in the public estimation. Conscious of its integrity, it must desire to be scrutinized by the intelligent and candid, and if it regards its own preservation, the first objects of its policy should be to diffuse knowledge among the people, and to cultivate that inflexible virtue, which corresponds with its institution, and can alone give to it stability.

We shall not fail to bestow on those subjects particularly committed to us, that serious attention which their importance to the interests of society demands.

By the majority of the Grand Jury,
HENRY LEE, *Foreman.*

May 26th, 1796.

The above address having been presented to the Judges out of Court, the following reply was given:

To Henry Lee, Esq.

Sir:—The sentiments contained in the address you have done us the honor to present, give us great satisfaction. They breathe a spirit of union and republicanism, which the situation of the United States peculiarly demands, and which appears with peculiar dignity and weight, in those who have so eminently contributed to the establishment of both. Such an example must produce the happiest effects on many, who, though they highly value the liberty and reputation of their country, too slightly estimate the dangers to which they are exposed, when a temper of indiscriminate distrust is substituted for a wise and discreet jealousy, and unavoidable differences of opinion are suffered to rankle into personal animosity and ill will. But we trust, and doubt not, that, as the people of the different States become better acquainted with each other, a great deal of unfortunate prejudice which still prevails, will be done away, and that every day will more strongly cement that union so essential to the prosperity of all.

We have the honor to be,
With the highest respect, Sir,
Your most obedient, and
Most faithful servants,
JAS. IREDELL.
C. GRIFFIN.

Richmond, May 27, 1796.

Memorandum concerning the Granville claim to lands in North Carolina.

The whole country which was afterwards divided into North and South Carolina, was originally a proprietary one, by charter from the Crown of Great Britain.

The proprietors were:

The Earl of Carendon,   Lord Ashley,
The Duke of Albemarle,   Sir George Carteret, and
The Earl of Craven,   Sir John Colleton.
Lord Berkley,

All the above proprietors or their descendants sold to the Crown except Sir George Carteret or his: and the country was divided into North and South Carolina.

The share belonging to the Carteret family was in North Carolina, and formed a most considerable or valuable part of it.

In November, 1777, the Assembly opened a land office for the disposal of vacant lands, which were to be entered on the terms presented in the act, and grants to issue accordingly.

See. p. 292, this act, and particularly the 3d Sec. p. 296, the 16 and 17 Sec.

See p. 367, Chap. 6.

At the same session they passed a confiscation act, which see p. 341. This confiscation, it will be observed, was conditional: read the 2d Sec.

See p. 364, act, after the time for performance of the condition elapsed.

P. 379, another act on the subject—especially naming some, and including others by general words.

P. 302, declaring entries void of any land comprised within the confiscation acts.

There are subsequent acts on the subject, particularly directing sales, &c., but none that are deemed material to the present inquiry.

The act of confiscation as to lands, is in p. 12.

The material parts of it to be considered in this case are the 2d, 3d, and 4th Sections.

See as exception, p. 453, Sec. 9.

Whether a descent hath been in fact lost of the old proprietary title since the Revolution, I don't know.—But I think it highly probable.

From the clause above referred to in the entry law, and that which says "all entries of confiscation lands shall be void," it seems as if the Assembly considered the old proprietary estate as held in the nature of a *Royal interest* and not as a *private estate.*

But query if an actual confiscation by *name* could be stronger than the directions of that act to show *the will of the State and to exercise it,* which circumstances, in case of an actual confiscation, have been usually deemed sufficient.

The *words* of the confiscation act are undoubtedly large enough, taken by themselves, to comprehend this case, whatever may be the effect of a general confiscation act not naming the parties.

See Mr. Johnston's letter to Mr. Jefferson—Message, &c. p. 137.

The verdict, to my knowledge, was given *agreeable to the direction, and with the unanimous approbation,* of the Judges of the Superior Court of North Carolina.

The deeds of gift mentioned in the case, I believe were executed while he was on board a flag of truce in the harbor of Newbern, while the Assembly was sitting, *and before the act of confiscation was actually passed, but when it was in contemplation.*

It was alleged, if I recollect right, that the deeds were void.

1. Because it was said they were executed *upon* the act, and dated *before* it—of this I don't recollect any proof.

2. Because Mr. Cornell was not a citizen of the United States, and therefore *could neither hold nor convey.*

3. Because the deeds being in contemplation of the act, and to evade it, were *void,* as being fraudulent.

Note: In the then act (1777), *Mr. Cornell was not named,* though comprehended within a general description.

He was not specially named in any act till October, 1779.

I was present during the above trial (having received a retaining fee in the case, on behalf of the purchasers under the act, though particular circumstances prevented my being fully engaged).

If there was time Mr. Bryant or Mr. LeRoy, of New York, could give a particular account of this case.

I think the above account is correct, but cannot positively vouch for it.

It does not occur to me that any doubt was suggested but that *if the deeds had been executed after the act of confiscation had actually passed, they would have been void.*

B. Com. Descent not cast on an alien propter defectum sanguinis.

CHAPTER XXX.
ÆT. 45—46.

COL. DAVIE TO IREDELL. SUPREME COURT, FEBRUARY TERM. CLOSING SCENES OF WASHINGTON'S ADMINISTRATION. LETTER FROM JUDGE PATTERSON. MIDDLE CIRCUIT. CHARGE TO GRAND JURY AT PHILADELPHIA. CHARGE AT RICHMOND, AND PRESENTMENT OF MR. CABELL. LETTERS FROM COL. DAVIE, GOV. JOHNSTON, JNO. MILLER, T. PICKERING, ETC.

COL. DAVIE TO IREDELL.

HALIFAX, February 1st, '97.

MY DEAR SIR:—The statement I sent you from Raleigh, and which came from pretty good authority in Philadelphia, was calculated upon mistaken data. The result, however, has been really the same. Mr. Blount has informed some of his *factionary correspondents* here, that the votes of Vermont will be probably set aside, and that this measure will defeat the election of Adams; but should Vermont have acted so unadvisedly, I flatter myself the majority of the States would confirm the election.

Our Assembly voted the Address to the President unanimously: it is indeed very indifferently written, but is warm, affectionate and respectful; and will surely contradict in plain and strong terms the representative language, and conduct, of some of our members of Congress; and let *Posterity* (for whose good opinion these gentlemen appear to be anxious) see that they were actuated by their own factious views, not the sense or feelings of their constituents. It is now clear that this unprincipled faction are determined to embitter even the *last drop* of the Presidential cup; and although their public conduct appears to receive its direction from personal animosity, I think it is not to be expected that their political principles or dispositions will be meliorated by their late disappointment.

The Virginia resolutions were disposed of by our Assembly, by making them the order of the day at the next session.

I confess to you I feel some uneasiness respecting the present aspect of our affairs with the French: these madmen possess nothing upon which you can certainly calculate, no moral principle, no fixed political data: they seem to have no system but anarchy, no plan but plunder and military tyranny.

Peace is indeed essential to American prosperity, and it is with great regret I observe our newspapers, as well as members of Congress, desert us on the very verge of a war with France. I beg that you will let me know what are our real prospects from that nation, &c.

WM. R. DAVIE.

SUPREME COURT—FEBRUARY TERM.

IREDELL TO MRS. IREDELL.

PHILADELPHIA, February 9th, '97.

MY DEAR HANNAH:—I arrived here on Saturday extremely well. * * * Some very melancholy scenes have taken place among our friends in Front street. Mrs. Barclay died the evening before my arrival, and our excellent friend Mrs. Duffield that very morning; the former of a lingering illness, aggravated probably by a broken heart, and the latter very suddenly. You will see in the newspapers a dreadful account of the destruction of Brown's family (the printer). The circumstances were uncommonly affecting. His eldest daughter, who was one of the victims, I am told was very accomplished. Miss Mease is in pretty good health, but has had a most melancholy task the whole winter, which, she said, prevented her writing to you several times when she intended it. Her brothers John and Robert have both been most dangerously ill, and the grandfather has been for some time confined to his bed. Miss Stocker is now solely occupied with the thoughts of approaching matrimony, and her intended husband, a brother of Mr. Miller, who is married to her sister, is almost as impatient for it as herself. Miss Hewes, with very different attractions, is likewise soon to be married to a Mr. Potts. * * * I saw the President and Mrs. Washington on Tuesday, and am to dine there to-day. They are both extremely well. Mrs. Washington desired her best respects to you. Mr. Adams was yesterday declared in form President, and Mr. Jefferson Vice President. Mr. Adams made a short address, which I am told, was very touching. It is beyond a doubt that Mr. Jefferson will serve; and, I am told, during the election both gentlemen spoke with great personal esteem of each other, and that Mr. Jefferson declared he did not think the choice could fall on a fitter man than Mr. Adams. Mrs. Adams is not yet here. They are to reside in the house now occupied by Gen. Washington. We shall get no addition to our salary. It has not even been proposed, that I have heard. The Senate, I believe, were well inclined, but feared the proposition might defeat a measure of great moment, to take place immediately—raising the salaries of the President and Vice President, which, unless done at this session, cannot be done until four years afterwards. The Chief Justice has been sick the whole Court, and though better, is still unable to attend. A vessel from Bordeaux is just in, which brings an account of General Pinckney's safe arrival there. He was waited upon with great respect by the municipality, and, among other civilities, was presented with a box at the theatre during his stay. No account has been received from him at Paris. The negotiations for peace there had undergone a short suspension, but don't appear to have ceased. Miss Allen is *not* to be married to Mr. Greenleaf, though so confidently reported, &c.

February 10th.

I this moment see the following in Claypoole's paper of this morning—" A letter is in town, dated at Paris, November 27th, 1796, which mentions that a courier had been dispatched from thence, in order to negotiate for a general suspension of hostilities: the letter also mentions that it was expected a profound peace would immediately ensue."

February 17th.

* * * Our Court broke up on Monday last. The Middle Circuit is assigned to me—the Eastern to Mr. Ellsworth—the Southern to Mr. Chase. If you were only within two hundred miles of me, I could have spent some short time at home in the vacation between the Courts. As it is, it would be folly to attempt it. * * * The whole salary business is destroyed by the illiberality of the House of Representatives. I am told Mr. Adams will have to give £1000 a year for his house; but he says he shall live according to his income. The prospects of a general peace in Europe seem fair, though the French have lately had astonishing success in Italy—after prodigies of valor on both sides. I waited on Mrs. Lennox with Mrs. Pollock's letter. She had sent the locket to Mr. Lennox of New York, but would endeavor to get it back again. I did not wait upon her for several days, supposing she was too great a lady to be seen before our Court hours; but I found her without difficulty, "tête-à-tête"

with her husband in the parlor at an earlier hour than I supposed she had been out of bed. Mrs. Potts having honored me with an invitation to be of her party to the play this evening, I am going for the first time. The play is "The way to get married," which, it is said, was acted in London 29 nights without intermission, and since 250 nights. Miss Hewes is to be one of the company. I believe none of the company go for instruction, but for amusement. Mrs. Potts would like very well to attend for both, if there was to be added, "The way to get married the second time."

I am told to-night will be Mrs. Washington's last Drawing-Room. I intend going, if only for a few minutes, but shall be much moved. The Vice President's (upon a leave of absence) taking leave of the Senate, I am told, was a very affecting scene, the day before yesterday. His speech is published. It is hoped that great harmony will subsist between him and Mr. Jefferson, and that the violence of party spirit will subside. God grant it may! &c., &c.

February 24th.

* * * The President's birthday (the 22d) was celebrated here with every possible mark of attachment, affection and respect, rendered affecting beyond all expression, by its being in some degree a parting scene. Mrs. Washington was moved even to tears, with the mingled emotions of gratitude for such strong proofs of public regard, and the new prospect of the uninterrupted enjoyment of domestic life: she expressed herself something to this effect. I never saw the President look better, or in finer spirits, but his emotions were too powerful to be concealed. He could sometimes scarcely speak. Three rooms of his house were almost entirely full from 12 to 3, and such a crowd at the door it was difficult to get in. At the Amphitheatre at night it is supposed there were at least 1200 persons. The show was a very brilliant one, but such scrambling to go to supper that there was some danger of being squeezed to death. The Vice President handed in Mrs. Washington, and the President immediately followed. The applause with which they were received is indescribable. The same was shown on their return from supper. The music added greatly to the interest of the scene. The President staid till between 12 and 1. The Vice President till near 2. Both were serenaded with repeated huzzahs, long after they had been in bed. The latter slept so soundly that he knew nothing of it till next morning, though it is said "Yankee Doodle" was one of the tunes they played. I was at Mr. Bond's yesterday evening. He and Miss Bond, as also Mrs. Cushing, Mrs.

Wolcott, Mrs. Phillips, Miss Hewes, &c., desired to be remembered to you. Miss Hewes is certainly to be married soon to an industrious, sensible young man, named Potts, who superintends some iron works at a handsome salary. I was at a party at Mrs. Stocker's—one less crowded than usual, and really very agreeable. I was at one of the same kind at Mr. Miller's the other night. I have received great civilities from Mr. Buck's family, which is one of the most agreeable of the city. The misfortunes of Judge Wilson throw an unfortunate gloom over his house, though I have been there two or three times, and have experienced all their former kindness. ✱ ✱ ✱ Before I received your letter I inquired for Camille for you, but could not get a copy in the city. It is printing by subscription, and I will get one as soon as it can be had. I forgot to tell you that I think the new actors (whom I saw one night only), Mr. Cooper and Mr. Merry, very clever—the play (the "Way to get married,") has some interesting scenes, but the title is absurd—there is no matrimonial plot in it, and a clergyman at the end of a moral sermon might as well say, "Young ladies, this is the way to get married," &c.

March 3d.

✱ ✱ ✱ The bill for direct taxes has been given up, and a very small addition, I believe, made to the impost. To-day the Session closes, and the present Congress dies; and to-morrow, the new President and Vice President are to be sworn in. You will have seen what affecting proofs have been given to the present President, of the love of the people in every part of the Union. To-morrow the merchants here are to give him a grand dinner, which he wished, ineffectually, to decline. Neither can he prevent the Light Horse from escorting him out of the city, though when they waited upon him to know when he would leave it, he earnestly requested that he might be permitted to go privately, &c.

Such a succession of frolickings as some people have in this city, is really disgusting. This evening is Mrs. Washington's last drawing-room, and a very crowded one it will be, though extremely exciting to a person of any sensibility. I saw her on Tuesday, when she was complaining a little of indisposition. I have a thousand compliments for you, which I can't remember, &c.
JAS. IREDELL.

The official oath, on the 4th March, was administered to President Adams by the Chief Justice, attended by two of his brethren, of whom Judge Iredell was one.

JUDGE PATTERSON TO IREDELL.

NEW BRUNSWICK, March 7th.

DEAR SIR:—I acknowledge the receipt of your letter of the 4th of this month; and am sorry that any alterations have taken place in the bill concerning the Circuit Courts. I wish it had passed in its original shape; but that not being the case, we must make the best of it we can. It is certainly right, that we should be accommodating to each other; for in this way we shall facilitate our official duty, and render its burden more supportable. I shall with much pleasure attend the Court at New Castle in your stead; but being ignorant of the day on which it is to be held, you will be pleased to ascertain the time, and inform me of it. If convenient, I shall be happy to see you with us for a few days before the opening of the Court at Trenton. I returned from Philadelphia with a bad cold, of which I am not yet entirely rid.

I am much pleased that Mr. Adams and Mr. Jefferson lodge together. The thing looks well: it carries conciliation and healing with it, and may have a happy effect on parties. Indeed, my dear sir, it is high time that we should be done with parties. In the present crisis, they injure us materially; they weaken, and render us contemptible; they make us the sport of every foreign breeze that blows. We must unite; we must consult our own interest, and look to ourselves; and then foreign influence, intrigue, and politics will cease to agitate and rend us. If we were one and true to ourselves, we should be in peace at home, and respected abroad; we should not be plundered, and despoiled on the ocean, nor insulted on the very ground where we live. It is, however, a consoling idea that we are becoming right very fast; I hope that, in a short time, we shall have no interest or views but what are purely American. In this wish will all wise heads and honest hearts unite.

I have written to Judge Chase, and inclosed the necessary route and directions. Yours sincerely,
WM. PATTERSON.

IREDELL TO MR. SAMUEL TREDWELL.

PHILADELPHIA, March 10th, '97.

MY DEAR SIR:—I was very happy to see your brother, Mr. Adam Tredwell, last Sunday, and to hear by him the agreeable intelligence that you were all well.* He was in perfect health

---
* Mr. A. Tredwell thought the people of Edenton, North Carolina, "the most agreeable he had ever seen." Letter from Mrs. E. Tredwell, of New York.

---

himself, and proceeded forward to New York on Monday. We have lately had no authentic news from Europe. A rumor of peace from the West Indies is too agreeable to be credited without further confirmation. There is every appearance of harmony between the President and Vice President, who lodge together, and appear on very friendly terms. God grant it may continue, and serve to allay that vile party-spirit which does so much injury to our country. I was present at the affecting scene on Saturday when the new President was sworn in. The speech he made on that occasion has, I am told, given the highest satisfaction even to some gentlemen who before had strong prejudices against him. General Washington attended as a private gentleman, and was the first after the President's return to wait upon him, though such an immense concourse of people attended him, that it was with some difficulty he reached the lodgings. They waited for him until he came out, and then accompanied him to his own house with unbounded applause. He, as well as the President and Vice President, was received with the warmest shouts of approbation as they entered and went out of the room where the qualification took place. General Washington and his family left town yesterday. ✱ ✱ ✱ I went last night to hear Mr. Fennell read and recite. He is clever, but by no means equalled my expectation. Our countrywoman, Mrs. Biddle, gave a party and dance the night before last, at which I was present, and shared in the dancing till ten o'clock. The two Mrs. Blounts and Governor Blount were there. Mrs. Wm. Blount very nearly lost her life by a miscarriage, but as she danced a good deal that night, you may be assured she is pretty well recovered. She is a very agreeable woman, &c., &c.
JAS. IREDELL.

CIRCUIT COURT.

Judge Iredell, after attending, as I suppose, the Court at Trenton, opened the Circuit Court at Philadelphia with the following charge to the Grand Jury, which is copied from a Philadelphia paper with the request of the Jury for its publication.

Circuit Court of the United States for the Pennsylvania District.

The Grand Inquest have listened to the Charge, this day deliverd by the Court, with much pleasure; the sentiments therein contained are perfectly congenial with their own, and they think with the interests, honor, and happiness of the United States. Thus impressed, they take the liberty of requesting a copy, for the purpose of making it known to the public through the medium of the press.
J. COWPERTHWAIT, F. M.

April 11, 1797.

A CHARGE

Delivered to the Grand Jury of the United States, for the District of Pennsylvania, in the Circuit Court of the United States, held at the City of Philadelphia, April 11th, 1797. By JAMES IREDELL, *one of the Associate Justices of the Supreme Court of the United States.*

[Published at the request of the Grand Jury.]

GENTLEMEN OF THE GRAND JURY:—

Though occasions like the present so frequently occur, yet so great is the importance of the high trust reposed in you, that it never ought to be entered upon without the most serious reflection on the duties it enjoins. The administration of justice is in every particular deeply interesting to the community; but when it affects the life or liberty of any individual, by inflexible laws which either endanger the safety or promote the security of all, it is a subject upon which none can be indifferent, much less those to whom that administration is intrusted. A sense of duty in a well disposed mind would indeed induce an equal endeavor to do justice in a single case which could be productive of neither good nor evil as an example, and were the person who was the object of it no otherwise to be regarded than as an individual accused of a crime of which it remained to be proved that he was guilty. An individual so circumstanced would, in the eyes of God and man, be an object of consideration entitled to all the attention we could bestow upon a fellow-creature claiming the common rights of a man, to be deemed innocent until clear proof could be adduced against him. But happy is that country, where the security of each individual depends, not on a strict and undeviating regard to justice alone, arising from a principle of moral duty which the passions of men are too apt to control or weaken; but where the security of each depends on the security of all, and no man can do an act of injustice to another, however indifferent or even obnoxious to him, without exposing himself, his family, his friends to a danger of the like injustice on some future occasion. The ties of interest thus co-operating with the ties of duty, cannot but have a most powerful effect.

Whatever may be the condition of other countries, the situation of our own has long been such that we must all stand or fall together. We have no men distinguished by any exclusive political advantages from the rest of their fellow-citizens; no one man

VOL. II.—32

who possesses any political power, but such as is held by the delegation of his fellow-citizens, and in trust for the whole of which he himself is a part; none who will not feel the benefit of good laws, and the mischief of bad ones. There is no office to which a competent responsibility is not annexed. We have thus every security against partial oppression which can be provided by the laws of any community.

If ever any government was entitled to confidence, and the laws of any government to a cheerful and ready obedience, the government of the United States, and the laws enacted under their authority, surely are. In every stage of their progress, the people of these States have not only been nominally, but in reality the origin of all power. Representatives of the people first established or sanctioned the governments of the several States, some of which have been since with equal solemnity and deliberation altered. Representatives of the people in each State have established the government of the United States, and this has been done by the unanimous concurrence of all the States in the Union. These several solemn acts have, in every instance, taken place without any kind of tumult or confusion, deliberately, voluntarily, uninfluenced by the artifices, unawed by the coercion of any foreign power, and owing their whole force and efficacy to the genuine good sense, moderation, patriotism, and discerning foresight of the people themselves. The world had never before seen such an example, and certainly no people could undergo such various, important and critical changes, with greater order, and a stricter degree of justice, than have uniformly characterized these illustrious scenes. Experience has justified the wisdom of their institutions. They have been found not only highly conducive to public prosperity, but the strongest support of individual and private justice. The political liberty and independence of our country have not only hitherto been preserved inviolate, (God grant they may ever remain so,) but individual and personal liberty has been sacredly protected. The humblest condition is secure where no offence has been committed. The greatest cannot shield an oppressor from punishment.

Such, however, is the lot of man, so incessantly are exertions necessary to preserve as well as to acquire any good whatever, much more any lasting political good, that an indolent enjoyment of it is never permitted with impunity. Vice will ever be at war with virtue, and the selfish part of mankind constantly opposed to the generous and disinterested. An immediate good, though of the slightest kind, will often be preferred to the most important which is a little distant. Private interests will be magnified: public ones, though unavoidably comprehending the latter, regarded as of comparative insignificance; and the prevailing indifference of scattered members of the community endanger not only the prosperity, but the safety of the whole. To counteract these tendencies, laws are necessary, compelling bad members of the community to do their share of the duty of the whole; providing not only for immediate, but guarding against remote dangers; consulting as much as possible the interest of each, but when necessary, without scruple, making a lesser good subservient to a greater; and combining, in one general system, every practicable means of promoting the public welfare consistently with the personal safety, interest, and happiness of each individual entitled to partake of it.

The laws of the United States, as contradistinguished from those of each State in the Union, have one characteristical mark of distinction. Every thing that concerns one State alone, is governed by the laws of that State. Every thing that concerns the United States is governed by the laws of the United States. This principle no one can deny to be proper; but as the concerns of a single State are more simple and obvious than those of the Union at large, they are apt to create a stronger attachment, and to be viewed with less jealousy than those of the other, as if one State could long be safe, much less prosperous, without a connection with the rest in those great points upon which their common interest and safety unquestionably depend.

All the objects of the Union are undoubtedly of great importance, but none certainly are so critical as the relations of this country to foreign powers. The true desire of all men who love their country, and understand its real interest, must be to be upon friendly terms with all of them, to perform our duty faithfully to each whether arising from the Law of Nations generally, or any special treaties or conventions in particular, cordially to wish the success of liberty, justice and virtue, when struggling with oppression in any shape or upon any pretences whatsoever, but to regard as our first duty the maintenance of the independence, the defence of the honor, the pursuit of the interest of our own country, whose rights we are by the most sacred ties bound to preserve, and whose interests (as is the case also with every country) we are alone competent to decide upon. Not only history, but experience must have convinced us what erroneous ideas independent nations are apt to entertain of each other, how incompetent therefore they are for the most part to judge of each other's internal situation, and consequently that it is no less the dictate of prudence and wisdom than of duty to forbear any active interference with what does not particularly concern us, upon an idle conjecture of remote and imaginary contingences which are constantly eluding the foresight of the most sagacious of men. Nevertheless, as ambition is constantly active, as the rulers of nations are not always actuated by patriotism and duty alone, but in disregard of their real interest will frequently aim at the gratification of injurious and destructive passions, to the prejudice of the rest of mankind, a principle of self-defence requires that each government should be perpetually on its guard against the machinations of others, and at the same time that it sacredly regards the rights of other nations, be prepared to resist all attacks, and resent all insults committed against its own. To do this with a proper mixture of temper and firmness, to preserve real independence without pride, to conciliate without meanness, and by a prudent forbearance where forbearance is practicable, to leave an opening for an honorable reparation where reparation can be made if any injury is committed, is a duty which all nations owe not only to the peace and happiness of their own country, but to mankind at large who have suffered incalculable evils from wars, which have had their origin in pride or ambition alone without regard to any thing but the dictates of violent, impetuous passions, kept under no restraint, governed by no principle and indulged without any remorse. The constitution of our country fortunately guards us against wars of such a description, since our government can voluntarily engage in no war, nor permit any act of hostility, but by the authority of the Congress of the United States, who are so constituted as to form a most powerful check on the temporary ambitious delusion which at certain times unaccountably actuates even a people generally temperate and wise. Standing therefore for the most part upon defensive, we stand upon safer ground than most other nations, and may have the satisfaction to hope that if the peace of our country should be unhappily interrupted, it will be by the misguided ambition or unqualified injustice of some other government, and not provoked by any unwarranted hostilities of our own.

The Congress of the United States having alone the authority to declare war, or permit any act of hostility, it is evident that until they exercise this authority, it is the duty of the citizens of the United States to forbear any hostile act to any power whatever. When any injury is sustained it will be proper to prefer a complaint to the government, which will undoubtedly bestow every possible attention upon it; but what other proceedings the case may require must be left to the respective branches of the government, to whose discretion the proper remedy is confided. There can be no reason to doubt that every means will be pursued for relief which the nature of the case requires, and the condition and circumstances of our country admit of.

As there was reason to fear, early in the present unfortunate contest in Europe, that some of the citizens of the United States, unacquainted with the Law of Nations, and therefore ignorant of the duties incumbent upon them in a case altogether new to our country, or impelled by an unprincipled love of plunder, might dishonor the character of the government, and endanger the public peace, by giving hostile assistance to some one of the powers at war, a proclamation was issued by the President, informing all of the duties incumbent upon them in this important case, and of the consequences that would follow a disregard of them. The object in effect was, to preserve that peace which the President was bound upon every tie of honor and duty to maintain inviolate to the utmost of his power, until Congress thought proper (if they deemed it expedient at all) to authorize any species of hostility; to maintain, in short, due obedience to the laws of the country then actually in being. This proclamation, which for a time was the subject of an absurd clamor, of which most of the promoters seem at present to be heartily ashamed, had the decided approbation of both Houses of Congress, and the policy of it (which they alone could alter) they have persevered in to the present hour, notwithstanding all the artifices used to shake them from a purpose so essential to their country's welfare. But as it was highly expedient to enforce the observance of duties so important in their nature, and which too general a disposition had been shown to disregard, the legislature thought proper, by an express law, to detail a series of prohibitions, which though existing in effect before might otherwise be the subject of doubt and controversy, and to substitute a precise and positive direction as to punishments for one too vague and indefinite to be regarded with equal confidence and respect. This law was passed in the year 1794 for a limited time, and at the last session was re-enacted with a further limitation. As temptations may yet occur for its violation, and our legal condition is still the same as when the law was originally passed, and lately re-enforced, and must remain so until Congress shall think proper to alter it, I will read you its several provisions, recommending them earnestly to your attention as of the highest moment to be exactly observed.

[Here the provisions in the act were read.]

The observations I have made relative to circumstances at the present time are so highly important that I thought them deserving of your attention in preference to any other. It is full time that any men who have been deluded by inconsiderate foreign attachments of any kind, and in the fervor of their zeal lost sight of their own country, should seriously reflect on the duties they owe to it, and the great stake intrusted to them as well as the rest of their countrymen to preserve. God forbid that it ever should be said of the United States, that after having succeeded in one of the noblest and most difficult contests ever maintained by men; after obtaining unexampled freedom with a degree of order and justice unparalleled in the history of the world; after having peaceably submitted to irregular and imperfect governments of their own formation, though under many disadvantages both of a private and a public nature; after establishing new ones calculated to remedy former defects, and undergoing this change as well as all the former with a moderation and order surprising even to themselves, and which had never been supposed practicable before; after experiencing the most happy effects—effects exceeding their most sanguine expectations, from the last change (calculated to perpetuate their freedom and happiness, I trust for ages to come); that in the wantonness of success, instead of preserving with vigilance what had been with so much difficulty and such extraordinary marks of providence acquired, they lost it all by an infatuated disregard of the most formidable danger to which their situation can ever expose them, that of foreign influence, blindly yielded to by some, and supinely unattended to by others, until a fatal catastrophe involved them in one common ruin, a deplorable example of the vanity, presumption, and folly of mankind! May God in his mercy preserve us from this ruinous and disgraceful fate, and on the contrary enable this country, in addition to other illustrious examples it has had the glory to exhibit, to present the spectacle of a people, who, knowing what freedom is, and wishing and respecting independence in others, know how to preserve it themselves, and at all hazards will defend it against all attacks whether covert or open, from without as well as from within, whatever force may annoy, whatever temptations may assail it!

IREDELL TO MRS. IREDELL.

PHILADELPHIA, April 28th.

MY DEAR HANNAH:—Miss Mease is now making a dress for Helen. She is well and lives a very retired life with her grandfather, though many ladies of her acquaintance pay her great attention, our amiable friend, Mrs. Wolcott, among the number: * * * * Poor old Mrs. Yorke has been made very happy by the arrival of her daughter Mrs. Humphries, and her husband and seven children. They have come here to reside from Nova Scotia. He joined the British during the war. Mrs. Humphries is very like her sister, but handsomer, and the family in general is a very agreeable one. Our Court is still sitting, owing to unexpected business, but I imagine we shall break up to-day. No public news, but that an official letter has been received from Mr. Pinckney, at Amsterdam. He received a written order to quit France, the day after the account arrived of Buonaparte's victories, &c., &c.

JAMES IREDELL.

GOV. JOHNSTON TO IREDELL.

WILLIAMSTON, May 3d.

MY DEAR SIR:—I am not much disappointed that your uncle has disinherited you in favor of your brother. I had heard of his declaration to that purpose. Whenever old men form a resolution founded either on religious or political prejudices, however erroneous or unjust, they have seldom liberality or courage enough to alter it, even though sensible of their error. * * * Our "ci-devant" friends, by their late conduct, give us no reason to hope a speedy return of a good understanding. There is no instance of such conduct in the annals of modern civilized nations. Nothing can be more odious and despicable than that republican pride and haughtiness which they affect on all occasions: it can only be assumed towards us at this time because they find it more convenient to supply themselves with indispensable articles from this country by rapine and plunder than in a fair course of commerce. I was last week at Halifax. All our old acquaintances were well. I did not see Col. M'Culloh. There was little said on politics except by the friends of the Government. The conduct of the French is universally execrated; indeed, I have heard no one attempt to justify it, though the Jacobins say we shall have no war with them. I do not believe that there are in America two more promising children than your two eldest; it is not so easy to say what the youngest will be, though the seeds of a strong understanding are apparent, &c., &c.

SAM. JOHNSTON.

IREDELL TO MR. SAMUEL TREDWELL.

ANNAPOLIS, May 12th.

DEAR SIR:— * * * People's expectation is all alive as to the approaching meeting of Congress. I doubt not every honorable effort will be made to avoid extremities, though it is difficult to conjecture what measures may be found necessary. I think it highly possible that Mr. Pinckney may be appointed Envoy Extraordinary (though I believe he had as full powers before without the name). The report that he was rejected because he was not appointed Envoy Extraordinary before must be groundless, because it was at first agreed to receive him, and the ceremonial of his reception was fixed. Besides, that it is scarcely to be imagined a Minister, with full powers to explain, as well as to negotiate, should be rejected merely on account of a name. The country, I presume, will be put in a strong posture of defence. As to any measures for protecting *trade*, though nothing can be more distressing than its present situation, great deliberation will be required before any exceptionable ones can be adopted. Whatever may be done, I am convinced every honorable method will be pursued to avoid hostilities if possible, as I am sure nothing can be more false than the report that the Government or any part of it wish to provoke war. But some men suppose none possess sense or common honesty but themselves, &c., &c.

JAMES IREDELL.

From Annapolis Judge Iredell proceeded to Richmond. He arrived there at a period of great political excitement. Washington had gone into retirement; and a new President had succeeded: the passions, whose turbulence had been awed, and in a measure suppressed by the majesty of that great man, now blazed with the fiercest flames. Mr. Adams' public services, though illustrious and valuable, were not such as strike the masses. The deference of a distinction between the President and his cabinet was personal to Washington, and expired with his official term. Nowhere was the opposition to the Government more violent than in Virginia: nowhere was it directed by so much ability, such consummate skill, such sleepless animosity. Though in a minority, the Federalists were by no means powerless; but their cause was sustained by the most potent eloquence, and formidable talents. No man could well be neutral. The air was darkened with missiles: and every object that could be used as a projectile, even dirt and garbage, was unscrupulously employed by the combatants. Not only was the Executive, but every department of Government, the subject of ceaseless assault: wherever a point was uncovered, there was promptly launched by some stout arm a well-directed bolt. No man, however discreet, or however spotless his robes, could well hope to pass through that scene of strife, and escape without a blow, or a stain upon his garments.

On the 22d of May, Judge Iredell delivered the following Charge to the Grand Jury, in the Circuit Court. The charge had been deliberately written in Philadelphia, and previously delivered at Annapolis.

A CHARGE

Delivered to the Grand Jury of the United States, for the District of Virginia, in the Circuit Court of the United States, held at Richmond, May 22d, 1797, by JAMES IREDELL, *one of the Associate Justices of the Supreme Court of the United States.*

[Published at the Request of the Grand Jury.]

GENTLEMEN OF THE GRAND JURY:—

The frequent returns of courts of justice naturally occasion us to reflect on the origin from which they flow. However painful such review may be to some nations, to us it can afford nothing but satisfaction and gratitude. We trace the origin of ours as well as of every other authority to the purest source from which any authority can be derived, the spontaneous but deliberate grant of the people themselves for whose benefit it is established. Liberty to a considerable degree had subsisted in other ages and other countries, but such an exercise of it as this (notwithstanding the fanciful opinion of some ingenious writers) probably first took place in our own. The attempt was noble, and the success hitherto has been beyond all expectation. Whether its blessings are to be preserved or lost, must, in no small degree, depend on the conduct of the people themselves.

If they wish for good laws, they must choose able and disinterested men to make them. If they wish for officers adequate to their stations in the other departments of government, it is in their power directly or indirectly to secure them by a discreet and judicious exercise of the choice with which they are invested. If in any particular their confidence should be abused, a plain and adequate remedy is provided. After a stated interval their legislators may be changed. Without any delay but such as the occasion must require, any public officer who has misbehaved is liable to trial, punishment, and disgrace. To this may be added, what probably is not the weakest restraint, the general odium that must attend a manifest departure from duty in an important public employment.

The people at large having these securities for the faithful discharge of offices of public trust, it is fit that those whom they select as their officers should have some security on their part. It is not to be presumed, that men, chosen as they are, should be remarkably deficient either in ability or integrity, and therefore they have a right to expect that their conduct should not immediately be condemned merely because some persons are ready to find fault with it. The task they have to perform is of no common magnitude, both as to difficulty and importance. If in the small concerns of private life, few men can conduct themselves with strict regularity and exactness, and unexpected difficulties will disconcert even the most orderly and discreet, can we conceive the path perfectly plain and obvious for the government of millions of men, who, though possessing one common and united interest, have an infinite variety of private views, tending to divert them from the great object of union, even if their understandings and dispositions were perfectly alike. But if to this we add the various degrees of their understanding, their different means of improvement and information, the delusive and dangerous passions by which many are guided, the activity of bad citizens, the supineness of good, until some critical alarm alike actuates both to a struggle which may endanger the government at the moment when its utmost energies are necessary, we cannot wonder at the diversity of opinion which prevails in respect to most public measures, nor at the consequences which follow from rival sentiments, too apt to disturb the temper even of the best minds, but which, unavoidably, give a full scope to the passions of weak, arrogant, or unprincipled men, who either make no allowances for difficulties which weak minds never perceive ; or, from an excess of vanity and presumption, suppose none can surmount them but themselves; or, with views too base to be avowed, hesitate not to gratify malignant or grovelling purposes of their own, without the slightest independent regard to the honor, the interest, or even the safety of their country. Such causes must often produce great agitation in any country, but must operate with increased and dangerous vigor in one like our own, composed of many powerful States, to a great degree independent of each other, having either real or imaginary differences of local interest, and with little other effectual cement to bind them together but a sense of foreign external danger, which with respect to many will be apt to operate but too weakly until it has increased to a magnitude which astonishes and confounds them.

Considerations like these are calculated to impress upon the mind that salutary caution with which all public measures ought to be discussed. If it be a point of duty or justice we need inquire no farther : policy is out of the question : the duty must be performed.—Justice must be satisfied, at all risks. Men would be for ever unjust, and morality would be a name, if exceptions were once admitted upon any principle whatever, to a strict observance of it. If a subject of policy is in question, nothing affords greater room for real differences of opinion. The wisest men, with the best motives, have been always divided on such questions, and always will be—because nothing is more fallible than human judgment when it extends its views into a futurity, for the greatest part so impenetrably hid from the sight of man. All political measures must be grounded on such views, and consequently must partake of the imperfection of the grounds on which they are adopted. Diffidence, therefore, as to any point of policy, is becoming the ablest men, and they are generally the best disposed to entertain it. Some mode of decision however must take place. Can we desire a better than that it should be such a decision as the people themselves have deliberately thought best adapted to the case ? It is indeed, as well as all other political subjects, a natural and proper object of their review. For their own sake, that review ought to be conducted with temper and moderation, lest they should themselves suffer by a precipitate and erroneous judgment. Before they condemn any one measure, where some measure was necessary, they ought to be very sure that a better could be adopted. None can be adopted without some inconveniences,—few, perhaps, without some advantages. It is the part of wisdom to weigh one against the other, and decide in favor of that measure where the advantages are greatest, the inconveniences fewest. Any other mode of considering great questions of public policy is idle and insignificant. If, after all, any individual disapproves of the voice of his country, what does duty and common modesty require of him ? To be perfectly confident he is right in his opinion, and those intrusted to decide are wrong ! Who is the man entitled to so arrogant an estimation of his own abilities? Is he rashly to determine, that the measure has been adopted from some dishonest motive ? What right has any one man to charge another with dishonesty without proof ? Let him prove and punish if he can—if he can do neither, but will indulge in atrocious calumny, he must stand in the view of his fellow-citizens as a slanderer, and incur the suspicion, that his readiness to suspect others of dishonorable intentions has probably arisen from something in the texture of his own mind which led him to ascribe worthless motives as the most natural inducement of action. The part, surely, for every man who loves his country, but who disapproves of any public authoritative decision, is to submit to it with diffidence and respect, considering the many chances there are that his own opinion may be really wrong, though he cannot perceive it to be so—that whether it be or not he does not live in a despotic government where any one man's opinion, not even his own, is to decide for all others ; and that the very basis of all republican governments in particular is, the submission of a minority to the majority where a majority are constitutionally authorized to decide. For a man to call himself a republican without entertaining this sentiment, is folly. To be one, without acting upon it, is impossible.

Since, therefore, the plainest dictates of duty, and the principles of republicanism itself, which, in their due application, ennoble the human mind, though nothing can more disgrace it than the abuse of them, require of us all to obey the laws of our country, it is incumbent on us to take care that an obligation so important be not rendered merely nominal, but that every individual shall perform his share of the common trust, or answer for his neglect of it. Many instances of neglect or indifference towards it, which may have great effects on the happiness of his country, are of a nature not punishable by human laws, and the punishment of them, therefore, must be left to the conscience of the individual, and the reproach which a violation of the rules of morality, though unaccompanied by any human sanction, seldom fails to draw upon it. There are, however, others of so serious a nature, and so directly tending either to destroy or injure the society at large, that laws are provided by it for their punishment, and without such laws, and a due execution of them, no society could subsist; for an idea that all men will support voluntarily any government however excellent, or cheerfully obey any laws however wise, is ridiculous. But as it is of great moment to establish some laws containing penal sanctions, so it is also of the highest importance that the execution of these should be provided for in such a manner as to secure as much as possible the conviction only of the guilty, leaving innocence nothing to fear. The mode of prosecution, so long adopted in our country, probably contains this security in its utmost extent. Accusation by one jury—trial by another—the trial being altogether public—witnesses adduced face to face—the prisoner under no restraint but from mere confinement—challenges to a considerable number, in all capital cases, to set aside jurors even for momentary dislike— the jury not being a permanent but an occasional body, liable to be associated either as members of the community, or as individuals who may be subjected to a similar prosecution, by their own precedents—all these circumstances probably provide as great a security for innocence as is compatible with avoiding a total immunity for guilt. With us happily this is no theoretic speculation : none of us can remember a time when these privileges were not in a great degree familiar to us. So familiar indeed, that knowing scarcely any thing of oppressive prosecutions but from the history of other countries, we are too apt to undervalue this inestimable blessing in our own.

To you, gentlemen, are committed prosecutions for offences against the United States. The object is the preservation of a union, without which undoubtedly we should not now be enjoying the rights of an independent people, and without the support of which it is in vain to think we can continue to enjoy them. This country has great energies for defence, and by supporting each other might defy the world. But if we disunite, if we suffer differences of opinion to corrode into enmity, jealousy to rankle into distrust, weak men to delude by their folly, abandoned men to disturb the order of society by their crimes, we must expect nothing but a fate as ruinous as it would be disgraceful, that of inviting some foreign nation to foment and take advantage of our internal discords, first making us the dupe and then the prey of an ambition we excited by our divisions, and to which those divisions, if continued, must inevitably give success. So critical and peculiar is our situation, that nothing can save us from this as well as every other external danger, but constant vigilance to guard against even the most distant approaches of it, and being at all times ready to provide adequate means of defence. Our government is so formed, that that vigilance can always be exerted, and those means, when necessary, be drawn forth. To rely upon these is not only our indispensable duty, but the only chance of securing that union of spirit and exertion, without which in a moment of danger no efforts can be of any avail. For twenty-one years that union has preserved us through multiplied dangers, and more than once rescued us from impending ruin. I trust it will still display itself with its wonted efficacy, and that no threats, no artifices, no idle devotion to names without meaning, or to professions without sincerity, will be capable of weakening by any impression on a sensible people a cement essential to their existence.

I deliver this general address, not knowing of any particular offences likely to come before you. The sentiments have flowed warmly from my heart, and I flatter myself are not uncongenial to your own. The present situation of our country is such as requires the exertion of all good men to support and save it. I enter into no particulars, as the legislature of the United States are now assembled, and for whose decision every worthy citizen must wait with solicitude and respect. In the mean time it is of the utmost consequence that every man should sacredly obey the laws of the country actually in being. They cannot be altered, nor the observance of them in any instance dispensed with, without the authority of the Congress of the United States, in any exigence however great, in any situation however alarming. There is no occasion to doubt but that the whole proceedings of that most respectable body, will be conducted with a degree of temper and firmness suited to the important and trying situation which called them together, and that the great object of all their deliberations will be, if possible, to preserve the peace, at the same time that they maintain inviolably the honor, the interest, and the independence of their country.

The charge was animated, perhaps too warm ; but no fair-minded man can read it, and discover the judicial finger uplifted to point out to the jury a victim for their vengeance, or detect evidence of malice towards any individual. It was but natural, that even judicial *ice* should thaw in that heated atmosphere, and in the process evolve some latent heat ! but the wise precaution of the Judge, in the preparation of his charge, had avoided the danger and possibility of excitement by contagion.

It had been the custom in the South, a custom which still prevails, for juries to make a presentment of whatever they esteemed a grievance of a public nature, without any reference to the power of the Court to punish, to abate, or prevent. On this occasion the Jury presented " as a real evil the circular letters of several members of the late Congress, and particularly letters with the signature of Samuel J. Cabell, endeavoring at a time of real public danger to disseminate unfounded calumnies against the happy government of the United States, and thereby to separate the people therefrom, and to increase or produce a foreign influence ruinous to the peace, happiness, and independence of these United States." It may be necessary to inform the unprofessional reader, that such a presentment could not be the foundation of any criminal proceeding in that Court. Mr. Cabell was indignant, and made an angry retort assailing the jury, the judge, and the Court of which he was an associate. The anti-federal leaders came to his succor, with threats of vengeance. It was proposed to bring the matter before the House of Representatives as a breach of privileges ; but the federal majority in that branch of Congress deterred. Jefferson urged Monroe to present the matter to the State Legislature ; but the latter doubted their jurisdiction. Jefferson was inclined to proceed ultimately " by some legal process, whether against Iredell or the grand-jurymen does not appear, before the State tribunals ;" and suggested the propriety of reviving a law of *"premunire"* against all citizens, attempting to carry their causes before any other than the State courts, when those other courts had no cognizance. "As happens too often with champions of natural rights, in his eagerness to protect Cabell and the opposition members, Jefferson seems quite to have forgotten the rights of every body else. The presentment of the grand jury, which had so excited his indignation, was either an official act within their province, or it was extra-official ; in other words, a joint expression of opinion by so many individuals. If a proper official act, then it could not be questioned either in the Virginia General Assembly, or in any State court. Suppose, on the other hand, that it was extra-official, yet surely the gentlemen composing the grand jury had as good a natural right to correspond with their fellow-citizens on their joint interests as Mr. Cabell or any other opposition representative."* As soon as Judge Iredell was apprised of Mr. Cabell's attack, he published the following card. As a vindication, it is thorough and complete.

TO THE PUBLIC.

Having seen with great surprise in some of the public newspapers an attack upon my judicial character, signed with the name of Mr. *Cabell*, a Member of Congress, I think it proper to take some notice of it, on account of a mistake in point of fact which he seems to have committed. From the tenor of his observations, any one would conclude that I wrote the charge he condemns with a view to draw forth a censure upon him or some other Members of Congress who had written circular letters to their constituents. The truth is, I never knew that Mr. *Cabell* had written any circular letter at all, until I heard the presentment read in Court, nor have I seen the letter alluded to to this hour. I had indeed seen printed letters of one or two other Members of Congress from the same State, but had them not in my thoughts when I prepared that charge, which I wrote deliberately in Philadelphia, in order to be delivered in Maryland and Virginia. The same charge was delivered substantially in both States, and without a view to any particular person. With regard to the sentiments of that charge, I am ready on all proper occasions to vindicate every word of it, as well as the propriety of delivering such a charge on such an occasion. In the mean time, I have a right to expect, that if the charge be censured, it shall be censured for what it really contains, and not for what exists merely in the imagination of the censurer. I have no hesitation in saying, that if it has the tendency Mr. *Cabell* ascribes to it, it does, in my opinion, deserve a severer censure than any he has bestowed upon it.

The conduct of the Court after the presentment has incurred Mr. *Cabell's* censure. It is difficult to say what can escape it if

---

* Hildreth, Hist. U. S. Vol. 2, 2d series. Letter from Jefferson to Monroe, Sept. 7th, '97.—Mem. & Cor., vol. 3. p. 365.

---

the conduct of the Court on that occasion cannot. They knew not such a presentment was in contemplation. It was brought into Court the same day that the charge was delivered, and without any adjournment having taken place, and agreeably to the usual practice, I presume, in Virginia, (though different from that in some other States,) was read by the Clerk without even being seen by the Court. None of the circular letters which were the object of the presentment was produced to the Court, nor in possession of the Judges. The jury were asked if they had any business to require their attention longer, or if they wished to stay to consider of any. They answered in the negative. The attorney for the United States was asked if he wished them to be detained longer. He declared he knew of no occasion for it. They were then discharged. Were the Court to catechize the jury for their censure of a publication which they themselves had never seen ? or to direct a prosecution upon a publication without knowing the contents of it ? Ought they in any instance indeed to direct a prosecution in the presence of the attorney, within whose particular department it lies, and when no occasion calls for their immediate interposition ? Were they to interfere unnecessarily, they might justly be charged with becoming parties to a prosecution, and incapacitating themselves from the impartial conduct of judges afterwards. Whatever might be the intention of the jury, which was composed of very respectable men, it has been a frequent practice in some of the Southern States for grand juries to present what they considered as grievances though they could not be the foundation of a criminal prosecution in the court. I have known such presentments containing very heavy charges against the government itself. It never occurred to me to be proper to suppress a practice which I found established, whether the exercise of it was agreeable to my private sentiments or not ; and I incline to think, had the grand jury at *Richmond*, instead of presenting those circular letters, presented any obnoxious act of the government, and the court by an exertion of power had arbitrarily suppressed the presentment, it would have been the subject of a very virulent—and possibly a very just—invective, by some of those persons who have no scruple in condemning the court for not interfering with this.

With regard to the illiberal epithets Mr. *Cabell* has bestowed, not only on me, but on the other judges of the Supreme Court, I leave him in full possession of all the credit he can derive from the use of them. I defy him or any man to show, that in the exercise of my judicial character, I have been ever influenced in the slightest degree by any man, either in or out of office, and I assure him I shall be as little influenced by this new mode of attack by a Member of Congress as I can be by any other.

JAS. IREDELL.*

Edenton, North Carolina.

IREDELL TO MRS. IREDELL.

RICHMOND, May 25th, 1797.

MY DEAR HANNAH:— * * * Mrs. Tredwell does me honor in wishing me to name her child ; but I don't think it fair to accept of her offer. If she liked your name as well as yourself, I would mention that ; and then should wish Iredell added to it. Next to that my real wish (if expressed) would be to have the child called after your sister—" Annie Johnston"—a person and a name I never think of without inexpressible emotion—an emotion too painful to dwell upon. God knows with what love and respect I cherish her memory : Heaven never produced any more worthy of it. But say nothing of this to Mrs. Tredwell.

I inclose a copy of the President's speech, which has been read here with the highest admiration, and approved even by his old political opponents. You will find by a presentment of our grand jury, composed of many of the most respectable men in the state, a temper highly suitable to our present situation. There is such an immensity of business to do here, that I cannot even conjecture when I can get away. For a great deal of it I am to thank Judge * * *, who failed to attend the last term. I expect to be detained at least a fortnight or three weeks, for I am resolved to have no neglect chargeable on me, anxious as I am beyond expression to be with you and our dear children. I am in court every day from ten till four or five, &c.

JAS. IREDELL.

COL. DAVIE TO IREDELL.

HALIFAX, June 25th, '97.

MY DEAR SIR :— * * * * I have often occasion to regret that the few men with whom my heart has formed attachments are scattered over the earth by business or accident ; and that the vagabond life of a lawyer, of which I am heartily sick, deprives me even of the satisfaction of a regular correspondence ; and I look forward with some anxiety to that period when this last inconvenience will be done away.

On my return to this place on Monday last, I received the

---

* June 21st, 1797.

Virginia Gazette, containing the publications occasioned by your charge, and the presentment of the grand jury of that district; this solemn evidence of a change of the public sentiment has given a serious alarm to the whole faction; and they will now move heaven and earth to secure them from merited odium; and draw back the public mind within the sphere of French influence, where, to the great misfortune of this country, it has been a long time stationary.

It will hardly be denied in this country that all measures, whether of public or private men, which have a direct tendency to destroy or disturb the peace, good government, and happiness of the community, are strictly within the inquest of a grand jury, and of course, proper objects for a judge's charge; and surely the greatest evil with which we were threatened at the present alarming crisis, was the disorganizing effect of the correspondence of certain members of Congress, the baneful influence of which is visible in every part of the Southern States.

I congratulate you upon the present prospect of peace in Europe. The peace between the Emperor and the French appears to be well authenticated, and I hope that with England will soon follow, which will release us from all difficulties. Our embarrassments with France seem to arise mainly from their system of destroying the British commerce, which will terminate with peace, &c., &c.

January 28th.

* * * * I received your letter of the 19th, by Mr. Peter Brown, and feel myself greatly obliged to you for the professional communications it contains.

As the opinion and determination with regard to interest is a matter of great importance, and is somewhat novel here, I would be greatly obliged to you, to give me the grounds of this opinion, or permit the bearer, Mr. Littlejohn, to copy your argument or order on this subject; for my own part, I know of no regular authority that would warrant a deduction on account of the war merely, and in the case of British subjects, I suppose they would recover interest under what may be termed their *Treaty-rights.*

The case with respect to the statute of limitations is so briefly stated, that I am not certain if I understand it correctly. I think the dismission of the ejectment suits under these circumstances of fraud perfectly right: no precedent, I suppose, could be found for the practice, but nothing else could be done, and it is a suit always in the power of the court.

Congress appear to me to have acquired some accession of principle, but to have degenerated in point of dignity: loose conversations instead of solemn debates, and personalities instead of argument disgrace the proceedings of every day, &c., &c.

WM. R. DAVIE.

GOV. JOHNSTON TO IREDELL.

July 5th.

MY DEAR SIR:—I have read Mr. Cabell's very illiberal and unprovoked attack upon you, and your answer, than which nothing could be more proper, if it was proper to give it any answer at all. I am sensible of the difficulty with which a man of warm feelings and conscious integrity submits to bear, without a reply, unmerited censure: yet I am not certain but that it is more suitable to the dignity of one placed in a high and respectable department of State, to consider himself bound to answer only when called upon constitutionally before a proper tribunal; otherwise it may happen that too much of that time and attention which he owes to the duties of his office will be wasted in answering the attacks of every vain or wicked man, who takes it into his head that he has a talent for writing: it is besides very difficult to say how a contest of this kind is to be decided, for, after innumerable replications and rejoinders, fresh matter will continually arise to keep it alive. As to Mr. Cabell's putting his name to his publication, I do not consider that that circumstance entitles him to more respect than if he had written under a fictitious signature: it is an evidence rather of his confidence than his candor.

I am very much concerned for the situation in which the British nation appears to be placed, as it is of importance to the American commerce that the British navy should support a considerable degree of respectability. Even at this time, I think they have more to apprehend from their domestic dissensions than from their foreign enemies, &c., &c.

SAM. JOHNSTON.

HON. O. WOLCOTT TO IREDELL.

PHILA., July 12th.

MY DEAR SIR:—* * * * We have no news since that of Mr. Blount. How shocking the idea is, that in the bosom of our country, even in our *Senate*, native citizens are found, who treasonably conspire to plunge us in war!!! &c., &c.

OLIVER WOLCOTT.

SUPREME COURT.—AUGUST TERM.

Judge Iredell attended at this term, but no case of extraordinary interest was tried.

IREDELL TO MRS. IREDELL.

PHIL., August 11th, '97.

MY DEAR HANNAH:—I arrived here in perfect health, though with extreme difficulty, on Sunday last, there having been such violent torrents of rain for several days that the whole country, almost, was in a state of inundation, and some parts of the road for a time absolutely impassable. We were so fortunate, however, as to arrive within one day of the destined time, and I had very agreeable company, enabling me to pass my time with great cheerfulness. I found Mr. Chase at Baltimore, and he had been so obliging, depending on my punctuality, to take a place for me. All the judges are here but Wilson, who, unfortunately, is in a manner absconding from his creditors—his wife with him—the rest of the family here! What a situation! It is supposed his object is to wait until he can make a more favorable adjustment of his affairs than he could in a state of arrest. Our court will not last longer than next week. * * * * Your friends here are in general well. I am to dine at Mr. Bond's to-day. Major Butler and his daughters are in town. Miss Mease is well, and Robert is much better; but poor John is certainly irrecoverable, and cannot last much longer. His father was married on Tuesday last, to a Miss Simmonds, about thirty, who bears a very good character, and is said to be worth about £1500, *settled on herself.* She discovers a disposition, I am told, to be kind to the family. * * * Miss Socker is still unmarried. * * * I found Luther Martin and his daughters here, and he being obliged immediately to go to Maryland, I am to conduct them to Baltimore. Miss Martin was much pleased with Annie's letter, &c., &c.

JAS. IREDELL.

GOV. JOHNSTON TO IREDELL.

30th August.

MY DEAR SIR:—* * * There has never been a more promising prospect of plenty than our crops now exhibit. I have seen Monroe's contemptible performance addressed to the Secretary of State. He is an example to show how careful government should be to intrust important affairs of state to none but men of great minds, who, on all occasions, will prefer the true interest of government to all paltry personal, or party considerations. This wretch would not hesitate to disclose the most secret and confidential trusts, committed to him by his superiors, if by that means he could lessen them in the public eye, even though it contributed nothing to his own justification.

I have seen Mr. Fox's speech in support of Mr. Gray's motion for a Parliamentary reform. I cannot take it upon me to decide whether it would have been good policy to concur with the motion, though there is much good sense in the arguments offered by Mr. Fox, delivered with an uncommon degree of insinuating modesty. I very sincerely deplore the melancholy state of affairs in that devoted country, nor do I see from what quarter they can look for relief, &c.

SAM. JOHNSTON.

JNO. MILLER TO IREDELL.

PHILA., Oct. 30th, '97.

HON. SIR:—* * * * This city has had another stroke (*yellow fever*) but much lighter than that in '93. It is now happily over, since the 24th or 25th; the several committees are dissolved; and those who fled to the neighboring villages, and the country, are returned or on the way. Isabella (*Mease*) was invited to Germantown, by Mrs. Dr. Belton, who was lonely, her husband being daily in the city; and when the disorder took place she remained there, till Mr. and Mrs. Hopkinson asked her to visit Easton with them, as a Supreme Court was to be held there on the 2d of this month. She accepted the invitation: visited Bethlehem, and every town or place of note on the way: and during the sitting of the court, she, with other young persons like herself, crossed the Blue Mountain on horseback, and explored the hill country and lands beyond. She gave me a long account of her little excursion, of at least 100 miles, the manners and customs of the people, &c. She returned to her old lodgings in Germantown, till all was safe here, when she came home in good health, more fresh and lusty by several pounds than when she took her journey. We continued to keep house in Spruce-street (No. 105); it was airy both in front and back, and we were not fearful, though several died around us. Happily we enjoyed good health until 17th Sept., when I met with an accident by falling in a trap-door in the kitchen. I was in an inch of my eternal home, but my God spared my life, and prolonged it a little longer in a world of sin and sorrow. I am now in my usual good health, and as much so as I was forty years ago, except, what may be expected to attend a person of my years, more feebleness and inactivity. Temperance and exercise are the two doctors I have long employed, and I recommend them to all my good friends as the best in Philadelphia, or elsewhere.

You heard of the death of my poor John. It was God's pleasure: every thing is for the best. * * *

Poor James has been a little sick in body, but more in mind, I believe. Many blame him for the late epidemic; and Porcupine publishes hard things and false things.* The doctors all abuse each other. Rush talks of moving to New York, and leaving them all. All that James or any body can do is to see if the persons on deck are well and clear of any catching disorder, and what may be in the hold is not in his jurisdiction. Some say the disorder was imported: others not. I believe Almighty God sent it as a rod to put us more in mind of our duty, of which we are too much remiss in this city, &c., &c.

Your obliged humble servant,
JOHN MILLER.†

A letter from Mr. Timothy Pickering, Nov. 2d, contains a request for a copy of Judge Iredell's Revisal of the Laws of North Carolina, for Professor Ebeling, of Hamburg, "who is writing an elaborate work concerning America."

* Wm. Cobbett.
† I have taken some liberties with this letter, preserving, however, the sense.

CHAPTER XXXI.

ÆT. 46–47.

SUPREME COURT, FEBRUARY TERM. SOUTHERN CIRCUIT, SPRING TERM. ADDRESS TO GRAND JURY AT CHARLESTON. JOHN RUTLEDGE. SUPREME COURT, AUGUST TERM. DEATH OF JUDGE WILSON. LETTERS FROM DAVID STONE, GOV. JOHNSTON, JUDGE CUSHING, BISHOP WHITE, CHARLES LEE, WILLIAM RAWLE, GEN. STEELE, AND JUDGE WASHINGTON.

GOV. JOHNSTON TO IREDELL.

WILLIAMSTON, January 27th, 1798.

MY DEAR SIR:— * * * I cannot but be pleased with Admiral Duncan's success and promotion. In this I hope I am not guilty of an unjustifiable breach of neutrality, for, beside the partiality it is natural to entertain for our relations, I have long had a very high respect for his personal character.

I have lately heard nothing of the proceedings in Congress, nor of what our Commissioners were doing at Paris; if the latter have done any thing to the purpose, I shall be agreeably disappointed, &c., &c.

SAM. JOHNSTON.

SUPREME COURT.—FEBRUARY TERM.

IREDELL TO MRS. IREDELL.

PHILADELPHIA, February 5th, 1798.

MY DEAR HANNAH:—I arrived here perfectly well, though much fatigued, on Friday last. Our Court is to begin to-day, but we have barely a *quorum*, consisting of Cushing, Patterson, Chase, and myself. The Chief Justice is, unfortunately, now in very bad health, and we have no reason to expect he can attend.

* * * Peter escaped the yellow fever, and attends me.* Many imagine the deaths, in proportion to the people who remained, were as numerous as in 1793, and the disorder is said to have been accompanied with more malignant symptoms. It also spread into the country. * * * I went to Market-street meeting-house yesterday, and going up to speak to the President in his pew, whom I had not seen, he asked me to take a family-dinner with him and Mr. Cushing, and I found none else there. The President's family are all well; but Mrs. Smith, who is with him, looks much dejected. I know not what has become of her husband.† I alighted out of the stage to inquire for Mrs. Wilson, and found her and all his family at his house in Market-street. She was very well, but extremely affected in seeing me; and finding Mr. Wilson was not coming, she burst into tears. His family are all well.

February 8th.

Our Court has been busily employed every day, from ten till three. Your friends are generally well. The present Mrs. Mease has behaved in the kindest manner possible to her husband's children. Though a very lusty woman, she has a very pleasing countenance. The Stocker family are all well, but Miss Stocker unmarried, though her swain seems very constant. Mrs. Stedman is much recovered. Dr. Duffield's family are all well. John Barclay, it is said, is going to be married to a rich, agreeable widow, worth £100,000—a Mrs. Fisher, of Delaware State, the widow of a brother of the first wife; and Nelly Barclay to Mr. Cochran, a young, handsome, and respectable member of Congress from New York, six feet six inches high. Blackbourn, the Anthonys, and Butlers, are all well. Mrs. Wilson thinks of returning with me, which I suppose will be soon after the rising of this Court, for I take it for granted I shall go the Southern Circuit.

Not the least public news from abroad. You will have heard of the base conduct of Lyon, the member from Vermont, to a most respectable member, Mr. Griswold, from Connecticut. I am afraid two-thirds cannot be got to expel him,‡ &c., &c.

* When Judge Iredell returned to North Carolina to reside, his servants, whom he had taken to Philadelphia, remained there. "But whenever he went there (Phil.) his old body-servant, Peter, always came to wait on him, and was treated with the utmost confidence and kindness; he received more than usual wages, and I have heard him say he obtained more from 'Master,' for the short time he attended him there, than he did for the balance of the year, and that what he did get was by hard work—sawing wood."—*Letter from Jas. C. Johnston, Esq.*

† Wm. S. Smith was son-in-law to President Adams: he had recently failed for a large amount, under circumstances not very reputable: he was soon nominated Adjutant-General, with the rank of Brigadier, but rejected by the Senate.—*Hildreth*.

‡ Lyon, while the House was in session, being insulted by Griswold, spat in his face; subsequently Griswold, approaching Lyons, as he sat in his seat, made an attack on him with a cane.

SOUTHERN CIRCUIT.—SPRING TERM.

WILLIAMSTON, April 10th.

You will doubtless be surprised to receive a letter from me of this date from this place. I found it impossible to cross Tar River at Tarborough, or to proceed in any other direction. I left Mr. Johnston's with very little hope on Saturday, but resolved to make every effort in my power to get on. I proceeded accordingly, with a letter to Col. Mayo to assist me on the road if necessary. I was soon informed that all the bridges had been broken up, but that he had been repairing two that morning, and I reached his house (18 miles hence) without any difficulty. He told me he suspected the bridges in a great swamp called Coneta had been carried away, but recommended me to call on Mr. Pippin, on this side of it, and request his advice and assistance. I had proceeded several miles, when Col. Mayo overtook me, in order that he might speak to Mr. Pippin himself. We found the bridges were gone, but he thought, with the aid of two negroes, whom he lent me, I might get safely through; and they both assured me, after passing that swamp, there was no obstacle to my passing safely to the banks of the river; for, though I should have to go through a great deal of water, none of it was very deep. We got through the swamp with some difficulty, having in some places to plunge through very deep holes where the bridges had been. I then thought all my difficulties over, and proceeded on in high spirits. I found the water in one or two swamps much deeper than I expected, and began to be a little alarmed at my situation. Still, however, I went on, having full confidence in the information I had received. At length, when I suppose we had got within about a mile of the river, we entered a very long swamp, that had a most formidable appearance. I directed Hannibal, who was before, to proceed with great precaution, and if the water grew very deep, to stop. He did, and I directed him to return immediately; and I afterwards discovered that in two minutes he would have been in swimming water. In that swamp it was swimming water for 40 yards; and in another, a little beyond, for 100. I then found myself in a very disagreeable situation. It was impossible to return without the two negroes I had parted with, I knew of no house near where I could go, and the night was advancing fast. After going back some distance, I saw a house not very far off on my left, to which I went; and there, luckily, I found a most obliging man and his wife, a Mr. and Mrs. Ford, who had lately removed from the neighborhood of Halifax—people apparently poor, but singularly kind and hospitable. The river was higher than it had been known for 20 years, and was then rising. If it fell, Mr. Ford told me, it would be two or three days before the swamps would be passable without swimming, and I saw no possibility of crossing with my chair and horses without great risk and delay, and had every reason to believe that every road beyond Tarborough would be impracticable for some time. I then inquired if I could take any other road, even that to Halifax, but found insurmountable obstacles. Calculating the time I had to spare, I was convinced there was not the slightest probability of my getting to Savannah in time, and being in a private house, where I could not prevail upon the family to receive any remuneration, not a single tavern between that and this place, on the only passable road, I at length, with inexpressible reluctance, gave up the attempt to reach Savannah. I informed the District Judge of my situation by a letter to be sent by Tarborough, and I returned here, Mr. Ford lending me two negroes to assist me through the dangerous swamp of Coneta. * * * I am here shut up on every side, but hope soon to be able to travel. I think I shall arrive some days at Charleston before the court will meet, &c., &c.

CAMDEN, May 1st.

* * * The day is so dull that it has not inspired me with a proper tune for May-morning, though I have thought about it. * * * I am told that our old friend Mrs. Chesnutt (Miss Mary Cox that was) is in town, and well; and I propose waiting on her this afternoon. A family on the road, at whose house I staid the other night, and where I had frequently been, had heard so circumstantial an account of my death some time ago, that they took me for a brother of mine, and it was with some difficulty I could convince them that their information was ill-founded; the satisfaction they expressed in finding the report false was very grateful to me. I was overtaken at the house where I staid last night by an itinerant Methodist preacher, who appears to be a very worthy, good man, but extremely weak. We travelled here together. He, and hundreds more, are employed by the Society, to go constantly about preaching; they receive their travelling expenses, and $64 a year to find them in every thing. They are all, I find, under regular discipline, and receive precise orders, and are governed by certain rules agreed upon at a stated meeting of the Society, which is usually held at Baltimore. Bishops Coke and Asbury act in conjunction, as Wesley acted singly before. Such a society, under artful men, might do a great deal of mischief. He seems to be a good government-man, which I hope is the fashion of the Society, &c.

CHARLESTON, May 5th.

* * * I begin to receive the usual civilities of this agreeable place. Mr. Edward Rutledge called on me, and left an invitation to dine with him to-day, and I have another for Thursday next. I hope not to be detained here above ten days, which will enable me to have an easy ride to Raleigh.

May 8th.

Our Court began yesterday, and there is so little business to do, that I have no doubt I shall leave this city early next week. I dined out yesterday, and still have three dinners ahead. A very large and respectable meeting here on Saturday last, passed unanimous and strong resolutions in support of Government; and an address to the President and Congress; and opened a subscription, which it is supposed will amount to $20,000, for an additional sum to that granted by Congress for fortifying the harbor. French privateers are every day off the Bar; and have not only taken vessels, but some of the men have landed, and taken provisions against the will of the owners, for which they have, in one or two instances, paid less than the value. One or two Spanish privateers have also begun to plunder; and one had the insolence, the other day, to fire on a vessel in the harbor of St. Mary, Georgia. The Grand Jury did me the honor to thank me for my Charge, and it is this day published, at their request. I have not yet seen Mr. Izard, but intend waiting on him. He is unfortunately in a very dangerous way with a palsy, which has almost deprived him of the use of one side. I am told Mr. John Rutledge is quite recovered. He was from home when I arrived, but called on me yesterday evening, when I was unluckily from home. * * * Tell Mrs. Wilson I frequently remember her admonition about exclamation and swearing, and am sure I have improved by it; but the vile roads I had to pass, sometimes, unavoidably, made me transgress, &c., &c.

JAS. IREDELL.

CHARGE AT CHARLESTON, MAY 7, 1798.

GENTLEMEN OF THE GRAND JURY:—

The duty you are now called upon to perform is to present offences committed against the United States. These may be distributed, in a general point of view, into the following classes:

1. Offences against the United States, as one of the nations of the world.

2. Offences against the United States, as having the sole care of all concerns with foreign powers.

3. Offences against the United States, relative to their connection among themselves.

Under the first head are comprised such offences as are deemed to be committed against the universal law of society, and the punishment of which does not belong to one nation more than another, because committed out of the limits of any. Such, for instance, are the crimes of murder or piracy, committed on the high seas. These crimes are so atrocious in their nature, and would be so terrible in their consequences, if they were to be committed with impunity, that all nations concur in punishing them; but as the right belongs equally to all, each hath an equal right, if it can apprehend the offender, and procure sufficient testimony, to apprehend and bring him to trial. And as this is an object of great national concern, and might give rise to abuses for which one nation would be accountable to another, it belongs to the United States, to whom all national concerns in which the different States are interested are intrusted.

The two remaining classes of offences more immediately relate to the principal objects for which the government of the United States was formed. These are well expressed in the dignified introductory words to the constitution itself, where the objects of it are declared to be, "To form a more perfect union, establish justice, insure domestic tranquillity, provide for the common defence, promote the general welfare, and secure the blessings of liberty to ourselves and our posterity." The attainment of these important purposes required common counsels, united strength, and inflexible principles, from which no deviation should be permitted, where private morality and public faith could not without perfidy admit of any. Not only the objects are among the noblest that ever were deliberately provided for by any nation, but the government itself is so constituted as to secure the highest probability that they will be in fact the leading objects of its pursuit. This, however, will not prevent great clamor and discontent. A virtuous conduct will ever be hated by vicious men, justice by the unjust, impartiality by those who from sinister motives wish partial measures to be pursued, and men of the best intentions are liable to be deceived by artful intentional misrepresentation. Some measures, too, however proper they may in reality be, will sometimes appear so doubtful in their nature, and so uncertain in their consequences, that men of equal understandings, and hearts and intentions equally uncorrupt, will differ in opinion, and in proportion to the importance of the measures will differ with zeal concerning them. All these are unavoidable consequences of difficult situations, which are to be provided for with so limited a foresight as the ablest of mankind possess. There is no expedient to prevent that anarchy which all such causes would lead to, but by enabling, by regular and constitutional authority, a delegated number, as the nature of each case may require, to direct the conduct of the whole. Those who know the value of regularity and order, and have a proper abhorrence of confusion, well knowing it is the most dangerous enemy even to liberty itself, will readily submit to such a decision in each case as the constitution sanctions, however different it may be from their own private opinion, and with whatever confidence they may believe their own opinion to be right. In many cases, most men, whose vanity does not destroy all distrust in themselves, and all respect for others, will suppose it possible, at least that they may themselves be mistaken as well as other men, and therefore will exercise some caution, lest with unpardonable arrogance, as well as want of duty, they counteract the execution of measures as judicious as they are obligatory. It is however necessary, whatever may be the conduct or motives of individuals, that laws when constitutionally made should be obeyed. The safety and interest of the whole are not to be sacrificed to the caprice, the want of patriotism, or deliberate disaffection of a few. Every law, therefore, must have some sanction annexed to it, which ought to be more or less rigorous as the nature of the case requires. Some of these sanctions are merely fines and penalties, for which prosecutions of a civil nature are carried on. In others the punishment goes beyond these, and then the offence partakes of the nature of a crime presentable by a Grand Jury, and after trial and conviction by another jury, punishable as the law has particularly prescribed.

Besides offences of this description, there are others of a kind immoral in their own nature, presentable by a Grand Jury of the United States, if committed within any place under the peculiar jurisdiction of the United States, and not of any particular State. Such as murder, or larceny, within any fort, arsenal, dock-yard, or magazine, under the exclusive jurisdiction of the United States. So also are other crimes, if committed in the course of the execution of an authority of the United States. Such as perjury in any suit depending in one of their courts. I specify these merely as examples, not thinking an exact enumeration of each kind to be at present material. From these instances you may form a judgment of the whole.

With respect to the manner in which your inquiries are to be conducted, a very few observations will be sufficient. You are, among other things, directed to keep secret your own counsel and that of the United States. This has been considered by some as an arbitrary regulation, and unfavorable to the person accused. It appears to me, however (for which I have the sanction of very high authority), to be founded on the strongest principles of reason and justice. If any person knew of an important prosecution depending against him, he might make his escape, and thus elude it altogether, in a case possibly of great moment to the public. At the same time, considering all circumstances, this course of proceeding is more favorable to the person accused himself, than if he was permitted to know of the prosecution, and defend himself before the Grand Jury ; because in that case he would appear with greater disadvantage before the jury who were to pronounce finally on his fate. They would be naturally biassed in favor of a decision already given by another jury, perhaps of a greater number than their own, at least in all probability equally enlightened and upright as themselves, and bound by the most sacred obligations of religion and justice, as much as themselves, to decide impartially between the public and him. In that case, too, there could be no room for the suggestion that they found on probable evidence only, because another jury was to convict or acquit him, for though that would be a very good argument when the evidence only on one side could be received, it could not apply if there had been an opportunity of hearing both. It is also to be considered, that the accused, though he may suffer unjustly by a false accusation, has in the present method every chance for escaping, not only punishment, but odium, which an innocent man can wish for. He has in the first instance to rely on the integrity and discernment of the Grand Jury, who, when partial evidence alone is given will naturally scrutinize it with great particularity. Though they may deem, and I suppose ought to deem, probable evidence alone sufficient, they will consider the probability should not be a light one, but amounting nearly to a moral certainty, admitting the evidence to be true, because, if not absolutely false, evidence on one side is apt to give a color which opposite evidence can do away. If, however, the Grand Jury should be deceived by evidence too plausible to be rejected, yet when the defence is heard, if the person accused can entirely take off its force, no imputation can lie either on him or the Grand Jury. Much less can any lie on either, if direct perjury has been committed. So that it can rarely happen to any man entirely innocent, that his acquittal by the jury who is finally to try him does not restore his reputation, as well as secure his safety. You certainly are not confined to prosecutions commenced by the Attorney of the United States, or to such evidence as he may lay before you ; but if you are possessed of information which he is not, it will be safest to consult with him and avail of his legal assistance, without which your best intentions might be frustrated. Upon this subject I think it only necessary to add, that twelve at least should agree upon any bill.

The present situation of our country is alarming to a very great degree. But it is only alarming for want of that spirit of union which alone procured us peace and independence, and without which it is impossible to preserve either, or save ourselves from ruin and contempt. We have a government formed and calculated to cherish, and with the best intentions to preserve it ; but in vain are all the efforts of the government if the people do not coöperate, each in his several station, in its support. They have every blessing to preserve by it, and every danger to dread from supineness or indifference. May they be sensible in time of the great crisis which requires their exertions ! and by that manliness, virtue, and intrepidity, which have so often saved their country, when on the verge of ruin, extricate it with equal honor and success from its present difficulties !

IREDELL TO MRS. IREDELL.

CHARLESTON, May 11th, '98.

MY DEAR HANNAH :— * * * Our Court will probably end to-day—certainly to-morrow—and I intend to leave on Monday. I continue to receive the greatest attention. I have dined only once at my lodgings, and have engagements for every day that I am to stay. Mr. John Rutledge has repeatedly pressed me to stay at his house, which however I have declined, as I had previously engaged lodgings (at Mrs. Smith's). I have a number of kind invitations from many gentlemen, to take their houses on my return. I have accepted of three, so that I shall not move very rapidly for the first three or four days. * * * Mr. Rutledge is perfectly recovered, and in such high spirits that he, and another gentleman, and myself, outsat all the rest of the company at a friend's house, till near 11 o'clock. *He remarked, with surprise, that I never swore,* which seems to be an equal proof of my former sin, and present reformation. He himself, and most of the gentlemen here, swear a good deal. I am glad to hear that Judge Wilson and his wife are well, but am still a little uneasy about that *writ.* Present my best respects to them particularly, &c.

May 12th.

Our Court ended this morning. * * * The weather is so cold to-day the thermometer is at 68°; the other day it was at 85°. I have just come from sitting an hour with Mr. Izard. He and Mrs. I. seemed very glad to see me. The palsy under which he labors is too visible. His face is a good deal affected by it ; but his understanding seems perfectly good. I am to dine to-day with Mr. J. Rutledge, who has invited a number of other gentlemen. This week, I am told, is the first time he has broke from his retirement, &c.

STATESBURY (22 miles from Camden), S. C., May 18th.

I am thus far on my return, in perfect health, having broken away with great difficulty from the agreeable hospitality of Charleston, and the road I have passed from it. I left Charleston on Monday, and spent a delightful day at Mr. Roger Smith's, only about nine miles from town, upon Ashley River, and by far the handsomest place I have seen in the whole State. This gentleman is married to a sister of Mr. Rutledge's, and has a very large and agreeable family. Mr. Rutledge came out with me, and we had other company from town specially invited. Mr. Rutledge has lived so much in retirement that, though very fond of his sister, and the whole family, they had not seen him for a long time ; and it was truly affecting to witness their meeting, and how happy they all seemed to be. Mr. Rutledge himself was in the highest spirits the whole day, and prolonged his stay as long as he could. I staid there that night, and the next morning went to Mr. Bee's (about 12 miles), where I passed the remainder of the day, receiving every possible degree of kindness. I was at two private houses afterwards, but came along with great rapidity. * * * * * Considering that Mr. Rutledge had lived totally recluse before my arrival, his attention, his friendship, I could almost say his affection to me, was conspicuous in a remarkable degree. I saw frequently your old acquaintance, Mrs. Eveleigh that was, now Mrs. Edward Rutledge. They both look as young as ever I saw them, and are supposed by their acquaintances to be extremely happy with each other. He had courted her before either was married, but being then a young man without fortune, her father would not consent to the match. Mr. Izard's handsome daughter, whom you saw in Philadelphia, is soon to be married to a young gentleman of the name of Deas, with whom I am not acquainted, &c.

May 19th.

I went yesterday afternoon to see our old friend, Mrs. McNair, who lives within two miles of this place. She seemed very happy to see me, and much obliged to me for coming. She has but lately returned from Savannah, with her daughter Mary, and her son Richard, who is settled and married there. * * * Her situation is very pleasant, and she tells me she lives comfortably, though not affluently. Within two miles of her lives Mr. Silvester, a brother of Mrs. Kings, who has a very handsome property. Mrs. McNair speaks highly of him. She wished very much for me to stay all night, but that I had not prepared for. I am detained here by rain to-day, &c., &c.

JAS. IREDELL.

MISS MEASE TO IREDELL.

PHILADELPHIA, 7th June, '98.

DEAR SIR :—You judged rightly in supposing it would give me pleasure to hear from you during your southern tour. At all times intelligence of you and your worthy family will be highly interesting to me. My afflictions, however great, are lessened by the knowledge of the happiness of my friends. I was at one time very anxious for your arrival at Savannah : but now the object for whom I was solicitous no longer requires my care : he is gone to a world free from care and troubles. With inexpressible grief I write it—my poor brother survived his voyage but two weeks. In a strange country, surrounded by strangers, he, who had been accustomed from his cradle to the most affectionate and tender attentions, was doomed to breathe his last, and I have no doubt suffered under the reflection.* * * Our number is diminishing fast : three invaluable ones snatched away in the space of eighteen months ! My remaining brothers have both joined the army : Thomas in the foot and James in the horse. In the space of another year I may be left *alone* in this miserable world. Grandmamma is not well, but I hope it is only the warm weather. My friends tell me she declines fast : thank God, I do not perceive it ; and am sure I watch her too closely to be deceived. Grandpapa knows not what sickness is, though he sometimes thinks from his great age (78) he ought to complain —however his constant spirits soon make him forget. They both desire to be remembered to you and Mrs. Iredell.

My brother James has, much to my satisfaction, resigned the situation of port-physician. He tried it for four years, and never escaped sickness in the fall, generally of the most violent kind. The Assembly last winter passed such an inconsistent, foolish law, that a physician, who would undertake to obey it, would risk reputation, health, and every comfort. Your friends are all well—Mrs. Stocker's, Mrs. Phillips', and Mrs. Austin's family. I have no acquaintance with the gentleman to whom Miss Duffield is married ; but my brother James bids me assure you that he is a worthy man, and esteemed eminent in his profession. Mr. and Mrs. Ritchie are obliged to you for your kind remembrance.

VOL. II.—34

Mr. and Mrs. Hopkinson, and Judge Glen, send their best respects to you. My love, &c. Mrs. Iredell does not know how much I esteem her, and how much I would value a letter from her, or I am sure she would write me. With great respect, &c.

Your obliged friend,
I. E. MEASE.

DAVID STONE TO IREDELL.

David Stone, of Bertie, after graduating with distinction at Princeton, N. J., read law with Colonel Davie. From "his assiduity in his profession, and his deep and varied attainments," he soon rose to distinction. Commended by his address, and the sweetness of his manners, he became popular; and was often selected by the people of his county to represent them in the Assembly. Elected a Judge of the Superior Court of North Carolina, he resigned in '98; and, by an advertisement in the Edenton Gazette, announced himself a candidate for Congress. He was warmly supported by the leading Federalists, and carried the District by a very respectable majority. He was elected United States Senator in 1801, and served until 1806, when he was again made a Judge. In 1808, he was elected Governor of the State; and, in 1813, United States Senator again. He was regarded by his friends as a decided republican; but disappointed their hopes by his condemnation of the embargo, &c., during the war of 1812-14. He was undoubtedly a man of talents of a very high order, and possessed of the requisite energy and industry to render them valuable to himself, and the State.*

BERTIE, 2d of July.

DEAR SIR:—You will oblige me still further by accepting my best wishes for the interest you are pleased to take in my election. I am fully convinced, as you state, that the only just cause of censure to an address in the public papers arises from the *manner* in which the thing may be done. And indeed when an election is to be made by people scattered over so extensive a country as the whole district of Edenton, I apprehend there is no mode by which so effectually to obviate misrepresentation as by a declaration made in that manner.

* Wheeler. One of Gov. Stone's daughters married the late Mr. Robert Cowan, of Wilmington, one who combined the playfulness of a child with the proper dignity of a man; active, foremost in the fox-chase, gayest with the gay, hospitable, generous, and brave, his life well taught the admirable lesson that men owe a duty to society, and that the promotion of others' happiness reacts with a blessed influence, and has a double virtue.

Besides, on the present occasion I should be wanting in respect to my friends, not to second their endeavors by any thing that is proper for me to do, especially since by their attention to my interest they have been diverted from others who would have been more diligent. I will thank you to make my best respects to Mrs. Iredell, and to believe

I am your obliged and obt. servant,
DAVID STONE.

GOV. JOHNSTON TO IREDELL.

HERMITAGE, 5th July, '98.

MY DEAR SIR:—* * * I am very closely engaged in making hay, and have hitherto succeeded very well, but regret that I cannot have so great a share in it *personally* as I wish. The weather has been for some days so intensely warm that there was no bearing the heat of the sun long at one time without great inconvenience.

I feel a very sensible gratification in the desire expressed by my friends that I should represent this district in Congress; but I flatter myself that all who are acquainted with the melancholy state of my domestic situation will readily excuse my declining to accept this mark of their confidence, and that no one will attribute it to any deficiency of that patriotic zeal which has ever induced me to obey the public call whenever my services were thought necessary.

Can any thing be more contemptible than the French Minister's letter to our Envoys? I have not yet seen their reply. It gave me great pleasure to see the honorable reception, which your friend Mr. Marshall received on his return to Philadelphia. I have not yet heard of Mr. Pinckney's return, nor can I conceive at present what motive could induce Mr. Gerry to remain behind. I hope the President will see cause to recall him before he has an opportunity of doing any thing injurious to his country or disgraceful to himself. I have no doubt the French politicians have discovered his weak side, and that they will direct their attacks accordingly, &c., &c.

SAM. JOHNSTON.

COL. DAVIE TO IREDELL.

HALIFAX, July 22d.

MY DEAR SIR:—I have the pleasure to acknowledge your letter of the 11th instant, and am clearly of opinion with you that Mr. Gerry's remaining in Paris was highly impolitic and unjustifiable, in any other point of view than that of a prisoner: the consequences of his ill-judged measure have already appeared in Congress and in the Jacobin papers. * * * * *

It is said that the population and military strength of the State (N. C.), and its great importance towards the defence of our two weak Southern neighbors, would naturally give it that consequence in war, which it has lost by its *representation* in peace; this is probable enough, but it must be felt before it will be acknowledged. The elections go on tolerably well. There will in any event as to those who are doubtful be an important change in favor of Government.

I hope the Assembly will see the importance of appointing a man of business and energy Governor: in time of war it is the most important office in the State: in time of peace its duties may be performed by any body, even A. M. (Alex. Martin).

I observe there is a book published entitled "American law cases." If it has any merit please procure it for me, &c., &c.

WM. R. DAVIE.*

GOV. JOHNSTON TO IREDELL.

July 28th.

DEAR SIR:—* * * I feel very much for Judge Wilson. I hear that he has been ill. What upon earth will become of him and that unfortunate lady who has attached herself to his fortunes? He discovers no disposition to resign his office. Surely, if his feelings are not rendered altogether callous by his misfortunes, he will not suffer himself to be disgraced by a conviction on an impeachment.

Be pleased to present my respects to the President, and such others of my acquaintance at Philadelphia as may inquire for me. By the bye, I think the President might have given a more civil answer to the Franklin address, which was couched in very decent terms: though they did not come in till the 11th hour, yet according to Scripture rule—and the President is a good Christian—they were entitled to their *penny*, &c., &c.

SAM. JOHNSTON.

SUPREME COURT.—AUGUST TERM.

Among others, the interesting case of Wilson *vs.* Daniels came up for trial. By the judiciary act the Court only had jurisdiction when the matter in dispute exceeded the value of $2000. The

* Colonel Davie was soon appointed a Brigadier General in the Provisional Army.

main question presented by the record was whether "the matter in dispute" was of sufficient value to give jurisdiction. The judgment was in an action of debt for the penalty of £60,000; but the real and operative judgment of the Circuit Court was only for the sum due, amounting to 1800 dollars. The majority of the Court concurred in considering the judgment as a judgment at common law for the full penalty; and therefore that the Court had jurisdiction. Judge Iredell dissented, and, as was his wont, sustained his position by the strictest legal as well as logical deductions: his dissenting opinion proved to be the true construction of the law, as subsequently laid down by the Supreme Court in several cases.*

IREDELL TO MRS. IREDELL.

PHILADELPHIA, August 6th.

MY DEAR HANNAH:—I arrived here on Saturday, and am perfectly recruited from my journey. I find that there is a good deal of important business depending, so that I despair of getting away as soon as I had hoped. All the Judges are in town except Judge Wilson, and all tolerably well, though Mr. Chase has been very ill again and still has something of the sciatica. A most astonishing discovery of a private nature was made here on Saturday just after my arrival. Mr. Thomas, Judge Wilson's Attorney, and who had been universally thought an honest man (though some suspicions, however, have been entertained of him lately), absconded, after having defrauded among others some of his most intimate friends, by taking up money on forged checks on the bank. It is now supposed that he has done it for a long time, but that he contrived to pay the money before the checks were presented. The frauds are supposed to amount to upwards of $6000. There is not the smallest doubt as to the fact, and the whole city is greatly agitated by it. His poor wife, who is a very amiable woman, far advanced in her pregnancy, dropped down senseless, and remained in that condition for an hour, when the officers of justice came to search for him. Before he went away, he assigned all his effects to Mr. Edward Tylman, and others. I am afraid this must unavoidably add to Judge Wilson's distresses, though I have as yet no particulars. One of his friends, I expect, will write a letter to accompany this. It is an event as surprising as affecting. Until lately, though a most violent partisan, he was thought so able and honest a lawyer that both parties indiscriminately employed him, and it is supposed that his practice

* 3d Dallas. Van Santvoord.

at one time amounted to £3000 a year. Judge Wilson's family are all well. * * * Our old friend Miss Hewes (now Mrs. Potts) has turned Quaker. August 9th. There being some appearance of the Yellow Fever in Water-street, between the Bridge and Walnut street, the lawyers agreed to continue most of the causes, and our Court broke up yesterday, &c., &.

JAS. IREDELL.

IREDELL TO MISS GRAY.

EDENTON, N. C., August 25th, '98.

DEAR MADAM:—At the desire of our dear and unfortunate sister, Mrs. Wilson, who is in good health but extreme affliction, I have the pain to acquaint you that Judge Wilson died here on the night of the 21st instant, a few hours after my arrival. Though he had been at times in very bad health, evidently occasioned by distress of mind owing to his pecuniary difficulties, yet the illness of which he died was of short duration, though very sharp: the greater part of the time he was in a state of delirium, during which he would not suffer many things to be done for him which were advised, and might possibly have restored him. Your sister with her usual goodness never quitted him, day or night, until his death was plainly approaching; and then she was parted from him with great difficulty. It is a mercy for which her friends cannot be too thankful, that her health has been so well preserved in such a constant state of anxiety, trouble, and want of rest, as she endured before his death. She was so obliging as to comply with Mrs. Iredell's and my earnest wishes in coming to our house the very next day after this unfortunate event happened: and though for some time her mind was agitated to a most affecting degree, yet I have the satisfaction to assure you that she is now much more composed, and we are at present without any apprehensions about her health. You may be assured of the utmost tenderness and care being shown her by Mrs. I. and myself, who will feel no small satisfaction, though attended by such melancholy circumstances, in enjoying her society as long as it can be afforded to us, looking forward with concern only to the moment of separation, which we shall feel most painfully. Mrs. W. requested I would write to you and not to her mamma, in order that you may prepare her for the intelligence, to prevent her being too suddenly surprised. How painful it is to me, that a correspondence with which you so kindly honored me, on an occasion so very different, should be renewed for so melancholy a purpose! &c., &c.

JAS. IREDELL.

Mrs. Wilson was the daughter of Mr. Ellis Gray of Boston: she was the Judge's second wife; and, after his death, married Dr. Thomas Bartlett of Boston, whom she accompanied to England, where she died in 1807. Mrs. Wilson remained for some time with Judge Iredell, until she was escorted home by a Mr. Wallace, a member of the bar of Philadelphia, and, probably, their agent on this occasion. By the failure of some speculations in lands Judge Wilson had been ruined. His object was to gain time. He was long deluded by the hope that he could retrieve his affairs. He was in his latter years much at Edenton, and often Judge Iredell's guest. The remote situation of the town, and the certainty of his colleague's sympathy, doubtlessly attracted him: the former promised escape from general observation, the latter consolation. It has been elsewhere remarked that Judge Iredell was not wise in a merely worldly point of view, in the sense of a tradesman: misfortune, so far from repelling, attracted him; he measured his beneficence by the need, not by the merit of its subject; and was content to discharge his duty as a man, and a brother, leaving to others the task of moral inquisition, and punishment. The tenderness of Judge Iredell's letter to Miss Gray contrasts singularly with the coldness and caution of one written him by Mr. Bird Wilson, subsequently, I believe, distinguished as the Rev. Dr. Bird Wilson. This gentleman had no inclination to meddle with Judge Wilson's estate: creditors, at Edenton, for articles furnished or services rendered were referred to such creditors as might obtain letters of administration: and Judge Iredell was politely thanked for his attention to Mrs. Wilson, though at the same time reminded that she was only connected with Mr. Bird Wilson by marriage. Mr. Bird Wilson, I presume, was the Judge's *son* by his first marriage.

BISHOP WHITE TO IREDELL.

NEAR PHILADELPHIA.

DEAR SIR:—The melancholy tidings, of which your letter was intended to give me the first information, had been communicated to me by a gentleman from the city, on the 5th instant. In consequence of the intelligence, my daughter the next morning wrote to Miss Wilson, now at Dr. Thomas Redman's; and it was my servant's carrying of her letter to the Post Office, that brought me yours, which had probably been there some days. I have written to Polly, to acquaint her with the few particulars of your letter, which it was material for her to know; and the letter itself I have enclosed to Mr. Bird Wilson at Pottsgrove. It can-

not be now unknown to Mrs. Wilson, although it must have been so when you wrote, that the family have shut up the house, and are dispersed in consequence of the prevailing fever. I sympathize most tenderly with them all on the mournful occasion; and shall not be wanting in any attentions and services, which can tend to alleviate their sorrows. My family desire with me to be affectionately remembered to Mrs. Wilson. You do not mention when she intends to return; nor do I know of any appearance of such a speedy decline of the fever, as shall render the city safe to her. Great as the late calamity is in itself on her and the other members of the distressed family, it is certainly aggravated by the event, which separates them at the present crisis. I doubt not, sir, it will be a consolation to the children, that, in the extremity of Mrs. Wilson's distress, she found a reception under your hospitable roof. With my respectful compliments to Mrs. Iredell,

I am, sir, with respect and esteem,
Your affectionate humble servant,
WM. WHITE.

Upon the back of a letter from Mr. Joseph Anthony of Philadelphia, dated September 11th, and introducing Mr. Wallace, is endorsed in Judge Iredell's handwriting—"a most excellent man, and whose merit, kindness and regard for me, I shall ever cherish with the utmost warmth and respect."

HON. CHARLES LEE TO IREDELL.

ALEXANDRIA, 20th September.

DEAR SIR:—Accept my thanks for your obliging favor of the 8th. The change in North Carolina is most pleasing, and with so good an example before Virginia I trust this State will amend her representation also. General Marshall is a candidate in Richmond district—Mr. B. Washington in Westmoreland—General Blackwell in Nicholas's district—Levin Powell in Brent's —Wm. Cabel, a federalist, in Cabel's district, &c.

Some or most of these, I think, will succeed. Nothing can be more distressing than (*the situation of*) the citizens of Philadelphia, where the pestilence now rages with increased and increasing fatality. In New York it is very terrible also, and in several of the towns to the eastward it makes its appearance. I think Congress ought not to hold its session in Philadelphia next winter, for though the fever shall be extinguished by the frost, it is impossible but the city must be very unhealthy in some other way, as the consequence of its desertion and the present fever.

General Washington is well, but not so firm in his health as usual. With very great regard and esteem,

I am, sir, very respectfully,
CHARLES LEE.[*]

WM. RAWLE TO IREDELL.

PHILADELPHIA, September 26th, '98.

DEAR SIR:—I had the pleasure of receiving this day yours of the 16th. It is a happy circumstance for Mrs. Wilson, and must be most grateful to her near connections, that she met with such friends as Mrs. Iredell and you in the moment of her sorrow. * * *

I am sorry to hear that your part of the world has also experienced an epidemic disease. It is more malignant in Philadelphia than in 1793. Our only safety is in flight. Hilary Baker, Esq., mayor of the city, an excellent magistrate, fell a victim to it last night.

I removed the residue of my family very soon after the Supreme Court rose, to a house I purchased in the autumn of Vosy on the banks of the Schuylkill, and have now no sort of intercourse with the town, my letters coming and going through Germantown.

Your account of the election is a consolation in the midst of our misfortunes. I fear we shall not reform our representation much. Gallatin will again dishonor and disturb us, from the impolitic division of the federal interest in that election district between two very valuable men, one of whom ought to withdraw.

I am, dear sir, with warmest wishes for the restoration of health to yourself and family,

Your sincere friend and obedient servant,
W. RAWLE.[†]

GOV. JOHNSTON TO IREDELL.[‡]

RALEIGH, 28th November, 1798.

MY DEAR SIR:—Nothing of importance except the election of a Mr. Wm. White, of Lenoir county, to succeed Glascow, has been done in the Assembly since I last wrote you; nor is there any bill of a public nature before the House of any importance. Davie arrived here last evening, but I have not yet seen him: he has been engaged all day reviewing the militia of this place. He is spoken of for Governor, but I have not heard with certainty whether he means to

---

[*] Brother to Gov. Lee: Attorney-General United States, &c.
[†] William Rawle, an eminent lawyer: vid. "Brown's Forum."
[‡] Governor Johnston was Senator from Martin county?

accept it. I heartily wish he may. Mr. Martin is still endeavoring to secure his election in the Senate: it is said by some that he will meet with a strong opposition on account of having so often voted against the measures of the General Government. I have not heard who are the candidates against him, for Alfred Moore prefers being a Judge, and will undoubtedly be elected.

Major Pinckney left this place this morning, before I heard he was in town, on his way to Philadelphia.

I have spoke to some of the members about addressing the President, and find it pretty generally approved; but I have waited for Davie before I introduced it, that I might avail myself of his influence in the House of Commons, in hopes of getting an unanimous vote for it. All the members with whom I have conversed are wonderfully federal—I say wonderful because I never conceived it possible there could be so universal a conversion in so short a space, &c.

SAM. JOHNSTON.

GEN. STEELE TO IREDELL.

In '88 Gen. Steele was a very distinguished member of the Convention, on the adoption of the Federal Constitution: and in 1790 member of Congress. He was universally regarded as a very enlightened politician, and accomplished gentleman. He was appointed by Washington first Comptroller of the Treasury, which office he now filled.*

TRENTON, November 9th.

DEAR SIR:— * * * * We have nothing new from abroad. Every thing respecting our dispute with "*the great nation,*" remains (as for some time past) in doubt and uncertainty. The hope of peace tends to keep up the influence of the opposition party in the Middle States, and consequently our danger is not less alarming than at any former period.

General Pinckney is here in good health and spirits. His magnanimous conduct on the score of rank, and the manner in which he accepted the appointment of Major-General raised him very much in our esteem. In making out their commissions the President determined that they should rank in the following order—Hamilton 1st, Pinckney 2d, Knox 3d, which the latter resented, and sent on a notice that he would not serve under either of the other two, they being as he styled them his "juniors." The President therefore will make a new appointment. In the

* Wheeler.

late war General P. stood higher in rank than Colonel Hamilton; but on this occasion he nobly observed that when our country is in danger, it is not a fit time to be employed in discussing trivial questions.

The public officers will return in the course of this week after an absence of near three months. In going back (although my family and immediate connections have all escaped), I can hardly describe to you my sensations. It is literally going not to a house of mourning; but to a whole city in the state of the deepest sorrow and distress, &c.

JOHN STEELE.

JUDGE CUSHING (Supreme Court U. S.) TO IREDELL.

BALTIMORE, November 9th, '98.

DEAR SIR:—I received your favor of the 28th last, and am obliged by your attention in bespeaking us lodgings at Mrs. Gilbert's. We heartily sympathize with you in your trouble of indisposition in your family; and with Mrs. Wilson in her greater troubles. Hers will be mitigated by your kindness. Mrs. Cushing joins me in sincere regards to you and Mrs. Iredell, Gov. and Mrs. Johnston, Mrs. Wilson, and Mrs. Iredell. We arrived on Monday the 5th, and purpose setting out to-morrow for Richmond. The Court here was short, sat but two days—no civil business—a short trial for stealing a bank-bill out of a letter by a letter-carrier in the city. The proof failed in two material points—no proof of his receiving the letter, nor of any money being in the letter.

Day before yesterday I had the pleasure of shaking hands with General Washington, who was escorted into town in the morning by the light horse, reviewed several volunteer companies of foot, and soon passed out of town, and onward for Trenton to meet the President as it is said.

You have heard that Mr. Bushrod Washington is appointed to the bench, and I am told he has gone on for the Southern Circuit, and hope it is so.

From Philadelphia we went the 9th August, and spent a month at Middletown, Connecticut, and then came on, passing King's ferry, forty-six miles above the city of New York, and in short, cautiously went as much out of the way of infectious places as we could. I hope the weather and frost will soon put an end to that ravaging disorder.

As to elections—I believe the cause of liberty, of government,

and of order and decency, will be strengthened rather than weakened, this trial, upon the whole.

Your affectionate, humble servant,

WM. CUSHING.

GOV. JOHNSTON TO IREDELL.

RALEIGH, November 21st.

MY DEAR SIR:— * * * Mr. Martin is here, and, from present appearances, I think will be re-elected in the Senate. He is *wonderfully federal*; and Alfred Moore much less popular than I had reason to expect, though I believe he may be appointed a Judge, which his friends say he will accept. Davie is talked of for Governor, and will meet with no opposition if he inclines to accept it. * * * I was very much surprised to find even Gov. Ashe so perfectly anti-Gallican; but it is the fashion, and no one pretends to be otherwise, &c.

December 4th.

* * * I can think of nothing else at present except a bill just introduced to remove the Supreme Court from Hillsborough to this place. * * *

I keep my health perfectly well, but am convinced that neither I nor any one in the same situation can do much public service, without forming extensive connections something like a party, aided by a conduct calculated to establish a pretty general confidence, and this is not to be effected in a single session, &c., &c.

SAM. JOHNSTON.

JUDGE WASHINGTON (S. C. U. S.) TO IREDELL.

RALEIGH, December 5th.

DEAR SIR:—I received with much pleasure your polite and obliging letter by Mr. Coleman, for which I very sincerely thank you.

When I left Richmond, I then meditated a visit to you, not knowing but that Edenton was contiguous to the route which I should have to take. But when I reached Petersburg, and entered into conversation with those who very kindly undertook to direct the course of my journey, I found that it would be impracticable to reach Augusta in time for the Court, unless I pursued a more direct road than that which led through your town. I was consequently obliged to abandon my first intention, and this I did with considerable regret.

I left home within five days after I received my commission, and yet it was not possible for me to reach Charleston in time to hold Court there, in consequence of which I went at once to Augusta.

The fate of the Toulon fleet had reached us before Mr. Collins's arrival, and in such a shape as to have gained entire credit here. I wish we could as certainly rely upon the enmity of the Turkish Government to this expedition; there would in that case remain very (*little*) doubt upon my mind as to the fate of the army. My own opinion and hope is, that Buonaparte will be vigorously and successfully opposed.

I wish I could contrive it (*so*) as to meet at Alexandria, as we are going on to Philadelphia. I should feel very happy in having your company. I shall set off so as to reach Philadelphia a day or two before the meeting of the Court.

With best wishes I am, dear sir,

Very sincerely and respectfully yours,

BUSHROD WASHINGTON.

GOV. JOHNSTON TO IREDELL.

RALEIGH, December 9th.

MY DEAR SIR:— * * * * I have procured a committee to take Court laws into consideration, but have yet made no progress in the business. I am obliged to proceed with extreme caution: being a stranger to most of the members, they view me with a jealous eye. The plan now in agitation, though nothing is yet before the committee, is to allot two districts to each Judge, who is to have power to decide in all cases both in law and equity, with an appeal or writ of error to a Court of Errors and Appeals, to consist of all the Judges, who are to meet twice every year at this place to decide finally. I favor this plan. Mr. Davie, before he was appointed Governor, drew up a bill, erecting a jurisdiction to inquire into certain frauds in the land office: but this Court too is to be held by the Judges of the Superior Court: whether it will ever be matured into a law, or if it is, whether any good will arise from it, is very uncertain. We are very much at a loss for men of business, and more so since Mr. Davie has left the Commons. There are some men of very good understanding in both houses. Riddick from Gates has more influence than any man in the Senate: he seems generally disposed to do what is right, but will go about it his own way. I hope very little good from the session, principally from the important business being so long delayed. I did not dare to risk any thing on my own credit, being only just now beginning to gain a little confidence. Smith or Franklin will be Senator: it is uncertain which. Baker would certainly have been elected had not doubts arisen respecting his political principles. Judge Williams will not resign: it is in contemplation to appoint another Judge, and stop the payment of his salary, &c., &c.

December 23d.

I hope to leave this the 25th, as it is expected the business will be closed to-morrow. I took some pains to establish a Court of Errors and Appeals, and carried it through the Senate, but it failed in the Commons with almost every other useful act of a public nature. It would exceed the limits of a letter to give you a detail of the business of the session: I cannot, however, omit to inform you that an address to the President has been some days before the House of Commons without being acted on, and I fear will come to nothing, though I believe it would pass without opposition in the Senate. Two or three days ago the Governor laid before the House of Commons a string of resolves from Kentucky, prefaced with a most indecent and violent philippic on the measures of the General Government. The Commons sent them up to the Senate, who, after, *with great impatience*, hearing them read, ordered them to lie on the table; and I believe, in the temper they were then in, might easily have been prevailed on to have thrown them into the fire, which was proposed in whispers by several near me, &c., &c.

December 24th.

I have only time to inform you that a very decent Address to the President has passed both Houses: unanimously in the Senate, and by a respectable majority in the Commons. I regret that it is not more pointed with respect to the high esteem which is generally entertained for the President's great abilities and integrity; but this could not be done without touching the feelings of the electors who voted against him, one of whom was on the committee which prepared the Address.

December 30th.

After I wrote you on the 24th, a resolve came up to the Senate proposing to give it in charge to our Senators and Representatives in Congress to use their influence to procure the repeal of the Alien and Sedition Acts, which was rejected by the yeas and nays—31 to 8, &c., &c.

SAM. JOHNSTON.

CHAPTER XXXII.
ÆT. 47—48.

SUPREME COURT, FEBRUARY TERM. MIDDLE CIRCUIT, SPRING TERM. LETTERS FROM GOV. JOHNSTON, REV. A. BOYD, GEN. DAVIE, GEN. STEELE, JUDGE CHASE, JNO. MILLER, JUDGE WASHINGTON, MRS. WILSON, &C. DEATH. CONCLUSION.

IREDELL TO MRS. IREDELL.

January 24th, '99.

MY DEAR HANNAH:— * * * Hitherto we have been very fortunate, having had very fine weather, and very agreeable. Could I have ventured to stay at Alexandria, I should probably have seen General Washington, as he was to be in town the next day. He and his family are well, and Miss Custis is going to be married to a Major Lewis, a respectable widower, who is a nephew of Gen. Washington. The clothes were purchased the other day. * * * The President has not only issued the spirited orders published in regard to any British Men of War taking men from our armed ships, but, I am told, has displaced Captain Phillips, who gave up his men to Commodore Loring. The General Assembly of Virginia are pursuing steps which directly lead to a civil war; but there is a respectable minority struggling in defence of the General Government, and the Government itself is fully prepared for any thing they can do, resolved, if necessary, to oppose force to force, &c., &c.

JAS. IREDELL.

SUPREME COURT—FEBRUARY TERM.

Judge Iredell sat in the Supreme Court at this term for the last time. The most interesting case decided was that of Sims *vs.* Irvine. Judge Iredell concurred in the judgment of the Court, but for *different reasons*, which, with his usual "keen, subtle, logical argumentation," he proceeded to assign in one of his "best and most carefully written opinions." It is not clear how the Chief Justice, who very briefly delivered the opinion of the Court, could have well differed from Judge Iredell, or by another mode of reasoning could have arrived at precisely the same result.*

GOV. JOHNSTON TO IREDELL.

February 1st.

MY DEAR SIR:— * * * I congratulate you on the destruction of the Brest Fleet. I fear the rascally Government of France will continue the war till no power in Europe will possess a ship of the line but Great Britain. It would indeed be most unfortunate if any one power should obtain so decided a superiority at sea as to enable it to dictate to the whole of the mercantile world, without a rival capable of opposing it when it usurped and exercised powers incompatible with the rights of others. Were the French only to suffer, it would be of little moment. They will deserve it for their unpardonable and unparalleled insolence. I have somewhere seen it remarked that "Fortune is not only blind herself, but also renders blind all those whom she embraces." This is the only way to account for the conduct of the French Directory to America, and for Buonaparte's wild-goose expedition, &c., &c.

SAM. JOHNSTON.

REV. ADAM BOYD TO IREDELL.

AUGUSTA, 8th February.

DEAR SIR:—I should have replied ere this to your last favor; but sickness has oppressed me so long that I have been obliged to omit my answer.

I carefully delivered your compliments as desired, and they were very cordially received. In fact, it gave me a very sensible pleasure to find you stand so high in esteem here, for parties have made many deserving characters to be passed by as of little or no worth. However I hope the same mind will be amongst us all, much more than for some time past it has been. Unanimity and concord are blessings in public and private life. At present they are necessary in a very particular manner. Such are the convulsions of the times, that I fear we shall not escape undisturbed. Let the storm come from either point, unanimity is essential to our preservation.

The broken state of my health has put it out of my power to attend, as I ought, to my lands in the West. Gen. Armstrong has written me, that he has the title of the land I offered Mr. Allen. Lately I have requested a gentleman there to apply for it, and to send it down to Major Pleasant Henderson. As to the other tract they tell me a lawsuit is inevitable. I wish I could sell my right at almost any price. Lawsuits and threescore but illy agree. I wish very much to go into North Carolina; but two difficulties occur: ill health or weakness, and the danger of losing my parish, now become a support which I require; for my credulity has given to design an opportunity of robbing me, so that I am almost naked. We have no occurrences worth repeating. The Assembly is sitting, but I have not heard any of their proceedings.

I beg the favor of you to remember me in a friendly manner to Mr. Allen and Mr. Johnston, and all my old esteemed friends.

Whether I shall ever again have the pleasure of seeing you, is very doubtful. But at all events, with real friendship founded on worth, I wish you a life of prosperity, and such a close of it, as shall place you with blessed choirs in heaven. Amen.

Affectionately and respectfully yours,

A. BOYD.

GOV. JOHNSTON TO IREDELL.

16th February.

MY DEAR SIR:— * * * How do you like the Carolina Address, and what does the President mean, in his answer, when he recommends that we should prevent the French from hurting themselves?

Mr. Gerry's conduct in remaining in Paris and entering into that kind of correspondence with the Secretary of Foreign Affairs was unfortunate, both as it respected the honor and interest of the country and his own reputation: nor am I much better pleased with Mr. Pinckney's remarks on the conduct of the French Cabinet—the thing might have done very well in debate from a member in a speech, but some parts of it were certainly too frivolous to be communicated in a solemn message from the President, particularly when so much stress is laid on a private letter from Joel Barlow to his friends.

By the last packet I received a letter from our cousin Mr. James Ferrier, dated in November last.* He is promoted to the rank of Major-General in the Army. His daughter, who is his only

---

* Van Santvoord's "Lives of the Chief Justices." 3d Dallas.

* Mr. Ferrier, of G. B.

child, is married to a gentleman of the name of Armstrong, of a handsome, independent fortune. By his account it would appear that the rebellion in Ireland is entirely quelled. He likewise informs me that the dispute between my Uncle's legatees and Mr. Rutherford's children had been left to arbitration—to two merchants of London, who had awarded "that they had received considerably more than their share of our Uncle's legacy and effects; and that the moneys in the hands of Anderson's Executors (including what was received in England) should be divided among the other legatees." He informs me that he had scarcely got into winter-quarters, after a pretty active campaign, in which, says he, "I believe we have succeeded in convincing the French of the inutility of their efforts against this country after four unsuccessful attempts. All their friends here, composed of restless and intriguing spirits (not a man of real rank or property among them), and a great number of poor, ignorant, deluded peasants, are entirely and completely discovered, got under, and suppressed," &c., &c.

SAM. JOHNSTON.

IREDELL TO MRS. WILSON.

MY DEAR MADAM:—Having accidentally met with a very neat edition of Thomson's Seasons, I take the liberty of requesting your acceptance of it, in the hope not only that you may enjoy frequently the pleasure of reading so excellent an author in a dress something better than usual, but that it may sometimes be the means of recalling to your recollection the person who presented it. You will, I flatter myself, forgive this selfish motive, for the sake of the former, and in consideration of the earnest wish I naturally feel to live with some esteem in your memory as long as I possibly can.

I am ever, my dear Madam,
With the greatest respect,
Your obedient servant,
JAS. IREDELL.

IREDELL TO MRS. IREDELL.

PHILA., March 14th.

MY DEAR HANNAH:— * * * We have had the most uncomfortable weather I ever knew at the same season—scarcely one dry day—almost perpetual snows, which I hope, however, will occasion a pleasant and healthy summer. * * * When I first came here it was said there had been one or two cases of yellow fever, but as Dr. Rush's vision is certainly jaundiced I impute the suspicion principally to that cause. For some weeks I have not heard the name mentioned except as connected with fears for the summer. Miss Emily Rush, Dr. Rush's daughter, about twenty, was married on Tuesday night to a young gentleman of Canada, of the name of Cuthbert. They had been engaged for some years, and he had gone to England, and owing to some dissatisfaction with his conduct, his letters and picture were returned, and a sharp letter breaking off the match sent to him. He returned to Canada, came on in December, was peremptorily and indignantly rejected, but having pretty good talents at perseverance, he returned to the charge, and at length carried off the lady. It was a very splendid wedding; upwards of forty were invited to it, among whom were Mr. and Mrs. Liston.* I thought I had mentioned Mr. Bond's family. Perhaps I forgot Mr. Wolcott's, though I dined there soon after I came to town. I don't think Mrs. Wolcott looks well, though she has her usual amiable sweetness. Mrs. Cadwallader's family are well. Mr. Abercrombie has lately had an 8th child—a son. The old lady is still living. I had an invitation to attend Mrs. Potts to the play. I went with great reluctance, for it was a very bad night. There was a very thin house, only two performers worth looking at, and the room intolerably cold. Mrs. Merry performed exceedingly well. Maria Potts was there, and with as easy an assurance as Mrs. Bingham could have possessed. How I then thought of the lovely diffidence of my Annie! * * * I went to meeting with Miss Mease, on Sunday, to hear a promising young man on trial. The doctor denies paying his addresses, and I am sure has no chance of the father's consent, and I am very much of your opinion as to his temper. It is certain, however, he visits the Miss Butlers very often. The President left town on Tuesday, a few days sooner than it was expected he would go, and I conjecture on account of Mrs. Adams' illness, for he told me last week she was very ill. I shall have business enough at the Court here, for an Insurrection has begun in Northampton county (that in which Bethlehem is) on account of the Land Tax Act. A body of armed men, between 80 and 100, in military array, forming one troop of horse and two companies of foot, rescued from the marshal 23 prisoners he had taken. Very active civil and military measures are taking, and I don't doubt it can be easily suppressed, and some of the insurgents punished. One of the Miss Butlers, whom I found at home by herself the other evening, and with whom I had not particularly conversed before, of her own accord spoke highly of James Johnston, said he was universally respected and beloved, and her

---
* English Minister.

---

compliments to his appearance would have satisfied any mother who had anxiety about that particular. All accounts agree in the same character of him—without any concert, &c., &c.

March 7th.

* * * Our chief justice set off for Georgia, by land, yesterday morning. I dined with young Miller and his wife on Tuesday, and delivered your congratulations, &c.: she seemed much pleased on the occasion, and desired her kindest compliments to you and Mrs. Tredwell. So have many others. I went to a ball at the British Minister's, at night, in company with Miss Mease, and her brother, the doctor. A Mrs. Craike was to have gone in company, but the weather being severe, declined it. We had, however, the benefit of her carriage, the first I have visited in since I have been in the city. Company visit him every Tuesday evening, and every other Tuesday they have a ball. He had spoke to me about going two or three times before, but some prior engagement or indisposition prevented. Mrs. Liston was extremely unwell, but exerted herself with pain. Miss Bond was, I believe, for the first time absent on account of a severe cold, which is, however, better. We have had a severe winter, and most abominable walking. I dined yesterday for the second time at Mrs. Phillips's. Government has yet received no official account of the *Tales of the Tubs* from Charleston, but I don't doubt it is a very serious affair, &c.

JAS. IREDELL.

JUDGE CHASE (U. S. Sup. Ct.) TO IREDELL.

BALTIMORE, 17th March.

MY DEAR SIR:—For five weeks after you left me I was confined to my bed-chamber and then to my bed. For some days I was very ill. I was so very weak that I could not walk across my room without assistance: it is fourteen days, this day, since I came below stairs, and I have been only able, this last week, to go in a close carriage into the city for exercise. I have not the least hope of being able to travel in time to attend the Circuit Court at New York, on the 1st day of next month. A relapse would be fatal. My cough is still bad, and the spitting continues. My lungs are so weak that I cannot bear any but very gentle exercise. I have not attempted to write a line before yesterday to my daughter, at Norfolk. I shall request the favor of Judge Patterson to hold Court for me at New York. If he can and I should be able, I will be at New Haven by the 13th of April, and finish the other parts of the circuit. Judge Washington sent me your favor of the 21st Feb., which my son read to me in bed: it would have given me great pleasure to have seen that gentleman, but I should not, if I had been in health, as he left the city, in the wagon, the next morning.

The *special verdict* in the case of Sims *vs.* Irvine, was taken under my direction, and in my opinion the plaintiff had a clear title. In the case of Russell *vs.* Clark, I gave an opinion when the case was before the Court on the (*exception ?*) to the evidence, that the parol evidence was inadmissible to *contradict*, to *add to*, or to diminish the *written* agreement—this by the common law, before the statute of frauds. From my memory of the bill of exceptions, I do not see how the Court could give any opinion as to the legal operation of the letters: they were general and *unlimited* letters of credit, or only of *recommendation*. You say the Court differed in opinion, but do not mention in what manner.* I had considered the law, and I had taken up an opinion that the letters did not amount to an *unlimited credit.*

I received just now your letter of the 14th inst. I am concerned to hear of the Insurrection in Northampton. I hope a body of horse and foot are ordered to seize the insurgents.

Mrs. Chase and my son join me in wishing you every felicity in this life. I am, dear sir, with great respect and esteem,

Your affectionate and obedient servant,
SAML. CHASE.

ROBT. LENOX TO IREDELL.

NEW YORK, 20th March, '99.

DEAR SIR:—Your much esteemed favor of the 16th inst. was yesterday handed me by Capt. Blair, who, I rejoice, has succeeded in getting the appointment of Lieutenant in the Navy; and, as he expected no higher station, I think it just as well.† * * *

I am happy to see the exertions that are making to quell the rebellion in Pennsylvania, and I hope the promoters will continue to resist till they put it fairly in the power of government to make examples of them; for, rest assured, these are so many means formed to feel the pulse of the country, and preparatory to the grand "fête" when the *great Leaders* are to appear. I am very truly,

Your most obedient servant,
ROBT. LENOX.

---
* Mr. Dallas states in a note to his report of the case, that Iredell, Patterson, and Washington, held that the letters did not, of themselves, import an undertaking: the Chief Justice and Cushing *contra*. 3d Dallas.
† George Blair, nephew to Mrs. Iredell.

Gov. Johnston to Iredell.

Hermitage, March 23d.

My dear Sir :— * * * * It appears to me very extraordinary that the President should at this time appoint Ministers to treat with the French Republic, unless he has better grounds for it than that frivolous and equivocal letter published in the newspapers, said to be written by citizen Talleyrand to citizen Pichon, and without any kind of apology for their unhandsome treatment of our Ministers on former occasions : at the same time, I cannot presume to censure the President's measures, as it is not probable that the public are in possession of the whole of his information, &c., &c.

SAM. JOHNSTON.

Iredell to Mrs. Iredell.

Phila., March 28th.

My dear Hannah :— * * * * The insurrection still remains in the same situation. Troops preparing to march, and I suppose soon there will be a formidable force. It is impossible they can resist it : they will not be trifled with as heretofore. I am just going to dine with Mrs. Bond. Notwithstanding the civilities I receive, I am heartily tired, I assure you : but my idle time is now closing, and I shall soon have enough to occupy me. Poor Nelly Barclay that was, who married a very respectable young gentleman of the name of Cochran, a member of Congress, died on Sunday last, universally regretted. She had been long in an ill state of health, but a few weeks ago Dr. Rush gave strong hopes of her recovery. * * * She retained her senses to the last, and expired with perfect resignation in the arms of her father, who had been sent for by express. She died in a lodging-house in Third, near Walnut street. I called at Mrs. Cox's the evening after her death, and found Theodosia in very great distress for this event. She had been her most intimate friend. She and Mrs Wolcott, whom I saw the same evening, desired their kindest remembrance to you, &c., &c.

JAS. IREDELL.

CIRCUIT COURT.—SPRING TERM.

The Circuit Court was held at Philadelphia by Judge Iredell, and Peters, District Judge. At this term of the Court, Fries, and many other of the insurgents, were indicted. At the opening of the Court, April 11th, Judge Iredell delivered the following "luminous and pointed charge," which presently, in conformity with the wish of the grand jury, appeared in "Claypoole's American Daily Advertiser."

A CHARGE

Delivered to the Grand Jury of the United States, for the District of Pennsylvania, in the Circuit Court of the United States for the said district, held in the city of Philadelphia, April 11, 1799, by JAMES IREDELL, *one of the Associate Justices of the Supreme Court of the United States.*

[Published at the Request of the Grand Jury.]

Gentlemen of the Grand Jury,

The important duties you are now called upon to fulfil, naturally increase with the increasing difficulties of our country. But however great those difficulties may be, I am persuaded you will meet them with a firm and intrepid step, resolved, so far as you are concerned, that no dishonor or calamity (if any such should await us) shall be ascribable to a weak or partial administration of justice.

If ever any people had reason to be thankful for a long and happy enjoyment of peace, liberty, and safety, the people of these States surely have. While every other country almost has been convulsed with foreign or domestic war, and some of the finest countries on the globe have been the scene of every species of vice and disorder, where no life was safe, no property was secure, no innocence had protection, and nothing but the basest crimes gave any chance for momentary preservation, no citizen of the United States could truly say that in his own country any oppression had been permitted with impunity, or that he had any grievance to complain of, but that he was required to obey those laws which his own representatives had made, and under a government which the people themselves had chosen. Yet in the midst of this envied situation, we have heard the government as grossly abused as if it had been guilty of the vilest tyranny, as if common sense or common virtue had fled from our country, and those pure principles of republicanism, which have so strongly characterized its councils, could only be found in the happy soil of France, where the sacred fire is preserved by five Directors on ordinary occasions, and three on extraordinary ones—who, with the aid of a Republican army, secure its purity from violation by the Legislative representatives of the people.—The external conduct of that government is upon a par with its internal.—Liberty, like the religion of Mahomet, is propagated by the sword. Nations are not only compelled to be free, but to be free on the French model, and placed under French guardianship. French arsenals are the repository of their arms, French treasuries of their money, the city of Paris of their curiosities ; and they are honored with the constant support of French enterprises in any other part of the world. Such is the progress of a power which began by declarations that it abhorred all conquests for itself, and sought no other felicity but to emancipate the world from tyrants, and leave each nation free to choose a government of its own. Those who take no warning by such an awful example, may have deeply to lament the consequences of neglecting it.

The situation in which we now stand with that country is peculiarly critical. Conscious of giving no real cause of offence, but irritated with injuries, and full of resentment for insults ; desirous of peace, if it can be preserved with honor and safety, but disdaining a security equally fallacious and ignominious at the expense of either ; still holding the rejected Olive Branch in one hand, but a sword in the other—we now remain in a sort of middle path between peace and war, where one false step may lead to the most ruinous consequences, and nothing can be safely relied on but unceasing vigilance, and persevering firmness in what we think right, leaving the event to heaven, which seldom suffers the destruction of nations, without some capital fault of their own.

Among other measures of defence and precaution which the exigency of the crisis, and the magnitude of the danger, suggested to those to whom the people have intrusted all authority in such cases, were certain acts of the legislature of the United States, not only highly important in themselves, but deserving of the most particular attention, on account of the great discontent which has been excited against them, and especially as some of the State legislatures have publicly pronounced them to be in violation of the Constitution of the United States. I deem it my duty, therefore, on this occasion to state to you the nature of those laws, which have been grossly misrepresented, and to deliver my deliberate opinion as a Judge, in regard to the objections arising from the constitution.

The acts to which I refer you will readily suppose to be what are commonly called the Alien and Sedition acts. I shall speak of each separately, so far as no common circumstances belonging to them may make a joint discussion proper.

I. *The Alien Laws,* there being two.

To these Laws, in particular, it has been objected,

1. That an Alien ought not to be removed on suspicion, but on proof of some crime.

2. That an Alien coming into the country on the faith of an act stipulating that in a certain time, and on certain conditions, he may become a citizen, to remove him in an arbitrary manner before that time, would be a breach of public faith.

3. That it is inconsistent with the following clause in the constitution, (Art. 1, sec. 9.)

"The migration or importation of such persons as any of the States now existing shall think proper to admit, shall not be prohibited by the Congress prior to the year one thousand eight hundred and eight ; but a tax or duty may be imposed on such importation, not exceeding ten dollars for each person."

With regard to the first objection, viz.: "That an alien ought not to be removed on suspicion, but on proof of some crime." It is believed that it never was suggested in any other country, that *aliens* had a right to go into a foreign country, and stay at their will and pleasure without any leave from the government. The law of nations undoubtedly is, that when an alien goes into a foreign country, he goes under either an express or implied safe conduct. In most countries in Europe, I believe, an express passport is necessary for strangers. Where greater liberality is observed, yet it is always understood that the government may order away any alien whose stay is deemed incompatible with the safety of the country. Nothing is more common than to order away, on the eve of a war, all aliens or subjects of the nation with whom the war is to take place. Why is that done, but that it is deemed unsafe to retain in the country, men whose prepossessions are naturally so strong in favor of the enemy that it may be apprehended they will either join in arms, or do mischief by intrigue in his favor? How many such instances took place at the beginning of the war with Great Britain, nobody then objecting to the authority of the measure, and the expediency of it being alone in contemplation ! In cases like this, it is ridiculous to talk of a crime, because perhaps the only crime that a man can then be charged with, is his being born in another country, and having a strong attachment to it. He is not punished for a crime that he has committed, but deprived of the power of committing one hereafter, to which even a sense of patriotism may tempt a warm and misguided mind. Nobody who has ever heard of Major Andre, that possesses any liberality of mind, but must believe that he did what he thought right at the time, though in my opinion it was a conduct in no manner justifiable. Yet how fatal might his success have proved ! If men, therefore, of good characters, and held in universal estimation for integrity, can be tempted when a great object is in view, to violate the strictest duties of morality, what may be expected from others who have neither character nor virtue, but stand ready to yield to temptations of any kind? The opportunities during a war of making use of men of such a description are so numerous and so dangerous, that no prudent nation would ever trust to the possible good behaviour of many of them. Indeed, most of those who oppose this law seem to admit that as to *alien enemies* the interposition may be proper, but they contend it is improper before a war actually takes place to exercise such an authority, and that as to *neutral aliens* it is totally inadmissible. To be sure the two latter instances are not quite so plain, but the objection I am considering belongs equally to them all, for if an alien cannot be removed but on conviction of a crime, then an alien enemy ought not to be removed but on conviction of treason, or some other crime showing the necessity of it. If, however, we are not blind to what is evident to all the rest of the world, equal danger may be apprehended from the citizens of a hostile power before war actually declared as after, perhaps more, because less suspicion is entertained; and some citizens of a neutral power are equally dangerous with the others. What has given France possession of the Netherlands, Geneva, Switzerland, and almost all Italy, and enables her to domineer over so many other countries, lately powerful and completely independent, but that her arts have preceded her arms; the smooth words of amity, peace, and universal love by seducing weak minds, have led to an unbounded confidence which has ended in their destruction, and they have now to deplore the infatuation which led them to court a fraternal embrace from a bosom in which a dagger was concealed! In how many countries, alien friends as to us, dependent upon them, are there warm partisans not nominally French citizens, but completely illuminated with French principles, electrified with French enthusiasm; and ready for any sort of revolutionary mischief! Are we to be guarded against the former and exposed to the latter? No, gentlemen. If with such examples before their eyes, Congress had either confined their precaution to a war in form, or to citizens of France only, losing all sense of danger to their country in a regard to nominal distinctions, they would probably justly have deserved the charge of neglecting their country's safety in one of its most essential points, and hereafter the very men who are now clamorous against them for exercising a judicious foresight, might too late have had reason to charge them (as many former infatuated governments in Europe may now fairly be charged by their miserable, deluded fellow-citizens) as the authors of their country's ruin. But those who object to this law seem to pay little regard to considerations of this kind, and to entertain no other fear but that the President may exercise this authority for the mere purpose of abusing it. There is no end to arguments or suspicions of this kind. If this power is proper it must be exercised by somebody. If, from the nature of it, it could be exercised by so numerous a body as Congress, yet as Congress are not constantly sitting, it ought not to be exercised by them alone. If they are not to exercise it, who so fit as the President? What interest can he have in abusing such an authority? But on this occasion, as on others of the like kind, gentlemen think it sufficient to show, not that a power is likely to be abused (which is all that can be prudently guarded against), but that it possibly may, and therefore to guard against the possibility of an abuse of power, the power is not at all to be exercised. The argument would be just as good against his acknowledged powers, as any others that the legislature may occasionally confide to him. Suppose he should refuse to nominate to any office, or to command the army or navy, or should assign frivolous reasons against every law so that no law could be passed but with the concurrence of two-thirds of both houses! Suppose Congress should raise an army without necessity, lay taxes where there was no occasion for money, declare war from mere caprice, lay wanton and oppressive restraints on commerce, or in a time of imminent danger trifle with the safety of their country, to gain a momentary breath of popularity at the hazard of their country's ruin! All this they *may* do. Does any man of candor, who does not believe every thing they do wrong, apprehend that any of these things will be done? They have the *power* to do them, because the authority to pass very important and necessary acts of legislation on all those subjects, and in regard to which discretion must be left, unavoidably implies that as it may be exercised in a right manner, it may, if no principle prevent it, be exercised in a wrong one. If the State legislatures should combine to choose no more Senators, they may abolish the constitution without the danger of committing treason. If, to prevent a House of Representatives being in existence, they should keep no law in being for a similar branch of their own, deeming the abolition of the Government of the United States cheaply purchased by such a sacrifice, they may do this. They have the same power over the election of a President and Vice President. What is the security against abuse in any of these cases? None, but the precautions taken to procure a proper choice, which, if well exercised, will at least secure the public against a wanton abuse of power, though nothing can secure them absolutely against the common frailty of men, or the possibility of bad men, if accidentally invested with power, carrying it into a dangerous extreme. We must trust some persons, and as well as we can submit to any collateral evil which may arise from a provision for a great and indispensable good that can only be obtained through the medium of human imperfection. At the same time it may be observed, that in the case of the President, or any executive or judicial officer wantonly abusing his trust, he is liable to impeachment, and there are frequent opportunities of changing the members of the legislature if their conduct is not acceptable to their constituents.

The clause in the constitution, declaring that the trial of all crimes, except by impeachment, shall be by jury, can never in reason be extended to amount to a permission of perpetual residence of all sorts of foreigners unless convicted of some crime, but is evidently calculated for the security of any citizen, a party to the instrument, or even of a foreigner if resident in the country, who, when charged with the commission of a crime against the municipal laws for which he is liable to punishment, can be tried for it in no other manner.

The second objection is, "That an alien coming into the country, on the faith of an act stipulating that in a certain time and on certain conditions he may become a citizen, to remove him in an arbitrary manner before that time would be a breach of public faith."

With regard to this it may be observed, that undoubtedly the faith of government ought under all circumstances, and in all possible situations, to be preserved sacred. If, therefore, in virtue of this law, all aliens from any part of the world had a right to come here, stay the probationary time, and become citizens, the act in question could not be justified, unless it could be shown that a real (not a pretended) overruling public necessity, to which all inchoate acts of legislation must forever be subject, occasioned a partial repeal of it. But there are certain conditions, without which no alien can ever be admitted, if he stay ever so long; and one is, that during a limited time (two years in the case of aliens then resident; five in the case of aliens arriving after) *he has behaved as a man of good moral character, attached to the principles of the Constitution of the United States, and well disposed to the good order and happiness of the same.* If his conduct be different, he is no object of the naturalization law at all, and consequently no implied compact was made with him. If his conduct be conformable to that description, he is no object of the alien law to which the objection is applied, because he is not a person whom the President is empowered to remove, for such a person could not be deemed dangerous to the peace and safety of the United States, nor could there be reasonable grounds to suspect such a man of being concerned in any treasonable or secret machinations against the government; in which cases alone the removal of any alien friend is authorized. Besides any alien coming to this country must or ought to know, that this being an independent nation, it has all the rights concerning the removal of aliens which belong by the law of nations to any other; that while he remains in the country in the character of an alien, he can claim no other privilege than such as an alien is entitled to; and consequently, whatever risk he may incur in that capacity is incurred voluntarily, with the hope that in due time by his unexceptionable conduct, he may become a citizen of the United States. As there is no end to the ingenuity of man, it has been suggested that such a person, if not a citizen, is a denizen, and therefore cannot be removed as an alien. A denizen in those laws from which we derive our own, means a person who has received letters of denization from the king, and under the royal government such a power might undoubtedly have been exercised. This power of denization is a kind of partial naturalization, giving some, but not all the privileges of a natural born subject. He may take lands by purchase or devise, but cannot inherit. The issue of a denizen born *before* denization cannot inherit; but if born *after* may, the ancestor having been able to communicate to him inheritable blood. But this power of the crown was thought so formidable, that it is expressly provided by act of parliament, that no denizen can be a member of the Privy Council, or of either House of Parliament, or have any office of trust, civil or military, or be capable of any grant of lands from the crown. Upon the dissolution of the royal government, the whole authority of naturalization, either whole or partial, belonged to the several States, and this power the people of the States have since devolved on the Congress of the United States. Denization therefore (in the sense here used) is a term unknown in our law, since the right was not derived from any general legislative authority, but from a special prerogative of the crown, to which parliamentary restrictions afterwards were applied. So much so, that if an act of Parliament had passed, giving certain rights to an alien with restrictions exactly similar to those of a denizen, I imagine he would not have been called a denizen, because the royal authority was not the source from which his rights were derived. As to acts of naturalization themselves, they are liable in England, by an express law, to certain limitations, one of which is, that the person naturalized is incapable of being a member of the Privy Council, or either House of Parliament, or of holding offices or grants from the crown. Yet I never heard, nor do believe that such a person was ever called a denizen; for which, as there is no foundation in precedent, or in the Constitution of the United States,

I presume it is a distinction without solidity. Fixed principles of law cannot be grounded on the airy imagination of man.

The third objection is, "That it is inconsistent with the following clause in the constitution, viz.:

"The migration or importation of such person as any of the States now existing shall think proper to admit, shall not be prohibited by the Congress prior to the year one thousand eight hundred and eight, but a tax or duty may be imposed on said importation not exceeding ten dollars for each person."

I am not satisfied, as to this objection, that it is sufficient to overrule it, to say the words do not express the real meaning, either of those who formed the constitution, or those who established it, although I do verily believe in my own mind that the article was intended only for slaves, and the clause was expressed in its present manner to accommodate different gentlemen, some of whom could not bear the name *slaves*, and others had no objection to it. But, though this probably is the real truth, yet, if in attempting to compromise, they have unguardedly used expressions that go beyond their meaning, and there is nothing but private history to elucidate it, I shall deem it absolutely necessary to confine myself to the written instrument. Other reasons may make the point doubtful, but at present I am inclined to think it must be admitted that Congress, prior to the year 1808, cannot prohibit the migration of free persons to a particular State, existing at the time of the constitution, which such State shall, by law, agree to receive. The States then existing, therefore, till 1808, may (we will say) admit the migration of persons to their own States, without any prohibitory act of Congress.—This they may do upon principles of general policy, and in consistence with all their other duties. The States are expressly prohibited from entering into an engagement or contract with another State, or engaging in war, unless actually invaded, or in such imminent danger as will not admit of delay. The avenues to foreign connection being thus carefully closed, it will scarcely be contended that in the case of a war, a State could, either directly or indirectly, permit the migration of enemies. If they did, the United States could certainly without any impeachment of the general right of allowing migration, in virtue of their authority to repel invasion, prevent the arrival of such. And as such invasion may be attempted without a formal war, and Congress have an express right to *protect* against invasion, as well as to *repel* it, I presume Congress would also have authority to prevent the arrival of any enemies, coming in the disguise of friends, to invade their country. But, admitting the right to permit migration in its full force, the persons migrating on their authority must be subject to the laws of the country, which consist not only of those of the particular State but of the United States. While aliens, therefore, they must remain in the character of aliens ; and, of course, upon the principles I have mentioned, be subject to a power of removal, in certain cases recognized in the law of nations ; nor can they cease to be in this situation, until they become citizens of the United States ; in which case they must obey the laws of the Union as well as of the particular State they reside in. But, gentlemen argue as if because the States had a right to permit migration, the migrants were under a sort of special protection of the State admitting it, lest the United States, merely to disappoint the purpose of migration, should exercise an arbitrary authority of removal without any cause at all. It would be just as consistent to say, that if such migrant was charged with a murder on the high seas, or in any fort or arsenal of the United States, he should not be tried for it in a court of the United States, lest the court and juries, out of ill will to the State, should combine to procure his conviction and punishment, in all events, to defeat the State law. The two powers may undoubtedly be made compatible, if the legislatures of the particular States, and the government of the United States, do their duty, without which presumption not an authority given by the constitution can exist. They surely are more compatible than the collateral powers of taxation, which, under each government, go to an unlimited extent, but the very nature of which forbids any other limitation than a sense of moral right and justice. If we scepticize in the manner of some gentlemen on this subject, suppose each legislature should tax to the amount of 19s. in the pound. Each has the power ; but is such an exercise of it more apprehended than we apprehend an earthquake to swallow us all up, at this very moment ? All systems of government suppose they are to be administered by men of common sense and common honesty. In our country, as all ultimately depends on the voice of the people, they have it in their power, and it is to be presumed they generally will choose men of this description : but if they will not, the case to be sure is without remedy. If they choose fools, they will have foolish laws. If they choose knaves, they will have knavish ones. But this can never be the case until they are generally fools or knaves themselves, which, thank God, is not likely ever to become the character of the American people.

Having said what I thought material as to the alien laws, upon the subject of the particular objections to them, I now proceed to discuss the objections which have been made to what is called the Sedition Act, one of which equally applies to the alien laws as well as to this. But I think it proper previously to read the law itself.

The objections (so far as I have heard them) to this act are as follows :

1. (And this applies to the alien law also) That there is no specific power given to pass an act of this description, though in the particular specific powers given there is authority conveyed as to other offences specially named.

2. That this law is not warranted by a clause in the constitution, conveying legislative authority, which, after designating particular objects, adds :

"And to make all laws which shall be necessary and proper for carrying into execution the foregoing powers, and all other powers vested by this constitution in the government of the United States, or in any department or officer thereof "—Because it is not necessary and proper to pass any such law in order to carry into execution any of those powers.

3. That, admitting the former positions are not maintainable, yet the exercise of this authority is incompatible with the following amendment to the constitution, viz. :

"Congress shall make no law respecting an establishment of religion, or prohibiting the full exercise thereof ; or abridging the freedom of speech, or of the press, or the right of the people peaceably to assemble, and to petition the government for a redress of grievances."

With regard to the first objection, I readily acknowledge, that soon after the constitution was proposed, and when I had taken a much more superficial view of it than I was sensible of at the time, I did think Congress could not provide for the punishment of any crimes but such as are specifically designated in the particular powers enumerated. I delivered that opinion in the Convention of North Carolina, in the year 1788, with a perfect conviction, at the time, that it was well founded. But I have since been convinced it was an erroneous opinion, and my reasons for changing it I shall state to you as clearly as I am able.

It is in vain to make any law unless some sanction be annexed to it, to prevent or punish its violation. A law without it might be equivalent to a good moral sermon, but bad members of society would be as little influenced by one as the other. It is, therefore, necessary and proper, for instance under the Constitution of the United States, to secure the effects of all laws which impose a duty on some particular persons, by providing some penalty or punishment if they disobey. The authority to provide such is conveyed by the following general words in the constitution, at the end of the objects of legislation particularly specified : "To make all laws which shall be necessary and proper for carrying into execution the foregoing powers, and all other powers vested by this constitution in the government of the United States, or in any department or officer thereof." A penalty alone would not in every case be sufficient, for the offender might be rich and disregard it, or poor, though a wilful offender, and unable to pay it. A fine, therefore, will not always answer the purpose, but imprisonment must be in many cases added, though a wise and humane legislature will always dispense with this, where the importance of the case does not require it. But if it does, from the very nature of the punishment, it becomes a *criminal*, and not a *civil* offence ; the grand jury must indict, before the offender can be convicted.

This general position may be illustrated by a variety of instances under the penal code of the United States, which have, I believe, never been objected to as unconstitutional, though there have never been wanting penetrating and discerning members who were ready enough to take exceptions where they found any plausible ground for them. I shall enumerate a few.

In the act entitled, an act for the punishment of certain crimes against the United States (vol. I. Swift's edition, p. 100,) among other crimes specified, are the following :

Murder or larceny in a fort belonging to the United States. Misprision of felony committed in any place under the sole and exclusive jurisdiction of the United States. Stealing or falsifying a record of any court of the United States. Perjury in any court of the United States. Bribing a judge of the United States. Obstructing the execution of any kind of process issuing from a court of the United States.

In the collection act, 1 vol. p. 237, it is provided, that in all cases where an oath is by that act required from a master or other person having command of a ship or vessel, or from an owner or assignee of goods, wares, and merchandise, his or her factor, or agent, if the person so swearing shall swear falsely, such persons shall, on indictment and conviction thereof, be punished by fine or imprisonment, or both, in the discretion of the court, before whom such conviction shall be had, so as the fine shall not exceed one thousand dollars, and the term of imprisonment shall not exceed twelve months.

In the act laying duties on distilled spirits, (vol. i. p. 324,) in the 39th section it is provided as follows :

"If any supervisor, or other officer of inspection, in any criminal prosecution against them, shall be convicted of oppression or extortion in the execution of his office, he shall be fined not exceeding five hundred dollars, or imprisoned not exceeding six months, or both, at the discretion of the court ; and shall also forfeit his office."

VOL. II—36

These instances deserve great consideration; because I believe no candid man will deny that these provisions were constitutional exercises of authority, within the scope of the general authority conveyed, though not specially named as objects which it should be competent for Congress to provide for. And they certainly derive weight from the consideration, that the principle of them (which I believe was the case) was never objected to, though the expediency of some of the provisions may have been.

In further illustration of this subject, I shall state a case which was determined in this court—The United States against *Worrell*, published in Mr. *Dallas's* Reports, p. 384, where there was an indictment against the defendant for attempting to bribe Mr. *Coxe*, the Commissioner of the Revenue. The defendant was found guilty, and afterwards a motion was made in arrest of judgment, assigning, together with some technical objections, this general one, that the court had no cognizance of the offence, because no act of Congress had passed creating the offence and prescribing the punishment, but it was solely on the foot of the common law. The very able and ingenious gentleman who is the reporter of that case, and was the defendant's counsel in it, in the course of his argument, makes the following observations, part of which are remarkably striking and pertinent to my present subject: "In relation to crimes and punishments, the objects of the delegated power of the United States are enumerated and fixed. Congress may provide for the punishment of counterfeiting the securities and current coin of the United States; and may define and punish piracies and felonies committed on the high seas, and offences against the law of nations. Art. i. § 8. And so, likewise, *Congress may make all laws which shall be necessary and proper for carrying into execution the powers of the General Government*. But here is no reference to a common law authority: Every power is matter of definite and positive grant; and the very powers that are granted cannot take effect until they are exercised through the medium of a law. Congress had *undoubtedly* a power to make a law, which should render it criminal to offer a bribe to the Commissioner of the Revenue; but not having made the law, the crime is not recognized by the Federal code, constitutional or legislative; and consequently, it is not a subject on which the judicial authority of the Union can operate." So far the observations of the defendant's counsel. Judge *Chase*, who, on that occasion, differed from Judge *Peters*, as to the common law jurisdiction of the court, held, that under the 8th section of the first article, which I am now considering, although bribery is not among the crimes and offences specially mentioned, it is certainly included in that general provision; and Congress might have passed a law on the subject, which would have given the court cognizance of the offence. Judge Peters was of the opinion, that the defendant was punishable at common law; but that it was competent for Congress to pass a legislative act on the subject.

I conclude, therefore, that the first objection is not maintainable.

With regard to the second objection, which is, That this law is not warranted by that clause in the Constitution authorizing Congress to pass all laws which shall be necessary and proper for carrying into execution the powers specially enumerated, and all other powers vested by the Constitution in the Government of the United States, or in any department or officer thereof; because it is not necessary and proper to pass any such law in order to carry into execution any of those powers, it is to be observed, that from the very nature of the power it is and must be discretionary. What is necessary and proper in regard to any particular subject, cannot, before an occasion arises, be logically defined, but must depend upon various extensive views of a case which no human foresight can reach. What is necessary and proper in a time of confusion and general disorder, would not perhaps be necessary and proper in a time of tranquillity and order. These are considerations of policy, not questions of law, and upon which the Legislature is bound to decide according to its real opinion of the necessity and propriety of any act particularly in contemplation. It is, however, alleged, that the necessity and propriety of passing collateral laws for the support of others is confined to cases where the powers are delegated, and does not extend to cases which have a reference to general danger only. The words are general, "for carrying into execution the special powers previously enumerated, and all other powers vested by the Constitution in the Government of the United States, or any department or officer thereof." If therefore there be any thing necessary and proper for carrying into execution any or all of those powers, I presume that may be constitutionally enacted. Two objects are aimed at by every rational government, more especially by free ones. 1. That the people may understand the laws and voluntarily obey them. 2. That if this be not done by any individual, he shall be compelled to obey them, or punished for disobedience. The first object is undoubtedly the most momentous, for as the legitimate object of every government is the happiness of the people committed to its care, nothing can tend more to promote this than that by a voluntary obedience to the laws of the country, they should render punishments unnecessary. This can never be the case in any country but a country of slaves, where gross misrepresentation prevails, and any large body of the people can be induced to believe that laws are made either without authority or for the purpose of oppression. Ask the great body of the people who were deluded into an insurrection in the western parts of Pennsylvania, what gave rise to it? They will not hesitate to say, that the government had been vilely misrepresented, and made to appear to them in a character directly the reverse of what they deserved. In consequence of such misrepresentations, a civil war had nearly desolated our country, and a certain expense of near two millions of dollars was actually incurred, which might be deemed the price of libels, and among other causes made necessary a judicious and moderate land tax, which no man denies to be constitutional, but is now made the pretext of another insurrection. The liberty of the press is indeed valuable. Long may it preserve its lustre! It has converted barbarous nations into civilized ones, taught science to rear its head, enlarged the capacity, increased the comforts of private life, and, leading the banners of freedom, has extended her sway where her very name was unknown. But as every human blessing is attended with imperfection, as what produces by a right use the greatest good, is productive of the greatest evil in its abuse, so this, one of the greatest blessings ever bestowed by Providence on his creatures, is capable of producing the greatest good or the greatest mischief. A pen in the hand of an able and virtuous man, may enlighten a whole nation, and by observations of real wisdom, grounded on pure morality, may lead it to the path of honor and happiness. The same pen in the hands of a man equally able, but with vices as great as the other's virtues, may, by arts of sophistry easily attainable, and inflaming the passions of weak minds, delude many into opinions the most dangerous, and conduct them to actions the most criminal. Men who are at a distance from the source of information must rely almost altogether on the accounts they receive from others. If their accounts are founded in truth, their heads or hearts must be to blame if they think or act wrongly. But if their accounts are false, the best head and the best heart cannot be proof against their influence; nor is it possible to calculate the combined effect of innumerable artifices, either by direct falsehood, or invidious insinuations, told day by day, upon minds both able and virtuous. Such being unquestionably the case, can it be tolerated in any civilized society that any should be permitted with impunity to tell falsehoods to the people, with an express intention to deceive them, and lead them into discontent, if not into insurrection, which is so apt to follow? It is believed no government in the world ever was without such a power. It is unquestionably possessed by all the State Governments, and probably has been exercised in all of them: sure I am it has in some. If necessary and proper for them, why not equally so, at least, for the Government of the United States, naturally an object of more jealousy and alarm, because it has greater concerns to provide for? Combinations to defeat a particular law are admitted to be punishable. Falsehoods in order to produce such combinations, I should presume, would come within the same principle, as being the first step to the mischief intended to be prevented; and if such falsehoods with regard to one particular law are dangerous, and therefore ought not to be permitted without punishment, why should such which are intended to destroy confidence in government altogether, and thus induce disobedience to every act of it? It is said, libels may be rightly punishable in Monarchies, but there is not the same necessity in a Republic. The necessity in the latter case, I conceive greater, because in a Republic more is dependent on the good opinion of the people for its support, as they are directly or indirectly the origin of all authority, which of course must receive its bias from them. Take away from a Republic the confidence of the people, and the whole fabric crumbles into dust.

I have only to add, under this head, that in order to obviate any probable ill use of this large discretionary power, the constitution and certain amendments to it, have prohibited in express words the exercise of some particular authorities which otherwise might be supposed to be comprehended within them. Of this nature, is the prohibitory clause relating to the present object which I am to consider under the next objection.

3. That objection is, That the act is in violation of this Amendment of the Constitution. (3d vol. Swift's edition, p. 455, Article 3d.)

"Congress shall make no law respecting an establishment of religion, or prohibiting the free exercise thereof; or abridging the freedom of speech, or of the press; or the right of the people peaceably to assemble, and to petition the government for a redress of grievances."

The question then is,

Whether this law has abridged the Freedom of the Press.

Here is a remarkable difference in expressions as to the different objects in the same clause. They are to make no law *respecting* an establishment of religion, or prohibiting the free exercise thereof; or *abridging* the freedom of speech, or of the press. When as to one object they entirely prohibit any act whatever, and as to another object only limit the exercise of the power, they must in reason be supposed to mean different things. I presume, therefore, that Congress may make a law *respecting* the press, provided the law be such as not to *abridge its freedom*. What might be deemed the Freedom of the Press, if it had been a new subject, and never before in discussion, might indeed admit of some controversy. But so far as precedent, habit, laws and practices are concerned, there can scarcely be a more definite meaning than that which all these have affixed to the term in question.

We derive our principles of law originally from England. There the press, I believe, is as free as in any country of the world, and so it has been for near a century. The definition of it is, in my opinion, nowhere more happily or justly expressed than by the great Author of the Commentaries on the Laws of England, which book deserves more particular regard on this occasion, because for near thirty years it has been the manual of almost every student of law in the United States, and its uncommon excellence has also introduced it into the libraries, and often to the favorite reading of private gentlemen; so that his views of the subject could scarcely be unknown to those who framed the amendment to the Constitution, and if they were not, unless his explanation had been satisfactory, I presume the amendment would have been more particularly worded, to guard against any possible mistake. His explanation is as follows:

"The Liberty of the press is indeed essential to the nature of a free state: And this consists in laying no *previous* restraints upon publications, and not in freedom from censure for criminal matter when published. Every freeman has an undoubted right to lay what sentiments he pleases before the public; to forbid this, is to destroy the freedom of the press, but if he publishes what is improper, mischievous, or illegal, he must take the consequence of his own temerity. To subject the press to the restrictive power of a licenser, as was formerly done, both before and since the Revolution, is to subject all freedom of sentiment to the prejudices of one man, and make him the arbitrary and infallible judge of all controversial points in learning, religion, and government. But to punish (as the law does at present) any dangerous or offensive writings, which, when published, shall on a fair and impartial trial be adjudged of a pernicious tendency, is necessary for the preservation of peace and good order, of government and religion, the only solid foundations of civil liberty. Thus the will of individuals is still left free; the abuse only of that free will is the object of legal punishment. Neither is any restraint hereby laid upon freedom of thought or inquiry: liberty of private sentiment is still left: the disseminating, or making public, of bad sentiments, destructive of the ends of society, is the crime which society corrects. A man (says a fine writer on this subject) may be allowed to keep poisons in his closet, but not publicly to vend them as cordials. And to this we may add, that the only plausible argument heretofore used for the restraining the just freedom of the press, "that it was necessary to prevent the daily abuse of it," will entirely lose its force when it is shown (by a reasonable exercise of the laws) that the press cannot be abused to any bad purpose, without incurring a suitable punishment: whereas it never can be used to any good one, when under the control of an inspector. So true will it be found, that to censure the licentiousness, is to maintain the liberty of the press." 4 Black. Com. 151.

It is believed, that in every State in the Union the common law principles concerning libels apply; and in some of the States words similar to the words of the amendment are used in the constitution itself, or a contemporary bill of rights of equal authority, without ever being supposed to exclude any law being passed on the subject. So that there is the strongest proof that can be of a universal concurrence in America on this point, that the freedom of the press does not require that libellers shall be protected from punishment.

But in some respects the acts of Congress are much more restrictive than the principles of the common law, or than perhaps the principles of any State in the Union. For under the law of the United States the truth of the matter may be given in evidence, which at common law in criminal prosecutions was held not to be admissible; and the punishment of fine and imprisonment, which at common law is discretionary, is limited in point of severity, though not of lenity. It is to be observed too, that by the express words of the act both malice and falsehood must combine in the publication, with the seditious intent particularly described. So that if the writing be false, yet not malicious, or malicious, and not false, no conviction can take place. This therefore fully provides for any publication arising from inadvertency, mistake, false confidence, or any thing short of a wilful and atrocious falsehood. And none surely will contend that the publication of such a falsehood is among the indefeasible rights of men, for that would be to make the freedom of liars greater than that of men of truth and integrity.

I have now said all I thought material on these important subjects. There is another upon which it is painful to speak, but the notoriety as well as the official certainty of the fact, and the importance of the danger make it indispensable. Such incessant calumnies have been poured against the government for supposed breaches of the constitution, that an insurrection has lately begun for a cause where no breach of the constitution is or can be pretended. The grievance is the land tax act, an act which the public exigencies rendered unavoidable, and is framed with particular anxiety to avoid its falling oppressively on the poor, and in effect the greatest of it must fall on rich people only. Yet arms have been taken to oppose its execution: officers have been insulted: the authority of the law resisted: and the government of the United States treated with the utmost defiance and contempt. Not being thoroughly informed of all particulars, I cannot now say within what class of offences these crimes are comprehended. But as some of the offenders are committed for treason, and many certainly have been guilty of combinations to resist the laws of the United States, I think it proper to point your attention particularly to those subjects. The provisions in regard to the former, so far as they may at present be deemed material or instructive, are as follows:

[Here the passages referred to were read.]

The only species of treason likely to come before you is that of levying war against the United States. There have been various opinions, and different determinations on the import of those words. But I think I am warranted in saying, that if in the case of the insurgents who may come under your consideration, the intention was to prevent by force of arms the execution of any act of the Congress of the United States altogether, (as for instance the land tax act, the object of their opposition,) any forcible opposition calculated to carry that intention into effect was a levying of war against the United States, and of course an act of treason. But if the intention was merely to defeat its operation in a particular instance, or through the agency of a particular officer, from some private or personal motive, though a high offence may have been committed, it did not amount to the crime of treason. The particular motive must however be the sole ingredient in the case, for if combined with a general view to obstruct the execution of the act, the offence must be deemed treason.

With regard to the number of witnesses in treason, I am of opinion that two are necessary on the indictment as well as upon the trial in court. The provision in the constitution, that the two witnesses must be to the same overt-act (or actual deed constituting the treasonable offence) was in consequence of a construction which had prevailed in England, that though two witnesses were required to prove an act of treason, yet if one witness proved one act, and another witness another act of the same species of treason (as for instance that of levying war), it was sufficient; a decision which has always appeared to me contrary to the true intention of the law which made two witnesses necessary—this provision being, as I conceived, intended to guard against fictitious charges of treason, which an unprincipled government might be tempted to support and encourage, even at the expense of perjury, a thing much more difficult to be effected by two witnesses than one.

An act of Congress which I have already read to you (that commonly called the Sedition Act) has specially provided in the manner you have heard against combinations to defeat the execution of the laws. The combinations punishable under this act must be distinguished from such as in themselves amount to treason, which is unalterably fixed by the constitution itself. Any combinations, therefore, which before the passing of this act would have amounted to treason, still constitute the same crime. To give the act in question a different construction, would do away altogether the crime of treason as committed by levying war, because no war can be levied without a combination for some of the purposes stated in the act, which must necessarily constitute a part though not the whole of the offence.

Long, gentlemen, as I have detained you, for which the great importance of the occasion, I trust, is a just apology, it will be useful to recollect, that ever since the first formation of the present government, every act which any extraordinary difficulty has occasioned, has been uniformly opposed before its adoption, and every art practised to make the people discontented after it; without any allowance for the necessity which dictated them, some seem to have taken it for granted that credit could be obtained without justice, money without taxes, and the honor and safety of the United States only preserved by a disgraceful foreign dependence. But, notwithstanding all the efforts made to vilify and undermine the government, it has uniformly rose in the esteem and confidence of the people. Time has disproved arrogant predictions; a true knowledge of the principles and conduct of the government has rectified many gross misrepresentations; credit has risen from its ashes; the country has been found full of resources, which have been drawn without oppression, and faithfully applied to the purposes to which they were appropriated; justice is impartially administered; and the only crime which is fairly imputable is, that the minority have not been suffered to govern the majority, to which they had as little pretension upon the ground of superiority of talents, patriotism, or general probity, as upon the principles of republicanism, the perpetual theme of their declamation. If you suffer this government to be destroyed, what chance have you for any other? A scene of the most dreadful confusion must ensue. Anarchy will ride triumphant, and all lovers of order, decency, truth and justice, be trampled under foot. May that God whose peculiar providence seems often to have interposed to save these United States from destruction, preserve us from this worst of all evils! And may the inhabitants of this happy country deserve his care and protection by a conduct best calculated to obtain them!

PHILADELPHIA, May 15th, 1799.

SIR,

The Grand Jury of the Circuit Court of the district of Pennsylvania have heard with great satisfaction the charge delivered to them, on the opening of the court.

At a time like the present, when false philosophy and the most dangerous and wicked principles are spreading with rapidity, under the imposing garb of Liberty, over the fairest countries of the Old World—they are convinced, that the publication of a Charge, fraught with such clear and just observations on the nature and operation of the constitution and laws of the United States, will be highly beneficial to the citizens thereof.

With these sentiments strongly impressed on their minds, they unanimously request that a copy of the said charge may be delivered to them, for publication; especially for the information of those who are too easily led, by the misrepresentations of evil disposed persons, into the commission of crimes, ruinous to themselves, and against the peace and dignity of the United States.

ISAAC WHARTON, Foreman,   JOHN CRAIG,
J. ROSS,   SAMUEL COATES,
EDWARD PENNINGTON,   DAVID H. CONYNGHAM,
PHILIP NICKLIN,   JOHN PEROT,
JOSEPH PARKER NORRIS,   JAMES C. FISHER,
BENJ. W. MORRIS,   DANIEL SMITH,
THOMAS M. WILLING,   GIDEON HILL WELLS,
ROBERT RALSTON,   WM. MONTGOMERY,
            W. BUCKLEY.

Hon. Judge Iredell.

To the Gentlemen of the Grand Jury of the United States, for the District of Pennsylvania.

GENTLEMEN,

I receive with great sensibility the honor of this address, from gentlemen whom I personally respect so much. Believing, as I have long done, that the constitution and laws of the United States afford the highest degree of rational liberty which the world ever saw, or of which perhaps mankind are capable, I have seen with astonishment and regret, attempts made in the pursuit of visionary chimeras, to subvert or undermine so glorious a fabric, equally constructed for public and private security. It cannot but be extremely pleasing to me, that the sentiments on this subject I delivered in my charge, should meet with your entire approbation; and as you are pleased to suppose the publication of them may be of some service in correcting erroneous opinions, I readily consent to it, considering your sanction of them as giving them an additional value, which will increase the hope of their producing a good effect.

JAMES IREDELL.

PHILADELPHIA, May 15th, 1799.

IREDELL TO MRS. IREDELL.

PHILADELPHIA, April 11th, '99.

MY DEAR HANNAH:— * * * Our Court here is to begin to-day, and there is an immensity of business both civil and criminal. We expect to try some of the insurgents. Some are committed for treason. There is a respectable force now among them, taking up some of them every day. I expect to sit alone for about a week, Judge Peters having gone into that county to take examinations and issue warrants, &c. Your friends are well in general, except Mr. Phillips, who has a flying gout that frequently deranges him. Mrs. Wilson desires her love to you. * * * I am to dine to-day at Major Butler's with his son and daughters upon an invitation from "Thomas Butler," to take a "family dinner" with him. With all his democratical folly he has as much aristocratical pride as his father: he is very studious, but I have had no opportunity of judging of his understanding. * * * I wish you would send me my spectacles and the six last volumes of Gibbon, &c., &c.

April 18th.

Soon after I closed my letter to you last week, I heard of a *very extraordinary event*, which had taken place the night before (10th instant). Count Tilly, an eminent French nobleman, about forty or forty-five, a very dissipated man, and immensely in debt, but distinguished for being remarkably handsome, eloped with Maria Bingham (the only unmarried daughter), and was married to her at half after one in the morning, at a Universalist Minister's of the name of Jones; and at five in the morning they were found in bed at a milliner's of the name of Jones, the corner of Market and South streets. She was taken to her father's house, where she has ever since remained, but it is generally believed the marriage is a valid one. Her mother for a long time was in a state of distraction, and could only be composed by laudanum. Only two days before, it is said, her father had cautioned her about him. Now that the mischief is irreparable, she feels great contrition (though she did not at first), and would submit to any thing if it was possible to undo what she has done. What a deplorable event; but the too natural consequence of unbounded prosperity, and dissipation. He is taking legal steps to claim her. It is also reported that when her sister was married Mr. Bingham settled £500 a year on each of his daughters. A woman, servant in the house, was the agent; and was ordered to wake Mrs. Bingham at daylight, and inform her of the event, &c., &c.

JAS. IREDELL.

GOV. JOHNSTON TO IREDELL.

EDENTON, April 13th.

MY DEAR SIR:— * * * * Judge Moore and Judge Haywood attend this Court, and are despatching business with assiduity. Moore gives pretty general satisfaction, though some complain that he pays too little deference to principles founded on respectable decisions, and that he is inclined to eccentricity or novelty. I have not attended the Court; but, from all I can learn, I flatter myself he will prove a valuable addition to the Bench. The Land-tax, &c., are submitted to in this country without a murmur, and the only difficulty will be to find money to pay it, &c.

HERMITAGE, April 20th.

* * * The Court was then sitting, and I was sorry to learn that Judge Moore, by a strange inconsistency, and eccentricity of conduct, did not afford that satisfaction that was expected of him. * * * I beg to be presented to Mr. and Mrs. Wolcott: few things could give me more pleasure than to hear that she had recovered her health. * * * I hope by my next from you I shall learn that there is an end of the insurrection without bloodshed, &c., &c.

SAM. JOHNSTON.

IREDELL TO MRS. IREDELL.

PHILADELPHIA, April 25th.

MY DEAR HANNAH:— * * * Mrs. Phillips desires her love to you. Her son is soon to be married to a very fine, handsome girl, with a large fortune; her name is Smith, and she is nominally a Quaker.

Count Tilly is trying by law to recover his wife. Upon a writ called a *Habeas Corpus*, directed to Mr. Bingham to deliver her up, there was a hearing yesterday before Mr. Coxe, one of the State Judges. The father returned that she was not in his custody, &c., and Lewis, on behalf of Mr. Bingham, satisfied the Judge that the writ had not been issued in a proper manner. He has never been with his wife since the first night, and where she is now I don't know.

A series of most melancholy events have lately happened in Mr. McCall's family. Mr. George McCall, the eldest son, who bore a most excellent character, was married to a daughter of Mr. Clymer, a lovely young lady, highly respected and beloved: they were supposed to be a most happy couple. She has been for some months in a declining situation, during which he attended her with the utmost tenderness, giving her with his own hands all the medicines she took. On the 17th instant, when he was apparently in perfect health, he fell down dead in his father's yard. His father was then extremely ill, and it was necessary to conceal this event from him, which his wife, by uncommon exertion, though in all the agony of a mother's distress, contrived to do. He died, nevertheless, two or three days ago, and his unfortunate daughter-in-law the evening before last, leaving two children, and only about the age of 23. They concealed her husband's death from her as long as they could, but after it was fully disclosed to her, she was fond of hearing the most minute circumstances. Never, I believe, were two persons more regretted by their friends than this young gentleman and lady. Miss Bond, and many others who knew them well speak of them in the highest terms.

Though our Court has been constantly employed whenever there was business to do, and several bills have been found for treason, none of the trials can come on before Monday next. As I believe Mr. Chase has been detained by indisposition from going on to the eastward, I have written to him to see if he can attend at Annapolis for me, so as to enable me to finish the business here at this Term. Otherwise, I am afraid, a special Court will be unavoidable. But, at all events, I shall be at Richmond the 22d May. The insurrection is completely suppressed, and the troops returned. I suppose there are at least two hundred people attending the Court on that account, &c.

May 11th.

* * * The extraordinary fatigue I underwent made my head ache a little yesterday, though it did not prevent my attending the Court; but, as we adjourned early, I am quite refreshed to-

day, and the indisposition of the Attorney for the District allows me a kind of holiday, which will prove a great relief. The man tried for high treason, after a trial of nine days, was convicted. The Jury went out about eight o'clock, and, at their request, we adjourned till ten. Though we were punctual to a moment, the Court was so full that we could hardly get to our seats. The Jury, soon afterwards, were announced, and after the Clerk put the usual question whether he was guilty or not guilty, the foreman, after a most solemn pause, and in a very affecting tone of voice, pronounced him guilty, which had evidently a sensible effect on every person present. Though Mr. Peters and myself were clear that such ought to be the verdict, we both felt a great deal when it was actually pronounced. I could not bear to look upon the poor man, but, I am told, he fainted away. He behaved through the whole trial with great modesty and propriety. He now lies in the deepest distress, prostrate on the earth; but acknowledges the fairness of his trial, and the justice of the verdict. I dread the task I have before me in pronouncing sentence on him.

Having been strongly advised to remain here as long as I possibly can, for the sake of these trials, I have written to the District Judge and the Marshal to adjourn the Court at Richmond from day to day, till the 25th, when if I am alive and well I shall certainly be there. Six trials for treason, and many for misdemeanors, still remain. I expect one more of the former; but, as the points of law are all settled, I hope it will not be very long.

There is a young man here who takes a large picture, and gives a miniature print and twelve copies for 25 dollars, and as many more copies as are desired at a dollar a dozen. I have availed myself of the opportunity to oblige some of my friends, (as I hope it will do,) and now send the large picture and sixteen copies of the small one.* *Keep secret now what I am going to tell you.* I have had James Johnston drawn; and it is a most excellent and beautiful likeness. I intend the original for Mrs. Johnston, reserving a few copies for myself. * * * I availed myself of an early adjournment last night to go and see my Front-street acquaintance, and fell in with all of them almost at Mrs. Clem. Stocker's, &c., &c.

May 16th.

* * * My stay here does not arise from the difficulty of tearing myself from Philadelphia, but from the immense weight and importance of the criminal business of this Court, the greatest

* St. Memin, Artist.

part of which I must yet leave undone. It has oppressed me beyond measure, though my health is tolerably good. The other day when Fries was brought up to receive his sentence, his counsel moved for a new trial, which has occasioned an additional delay of more than two days. I hope it will be finished to-day. Mrs. Wilson is extremely pleased with your letter, and I think it extremely well written. I thank my dear Annie for hers, and regret I cannot now answer it, as my head is entirely taken up with law points, which require all my attention, &c., &c.

May 19th.

The business of the Court was so protracted it was utterly impossible for me to get away yesterday. Evidence at length was produced so irrefragable of one of the persons having made strong, prejudiced declarations against Fries, previous to his trial, that contrary to my wishes, bias, and inclination, I was at length compelled to vote for his having a new trial, and Judge Peters, with some hesitation, acquiesced. Four others were yesterday sentenced to fine and imprisonment,† &c., &c.

JAS. IREDELL.

GOV. JOHNSTON TO IREDELL.

May 25th.

MY DEAR SIR:— * * * I think your determination to continue the Court at Philadelphia was judicious. I congratulate you on the election of Gen. Lee, and Gen. Marshall. I observe some other changes in the representation from Virginia; but, not being acquainted with the political principles of the gentlemen who are returned, cannot decide how far they may be for the better, but think it a little more than an equal chance that they cannot be for the worse.

Present my best respects to Judge Griffin. I know no one else in Richmond that I can at present recollect, except Mr. Randolph, and him I would wish to forget.

I am glad you have got away from the land of *treason* to the land of *sedition*—the change is something for the better. Here you will find nothing but order, and almost universal acquiescence in the measures of government, &c., &c.

SAM. JOHNSTON.

MRS. WILSON TO IREDELL.

June 7th.

I was very happy to hear of your safe arrival at Richmond. You had delightful weather, and with agreeable company you

† Fries was convicted on a second trial, but pardoned by the President

must have had a charming ride. The pleasure of hearing from my dear Mrs. Iredell, and the children, must have added much to your happiness.

At the time I received your last letter, I thought I would answer it immediately, and then had enough for a page or two; but I have postponed it till I have scarcely any thing to say: however, as I told you what you had to expect, I shall make no apology. Remember you promised to be satisfied with merely one line, merely to know the state of my health, so that what I write in addition will be a disappointment.

My lovely young friend, as you justly call her, is writing to Boston. Mr. and Mrs. Breck have gone to pass two or three days in the country. We spend our time in the same manner we did before you left us—our mornings in our chambers. We have generally visitors in the evening. We had some charming music last evening from Eliza Redman. Mr. Hoe was of the party. He returned last week from New York, and inquired after you; he would certainly have called to see you, had he not left town unexpectedly. Miss Duché was married last Thursday week: I dined with her on Monday at Dr. White's; she was not as lively as usual, the thought of parting with her sister, to go entirely among strangers, being very painful to her. They go tomorrow to New Port for the summer. Anna and the boys desire their best respects to you, and thank you for your kind remembrance. When you write to Mrs. Iredell, present me affectionately to her and the children. I intend writing her very soon.

Your sincere friend,
H. WILSON.*

CHIEF JUSTICE ELLSWORTH TO IREDELL.

RALEIGH, June 10th.

DEAR SIR:—I thank you very sincerely for your letter from Richmond, and for the great pleasure I had in reading your luminous and pointed charge. That you left a great deal of business undone at Philadelphia, was doubtless a public misfortune, but it was a still greater that it became necessary to undo what had been done.

I hope this will find you very happy with your family, and that you will be abundantly recruited at August Term. Give my best respects to our common friend, Mr. Johnston, and believe me to be, very truly,

Your humble servant,
OLIVER ELLSWORTH.

* Widow of Judge Wilson.

GEN. DAVIE TO IREDELL.

HALIFAX, June 17th.

DEAR SIR:—I had the pleasure to receive, by Capt. Hamilton, your letter of the 20th of May, and with it your portrait, for which I beg you to accept of my thanks; it is a fine likeness, and nothing could have been more acceptable. * * * It was a very fortunate circumstance, in our present situation, that the insurrection in Pennsylvania had made so little progress, and so few proselytes; more examples than one would have been indispensable, had their treasonable designs taken a wider spread. Thus the last scene of every rebellion becomes the most afflictive to humanity.

I am greatly obliged to you for the copy of your charge; it is extremely well written, and the times called for every sentiment it contained. A Jacobin convinced, as Butler says, "against his will, is of the same opinion still;" he will never acknowledge his errors; and, I believe, would even die, obstinately professing his vile creed; but I cannot help hoping, that the great body of the people, who have been misled by an ill-placed confidence in these "illuminati," will examine the question for themselves, and now gradually correct their blunders. Virginia is the only State of which I despair; and I feel much anxiety to hear from yourself the result of the observations you had it in your power to make, during the time you were among them. My opinion, collected from some gentlemen who have been lately travelling in that State, and others who were at the Petersburg races, presents a melancholy picture of that country. These gentlemen returned with a firm conviction, that the leaders there were determined upon the overthrow of the General Government; and if no other measure would effect it, that they would risk it upon the chance of war. I understand that some of them talked of "seceding from the Union," while others boldly asserted the policy and practicability of "severing the Union;" alleging that Pennsylvania would join them; that Maryland would be compelled to change her politics with her situation; that the submission and assistance of North Carolina was counted on as a matter of course; and that the two Southern States would follow. As it was shortly after the election, these may have been the momentary effusions of goaded and disappointed ambition, and may end in nothing more than the miserable howlings of a baffled and sinking faction. At present, however, I am strongly induced to think their designs go further than this sort of natural relief to their chagrin. I beg you to let me hear from you on this subject.

VOL. II.—37

I shall be happy to find that I am mistaken with respect to our neighbors.

The death of P. Henry, at this critical period, is much to be lamented. Had he lived, I am persuaded he would have convinced the people of Virginia, that it was the conduct of their Legislature, not any change in his opinions that was the proper subject of regret, and over which the patriot would wish to drop a tear, that might blot out its memory for ever. Thus the Jacobins affect now to treat his last political opinions.

I have written to our friend, Mr. Johnston, urging him to serve again in the Assembly. I am very anxious that he should, as I have some reason to believe, that a plan is laid to produce a coöperation, if possible, with the Legislature of Virginia, and this I think he could defeat. I hope you will add your influence to mine, and that he may be induced to serve, &c., &c.

WM. R. DAVIE.

GEN. STEELE TO IREDELL.

PHILADELPHIA, June 27th.

DEAR SIR:—While you were at Richmond I could only inform you generally that despatches had been received from our agent, Dr. Stephens, at St. Domingo. The contents of some of them were not fully known, owing to the temporary absence of Col. Pickering, and such as were known did not give entire satisfaction. Since, however, things have assumed a more favorable appearance, and I have now the pleasure to inform you, that the trade will be opened in a few weeks, upon terms highly beneficial to our mercantile interest, and under circumstances peculiarly gratifying to us as a nation. These circumstances, although flattering as they respect the character of the American Government, cannot be published with propriety at the present time, and perhaps they ought not, during the war; but they speak a lesson to all the powers possessing colonies in the West Indies, which cannot fail to be understood, and consequently to produce more respectful treatment from them hereafter.

The jealousies and disputes which have subsisted for some time past between the two principal chiefs are coming fast to a crisis. Toussaint, it is thought, will in a short time expel Rigaud and his adherents, and with them the influence of the Directory. This, although apparently certain, will not be without much bloodshed, and a general peace might perhaps prevent it. Nothing else, I believe, can. The yellow chiefs are attached to France; the blacks think only of the prosperity of the Island, and seem determined, at all hazards, to adopt the means most likely to ensure it permanently.

This letter is noted *private*, as I intend it for your own eye only. Its contents ought not to be known as coming from an officer here, until after the proclamation of the President is published. This is intended to be so distributed as to be promulgated at all the Custom Houses in the Union on the same day. That day is not far distant.

The Aurora, as you may have seen, asserts that citizen Fayette is to be here, in the character of an Envoy Extraordinary, in the ensuing month. As nothing is more likely, this is generally believed. The Government has, however, received nothing official on that head. The thing is rendered probable by a variety of circumstances, &c., &c.

JNO. STEELE.

GOV. JOHNSTON TO IREDELL.

June 30th.

MY DEAR SIR:— * * * * Lest I should not have another opportunity of writing to you before you go, let me entreat you, carefully, and in defiance of every consequence, to avoid, by every means in your power, the most distant probability of taking the infection of that fatal fever. Your life is an object of more important consideration to the public than any temporary omission of your official duties, to say nothing of what you owe to your friends, and more particularly your family—a family truly worthy of all that affection you so sensibly feel, and which, from every present appearance, will be a comfort to you while you live, and do honor to your memory when you are no more. You are pleased to say that you will be perfectly satisfied to see your son such as mine, when he attains the same age. If I am not very much out of my judgment, you have nothing to apprehend on that score. Your James really appears to me, not only the most promising boy of his age I ever knew, but more so than I ever expected to see one. As to my James, permit me to use the words of Cicero in his letter to Brutus: "As to my son, if his merit be really as great as you write, I rejoice at it, as much as I ought to do; or if you make it greater than it is, because you love him, even that also gives me an incredible joy, to find that he is beloved by you." Adieu! &c., &c.

SAM. JOHNSTON.

Judge Iredell was prevented by indisposition from attending the August Term of the Supreme Court. "The place that knew him was soon to know him no more." The very arduous labors of his recent Circuit had seriously impaired his health; and if his vacation restored him to the comforts of home, it brought little relaxation to his active brain, and industrious fingers. In the sickly region in which he lived, he had had frequent and severe attacks of illness; the pillars of his constitution, often rudely shaken in his youth, began now to totter to their fall. He could well have exclaimed, "Sæpe sinistra cava prædixit ab ilice cornix," and yet he imposed no restraint upon his toil. The quick eye of his wife soon detected the faded cheek and the wasting form; but he regarded not her tender monitions. No lawyer had a more lively sense of the duty every individual owes his profession. The thought of death but stimulated his energies; and he was resolute so to prepare that, at the right time, he might plead to every demand, "solvit ad diem." His unfinished legal treatises engaged his unremitting attention, and with flagging strength, but indomitable purpose, he prosecuted his work.

GEN. STEELE TO IREDELL.

PHILADELPHIA, August 5th.

DEAR SIR:— * * * * You heard, I suppose, of General Davie's appointment to succeed Mr. Henry in the embassy to the *Great Nation*. I can say nothing further on this subject, except that the President lately received, through the hands of Mr. Murray, the assurance from the Directory required by the Message of February last, explaining the objects of the nomination. The assurance is in the old style, and though far from being what it ought to be, is nevertheless such as I suppose the President will consider himself bound to admit. You must therefore not be surprised, if you should hear of the new envoys being ordered to prepare for their departure. I confess I do not forebode any good from it, and on that account lament that the measure has been adopted. Three solemn embassies, composed of our most distinguished citizens, to be obliged to go to Paris in succession, to beg peace and reconciliation with a Government whose enmity is now unanimously considered less dangerous than their friendship, may serve to show our passion for humility and submission; but it is impossible to think that as a nation our honor can be preserved, or our interests promoted, by such condescensions.

Do me the favor to present my respects to Mrs. Iredell and family, and be assured of the great veneration and affection with which I am, dear sir,

Your obliged friend and humble servant,

JNO. STEELE.

MRS. WILSON TO IREDELL.

SPRING-HILL, Aug. 7th.

You do not know how much we were all disappointed in not seeing you on Sunday. We went to the Baptist meeting at Bustleton with the expectation of meeting you. I concluded that you had waited a day in Baltimore for Mr. Chase, for I thought if you had a day to spare, you would divide it between your mother and us. * * *

Every individual of the family felt the disappointment, even Charles and George expressed their regret. Anna and myself have been practising Pauvre Tague, and endeavoring to get the evening hymn, in anticipation of your arrival. We intended to take you to the most pleasant walks, and to point out the beauties of the place, which I assure you are many. * * * *

Mr. and Mrs. Hill have gone to Bordentown to pass the remainder of the summer. They have lost their dear little baby: it was one of the most lovely infants I ever saw. You would be astonished at the composure with which they speak of it as a little angel, removed from this world to a better. Though it is a severe trial to their fortitude, it is one happy effect of their religion, that it teaches them perfect resignation to the will of heaven.* How happy for us to think, "whatever is, is right;" but in the height of affliction, how difficult! * * *

Mr. Wikoff was here Sunday. I sent a message to Mr. Patterson and Mr. Washington, to request them to come out and pass a few days with us. Mr. Buck says it will give him great pleasure to see you. How much we all regret your absence! You say you think it a pity Mrs. Pollock is not thirty years younger. For the sake of your own sex I do not know if you ought to wish it. I think she would attach many by her pleasing manners. Though there are some disagreeable traits in her character, they are not easily discovered by a transient acquaintance. Upon the whole, I think her a very clever woman, but not one you would wish a friend to be connected with. Mr. Stoughton, who, it was said, addressed her, is engaged to Mrs. Dininville, the little, lively woman you saw at Mr. Buck's two winters ago. I do not know what you will say to the length of this letter. It is with writing as with talking: when a woman once begins, she never knows when to leave off, &c., &c.

H. WILSON.

---

* Hon. Wm. H. Hill, of North Carolina.

JNO. MILLER TO IREDELL.

PHILADELPHIA, Aug. 8th.

WORTHY SIR :—The letter your honor was pleased to write me on the 27th ultimo, was duly received, and found our family in the usual way, except my poor wife! She is low indeed, confined to her bed, and, by every appearance, will soon be launched into the vast ocean of eternity, that hath neither shore nor bottom. Well, sir, she has ever been a pious woman, industrious for both worlds, and will shortly leave a world of sin and sorrow, to enjoy a crown of glory, and be for ever with her God. We entered into the marriage state on the 21st Oct., '41, and have lived in perfect unison, love, and conjugal happiness for a long series of years, but must now part! She will, before many days, take up her abode in Pine Street Church-yard, near neighbor to my dear Mrs. Mease and her son, there to remain until the trump of God shall call—"Prepare to meet your God, O Israel." But here, here, sir, I am doomed to spend my solitary hours, and wakeful nights—no one to comfort me when I am near my departure to see my father, God.

I can't be long here; no, my sands are nearly all run out, and death, that king of terrors, and terror of kings, will soon make me a visit, and then at his summons I must appear. But oh! how shall I appear,

"When all my secret sins will be revealed,
Nor the minutest circumstance concealed."

At present, sir, my health is agreeable. I have no just cause to complain, but my spirits are low. Isabella is every hour with her dear grandmother, and renders her every service in her power. * * * * Pardon me for dwelling so long on this mournful subject.

I hope we shall have a healthful summer here. Both this city and New York were threatened last month, but our fears are now all subsided. I will give you an account of the burials for some days. You know I am a scribbling old fellow. * * * *

I have not been up at the City Hall since the Court began, as the Hon. James Iredell was not there. All join in love to you and Mrs. Iredell. Adieu! may heaven bless and preserve you! So says, and so prays,

Your most obt. humble serv't,

JNO. MILLER.

JUDGE WASHINGTON TO IREDELL.

ALEXANDRIA, August 20th.

DEAR SIR :—Upon my arrival at Baltimore, about the first of the month, I heard from Judge Chase, with great concern, that you were too much indisposed to attend the Supreme Court. The fatigue to which you had been exposed during the Circuit was well calculated to produce this consequence, and you would have acted imprudently, I think, to venture upon so long a journey in your then state of health. It will afford me very sincere pleasure to hear of your recovery.

Judge Cushing was seized upon the road by an indisposition, so severe as to prevent his proceeding. Fortunately there was no business brought on which involved any question of importance or difficulty, and the term was consequently short. I went from and returned to Baltimore with our brother Chase, whose excellent flow of spirits and good sense, rendered pleasant a journey which would otherwise have been fatiguing and disagreeable.

Being allotted to the Middle Circuit, I shall have to re-try the many perplexing cases, which engaged so much of your time at Philadelphia in the spring. I can easily foresee that the trials will be rather lengthened than curtailed, unless the same Judge presided who was present at the former trials. To avoid unnecessary prolixity, so far as may consist with perfect justice to both sides, I could wish if possible to be made acquainted with the circumstances attending the insurgent cases (particularly that of Fries); the mode in which the trials were conducted, and the points made and decided. This may in many instances prevent unnecessary discussions, and may aid in the better understanding of such as are important. If you can without much inconvenience forward to me at Philadelphia an abstract from your notes, relative to those cases, it will much oblige me. I shall be at that place about the 20th of September, on my way to Trenton ; should your letter arrive after I have gone through, I will direct it to be forwarded to me.

Your letter to me from Philadelphia in the spring was answered shortly after, but unfortunately I directed it to Annapolis, where I supposed you would be. In the post-office at that place I suppose it still is.

Mr. Buck's family, with Mrs. Wilson, were in the country, so that I did not see them. I received a message from them, but could not find an opportunity of riding out. They are all well.

With best respects for yourself and family, I am, dear sir,

Very sincerely yours,

BUSHROD WASHINGTON.

GEN. DAVIE TO IREDELL.

HALIFAX, Sept. 18th.

DEAR SIR :— * * * * I should have been happy to have availed myself of the assistance and company of Mr. Griffin, and particularly of rendering an acceptable service to a gentleman you esteem, had not the appointment been made before the receipt of your letter.*

The appointment of Envoy is highly honorable to me, and under any other circumstances would have been certainly agreeable ; but the unknown and ever-varying situation of the Government to which we are addressed, its strange, unparalleled character, and unsettled policy, connected with the probable events of the present campaign, furnish no "data" on which we can calculate the issue of our mission, and must cast the reputation of those concerned in it entirely upon *chance;* and your sensibility will easily anticipate the anxiety I feel under these circumstances.

You have no doubt seen the letters of B——, Col. of the Hussars at Lichten, respecting the assassination of B—— and R——, at Rastadt ; the circumstances are so strong that little doubt is left upon my mind of the real authors of that horrid deed. Can man support, or Providence permit, a government to exist, capable of such atrocious villany ? &c., &c.

WM. R. DAVIE.

A. B. POLLOK TO IREDELL.

NEWPORT, R. I., Sept. 25th.

DEAR SIR :— * * * * * We have a most excellent minister in our Episcopal church here, and one of the best orators in America. Mrs. Williams always attends, though brought up a Presbyterian : she has so charitable a mind that I find her well pleased with my church. * * * * The town has been very crowded in consequence of the distress of the great cities. Lodgings and provisions are very high. Your recollection of Mrs. Lopez's family gives them great pleasure. They beg me to present their best respects to you. Neither the Beauty nor any of her sisters are yet married. Gen. Pinckney, lady and family, are here. She is in very bad health. I think them all very agreeable. She enjoys most excellent spirits. We are every day highly entertained by her and the young ladies, with accounts of their residence in France. I hope Mrs. W. will keep a journal, as I cannot recollect half. Mr. Kinloch's family is not here. Col. Hamilton's family have been here, but are now in Boston, &c., &c.

A. B. POLLOK.

Judge Iredell's indisposition, baffling the skill of his physician, began now to assume a fatal character. The shadows were deepening around him ; the night was at hand. At his residence, in Edenton, he expired on the 20th day of October. He had borne with Christian fortitude the pangs that attended the parting of the soul and the body ; and, as his reward, hope accompanied and supported him through "the dark valley," that every man must tread, if not with fear, at least with awe.

The grief of his family was but natural ; but the tears of his servants, and the lamentation of a whole community, constituted a tribute to his merit, honorable indeed.

In the old church at Edenton, thronged with every class, free and bond, old and young, the Rt. Rev. Charles Pettigrew, Bishop of the Diocese of North Carolina, delivered over the body of his departed friend a funeral discourse, from which the following extracts are taken.*

"The melancholy occasion of this funeral solemnity evinces to us, that death is no respecter of persons ; that, regardless of distinction, he treats with equal impartiality the righteous and the wicked, the useful and the useless members of society. The worthy personage, whose death we this day deplore, stands not in need of my feeble efforts to adorn, or to establish his character ; yet there is, alas ! an unavailing duty which I wish to discharge to his memory. And now, that we may not be deficient in point of reflection, nor inattentive to an example so worthy of imitation, I must request your attention a few moments longer.

"But how or where shall I begin ? for I confess my embarrassment, from conscious inability to do that *justice* which *I wish*, to so worthy a character, unless I were possessed of more full and exact information. Sensible of the *delicacy* of the subject, I shall endeavor to avoid *extremes*, and to observe a *just medium*. I must, however, confide in the *indulgence* of my audience, whose *partiality* to the memory and well-known character of the deceased, may raise in them, on this occasion, the highest expectations.

"Judge Iredell was born in Europe of respectable parentage. He came to this country in early life. I am not able to be particular with respect to his family. I recollect to have seen a

---

* Judge Griffin, of Virginia, had, through Judge Iredell, applied for the post of Secretary for his son.

* For biographical notice of Bishop Pettigrew, see Appendix.

younger brother of his in London, about twenty years ago. He appeared to be a very promising youth. He belonged to one of the Inns of the Temple, where he was then prosecuting the study of the law. But having a Christian education, and retaining a partiality to the study of divinity, he afterwards entered into holy orders, as I have been informed; and now, if alive, fills a dignified station in the Church.

"In the Judge was, perhaps, verified the observation of a wise monarch of antiquity: 'Train up a child in the way he should go, and when he is old he will not depart from it.' Although he did not take the turn which that brother took, yet he still appears to have retained his belief and veneration of the Christian religion. Indeed I know from his lips, in a conversation which I had with him long before death, that he could not well brook the idea of men who hold principles confessedly inimical to the Christian religion, getting into offices and places of high trust and responsibility. From the sacred influence of religion on his own mind, to qualify him for so conspicuous a discharge of public trusts, and in different grades of advancement, he was capable of setting a true estimate on that religion, not only as the best and surest foundation for good government, together with security for life and property, but also the *safest* and best foundation whereon to rest our hopes of a happy and glorious immortality beyond the grave.

"What, my friends, but the meliorating influence of this religion upon the mature faculties of a well-informed and judicious mind, could have rendered him so humane, so sympathetic, so charitable, so humble, and so easy of access? What but a just sense of his duty to God, and a proper regard to man, united with strict honor and integrity, could have made him so conscientious a lawyer, so accurate and just a judge? What else but these could have made him in every view so perfectly consistent and finished a character? As his countenance was expressive, so his understanding was clear, and his judgment strong and accurate. When an attorney at the bar, he practised with intense study, and close application to the business of his profession. By this means he acquired a profound knowledge and acquaintance with the constitution and municipal laws of this country, which qualified him for eminence in a more exalted sphere.

"When chosen a delegate to our State Convention for the purpose of examining and adopting the Federal Constitution, he distinguished himself, by taking a decided and active part in that business. In the warmest and most interesting debates we find him exerting his powers with the spirit and firmness of the patriot, and at the same time with that moderation which characterizes the enlightened and able statesman.

"He acted some time in the office of Attorney General, in which he conducted himself with his usual propriety and address. He was also appointed a member of the honorable Council of State, under the administration of Governor Johnston. Likewise one of the Judges of our Superior Courts of Law and Equity, in which capacities he acquitted himself with reputation and honor. He was appointed by the General Assembly to revise the laws of this State, which trust he executed with such fidelity and care as secured to him the approbation and esteem of the public at large. Such *wisdom* and *integrity*, however *modest*, cannot escape the public eye, and must ever continue to rise, by a rapid gradation. He was accordingly called to fill the seat of justice in a higher tribunal. By a federal appointment he was made one of the Judges of that Court. This was to him, I believe, a sphere of eminence, from which he shone with peculiar lustre.

"I am persuaded that the justness and propriety of sentiment, together with that elegant simplicity and ease, which characterize the productions of his pen, will long do honor to the memory of the Judge.

"In the run of above twenty years *I have often heard high encomiums on the merit of this great and good man; but never, in a single instance, have I heard his character traduced, or his integrity called in question.*

"I am indeed astonished, when I consider the depravity of the multitude, and the proneness of human nature to envy and detraction, that one in so many different spheres of elevation could preserve his reputation so fair and unblemished. This, perhaps, would have been morally impossible, had this great and good man betrayed a consciousness of that dignity which his office conferred. But Judge Iredell was eminently superior to *this weakness*, while no man supported the dignity of office better than he did. That ease with which he conducted himself, that affability and politeness, flowing from true benevolence, which were so natural to him at all times, and on all occasions, disarmed his enemies (if he had an enemy, and who is without them?), and made even envy conceal her darts.

"As a friend he was sincere and transparent, easy and familiar. But taken in a conjugal and domestic view, we behold in him the tender and loving husband, the kind and indulgent father, the affectionate brother, and the humane master, who in each of these respects is, perhaps, equalled by few, and excelled by none. This State may very justly lament the loss of one of its brightest ornaments, and the United States of a useful and valuable character. Our duty is resignation to the unerring will of heaven. Let us imitate those virtues which shine with so distinguishing a lustre in his character; and let us with diligence prepare to follow to that unknown world, from whose 'drear bourn no traveller returns,' and where Christian charity persuades us that he now enjoys the happy fruits of a virtuous and useful life."

Such was the testimony borne to Judge Iredell's character as a man, where that character was best known, by one, the odor of whose sanctity still lingers about the place of his ministration. What more need be added?

Judge Iredell left unfinished at his death two legal treatises. One of these, "An Essay on the Law of Pleading in Suits at Common Law," consists of 1229 pages, constituting four volumes, folio, of closely written manuscript; the other, "The Doctrine of the Laws of England concerning Real Property, so far as it is in use or force in the State of North Carolina," extends to 365 pages. Had he lived a few years longer to complete these works, he would, in point of time, have anticipated "Chitty on Pleading," and the many essays on real property which have issued from the American press.

As a Judge, Iredell was, undoubtedly, the *ablest*, and *most learned* who sat upon the bench in his day. For profundity and variety of attainment, and for keen, subtle, yet vigorous logic, he had no equal. Mr. Vansantvoord says, "As a constitutional lawyer, Judge Iredell had no superior upon the bench."* Again the same writer says, in speaking of Judge Patterson, "In most of those qualities which constitute a successful judge, he was inferior to none of his colleagues, and perhaps was not equalled by any, save his brethren, Iredell and Chase. His intellect, though less accurate and logical than that of the former, and less bold and self-reliant than that of the latter, was original, comprehensive, discriminating, and strong." Chief Justice Marshall, who was always remarkable for the precision of his language, in a letter to Judge Murphy, in 1827; wrote, "*I always thought him a man of real talent.*" But why multiply authorities?† Let the Judge's fame, fairly won by himself, rest upon his speeches, his writings, and his judicial opinions! I have not attempted to raise it upon any fictitious basis. Removing the dust and lifting the statue from a recumbent position, I have but elevated it upon its own sculptured pedestal. For many years the evidences of his merit have, in a great measure, slumbered in the obscurity of a private office. Meanwhile, the laudable activity and industry of Northern artists have crowded with Northern groups the historical canvas: one city alone claims "one hundred orators," and many a village hero has been inflated into a celebrity. Of this I do not complain. Reverence for the dead is a commendable sentiment: even when characterized by a narrow and exclusive devotion to immediate ancestors, I can pardon it for a redeeming amiability. I honor the memory of the illustrious men of New England; and can even admire the genius and the enterprise that can dignify trifles, and exalt mediocrity. As a Southern man, I simply demand admission into the National Pantheon for those who have vindicated their right by ability, virtue, and patriotism.

A very accomplished gentleman, in a letter to me, says: "It seems to me that the Judges of the Supreme Court naturally divide into two classes,—the statesmen, and the jurists—strictly considered. Of the former Chief Justice Marshall was unquestionably the first, but almost too exclusively a statesman to discharge that portion of his duties which related to mere private rights. Judge Story was probably at the head of the latter class; yet he, unfortunately, was entirely deficient in those broad political views, which so eminently distinguished his Chief; and bold as the assertion may seem, he appeared to me devoid of that originality and force so requisite to the statesman. Indeed his law treatises seem fast disappearing from the shelf of authority, with the single exception of his 'Conflict of Laws,' which will always be valuable as a Digest and Index of that learning. Judge Iredell was a happy combination of both; his decisions upon questions of private right need no remark; it is as a constitutional lawyer, second only to Marshall, that his position should be vindicated. The opinion given by him in Chisholm *vs.* the State of Georgia was a masterpiece, and proved him to be the only statesman on the bench at that period; his argument was certainly in accordance with the principles of all government, and showed an insight into the depths of our constitutional system, quite outside of the comprehension of his associates. His reputation might rest upon that alone."*

Judge Iredell's body was, finally, deposited at Hayes, in the private burial-ground of Gov. Johnston. The spot is marked by an appropriate monument, upon which is the following inscription:

---

* Lives of the Chief Justices.
† In Philadelphia, where the Judge was well known, "he was universally esteemed and regretted."—*Brown's* "*Forum.*"

* Judge Iredell was below the average stature: he had large hazel eyes: his hair was black; and he was very quick in his walk, and movements. He lived entirely on his salary, which was most *judiciously* and *economically* managed by his wife.—*Letter from Jas. C. Johnston, Esq.*

"IN MEMORY OF
JAMES IREDELL,
BORN AT LEWES, SUSSEX COUNTY,
ENGLAND,
OCTOBER 5th, 1750,
EMIGRATED TO NORTH CAROLINA
IN 1768,
DIED AT EDENTON, OCTOBER 20th,
1799,
HAVING FILLED,
HONORABLY TO HIMSELF AND USEFULLY
TO HIS COUNTRY,
VARIOUS IMPORTANT CIVIL OFFICES.
HE WAS
AT THE TIME OF HIS DEATH
ONE OF THE ASSOCIATE JUSTICES
OF THE SUPREME COURT
OF THE UNITED STATES.
HE WAS
EXEMPLARY IN THE PURITY OF
HIS LIFE,
AND MOST AFFECTIONATE, KIND,
AND BENEVOLENT
IN ALL HIS DOMESTIC AND SOCIAL
RELATIONS."

APPENDIX TO VOL. II.

BIOGRAPHICAL NOTICE OF THE RT. REV. CHARLES PETTIGREW, FIRST BISHOP OF THE DIOCESE OF NORTH CAROLINA.*

The Rev. Charles Pettigrew was descended from a gentleman's family, originally from and still resident in Scotland, a branch of which removed, very many years ago, to County Tyrone, Ireland,—extinct at present, except in the persons of two ladies. He was of this branch. His father seems to have fallen out bitterly with his people—why, was never known, but probably on account of difference in religion, for he came to this country a dissenter of the dissenters, and so strict was he that his doors were always religiously closed on Sunday. On one occasion the Indians, on Sunday, having made an irruption into the settlement, passed by his house as uninhabited, while the neighbors met the usual fate,—an occurrence which, doubtless, did no little to steady the faith of his family. He followed the usual course of the Irish emigration, landing in Pennsylvania, and halting finally in North Carolina. The Rev. Mr. Pettigrew was indebted for his education, having parted from his father, to the Rev. Mr. Patillo, and the Rev. Mr. Waddell, Wirt's famous blind orator, who seem to have taken a great fancy to him in his youth, as appears from their correspondence, wherein allusion is made to presents of Greek books, received while at the Grammar School. Having but little besides his intellect, he became a teacher. The date of his appointment to the public school in Edenton is June, 1773, and under the seal of Governor Martin. Uniting to his inheritance of piety a lively intellect, and a considerable degree of literary cultivation; and having, moreover, returned to the faith of his forefathers, he was persuaded to enter the ministry; and accordingly, in the winter of 1774-5 made a voyage to London, where he was ordained by the Bishop of that city, his diocesan, assisted by the Bishop of Rochester. He immediately entered upon his function with zeal, for which there was much room during the war; and the death of the Rev. Mr. Earll shortly afterwards cast upon him the care of all that section. By his marriage with Mary, daughter of Col. John Blount, he became allied with the old Provincial Aristocracy, and thus had

---

* All that there is of excellence in this sketch must be ascribed to a friend, whose modesty forbids further allusion.

---

the sphere of his usefulness much enlarged. In a letter, dated 1789, he alludes to his former habit of preaching to great crowds, and states that he was compelled to give it up, because it almost inevitably produced a fever.

During all this period he seems to have been not so much at the head of the Episcopal Church, as of religion in general, for there are various letters to him from Edward Dromgoole, and other Methodists, who either resided in or travelled through that region, and also from Lutherans, &c., giving him an account of their movements, and requesting his attendance at their meetings. Indeed the Church Establishment having been dissolved, and all religious organization broken down, the enemies of the evil one fought together, with no other bond of union than that of a common foe.

In his politics he was a Whig. After the peace he received various invitations from the neighboring parts of Virginia, which were declined. In 1789 Bishop White suggested to Gov. Johnston the propriety of organizing the Church in North Carolina; but he, deeming any ecclesiastical interference inconsistent with his position, referred the whole matter to Mr. Pettigrew, who requested the clergy to meet at Tarborough, in June, 1790. The apathy on this subject was great, for it was not until a flood of letters had been written, and various small conventions held, that one could be assembled sufficiently universal to organize the Church. In May, 1794, such a convention was held at Tarborough, at which a constitution was framed and adopted, and Mr. Pettigrew selected as Bishop. With regard to this honor he sincerely said, "nolo episcopari;" the state of his health seemed absolutely to forbid it; but in the depressed state of the Church, and the scattered situation of its ministers, the acceptance of this post was deemed by his fellow-Christians a duty, and he yielded. Various alarms of yellow fever at Norfolk and Philadelphia, with their accompanying quarantine, cutting off all communication, prevented him from meeting the General Convention for some years, and in the latter part of his life declining health rendered him unequal to the exertion. Though he was thus unable to put the finishing stroke to the foundation, yet his labors in rescuing the ministers and their parishes from the disconnected state in which they were disposed to continue, and in increasing and diffusing a zeal for religion, were of great service, not only in the cause of the Church, but of Christianity in general.

About the same time another matter of general concern agitated the State, in which Mr. Pettigrew took great interest, and acted a leading part, —the establishment of a University. Such was his conviction of the importance of the measure, and his zeal for its success, that once being compelled to choose between the General Convention and a meeting of the friends of the University, he preferred the latter. On this subject there is a very good communication from him in the Archives of the University.

His literary attainments, though considerable for the time, were probably not very deep; but he had quite a classical taste. His favorite Latin author in youth was (judging from his quotations) Horace, and subsequently Virgil. His written style is easy; and his oratory, from all accounts, eloquent, but at the same time chaste, for he had a horror of *physical* religion. One gift he had by nature, to a considerable extent,—that of poetry; many scraps, rough drafts of odes, and poems on all sorts of subjects, and in all kinds of metre, either quite lively or the reverse, are still in existence. His turn for variety of metre probably produced or was produced by his partiality for Horace.

As a Christian he was as nearly without serious fault as is possible, for though he lived in an age when the clergy were rarely popular, and always subjected to harsh criticism, none, except the Baptists, ever said aught to his discredit. The manner in which he discharged the very onerous duties of his calling, in a sickly country, was exemplary; and in that day a clergyman who had three or four counties under his charge was far from having a sinecure.

About 1794 he began to reside at the Plantations of Bonarva and Belgrade, now the property of his grandsons, on and near Lake Scuppernong; and there he built Pettigrew's Chapel, which he presented to the church. From the above date until his death, in 1807, he refused to receive any compensation for his services. Indeed, he had always, even under the Establishment, forbidden the collection of any thing from the Quakers. An enlightened, cheerful, and consistent Christianity pervaded his whole life, and particularly characterized him in his domestic relations, and never was the duty of a Christian gentleman more elegantly set forth than in his letter of advice to his son at college, in 1797, when he believed himself approaching dissolution. As a curious instance of the opinion then entertained, it may be mentioned, that he therein advised him to make arrangements for procuring white labor, as a change might take place sooner than was expected.

His health was always delicate, but his cheerfulness of temper never forsook him. It was impossible to be with him without catching his sprightliness.

His marriage placed him in comparatively affluent circumstances, but, as might be expected, he was an indifferent manager of worldly concerns, though his own opinion of his skill was probably different. He died in 1807, leaving a widow, of the second marriage, formerly Miss Mary Lockhart, and one son. His remains repose in the family sepulchre at Bonarva.

The Bishop's only son, the Hon. Ebenezer Pettigrew, represented the Edenton District in Congress in 1835-7, and was distinguished for his intelligence, his purity, and his refined manners.

IREDELL TO HEWES.*

EDENTON, June 28th, 1775.

DEAR SIR:—I had the pleasure to receive your letter by Capt. Gillies, and thank you for the communication of public affairs you were pleased to give me, and for your obliging desire to transmit more, had it been (as it very properly was not) permitted. Far from being unreasonably impatient at the delay of Congress, I am much pleased they proceed with so great deliberation, for certainly no public body had ever objects of more magnitude to decide on. I believe I may add, few have had men of more wisdom than several among you to consider them. I yet conceive (lost as every thing seems to be to truth and reason) great hopes from the wise determinations of Congress. They will, I am persuaded, act in so decisive

---

* Member of the Cont. Congress, and Signer of the Declaration of Independence.

VOL. II.—38

a manner, that at the same time they prepare for a general defence in the last extremity, they will open a way to reconciliation, which it will be highly dishonorable on the part of Great Britain not to meet. Men who have committed injuries have no right to give themselves airs about tumults too naturally excited by them; much less can they with any grace do it when the whole tenor of their conduct proves a consciousness that they have been originally in the wrong. A very pretty story, that a man may not give another a box on the ear, who attempted his life! And *liberty*, to all men of feeling, is dearer than *life*. I much wish to know the opinion formed by Congress of Lord Chatham's Reconciliatory Bill. According to my poor ideas of the subject, it would afford a happy and honorable basis for both countries. It is framed with much judgment to remove difficulties on both sides of the question, and reconcile *substantially* the honest views of the two parties in opinion. Would to heaven it had succeeded! Heaven grant it may yet succeed, or something equally promising! All our hopes of any speedy happiness must at last centre *somewhere* in England. If, by the moderation and equity of our proposals, strong friends can be found on that side of the water, all may yet be well at no great distance of time. But, abstracted from this prospect, I see nothing but the most dreadful and miserable scenes in view. I rely *much, very much*, on Congress. They have the greatest trust under their care any set of men can hold. The happiness of millions depends upon their firmness and prudence. They have indeed great difficulties to contend with, but "the greater the difficulty the more the glory in surmounting it." In a letter I have from Mr. McCulloh to-day is the following passage, which I take leave to transcribe. (Speaking of Lord North's conciliatory motion:) "It pleases here, though it means nothing; at the same time Administration declare they have no design to tax America, and I truly believe they wish themselves out of the scrape." I really believe so too, and have long done so, and therefore the more earnestly wish to see things going on in the train of negotiation. Mr. M. desires his best compliments to you. For all provincial and committee intelligence, I refer to M. Bondfield, and your other correspondents who are in the secret. I shall only say that things were going on tantivy to licentiousness for awhile, but have lately received a curb from the spirited interposition of some of the old members of our committee, and the introduction of Mr. Johnston into a new one which has been appointed.* You have been much wanted here to keep the spirit of liberty from wandering beyond its bounds.

I am much obliged to you for your attention to the memorandum I took the liberty to trouble you with.

I must beg you to make my best respects to Mr. Hooper, who I hope will find as much health as *I am sure he will honor at the Congress*. Heaven direct your councils! God forbid I should wish your ardor to be improperly checked, but I hope in God all prospects of peace will not be despaired of.

Your little girl has wrote you another epistle, which I inclose.† She

* The allusion is, I suppose, to the mobbing of Mr. Pollok, an act condemned by Hooper, vol. 1, p. 269. Vid. letter from Mrs. Pollok to Hewes.—p. 602, v. 2.

† Miss Helen Blair.

has been lately very ill, but all this she will tell you. Mrs. Iredell joins in kindest wishes for your happiness, with, dear sir,

Your ever respectful, affect. and obliged,

JAMES IREDELL.

Iredell to Hewes.

Edenton, April 29th, 1776.

Dear Sir:—I had a few days ago the favor of receiving your letter of the 26th of March, which I believe came by Mr. Hooper, but I had not the pleasure of seeing him, as I was not at Halifax. It gives me great concern to hear of your ill state of health. I wish it was possible for you to avoid such incessant application, as I am sure you have not strength enough of constitution to bear it well. I am persuaded your situation admits not of much relaxation, but I hope you will pay as particular attention to your health as is consistent with it. By sedulously laying hold of every opportunity for this purpose, great things might be effected. I showed Nelly your letter. She was so much affected by it that she was obliged to leave the room. No circumstance in life could have made her more happy than the present of your picture; but the manner in which you mentioned it quite damped the joy such agreeable intelligence would otherwise have afforded her.

I am under great obligations to you and General Washington for the great kindness you both did me about my letter. My receiving no answer to it, as it happens, is no disappointment to me. *I have now no thought or wish of going home. My mind is raised above the sordid idea of providing for myself. I am impatient to be attached to my friends in the noblest of all causes—a struggle for freedom. It is a cause I have long honored, and which, since things are come to extremity, I deem it my duty to engage in. I have no merit from so doing. My soul follows its natural inclination, and gratifies its most favorite passion. In a cause I believe so just, and with friends I so highly honor, I could face danger with intrepidity, and embrace any fate with pleasure. I should not wish to survive the ruin of my country, and should think myself disgraced in pusillanimously deserting the support of her fallen fortunes.** The pride and arrogance of our oppressors is insufferable, and the fury of their conduct can rationally have no other effect than to kindle our resentment into a fiercer flame. When I wrote you my last letter, we had accounts of a favorable disposition towards us, and I warmly wished an occasion might be offered to restore peace and harmony once more to this distracted Empire. I felt for the dangers of my native country, and was miserable in the fear of its being sacrificed to the pride and insolence of a set of tyrants. This made me hope that if the great point could be secured, slight circumstances of ill-appearance might be passed over. But things now wear a quite different face. The Ministry do not appear the only blood-thirsty men in the nation. They are stimulated by some of the meanest wretches in the creation;—men who regard liberty only for themselves, and would tyrannize over others. It is difficult at this distance to judge properly. But I really fear a major-

* The Italics are not in the original.

ity of the nation are against us. The contemptible principles of self-interest (however mistakenly pursued), the hopes of plundering us, the desire of unlimited taxation to ease themselves, appear to me to carry away multitudes. Unhappy it is that the virtuous and noble minority, who prefer principles of equity and honor to the savage desire of plunder and devastation, must follow the fortunes of the rest. But so it is; and the county of *Berks* must be among the number.*

The tyranny and infatuation of the Ministry have driven us to the brink of a precipice. Scarcely any hope of a reconciliation can now be entertained. I see things in the most melancholy aspect. But it is necessary to be firm, and to prepare for all events with fortitude. My first attachment is to the liberty and welfare of America; my next to the happiness of Great Britain. If these can yet be found compatible, most happy should I be in seeing the blessed union; if they cannot, notwithstanding the extreme bitterness of the struggle, it would be our duty to support the former against the latter. "Ye gods, what havock does ambition make among your works."

You will undoubtedly have regular accounts from Halifax. Little has yet been done but the passing an order to raise four new regiments, and three companies of light-horse. A fifth regiment I hear is in contemplation. They are very busy now in framing a constitution for us, and they proceed with great delicacy in it. A variety of plans is offered, and night and day *wise* and *unwise* heads are ruminating upon them. I need give no particulars, because it is impossible that you should not have regular and frequent intelligence thence.

I inclose you some hair of both Mrs. Iredell's sisters, part of which, according to your request, is intended for you. Mrs. Iredell is extremely obliged to you for your kind care about the locket, and wishes both kinds of hair to be plaited together in a plain manner.

I shall probably, now that I mean to free myself from all restraint, and as you pay no postage, trouble you with frequent letters. I at the same time make it a condition that you use no ceremony, and never write to me but when you are quite "degagé" and easy. I shall wish for your letters, but I shall be more anxious for your health, and it would make me unhappy if I had any reason to think that I was concerned in your loss of it.

But I forgot to tell you a smart action lately performed at our bar. There were two tenders there going out with some prizes they had taken; two of the vessels were too late for the tide, and obliged to wait, and one tender remained with them; in the night time a number of the pilots and others boarded the tender in boats, and carried her and the prizes immediately up to Newbern. Old G——† had the command of the tender, and having been thinned of men to put on board the prizes, had only with him three or four negroes; hearing the noise of the oars just as they approached near the vessel, he ordered the negroes to fire, but upon a gun being presented at him (which snapped in the pan) he immediately delivered the vessel up. J. Buchanan and A. Campbell owned one of the vessels that were thus retaken, and were going out to Madeira.

* There is some doubt about the word Berks.

† Goodrich?

Mrs. Blair and Mrs. Iredell desire their best compliments to you, and join with me in most earnest wishes for the re-establishment of your health. And they add their requests to mine, that you will improve every moment for the truly valuable purpose of putting it on a good footing.

Adieu! my dear sir. May heaven bless you! I am at all times, with the greatest sincerity and high respect,

Your most affect. and obt. servant,

JAS. IREDELL.

Iredell to Hewes.

Edenton, June 9th, 1776.

Dear Sir:—I begin to be troublesome, I fear. I wrote you only last week, and now am about it again. I have not, however, much to say; and certainly should not have wrote at all if you had any postage to pay, but as this is not the case, I hazard a few lines. We have a report, by credible people from Newbern, that the King's troops have all left Cape Fear. Gen. Lee, about 10 minutes before he set off from Newbern to go there, received a letter which gave him reason to apprehend they intended it; and since, it is said, undoubted information had arrived that they were actually gone. The place of their destination is uncertain; it seems most probable that they are gone either to South Carolina or Virginia, or perhaps in separate bodies to both; it is conjectured by some, that they may perhaps attempt landing between Cape Fear and Charles-Town, and that way penetrating into the back country. There are about 300 lighthorse established between Cross Creek and the only place where it is imagined they could attempt landing (the name of which I have forgotten, but where it seems there is very shallow water at a great distance from the shore). These lighthorse will be able to discover, and give intelligence. Gen. Lee staid only one day at Newbern, and his Virginia Regiment marched directly from Halifax to Cape Fear by the upper road. I have always been cautious in mentioning any report I hear at these times, when so many idle and false ones are continually propagated; but I thought I had extremely good authority for mentioning that Gen. Lee intended to rendezvous his troops for the present at Newbern. I believe, however, I had the caution to tell it you only as *a report*, a word for which great allowances must be made now-a-days. *I inclose you copies of an address from the people of Newbern to the General, and his answer, for the sake of the latter, wherein he does an honor to this Province I am not a little proud of. Comparative compliments must always have some better grounds than absolute ones.*

Mr. Smith is at Williamsburg, or some other place in Virginia. He went a few days ago. You will undoubtedly hear fully from him there.

I wish much to know the truth about the people of Maryland. We are told, they refused to alter their form of government, and this is construed by many as a proof of *great disaffection*. I only consider it in the light of unwillingness to come into this measure, and independency which may be the consequence, until the very last necessity, which they choose to make themselves judges of. I can never believe they will be guilty of such abandoned infamy as to desert a cause they were so forward to engage in. *At the same time, I do really think there is an evident indecency and incongruity (and have long so) in conducting business in the name of the King, when we are in arms against him;* and the direction of the Congress on this subject I conceive ought to be obeyed. For there is, as I conceive, this material difference between such a conduct and an express declaration of independence; that in the former case a reconciliation is *practicable;* in the other, any hopes or intention of it absolutely renounced. *With respect to the latter, I do clearly think, that a majority of voices alone ought not (indeed they cannot) carry it, but it must be individually consented to by each Province.* But the former being a mere incident of the original purpose of the Confederacy, calculated for conducting it with more dignity, and still having in view a re-union as *possible,* I think it was a proper object of the Congress' attention, and ought universally to be obeyed. Our situation is so unhappy, that a declaration of *absolute independence* may become necessary, before a distant body can be collected, and therefore I think the members of the Congress ought to have full powers to declare it, when the melancholy exigence shall arrive. I do not view the subject as a matter of *ambition;* in my opinion it is criminal and impolitic to consider it in that light; but as a matter of *necessity;* and in that case, in spite of every consequence (and very bad ones may be dreaded), *I should not hesitate an instant in acceding to it.*

Nelly was so ambitious to thank you for your picture, in a long letter, that she had not finished it when the Post went away. I now inclose it. Your negroes have been coming to see your picture, and were transported with it. I met Cam at the door one day, and brought him in. He was in a perfect ecstasy—"Master, every bit," says he,—"ah! the old gentleman is grown handsome." Mr. Smith has made a gentleman of him once more: he has carried him to Virginia.

Nelly has wrote you that Mr. Allen went away from here some little time ago for the Augusta Springs. He has had, poor fellow! a terrible time of it, but was pretty well recovered when he went from here, enough so to travel with ease. And in a letter Mr. Smith received from him a few day ago, he mentioned he was much better, and had procured letters of introduction to many on the road, from gentlemen to whom he carried letters, and who had shown him great civilities.

I repeat again, that if you excuse my scribbling to you so much, it is all I expect and hope for, unless when you find yourself in a disposition and leisure enough to relieve yourself from a labyrinth of politics, by either railing or laughing, you will do me the honor to do it with me.

May God grant you better health, and every felicity, is the constant and anxious wish of, dear sir,

Your most obliged and faithful servant,

JAS. IREDELL.

HON. CHARLES JOHNSON TO IREDELL.*

STRAWBERRY-HILL, January 14th, 1788.

DEAR SIR:—I return you the papers containing the Federalist, and am much obliged to you for communicating them to me. I observe that No. 13 of the papers, containing No. 6 of the Federalist, is wanting, and cannot be certain whether it came with the rest or not, as I was at the time

* Mr. Johnson's grandson, Dr. Chas. E. Johnson, is the husband of one of Judge Iredell's grand-daughters.

of receiving them in too much pain to look them over. Although it has already been looked for, yet if it was sent—which please let me know—I will cause another search to be made for it.

The Federalist appears to me to be elegantly written; the author displays a most comprehensive imagination, and great extent of political knowledge. But I am surprised that he should have thought it necessary to take so much pains to establish, what appears at the first glance, at least to me, an incontrovertible truth, which is—that the States, united under one efficient government, properly balanced, will be much more powerful, have much fewer causes either of internal or external quarrel, and will be able to procure greater commercial advantages, more respectability and credit, than the States disunited into distinct, independent governments, or separate confederacies. Either of these ideas seem so absurd that I must believe they can have few partisans; and had not the Federalist taken so much pains to refute them, I could scarce imagine they could have been at all entertained.

If he means to exhaust the subject, and is equally copious upon each article, he will undoubtedly afford a great fund of entertainment. I shall be particularly desirous to see those numbers that treat of the additional security which the adoption of the new Constitution will afford to the republican form of government, to liberty and property; and that will satisfactorily answer all the objections of importance that shall have made their appearance against it. This is part of the task he has set himself in his first number, and it will afford great room for the exertion of his excursive genius and reasoning powers, as some very weighty objections have already arisen, and still more may possibly arise when the subject comes to be more fully and unprejudicedly investigated. For certainly there are few men acquainted with the great, respected, I may almost say adored, characters who formed the late convention, who did not view the new Constitution with an eye strongly prejudiced in its favor. There are, nevertheless, great defects found in it: ought they not to be more attended to even on that account?

For my part I will candidly, and in confidence, declare to you that it is a doubtful point with me, and which I cannot yet bring to a decision, whether it will be better to receive the new Constitution, with all its seeming imperfections on its head, or run the risk of obtaining another Convention, which may revise and amend, expunge those articles that seem repugnant to the liberties of the people—secure our political liberty by separating the executive, legislative, and judicial powers—affix responsibility to every office—and explicitly secure the trial by jury, according to former usage—the liberty of the press, with all the other rights of the individual which are not necessary to be given up to government, and which ought not and cannot be required for any good purpose. Surely, if there is no immediate, impending danger to prevent the adoption of the measure, it is most devoutly to be wished. This requisite information might easily, as I conceive, be obtained from Congress, as they must be acquainted, by the communications of their ambassadors, with the general aspect of affairs in Europe. I have already said that I have formed no decided opinion; the subject I conceive of too great magnitude, and above me. I only venture my doubts without any apprehension of your placing me in any of our friend

Dr. W.'s classes, the burden of each verse of which, if I remember rightly, is, "the government is not for him." *

The gout still continues a kind of desultory skirmishing, sometimes forcing one or the other of my outworks; but soon leaving them. This makes me imagine that only its advance, composed of light troops and hussars, have yet made their appearance; and induces me to believe that I have still a heavy, serious attack from the main army to sustain. But as the citadel is in pretty good order, the garrison in tolerable spirits, no scarcity of provision or ammunition, and the assistance of able engineers to be had if requisite, I am determined to hold out to the last extremity, and dispute the ground inch by inch; and I flatter myself that, by a vigorous defence, I shall compel the enemy to raise the siege. When, if they do no considerable damage to the body of the place, I am in hopes speedily to repair the outworks, and put the whole fort in a proper state of defence against the next attack.

I would apologize for taking up so much of your time, but know your good nature will excuse greater intrusions. The truth is, I am quite fatigued with reading, and having taken up the pen, found some relief from weariness, and even pain, by having my attention taken off from it,—so, though the tedious length of this letter may tire you, yet your humanity will be gratified by the consideration that you have been the means of administering relief to the weary and heavy laden. Mrs. Johnson still continues indisposed. Tom, the night before last, had a return of the fever and ague, but is now again pretty well; the rest of the family are in good health. With real regard, I am, dear sir,

Your most obt. and obliged serv't,

CHAS. JOHNSON.

FAYETTEVILLE, 14th Nov., 1788.

DEAR SIR:—Expecting this will find you at Newbern, I cannot deny myself the pleasure of writing you. And in the first place permit me to congratulate you on the birth of your son, and to assure you that I participate the pleasure you so feelingly describe your family to have felt on that joyful event. You will perceive, by what I have said, that the Governor was kind enough to show me your letter.† In it I recognize the genuine, parental affection, which every person of sensibility must feel on a similar occasion. Long, very long, may you continue to enjoy the blessings of domestic felicity.

I shall now recur to the present scene, though nothing of any consequence has yet occurred. On the day appointed a House was formed. We have since chosen our officers of State, a list of whom is inclosed. An attempt has been made to bring on the business of a new Convention. *It was introduced in our House by General Caswell,* as we counted upon carrying the resolution there, and expected that the question being carried in the Senate would add greater weight to it in the Commons, where we were most dubious of our strength. But Wilie Jones, with his usual adroitness in the finesse of the House, set forth the necessity of a conference, and moved the previous question, which be carried by a very great majori-

* Dr. Williamson.

† Gov. Johnston.

ty indeed—at least four to one—so few were there that could understand the nature, meaning and extent of the previous question. To evince clearly how much that party excels ours in all the mysteries of political manœuvre, I need only mention that the very measure proposed by Wilie Jones (that of a conference of both Houses) after he had defeated the resolution introduced by Gen. Caswell, was rejected by the Antifederal party, with Parsons at their head. You will perceive that this afforded no great cause for triumph, though they exult extremely; nor do I think it by any means a fair trial of strength. The business will again be brought on, and I hope with more success—at least we must endeavor to have fairer play. A great number of petitions have been presented, many from counties formerly anti-constitutional. Another circumstance will operate for a new convention; many want to reconsider the seat of government—even this must be risked. Many bills of a public nature are introduced, but their fate being uncertain, I shall not trouble you with their titles. I declined being nominated to my former honorable office, lest another Assembly may be called the present year, and Chowan deprived of a representation. All your friends here are well. We live in the same house, and have a great plenty of venison, turkeys, and every thing else. The town of Fayette has converted your old friend C. into a Fayette-villian; it operates like the charms of Circe.

I am, dear sir, yours sincerely,

CHAS. JOHNSON.

NOTES.

1. To the Assembly of '86–7, Judge Ashe addressed a letter, defensive of himself and colleagues, in which he animadverted severely on the bar. An answer soon appeared, signed by James Iredell, Wm. Cumming, Sam. Johnston, Alfred Moore, Wm. R. Davie, Jno. Stokes, Wm. Hooper, Archibald Maclaine, Jno. Hay, and James Spiller. My kinsman, Hon. Jno. B. Ashe, of Texas, has forwarded to me so much of the original of the Judge's rejoinder as has been preserved; it is dated Aug. 30th, 1787. In it the Judge says, that none of his communication to the Assembly was intended to apply to Moore, Iredell, and Johnston. Of Iredell he says: "having from our first acquaintance been in intimacy with him, and having once been happy in his assistance upon the bench, and knowing his merits (truth and not compliment draws this from me), and pained at the apprehension of his uneasiness," &c. The rejoinder thus concludes: "that in my turn I would plainly tell him (*Mr. Penn*), that, though there were several gentlemen of the bar, in whose acquaintance and friendship I had been happy, yet, if they thought proper to withdraw themselves, I should have no objection, for that I was independent in principle, in person, and in purse, and should neither court their love, nor fear their enmity."

2. In speaking of the refinement of society at Wilmington, in 1774, in Vol I., I omitted to mention that a resident of that town was the author of the earliest American drama, "The Prince of Parthia." Wilmington was the home of Thomas Godfrey's choice and manhood; and his remains lie in St. James' Church-yard, not very far from the grave of Harnett. Many

of the minor pieces in his collection of poems, abound in local allusions. In the same connection I will state that Wm. S. Hasell, at Yale College, Sept. 11th, 1799, recited "Alfred, an Historical Poem," a very creditable production, considering the era, and viewed in relation to cotemporaneous efforts. The poem appears, by mistake, in the "Charleston Book" (1845). Hasell was a native of Wilmington, and is interred in its immediate vicinity, in the family burial-ground. The ancient mansions at Hillton, and Hyrnham; Lillington Hall, and the residence of Dr. Thos. H. Wright; the ruins at Swann's-Point; the monuments about the old church at Brunswick; and similar memorials at Orton and Lilliput, indicate a degree of taste and wealth that has not been rivalled since the Revolution.

Mrs. Pollok to Joseph Hewes.

Edenton, Decem. 23d, 1775.

Sir:—You will no doubt be surprised at receiving a Letter from me, but such is the unhappy Situation of my mind at present, that I feel a kind of negative satisfaction in having an opportunity by the return of the Express to Inform you the Particulars of our unkind reception we met with on our return to Edenton—so unexpected and so unmerited—not one person in my Family knows of my writing so must intreat you do not Let Mr. P. know of it. Coll Howe who seem'd shock'd beyond measure at our Sufferings, told me he had wrote to you; but alas no person could Let you know the circumstances in so clear a manner as myself; who most Solemnly declare to you, the following to be truth, as I expect to answer before the great Creator of the Universe—after we Left you att Philda we had a most agreeable Journey to Anapolis—from whence we intended going by land home but not being able to get horses and ours much fatigu'd, we were perswaded by our friends there, to get a boat and go down to the mouth of Potowmack. We took their advice, but the wind springing up it blue so hard, and the seas run so high, out of Potowmack, that we were obliged to go right before it, and attempt running to Suffolk; which we shou'd have accomplis'd without being stopd by the men of war —but in the mouth of Nansamond we got fast on an oyster bank, and there remaind part of two days and a night before we got assistance from the shore to get our horses out and proceed to Suffolk about twelve miles off; at Last we arrived, thankful was I to be thus nigh the End of my Journey; Mr. Donaldson came to the Tavern and took us to his house, during our stay which was only one day and two nights General was the conversation, but unluckily Mr. Pollok said that he heard a gentleman in Anapolis tell Major Junipher who is presidint of the counsel of safety that his Brother in a Letter from London in a jocular way said, he thought matters might be easily settled by hanging half a Dousen on each side the Question, Major Junipher Immediately made answer poor Lord Chatham he suppos'd wou'd be one—this was all—which was nothing more than a member of the Congress might have said—but a narrow Sould wretch one Major Smith who Lives on Tar river happening to be present went to Wells Cooper and told heaven knows what, that Mr. Pollok shou'd say they must be all Hang'd, as soon as we had Left Suffolk Wells Cooper came over to Mr. Donaldson swore if we had not gone away as we did he wou'd have blown out Mr. P. Brains burnt our carriage &c. &c. had D.

Hamilton and Mr. Donaldson on their oath to declare what they knew, which ammounts just to the above conversation; however Mr. Cooper sent to our commite to have Mr. Pollok taken up, and sent to every house we stop'd at on the road to know what Mr. Pollok said the particulars too tedious for a Letter and will give you them when we meet, nothing tho' in the Least Blamable, Mr. Roy he call'd a fool and such Like stuff—these matters however was carried on with so much secrecy that no person ever knew of it, or if they did was made to beleive Mr. Polloks crimes were of such a nature that they were Intimidated. and Injoying ourselves at home nursing a violent cold we had got coming down the Bay. Mr. P. did not go out for some days after our arrival, but finding himself better we paid a morning visit one morn'g to Mr. Maxwell a gentleman from York married to a distant connection of Mr. P. and Lodged at Mr. Hardys much Indisposed—whilst we was there a Mr. Blackburn came into the house, and addressing himself to Mr. P. you are order'd not to Leave the Town before you make your appearance before the committe—Mr. P. was much surprised and asked him what he ment; he again told him the message. Mr. Pollok said he had no Intention of leaving the Town—but tell the Committe I shall go where I please, nor shall I wait on them. Consider the Insult and concious Innocence to a man of spirit who cou'd have done otherways? Immeditably a Body of men about one Hundred and fifty or more commanded by Captn Tool was order'd to go to Mr. Hardys and take Mr. Pollok prisoner. Mr. P. refused to go on that Captn Tool order'd a party of his men to seize Mr. P. and himself attempting to collar Mr. P. I fell on my knees to him, intreated he wou'd go without force, for what cou'd an unarm'd man do against numbers, he comply'd with my Intreaty and went prisoner to the court house—please to observe all this was done by the express order of Mr. Benbury for what reason I know not—think of the distress I must be in not allow'd to know what the cause of all this was, I went to the court house after waiting about an hour at Mr. Hardys to know the fate of poor Mr. Pollok—when I came there I saw him at the door but it being surrounded with a great number of armed men I attempted to enter but was pulled off and used in a savage manner by them, who where call'd too by their officers in the street to Push me down and pull me off till one gardmen with more Humanity than the rest told them to let me alone, and gave me his arm into Hornibloe where I was order'd by the committe to be search'd for arms, I told them they were welcome to search me that I might be a fool, but was not a mad woman to carry arms to Mr. Pollok who was so much Enrag'd I knew wou'd make use of them, in short the Ill treatment I met with from committe and officers has yet been unequalled—after keeping Mr. Pollok under confinement part of two days and one night he was tryed before the committe and discharg'd —I know nothing from himself but have been told he sign'd the assosiation and tis more than probable Look'd on it as compulsary situated as he then was, and perhaps told some Individuals things they did not like, but consider how little presence of mind a man has in the midst of people who did every thing to enrage him to have an excuse for their future conduct; however had they acted according to order some proper person might have presented the assosiation had Mr. Pollok refused then to sign he merited what censure they thought proper—but moderate measures seem'd Intirely

Exploded and a worthy member of Siciety was with his Family to be sacrificed to the caprice of a malicious few whose own private resentment was to be sanctified by the public good—in order to accomplish which the persons who I shall give you a list of, by the most scandelous arts got a Number of Soldiers out of their Barracks who did not know Mr. Pollok, told them he was a Scotchman, and an Enemy to America made them allmost drunk and that night on which Mr. P. was discharged and once more in his own bed in Security (for strange it was) but not a person who wish'd us well knew of it, Mr. Pollok and myself having bad colds had taken a dose of yapon and about two o'clock being in a profuse perspiration we was awak'd by Jacks coming into the room and telling us that Mr. Hall with a great number of arm'd men was at our door and must see his master directly Mr. P. told him to go and ask what he wanted they Immediately call'd bring him out or down with the house, I then jump'd out of bed to open the door to speak to them, but before I cou'd get it open'd they chopp'd it down with their axes in my face and guns pointed, I beg'd to know what Mr. P. had done thought he was discharg'd, and asked by what Authority they commited such an outrage; they told me by an arbitary Authority. I used every argument I cou'd think of but in vain, bring him out or down with the house Mr. C. Hall keep repeating, the House was surrounded with more than two hundred men no Possibility of Mr. P.s getting out, all the arms we had I had carried out of the house when I returned from Mr. Hardys, for I well knew had Mr. Pollok any he wou'd have lost his life rather than submited to such usuage; in short, their promising no Insult shou'd be offer'd to his person; made me on my knees beg him to accompany them to the court House to speak to those officers he had offended; and who were so little of the gentleman, as ruffian like, so unequally attack an unarm'd man at that unseasonable hour: at Last he comply'd with my request and went with them, two men who staid behind and seem'd to have a little more feeling than the rest, told me I need not be so uneasy for the worst that wou'd be done to Mr. Pollok wou'd be to Tar and Feather him—Heavens can they do any thing worse death would be more mercifull—I flew out of the house little clothing upon me the coldest night we have had this year, screaming for Mr. Pollok all over the streets some time bare footed—at last I found Him standing in the midst of hundreds before the Court house, all the commanding officers except Captn Tool were not in Town—gone out on purpose it is well known I sent Mr. Corrie of N york to beg him to come and disperse them, I waited till he might have come over, and over—at last went myself, and after waiting a considerable time screaming enough to raise the dead, he came down but used no means proper to disperce the mob in short all were combined to make Mr. Pollok a Sacrifice, and when they had done that, now says Clem Hall Let us burn the coach, which they did—then Merceracu proposed to return and break open the cellers, which they return'd to do but the store house being open'd and no Liquors there as ours had not arrived Mr. Pollok gave them a sum of money and they went away. I had been Taken in strong convultions at Hornibloes they brought me home, but I remaind that night and next day so bad that it was with difficulty Life was preserved in me, and certain I am that my being in uncommon good health, was all that saved me and the kindness I received from Mr. Johnstons Family, who on a bed had me carried round and there I was at

least more secure, but no person hardly thought I should have the use of my limbs again, we staid there near three weeks Expecting to hear every morning the house was down as it was a determin'd point with Clem Hall. I need not point out to you the daring Insult offered to the Commite Mr. Lamb a member of that with some others is said to have Patronized this affair, I was promised by Mr. Gray and some others that Hall and some more shou'd be made Examples of but tis now gone over; and I remain in an unhappy situation; every night allarm'd at the least noise Expecting to be turned out of my bed or the house pull'd down over me. Mr. Pollok never speaks on the occasion only to blame me for perswading him to go with the mob, and sending away his arms. Oh Mr. Hewes I am sure those feelings of Humanity so predominant in your breast must be shock'd —do consider—do use that power Invested in you towards the security of civil peace. Let not a respectable member of society be made a victim to a Barberous few, I am sure you never thought Soldiers necessary in this part of Carolina nor cou'd you have thought they were to be paid to ruin Individuals, or disturb the peace of society—to you I look for justice: surely you will not suffer Authority thus to be trampled under foot, none are safe, all as guilty as Mr. Pollok. May the Almighty direct your Counsels for the Happiness and peace of America is the sincere wish of Sir your

Sincere Friend, A. POLLOK.

These persons I mention to you are accused by good evidence I beg you will keep the List and shou'd find them guilty you will be a judge of their merits the affronts to some of them which the pretend to have received I will give you at large when we meet and you will find them false.

Thomas Jones painter the blacksmith Clem Hall young Ned Vail, Micheal Payne, an Ensign in Capt. Blount's, Joseph Worth, Boyd, Blackburn, and many others.

I fear this is Scarcely Ledgable but when you reflect on the agitation of my mind on a retrospective view of my sufferings I know you will excuse all.